MARKET SHARE REPORTER

ISSN 1052-9578

MARKET SHARE REPORTER

AN ANNUAL COMPILATION

OF REPORTED MARKET SHARE

DATA ON COMPANIES,

PRODUCTS, AND SERVICES

2013

Volume 2
ROBERT S. LAZICH, Editor

GALE
CENGAGE Learning

Detroit • New York • San Francisco • New Haven, Conn • Waterville, Maine • London

Market Share Reporter 2013

Robert S. Lazich, Editor

Project Editor: Virgil L. Burton III

Editorial: Joyce P. Simkin, Monique D. Magee

Manufacturing: Rita Wimberley

Product Management: Jenai Drouillard

For product information and technology assistance, contact us at **Gale Customer Support, 1-800-877-4253.**
For permission to use material from this text or product, submit all requests online at **www.cengage.com/permissions.**
Further permissions questions can be emailed to **permissionrequest@cengage.com**

While every effort has been made to ensure the reliability of the information presented in this publication, Gale, a part of Cengage Learning, does not guarantee the accuracy of the data contained herein. Gale accepts no payment for listing; and inclusion in the publication of any organization, agency, institution, publication, service, or individual does not imply endorsement of the editors or publisher. Errors brought to the attention of the publisher and verified to the satisfaction of the publisher will be corrected in future editions.

EDITORIAL DATA PRIVACY POLICY. Does this publication contain information about you as an individual? If so, for more information about our editorial data privacy policies, please see our Privacy Statement at www.gale.com.

Gale
27500 Drake Rd.
Farmington Hills, MI, 48331-3535

ISBN-13: 978-1-4144-5981-3 (2 vol. set)   ISBN-10: 1-4144-5981-5 (2 vol. set)
ISBN-13: 978-1-4144-5982-0 (vol. 1)   ISBN-10: 1-4144-5982-3 (vol. 1)
ISBN-13: 978-1-4144-5983-7 (vol. 2)   ISBN-10: 1-4144-5983-1 (vol. 2)

ISSN 1052-9578

Printed in Mexico
1 2 3 4 5 6 7 16 15 14 13 12

TABLE OF CONTENTS

Table of Topics . . . . **vii**
Acronyms and Abbreviations . . . . **xvii**
Introduction . . . . **xxi**

Volume I
General Interest and Broad Topics 1
SIC 01 - Agricultural Production - Crops 14
SIC 02 - Agricultural Production - Livestock 29
SIC 07 - Agricultural Services 35
SIC 08 - Forestry 36
SIC 09 - Fishing, Hunting, and Trapping 37
SIC 10 - Metal Mining 39
SIC 12 - Coal Mining 48
SIC 13 - Oil and Gas Extraction 50
SIC 14 - Nonmetallic Minerals, Except Fuels 57
SIC 15 - General Building Contractors 64
SIC 16 - Heavy Construction, Except Building 71
SIC 17 - Special Trade Contractors 73
SIC 20 - Food and Kindred Products 77
SIC 21 - Tobacco Products 224
SIC 22 - Textile Mill Products 232
SIC 23 - Apparel and Other Textile Products 241
SIC 24 - Lumber and Wood Products 255
SIC 25 - Furniture and Fixtures 261
SIC 26 - Paper and Allied Products 267
SIC 27 - Printing and Publishing 282
SIC 28 - Chemicals and Allied Products 293
SIC 29 - Petroleum and Coal Products 367
SIC 30 - Rubber and Misc. Plastics Products 371
SIC 31 - Leather and Leather Products 381
SIC 32 - Stone, Clay, and Glass Products 385
SIC 33 - Primary Metal Industries 394
SIC 34 - Fabricated Metal Products 405
SIC 35 - Industry Machinery and Equipment 422

Volume II
SIC 36 - Electronic and Other Electric Equipment 461
SIC 37 - Transportation Equipment 500
SIC 38 - Instruments and Related Products 532
SIC 39 - Miscellaneous Manufacturing Industries 554
SIC 40 - Railroad Transportation 570
SIC 41 - Local and Interurban Passenger Transit 571
SIC 42 - Trucking and Warehousing 573
SIC 43 - Postal Service 577
SIC 44 - Water Transportation 578
SIC 45 - Transportation by Air 581

SIC 46 - Pipelines, Except Natural Gas 587
SIC 47 - Transportation Services 588
SIC 48 - Communications 590
SIC 49 - Electric, Gas, and Sanitary Services 615
SIC 50 - Wholesale Trade - Durable Goods 621
SIC 51 - Wholesale Trade - Nondurable Goods .628
SIC 52 - Building Materials and Garden Supplies 632
SIC 53 - General Merchandise Stores 634
SIC 54 - Food Stores 639
SIC 55 - Automotive Dealers and Service Stations 651
SIC 56 - Apparel and Accessory Stores 654
SIC 57 - Furniture and Homefurnishings Stores .659
SIC 58 - Eating and Drinking Places 666
SIC 59 - Miscellaneous Retail 672
SIC 60 - Depository Institutions 687
SIC 61 - Nondepository Institutions 699
SIC 62 - Security and Commodity Brokers 705
SIC 63 - Insurance Carriers 709
SIC 64 - Insurance Agents, Brokers, and Service 730
SIC 65 - Real Estate 731
SIC 67 - Holding and Other Investment Offices .736
SIC 70 - Hotels and Other Lodging Places 738
SIC 72 - Personal Services 741
SIC 73 - Business Services 745
SIC 75 - Auto Repair, Services, and Parking 770
SIC 76 - Miscellaneous Repair Services 774
SIC 78 - Motion Pictures 777
SIC 79 - Amusement and Recreation Services 781
SIC 80 - Health Services 793
SIC 81 - Legal Services 800
SIC 82 - Educational Services 801
SIC 83 - Social Services 804
SIC 84 - Museums, Botanical, Zoological Gardens 807
SIC 86 - Membership Organizations 809
SIC 87 - Engineering and Management Services .812
SIC 92 - Justice, Public Order, and Safety 818
SIC 94 - Administration of Human Resources 819
SIC 95 - Environmental Quality and Housing 820
SIC 96 - Administration of Economic Programs .821
SIC 97 - National Security and International Affairs 822

Indexes

Source Index 823
Place Names Index 863
Products, Services, Names, and Issues Index 877
Company Index 895
Brands Index 945

Appendix I - Industrial Classifications

SIC Coverage 967
NAICS Coverage 977
ISIC Coverage 989
Harmonized Code Coverage 995

Appendix II - Annotated Source List 997

TABLE OF TOPICS

The *Table of Topics* lists all topics used in *Market Share Reporter* in alphabetical order. One or more page references follow each topic; the page references identify the starting point where the topic is shown. The same topic name may be used under different SICs; therefore, in some cases, more than one page reference is provided. Roman numerals indicate volume number.

Abrasives, pp. I-392-393

Access Equipment, p. I-431

Accounting Services, p. II-813

Acetic Acid, p. I-353

Acoustical Instruments, p. II-535

Activated Carbon, p. I-297

Acute Care, p. II-805

Adhesives and Sealants, pp. I-358-359

Adult Incontinence Products, p. I-274

Adult Living Facilities, p. II-805

Advanced Ceramics, p. I-390

Advertising, pp. II-745-749

Aeronautical, Nautical and Navigational Instruments, p. II-532

Aerosols, p. I-361

Aerospace and Defense, pp. II-527-529

Agents, p. II-781

Aggregate, p. I-57

Agricultural Products, p. I-357

Agricultural Retailing, p. II-633

Air Care, pp. I-362-363

Air Cargo, p. II-585

Air Purification Equipment, p. I-457

Aircraft, pp. II-518-519

Aircraft and Aeronautical Equipment Wholesalers, p. II-625

Aircraft Insurance, p. II-717

Aircraft Maintenance, Repair and Overhaul, pp. II-519-520

Aircraft Parts, p. II-521

Airlines, pp. II-581-585

Airports, p. II-585

Alcoholic Beverages, pp. I-180-181

Alkalies and Chlorine, p. I-294

Allied Line Insurance, p. II-717

Alumina, p. I-399

Aluminum, pp. I-399-400, 402-403

Aluminum Foil Pans, p. I-402

Aluminum Sheet, Plate and Foil, p. I-402

Ambulance Services, p. II-571

Amusement Parks, p. II-787

Analgesics, pp. I-306-311, 672

Analytical and Life Science Instruments, p. II-532

Anchor Handling Tug Supply Vessels, p. I-428

Animal Health, p. I-311

Animal Slaughtering, p. I-88

Anodes, p. II-494

Antifreeze, p. I-363

Antimony, p. I-45

Apartments, p. II-732

App Stores, p. II-664

Apparel, pp. I-241-243, 245-247

Apparel Accessories, pp. I-249-250

Apparel Agents and Brokers, p. II-629

Apparel Retailing, pp. II-654-657

Apparel Wholesalers, p. II-629

Appliance Repair, p. II-774

Appliance Retailing, pp. II-662-663

Appliances, pp. II-465-466

Apprenticeship Training, p. II-803

Aquaculture, p. I-34

Arcade, Food and Entertainment Complexes, pp. II-786-787

Architectural Services, pp. II-812-813

Armored Vehicles and Tank Parts, pp. II-530-531

Art, Drama, and Music Schools, p. II-781

Art Goods Wholesalers, p. II-631

Artificial Insemination, p. I-35

Artificial Insemination Equipment, p. I-424

Artificial Sweeteners, p. I-353

Arts, Crafts and Sewing Stores, p. II-682

Arts and Crafts, p. II-561

Asbestos, p. I-61

Asian Foods, p. I-213

Asphalt Paving, p. I-367

Asphalt Shingles, pp. I-367-368

Auction Houses, p. II-807

Audio and Video Media Reproduction, p. II-778

Audio Production Studios, p. II-765

Auto Dealerships, p. II-651

Auto Insurance, pp. II-717-719

Auto Loans, p. II-700

Auto Parts, pp. II-511-517

Auto Parts Stores, p. II-651

Auto Rental, p. II-770

Automated Teller Machines, p. I-456

Automated Tire Inflation Systems, p. I-442

Automobile and Motorcycle Wholesalers, p. II-621

Automobile Clubs, p. II-811

Automotive Ceilings, p. I-239

Automotive Electronics, p. II-499

Automotive Repair, pp. II-771-772

Automotive Seating, pp. I-265-266

Automotive Treatments, p. I-363

Autonomous Underwater Vehicles, p. II-535

Autos, pp. II-500-507

Baby Care, pp. I-1, 331, II-567

Baby Food, p. I-111

Baby Wipes, p. I-274

Backpacks, p. I-254

Bacon, p. I-91

Bagels, pp. I-144-145

Bakeries, p. II-650

Bakery Products, pp. I-145-149

Bakeware, pp. I-1, 387

Baking Mixes and Prepared Food, p. I-213

Bank Holding Companies, p. II-736

Banking, pp. II-687-697

Barbecue Sauces, p. I-116
Barite, p. I-61
Batteries, pp. II-496-498
Battery Separators, p. II-494
Bauxite, pp. I-45, 297
Bearings, pp. I-414, 441-442
Bed and Breakfasts, p. II-738
Bedding, pp. I-263-264
Bedding Stores, p. II-660
Beef, p. I-29
Beer, pp. I-181-185
Beer, Wine, and Liquor Stores,
   p. II-677
Beer and Ale Wholesalers, p. II-631
Behavioral Health, p. II-797
Belts, p. I-250
Bentonite, p. I-59
Beverages, p. I-181
Beverageware, p. I-387
Bicycle Retailing, p. II-678
Bicycles, p. II-525
Biological Products, p. I-316
Bioplastics, p. I-299
Biotechnology, pp. I-316-317
Bleach, p. I-324
Blinds and Shades, pp. I-250-251
Blood and Organ Banks, p. II-798
Blood Pressure Kits, p. I-317
Blow Molding, p. I-379
Blowers, p. I-442
Blu-Ray DVD Replication Machines,
   p. I-438
Boat Dealers, p. II-652
Boat Repair Services, p. II-775
Boats, pp. II-522-524
Body Scrubbers, p. II-567
Boilers, p. I-412
Bolts, Nuts, Screws, Rivets and
   Washers, pp. I-413-414
Book Printing, p. I-289
Book Retailing, pp. II-678-679
Books, pp. I-285-287
Boron, p. I-297
Bottled Tea, p. I-190
Bottled Water, pp. I-191-193
Bowling Alleys, p. II-782
Boxes, pp. I-270-271
Bread, pp. I-150-151
Bread Retailing, p. II-650
Breakfast/Cereal/Snack Bars,
   pp. I-156-157
Breath Fresheners, p. I-157
Bridge and Tunnel Construction,
   p. I-71

Broilers, pp. I-31-32
Brooms, Brushes and Mops,
   pp. II-564-565
Browning and Cooking Sprays,
   p. I-178
Building Exterior Cleaning, p. II-753
Building Inspection Services,
   p. II-766
Building Leasing, pp. II-731, 733
Building Materials, p. I-1
Buns and Rolls, p. I-151
Burglary Insurance, p. II-719
Bus and Recreational Vehicle Whole-
   salers, p. II-621
Buses, pp. II-509, 571
Business Associations, p. II-809
Business Coaching, p. II-766
Business Processing Outsourcing,
   p. II-762
Butter, pp. I-97-98
c-Si Cell Equipment, p. I-409
Cabinets, pp. I-256-257
Cable, p. I-444
Cable Television, pp. II-612-613
Cadmium, p. I-400
Calculators, p. I-456
Camcorder and Digicam Retailing,
   p. II-681
Camera Stores, p. II-681
Cameras, pp. II-550-551
Candles, p. II-568
Canned Food, pp. I-112-113, 116-
   118
Canned Food Wholesalers, p. II-629
Capacitors, pp. II-493-494
Caps and Closures, p. I-415
Car Audio Retailing, p. II-663
Car Transportation, p. II-589
Car Washes, p. II-772
Carbon Black, p. I-361
Carbon Nanotubes, p. II-465
Carbon Paper and Inked Ribbon,
   p. II-564
Carburetors, Pistons, Rings and
   Valves, p. I-460
Carpet Cleaning Services, p. II-742
Carpets and Rugs, pp. I-237-238
Carsharing, p. II-766
Casinos, p. II-789
Caskets, p. II-566
Castings, p. I-404
Catalog Retailing, p. II-682
Cathodes, p. II-494
Cattle, p. I-30

CD-R Media, p. II-499
Celebrity and Sports Agents,
   p. II-783
Cellular Phone Accessories, p. I-2
Cellular Phones, pp. II-481-482
Cement, pp. I-388-389
Cemeteries, p. II-735
Ceramic Tile, p. I-390
Cereal, pp. I-136-137
Chain Saws, p. I-407
Chalk, p. II-562
Charcoal, p. I-363
Charities, p. II-805
Cheese, pp. I-99-102
Chemicals, pp. I-293-294
Chicken, p. I-95
Child Care, p. II-804
China, Glassware, and Crockery
   Wholesalers, p. II-622
Chip Cards, p. II-488
Chiropractors, p. II-794
Chocolate, pp. I-170-173
Chocolate Retailing, p. II-649
Christmas, p. I-2
Christmas Trees, p. I-2
Churches, p. II-810
Cigarettes, pp. I-227-230
Cigars, p. I-230
Circuit Breakers, p. II-463
Civic Organizations, p. II-809
Claims Adjusting, p. II-730
Clay, p. I-59
Clay Bricks and Blocks, p. I-390
Cleaning Products, pp. I-324-327
Clocks, p. II-552
Closet Storage, p. I-3
Cloud Computing, p. I-447
Coal, p. I-48
Coal Wholesalers, p. II-624
Coated Fabrics, p. I-239
Coated Paper, pp. I-271-272
Cobalt, p. I-43
Cocoa, pp. I-173-174
Coffee, pp. I-201-204
Coffee, Tea and Powdered Drink
   Wholesalers, p. II-630
Coffee and Snack Shops, p. II-666
Coffee Creamers, p. I-102
Coffee Drinks, p. I-204
Collection Services, p. II-750
College Book Stores, p. II-679
Colleges and Universities, p. II-802
Colored Pencils, p. II-562
Comic Books, p. I-283

Commercial Laundries, p. II-742

Commercial Line Insurance, p. II-719

Commercial Photography, p. II-751

Commercial Vehicles, pp. II-509-510

Commodity Contracts, p. II-707

Communication Equipment Repair, p. II-775

Communications Equipment Wholesalers, p. II-624

Community Food Services, p. II-804

Composite Wood, p. I-259

Compressors, p. I-442

Computer and Office Machine Repair, p. II-763

Computer Data Storage, pp. I-452-453

Computer Facilities Management Services, p. II-763

Computer Peripheral Wholesalers, p. II-623

Computer Peripherals, p. I-453

Computer Printers, pp. I-453-455

Computer Rental and Leasing, p. II-763

Computer Repair and Maintenance, p. II-763

Computer Retailing, p. II-664

Computer Systems Design, p. II-764

Computers, pp. I-448-451

Concerts, p. II-781

Concessions, p. II-790

Concrete Contracting, p. I-75

Concrete Pipe and Block, p. I-391

Condiments, p. I-126

Condoms, p. I-376

Confectionery Products, pp. I-157-168

Construction, p. I-64

Construction Equipment, pp. I-426-428

Consulting Services, p. II-816

Consumer Electronics, pp. II-475-477

Consumer Electronics Repair and Maintenance, pp. II-774-775

Consumer Spending, p. I-3

Contact Lenses, pp. II-548-549

Container Leasing, p. II-755

Containerboard, p. I-269

Containers and Pallets, p. I-258

Contract Research Organizations, p. II-814

Contractors, p. I-71

Convenience Stores, pp. II-635-636

Convention and Visitors Bureaus, p. II-766

Conveyors, p. I-431

Cookie Dough, p. I-139

Cookies, pp. I-152-154

Cooking and Salad Oils, p. I-178

Cooking Equipment, pp. II-466-468

Cooking Sauces, p. I-126

Cookware, p. I-415

Copper, pp. I-39-40, 398-399

Copper Foundries, p. I-404

Copper Wire, p. I-404

Cork, p. I-260

Corn, pp. I-16-17

Corn Flour, p. I-140

Correctional Products, p. II-562

Cosmetic Storage, p. I-379

Cosmetics, pp. I-331-333

Cosmetics, Beauty Supplies, and Perfume Stores, p. II-686

Costume Jewelry, p. II-564

Cottage Cheese, p. I-105

Cotton, pp. I-18, 35

Cough Syrup, p. I-168

Countertops, pp. I-255-256

Couplings, p. I-419

Coupons, p. I-3

Court Reporting Services, p. II-752

Crackers, p. I-154

Cranes, Hoists and Monorail Systems, pp. I-432-433

Crayons, p. II-563

Cream Cheese, p. I-102

Credit Cards, p. II-699

Credit Reporting Agencies, p. II-750

Credit Unions, p. II-698

Croutons, p. I-152

Cruise Lines, p. II-579

Crushed Stone, p. I-57

Custodial Equipment Wholesalers, p. II-625

Cutlery, p. I-406

Cyclic Crude, p. I-352

Dairy Alternatives, p. I-106

Dairy Foods, p. I-97

Dairy Product Wholesalers, pp. II-629-630

Dance Schools, p. II-781

Data Processing and Hosting, p. II-762

Data Processing and Outsourcing, p. II-762

Dating Services, p. II-743

Debit Cards, pp. II-699-700

Debt Collection Agencies, p. II-750

Decking, p. I-259

Decorated Apparel, p. I-254

Defense, p. II-822

Demolition Work, p. I-76

Dental Equipment, pp. II-547-548

Dental Implants, p. II-548

Dental Laboratories, p. II-797

Dental Tools, p. II-469

Dentists, p. II-793

Deodorants, p. I-334

Department Stores, p. II-635

Design Industry, p. II-812

Desserts, p. I-214

Diagnostic Imaging, p. II-548

Diagnostics, p. I-317

Dialysis Industry, p. II-798

Diamonds, pp. I-61-62

Diapers, pp. I-274-275

Diesel Cars, p. II-507

Diet Foods, p. I-214

Digital Cameras, p. II-551

Digital Film Projectors, p. II-549

Digital Video Recorders, p. II-613

Dimension Stone, p. I-57

Dip Mixes, p. I-214

Dips, p. I-106

Direct-Broadcast Satellite Equipment, p. II-483

Direct Marketing, p. II-750

Direct Selling, p. II-683

Directories and Mailing Lists, p. I-289

Dishwashers, p. II-471

Dishwashing Detergents, pp. I-318-320

Disposable Plates and Bowls, p. I-275

Doctors, p. II-793

Document Preparation, pp. II-766-767

Dog Parks, p. II-820

Dollar Stores, p. II-637

Doors, p. I-411

Dredging, p. I-72

Dried and Dehydrated Foods, p. I-214

Dried Cranberries, p. I-125

Drill Pipe, pp. I-397-398

Drinking Places, p. II-671

Drive-In Theaters, p. II-779

Drug Stores, pp. II-672-676

Drug Wholesalers, p. II-628

Drugs, pp. I-311-315
Dry, Condensed and Evaporated Products, pp. I-102-103
Dry Packaged Dinners, pp. I-215-216
Drywall Contracting, p. I-74
Ducts, p. I-413
DVD Retailing, p. II-664
E-Books, pp. I-287, II-679
E-Reader Displays, p. II-495
E-Readers, p. II-477
Ear Care, p. I-334
Earthquake Insurance, pp. II-719-720
Education, p. II-801
Educational Services, p. II-803
Eggs, p. I-32
Electric Vehicles, pp. II-507-508
Electrical Contracting, p. I-73
Electrical Equipment, p. II-464
Electrical Equipment and Wiring Wholesalers, p. II-624
Electrical Transmission and Distribution Equipment, p. II-461
Electricity, pp. II-615-617
Electronic Commerce, pp. II-598-599
Electronic Components, p. II-495
Electronic Ink, p. II-495
Electronic Manufacturing Services, p. II-461
Electronic Trainers and Teaching Machines, p. II-485
Electronics Distribution, p. II-624
Electronics Retailing, p. II-663
Electroplating and Polishing, p. I-416
Elevators and Escalators, p. I-431
Embroidery Shops, p. I-254
Emergency Department Contractors, p. II-799
Employment Services, p. II-816
Energy Drinks, pp. I-193-194
Energy Shots, p. I-194
Engineered Wood Products, p. I-259
Engineering Services, p. II-812
Engines, pp. I-422-424
English Muffins, p. I-152
Entertainment, p. I-3
Equines, p. I-33
Ethanol, p. I-353
Ethnic Food, p. I-216
Ethylene, p. I-354
Excavation and Foundation Work, p. I-76

Excess and Surplus Insurance, p. II-720
Excipients, p. I-315
Executive Search Industry, pp. II-816-817
Explosives, p. I-360
Explosives Trace Detection, p. II-534
Express Delivery Services, p. II-575
Eye Care, p. I-334
Eyewear, pp. II-549-550
Fabric Mills, p. I-233
Fabric Softeners, pp. I-327-328
Fabricated Metal Products, p. I-396
Facial Tissue, p. I-276
Family Planning Centers, p. II-799
Fans, p. I-443
Farm Loans, p. II-700
Farm Machinery, pp. I-424-425
Farm Warehousing and Storage, p. II-576
Farmers Markets, p. II-649
Farms, p. I-34
Fasteners, Buttons, Needles and Pins, p. II-564
Fats and Oils, pp. I-176-177
Federal Contracting, p. II-821
Feedlots, p. I-29
Feldspar, p. I-59
Feminine Hygiene Products, pp. I-276-277
Fencing, p. I-396
Ferroalloy Products, p. I-396
Ferrochrome, p. I-396
Fertilizers, pp. I-355-357
Fibers, p. I-303
Film, p. II-551
Film Distribution, p. II-778
Filters, pp. I-444-445
Financial Information, p. II-707
Financial Transactions, p. II-698
Fine Arts Schools, p. II-801
Fire and Allied Insurance, p. II-720
Fire Safety Equipment Wholesalers, p. II-627
First Aid Products, pp. II-541-542
Fish Markets, p. II-649
Fishing, p. I-37
Flat Panel Displays, p. II-495
Flatware, p. II-555
Flavorings and Fragrances, p. I-354
Fleet Management, p. II-770
Flood Insurance, p. II-720
Floor Care Equipment, p. II-472

Flooring, pp. I-4, 255, II-566, 622, 659-660
Florist and Nursery Supply Wholesalers, p. II-631
Florists, p. II-684
Flour, p. I-136
Flowers and Plants, p. I-27
Fluid Power, p. I-460
Folding Campers, p. II-530
Food Additives, p. I-216
Food and Drinks, pp. I-77-84
Food Colorings and Flavorings, p. I-198
Food Containers, p. I-270
Food Machinery, p. I-438
Food Preservatives, p. I-217
Food Specialties, p. I-217
Foodservice, pp. II-666-667
Foodservice Disposables, pp. I-270-271
Foodservice Equipment and Supplies, p. II-625
Foot Care, p. I-335
Footwear, pp. I-373-375, 381-382
For-Profit Education, p. II-802
Forestry, p. I-36
Forgings, p. I-394
Foundries, pp. I-404, II-488
Fractional Jet Industry, p. II-520
Fragrances, pp. I-335-336
Franchises, p. II-736
Fresh-Cut Fruit, p. I-217
Fresh-Cut Vegetables, p. I-218
Frozen Desserts, pp. I-103-104
Frozen Foods, pp. I-130-135
Frozen Fruit, p. I-129
Frozen Pies, p. I-155
Frozen Pizza, pp. I-135-136
Frozen Vegetables, pp. I-129-130
Fruit, pp. I-22-27
Fruit and Vegetable Markets, p. II-649
Fruit and Vegetable Wholesalers, p. II-630
Fruit Drink Mixes, p. I-218
Fruits and Vegetable Processing, p. I-118
Fuel Cells, p. I-410
Functional Beverages, p. I-194
Functional Foods, p. I-84
Funeral Services, p. II-743
Fur, p. I-249
Furniture, pp. I-261-263
Furniture Rental, p. II-755

Furniture Stores, p. II-659

Furniture Upholstery and Repair, p. II-775

Furniture Wholesalers, p. II-622

Gambling, p. II-790

Garbage, Trash and Leaf Bags, p. I-272

Garlic Spreads, p. I-198

Garment Repair and Alterations, p. II-767

Garnets, p. I-62

Gas and Fire Detection Equipment, pp. II-485-486

Gas Cans, p. I-378

Gas Stations, p. II-652

Gaskets, Packing and Sealing Devices, pp. I-375-376

Gearboxes, p. I-414

Gears, p. I-444

Gemstones, p. I-62

Generators, p. II-464

Geosynthetics, p. I-62

Germanium, p. I-401

Gift, Card and Novelty Stores, pp. II-681-682

Glass, pp. I-385-387

Glass Containers, p. I-387

Glassware, p. I-387

Glazing and Curtain Wall Contracting, p. I-75

Gloves and Mittens, pp. I-249-250

Glue, p. I-359

Gluten-Free Products, p. I-85

Gold, pp. I-41-42

Golf Courses, p. II-786

Government Building Construction, p. I-69

Government Contracting, p. II-822

Government Spending, p. II-819

Grain and Field Bean Wholesalers, p. II-630

Granola Bars, p. I-168

Graphic Design, p. II-752

Graphite, pp. I-62, II-465

Gravy Mixes, p. I-218

Great Lakes Transportation, p. II-579

Green Design, p. II-812

Greeting Cards, pp. I-292, II-680

Grocery Stores, pp. II-639-648

Grocery Wholesalers, p. II-629

Guided Missile and Space Vehicle Parts, p. II-529

Gum, pp. I-174-175

Guns and Ammunition, p. I-416

Gym and Exercise Equipment, pp. II-558-559

Gyms, p. II-785

Gypsum, p. I-63

Hair Accessories, p. II-568

Hair and Nail Salons, p. II-742

Hair Care, pp. I-336-339

Hair Loss and Treatment, p. II-744

Halloween, p. I-5

Hammers, p. I-408

Hand Tools, p. I-408

Handbag, Luggage and Accessory Stores, p. II-682

Handbags and Purses, p. I-384

Hardware Stores, pp. II-632-633

Hardwood, p. I-257

Hats and Caps, p. I-249

Headsets, p. II-482

Health Food Stores, p. II-676

Health Insurance, pp. II-713-716

Health Publishing, p. I-289

Healthcare Management Consulting, p. II-817

Hearths, p. I-458

Heating and Cooling, pp. I-458-459, 469

Heavy Equipment Rental, p. II-754

Heavy Industrial Facility Construction, p. I-72

Helicopters, pp. II-520-521

Hides, Skins, and Pelts Wholesalers, p. II-630

High-Fructose Corn Syrup, p. I-156

Historical Sites, p. II-807

Hobby Industry, p. II-556

Hogs, pp. I-30-31

Home Electronics and Appliance Wholesaling, p. II-624

Home Health Care, p. II-797

Home Health Care Equipment Rental, p. II-754

Home Improvement Stores, p. II-632

Home Organization Products, pp. I-5-6

Home Repair Industry, p. II-775

Home Shopping, p. II-683

Home Video industry, p. II-780

Homefurnishings, pp. I-251-253, 660-661

Homeland Security, p. II-534

Homeowners Insurance, pp. II-721-724

Hospice Care, p. II-796

Hospitals, pp. II-796-797

Hot Dogs, p. I-92

Hotel Construction, p. I-70

Hotels, pp. II-738-739

Human Machine Interfaces, p. I-445

Hunting, p. I-38

Hybrid Cars, p. II-508

Hydroelectric Power, p. II-617

Hypermarkets, p. II-635

Ice, p. I-211

Ice Cream, pp. I-104-105

Incinerators, p. II-618

Indium, p. I-297

Inductors, p. II-461

Industrial Feed, p. I-144

Industrial Gases, pp. I-295-296

Industrial Laundries, p. II-742

Industrial Laundries and Linen Suppliers, p. II-741

Industrial Machinery, pp. I-423, 460

Industrial Trucks, Tractors and Stackers, p. I-433

Infant Formula, pp. I-113-114

Information Technology, pp. II-762-763

Injection Molding, p. I-379

Ink, p. I-360

Inorganic Chemicals, p. I-298

Inorganic Dyes and Pigments, p. I-296

Insect Repellents, p. I-364

Institutional Cleaning, p. I-320

Institutional Furniture, p. I-265

Insulation, p. I-393

Insurance, pp. II-709-712

Inter-Dealer Brokers, p. II-707

Internet, p. II-600

Internet Protocol Television, p. II-613

Internet Service Providers, pp. II-601-602

Internet Sites, pp. II-602-608

Investment Banking, pp. II-705-706

Iodine, p. I-298

IPOs, p. II-706

Iron Ore, p. I-39

Iron Ore Pellets, p. I-398

Iron Oxide, p. I-296

Irradiation Apparatus, p. II-548

Isocyanates, p. I-352

Jams and Jellies, pp. I-118-119

Janitorial Equipment and Supplies, p. I-6

Janitorial Services, p. II-753

Jewelry, p. II-554

Jewelry, Watch and Silverware
  Wholesalers, p. II-627
Jewelry Materials and Lapidary
  Work, p. II-555
Jewelry Retailing, p. II-680
Job Training and Career Counseling,
  p. II-804
Juices, pp. I-119-123
Juvenile Product Retailing, p. II-686
Kaolin, p. I-59
Ketchup, p. I-124
Kilns, p. I-438
Knitting Mills, pp. I-235-236
Lab Testing, p. II-814
Labels, p. I-290
Laboratory Instruments, pp. II-532-
  533
Lace, Embroidery and Ribbons,
  p. I-237
Ladders, p. I-421
Laminates, p. I-377
Lamps, pp. II-472-473
Land Ownership, p. I-36
Landfills, p. II-618
Landscaping Products, p. I-6
Landscaping Services, p. I-35
Language Instruction, p. II-803
Language Services, p. II-767
Lard, p. I-88
Lasers, p. II-488
Laundromats and Drycleaners,
  p. II-741
Laundry Aids, pp. I-328-329
Laundry and Garment Services,
  p. II-741
Laundry Detergents, pp. I-320-321
Laundry Equipment, pp. II-468-469
Laundry Routes, p. II-742
Laundry Storage, p. I-6
Lawn and Garden Consumables,
  p. I-357
Lawn and Garden Equipment,
  pp. I-425-426
Lead, pp. I-40-41
Leather Tanning and Finishing,
  p. I-381
Legal & Regulatory Publishing,
  p. I-290
Legal Services, p. II-800
Lens Shutters, p. II-551
Lenses, p. II-550
Liability Insurance, pp. II-724, 728
Libraries, p. II-802
Licensed Merchandise, p. I-7

Life Insurance, p. II-712
Life Sciences, p. II-816
Lift Trucks, p. I-433
Light Bulbs, p. II-474
Light Vehicles, p. II-508
Lighters, p. II-568
Lighting, pp. II-473-474
Lighting Fixtures, p. II-475
Lime, pp. I-391-392
Limousine Services, p. II-571
Linear Motion Technology, p. II-533
Linens and Draperies Wholesalers,
  p. II-622
Lingerie, p. I-248
Lip Care, pp. I-339-340
Liquor, pp. I-187-190
Lithium, p. I-298
LNG Tankers, p. II-578
Lobbying Groups, p. II-810
Locker Accessories, p. II-568
Locksmiths, p. II-776
Logging, p. I-255
Logistics, p. II-573
Low-Voltage Products, p. II-462
Lubricants, pp. I-368-369
Luggage, pp. I-382-384
Lumber Agents and Brokers,
  p. II-622
Lumber and Building Materials,
  p. II-632
Lunch Meat, pp. I-92-93
Luxury Goods, pp. I-7-8
Machine Shops, p. I-460
Machine Tools, pp. I-434-435
Machinery Repair and Maintenance,
  p. II-776
Magazines, pp. I-283-284, 684-685
Malpractice Insurance, p. II-724
Malt, p. I-185
Malt Beverages, p. I-185
Manganese, p. I-396
Manufactured Home Leasing,
  p. II-733
Manufactured Homes, p. I-258
Margarine, Spreads and Butter,
  p. I-98
Margarines, Spreads and Butter,
  pp. I-98-99
Marinas, p. II-580
Marine Insurance, pp. II-724-725
Marine Machinery Wholesalers,
  p. II-626
Markers, p. II-563
Marketing Research, p. II-814

Marking Devices, p. II-564
Masonry Contracting, pp. I-73-74
Massively Multiplayer Online Role-
  Playing Games, p. II-608
Materials Handling Equipment,
  pp. I-433-434
Materials Handling Equipment
  Wholesalers, p. II-625
Materials Recovery, p. II-619
Mayonnaise and Sandwich Spreads,
  p. I-126
Measuring, Testing and Navigational
  Instruments, p. II-533
Meat, pp. I-89-91
Meat Sauces and Marinades, p. I-124
Meat Snacks, p. I-93
Medical Beds, p. I-266
Medical Case Management, p. II-799
Medical Equipment Maintenance,
  p. II-774
Medical Equipment Rental and Leas-
  ing, p. II-754
Medical Products, pp. II-536-541,
  543-544
Medium-Density Fiberboard,
  p. I-260
Membrane Technologies, pp. I-445-
  446
Memory Cards, p. II-487
Metal Cans, p. I-405
Metal Coating and Engraving,
  p. I-416
Metal Containers, p. I-405
Metal Foil, p. I-421
Metal Powders, p. I-421
Metal Sales Offices Wholesalers,
  p. II-623
Metal Tanks, p. I-413
Metalworking Fluids, p. I-370
Meteorological Services, p. II-767
Meters and Test Devices, pp. II-533-
  534
Mexican Foods, p. I-218
Mexican Sauces, p. I-124
Micro Reaction Technology, p. I-439
Milk, pp. I-106-109
Milkshakes, p. I-109
Mill Rolls, p. I-394
Millwork, p. I-256
Miniature Golf Courses, p. II-786
Mining Equipment, p. I-428
Mink, p. I-33
Mints, p. I-169
Moist Towelettes, p. I-277

Molds, p. I-436

Molybdenum, p. I-46

Mortgage Guaranty Insurance, p. II-729

Mortgage Loans, pp. II-701-703

Motion Pictures, pp. II-777, 779

Motor Vehicle Stampings, p. I-412

Motor Vehicle Towing, p. II-773

Motorcoaches, p. II-571

Motorcycle and Powersports Dealers, p. II-653

Motorcycles, pp. II-526-527

Motorhomes, pp. II-517-518

Motors, p. II-465

Movie Theaters, pp. II-779-780

Multifamily Construction, p. I-69

Multifamily Lending, p. II-704

Multiperil Insurance, pp. II-725-726

Multiple Peril Insurance, p. II-726

Municipal Building Construction, p. I-70

Museums, p. II-807

Mushrooms, p. I-28

Music, pp. II-480-481

Music Retailing, p. II-665

Musical Instrument Stores, p. II-665

Musical Instruments, pp. II-555-556

Mustard, p. I-127

Nail Care, p. I-340

Nails, Staples, Tacks, Spikes and Brads, p. I-397

Nasal Care, p. I-340

National Parks, p. II-807

Natural Gas, p. I-50

Natural Gas Liquids, p. I-53

Networking Equipment, pp. II-486-487

Networks, p. II-761

News Syndicates, p. II-765

Newspapers, pp. I-282-283

Nickel, pp. I-44, 403

Nightclubs, p. II-671

Non-Lethal Weapons, p. I-417

Nonferrous Metal Shaping, p. I-403

Nonwoven Fabrics, pp. I-239-240

Nuclear Energy, p. II-617

Nursing Care, p. II-796

Nutraceuticals, p. I-304

Nutrition Bars, pp. I-169-170

Nuts, pp. I-24, 175-176

Office Equipment Wholesalers, p. II-623

Office Furniture, p. I-264

Office Furniture Retailing, p. II-659

Office Machinery, p. I-456

Office Machinery Rental and Leasing, p. II-755

Office Space Construction, p. I-70

Office Stationery Wholesaling, p. II-628

Office Supplies, p. I-274

Oil, pp. I-51-52

Oil and Gas, p. I-52

Oil and Gas Equipment, pp. I-428-430

Oil and Gas Pipeline Construction, p. I-72

Oil and Gas Wells, pp. I-53-54

Oil Change Industry, p. II-773

Oil Field Services, pp. I-54-56

Oilseeds, p. I-177

Olive Oil, p. I-179

Online Brokers, p. II-708

Online Gaming, p. II-608

Online Movies, p. II-780

Online Music, p. II-609

Online Ticketing, p. II-791

Online Video, p. II-609

Operating Room Equipment, p. I-266

Ophthalmic Goods, p. II-550

Optical Goods Stores, p. II-685

Optometrists, pp. II-794-795

Oral Care, pp. I-341-343

Orchestras and Chamber Music Groups, p. II-782

Ordnance, p. I-417

Organic Chemicals, p. I-354

Organic Food Retailing, p. II-649

Organic Foods, pp. I-85-86

Oriented Strand Board, p. I-260

Original Design Manufacturing, p. II-461

Orthopedic Appliances, pp. II-544-545

Oscillators, p. II-489

Outdoor Furniture and Grills, p. I-8

Outlet Centers, p. II-637

Outpatient Mental Health & Substance Abuse Centers, p. II-798

Packaged Food, pp. I-86-87

Packaging, pp. I-8-11

Packaging Machinery, pp. I-443-444

Packing and Crating, p. II-589

Paint Stores, p. II-632

Painting Contracting, p. I-73

Paints and Coatings, pp. I-350-352

Palladium, p. I-46

Pantyhose, p. I-234

Paper, pp. I-267-268

Paper Bags, pp. I-273-274

Paper Machinery, p. I-438

Paper Towels, pp. I-277-278

Paperboard, p. I-269

Parking Lots and Garages, p. II-771

Pasta, pp. I-211-213

Patents, p. II-736

Patient Handling Equipment, p. I-266

Pawnshops, p. II-677

Pay Television, pp. II-613-614

Payment Cards, p. II-487

Payment Terminals, p. I-456

Payroll Services, p. II-813

PBIED and VBIED Equipment, p. II-535

PC Cameras, p. I-455

Peanut Butter, p. I-219

Pencils, p. II-563

Pens, pp. II-560-561

Pensions, p. II-729

People Screening Technologies, p. II-535

Performing Arts Companies, p. II-782

Personal Care Products, pp. I-343-346

Personal Digital Assistants, p. I-451

Personal Line Insurance, p. II-726

Personal Watercraft, p. II-531

Pest Control, pp. II-752-753

Pesticides, p. I-358

Pet Food, pp. I-140-143

Pet Groomers, p. II-686

Pet Products, p. II-569

Pet Stores, p. II-686

Petrochemicals, p. I-353

Petroleum Products Wholesalers, p. II-631

Petroleum Refining, p. I-367

Pets, p. I-11

Pharmacy Benefit Managers, p. II-676

Phosphate Rock, p. I-60

Photofinishing, p. II-765

Photography, p. II-742

Photovoltaics, p. I-410

Pipe, p. I-11

Pipelines, p. II-587

Pizza, p. I-219

Pizza Dough, p. I-139

Pizza Kits, p. I-219

Planning and Development Organizations, p. II-767

Plaster Contracting, p. I-73

Plastic Bags, p. I-273

Plastic Film and Sheet, pp. I-376-377

Plastic Pipe, p. I-378

Plastic Plates, Sheets and Shapes, p. I-377

Plastic Products, p. I-379

Plastics, pp. I-299-301

Plastics Machinery, p. I-439

Plate Work, p. I-416

Platinum, pp. I-46, 401

Plumbing Products, pp. I-391, 409

Podiatrists, p. II-795

Polishes, p. I-329

Political Action Committees, p. II-810

Polyester, p. I-301

Polyurethane Foam, p. I-378

Pork, pp. I-95-96

Portable Navigation Devices, p. II-532

Portable Toilet Rental, p. II-755

Ports, p. II-580

Postal Service, p. II-577

Potash, p. I-60

Potassium Sulfate, p. I-364

Potatoes, p. I-20

Poultry, p. I-96

Poultry Wholesalers, p. II-630

Power Products, p. II-462

Power Tools, p. I-436

Power Toothbrushes, p. II-469

Precipitated Silica, p. I-58

Prefabricated Buildings, p. I-413

Prefabricated Housing, p. I-258

Pregnancy Tests, p. I-317

Prepaid Cards, p. II-698

Prescription Dispensing, pp. II-676-677

Printed Circuit Boards, pp. II-487-488

Printing, pp. I-290-292

Prisons, p. II-818

Projectors, p. II-551

Promotional Auditing, p. II-815

Promotional Industry, p. II-751

Promotional Products, pp. I-11-12

Propane Retailing, p. II-683

Property Insurance, pp. II-726-727

Proppants, pp. I-58-59

Public Relations Industry, p. II-817

Publishing, p. I-282

Pulp, p. I-267

Pumps, pp. I-440-441

Purpose-Built Backup Appliances, p. I-453

PV Equipment, p. I-410

Quick Printing, p. II-751

Racetracks, pp. II-784-785

Radio Broadcasting, pp. II-611-612

Radios, p. II-484

Railroad Car Rental and Leasing, p. II-755

Railroad Equipment, pp. II-524-525

Railroads, p. II-570

Raisins, p. I-125

Rare Earth, pp. I-46-47

Razor Blades, pp. I-406-407

Ready Meals, p. I-219

Ready-Mix Concrete, p. I-389

Real Estate, pp. II-732-734

Real Estate Investment Trusts, p. II-737

Recreational and Vacation Camps, p. II-740

Recyclable Material Wholesalers, p. II-626

Refractories, pp. I-390, 393

Refrigerated and Frozen Foods, p. I-88

Refrigerated Warehousing, p. II-576

Refrigeration Equipment Wholesalers, p. II-624

Refrigerators, p. II-468

Rehabilitation Hospitals, p. II-797

Reinsurance Industry, p. II-730

Relays and Controls, p. II-465

Religion, p. II-810

Remediation and Environmental Cleanup Services, p. II-620

Remodeling, pp. I-64-65

Remote Controllers, p. II-484

Remotely Operated Vehicles, p. II-536

Renewable Energy, p. II-615

Repossession Services, p. II-768

Research & Development, pp. II-815-816

Residential Construction, pp. I-65-69

Restaurants, pp. II-668-671

Retail Space Construction, p. I-70

Retailers, p. II-634

Retailing, p. II-634

Reverse Mortgages, p. II-704

RFID Tags, p. II-487

Rice, pp. I-15-16, 137-139

Road and Highway Construction, p. I-71

Robotics, p. I-446

Roofing Contracting, p. I-74

Roofing Materials, p. I-368

Rooming and Boarding Houses, p. II-739

Rope, Cordage and Twine, p. I-240

Rubber, pp. I-301-302

RV Parks, p. II-740

Salad Dressing Mixes, p. I-220

Salad Dressings, p. I-127

Salads, p. I-220

Salt, pp. I-364-365

Sand and Gravel, p. I-58

Sanitary Paper Products, pp. I-278-279

Sanitaryware, p. I-408

Sapphire Ingots, p. II-496

Satellite Broadcasting, p. II-614

Satellites, p. II-484

Sauces, pp. I-127-128

Sausage and Ham, p. I-94

Saw Blades, p. I-408

Saw Chains, p. I-437

Scanners, p. I-455

School Buses, p. II-572

School Construction, p. I-70

School Publishing, p. I-287

Schools, p. II-801

Scissors, p. I-407

Screening Equipment, p. I-428

Seafood, pp. I-199-201

Sealants and Caulk, p. I-360

Seals, p. I-376

Seasonings, pp. I-198-199

Secured Logistics, p. II-764

Security Industry, pp. I-12, II-764-765

Seeds, p. I-14

Seedstock, p. I-29

Self Storage Industry, p. II-576

Semiconductor Equipment, p. I-439

Semiconductors, pp. II-489-492

Senior Living Services, p. II-805

Septic Tank Services, p. II-776

Servers, p. II-762

Set-Top Decoder Boxes, p. II-484

Sewing Machines, p. II-472

Shale Gas, pp. I-52-53

Shapewear, p. I-248

Shaving Cream, p. I-346

Sheeps and Goats, p. I-31

Sheet Metal Contracting, p. I-74

Ship Building, p. II-522

Shipping, pp. I-12, II-578

Shipping Containers, p. I-413

Shoe and Leather Goods Repair,
p. II-743

Shoe Retailing, pp. II-657-658

Shopping Center Leasing, p. II-732

Shortening, p. I-179

Showcases, Partitions, Shelving and
Lockers, p. I-265

Siding, p. I-13

Sightseeing Tours, p. II-579

Sightseeing Transportation, p. II-572

Sign and Transportation Reflective
Materials, p. II-565

Sign Painting and Lettering Shops,
p. II-749

Signs, pp. II-565-566

Silicon, p. I-401

Silicon Timing Industry, p. II-493

Silicon Wafers, p. II-493

Silk, p. I-34

Silver, pp. I-42-43

Skating Rinks, p. II-791

Ski and Snowboard Resorts,
p. II-791

Skin Care, pp. I-346-349

Slippers, pp. I-381-382

Slot Machines, p. II-787

Small Appliances, pp. II-470-471

Smart Meters, p. II-534

Smartphones, pp. II-482-483

Smokeless Tobacco, p. I-231

Smoothies, p. I-124

Snacks, pp. I-205-211

Snow Removal Contractors, p. II-620

Snowmobiles, p. II-531

Snuff, p. I-231

Soap, pp. I-322-323

Socks, p. I-234

Soda Ash, p. I-60

Soft Drinks, pp. I-194-197

Software, pp. II-756-760

Software Retailing, p. II-681

Softwood, p. I-257

Solar Cell Metal Paste, p. I-360

Solar Panels, pp. I-410-411

Solar Power, p. II-617

Solid-State Voice Recorders,
p. II-484

Sound Recording Studios, p. II-778

Soup, pp. I-114-116, 125-126

Soybeans, pp. I-17-18

Special Events Industry, p. II-768

Spices, pp. I-220-221

Sporting Goods, pp. II-559-560

Sporting Goods Stores, p. II-678

Sports, pp. II-783-784, 787-788

Sports and Recreation Instruction,
pp. II-791-792

Sports Bras, p. I-248

Sports Drinks, p. I-197

Sportswear, pp. I-244-245

Spreads, p. I-124

Springs, p. I-419

Staffing Industry, p. II-756

Stain Removers, pp. I-329-330

Stationery, p. I-281

Steel, pp. I-394-395, 397

Steel Framing, p. I-75

Stem Cells, p. I-318

Stock Exchanges, p. II-707

Structural Metal, p. I-411

Student Loans, p. II-700

Styrene, p. I-355

Sugar, pp. I-155-156

Sugar Substitutes, p. I-156

Sugarbeets, p. I-19

Sugarcane, p. I-20

Sun Care, pp. I-349-350

Sunglasses Stores, p. II-685

Supercenters, p. II-637

Supplements, pp. I-304-305

Surfactants, p. I-330

Surgical Supplies, pp. II-545-546

Sweeteners, p. I-221

Swimming Pool Construction,
p. I-76

Swimming Pools, p. II-626

Switchgear, p. II-463

Tableware, p. I-391

Taco Sauces, p. I-125

Talent Agents, p. II-782

T&D Equipment, p. II-462

Tank Barges, p. II-578

Tanker Fleets, p. II-578

Tape, p. I-273

Tax & Accounting Publishing,
p. I-290

Tax Preparation, p. II-743

Tea, pp. I-221-222

Teaware, p. I-387

Telecommunications Equipment,
p. II-485

Telemarketers and Call Centers,
p. II-768

Telephone Services, p. II-598

Telephones, p. II-483

Television Broadcasting, p. II-612

Television Shows, pp. II-777-778

Televisions, pp. II-478-480

Temporary Tattoos, p. I-365

Terminal Operators, p. II-580

Test Preparation, p. II-803

Textbooks, pp. I-288, II-679

Textile Finishing, p. I-237

Textile Machinery, p. I-437

Textiles, pp. I-232-233

Theatrical Entertainment, p. II-782

Thermal Management, p. I-443

Thread, Yarn and Fibers, pp. I-238-
239

Timeshares, pp. II-768-769

Tin, pp. I-401-402

Tire Retailing, p. II-652

Tire Retreading, p. II-771

Tires, pp. I-371-373, 621

Title Abstract and Settlement
Offices, p. II-734

Title Insurance, p. II-729

Tobacco, pp. I-19, 224-227

Tobacco Retailing, p. II-684

Tobacco Wholesalers, p. II-631

Toilet Tissue, p. I-280

Toll Roads and Weighing Stations,
p. II-589

Toothbrushes, p. II-565

Tortillas, p. I-222

Tour Operators, p. II-588

Tourism, p. II-588

Tourist Attractions, p. II-808

Towing, p. II-580

Toy and Hobby Goods Wholesalers,
p. II-626

Toys and Games, pp. II-556-558

Toys and Games Retailing, p. II-681

Trade Shows and Event Planning,
p. II-769

Trading Stamp Services, p. II-769

Train, Subway and Transit Cars,
p. II-525

Transformers, pp. II-462-463

Transmission Supplies Wholesalers,
p. II-621

Transportation Arrangement,
p. II-589

Travel Arrangers, p. II-588

Travel Trailers, p. II-530

Truck Rental, p. II-770

Trucking, pp. II-573-575

Trucks, p. II-510

Trust, Fiduciary, and Custody Activities, p. II-736
Turbines, p. I-423
Turkeys, pp. I-32-33, 96
Twitter, p. II-809
Uninterruptible Power Equipment, p. II-463
Uninterruptible Power Supplies, p. II-464
Unions, p. II-809
U.S. Department of Education, p. II-819
Uranium, pp. I-44-45
Used Car Retailing, p. II-651
Used Merchandise Stores, pp. II-677-678
Utensils, Pots and Pans, p. I-415
Utilities, p. II-618
Utility Construction, p. I-72
Utility Vehicles, p. II-531
Vacation Homes, p. II-734
Vaccines, p. I-318
Vacuum Cleaners, p. II-471
Valves, pp. I-417-420
Valves and Fittings Wholesalers, p. II-625
Valves and Hoses, p. I-418
Vegetable Oils, p. I-179
Vegetables, pp. I-20-22
Vehicle Leasing, p. II-770
Vending Machines, pp. I-457, II-683
Vessel Rental and Leasing, p. II-756
Veterinary Services, p. I-35
Video Game Consoles, p. II-558
Video Game Digital Distribution, p. II-609
Video Game Software, pp. II-760-761
Vinyl Acetate Monomer, p. I-355
Vitamins, pp. I-305-306
Vitamins and Supplements, p. II-677
Vocational Rehabilitation Services, p. II-804
Voice Over Internet Protocol, p. II-610
Wall Coverings, p. I-13
Wallboard, p. I-392
Warehouse Clubs, pp. II-637-638
Warehousing and Storage, p. II-576
Waste Glass Processing, p. I-439
Waste Treatment and Disposal, p. II-619
Watch, Clock, and Jewelry Repair, p. II-774

Watches, pp. II-552-553
Water, p. II-618
Water Softeners, pp. I-365-366
Water Softeners and Treatments, p. I-358
Water Supply and Irrigation, p. II-620
Water Transportation, p. II-579
Water Treatment Equipment, pp. I-446-447
Water Well Drilling, p. I-75
Waterproof-Breathable Fabrics, p. I-250
Wearable-Cams, p. II-552
Weight Control Products, pp. I-315-316
Weight Loss Services, p. II-744
Welding Equipment, p. I-437
Wheat, p. I-15
Whiteboards, p. II-569
Windows, p. I-256
Wine, p. I-186
Wipes, p. I-280
Wire and Cable, p. I-420
Wire Bonding Equipment, p. I-439
Wireless Payments, pp. II-610-611
Wireless Services, pp. II-590-598
Wireless Towers, p. II-485
Woodworking Machinery, pp. I-437-438
Workers Compensation Insurance, pp. II-727-728
Writing Instruments, p. II-561
Yellow Pages Publishing, p. I-290
Yogurt, pp. I-109-110
Zinc, pp. I-41, 403

ACRONYMS AND ABBREVIATIONS

3-D	Three dimension
ABS	Acylonitrile butadiene styrene (a plastic)
AC	Alternating current
ACT	American College Test
ADHD	Attention deficit hyperactivity disorder (medicine)
ADSL	Asymmetric digital subscriber line (telecommunications)
ADW	Automated deposit wagering
AFH	Away from home
AG	Arbeitsgruppe (German for Working Group)
ALC	Automatic level control
APU	Auxiliary power unit (power source in vehicles not involved in locomotion)
ARRA	American Recovery and Reinvestment Act of 2009
ART	Assisted reproductive technologies
ATE	Automatic test equipment or advanced technology engine
ATV	All-terrain vehicle
B/W	Black and white
CAD/CAM	Computer aided design/computer aided manufacturing
CAFE	Corporate average fuel economy
CARG	Compounded annual growth rate
CD	Compact disk (electronic storage device) or certificate of deposit (banking)
CFL	Compact fluorescent lamp
CIGS	Copper, Indium, Gallium, Selenide
CIS	Copper, Indium, Sulphur
CMBS	Commercial Mortgage-Backed Secutiries
CMOS	Complementary Metal Oxide Silicon
CPO	Crude palm oil

Crore	Indian word signifying 10 million, used ahead or behind other numbers to modify these
CRT-D	Cardiac Resynchonization Therapy-Defibrillators
CVT	Continuously variable transmission
CWT	Hundredweight (100 pounds)
DAB	Digital audio broadcasting
DCI	Digital Camera Initiatives (film and entertainment industry standard for cameras)
DCS	Distributed control system (control system with multiple nodes spatially separated)
DISMO	Distilled monoglyerides
DKK	Danish Krone (currency)
DMFC	Direct methanol fuel cell
DRAM	Dynamic random access memory
D-SLR	Digital single-lens reflex (camera)
DVD	Digital video disk
DVR	Digital video recorder
DWT	Deadweight (carrying capacity of ships, usually given in metric tons)
E85	Fuel containing 85% ethanol, 15% gasoline
ECNs	Electronic Communications Networks
EEA	European Economic Area, the EU plus a selection of other European countries
EFT	Electronic funds transfer
EMEA	Europe, Middle East, and Africa
ERP	Enterprise resource planning
ERTMS	European Railway Traffic Management System
ETCS	European Train Control System
EU	European Union
FABLESS	Not fabricated or fabricationless

FDA	Food & Drug Administration	JPEG	Joint Photographic Experts Group (file format and file extension)
FHA	Federal Housing Administration	KGaA	Kommanditgesellschaft auf Aktien (German corporate form based on shares)
FHP	Fractional horsepower		
FTTH	Fiber-to-the-home (fiber optic fiber replacing copper wire in communications)	KW	Kilowatts
GC	Gas chromatography	LCD	Liquid crystal display
GC - MS	Gas chromatography - mass spectrometry	LDPE	Low-density polyethylene
GLA	Gross leasable area	LED	Light-emitting diode
GmbH	Gesellschaft mit beschraenkter Haftung (German limited liability corporation)	LLDPE	Linear low-density polyethylene
		LT	Long ton (2,240 pounds)
GNMA	Government National Mortgage Association	LTL	Less than truckload (transportation)
		M&E	Mergers and acquisitions
GNSS	Global navigation satellite system	MCOT	Mobile cardiac outpatient telemetry
GSA	General Service Administration	MEMS	Micro-electromechanical systems
GSE	Government Sponsored Enterprise	MLB	Major League Baseball
HCFC	Hydrochlorofluorocarbon	MLCC	Multilayer Ceramic Capacitor
HDD	High-density disk	MLO	multiple-location collision repair operator
HDPE	High-density polythylene		
HFCS	High fructose corn sweetener	MMDS	Multichannel, multipoint distribution services (television distribution system)
HMI	Human Machine Interface		
HID	High-intensity discharge	MNR/EPR	Nuclear Magnetic Resonance/Electronic Paramagnetic Resonance
HIV/AIDS	Human immunodeficiency virus/Acquired immunodeficiency syndrome	MP3	Moving Picture Experts Group Layer-3 Audio (audio file format/extension)
HVAC	Heating, ventilation, and air conditioning	MRI	Magnetic resonance imaging (diagnostic instrument)
HVACR	Heating, ventilation, air conditioning and refrigeration		
		MRO	Maintenance, repair and overhaul
IBD	Irritable bowel disease	MT	Metric ton (1,000 kilograms or 2,205 pounds)
IC	Integrated circuit (electronics) or independent contractor (labor markets)		
		MW	Megawatts
ICD	Implantable cardiac defibrillator	NAFTA	North American Free Trade Area
IED	Improvised explosive device	NAICS	North American Industrial Classification System
IOL	Intraocular lens or Implantable lenses (optics)		
		NASA	National Aeronautical and Space Administration
IPTV	Internet protocol television (digitally delivered television)		
		NBA	National Basketball Association
IQF	Individually quick frozen	NC	Numerically controlled
ITC	Investment tax credit	NDT	Nondestructive testing
IVD	In vitro diagnostics	NEC	Not elsewhere classified (Census abbreviation)
IVF	In vitro fertilization		

NFL	National Footbal League	Renminbi	Chinese currency with the same meaning as Yuan
NHL	National Hockey League		
NIMH	Nickel, metal hydride	RES	Renewable energy standard
NPCC	Nano-Precipitated Calcium Carbonate	RF	Radio frequency
NSK	Not specified by kind (Census abbreviation)	ROV	Remotely operated vehicle
		Rs	Rupees (India's currency)
OCTG	Oil country tubular goods (pipe and tube used in the petroleum industry)	RTD	Ready-to-drink
		SA	Service Assurance or, in many parts of the world, a corporate designation translated as Autonomous Society
OCTG	Oil Country Tubular Goods		
OEM	Original equipment manufacturer		
OLED	Organic light-emitting diode or device	SAAR	Seasonally adjusted annualized rate
OSB	Oriented strandboard (wood board similar in function but differently made than plywood)	SAR	Saudi Arabian Riyal
		SAT	Scholastic Achievement Test
		SB	Styrene butadiene (latex)
OTC	Over the counter	SC	Supercalendered paper, uncoated and mechanically compressed
PAAS	Platform as a Service		
PACS	Picture Archiving and Communications Systems	SIC	Standard Industrial Classification (replaced by NAICS)
PAN	Polyacrylonitrile	SKU	Stock keeping unit (accounting, warehousing)
PCM	Phase Change Materials		
PDF	Portable document format	SLR	Single lense reflex (camera)
PEMFC	Protein exchange membrane fuel cell	SME	Small and Medium Enterprise
PET	Polyethylene terephthalate	SONET/SDH	Synchronous Optical Network/ Synchronous Digital Hierarchy
PLC	Programmable logic controller (computers)	SSRI/SNRI	Selective serotonin inhibitors/serotonin-norepinephrine reuptake inhibitors (pharmaceuticals)
PLD	Programmable Logic Displays		
PLM	Product lifecycle management	ST	Short ton (2,000 pounds)
PLU	Primary logical unit	SUV	Sport utility vehicle
PND	Portable navigation device	T&D	Transmission and distribution
POC	Point of care (medical practice)	TEU	Twenty-foot equivalent units
POL	Physician office laboratories	TAM	Total available market
POS	Point-of-sale or point and shoot	UAE	United Arab Emirates
PPV	Pay-per-view (television expression)	UAS	Unmanned aerial system (military)
PSA	Pressure Sensitive Adhesive	UGV	Unmanned ground vehicle (military)
PV	Photovoltaic	UK	United Kingdom
PVA	Polyvinyl acetate	USV	Unmanned surface vehicle (military)
PVC	Polyvinyl chloride (a plastic)	UUV	Unmanned underwater vehicle (military)
QSR	Quick-service restaurant	VA	Veterans Affairs

VCM	Vinyl chloride monomer (a plastic)
VOD	Video-on-demand (television expression)
VOIP	Voice over Internet protocol
VPN	Virtual private network
VSAT	Very small aperture terminal
WAN	Wide area network
WCDMS	Wide division code multiple access
WLAN	Wireless local area network

SIC 36 - Electronic and Other Electric Equipment

★ 1991 ★

Electronic Manufacturing Services

SIC: 3600; NAICS: 33431, 334417

Top EMS Firms Worldwide, 2010

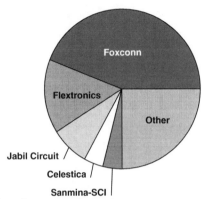

Market shares are shown in percent.

Foxconn	44.0%
Flextronics	15.0
Jabil Circuit	8.0
Celestica	4.0
Sanmina-SCI	4.0
Other	25.0

Source: *Seri Quarterly*, January 2012, p. 16, from International Data Corp.

★ 1992 ★

Original Design Manufacturing

SIC: 3600; NAICS: 33431, 334417

Top ODS Firms Worldwide, 2010

Market shares are shown in percent.

Quanta	27.0%
Compal	21.0
Wistron	14.0
Inventec	9.0
Pegatron	8.0
Other	21.0

Source: *Seri Quarterly*, January 2012, p. 16, from International Data Corp.

★ 1993 ★

Electrical Transmission and Distribution Equipment

SIC: 3612; NAICS: 335311

Top Electrical Transmission and Distribution Equipment Makers, 2010

The industry was valued at $20.1 billion.

Siemens	9.0%
Eaton Corp.	8.3
Schneider Electric	8.0
General Electric Co.	7.3
ABB Ltd.	6.7
Other	60.7

Source: "Electric Transmission & Distribution Equipment." [online] from http://www.freedoniagroup.com [Published May 2011], from Freedonia Group.

★ 1994 ★

Inductors

SIC: 3612; NAICS: 334416

Electronic Coil, Transformer, and Other Inductor Manufacturing, 2007

Data show the percent of industry sales held by the largest 4, 8, 20 and 50 firms in the sector. There are approximately 299 firms operating in the industry generating employment for 11,524 people.

4 largest companies	33.3%
8 largest companies	44.1
20 largest companies	57.6
50 largest companies	74.0

Source: "2007 Economic Census." [online] from http://www.census.gov/econ/concentration.html [Accessed August 12, 2011], from U.S. Bureau of the Census.

★ 1995 ★
Low-Voltage Products
SIC: 3612; NAICS: 335311

Low-Voltage Products Market Worldwide, 2010

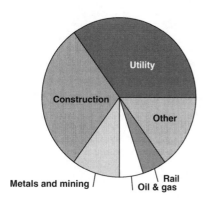

The industry was estimated to be worth $60 billion.

Utility	35.0%
Construction	30.0
Metals and mining	10.0
Oil & gas	5.0
Rail	5.0
Other	15.0

Source: "Power Products Market Information." [online] from http://www02.abb.com [Published November 4, 2011].

★ 1996 ★
Low-Voltage Products
SIC: 3612; NAICS: 335311

Top Low-Voltage Motor Drive Makers Worldwide, 2009

Market shares are shown in percent.

ABB Ltd.	17.5%
Siemens	14.0
Schneider Toshiba	8.5
Danfoss	6.0
Rockwell Automation	6.0
Yaskawa	5.0
Vacon	4.5
Converteam	4.0
Mitsubishi Electric	4.0
Fuji	3.5
Other	27.0

Source: "Vacon - the AC Drives Company." [online] from http://www.vacon.com [Published August 31, 2011], from IMS Research and Vacon estimates.

★ 1997 ★
Power Products
SIC: 3612; NAICS: 335311

Power Products Market Worldwide, 2010

The industry was estimated to be worth $55 billion.

Industries	40.0%
Utility distribution	25.0
Utility transmission	25.0
Power generation	10.0

Source: "Power Products Market Information." [online] from http://www02.abb.com [Published November 4, 2011].

★ 1998 ★
T&D Equipment
SIC: 3612; NAICS: 335311

Top Markets for Electric Power Transmission and Distribution Equipment, 2003, 2008 and 2013

Figures are in millions of dollars.

	2003	2008	2013
Office	$ 399	$ 490	$ 1,340
Mercantile and service . . .	405	495	550
Warehouse and other	330	395	440
Lodging	167	235	275
Food sales and service . . .	95	120	140

Source: *Business Economics*, October 2011, p. 24, from Freedonia Group.

★ 1999 ★
Transformers
SIC: 3612; NAICS: 335311

Electric Power and Specialty Transformer Manufacturing, 2010

Total shipments were valued at $5.16 billion. "NSK" stands for Not Specified by Kind.

	($ 000)	Share
Power and distribution transformers, except parts . . .	$ 3,226,134	62.56%
Power, distribution, and specialty transformer mfg, nsk, total . .	666,418	12.92
Power regulators/boosters/other trans./parts, all transformers . .	500,308	9.70
Specialty transformers, except fluorescent lamp ballast . . .	420,422	8.15

Continued on next page.

★ 1999 ★

[Continued]

Transformers

SIC: 3612; NAICS: 335311

Electric Power and Specialty Transformer Manufacturing, 2010

Total shipments were valued at $5.16 billion. "NSK" stands for Not Specified by Kind.

	($ 000)	Share
Commercial/institutional/industrial general-purpose trans, all volts.	$ 290,317	5.63%
Fluorescent lamp ballasts . . .	53,017	1.03

Source: "Annual Survey of Manufactures." [online] from http://www.census.gov/manufacturing/asm/index.html [Accessed January 18, 2012], from U.S. Department of Commerce.

★ 2000 ★

Transformers

SIC: 3612; NAICS: 335311

Leading Transformer/Substation Makers in India, 2011

Market shares are shown for fiscal year 2011.

Tata projects	13.0%
KEC	9.0
Sterlite Tech	9.0
Areva T&D	4.0
EMC	4.0
Gammon	4.0
Siemens Electric S.A.	4.0
IVRCL	3.0
Kalpataru Power	3.0
Other	47.0

Source: "India Capital Goods Sector." [online] from http://doc.research-and-analytics.csfb.com [Published March 31, 2011], from Powergrid.

★ 2001 ★

Circuit Breakers

SIC: 3613; NAICS: 335313

Power Circuit Breakers, 2006-2010

Shipments are shown in millions of dollars.

2008	$ 729.7
2009	696.6
2010	685.3
2007	579.9
2006	576.2

Source: "Current Industrial Reports." [online] from http://www.census.gov/manufacturing/cir/index.html [Accessed August 15, 2011], from U.S. Bureau of the Census.

★ 2002 ★

Switchgear

SIC: 3613; NAICS: 335313

Shipments of Mechanical Switches for Electronic Circuitry, 2006-2010

Shipments are shown in millions of dollars.

2007	$ 662
2006	645
2008	581
2009	396
2010	360

Source: "Current Industrial Reports." [online] from http://www.census.gov/manufacturing/cir/index.html [Accessed August 15, 2011], from U.S. Bureau of the Census.

★ 2003 ★

Switchgear

SIC: 3613; NAICS: 335313

Shipments of Switchgear (Except Ducts), 2006-2010

Shipments are shown in millions of dollars.

2008	$ 3,753.2
2009	3,317.5
2010	3,254.6
2007	3,226.4
2006	2,944.7

Source: "Current Industrial Reports." [online] from http://www.census.gov/manufacturing/cir/index.html [Accessed August 15, 2011], from U.S. Bureau of the Census.

★ 2004 ★

Uninterruptible Power Equipment

SIC: 3613; NAICS: 335313

Top Uninterruptible Power Equipment Suppliers Worldwide, 2010

Market shares are shown in percent.

Schneider Electric S.A.	26.0%
Eaton Corp.	12.0
Emerson	9.0
Chloride Power	4.0
Mitsubishi Electric	4.0
Piller	3.0
Riello UPS	3.0
Socomec	3.0
Toshiba	3.0
Other	33.0

Source: "Schneider Electric." [online] from http://www.research.hsbc.com [Published September 23, 2010], from Frost & Sullivan.

★ 2005 ★
Uninterruptible Power Supplies
SIC: 3613; NAICS: 335313

Top UPS Makers, 2010

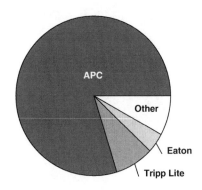

Market shares are shown in percent.

APC	79.2%
Tripp Lite	8.2
Eaton	4.3
Other	8.3

Source: *CRN*, March 23, 2011, p. NA, from NPD Group Inc.

★ 2006 ★
Electrical Equipment
SIC: 3621; NAICS: 335312

Top Electrical Equipment Makers, 2010

The industry generated revenues of $33.3 billion in 2010.

Eaton Corp.	7.0%
General Electric Co.	7.0
Rockwell Automation Inc.	7.0
Siemens A.G.	6.0
ABB Ltd.	5.5
Baldor	3.2
Schneider Electric S.A.	2.6
Other	62.7

Source: "General Electric Company." [online] from http://www.docstoc.com [Published June 20, 2010], from IBIS-World.

★ 2007 ★
Generators
SIC: 3621; NAICS: 335312

Top Generator Makers Worldwide, 2009

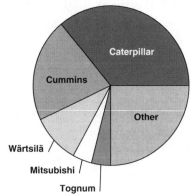

Market shares are shown in percent.

Caterpillar	36.0%
Cummins	21.0
Wärtsilä	10.0
Mitsubishi	4.0
Tognum	4.0
Other	25.0

Source: "Electrical." [online] from http://www.bostonstrate-gies.com/clientlogin/rawmaterials/ElectricalFeb.pdf [Published January 2010], from Boston Strategies International.

★ 2008 ★
Generators
SIC: 3621; NAICS: 335312

Top Makers of Generators Worldwide, 2010

Market shares are estimated in percent.

ABB Ltd.	10.0-20.0%
Emerson	10.0-20.0
Brush HMA	5.0-10.0
Cummins	5.0-10.0
Hyundai Heavy Industries	5.0-10.0
WEG	5.0-10.0
Converteam	0.0-5.0
Siemens A.G.	0.0-5.0
Other	40.0-50.0

Source: "GE Energy/Converteam." [online] from http://ec.europa.eu [Published July 25, 2011], from IMS Research and Goulden estimates.

★ 2009 ★

Motors

SIC: 3621; NAICS: 335312

Electric Motor Market Worldwide, 2009

Regions are ranked by revenues in millions of dollars.

	($ mil.)	Share
North Asia	$ 34,936	55.8%
East Asia	11,131	17.8
North America	6,210	9.9
Western Europe	5,680	9.1
Latin America	2,561	4.1
South Asia	1,116	1.8
Eastern Europe	845	1.3
Africa	168	0.3

Source: "International Copper Association." [online] from http://industrial-energy.lbl.gov/files/industrial-energy [Published September 11, 2011], from Frost & Sullivan.

★ 2010 ★

Carbon Nanotubes

SIC: 3624; NAICS: 335991

Carbon Nanotube Composite Market, 2008

The global industry was valued at $18.7 billion. The United States claims nearly 40% of the market.

Construction	45.0%
Marine	20.0
Corrosion	12.0
Transportation	12.0
Consumer products	5.0
Electrical	4.0
Others	2.0

Source: "Frost & Sullivan's Study on Potential Market for Carbon Nanomaterials Applications." [online] from http://www.frost.com [Published February 28, 2011], from Frost & Sullivan.

★ 2011 ★

Graphite

SIC: 3624; NAICS: 335991

Leading Fine Grain, High Density Graphite Producers in China, 2010

Companies are ranked by annual production in metric tons.

Xuzhou Carbon Co.	20,000
Beijing XinCheng Sci-Tech Development Inc.	15,000
China Carbon Graphite Group	15,000
Jieshi Carbon Material Co.	10,000
Shanghai Carbon Co.	2,000
Chengdu Rongguang Carbon	1,000

Source: "Fine Grain, High Density Graphite." [online] from http://www.bis.doc.gov [Published April 2010], from company reports.

★ 2012 ★

Relays and Controls

SIC: 3625; NAICS: 335314

Relay and Industrial Control Manufacturing, 2010

Total shipments were valued at $8.28 billion. "NSK" stands for Not Specified by Kind.

	($ 000)	Share
General-purpose industrial controls	$ 3,511,146	42.41%
Specific-purpose industrial controls	2,294,845	27.72
Relays, elect. circ., ind. control overload, & switchgear type	1,051,146	12.70
Parts for industrial controls and motor-control accessories	712,388	8.61
Relay and industrial control manufacturing, nsk, total	708,823	8.56

Source: "Annual Survey of Manufactures." [online] from http://www.census.gov/manufacturing/asm/index.html [Accessed January 18, 2012], from U.S. Department of Commerce.

★ 2013 ★

Appliances

SIC: 3630; NAICS: 335212, 335221, 335222

Appliance Demand Worldwide, 2010

Total demand was placed at 334.2 million units. India is expected to be the fastest-growing market, fueled by rising standards of living and home ownership. These factors will drive other developing markets in Africa and the Middle East.

Asia-Pacific	42.0%
Western Europe	18.0
North America	16.0
Other	23.0

Source: "World Major Household Appliances." [online] from http://www.freedoniagroup.com [Published November 2011], from Freedonia Group.

★ 2014 ★

Appliances

SIC: 3630; NAICS: 335221, 335222, 335224

Top Appliance Makers, 2009-2010

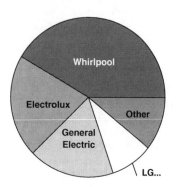

One of the major trends in this market has been the growth of smart appliances, which can connect to wireless networks. This allows appliances to do everything from connect to repair staff to play music. Smart appliances are expected to completely replace traditional appliances by 2020, according to Zpryme Research & Consulting. Because of this, electronics firms such as LG and Samsung are seen as having something of an advantage as they look to grow share in the appliance market. Indeed, while Samsung had less than 1% of the market in 2010, Zpryme Research & Consulting expects it to add eight to twelve percentage points in the coming years.

	2009	2010
Whirlpool	41.6%	41.5%
Electrolux	21.6	20.8
General Electric	22.5	18.4
LG Electronics	7.0	8.7
Other	7.3	10.6

Source: *BusinessWeek*, January 26, 2011, p. NA, from IBISWorld.

★ 2015 ★

Appliances

SIC: 3630; NAICS: 335221, 335222, 335224

Top Appliance Makers Worldwide, 2010

Market shares are shown in percent.

Whirlpool	15.0%
Electrolux	12.0
Bosch Siemens	10.0
LG Electronics	8.0
Samsung	8.0
Haier Group	7.0

General Electric	5.0%
Other	35.0

Source: *Wall Street Journal*, April 28, 2011, p. B6, from KeyBanc Capital Markets.

★ 2016 ★

Cooking Equipment

SIC: 3631; NAICS: 335221

Barbecue Grill Market, 2011

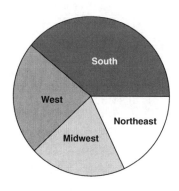

Total spending was $1.3 billion. Warehouse centers claimed 51.3% of the market, mass merchants 20.0%, department stores 8.5%, specialty stores 6.4%, hardware stores 4.0% and other sectors 13.8%.

South	38.9%
West	22.8
Midwest	19.8
Northeast	18.4

Source: *Home Channel News*, July 4, 2011, p. 58, from NPD Group Inc.

★ 2017 ★

Cooking Equipment

SIC: 3631; NAICS: 335221

Household Cooking Appliance Manufacturing, 2010

Total shipments were valued at $3.74 billion. "NSK" stands for Not Specified by Kind.

	($ 000)	Share
Electric household ranges, ovens, surface cooking units/equip.	$ 1,895,416	50.67%
Gas household ranges/ovens/ surface cooking units, & equip.	1,121,033	29.97

Continued on next page.

★ 2017 ★

[Continued]

Cooking Equipment

SIC: 3631; NAICS: 335221

Household Cooking Appliance Manufacturing, 2010

Total shipments were valued at $3.74 billion. "NSK" stands for Not Specified by Kind.

	($ 000)	Share
Household cooking appliance manufacturing, nsk, total . . .	$ 12,945	0.35%
Other household ranges and cooking equipment	711,048	19.01

Source: "Annual Survey of Manufactures." [online] from http://www.census.gov/manufacturing/asm/index.html [Accessed January 18, 2012], from U.S. Department of Commerce.

★ 2018 ★

Cooking Equipment

SIC: 3631; NAICS: 335221

Kitchen Appliance Market Worldwide, 2010

Data are in billions of dollars.

	($ bil.)	Share
Brazil	$ 3.0	24.79%
China	1.5	12.40
North America	1.5	12.40
Japan	1.1	9.09
Russia	0.5	4.13
Germany, Austria and Switzerland .	0.4	3.31
France	0.4	3.31
United Kingdom and Ireland . . .	0.4	3.31
India	0.3	2.48
Other	3.0	24.79

Source: "Philips - Building Global Category Leadership." [online] from http://www.newscenter.philips.com [Accessed April 1, 2012], from GfK and Euromonitor.

★ 2019 ★

Cooking Equipment

SIC: 3631; NAICS: 335221

Top Makers of Electric Ranges, 2008

Market shares are shown based on shipments.

General Electric	47.0%
Whirlpool	29.0

Electrolux (Frigidaire)	8.0%
Other	16.0

Source: "Appliance Market Research Report." [online] from http://www.appliancemagazine.com [Published January 2010], from *Appliance* estimates and company reports.

★ 2020 ★

Cooking Equipment

SIC: 3631; NAICS: 335221

Top Makers of Gas Ranges, 2008

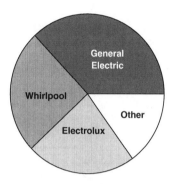

Market shares are shown based on shipments.

General Electric	37.0%
Whirlpool	25.0
Electrolux (Frigidaire)	23.0
Other	15.0

Source: "Appliance Market Research Report." [online] from http://www.appliancemagazine.com [Published January 2010], from *Appliance* estimates and company reports.

★ 2021 ★

Cooking Equipment

SIC: 3631; NAICS: 335221

Top Makers of Microwave Ovens, 2008

Market shares are shown based on shipments. Figures exclude combination ranges.

LG Electronics	33.0%
Samsung	15.0
Sharp	15.0
Other	37.0

Source: "Appliance Market Research Report." [online] from http://www.appliancemagazine.com [Published January 2010], from *Appliance* estimates and company reports.

★ 2022 ★

Cooking Equipment

SIC: 3631; NAICS: 335221

Top Microwave Oven Makers in India, 2009-2010

Market shares are shown based on sales of 1.25 million units. Convection ovens claimed nearly half of all sales (49.4%), grills claimed 31.3% and solo grills 19.1%.

LG Electronics	31.79%
Samsung	15.89
Whirlpool	10.33
IFB	9.94
Onida	9.94
Videocon	8.89
Godrej	7.95
Koryo	3.89

Source: *TV Veopar Journal*, April 2011, p. 75.

★ 2023 ★

Refrigerators

SIC: 3632; NAICS: 335222

Shipments of Household Refrigerators, 2006-2010

Shipments are shown in millions of dollars. Figures include combination refrigerator-freezers.

2008	$ 5,891.1
2010	5,466.0
2007	5,439.6
2006	5,427.4
2009	5,187.5

Source: "Current Industrial Reports." [online] from http://www.census.gov/manufacturing/cir/index.html [Accessed August 15, 2011], from U.S. Bureau of the Census.

★ 2024 ★

Refrigerators

SIC: 3632; NAICS: 335222

Top Makers of Refrigerators, 2008

Market shares are shown based on shipments.

Whirlpool	33.0%
General Electric	27.0
Electrolux (Frigidaire)	23.0
Other	17.0

Source: "Appliance Market Research Report." [online] from http://www.appliancemagazine.com [Published January 2010], from *Appliance* estimates and company reports.

★ 2025 ★

Refrigerators

SIC: 3632; NAICS: 335222

Top Refrigerator and Freezer Makers in China, 2009

Market shares are shown in percent.

Qingdao Haier Co. Ltd.	11.0%
Guangdong Kelon Electrical Holdings Co. Ltd.	3.0
Henan Xinfel Electric Co. Ltd.	3.0
Hefel Melling Co. Ltd.	2.7
Other	80.3

Source: "Household Refrigerator and Freezer Manufacturing in China." [online] from http://www.docin.com/p-80616558.html [Published December 2009], from IBISWorld.

★ 2026 ★

Refrigerators

SIC: 3632; NAICS: 335222

Top Refrigerator Makers in India, 2009-2010

Market shares are shown based on sales of 7.3 million units.

LG Electronics	25.34%
Samsung	18.49
Whirlpool	18.49
Godrej	16.44
Videocon Group	16.44
Other	4.80

Source: *TV Veopar Journal*, April 2011, p. 75.

★ 2027 ★

Laundry Equipment

SIC: 3633; NAICS: 335224

Top Makers of Electric Dryers, 2008

Market shares are shown based on shipments.

Whirlpool	70.0%
General Electric	16.0
Electrolux	8.0
Other	6.0

Source: "Appliance Market Research Report." [online] from http://www.appliancemagazine.com [Published January 2010], from *Appliance* estimates and company reports.

★ **2028** ★

Laundry Equipment

SIC: 3633; NAICS: 335224

Top Makers of Washing Machines, 2008

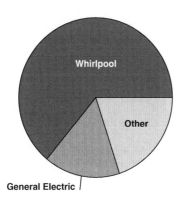

Market shares are shown based on shipments.

Whirlpool	64.0%
General Electric	16.0
Other	20.0

Source: "Appliance Market Research Report." [online] from http://www.appliancemagazine.com [Published January 2010], from *Appliance* estimates and company reports.

★ **2029** ★

Laundry Equipment

SIC: 3633; NAICS: 335224

Top Makers of Washing Machines in India, 2009-2010

Market shares are shown based on sales of 3.8 million units.

LG Electronics	28.95%
Samsung	18.68
Videocon Group	15.79
Whirlpool	15.74
Godrej	6.58
IFB	4.21
Other	10.05

Source: *TV Veopar Journal*, April 2011, p. 69.

★ **2030** ★

Dental Tools

SIC: 3634; NAICS: 335211

Top Dental Accessory/Tool Bars, 2010

Brands are ranked by drug store sales for the 52 weeks ended December 26, 2010.

	($ mil.)	Share
Waterpik	$ 31.0	7.41%
Sonicare	24.1	5.76

	($ mil.)	Share
Dentek	$ 22.1	5.28%
Sunstar G-U-M Go Betweens	16.1	3.85
Braun Oral-B Precision Clean	14.4	3.44
Oral-B Dual Action	12.2	2.92
Sonicare Proresults	11.1	2.65
Private label	52.1	12.45
Other	235.3	56.24

Source: *Chain Drug Review*, June 27, 2011, p. 168, from SymphonyIRI Group Inc.

★ **2031** ★

Heating and Cooling

SIC: 3634; NAICS: 333414

Shipments of Water Heaters, except Electric, 2006-2010

Shipments are shown in millions of dollars.

2007	$ 1,571.8
2008	1,547.0
2010	1,524.5
2009	1,452.0
2006	902.8

Source: "Current Industrial Reports." [online] from http://www.census.gov/manufacturing/cir/index.html [Accessed August 15, 2011], from U.S. Bureau of the Census.

★ **2032** ★

Power Toothbrushes

SIC: 3634; NAICS: 335211

Top Power Toothbrush Brands, 2011

Market shares are shown based on drug store sales for the 52 weeks ended March 20, 2011.

Sonicare Essence	12.38%
Oral-B Pulsar	10.37
Arm & Hammer Spinbrush PC	8.67
Oral-B Crossaction Power Max	6.99
Sonicare Flexcare	5.48
Crest Spoonbrush Pro White	5.46
Sonicare	4.58
Oral-B Pro Health	3.95
Colgate 360	3.83
Private label	3.35
Other	34.94

Source: *DrugStore Management*, Annual 2011-2012, p. 112, from SymphonyIRI Group Inc.

★ 2033 ★

Small Appliances

SIC: 3634; NAICS: 335211

Electric Kettle Sales, 2010

Discount stores claimed 64% of the market, specialty stores 16%, department stores 10% and other channels 10%. The industry has enjoyed double-digit growth lately, jumping from $60 million in 2007 to $83 million in 2010.

Plastic	55.0%
Stainless steel	40.0
Glass	5.0

Source: *HomeWorld Business*, January 2011, p. 40, from *HomeWorld Business* research.

★ 2034 ★

Small Appliances

SIC: 3634; NAICS: 335211

Popcorn Maker Sales, 2006-2010

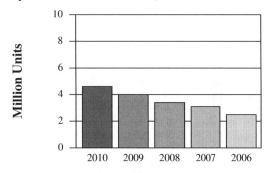

Retail sales are shown in millions of units. Total sales grew from $55.3 million to $99.4 million. Discount stores claimed 44% of the market, warehouse clubs claimed 15%, department stores 13% and other sectors 28%.

2010	4.6
2009	4.0
2008	3.4
2007	3.1
2006	2.5

Source: *HomeWorld Business*, January 2011, p. 10, from *HomeWorld Business* research.

★ 2035 ★

Small Appliances

SIC: 3634; NAICS: 335211

Portable Fan Sales by Type, 2010

A total of 35.1 million units were sold in 2010, valued at $532 million.

Stand/tower	42.0%
Table	16.0

Box	15.0%
Floor	14.0
Personal/clip	11.0
Window	2.0

Source: *HomeWorld Business*, January 2011, p. 100, from *HomeWorld Business* research.

★ 2036 ★

Small Appliances

SIC: 3634; NAICS: 335211

Retail Sales of Personal Massagers, 2010

A total of 12.0 million units were sold in 2010, valued at $373.9 million.

Back/body	50.0%
Handheld	35.0
Foot	15.0

Source: *HomeWorld Business*, January 2011, p. 92, from *HomeWorld Business* research.

★ 2037 ★

Small Appliances

SIC: 3634; NAICS: 335211

Retail Sales of Selected Home Appliances, 2008-2010

Retail sales are shown in millions of dollars.

	2008	2009	2010
Blenders	$ 594.70	$ 577.80	$ 576.10
Portable fans	515.00	527.00	532.00
Air cleaners	536.70	518.20	525.70
Coffeemakers	501.80	501.30	481.40
Massagers	391.20	381.40	373.90
Irons	389.20	357.10	352.60
Hair dryers	345.10	332.20	332.30
Toaster ovens	341.70	336.80	332.00
Compact refrigerators . .	298.60	290.10	299.10
Deep fryers	275.40	285.30	283.90
Vacuum sealers . . .	262.20	259.20	266.90
Bath scales	245.30	251.50	257.80
Tabletop convention ovens	253.10	248.30	250.10
Toasters	264.48	255.88	249.38
Slow cookers	192.10	205.80	219.10
Espresso machines . .	129.50	132.30	136.20

Source: *HomeWorld Business*, January 2011, p. 10, from *HomeWorld Business* research.

★ 2038 ★

Small Appliances

SIC: 3634; NAICS: 335211

Single-Serve Coffeemaker Sales, 2006-2010

The single-serve coffeemaker industry is one of the fastest-growing sectors of the housewares market. Sales are shown in millions of units. In dollar sales, the market grew from $111 million to $505 million. Specialty stores claimed 34% of the market, discount stores 31% and other sectors 35%.

2010	4.1
2009	2.7
2008	1.8
2007	1.7
2006	1.2

Source: *HomeWorld Business*, January 2011, p. 36, from *HomeWorld Business* research.

★ 2039 ★

Small Appliances

SIC: 3634; NAICS: 335211

Top Humidifer/Vaporizer Brands, 2011

Brands are ranked by sales at drug stores, supermarkets and mass merchandisers (excluding Wal-Mart) for the 12 weeks ended January 22, 2012.

	($ mil.)	Share
Vicks	$ 23,592.3	46.44%
Holmes	7,096.9	13.97
Honeywell	3,795.5	7.47
Crane	3,083.2	6.07
Honeywell Easy Care	1,250.1	2.46
Safety 1st	641.0	1.26
Protec	405.5	0.80
Private label	8,566.5	16.86
Other	2,371.3	4.67

Source: *Drug Store News*, March 12, 2012, p. 2, from SymphonyIRI Group Inc.

★ 2040 ★

Small Appliances

SIC: 3634; NAICS: 335211

Top Makers of Electric Housewares, 2008

Market shares are shown based on shipments. Figures include blenders, can openers, coffee makers, food choppers/mincers, food processors, hand mixers, irons, stand mixers, toaster ovens, toasters and waffle irons.

Applica (Windmere/Black & Decker)	22.0%
Hamilton Beach brand	21.0

Jarden Corp.	19.0%
Cuisinart	8.0
Salton	7.0
Krups	3.0
Whirlpool (KitchenAid)	3.0

Source: ''Appliance Market Research Report.'' [online] from http://www.appliancemagazine.com [Published January 2010], from *Appliance* estimates and company reports.

★ 2041 ★

Vacuum Cleaners

SIC: 3635; NAICS: 335212

Vacuum Cleaner Sales by Type, 2008-2010

Sales are shown in millions of units. In 2010, upright models claimed 69% of the total, handhelds 18% and sticks 13%.

	2008	2009	2010
Upright	18.8	18.6	19.3
Handheld	5.7	5.5	5.1
Stick	3.5	3.4	3.5

Source: *HomeWorld Business*, January 2011, p. 106, from *HomeWorld Business* research.

★ 2042 ★

Dishwashers

SIC: 3639; NAICS: 335228

Top Makers of Dishwashers, 2008

Market shares are shown based on shipments.

Whirlpool	49.0%
General Electric	27.0
Electrolux	18.0
BSH	5.0
Other	1.0

Source: ''Appliance Market Research Report.'' [online] from http://www.appliancemagazine.com [Published January 2010], from *Appliance* estimates and company reports.

★ 2043 ★

Floor Care Equipment

SIC: 3639; NAICS: 333298

Household Floor Care Appliance Market, 2010

The industry was valued at 32 million units.

Vacuum cleaners	91.0%
Shampooers and steam cleaners	8.6
Polishers and waxers	0.5

Source: "Household Floor Care Appliances - U.S." [online] from http://www.freedoniagroup.com [Published September 2011], from Freedonia Group.

★ 2044 ★

Floor Care Equipment

SIC: 3639; NAICS: 333298

Top Makers of Floor Care Equipment, 2008

Market shares are shown based on shipments. Figures include vacuum cleaners and shampoo/steam cleaners.

TTI Floor Care North America	33.0%
Bissell	24.0
Electrolux (Eureka)	19.0
Dyson	5.0
Panasonic (Kenmore)	5.0
Euro Pro (Fantom)	4.0
Oreck	4.0

Source: "Appliance Market Research Report." [online] from http://www.appliancemagazine.com [Published January 2010], from *Appliance* estimates and company reports.

★ 2045 ★

Floor Care Equipment

SIC: 3639; NAICS: 333298

Top Makers Worldwide of Floor Care Equipment, 2010

The industry was valued at $5 billion.

Nilfisk Advance	17.0%
Tennant	15.0
Hako	10.0
Karcher	6.0
Other	52.0

Source: "Tennant Corp." [online] from http://phx.corporate-ir.net [Published January 2011], from company estimates.

★ 2046 ★

Sewing Machines

SIC: 3639; NAICS: 333298

Sewing Machine Market, 2010

The home sewing machine market has weathered a number of challenges in recent years. The economic downturn meant less discretionary spending and the delay of new machine purchases. However, this same downturn prompted more consumers to mend clothes and explore other do-it-yourself sewing projects.

Singer	43.0%
Brother	29.0
Other	28.0

Source: "Sewing Machine Brands." [online] from http://www.consumereports.org [Accessed October 1, 2011].

★ 2047 ★

Lamps

SIC: 3641; NAICS: 33511

Lamp Demand, 2010

Demand for lamps is projected to decline nearly two percent annually in unit terms through 2015 as the market adjusts to the regulations which will effectively ban the sale of general service incandescent lamps starting in 2012. Compact fluorescent lamps (CFLs) and halogen lamps are expected to replace most incandescents. Since both CFLs and halogen lamps have much longer lives than incandescent lamps, the average replacement rate for lamps will decrease over time, depressing unit demand.

Fluorescent	42.0%
Incandescent	25.0
Halogen	15.0
Other	18.0

Source: "Lamps." [online] from http://www.freedoniagroup.com [Published August 2011], from Freedonia Group.

★ **2048** ★

Lamps

SIC: 3641; NAICS: 33511

Top Lamp Makers, 2010

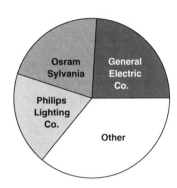

Market shares are shown in percent. The value of the lamp market is expected to increase 1.1% annually from $5.9 billion in 2010 to $6.1 billion in 2015. Fluorescent lamps claimed 42% of demand in 2010, incandescent 24%, halogen 15% and other types 19%.

General Electric Co.	24.3%
Osram Sylvania	20.9
Philips Lighting Co.	19.1
Other	35.7

Source: "Lamps." [online] from http://www.freedoniagroup.com [Published August 2011], from Freedonia Group.

★ **2049** ★

Lighting

SIC: 3641; NAICS: 33511

General Lighting Market, 2011

The market was valued at 52 billion euros and exclude automotive lighting. Acuity, Cooper, Hubbell and Philips control the overall market. Outside of the United States, the market is much more fragmented. Key reasons for this include low capital, scale and technology requirements.

Fixtures	70.0%
Light source	24.0
Ballasts/control gear	6.0

Source: "LED Lighting." [online] from http://www.research.hsbc.com [Published December 13, 2011], from Frost & Sullivan.

★ **2050** ★

Lighting

SIC: 3641; NAICS: 33511

General Lighting Market Worldwide, 2010, 2016 and 2020

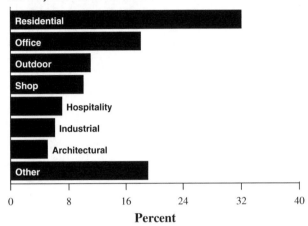

Percent

Market shares are shown based on units.

	2010	2016	2020
Residential	21.0%	28.0%	32.0%
Office	8.0	13.0	18.0
Outdoor	7.0	10.0	11.0
Shop	5.0	9.0	10.0
Hospitality	4.0	5.0	7.0
Industrial	8.0	5.0	6.0
Architectural	3.0	4.0	5.0
Other	24.0	26.0	19.0

Source: "Lighting the Way." [online] from http://img.ledsmagazine.com/pdf/LightingtheWay.pdf [Accessed May 1, 2012], from McKinsey Global.

★ **2051** ★

Lighting

SIC: 3641; NAICS: 33511

General Lighting Market Worldwide by Technology, 2010, 2016 and 2020

Market shares are shown based on units. LED - Light Emitting Diode. CFL - Compact Fluorescent Lamp. LFL - Linear Fluorescent Lamp. HID - High Intensity Discharge.

	2010	2016	2020
LED	1.0%	22.0%	46.0%
CFL	17.0	25.0	19.0
LFL	16.0	20.0	18.0
Halogen	12.0	22.0	12.0
HID	2.0	2.0	2.0
Incandescent	52.0	9.0	2.0

Source: "Lighting the Way." [online] from http://img.ledsmagazine.com/pdf/LightingtheWay.pdf [Accessed May 1, 2012], from McKinsey Global.

★ 2052 ★
Lighting
SIC: 3641; NAICS: 33511

Lighting Market Worldwide, 2010, 2012 and 2014

Demand is shown in millions of dollars.

	2010	2012	2014
China	$ 5,950	$ 7,050	$ 8,200
Western Europe	4,700	5,150	5,650
United States	3,850	4,300	5,400
Japan	4,000	4,350	4,600
Other	11,500	13,500	15,000

Source: ''NVC Lighting Holding Ltd.'' [online] from http://www.research.hsbc.com [Published July 9, 2010], from Freedonia Group.

★ 2053 ★
Lighting
SIC: 3641; NAICS: 33511

Top Lighting and Bulb Makers, 2009

The industry generated revenues of $1.7 billion in 2010.

Koninklijke Philips Electronics N.V.	30.0%
Siemens A.G.	30.0
General Electric Co.	28.0
Other	12.0

Source: ''General Electric Company.'' [online] from http://www.docstoc.com [Published June 20, 2010], from IBISWorld.

★ 2054 ★
Lighting
SIC: 3641; NAICS: 33511

Top Lighting Makers Worldwide, 2010

Market shares are shown in percent.

Philips Lighting Co.	29.0%
Osram	19.0
General Electric Co.	9.0
Sylvania	5.0
Other	38.0

Source: ''Lighting.'' [online] from http://www.havells.com/Admin/Forms/Brochures [Published March 2011], from company reports and ICRA Ltd.

★ 2055 ★
Lighting
SIC: 3641; NAICS: 33511

Top Makers of ECG Lighting in the EEA, 2010

ECG refers to electronic control gear, otherwise known as fluorescent lighting. EEA stands for the European Economic Area, which consists of the 25 European Union countries as well as Iceland, Lichtenstein and Norway.

Osram	30.0-40.0%
Philips	20.0-30.0
Tridonic/Zumtobel	10.0-20.0
Other	0.0-30.0

Source: ''Osram/Siteco Lighting.'' [online] from http://ec.europa.eu [Published June 22, 2011].

★ 2056 ★
Light Bulbs
SIC: 3643; NAICS: 335931

Top Light Bulb Brands, 2011

Market shares are shown based on sales at supermarkets, drug stores and mass merchandisers (excluding Wal-Mart) for the 52 weeks ended August 7, 2011.

GE	28.8%
GE Reveal	14.0
GE Energy Smart	9.7
Sylvania	9.3
Sylvania Double Life	3.4
Sylvania Super Saver	1.8
GE Soft White	1.7
Philips Duramax	1.6
GE Longer Life	1.4
Private label	15.5
Other	12.8

Source: *2011-2012 Nonfoods Handbook - A Supplement to Grocery Headquarters*, Annual 2011-2012, p. 17, from SymphonyIRI Group Inc.

★ 2057 ★
Light Bulbs
SIC: 3643; NAICS: 335931

Top Light Bulb Makers, 2011

Market shares are shown based on sales at supermarkets, drug stores and mass merchandisers (excluding Wal-Mart) for the 52 weeks ended August 7, 2011.

General Electric Co.	59.2%
Osram Sylvania	16.2
North American Philips Light	3.0

Continued on next page.

★ 2057 ★

[Continued]

Light Bulbs

SIC: 3643; NAICS: 335931

Top Light Bulb Makers, 2011

Market shares are shown based on sales at supermarkets, drug stores and mass merchandisers (excluding Wal-Mart) for the 52 weeks ended August 7, 2011.

Feit Electric Co.	2.6%
Energizer Holdings	0.4
Philips Lighting Co.	0.4
Technical Consumer Products	0.4
First Alert/Powermate	0.3
Globe Electric Co.	0.2
Private label	15.5
Other	1.8

Source: *2011-2012 Nonfoods Handbook - A Supplement to Grocery Headquarters*, Annual 2011-2012, p. 17, from SymphonyIRI Group Inc.

★ 2058 ★

Lighting Fixtures

SIC: 3645; NAICS: 335121

Top Lighting Fixture Makers Worldwide, 2010

Market shares are shown in percent.

Zumtobel	11.0%
Philips Lighting Co.	7.0
General Electric Co.	2.0
Sylvania	2.0
Other	78.0

Source: "Lighting." [online] from http://www.havells.com/Admin/Forms/Brochures [Published March 2011], from company reports.

★ 2059 ★

Consumer Electronics

SIC: 3651; NAICS: 33431

Audio and Video Equipment Manufacturing, 2009

Total shipments were valued at $2.87 billion. "NSK" stands for Not Specified by Kind.

	($ 000)	Share
Speakers and commercial sound equipment	$ 984,042	34.30%
Audio and video equipment manufacturing, nsk, total	833,734	29.06
Automotive audio equipment (excluding speakers)	305,713	10.66

	($ 000)	Share
Television receivers, including combination models	$ 126,478	4.41%
Other consumer audio and video equipment	619,227	21.58

Source: "Annual Survey of Manufactures." [online] from http://www.census.gov/manufacturing/asm/index.html [Accessed January 18, 2012], from U.S. Department of Commerce.

★ 2060 ★

Consumer Electronics

SIC: 3651; NAICS: 33431

Global Consumer Electronics Market, 2008 and 2011

The industry is projected to climb from 556 billion euros in 2008 to 668 billion euros in 2011.

	2008	2011
Europe	35.0%	28.0%
North America	21.0	21.0
China	10.0	13.0
South America	9.0	12.0
Japan	9.0	8.0
Middle East	5.0	6.0
Other Asia-Pacific	5.0	6.0

Source: "World Market of Consumer Technics." [online] from http://www1.messe-berlin.de/vip8_1/website/Internet/Internet/www.ifa-gpc [Accessed November 1, 2011], from GfK and Consumer Electronics Association.

★ 2061 ★

Consumer Electronics

SIC: 3651; NAICS: 33431

Global Consumer Electronics Market by Product, 2008 and 2011

The industry is projected to climb from 556 billion euros in 2008 to 668 billion euros in 2011.

	2008	2011
Mobile computers	14.0%	16.0%
Smartphones	6.0	16.0
LCD televisions	13.0	15.0
Mobile phones	20.0	12.0
Desktop computers	9.0	7.0
Tablet computers	0.0	3.0
Other	37.0	30.0

Source: "Gfk: Growth from Knowledge." [online] from http://www.gfk.com [Published September 28, 2011], from GfK and Consumer Electronics Association.

★ 2062 ★
Consumer Electronics
SIC: 3651; NAICS: 33431

Top Brands of Blu-Ray DVD Players, 2011

Market shares are shown based on dollar sales for November 2010 through April 2011. The top brands in order of market share were Sony, Samsung, LG, Panasonic, Toshiba, Vizio, Sharp, Phillips, Memorex and Denon.

Top 10 brands	91.9%
Other	8.1

Source: *Twice*, July 5, 2011, p. 17, from NPD Group Inc.

★ 2063 ★
Consumer Electronics
SIC: 3651; NAICS: 33431

Top Brands of Camcorders, 2011

Market shares are shown based on dollar sales for November 2010 through April 2011. The top brands in order of market share were Sony, Pure Digital, Canon, Kodak, Panasonic, JVC, Samsung, Vivitar, Sanyo and GoPro.

Top 10 brands	94.0%
Other	6.0

Source: *Twice*, July 5, 2011, p. 14, from NPD Group Inc.

★ 2064 ★
Consumer Electronics
SIC: 3651; NAICS: 33431

Top Brands of CD Boomboxes, 2011

Market shares are shown based on dollar sales for November 2010 through April 2011. The top brands in order of market share were Sony, GPX, Jensen, Emerson, Memorex, Coby, RCA, Disney, Phillips and JVC.

Top 10 brands	91.2%
Other	8.8

Source: *Twice*, July 5, 2011, p. 17, from NPD Group Inc.

★ 2065 ★
Consumer Electronics
SIC: 3651; NAICS: 33431

Top Brands of Home CD Players, 2011

Market shares are shown based on dollar sales for November 2010 through April 2011. The leaders in the market were Sony, Onkyo, Denon, Yamaha and Pioneer.

Top 10 brands	81.1%
Other	18.9

Source: *Twice*, July 5, 2011, p. 14, from NPD Group Inc.

★ 2066 ★
Consumer Electronics
SIC: 3651; NAICS: 33431

Top Brands of Home Speakers, 2011

Market shares are shown based on dollar sales for November 2010 through April 2011. The top brands in order of market share were Klipsch, Polk, Definitive, Bose, Bowers & Wilkins, Mirage, Energy, Yamaha, Sony and Sonance.

Top 10 brands	70.5%
Other	29.5

Source: *Twice*, July 5, 2011, p. 14, from NPD Group Inc.

★ 2067 ★
Consumer Electronics
SIC: 3651; NAICS: 33431

Top Brands of In-Dash CD Players, 2011

Market shares are shown based on dollar sales for November 2010 through April 2011. The top brands in order of market share were Kenwood, Pioneer, Sony, Alpine, JVC, Clarion, Dual Audio, Boss, Pyle, and Jensen.

Top 10 brands	99.0%
Other	1.0

Source: *Twice*, July 5, 2011, p. 17, from NPD Group Inc.

★ 2068 ★
Consumer Electronics
SIC: 3651; NAICS: 33431

Top Brands of Portable Audio Products, 2011

Market shares are shown based on dollar sales for November 2010 through April 2011. The top brands in order of market share were Apple, Sony, Monster, Bose, Skullcandy, Griffin Technology, iHome, Phillips, Belkin and SanDisk.

Top 10 brands	81.3%
Other	18.7

Source: *Twice*, July 5, 2011, p. 17, from NPD Group Inc.

★ **2069** ★

Consumer Electronics

SIC: 3651; NAICS: 33431

Top Brands of Shelf Systems, 2011

Market shares are shown based on dollar sales for November 2010 through April 2011. The top brands in order of market share were Sony, Sharp, Panasonic, RCA, Crosley, Innovative Technology, GPX, Phillips, JVC and Yamaha.

Top 10 brands	95.9%
Othe	4.1

Source: *Twice*, July 5, 2011, p. 14, from NPD Group Inc.

★ **2070** ★

Consumer Electronics

SIC: 3651; NAICS: 33431

Top Camcorder Brands in Canada, 2010

Sony was the leader in the market with a 27.9% share, followed by JVC with 18.8%. Electronics and appliance specialty stores claimed 46.8% of the market.

Handycam	27.9%
JVC	18.8
Canon	9.1
Kodak	8.1
Flip Video	3.0
Panasonic	2.5
Samsung	2.0
Other	28.7

Source: "Camcorders in Canada." [online] from http://www.scribd.com [Published September 2011], from Euromonitor.

★ **2071** ★

Consumer Electronics

SIC: 3651; NAICS: 33431

Top Car Audio Brands in China, 2009

Market shares are shown in percent.

Sony	36.0%
Pioneer	12.0
Other	52.0

Source: "Car Audio Market - The Lack of Voice." [online] from http://weihua.articlesbase.com [Published July 13, 2010].

★ **2072** ★

Consumer Electronics

SIC: 3651; NAICS: 33431

Top DVD Player Makers in India, 2009-2010

Market shares are shown based on sales of 4.5 million units in the organized sector. The organized sector represents approximately 75% of the market. The unorganized sector jumped from 20% in 2009 to 25% in 2010.

Philips	20.0%
LG	18.0
Onida	11.0
Samsung	7.0
Sony	5.5
Modern Retail	5.0
Oscar	4.5
Videocon	4.5
Other	24.5

Source: *TV Veopar Journal*, April 2011, p. 67.

★ **2073** ★

Consumer Electronics

SIC: 3651; NAICS: 33431

Top TV/DVD and Video Equipment Makers in China, 2011

The industry generated revenues of $56.7 billion. LCD/plasma televisions claimed 62.5% of the total, DVD players 17.6%, digital video cameras 8.3%, CRT televisions 5.4% and other 6.2%.

TCL Corp.	8.5%
Skyworth Group	7.0
Hisense Group	6.7
Sichuan Changhong Electronics Corp.	5.1
Konka Group Co. Ltd.	4.1
Other	68.6

Source: "TV, DVD and Video Equipment Manufacturing in China." [online] from http://www.docin.com [Published August 2011], from IBISWorld.

★ **2074** ★

E-Readers

SIC: 3651; NAICS: 33431

Top E-Reader Vendors Worldwide, 2010

Market shares are shown for the third quarter of the year.

Amazon	41.5%
Pandigital	16.1
Barnes & Noble	15.4

Continued on next page.

★ 2074 ★

[Continued]

E-Readers

SIC: 3651; NAICS: 33431

Top E-Reader Vendors Worldwide, 2010

Market shares are shown for the third quarter of the year.

Sony	8.2%
Other	10.4

Source: "No Surprise: U.S. is 75% of Global e-Reader Market." [online] from http://publishingperspectives.com [Published January 11, 2011], from International Data Corp.

★ 2075 ★

Televisions

SIC: 3651; NAICS: 33431

Television Sales by Type Worldwide, 2011

Market shares are shown based on units shipped during the third quarter of 2011.

LCD	83.1%
CRT	10.2
Plasma	6.7

Source: *Investor's Business Daily*, November 22, 2011, p. A4, from DisplaySearch.

★ 2076 ★

Televisions

SIC: 3651; NAICS: 33431

Television Shipments by Type Worldwide, 2012

According to the source, people now replace their television set every 6.9 years. LCD stands for liquid crystal display. CRT stands cathode ray tube.

LCD	88.5%
Plasma	5.3
Other and CRT	6.2

Source: *Investor's Business Daily*, May 31, 2012, p. A4, from DisplaySearch.

★ 2077 ★

Televisions

SIC: 3651; NAICS: 33431

Top 3-D Television Makers in Mexico, 2011

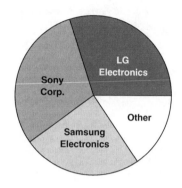

Market shares are shown in percent.

LG Electronics	33.0%
Sony Corp.	32.6
Samsung Electronics	27.1
Other	17.3

Source: *AsiaPulse News*, February 8, 2012, p. NA, from NPD Group Inc.

★ 2078 ★

Televisions

SIC: 3651; NAICS: 33431

Top Brands of 3-D LCD Televisions, 2011

Market shares are shown based on dollar sales for November 2010 through April 2011. The top five brands in order of market share were Samsung, Sony, LG, Toshiba and Sharp.

Top 5 brands	99.3%
Other	0.7

Source: *Twice*, July 5, 2011, p. 12, from NPD Group Inc.

★ 2079 ★

Televisions

SIC: 3651; NAICS: 33431

Top Brands of Direct-View Televisions, 2011

Market shares are shown based on dollar sales for November 2010 through April 2011. The top ten brands in order of market share were Disney, Sansui, Haier, RCA, Samsung, Magnavox, Sony, Toshiba, Sylvania and Panasonic.

Top 10 firms	45.5%
Other	54.5

Source: *Twice*, July 5, 2011, p. 12, from NPD Group Inc.

★ 2080 ★

Televisions

SIC: 3651; NAICS: 33431

Top Brands of Portable Televisions, 2011

Market shares are shown based on dollar sales for November 2010 through April 2011. The top ten brands in order of market share were Axion Technology, Haier, Eviant, Sharper Image, Jensen, Viore, Access HD, Phillips, Coby and RJ Technology.

Top 10 firms	71.9%
Other	28.1

Source: *Twice*, July 5, 2011, p. 12, from NPD Group Inc.

★ 2081 ★

Televisions

SIC: 3651; NAICS: 33431

Top Flat Panel Television Makers Worldwide, 2011

Market shares are shown for the fourth quarter of 2011.

Samsung	26.3%
LG Electronics	13.4
Sony	9.8
Panasonic	6.9
Sharp	5.9
Other	37.7

Source: ''2011 TV Shipments Fall After Six Consecutive Years of Growth.'' [online] from http://www.displaysearch.com [Published March 14, 2012], from DisplaySearch.

★ 2082 ★

Televisions

SIC: 3651; NAICS: 33431

Top LCD Television Makers, 2011

Market shares are shown for the fourth quarter of 2011.

Samsung	23.6%
Vizio	15.4
LG Electronics	12.4
Sony	8.0
Toshiba	7.8
Other	32.8

Source: *Investor's Business Daily*, April 5, 2012, p. A4, from IHS iSuppli.

★ 2083 ★

Televisions

SIC: 3651; NAICS: 33431

Top LCD Television Makers (19"-30"), 2010

Market shares are shown in percent.

Viewsonic	21.9%
Samsung	21.1
Vizio	11.7
Other	45.3

Source: *CRN*, March 23, 2011, p. NA, from NPD Group Inc.

★ 2084 ★

Televisions

SIC: 3651; NAICS: 33431

Top LCD Television Makers (30" or More), 2010

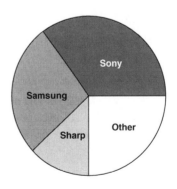

Market shares are shown in percent.

Sony	35.1%
Samsung	26.9

Continued on next page.

★ 2084 ★

[Continued]

Televisions

SIC: 3651; NAICS: 33431

Top LCD Television Makers (30" or More), 2010

Market shares are shown in percent.

Sharp	12.6%
Other	25.4

Source: *CRN*, March 23, 2011, p. NA, from NPD Group Inc.

★ 2085 ★

Televisions

SIC: 3651; NAICS: 33431

Top Television Exporters Worldwide, 2010

Total exports were valued at $99.6 billion. The United States was the largest importer with a 30.6% share.

China	22.2%
Mexico	20.4
Slovakia	7.5
Poland	7.3
Hungary	5.9
Malaysia	4.9
United States	3.8
Netherlands	3.4
Other	24.6

Source: ''2010 International Trade Statistics Yearbook.'' [online] from http://comtrade.un.org/pb/CommodityPagesNew.aspx?y2010 [Accessed April 1, 2012], from UN Comtrade.

★ 2086 ★

Televisions

SIC: 3651; NAICS: 33431

Top Television Makers in India, 2010

Market shares are shown based on sales of 18 million units.

ELCOT	27.78%
LG Electronics	20.56
Vid Group	17.22
Samsung	12.78
Onida	7.78
Other	13.88

Source: *TV Veopar Journal*, April 2011, p. 52.

★ 2087 ★

Music

SIC: 3652; NAICS: 334612, 51222

Best-Selling Albums, 2011

Albums are ranked by millions of units sold.

21, Adele	5.82
Christmas, Michael Bublé	2.45
Born This Way, Lady Gaga	2.10
Tha Carter IV, Lil Wayne	1.92
My Kinda Party, Jason Aldean	1.58
Sigh No More, Mumford & Sons	1.42
Take Care, Drake	1.25
Under the Mistletoe, Justin Bieber	1.25
Watch the Throne, Jay-Z and Kanye West . . .	1.23
Own the Night, Lady Antebellum	1.20

Source: *USA TODAY*, January 5, 2012, p. C1, from Nielsen SoundScan.

★ 2088 ★

Music

SIC: 3652; NAICS: 334612, 51222

Best-Selling Digital Artists, 2011

Data show millions of units sold from January 3, 3011-January 1, 2012.

Katy Perry	15.18
Adele	14.24
Rihanna	13.91
Glee cast	13.58
Lady Gaga	12.76
Lil Wayne	12.32
LMFAO	10.50
Bruno Mars	10.44
Eminem	9.26
Chris Brown	8.77

Source: ''Nielsen Company and Billboard's 2011 Music Industry Report.'' [online] from http://www.businesswire.com [Published January 5, 2012], from Nielsen SoundScan.

★ 2089 ★

Music

SIC: 3652; NAICS: 334612, 51222

Music Sales by Genre, 2011

Data are from January 3, 3011-January 1, 2012.

	(000)	Share
Rock	105,685	26.36%
R&B	55,435	13.83
Alternative	55,032	13.73
Country	42,923	10.71

Continued on next page.

★ 2089 ★

[Continued]

Music

SIC: 3652; NAICS: 334612, 51222

Music Sales by Genre, 2011

Data are from January 3, 3011-January 1, 2012.

	(000)	Share
Metal	32,206	8.03%
Rap	28,251	7.05
Christian/gospel	23,734	5.92
Soundtrack	13,232	3.30
Latin	11,814	2.95
Jazz	11,077	2.76
Electronic	10,049	2.51
Classical	9,566	2.39
New Age	1,929	0.48

Source: "Nielsen Company and Billboard's 2011 Music Industry Report." [online] from http://www.businesswire.com [Published January 5, 2012], from Nielsen Company.

★ 2090 ★

Music

SIC: 3652; NAICS: 334612, 51222

Top Music Firms, 2010-2011

Data are from January 3, 3011-January 1, 2012. Data include both current and catalog albums.

	2010	2011
Universal Music Group	30.84%	29.85%
Sony Music Entertainment	27.95	29.29
Warner Music Group	20.01	19.13
EMI	10.18	9.62
Other	11.02	12.11

Source: "Nielsen Company and Billboard's 2011 Music Industry Report." [online] from http://www.businesswire.com [Published January 5, 2012], from Nielsen SoundScan.

★ 2091 ★

Music

SIC: 3652; NAICS: 334612, 51222

Top Music Firms Worldwide, 2010

Market shares are shown in percent.

Universal Music Group	28.7%
Independents	23.2
Sony Music Entertainment	23.0
Warner Music Group	14.9
EMI	10.2

Source: *Financial Times*, February 18, 2012, p. 12, from *Music & Copyright*.

★ 2092 ★

Music

SIC: 3652; NAICS: 334612, 51222

Top Music Publishers Worldwide, 2010

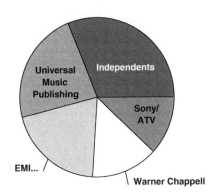

Market shares are shown in percent.

Independents	31.4%
Universal Music Publishing	22.6
EMI Music Publishing	19.7
Warner Chappell	13.9
Sony/ATV	12.5

Source: *Financial Times*, November 8, 2011, p. 19, from *Music & Copyright* and Enders Analysis.

★ 2093 ★

Cellular Phones

SIC: 3661; NAICS: 33421

iPhone Sales by Year, 2007-2011

Sales are shown in millions of units. Data for 2011 are for the first nine months.

2011	95.2
2010	40.0
2009	20.7
2008	11.6
2007	1.4

Source: *Wall Street Journal*, July 25, 2011, p. C10, from company reports.

★ 2094 ★

Cellular Phones

SIC: 3661; NAICS: 33421

Top Cell Phone Makers in Japan, 2012

Market shares are shown for February 2012.

Sharp	23.50%
Panasonic	13.80
Fujitsu	11.80

Continued on next page.

★ 2094 ★

[Continued]

Cellular Phones

SIC: 3661; NAICS: 33421

Top Cell Phone Makers in Japan, 2012

Market shares are shown for February 2012.

NEC	9.70%
Other	41.52

Source: *Investor's Business Daily*, April 25, 2012, p. A5, from comScore.

★ 2095 ★

Cellular Phones

SIC: 3661; NAICS: 33421

Top Cellular Phone Makers Worldwide, 2010-2011

Total shipments are expected to increase from 1.39 billion in 2010 to 1.54 billion in 2011.

	2010	2011
Nokia	32.6%	27.0%
Samsung	20.1	21.3
LG Electronics	8.4	5.7
ZTE	3.6	4.3
Apple Inc.	3.4	6.0
Other	31.9	35.7

Source: "Worldwide Mobile Phone Market Maintains Its Growth Trajectory in the Fourth Quarter." [online] from http://www.idc.com [Press release February 1, 2012], from International Data Corp.

★ 2096 ★

Headsets

SIC: 3661; NAICS: 33421

Top Brands of Cellular Headsets, 2011

Market shares are shown based on dollar sales for November 2010 through April 2011. The top 10 brands were Plantronics, Motorola, Aliph, Samsung, Jabra, BlueAnt Wireless, LG, Just Wireless, ESI and Bose.

Top 10 brands	86.8%
Other	13.2

Source: *Twice*, July 5, 2011, p. 14, from NPD Group Inc.

★ 2097 ★

Headsets

SIC: 3661; NAICS: 33421

Top Brands of PC Headset and Microphones, 2011

Market shares are shown based on dollar sales for November 2010 through April 2011. The top 10 brands were Logitech, Plantronics, Creative Labs, Razer, Microsoft, Cyber Acoustics, General Electric, Sennheiser, Blue Microphone and Steel Series.

Top 10 firms	85.1%
Other	14.9

Source: *Twice*, July 5, 2011, p. 14, from NPD Group Inc.

★ 2098 ★

Smartphones

SIC: 3661; NAICS: 33421

Smartphone Sales Worldwide, 2008-2014

Sales are shown in millions of units. Data for 2011-2014 are projected.

2014	999.7
2013	832.5
2012	652.7
2011	467.6
2010	298.8
2009	172.4
2008	139.3

Source: *USA TODAY*, September 6, 2011, p. 2B, from Gartner Inc.

★ **2099** ★
Smartphones
SIC: 3661; NAICS: 33421

Smartphone Shipments Worldwide by Region, 2011, 2012 and 2016

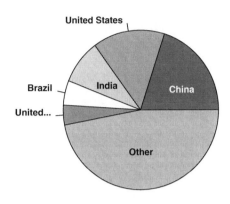

China is expected to surpass the United States to become the largest market for smartphones in 2012. Figures are shown based on unit shipments and projected for 2012 and 2016.

	2011	2012	2016
China	18.2%	20.7%	20.2%
United States	21.3	20.6	15.3
India	2.2	2.9	9.3
Brazil	1.8	2.3	4.7
United Kingdom	5.3	4.5	3.7
Other	51.2	49.0	46.8

Source: *Investor's Business Daily*, March 16, 2012, p. A4, from International Data Corp.

★ **2100** ★
Smartphones
SIC: 3661; NAICS: 33421

Top Smartphone Makers Worldwide, 2010-2011

Total shipments are expected to climb from 304.7 million in 2010 to 491.4 million in 2011.

	2010	2011
Samsung	7.5%	19.1%
Apple Inc.	15.6	19.0
Nokia	32.9	15.7
Research in Motion	16.0	10.4
HTC	7.1	8.9
Other	20.9	26.9

Source: "Smartphone Market Hits All-Time Quarterly High." [online] from http://www.idc.com [Press release February 6, 2012], from International Data Corp.

★ **2101** ★
Telephones
SIC: 3661; NAICS: 33421

Top Brands of Corded Telephones, 2011

Market shares are shown based on dollar sales for November 2010 through April 2011. The top 10 brands were AT&T, RCA, Clarity, Panasonic, Clarity, Crosley, Uniden, Plantronics, Ameriphone, Cortelco Kellogg and General Electric.

Top 10 firms	84.3%
Other	15.7

Source: *Twice*, July 5, 2011, p. 12, from NPD Group Inc.

★ **2102** ★
Telephones
SIC: 3661; NAICS: 33421

Top Brands of Cordless Telephones, 2011

Market shares are shown based on dollar sales for November 2010 through April 2011. The top 10 brands were Vtech, AT&T, Uniden, Panasonic, RCA, Clarity, Plantronics, Siemens, Motorola and Ooma Inc.

Top 10 firms	92.1%
Other	7.9

Source: *Twice*, July 5, 2011, p. 14, from NPD Group Inc.

★ **2103** ★
Direct-Broadcast Satellite Equipment
SIC: 3663; NAICS: 33422

Top Brands of Direct-Broadcast Satellite Equipment, 2011

Market shares are shown based on dollar sales for November 2010 through April 2011. The top brands in order of market share were DirecTV, Pro Brand and RCA.

Top three brands	98.7%
Other	1.3

Source: *Twice*, July 5, 2011, p. 14, from NPD Group Inc.

★ 2104 ★

Radios

SIC: 3663; NAICS: 33422

Top Radio Receiver Exporters Worldwide, 2010

Total exports were valued at $16 billion.

China	23.8%
Malaysia	10.9
Hong Kong	7.0
Portugal	6.8
Thailand	6.8
United States	6.5
Mexico	6.1
Other	32.1

Source: "2010 International Trade Statistics Yearbook." [online] from http://comtrade.un.org/pb/CommodityPagesNew. aspx?y2010 [Accessed April 1, 2012], from UN Comtrade.

★ 2105 ★

Remote Controllers

SIC: 3663; NAICS: 33422

Top Brands of Remote Controllers, 2011

Market shares are shown based on dollar sales for November 2010 through April 2011. The top brands in order of market share were Logitech, Universal Remote Controller Inc., RCA, Sony, General Electric, Jasco, DirecTV, TIVO, Phillips and Acoustic Research.

Top 10 brands	92.2%
Other	7.8

Source: *Twice*, July 5, 2011, p. 17, from NPD Group Inc.

★ 2106 ★

Satellites

SIC: 3663; NAICS: 33422

Global Satellite Launches by Operator Technology, 2010-2019

A total of 230 earth observation satellites are forecast to be launched during this period.

	Satellites	Share
Leading space programs	99	43.04%
Commercial	47	20.43
Emerging	42	18.26
In development	33	14.35
Dual use	9	3.91

Source: *Earth Imaging Journal*, January-February 2011, p. 19, from Euroconsult.

★ 2107 ★

Set-Top Decoder Boxes

SIC: 3663; NAICS: 33422

Top Brands of Digital Set-Top Decoder Boxes, 2011

Market shares are shown based on dollar sales for November 2010 through April 2011. The top brands in order of market share were Digital Stream, Apex, Magnavox, Access and RCA.

Top five brands	47.4%
Other	52.6

Source: *Twice*, July 5, 2011, p. 14, from NPD Group Inc.

★ 2108 ★

Set-Top Decoder Boxes

SIC: 3663; NAICS: 33422

Top Makers Worldwide of Set-Top Boxes, 2010

Companies are ranked by shipments in millions of units.

Pace	20.7
Motorola	19.0
Technicolor	12.9
SA Cisco	11.2
Samsung	8.7
Echostar	8.2
Humax	6.5
Skyworth	6.5
Coship	4.6
Handan	3.0

Source: *Screen Digest*, June 2011, p. 177, from IHS Screen Digest.

★ 2109 ★

Solid-State Voice Recorders

SIC: 3663; NAICS: 33422

Top Brands of Solid State Voice Recorders, 2011

Market shares are shown based on dollar sales for November 2010 through April 2011. The top brands in order of market share were Olympus, Sony, RCA, Phillips and Coby.

Top five brands	99.4%
Other	6.0

Source: *Twice*, July 5, 2011, p. 17, from NPD Group Inc.

★ 2110 ★

Telecommunications Equipment

SIC: 3663; NAICS: 33422

Broadcast and Wireless Communications Equipment, 2007

Data show the percent of industry sales held by the largest 4, 8, 20 and 50 firms in the sector. There are approximately 844 firms operating in the industry generating employment for 94,059 people.

4 largest companies	45.2%
8 largest companies	60.2
20 largest companies	76.1
50 largest companies	86.7

Source: "2007 Economic Census." [online] from http://www.census.gov/econ/concentration.html [Accessed August 12, 2011], from U.S. Bureau of the Census.

★ 2111 ★

Telecommunications Equipment

SIC: 3663; NAICS: 33422

Top Telecom Equipment Makers, 2010

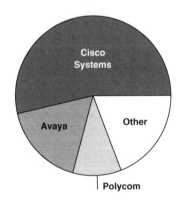

Market shares are shown based on volume.

Cisco Systems	53.0%
Avaya	17.3
Polycom	10.5
Other	19.2

Source: *CRN*, March 23, 2011, p. NA, from NPD Group Inc.

★ 2112 ★

Wireless Towers

SIC: 3663; NAICS: 33422

Leading Wireless Tower Companies, 2011

Companies are ranked by number of towers.

Crown Castle	22,251
American Tower	21,644

AT&T Towers	10,312
SBA Communications	9,290
T-Mobile Towers	8,782
United States Cellular Co.	4,802
Global Tower Partners	4,150
TowerCo	3,295
Mobilitie	2,586
Verizon Wireless	1,400

Source: "America's Top Tower Companies." [online] from http://www.wirelessestimator.com [Accessed April 17, 2012], from company reports.

★ 2113 ★

Electronic Trainers and Teaching Machines

SIC: 3669; NAICS: 33429

Shipments of Electronic Trainers and Simulators, Teaching Machines and Teaching Aids, 2006-2010

Shipments are shown in millions of dollars. Figures include kits.

2006	$ 1,030.0
2008	822.5
2007	776.7
2009	727.7
2010	708.6

Source: "Current Industrial Reports." [online] from http://www.census.gov/manufacturing/cir/index.html [Accessed August 15, 2011], from U.S. Bureau of the Census.

★ 2114 ★

Gas and Fire Detection Equipment

SIC: 3669; NAICS: 33429

Top Fire Suppression Equipment Makers Worldwide, 2009

Market shares are shown in percent.

Tyco	17.0%
UTC	14.0
Minimax	7.0
Amerex	6.0
Idex	5.0
Other	51.0

Source: "Safety and Security." [online] from http://www.bostonstrategies.com/clientlogin/rawmaterials/Safety090724.pdf [Published July 2009], from Boston Strategies International.

★ 2115 ★
Gas and Fire Detection Equipment
SIC: 3669; NAICS: 33429

Top Gas & Fire Detection Equipment Makers Worldwide, 2009

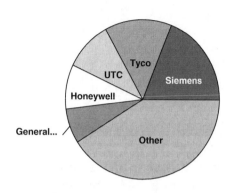

Market shares are shown in percent.

Siemens	19.0%
Tyco	14.0
UTC	10.0
Honeywell	9.0
General Electric	7.0
Other	41.0

Source: "Safety and Security." [online] from http://www.bostonstrategies.com/clientlogin/rawmaterials/Safety090724.pdf [Published July 2009], from Boston Strategies International.

★ 2116 ★
Networking Equipment
SIC: 3669; NAICS: 33429

Leading Home Networking Equipment Makers, 2010

Market shares are estimated in percent.

Netgear	30.0%
Linksys	26.0
Apple Inc.	6.0
Belkin	6.0
D-Link	6.0
Other	26.0

Source: *Investor's Business Daily*, June 23, 2011, p. A5, from RBC Capital Markets.

★ 2117 ★
Networking Equipment
SIC: 3669; NAICS: 33429

Leading Home Networking Equipment Makers in Europe, 2010

Market shares are estimated in percent.

Netgear	30.0%
AVM	24.0
D-Link	14.0
Buffalo	6.0
WD	6.0
Linksys	4.0
Other	16.0

Source: *Investor's Business Daily*, June 23, 2011, p. A5, from RBC Capital Markets.

★ 2118 ★
Networking Equipment
SIC: 3669; NAICS: 33429

Top Makers of Wi-Fi Networking Equipment Worldwide, 2011

Market shares are shown based on unit shipments for the first quarter of 2011.

TP-LINK	26.0%
Netgear	19.0
D-Link	17.0
Linksys	7.0
Pace	5.0
Other	26.0

Source: "802.11n-Enables Wi-Fi Networking Equipment Unit Shipments Increase 17%, Q2'11 over Q1'11." [online] from http://instat-com [Press release September 27, 2011], from In-Stat.

★ 2119 ★
Networking Equipment
SIC: 3669; NAICS: 33429

Top Network Security Hardware Makers, 2010

Market shares are shown based on volume.

Cisco Systems	33.5%
SonicWall	11.9
Blue Coat Systems	9.8
Other	44.8

Source: *CRN*, March 23, 2011, p. NA, from NPD Group Inc.

★ 2120 ★

Networking Equipment

SIC: 3669; NAICS: 33429

Top Wired/Wireless Router Makers, 2010

Market shares are shown based on volume.

Cisco Systems/Linksys	80.6%
D-Link	4.2
Netgear	3.6
Other	11.6

Source: *CRN*, March 23, 2011, p. NA, from NPD Group Inc.

★ 2121 ★

Payment Cards

SIC: 3669; NAICS: 33429

Top Payment Card Makers Worldwide, 2010

Companies are ranked by shipments in millions of units.

	(mil.)	Share
Gemalto	629	12.94%
G&D	592	12.18
Oberthur	459	9.44
CPI	453	9.32
Perfect	425	8.74
Versatile	381	7.84
Toppan	167	3.44
IntelCav	132	2.72
AbaciCard	102	2.10
Morpho	88	1.81
Other	1,432	29.47

Source: "Shipments of Payment Cards Worldwide 2010." [online] from http://www.nilsonreport.com [Published October 2011], from *Nilson Report*.

★ 2122 ★

RFID Tags

SIC: 3669; NAICS: 33429

Global RFID Market, 2008, 2013 and 2018

Market shares are shown based on revenues.

	2008	2013	2018
East Asia	52.9%	36.3%	40.6%
North America	25.5	34.5	29.2
Europe	18.1	23.6	24.7
Other	3.4	5.5	5.5

Source: "RFID: Prospects for Europe." [online] from http://ftp.jrc.es/EURdoc/JRC58486.pdf [Accessed February 20, 2012], from IdTechEX.

★ 2123 ★

Memory Cards

SIC: 3672; NAICS: 334412

Top Brands of Memory Cards, 2011

Market shares are shown based on dollar sales for November 2010 through April 2011. The top brands in order of market share were SanDisk, PNY Electronics, Lexar Media, Transcend, Dane-Elec, Sony, Kodak, Kingston Technology, Delkin Devices, Eye-Fi.

Top 10 brands	88.8%
Other	11.2

Source: *Twice*, July 5, 2011, p. 18, from NPD Group Inc.

★ 2124 ★

Printed Circuit Boards

SIC: 3672; NAICS: 334412

Printed Circuit Board Production Worldwide, 2010-2012

Production are ranked by sales in millions of dollars. China is expected to have 44% of the market in 2012.

	2010	2011	2012
China	$ 22,185	$ 24,740	$ 27,000
Japan	9,895	9,260	8,470
Taiwan	7,076	7,320	7,510
South Korea	6,087	6,520	6,650
America	3,439	3,525	3,595
Europe	2,963	3,275	3,310
Other	3,437	3,670	4,105

Source: "World PCB Production." [online] from http://www.tpca.org.tw/download.aspx?dlfnTPCAShow_Market.pdf [Accessed February 14, 2012], from N.T. Information.

★ 2125 ★

Printed Circuit Boards

SIC: 3672; NAICS: 334412

Shipments of Bare Printed Circuit Boards, 2006-2010

Shipments are shown in millions of dollars.

2008	$ 5,269
2006	4,933
2007	4,443
2010	4,335
2009	4,113

Source: "Current Industrial Reports." [online] from http://www.census.gov/manufacturing/cir/index.html [Accessed August 15, 2011], from U.S. Bureau of the Census.

★ 2126 ★
Printed Circuit Boards
SIC: 3672; NAICS: 334412

Top Printed Circuit Board Makers Worldwide, 2010

Companies are ranked by sales in millions of dollars.

Unimicron Group	$ 2,179
Ibiden	2,110
Nippon Mektron	2,106
Tripod	1,370
TTM Technologies	1,366
SEMCO	1,282
Nanya PCB	1,158
Foxconn	1,148
KB PCB Group	1,122
Shinko Denki	1,003

Source: "World PCB Production." [online] from http://www.tpca.org.tw/download.aspx?dlfnTPCAShow_Market.pdf [Accessed February 14, 2012].

★ 2127 ★
Chip Cards
SIC: 3674; NAICS: 334413

Top Makers Worldwide of Chip Cards, 2010

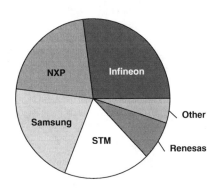

Market shares are shown in percent.

Infineon	27.0%
NXP	21.0
Samsung	21.0
STM	18.0
Renesas	8.0
Other	5.0

Source: "Deutsche Bank European TMT Conference." [online] from http://www.equitystory.com [Published September 7, 2011], from Strategy Analytics.

★ 2128 ★
Foundries
SIC: 3674; NAICS: 334413

Top Semiconductor Foundry Firms Worldwide, 2010-2011

Industry revenues increased from $28.3 billion in 2010 to $29.7 billion in 2011.

	2010	2011
TSMC	47.1%	48.8%
UMC	13.5	12.1
GlobalFoundries	12.4	12.0
SMIC	5.5	4.4
TowerJazz	1.8	2.1
IBM Microelectronics	1.8	1.8
Vanguard International	1.8	1.7
Fongbu HiTek	1.8	1.6
Powerchip Technology	0.5	1.4
Other	12.4	12.3

Source: *EE Times*, April 2, 2012, p. NA, from Gartner Inc.

★ 2129 ★
Lasers
SIC: 3674; NAICS: 334413

Global Laser Revenues by Application, 2011

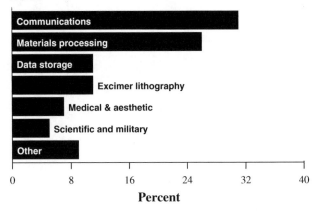

The industry generated revenues of $7.46 billion in 2011.

Communications	31.0%
Materials processing	26.0
Data storage	11.0
Excimer lithography	11.0
Medical & aesthetic	7.0
Scientific and military	5.0
Other	9.0

Source: *Laser Focus World*, January 2012, p. NA, from Strategies Unlimited.

★ 2130 ★
Oscillators
SIC: 3674; NAICS: 334413

Top Makers of Oscillators and High-End Crystals Worldwide, 2009

Market shares are shown in percent.

Epson Toycom	22.0%
NDK	16.0
Kyocera Kinseki	10.0
KDS	9.0
TXC	8.0
Ventron	5.0
Hosonic	3.0
Rakon	3.0
Pericom	2.0
TEW	2.0
Other	20.0

Source: "TXC Corp." [online] from https://mm.jpmorgan.com [Published September 1, 2010], from J.P. Morgan.

★ 2131 ★
Semiconductors
SIC: 3674; NAICS: 334413

Desktop PC Market Worldwide, 2011

Market shares are shown based on unit shipments for the third quarter of 2011.

Intel	75.8%
AMD	24.1

Source: *Business Wire*, November 3, 2011, p. NA, from International Data Corp.

★ 2132 ★
Semiconductors
SIC: 3674; NAICS: 334413

Global Semiconductor Sales, 2012

Total sales for the year-to-date were $301 billion.

Asia-Pacific	54.0%
Americas	19.0
Japan	14.5
Europe	12.5

Source: *Investor's Business Daily*, June 11, 2012, p. A4, from Semiconductor Industry Association.

★ 2133 ★
Semiconductors
SIC: 3674; NAICS: 334413

Notebook PC Market Worldwide, 2011

Market shares are shown based on unit shipments for the third quarter of 2011.

Intel	82.3%
AMD	17.6
Via Technologies	0.1

Source: *Investor's Business Daily*, November 4, 2011, p. A4, from International Data Corp.

★ 2134 ★
Semiconductors
SIC: 3674; NAICS: 334413

PC Server/Workstation Processor Market Worldwide, 2011

Market shares are shown based on unit shipments for the third quarter of 2011.

Intel	95.1%
AMD	4.9

Source: *Business Wire*, November 3, 2011, p. NA, from International Data Corp.

★ 2135 ★
Semiconductors
SIC: 3674; NAICS: 334413

Shipments of Crystals, Filters, Piezoelectric and Other Related Electronic Devices, 2006-2010

Shipments are shown in millions of dollars.

2006	$ 754
2007	689
2008	656
2009	570
2010	544

Source: "Current Industrial Reports." [online] from http://www.census.gov/manufacturing/cir/index.html [Accessed August 15, 2011], from U.S. Bureau of the Census.

★ 2136 ★
Semiconductors
SIC: 3674; NAICS: 334413

Top DRAM Makers Worldwide, 2011

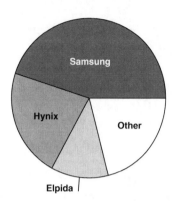

Market shares are shown for the third quarter of 2011. DRAM stands for Dynamic Random Access Memory.

Samsung	45.0%
Hynix	22.0
Elpida	12.0
Other	21.0

Source: *New York Times*, February 27, 2012, p. NA, from iSuppli.

★ 2137 ★
Semiconductors
SIC: 3674; NAICS: 334413

Top DRAM Module Suppliers Worldwide, 2010

Market shares are shown based on revenues. Data are for third party suppliers.

Kingston Technology	46.04%
A-Data Technology	6.92
Ramaxel Technology	6.73
Smart Modular Technologies	6.08
Crucial Technology	5.77
Corsair Memory	3.16
Apacer Technology	2.98
MA Labs	2.95
Kingmax Semiconductor	2.84
PQI	2.71
Other	13.81

Source: "Marketshare Chart." [online] from http://www.kingston.com/company/marketshare.asp [Published May 2011], from iSuppli.

★ 2138 ★
Semiconductors
SIC: 3674; NAICS: 334413

Top Makers Worldwide of Automotive Semiconductors, 2010

Market shares are shown in percent.

Renesas	14.0%
Infineon	9.0
Freescale	8.0
STMicro	8.0
NXP	7.0
Other	54.0

Source: "Deutsche Bank European TMT Conference." [online] from http://www.equitystory.com [Published September 7, 2011], from Strategy Analytics.

★ 2139 ★
Semiconductors
SIC: 3674; NAICS: 334413

Top Microcontroller Makers Worldwide, 2010

Market shares are shown in percent.

Renesas	28.1%
Freescale	9.3
Samsung	7.8
Infineon	6.9
Atmei	6.1
Microchip	6.0
Other	35.8

Source: "Microcontroller Solutions Group." [online] from http://phx.corporate-ir.net [Published June 2011], from IHS iSuppli.

★ 2140 ★
Semiconductors
SIC: 3674; NAICS: 334413

Top Microprocessor Makers Worldwide, 2011

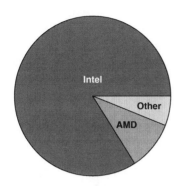

Market shares are shown for the third quarter of 2011.

Intel	83.7%
AMD	10.2
Other	6.1

Source: *Wall Street Journal*, December 13, 2011, p. C10, from IHS iSuppli.

★ 2141 ★
Semiconductors
SIC: 3674; NAICS: 334413

Top NAND Flash Memory Makers Worldwide, 2011

Market shares are shown for the fourth quarter of 2011.

Samsung	36.9%
Toshiba	31.1
Micron	18.8
Hynix	12.8
Powerchip	0.5

Source: *Investor's Business Daily*, March 26, 2012, p. A6, from IHS iSuppli.

★ 2142 ★
Semiconductors
SIC: 3674; NAICS: 334413

Top Power Semiconductor Makers Worldwide, 2010

Market shares are shown in percent.

Infineon	11.0%
Mitsubishi	7.0
STMicro	7.0

Toshiba	7.0%
Vishay	6.0

Source: "Deutsche Bank European TMT Conference." [online] from http://www.equitystory.com [Published September 7, 2011], from Strategy Analytics.

★ 2143 ★
Semiconductors
SIC: 3674; NAICS: 334413

Top Semiconductor Makers, 2010

The industry generated total revenues of $51.9 billion in 2010.

Intel	14.7%
Samsung Electronics	9.6
Texas Instruments	6.0
Toshiba Corp.	5.0
Other	64.7

Source: *Datamonitor Industry Market Research*, November 11, 2011, p. NA, from Datamonitor.

★ 2144 ★
Semiconductors
SIC: 3674; NAICS: 334413

Top Semiconductor Makers in France, 2010

The industry generated total revenues of $3.4 billion in 2010.

Samsung Electronics	30.0%
Intel	23.3
Texas Instruments	19.9
STMicroelectronics	7.4
Other	19.4

Source: *Datamonitor Industry Market Research*, November 11, 2011, p. NA, from Datamonitor.

★ 2145 ★
Semiconductors
SIC: 3674; NAICS: 334413

Top Semiconductor Makers in Japan, 2010

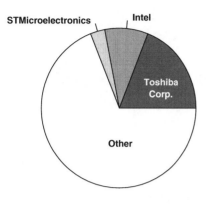

The industry generated total revenues of $48.6 billion in 2010.

Toshiba Corp.	19.3%
Intel	9.3
STMicroelectronics	2.7
Other	68.7

Source: *Datamonitor Industry Market Research*, November 11, 2011, p. NA, from Datamonitor.

★ 2146 ★
Semiconductors
SIC: 3674; NAICS: 334413

Top Semiconductor Makers Worldwide, 2011

Market shares are shown based on revenues of $312.7 billion.

Intel	15.9%
Samsung Electronics	9.3
Texas Instruments	4.5
Toshiba Corp.	4.3
Renesas	3.6
Qualcomm	3.2
STMicroelectronics	3.1
Hynix	2.8
Broadcom	2.3
Micron Technology	2.3
AMD	2.1
Infineon Technologies	1.7
Sony	1.6
Other	39.3

Source: "Intel Reasserts Semiconductor Market Leadership in 2011." [online] from http://www.isuppli.com [Published December 1, 2011], from IHS iSuppli.

★ 2147 ★
Semiconductors
SIC: 3674; NAICS: 334413

Top Semiconductor TAM Makers Worldwide, 2011

Leading electronic equipment manufacturers remained the center of the semiconductor world in 2011, accounting for $105.6 billion of semiconductors on a design total available market (TAM) basis. Design TAM represents the total silicon content in all products designed by a certain electronic equipment manufacturer or in a certain region, while purchasing TAM represents the total silicon content purchased directly by a certain electronic equipment manufacturer or in a certain region. Design TAM is a useful index for semiconductor vendors when they are considering how to allocate their sales or field application engineer resources by customer or region. Purchasing TAM is a useful index for semiconductor vendors when they are considering how to establish an efficient distribution network by customer or region. According to Gartner, the major growth drivers in 2011 were smartphones, media tablets and solid-state drives.

Apple Inc.	5.7%
Hewlett-Packard Co.	5.5
Samsung Electronics	5.5
Dell	3.2
Nokia	3.0
Sony	2.7
Lenovo	2.5
Toshiba Corp.	2.5
LG Electronics	2.2
Panasonic	2.1
Other	65.0

Source: "Gartner Says Apple Became the Top Semiconductor Customer in 2011." [online] from http://www.gartner.com [Press release January 24, 2012], from Gartner Inc.

★ 2148 ★

Silicon Timing Industry

SIC: 3674; NAICS: 334413

MEMS-Based Silicon Timing Market Worldwide, 2010

According to SiTime, the silicon MEMS timing market is growing at a CAGR of 66.4% per year from 2011-2016. This growth is the result of company's adopting the MEMS-based technology over legacy quartz products. The company reported shipping more than 50 million oscillators, clock generators and resonators since its inception.

SiTime	85.0%
Discera	15.0

Source: ''Revolutionizing the Timing Market Silicon Replaces Quartz.'' [online] from http://www.i-micronews.com/upload/./Microtech-SiTime%20June%202010.pdf [Published June 2010], from Yole Developpement.

★ 2149 ★

Silicon Wafers

SIC: 3674; NAICS: 334413

Top Makers of Silicon Wafers Worldwide, 2011

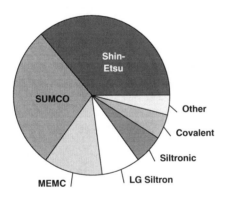

Market shares are shown in percent.

Shin-Etsu	36.0%
SUMCO	29.0
MEMC	12.0
LG Siltron	8.0
Siltronic	6.0
Covalent	5.0
Other	4.0

Source: ''Supply Chain Management in Electronics Industry.'' [online] from http://www.sematech.org [Accessed October 1, 2011], from iSuppli.

★ 2150 ★

Capacitors

SIC: 3675; NAICS: 334414

Top Makers of Aluminum Electrolytic Capacitors Worldwide, 2011

Market shares are shown in percent.

Nippon Chemi-con	25.0%
Nichicon	18.0
Panasonic	15.0
Rubycon	15.0
Other	27.0

Source: ''Supply Chain Management in Electronics Industry.'' [online] from http://www.sematech.org [Accessed October 1, 2011], from iSuppli.

★ 2151 ★

Capacitors

SIC: 3675; NAICS: 334414

Top Makers of Ceramic Capacitors Worldwide, 2011

Market shares are shown in percent.

Murata	30.0%
Kyocera	15.0
TDK	15.0
Taiyo-yuden	10.0
Other	30.0

Source: ''Supply Chain Management in Electronics Industry.'' [online] from http://www.sematech.org [Accessed October 1, 2011], from iSuppli.

★ 2152 ★
Capacitors
SIC: 3675; NAICS: 334414

Top Makers of Tantalum Electrolytic Capacitors Worldwide, 2011

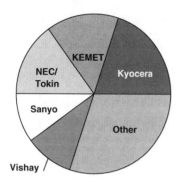

Market shares are shown in percent.

Kyocera	20.0%
KEMET	15.0
NEC/Tokin	15.0
Sanyo	10.0
Vishay	10.0
Other	30.0

Source: "Supply Chain Management in Electronics Industry." [online] from http://www.sematech.org [Accessed October 1, 2011], from iSuppli.

★ 2153 ★
Anodes
SIC: 3679; NAICS: 334419

Top Makers of Anodes Worldwide, 2010

An anode is an electrode through which electric current flows into a polarized electrical device.

Hitachi Chemical	35.0%
Nippon Carbon	16.0
BTR New Materials	12.0
JFE Chemical	10.0
Mitsubishi Chemical	8.0
Other	19.0

Source: "Samsung SDI." [online] from https://mm.jpmorgan.com [Published April 6, 2011], from J.P. Morgan estimates and company data.

★ 2154 ★
Battery Separators
SIC: 3679; NAICS: 334419

Top Makers of Battery Separators Worldwide, 2010

Market shares are shown in percent.

Asahi Kasei	29.0%
Celgard	24.0
Tonen	24.0
Ube Industries	10.0
SK Energy	9.0
Other	4.0

Source: "Samsung SDI." [online] from https://mm.jpmorgan.com [Published April 6, 2011], from J.P. Morgan estimates and company data.

★ 2155 ★
Cathodes
SIC: 3679; NAICS: 334419

Top Makers of Cathodes Worldwide, 2010

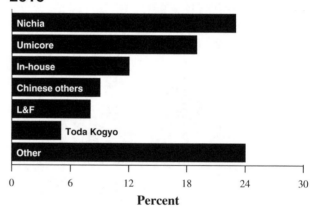

A cathode is an electrode through which electric current flows out of a polarized electrical device.

Nichia	23.0%
Umicore	19.0
In-house	12.0
Chinese others	9.0
L&F	8.0
Toda Kogyo	5.0
Other	24.0

Source: "Samsung SDI." [online] from https://mm.jpmorgan.com [Published April 6, 2011], from J.P. Morgan estimates and company data.

★ 2156 ★
E-Reader Displays
SIC: 3679; NAICS: 33431

E-Reader Display Market, 2010

An estimated 12 million e-readers are expected to be shipped in 2010.

E Ink Holdings	90.0%
Other	10.0

Source: "E Ink Holdings Inc." [online] from https://mm.jpmorgan.com [Published January 19, 2011].

★ 2157 ★
Electronic Components
SIC: 3679; NAICS: 334419

Top Electrical Component Makers Worldwide, 2010

Market shares are shown in percent.

Schneider Electric S.A.	22.3%
ABB Ltd.	10.1
Siemens	4.8
Furukawa Electric	4.0
Other	58.9

Source: *Datamonitor Industry Market Research*, May 20, 2011, p. NA, from Datamonitor.

★ 2158 ★
Electronic Components
SIC: 3679; NAICS: 334419

Top Electronic Apparatus and Other Components Makers, 2010

The industry generated revenues of $10 billion in 2010.

Varian Medical Systems Inc.	11.0%
Eaton Corp.	10.0
Emerson Electric Co.	10.0
General Electric Co.	6.0
Schneider Electric S.A.	5.0
Other	58.0

Source: "General Electric Company." [online] from http://www.docstoc.com [Published June 20, 2010], from IBISWorld.

★ 2159 ★
Electronic Components
SIC: 3679; NAICS: 334419

Top Electronic Component Firms Worldwide, 2011

The industry generated revenues of $163.5 billion in 2011. Power cables claimed 61.2% of the total and switchgear 38.7%.

Schneider Electric	15.8%
ABB Ltd.	9.7
Siemens	4.1
Furukawa Electric	3.7
Other	66.7

Source: *Datamonitor Industry Market Research*, February 24, 2012, p. NA, from Datamonitor.

★ 2160 ★
Electronic Ink
SIC: 3679; NAICS: 33431

E-Reader Frontplane Market Worldwide, 2010

Market shares are shown for the fourth quarter 2010. It also controls 78% of the display market.

E Ink Holdings	96.0%
Other	4.0

Source: *Touch Panel*, May 2011, p. 1, from IMS Research.

★ 2161 ★
Flat Panel Displays
SIC: 3679; NAICS: 33431

Top Flat Panel Display Producing Nations Worldwide, 2015

Market shares are projected based on surface produced.

Korea	46.0%
Taiwan	36.0
China	11.0
Japan	7.0

Source: "Ambition 2015 Objective." [online] from http://www.airliquide.com [Published December 2010], from DisplaySearch.

★ 2162 ★
Sapphire Ingots
SIC: 3679; NAICS: 334419

Top Makers of Sapphire Ingots Worldwide, 2011

Sapphire ingots are used to make LED chips.

Sapphire Tech	29.0%
Rubicon	27.0
Monocrystal	21.0
Kyocera	8.0
Namiki	8.0
ACME	7.0

Source: "LED Industry." [online] from http://www.docstoc.com [Published March 28, 2011], from J.P. Morgan estimates.

★ 2163 ★
Batteries
SIC: 3691; NAICS: 335911

Battery Demand, 2010

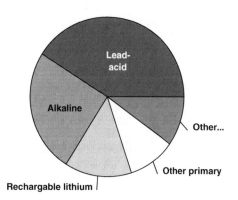

Sales are projected to increase from $13.2 billion in 2010 to $16.7 billion in 2015.

Lead-acid	41.0%
Alkaline	25.0
Rechargable lithium	14.0
Other primary	10.0
Other secondary	10.0

Source: "Batteries." [online] from http://www.freedoniagroup.com [Published September 2011], from Freedonia Group.

★ 2164 ★
Batteries
SIC: 3691; NAICS: 335911

Battery Sales by Type, 2011

Data show sales at supermarkets, drug stores and mass merchandisers (excluding Wal-Mart) for the 52 weeks ended June 12, 2011.

	($ mil.)	Share
Alkaline	$ 456.4	85.18%
NICD/NIMD/Lith-Ion/Lead Acid .	15.5	2.89
Zinc Air	12.5	2.33
Other	51.4	9.59

Source: *Supermarket News*, August 15, 2011, p. NA, from SymphonyIRI Group Inc.

★ 2165 ★
Batteries
SIC: 3691; NAICS: 335911

Lithium Polymer Battery Market Worldwide, 2010

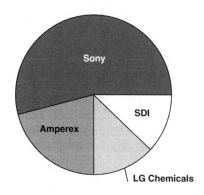

Market shares are shown based on capacity.

Sony	54.0%
Amperex	21.0
LG Chemicals	13.0
SDI	12.0

Source: "Samsung SDI." [online] from https://mm.jpmorgan.com [Published April 6, 2011], from J.P. Morgan estimates and company data.

★ 2166 ★

Batteries

SIC: 3691; NAICS: 335911

Top Battery Brands, 2011

Market shares are shown based on sales at supermarkets, drug stores and mass merchandisers (excluding Wal-Mart) for the 52 weeks ended August 13, 2011.

Energizer	39.4%
Duracell	38.4
Rayovac	0.1
Private label	0.2
Other	21.9

Source: *2011-2012 Nonfoods Handbook - A Supplement to Grocery Headquarters*, Annual 2011-2012, p. 17, from Nielsen Company.

★ 2167 ★

Batteries

SIC: 3691; NAICS: 335911

Top Battery Makers, 2011

Market shares are shown based on sales at supermarkets, drug stores and mass merchandisers (excluding Wal-Mart) for the 52 weeks ended August 7, 2011.

Procter & Gamble Co.	40.0%
Energizer Holdings	39.0
Other	21.0

Source: ''Procter & Gamble.'' [online] from http://www.trinity.edu/smf/inc/reports/fl2011/pg.pdf [Published November 8, 2011], from SymphonyIRI Group Inc.

★ 2168 ★

Batteries

SIC: 3691; NAICS: 335911

Top Household Battery Brands, 2011

Market shares are shown based on sales at supermarkets, drug stores and mass merchandisers (excluding Wal-Mart) for the 52 weeks ended August 13, 2011.

Duracell CopperTop	35.1%
Energizer Max	27.0
Duracell Ultra + Pix	4.6
Energizer Lithium	4.6
Private label	19.4
Other	9.3

Source: *2011-2012 Nonfoods Handbook - A Supplement to Grocery Headquarters*, Annual 2011-2012, p. 17, from Nielsen Company.

★ 2169 ★

Batteries

SIC: 3691; NAICS: 335911

Top LiB Suppliers Worldwide, 2015

Market shares are projected.

Aone	26.0%
LG Chemical	18.0
Panasonic Sanyo	15.0
A123 Systems	14.0
SB LiMotive	6.0
GS Yuasa	2.0
Hitachi	2.0
Other	27.0

Source: ''A123 Investor Presentation.'' [online] from http://files.shareholder.com [Published August 2011], from Roland Berger.

★ 2170 ★

Batteries

SIC: 3691; NAICS: 335911

Top LiB Suppliers Worldwide (Trucks and Buses), 2015

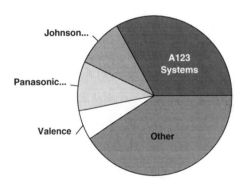

Market shares are projected.

A123 Systems	33.0%
Johnson Controls	10.0
Panasonic Sanyo	10.0
Valence	6.0
Other	41.0

Source: ''A123 Investor Presentation.'' [online] from http://files.shareholder.com [Published August 2011], from Roland Berger.

★ 2171 ★
Batteries
SIC: 3691; NAICS: 335911

Top Lithium Battery Markets Worldwide, 2010

Market shares are shown based on volume.

Laptop PCs	43.0%
Mobile phones	39.0
Digital cameras and video cameras	5.0
Power tools	2.0
Other general	11.0

Source: "LIB Materials Industry." [online] from http://gold-estate.com/content/Lithium/LiB12611.pdf [Published January 26, 2011], from Deutsche Securities.

★ 2172 ★
Batteries
SIC: 3691; NAICS: 335911

Top Makers Worldwide of Lithium-Ion Batteries, 2011

Market shares are shown for the first quarter of 2011.

Samsung	25.4%
Sanyo	18.4
LG Chemical	17.3
Sony	7.9
Panasonic	4.9
Other	26.1

Source: "Korea Tops Global Lithium-Ion Battery Market in 2nd Quarter." [online] from http://www.korea.net [Published September 7, 2011], from Techno Systems Research.

★ 2173 ★
Batteries
SIC: 3691; NAICS: 335911

Top Makers Worldwide of Lithium-Ion Power Tool Cells, 2007

Market shares are shown in percent.

Sony	39.0%
Panasonic Sanyo	16.0
E-One	14.0
A123 Systems	13.0
SDI	10.0
LG Chemical	5.0
Other	3.0

Source: "Power Tool Batteries." [online] from http://www.el-sevierdirect.com/brochures/ecps/PDFs/PowerTools_Batteries.pdf [Accessed September 1, 2011], from Avicenne.

★ 2174 ★
Batteries
SIC: 3691; NAICS: 335911

Top Specialty Battery Brands, 2011

Market shares are shown based on sales at supermarkets, drug stores and mass merchandisers (excluding Wal-Mart) for the 52 weeks ended August 13, 2011.

Energizer	47.4%
Duracell	35.8
Rayovac	5.5
Private label	10.2
Other	1.1

Source: *2011-2012 Nonfoods Handbook - A Supplement to Grocery Headquarters*, Annual 2011-2012, p. 17, from Nielsen Company.

★ 2175 ★
Batteries
SIC: 3691; NAICS: 335911

Top Zinc Air Battery Brands, 2011

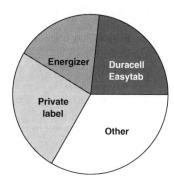

Market shares are shown based on sales of $56.8 million at supermarkets, drug stores and mass merchandisers (excluding Wal-Mart) for the 52 weeks ended October 3, 2011.

Duracell Easytab	23.1%
Energizer	18.5
Private label	25.0
Other	33.4

Source: *Progressive Grocer*, November 2011, p. NA, from Information Resources Inc.

★ 2176 ★
Automotive Electronics
SIC: 3694; NAICS: 336322

Other Motor Vehicle Electric Equipment Manufacturing, 2010

Total shipments were valued at $10.88 billion. "NSK" stands for Not Specified by Kind.

	($ 000)	Share
Electrical and electronic equipment, motor vehicles . .	$ 4,311,596	39.63%
Cranking motors (starters) . . .	1,579,603	14.52
Electrical engine equipment, all other types, complete . . .	1,566,715	14.40
Ignition wiring harness and electrical cable sets	1,368,174	12.58
Alternators, generators, and regulators, battery charging . .	810,700	7.45
Spark plugs, internal combustion engines	285,980	2.63
Parts for electrical and electronic engine equipment	260,364	2.39
Other motor vehicle electrical/ electronic equip. mfg, nsk, total	695,128	6.39

Source: "Annual Survey of Manufactures." [online] from http://www.census.gov/manufacturing/asm/index.html [Accessed January 18, 2012], from U.S. Department of Commerce.

★ 2177 ★
CD-R Media
SIC: 3695; NAICS: 334613

Top Blank CD-R Brands, 2011

Market shares are shown based on supermarket sales for the 52 weeks ended March 20, 2011.

Memorex	60.76%
Sony	10.93
TDK	9.47
Fuji	7.73
Maxell	7.38
Staples	1.77
Imation	1.20
Fujifilm	0.50
Innovera	0.15
Kodak	0.08
Other	0.03

Source: *Non-Foods Management*, Annual 2011-2012, p. 176, from SymphonyIRI Group Inc.

★ 2178 ★

Autos

SIC: 3711; NAICS: 336111

Auto and Light Truck Production by State, 2010

Market shares are shown based on production of 7.63 million vehicles.

Michigan	20.8%
Ohio	14.5
Indiana	11.7
Kentucky	9.7
Alabama	9.1
Missouri	6.9
Texas	5.7
Kansas	4.1
Illinois	4.0
Other	13.5

Source: *Automotive News*, July 25, 2011, p. 3, from Automotive News Data Center and company sources.

★ 2179 ★

Autos

SIC: 3711; NAICS: 336111

Auto Production by Powertrain, 2010, 2015 and 2020

Market shares are shown in percent.

	2010	2015	2020
Gas	95.3%	90.4%	88.0%
Hybrid	2.4	3.5	4.4
Diesel	2.3	3.5	3.3
Plugin	0.0	1.4	2.3
Full electric	0.0	1.2	2.0

Source: "U.S. Autos & Auto Parts." [online] from http://www.ceres.org [Published March 14, 2011], from Baum & Associates.

★ 2180 ★

Autos

SIC: 3711; NAICS: 336111

Best-Selling Autos, 2011

Vehicles are ranked by unit sales.

Ford F-series	584,817
Chevrolet Silverado	415,130
Toyota Camry	308,510
Nissan Altima	268,981
Ford Escape	254,293
Ford Fusion	248,067
Dodge Ram	244,763
Toyota Corolla/Matrix	240,259
Honda Accord	235,625
Chevrolet Cruze	231,732

Source: *Automotive News*, January 9, 2012, p. 35, from Automotive News Data Center.

★ 2181 ★

Autos

SIC: 3711; NAICS: 336111

Best-Selling Entry-Luxury Autos, 2011

Data show unit sales.

BMW 3 Series	94,371
Mercedes-Benz C-Class	69,314
Nissan Maxima	58,737
Infiniti G	58,246
Cadillac CTS	55,042
Audi A4/A5	50,619
Lexus ES	40,873

Source: "Sales Charts of the Top 10 Best-Selling Cars of 2011 and December 2011, by Class." [online] from http://www.examiner.com [Accessed March 20, 2012].

★ 2182 ★

Autos

SIC: 3711; NAICS: 336111

Best-Selling Luxury SUVs, 2011

Data show unit sales.

Mercedes-Benz GL	25,139
Range Rover Sport	15,333

Continued on next page.

★ 2182 ★

[Continued]

Autos

SIC: 3711; NAICS: 336111

Best-Selling Luxury SUVs, 2011

Data show unit sales.

Cadillac Escalade	15,079
Infiniti QX	13,428
Porsche Cayenne	12,978
Lexus GX	11,609
Range Rover	9,761

Source: "Sales Charts of the Top 10 Best-Selling Cars of 2011 and December 2011, by Class." [online] from http://www.examiner.com [Accessed March 20, 2012].

★ 2183 ★

Autos

SIC: 3711; NAICS: 336111

Best-Selling Mainstream Compact Autos, 2011

Data show unit sales.

Toyota Corolla/Matrix	240,259
Chevrolet Cruze	232,588
Honda Civic	221,235
Hyundai Elantra/Touring	186,381
Volkswagen Jetta/Sportswagen	177,360
Ford Focus	175,717
Toyota Prius/Prius V	135,343

Source: "Sales Charts of the Top 10 Best-Selling Cars of 2011 and December 2011, by Class." [online] from http://www.examiner.com [Accessed March 20, 2012].

★ 2184 ★

Autos

SIC: 3711; NAICS: 336111

Best-Selling Midsize Autos, 2011

Data show unit sales.

Toyota Camry	308,510
Nissan Altima	268,981
Honda Accord/Crosstour	253,599
Ford Fusion	248,067
Hyundai Sonata	225,961
Chevrolet Malibu	204,808
Chevrolet Impala	171,434

Source: "Sales Charts of the Top 10 Best-Selling Cars of 2011 and December 2011, by Class." [online] from http://www.examiner.com [Accessed March 20, 2012].

★ 2185 ★

Autos

SIC: 3711; NAICS: 336111

Best-Selling Small Luxury Cars, 2011

Market shares are shown in percent.

BMW 3 series	18.0%
Mercedes-Benz C-Class	13.0
Infiniti G	11.0
Cadillac CTS	10.0
Lexus ES	8.0
Audi A4/S4	7.0
Acura TL	6.0
Hyundai Genesis	6.0
Lexus IS	6.0
Other	15.0

Source: *Automotive News*, April 2, 2012, p. 40, from Automotive News Data Center.

★ 2186 ★

Autos

SIC: 3711; NAICS: 336111

Best-Selling Vans, 2011

Data show unit sales.

Ford E-Series	116,874
Toyota Sienna	111,429
Dodge Grand Caravan	110,862
Honda Odyssey	107,068
Chrysler Town & Country	94,320
Chevrolet Express	71,943
Ford Transit Connect	31,943

Source: "Sales Charts of the Top 10 Best-Selling Cars of 2011 and December 2011, by Class." [online] from http://www.examiner.com [Accessed March 20, 2012].

★ 2187 ★

Autos

SIC: 3711; NAICS: 336111

Largest Government Fleets, 2010

Agencies or departments are ranked by size of fleet.

Department of Homeland Security	54,972
Department of Agriculture	45,110
Department of Justice	41,002
Department of the Interior	34,007
Department of Energy	15,108
Department of Veterans Affairs	14,704
Department of State	11,799
Department of Transportation	6,163

Continued on next page.

★ 2187 ★

[Continued]

Autos

SIC: 3711; NAICS: 336111

Largest Government Fleets, 2010

Agencies or departments are ranked by size of fleet.

Department of Health and Human Services	4,297
National Aeronautics and Space Administration	3,764

Source: *Government Fleet*, Fact Book 2011, p. 32, from U.S. General Services Administration.

★ 2188 ★

Autos

SIC: 3711; NAICS: 336111

Passenger Car Sales in China, 2010

Market shares are shown based on sales volume. Mid-to-upper end cars generated sales of 8.43 million. Volks-wagen claimed 17.9%, Hyundai 8.7%, Honda 7.7% and other brands 65.7%. Luxury cars sold 770,000. Audi sold 29.3%, BMW 21.9%, Benz 19.2% and other brands 29.6%. Ultra-luxury cars sold 73,000. Land Rover & Jaguar claimed 58.1%, Porsche 30.8% and other brands 11.1%.

East China	33.2%
North China	19.8
Southwest China	12.9
South China	10.9
Central China	10.3
Northeast China	7.2
Northwest China	5.7

Source: "Industry Overview." [online] from http://www.hkexnews.hk/listedco/listconews/sehk/2011/1202/01293_1217327/E113.pdf [Accessed December 1, 2011], from Euromonitor.

★ 2189 ★

Autos

SIC: 3711; NAICS: 336111

Top Auto Brands in Australia, 2011

Brands are ranked by unit sales.

Toyota	181,624
Holden	126,095
Ford	91,243
Mazda	88,333
Hyundai	87,008
Nissan	67,926
Mitsubishi	61,108
Volkswagen	44,740

Subaru	34,011
Honda	30,107

Source: "New Vehicle Sales Top the Million Mark in 2011." [online] from http://www.fcau.com.au [Published January 5, 2012], from VFACTS.

★ 2190 ★

Autos

SIC: 3711; NAICS: 336111

Top Auto Brands in France, 2011

Data show unit sales.

Renault Clio	123,827
Peugeot 207	103,332
Citroën C3	79,364
Renault Mégane	78,858
Renault Twingo	68,236
Renault Scénic	66,362
Peugeot 308	62,279
VW Polo	53,586
Peugeot 3008	53,302

Source: "France Full Year 2011." [online] from http://bestsellingcarsblog.com [Published January 21, 2012].

★ 2191 ★

Autos

SIC: 3711; NAICS: 336111

Top Auto Brands in Israel, 2010

Data show unit sales.

	Units	Share
Mazda	31,819	14.7%
Hyundai	30,453	14.1
Toyota	22,289	10.3
Suzuki	12,218	5.6
Volkswagen	11,514	5.3
General Motors	11,049	5.1
Ford	10,263	4.7
Kia	9,513	4.4
Mitsubishi	8,432	3.9
Honda	8,275	3.8

Source: "Car Sales Israel 2011." [online] from http://raycee-1234.blogspot.com/2012/01/car-sales-israel-2010.html [Published January 21, 2012], from Israel Vehicle Importers Association.

★ **2192** ★

Autos

SIC: 3711; NAICS: 336111

Top Auto Brands in Lebanon, 2010

Data show unit sales.

Kia	6,494
Nissan	5,663
Hyundai	4,152
Toyota	3,103
Chevrolet	1,338
Mitsubishi	1,287
Renault	1,145
Peugeot	970
Mazda	946
BMW	816

Source: "Car Sales Lebanon 2010." [online] from http://raycee1234.blogspot.com/2012/01/car-sales-lebanon-2010.html [Published January 21, 2012], from databank.com.lb.

★ **2193** ★

Autos

SIC: 3711; NAICS: 336111

Top Auto Brands in Malaysia, 2011

Data show unit sales.

	Units	Share
Perodua Myvi	81,904	13.6%
Proton Saga	74,258	12.4
Perodua Viva	60,675	10.1
Proton Persona	46,415	7.7
Perodua Alza	37,402	6.2
Toyota Vios	29,820	5.0
Toyota Hilux	21,471	3.6
Toyota Exora	21,064	3.5
Nissan Grand Livinia	12,204	2.0
Honda City	10,995	1.8

Source: "Malaysia Full Year 2011." [online] from http://best-sellingcarsblog.com/2012/02/13/malaysia-full-year-2011-perodua-myvi-and-proton-saga-rule/ [Published February 13, 2012], from http://www.motortrader.com.my.

★ **2194** ★

Autos

SIC: 3711; NAICS: 336111

Top Auto Brands in Morocco, 2011

Data show unit sales for the first nine months of the year.

	Units	Share
Renault Kangoo	8,884	11.8%
Dacia Logan	8,826	11.8
Dacia Sandero	4,657	6.2
Dacia Duster	3,698	4.9
Peugeot Partner	2,465	3.3%
Citroën Berlingo	2,448	3.3
Peugeot 206	2,132	2.8
Ford Focus	1,882	2.5
Fiat Punto	1,785	2.4

Source: "Morocco September 2011." [online] from http://best-sellingcarsblog.com/2011/11/03/morocco-september-2011-renault-kangoo-reclaims-leadership [Published November 3, 2011], from http://www.lavieeco.com.

★ **2195** ★

Autos

SIC: 3711; NAICS: 336111

Top Auto Brands in Turkey, 2011

Data show unit sales.

	Units	Share
Renault	94,400	15.9%
Ford	58,800	9.9
Fiat	57,800	9.7
Volkswagen	55,550	9.4
Opel	52,600	8.9
Hyundai	46,450	7.8
Toyota	36,650	6.2
Chevrolet	23,600	4.0
Nissan	18,600	3.1
Dacia	17,900	3.0

Source: "Car Sales Turkey 2011." [online] from http://raycee-1234.blogspot.com/2012/01/car-sales-lebanon-2010.html [Published January 21, 2012], from ODD.

★ **2196** ★

Autos

SIC: 3711; NAICS: 336111

Top Auto Makers, 2011

General Motors includes Buick, Cadillac, Chevrolet and GMC. Ford includes Ford, Lincoln and Mercury. Chrysler includes Dodge, Fiat, Jeep and Ram. Volkswagen includes Audi and Bentley. BMW includes Mini and Rolls-Royce. Toyota includes Lexus and Scion. Honda includes Acura. Nissan includes Infiniti. Daimler includes Mercedes-Benz, Maybach and Smart.

General Motors Corp.	19.6%
Ford	16.8
Toyota Motor	12.9
Chrysler	10.7
Honda	9.0
Nissan	8.2
Hyundai	5.1

Continued on next page.

★ 2196 ★

[Continued]

Autos

SIC: 3711; NAICS: 336111

Top Auto Makers, 2011

General Motors includes Buick, Cadillac, Chevrolet and GMC. Ford includes Ford, Lincoln and Mercury. Chrysler includes Dodge, Fiat, Jeep and Ram. Volkswagen includes Audi and Bentley. BMW includes Mini and Rolls-Royce. Toyota includes Lexus and Scion. Honda includes Acura. Nissan includes Infiniti. Daimler includes Mercedes-Benz, Maybach and Smart.

Kia Motors	3.8%
Volkswagen	3.5
BMW	2.4
Daimler	2.1
Subaru	2.1
Mazda	2.0
Mitsubishi	0.6
Volvo	0.5

Source: *Detroit Free Press*, January 5, 2012, p. NA, from Autodata.

★ 2197 ★

Autos

SIC: 3711; NAICS: 336111

Top Auto Makers in Argentina, 2010

Market shares are shown based on sales.

Volkswagen	22.4%
General Motors Corp.	17.2
Renault	15.0
PSA Peugeot Citroën	13.4
Ford	13.1
Fiat	10.6
Toyota	5.1
Mercedes	2.2
Other	1.0

Source: *Argentina Autos Report*, July 2011, p. 20, from Asociation de Fabricacion de Automotores de Argentina.

★ 2198 ★

Autos

SIC: 3711; NAICS: 336111

Top Auto Makers in Canada, 2010-2011

Market shares are shown for the first nine months of the year.

	2010	2011
Hyundai	11.2%	13.1%
Toyota Motor	13.6	11.8
General Motors Corp.	11.6	11.5

	2010	2011
Ford	8.6%	10.5%
Honda	11.6	9.8
Mazda	9.3	8.2
Nissan	7.6	6.8
Volkswagen	5.2	6.4
Chrysler	3.9	4.8

Source: "Global Auto Report." [online] from http://www.scotiacapital.com/English/bns_econ/bns_auto.pdf [Published November 29, 2011], from Association of International Automobile Manufacturers of Canada.

★ 2199 ★

Autos

SIC: 3711; NAICS: 336111

Top Auto Makers in China, 2012

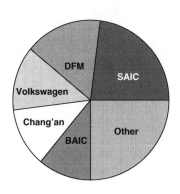

Market shares are shown for the first three months of the year.

SAIC	23.0%
DFM	16.0
Volkswagen	13.0
Chang'an	12.0
BAIC	11.0
Other	25.0

Source: *Financial Times*, April 23, 2012, p. 17, from LMC Automotive.

★ 2200 ★

Autos

SIC: 3711; NAICS: 336111

Top Auto Makers in Europe, 2011

Data show share of new registrations for the EU-27 and the European Free Trade Association.

Volkswagen	21.6%
PSA	13.2
Scania	10.1

Continued on next page.

★ **2200** ★

[Continued]

Autos

SIC: 3711; NAICS: 336111

Top Auto Makers in Europe, 2011

Data show share of new registrations for the EU-27 and the European Free Trade Association.

Ford	8.3%
General Motors Corp.	8.1
Japanese brands	7.7
Daimler Chrysler	5.6
BMW	5.1
Other	20.3

Source: "New Registrations in Europe." [online] from http://www.acea.be [Accessed January 16, 2012], from European Automobile Manufacturers Association.

★ **2201** ★

Autos

SIC: 3711; NAICS: 336111

Top Auto Makers in Germany, 2011

Companies are ranked by unit sales. Total sales were 3,173,634.

	Units	Share
Volkswagen	686,722	21.64%
BMW, Mini	297,439	9.37
Mercedes	285,651	9.00
Opel	254,651	8.02
Audi	250,708	7.90
Ford	230,939	7.28
Renault, Dacia	160,366	5.05
Skoda	142,611	4.49
Other	864,547	27.24

Source: "2011 Full Year Top-Selling Car Brands and Manufacturers in Germany." [online] from http://cars.european-traveler.com/germany [Published January 3, 2012], from Kraftfahrt-Bundesamt.

★ **2202** ★

Autos

SIC: 3711; NAICS: 336111

Top Auto Makers in India, 2011

Market shares are shown for the third quarter of 2011.

Maruti Suzuki	34.3%
Hyundai India	15.8
Tata Motors	14.6
Mahindra and Mahindra	12.0
Other	23.3

Source: "Maruti Suzuki: Will it Sustain Leadership?" [online] from http://www.inin.co.in [Accessed April 1, 2012].

★ **2203** ★

Autos

SIC: 3711; NAICS: 336111

Top Auto Makers in Italy, 2010

The new car market was valued at $57.2 billion.

Fiat	31.2%
Volkswagen	12.4
PSA	10.7
Ford	7.7
Other	38.0

Source: *Datamonitor Industry Market Research*, October 20, 2011, p. NA, from Datamonitor.

★ **2204** ★

Autos

SIC: 3711; NAICS: 336111

Top Auto Makers in Japan, 2011

Total sales were 4.2 million. The Toyota Prius was the top-selling brand.

	Units	Share
Toyota	1,157,383	27.56%
Nissan	591,370	14.08
Suzuki	552,903	13.16
Daihatsu	548,279	13.05
Honda	503,532	11.99
Mazda	189,925	4.52
Subaru	158,701	3.78
Mitsubishi	147,624	3.51
Other	350,283	8.34

Source: "2011 Full Year Best-Selling Car Models in Japan." [online] from http://cars.european-traveler.com/tag/2011 [Published January 11, 2012], from Japan Automobile Dealers Association.

★ **2205** ★

Autos

SIC: 3711; NAICS: 336111

Top Auto Makers in Norway, 2010

The new car market was valued at $3.7 billion.

Volkswagen	24.2%
Ford	17.4
Toyota	14.8
PSA	8.3
Other	35.3

Source: *Datamonitor Industry Market Research*, October 20, 2011, p. NA, from Datamonitor.

★ 2206 ★

Autos

SIC: 3711; NAICS: 336111

Top Auto Makers in Switzerland, 2011

Total sales were 318,958 vehicles.

	Units	Share
Volkswagen	40,594	12.73%
Audi	18,502	5.80
Ford	18,400	5.77
Renault	18,323	5.74
BMW	17,532	5.50
Skoda	17,470	5.48
Opel	15,978	5.01
Peugeot	15,186	4.76
Mercedes	14,037	4.40
Other	142,936	44.81

Source: "2011 Full Year Best-Selling Car Brands and Manufacturers in Switzerland." [online] from http://cars.european-traveler.com/tag/2011 [Published January 5, 2012], from Auto Schweiz.

★ 2207 ★

Autos

SIC: 3711; NAICS: 336111

Top Auto Makers in Taiwan, 2010

The new car market was valued at $9 billion.

Kuozui	27.2%
CMC	15.3
Yulon Motor Co. Ltd.	13.6
Ford	9.7
Other	34.2

Source: *Datamonitor Industry Market Research*, October 20, 2011, p. NA, from Datamonitor.

★ 2208 ★

Autos

SIC: 3711; NAICS: 336111

Top Auto Makers in the Netherlands, 2010

The new car market was valued at $13 billion.

Volkswagen	14.2%
PSA	13.4
Ford	11.6
Renault	9.5
Other	51.3

Source: *Datamonitor Industry Market Research*, October 20, 2011, p. NA, from Datamonitor.

★ 2209 ★

Autos

SIC: 3711; NAICS: 336111

Top Auto Makers in the United Kingdom, 2011

Total sales were 1.94 million vehicles.

	Units	Share
Ford	265,894	13.7%
Vauxhall	234,710	12.0
Volkswagen	179,290	9.2
BMW	116,642	6.0
Audi	113,797	5.8
Nissan	96,249	4.9
Peugeot	94,989	4.8
Mercedes-Benz	81,873	4.2
Toyota	73,589	3.7

Source: "2011 Full Year Best-Selling Car Brands and Marques in the U.K." [online] from http://cars.european-traveler.com/tag/2011/ [Published January 7, 2012], from Society of Motor Manufacturers and Traders.

★ 2210 ★

Autos

SIC: 3711; NAICS: 336111

Top Makers Worldwide of Low-Cost Autos, 2015

The definition of a low-cost car varies by region. In India, the price of such a vehicle is less than $5,000. In Eastern Europe, it is less than $10,000.

Renault-Nissan Group	22.4%
Volkswagen	14.8
Suzuki Group	11.7
Chinese VMs	8.7
Indian manufacturers	7.8
Toyota	7.6
Hyundai Group	7.4
Other	19.6

Source: "Strategic Analysis of the Global Market for Low-Cost Chassis Systems." [online] from http://www.hqpec.com [Published March 2009], from Frost & Sullivan.

★ **2211** ★

Autos

SIC: 3711; NAICS: 336111

Top New Vehicle Markets Worldwide, 2012, 2014 and 2016

Polk expects China to make the largest contribution to global sales growth for new vehicles, with an anticipated 16% increase over 2011. Polk analysts anticipate much of this growth to occur outside of the large metropolitan cities of Shanghai and Beijing. The luxury segment in the U.S. market in 2012 is expected to be the fastest-growing segment, with more than 14% growth. Data show sales in millions of units.

	2012	2014	2016
Europe	19.0	21.5	23.7
China	17.9	20.6	23.6
United States	13.7	15.6	16.3
Japan	4.5	4.9	4.8
Brazil	3.6	3.9	4.3
Other	19.0	21.6	25.6

Source: "Polk Forecasts Global New Vehicle Auto Sales to Reach 77.7M in 2012." [online] from http://www.greencarcongress.com [Published January 3, 2012], from Polk & Co.

★ **2212** ★

Autos

SIC: 3711; NAICS: 336111

Top Passenger Car Markets Worldwide, 2009-2010

Figures are in millions of units.

	2009	2010
China	10.33	13.76
United States	5.46	5.65
Japan	3.92	4.21
Brazil	3.01	3.33
Germany	3.81	2.92
France	2.30	2.25
United Kingdom	2.00	2.03
Italy	2.16	1.96
Russia	1.47	1.91
India	1.43	1.87

Source: "Industry Overview." [online] from http://www.hkexnews.hk/listedco/listconews/sehk/2011/1202/01293_1217327/E113.pdf [Accessed December 1, 2011], from Euromonitor.

★ **2213** ★

Autos

SIC: 3711; NAICS: 336111

Top Passenger Car Sectors, 2011

Market shares are shown in percent.

Mid-sized	51.8%
Small	27.9
Upscale	12.3
Sporty	5.0
Alternative power	2.9

Source: *Automotive News*, January 9, 2012, p. 42, from Automotive News Data Center.

★ **2214** ★

Diesel Cars

SIC: 3711; NAICS: 336111

Top Clean Diesel Car Brands, 2011

Data show unit sales.

VW Jetta	51,530
Volkswagen Golf	9,768
BMW X5	7,378
Mercedes GL320	5,782
Mercedes ML320	5,020
Volkswagen Passat	4,032
VW Touareg	3,633
BMW 335d	3,583

Source: "December 2011 Dashboard: Sales Still Climbing." [online] from http://www.hybridcars.com [Published January 9, 2012], from Baum & Associates.

★ **2215** ★

Electric Vehicles

SIC: 3711; NAICS: 336111

Top Electric Vehicle Makers, 2015

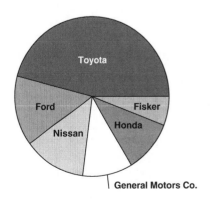

A projected 456,000 vehicles are expected to be sold.

Toyota	39.0%
Ford	12.0

Continued on next page.

★ 2215 ★

[Continued]

Electric Vehicles

SIC: 3711; NAICS: 336111

Top Electric Vehicle Makers, 2015

A projected 456,000 vehicles are expected to be sold.

Nissan	11.0%
General Motors Co.	9.0
Honda	9.0
Fisker	5.0

Source: "U.S. Autos and Auto Parts." [online] from http://www.ceres.org/resources/reports/electric-vehicles-report [Published February 23, 2011], from Baum & Associates and CIRA.

★ 2216 ★

Electric Vehicles

SIC: 3711; NAICS: 336111

Top Markets for Electric Vehicles Worldwide, 2011

Regions are ranked by estimated supply.

	Units	Share
Japan	532,160	52.3%
United States	274,562	27.0
11 EU countries	163,131	16.0
Korea	16,269	1.6
China	13,587	1.3
Australia	9,413	0.9
Other	15,000	1.5

Source: "World Electric Vehicle Market Exceeds One Million Units This Year." [online] from http://www.solarenergy.com [Press release November 11, 2011], from Solar & Energy and auto associations.

★ 2217 ★

Electric Vehicles

SIC: 3711; NAICS: 336111

Top Plug-In Electric Car Brands, 2011

Data show unit sales.

Nissan Leaf	9,674
Chevrolet Volt	7,671
Smart ED	388
Mitsubishi i	80

Source: "December 2011 Dashboard: Sales Still Climbing." [online] from http://www.hybridcars.com [Published January 9, 2012], from Baum & Associates.

★ 2218 ★

Hybrid Cars

SIC: 3711; NAICS: 336111

Top Hybrid Car Brands, 2011

Data show unit sales.

Toyota Prius	136,463
Hyundai Sonata	19,673
Honda Insights	15,549
Lexus CT 200h	14,381
Honda CR-Z	11,330
Ford Fusion	11,286
Lexus RX400/450h	10,723
Ford Escape	10,089
Lincoln MKZ Hybrid	5,739

Source: "December 2011 Dashboard: Sales Still Climbing." [online] from http://www.hybridcars.com [Published January 9, 2012], from Baum & Associates.

★ 2219 ★

Light Vehicles

SIC: 3711; NAICS: 336112

Light-Vehicle Market by Engine Type, 2007, 2009, 2011

Data for 2011 are for the first six months of the year.

	2007	2009	2011
4-cylinder	31.0%	40.0%	43.0%
6-cylinder	40.0	36.0	37.0
8-cylinder	26.0	23.0	18.0
Other	3.0	1.0	2.0

Source: *Automotive News*, July 25, 2011, p. 18, from IHS Automotive.

★ 2220 ★

Light Vehicles

SIC: 3711; NAICS: 336112

Light Vehicle Sales, 2007-2015

Sales are shown in millions of units. Data for 2013 and 2015 are forecasts.

2015	16.2
2007	16.1
2013	14.7
2011	12.6
2009	10.4

Source: *Financial Times*, January 14, 2012, p. 9, from Polk & Co.

★ 2221 ★
Buses
SIC: 3713; NAICS: 336211

Global Bus Market, 2010

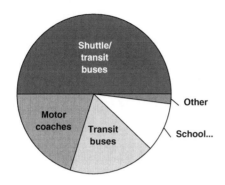

Market shares are shown in percent.

Shuttle/transit buses	50.0%
Motor coaches	20.0
Transit buses	18.0
School buses	10.0
Other	2.0

Source: "Investor Overview." [online] from http://www.fisher-coachworks.com/pdf/investor_overview_web.pdf [Published January 2010], from Freedonia Group.

★ 2222 ★
Buses
SIC: 3713; NAICS: 336211

Top Bus and Coach Brands in the United Kingdom, 2010

Market shares are shown in percent.

Alexander Dennis	26.94%
Volvo Bus	17.54
Scania	17.20
Optare	8.65
Iris Bus	7.28
Other	22.39

Source: *United Kingdom Autos Report*, July 2011, p. 44, from Society of Motor Manufacturers and Traders.

★ 2223 ★
Buses
SIC: 3713; NAICS: 336211

Transit Bus Production Worldwide, 2020

Total production is forecast to be 197,745 vehicles.

China	17.0%
Brazil	16.0

Korea	12.0%
Western Europe	12.0
India	9.0
Japan	7.0
North America	5.0
Russia	4.0
Other	18.0

Source: "Commercial Vehicle Outlook Conference 2011." [online] from http://www.hdma.org [Accessed September 1, 2011], from Heavy Duty Trucking Association.

★ 2224 ★
Commercial Vehicles
SIC: 3713; NAICS: 336211

Top Commercial Vehicle Makers in North America, 2010

Market shares are shown in percent.

Stoneridge	26.0%
Continental	25.0
Hella	9.0
Phoenix	9.0
Wabco	4.0
Other	27.0

Source: "Continental Fact Book Fiscal Year 2010." [online] from http://www.conti-online.com [Accessed September 1, 2011], from Continental estimates.

★ 2225 ★
Commercial Vehicles
SIC: 3713; NAICS: 336211

Top Commercial Vehicle Makers Worldwide, 2010

Market shares are shown in percent.

Continental	37.0%
Stoneridge	10.0
Yazaki	7.0
Actia	4.0
Bosch	4.0
Wabco	4.0
Harbin	3.0
Other	31.0

Source: "Continental Fact Book Fiscal Year 2010." [online] from http://www.conti-online.com [Accessed September 1, 2011], from Continental estimates.

★ 2226 ★
Commercial Vehicles
SIC: 3713; NAICS: 336211

Top Heavy Commercial Vehicle Brands in the United Kingdom, 2010

Market shares are shown in percent.

Daf Trucks	23.75%
Mercedes	18.08
Scania	12.96
Volvo Trucks	11.47
MAN	9.98
Other	23.76

Source: *United Kingdom Autos Report*, July 2011, p. 44, from Society of Motor Manufacturers and Traders.

★ 2227 ★
Trucks
SIC: 3713; NAICS: 336211

Multi-Purpose Vehicle Production Worldwide, 2020

Total production is forecast to be 3.22 million vehicles.

China	41.0%
Western Europe	17.0
North America	12.0
India	9.0
Brazil	6.0
Russia	4.0
Other	18.0

Source: ''Commercial Vehicle Outlook Conference 2011.'' [online] from http://www.hdma.org [Accessed September 1, 2011], from Heavy Duty Trucking Association.

★ 2228 ★
Trucks
SIC: 3713; NAICS: 336211

Top Truck Makers (Class 6), 2011

Market shares are shown in percent.

International	39.8%
Freightliner	33.8
Ford	12.7
Hino USA	9.7
Kenworth	2.1
Nissan	1.1
Peterbilt	0.4
Mitsubishi Fuso	0.3

Source: *Today's Trucking*, March 2012, p. NA.

★ 2229 ★
Trucks
SIC: 3713; NAICS: 336211

Top Truck Makers (Class 7), 2011

Market shares are shown in percent.

International	37.7%
Freightliner	26.2
Ford	9.0
Peterbilt	7.1
Kenworth	6.5
Hino USA	2.7
Nissan	0.7
Mitsubishi Fuso	0.1

Source: *Today's Trucking*, March 2012, p. NA.

★ 2230 ★
Trucks
SIC: 3713; NAICS: 336211

Top Truck Makers (Class 8), 2011

Market shares are shown in percent.

Freightliner	30.5%
International	21.0
Peterbilt	14.3
Kenworth	13.2
Volvo	12.2
Mack	7.5
Western Star	1.2

Source: *Today's Trucking*, March 2012, p. NA.

★ 2231 ★
Trucks
SIC: 3713; NAICS: 336211

Truck Sales Worldwide, 2006 and 2011

Market shares are shown by region.

	2006	2011
China	23.0%	53.0%
India	12.0	12.0
North America	29.0	11.0
Western Europe	15.0	8.0
Central/South America	4.0	7.0
Central/Eastern Europe	9.0	5.0
Other	8.0	4.0

Source: *Investor's Business Daily*, March 5, 2012, p. A8, from J.D. Power, Citigroup and Marketsmith.com.

★ 2232 ★
Auto Parts
SIC: 3714; NAICS: 33635

Mechanical Power Transmission Equipment Manufacturing, 2007

Data show the percent of industry sales held by the largest 4, 8, 20 and 50 firms in the sector. There are approximately 207 firms operating in the industry generating employment for 16,328 people.

4 largest companies	26.9%
8 largest companies	45.9
20 largest companies	68.5
50 largest companies	88.2

Source: ''2007 Economic Census.'' [online] from http://www.census.gov/econ/concentration.html [Accessed August 12, 2011], from U.S. Bureau of the Census.

★ 2233 ★
Auto Parts
SIC: 3714; NAICS: 336211

Motor Vehicle Body Manufacturing, 2007

Data show the percent of industry sales held by the largest 4, 8, 20 and 50 firms in the sector. There are approximately 754 firms operating in the industry generating employment for 48,217 people.

4 largest companies	23.6%
8 largest companies	34.6
20 largest companies	52.6
50 largest companies	71.3

Source: ''2007 Economic Census.'' [online] from http://www.census.gov/econ/concentration.html [Accessed August 12, 2011], from U.S. Bureau of the Census.

★ 2234 ★
Auto Parts
SIC: 3714; NAICS: 33633

Motor Vehicle Steering and Suspension Parts, 2007

Data show the percent of industry sales held by the largest 4, 8, 20 and 50 firms in the sector. There are approximately 221 firms operating in the industry generating employment for 35,511 people.

4 largest companies	32.7%
8 largest companies	49.4
20 largest companies	73.5
50 largest companies	93.3

Source: ''2007 Economic Census.'' [online] from http://www.census.gov/econ/concentration.html [Accessed August 12, 2011], from U.S. Bureau of the Census.

★ 2235 ★
Auto Parts
SIC: 3714; NAICS: 336312

Top Actuator Makers Worldwide, 2010

Market shares are shown in percent.

Continental	25.0%
Bosch	20.0
TRW	13.0
Advics	10.0
Mando	6.0
Akebono	5.0
KDAC	3.0
SABS	3.0
Other	15.0

Source: ''Continental Fact Book Fiscal Year 2010.'' [online] from http://www.conti-online.com [Accessed September 1, 2011], from Continental estimates.

★ 2236 ★
Auto Parts
SIC: 3714; NAICS: 336312

Top Actuators Makers in North America, 2010

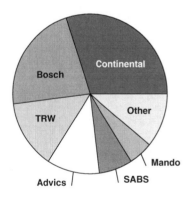

Market shares are shown in percent.

Continental	30.0%
Bosch	22.0
TRW	14.0
Advics	11.0
SABS	7.0
Mando	5.0
Other	11.0

Source: ''Continental Fact Book Fiscal Year 2010.'' [online] from http://www.conti-online.com [Accessed September 1, 2011], from Continental estimates.

★ 2237 ★
Auto Parts
SIC: 3714; NAICS: 336322

Top Advanced Driver Assistance System Makers in North America, 2010

Market shares are shown in percent.

Valeo	23.0%
Hella	14.0
Autoliv	12.0
Continental	10.0
Denso	9.0
Gentex	8.0
Hitachi	4.0
Honda Elesys	3.0
Other	17.0

Source: "Continental Fact Book Fiscal Year 2010." [online] from http://www.conti-online.com [Accessed September 1, 2011], from Continental estimates.

★ 2238 ★
Auto Parts
SIC: 3714; NAICS: 336322

Top Advanced Driver Assistance System Makers Worldwide, 2010

Market shares are shown in percent.

Continental	20.0%
Denso	18.0
Bosch	10.0
Autoliv	7.0
Delphi	7.0
Hitachi	6.0
Valeo	6.0
Hella	5.0
Honda Elesys	4.0
Other	11.0

Source: "Continental Fact Book Fiscal Year 2010." [online] from http://www.conti-online.com [Accessed September 1, 2011], from Continental estimates.

★ 2239 ★
Auto Parts
SIC: 3714; NAICS: 336322

Top Air Bag Electronics Makers in North America, 2010

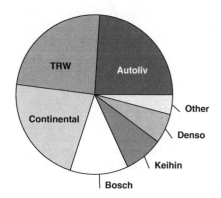

Market shares are shown in percent.

Autoliv	24.0%
TRW	24.0
Continental	22.0
Bosch	12.0
Keihin	8.0
Denso	6.0
Other	4.0

Source: "Continental Fact Book Fiscal Year 2010." [online] from http://www.conti-online.com [Accessed September 1, 2011], from Continental estimates.

★ 2240 ★
Auto Parts
SIC: 3714; NAICS: 336322

Top Air Bag Electronics Makers Worldwide, 2010

Market shares are shown in percent.

Continental	27.0%
Bosch	19.0
Autoliv	16.0
TRW	15.0
Denso	12.0
Other	11.0

Source: "Continental Fact Book Fiscal Year 2010." [online] from http://www.conti-online.com [Accessed September 1, 2011], from Continental estimates.

★ 2241 ★
Auto Parts
SIC: 3714; NAICS: 336211, 336312, 336322

Top Auto Parts Firms in North America, 2011

Firms are ranked by original equipment sales in millions of dollars.

Magna International Inc.	$ 14,716
Johnson Controls Inc.	7,874
Continental	5,799
Bosch	5,565
Denso	5,464
Delphi Automotive Systems L.L.C.	5,133
Lear Corp.	4,955
Faurecia	4,725
TRW	4,621
Cummins Inc.	4,136
Mobis North America	3,811
Dana Holding Corp.	3,416

Source: *Automotive News*, May 21, 2012, p. NA.

★ 2242 ★
Auto Parts
SIC: 3714; NAICS: 336399

Top Automotive Exterior Firms Worldwide, 2010

The industry was valued at 4.0 billion euros.

Faurecia	28.0%
Plastic Omnium	19.0
Peguform	13.0
Magnum	11.0
Rehau	8.0
Other	21.0

Source: "Faurecia 2011-2015 Targeting Profitable Growth." [online] from http://www.faurecia.com [Published November 7, 2011], from Roland Berger analysis.

★ 2243 ★
Auto Parts
SIC: 3714; NAICS: 336399

Top Automotive Interior System Firms Worldwide, 2010

The industry was valued at 19 billion euros.

Faurecia	15.0%
Johnson Controls Inc.	12.0
International Automotive Components	10.0
Visteon	10.0

Magna	7.0%
Other	46.0

Source: "Faurecia 2011-2015 Targeting Profitable Growth." [online] from http://www.faurecia.com [Published November 7, 2011], from Roland Berger analysis.

★ 2244 ★
Auto Parts
SIC: 3714; NAICS: 336211

Top Body and Security Interior Makers Worldwide, 2010

Market shares are shown in percent.

Continental	21.0%
Denso	10.0
Delphi	8.0
Hella	6.0
Lear	6.0
Bosch	5.0
Omron	4.0
Other	41.0

Source: "Continental Fact Book Fiscal Year 2010." [online] from http://www.conti-online.com [Accessed September 1, 2011], from Continental estimates.

★ 2245 ★
Auto Parts
SIC: 3714; NAICS: 336312

Top Compressor Makers in China, 2010

The compressor puts the refrigerant under pressure and sends it to the condensing coils. The industry was valued at 14.3 million units, worth 8.7 billion renminbi.

Sanden	33.0%
Denso	17.7
Visteon	11.8
Valeo	10.4
Delphi	9.7
Other	17.3

Source: "Industry Overview." [online] from http://iis.aastocks. com/20110630/001231091-10.PDF [Accessed September 1, 2011], from Frost & Sullivan.

★ 2246 ★
Auto Parts
SIC: 3714; NAICS: 336322

Top Condenser Makers in China, 2010

The condenser changes the phase of the refrigerant from gas to liquid and expels heat removed from the car. The industry was placed at 13.8 million units, valued at 2.8 billion renminbi.

Denso	16.5%
Delphi	12.2
Visteon	11.1
Valeo	8.2
Calsonic Kansei	6.9
Other	45.0

Source: "Industry Overview." [online] from http://iis.aastocks. com/20110630/001231091-10.PDF [Accessed September 1, 2011], from Frost & Sullivan.

★ 2247 ★
Auto Parts
SIC: 3714; NAICS: 33634

Top Electronic Brake System Makers in North America, 2010

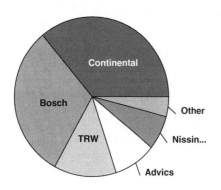

Market shares are shown in percent.

Continental	36.0%
Bosch	31.0
TRW	13.0
Advics	9.0
Nissin Kogyo	7.0
Other	4.0

Source: "Continental Fact Book Fiscal Year 2010." [online] from http://www.conti-online.com [Accessed September 1, 2011], from Continental estimates.

★ 2248 ★
Auto Parts
SIC: 3714; NAICS: 33634

Top Electronic Brake System Makers Worldwide, 2010

Market shares are shown in percent.

Continental	33.0%
Bosch	30.0
Advics	10.0
TRW	8.0
Mando	5.0
Nissin Kogyo	5.0
Mobis	4.0
Other	5.0

Source: "Continental Fact Book Fiscal Year 2010." [online] from http://www.conti-online.com [Accessed September 1, 2011], from Continental estimates.

★ 2249 ★
Auto Parts
SIC: 3714; NAICS: 336399

Top Emission Control Technology Firms Worldwide, 2010

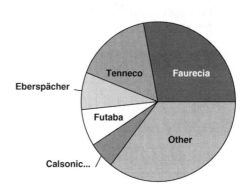

The industry was valued at 20 billion euros.

Faurecia	26.0%
Tenneco	15.0
Eberspächer	7.0
Futaba	7.0
Calsonic Kansei	5.0
Other	33.0

Source: "Faurecia 2011-2015 Targeting Profitable Growth." [online] from http://www.faurecia.com [Published November 7, 2011], from Roland Berger analysis.

★ 2250 ★
Auto Parts
SIC: 3714; NAICS: 336322

Top Evaporator Makers in China, 2010

The evaporator is used to remove heat from the inside of the vehicle. The industry was valued at 13.4 million units, worth 2.1 billion renminbi.

Denso	18.0%
Valco	13.9
Delphi	11.7
Behr	10.2
Visteon	10.1
Other	36.2

Source: "Industry Overview." [online] from http://iis.aastocks. com/20110630/001231091-10.PDF [Accessed September 1, 2011], from Frost & Sullivan.

★ 2251 ★
Auto Parts
SIC: 3714; NAICS: 33634

Top Foot Control Makers in the EEA, 2010

Market shares are estimated. EEA stands for the European Economic Area and consists of Lichtenstein, Iceland, Norway and the 27 EU member states.

Cimos	10.0-20.0%
Gestamp	10.0-20.0
Batz	5.0-10.0
Magnetti Marelli	5.0-10.0
TKMF (Sofedit)	5.0-10.0
Brano	0.0-5.0
Ficosa	0.0-5.0
ZF	0.0-5.0
Other	30.0-40.0

Source: "Regulation Merger Procedure." [online] from http:// ec.europa.eu [Published July 18, 2011], from Gestamp's internal estimates.

★ 2252 ★
Auto Parts
SIC: 3714; NAICS: 33634

Top Foundation Brake System Makers in North America, 2010

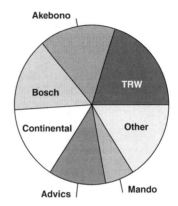

Market shares are shown in percent.

TRW	20.0%
Akebono	16.0
Bosch	15.0
Continental	15.0
Advics	12.0
Mando	6.0
Other	16.0

Source: "Continental Fact Book Fiscal Year 2010." [online] from http://www.conti-online.com [Accessed September 1, 2011], from Continental estimates.

★ 2253 ★
Auto Parts
SIC: 3714; NAICS: 33634

Top Foundation Brake System Makers Worldwide, 2010

Market shares are shown in percent.

TRW	25.0%
Continental	21.0
Advics	10.0
Akebono	9.0
Bosch	9.0
Mando	6.0
Other	20.0

Source: "Continental Fact Book Fiscal Year 2010." [online] from http://www.conti-online.com [Accessed September 1, 2011], from Continental estimates.

★ 2254 ★
Auto Parts
SIC: 3714; NAICS: 33634

Top Hinge and Control Makers in the EEA, 2010

Market shares are estimated. EEA stands for the European Economic Area and consists of Lichtenstein, Iceland, Norway and the 27 EU member states.

Gestamp	40.0-50.0%
Cimos	5.0-10.0
ISE	5.0-10.0
Multimatic	5.0-10.0
Flex 'n Gale	0.0-5.0
Gammastamp	0.0-5.0
TKMF	0.0-5.0
Other	15.0-20.0

Source: "Regulation Merger Procedure." [online] from http://ec.europa.eu [Published July 18, 2011], from Gestamp's internal estimates.

★ 2255 ★
Auto Parts
SIC: 3714; NAICS: 336211

Top Infotainment and Connectivity Makers Worldwide, 2010

Market shares are shown in percent.

Harman	10.0%
Panasonic	10.0
Continental	9.0
Clarion	7.0
Denso	7.0
Magnetti Marelli	7.0
Bosch	6.0
Other	44.0

Source: "Continental Fact Book Fiscal Year 2010." [online] from http://www.conti-online.com [Accessed September 1, 2011], from Continental estimates.

★ 2256 ★
Auto Parts
SIC: 3714; NAICS: 336211

Top Instrumentation & Driver HMI Interior Makers Worldwide, 2010

Market shares are shown in percent. HMI stands for Human Machine Interface.

Continental	19.0%
Denso	12.0
JCI	6.0
Valeo	6.0
Nippon Seiki	5.0

Visteon	4.0%
Yazaki	4.0
Other	44.0

Source: "Continental Fact Book Fiscal Year 2010." [online] from http://www.conti-online.com [Accessed September 1, 2011], from Continental estimates.

★ 2257 ★
Auto Parts
SIC: 3714; NAICS: 336322

Top Makers of Crash Active Head Rests in the EEA, 2009

Market shares are estimated in percent. The EEA stands for the European Economic Area and consists of Iceland, Liechtenstein, Norway and the 27 EU Member states.

Grammar	20.0-30.0%
Johnson Controls Inc.	20.0-30.0
Keiper	20.0-30.0
CRH	0.0-5.0
Other	0.0-40.0

Source: "JCI/CRH Merger Procedure." [online] from http://ec.europa.eu [Published January 14, 2011].

★ 2258 ★
Auto Parts
SIC: 3714; NAICS: 33634

Top Makers of Electric Parking Brakes in Europe, 2008

An estimated three million vehicles had an electric parking brake in 2008, a figure expected to rise to 11 million by 2015.

TRW	50.60%
Küster	45.15
SVDO	1.45
Other	2.80

Source: *Automobil Industrie*, September 2009, p. NA.

★ 2259 ★
Auto Parts

SIC: 3714; NAICS: 33634

Top Makers of Length Adjusters in the EEA, 2009

Market shares are estimated in percent. The EEA stands for the European Economic Area and consists of Iceland, Liechtenstein, Norway and the 27 EU Member states.

CRH	10.0-20.0%
Keiper	10.0-20.0
Brose	5.0-10.0
Johnson Controls Inc.	5.0-10.0
Lear	0.0-5.0
Other	30.0-65.0

Source: ''JCI/CRH Merger Procedure.'' [online] from http://ec.europa.eu [Published January 14, 2011], from CSM Worldwide.

★ 2260 ★
Auto Parts

SIC: 3714; NAICS: 33634

Top Powertrain Diesel Injection System Makers Worldwide, 2010

Market shares are shown in percent.

Bosch	55.0%
Continental	16.0
Delphi	14.0
Denso	12.0
Other	3.0

Source: ''Continental Fact Book Fiscal Year 2010.'' [online] from http://www.conti-online.com [Accessed September 1, 2011], from Continental estimates.

★ 2261 ★
Auto Parts

SIC: 3714; NAICS: 33635

Top Powertrain Gasoline Injection System Makers Worldwide, 2010

Market shares are shown in percent.

Bosch	29.0%
Continental	22.0
Denso	17.0
Hitachi	10.0
Keihin	6.0
Delphi	5.0
Magnetti Marelli	4.0
Other	7.0

Source: ''Continental Fact Book Fiscal Year 2010.'' [online] from http://www.conti-online.com [Accessed September 1, 2011], from Continental estimates.

★ 2262 ★
Auto Parts

SIC: 3714; NAICS: 33635

Top Transmission Control Unit Makers Worldwide, 2010

Market shares are shown in percent.

Continental	45.0%
Bosch	19.0
Visteon	11.0
Aisin Seiki	8.0
Keihin	6.0
Delphi	5.0
Denso	4.0
Other	2.0

Source: ''Continental Fact Book Fiscal Year 2010.'' [online] from http://www.conti-online.com [Accessed September 1, 2011], from Continental estimates.

★ 2263 ★
Motorhomes

SIC: 3716; NAICS: 336213

Top Motorhome Makers (Class A), 2011

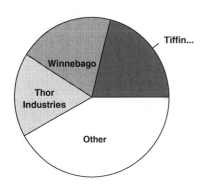

Market shares are shown for the first eight months of the year.

Tiffin Motorhomes Inc.	20.8%
Winnebago	20.2
Thor Industries	17.4
Other	41.6

Source: *RV Business*, October 2011, p. NA, from Statistical Surveys Inc.

★ 2264 ★
Motorhomes
SIC: 3716; NAICS: 336213

Top Motorhome Makers (Class C), 2011

Market shares are shown for the first eight months of the year.

Thor Industries	26.3%
Forest River's Coachmen	19.0
Winnebago	16.6
Other	38.1

Source: *RV Business*, October 2011, p. NA, from Statistical Surveys Inc.

★ 2265 ★
Aircraft
SIC: 3721; NAICS: 336411

Aircraft Manufacturing, 2010

Total shipments were valued at $83.73 billion. "NSK" stands for Not Specified by Kind.

	($ 000)	Share
Aircraft, civilian	$ 36,755,994	43.90%
Aircraft, military (incl. U.S. mil./aircraft built to mil. specs)	29,578,839	35.33
All other aeronautical services on complete aircraft	9,422,835	11.25
Modification, conversion, & overhaul of prev. accepted aircraft	7,550,458	9.02
Aircraft manufacturing, nsk, total	418,566	0.50

Source: "Annual Survey of Manufactures." [online] from http://www.census.gov/manufacturing/asm/index.html [Accessed January 18, 2012], from U.S. Department of Commerce.

★ 2266 ★
Aircraft
SIC: 3721; NAICS: 336411

Airplane Shipments Worldwide, 2010-2011

Total shipments fell from 1,932 in 2010 to 1,865 in 2011. The market was valued at $19 billion.

	2010	2011	Share
Pistons	873	860	46.11%
Business jets	727	681	36.51
Turboprops	332	324	17.37

Source: "2011 General Aviation Statistical Databook & Industry Outlook." [online] from http://www.gama.org [Accessed April 19, 2012], from General Aviation Manufacturers Association.

★ 2267 ★
Aircraft
SIC: 3721; NAICS: 336411

New Aircraft Deliveries Worldwide, 2011-2030

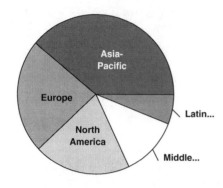

Figures are in billions of dollars. A total of 23,370 single-aisle jets, valued at $1.9 trillion, are expected to be delivered during this period. The market consists of 7,330 twin-aisle jets, valued at $1.77 trillion, 820 large (jumbo) craft valued at $270 billion and 1,980 regional jets, valued at $70 billion.

	($ bil.)	Share
Asia-Pacific	$ 1,510	39.22%
Europe	880	22.86
North America	760	19.74
Middle East	450	11.69
Latin America	250	6.49

Source: *Financial Times*, June 18, 2011, p. 10, from Ascend and Boeing.

★ 2268 ★
Aircraft
SIC: 3721; NAICS: 336411

Special Light-Sport Aircraft Market, 2011

Manufacturers are ranked by number of aircraft produced for the first six months of the year. Data are only for fixed wing airplanes.

	Aircraft	Share
Flight Design	333	16.0%
Czech Sport Aircraft	177	8.5
CubCrafters	168	8.1
American Legend	162	7.8
Tecnam	141	6.8
Remos	121	5.8
Cessna	102	4.9

Continued on next page.

★ 2268 ★

[Continued]

Aircraft

SIC: 3721; NAICS: 336411

Special Light-Sport Aircraft Market, 2011

Manufacturers are ranked by number of aircraft produced for the first six months of the year. Data are only for fixed wing airplanes.

	Aircraft	Share
Jabiru USA	102	4.9%
Evektor	92	4.4

Source: "First Half 2011 LSA Market Report." [online] from http://www.bydanjohnson.com [Published July 21, 2011], from FAA database research by Jan Fridirich.

★ 2269 ★

Aircraft

SIC: 3721; NAICS: 336411

Top Aircraft, Engine and Parts Makers, 2010

The industry generated revenues of $130.1 billion in 2010.

Boeing	20.2%
Lockheed Martin Corp.	9.1
United Technologies Corp.	7.1
General Electric Co.	6.8
Other	56.8

Source: "General Electric Company." [online] from http://www.docstoc.com [Published June 20, 2010], from IBISWorld.

★ 2270 ★

Aircraft

SIC: 3721; NAICS: 336411

Top Airplane Makers Worldwide, 2011

Companies are ranked by billings in millions of dollars.

Bombardier	$ 5,898.9
Gulfstream	4,904.6
Dassault	2,703.9
Cessna	1,761.9
Hawker Beechcraft Corp.	1,354.3
Embraer	1,004.5
Airbus	695.0
Liberty Aerospace	668.0

Source: "General Aviation Airplane Shipment Report." [online] from http://www.gama.org [Published April 19, 2012], from General Aviation Manufacturers Association.

★ 2271 ★

Aircraft

SIC: 3721; NAICS: 336411

Top Makers of Business Aircraft Worldwide, 2011

Market shares are shown based on number of aircraft manufactured.

Citation	33.0%
Learjet	13.0
Falconer	11.0
Gulfstream	11.0
Challenger	10.0
Hawker	10.0
Embraer	3.0
Other	9.0

Source: "Aerospace and Defense." [online] from http://bizavnews.ru/images/bizavweek/JPMorgan_Investment_Research_02.2012.pdf [Published February 16, 2012], from Teal Group and J.P. Morgan.

★ 2272 ★

Aircraft

SIC: 3721; NAICS: 336411

Top Makers of Heavy Jets Worldwide, 2010

Heavy jets claimed 54% of the overall jet market.

Bombardier	34.0%
Gulfstream	29.0
Dassault	24.0
Embraer	7.0
Other	6.0

Source: "Aerospace and Defense." [online] from http://bizavnews.ru/images/bizavweek/JPMorgan_Investment_Research_02.2012.pdf [Published February 16, 2012], from Teal Group and J.P. Morgan.

★ 2273 ★

Aircraft Maintenance, Repair and Overhaul

SIC: 3721; NAICS: 336411

MRO Industry Worldwide, 2011

Engine overhaul claimed $21.8 billion of the total, component MRO $11 billion, airframe/heavy maintenance $10.7 billion and line maintenance $9.5 billion.

	($ bil.)	Share
North America	$ 17.2	32.45%
Asia-Pacific	13.3	25.09
Europe	12.8	24.15
Middle East	2.9	5.47
South America	2.6	4.91

Continued on next page.

★ 2273 ★

[Continued]

Aircraft Maintenance, Repair and Overhaul

SIC: 3721; NAICS: 336411

MRO Industry Worldwide, 2011

Engine overhaul claimed $21.8 billion of the total, component MRO $11 billion, airframe/heavy maintenance $10.7 billion and line maintenance $9.5 billion.

	($ bil.)	Share
C.I.S.	$ 2.4	4.53%
Africa	1.8	3.40

Source: "India as an MRO Destination: Myth or Reality." [online] from http://www.slideshare.net [Published September 21, 2011], from Secondary Search.

★ 2274 ★

Aircraft Maintenance, Repair and Overhaul

SIC: 3721; NAICS: 336411

Top Aircraft Maintenance, Repair and Overhaul Firms, 2010

The industry generated revenues of $18.4 billion in 2010.

General Electric Co.	4.8%
Boeing	4.6
General Dynamics Corp.	4.6
United Technologies Corp.	3.9
BBA Aviation PLC	3.5
AAR Corp.	2.7
Other	75.9

Source: "General Electric Company." [online] from http://www.docstoc.com [Published June 20, 2010], from IBISWorld.

★ 2275 ★

Fractional Jet Industry

SIC: 3721; NAICS: 336411

Fractional Jet Market, 2011

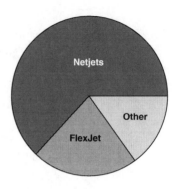

Fractional ownership refers to the ownership of a portion of an aircraft, as opposed to owning the entire plane. The owners then have access to it for a specific number of days or hours. NetJets offered the first program in 1986. Jon Peddie places NetJet's share at 57%.

Netjets	63.0%
FlexJet	22.0
Other	15.0

Source: *Montreal Gazette*, October 22, 2011, p. NA, from NetJets.

★ 2276 ★

Helicopters

SIC: 3721; NAICS: 336411

Top Civil Helicopter Makers Worldwide, 2009

Market shares are shown in percent.

Eurocopter	53.0%
AGW	18.0
Bell	15.0
Sikorsky	6.0
MDHI	4.0
Other	4.0

Source: "Aerospace Global Report 2010." [online] from http://www.imap.com/imap/media/resources/Aerospace_8_1FED752787A1E.pdf [Accessed September 1, 2011], from Eurocopter and Clearwater.

★ 2277 ★

Helicopters

SIC: 3721; NAICS: 336411

Top Military Helicopter Makers Worldwide, 2009

Market shares are shown in percent.

Sikorsky	31.0%
Eurocopter	21.0
Russia	14.0
Bell	11.0
Boeing	10.0
AgustaWestland	6.0
Japan	3.0
Halliburton	2.0
Other	2.0

Source: "Aerospace Global Report 2010." [online] from http://www.imap.com/imap/media/resources/Aerospace_8_1FED752787A1E.pdf [Accessed September 1, 2011], from Eurocopter and Clearwater.

★ 2278 ★

Aircraft Parts

SIC: 3724; NAICS: 336412

Aircraft Engine and Engine Parts Manufacturing, 2010

Total shipments were valued at $26.07 billion. "NSK" stands for Not Specified by Kind.

	($ 000)	Share
Aircraft engine parts and accessories	$ 11,094,922	42.56%
Aircraft engines, civilian	6,788,698	26.04
Aeronautical services on aircraft engines	4,632,660	17.77
Aircraft engines, military (incl. engines built to mil. specs)	3,098,822	11.89
Aircraft engine and engine parts manufacturing, nsk, total	450,818	1.73

Source: "Annual Survey of Manufactures." [online] from http://www.census.gov/manufacturing/asm/index.html [Accessed January 18, 2012], from U.S. Department of Commerce.

★ 2279 ★

Aircraft Parts

SIC: 3724; NAICS: 336412

Other Aircraft Parts and Equipment, 2010

Total shipments were valued at $31.32 billion. "NSK" stands for Not Specified by Kind.

	($ 000)	Share
Aircraft parts and auxiliary equipment	$ 23,915,640	76.36%
Aircraft propellers and helicopter rotors	2,849,728	9.10
Research and development on aircraft parts, except engines	2,813,144	8.98
Other aircraft parts and auxiliary equipment mfg, nsk, total	1,743,007	5.56

Source: "Annual Survey of Manufactures." [online] from http://www.census.gov/manufacturing/asm/index.html [Accessed January 18, 2012], from U.S. Department of Commerce.

★ 2280 ★

Aircraft Parts

SIC: 3724; NAICS: 336412

Top Aircraft Engine Makers Worldwide, 2011

Market shares are shown based on deliveries.

	Units	Share
CFM International	1,178	58.0%
IAE	364	18.0
General Electric	242	12.0
Rolls-Royce	166	8.0
Engine Alliance	48	2.0
Pratt & Whitney	38	3.0

Source: *Airline Business*, April 2012, p. 38.

★ 2281 ★
Ship Building
SIC: 3731; NAICS: 336611

Ship Building Market, 2010

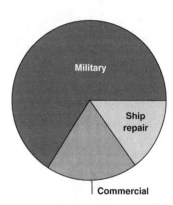

The United States is a small player in the ship building market, an industry dominated by South Korea, Japan, Europe and China. The Southeast claimed 42.2% and the Western regions 23.3% of all establishments.

Military	66.0%
Commercial	19.0
Ship repair	15.0

Source: "Marine Market in the United States." [online] from http://www.nzte.govt.nz [Published June 2011], from IBIS-World.

★ 2282 ★
Ship Building
SIC: 3731; NAICS: 336611

Shipyard Revenues Worldwide, 2004, 2009 and 2014

Figures are in millions of dollars.

	2004	2009	2014
Military self-propelled construction	$ 7,085	$ 8,940	$ 12,500
Military ship repair . . .	3,115	3,010	3,700
Non-military self-propelled construction	1,710	2,660	3,100
Non-propelled ship construction	765	1,870	2,300
Non-military ship repair . .	700	1,120	2,200

Source: "Nova Scotia's Ocean Technologies." [online] from http://www.cggc.duke.edu/pdfs/2012-03-05_Nova%20Scotia-%20OTReport.pdf [Published March 5, 2012], from Freedonia Group.

★ 2283 ★
Ship Building
SIC: 3731; NAICS: 336611

Top Ship Builders, 2009-2011

Market shares show percent of compensated gross tonnage of new orders. Figures for 2011 are for the first half of the year. CESA stands for the Community of European Shipyards Associations.

	2009	2010	2011
China	28.2%	36.5%	35.6%
South Korea	32.6	28.9	33.6
Japan	21.7	19.0	19.0
CESA	8.8	7.7	5.3
EU-27	8.2	7.2	4.8
Philippines	0.7	1.2	1.2
Vietnam	0.8	1.1	1.0

Source: "Ship Building Market Monitoring." [online] from http://www.cesa.eu [Published September 2011], from Community of European Shipyards Associations.

★ 2284 ★
Ship Building
SIC: 3731; NAICS: 336611

Top Ship Building Firms, 2011

The industry generated revenues of $19.1 billion in 2011. Military ships claimed 66% of the total, commercial ships claimed 19% and ship repairing 15%.

General Dynamics	35.7%
Huntington Ingalls Industries Inc.	34.5
Other	19.8

Source: "Ship Building in the U.S." [online] from http://www.ibisworld.com [Published July 2011], from IBISWorld.

★ 2285 ★
Boats
SIC: 3732; NAICS: 336612

Boat Building, 2010

Total shipments were valued at $5.05 billion. "NSK" stands for Not Specified by Kind.

	($ mil.)	Share
Motorboats, outboard, including commercial and military . . .	$ 1,737.85	34.42%
Motorboats, inboard, including commercial and military	1,277.28	25.30
Inboard-outdrive boats, including commercial and military	983.97	19.49

Continued on next page.

★ 2285 ★

[Continued]

Boats

SIC: 3732; NAICS: 336612

Boat Building, 2010

Total shipments were valued at $5.05 billion. "NSK" stands for Not Specified by Kind.

	($ mil.)	Share
Boat building, nsk, total	$ 530.56	10.51%
Boats, all other types, except military and commercial . . .	519.85	10.30

Source: "Annual Survey of Manufactures." [online] from http://www.census.gov/manufacturing/asm/index.html [Accessed January 18, 2012], from U.S. Department of Commerce.

★ 2286 ★

Boats

SIC: 3732; NAICS: 336612

Boat Production, 2010

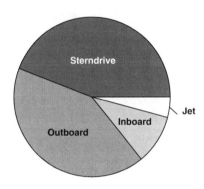

The boating industry is highly competitive, with the top 50 companies claiming approximately three-quarters of the market. Sales of boats fell from 59,602 in 2009 to 45,761 in 2010 due to the economic recession. However, attendance at boat shows did increase over the same period as did participation in boating activities.

Sterndrive	53.0%
Outboard	50.0
Inboard	12.0
Jet	5.0

Source: "Marine Products Corporation." [online] from http://www.freeman.tulane.edu [Published March 15, 2011].

★ 2287 ★

Boats

SIC: 3732; NAICS: 336612

Boat Propellor Market in China, 2009

Market shares are shown in percent.

Hyundai Heavy Industries	90.0%
Other	10.0

Source: "Hyundai Heavy Industries." [online] from http://www.hhiir.com/upload/presentation/Woori%20conference.pdf [Published March 28, 2011].

★ 2288 ★

Boats

SIC: 3732; NAICS: 336612

Top Boat Makers, 2009

The industry was valued at $4.2 billion in 2010. Genamar declared bankruptcy the same year.

Brunswick Marine Group	24.5%
Genmar Group	16.3
Marine Products Corp.	1.9
Other	57.3

Source: "Marine Market in the United States." [online] from http://www.nzte.govt.nz [Published June 2011], from IBISWorld.

★ 2289 ★

Boats

SIC: 3732; NAICS: 336612

Top Deck Boat Makers, 2010

Market shares are shown for January-June 2010.

Nautic Global Group	31.7%
Brunswick Marine Group	20.0
Tracker Marine	14.4
Marine Products	10.3
Starcraft Marine	5.4
Nautic Star	3.4
Four Winns	2.3
Regal	1.9
Glastron	1.8
Other	8.8

Source: *Soundings*, September 29, 2011, p. NA, from Statistical Surveys Inc.

★ 2290 ★
Boats
SIC: 3732; NAICS: 336612

Top Fiberglass Boat Makers, 2011

Market shares are shown for January-June 2011.

Sea Ray	4.9%
Carolina Skiff	4.7
Ranger	4.6
Bayliner	4.2
Nitro	3.5
Yamaha Jet	3.3
Tahoe	3.2
Hurricane	2.8
Other	68.8

Source: *Soundings*, September 29, 2011, p. NA, from Statistical Surveys Inc.

★ 2291 ★
Boats
SIC: 3732; NAICS: 336612

Top Luxury Motorboat Makers Worldwide, 2004

Companies are ranked by sales in millions of dollars.

Brunswick Marine Group	$ 2,771
Genmar Group	1,000
Ferretti Group	692
Azimut Benetti Group	565
Sunseeker International Ltd.	255
Princess Yachts Intl. Ltd.	195

Source: "Nova Scotia's Ocean Technologies." [online] from http://www.cggc.duke.edu/pdfs/2012-03-05_Nova%20Scotia-%20OTReport.pdf [Published March 5, 2012], from KPMG-U.K. DTI.

★ 2292 ★
Boats
SIC: 3732; NAICS: 336612

Top Ski Boat Makers, 2011

Market shares are shown for January-June 2011.

MasterCraft	24.3%
Malibu	22.9
Skier's Choice	16.0
Correct Craft	14.8
Tige	6.6
Axis Wake Research	5.9
Fineline	3.4
M.B. Sports	3.3
Other	2.8

Source: *Soundings*, September 29, 2011, p. NA, from Statistical Surveys Inc.

★ 2293 ★
Boats
SIC: 3732; NAICS: 336612

Top Superyacht Producing Nations, 2011

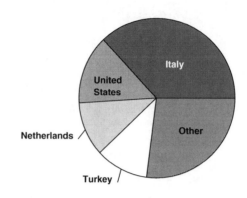

The United States has experienced a small drop in total number of deliveries, falling from 21 in 2009 to 20 in 2010.

Italy	37.0%
United States	14.0
Netherlands	11.0
Turkey	11.0
Other	27.0

Source: "Marine Market in the United States." [online] from http://www.nzte.govt.nz [Published June 2011], from IBIS-World.

★ 2294 ★
Railroad Equipment
SIC: 3743; NAICS: 33651

Leading Makers Worldwide of Rolling Stock, 2010 and 2020

Market shares are shown in percent.

	2010	2020
Alstom	35.0%	30.0%
Shinkansen	32.0	21.0
Siemens	16.0	18.0
Bombardier - Talgo	14.0	16.0
Other	3.0	5.0

Source: "Global High Speed Rail Market on the Fast Track for Business Development." [online] from http://www.docstoc.com [Published April 13, 2011], from Frost & Sullivan.

★ 2295 ★

Railroad Equipment

SIC: 3743; NAICS: 33651

Top Purchasers of Passenger Rail Cars in North America, 2010

Companies are ranked by number of new or rebuilt cars purchased or delivered.

New York (NYC Transit)	602
Amtrak	365
New York/New Jersey (PATH)	170
Montreal (AMT)	87
Salt Lake City (UTA)	50
Denver (RTD)	28
Maryland (MARC)	28
Los Angeles (LACMTA)	26
New Orleans	24
Connecticut (DOT/N.Y. MTA)	22

Source: *Railway Age*, January 2011, p. 52.

★ 2296 ★

Train, Subway and Transit Cars

SIC: 3743; NAICS: 33651

Top Train, Subway and Transit Car Makers, 2010

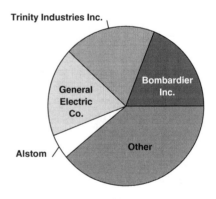

Trinity Industries Inc.

General Electric Co.

Bombardier Inc.

Alstom

Other

The industry generated revenues of $13.7 billion in 2010.

Bombardier Inc.	19.2%
Trinity Industries Inc.	18.6
General Electric Co.	17.6
Alstom	5.2
Other	39.4

Source: "General Electric Company." [online] from http://www.docstoc.com [Published June 20, 2010], from IBIS-World.

★ 2297 ★

Bicycles

SIC: 3751; NAICS: 336991

Bicycle Market, 2010

The market was valued at $3.2 billion. Trek, Specialized, Giant, Haro, Electra and Raleigh were the top brands, in order. Mass merchants claimed 75.5% of retail sales, bike shops 15.5% and chain stores 6.0%.

Road	37.8%
Hybrids	15.5
26-inch full suspension MTB	9.4
26-inch comfort	4.6
29er front suspension MTB	3.9
20/24-inch BMX/freestyle	2.7
29er full suspension MTB	2.6
24-inch juvenile	1.8
26-inch cruiser	1.6

Source: *Bicycle Retailer & Industry News*, July 1, 2011, p. 29, from U.S. Department of Commerce.

★ 2298 ★

Bicycles

SIC: 3751; NAICS: 336991

Top Bicycle Makers in China, 2011

Standard bicycles claimed 37.4% of the total, mountain bikes 34%, cross-country 12% and handicapped bikes 8.0%. Wholesalers represented 39% of the market by channel, direct sales specialty stores 14.5%, supermarkets/department stores 9%, medical equipment stores 6%, outdoor retailers and sporting goods stores 5.5% and other bike shops 26%.

Giant (China) Co. Ltd.	5.6%
Tianjin Fujita Group Co. Ltd.	4.0
HL Corp. (Shenzhen)	2.6
Shimano Group	2.5
Guangdong Tandem Industries Co. Ltd.	2.2
Other	83.1

Source: "Bicycle Manufacturing in China." [online] from http://www.docin.com/p-313015406.html [Published September 2011], from IBISWorld.

★ 2299 ★

Bicycles

SIC: 3751; NAICS: 336991

U.S. Bicycle Imports, 2010-2011

Data are imports through December 2011 year-to-date.

	2010	2011	Share
China	18,851,224	14,643,321	93.58%
Taiwan	823,018	878,347	5.61

Continued on next page.

★ 2299 ★

[Continued]

Bicycles

SIC: 3751; NAICS: 336991

U.S. Bicycle Imports, 2010-2011

Data are imports through December 2011 year-to-date.

	2010	2011	Share
Canada	7,364	16,397	0.10%
Italy	3,227	3,893	0.02
Other	80,739	106,157	0.68

Source: *Bicycle Retailer & Industry News*, March 1, 2012, p. 49, from U.S. Department of Commerce.

★ 2300 ★

Motorcycles

SIC: 3751; NAICS: 336991

Global Motorcycle Market, 2008

Market shares are shown in percent.

Asia	43.4%
China	32.8
Europe	5.4
North America	2.5
Japan	1.1
Other	14.8

Source: *Greece Autos Report*, July 2011, p. 35, from Yamaha Motor.

★ 2301 ★

Motorcycles

SIC: 3751; NAICS: 336991

Motorcycle and Scooter Sales by Year, 2002-2010

Data are in thousands of units.

2006	1,190
2007	1,124
2005	1,089
2008	1,087
2003	996
2004	965
2002	936
2009	843
2010	696

Source: "Motorcycles and Motor Scooters." [online] from http://www.profile-america.com/images/Motorcycles%20and%20Motor%20Scooters.pdf [Accessed May 1, 2012], from Motorcycle Industry Council and press releases.

★ 2302 ★

Motorcycles

SIC: 3751; NAICS: 336991

Top Motorcycle Brands in France, 2010

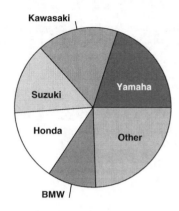

France is the second largest market in Europe for new motorcycles and mopeds and the fourth largest in terms of number of motorcycles on the road. Road motorcycles claimed 70.7% of the market for motorcycles with more than 125cc, scooters claimed 11.4%, all terrain 10.3% and custom bikes 7.6%.

Yamaha	18.4%
Kawasaki	14.9
Suzuki	13.3
Honda	13.1
BMW	8.8
Other	21.5

Source: "Motorcycle Brief." [online] from http://www.export.gov [Published June 2011], from *Le Journal Moto du Net*.

★ 2303 ★

Motorcycles

SIC: 3751; NAICS: 336991

Top Motorcycle Makers, 2010

The industry generated revenues of $4.5 billion.

Honda	39.8%
Harley Davidson	29.9
Yamaha	10.7
Suzuki	10.3
Other	9.3

Source: *Datamonitor Industry Market Research*, October 31, 2011, p. NA, from Datamonitor.

★ **2304** ★
Motorcycles
SIC: 3751; NAICS: 336991

Top Motorcycle Makers in India, 2011

Market shares are shown for the second quarter of 2011.

Hero MotoCorp	55.0%
Bajaj Auto	26.8
TVS	6.8
Honda Motorcycles	6.5
Other	4.9

Source: "Indian Two-Wheeler Industry." [online] from http://www.icra.in/Files/ticker/Indian%202W%20Industry.pdf [Published November 2011], from Society of Indian Automobile Manufacturers and ICRA Ltd.

★ **2305** ★
Motorcycles
SIC: 3751; NAICS: 336991

Top Motorcycle Makers in Japan, 2011

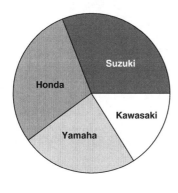

Companies are ranked by production of unit shipments for the first six months of the year.

	Units	Share
Suzuki	92,533	30.58%
Honda	88,765	29.33
Yamaha	73,317	24.23
Kawasaki	47,939	15.84

Source: "Motorcycle Sales Statistics." [online] from http://www.webbikeworld.com/motorcycle-news/statistics/motorcycle-sales-statistics.htm [Accessed January 1, 2012], from Japan Automobile Manufacturers Association.

★ **2306** ★
Aerospace and Defense
SIC: 3761; NAICS: 336414, 541711, 541712

Aerospace Orders by Type, 2011

Total spending is projected to be worth $218.1 billion.

Military	30.5%
Civil	22.8
Space	21.3
Related products and services	13.7
Missiles	11.7

Source: "2011 Year End Review and Forecast." [online] from http://www.aia-aerospace.org/assets/YE_Analysis.pdf [Accessed January 2, 2012], from Aerospace Industries Association.

★ **2307** ★
Aerospace and Defense
SIC: 3761; NAICS: 336414, 541711, 541712

Top Aerospace and Defense Firms, 2010

The industry generated total revenues of $510.4 billion in 2010.

Boeing	7.5%
BAE Systems PLC	3.1
EADS	1.4
Finmeccanica	1.1
Other	86.9

Source: *Datamonitor Industry Market Research*, November 17, 2011, p. NA, from Datamonitor.

★ **2308** ★
Aerospace and Defense
SIC: 3761; NAICS: 336414, 541711, 541712

Top Aerospace and Defense Firms in China, 2010

The industry generated total revenues of $106.7 billion in 2010.

EADS	4.5%
Boeing	2.9
Mitsubishi Heavy Industries Ltd.	1.8
Xi'An Aircraft International Corp.	1.5
Other	89.3

Source: *Datamonitor Industry Market Research*, November 17, 2011, p. NA, from Datamonitor.

★ 2309 ★
Aerospace and Defense
SIC: 3761; NAICS: 336414, 541711, 541712

Top Aerospace and Defense Firms in France, 2010

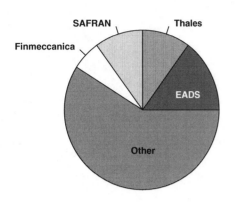

The industry generated total revenues of $38.4 billion in 2010.

EADS	15.2%
Thales	10.1
SAFRAN	9.6
Finmeccanica	6.2
Other	58.8

Source: *Datamonitor Industry Market Research*, November 17, 2011, p. NA, from Datamonitor.

★ 2310 ★
Aerospace and Defense
SIC: 3761; NAICS: 336414, 541711, 541712

Top Aerospace and Defense Firms in Germany, 2010

The industry generated total revenues of $34.9 billion in 2010.

EADS	20.4%
Lockheed Martin Corp.	4.3
Boeing	3.4
Finmeccanica	2.7
Other	69.1

Source: *Datamonitor Industry Market Research*, November 17, 2011, p. NA, from Datamonitor.

★ 2311 ★
Aerospace and Defense
SIC: 3761; NAICS: 336414, 541711, 541712

Top Aerospace and Defense Firms in India, 2010

The industry generated total revenues of $24 billion in 2010.

EADS	6.5%
Boeing	4.5
Mitsubishi Heavy Industries Ltd.	1.8
Finmeccanica	1.3
Other	85.9

Source: *Datamonitor Industry Market Research*, November 17, 2011, p. NA, from Datamonitor.

★ 2312 ★
Aerospace and Defense
SIC: 3761; NAICS: 336414, 541711, 541712

Top Aerospace and Defense Firms in Italy, 2010

The industry generated total revenues of $14.8 billion in 2010.

Finmeccanica	33.8%
EADS	12.4
Lockheed Martin Corp.	4.3
Boeing	3.4
Other	46.0

Source: *Datamonitor Industry Market Research*, November 17, 2011, p. NA, from Datamonitor.

★ 2313 ★
Aerospace and Defense
SIC: 3761; NAICS: 336414, 541711, 541712

Top Aerospace and Defense Firms in Japan, 2010

The industry generated total revenues of $41.4 billion in 2010.

Mitsubishi Heavy Industries Ltd.	40.7%
EADS	6.5
Boeing	4.5
Finmeccanica	1.3
Other	47.1

Source: *Datamonitor Industry Market Research*, November 17, 2011, p. NA, from Datamonitor.

★ 2314 ★
Aerospace and Defense
SIC: 3761; NAICS: 336414, 541711, 541712

Top Aerospace and Defense Firms in Mexico, 2010

The industry generated total revenues of $2.4 billion in 2010.

Boeing	7.2%
Lockheed Martin Corp.	4.3
BAE Systems PLC	2.9
EADS	1.4
Other	84.2

Source: *Datamonitor Industry Market Research*, November 17, 2011, p. NA, from Datamonitor.

★ 2315 ★
Aerospace and Defense
SIC: 3761; NAICS: 336414, 541711, 541712

Top Aerospace and Defense Firms in South Africa, 2010

The industry generated total revenues of $4.1 billion in 2010.

EADS	15.0%
Boeing	11.5
Lockheed Martin Corp.	6.2
Rolls-Royce	4.1
Other	63.1

Source: *Datamonitor Industry Market Research*, November 17, 2011, p. NA, from Datamonitor.

★ 2316 ★
Aerospace and Defense
SIC: 3761; NAICS: 336414, 541711, 541712

Top Aerospace and Defense Firms Worldwide, 2010

The industry generated total revenues of $1.0 billion in 2010.

Boeing	6.0%
EADS	5.7
Lockheed Martin Corp.	4.3
BAE Systems PLC	3.2
Other	80.8

Source: *Datamonitor Industry Market Research*, November 17, 2011, p. NA, from Datamonitor.

★ 2317 ★
Aerospace and Defense
SIC: 3761; NAICS: 336414

Top Defense Firms, 2011

Companies are ranked by value of contracts in billions of dollars.

Lockheed Martin Corp.	$ 17.34
Northrop Grumman	10.80
Boeing	8.40
Raytheon Co.	6.20
General Dynamics Corp.	5.49
Science Applications International Corp. . .	5.15
Hewlett-Packard Co.	3.83
L-3 Communications Corp.	3.81
Booz Allen Hamilton	3.71
KBR Inc.	3.54

Source: *Washington Technology*, Annual 2011, p. NA.

★ 2318 ★
Guided Missile and Space Vehicle Parts
SIC: 3769; NAICS: 336419

Other Guided Missile and Space Vehicle Parts, 2010

Total shipments were valued at $2.53 billion. "NSK" stands for Not Specified by Kind. Figures exclude propulsion units.

	($ 000)	Share
Missile and space vehicle components/parts/ subassemblies	$ 2,153,581	85.00%
Research/development, missile/ space vehicle parts/components	305,237	12.05
Other guided missile and space vehicle parts, nsk, total	74,888	2.96

Source: "Annual Survey of Manufactures." [online] from http://www.census.gov/manufacturing/asm/index.html [Accessed January 18, 2012], from U.S. Department of Commerce.

★ 2319 ★
Folding Campers
SIC: 3792; NAICS: 336214

Top Folding Camper Makers, 2011

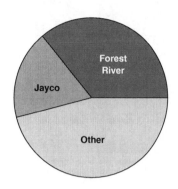

Market shares are shown for the first eight months of the year.

Forest River	36.0%
Jayco	18.1
Other	45.9

Source: *RV Business*, October 2011, p. NA, from Statistical Surveys Inc.

★ 2320 ★
Travel Trailers
SIC: 3792; NAICS: 336214

Top Travel Trailer Makers, 2011

Market shares are shown for the first eight months of the year.

Thor Industries	33.4%
Forest River	22.2
Jayco	14.0
Other	40.4

Source: *RV Business*, October 2011, p. NA, from Statistical Surveys Inc.

★ 2321 ★
Travel Trailers
SIC: 3792; NAICS: 336214

Top Truck Trailer Makers in North America, 2011

Companies are ranked by output. Market shares are shown based on the top 25 firms.

	Units	Share
Wabash National Corp.	46,526	21.56%
Great Dane Limited Partnership	39,000	18.07
Utility Trailer Manufacturing	33,289	15.42
Hyundai Translead	25,350	11.75
Stoughton Trailers	12,000	5.56
Vanguard National Trailer Corp.	8,184	3.79
MANAC	6,500	3.01
Strick Corp.	5,200	2.41
Wilson Trailer Co.	5,000	2.32
Timpte Inc.	3,583	1.66
Other	31,183	14.45

Source: *Trailer/Body Builders*, February 1, 2012, p. NA.

★ 2322 ★
Armored Vehicles and Tank Parts
SIC: 3795; NAICS: 336992

Military Armored Vehicle, Tank, and Tank Component Manufacturing, 2007

Data show the percent of industry sales held by the largest 4, 8, 20 and 50 firms in the sector. There are approximately 61 firms operating in the industry generating employment for 13,924 people.

4 largest companies	81.8%
8 largest companies	93.7
20 largest companies	98.0
50 largest companies	99.9

Source: "2007 Economic Census." [online] from http://www.census.gov/econ/concentration.html [Accessed August 12, 2011], from U.S. Bureau of the Census.

★ **2323** ★
Armored Vehicles and Tank Parts
SIC: 3795; NAICS: 336992

Top Tank and Armored Vehicle Firms, 2011

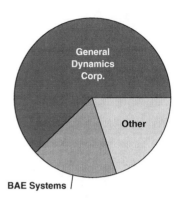

The industry generated revenues of $10.0 billion in 2011. While the government is expected to cut funding on tank and armored vehicle manufacturing, demand from foreign governments will help offset a major decline.

General Dynamics Corp.	62.0%
BAE Systems	17.6
Other	20.4

Source: "Tank & Armored Vehicle Manufacturing in the U.S." [online] from http://www.ibisworld.com [Published August 2011], from IBISWorld.

★ **2324** ★
Personal Watercraft
SIC: 3799; NAICS: 336999

Top Personal Watercraft Makers, 2011

Market shares are shown for year-to-date 2011.

Bombardier	44.8%
Yamaha	42.0
Honda	11.6
Hydrospace	1.6

Source: *Soundings*, September 29, 2011, p. NA, from Statistical Surveys Inc.

★ **2325** ★
Snowmobiles
SIC: 3799; NAICS: 336999

Top Snowmobile Makers, 2010-2011

A total of 51,796 units were sold in 2010-2011. Approximately 1.5 million snowmobiles were registered, with Michigan, Minnesota and Wisconsin claiming the most registrations. The average snowmobiler is 44 years of age and has an annual household income of $68,000.

Bombardier	40.0%
Arctic Cat	24.0
Polaris Industries	24.0
Other	12.0

Source: "Snowmobiles." [online] from http://www.mediacenteronline.com [Accessed November 1, 2011], from International Snowmobile Association.

★ **2326** ★
Utility Vehicles
SIC: 3799; NAICS: 336999

Top UTV Makers in North America, 2010

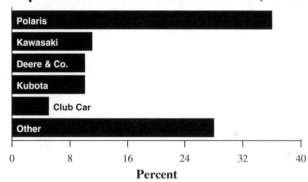

A total of 239,200 units were sold in Canada and United States.

Polaris	36.0%
Kawasaki	11.0
Deere & Co.	10.0
Kubota	10.0
Club Car	5.0
Other	28.0

Source: *Dealernews*, July 28, 2011, p. NA, from Power Products Marketing.

SIC 38 - Instruments and Related Products

★ 2327 ★
Aeronautical, Nautical and Navigational Instruments
SIC: 3812; NAICS: 334511

Aeronautical, Nautical and Navigational Instruments (Except Aircraft Engine Instruments), 2006-2010

Shipments are shown in millions of dollars.

2008	$ 3,678.3
2007	3,371.3
2009	3,295.0
2010	2,972.1
2006	2,838.6

Source: "Current Industrial Reports." [online] from http://www.census.gov/manufacturing/cir/index.html [Accessed August 15, 2011], from U.S. Bureau of the Census.

★ 2328 ★
Portable Navigation Devices
SIC: 3812; NAICS: 334511

Top Brands of Portable Navigation Devices, 2011

Market shares are shown based on dollar sales for November 2010 through April 2011. The top brands in order of market share were Garmin, TomTom, Magellan, Kenwood, Pioneer, Mio, Alpine, Clarion, Rosen and Sony.

Top 10 brands	98.0%
Other	2.0

Source: *Twice*, July 5, 2011, p. 17, from NPD Group Inc.

★ 2329 ★
Analytical and Life Science Instruments
SIC: 3821; NAICS: 337127

Analytical and Scientific Instruments, Except Optical, 2006-2010

Shipments are shown in millions of dollars.

2010	$ 11,266.6
2008	11,082.5
2009	10,214.6

2007	$ 9,225.1
2006	8,393.6

Source: "Current Industrial Reports." [online] from http://www.census.gov/manufacturing/cir/index.html [Accessed August 15, 2011], from U.S. Bureau of the Census.

★ 2330 ★
Analytical and Life Science Instruments
SIC: 3821; NAICS: 333994

Top Analytical and Life Science Instrument Firms, 2010

Companies are ranked by revenues in millions of dollars.

Thermo Fisher Scientific	$ 2.84
Life Technologies	2.67
Agilent Technologies	2.61
Waters	1.64
Danaher	1.45
PerkinElmer	1.24
Shimadzu	1.24
Bruker	1.23
General Electric	1.04
Becton Dickinson	1.01
Sigma-Aldrich	0.88
Illumina	0.87
Merck KGaA	0.87

Source: *Instrument Business Outlook*, April 15, 2011, p. 1.

★ 2331 ★
Laboratory Instruments
SIC: 3821; NAICS: 333298

Analytical Laboratory Instrument Manufacturing, 2007

Data show the percent of industry sales held by the largest 4, 8, 20 and 50 firms in the sector. There are approximately 578 firms operating in the industry generating employment for 34,282 people.

4 largest companies	32.3%
8 largest companies	48.7

Continued on next page.

★ 2331 ★

[Continued]

Laboratory Instruments

SIC: 3821; NAICS: 333298

Analytical Laboratory Instrument Manufacturing, 2007

Data show the percent of industry sales held by the largest 4, 8, 20 and 50 firms in the sector. There are approximately 578 firms operating in the industry generating employment for 34,282 people.

20 largest companies	67.9%
50 largest companies	82.8

Source: "2007 Economic Census." [online] from http://www.census.gov/econ/concentration.html [Accessed August 12, 2011], from U.S. Bureau of the Census.

★ 2332 ★

Laboratory Instruments

SIC: 3821; NAICS: 337127

Top Makers Worldwide of Gene Sequencing Tools, 2010

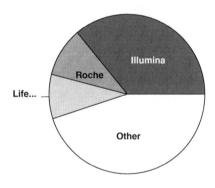

LifeSciences is a subsidiary of Roche.

Illumina	36.0%
Roche	10.0
Life Sciences	9.0
Other	45.0

Source: *Investor's Business Daily*, June 29, 2011, p. A5, from Maxim Group.

★ 2333 ★

Measuring, Testing and Navigational Instruments

SIC: 3821; NAICS: 333999

Measuring, Testing and Navigational Instrument Manufacturing, 2010

The industry generated revenues of $103.3 billion.

Search, detection and navigation instruments .	50.1%
Electricity measuring and testing instruments .	14.1

Analytical laboratory instruments	9.5%
Industrial process control instruments	8.6
Totalizing fluid meter and counting devices . .	6.4
Other	11.3

Source: "Measuring, Testing & Navigational Instrument Manufacturing in the U.S." [online] from http://www.ibisworld.com [Published November 2009], from IBISWorld.

★ 2334 ★

Linear Motion Technology

SIC: 3824; NAICS: 334514

Top Makers Worldwide of Linear Motion Technology, 2009

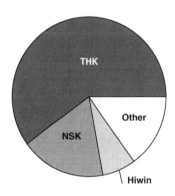

Market shares are shown in percent.

THK	60.0%
NSK	18.0
Hiwin	7.0
Other	15.0

Source: "Hiwin." [online] from https://mm.jpmorgan.com [Published March 12, 2011], from J.P. Morgan.

★ 2335 ★

Meters and Test Devices

SIC: 3824; NAICS: 334514

Shipments of Counting Devices, 2006-2010

Shipments are shown in millions of dollars.

2010	$ 627.2
2009	588.2
2008	579.7
2007	576.3
2006	533.6

Source: "Current Industrial Reports." [online] from http://www.census.gov/manufacturing/cir/index.html [Accessed August 15, 2011], from U.S. Bureau of the Census.

★ 2336 ★
Smart Meters
SIC: 3824; NAICS: 334514

Top Smart Meter Product and Service Makers, 2011

The industry was valued at $2.6 billion in 2011. Automatic meter infrastructure is expected to claim 48% of the total in 2016, automatic meter reading 19%, installation and systems integration 17% and parts and accessories 16%.

Itron Inc.	19.7%
Toshiba	10.6
Sensus USA	9.6
Elseter	8.5
General Electric Co.	5.8
Other	45.8

Source: "Smart Meters." [online] from http://www.freedonia-group.com [Published February 2012], from Freedonia Group.

★ 2337 ★
Smart Meters
SIC: 3824; NAICS: 334514

Top Smart Meter Vendors Worldwide, 2011

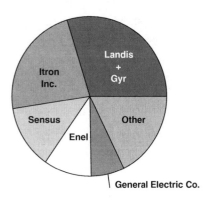

Market shares are shown for the first quarter of 2011.

Landis + Gyr	30.0%
Itron Inc.	22.9
Sensus	13.0
Enel	9.9
General Electric Co.	6.7
Other	17.5

Source: "Worldwide Smart Meter Market Continues to Grow With First Quarter 2011." [online] from http://www.watereffi-ciency.net/the-latest/smart-meter-market.aspx [Published June 14, 2011], from *IDC's Worldwide Quarterly Smart Meter Tracker.*

★ 2338 ★
Meters and Test Devices
SIC: 3825; NAICS: 334515

Shipments of Electrical Integrating Instruments, 2006-2010

Value of shipments are shown in millions of dollars.

2010	$ 1,631.0
2009	1,221.0
2008	1,087.5
2007	962.9
2006	872.1

Source: "Current Industrial Reports." [online] from http://www.census.gov/manufacturing/cir/index.html [Accessed August 15, 2011], from U.S. Bureau of the Census.

★ 2339 ★
Explosives Trace Detection
SIC: 3826; NAICS: 334516

Global ETD Market, 2011-2016

Explosives Trace Detection (ETD) is technology used at security checkpoints around the country to screen carry-on baggage and passengers for traces of explosives. Officers may swab a piece of luggage or passenger hands and then use ETD technology to test for explosives. The swab is placed inside the ETD unit which analyzes the content for the presence of potential explosive residue.

United States	42.0%
United Kingdom, Germany, France, Italy, Spain	19.0
China and India	16.0
Japan, Korea, Australia, Malaysia and Singapore	6.0
Turkey, Israel, Saudi Arabia and the United Arab Emirates	6.0
Brazil, Argentina and Mexico	4.0
Other	7.0

Source: "Explosives Trace Detection." [online] from http://www.homelandsecurityresearch.com [Accessed April 1, 2012], from Homeland Security Research.

★ 2340 ★
Homeland Security
SIC: 3826; NAICS: 334516

Federal Homeland Security Market, 2014

Market shares are shown in percent.

Department of Homeland Security	58.5%
Department of Defense	21.5
Department of Health and Human Services	5.7

Continued on next page.

★ **2340** ★

[Continued]

Homeland Security

SIC: 3826; NAICS: 334516

Federal Homeland Security Market, 2014

Market shares are shown in percent.

Department of Justice 5.1%
Other 9.3

Source: "People Screening Technologies." [online] from
http://www.homelandsecurityresearch.com [Accessed April 1,
2012], from Homeland Security Research.

★ **2341** ★

PBIED and VBIED Equipment

SIC: 3826; NAICS: 334516

Standoff PBIED and VBIED Detection Market, 2011

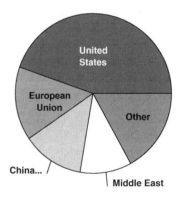

*Market shares are shown in percent. PBIED and
VBIED stands for Standoff Person-Borne and Vehicle-
Borne Explosives and Weapon Detection.*

United States 42.0%
European Union 14.0
China, India and Japan 12.0
Middle East 10.0
Other 16.0

Source: "Standoff Person-Borne and Vehicle-Borne Explosives & Weapon Detection." [online] from http://www.home-
landsecurityresearch.com [Accessed April 1, 2012], from
Homeland Security Research.

★ **2342** ★

People Screening Technologies

SIC: 3826; NAICS: 334516

People Screening Market Worldwide, 2016

Market shares are shown in percent.

United States 33.0%
China, India and Japan 20.0
European Union 18.0
Middle East 11.0
Other 18.0

Source: "People Screening Technologies." [online] from
http://www.homelandsecurityresearch.com [Accessed April 1,
2012], from Homeland Security Research.

★ **2343** ★

Acoustical Instruments

SIC: 3829; NAICS: 334519

Top Underwater Acoustical Instrument Makers Worldwide, 2010

Companies are ranked by sales in millions of dollars.

Teledyne Technologies Inc.. . . . . $ 1,644.2
Thales Underwater System PTY 952.2
Kongsber Maritime 834.7
Sercel Underwater Acoustics Division . . .   638.9
Atlas Elektronik 579.9
Raytheon Systems 337.9
General Dynamics Canada 203.1
Thales Underwater System Ltd. 194.5
Seamap U.K. 66.8
Lockheed Martin Corp. 62.0

Source: "Nova Scotia's Ocean Technologies." [online] from
http://www.cggc.duke.edu/pdfs/2012-03-05_Nova%20Scotia-
%20OTReport.pdf [Published March 5, 2012], from CBGGC
Ocean Technology Database and Hoover's.

★ **2344** ★

Autonomous Underwater Vehicles

SIC: 3829; NAICS: 334519

Top AUV Makers Worldwide, 2000-2010

Companies are ranked by number of units sold.

Teledyne Webb Research   192
Kongsberg Hydroid Inc.   150
Kongsberg Defense Systems   101
OceanServer Technology Inc.   101
iRobot Corp.   61
Kongsberg Maritime AS   25

Continued on next page.

★ 2344 ★

[Continued]

Autonomous Underwater Vehicles

SIC: 3829; NAICS: 334519

Top AUV Makers Worldwide, 2000-2010

Companies are ranked by number of units sold.

ECA S.A.	24
Teledyne Gavia ehf	20

Source: "Nova Scotia's Ocean Technologies." [online] from http://www.cggc.duke.edu/pdfs/2012-03-05_Nova%20Scotia-%20OTReport.pdf [Published March 5, 2012], from CBGGC Ocean Technology Database and Hoover's.

★ 2345 ★

Remotely Operated Vehicles

SIC: 3829; NAICS: 334519

Deepsea Remotely Operated Vehicle Market Worldwide, 2010

Market shares are shown in percent.

Schilling Robotics	75.0%
Other	25.0

Source: *World Oil*, October 2011, p. NA.

★ 2346 ★

Remotely Operated Vehicles

SIC: 3829; NAICS: 334519

Top ROV Makers Worldwide, 2000-2010

Companies are ranked by number of units sold.

SeaBotix Inc.	845
VideoRay L.L.C.	820
ECA S.A.	476
Deep Ocean Engineering	470
Saab Seaeye Ltd.	441
Mitsui Engineering & Shipbuilding	301
SMD Ltd.	297
Oceaneering International Inc.	212

Source: "Nova Scotia's Ocean Technologies." [online] from http://www.cggc.duke.edu/pdfs/2012-03-05_Nova%20Scotia-%20OTReport.pdf [Published March 5, 2012], from CBGGC Ocean Technology Database and Hoover's.

★ 2347 ★

Medical Products

SIC: 3841; NAICS: 339112

Global Medical Equipment and Supplies Industry, 2010

North America claimed 48% of the market, Europe 33% and the Asia-Pacific region 19%.

Disposable equipment and supplies	40.0%
In vitro diagnostics	11.0
Otologic and technical aids	11.0
Dental surgery and equipment	10.0
Ophthalmic equipment	10.0
Other	18.0

Source: "Healthcare Equipment & Supplies Global Report 2012." [online] from http://www.clearwatercf.com [Accessed October 1, 2011], from Datamonitor.

★ 2348 ★

Medical Products

SIC: 3841; NAICS: 339112

Top Color Ultrasound Makers in China, 2010

Market shares are estimated.

General Electric	25.0%
Philips	23.0
Siemens	12.0
Other	40.0

Source: "Seizing China's MedTech Opportunities." [online] from http://www.medcitynews.com/wordpress/wp-content/uploads/China-MedTech.pdf [Published January 6, 2012], from Citi Investment Research.

★ 2349 ★

Medical Products

SIC: 3841; NAICS: 339112

Top Dialysis Product Makers Worldwide, 2010

The market includes dialyzers, hemodialysis machines, concentrates and dialysis solutions and products for periotoneal dialysis.

Fresenius	33.0%
Baxter	19.0
Gambro	15.0
Other	33.0

Source: "Fresenius Annual Report 2010." [online] from http://annualreport2010.fresenius.com [Accessed April 13, 2012].

★ 2350 ★
Medical Products
SIC: 3841; NAICS: 339112

Top Digital Subtraction Angiography Makers in China, 2010

Market shares are estimated.

General Electric Co. 24.0%
Siemens 22.0
Philips 19.0
Other 35.0

Source: "Seizing China's MedTech Opportunities." [online] from http://www.medcitynews.com/wordpress/wp-content/uploads/China-MedTech.pdf [Published January 6, 2012], from Citi Investment Research.

★ 2351 ★
Medical Products
SIC: 3841; NAICS: 339112

Top Drug-Coated Stent Makers Worldwide, 2012-2014

Market shares are projected.

	2012	2013	2014
Abbott Laboratories	38.0%	39.0%	40.0%
Boston Scientific	41.0	39.0	38.0
Medtronic	18.0	19.0	19.0
Other	3.0	3.0	3.0

Source: "J&J's Heart Stent Sales, Market Share Declining." [online] from http://seadev.bonnint.net/category/money_news_articles [Published June 15, 2011], from Jefferies & Co. and Johnson & Johnson.

★ 2352 ★
Medical Products
SIC: 3841; NAICS: 339112

Top Drug-Eluting Stent Makers in China, 2009

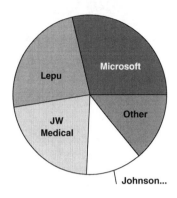

Market shares are estimated.

Microsoft 28.9%
Lepu 23.5
JW Medical 22.0
Johnson & Johnson 11.6
Other 14.0

Source: "China Healthcare Sector." [online] from http://download.bioon.com.cn/upload/201105/17235814_9161.pdf [Published December 3, 2010], from Citi Investment Research.

★ 2353 ★
Medical Products
SIC: 3841; NAICS: 339112

Top Insulin Makers in China, 2010

Market shares are shown in percent.

Novo Nordisk 63.0%
Lilly 13.0
Shanghai Fosum 12.0
Sanofi-Aventis 5.0
Other 7.0

Source: "China Healthcare Sector." [online] from http://doc.research-and-analytics.csfb.com [Published May 31, 2011], from IMS Health.

★ 2354 ★
Medical Products
SIC: 3841; NAICS: 339112

Top Major CT Makers in China, 2010

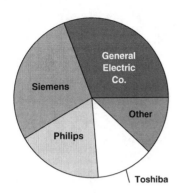

Market shares are estimated.

General Electric Co.	30.6%
Siemens	27.5
Philips	17.6
Toshiba	12.3
Other	12.0

Source: "Seizing China's MedTech Opportunities." [online] from http://www.medcitynews.com/wordpress/wp-content/uploads/China-MedTech.pdf [Published January 6, 2012], from Citi Investment Research.

★ 2355 ★
Medical Products
SIC: 3841; NAICS: 339112

Top Makers of Ambulatory Pumps, 2009

The industry is based on $174.6 million in manufacturer revenues.

Smiths Medical	20.2%
Abbott Laboratories	15.0
Cardinal Health	10.9
Other	53.9

Source: "Market for Home Care Products." [online] from http://www.docin.com [Published December 2010], from Kalorama Information.

★ 2356 ★
Medical Products
SIC: 3841; NAICS: 339112

Top Makers of Nebulizers, 2009

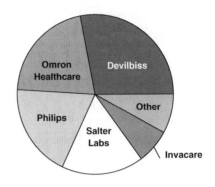

Nebulizers dispense liquid medication in a fine mist for inhalation deep into the lungs. The industry is based on $117.2 million on manufacturer revenues.

Devilbiss	27.7%
Omron Healthcare	20.6
Philips	19.2
Salter Labs	16.9
Invacare	7.3
Other	8.3

Source: "Market for Home Care Products." [online] from http://www.docin.com [Published December 2010], from Kalorama Information.

★ 2357 ★
Medical Products
SIC: 3841; NAICS: 339112

Top Makers of Oxygen Concentrators, 2009

The industry is based on $166.8 million in manufacturer revenues.

Invacare	43.2%
Philips	30.3
Devilbiss	14.4
AirSep	7.2
Other	4.9

Source: "Market for Home Care Products." [online] from http://www.docin.com [Published December 2010], from Kalorama Information.

★ 2358 ★
Medical Products
SIC: 3841; NAICS: 339112

Top Makers of Peripheral Vascular Devices Worldwide, 2010

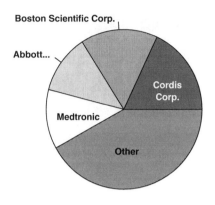

The market was forecast to climb from $4.3 billion in 2010 to $5.3 billion in 2017. The United States claimed 45% of the global market.

Cordis Corp.	18.0%
Boston Scientific Corp.	16.0
Abbott Laboratories	12.0
Medtronic	12.0
Other	42.0

Source: *Business Wire*, July 22, 2011, p. NA, from companies-andmarkets.com.

★ 2359 ★
Medical Products
SIC: 3841; NAICS: 339112

Top Makers of Plasma and Plasma-Derived Products Worldwide, 2010

The industry was valued at $8.8 billion.

Baxter	33.7%
CSL Plasma	23.6
Octapharma	11.8
Talecris	11.4
Grifols	7.6
Other	11.9

Source: "Blood Products and Blood Testing Markets." [online] from http://www.docin.com [Published February 2011], from Kalorama Information.

★ 2360 ★
Medical Products
SIC: 3841; NAICS: 339112

Top Makers Worldwide of ICDs and CRT-Ds, 2010

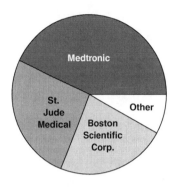

ICD stands for Implantable Cardiac Defibrillators. CRT-D stands for Cardiac Resynchonization Therapy-Defibrillators.

Medtronic	43.0%
St. Jude Medical	26.0
Boston Scientific Corp.	23.0
Other	8.0

Source: "Implantable Cardioverter Defibrillators and Cardiac Resynchronization." [online] from http://www.free-press-release.com/news/print-1321006002.html [Published November 11, 2011], from GlobalData.

★ 2361 ★
Medical Products
SIC: 3841; NAICS: 339112

Top Medical Device Firms Worldwide, 2010

Companies are ranked by sales in billions of dollars.

Johnson & Johnson Co.	$ 24.6
GE Healthcare	16.9
Siemens Healthcare	16.7
Medtronic	15.8
Baxter International	12.8
Philips Healthcare	11.4
Abbott Laboratories	9.3
Cardinal Health	8.8
Covidien	8.4
Boston Scientific	7.8
Becton Dickinson	7.4
Stryker	7.3
B. Braun	5.9

Continued on next page.

★ 2361 ★

[Continued]

Medical Products

SIC: 3841; NAICS: 339112

Top Medical Device Firms Worldwide, 2010

Companies are ranked by sales in billions of dollars.

St. Jude Medical	$ 5.2
Toshiba	4.6

Source: *Medical Product Outsourcing*, July-August 2011, p. NA.

★ 2362 ★

Medical Products

SIC: 3841; NAICS: 339112

Top Medical Device Makers in China, 2011

The industry generated revenues of $5.9 billion. CT endoscopes claimed 20% of the market, X-ray equipment 17.4%, MRI equipment 14.6%, endoscopes and medical nuclear equipment 13% and other sectors 35%.

GE Healthcare	19.0%
Siemens Ltd. China Medical Solutions Group .	14.0
Shenzhen Mindray Bio-Medical Electronics Co. Ltd.	11.3
Shinva Medical Instrument Co. Ltd.	3.5
Other	52.2

Source: "Medical Device Makers in China." [online] from http://www.docin.com [Published June 2011], from IBIS-World.

★ 2363 ★

Medical Products

SIC: 3841; NAICS: 339112

Top Medical Instrument and Supply Makers, 2010

The industry generated revenues of $89.4 billion in 2010.

Johnson & Johnson Co.	13.5%
General Electric Co.	10.2
Medtronic	8.9
Baxter International Inc.	7.0
Covidien PLC	6.3
Other	54.1

Source: "General Electric Company." [online] from http://www.docstoc.com [Published June 20, 2010], from IBIS-World.

★ 2364 ★

Medical Products

SIC: 3841; NAICS: 339112

Top MRI Makers in China, 2010

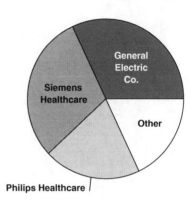

Market shares are estimated.

General Electric Co.	32.0%
Siemens Healthcare	30.0
Philips Healthcare	20.0
Other	18.0

Source: "Seizing China's MedTech Opportunities." [online] from http://www.medcitynews.com/wordpress/wp-content/uploads/China-MedTech.pdf [Published January 6, 2012], from Citi Investment Research.

★ 2365 ★

Medical Products

SIC: 3841; NAICS: 339112

Top Patient Monitor Equipment Makers in China, 2010

Market shares are estimated.

Mindray	44.4%
Philips Healthcare	16.3
Goldway	11.0
General Electric Co.	8.4
Other	19.9

Source: "Seizing China's MedTech Opportunities." [online] from http://www.medcitynews.com/wordpress/wp-content/uploads/China-MedTech.pdf [Published January 6, 2012], from Citi Investment Research.

★ 2366 ★
Medical Products
SIC: 3841; NAICS: 339112

Top Patient Monitoring Device Makers in China, 2009

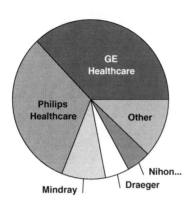

Market shares are estimated.

GE Healthcare	37.0%
Philips Healthcare	32.0
Mindray	9.0
Draeger	5.0
Nihon Kohden	5.0
Other	12.0

Source: "China Healthcare Sector." [online] from http://download.bioon.com.cn/upload/201105/17235814_9161.pdf [Published December 3, 2010], from Citi Investment Research.

★ 2367 ★
Medical Products
SIC: 3841; NAICS: 339112

Top Personal Thermometer Brands, 2011

Brands are ranked by sales at drug stores, supermarkets and mass merchandisers (excluding Wal-Mart) for the 12 weeks ended January 22, 2012.

	($ 000)	Share
Braun Thermoscan	$ 3,960.9	14.39%
Comfort Scanner	2,559.3	9.30
Vicks Speed Read	1,864.7	6.78
Vicks	1,799.7	6.54
Vicks Comfort Flex	1,294.3	4.70
Geratherm	708.7	2.58
BD	512.7	1.86
Private label	11,453.0	41.62
Other	3,365.1	12.23

Source: *Drug Store News*, March 12, 2012, p. 2, from SymphonyIRI Group Inc.

★ 2368 ★
Medical Products
SIC: 3841; NAICS: 339112

Top Sleep Apnea Product Makers Worldwide, 2010

The global sleep apnea diagnostic systems market was valued at $205.6 million in 2010, and is expected to grow to reach a market value of $284 million in 2017. This growth will be driven by the growth of the home sleep testing market. The aging population and increasing prevalence of sleep apnea are expected to drive demand for sleep apnea diagnostic systems in the future. Growth will also come from technological advancements such as enhanced portability, improved ergonomics, miniaturization, and wireless communication in sleep apnea diagnostic systems.

CareFusion Corp.	21.0%
Philips Respironics	16.0
Embla Systems	8.0
Other	55.0

Source: "Sleep Apnea Diagnostic Systems." [online] from http://www.marketshare.com [Published December 19, 2011], from GlobalData.

★ 2369 ★
First Aid Products
SIC: 3842; NAICS: 339113

Top Brands of Adhesive Bandages and First Aid Tape, 2012

Market shares are shown based on sales at supermarkets, drug stores and mass merchandisers (excluding Wal-Mart) for the 52 weeks ended April 15, 2012.

Band-Aid	45.0%
Private label	39.4
Other	15.6

Source: *New York Times*, May 22, 2012, p. NA, from SymphonyIRI Group Inc.

★ 2370 ★
First Aid Products
SIC: 3842; NAICS: 339113

Top Cotton Ball/Swab Brands, 2012

Market shares are shown based on sales at supermarkets, drug stores and mass merchandisers (excluding Wal-Mart) for the previous 12 months.

	($ mil.)	Share
Q-Tips	$ 92.3	32.78%
Swisspers Supreme	2.1	0.75
Swiss Beauty	2.0	0.71

Continued on next page.

★ 2370 ★
[Continued]
First Aid Products
SIC: 3842; NAICS: 339113
Top Cotton Ball/Swab Brands, 2012

Market shares are shown based on sales at supermarkets, drug stores and mass merchandisers (excluding Wal-Mart) for the previous 12 months.

	($ mil.)	Share
Swisspers	$ 1.6	0.57%
Q-Tips Precision Cloud	0.4	0.14
Coralite	0.3	0.11
Private label	171.9	61.04
Other	11.0	3.91

Source: *MMR*, April 16, 2012, p. 99, from SymphonyIRI Group Inc.

★ 2371 ★
First Aid Products
SIC: 3842; NAICS: 339113
Top First Aid Bandage Brands, 2011

Brands are ranked by supermarket, drug store and mass merchandiser sales for the 12 weeks ended April 17, 2011.

	($ mil.)	Share
Band-Aid	$ 17.8	14.24%
Band-Aid Comfort Flex	7.7	6.16
3M Nexcare	6.4	5.12
Band-Aid Tough Strips	5.8	4.64
Private label	48.2	38.56
Other	39.1	31.28

Source: *Drug Store News*, July 11, 2011, p. 33, from SymphonyIRI Group Inc.

★ 2372 ★
First Aid Products
SIC: 3842; NAICS: 339113
Top First Aid Kit Brands, 2011

Market shares are shown based on drug store sales of December 25, 2011.

Johnson & Johnson	28.7%
Safety 1st Hospital's Choice	10.8
Johnson & Johnson 1st Aid to Go	8.3
Johnson & Johnson Safe Travels	5.4
First Aid Only	4.7
BleedArrest	4.3
Other	37.8

Source: *Chain Drug Review*, February 13, 2012, p. 24, from SymphonyIRI Group Inc.

★ 2373 ★
First Aid Products
SIC: 3842; NAICS: 339113
Top First Aid Ointments/Antiseptics, 2010

Brands are ranked by drug store sales in millions of dollars for the 52 weeks ended December 26, 2010.

	($ mil.)	Share
Neosporin	$ 101.1	26.64%
Mederma	28.2	7.43
Hibiclens	10.5	2.77
Polysporin	9.4	2.48
Neosporin Neo To Go	6.8	1.79
Bactine	5.9	1.55
S&D	5.7	1.50
Private label	211.9	55.84

Source: *Chain Drug Review*, June 27, 2011, p. 166, from SymphonyIRI Group Inc.

★ 2374 ★
First Aid Products
SIC: 3842; NAICS: 339113
Top Heat/Ice Pack Brands, 2011

Market shares are shown based on drug store sales for the 52 weeks ended March 20, 2011.

Thermacare	26.03%
Bed Buddy	3.55
Thermalon	3.26
Precise	3.19
Cryo Max	2.80
Thermipaq	2.58
Ace	2.30
Be Kool	2.12
Therma Med	1.77
Private label	40.86
Other	11.54

Source: *DrugStore Management*, Annual 2011-2012, p. 108, from SymphonyIRI Group Inc.

★ 2375 ★
First Aid Products
SIC: 3842; NAICS: 339113
Top Muscle Support Device Brands, 2010

Brands are ranked by drug store sales for the 52 weeks ended December 26, 2010.

	($ mil.)	Share
Futuro	$ 62.1	13.97%
Ace	40.3	9.06

Continued on next page.

★ 2375 ★

[Continued]

First Aid Products

SIC: 3842; NAICS: 339113

Top Muscle Support Device Brands, 2010

Brands are ranked by drug store sales for the 52 weeks ended December 26, 2010.

	($ mil.)	Share
Futuro Sport	$ 22.5	5.06%
Mueller Sport Care	19.2	4.32
Jobst	11.0	2.47
ACE Tekzone	7.3	1.64
Sport Aid	7.3	1.64
Futuro Infinity	7.0	1.57
Truform	6.6	1.48
Private label	94.0	21.14
Other	167.3	37.63

Source: *Chain Drug Review*, June 27, 2011, p. 176, from SymphonyIRI Group Inc.

★ 2376 ★

Medical Products

SIC: 3842; NAICS: 339113

Home Health Care Product Market, 2010, 2012 and 2014

Data show manufacturer shipments in millions of dollars. "Other" includes lifts, seating and positioning devices. Wheelchairs are the leading sector, and while manufacturers have introduced a number of technological improvements, many of these changes have been discontinued, according to the source. Bathroom safety products such as grab rails and seats have become popular and are sold in many retail channels. The popularity of bariatric chairs is a growing trend. Invacare was the leader in the market with a 20.9% share, followed by Sunrise with a 12.5%.

	2010	2012	2014
Wheelchairs	$ 1,517.9	$ 1,462.1	$ 1,314.5
Bathroom safety supplies	519.7	616.4	733.7
Home care beds . . .	343.0	278.0	286.1
Ambulatory aids . . .	222.1	234.9	221.4
Other	152.0	175.1	202.6

Source: "Market for Home Care Products." [online] from http://www.docin.com [Published December 2010], from Kalorama Information.

★ 2377 ★

Medical Products

SIC: 3842; NAICS: 339113

Mobility Aids, 2010, 2012 and 2014

Data show manufacturer shipments in millions of dollars. Scooters became popular in the late 1990s, boosted in part by Medicare reimbursement and the appeal of the device's technological sophistication. Walkers and canes remain very popular, with some users owning more than one. In 2014, scooters are projected to claim 54% of the market, canes and walking sticks 2%, walkers 18% and crutches 7%.

	2010	2012	2014
Scooters	139.6	143.2	121.2
Canes and walking sticks . .	33.1	38.3	44.6
Walkers	38.2	40.4	40.8
Crutches	11.2	12.9	14.8

Source: "Market for Home Care Products." [online] from http://www.docin.com [Published December 2010], from Kalorama Information.

★ 2378 ★

Medical Products

SIC: 3842; NAICS: 334510

Top Makers of Hearing Aid Implants Worldwide, 2010

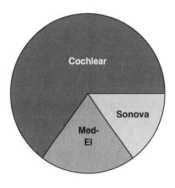

Market shares are shown in percent.

Cochlear	65.0%
Med-El	20.0
Sonova	15.0

Source: *Wall Street Journal*, September 13, 2011, p. B5, from Nomura Research.

★ 2379 ★
Medical Products
SIC: 3842; NAICS: 339113

Top Respirator Makers Worldwide, 2009

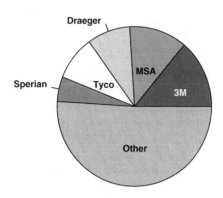

Market shares are shown in percent.

3M	14.0%
MSA	12.0
Draeger	9.0
Tyco	9.0
Sperian	5.0
Other	51.0

Source: "Safety and Security." [online] from http://www.bostonstrategies.com/clientlogin/rawmaterials/Safety090724.pdf [Published July 2009], from Boston Strategies International.

★ 2380 ★
Orthopedic Appliances
SIC: 3842; NAICS: 339113

Top Orthobiologics Makers Worldwide, 2010

The industry was valued at $4.5 billion.

Medtronic	19.0%
Genzyme	11.0
Synthes	7.0
Nephew	4.0
Johnson & Johnson Co.	3.0
Other	55.0

Source: "Stryker Fact Book 2010-2011." [online] from http://hx.corporate-ir.net [Accessed October 1, 2011].

★ 2381 ★
Orthopedic Appliances
SIC: 3842; NAICS: 339113

Top Orthopedic Appliance Makers Worldwide, 2010

Spinal devices claimed 18% of the market, knees 17%, trauma and craniomaxillofacial 16%, hips 14% and other products 54%.

Stryker Corp.	15.0%
Johnson & Johnson Co.	13.0
Zimmer	10.0
Medtronic	9.0
Synthes	9.0
Smith & Nephew	8.0
Biomet	6.0
Other	30.0

Source: "Stryker Fact Book 2010-2011." [online] from http://hx.corporate-ir.net [Accessed October 1, 2011].

★ 2382 ★
Orthopedic Appliances
SIC: 3842; NAICS: 339113

Top Orthopedic Reconstructive Implant Makers Worldwide, 2010

The industry was valued at $13.7 billion.

Zimmer	24.0%
Johnson & Johnson Co.	22.0
Stryker Corp.	19.0
Biomet	12.0
Smith & Nephew	11.0
Other	12.0

Source: "Stryker Fact Book 2010-2011." [online] from http://hx.corporate-ir.net [Accessed October 1, 2011].

★ 2383 ★
Orthopedic Appliances
SIC: 3842; NAICS: 339113

Top Spinal Implant Makers in China, 2009

Market shares are estimated.

Medtronic	13.3%
Johnson & Johnson (DePuy)	11.1
Shandong Weigao	8.1
Synthes Inc.	7.4
Stryker Corp.	5.7
Other	62.4

Source: "China Healthcare Sector." [online] from http://download.bioon.com.cn/upload/201105/17235814_9161.pdf [Published December 3, 2010], from Citi Investment Research.

★ 2384 ★
Orthopedic Appliances
SIC: 3842; NAICS: 339113

Top Spinal Implant Makers Worldwide, 2010

The industry was valued at $7.2 billion.

Medtronic	35.0%
Johnson & Johnson Co.	14.0
Synthes	13.0
Stryker	9.0
Nuvasive	7.0
Globus	4.0
Other	17.0

Source: "Stryker Fact Book 2010-2011." [online] from http://hx.corporate-ir.net [Accessed October 1, 2011].

★ 2385 ★
Orthopedic Appliances
SIC: 3842; NAICS: 339113

Top Trauma and Craniomaxillofacial Implant Makers Worldwide, 2010

The industry was valued at $6.2 billion.

Synthes Inc.	38.0%
Stryker	16.0
Smith & Nephew	7.0
Johnson & Johnson Co.	5.0
Biomet	4.0
Zimmer	4.0
Other	26.0

Source: "Stryker Fact Book 2010-2011." [online] from http://hx.corporate-ir.net [Accessed October 1, 2011].

★ 2386 ★
Orthopedic Appliances
SIC: 3842; NAICS: 339113

Top Trauma Makers in China, 2009

Market shares are estimated.

Synthes Inc.	13.8%
Trauson	8.4
Kanghui Medical	5.1
Shandongh Weigao	3.6
Beijing Libeier	2.7
Other	66.4

Source: "China Healthcare Sector." [online] from http://download.bioon.com.cn/upload/201105/17235814_9161.pdf [Published December 3, 2010], from Citi Investment Research.

★ 2387 ★
Surgical Supplies
SIC: 3842; NAICS: 339113

Disposable Medical Supply Market, 2011

The industry was valued at $37.8 billion in 2011.

Drug delivery products	25.0%
Wound management products	23.0
Nonwoven medical disposables	13.0
Other	39.0

Source: "Disposable Medical Supplies." [online] from http://www.freedoniagroup.com [Published March 2012], from Freedonia Group.

★ 2388 ★
Surgical Supplies
SIC: 3842; NAICS: 339113

Global Wound Care Market, 2010

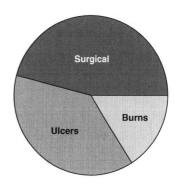

The market was valued at $15 billion.

Surgical	46.0%
Ulcers	38.0
Burns	16.0

Source: *Medical Product Outsourcing*, November/December 2011, p. NA, from Marketresearch.com.

★ 2389 ★
Surgical Supplies
SIC: 3842; NAICS: 339113

Top Endoscopy Makers Worldwide, 2010

The industry was valued at $23.5 billion.

Johnson & Johnson Co.	20.0%
Olympus	17.0
Covidien	13.0
Boston Scientific	7.0
Karl Storz	4.0
Smith & Nephew	4.0

Continued on next page.

★ 2389 ★

[Continued]

Surgical Supplies

SIC: 3842; NAICS: 339113

Top Endoscopy Makers Worldwide, 2010

The industry was valued at $23.5 billion.

Stryker	4.0%
Other	32.0

Source: ''Stryker Fact Book 2010-2011.'' [online] from http://hx.corporate-ir.net [Accessed October 1, 2011].

★ 2390 ★

Surgical Supplies

SIC: 3842; NAICS: 339113

Top Makers of Disposable Medical Products Worldwide, 2009

The industry is projected to grow from $124.9 billion in 2009 to $164 billion in 2014.

Johnson & Johnson Co.	8.7%
Covidien	5.3
BD	3.6
Kimberly-Clark Corp.	2.6
B. Braun	2.2
Other	77.6

Source: ''World Disposable Medical Supplies.'' [online] from http://www.freedoniagroup.com [Published December 2010], from Freedonia Group.

★ 2391 ★

Surgical Supplies

SIC: 3842; NAICS: 339113

Top Makers of Surgical Drapes in Europe, 2008

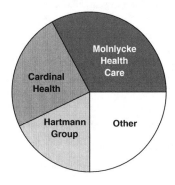

Market shares are shown in percent.

Molnlycke Health Care	33.0%
Cardinal Health	24.0

Hartmann Group	18.0%
Other	25.0

Source: ''Surgical Drapes, Gowns and Gloves Market in Europe.'' [online] from http://www.sicherheitimop.at/documents/SurgicalDrapesEuropeFSDec2009.pdf [Published December 2009], from Frost & Sullivan.

★ 2392 ★

Surgical Supplies

SIC: 3842; NAICS: 339113

Top Makers of Surgical Gloves in Europe, 2008

Market shares are shown in percent.

Ansell Health	30.0%
Molnlycke Health Care	25.0
Sempermed	25.0
Other	20.0

Source: ''Surgical Drapes, Gowns and Gloves Market in Europe.'' [online] from http://www.sicherheitimop.at/documents/SurgicalDrapesEuropeFSDec2009.pdf [Published December 2009], from Frost & Sullivan.

★ 2393 ★

Surgical Supplies

SIC: 3842; NAICS: 339113

Top Makers of Surgical Gowns in Europe, 2008

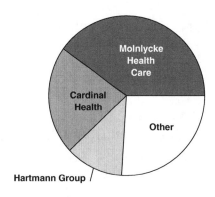

Market shares are shown in percent.

Molnlycke Health Care	40.0%
Cardinal Health	22.0
Hartmann Group	12.0
Other	26.0

Source: ''Surgical Drapes, Gowns and Gloves Market in Europe.'' [online] from http://www.sicherheitimop.at/documents/SurgicalDrapesEuropeFSDec2009.pdf [Published December 2009], from Frost & Sullivan.

★ 2394 ★
Dental Equipment
SIC: 3843; NAICS: 339114

Dental Equipment and Supplies Manufacturing, 2010

Total shipments were valued at $4.61 billion. "NSK" stands for Not Specified by Kind.

	($ 000)	Share
Dental equipment and supplies, professional	$ 3,105,150	67.31%
Dental equipment and supplies, laboratory	1,115,576	24.18
Dental equipment and supplies manufacturing, nsk, total	392,693	8.51

Source: "Annual Survey of Manufactures." [online] from http://www.census.gov/manufacturing/asm/index.html [Accessed January 18, 2012], from U.S. Department of Commerce.

★ 2395 ★
Dental Equipment
SIC: 3843; NAICS: 339114

Top Makers of Bench Lathes, 2010

Bench lathes are used in the dental lab for bulk grinding of acrylic and stone.

Redwing	72.0%
Baldor	25.0
KaVo	11.0
Buffalo	2.0

Source: "2010 USAF Dental Laboratory Equipment/Product Survey." [online] from http://airforcemedicine.afms.mil [Published June 2011], from USAF Dental Equipment & Consultation Service.

★ 2396 ★
Dental Equipment
SIC: 3843; NAICS: 339114

Top Makers of Burnout Ovens, 2010

A burnout oven is used for wax elimination, preheating and heat treatment.

Jelrus	33.0%
Jelenko	19.0
Ney	18.0
Whip Mix	18.0
KaVo	10.0
Dentsply	1.0
Intratech	1.0

Source: "2010 USAF Dental Laboratory Equipment/Product Survey." [online] from http://airforcemedicine.afms.mil [Published June 2011], from USAF Dental Equipment & Consultation Service.

★ 2397 ★
Dental Equipment
SIC: 3843; NAICS: 339114

Top Makers of Electric Waxers, 2010

Electric waxers are designed to increase a waxer's production by eliminating going back and forth with an instrument to a flame.

Kerr	64.0%
Renfert	35.0
Whip Mix	1.0

Source: "2010 USAF Dental Laboratory Equipment/Product Survey." [online] from http://airforcemedicine.afms.mil [Published June 2011], from USAF Dental Equipment & Consultation Service.

★ 2398 ★
Dental Equipment
SIC: 3843; NAICS: 339114

Top Makers of Handpieces (High-Speed), 2010

High-speed handpieces are routinely used to grind and share porcelain restorations in the dental laboratory.

KaVo	24.0%
NSK	18.0
Brassler	14.0
Ney	14.0
Bien Air	8.0
Jelenko	6.0
Shofu	6.0
Other	10.0

Source: "2010 USAF Dental Laboratory Equipment/Product Survey." [online] from http://airforcemedicine.afms.mil [Published June 2011], from USAF Dental Equipment & Consultation Service.

★ 2399 ★
Dental Equipment
SIC: 3843; NAICS: 339114

Top Makers of Lathes (Stand-Up Polishers), 2010

Stand-up lathes are generally used to smooth and polish acrylic appliances.

KaVo	83.0%
Nevin	8.0
Nobilium	6.0
Baldor	3.0

Source: "2010 USAF Dental Laboratory Equipment/Product Survey." [online] from http://airforcemedicine.afms.mil [Published June 2011], from USAF Dental Equipment & Consultation Service.

★ 2400 ★
Dental Equipment
SIC: 3843; NAICS: 339114

Top Makers of Porcelain Systems, 2010

Market shares are shown in percent.

VM-13	72.0%
Omega 900	7.0
VMK 95	7.0
IPSd.Sign	5.0
Other	13.0

Source: "2010 USAF Dental Laboratory Equipment/Product Survey." [online] from http://airforcemedicine.afms.mil [Published June 2011], from USAF Dental Equipment & Consultation Service.

★ 2401 ★
Dental Implants
SIC: 3843; NAICS: 339114

Global Dental Implant Market, 2010

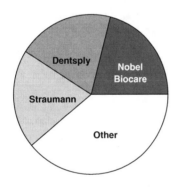

The industry was valued at $3 billion.

Nobel Biocare	21.0%
Dentsply	20.0
Straumann	20.0
Other	39.0

Source: "Dentsply Acquires Astra Tech for $1.8B." [online] from http://www.drbicuspid.com [Published June 22, 2011], from Robert W. Baird.

★ 2402 ★
Diagnostic Imaging
SIC: 3844; NAICS: 334517

Global Diagnostic Market, 2010

The global diagnostic imaging market is expected to grow from $20.7 billion in 2010 to $26.6 billion by 2016, at an estimated CAGR of 4.2% from 2011 to 2016. The market is being driven by an increasing aging population and widening applications of diagnostic imaging.

X-ray	34.0%
Ultrasound	21.0
CT scan	19.5
MRI	18.5
Nuclear medicine	7.0

Source: *PR Newswire*, July 25, 2011, p. NA, from MarketsandMarkets.

★ 2403 ★
Irradiation Apparatus
SIC: 3844; NAICS: 334517

Irradiation Apparatus Manufacturing, 2007

Data show the percent of industry sales held by the largest 4, 8, 20 and 50 firms in the sector. There are approximately 168 firms operating in the industry generating employment for 15,533 people.

4 largest companies	58.2%
8 largest companies	75.7
20 largest companies	89.7
50 largest companies	96.5

Source: "2007 Economic Census." [online] from http://www.census.gov/econ/concentration.html [Accessed August 12, 2011], from U.S. Bureau of the Census.

★ 2404 ★
Contact Lenses
SIC: 3851; NAICS: 339115

Contact Lens Market in the United Kingdom, 2010

Total sales were 557 million contact lenses.

Daily disposable	58.0%
Silicon hydrogel	27.0
Soft frequent replacement	9.0
Rigid	5.0
Soft traditional	2.0

Source: *Optician*, May 13, 2011, p. NA, from Association of Contact Lens Manufacturers.

★ 2405 ★
Contact Lenses
SIC: 3851; NAICS: 339115
Top Soft Contact Lens Makers, 2011

Market shares are estimated.

Johnson & Johnson Co.	42.0%
Ciba Vision	25.0
CooperVision	21.0
Bausch & Lomb	14.0

Source: "Contact Lenses." [online] from http://www.clspectrum.com/articleviewer.aspx?articleid106550 [Published January 1, 2012], from Robert W. Baird.

★ 2406 ★
Contact Lenses
SIC: 3851; NAICS: 339115
Top Soft Contact Lens Makers Worldwide, 2010

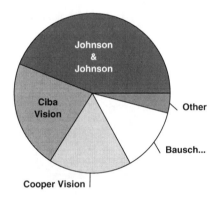

Market shares are shown in percent.

Johnson & Johnson Co.	44.0%
Ciba Vision	22.0
Cooper Vision	17.0
Bausch & Lomb	13.0
Other	4.0

Source: "Cooper Investor Presentation." [online] from http://files.shareholder.com/downloads [Published December 8, 2011], from market research data.

★ 2407 ★
Digital Film Projectors
SIC: 3851; NAICS: 339115
Top Digital Cinema Projector Makers Worldwide, 2011

Market shares are shown in percent.

Christie	50.0%
Barco	40.0
NEC	10.0

Source: "Christie has 50% Share of DLP Cinema Market." [online] from http://www.installationeurope.com [Published December 14, 2011].

★ 2408 ★
Eyewear
SIC: 3851; NAICS: 339115
Retail Eyewear Sales, 2008

Data are in millions of dollars.

	($ mil.)	Share
Prescription eyeglasses	$ 16,028.9	72.97%
Contact lenses	3,210.9	14.62
Non-prescription eyeglasses/ sunglasses	1,934.8	8.81
Other	791.7	3.60

Source: "U.S. Eyewear Market." [online] from http://www.packagedfacts.com [Published June 2009], from Packaged Facts.

★ 2409 ★
Eyewear
SIC: 3851; NAICS: 339115
Top Eyeglass Frame and Sunglass Makers Worldwide, 2008

Shares are shown for the wholesale market.

Luxottica	42.9%
Safilo	18.1
Marchon	6.6
Silohuette	3.2
De Rigo	3.0
Other	26.2

Source: "U.S. Eyewear Market." [online] from http://www.packagedfacts.com [Published June 2009], from Packaged Facts.

★ 2410 ★
Eyewear
SIC: 3851; NAICS: 339115

Top Eyewear Makers Worldwide, 2008

The wholesale industry was valued at $63.8 billion in 2008.

Luxottica	14.8%
Essilor	12.5
Johnson & Johnson Co.	10.2
Carl Zeiss	5.3
Ciba Vision	4.9
Hoya	4.6
Safilo	4.2
Cooper Vision	3.6
Other	39.9

Source: "U.S. Eyewear Market." [online] from http://www.packagedfacts.com [Published June 2009], from Packaged Facts.

★ 2411 ★
Lenses
SIC: 3851; NAICS: 339115

Lense Manufacturing in Europe, 2011

Data are based on the top five markets of France, Germany, Italy, Spain and the United Kingdom. Mineral and carbonates both saw shares fall from 2006, when they had shares of 9.8% and 6.3%, respectively. Essilor held approximately 42% of the market by volume.

Plastic	89.3%
High-index lenses	18.2
Mineral	4.7
Polycarbonate	4.7
Trives	1.3

Source: "The European Optical Market 2010-2011." [online] from http://www.swv4u.com/173.html?filetl_files/references/2011.pdf [Accessed May 1, 2012], from Strategy With Vision.

★ 2412 ★
Ophthalmic Goods
SIC: 3851; NAICS: 339115

Ophthalmic Goods Manufacturing, 2010

Total shipments were valued at $5.68 billion. "NSK" stands for Not Specified by Kind.

	($ 000)	Share
Ophthalmic fronts, temples, and focal and contact lenses	$ 3,475,785	61.16%
Ophthalmic goods, other types	1,971,023	34.68
Ophthalmic goods manufacturing, nsk, total	236,663	4.16

Source: "Annual Survey of Manufactures." [online] from http://www.census.gov/manufacturing/asm/index.html [Accessed January 18, 2012], from U.S. Department of Commerce.

★ 2413 ★
Cameras
SIC: 3861; NAICS: 333315

Top Digital Still Camera Makers, 2011

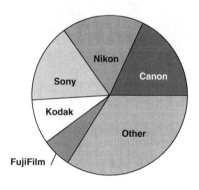

Market shares are shown for the first six months of the year.

Canon	18.0%
Nikon	17.0
Sony	16.0
Kodak	9.0
FujiFilm	6.0
Other	34.0

Source: *Wall Street Journal*, December 19, 2011, p. B1, from International Data Corp.

★ 2414 ★
Cameras
SIC: 3861; NAICS: 333315

Top Disposable Camera Brands, 2011

Market shares are shown based on drug store sales for the 52 weeks ended March 20, 2011.

Kodak Power Flash	22.65%
Kodak Fun Saver	17.15
Fuji Quicksnap Flash	4.79
Kodak Max Sport	4.65
Kodak Max Zoom	3.32
Private label	42.76
Other	4.68

Source: *DrugStore Management*, Annual 2011-2012, p. 223, from SymphonyIRI Group Inc.

★ 2415 ★
Digital Cameras
SIC: 3861; NAICS: 333315

Top Digital Camera Makers Worldwide, 2010

Market shares are shown in percent.

Canon	19.0%
Sony	17.9
Nikon	12.6
Samsung	11.1
Panasonic	7.6
Kodak	7.4
Olympus	6.1
Fuji	4.9
Casio	4.0
Pentax	1.5
Vivitar	1.2
Other	6.7

Source: "2010 Worldwide Digital Camera Market Shares by Vendor." [online] from http://nikonrumors.com [Published April 15, 2011], from International Data Corp. Japan.

★ 2416 ★
Film
SIC: 3861; NAICS: 325992

Top Cinematographic Film Exporters Worldwide, 2010

Total exports were valued at $638.9 million.

Canada	45.5%
Italy	17.9
Thailand	6.3
United States	4.9
India	4.5

Bulgaria	3.3%
United Kingdom	3.1
Other	14.5

Source: "2010 International Trade Statistics Yearbook." [online] from http://comtrade.un.org/pb/CommodityPagesNew.aspx?y2010 [Accessed April 1, 2012], from UN Comtrade.

★ 2417 ★
Film
SIC: 3861; NAICS: 325992

Top Conventional Film Brands, 2011

Market shares are shown based on supermarket sales for the 52 weeks ended March 20, 2011.

Fuji Superia Xtra	29.64%
Kodak Gold	16.91
Kodak Ultra Max	11.04
Fuji Super HQ	9.97
Kodak Ultra	7.34
Kodak Gold Max	5.03
Fujifilm	3.69
Kodak Advantix	2.56
Private label	4.57
Other	9.25

Source: *Non-Foods Management*, Annual 2011-2012, p. 176, from SymphonyIRI Group Inc.

★ 2418 ★
Lens Shutters
SIC: 3861; NAICS: 325992

Top Brands of 35mm Lens Shutters, 2011

Market shares are shown based on dollar sales for November 2010 through April 2011. The top brands in order of market share were Lomographic, Olympus, Nikon, Vivitar and Polaroid.

Top five brands	42.6%
Other	57.4

Source: *Twice*, July 5, 2011, p. 18, from NPD Group Inc.

★ 2419 ★
Projectors
SIC: 3861; NAICS: 333315

Large-Venue Projector Market, 2010

Market shares are shown in percent.

Houses of Worship	45.91%
Corporate	24.59

Continued on next page.

★ 2419 ★

[Continued]

Projectors

SIC: 3861; NAICS: 333315

Large-Venue Projector Market, 2010

Market shares are shown in percent.

Education	21.31%
Museums	8.19

Source: *Systems Contractor News*, October 2011, p. 54.

★ 2420 ★

Wearable-Cams

SIC: 3861; NAICS: 325992

Wearable-Cam Market, 2010

The company is estimated to have generated revenues of $15 million and sold 800,000 cams.

GoPro	90.0%
Other	10.0

Source: *Inc.*, February 2012, p. 52.

★ 2421 ★

Clocks

SIC: 3873; NAICS: 334518

Clock Production in Japan, 2011

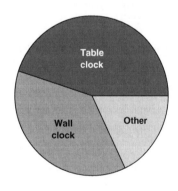

The industry was valued at 25.6 billion yen.

	(bil.)	Share
Table clock	¥ 11.4	45.06%
Wall clock	9.3	36.76
Other	4.6	18.18

Source: "Japanese Watch & Clock Industry in 2011." [online] from http://www.jcwa.or.jp/eng/statistics/industry_11.html [Accessed April 30, 2012], from Japanese Watch & Clock Association.

★ 2422 ★

Watches

SIC: 3873; NAICS: 334518

Global Watch Production, 2011

Total production was 1.05 billion pieces.

Analog quartz	81.0%
Digital quartz	17.0
Mechanical watch	2.0

Source: "Japanese Watch & Clock Industry in 2011." [online] from http://www.jcwa.or.jp/eng/statistics/industry_11.html [Accessed April 30, 2012], from Japanese Watch & Clock Association.

★ 2423 ★

Watches

SIC: 3873; NAICS: 334518

Top Mechanical Movement Makers Worldwide, 2011

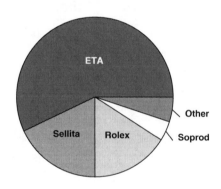

A movement contains all the moving parts of a watch. The industry is expected to produce 5.5 million units. ETA's main customers include Swatch Group brands, Richemont Group and LVMH Group.

ETA	57.0%
Sellita	18.0
Rolex	16.0
Soprod	4.0
Other	5.0

Source: *Financial Times*, September 10, 2011, p. 2, from Kepler Capital Markets.

★ 2424 ★
Watches
SIC: 3873; NAICS: 334518

Top Watch Makers Worldwide, 2010

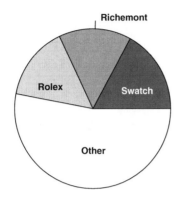

Market shares are shown in percent.

Swatch 17.4%
Richemont 14.7
Rolex 14.7
Other 53.2

Source: ''Chinese Demand Fuels Swiss Watch Success.'' [on-line] from http://www.thelocal.ch/1875/20111128 [Published November 28, 2011], from Bank Vontobel.

SIC 39 - Miscellaneous Manufacturing Industries

★ 2425 ★

Jewelry

SIC: 3911; NAICS: 339911

Jewelry (except Costume) Manufacturing, 2007

Data show the percent of industry sales held by the largest 4, 8, 20 and 50 firms in the sector. There are approximately 1,652 firms operating in the industry generating employment for 27,442 people.

4 largest companies	28.5%
8 largest companies	38.4
20 largest companies	55.2
50 largest companies	69.0

Source: "2007 Economic Census." [online] from http://www.census.gov/econ/concentration.html [Accessed August 12, 2011], from U.S. Bureau of the Census.

★ 2426 ★

Jewelry

SIC: 3911; NAICS: 339911

Jewelry (except Costume) Manufacturing, 2010

Total shipments were valued at $6.09 billion. "NSK" stands for Not Specified by Kind.

	($ 000)	Share
Jewelry, gold and platinum . . .	$ 4,384,116	71.99%
All other jewelry and personal goods (excluding costume) . .	967,134	15.88
Jewelry (except costume) manufacturing, nsk, total . . .	739,056	12.13

Source: "Annual Survey of Manufactures." [online] from http://www.census.gov/manufacturing/asm/index.html [Accessed January 18, 2012], from U.S. Department of Commerce.

★ 2427 ★

Jewelry

SIC: 3911; NAICS: 339911

Jewelry Industry in China, 2011 and 2015

Data show retail value in billions of Hong Kong dollars. "Gem-set" refers to jewelry with diamonds or gemstones.

	2011	2015	Share
Gold products	220.5	843.1	54.50%
Gem-set jewelry	117.4	385.0	24.89
Platinum/karat gold products .	85.1	318.9	20.61

Source: "Riding the Luxury Boom." [online] from http://www.clsa.com [Published December 21, 2011], from Frost & Sullivan.

★ 2428 ★

Jewelry

SIC: 3911; NAICS: 339911

Jewelry Sales, 2010

Market shares are shown in percent.

Diamond jewelry	43.0%
Pearl jewelry	31.0
Watches	12.0
Carat gold jewelry	9.0
Loose gemstones	5.0
Pearl jewelry	3.0

Source: *IDEX Magazine*, May 31, 2011, p. NA, from U.S. Bureau of the Census.

★ 2429 ★

Flatware

SIC: 3914; NAICS: 332211

Cutlery and Flatware (except Precious) Manufacturing, 2007

Data show the percent of industry sales held by the largest 4, 8, 20 and 50 firms in the sector. There are approximately 133 firms operating in the industry generating employment for 4,906 people.

4 largest companies	68.0%
8 largest companies	82.2
20 largest companies	94.0
50 largest companies	98.5

Source: "2007 Economic Census." [online] from http://www.census.gov/econ/concentration.html [Accessed August 12, 2011], from U.S. Bureau of the Census.

★ 2430 ★

Flatware

SIC: 3914; NAICS: 332211

Retail Flatware Sales, 2006-2010

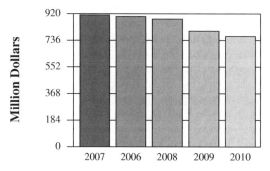

Flatware saw declining sales in the tightening economy. Unlike many tabletop items that chip or break, flatware doesn't need to be replaced regularly. As well, the category lacks marketing to entice consumers into making new purchases. Discount stores claimed 50% of the market, specialty stores 28%, department stores 11% and other sectors 11%.

2007	$ 907.8
2006	898.8
2008	880.6
2009	801.3
2010	761.2

Source: *HomeWorld Business*, January 2011, p. 160, from *HomeWorld Business* research.

★ 2431 ★

Jewelry Materials and Lapidary Work

SIC: 3915; NAICS: 339913

Jewelers' Material and Lapidary Work Manufacturing, 2007

Data show the percent of industry sales held by the largest 4, 8, 20 and 50 firms in the sector. There are approximately 224 firms operating in the industry generating employment for 3,380 people.

4 largest companies	56.1%
8 largest companies	68.0
20 largest companies	84.4
50 largest companies	94.4

Source: "2007 Economic Census." [online] from http://www.census.gov/econ/concentration.html [Accessed August 12, 2011], from U.S. Bureau of the Census.

★ 2432 ★

Jewelry Materials and Lapidary Work

SIC: 3915; NAICS: 339913

Jewelers' Material and Lapidary Work Manufacturing, 2010

Total shipments were valued at $1.06 billion. "NSK" stands for Not Specified by Kind.

	($ 000)	Share
Lapidary work, except for watch jewels	$ 513,437	48.21%
Jewelers' findings and materials, precious metal	320,384	30.08
Jewelers' material and lapidary work manufacturing, nsk, total . .	69,212	6.50
Other jewelers' findings and materials	161,952	15.21

Source: "Annual Survey of Manufactures." [online] from http://www.census.gov/manufacturing/asm/index.html [Accessed January 18, 2012], from U.S. Department of Commerce.

★ 2433 ★

Musical Instruments

SIC: 3931; NAICS: 339992

Best-Selling Music Product Categories, 2008 and 2010

Categories are ranked by retail sales in millions of dollars.

	2008	2010	Share
Fretted instruments and related products	$ 1,693	$ 1,430	23.17%
Pro audio and related products	1,535	1,305	21.14

Continued on next page.

★ 2433 ★

[Continued]

Musical Instruments

SIC: 3931; NAICS: 339992

Best-Selling Music Product Categories, 2008 and 2010

Categories are ranked by retail sales in millions of dollars.

	2008	2010	Share
Recording products	$ 604	$ 549	8.90%
Print music	597	545	8.83
School music products . . .	609	531	8.60
Percussion	518	478	7.74
Pianos	444	472	7.65
General accessories	445	435	7.05
Electronic music products . .	238	226	3.66
Portable keyboards	176	201	3.26

Source: *Music Trades*, April 2011, p. 67.

★ 2434 ★

Musical Instruments

SIC: 3931; NAICS: 339992

Largest Music and Audio Product Suppliers, 2011

Firms are ranked by revenues in millions of dollars.

Fewer Musical Instruments	$ 700.5
Harman Professional	613.2
Yamaha Corporation of America	538.8
Shore Inc.	427.0
Inway Musical Instruments	346.2
Jam Industries	290.0
Gibson Guitar Corp.	285.0
Avid Pro Audio	275.0
Numark Industries	251.4
Peavey Electronics Corp.	185.5

Source: *Music Trades*, April 2012, p. 98.

★ 2435 ★

Toys and Games

SIC: 3942; NAICS: 339931

Doll and Stuffed Toy Manufacturing, 2007

Data show the percent of industry sales held by the largest 4, 8, 20 and 50 firms in the sector. There are approximately 87 firms operating in the industry generating employment for 1,150 people.

4 largest companies	56.9%
8 largest companies	70.6

20 largest companies	86.1%
50 largest companies	97.8

Source: "2007 Economic Census." [online] from http://www.census.gov/econ/concentration.html [Accessed August 12, 2011], from U.S. Bureau of the Census.

★ 2436 ★

Toys and Games

SIC: 3942; NAICS: 339931

Fashion Doll Market, 2011

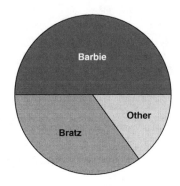

MGA Entertainment released the Bratz dolls in 2001, challenging Mattel's near monopoly of the market through its Barbie brand. The two companies spent much of the next decade in court over charges that MGA infringed on Mattel's copyright. However, in March 2012, Mattel announced plans to drop the suit.

Barbie	50.0%
Bratz	35.0
Other	15.0

Source: *Macleans*, March 14, 2012, p. NA.

★ 2437 ★

Hobby Industry

SIC: 3944; NAICS: 339932

Hobby Industry, 2010

The industry was valued at $2.45 billion in 2010, up 9.7% from 2007. This is a small part of the overall $24 billion craft and hobby industry. General hobby products include paint, hobby knife blades and airbrushes.

	($ mil.)	Share
Model railroading	$ 708	28.87%
General hobby	629	25.65
Radio controlled products	605	24.67
Plastics kits and diecast	510	20.80

Source: *Model Railroad News*, April 29, 2011, p. NA, from Hobby Manufacturers Association.

★ 2438 ★
Toys and Games
SIC: 3944; NAICS: 339932

Top Discovery/Infant Toy Makers, 2010

The industry was valued at $323 million in 2010.

Kids II	41.3%
Mattel Inc.	12.5
Kid Brands	9.1
Munchkin Bottling	9.1
Other	28.0

Source: "Infant, Toddler and Preschool Furnishings Toys, Accessories in the U.S." [online] from http://www.packagedfacts.com [Published November 2010], from Packaged Facts and SymphonyIRI Group Inc.

★ 2439 ★
Toys and Games
SIC: 3944; NAICS: 339932

Top Makers of Games and Puzzles, 2009

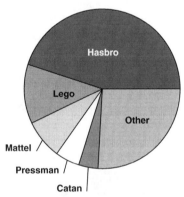

Market shares are shown based on online sales only. Hasbro controlled 60% of the market across all channels.

Hasbro	45.1%
Lego	12.4
Mattel	7.5
Pressman	5.0
Catan	3.6
Other	26.4

Source: "Lego Toys With Hasbro's U.S. Games Monopoly." [online] from http://www.toydirectory.com [Published August 2010], from Lutz Muller.

★ 2440 ★
Toys and Games
SIC: 3944; NAICS: 339932

Top Toy and Game Markets Worldwide, 2010

The industry was valued at $83.3 billion.

United States	26.3%
Japan	7.5
China	6.7
United Kingdom	5.4
France	4.9
Germany	4.0
Brazil	3.9
Australia	2.8
India	2.7
Canada	2.5
Other	33.3

Source: "Toy Markets in the World Annual 2010." [online] from http://www.toyassociation.org/AM/PDFs/Trends/Toy-Markets11.pdf [Published October 17, 2011], from NPD Group Inc.

★ 2441 ★
Toys and Games
SIC: 3944; NAICS: 339932

Top Toy and Game Sectors, 2011

The retail industry was valued at $22 billion in 2011.

Plush	30.5%
Infant/pre-school	16.1
Activity toys	15.1
Dolls	12.2
Games and puzzles	9.5
Ride-ons	5.0
Other	11.3

Source: *Datamonitor Industry Market Research*, January 31, 2012, p. NA, from Datamonitor.

★ 2442 ★
Toys and Games
SIC: 3944; NAICS: 339932

Top Toy and Game Sectors Worldwide, 2011

The industry was valued at $78 billion in 2011.

Plush	28.2%
Infant/pre-school	15.4
Activity toys	14.7
Dolls	12.7
Games and puzzles	11.9

Continued on next page.

★ 2442 ★

[Continued]

Toys and Games

SIC: 3944; NAICS: 339932

Top Toy and Game Sectors Worldwide, 2011

The industry was valued at $78 billion in 2011.

Ride-ons	6.3%
Other	10.3

Source: *Datamonitor Industry Market Research*, January 31, 2012, p. NA, from Datamonitor.

★ 2443 ★

Toys and Games

SIC: 3944; NAICS: 339932

Top Toy Makers, 2010

Toys generated sales of $21.8 billion in 2010, a 2% increase over the year.

Mattel	16.0%
Hasbro	10.0
Other	74.0

Source: *Barron's*, August 27, 2011, p. NA, from Toy Industry Association.

★ 2444 ★

Video Game Consoles

SIC: 3944; NAICS: 339932

Video Game Console Market, 2011

Platforms are ranked by unit sales.

	(mil.)	Share
Xbox 360	7.41	28.79%
Nintendo Wii	4.87	18.92
PlayStation 3	4.46	17.33
Nintendo 3DS	4.14	16.08
Nintendo DS	3.62	14.06
PlayStation Portable	1.24	4.82

Source: "USA Yearly Chart." [online] from http://www.vg-chartz.com/yearly/2011/USA [Accessed March 20, 2012].

★ 2445 ★

Gym and Exercise Equipment

SIC: 3949; NAICS: 33992

Consumer Fitness Equipment Sales, 2008-2010

Wholesale shipments fell from $1.04 billion in 2008 to $970 million in 2009 then rose to $1.02 billion in 2010. Major players include Life Fitness, Star Trac, Matrix Fitness and Cybex International.

	2008	2009	2010
Treadmills	27.3%	25.9%	26.8%
Elliptical machines	21.6	22.6	23.7
Exercise cycles	10.8	10.8	10.8
Home gyms	7.3	6.2	6.0
Ab machines	6.4	6.1	5.9
Free weights	5.2	5.1	4.9
Exercise benches	3.8	3.7	3.6
Rowing machines	1.8	1.8	1.7
Ski machines	1.1	1.1	1.0
Other	14.5	16.8	15.7

Source: "Health, Nutrition & Fitness Report." [online] from https://www.acg.org/assets/10/documents/Health__Nutrition_ &_Fitness_Report.pdf [Published Spring 2012], from Sporting Goods Manufacturers Association.

★ 2446 ★

Gym and Exercise Equipment

SIC: 3949; NAICS: 33992

Gym and Exercise Equipment Sales, 2011

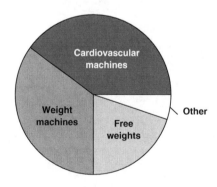

The industry generated revenues of $4.0 billion. There were 471 establishments providing employment to 12,781 people.

Cardiovascular machines	40.0%
Weight machines	35.0

Continued on next page.

★ 2446 ★

[Continued]

Gym and Exercise Equipment

SIC: 3949; NAICS: 33992

Gym and Exercise Equipment Sales, 2011

The industry generated revenues of $4.0 billion. There were 471 establishments providing employment to 12,781 people.

Free weights	20.0%
Other	5.0

Source: "Gym and Exercise Equipment Manufacturing in the U.S." [online] from http://www.ibisworld.com [Published July 2011], from IBISWorld.

★ 2447 ★

Gym and Exercise Equipment

SIC: 3949; NAICS: 33992

Hydration Belt Market, 2009

The company has 85% of the running store channel and controls 90% of the triathlon market.

FuelBelt	85.0%
Other	15.0

Source: *TriAthlete Magazine*, September 2009, p. 50.

★ 2448 ★

Sporting Goods

SIC: 3949; NAICS: 33992

Football Helmet Market, 2009

The two companies have more than 90% of the market. Rawlings returned to the helmet market after twenty years and is expected to claim 6-7% of the market in its first year. According to the Sporting Goods Manufacturers Association, sales increased from $308 million in 2009 to $327 million in 2010.

Schutt Sports/Riddell	90.0%
Other	10.0

Source: *St. Louis Post-Dispatch*, September 18, 2011, p. NA.

★ 2449 ★

Sporting Goods

SIC: 3949; NAICS: 33992

Sporting Goods Industry Worldwide, 2010

The industry generated revenues of $64.9 billion in 2011.

Ball sports	23.68%
Adventure sports	23.52

Fitness	17.73%
Golf	17.72
Winter sports	9.05
Racket sports	8.26
Other	0.24

Source: *Datamonitor Industry Market Research*, February 2, 2012, p. NA, from Datamonitor.

★ 2450 ★

Sporting Goods

SIC: 3949; NAICS: 33992

Top Athletic/Outdoor Gear and Apparel Firms, 2005

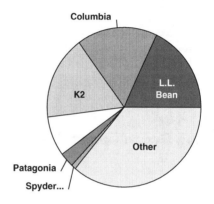

Market shares are shown in percent.

L.L. Bean	18.0%
Columbia	17.0
K2	17.0
The North Face	8.0
Patagonia	3.0
Spyder Active Sports Inc.	1.0
Other	36.0

Source: "North Face Inc: Market Segmentation and Target Market Selection." [online] from http://www.docstoc.com/docs/84899987/The-North-Face_-Inc [Published March 21, 2007], from VFC Corp.

★ 2451 ★

Sporting Goods

SIC: 3949; NAICS: 33992

Top Fishing Equipment Brands, 2011

Market shares are shown based on percent of all purchases in selected categories.

Plano (tackle boxes)	45.8%
Cabela (fly combo)	31.5
Rapela (fishing knives)	25.2
Frabill (landing nets)	24.5
Scientific Angler (fly lines)	23.8

Continued on next page.

★ 2451 ★

[Continued]

Sporting Goods

SIC: 3949; NAICS: 33992

Top Fishing Equipment Brands, 2011

Market shares are shown based on percent of all purchases in selected categories.

Shimano (reels)	21.4%
Orvis (fly rods)	16.5
Strike King (spinner bait)	16.4
Rapela (hard bait)	15.2
Zoom (soft bait)	15.2
Berkley Trilene (fishing lines)	13.1
Shakespeare (rods)	9.6

Source: "Top Fishing Equipment Brands for 2011." [online] from http://www.southwickassociates.com [Press release February 27, 2012], from Southwick Associates.

★ 2452 ★

Sporting Goods

SIC: 3949; NAICS: 33992

Top Sporting Goods Categories, 2010

Sales are projected in millions of dollars. Total spending was $24.56 billion.

	($ mil.)	Share
Hunting and firearms	$ 5,165	43.28%
Fishing tackle	1,861	15.59
Exercise	1,526	12.79
Optics	1,091	9.14
Snow skiing	516	4.32
Archery	383	3.21
Baseball and softball	378	3.17
Tennis	364	3.05
Skin diving	350	2.93
Camping	300	2.51

Source: "Sporting Goods Sales by Product Category." [online] from http://www.statab.com [Accessed April 1, 2012], from National Sporting Goods Association.

★ 2453 ★

Sporting Goods

SIC: 3949; NAICS: 33992

Top Sporting Goods Makers in China, 2011

The industry generated revenues of $15.7 billion in 2011. Athletic equipment claimed 32.2% of the total, fitness equipment 29.0%, balls 11.6%, sports protection equipment 7.7% and other products 19.5%.

Zhongshan Worldmark Sporting Goods Co. Ltd.	4.4%
Taishan Sports Industry Group Co. Ltd. . . .	2.5

Guangwei Group Co. Ltd.	2.1%
Daito-Osin Healthcare Manufacturing Co. Ltd. .	1.8
Johnson Health Ted (Shanghai) Co. Ltd. . . .	1.8
Other	87.4

Source: "Sports Equipment Manufacturing in China." [online] from http://www.docin.com [Published September 2011], from IBISWorld.

★ 2454 ★

Pens

SIC: 3951; NAICS: 339992

Top Luxury Pen Makers Worldwide, 2010

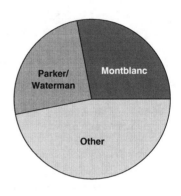

Market shares are shown in percent.

Montblanc	28.0%
Parker/Waterman	25.0
Other	47.0

Source: *Wall Street Journal*, February 2, 2011, p. NA.

★ 2455 ★

Pens

SIC: 3951; NAICS: 339941

Top Pen Brands, 2011

Brands are ranked by sales at supermarkets, drug stores and discount stores (excluding Wal-Mart) for the 12 weeks ended July 10, 2011.

	($ mil.)	Share
Pilot G2	$ 4.4	13.29%
Sanford Sharpie	2.1	6.34
Uni Ball Signo 207	1.5	4.53
Paper Mate Profile	1.4	4.23
Pilot Easy Touch	1.3	3.93
Paper Mate & Write	1.0	3.02
Pilot Precise V5	0.9	2.72
BIC Cristal	0.8	2.42
Paper Mate Flair	0.8	2.42

Continued on next page.

★ 2455 ★

[Continued]

Pens

SIC: 3951; NAICS: 339941

Top Pen Brands, 2011

Brands are ranked by sales at supermarkets, drug stores and discount stores (excluding Wal-Mart) for the 12 weeks ended July 10, 2011.

	($ mil.)	Share
BIC Velocity	$ 0.6	1.81%
Private label	1.7	5.14
Other	16.6	50.15

Source: *MMR*, September 5, 2011, p. 18, from SymphonyIRI Group Inc.

★ 2456 ★

Pens

SIC: 3951; NAICS: 339941

Top Pen Makers, 2010

Companies are ranked by sales at supermarkets, drug stores and discount stores (excluding Wal-Mart) for the 12 weeks ended December 26, 2010.

	($ mil.)	Share
Newell Rubbermaid	$ 12.8	30.62%
BIC	5.8	13.88
Pilot	2.8	6.70
Pentel	1.9	4.55
Joseph Enterprises	1.7	4.07
Zebra Pen	1.2	2.87
Mega Brands	0.9	2.15
Sanrio	0.7	1.67
Jakks Pacific	0.5	1.20
Private label	2.4	5.74
Other	11.1	26.56

Source: *Drug Store News*, February 28, 2011, p. NA, from SymphonyIRI Group Inc.

★ 2457 ★

Writing Instruments

SIC: 3951; NAICS: 339941

Pen and Mechanical Pencil Manufacturing, 2007

Data show the percent of industry sales held by the largest 4, 8, 20 and 50 firms in the sector. There are approximately 80 firms operating in the industry generating employment for 4,372 people.

4 largest companies	57.7%
8 largest companies	71.1
20 largest companies	88.7%
50 largest companies	99.2

Source: "2007 Economic Census." [online] from http://www.census.gov/econ/concentration.html [Accessed August 12, 2011], from U.S. Bureau of the Census.

★ 2458 ★

Writing Instruments

SIC: 3951; NAICS: 339941

Top Makers of Writing Instruments and Related Products Worldwide, 2009

Pens claimed 56% of the market, markers 16%, coloring 14%, correctional products 7%, mechanical products 6% and glue 2% and other sectors 6%.

Newell Rubbermaid	13.0%
BIC	10.0
Pilot	6.0
Crayola	3.0
Mitsubishi	3.0
Pentel	3.0
Zebra Pen	3.0
Other	60.0

Source: "Group Presentation for Investors." [online] from http://www.bicworld.com [Published August 2011], from company reports.

★ 2459 ★

Arts and Crafts

SIC: 3952; NAICS: 339942

Best-Selling Craft Sectors, 2010

The CHA U.S. A&U Study found that 56% of U.S. households crafted at least once during 2010, contributing to the $29.2 billion U.S. craft and hobby industry. Measured by millions of households participating, drawing was the most popular art and craft activity with 21.1 million households engaging in it in 2010, followed by scrapbooking with 18.4 million and crocheting with 17.4 million households. Sales are shown in millions of dollars.

	($ mil.)	Share
Woodworking/wood crafts	$ 3,322	11.38%
Drawing	2,078	7.12
Food crafting	2,001	6.85
Jewelry making	1,446	4.95
Scrapbooking and memory crafts	1,440	4.93
Floral decorating	1,303	4.46
Crocheting	1,062	3.64
Card making	1,040	3.56
Home decor crafts (non-sewing)	948	3.25

Continued on next page.

★ 2459 ★

[Continued]

Arts and Crafts

SIC: 3952; NAICS: 339942

Best-Selling Craft Sectors, 2010

The CHA U.S. A&U Study found that 56% of U.S. households crafted at least once during 2010, contributing to the $29.2 billion U.S. craft and hobby industry. Measured by millions of households participating, drawing was the most popular art and craft activity with 21.1 million households engaging in it in 2010, followed by scrapbooking with 18.4 million and crocheting with 17.4 million households. Sales are shown in millions of dollars.

	($ mil.)	Share
Wedding crafts	$ 803	2.75%
Other	13,757	47.11

Source: "CHA Announces 2010 Craft Industry Statistics." [online] from http://craftandhobby.wordpress.com/2011/04/06/cha-announces-2010-craft-industry-statistics [Published April 6, 2011], from *2010 CHA U.S. Attitude & Usage Study.*

★ 2460 ★

Chalk

SIC: 3952; NAICS: 339942

Top Chalk Brands, 2011

Brands are ranked by sales at drug stores, supermarkets and mass merchandisers (excluding Wal-Mart) for the 22 weeks ended November 27, 2011.

	($ 000)	Share
Crayola	$ 538.6	37.34%
Crayola Sidewalk	466.0	32.30
Crayola Glow	184.4	12.78
Rose Art	57.3	3.97
Jaru	25.9	1.80
Omni Party	21.8	1.51
Private label	54.8	3.80
Other	93.8	6.50

Source: *Drug Store News*, January 30, 2012, p. NA, from SymphonyIRI Group Inc.

★ 2461 ★

Colored Pencils

SIC: 3952; NAICS: 339942

Top Colored Pencil Brands, 2011

Brands are ranked by sales at drug stores, supermarkets and mass merchandisers (excluding Wal-Mart) for the 12 weeks ended November 27, 2011.

	($ 000)	Share
Crayola	$ 3,401.5	61.42%
Crayola Twistables	817.9	14.77
Rose Art	552.7	9.98
Dixon	156.9	2.83
Crayola Pip Squeaks	89.0	1.61
Playskool	45.7	0.83
Private label	314.3	5.67
Other	160.5	2.90

Source: *Drug Store News*, January 30, 2012, p. NA, from SymphonyIRI Group Inc.

★ 2462 ★

Correctional Products

SIC: 3952; NAICS: 339942

Top Correctional Product Makers, 2010

Companies are ranked by sales at supermarkets, drug stores and discount stores (excluding Wal-Mart) for the 12 weeks ended December 26, 2010.

	($ mil.)	Share
BIC	$ 2,137.8	63.88%
Sanford Ink	1,000.0	29.88
American Tombow	5.7	0.17
Bangkit (U.S.A.)	3.2	0.10
Pentel	3.3	0.10
3M	1.9	0.06
Encore Sales	0.7	0.02
SK Merch	0.6	0.02
Promotions Unlimited	0.5	0.01
Private label	192.2	5.74
Other	0.9	0.03

Source: *Drug Store News*, February 28, 2011, p. NA, from SymphonyIRI Group Inc.

★ **2463** ★

Crayons

SIC: 3952; NAICS: 339942

Top Crayon Brands, 2011

Market shares are shown based on supermarket sales for the 52 weeks ended March 20, 2011.

Crayola	79.75%
Crayola Twistables	8.40
Crayola Telescoping Tower	2.19
Crayola Beginnings	1.42
Rose Art	1.30
Cra-Z-Art	0.75
Staples	0.64
Crayola Twist Slick Stix	0.54
Nick Jr. Dora The Explorer	0.46
Private label	1.77
Other	2.78

Source: *Non-Foods Management*, Annual 2011-2012, p. 176, from SymphonyIRI Group Inc.

★ **2464** ★

Pencils

SIC: 3952; NAICS: 339941

Top Pencil Brands, 2011

Brands are ranked by sales at supermarkets, drug stores and discount stores (excluding Wal-Mart) for the 12 weeks ended July 10, 2011.

	($ mil.)	Share
BIC	$ 1.5	11.03%
Paper Mate Clearpoint	1.3	9.56
Paper Mate	0.6	4.41
BIC Matic Grip	0.5	3.68
Dixon Ticonderoga	0.5	3.68
Paper Mate & Write	0.5	3.68
Ticonderoga	0.4	2.94
BIC Velocity	0.3	2.21
Paper Mate Comfort	0.3	2.21
Paper Mate Write Bros.	0.2	1.47
Private label	1.6	11.76
Other	5.9	43.38

Source: *MMR*, September 5, 2011, p. 21, from SymphonyIRI Group Inc.

★ **2465** ★

Pencils

SIC: 3952; NAICS: 339941

Top Pencil Makers, 2010

Companies are ranked by sales at supermarkets, drug stores and discount stores (excluding Wal-Mart) for the 12 weeks ended December 26, 2010.

	($ mil.)	Share
Newell Rubbermaid	$ 5.8	29.29%
BIC	4.3	21.72
Devrian Global Industries	1.6	8.08
Dixon Ticonderoga	1.3	6.57
Pentel	1.1	5.56
Mega Brands	0.9	4.55
Sanrio	0.6	3.03
Raymond Geddes & Co.	0.4	2.02
Zebra Pen	0.3	1.52
Private label	2.1	10.61
Other	1.4	7.07

Source: *Drug Store News*, February 28, 2011, p. NA, from SymphonyIRI Group Inc.

★ **2466** ★

Markers

SIC: 3953; NAICS: 339943

Top Marker Brands, 2011

Brands are ranked by sales at supermarkets, drug stores and discount stores (excluding Wal-Mart) for the 12 weeks ended July 10, 2011.

	($ mil.)	Share
Sanford Sharpie	$ 7.8	22.61%
Crayola	4.9	14.20
Crayola Color Wonder	3.7	10.72
Crayola Color	2.4	6.96
Sanford Expo	1.9	5.51
BIC Mark It	1.3	3.77
Crayola Pip Squeaks	1.1	3.19
Sanford Expo 2	0.9	2.61
Sanford Sharpie Accent	0.9	2.61
Sanford Sharpie Rt	0.6	1.74
Private label	0.6	1.74
Other	8.4	24.35

Source: *MMR*, September 5, 2011, p. 18, from SymphonyIRI Group Inc.

★ 2467 ★
Marking Devices
SIC: 3953; NAICS: 339943

Marking Device Manufacturing, 2007

Data show the percent of industry sales held by the largest 4, 8, 20 and 50 firms in the sector. There are approximately 390 firms operating in the industry generating employment for 4,896 people.

4 largest companies	28.0%
8 largest companies	42.8
20 largest companies	61.3
50 largest companies	78.0

Source: "2007 Economic Census." [online] from http://www.census.gov/econ/concentration.html [Accessed August 12, 2011], from U.S. Bureau of the Census.

★ 2468 ★
Carbon Paper and Inked Ribbon
SIC: 3955; NAICS: 339944

Carbon Paper and Inked Ribbon Manufacturing, 2007

Data show the percent of industry sales held by the largest 4, 8, 20 and 50 firms in the sector. There are approximately 50 firms operating in the industry generating employment for 1,730 people.

4 largest companies	66.2%
8 largest companies	85.7
20 largest companies	96.5
50 largest companies	100.0

Source: "2007 Economic Census." [online] from http://www.census.gov/econ/concentration.html [Accessed August 12, 2011], from U.S. Bureau of the Census.

★ 2469 ★
Costume Jewelry
SIC: 3961; NAICS: 339914

Costume Jewelry and Novelty Manufacturing, 2007

Data show the percent of industry sales held by the largest 4, 8, 20 and 50 firms in the sector. There are approximately 554 firms operating in the industry generating employment for 5,442 people.

4 largest companies	23.9%
8 largest companies	36.8
20 largest companies	55.4
50 largest companies	72.5

Source: "2007 Economic Census." [online] from http://www.census.gov/econ/concentration.html [Accessed August 12, 2011], from U.S. Bureau of the Census.

★ 2470 ★
Fasteners, Buttons, Needles and Pins
SIC: 3965; NAICS: 339993

Fastener, Button, Needle and Pin Manufacturing, 2007

Data show the percent of industry sales held by the largest 4, 8, 20 and 50 firms in the sector. There are approximately 174 firms operating in the industry generating employment for 5,501 people.

4 largest companies	49.1%
8 largest companies	62.3
20 largest companies	78.4
50 largest companies	92.7

Source: "2007 Economic Census." [online] from http://www.census.gov/econ/concentration.html [Accessed August 12, 2011], from U.S. Bureau of the Census.

★ 2471 ★
Fasteners, Buttons, Needles and Pins
SIC: 3965; NAICS: 339993

Fastener, Button, Needle and Pin Manufacturing, 2009

Total shipments were valued at $652.93 million. "NSK" stands for Not Specified by Kind.

	$ (000)	Share
Buckles, fasteners (excl slide fasteners), needles, and pins . .	$ 348,507	53.38%
Zippers and slide fasteners	166,306	25.47
Buttons & button parts, incl button backs, blanks, & molds	107,539	16.47
Fastener, button, needle, and pin manufacturing, nsk, total	30,577	4.68

Source: "Annual Survey of Manufactures." [online] from http://www.census.gov/manufacturing/asm/index.html [Accessed January 18, 2012], from U.S. Department of Commerce.

★ 2472 ★
Brooms, Brushes and Mops
SIC: 3991; NAICS: 339994

Broom, Brush, and Mop Manufacturing, 2009

Total shipments were valued at $1.95 billion. "NSK" stands for Not Specified by Kind.

	($ 000)	Share
Brushes, other types	$ 960,451	49.28%
Brooms, mops, and dusters . . .	613,544	31.48

Continued on next page.

★ 2472 ★

[Continued]

Brooms, Brushes and Mops

SIC: 3991; NAICS: 339994

Broom, Brush, and Mop Manufacturing, 2009

Total shipments were valued at $1.95 billion. "NSK" stands for Not Specified by Kind.

	($ 000)	Share
Brushes & holders/pads/roller frames/rollers, paint/varnish	$ 327,055	16.78%
Broom, brush, and mop manufacturing, nsk, total	47,749	2.45

Source: "Annual Survey of Manufactures." [online] from http://www.census.gov/manufacturing/asm/index.html [Accessed August 8, 2011], from U.S. Department of Commerce.

★ 2473 ★

Brooms, Brushes and Mops

SIC: 3991; NAICS: 339994

Top Cleaning Tool Makers, 2011

Market shares are shown based on sales at supermarkets, drug stores and mass merchandisers (excluding Wal-Mart) for the 52 weeks ended August 7, 2011.

Procter & Gamble Co.	37.8%
The Libman Co.	10.3
Onecare	6.8
3M	6.1
Freudenberg Household Products	5.1
Quickie Manufacturing Corp.	3.8
Clorox Co.	3.5
Butler Home Products Co.	3.3
S.C. Johnson & Son	2.3
Other	21.0

Source: *2011-2012 Nonfoods Handbook - A Supplement to Grocery Headquarters*, Annual 2011-2012, p. 17, from SymphonyIRI Group Inc.

★ 2474 ★

Toothbrushes

SIC: 3991; NAICS: 339994

Top Manual Toothbrush Brands, 2012

Market shares are shown based on sales at supermarkets, drug stores and mass merchandisers (excluding Wal-Mart) for the previous 12 months.

	($ mil.)	Share
Colgate 360	$ 41.8	8.91%
Oral-B Crossaction Pro Health	39.7	8.46

	($ mil.)	Share
Oral-B Complete Advantage	$ 30.7	6.54%
Oral-B Indicator	20.8	4.43
Oral-B Advantage 3D White	20.4	4.35
Colgate Extra Clean	14.8	3.15
Colgate Wisp	14.1	3.00
Colgate Max White	12.4	2.64
Colgate Wave	12.2	2.60
Private label	63.3	13.49
Other	199.1	42.42

Source: *MMR*, April 16, 2012, p. 99, from SymphonyIRI Group Inc.

★ 2475 ★

Toothbrushes

SIC: 3991; NAICS: 339994

Top Manual Toothbrush Makers, 2010

Market shares are shown in percent.

Procter & Gamble Co.	39.0%
Colgate	33.0
Other	28.0

Source: "The Deal 2010 - P&G's Acquisition of Reckitt Benckiser." [online] from http://www.slideshare.net [Accessed May 1, 2012], from Credit Suisse estimates.

★ 2476 ★

Sign and Transportation Reflective Materials

SIC: 3993; NAICS: 33995

Sign and Transportation Reflective Materials Market, 2011

The company claims 70-100% of the market.

3MAE	70.0-100.0%
Other	0.0-30.0

Source: *Finance & Commerce*, December 6, 2011, p. NA, from Avery Dennison.

★ 2477 ★

Signs

SIC: 3993; NAICS: 33995

Electric Sign Sales by Type, 2010

Market shares are shown in percent.

Fluorescent	41.3%
LED	40.1
Neon	17.9
Other	0.7

Source: *Signs of the Times*, July 2011, p. 6.

★ 2478 ★
Signs
SIC: 3993; NAICS: 33995

Leading Billboard and Sign Makers, 2011

The industry was valued at $12 billion in 2011. Alternative displays claimed 55% of the total, billboards 30% and transit displays 15%.

Daktronics Inc.	3.7%
Brady Corp.	0.9
Young Electric Sign Company	0.9
Other	94.5

Source: "Billboard and Sign Manufacturing in the U.S." [online] from http://www.ibisworld.com [Published August 2011], from IBISWorld.

★ 2479 ★
Caskets
SIC: 3995; NAICS: 339995

Top Casket Makers, 2010

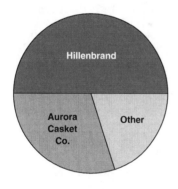

The industry was valued at $1.3 billion.

Hillenbrand	50.0%
Aurora Casket Co./Matthews International	30.0
Other	20.0

Source: *Indianapolis Business Journal*, April 4, 2011, p. 15.

★ 2480 ★
Flooring
SIC: 3996; NAICS: 326192

Resilient Floor Sales, 2010

Total sales were valued at $2.2 billion.

Vinyl composite tile	31.6%
Vinyl sheet	31.3
Luxury vinyl tile	21.9
Fiberglass-backed sheet	5.4
Rubber	1.8

Linoleum	1.6%
Cork	0.4
Other	6.0

Source: *Floor Covering Weekly*, July 18, 2011, p. 18, from Catalina Research and U.S. Department of Commerce.

★ 2481 ★
Flooring
SIC: 3996; NAICS: 326192

Top Laminated Flooring Brands in China, 2009

Market shares are shown based on sales of 16.1 billion renminbi.

Power Dekor	11.3%
Nature	7.2
Vohringer	4.8
Der	4.0
YangZi Flooring	4.0
Other	68.7

Source: "Industry Overview." [online] from http://corpsv. etnet.com.hk/data/documents/ipo/LTN20110516025/113_e. pdf [Accessed September 1, 2011], from Frost & Sullivan.

★ 2482 ★
Flooring
SIC: 3996; NAICS: 326192

Top Makers of Hard Surface Flooring, 2010

The industry is forecast to grow from $7.0 billion in 2010 to $11 billion in 2015. Nonresidential flooring is expected to be the fastest-growing sector during this period. Vinyl claimed 46% of the market in 2010, tile 21%, wood 12%, laminate 14% and other products 7%.

Mohawk	17.0%
Armstrong	14.9
Shaw Industries	5.7
Mannington	5.0
Tarkett	4.3
Other	53.1

Source: "Hard Surface Flooring." [online] from http://www. freedoniagroup.com [Published July 2011], from Freedonia Group.

★ 2483 ★
Baby Care
SIC: 3999; NAICS: 339999

Top Baby Care Brands, 2011

Market shares are shown based on sales at supermarkets, drug stores and mass merchandisers (excluding Wal-Mart) for the 52 weeks ended August 7, 2011.

Munchkin	9.1%
Playtex Diaper Genie Li Elite	7.1
Safety 1st	6.0
First Years	5.4
Boppy	4.0
Graco Nautilus	3.3
Evenflo	3.1
Cosco Scenera	2.9
Fisher Price	2.8
Goldbug Eddie Bauer	2.4
Other	53.9

Source: *2011-2012 Nonfoods Handbook - A Supplement to Grocery Headquarters*, Annual 2011-2012, p. 17, from SymphonyIRI Group Inc.

★ 2484 ★
Baby Care
SIC: 3999; NAICS: 326199

Top Baby Care Firms in China, 2009

Market shares are shown based on volume.

Johnson & Johnson Co.	61.0%
Tianjing Yumeljing	9.0
Henkel	7.0
Other	23.0

Source: "China Consumer Staples." [online] from http://search.deutsche-bank.de [Published November 19, 2010], from Euromonitor and Deutsche Bank.

★ 2485 ★
Baby Care
SIC: 3999; NAICS: 339999

Top Baby Care Vendors, 2011

Market shares are shown based on sales at supermarkets, drug stores and mass merchandisers (excluding Wal-Mart) for the 52 weeks ended August 7, 2011.

Dorel Juvenile Group	16.4%
Graco	13.6
Munchkin Inc.	10.9
Playtex Products Inc.	8.0
Learning Curve Brands	7.7
Summer Infant Products	5.7
Fisher Price	4.6
Boppy Co.	4.1

Goldbug	2.7%
Other	26.3

Source: *2011-2012 Nonfoods Handbook - A Supplement to Grocery Headquarters*, Annual 2011-2012, p. 17, from SymphonyIRI Group Inc.

★ 2486 ★
Baby Care
SIC: 3999; NAICS: 339999

Top Branded Baby Accessory Makers, 2010

The industry was valued at $6.3 billion in 2010 and includes car seats, baby monitors, nursery pillows and related products.

Dorel Industries	22.8%
Newell Rubbermaid Inc.	14.1
Western Presidio/Evenflo Co. Inc.	13.9
RC2 Corp.	10.0
Munchkin Inc.	8.0
Energizer Holdings/Playtex Products Inc.	6.8
Mattel Inc.	4.3
Other	20.1

Source: "Juvenile Products." [online] from http://www.capstonellc.com [Published Fourth Quarter 2011], from Packaged Facts and SymphonyIRI Group Inc.

★ 2487 ★
Body Scrubbers
SIC: 3999; NAICS: 339999

Top Body Scrubber Brands, 2011

Brands are shown based on sales at supermarkets, drug stores and mass merchandisers (excluding Wal-Mart) for the 12 weeks ended December 25, 2011.

	($ mil.)	Share
Body Image Body	$ 2.1	9.17%
Body Benefits	1.6	6.99
Axe Detailer	1.4	6.11
Bath Essentials	0.9	3.93
Dove Men + Care	0.7	3.06
Razz	0.6	2.62
Private label	10.4	45.41
Other	5.2	22.71

Source: *MMR*, January 23, 2012, p. 13, from SymphonyIRI Group Inc.

★ 2488 ★
Candles

SIC: 3999; NAICS: 339999

Top Candle Brands, 2011

Brands are ranked by sales at supermarkets, drug stores and mass merchandisers (excluding Wal-Mart) for the 12 weeks ended April 17, 2011.

	($ mil.)	Share
Glade	$ 17.1	12.61%
Betty Crocker	5.3	3.91
Reed's	5.2	3.83
Village Candle	4.3	3.17
Febreze	3.7	2.73
Cake Mate	3.5	2.58
Glade 2 in 1	3.2	2.36
Chesapeake Bay Candle	3.0	2.21
Everyday Essentials	2.9	2.14
Private label	18.9	13.94
Other	68.5	50.52

Source: *MMR*, June 20, 2011, p. 96, from SymphonyIRI Group Inc.

★ 2489 ★
Hair Accessories

SIC: 3999; NAICS: 326199

Top Hair Accessory Brands, 2011

Market shares are shown based on drug store sales for the 52 weeks ended March 20, 2011.

Scunci	18.60%
Conair	12.61
Scunci No Slip Grip	8.20
Conair Styling Essentials	7.64
Scunci No Damage	5.35
Scunci Effortless Beauty	5.11
Revlon	3.30
Goody	3.10
Goody Ouchless	2.32
Private label	7.87
Other	24.90

Source: *DrugStore Management*, Annual 2011-2012, p. 223, from SymphonyIRI Group Inc.

★ 2490 ★
Lighters

SIC: 3999; NAICS: 339999

Top Lighter Brands, 2011

Market shares are shown based on supermarket sales for the 52 weeks ended March 20, 2011.

BIC	57.29%
Scripto Aim N Flame II	5.41

BIC Limited Edition	4.40%
Calico	2.36
BIC Luminere	1.99
Power Striker	1.56
Scripto Wind Resistant	1.41
BIC Sure Start	1.04
Private label	9.69
Other	4.85

Source: *Non-Foods Management*, Annual 2011-2012, p. 176, from SymphonyIRI Group Inc.

★ 2491 ★
Lighters

SIC: 3999; NAICS: 326199

Top Lighter Makers, 2011

Market shares are shown based on sales at supermarkets, drug stores and mass merchandisers (excluding Wal-Mart) for the 52 weeks ended August 7, 2011.

BIC Corp.	66.7%
Scripto Tokai	7.7
Westco Products Group	2.4
Beacon Power	2.3
Ace Products USA	2.0
Gibson Enterprises	1.4
Zippon Manufacturing Co.	1.2
New York Lighter Co.	1.1
Jarden Home Brands	1.0
Private label	8.5

Source: *2011-2012 Nonfoods Handbook - A Supplement to Grocery Headquarters*, Annual 2011-2012, p. 17, from SymphonyIRI Group Inc.

★ 2492 ★
Locker Accessories

SIC: 3999; NAICS: 339999

Locker Accessory Market, 2011

The industry saw sales of $30 million. It includes adjustable shelves and accessory kits.

LockerMate	71.0%
Other	29.0

Source: *Fort Worth Star-Telegram*, May 1, 2011, p. NA, from It's Academic.

★ 2493 ★
Pet Products
SIC: 3999; NAICS: 339999

Top Pet Product Makers in Japan, 2009

The pet products market includes sanitation products, grooming products, training products, apparel, toys and accessories. Total sales were $1.9 billion, making Japan the second largest market worldwide after the United States. There were an estimated 21.5 million cats and dogs living in Japan in 2010. Poodles were the top dog breed.

IrisOhyama	10.7%
Unicharm Pet Care	9.7
Lion Shoji	3.3
C's lshishara	3.1
Yamahisa	2.9
DoggyMan	2.7
Johnny Trading	1.4
Other	66.2

Source: "Japan: Pet Products Industry." [online] from http://www.export.gov [Published November 2011], from Yano Research Institute.

★ 2494 ★
Pet Products
SIC: 3999; NAICS: 326199

Top Rawhide Dog Chew Brands, 2011

Market shares are shown based on drug store sales for the 52 weeks ended March 20, 2011.

Dingo Meat in the Middle	15.18%
Dingo	8.40
Waggin' Train Meat Blast	7.40
Hartz	7.21
Hartz American BFHD	5.78
Dingo Goof Balls	5.23
Hartz Americas Prime	5.06
Dingo Dynostix	4.81
Dingo Bone	2.93
Private label	5.33
Other	32.67

Source: *DrugStore Management*, Annual 2011-2012, p. 223, from SymphonyIRI Group Inc.

★ 2495 ★
Whiteboards
SIC: 3999; NAICS: 339999

Global Interactive Whiteboard Sales by Region, 2010 and 2013

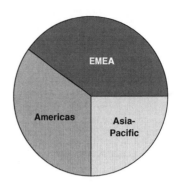

Data are in thousands of units.

	2010	2013	Share
EMEA	309	558	39.6%
Americas	427	496	35.2
Asia-Pacific	158	355	25.2

Source: "Smart Technologies." [online] from http://abea-4cueer.client.shareholder.com [Published January 11, 2011], from Futuresource Consulting.

★ 2496 ★
Whiteboards
SIC: 3999; NAICS: 339999

Interactive Whiteboard Market Worldwide, 2010

Smart Technologies is the leader in whiteboards, which are glossy white boards used for non-permanent writing. Market shares are for the 12 months ended September 30, 2010.

	Smart's Share	Closest Competitor
Americas	62.0%	24.0%
World	47.0	21.0
EMEA	42.0	24.0
Asia-Pacific	19.0	12.0

Source: "Smart Technologies." [online] from http://abea-4cueer.client.shareholder.com [Published January 11, 2011], from Futuresource Consulting.

SIC 40 - Railroad Transportation

★ 2497 ★
Railroads
SIC: 4011; NAICS: 482111

Railroad Shipping, 2010

Distribution is shown based on tons.

Coal	44.0%
Chemicals	10.1
Farm products	8.6
Non-metallic minerals	6.6
Food and related products	5.9
Intermodal shipments	5.9
Other	18.9

Source: *Financial Times*, August 23, 2011, p. 13, from American Association of Railroads.

★ 2498 ★
Railroads
SIC: 4011; NAICS: 482111

Top Freight Rail Transporters in China, 2011

The industry generated revenues of $30.1 billion. Between 2006 and 2010, the Chinese government provided funds to expand the rail network to over 90,000 kilometers. By 2020, the network is expected to be over 120,000 kilometers. The need for coal helped drive the growth of the market.

Taiyuan Railway Administration	14.0%
Shenyang Railway Administration	10.0
Beijing Railway Administration	9.0
Shanghai Railway Administration	7.0
Guangzhou Railway Group	5.0
Other	55.0

Source: "Freight Rail Transportation in China." [online] from http://www.docin.com [Published September 2011], from IBISWorld.

★ 2499 ★
Railroads
SIC: 4011; NAICS: 482111

Top Railroads in North America, 2009

Companies are ranked by operating revenues in millions of dollars.

BNSF Railway	$ 14,124
Union Pacific	14,117
CSX Transportation	8,170
Norfolk Southern	7,969
Canadian National Railway	6,451
Canadian Pacific	3,828
Ferrocarril Mexicano	914
Kansas City Southern	860
Kansas City Southern de México	616

Source: "Class 1 Railroad Statistics." [online] from http://www.aar.org [Published June 17, 2011], from American Association of Railroads.

SIC 41 - Local and Interurban Passenger Transit

★ 2500 ★
Ambulance Services
SIC: 4119; NAICS: 62191

Ambulance Market, 2010

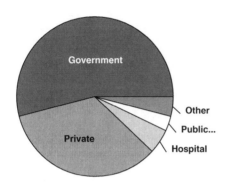

Total spending was valued at $14 billion in 2010. In the private sector, AMR claimed 21% and Rural/Metro 10% and other companies 69% of the total.

Government	54.0%
Private	34.0
Hospital	5.0
Public utility	3.0
Other	4.0

Source: "Rural/Metro Corporation." [online] from http://files.shareholder.com/downloads/RURL/2Q11_Investor__Presentation.pdf [Accessed February 20, 2012], from U.S. Bureau of the Census and association reports.

★ 2501 ★
Limousine Services
SIC: 4119; NAICS: 48532

Largest Limo Fleets, 2010

Companies are ranked by size of fleet, which includes limos, sedans, SUVs, vans and motorcoaches.

Dav El Chauffered Transportation	779
Empire CLS Worldwide	725
Tristar Worldwide Chauffeur Services	526
Music Express	376
Bell Trans	373
ExecuCar	325

Transtyle Transportation	246
Metro Cars	231
Flyte Tyme Worldwide Transportation	226
Commonwealth Worldwide Chauffered Transportation	218

Source: *Limousine, Charter & Tour*, August 2011, p. 18.

★ 2502 ★
Buses
SIC: 4141; NAICS: 48551

Largest Transit Bus Fleets in North America, 2011

Companies are ranked by size of fleet.

MTA New York City Transit	4,336
Metro	2,515
New Jersey Transit Corp.	2,371
Toronto Transit Commission	2,066
Coast Mountain Bus Co.	1,891
King County DOT/Metro Transit	1,870
Pace Suburban Bus	1,856
Montreal Urban Transit	1,782
Chicago Transit Authority	1,781
Washington Area Metropolitan Transit Authority	1,492

Source: *Metro Magazine*, September-October 2011, p. 24.

★ 2503 ★
Motorcoaches
SIC: 4141; NAICS: 48551

Top Motorcoach Operators, 2010

Companies are ranked by total buses and coaches.

FirstGroup America	9,175
Coach USA/Coach Canada	1,717
Academy Express	639
Pacific Western Transportation	460
Royal Highway Tours	419
Easton Coach Co.	319
Peter Pan Bus Lines	257
Roberts Hawaii	228

Continued on next page.

★ 2503 ★

[Continued]

Motorcoaches

SIC: 4141; NAICS: 48551

Top Motorcoach Operators, 2010

Companies are ranked by total buses and coaches.

Arrow Stage Lines	215
Mears Transportation	204

Source: *Metro Magazine*, Annual Fact Book 2012, p. 24.

★ 2504 ★

Sightseeing Transportation

SIC: 4141; NAICS: 48551

Top Sightseeing Transportation Firms, 2011

The industry generated revenues of $1.9 billion in 2011. Buses claimed 40% of the total, water 37%, charter fishing 11%, scenic rail 9% and other sectors 3%. Industry revenues declined 5.1% from 2006-2011 as the economic downturn prompted consumers to cut their travel spending. A total of 2,078 businesses provided employment to more than 20,400 people.

Stagecoach	2.3%
Gray Line	1.3
Trailways Transportation Systems	1.0
Other	95.4

Source: "Sightseeing Transportation in the U.S." [online] from http://www.ibisworld.com [Published August 2011], from IBISWorld.

★ 2505 ★

School Buses

SIC: 4151; NAICS: 48541

Top School Bus Fleet Firms, 2011

Firms are ranked by size of fleet.

First Student Inc.	57,400
National Express Corp.	17,408
Student Transportation Inc.	7,220
Atlantic Express Transportation Corp. . . .	5,477
Illinois Central School Bus Co.	3,400
Petermann Ltd.	3,351
Cook-Illinois Corp.	2,275
George Krapf Jr. & Sons Inc.	1,323
WE Transport	1,200
Lamers Bus Lines Inc.	1,124

Source: *School Bus Fleet*, Annual Fact Book 2012, p. 44.

SIC 42 - Trucking and Warehousing

★ 2506 ★

Logistics

SIC: 4210; NAICS: 48411, 484121, 484122

Top Logistics Providers Worldwide, 2010

Companies are ranked by revenues in millions of dollars.

DHL Logistics	$ 35,208
Kuehne & Nagel	19,420
DB Schenker Logistics	18,245
CEVA Logistics	9,070
C.H. Robinson Worldwide	7,576
DSV	7,570
Panalpina	6,880
SNCF Geodis	6,125
UPS Supply Chain Solutions	6,022
Expeditors International	5,968

Source: *Journal of Commerce*, March 14, 2011, p. NA.

★ 2507 ★

Trucking

SIC: 4212; NAICS: 48422

Dump Trucking, 2007

Data show the percent of industry sales held by the largest 4, 8, 20 and 50 firms in the sector. There are approximately 17,027 firms operating in the industry generating employment for 97,428 people.

4 largest firms	2.4%
8 largest firms	3.9
20 largest firms	7.0
50 largest firms	11.9

Source: "2007 Economic Census." [online] from http://www.census.gov/econ/concentration.html [Accessed August 12, 2011], from U.S. Bureau of the Census.

★ 2508 ★

Trucking

SIC: 4212; NAICS: 48422

Leading Flatbed/Heavy Specialized Carriers, 2010

Companies are ranked by revenues in millions of dollars.

Landstar System	$ 744.0
TransForce Inc.	425.0
United Vision Logistics	373.4
Mercer Transportation	363.6
Contains Group	347.9
TMC	347.0
Anderson Trucking Service	332.5
Greatwide Logistics Services	216.8
Maverick USA	200.1
Lone Star Transportation	198.0

Source: *Transport Topics*, Annual 2011, p. 24.

★ 2509 ★

Trucking

SIC: 4212; NAICS: 48422

Leading Intermodal/Drayage Carriers, 2010

Companies are ranked by revenues in millions of dollars.

J.B. Hunt Intermodal	$ 2,141.2
Hub Group	1,285.1
Pacer International	1,081.5
RoadLink	297.0
US 1 Industries	210.7
Consolidated Fastfrate Inc.	196.0
Bridge Terminal Transport	192.5
Evans Network of Cos.	178.7
Trailer Bridge Inc.	118.1
Universal Truckload Services	87.8

Source: *Transport Topics*, Annual 2011, p. 24.

★ 2510 ★
Trucking
SIC: 4212; NAICS: 48411

Leading Refrigerated Transporters, 2010

Companies are ranked by revenues in millions of dollars.

Marten Transport Ltd.	$ 516.9
Stevens Transport Inc.	508.9
Frozen Food Express Industries	368.8
KLLM Transport Services L.L.C.	280.9
John Christner Trucking L.L.C.	242.0
Southern Refrigerated Transport Inc.	165.1
May Trucking Co.	145.9
WEL Companies Inc.	126.0
Pride Transport Inc.	82.7
Continental Express Inc.	56.5

Source: *Refrigerated Transporter*, June 2011, p. 1.

★ 2511 ★
Trucking
SIC: 4212; NAICS: 48422

Leading Tank/Bulk Carriers, 2010

Companies are ranked by revenues in millions of dollars.

Kenan Advantage Group	$ 772.4
Quality Distribution Inc.	686.5
Trimac Group	579.5
A&R Logistics	212.0
Superior Bulk Logistics	207.0
Groendyke Transport	191.0
Schneider National Bulk Carriers	175.9
Ruan Transport Corp.	172.1
Foodliner Inc./Quest Logistics	166.8
Enterprise Transportation Co.	151.3

Source: *Transport Topics*, Annual 2011, p. 24.

★ 2512 ★
Trucking
SIC: 4212; NAICS: 48411

Top Less-Than-Truckload Carriers, 2010

Companies are ranked by revenues in millions of dollars.

FedEx Freight	$ 4,421
Con-Way Freight	3,026
YRC National	2,642
UPS Freight	2,002
ABF Freight System	1,395

Old Dominion Freight Line	$ 1,377
Estes Express Lines	1,352
YRC Regional	1,257
R+L Carriers	1,077
Saia Motor Freight Line	836

Source: *Logistics Management*, April 2011, p. NA, from S.J. Consulting Group Inc.

★ 2513 ★
Trucking
SIC: 4212; NAICS: 48411

Top Truckload Carriers, 2010

Companies are ranked by revenues in millions of dollars.

Swift Transportation	$ 2,631
Schneider National	2,350
Werner Enterprises	1,542
U.S. Xpress Enterprises	1,450
J.B. Hunt Transport Services	1,386
Prime Inc.	1,019
Crete Carrier Corp.	841
C.R. England	835
CRST International	692
Knight Transportation	659

Source: *Logistics Management*, April 2011, p. NA, from S.J. Consulting Group Inc.

★ 2514 ★
Trucking
SIC: 4214; NAICS: 48411

Leading Household Goods/Commercial Delivery Carriers, 2010

Companies are ranked by revenues in millions of dollars.

Sirva Inc.	$ 1,731.9
UniGroup Inc.	1,520.0
Atlas World Group	759.9
Suddath Cos.	281.5
Graebel Cos.	266.0
Specialized Transportation Inc.	230.7
Arpin Van Lines	180.7
Wheaton Van Lines	160.0
Bekins Holding Corp.	91.2
Furniture Transportation Group	82.7

Source: *Transport Topics*, Annual 2011, p. 24.

★ 2515 ★

Trucking

SIC: 4214; NAICS: 48411

Leading Motor Vehicle Carriers, 2010

Companies are ranked by revenues in millions of dollars.

Allied System Holdings	$ 528.0
United Road	285.0
Jack Cooper Transport	275.0
Cassens Transport	177.7
The Waggoners Trucking	162.0

Source: *Transport Topics*, Annual 2011, p. 24.

★ 2516 ★

Express Delivery Services

SIC: 4215; NAICS: 49211, 49221

Top Express Delivery Firms in Eastern Europe, the Middle East and Africa, 2010

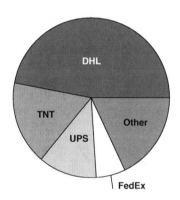

Market shares are shown in percent.

DHL	47.0%
TNT	17.0
UPS	12.0
FedEx	6.0
Other	18.0

Source: "Credit Suisse Business Services Conference." [online] from http://www.dp-dhl.com [Published December 6, 2011], from Market Intelligence.

★ 2517 ★

Express Delivery Services

SIC: 4215; NAICS: 49211, 49221

Top Express Delivery Firms in Europe, 2010

Market shares are shown in percent.

DHL	38.0%
UPS	23.0
TNT	16.0
FedEx	11.0
Other	12.0

Source: "Credit Suisse Business Services Conference." [online] from http://www.dp-dhl.com [Published December 6, 2011], from Market Intelligence.

★ 2518 ★

Express Delivery Services

SIC: 4215; NAICS: 49211, 49221

Top Express Delivery Firms in the Americas, 2010

Market shares are shown in percent.

FedEx	51.0%
UPS	32.0
DHL	13.0
Other	4.0

Source: "Credit Suisse Business Services Conference." [online] from http://www.dp-dhl.com [Published December 6, 2011], from Market Intelligence.

★ 2519 ★

Express Delivery Services

SIC: 4215; NAICS: 49211, 49221

Top Express Delivery Firms in the Asia-Pacific Region, 2010

Market shares are shown in percent.

DHL	36.0%
FedEx	21.0
UPS	10.0
TNT	6.0
Other	26.0

Source: "Credit Suisse Business Services Conference." [online] from http://www.dp-dhl.com [Published December 6, 2011], from Market Intelligence.

★ 2520 ★
Farm Warehousing and Storage
SIC: 4221; NAICS: 49313

Top Farm Product Storage and Warehousing Firms, 2011

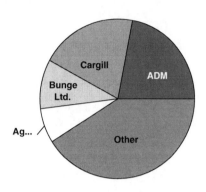

The industry generated revenues of $865.4 million in 2011. A total of 623 businesses provided employment to more than 6,400 people.

ADM	22.0%
Cargill	19.6
Bunge Ltd.	10.3
Ag Processing Inc.	7.0
Other	41.1

Source: "Farm Product Storage & Warehousing in the U.S." [online] from http://www.ibisworld.com [Published August 2011], from IBISWorld.

★ 2521 ★
Refrigerated Warehousing
SIC: 4222; NAICS: 49312

Leading Refrigerated Warehousing Firms Worldwide, 2012

Firms are ranked by capacity in millions of cubic meters. Total capacity was 89.2 billion.

	(mil.)	Share
Americold Logistics L.L.C. and China		
Merchants Americold	25.70	28.81%
Millard	7.85	8.80
Swire Cold Storage	7.66	8.59
Preferred Freezer Services	6.09	6.83
Nichirei Logistics, Euofrigo, Frigo		
Logistics. HIWA Rotterdam	4.31	4.83
Partner Logistics	3.61	4.05
VersaCold	3.32	3.72
Castle & Cooke Cold Storage	3.16	3.54

	(mil.)	Share
Kloosbeheer B.V.	3.03	3.40%
Other	24.47	27.43

Source: "IARW Global Top 25 List." [online] from http://www.gcca.org [Published May 2012], from International Association of Refrigerated Warehouses.

★ 2522 ★
Self Storage Industry
SIC: 4225; NAICS: 49311

Top Self Storage Firms, 2011

Firms are ranked by millions of square feet of rentable space.

Public Storage Inc.	139.0
Extra Space Storage	59.0
U-Haul International Inc.	36.2
U-Store-It Trust Inc.	29.0
Sovran Self Storage Inc.	24.7
OB Cos - Simply Self Storage	9.5
Derrel's Mini Storage Inc.	9.4
StorageMart	8.3
Platinum Storage Group	7.4
Dahn Corp.	6.4

Source: *Inside Self-Storage*, April 2011, p. NA.

★ 2523 ★
Warehousing and Storage
SIC: 4226; NAICS: 49319

Specialized Goods Warehousing and Storage, 2007

Data show the percent of industry sales held by the largest 4, 8, 20 and 50 firms in the sector. There are approximately 1,423 firms operating in the industry generating employment for 38,474 people.

4 largest firms	22.0%
8 largest firms	35.7
20 largest firms	53.0
50 largest firms	70.1

Source: "2007 Economic Census." [online] from http://www.census.gov/econ/concentration.html [Accessed August 12, 2011], from U.S. Bureau of the Census.

SIC 43 - Postal Service

★ 2524 ★

Postal Service

SIC: 4311; NAICS: 49111

Shipments of Mail, 2011-2020

Data show the projected decline in shipments of mail in billions of pieces. Data include first class mail, standard mail, periodicals and other items. The Postal Service made news in September 2011 when the Postmaster General announced that the U.S. Postal Service was nearing bankruptcy due to competition and retiree obligations.

2011	167
2012	161
2013	156
2014	153
2015	151
2016	147
2017	143
2018	141
2019	137
2020	133

Source: ''USPS Financial Future.'' [online] from https://ribbs. usps.gov/webinar/CustomerWebinar.pdf [Published October 5, 2011], from U.S. Postal Service.

★ 2525 ★

Postal Service

SIC: 4311; NAICS: 49111

Top Postal Service Suppliers, 2011

Suppliers are ranked by contracts in millions of dollars.

FedEx	$ 1,495.5
Kalitta Air L.L.C.	548.7
Northrop Grumman	410.6
Pat Salmon & Sons Inc.	136.6
Wheeler Bros. Inc.	128.5
Campbell Ewald	126.3
Accenture	125.2
Mail Contractors of America Inc.	116.6
IBM	108.2
United Airlines	102.8

Source: ''Top U.S. Postal Service Suppliers.'' [online] from http://www.huschblackwell.com [Accessed April 1, 2012], from U.S. Postal Service.

SIC 44 - Water Transportation

★ 2526 ★

LNG Tankers

SIC: 4412; NAICS: 483111

Largest LNG Tanker Fleet Firms Worldwide, 2010

Companies are ranked by volume share at the end of December 2010.

Project/Major	23.8%
QGTC	14.7
Mitsui O.S.K. Lines	7.1
NYK Line	7.1
MISC	6.6
South Korean lines	5.0
Teekay Shipping	3.7
"K" Line	3.2
Other	28.8

Source: "NYK Fact Book 2011." [online] from http://www. nyk.com [Accessed April 28, 2011].

★ 2527 ★

Shipping

SIC: 4412; NAICS: 483111

Largest Fleets Worldwide, 2011

Market shares are shown based on TEUs (twenty-foot equivalent units) as of September 7, 2011.

	TEUs	Share
APM-Maersk	2,461,993	15.7%
Mediterranean Shipping Co.	2,033,207	13.0
CMA CGM Group	1,337,185	8.5
COSCO Container	650,840	4.2
Hapag-Lloyd	627,725	4.0
Evergreen Line	611,678	3.9
APL	596,415	3.8
CSCL	505,913	3.2
Hanjin Shipping	487,999	3.1
CSAV Group	452,641	2.9

Source: "Alphaliner - Top 100." [online] from http://www.al-phaliner.com/top100/index.php [Accessed September 8, 2011], from Alphaliner.

★ 2528 ★

Tank Barges

SIC: 4424; NAICS: 483113

Tank Barge Market, 2011

Companies are ranked by estimated number of tank barges operated as of March 2011.

	Barges	Share
Kirby Corp.	837	25.74%
American Commercial Lines L.L.C.	314	9.66
Canal Barge Company Inc.	211	6.49
Florida Marine	173	5.32
Ingram Barge Co.	172	5.29
Marathon Oil Corp.	172	5.29
Enterprise Products Partners	122	3.75
Higman Barge Lines Inc.	108	3.32
Blessey Marine Services	107	3.29
American River Transportation Co.	84	2.58
Other	952	29.27

Source: "Putting America's Waterways to Work." [online] from http://www.kirbycorp.com/documents/2011_Sept13.pdf [Published September 2011], from Informa Economics.

★ 2529 ★

Tanker Fleets

SIC: 4424; NAICS: 483113

Largest Tanker Fleet Firms Worldwide, 2011

Companies are ranked by dead-weight tonnage as of January 1, 2011.

Mitsui O.S.K. Lines	15,790
Fredriksen Group	15,583
NYK Line	11,665
Teekay Corporation	11,662
NIOC	10,667
SCF Group	10,230
MISC	8,572
Angelicoussis Group	8,084
Overseas Shipholding	7,530
China Shipping Group	6,939

Source: "NYK Fact Book 2011." [online] from http://www. nyk.com [Accessed April 28, 2011], from Clarkson's *Tanker Register 2011.*

★ 2530 ★
Great Lakes Transportation
SIC: 4432; NAICS: 483113

Top Commodities Transported on the Great Lakes-Saint Lawrence Basin, 2007

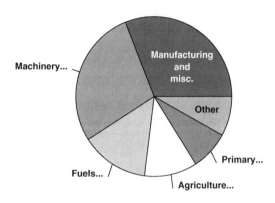

Market shares are shown based on value.

Manufacturing and misc. goods	31.0%
Machinery and transportation equipment . . .	28.0
Fuels and chemicals	14.0
Agriculture and food products	11.0
Primary and fabricated metal products	8.0
Other	8.0

Source: "Multimodal Freight Transportation Within the Great Lakes-Saint Lawrence Basin." [online] from http://www. duffphelps.com [Published February 7, 2012], from CPCS Transcom Limited.

★ 2531 ★
Cruise Lines
SIC: 4481; NAICS: 483112, 483114

Top Cruise Lines in North America, 2011

The industry was estimated at $17.4 billion.

Carnival	52.9%
Royal Carribean	27.6
Norwegian Cruise Line	9.6
Disney Cruise Line	3.3
MSC Cruises	1.6
Other	4.8

Source: "Market Share." [online] from http://www.cruisemarketwatch.com/blog1/market-share-2 [Accessed September 16, 2011].

★ 2532 ★
Cruise Lines
SIC: 4481; NAICS: 483112, 483114

Top Cruise Lines Worldwide (Excl. North America), 2011

The industry was estimated at $11.8 billion.

Carnival	51.6%
Royal Carribean	25.6
Norwegian Cruise Line	7.7
MSC Cruises	5.1
Disney Cruise Line	1.9
Louis Cruise Line	1.7
Other	8.4

Source: "Market Share." [online] from http://www.cruisemarketwatch.com/blog1/market-share-2 [Accessed September 16, 2011].

★ 2533 ★
Sightseeing Tours
SIC: 4489; NAICS: 48721

Excursion and Sightseeing Boats (including Dinner Cruises), 2007

Data show the percent of industry sales held by the largest 4, 8, 20 and 50 firms in the sector. There are approximately 813 firms operating in the industry generating employment for 10,065 people.

4 largest firms	20.2%
8 largest firms	26.8
20 largest firms	38.9
50 largest firms	54.3

Source: "2007 Economic Census." [online] from http://www.census.gov/econ/concentration.html [Accessed August 12, 2011], from U.S. Bureau of the Census.

★ 2534 ★
Water Transportation
SIC: 4489; NAICS: 483212

Other Water Passenger Transportation (including Water Taxi), 2007

Data show the percent of industry sales held by the largest 4, 8, 20 and 50 firms in the sector. There are approximately 185 firms operating in the industry generating employment for 1,310 people. Figures exclude ferries.

4 largest firms	34.7%
8 largest firms	51.7
20 largest firms	73.0
50 largest firms	86.3

Source: "2007 Economic Census." [online] from http://www.census.gov/econ/concentration.html [Accessed August 12, 2011], from U.S. Bureau of the Census.

★ 2535 ★
Ports
SIC: 4491; NAICS: 48831

Top Ports Worldwide, 2010

Ports are ranked by traffic in millions of twenty-foot equivalent units.

Ningbo-Zhoushan, China	131.40
Shanghai, China	29.07
Singapore	28.43
Hong Kong, China	23.70
Shenzhen, China	22.51
Busan, South Korea	14.19
Guangzhou Harbor, China	12.55
Qingdao, China	12.01
Dubai, United Arab Emirates	11.60
Rotterdam, Netherlands	11.14

Source: ''Top 50 World Container Ports.'' [online] from http://www.worldshipping.org/about-the-industry/global-trade/top-50-world-container-ports [Accessed June 1, 2012], from World Shipping Council.

★ 2536 ★
Terminal Operators
SIC: 4491; NAICS: 48831

Largest Container Terminal Operators Worldwide, 2009

Market shares are shown in percent.

Hutchinson Port Holdings	13.6%
APM Terminals	12.0
PSA International	11.7
DP World	9.5
Cosco	6.9
MSC	3.5
Eurogate	2.5
Evergreen	1.8
SSA Marine	1.6
CMA CGM Group	1.5
Other	35.4

Source: ''Industry Overview.'' [online] from http://webapps.dpworld.com [Accessed November 1, 2011], from Drewry Shipping Consultants.

★ 2537 ★
Towing
SIC: 4492; NAICS: 48833

Inland Waterways Towing Transportation, 2007

Data show the percent of industry sales held by the largest 4, 8, 20 and 50 firms in the sector. There are approximately 132 firms operating in the industry generating employment for 6,118 people.

4 largest firms	58.2%
8 largest firms	69.1
20 largest firms	84.4
50 largest firms	95.6

Source: ''2007 Economic Census.'' [online] from http://www.census.gov/econ/concentration.html [Accessed August 12, 2011], from U.S. Bureau of the Census.

★ 2538 ★
Marinas
SIC: 4493; NAICS: 71393

Marina Industry Revenues, 2011

Marinas primarily offer docking and storage for pleasure craft owners. Marinas may also sell fuel and marine supplies, offer boat rental, sell fuel and provide sailing instruction. The industry generated revenues of $3.9 billion. There were approximately 4,060 enterprises in 2011.

Pleasure boat dockage, slip rental, launch fees and storage	40.0%
Fuel sales	18.0
Boat repair maintenance	15.0
Boat and marine equipment sales	10.0
Food and beverage sales	8.0
Other	9.0

Source: ''Marinas in the U.S.'' [online] from http://www.ibisworld.com [Published August 2011], from IBISWorld.

SIC 45 - Transportation by Air

★ 2539 ★
Airlines
SIC: 4512; NAICS: 481111
Airline Industry, 2010

Over the previous decade, the industry has faced many challenges, such as high oil prices and safety issues. Passengers have complained about flight delays and high fees. The industry generated revenues of $139.2 billion. A total of 2,258 businesses were operating in this industry.

Domestic mainline services	53.8%
Regional airline services	31.3
Air freight services	5.0
Other	9.9

Source: ''Domestic Airlines in the U.S.'' [online] from http://www.ibisworld.com [Published December 2010], from IBISWorld.

★ 2540 ★
Airlines
SIC: 4512; NAICS: 481111
Top Airlines, 2000 and 2010

Market shares are shown based on seats filled.

	2000	2010
United	15.4%	21.0%
Delta	16.3	20.9
Southwest	8.4	18.4
American	16.0	14.9
Other	43.9	24.8

Source: *New York Times*, October 19, 2011, p. B4, from Wolf Trahan & Co.

★ 2541 ★
Airlines
SIC: 4512; NAICS: 481111
Top Airlines, 2011

Market shares are shown for September 2010-August 2011.

United Continental	17.0%
Delta	16.3
Southwest	14.7%
American	13.3
US Airways	7.9
Other	30.8

Source: *Financial Times*, December 3, 2011, p. 10, from U.S. Bureau of Transportation.

★ 2542 ★
Airlines
SIC: 4512; NAICS: 481111
Top Airlines at Charlotte Douglas International, NC, 2011

Market shares are shown for November 2010-October 2011.

US Airways	56.03%
Mesa	8.45
Wisconsin	4.16
Delta	2.99
American	1.20
Other	27.16

Source: ''Carrier Shares.'' [online] from http://www.transtats.bts.gov [Accessed February 10, 2012], from U.S. Department of Transportation.

★ 2543 ★
Airlines
SIC: 4512; NAICS: 481111
Top Airlines at Chicago O'Hare International, IL, 2011

Market shares are shown for November 2010-October 2011.

United	27.01%
American	24.33
American Eagle	11.72
ExpressJet	5.56
SkyWest	4.50
Other	26.88

Source: ''Carrier Shares.'' [online] from http://www.transtats.bts.gov [Accessed February 10, 2012], from U.S. Department of Transportation.

★ 2544 ★
Airlines
SIC: 4512; NAICS: 481111

Top Airlines at Dallas/Fort Worth International Airport, TX, 2011

Market shares are shown for November 2010-October 2011.

American	71.95%
American Eagle	10.93
US Airways	3.31
Delta	2.40
United	1.25
Other	10.16

Source: "Carrier Shares." [online] from http://www.transtats.bts.gov [Accessed February 10, 2012], from U.S. Department of Transportation.

★ 2545 ★
Airlines
SIC: 4512; NAICS: 481111

Top Airlines at Denver International Airport, CO, 2011

Market shares are shown for November 2010-October 2011.

United	24.66%
Southwest	22.04
Frontier	18.23
SkyWest	10.69
Delta	4.01
Other	20.37

Source: "Carrier Shares." [online] from http://www.transtats.bts.gov [Accessed February 10, 2012], from U.S. Department of Transportation.

★ 2546 ★
Airlines
SIC: 4512; NAICS: 481111

Top Airlines at Detroit Wayne County Airport, MI, 2011

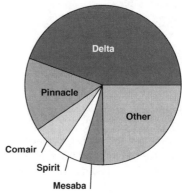

Market shares are shown for November 2010-October 2011.

Delta	44.74%
Pinnacle	14.81
Comair	6.26
Spirit	4.83
Mesaba	4.70
Other	24.66

Source: "Carrier Shares." [online] from http://www.transtats.bts.gov [Accessed February 10, 2012], from U.S. Department of Transportation.

★ 2547 ★
Airlines
SIC: 4512; NAICS: 481111

Top Airlines at Hartsfield-Jackson Atlanta International, GA, 2011

Market shares are shown for November 2010-October 2011.

Delta	62.87%
AirTran	17.17
Atlantic Southeast	11.74
Pinnacle	1.93
US Airways	1.40
Other	4.89

Source: "Carrier Shares." [online] from http://www.transtats.bts.gov [Accessed February 10, 2012], from U.S. Department of Transportation.

★ 2548 ★

Airlines

SIC: 4512; NAICS: 481111

Top Airlines at Heathrow Airport, United Kingdom, 2010

Market shares are shown based on the summer of 2010.

IAG	44.0%
BMI	8.6
Lufthansa	5.6
Aer Lingus	3.5
SAS	3.0
Virgin Atlantic	3.0
Other	32.3

Source: *Financial Times*, September 20, 2011, p. 19, from Airport Coordination Limited.

★ 2549 ★

Airlines

SIC: 4512; NAICS: 481111

Top Airlines at John F. Kennedy International, NY, 2011

Market shares are shown for November 2010-October 2011.

JetBlue	38.95%
Delta	20.96
American	17.07
United	3.66
American Eagle	2.95
Other	16.41

Source: "Carrier Shares." [online] from http://www.transtats. bts.gov [Accessed February 10, 2012], from U.S. Department of Transportation.

★ 2550 ★

Airlines

SIC: 4512; NAICS: 481111

Top Airlines at LaGuardia International, NY, 2011

Market shares are shown for November 2010-October 2011.

Delta	21.69%
American	16.28
US Airways	8.46
United	6.40
AirTran	5.39
Other	41.78

Source: "Carrier Shares." [online] from http://www.transtats. bts.gov [Accessed February 10, 2012], from U.S. Department of Transportation.

★ 2551 ★

Airlines

SIC: 4512; NAICS: 481111

Top Airlines at Logan International, MA, 2011

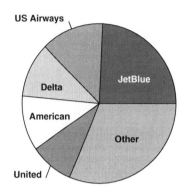

Market shares are shown for November 2010-October 2011.

JetBlue	24.35%
US Airways	13.26
Delta	11.37
American	11.05
United	8.78
Other	31.18

Source: "Carrier Shares." [online] from http://www.transtats. bts.gov [Accessed February 10, 2012], from U.S. Department of Transportation.

★ 2552 ★

Airlines

SIC: 4512; NAICS: 481111

Top Airlines at McCarran International, NV, 2011

Market shares are shown for November 2010-October 2011.

Southwest	42.52%
Delta	10.81
American	6.50
US Airways	6.48
United	5.62
Other	28.07

Source: "Carrier Shares." [online] from http://www.transtats. bts.gov [Accessed February 10, 2012], from U.S. Department of Transportation.

★ 2553 ★
Airlines

SIC: 4512; NAICS: 481111

Top Airlines at Philadelphia International, PA, 2011

Market shares are shown for November 2010-October 2011.

US Airways	38.88%
Southwest	13.16
Wisconsin	9.30
Delta	5.92
American	3.59
Other	29.16

Source: "Carrier Shares." [online] from http://www.transtats. bts.gov [Accessed February 10, 2012], from U.S. Department of Transportation.

★ 2554 ★
Airlines

SIC: 4512; NAICS: 481111

Top Airlines at Phoenix Sky Harbor International, AZ, 2011

Market shares are shown for November 2010-October 2011.

US Airways	38.13%
Southwest	32.69
Mesa	7.93
Delta	6.19
American	3.42
Other	11.64

Source: "Carrier Shares." [online] from http://www.transtats. bts.gov [Accessed February 10, 2012], from U.S. Department of Transportation.

★ 2555 ★
Airlines

SIC: 4512; NAICS: 481111

Top Airlines at Salt Lake City International, UT, 2011

Market shares are shown for November 2010-October 2011.

Delta	42.65%
SkyWest	31.38
Southwest	12.84
Mesaba	2.63
American	2.11
Other	8.39

Source: "Carrier Shares." [online] from http://www.transtats. bts.gov [Accessed February 10, 2012], from U.S. Department of Transportation.

★ 2556 ★
Airlines

SIC: 4512; NAICS: 481111

Top Airlines at Washington Dulles Airport, 2011

Market shares are shown for November 2010-October 2011.

United	40.02%
Mesa	6.37
JetBlue	6.15
ExpressJet	5.67
American	5.33
Other	36.46

Source: "Carrier Shares." [online] from http://www.transtats. bts.gov [Accessed February 10, 2012], from U.S. Department of Transportation.

★ 2557 ★
Airlines

SIC: 4512; NAICS: 481111

Top Airlines in India, 2011

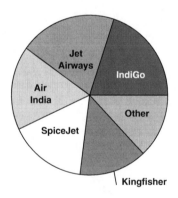

Market shares are shown in percent.

IndiGo	20.0%
Jet Airways	20.0
Air India	17.0
SpiceJet	16.0
Kingfisher	14.0
Other	13.0

Source: *Financial Times*, January 13, 2012, p. 12, from Thomson Reuters Datastream.

★ 2558 ★
Airlines
SIC: 4512; NAICS: 481111

Top Airlines in Japan, 2011

Market shares are shown based on passenger kilometers traveled.

All Nippon Airways	46.0%
Japan Airlines	36.0
Skymark	5.0
StarFlyer	1.0
Other	12.0

Source: *Financial Times*, April 16, 2012, p. 20, from Ministry of Land, Infrastructure, Transport and Tourism.

★ 2559 ★
Airlines
SIC: 4512; NAICS: 481111

Top Regional Airlines, 2010

Market shares are shown based on enplanements.

SkyWest Airlines	14.5%
ExpressJet	10.0
American Eagle	9.7
Atlantic Southeast	8.4
Pinnacle Airlines Corp.	6.6
Republic Holdings	6.6
Mesa Airlines	5.5
Horizon Air	4.1
Delta Air Lines	3.9
Mesaba Airlines	3.7
Other	27.0

Source: "Corporate Groups of Top 50 Regional Airlines." [online] from http://www.raa.org/Portals/0/IndustryStats/RAAChartsApr2011.pdf [Published April 2011], from OAG.

★ 2560 ★
Air Cargo
SIC: 4513; NAICS: 49211

Largest Air Cargo Operators Worldwide, 2009

Companies are ranked by capacity in millions of tons.

Korean Air	8,225
Cathay Pacific Airways	7,722
Lufthansa Cargo AG	6,660
Singapore Airlines	6,455
Emirates Airline	6,369
Federal Express	5,808
China Airlines	4,903
Air France	4,672

Cargolux	4,652
UPS	4,495

Source: "NYK Fact Book 2011." [online] from http://www.nyk.com [Accessed April 28, 2011], from International Air Travel Association.

★ 2561 ★
Air Cargo
SIC: 4513; NAICS: 49211

Top Air Cargo Airports Worldwide, 2010

Airports are ranked by cargo transport in millions of tons.

Hong Kong	4.16
Memphis, TN	3.91
Shanghai, China	3.22
Incheon, Korea	2.68
Anchorage, AK	2.64
Paris, France	2.39
Dubai, United Arab Emirates	2.27
Frankfurt, Germany	2.27
Louisville, KY	2.16
Tokyo, Japan	2.16

Source: "Cargo Traffic 2010 Final." [online] from http://www.airports.org [Published August 1, 2011], from Airports Council International.

★ 2562 ★
Airports
SIC: 4581; NAICS: 488111

Top Airport Operations Firms Worldwide, 2010

Market shares are shown in percent.

Aeropuertos Españoles y Navegación Aérea	4.3%
Aéroports de Paris	3.8
Grupo Ferrovial S.A.	3.7
Other	88.2

Source: "Global Airport Operations." [online] from http://retail.ibisworld.com [Published January 10, 2011], from IBISWorld.

★ 2563 ★
Airports
SIC: 4581; NAICS: 488111

Top Airports Worldwide, 2010

Airports are ranked by millions of passengers transported.

Atlanta, GA	89.3
Beijing, China	73.8

Continued on next page.

★ 2563 ★

[Continued]

Airports

SIC: 4581; NAICS: 488111

Top Airports Worldwide, 2010

Airports are ranked by millions of passengers transported.

Chicago, IL	66.7
London, England	65.8
Tokyo, Japan	64.2
Los Angeles, CA	59.0
Paris, France	58.1
Dallas/Ft. Worth, TX	56.9
Frankfurt, Germany	53.0
Denver, CO	52.2

Source: "Passenger Traffic 2010 Final." [online] from http://www.airports.org [Published August 1, 2011], from Airports Council International.

SIC 46 - Pipelines, Except Natural Gas

★ 2564 ★

Pipelines

SIC: 4612; NAICS: 48611

Leading Pipeline Operators by Crude Oil Deliveries, 2010

Companies are ranked by deliveries in trillions of barrels.

Plains Pipeline L.P.	637.3
Enbridge Energy L.P.	622.9
Shell Pipeline Company L.P.	511.4
Marathon Pipe Line L.L.C.	439.3
LOCAP L.L.C.	401.7
ExxonMobil Pipeline Co.	376.2
Enterprise Crude Pipeline L.L.C.	331.3
Sunoco Pipeline L.P.	315.3
Seaway Crude Pipeline Co.	266.4
Alyeska Pipeline Service Co.	225.2

Source: *Pipeline & Gas Journal*, November 2011, p. NA.

★ 2565 ★

Pipelines

SIC: 4612; NAICS: 48611

Pipeline Transportation of Crude Oil, 2007

Data show the percent of industry sales held by the largest 4, 8, 20 and 50 firms in the sector. There are approximately 395 firms operating in the industry generating employment for 6,551 people.

4 largest firms	55.1%
8 largest firms	78.8
20 largest firms	97.0
50 largest firms	100.0

Source: ''2007 Economic Census.'' [online] from http://www.census.gov/econ/concentration.html [Accessed August 12, 2011], from U.S. Bureau of the Census.

SIC 47 - Transportation Services

★ 2566 ★
Tourism
SIC: 4720; NAICS: 56151, 56152

Largest Tourism Markets Worldwide, 2010

Cities are ranked by thousands of visitors.

Hong Kong	19,973
Singapore	18,297
London, England	14,706
Macau	13,098
Bangkok	10,984
Antalya	10,641
Kuala Lumpur	10,351
New York City, NY	8,961
Paris, France	8,176
Istanbul, Turkey	8,124

Source: "Top 100 City Destinations Ranking." [online] from http://blog.euromonitor.com/2012/01 [Published January 2012], from Euromonitor.

★ 2567 ★
Tourism
SIC: 4720; NAICS: 56151, 56152

Top Visitors to China, 2009

Data show thousands of travelers.

Macau	14,439
Hong Kong	9,411
South Korea	1,031
Japan	893
Malaysia	890
Singapore	819
Thailand	581
United States	544
Vietnam	447
Australia	342

Source: "Around the World, Around the World." [online] from http://www.luxesf.com/wp-content/uploads/2011/10 [Published October 2011], from Euromonitor.

★ 2568 ★
Travel Arrangers
SIC: 4724; NAICS: 56151

Top Travel Arrangers, 2010

Companies are ranked by sales in millions of dollars.

Expedia Inc.	$ 25,960
American Express	25,700
Carlson Wagonlit Travel	24,300
BCD Travel	14,600
Priceline.com	13,600
Orbitz Worldwide	11,400
AAA Travel	3,440
Travel Leaders Group	1,790
Travelong	1,600
Altour International	1,200
Omega World Travel	1,180
Travel and Transport	1,150
Loyalty Travel Agency	865

Source: *Travel Weekly*, June 27, 2011, p. P6.

★ 2569 ★
Tour Operators
SIC: 4725; NAICS: 56152

Top Tour Operators, 2010

The industry generated revenues of $3.5 billion in 2010.

Flight Centre Ltd.	18.8%
The Mark Travel Corp.	9.3
American Tours International L.L.C.	4.9
Tauck Inc.	1.7
Extraordinary Vacations Group Inc.	1.4
Other	63.9

Source: "Tour Operators in the U.S." [online] from http://www.ibisworld.com [Published November 2011], from IBIS-World.

★ **2570** ★
Transportation Arrangement
SIC: 4731; NAICS: 48851

Arrangement of Transportation of Freight and Cargo, 2007

Data show the percent of industry sales held by the largest 4, 8, 20 and 50 firms in the sector. There are approximately 13,134 firms operating in the industry generating employment for 137,657 people.

4 largest firms	9.9%
8 largest firms	15.8
20 largest firms	23.8
50 largest firms	31.4

Source: ''2007 Economic Census.'' [online] from http://www.census.gov/econ/concentration.html [Accessed August 12, 2011], from U.S. Bureau of the Census.

★ **2571** ★
Packing and Crating
SIC: 4783; NAICS: 488991

Packing and Crating, 2007

Data show the percent of industry sales held by the largest 4, 8, 20 and 50 firms in the sector. There are approximately 1,395 firms operating in the industry generating employment for 16,354 people.

4 largest firms	14.6%
8 largest firms	21.7
20 largest firms	34.4
50 largest firms	50.5

Source: ''2007 Economic Census.'' [online] from http://www.census.gov/econ/concentration.html [Accessed August 12, 2011], from U.S. Bureau of the Census.

★ **2572** ★
Toll Roads and Weighing Stations
SIC: 4785; NAICS: 48849

Top Toll Road and Weighing Stations, 2011

There were a total of 1,237 businesses in the United States. They generated revenues of $1.9 billion.

New York State Thruway Authority.	36.4%
Delaware River Port Authority of Pennsylvania and New Jersey	15.0
Ohio Turnpike Commission	14.0
Macquarie Infrastructure L.L.C.	8.0
Other	26.6

Source: ''Toll Roads and Weighing Stations in the U.S.'' [online] from http://www.ibisworld.com [Published September 2011], from IBISWorld.

★ **2573** ★
Car Transportation
SIC: 4789; NAICS: 488999

Largest Car Transport Firms Worldwide, 2011

Companies are ranked by capacity of cars as of January 1, 2011.

	Capacity	Share
NYK Line	572,385	17.7%
Mitsui O.S.K. Lines	450,209	14.0
EUKOR	409,333	12.7
''K'' Line.	362,749	11.2
Wallenius Wilhelmsen Line . . .	323,108	10.0
Halliburton	285,025	8.8
Grimaldi	168,324	5.2
CCCS	152,122	4.7
Glovis	104,708	3.2
CSAV	70,211	2.2
N.M.C.C..	59,040	1.8
Other	279,781	8.5

Source: ''NYK Fact Book 2011.'' [online] from http://www.nyk.com [Accessed April 28, 2011], from Hesnes Shipping AS, *Car Carrier Market 2010.*

SIC 48 - Communications

★ 2574 ★
Wireless Services
SIC: 4812; NAICS: 51721, 517911

Largest Wireless Markets in Latin America, 2009

Countries are ranked by millions of subscribers.

Brazil	173.9
Mexico	83.5
Argentina	52.4
Colombia	42.1
Venezuela	28.1
Peru	24.7
Guatemala	17.3
Chile	16.4
Ecuador	13.6
Dominican Republic	8.6
Honduras	8.3
El Salvador	7.5

Source: *Latin Trade*, May-June 2011, p. 34, from International Telecommunication Union and *Latin Business Chronicle*.

★ 2575 ★
Wireless Services
SIC: 4812; NAICS: 51721, 517911

Top Wireless Firms, 2011

Market shares are shown in percent.

Verizon	34.0%
AT&T	31.0
Sprint	17.0
T-Mobile	11.0%
Other	7.0

Source: *Financial Times*, September 2, 2011, p. 12, from Thomson Reuters Datastream and UBS.

★ 2576 ★
Wireless Services
SIC: 4812; NAICS: 51721, 517911

Top Wireless Firms in Angola, 2011

Market shares are estimated based on subscribers for the first quarter of 2011.

Unitel	68.8%
Movicel	31.2

Source: *Southern Africa Telecommunications Report*, July 2011, p. 36, from Portugal Telecom and Business Monitor International.

★ 2577 ★
Wireless Services
SIC: 4812; NAICS: 51721, 517911

Top Wireless Firms in Argentina, 2010

Market shares are estimated based on subscribers for the fourth quarter of 2010.

Claro	35.4%
Telecom Personal	31.4
Movistar	31.0
Nextel Argentina	3.1

Source: *Argentina Telecommunications Report*, July 2011, p. 20, from Business Monitor International.

★ 2578 ★
Wireless Services
SIC: 4812; NAICS: 51721, 517911

Top Wireless Firms in Australia, 2010

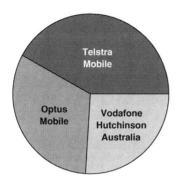

Market shares are estimated based on subscribers for the third quarter of 2010.

Telstra Mobile	41.9%
Optus Mobile	31.9
Vodafone Hutchinson Australia	26.2

Source: *Australia Telecommunications Report*, July 2011, p. 24, from Business Monitor International.

★ 2579 ★
Wireless Services
SIC: 4812; NAICS: 51721, 517911

Top Wireless Firms in Bahrain, 2010

Market shares are estimated based on subscribers for the fourth quarter of 2010.

Batelco	50.7%
Zain (MTC)	32.9
VIVA	16.5

Source: *Bahrain Telecommunications Report*, July 2011, p. 20, from company reports.

★ 2580 ★
Wireless Services
SIC: 4812; NAICS: 51721, 517911

Top Wireless Firms in Bangladesh, 2010

Market shares are shown as of December 2010.

Grameenphone	41.1%
Banglalink	26.5
Robi	22.5
Airtel Bangladesh	5.4

Citycell	2.5%
Teletalk	1.6

Source: *Bangladesh Telecommunications Report*, July 2011, p. 20, from Bangladesh Telecommunications and Regulatory Commission and Business Monitor International.

★ 2581 ★
Wireless Services
SIC: 4812; NAICS: 51721, 517911

Top Wireless Firms in Belgium, 2010

Market shares are shown for the fourth quarter of 2010.

Proximus	41.3%
Mobistar	32.2
BASE	26.5

Source: *Belgium Telecommunications Report*, July 2011, p. 20, from Business Monitor International.

★ 2582 ★
Wireless Services
SIC: 4812; NAICS: 51721, 517911

Top Wireless Firms in Belize, 2011

Market shares are shown based on subscribers as of March 2011.

Belize Telemedia	67.4%
Smart	32.6

Source: *Central America Telecommunications Report*, July 2011, p. 24, from Business Monitor International.

★ 2583 ★
Wireless Services
SIC: 4812; NAICS: 51721, 517911

Top Wireless Firms in Botswana, 2011

Market shares are estimated based on subscribers for the first quarter of 2011.

Mascom	54.1%
Orange	30.4
BTC	15.2
Other	0.3

Source: *Southern Africa Telecommunications Report*, July 2011, p. 40, from France Télécom and MTN.

★ 2584 ★
Wireless Services
SIC: 4812; NAICS: 51721, 517911

Top Wireless Firms in Bulgaria, 2010

Market shares are shown based on net additions for the fourth quarter of 2010.

Globul	67.7%
Mobiltel	24.3
Vivacom	8.0

Source: *Bulgaria Telecommunications Report*, July 2011, p. NA, from Business Monitor International and operators.

★ 2585 ★
Wireless Services
SIC: 4812; NAICS: 51721, 517911

Top Wireless Firms in Canada, 2010

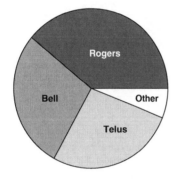

The industry is valued at $18 billion.

Rogers	39.0%
Bell	28.0
Telus	27.0
Other	6.0

Source: "CRTC: Broadband and Wireless Gaining Momentum in Canada." [online] from http://www.thetelecomblog. com [Published July 29, 2011], from CRTC.

★ 2586 ★
Wireless Services
SIC: 4812; NAICS: 51721, 517911

Top Wireless Firms in Chile, 2010

Market shares are shown based on the fourth quarter of 2010.

Movistar	41.6%
Entel PCS	35.8
Claro	22.6

Source: *Chile Telecommunications Report*, July 2011, p. 50, from Business Monitor International.

★ 2587 ★
Wireless Services
SIC: 4812; NAICS: 51721, 517911

Top Wireless Firms in China, 2011-2013

Market shares are projected.

	2011	2012	2013
China Mobile	76.9%	75.3%	74.5%
China Unicom	14.6	15.7	16.2
China Telecom	8.5	9.0	9.3

Source: "China in 2015." [online] from http://wpc.186f.edge-castcdn.net [Published January 1, 2011], from Credit Suisse estimates.

★ 2588 ★
Wireless Services
SIC: 4812; NAICS: 51721, 517911

Top Wireless Firms in Colombia, 2010

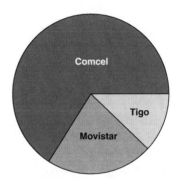

Market shares are shown based on subscribers for the fourth quarter of 2010.

Comcel	65.8%
Movistar	22.5
Tigo	11.7

Source: *Colombia Telecommunications Report*, July 2011, p. 26, from Business Monitor International and MinCom.

★ 2589 ★
Wireless Services
SIC: 4812; NAICS: 51721, 517911

Top Wireless Firms in Croatia, 2010

Market shares are shown based on subscribers for the fourth quarter of 2010.

T-Mobile Hrvatska	45.4%
Vipnet	43.0
Tele2	11.6

Source: *Croatia Telecommunications Report*, July 2011, p. 27, from Business Monitor International.

★ 2590 ★
Wireless Services
SIC: 4812; NAICS: 51721, 517911

Top Wireless Firms in Egypt, 2011

Market shares are estimated based on subscribers for the first quarter of 2011.

Vodafone Egyot	45.1%
Mobinil	42.5
Etisalat Misr	12.3

Source: *Egypt Telecommunications Report*, July 2011, p. 50, from operator results and Business Monitor International.

★ 2591 ★
Wireless Services
SIC: 4812; NAICS: 51721, 517911

Top Wireless Firms in El Salvador, 2011

Market shares are shown based on subscribers as of March 2011.

Tigo El Salvador (Millicom)	33.9%
Claro El Salvador (America Movil)	26.8
Movistar El Salvador (Telefónica)	23.5
Digicel El Salvador	14.8
Intelfon (RED)	0.9

Source: *Central America Telecommunications Report*, July 2011, p. 24, from Business Monitor International, company reports and SIGET.

★ 2592 ★
Wireless Services
SIC: 4812; NAICS: 51721, 517911

Top Wireless Firms in France, 2011

Market shares are estimated based on subscribers for the first quarter of 2011.

Orange	41.5%
SFR	32.8
Bouygues	17.4%
MVNOs	8.3

Source: *France Telecommunications Report*, July 2011, p. 30, from ARCEP and Business Monitor International.

★ 2593 ★
Wireless Services
SIC: 4812; NAICS: 51721, 517911

Top Wireless Firms in Germany, 2011

Market shares are estimated based on subscribers for the third quarter of 2010.

Vodafone Deutschland	33.79%
T-Mobile Deutschland	31.79
E-Plus	18.80
O2	15.70

Source: *France Telecommunications Report*, July 2011, p. 50, from Business Monitor International.

★ 2594 ★
Wireless Services
SIC: 4812; NAICS: 51721, 517911

Top Wireless Firms in Guatemala, 2011

Market shares are shown based on subscribers as of March 2011.

Tigo Guatemala (Millicom)	41.2%
Movistar Guatemala (Telefónica)	33.2
Claro Guatemala (America Movil)	25.6

Source: *Central America Telecommunications Report*, July 2011, p. 24, from Business Monitor International, company reports and SIGET.

★ 2595 ★
Wireless Services
SIC: 4812; NAICS: 51721, 517911

Top Wireless Firms in Honduras, 2011

Market shares are shown based on subscribers as of March 2011.

Tigo Honduras	49.1%
Digicel Honduras	27.9
Claro Honduras	22.2
Tegucel Sulacel	0.9

Source: *Central America Telecommunications Report*, July 2011, p. 24, from Business Monitor International, company reports and SIGET.

★ 2596 ★
Wireless Services
SIC: 4812; NAICS: 51721, 517911
Top Wireless Firms in Hong Kong, 2010

Market shares are estimated based on 2G and 3G subscribers as of December 2010.

CSL New World Mobility	33.4%
Hutchinson 3G HK Ltd.	23.9
China Mobile Hong Kong	19.5
PCCW Mobile	11.1
SmarTone	10.7
Other	1.4

Source: *Hong Kong Telecommunications Report*, July 2011, p. 50, from Business Monitor International.

★ 2597 ★
Wireless Services
SIC: 4812; NAICS: 51721, 517911
Top Wireless Firms in Hungary, 2010

Market shares are estimated based on subscribers for the fourth quarter of 2010.

T-Mobile Hungary	46.0%
Telenor (Pannon GSM)	30.3
Vodafone Hungary	23.7

Source: *Hungary Telecommunications Report*, July 2011, p. 24, from Business Monitor International.

★ 2598 ★
Wireless Services
SIC: 4812; NAICS: 51721, 517911
Top Wireless Firms in India, 2011

Market shares are as of May 2011.

Bharti	28.3%
Vodafone	23.6
Idea	15.9
BSNL	14.8

Aircel	9.7%
Other	7.7

Source: "Telecom Sector." [online] from http://web.angel-backoffice.com/research/archives/fundamental/company_reports [Published June 17, 2011], from Angel Research.

★ 2599 ★
Wireless Services
SIC: 4812; NAICS: 51721, 517911
Top Wireless Firms in Iran, 2010

Market shares are shown as of March 2010.

MCI	53.6%
MT Irancell	40.7
Taliya	5.3
Other	0.5

Source: *Iran Telecommunications Report*, August 2010, p. 10, from Business Monitor International.

★ 2600 ★
Wireless Services
SIC: 4812; NAICS: 51721, 517911
Top Wireless Firms in Ireland, 2011

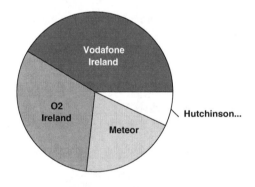

Market shares are estimated based on the fourth quarter 2010.

Vodafone Ireland	41.7%
O2 Ireland	31.9
Meteor	19.8
Hutchinson 3G Ireland	6.6

Source: *Ireland Telecommunications Report*, July 2011, p. 24, from Business Monitor International.

★ 2601 ★
Wireless Services
SIC: 4812; NAICS: 51721, 517911

Top Wireless Firms in Japan, 2011

Market shares are estimated based on mobile and PHS subscribers for the quarter ended March 2011.

NTT DoCoMo	46.7%
KDDI	26.6
Softbank Mobile	20.5
Willcom	3.0
eMobile	2.5
UQ Communications	0.7

Source: *Japan Telecommunications Report*, July 2011, p. 28, from Telecommunications Carrier Association.

★ 2602 ★
Wireless Services
SIC: 4812; NAICS: 51721, 517911

Top Wireless Firms in Jordan, 2010

Market shares are estimated based on subscribers for the fourth quarter of 2010.

Zain	35.7%
Orange	30.9
Umniah	30.7
xpress	2.6

Source: *Jordan Telecommunications Report*, July 2011, p. 28, from Business Monitor International.

★ 2603 ★
Wireless Services
SIC: 4812; NAICS: 51721, 517911

Top Wireless Firms in Malaysia, 2010

Market shares are shown based on subscribers as of fourth quarter 2010.

Maxis Communications	41.2%
Celcom	33.0
DiGi	25.8

Source: *Malaysia Telecommunications Report*, July 2011, p. 27, from Business Monitor International.

★ 2604 ★
Wireless Services
SIC: 4812; NAICS: 51721, 517911

Top Wireless Firms in Mauritius, 2011

Market shares are estimated based on subscribers for the first quarter of 2011.

Orange	53.9%
Emtel	37.9
MTML	8.2

Source: *Southern Africa Telecommunications Report*, July 2011, p. 50, from Millicom International Center and Business Monitor International.

★ 2605 ★
Wireless Services
SIC: 4812; NAICS: 51721, 517911

Top Wireless Firms in Mexico, 2011

Market shares are estimated based on subscribers for the fourth quarter of 2010.

Telcel	70.6%
TMM (Movistar)	21.6
Lusacell	4.0
Nextel	3.6

Source: *Mexico Telecommunications Report*, July 2011, p. 23, from Business Monitor International.

★ 2606 ★
Wireless Services
SIC: 4812; NAICS: 51721, 517911

Top Wireless Firms in Mozambique, 2011

Market shares are estimated based on subscribers for the first quarter of 2011.

Mcel	57.9%
Vodacom	42.1

Source: *Southern Africa Telecommunications Report*, July 2011, p. 50, from Millicom International Center and Business Monitor International.

★ 2607 ★
Wireless Services
SIC: 4812; NAICS: 51721, 517911

Top Wireless Firms in Namibia, 2011

Market shares are estimated based on subscribers for the first quarter of 2011.

MTC	74.8%
Leo	18.4
Telecom Namibia	6.8

Source: *Southern Africa Telecommunications Report*, July 2011, p. 50, from Millicom International Center and Business Monitor International.

★ 2608 ★
Wireless Services
SIC: 4812; NAICS: 51721, 517911

Top Wireless Firms in Norway, 2011

Market shares are shown based on subscribers for the first quarter of 2011.

Telenor Mobil	54.8%
NetCom	30.8
Other	15.1

Source: *Norway Telecommunications Report*, July 2011, p. 25, from Business Monitor International.

★ 2609 ★
Wireless Services
SIC: 4812; NAICS: 51721, 517911

Top Wireless Firms in Oman, 2010

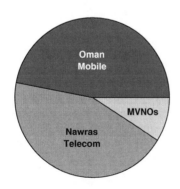

Market shares are shown based on subscribers for the fourth quarter of 2010.

Oman Mobile	46.7%
Nawras Telecom	44.1
MVNOs	9.2

Source: *Oman Telecommunications Report*, July 2011, p. 22, from Business Monitor International.

★ 2610 ★
Wireless Services
SIC: 4812; NAICS: 51721, 517911

Top Wireless Firms in Pakistan, 2010

Market shares are shown based on subscribers as of December 2010.

Mobilink	30.9%
Telenor	24.0
Ufone	19.7
Wrid Telecom	17.0
Zong	8.4

Source: *Pakistan Telecommunications Report*, July 2011, p. 22, from Business Monitor International.

★ 2611 ★
Wireless Services
SIC: 4812; NAICS: 51721, 517911

Top Wireless Firms in Panama, 2011

Market shares are shown based on subscribers as of March 2011.

+movil (Cable & Wireless)	37.2%
Movistar Panama (Telefónica)	36.2
Digicel Panama	24.3
Claro Panama (America Movil)	2.2

Source: *Central America Telecommunications Report*, July 2011, p. 24, from Business Monitor International and company reports.

★ 2612 ★
Wireless Services
SIC: 4812; NAICS: 51721, 517911

Top Wireless Firms in Peru, 2010

Market shares are shown based on subscribers for the fourth quarter of 2010.

Movistar	53.6%
Claro	41.5
Nextel	4.8

Source: *Peru Telecommunications Report*, July 2011, p. 22, from Business Monitor International.

★ 2613 ★
Wireless Services
SIC: 4812; NAICS: 51721, 517911
Top Wireless Firms in Saudi Arabia, 2010

Market shares are shown based on subscribers for the fourth quarter of 2010.

Vodacom	48.5%
MTN	36.1
Cell C	14.4
Virgin Mobile	0.6
8ta	0.4

Source: *Saudi Arabia Telecommunications Report*, July 2011, p. 22, from Business Monitor International.

★ 2614 ★
Wireless Services
SIC: 4812; NAICS: 51721, 517911
Top Wireless Firms in Singapore, 2011

Market shares are estimated based on subscribers for the first quarter of 2011.

SingTel Mobile	44.8%
StarHub	29.0
M1	26.2

Source: *Singapore Telecommunications Report*, July 2011, p. 22, from Business Monitor International.

★ 2615 ★
Wireless Services
SIC: 4812; NAICS: 51721, 517911
Top Wireless Firms in Spain, 2010

Market shares are shown based on subscribers for the first quarter of 2011.

Telefónica Moviles (Movistar)	43.4%
Vodafone	30.7
Orange	21.4
Yoigo	4.4

Source: *Spain Telecommunications Report*, July 2011, p. 41, from Business Monitor International.

★ 2616 ★
Wireless Services
SIC: 4812; NAICS: 51721, 517911
Top Wireless Firms in Switzerland, 2010

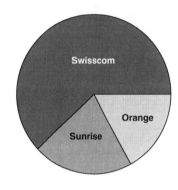

Market shares are shown based on subscribers for the fourth quarter of 2010.

Swisscom	62.1%
Sunrise	21.2
Orange	16.7

Source: *Switzerland Telecommunications Report*, July 2011, p. 20, from Business Monitor International.

★ 2617 ★
Wireless Services
SIC: 4812; NAICS: 51721, 517911
Top Wireless Firms in Thailand, 2010

Market shares are shown based on subscribers for the fourth quarter of 2010.

AIS	43.6%
DTAC	30.2
TrueMove	23.9

Source: *Thailand Telecommunications Report*, July 2011, p. 20, from Business Monitor International and National Telecommunications Commission.

★ 2618 ★
Wireless Services
SIC: 4812; NAICS: 51721, 517911
Top Wireless Firms in the Czech Republic, 2010

Market shares are shown based on subscribers for the fourth quarter of 2010.

T-Mobile	40.2%
Telefónica O2	35.5

Continued on next page.

★ 2618 ★
[Continued]
Wireless Services
SIC: 4812; NAICS: 51721, 517911
Top Wireless Firms in the Czech Republic, 2010

Market shares are shown based on subscribers for the fourth quarter of 2010.

Vodafone CZ	23.3%
U:fon	1.0

Source: *Czech Republic Telecommunications Report*, July 2011, p. 29, from Business Monitor International.

★ 2619 ★
Wireless Services
SIC: 4812; NAICS: 51721, 517911
Top Wireless Firms in Turkey, 2010

Market shares are shown based on subscribers for the fourth quarter of 2010.

Turkcell	54.2%
Vodafone	27.0
Avea	18.8

Source: *Turkey Telecommunications Report*, July 2011, p. 20, from Business Monitor International.

★ 2620 ★
Wireless Services
SIC: 4812; NAICS: 51721, 517911
Top Wireless Firms in Venezuela, 2010

Market shares are shown based on subscribers for the fourth quarter of 2010.

Movilnet	47.5%
Movistar	32.3
Digitel	20.2

Source: *Venezuela Telecommunications Report*, July 2011, p. 20, from Business Monitor International.

★ 2621 ★
Wireless Services
SIC: 4812; NAICS: 51721, 517911
Top Wireless Firms Worldwide, 2010

The industry generated revenues of $890.9 billion.

China Mobile	14.3%
Vodafone	8.0
O2	4.7
T-Mobile	2.7
Other	70.2

Source: *Datamonitor Industry Market Research*, November 2, 2011, p. NA, from Datamonitor.

★ 2622 ★
Telephone Services
SIC: 4813; NAICS: 51711, 517911
Leading Wired Telecom Firms, 2011

Market shares are shown based on fourth quarter subscribers.

AT&T	39.76%
Verizon	24.60
CenturyLink	9.60
Frontier	2.46
Windstream	1.97
Other	21.61

Source: "United States Telecommunications Report Second Quarter 2012." [online] from http://www.docin.com [Accessed June 1, 2012], from Business Monitor International.

★ 2623 ★
Telephone Services
SIC: 4813; NAICS: 51711, 517911
Pay Telephone Operators, 2007

Data show the percent of industry sales held by the largest 4, 8, 20 and 50 firms in the sector. There are approximately 521 firms operating in the industry generating employment for 1,915 people.

4 largest firms	27.7%
8 largest firms	38.2
20 largest firms	53.1
50 largest firms	69.6

Source: "2007 Economic Census." [online] from http://www.census.gov/econ/concentration.html [Accessed August 12, 2011], from U.S. Bureau of the Census.

★ 2624 ★
Electronic Commerce
SIC: 4822; NAICS: 51711
E-Commerce Market Worldwide, 2015

Internet penetration is increasing in developing markets, enlarging the potential for online commerce. Brazil is expected to move from the seventh largest market in 2012 to fourth in 2015. The United States claimed 24.9% of the market in 2011, making it the largest market, but China is expected to overtake it by 2015.

China	18.8%
United States	16.8
Japan	4.9
Brazil	4.3
Other	55.2

Source: *America's Intelligence Wire*, December 30, 2011, p. NA, from T-Index 2015 study by Translated.

★ 2625 ★
Electronic Commerce
SIC: 4822; NAICS: 51711
Online Payment Market in China, 2010

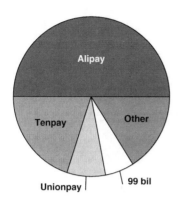

Market shares are shown for the third quarter of 2010.

Alipay	50.0%
Tenpay	20.0
Unionpay	8.0
99 bil	6.0
Other	16.0

Source: "China in 2015." [online] from http://wpc.186f.edge-castcdn.net [Published January 1, 2011], from Credit Suisse estimates.

★ 2626 ★
Electronic Commerce
SIC: 4822; NAICS: 51711
Top Online Retailers, 2010

Market shares are shown based on brand value.

Wal-Mart	9.9%
CVS (CVS Caremark)	2.7
Walgreens	2.5
Costco	2.2
Kroger	2.2
Target	1.9
Home Depot	1.8
Sam's Club	1.6
Other	75.1

Source: *Financial Times*, July 23, 2011, p. 10, from Thomson Reuters Datastream and Euromonitor.

★ 2627 ★
Electronic Commerce
SIC: 4822; NAICS: 51711
Top Online Spending Sectors, 2012-2013

Spending is shown in millions of dollars.

	2012	2013	Share
Computers	$ 57.8	$ 63.7	25.22%
Apparel	47.0	52.2	20.67
Housewares	31.8	35.6	14.09
Books, music, videos	16.4	18.4	7.28
Groceries	13.4	14.8	5.86
Personal care	9.1	10.1	4.00
Movies, events	8.9	9.9	3.92
Office products	7.5	8.2	3.25
Auto parts	5.9	6.8	2.69
Video games	5.1	6.6	2.61
Flowers	4.1	4.8	1.90
Other	19.4	21.5	8.51

Source: *Advertising Age*, February 27, 2012, p. NA, from Forrester Research.

★ 2628 ★
Electronic Commerce
SIC: 4822; NAICS: 51711
Top Social Commerce Sites in South Korea, 2010

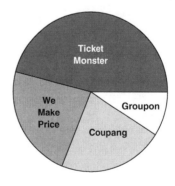

Market shares are shown in percent.

Ticket Monster	46.0%
We Make Price	23.0
Coupang	22.0
Groupon	9.0

Source: *Wall Street Journal*, June 1, 2011, p. B8, from company reports.

★ 2629 ★
Internet

SIC: 4822; NAICS: 51711

Bloggers Worldwide, 2010

A blog is a web site or a part of a web site with content updated regularly or from time to time. According to a February 16, 2011 estimate by Nielsen, there were over 156 million public blogs in existence.

United States	49.0%
European Union	29.0
Asia-Pacific	12.0
Canada and Mexico	7.0
South America	3.0

Source: "State of the Blogosphere 2010 Introduction." [online] from http://www.technorati.com [Accessed August 1, 2010], from Technorati.

★ 2630 ★
Internet

SIC: 4822; NAICS: 51711

Internet Domains Worldwide, 2011

Data show millions of domain names, as of April 2011.

	(mil.)	Share
.com	94.5	73.14%
.net	13.9	10.76
.org	9.2	7.12
.info	7.7	5.96
Other	3.9	3.02

Source: *Wall Street Journal*, June 21, 2011, p. B1, from ZookNIC Internet Intelligence.

★ 2631 ★
Internet

SIC: 4822; NAICS: 51711

Microblogging Market in China, 2011

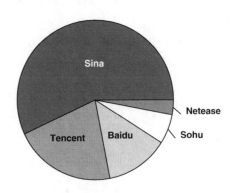

Microblogging is similar to blogging. However, microblogging files are smaller in size and might contain a few sentences or simply a video clip. Market shares are shown based on number of visitors for the first quarter of the year.

Sina	57.0%
Tencent	21.0
Baidu	13.0
Sohu	6.0
Netease	3.0

Source: *Wall Street Journal*, June 27, 2011, p. B11, from RedTech Advisors.

★ 2632 ★
Internet

SIC: 4822; NAICS: 51711

Top Internet Users Worldwide, 2011

Data show millions of users.

China	513.0
United States	231.9
Japan	94.2
India	83.2
Brazil	79.3
Russia	62.0
Germany	55.6
United Kingdom	45.5

Source: *Advertising Age*, February 27, 2012, p. NA, from eMarketer.

★ **2633** ★
Internet Service Providers
SIC: 4822; NAICS: 51711

Leading Broadband Firms, 2011

Market shares are shown based on fourth quarter subscribers.

Comcast	21.4%
AT&T	19.1
Time Warner	13.7
Verizon	10.2
CenturyLink	6.5
Cox	5.2
Charter Communications	4.8
Other	19.1

Source: "United States Telecommunications Report Second Quarter 2012." [online] from http://www.docin.com [Accessed June 1, 2012], from Business Monitor International and National Cable & Telecommunications Association.

★ **2634** ★
Internet Service Providers
SIC: 4822; NAICS: 51711

Top Broadband Firms in Argentina, 2011

Market shares are estimated based on subscribers for the first quarter of the year.

TASA	28.7%
Telecom Argentina	26.9
Cablevision	22.0
Other	2.3

Source: *Argentina Telecommunications Report*, July 2011, p. 20, from Business Monitor International and Indec.

★ **2635** ★
Internet Service Providers
SIC: 4822; NAICS: 51711

Top Broadband Firms in Australia, 2010

Market shares are shown as of June 2010.

VHA (wireless broadband)	24.3%
Telstra (fixed retail)	23.6
Telstra (wireless broadband)	17.3
Optus (On-net)	9.7

Source: *Australia Telecommunications Report*, July 2011, p. 50, from Business Monitor International.

★ **2636** ★
Internet Service Providers
SIC: 4822; NAICS: 51711

Top Broadband Firms in Chile, 2010

Market shares are shown based on subscribers as of September 2010.

Telefónica Chile	43.4%
VTR GlobalCom	38.2
CNT (Telsur)	5.0
Entel	1.2
Other	12.2

Source: *Chile Telecommunications Report*, July 2011, p. 50, from Business Monitor International and Subtel.

★ **2637** ★
Internet Service Providers
SIC: 4822; NAICS: 51711

Top Broadband Firms in Japan, 2011

Market shares are estimated based on the quarter ended March 2011.

	(000)	Share
Telecom Italia	7,194	51.46%
WIND Infostrada	2,030	14.52
Fastweb	1,746	12.49
Vodafone	1,700	12.16
Tiscali	541	3.87
Other	768	5.49

Source: *Japan Telecommunications Report*, July 2011, p. 56, from Business Monitor International.

★ **2638** ★
Internet Service Providers
SIC: 4822; NAICS: 51711

Top Business Internet Service Providers, 2011

Market shares are shown based on all Internet traffic in September 2011.

AT&T	20.0%
Verizon	12.0
CenturyLink	7.0
Comcast	5.0
Level 3	5.0
TW Telecom	5.0
Cogent	4.0
Sprint	4.0
Time Warner Cable	4.0

Continued on next page.

★ 2638 ★

[Continued]

Internet Service Providers

SIC: 4822; NAICS: 51711

Top Business Internet Service Providers, 2011

Market shares are shown based on all Internet traffic in September 2011.

Cox	3.0%
Other	31.0

Source: "AT&T Leads U.S. Biz ISP Market." [online] from http://www.marketingcharts.com/direct/att-leads-us-biz-isp-market-20081/comscore-biz-isp-sharejpg [Accessed June 1, 2012], from comScore.

★ 2639 ★

Internet Service Providers

SIC: 4822; NAICS: 51711

Top Fixed-Line Broadband Firms in Ireland, 2011

Market shares are estimated based on the fourth quarter 2010.

eircom	49.0%
UPC	20.0
Vodafone	16.0
Other	14.0

Source: *Ireland Telecommunications Report*, July 2011, p. 24, from Business Monitor International.

★ 2640 ★

Internet Service Providers

SIC: 4822; NAICS: 51711

Top Fixed-Line Broadband Firms in Pakistan, 2010

Market shares are shown based on subscribers as of December 2010.

NTC	95.6%
NayaTel	3.1
Worldcall	0.6
Other	0.7

Source: *Pakistan Telecommunications Report*, July 2011, p. 22, from Business Monitor International.

★ 2641 ★

Internet Service Providers

SIC: 4822; NAICS: 51711

Top Internet Service Providers Worldwide, 2011

The market was valued at $196.5 billion.

Nippon Telegraph & Telephone Corp.	9.6%
AT&T Inc.	7.9
Comcast	4.6
Time Warner Cable	2.7
Other	75.2

Source: "Internet Service Providers." [online] from http://www.docin.com/p-320610766.html [Published May 2011], from IBISWorld.

★ 2642 ★

Internet Sites

SIC: 4822; NAICS: 51711

Online Parking Reservation Market, 2011

ParkWhiz allows users to reserve off-street parking sites. The company has partnered with parking industry leaders LAZ Karp Associates, Imperial Parking Corp. and Ampco System Parking.

ParkWhiz	99.0%
Other	1.0

Source: *Crain's Chicago Business*, October 11, 2011, p. 4.

★ 2643 ★

Internet Sites

SIC: 4822; NAICS: 51711

Search Engine Market, 2012

Market shares are shown in percent.

	Feb.	March	April
Google	80.74%	80.70%	81.50%
Bing	8.78	8.99	8.41
Yahoo!	7.68	7.49	7.30
Ask	1.55	1.48	1.45
AOL	1.24	1.33	1.29

Source: "Search Engine Market Share." [online] from http://www.statowl.com/search_engine_market_share.php [Accessed June 1, 2012].

★ 2644 ★
Internet Sites
SIC: 4822; NAICS: 51711

Search Engine Market in Argentina, 2011

Market shares are shown for July 2011.

Google	89.4%
Other	10.6

Source: "Search Engine Market Share." [online] from http://www.chandlernguyen.com/2011 [Accessed December 1, 2011], from comScore.

★ 2645 ★
Internet Sites
SIC: 4822; NAICS: 51711

Search Engine Market in Brazil, 2010

Market shares are shown in percent.

Google	89.0%
Other	11.0

Source: "Google's Market Share by Country." [online] from http://visualeconomics.creditloan.com/2010-02-03-planet-google-from-philosophies-to-market-shares [Accessed December 1, 2011].

★ 2646 ★
Internet Sites
SIC: 4822; NAICS: 51711

Search Engine Market in Canada, 2011

Market shares are shown for July 2011.

Google	80.96%
Microsoft	8.60
Yahoo!	4.20
Ask	3.70

Source: "Search Engine Market Share." [online] from http://www.chandlernguyen.com/2011 [Accessed December 1, 2011], from comScore.

★ 2647 ★
Internet Sites
SIC: 4822; NAICS: 51711

Search Engine Market in Chile, 2010

Market shares are shown in percent.

Google	93.0%
Other	7.0

Source: "Google's Market Share by Country." [online] from http://visualeconomics.creditloan.com/2010-02-03-planet-google-from-philosophies-to-market-shares [Accessed December 1, 2011], from comScore.

★ 2648 ★
Internet Sites
SIC: 4822; NAICS: 51711

Search Engine Market in Colombia, 2011

Market shares are shown for July 2011.

Google	92.0%
Other	8.0

Source: "Search Engine Market Share." [online] from http://www.chandlernguyen.com/2011 [Accessed December 1, 2011], from comScore.

★ 2649 ★
Internet Sites
SIC: 4822; NAICS: 51711

Search Engine Market in Finland, 2010

Market shares are shown in percent.

Google	92.0%
Other	8.0

Source: "Google's Market Share by Country." [online] from http://visualeconomics.creditloan.com/2010-02-03-planet-google-from-philosophies-to-market-shares [Accessed December 1, 2011].

★ 2650 ★
Internet Sites
SIC: 4822; NAICS: 51711

Search Engine Market in Germany, 2010

Market shares are shown in percent.

Google	93.0%
Other	7.0

Source: "Google's Market Share by Country." [online] from http://visualeconomics.creditloan.com/2010-02-03-planet-google-from-philosophies-to-market-shares [Accessed December 1, 2011].

★ 2651 ★
Internet Sites
SIC: 4822; NAICS: 51711

Search Engine Market in Hong Kong, 2011

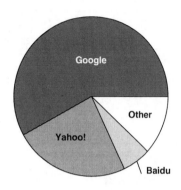

Market shares are shown for July 2011.

Google	58.02%
Yahoo!	23.51
Baidu	6.08
Other	12.39

Source: "Search Engine Market Share." [online] from http://www.chandlernguyen.com/2011 [Accessed December 1, 2011], from comScore.

★ 2652 ★
Internet Sites
SIC: 4822; NAICS: 51711

Search Engine Market in Italy, 2010

Market shares are shown in percent.

Google	90.0%
Other	10.0

Source: "Google's Market Share by Country." [online] from http://visualeconomics.creditloan.com/2010-02-03-planet-google-from-philosophies-to-market-shares [Accessed December 1, 2011].

★ 2653 ★
Internet Sites
SIC: 4822; NAICS: 51711

Search Engine Market in Poland, 2010

Market shares are shown in percent.

Google	95.0%
Other	5.0

Source: "Google's Market Share by Country." [online] from http://visualeconomics.creditloan.com/2010-02-03-planet-google-from-philosophies-to-market-shares [Accessed December 1, 2011].

★ 2654 ★
Internet Sites
SIC: 4822; NAICS: 51711

Search Engine Market in Romania, 2010

Market shares are shown in percent.

Google	95.0%
Other	5.0

Source: "Google's Market Share by Country." [online] from http://visualeconomics.creditloan.com/2010-02-03-planet-google-from-philosophies-to-market-shares [Accessed December 1, 2011].

★ 2655 ★
Internet Sites
SIC: 4822; NAICS: 51711

Search Engine Market in South Korea, 2011

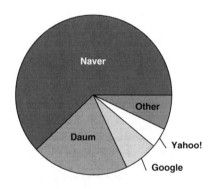

Market shares are shown for July 2011.

Naver	61.9%
Daum	19.7
Google	7.3
Yahoo!	4.1
Other	7.0

Source: "Search Engine Market Share." [online] from http://www.chandlernguyen.com/2011 [Accessed December 1, 2011], from comScore.

★ **2656** ★

Internet Sites

SIC: 4822; NAICS: 51711

Search Engine Market in the Netherlands, 2010

Market shares are shown in percent.

Google	95.0%
Other	5.0

Source: ''Google's Market Share by Country.'' [online] from http://visualeconomics.creditloan.com/2010-02-03-planet-google-from-philosophies-to-market-shares [Accessed December 1, 2011].

★ **2657** ★

Internet Sites

SIC: 4822; NAICS: 51711

Top Coupon and Daily Deal Sites, 2011

Sites are ranked by share of all visits.

Groupon	47.6%
Living Social	29.5
Eversave.com	10.6
Dealfind	3.6
Bloomspot	1.7
AmazonLocal	1.0
Kgbdeals	1.0
BuyWithMe	0.9
DealChicken.com	0.6
HalfOffDepot.com	0.5
Other	3.0

Source: *USA TODAY*, September 1, 2011, p. B1, from Experian Hitwise.

★ **2658** ★

Internet Sites

SIC: 4822; NAICS: 51711

Top Coupon Sites in China, 2011

Data show millions of unique visitors during the second quarter of 2011.

Lashou	53.9
Meituan	48.4
55tuan	36.5
24qun	31.4
Manzuo	18.1
Groupon.cn	17.2
GaoPeng	15.0
Didatuan	13.9
Ftuan	8.8

Source: *Wall Street Journal*, August 24, 2011, p. B1, from Analysys International and Bloomberg News.

★ **2659** ★

Internet Sites

SIC: 4822; NAICS: 51711

Top Diet Sites, 2009

The sites are ranked by revenues generated in millions of dollars.

Nutrisystem	$ 527
Weightwatchers.com	196
The Biggest Loser Club	63
Medifast	47
JillianMichaels.com	23
eDiets.com	19

Source: ''Online Dieting Represents a $910 Million Market.'' [online] from http://www.prweb.com/releases/2011/01/prweb4961684.htm [Published January 6, 2011], from Marketdata Enterprises.

★ **2660** ★

Internet Sites

SIC: 4822; NAICS: 51711

Top E-Card Sites, 2012

Sites are ranked by millions of unique visitors for February 2012.

Evite.com	6.9
American Greetings Interactive	3.4
MyFunCards.com	2.8
123Greetings.com	2.4
SomeEcards.com	2.4

Source: ''comScore Media Metrix Ranks Top 50 U.S. Web Properties for February 2012.'' [online] from http://www.comscore.com [Press release March 21, 2012], from comScore.

★ **2661** ★

Internet Sites

SIC: 4822; NAICS: 51711

Top Flash Sale Sites, 2011

Sites are ranked by thousands of visitors during October 2011.

Woot.com	1,881
Zulily.com	1,880
BeyondtheRack.com	1,183
Ideeli.com	1,149
Hautelook.com	1,098
OneKingsLane.com	923
Gilt.com	760
RueLALA.com	610

Source: *USA TODAY*, November 18, 2011, p. 2B, from comScore.

★ 2662 ★
Internet Sites

SIC: 4822; NAICS: 51711

Top Flowers, Gifts and Greetings Sites, 2012

Sites are ranked by millions of unique visitors for February 2012.

ProFlowers.com	5.4
AmericanGreetings.com	4.6
Gifts.com	3.6
1-800-Flowers.com	2.5
FTD.com	1.9

Source: ''comScore Media Metrix Ranks Top 50 U.S. Web Properties for February 2012.'' [online] from http://www.comscore.com [Press release March 21, 2012], from comScore.

★ 2663 ★
Internet Sites

SIC: 4822; NAICS: 51711

Top Internet Sites, 2012

Sites are ranked by millions of unique visitors for April 2012.

Google	188.9
Microsoft	171.1
Yahoo!	170.8
Facebook	158.6
AOL	110.8
Amazon	101.0
Wikimedia Foundation sites	85.4
Glam Media	80.9
Apple Inc.	79.1

Source: ''comScore Media Metrix Ranks Top 50 U.S. Web Properties for April 2012.'' [online] from http://www.comscore.com [Press release May 24, 2012], from comScore.

★ 2664 ★
Internet Sites

SIC: 4822; NAICS: 51711

Top Late-Night Show Sites, 2011

Market shares are shown based on visitors to the web sites.

The Daily Show	30.4%
The Colbert Report	11.9
Conan	11.5
The Tonight Show with Jay Leno	10.2
Nightline	8.7
Late Show with David Letterman	7.6
Late Night with Jimmy Fallon	5.6
Charlie Rose	3.0%
Chelsea Lately	2.7
The Soup	2.5
Other	5.9

Source: *New York Times*, May 9, 2011, p. B8.

★ 2665 ★
Internet Sites

SIC: 4822; NAICS: 51711

Top News Sites, 2012

Sites are ranked by millions of unique visitors for April 2012.

Yahoo!-ABC News	89.1
HPMG News	59.4
CNN Network	57.4
MSNBC Network	55.7
CBS News	39.3
USA Today	34.1

Source: ''comScore Media Metrix Ranks Top 50 U.S. Web Properties for April 2012.'' [online] from http://www.comscore.com [Press release May 24, 2012], from comScore.

★ 2666 ★
Internet Sites

SIC: 4822; NAICS: 51711

Top Online Dating Sites in China, 2010

Chinese dating sites saw an estimated 19 million visitors during 2010, according to Oppenheimer.

Jiayuan	44.0%
Zhenai	21.0
Baihe	16.0
Marry5	10.0
Other	9.0

Source: *Wall Street Journal*, July 5, 2011, p. C10, from iResearch and Oppenheimer & Co.

★ 2667 ★
Internet Sites

SIC: 4822; NAICS: 51711

Top Photo Sharing Sites, 2011

Sites are ranked by millions of unique visitors.

	(mil.)	Share
Flickr	31.5	29.4%
Photobucket	21.1	19.8
Instagram	11.0	10.2
Picasa Web Albums	9.1	8.5

Continued on next page.

★ 2667 ★

[Continued]

Internet Sites

SIC: 4822; NAICS: 51711

Top Photo Sharing Sites, 2011

Sites are ranked by millions of unique visitors.

	(mil.)	Share
Shutterfly	7.9	7.4%
Snapfish	5.4	5.0
TwitPic	4.9	4.6

Source: *New York Times*, April 16, 2012, p. B9, from Experian Hitwise.

★ 2668 ★

Internet Sites

SIC: 4822; NAICS: 51711

Top Real Estate Sites, 2011

Sites are ranked by millions of visitors.

Yahoo-Zillow	24.6
Move Inc. sites	15.6
Trulia	9.3
ForRent.com/Homes.com	6.7
MSN Real Estate	6.1

Source: *Investor's Business Daily*, June 17, 2011, p. A10, from comScore.

★ 2669 ★

Internet Sites

SIC: 4822; NAICS: 51711

Top Shipping Sites, 2011

Sites are ranked by millions of unique visitors as of October 2011.

UPS - United Parcel	14.4
U.S. Postal Service	13.0
FedEx	11.5
Stamps.com	1.2
DHL	0.6
Uline.com	0.6
Advanced Shipping Manager	0.3
Express Mail Services	0.2
Streamlite	0.2
iShip	0.1

Source: *New York Times*, December 12, 2011, p. B9, from comScore.

★ 2670 ★

Internet Sites

SIC: 4822; NAICS: 51711

Top Shopping Sites, 2011

Sites are ranked by millions of visitors for November 25-28, 2011.

	(mil.)	Share
Amazon	84.8	14.0%
Wal-Mart	56.6	9.0
Target	30.7	5.0
Best Buy	27.5	5.0
J.C. Penney	17.5	3.0
Sears	15.7	3.0
Kohls	14.4	2.0
Toys R Us	13.7	2.0
Macy's	13.5	2.0
Kmart	11.0	2.0

Source: *New York Times*, December 5, 2011, p. B8, from Experian Hitwise.

★ 2671 ★

Internet Sites

SIC: 4822; NAICS: 51711

Top Sites in Germany, 2011

Sites are ranked by millions of unique visitors.

Google	49.5
Facebook	39.8
Microsoft	35.2
eBay	27.9

Source: *Financial Times*, November 13, 2011, p. 12, from GP Bullhound.

★ 2672 ★

Internet Sites

SIC: 4822; NAICS: 51711

Top Sites in Russia, 2011

Sites are ranked by millions of unique visitors.

Mail.ru Group	38.0
Yandex	37.7
vKontakte	33.0
Google	29.8

Source: *Financial Times*, November 13, 2011, p. 12, from GP Bullhound.

★ 2673 ★
Internet Sites
SIC: 4822; NAICS: 51711

Top Social Networking Sites, 2011

Sites are ranked by millions of unique visitors as of July 2011.

Facebook	162
LinkedIn	33
MySpace	33
Twitter	33

Source: *USA TODAY*, September 13, 2011, p. B1, from comScore.

★ 2674 ★
Internet Sites
SIC: 4822; NAICS: 51711

Top Ticket Sites, 2011

Sites are ranked by millions of visitors for July 2011.

Ticketmaster	11.19
StubHub	3.93
Eventbrite	2.35
Eventful	1.74
Tickets	1.60
Zvents	1.26
Evenue.net	1.20
TicketsNow	1.11
FanSnap	0.73
Goldstar Events	0.67

Source: *New York Times*, August 29, 2011, p. B7, from Nielsen Company.

★ 2675 ★
Internet Sites
SIC: 4822; NAICS: 51711

Top Travel Sites, 2012

Sites are ranked by millions of unique visitors.

Google Maps	79.4
MapQuest	29.6
Yahoo!	15.2
TripAdvisor	13.2
Expedia	12.9
Priceline	12.2
Bing Maps	10.8

Source: *Investor's Business Daily*, May 30, 2012, p. A4, from NielsenWire.

★ 2676 ★
Internet Sites
SIC: 4822; NAICS: 51711

Top Video Sites, 2011

Sites are ranked by millions of visitors.

Google	152
Vevo	55
Facebook	51
Yahoo!	50
Viacom Digital	47
Microsoft	45
AOL	43
Hulu	31

Source: *Investor's Business Daily*, December 19, 2011, p. A5, from comScore.

★ 2677 ★
Massively Multiplayer Online Role-Playing Games
SIC: 4822; NAICS: 51711

Top MMORPG Makers Worldwide, 2009

A MMORPG (Massively Multiuser Online Role Playing Game) is a role playing game on the computer played by many people. Blizzard's World of Warcraft claimed 62% of the market in 2011.

Blizzard	22.0%
Shanda	12.0
Nexon	10.0
Netease	9.0
Ncsoft	7.0
Tencent	7.0
Other	33.0

Source: "Community Network Game Project." [online] from http://www.fines-cluster.eu [Published March 15, 2012], from Strategy Analytics.

★ 2678 ★
Online Gaming
SIC: 4822; NAICS: 51711

Top Facebook Games, 2011

Games are ranked by millions of monthly active users as of November 1, 2011. Developers are shown in parentheses.

CityVille (Zynga)	54.5
Sims Social (Electronic Arts)	38.3
Texas HoldEm Poker (Zynga)	29.9
Farmville (Zynga)	28.1
Empires & Allies (Zynga)	20.0

Source: *Wall Street Journal*, November 2, 2011, p. B1, from AppData.

★ 2679 ★
Online Music
SIC: 4822; NAICS: 51711

Online Music Spending Worldwide, 2010 and 2015

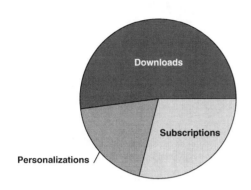

Total spending is projected to climb from $5.9 billion in 2010 to $6.3 billion in 2015. Sales are growing as consumers look to access their music through tablet computers, smartphones and other connected devices.

	2010	2015
Downloads	57.3%	52.4%
Personalizations	34.3	18.9
Subscriptions	8.4	28.7

Source: *Investor's Business Daily*, November 10, 2011, p. A4, from Gartner Inc.

★ 2680 ★
Online Video
SIC: 4822; NAICS: 51711

Top Online Video Providers in China, 2011

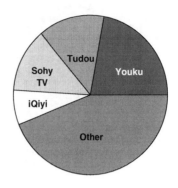

Market shares are shown for the fourth quarter of 2011. The industry was valued at 1.7 billion yen during this period. While China has long been a market for pirated materials, online providers have competed vigorously for the licensed content market. Youku agreed to acquire Tudou in a transaction valued at $684 million.

Youku	21.8%
Tudou	13.7
Sohy TV	13.3
iQiyi	6.9
Other	44.3

Source: *Wall Street Journal*, March 13, 2012, p. B4, from Analysys International.

★ 2681 ★
Video Game Digital Distribution
SIC: 4822; NAICS: 51711

Video Game Distribution Market, 2011

Data show the market for services that allow travelers to play games from their home console through their laptops.

Valve's Steam	70.0%
Spawn Lab's Impulse	10.0
Other	20.0

Source: ''Full Focus: GameStop and the Digital Future.'' [online] from http://www.nintendojo.com [Published April 23, 2011].

★ 2682 ★
Voice Over Internet Protocol
SIC: 4822; NAICS: 51711

Leading VOIP Providers, 2010

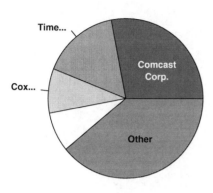

Voice Over Internet Protocol (VOIP) became commercially available in 2002. This service involves the making of phone calls over the Internet. This service is attractive to companies and users for a variety of reasons. For the provider, the cost of the infrastructure needed to make Internet calls is less than that needed to make land-line calls. For the user, calls are less expensive than land-line calls. While this industry is seen as being in its infancy, it already generated revenues of $12.3 billion in 2010.

Comcast Corp.	28.1%
Time Warner Cable Inc.	16.0
Cox Enterprises Inc.	9.3
Vonage Holdings Corp.	7.5
Other	39.1

Source: ''Voice Over Internet Protocol Providers in the U.S.'' [online] from http://www.ibisworld.com [Published June 2010], from IBISWorld.

★ 2683 ★
Voice Over Internet Protocol
SIC: 4822; NAICS: 51711

VOIP Subscribers Worldwide, 2010

A total of 120.4 million subscribers were reported during the fourth quarter of the year.

	(mil.)	Share
Western Europe	42.6	35.47%
Asia-Pacific	33.8	28.14
North America	30.7	25.56
South and East Asia	7.3	6.08
Latin America	4.3	3.58
Eastern Europe	1.4	1.17

Source: *Total Telecom*, July/August 2011, p. 20, from Point Topic.

★ 2684 ★
Wireless Payments
SIC: 4822; NAICS: 51711

Mobile Payment Transactions Worldwide, 2009-2014

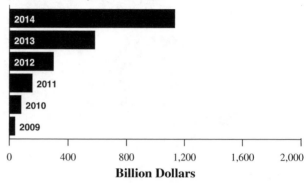

Billion Dollars

Data show volume in billions of dollars. The market's growth is expected to come from the popularity of smartphones, improved technology, the developments of apps, and customer needs.

2014	$ 1,130
2013	580
2012	298
2011	153
2010	78
2009	37

Source: ''Mobile Payments 2012.'' [online] from http://www.mobeyforum.org [Accessed May 1, 2012], from IE Market Research.

★ 2685 ★
Wireless Payments
SIC: 4822; NAICS: 51711

Top Operators of Mobile Financial Services, 2009

Market shares are shown in percent.

AT&T	35.0%
Verizon	24.0
T-Mobile	13.0
Sprint PCS	11.0
Nextel	2.0
Other	15.0

Source: *2010 EFT Data Book - A Supplement to ATM & Debit News*, September 24, 2009, p. 11, from Cellular Telecommunications Industry Association.

★ 2686 ★
Wireless Payments
SIC: 4822; NAICS: 51711

Wireless Cashless Payments in Small Ticket Self-Service Retail, 2011

The company controls 80% of the market for wireless, cashless payments for small ticket industries (excluding vending and kiosks).

USA Technologies	80.0%
Other	20.0

Source: "USA Technologies Company Overview." [online] from http://www.usatech.com/company_info/dl/USAT_company_overview.pdf [Published January 2012].

★ 2687 ★
Radio Broadcasting
SIC: 4832; NAICS: 515111, 515112

Internet Radio Market, 2011

Data show average active sessions among the top 20 stations and networks in the United States, Monday-Sunday 6AM-Midnight, September 2011. Terrestrial radio claimed 94.4% of all radio listening hours, Pandora 3.6% and other Internet radio 2.0%.

Pandora	66.0%
CBS	8.0
Clear Channel	8.0
Citadel	3.0
Slacker	3.0
Entercom	2.0
Other	10.0

Source: "Pandora." [online] from http://phx.corporate-ir.net [Published November 10, 2011], from Triton Digital.

★ 2688 ★
Radio Broadcasting
SIC: 4832; NAICS: 515111, 515112

Largest Talk Radio Audiences, 2011

Data show minimum weekly cumulative estimates for Monday-Sunday audiences, in millions. Numbers are based on sampling of Arbitron reports supported by other reliable indicators in rated and non-rated markets based on Spring 2011 data.

Rush Limbaugh	15.00
Sean Hannity	14.00
Michael Savage	9.00
Dave Ramsey	8.50
Glenn Beck	8.50
Mark Levin	8.50
Laura Ingraham	6.00
Neal Boortz	6.00
Doug Stephan	3.75
Jerry Doyle	3.75
Jim Bohannon	3.75
Michael Medved	3.75
Mike Gallagher	3.75

Source: *Talkers Magazine*, Annual 2011, p. NA, from Arbitron and *Talkers Magazine* research.

★ 2689 ★
Radio Broadcasting
SIC: 4832; NAICS: 515111, 515112

Producers of Taped Radio Programs, 2007

Data show the percent of industry sales held by the largest 4, 8, 20 and 50 firms in the sector. There are approximately 146 firms operating in the industry generating employment for 820 people.

4 largest firms	39.8%
8 largest firms	51.5
20 largest firms	67.9
50 largest firms	87.1

Source: "2007 Economic Census." [online] from http://www.census.gov/econ/concentration.html [Accessed August 12, 2011], from U.S. Bureau of the Census.

★ 2690 ★
Radio Broadcasting
SIC: 4832; NAICS: 515111, 515112

Sports Radio Market, 2005-2011

Data show the number of sports radio stations. Sports radio's market share grew from 2.1% to 3.4% during this period.

2011	677
2010	634
2009	587
2008	547
2007	530
2006	520
2005	500

Source: *SportsBusiness Journal*, February 13, 2012, p. NA, from Arbitron.

★ 2691 ★
Radio Broadcasting
SIC: 4832; NAICS: 515111, 515112

Top Radio Firms, 2010

Firms are ranked by revenues in millions of dollars.

Clear Channel Communications	$ 2,500
CBS Radio	1,400
Cumulus Media	1,000
Entercom	415
Cox Radio Inc.	385
Univision	334
Radio One Inc.	238
Emmis Communications	185
Hubbard Radio	177
Salem Communications Corp.	170

Source: *Radio Ink*, December 5, 2011, p. NA, from BIA/Kelsey.

★ 2692 ★
Television Broadcasting
SIC: 4833; NAICS: 51512

Leading Broadcast Television Firms, 2011

Firms are ranked by broadcast revenues in millions of dollars.

CBS Corp.	$ 5,615
Comcast Corp.	4,813
News Corp.	4,778
Walt Disney Co.	4,000
Univision Communications	1,769
Gannett Co.	770
Tribune Co.	767
Sinclair Broadcast Group	731
Hearst Corp.	711
Belo Corp.	649

Source: *Advertising Age*, October 3, 2011, p. 52, from AdAge DataCenter.

★ 2693 ★
Television Broadcasting
SIC: 4833; NAICS: 51512

Top Television Broadcasters, 2010

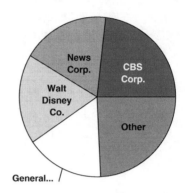

The industry generated revenues of $29.9 billion in 2010.

CBS Corp.	23.1%
News Corp.	18.5
Walt Disney Co.	18.5
General Electric Co.	16.1
Other	23.8

Source: "General Electric Company." [online] from http://www.docstoc.com [Published June 20, 2010], from IBISWorld.

★ 2694 ★
Cable Television
SIC: 4841; NAICS: 51521, 51711

Leading Cable Television Firms, 2011

Firms are ranked by cable broadcast revenues in millions of dollars.

Walt Disney Co.	$ 10,059
Time Warner	9,419
Viacom	6,476
Comcast Corp.	6,253
News Corp.	5,829
A&E Television Networks	2,774
Discovery Communications	2,363
Scripps Network Interactive	1,867
CBS Corp.	1,475
Liberty Media Corp.	1,247

Source: *Advertising Age*, October 3, 2011, p. 52, from AdAge DataCenter.

★ 2695 ★

Cable Television

SIC: 4841; NAICS: 51521, 51711

Top Cable Networks, 2010

Channels are ranked by millions of subscribers.

TBS	102.1
Discovery	101.9
ESPN	101.4
CNN	101.3
Food Network	101.3
USA Network	101.3
C-Span	100.9
ESPN2	100.9
HGTV	100.9
TLC	100.9
The Weather Channel	100.9
MTC	100.5
Fox News	100.4
Nickelodeon	100.4
Spike TV	100.4
TNT	100.4

Source: ''Top 25 Cable Programming Networks.'' [online] from http://www.ncta.com/Stats/TopMSOs.aspx [Accessed September 1, 2011], from SNL Kagan and *Economics of Basic Cable Networks.*

★ 2696 ★

Cable Television

SIC: 4841; NAICS: 51521, 51711

Top Cable Television Providers, 2011

Market shares are shown in percent.

Comcast Corp.	32.0%
Time Warner	14.0
Cox Enterprises	11.0
Charter Communications	5.0
Cablevision	3.0
Verizon	3.0
Other	33.0

Source: ''Cable and Satellite TV Industry.'' [online] from https://faculty.cit.cornell.edu/jl2545/4160/presentation/2012-presentation [Accessed May 1, 2012].

★ 2697 ★

Digital Video Recorders

SIC: 4841; NAICS: 51521, 51711

DVR Subscriptions, 2006-2014

Data show millions of subscribers.

2014	52.2
2012	46.4
2010	39.3

2008	29.8
2006	18.6

Source: *Broadcasting & Cable*, January 2, 2012, p. 32, from MagnaGlobal.

★ 2698 ★

Internet Protocol Television

SIC: 4841; NAICS: 51521, 51711

Top IPTV Providers Worldwide, 2010

Companies are ranked by millions of subscribers.

Free	3.53
France Telecom	1.98
Verizon	1.91
China Telecom	1.80
AT&T	1.04
PCCW	0.98
Neuf Cegetel	0.85
KPN Telecom	0.77
Hanaro Telecom	0.76
Korea Telecom	0.71

Source: ''Global IPTV Equipment Market and Provider Competition Analysis.'' [online] from http://www.frostchina.com [Published July 2009], from Frost & Sullivan.

★ 2699 ★

Pay Television

SIC: 4841; NAICS: 51521, 51711

Leading Pay Television Firms, 2011

Market shares are shown based on fourth quarter subscribers.

Comcast Corp.	22.1%
DirecTV	19.7
DISH Network	13.9
Time Warner Cable	12.0
AT&T	5.1
Verizon	4.7
Charter Communications	4.1
Cablevision	3.1
Other	14.8

Source: ''United States Telecommunications Report Second Quarter 2012.'' [online] from http://www.docin.com [Accessed June 1, 2012], from Business Monitor International and National Cable & Telecommunications Association.

★ 2700 ★
Pay Television
SIC: 4841; NAICS: 51521, 51711

Leading Pay Television Providers in Pan American Countries, 2010

Market shares are shown based on subscribers in Argentina, Venezuela, Colombia, Puerto Rico, Trinidad and Tobago, Ecuador, Peru and Chile as of September 30, 2010.

DirecTV PanAmericana	18.2%
Cablevisión	17.6
Telmex	13.1
Telefónica	7.4
VTR	5.1
Other	38.6

Source: "DirecTV PanAmericana." [online] from http://files. shareholder.com [Published December 2, 2010].

★ 2701 ★
Pay Television
SIC: 4841; NAICS: 51521, 51711

Top Multichannel Programming Distributors, 2011

Companies are ranked by millions of subscribers as of March 2011.

Comcast Corp.	22.76
DirecTV	19.40
DISH Network	14.19
Time Warner	12.35
Cox Communications Inc.	4.89
Charter Communications Inc.	4.49
Verizon	3.66
Cablevision	3.30
AT&T	3.20
Bright House Networks L.L.C.	2.17
Suddenlink Communications	1.21
Mediacom Communications Corp.	1.17
Insight Communications Co.	0.69

Source: "Top 25 Multichannel Video Programming Distributors." [online] from http://www.ncta.com/Stats/TopMSOs. aspx [Accessed September 1, 2011], from SNL Kagan.

★ 2702 ★
Satellite Broadcasting
SIC: 4841; NAICS: 51521, 51711

Top Satellite Television Providers, 2011

Market shares are shown in percent.

DirecTV	57.0%
DISH Network	37.0
Home2US Communications	1.0%
Other	6.0

Source: "Cable and Satellite TV Industry." [online] from https://faculty.cit.cornell.edu/jl2545/4160/presentation/2012-presentation [Accessed May 1, 2012].

SIC 49 - Electric, Gas, and Sanitary Services

★ 2703 ★
Electricity
SIC: 4900; NAICS: 221111, 221112, 221113
Global Power Generation, 2010

Market shares are shown in percent.

Nuclear	75.4%
Fossil-fired	9.8
Hydropower	7.9
Gas	5.5
Renewables	1.3

Source: *Financial Times*, November 15, 2011, p. 17, from company reports and Bloomberg.

★ 2704 ★
Renewable Energy
SIC: 4900; NAICS: 221111, 221112, 221113
Renewable Energy Spending Worldwide, 2010

Countries are ranked by new investment in renewable energy (large solar and wind farms and small residential solar installations). Spending on renewable energy increased 32% over 2009 to reach $211 billion. The boost can be attributed to soaring interest in renewables as well as the drop in solar cell prices.

China	$ 49.8
Germany	41.0
United States	29.6
Italy	13.8
Brazil	6.9
Canada	5.2
Spain	4.9
France	4.0
India	4.0
Czech Republic	3.6

Source: *USA TODAY*, July 8, 2011, p. 3B, from Bloomberg New Energy Finance and United Nations Environmental Programme.

★ 2705 ★
Electricity
SIC: 4911; NAICS: 221111, 221112, 221113
Electricity Generation, 2010 and 2035

Market shares are shown in percent.

	2010	2035
Coal	45.0%	39.0%
Natural gas	24.0	27.0
Nuclear	20.0	18.0
Renewables	10.0	16.0
Oil and other liquids	1.0	1.0

Source: "AEO2012 Early Release Overview." [online] from http://www.eia.gov/forecasts/aeo/er/pdf/0383er%282012%29.pdf [Accessed May 1, 2012], from U.S. Energy Information Administration.

★ 2706 ★
Electricity
SIC: 4911; NAICS: 221111, 221112, 221113
Energy Consumption, 2010 and 2035

Market shares are shown in percent.

	2010	2035
Oil and other liquids	37.0%	32.0%
Natural gas	25.0	25.0
Coal	21.0	20.0
Renewables	7.0	11.0
Nuclear	9.0	9.0
Liquid biofuels	1.0	4.0

Source: "AEO2012 Early Release Overview." [online] from http://www.eia.gov/forecasts/aeo/er/pdf/0383er%282012%29.pdf [Accessed May 1, 2012], from U.S. Energy Information Administration.

★ 2707 ★
Electricity
SIC: 4911; NAICS: 221111, 221112, 221113
Top Electricity Firms in China, 2010

The industry generated revenues of $355 billion in 2010.

China Southern Power Grid	52.3%
State Grid Corp. of China	47.7

Source: *Datamonitor Industry Market Research*, October 26, 2011, p. NA, from Datamonitor.

★ 2708 ★
Electricity
SIC: 4911; NAICS: 221111, 221112, 221113

Top Electricity Firms in Europe, 2010

The industry generated revenues of $567.4 billion in 2010.

FGC (RAO UESR)	15.5%
EdF	9.5
Enel S.p.A	2.9
E.ON AG	2.3
Other	69.8

Source: *Datamonitor Industry Market Research*, November 3, 2011, p. NA, from Datamonitor.

★ 2709 ★
Electricity
SIC: 4911; NAICS: 221111, 221112, 221113

Top Electricity Firms in France, 2010

The industry generated revenues of $50.7 billion in 2010.

EdF	77.2%
GdF-Suez	7.7
E.ON	4.4
Other	10.7

Source: *Datamonitor Industry Market Research*, October 26, 2011, p. NA, from Datamonitor.

★ 2710 ★
Electricity
SIC: 4911; NAICS: 221111, 221112, 221113

Top Electricity Firms in Germany, 2010

The industry generated revenues of $106.5 billion in 2010.

E.ON	17.0%
EnBW AG	12.4
RWE	10.4

Vattenfall	1.7%
Other	58.6

Source: *Datamonitor Industry Market Research*, October 26, 2011, p. NA, from Datamonitor.

★ 2711 ★
Electricity
SIC: 4911; NAICS: 221111, 221112, 221113

Top Electricity Firms in India, 2010

The industry generated revenues of $98.7 billion in 2010.

National Thermal Power Corp.	31.9%
Tata Power Company Ltd.	2.5
Reliance Energy Limited	1.6
Other	64.0

Source: *Datamonitor Industry Market Research*, October 26, 2011, p. NA, from Datamonitor.

★ 2712 ★
Electricity
SIC: 4911; NAICS: 221111, 221112, 221113

Top Electricity Firms in Japan, 2010

The industry generated revenues of $152 billion in 2010.

Tokyo Electric Power Company	30.8%
Kansai Electric Power Company	14.9
Chubu Electric Power Company	12.9
Kyushu Electric Power Company	8.8
Other	32.6

Source: *Datamonitor Industry Market Research*, November 3, 2011, p. NA, from Datamonitor.

★ 2713 ★
Electricity
SIC: 4911; NAICS: 221111, 221112, 221113

Top Electricity Firms in North America, 2010

The industry generated revenues of $440.8 billion in 2010.

CFE (Comision Federal de Electricided) . . .	4.8%
Hydro-Quebec Distribution	4.3
American Electric Power Company	3.9
Southern Company	3.7
Other	83.4

Source: *Datamonitor Industry Market Research*, October 26, 2011, p. NA, from Datamonitor.

★ 2714 ★
Electricity
SIC: 4911; NAICS: 221111, 221112, 221113

Top Electricity Firms in Russia, 2010

The industry generated revenues of $54.3 billion in 2010.

FGC (RAO UESR)	70.1%
RosEnergoAtom OAO	17.8
RusHydro	8.4
Other	3.7

Source: *Datamonitor Industry Market Research*, November 3, 2011, p. NA, from Datamonitor.

★ 2715 ★
Electricity
SIC: 4911; NAICS: 221111, 221112, 221113

Top Electricity Firms in the United Kingdom, 2010

The industry generated revenues of $57.6 billion in 2010.

EdF Energy U.K.	16.7%
RWE (nPower)	15.3
E.ON U.K. (formerly Powergen)	14.8
Centrica PLC	8.0
Other	45.2

Source: *Datamonitor Industry Market Research*, October 26, 2011, p. NA, from Datamonitor.

★ 2716 ★
Electricity
SIC: 4911; NAICS: 221111, 221112, 221113

Top Electricity Firms Worldwide, 2010

The industry generated revenues of $1.9 trillion in 2010.

China Southern Power Grid	11.8%
State Grid Corp. of China	10.7
FGC (RAO UESR)	3.7
Korea Electric Power Corp.	2.8
Other	71.0

Source: *Datamonitor Industry Market Research*, November 3, 2011, p. NA, from Datamonitor.

★ 2717 ★
Hydroelectric Power
SIC: 4911; NAICS: 221113

Top Nations by Hydroelectric Power, 2010

Market shares are shown based on total consumption of 775.6 million tons of oil equivalent.

Hong Kong	21.0%
Brazil	11.6
Canada	10.7
United States	7.6
Russia	4.9
Norway	3.4
Japan	2.5
Venezuela	2.2
Sweden	2.0
Other	34.1

Source: *BP Statistical Review of World Energy*, June 2011, p. 36.

★ 2718 ★
Nuclear Energy
SIC: 4911; NAICS: 221113

Top Nations by Nuclear Energy Consumption, 2010

Market shares are shown based on total consumption of 826.2 million tons of oil equivalent.

United States	30.7%
France	15.5
Japan	10.6
Russia	6.2
South Korea	5.3
Germany	5.1
Canada	3.2
Ukraine	3.2
Hong Kong	2.7
Other	17.5

Source: *BP Statistical Review of World Energy*, June 2011, p. 9.

★ 2719 ★
Solar Power
SIC: 4911; NAICS: 221113

Top States for Solar Power, 2010-2011

Data show the states with the most megawatts of electrical capacity from solar power installations.

	2010	2011	Share
California	259	542	33.27%
New Jersey	132	313	19.21

Continued on next page.

★ 2719 ★

[Continued]

Solar Power

SIC: 4911; NAICS: 221113

Top States for Solar Power, 2010-2011

Data show the states with the most megawatts of electrical capacity from solar power installations.

	2010	2011	Share
Arizona	63	273	16.76%
New Mexico	43	116	7.12
Colorado	54	91	5.59
Pennsylvania	47	88	5.40
New York	23	60	3.68
North Carolina	31	55	3.38
Texas	23	47	2.89
Nevada	61	44	2.70

Source: *USA TODAY*, March 14, 2012, p. 7A, from Solar Energy Industries Association and GTM Research.

★ 2720 ★

Utilities

SIC: 4931; NAICS: 221112

Top Electric Utilities, 2010

Firms are ranked by sales in millions of dollars.

Pacific Gas & Electric Co.	$ 10.7
Southern California Edison Co.	10.0
Florida Power & Light Co.	9.0
Georgia Power Co.	6.8
Virginia Electric & Power Co.	6.1
Duke Energy Carolinas L.L.C.	5.2
Consolidated Edison Co.-NY Inc.	5.1
Alabama Power Co.	4.6
Commonwealth Edison Co.	4.5
Progress Energy Florida Inc.	4.3

Source: "Top 10 U.S. Utilities by DSM Investment." [online] from http://smartgridresearch.org/wp-content/uploads/sgi_reports [Published March 2011], from U.S. Department of Energy.

★ 2721 ★

Water

SIC: 4941; NAICS: 22131

Top Water Companies, 2011

Companies are ranked by millions of people served.

American Water Works	16.80
CH2M Hill	4.00
Aqua America	3.00
California Water Service Corp.	2.18
SouthWest Water Company	1.42
Han's Technologies	1.13

American States Water Corp.	1.12
SJW Corp.	1.06
Utilities Inc.	1.05

Source: "Pinsent Mason Water Yearbook 2011-2012." [online] from http://wateryearbook.pinsentmasons.com [Accessed April 1, 2012], from Pinsent Mason.

★ 2722 ★

Incinerators

SIC: 4953; NAICS: 562211

Solid Waste Combustors and Incinerators, 2007

Data show the percent of industry sales held by the largest 4, 8, 20 and 50 firms in the sector. There are approximately 117 firms operating in the industry generating employment for 4,204 people.

4 largest firms	92.4%
8 largest firms	97.0
20 largest firms	98.9
50 largest firms	100.0

Source: "2007 Economic Census." [online] from http://www.census.gov/econ/concentration.html [Accessed August 12, 2011], from U.S. Bureau of the Census.

★ 2723 ★

Landfills

SIC: 4953; NAICS: 562212

Solid Waste Landfill Operation, 2007

Data show the percent of industry sales held by the largest 4, 8, 20 and 50 firms in the sector. There are approximately 1,501 firms operating in the industry generating employment for 21,766 people.

4 largest firms	56.1%
8 largest firms	63.2
20 largest firms	71.9
50 largest firms	81.3

Source: "2007 Economic Census." [online] from http://www.census.gov/econ/concentration.html [Accessed August 12, 2011], from U.S. Bureau of the Census.

★ 2724 ★
Materials Recovery
SIC: 4953; NAICS: 56292

Materials Recovery Facilities, 2007

This industry comprises establishments primarily engaged in operating facilities for separating and sorting recyclable materials from nonhazardous waste streams (i.e., garbage) and/or operating facilities where commingled recyclable materials, such as paper, plastics, used beverage cans, and metals, are sorted into distinct categories. Data show the percent of industry sales held by the largest 4, 8, 20 and 50 firms in the sector. There are approximately 1,133 firms operating in the industry generating employment for 15,803 people.

4 largest firms	33.3%
8 largest firms	38.2
20 largest firms	47.1
50 largest firms	59.9

Source: "2007 Economic Census." [online] from http://www.census.gov/econ/concentration.html [Accessed August 12, 2011], from U.S. Bureau of the Census.

★ 2725 ★
Waste Treatment and Disposal
SIC: 4953; NAICS: 562211

Hazardous Waste Collection, 2007

Data show the percent of industry sales held by the largest 4, 8, 20 and 50 firms in the sector. There are approximately 506 firms operating in the industry generating employment for 9,749 people.

4 largest firms	45.8%
8 largest firms	52.9
20 largest firms	65.3
50 largest firms	78.9

Source: "2007 Economic Census." [online] from http://www.census.gov/econ/concentration.html [Accessed August 12, 2011], from U.S. Bureau of the Census.

★ 2726 ★
Waste Treatment and Disposal
SIC: 4953; NAICS: 562211

Hazardous Waste Treatment and Disposal, 2007

Data show the percent of industry sales held by the largest 4, 8, 20 and 50 firms in the sector. There are approximately 751 firms operating in the industry generating employment for 34,444 people.

4 largest firms	44.6%
8 largest firms	59.2
20 largest firms	75.2
50 largest firms	87.5

Source: "2007 Economic Census." [online] from http://www.census.gov/econ/concentration.html [Accessed August 12, 2011], from U.S. Bureau of the Census.

★ 2727 ★
Waste Treatment and Disposal
SIC: 4953; NAICS: 562212

Top Waste Disposal Firms, 2010

Firms are ranked by revenues in millions of dollars.

Waste Management	$ 12,500
Republic Services Inc.	8,100
Veolia Environmental Services, North America Corp.	1,900
Clean Harbors	1,700
Covanta Energy Corp.	1,600
Stericycle Inc.	1,440
Progressive Waste Solutions Ltd.	1,430
Waste Connections	1,320
Newpark Resources Inc.	716
Recology Inc.	539
Casella Waste Systems Inc.	522
Rukpke Consolidated Companies Inc.	450
Waste Industries USA Inc.	397

Source: *Waste Age*, July 13, 2011, p. NA.

★ 2728 ★
Remediation and Environmental Cleanup Services
SIC: 4959; NAICS: 56291

Leading Providers of Remediation/Environmental Cleanup Services, 2009

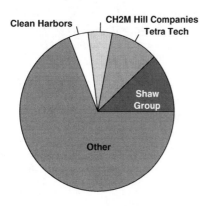

According to the source, the industry grew from $10.3 billion in 2004 to $13.8 billion in 2006, in the aftermath of Hurricane Katrina. In 2009, the industry was valued at $15.69 billion. More than 4,900 businesses operate in this sector, offering employment to nearly 91,000 people.

Shaw Group	12.0%
Tetra Tech	10.0
CH2M Hill Companies	5.3
Clean Harbors	4.0
Other	68.7

Source: ''BP Oil Spill: Cleanup Stocks to Watch.'' [online] from http://www.thestreet.com/story/10783927.html [Published June 15, 2010], from IBISWorld.

★ 2729 ★
Snow Removal Contractors
SIC: 4959; NAICS: 56179

Largest Snow Removal Contractors, 2009

Firms are ranked by revenues in millions of dollars.

Brickman Group	$ 122.8
USM	105.3
Lipinski Snow Services	30.7
Valleycrest Companies	30.0
Cintar Landscape Management	23.7
Arctic Snow & Ice Control	18.3
Ferrandino & Son	16.4
The True Green Cos.	13.1
Cenova	10.6
Professional Property Manintenance	9.5
True North Services	6.8

Source: *Snow Magazine*, October 2010, p. 46.

★ 2730 ★
Water Supply and Irrigation
SIC: 4971; NAICS: 22131

Top Water Supply and Irrigation System Firms, 2011

There were a total of 50,790 businesses operating in the United States during the year. They generated revenues of $62 billion.

American Water Works	4.9%
Aqua America	1.3
California Water Service Corp.	0.8
American States Water Corp.	0.6
Other	92.4

Source: ''Water Supply & Irrigation Systems in the U.S.'' [online] from http://www.ibisworld.com [Published February 2012], from IBISWorld.

SIC 50 - Wholesale Trade - Durable Goods

★ 2731 ★

Automobile and Motorcycle Wholesalers

SIC: 5012; NAICS: 42311

Automobile and Motorcycle Merchant Wholesalers, 2007

Data show the percent of industry sales held by the largest 4, 8, 20 and 50 firms in the sector. There are approximately 3,794 firms operating in the industry generating employment for 45,021 people.

4 largest firms	60.1%
8 largest firms	79.6
20 largest firms	93.6
50 largest firms	95.5

Source: "2007 Economic Census." [online] from http://www.census.gov/econ/concentration.html [Accessed August 12, 2011], from U.S. Bureau of the Census.

★ 2732 ★

Bus and Recreational Vehicle Wholesalers

SIC: 5012; NAICS: 42311

Bus and Recreational Vehicle Merchant Wholesalers, 2007

Data show the percent of industry sales held by the largest 4, 8, 20 and 50 firms in the sector. There are approximately 344 firms operating in the industry generating employment for 7,212 people.

4 largest firms	54.8%
8 largest firms	64.3
20 largest firms	73.4
50 largest firms	85.1

Source: "2007 Economic Census." [online] from http://www.census.gov/econ/concentration.html [Accessed August 12, 2011], from U.S. Bureau of the Census.

★ 2733 ★

Transmission Supplies Wholesalers

SIC: 5013; NAICS: 42312

Mechanical Power Transmission Supplies Merchant Wholesalers, 2007

Data show the percent of industry sales held by the largest 4, 8, 20 and 50 firms in the sector. There are approximately 1,582 firms operating in the industry generating employment for 16,308 people.

4 largest firms	48.0%
8 largest firms	60.4
20 largest firms	72.3
50 largest firms	81.9

Source: "2007 Economic Census." [online] from http://www.census.gov/econ/concentration.html [Accessed August 12, 2011], from U.S. Bureau of the Census.

★ 2734 ★

Tires

SIC: 5014; NAICS: 42313

Replacement Tire Shipments from Manufacturers, 2010

Local dealerships have fewer than 10 outlets in a single distribution area. Regional dealerships are independents with 10 or more outlets in at least two regions. National dealerships have more than 40 outlets in three or more regions.

National dealerships	33.0%
Local dealerships	22.0

Continued on next page.

621

★ 2734 ★

[Continued]

Tires

SIC: 5014; NAICS: 42313

Replacement Tire Shipments from Manufacturers, 2010

Local dealerships have fewer than 10 outlets in a single distribution area. Regional dealerships are independents with 10 or more outlets in at least two regions. National dealerships have more than 40 outlets in three or more regions.

General merchandise distributors	13.0%
Regional dealerships	11.0
Other	5.0

Source: *Tire Business*, February 13, 2012, p. 9, from Rubber Manufacturers Association.

★ 2735 ★

Furniture Wholesalers

SIC: 5021; NAICS: 42321

Household and Lawn Furniture Merchant Wholesalers, 2007

Data show the percent of industry sales held by the largest 4, 8, 20 and 50 firms in the sector. There are approximately 4,199 firms operating in the industry generating employment for 36,151 people.

4 largest firms	9.8%
8 largest firms	15.6
20 largest firms	25.1
50 largest firms	39.5

Source: ''2007 Economic Census.'' [online] from http://www.census.gov/econ/concentration.html [Accessed August 12, 2011], from U.S. Bureau of the Census.

★ 2736 ★

China, Glassware, and Crockery Wholesalers

SIC: 5023; NAICS: 42322

Household China, Glassware, and Crockery Merchant Wholesalers, 2007

Data show the percent of industry sales held by the largest 4, 8, 20 and 50 firms in the sector. There are approximately 649 firms operating in the industry generating employment for 8,260 people.

4 largest firms	26.3%
8 largest firms	37.8
20 largest firms	51.9
50 largest firms	70.3

Source: ''2007 Economic Census.'' [online] from http://www.census.gov/econ/concentration.html [Accessed August 12, 2011], from U.S. Bureau of the Census.

★ 2737 ★

Flooring

SIC: 5023; NAICS: 42322

Top Flooring Distributors, 2011

Firms are ranked by revenues in millions of dollars.

J.J. Haines & Co.	$ 275
BPI	191
NRF Distributors	145
CMH Space Flooring	140
William M. Bird & Co.	124
Apollo Distributing Co.	114
B.R. Funsten & Co.	106
Tri-West LTD	105
Ohio Valley Flooring	103
FlorStar Sales	102

Source: *Floor Covering Weekly*, October 17, 2011, p. 4.

★ 2738 ★

Linens and Draperies Wholesalers

SIC: 5023; NAICS: 42322

Linens, Domestics, Draperies, and Curtains Merchant Wholesalers, 2007

Data show the percent of industry sales held by the largest 4, 8, 20 and 50 firms in the sector. There are approximately 1,464 firms operating in the industry generating employment for 18,826 people.

4 largest firms	16.9%
8 largest firms	23.9
20 largest firms	38.8
50 largest firms	56.1

Source: ''2007 Economic Census.'' [online] from http://www.census.gov/econ/concentration.html [Accessed August 12, 2011], from U.S. Bureau of the Census.

★ 2739 ★

Lumber Agents and Brokers

SIC: 5031; NAICS: 42331

Lumber and Other Construction Materials Agents and Brokers, 2007

Data show the percent of industry sales held by the largest 4, 8, 20 and 50 firms in the sector. There are approximately 1,826 firms operating in the industry generating employment for 6,327 people.

4 largest firms	25.6%
8 largest firms	30.4
20 largest firms	36.5
50 largest firms	46.6

Source: ''2007 Economic Census.'' [online] from http://www.census.gov/econ/concentration.html [Accessed August 12, 2011], from U.S. Bureau of the Census.

★ 2740 ★

Office Equipment Wholesalers

SIC: 5044; NAICS: 42342

Office Equipment Merchant Wholesalers, 2007

Data show the percent of industry sales held by the largest 4, 8, 20 and 50 firms in the sector. There are approximately 6,415 firms operating in the industry generating employment for 140,472 people.

4 largest firms	45.4%
8 largest firms	59.3
20 largest firms	71.8
50 largest firms	78.3

Source: "2007 Economic Census." [online] from http://www.census.gov/econ/concentration.html [Accessed August 12, 2011], from U.S. Bureau of the Census.

★ 2741 ★

Computer Peripheral Wholesalers

SIC: 5045; NAICS: 42343

Computer and Computer Peripheral Equipment Merchant Wholesalers, 2007

Data show the percent of industry sales held by the largest 4, 8, 20 and 50 firms in the sector. There are approximately 9,635 firms operating in the industry generating employment for 276,716 people.

4 largest firms	33.0%
8 largest firms	44.2
20 largest firms	58.4
50 largest firms	72.1

Source: "2007 Economic Census." [online] from http://www.census.gov/econ/concentration.html [Accessed August 12, 2011], from U.S. Bureau of the Census.

★ 2742 ★

Computer Peripheral Wholesalers

SIC: 5045; NAICS: 42343

Computer and Peripheral Equipment For End Use Merchant Wholesalers, 2007

Data show the percent of industry sales held by the largest 4, 8, 20 and 50 firms in the sector. There are approximately 5,898 firms operating in the industry generating employment for 195,456 people.

4 largest firms	56.2%
8 largest firms	63.3

20 largest firms	72.0%
50 largest firms	82.0

Source: "2007 Economic Census." [online] from http://www.census.gov/econ/concentration.html [Accessed August 12, 2011], from U.S. Bureau of the Census.

★ 2743 ★

Computer Peripheral Wholesalers

SIC: 5045; NAICS: 42343

Computer and Peripheral Equipment For Resale Merchant Wholesalers, 2007

Data show the percent of industry sales held by the largest 4, 8, 20 and 50 firms in the sector. There are approximately 3,737 firms operating in the industry generating employment for 81,260 people.

4 largest firms	28.1%
8 largest firms	41.7
20 largest firms	61.7
50 largest firms	75.0

Source: "2007 Economic Census." [online] from http://www.census.gov/econ/concentration.html [Accessed August 12, 2011], from U.S. Bureau of the Census.

★ 2744 ★

Metal Sales Offices Wholesalers

SIC: 5051; NAICS: 42351

Ferrous Metal Sales Offices Merchant Wholesalers, 2007

Data show the percent of industry sales held by the largest 4, 8, 20 and 50 firms in the sector. There are approximately 3,575 firms operating in the industry generating employment for 30,693 people.

4 largest firms	41.0%
8 largest firms	50.4
20 largest firms	61.3
50 largest firms	70.7

Source: "2007 Economic Census." [online] from http://www.census.gov/econ/concentration.html [Accessed August 12, 2011], from U.S. Bureau of the Census.

★ 2745 ★
Coal Wholesalers
SIC: 5052; NAICS: 42352

Coal Merchant Wholesalers, 2007

Data show the percent of industry sales held by the largest 4, 8, 20 and 50 firms in the sector. There are approximately 265 firms operating in the industry generating employment for 2,499 people.

4 largest firms	44.5%
8 largest firms	61.6
20 largest firms	82.0
50 largest firms	93.4

Source: "2007 Economic Census." [online] from http://www.census.gov/econ/concentration.html [Accessed August 12, 2011], from U.S. Bureau of the Census.

★ 2746 ★
Communications Equipment Wholesalers
SIC: 5063; NAICS: 42361

Communications Equipment and Supplies Merchant Wholesalers, 2007

Data show the percent of industry sales held by the largest 4, 8, 20 and 50 firms in the sector. There are approximately 6,074 firms operating in the industry generating employment for 130,266 people.

4 largest firms	34.8%
8 largest firms	47.8
20 largest firms	64.2
50 largest firms	76.0

Source: "2007 Economic Census." [online] from http://www.census.gov/econ/concentration.html [Accessed August 12, 2011], from U.S. Bureau of the Census.

★ 2747 ★
Electrical Equipment and Wiring Wholesalers
SIC: 5063; NAICS: 42361

Electrical Equipment and Wiring Merchant Wholesalers, 2007

Data show the percent of industry sales held by the largest 4, 8, 20 and 50 firms in the sector. There are approximately 13,948 firms operating in the industry generating employment for 187,786 people.

4 largest firms	17.6%
8 largest firms	29.4
20 largest firms	41.7
50 largest firms	53.3

Source: "2007 Economic Census." [online] from http://www.census.gov/econ/concentration.html [Accessed August 12, 2011], from U.S. Bureau of the Census.

★ 2748 ★
Electronics Distribution
SIC: 5063; NAICS: 42361

Leading Electronics Distributors Worldwide, 2011

Market shares are shown in percent.

Ingram Micro	19.7%
Avnet	14.4
Tech Data Corp.	14.4
Other	51.5

Source: *Datamonitor Industry Market Research*, May 1, 2012, p. NA, from Datamonitor.

★ 2749 ★
Home Electronics and Appliance Wholesaling
SIC: 5064; NAICS: 42362

Top Home Entertainment and Appliance Wholesalers, 2010

The industry generated revenues of $88 billion in 2010.

Sony Corp.	11.5%
Panasonic Corp.	8.5
General Electric Co.	6.5
AB Electrolux	5.5
Other	67.0

Source: "General Electric Company." [online] from http://www.docstoc.com [Published June 20, 2010], from IBIS-World.

★ 2750 ★
Refrigeration Equipment Wholesalers
SIC: 5078; NAICS: 42374

Refrigeration Equipment and Supplies Merchant Wholesalers, 2007

Data show the percent of industry sales held by the largest 4, 8, 20 and 50 firms in the sector. There are approximately 1,318 firms operating in the industry generating employment for 13,158 people.

4 largest firms	27.1%
8 largest firms	37.5
20 largest firms	51.5
50 largest firms	67.6

Source: "2007 Economic Census." [online] from http://www.census.gov/econ/concentration.html [Accessed August 12, 2011], from U.S. Bureau of the Census.

★ 2751 ★
Materials Handling Equipment Wholesalers
SIC: 5084; NAICS: 42383

Materials Handling Equipment Merchant Wholesalers, 2007

Data show the percent of industry sales held by the largest 4, 8, 20 and 50 firms in the sector. There are approximately 3,800 firms operating in the industry generating employment for 65,729 people.

4 largest firms	10.8%
8 largest firms	15.7
20 largest firms	24.4
50 largest firms	37.3

Source: "2007 Economic Census." [online] from http://www.census.gov/econ/concentration.html [Accessed August 12, 2011], from U.S. Bureau of the Census.

★ 2752 ★
Valves and Fittings Wholesalers
SIC: 5085; NAICS: 42384

Industrial Valves and Fittings (Except Fluid-power) Merchant Wholesalers, 2007

Data show the percent of industry sales held by the largest 4, 8, 20 and 50 firms in the sector. There are approximately 1,224 firms operating in the industry generating employment for 15,051 people.

4 largest firms	12.9%
8 largest firms	21.0
20 largest firms	37.0
50 largest firms	55.9

Source: "2007 Economic Census." [online] from http://www.census.gov/econ/concentration.html [Accessed August 12, 2011], from U.S. Bureau of the Census.

★ 2753 ★
Custodial Equipment Wholesalers
SIC: 5087; NAICS: 42385

Custodial and Janitors' Equipment and Supplies Merchant Wholesalers, 2007

Data show the percent of industry sales held by the largest 4, 8, 20 and 50 firms in the sector. There are approximately 1,624 firms operating in the industry generating employment for 22,230 people.

4 largest firms	19.6%
8 largest firms	30.2

20 largest firms	45.8%
50 largest firms	59.6

Source: "2007 Economic Census." [online] from http://www.census.gov/econ/concentration.html [Accessed August 12, 2011], from U.S. Bureau of the Census.

★ 2754 ★
Foodservice Equipment and Supplies
SIC: 5087; NAICS: 42385

Top Foodservice Equipment and Supply Firms, 2010

Firms are ranked by annual sales in millions of dollars.

Edward Don & Co.	$ 552.0
TriMark USA Inc.	513.0
Wasserstrom Co.	457.0
Strategic Equipment & Supply Co.	224.0
The Boelter Companies	173.0
Bargreen-Ellingson Inc.	144.2
Hubert Co.	144.0
Singer Equipment Co.	126.6
Clark Associates	103.3
Stafford-Smith Inc.	101.0

Source: *Foodservice Equipment & Supplies*, March 28, 2011, p. NA.

★ 2755 ★
Aircraft and Aeronautical Equipment Wholesalers
SIC: 5088; NAICS: 42386

Aircraft and Aeronautical Equipment and Supply Merchant Wholesalers, 2007

Data show the percent of industry sales held by the largest 4, 8, 20 and 50 firms in the sector. There are approximately 1,668 firms operating in the industry generating employment for 27,086 people.

4 largest firms	38.8%
8 largest firms	48.7
20 largest firms	64.2
50 largest firms	76.8

Source: "2007 Economic Census." [online] from http://www.census.gov/econ/concentration.html [Accessed August 12, 2011], from U.S. Bureau of the Census.

★ 2756 ★
Marine Machinery Wholesalers

SIC: 5088; NAICS: 42386

Marine Machinery, Equipment, and Supplies Merchant Wholesalers, 2007

Data show the percent of industry sales held by the largest 4, 8, 20 and 50 firms in the sector. There are approximately 506 firms operating in the industry generating employment for 6,183 people.

4 largest firms	27.5%
8 largest firms	36.8
20 largest firms	51.9
50 largest firms	69.5

Source: "2007 Economic Census." [online] from http://www.census.gov/econ/concentration.html [Accessed August 12, 2011], from U.S. Bureau of the Census.

★ 2757 ★
Swimming Pools

SIC: 5091; NAICS: 42391

Swimming Pool Repair and Construction Market, 2011

The company is the leader with an estimated 33% of the market. It is also the world's largest distributor of swimming pool supplies, equipment and leisure products as well as one of the top three distributors of irrigation and landscape products in the United States. An estimated 70 million households have the room and the economic capacity for a pool, according to the source.

Pool Corp.	33.0%
Other	67.0

Source: "Pool Corp." [online] from http://www.zacks.com/ZER/zer_get_pdf.php?rZ869569&tPOOL&id21365 [Published May 2012].

★ 2758 ★
Toy and Hobby Goods Wholesalers

SIC: 5092; NAICS: 42392

Toy and Hobby Goods and Supplies Merchant Wholesalers, 2007

Data show the percent of industry sales held by the largest 4, 8, 20 and 50 firms in the sector. There are approximately 2,504 firms operating in the industry generating employment for 34,990 people.

4 largest firms	43.9%
8 largest firms	50.3

20 largest firms	59.5%
50 largest firms	70.3

Source: "2007 Economic Census." [online] from http://www.census.gov/econ/concentration.html [Accessed August 12, 2011], from U.S. Bureau of the Census.

★ 2759 ★
Recyclable Material Wholesalers

SIC: 5093; NAICS: 42393

Recyclable Material Merchant Wholesalers, 2007

Data show the percent of industry sales held by the largest 4, 8, 20 and 50 firms in the sector. There are approximately 7,377 firms operating in the industry generating employment for 104,671 people.

4 largest firms	16.1%
8 largest firms	23.4
20 largest firms	32.9
50 largest firms	43.6

Source: "2007 Economic Census." [online] from http://www.census.gov/econ/concentration.html [Accessed August 12, 2011], from U.S. Bureau of the Census.

★ 2760 ★
Recyclable Material Wholesalers

SIC: 5093; NAICS: 42393

Recyclable Paper and Paperboard Merchant Wholesalers, 2007

Data show the percent of industry sales held by the largest 4, 8, 20 and 50 firms in the sector. There are approximately 1,005 firms operating in the industry generating employment for 14,616 people.

4 largest firms	26.7%
8 largest firms	35.8
20 largest firms	49.5
50 largest firms	64.9

Source: "2007 Economic Census." [online] from http://www.census.gov/econ/concentration.html [Accessed August 12, 2011], from U.S. Bureau of the Census.

★ 2761 ★

Jewelry, Watch and Silverware Wholesalers

SIC: 5094; NAICS: 42394

Jewelry, Watch, Precious Stone and Silverware Merchant Wholesalers, 2007

Data show the percent of industry sales held by the largest 4, 8, 20 and 50 firms in the sector. There are approximately 7,317 firms operating in the industry generating employment for 48,811 people.

4 largest firms	7.3%
8 largest firms	11.2
20 largest firms	18.6
50 largest firms	28.7

Source: ''2007 Economic Census.'' [online] from http://www. census.gov/econ/concentration.html [Accessed August 12, 2011], from U.S. Bureau of the Census.

★ 2762 ★

Fire Safety Equipment Wholesalers

SIC: 5099; NAICS: 42399

Fire Extinguishers and Fire Safety Equipment Merchant Wholesalers, 2007

Data show the percent of industry sales held by the largest 4, 8, 20 and 50 firms in the sector. There are approximately 1,168 firms operating in the industry generating employment for 13,820 people.

4 largest firms	31.1%
8 largest firms	40.2
20 largest firms	49.1
50 largest firms	60.7

Source: ''2007 Economic Census.'' [online] from http://www. census.gov/econ/concentration.html [Accessed August 12, 2011], from U.S. Bureau of the Census.

SIC 51 - Wholesale Trade - Nondurable Goods

★ 2763 ★

Office Stationery Wholesaling

SIC: 5112; NAICS: 42412

Top Products Sold by Office Wholesalers, 2011

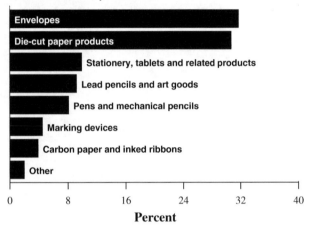

Percent

The industry has had many challenges in recent years, such as the recession, the rise of superstores and the increasing reliance on electronic communications. Because of these issues, revenues shrank 2.4% a year from 2006 to 2011. A total of 7,894 businesses generated revenues of $42.4 billion in 2011. By 2016, revenues are expected to be down to $41.3 billion. Some analysts have wondered if the market for printing paper, fax paper and stationery will be gone in 15 years. Office supply retailers claimed 35.7% of industry shipments, exports 15.7%, schools 15.4% and other sectors 33.2%. Industry leader Genuine Parts Company claimed an estimated 4% of the market, followed by United Stationers Inc. with an estimated 3.3%.

Envelopes	31.7%
Die-cut paper products	30.7
Stationery, tablets and related products	9.9
Lead pencils and art goods	9.2
Pens and mechanical pencils	8.1
Marking devices	4.5
Carbon paper and inked ribbons	3.9
Other	2.0

Source: "Office Stationery Wholesalers in the U.S." [online] from http://www.ibisworld.com [Published December 2011], from IBISWorld.

★ 2764 ★

Drug Wholesalers

SIC: 5122; NAICS: 42421

Drugs and Druggists' Sundries Merchant Wholesalers, 2007

Data show the percent of industry sales held by the largest 4, 8, 20 and 50 firms in the sector. There are approximately 8,535 firms operating in the industry generating employment for 259,412 people.

4 largest firms	43.9%
8 largest firms	55.7
20 largest firms	73.0
50 largest firms	84.2

Source: "2007 Economic Census." [online] from http://www.census.gov/econ/concentration.html [Accessed August 12, 2011], from U.S. Bureau of the Census.

★ 2765 ★

Drug Wholesalers

SIC: 5122; NAICS: 42421

General-line Drugs Merchant Wholesalers, 2007

Data show the percent of industry sales held by the largest 4, 8, 20 and 50 firms in the sector. There are approximately 4,764 firms operating in the industry generating employment for 86,938 people.

4 largest firms	74.6%
8 largest firms	79.4
20 largest firms	84.6
50 largest firms	90.1

Source: "2007 Economic Census." [online] from http://www.census.gov/econ/concentration.html [Accessed August 12, 2011], from U.S. Bureau of the Census.

★ 2766 ★
Apparel Agents and Brokers
SIC: 5131; NAICS: 42512

Apparel, Piece Goods and Notions Agents and Brokers, 2007

Data show the percent of industry sales held by the largest 4, 8, 20 and 50 firms in the sector. There are approximately 2,569 firms operating in the industry generating employment for 7,355 people.

4 largest firms	31.5%
8 largest firms	35.1
20 largest firms	41.0
50 largest firms	49.8

Source: "2007 Economic Census." [online] from http://www.census.gov/econ/concentration.html [Accessed August 12, 2011], from U.S. Bureau of the Census.

★ 2767 ★
Apparel Wholesalers
SIC: 5136; NAICS: 42432

Men's and Boys' Clothing and Furnishings Merchant Wholesalers, 2007

Data show the percent of industry sales held by the largest 4, 8, 20 and 50 firms in the sector. There are approximately 4,252 firms operating in the industry generating employment for 66,777 people.

4 largest firms	20.0%
8 largest firms	27.6
20 largest firms	41.2
50 largest firms	53.9

Source: "2007 Economic Census." [online] from http://www.census.gov/econ/concentration.html [Accessed August 12, 2011], from U.S. Bureau of the Census.

★ 2768 ★
Grocery Wholesalers
SIC: 5141; NAICS: 42441

General Line Grocery Merchant Wholesalers, 2007

Data show the percent of industry sales held by the largest 4, 8, 20 and 50 firms in the sector. There are approximately 2,547 firms operating in the industry generating employment for 128,987 people.

4 largest firms	39.5%
8 largest firms	52.6
20 largest firms	71.8%
50 largest firms	85.9

Source: "2007 Economic Census." [online] from http://www.census.gov/econ/concentration.html [Accessed August 12, 2011], from U.S. Bureau of the Census.

★ 2769 ★
Canned Food Wholesalers
SIC: 5142; NAICS: 42442

Nonperishable (Canned) Food Merchant Wholesalers, 2007

Data show the percent of industry sales held by the largest 4, 8, 20 and 50 firms in the sector. There are approximately 1,152 firms operating in the industry generating employment for 18,963 people.

4 largest firms	31.3%
8 largest firms	45.6
20 largest firms	62.6
50 largest firms	75.1

Source: "2007 Economic Census." [online] from http://www.census.gov/econ/concentration.html [Accessed August 12, 2011], from U.S. Bureau of the Census.

★ 2770 ★
Dairy Product Wholesalers
SIC: 5143; NAICS: 42443

Dairy Product (except Dried or Canned) Merchant Wholesalers, 2007

Data show the percent of industry sales held by the largest 4, 8, 20 and 50 firms in the sector. There are approximately 2,288 firms operating in the industry generating employment for 47,636 people.

4 largest firms	26.8%
8 largest firms	42.2
20 largest firms	63.3
50 largest firms	76.7

Source: "2007 Economic Census." [online] from http://www.census.gov/econ/concentration.html [Accessed August 12, 2011], from U.S. Bureau of the Census.

★ 2771 ★

Dairy Product Wholesalers

SIC: 5143; NAICS: 42443

Dairy Product (except Raw Milk) Merchant Wholesalers, 2007

Data show the percent of industry sales held by the largest 4, 8, 20 and 50 firms in the sector. There are approximately 2,177 firms operating in the industry generating employment for 46,036 people.

4 largest firms	26.1%
8 largest firms	43.3
20 largest firms	62.1
50 largest firms	75.3

Source: "2007 Economic Census." [online] from http://www.census.gov/econ/concentration.html [Accessed August 12, 2011], from U.S. Bureau of the Census.

★ 2772 ★

Fruit and Vegetable Wholesalers

SIC: 5148; NAICS: 42448

Fresh Fruit and Vegetable Merchant Wholesalers, 2007

Data show the percent of industry sales held by the largest 4, 8, 20 and 50 firms in the sector. There are approximately 5,074 firms operating in the industry generating employment for 104,749 people.

4 largest firms	8.8%
8 largest firms	15.0
20 largest firms	23.1
50 largest firms	32.4

Source: "2007 Economic Census." [online] from http://www.census.gov/econ/concentration.html [Accessed August 12, 2011], from U.S. Bureau of the Census.

★ 2773 ★

Coffee, Tea and Powdered Drink Wholesalers

SIC: 5149; NAICS: 42449

Coffee, Tea and Powdered Drink Mix Merchant Wholesalers, 2007

Data show the percent of industry sales held by the largest 4, 8, 20 and 50 firms in the sector. There are approximately 1,527 firms operating in the industry generating employment for 17,894 people.

4 largest firms	28.1%
8 largest firms	41.9
20 largest firms	59.1
50 largest firms	73.8

Source: "2007 Economic Census." [online] from http://www.census.gov/econ/concentration.html [Accessed August 12, 2011], from U.S. Bureau of the Census.

★ 2774 ★

Grain and Field Bean Wholesalers

SIC: 5153; NAICS: 42451

Grain and Field Bean Merchant Wholesalers, 2007

Data show the percent of industry sales held by the largest 4, 8, 20 and 50 firms in the sector. There are approximately 4,851 firms operating in the industry generating employment for 47,574 people.

4 largest firms	27.3%
8 largest firms	39.2
20 largest firms	56.7
50 largest firms	66.8

Source: "2007 Economic Census." [online] from http://www.census.gov/econ/concentration.html [Accessed August 12, 2011], from U.S. Bureau of the Census.

★ 2775 ★

Poultry Wholesalers

SIC: 5154; NAICS: 42452

Live Poultry Merchant Wholesalers, 2007

Data show the percent of industry sales held by the largest 4, 8, 20 and 50 firms in the sector. There are approximately 41 firms operating in the industry generating employment for 1,440 people.

4 largest firms	41.6%
8 largest firms	58.8
20 largest firms	87.4
50 largest firms	100.0

Source: "2007 Economic Census." [online] from http://www.census.gov/econ/concentration.html [Accessed August 12, 2011], from U.S. Bureau of the Census.

★ 2776 ★

Hides, Skins, and Pelts Wholesalers

SIC: 5159; NAICS: 42459

Hides, Skins, and Pelts Merchant Wholesalers, 2007

Data show the percent of industry sales held by the largest 4, 8, 20 and 50 firms in the sector. There are approximately 161 firms operating in the industry generating employment for 1,284 people.

4 largest firms	40.0%
8 largest firms	59.7
20 largest firms	80.4
50 largest firms	93.7

Source: "2007 Economic Census." [online] from http://www.census.gov/econ/concentration.html [Accessed August 12, 2011], from U.S. Bureau of the Census.

★ **2777** ★

Petroleum Products Wholesalers

SIC: 5172; NAICS: 42472

Petroleum Products Marketing Equipment Merchant Wholesalers, 2007

Data show the percent of industry sales held by the largest 4, 8, 20 and 50 firms in the sector. There are approximately 380 firms operating in the industry generating employment for 4,476 people.

4 largest firms	18.9%
8 largest firms	30.4
20 largest firms	48.8
50 largest firms	69.9

Source: ''2007 Economic Census.'' [online] from http://www.census.gov/econ/concentration.html [Accessed August 12, 2011], from U.S. Bureau of the Census.

★ **2778** ★

Beer and Ale Wholesalers

SIC: 5181; NAICS: 42481

Beer and Ale Merchant Wholesalers, 2007

Data show the percent of industry sales held by the largest 4, 8, 20 and 50 firms in the sector. There are approximately 2,142 firms operating in the industry generating employment for 105,889 people.

4 largest firms	14.0%
8 largest firms	19.1
20 largest firms	27.4
50 largest firms	37.6

Source: ''2007 Economic Census.'' [online] from http://www.census.gov/econ/concentration.html [Accessed August 12, 2011], from U.S. Bureau of the Census.

★ **2779** ★

Florist and Nursery Supply Wholesalers

SIC: 5193; NAICS: 42493

Flower, Nursery Stock & Florists' Supplies Merchant Wholesalers, 2007

Data show the percent of industry sales held by the largest 4, 8, 20 and 50 firms in the sector. There are approximately 4,218 firms operating in the industry generating employment for 58,864 people.

4 largest firms	7.5%
8 largest firms	12.1
20 largest firms	20.7
50 largest firms	33.5

Source: ''2007 Economic Census.'' [online] from http://www.census.gov/econ/concentration.html [Accessed August 12, 2011], from U.S. Bureau of the Census.

★ **2780** ★

Tobacco Wholesalers

SIC: 5194; NAICS: 42494

Leaf Tobacco Merchant Wholesalers, 2007

Data show the percent of industry sales held by the largest 4, 8, 20 and 50 firms in the sector. There are approximately 68 firms operating in the industry generating employment for 684 people.

4 largest firms	83.0%
8 largest firms	91.3
20 largest firms	97.0
50 largest firms	99.7

Source: ''2007 Economic Census.'' [online] from http://www.census.gov/econ/concentration.html [Accessed August 12, 2011], from U.S. Bureau of the Census.

★ **2781** ★

Art Goods Wholesalers

SIC: 5199; NAICS: 42499

Art Goods Merchant Wholesalers, 2007

Data show the percent of industry sales held by the largest 4, 8, 20 and 50 firms in the sector. There are approximately 3,758 firms operating in the industry generating employment for 30,044 people.

4 largest firms	5.7%
8 largest firms	10.4
20 largest firms	20.4
50 largest firms	33.3

Source: ''2007 Economic Census.'' [online] from http://www.census.gov/econ/concentration.html [Accessed August 12, 2011], from U.S. Bureau of the Census.

SIC 52 - Building Materials and Garden Supplies

★ 2782 ★
Home Improvement Stores
SIC: 5211; NAICS: 44411, 44419

Top Home Improvement Stores, 2011

Companies are ranked by sales in billions of dollars.

Home Depot	$ 67.9
Lowe's Companies	48.8
CCA Global Partners	10.1
Menards	8.3
Sherwin-Williams Co.	4.3
Tractor Supply	3.6
ProBuild Holdings Inc.	3.5
Fastenal	2.2
Abbey Carpet & Floor	2.1
Dal-Tile	1.9
84 Lumber Co.	1.4
ICI AkzoNobel Decorative Paints US	1.2

Source: *Home Channel News*, Top 500, 2011, p. NA.

★ 2783 ★
Lumber and Building Materials
SIC: 5211; NAICS: 44411, 44419

Top Lumber and Building Material Stores, 2011

A total of 51,813 businesses generated revenues of $101.2 billion. The collapse of the housing market has greatly affected the market, it but has also been affected by the rise of DIY spending, the rising price of lumber and the rise in remodeling spending. Professional contractors claimed 54.4% of the market, household consumers (homeowners) 30.2%, retailers for resale 4.5%, wholesalers for resale 3.4% and other 7.5%.

ProBuild Holdings Inc.	4.4%
Stock Building Supply Inc.	1.5
84 Lumber Co.	1.4
Other	92.7

Source: "Lumber & Building Material Stores in the U.S." [online] from http://lowes.retailforward.com [Published February 2011], from IBISWorld.

★ 2784 ★
Paint Stores
SIC: 5231; NAICS: 44412

Top Paint Store Chains in North America, 2010

Companies are ranked by store count.

Sherwin-Williams Co.	3,390
Akzo Nobel/ICI/Glidden	495
PPG Industries	392
Comex/Pro Paint Inc.	334
Kelly-Moore	162
Cloverdale/Rodda	111
Dun Edwards	108
Diamond Vogel	68
Benjamin Moore	65
Vista	49

Source: "Sherwin-Williams Company." [online] from http://investors.sherwin-williams.com [Published Second Quarter 2011], from *Chain Store Guide*, Rauch Guide and company reports.

★ 2785 ★
Hardware Stores
SIC: 5251; NAICS: 44413

Hardware Store Industry, 2012

A total of 15,903 businesses operate in this industry. Total revenues generated $22.1 billion. Do-it-yourself consumers claimed 69.5% of the market, contractors 19% and do-it-for-me consumers 11.5%.

Hardware, tools, plumbing and electrical supplies	58.1%
Lawn, garden and farm supplies	10.8
Paint and sundries	8.8
Lumber and other building materials	7.1
Other	15.2

Source: "Hardware Stores in the U.S." [online] from http://lowes.retailforward.com/RichMedia/RfMedia_634643927934460627.pdf [Published February 2012], from IBISWorld.

★ 2786 ★

Hardware Stores

SIC: 5251; NAICS: 44413

Leading Hardware Stores, 2010

Companies are ranked by sales in millions of dollars.

Ace Hardware	$ 834
Do-It-Best	454
True Value	411
Brookstone	69
Orchard Supply Hardware	39

Source: *HomeWorld Business*, September 19, 2011, p. 32, from *HomeWorld Business* estimates.

★ 2787 ★

Agricultural Retailing

SIC: 5261; NAICS: 44422

Top Agricultural Retailers, 2010

Firms are ranked by the number of outlets.

Agrium U.S. Rental	791
Growmark Inc.	663
Helena Chemical Company	334
Southern States Cooperative Inc.	211
Tennessee Farmers Cooperative	160
Wilbur-Ellis Company	156
MFA Inc.	130
J.R. Simplot	85
Jimmy Sanders Inc.	80
Harvest Land Co-Op	60

Source: *CropLife*, December 2011, p. NA.

SIC 53 - General Merchandise Stores

★ 2788 ★
Retailers
SIC: 5300; NAICS: 452111, 452112, 45291

Top Retailers of Consumer Packaged Goods, 2011

Market shares are shown in percent. The fastest-growing categories from 2010 to 2011 were energy drinks (16.7%), natural cheese (7.1%) and chocolate candy (6.6%).

Grocery stores	48.5%
Wal-Mart	19.4
Supercenters	18.4
Club stores	10.0
Convenience stores	9.8
Drug stores	5.8
Mass merchandisers	5.7
Dollar stores	1.8

Source: *Supermarket News*, March 19, 2012, p. 12, from SymphonyIRI Group Inc.

★ 2789 ★
Retailing
SIC: 5300; NAICS: 452111, 452112, 45291

Top Retail Sectors in Canada, 2011

Market shares are shown in percent. Costco was the leader in the warehouse sector. Canadian Tire, Wal-Mart Canada, Zellers, Giant Tiger Stores and Dollarama Stores were leaders in the mass merchandising sector. Alimentation Couche-Tard was the leader in the convenience store sector.

Grocery stores/supermarkets	63.5%
Mass merchandisers	11.7
Warehouse clubs	7.8
Drug stores	7.2
Convenience stores	6.0
Specialty stores	2.0
Gas stations	1.8

Source: "Canada Retail Food Sector Report." [online] from http://gain.fas.usda.gov [Published March 9, 2012], from Statistics Canada and ACNielsen.

★ 2790 ★
Retailing
SIC: 5300; NAICS: 452111, 452112, 45291

Top Retailers, 2010

Firms are ranked by retail sales in billions of dollars.

Wal-Mart	$ 307.7
Kroger	78.3
Target	61.2
Walgreen	61.2
Home Depot	60.1
Costco	58.9
CVS Caremark	57.6
Lowe's	48.1
Best Buy	37.1
Sears Holding	35.3
Safeway	33.2
Supervalu	30.9
Rite Aid	25.1
Publix	25.0
Macy's	24.8

Source: *Stores*, July 2011, p. NA, from Kantar Retail.

★ 2791 ★
Retailing
SIC: 5300; NAICS: 452111, 452112, 45291

Top Retailers in Mexico, 2009

Store-based retailers generated revenues of $2.9 billion in 2010.

Wal-Mart Stores Inc.	13.2%
Organizacion Soriana S.A. de C.V.	3.8
Fomento Economico Mexicano S.A. de C.V. (FEMSA)	2.7
Controladora Comercial Mexicana S.A. de C.V.	2.3
Other	77.0

Source: "Mexico: Market Concentration in Selected Agricultural and Food Subsectors." [online] from http://gain.fas.usda.gov [Published May 25, 2011], from Euromonitor.

★ 2792 ★
Department Stores
SIC: 5311; NAICS: 452111, 452112

Top Department Store Chains, 2010

Companies are ranked by retail sales in millions of dollars.

Sears	$ 35.36
Macy's	24.86
Kohl's	18.39
J.C. Penney	17.69
Nordstrom	9.62
Neiman Marcus	3.72
Belk	3.51
Bon-Ton	2.98

Source: *Stores*, July 2011, p. NA.

★ 2793 ★
Department Stores
SIC: 5311; NAICS: 452111, 452112

Top Department Stores in Japan, 2011

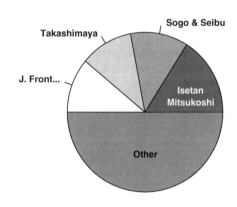

Market shares are shown in percent.

Isetan Mitsukoshi	15.8%
Sogo & Seibu	12.4
Takashimaya	11.1
J. Front Retailing	11.0
Other	49.7

Source: "7 And I Holdings Corporate Outline 2011." [online] from http://www.7andi.com/en/ir/pdf/corporate/2011_all.pdf [Accessed September 1, 2011], from Ministry of Economy, Trade and Industry.

★ 2794 ★
Hypermarkets
SIC: 5311; NAICS: 452111, 452112

Top Hypermarkets in China, 2008 and 2010

Market shares are shown in percent.

	2008	2010
Sun Art	10.6%	12.0%
Wal-Mart (incl. Trust Mart)	10.7	11.2
CRE	9.1	9.8
Carrefour	8.6	8.1
Shenzhen A-Best	5.2	4.0
Tesco	2.9	2.6
Renrenle	2.3	2.3
Other	50.6	50.2

Source: "Sun Art Retail Group." [online] from http://pg.jrj. com.cn/acc/Res%5CHK_RES%5CSTOCK%5C2011%5C8 %5C18%5Cf5468742-06ce-442f-a166-2763fd9f5bde.pdf [Published August 18, 2011].

★ 2795 ★
Convenience Stores
SIC: 5331; NAICS: 45299

Convenience Stores by State, 2011

Data are as of December 31, 2011.

	Outlets	Share
Texas	14,766	9.97%
California	10,763	7.27
Florida	9,510	6.42
New York	7,929	5.35
Georgia	6,535	4.41
North Carolina	6,269	4.23
Ohio	5,359	3.62
Michigan	4,865	3.28
Illinois	4,553	3.07
Virginia	4,512	3.05
Other	73,065	49.33

Source: *The Manufacturing Confectioner*, March 2012, p. 14, from Nielsen Convenience Industry Store Count and National Association of Convenience Stores.

★ 2796 ★
Convenience Stores
SIC: 5331; NAICS: 45299

Top Convenience Stores, 2010

According to the source, the industry continues to fragment. The top 100 retailers cumulatively experienced a decline of 63 stores from 2009 to 2010, while the total store industry store count grew by 1,800 stores (or 1.3%) in the past year. Alimentation Couche-Tard's store names include Circle K, Dairy Mart and Discount Beverage Outlet. Companies are ranked by number of stores.

7-Eleven Inc.	6,727
Shell Oil Products US/Motiva Enterprises L.L.C.	4,831
BP North America	4,718
Chevron Corp.	3,987
ExxonMobil Corp.	3,882
Alimentation Couche-Tard	3,480
Marathon Oil Co.	2,809
Sunoco Inc.	1,896
CITGO	1,776
Valero Energy Corp.	1,712
Casey's General Stores Inc..	1,667
The Pantry Inc.	1,667
Hess Corp.	1,287
ConocoPhillips Inc.	1,255

Source: *Convenience Store News*, May 23, 2011, p. NA, from Nielsen TDLinx.

★ 2797 ★
Convenience Stores
SIC: 5331; NAICS: 45299

Top Convenience Stores in Australia, 2010

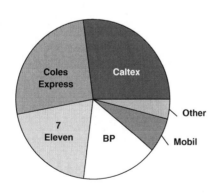

Market shares are shown in percent.

Caltex	27.3%
Coles Express	25.5
7 Eleven	19.7

BP	16.3%
Mobil	6.9
Other	4.3

Source: "Caltex Australia Limited." [online] from http://afr.com/rw/2009-2014/AFR/2011/05/09 [Published May 2011], from ACNielsen ScanTrack.

★ 2798 ★
Convenience Stores
SIC: 5331; NAICS: 45299

Top Convenience Stores in Japan, 2011

Market shares are shown in percent.

Seven-Eleven Japan	35.7%
Lawson	18.2
FamilyMart	17.4
Circle K Sunkus	10.3
Ministop	3.9
Other	14.5

Source: "7 And I Holdings Corporate Outline 2011." [online] from http://www.7andi.com/en/ir/pdf/corporate/2011_all.pdf [Accessed September 1, 2011], from Ministry of Economy, Trade and Industry.

★ 2799 ★
Convenience Stores
SIC: 5331; NAICS: 45299

Top Convenience Stores in Mexico, 2009

The industry generated revenues of $5.6 billion in 2010.

Fomento Economico Mexicano S.A. de C.V. (FEMSA)	73.9%
Seven & I Holdings Co. Ltd.	12.6
Grupo Modelo S.A. de C.V.	6.6
Other	6.9

Source: "Mexico: Market Concentration in Selected Agricultural and Food Subsectors." [online] from http://gain.fas.usda.gov [Published May 25, 2011], from Euromonitor.

★ 2800 ★
Convenience Stores
SIC: 5331; NAICS: 45299

Top Convenience Stores in Russia, 2010

Market shares are shown in percent.

Magnit	82.8%
Kvartal	11.0

Continued on next page.

★ 2800 ★

[Continued]

Convenience Stores

SIC: 5331; NAICS: 45299

Top Convenience Stores in Russia, 2010

Market shares are shown in percent.

Magnolia	4.2%
ABK	0.5
Other	1.5

Source: ''Russian Federation Retail Foods.'' [online] from http://gain.fas.usda.gov [September 2, 2011], from Euromonitor.

★ 2801 ★

Dollar Stores

SIC: 5331; NAICS: 45299

Top Dollar Store Chains, 2009

Companies are ranked by sales in billions of dollars.

	($ bil.)	Share
Dollar General	$ 11.8	42.91%
Family Dollar	7.4	26.91
Dollar Tree	5.2	18.91
Fred's	1.8	6.55
99 Cents Only	1.3	4.73

Source: ''Overview of the Retail Dollar Store Market.'' [online] from http://www.ats.agr.gc.ca/amr/4356-eng.pdf [Published May 2011].

★ 2802 ★

Outlet Centers

SIC: 5331; NAICS: 45299

Top Chains Primarily Tenanting Outlet Centers, 2010

Companies are ranked by number of stores. Apparel and shoe categories dominate the outlet sector, claiming 65% of the industry's chains and 72% of its stores. Linens and domestics dropped off the source's list, not having appeared since 2008.

Van Heusen	200
Nine West Outlet	198
L'eggs Hanes Bali Playtex	195
Bass Shoe Outlet	193
Gap Outlet	182
Carter's Outlets	173
Factory Brand Shoes	170
Ultra Diamond Outlet	170
Famous Footwear	169
Reebok/Rockport/Greg Norman	161

Source: *Value Retail News*, March 2011, p. 9.

★ 2803 ★

Supercenters

SIC: 5331; NAICS: 45299

Top Supercenter/Hypercenter Firms Worldwide, 2011

The industry generated revenues of $1.8 trillion.

Wal-Mart	23.2%
Carrefour S.A.	7.0
Tesco PLC	6.0
Metro A.G.	5.1
Other	58.7

Source: *Datamonitor Industry Market Research*, May 1, 2012, p. NA, from Datamonitor.

★ 2804 ★

Supercenters

SIC: 5331; NAICS: 45299

Top Superstores in Japan, 2011

Market shares are shown in percent.

Aeon Retail	12.2%
Ito-Yokado	10.5
UNY	6.0
Daiei	5.4
Other	65.9

Source: ''7 And I Holdings Corporate Outline 2011.'' [online] from http://www.7andi.com/en/ir/pdf/corporate/2011_all.pdf [Accessed September 1, 2011], from Ministry of Economy, Trade and Industry.

★ 2805 ★

Warehouse Clubs

SIC: 5331; NAICS: 45299

Top Warehouse Clubs in Mexico, 2009

The industry generated revenues of $7.8 billion in 2010.

Wal-Mart	77.1%
Controladora Comercial Mexicana S.A. de C.V.	13.2
Organizacion Soriana S.A. de C.V.	6.3
Casa Ley S.A. de C.V.	3.4

Source: ''Mexico: Market Concentration in Selected Agricultural and Food Subsectors.'' [online] from http://gain.fas.usda.gov [Published May 25, 2011], from Euromonitor.

★ 2806 ★
Warehouse Clubs
SIC: 5331; NAICS: 45299

Top Warehouse Clubs in North America, 2010

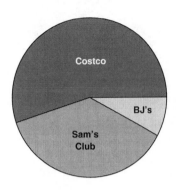

Clubs are ranked by North American sales in billions of dollars.

	($ bil.)	Share
Costco	$ 70.2	55.06%
Sam's Club	46.7	36.63
BJ's	10.6	8.31

Source: "An Insider's Guide to Retail Success 2011-2012." [online] from http://www.rx-edge.com/research%20pdfs/OTC_Health%5B1%5D.pdf [Accessed May 1, 2012], from Barclays Capital, Citigroup and Kantar Retail.

★ 2807 ★
Warehouse Clubs
SIC: 5331; NAICS: 45299

Top Warehouse Clubs in the North Central United States, 2010

Companies are ranked by number of outlets as of December 31, 2010.

	Outlets	Share
Sam's Club	163	73.09%
Costco	54	24.22
BJ's	6	2.69

Source: "Location Analysis." [online] from http://www.warehouseclubfocus.com/warehouse_club_industry/2011_selling_bjs_location_analysis.pdf [Accessed September 1, 2011], from *Warehouse Club* research.

★ 2808 ★
Warehouse Clubs
SIC: 5331; NAICS: 45299

Top Warehouse Clubs in the Northeastern United States, 2010

Companies are ranked by number of outlets as of December 31, 2010.

	Outlets	Share
BJ's	119	51.97%
Sam's Club	62	27.07
Costco	48	20.96

Source: "Location Analysis." [online] from http://www.warehouseclubfocus.com/warehouse_club_industry/2011_selling_bjs_location_analysis.pdf [Accessed September 1, 2011], from *Warehouse Club* research.

★ 2809 ★
Warehouse Clubs
SIC: 5331; NAICS: 45299

Top Warehouse Clubs in the Southeastern United States, 2010

Companies are ranked by number of outlets as of December 31, 2010.

	Outlets	Share
Sam's Club	130	49.06%
BJ's	69	26.04
Costco	66	24.91

Source: "Location Analysis." [online] from http://www.warehouseclubfocus.com/warehouse_club_industry/2011_selling_bjs_location_analysis.pdf [Accessed September 1, 2011], from *Warehouse Club* research.

SIC 54 - Food Stores

★ 2810 ★
Grocery Stores
SIC: 5411; NAICS: 44511

Grocery Sales by Channel, 2010 and 2015

Market shares are shown in percent.

	2010	2015
Traditional supermarkets	40.2%	34.1%
Supercenters	17.0	20.3
Convenience stores	15.4	15.8
Warehouse clubs	8.1	9.3
Drug stores	5.5	5.8
Limited-assortment stores	2.6	4.6
Super warehouse	1.9	2.4

Source: *Feedstuffs*, July 4, 2011, p. 6, from Willard Bishop.

★ 2811 ★
Grocery Stores
SIC: 5411; NAICS: 44511

Retail Food Sales, 2010

Market shares are shown based on sales at supermarkets, drug stores and mass merchandisers for the 52 weeks ended December 19, 2010. Wal-Mart data is also included in supercenters and mass merchandisers.

Grocery stores	49.4%
Wal-Mart	20.0
Supercenters	18.6
Drug stores	11.0
Club stores	9.4
Mass merchandisers	5.8
Dollar stores	1.7
Convenience stores	1.3

Source: *Refrigerated & Frozen Foods*, July 2011, p. 23, from SymphonyIRI Group Inc.

★ 2812 ★
Grocery Stores
SIC: 5411; NAICS: 44511

Top Grocery Retailers, 2011

Firms are ranked by sales in millions of dollars.

Wal-Mart	$ 311.0
Kroger	81.1
Costco	77.9
Safeway	41.0
Supervalu	37.9
Loblaw Cos.	30.6
Publix	25.1
Ahold USA	23.4
C&S Wholesale Grocers	19.3
Delhaize America	18.8
H.E. Butt Grocery Co.	16.1
Sobeys	15.6
7-Eleven Inc.	15.5
Meijer Inc.	14.2

Source: *Supermarket News*, Annual 2011, p. NA.

★ 2813 ★
Grocery Stores
SIC: 5411; NAICS: 44511

Top Grocery Stores in Atlanta, GA, 2010

Market shares are shown in percent.

Kroger	29.5%
Publix	23.5
Wal-Mart	22.5
Other	23.5

Source: *The Packer*, March 21, 2011, p. B7, from *Shelby Report*.

★ 2814 ★
Grocery Stores
SIC: 5411; NAICS: 44511

Top Grocery Stores in Bakersfield, CA, 2011

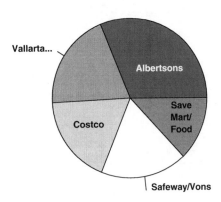

Market shares are shown in percent.

Albertsons	19.4%
Vallarta Supermarkets	11.9
Costco	10.9
Safeway/Vons	10.8
Save Mart/Food Maxx	8.3

Source: *Supermarket News*, April 25, 2011, p. NA, from Metro Market Studies.

★ 2815 ★
Grocery Stores
SIC: 5411; NAICS: 44511

Top Grocery Stores in Baltimore, MD, 2011

Market shares are shown in percent.

Giant Food	22.0%
Safeway	9.9
Shoppers	7.6
Food Lion/Bloom	6.4
Costco	5.5
Other	48.6

Source: *Supermarket News*, April 25, 2011, p. NA, from Metro Market Studies.

★ 2816 ★
Grocery Stores
SIC: 5411; NAICS: 44511

Top Grocery Stores in Birmingham-Hoover, AL, 2010

Market shares are shown based on area volume.

Wal-Mart	42.0%
Publix	17.0
Other	41.0

Source: *MMR*, June 20, 2011, p. 33.

★ 2817 ★
Grocery Stores
SIC: 5411; NAICS: 44511

Top Grocery Stores in Boston-Cambridge-Quincy, MA-NH, 2010

Market shares are shown based on area volume.

Stop & Shop	23.0%
Shaw's/Star Market	18.0
DeMoulas/Market Basket	17.0
Other	42.0

Source: *MMR*, June 20, 2011, p. 33.

★ 2818 ★
Grocery Stores
SIC: 5411; NAICS: 44511

Top Grocery Stores in Bridgeport-Stamford-Norwalk, CT, 2010

Market shares are shown based on area volume.

Stop & Shop	37.0%
ShopRite	13.0
Costco	9.0
Stew Leonard's	8.0
Other	32.0

Source: *MMR*, June 20, 2011, p. 33.

★ 2819 ★
Grocery Stores
SIC: 5411; NAICS: 44511

Top Grocery Stores in Bulgaria, 2010

Companies are ranked by sales in millions of dollars.

National Distributors (Cyprus) Ltd.	$ 85
Maxima	60
Familia (Equest)	45
Metro Group	30
Lidl & Schwarz	20
CBA Bulgaria	12

Continued on next page.

★ 2819 ★

[Continued]

Grocery Stores

SIC: 5411; NAICS: 44511

Top Grocery Stores in Bulgaria, 2010

Companies are ranked by sales in millions of dollars.

Fantastico	$ 11
Rewe AG (Germany)	11
Delta Maxi	8

Source: *Bulgaria Food & Drink Report*, July 2011, p. 71.

★ 2820 ★

Grocery Stores

SIC: 5411; NAICS: 44511

Top Grocery Stores in Canada, 2010

Firms are ranked by estimated sales in billions of dollars.

Loblaw Cos. Ltd.	$ 32.15
Sobeys	15.99
Metro	11.68
Costco Canada	6.88
Canada Safeway	6.85
Wal-Mart Canada	5.05
Co-ops	3.41
Overwaitea Food Group	2.97

Source: *Grocery Headquarters*, September 2011, p. 34, from CIBC World Markets, *Canadian Grocer* and *Annual Directory of Chains and Groups*.

★ 2821 ★

Grocery Stores

SIC: 5411; NAICS: 44511

Top Grocery Stores in Chicago-Naperville-Joliet, IL-IN-WI, 2010

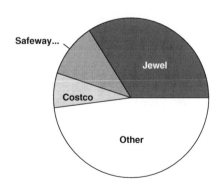

Market shares are shown based on area volume.

Jewel	34.0%
Safeway/Dominick's	11.0

Costco	7.0%
Other	48.0

Source: *MMR*, June 20, 2011, p. 33.

★ 2822 ★

Grocery Stores

SIC: 5411; NAICS: 44511

Top Grocery Stores in Cleveland-Elyria-Mentor, OH, 2010

Market shares are shown based on area volume.

Giant Eagle	29.0%
Wal-Mart	11.0
Heinen's	9.0
Other	51.0

Source: *MMR*, June 20, 2011, p. 33.

★ 2823 ★

Grocery Stores

SIC: 5411; NAICS: 44511

Top Grocery Stores in Dallas-Fort Worth-Arlington, TX, 2010

Market shares are shown based on area volume.

Wal-Mart	27.0%
Kroger	14.0
Safeway/Tom Thumb	12.0
Albertsons	8.0
Other	39.0

Source: *MMR*, June 20, 2011, p. 33.

★ 2824 ★

Grocery Stores

SIC: 5411; NAICS: 44511

Top Grocery Stores in Denver-Aurora, CO, 2010

Market shares are shown based on area volume.

King Soopers	32.0%
Safeway	19.0
Wal-Mart	14.0
Costco	10.0
Other	25.0

Source: *MMR*, June 20, 2011, p. 33.

★ 2825 ★
Grocery Stores
SIC: 5411; NAICS: 44511

Top Grocery Stores in Des Moines, IA, 2011

Market shares are shown in percent.

Hy-Vee	37.0%
Wal-Mart	33.0
Fareway	11.0
Affiliated Midwest	4.0
Super Target	4.0
Other	11.0

Source: *The Packer*, September 12, 2011, p. D1.

★ 2826 ★
Grocery Stores
SIC: 5411; NAICS: 44511

Top Grocery Stores in Detroit-Warren-Livonia, MI, 2010

Market shares are shown based on area volume.

Kroger	26.0%
Meijer	22.0

★ 2827 ★
Grocery Stores
SIC: 5411; NAICS: 44511

Top Grocery Stores in Fargo, ND, 2011

Market shares are shown in percent.

Hornbacher's/Supervalu	35.0%
Wal-Mart Supercenter	31.8
Coborn's/Little Duke's.	11.2
Sam's Club.	7.7
Sun Mart/Nash Finch	7.7
Other	6.6

Source: *Supermarket News*, April 25, 2011, p. NA, from Metro Market Studies.

★ 2828 ★
Grocery Stores
SIC: 5411; NAICS: 44511

Top Grocery Stores in Fresno, CA, 2010

Market shares are shown based on area volume.

Save Mart	29.0%
Costco	16.0
WinCo	11.0
Other	44.0

Source: *MMR*, June 20, 2011, p. 33.

★ 2829 ★
Grocery Stores
SIC: 5411; NAICS: 44511

Top Grocery Stores in Greece, 2010

Market shares are shown in percent.

Carrefour-Marinopoulos S.A.	9.2%
Alfa-Beta Vassilopoulos S.A.	5.5
Sklavenitis S&S S.A.	4.6
Lidl Hellas & Co. E.E.	4.3
Veropoulos Bros S.A.	3.0
Dimantis Masoutis S.A.	2.2
Atlantic S.A.	1.1
Metro S.A.	1.1
Other	70.0

Source: "Greece Retail Foods 2011." [online] from http://gain.fas.usda.gov [Published December 16, 2011], from Euromonitor.

★ 2830 ★

Grocery Stores

SIC: 5411; NAICS: 44511

Top Grocery Stores in Honolulu, HI, 2010

Market shares are shown based on area volume.

Food Land	22.0%
Costco	19.0
Times	17.0
Safeway	14.0
Don Quijote Food	9.0
Other	19.0

Source: *MMR*, June 20, 2011, p. 33.

★ 2831 ★

Grocery Stores

SIC: 5411; NAICS: 44511

Top Grocery Stores in Indianapolis, IN, 2010

Market shares are shown based on area volume.

Kroger	25.0%
Wal-Mart	22.0
Marsh	17.0
Meijer	10.0
Other	36.0

Source: *MMR*, June 20, 2011, p. 33.

★ 2832 ★

Grocery Stores

SIC: 5411; NAICS: 44511

Top Grocery Stores in Kansas City, MO, 2011

Market shares are shown in percent.

Wal-Mart	38.0%
AWG	23.0
Kroger	15.0

Hy-Vee	10.0%
Ball's	6.0
Other	8.0

Source: *The Packer*, September 12, 2011, p. D1.

★ 2833 ★

Grocery Stores

SIC: 5411; NAICS: 44511

Top Grocery Stores in Knoxville, TN, 2010

Market shares are shown based on area volume.

Wal-Mart	29.0%
Food City	22.0
Kroger	21.0
Other	28.0

Source: *MMR*, June 20, 2011, p. 33.

★ 2834 ★

Grocery Stores

SIC: 5411; NAICS: 44511

Top Grocery Stores in Lancaster, PA, 2010

Market shares are shown based on area volume.

Giant	27.0%
Weis Markets	23.0
Wal-Mart	9.0
Costco	8.0
Other	33.0

Source: *MMR*, June 20, 2011, p. 33.

★ 2835 ★

Grocery Stores

SIC: 5411; NAICS: 44511

Top Grocery Stores in Las Vegas-Paradise, NV, 2010

Market shares are shown based on area volume.

Wal-Mart	22.0%
Smith's Food & Drug	20.0
Albertsons	17.0
Other	41.0

Source: *MMR*, June 20, 2011, p. 33.

★ 2836 ★
Grocery Stores
SIC: 5411; NAICS: 44511

Top Grocery Stores in Los Angeles-Long Beach-Santa Ana, CA, 2010

Market shares are shown based on area volume.

Ralphs	16.0%
Safeway/Non's	13.0
Costco	11.0
Albertsons	10.0
Other	50.0

Source: *MMR*, June 20, 2011, p. 33.

★ 2837 ★
Grocery Stores
SIC: 5411; NAICS: 44511

Top Grocery Stores in Mexico, 2009

The industry generated revenues of $9.2 billion in 2010.

Wal-Mart	12.3%
Controladora Comercial Mexicana S.A. de C.V.	10.4
Organizacion Soriana S.A. de C.V.	7.2
Casa Ley S.A. de C.V.	3.9
H.E. Butt Grocery Co. (H-E-B)	3.2
Supermercados Organizados S.A. de C.V.	2.8
Other	60.2

Source: "Mexico: Market Concentration in Selected Agricultural and Food Subsectors." [online] from http://gain.fas.usda.gov [Published May 25, 2011], from Euromonitor.

★ 2838 ★
Grocery Stores
SIC: 5411; NAICS: 44511

Top Grocery Stores in Miami-Fort Lauderdale-Miami Beach, FL, 2010

Market shares are shown based on area volume.

Publix	52.0%
Winn-Dixie	10.0
Wal-Mart	9.0
Costco	8.0
Other	21.0

Source: *MMR*, June 20, 2011, p. 33.

★ 2839 ★
Grocery Stores
SIC: 5411; NAICS: 44511

Top Grocery Stores in Minneapolis, MN, 2011

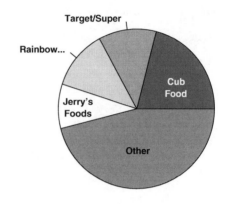

Market shares are shown in percent.

Cub Food	20.7%
Target/Super	11.9
Rainbow Foods	11.6
Jerry's Foods	9.3
Other	46.5

Source: *Supermarket News*, April 25, 2011, p. NA, from Metro Market Studies.

★ 2840 ★
Grocery Stores
SIC: 5411; NAICS: 44511

Top Grocery Stores in Nashville-Davidson-Murfreesboro, TN, 2010

Market shares are shown based on area volume.

Kroger	28.0%
Wal-Mart	22.0
Publix	17.0
Other	33.0

Source: *MMR*, June 20, 2011, p. 33.

★ 2841 ★
Grocery Stores
SIC: 5411; NAICS: 44511

Top Grocery Stores in Oklahoma City, OK, 2010

Market shares are shown based on area volume.

Wal-Mart	41.0%
Homeland	13.0

Continued on next page.

★ 2841 ★

[Continued]

Grocery Stores

SIC: 5411; NAICS: 44511

Top Grocery Stores in Oklahoma City, OK, 2010

Market shares are shown based on area volume.

Crest Foods	12.0%
Other	34.0

Source: *MMR*, June 20, 2011, p. 33.

★ 2842 ★

Grocery Stores

SIC: 5411; NAICS: 44511

Top Grocery Stores in Omaha, NE, 2011

Market shares are shown in percent.

Wal-Mart	35.0%
Hy-Vee	19.0
Affiliated Midwest	11.0
Nash Finch	8.0
Kroger	7.0
Other	20.0

Source: *The Packer*, September 12, 2011, p. D1.

★ 2843 ★

Grocery Stores

SIC: 5411; NAICS: 44511

Top Grocery Stores in Oregon, 2010

Market shares are shown in percent.

Safeway	22.0%
Fred Meyer	18.0
Wal-Mart	10.0
Albertsons	8.0
Costco	8.0
Other	34.0

Source: *Oregonian*, May 7, 2011, p. NA, from *Shelby Report*.

★ 2844 ★

Grocery Stores

SIC: 5411; NAICS: 44511

Top Grocery Stores in Philadelphia-Camden-Wilmington, PA-NJ-DE-MD, 2010

Market shares are shown based on area volume.

Acme	17.0%
Giant	12.0

Wawa	9.0%
Other	62.0

Source: *MMR*, June 20, 2011, p. 33.

★ 2845 ★

Grocery Stores

SIC: 5411; NAICS: 44511

Top Grocery Stores in Phoenix-Mesa-Scottsdale, AZ, 2010

Market shares are shown based on area volume.

Fry's	27.0%
Wal-Mart	18.0
Safeway	13.0
Bashas'	11.0
Costco	9.0
Other	22.0

Source: *MMR*, June 20, 2011, p. 33.

★ 2846 ★

Grocery Stores

SIC: 5411; NAICS: 44511

Top Grocery Stores in Pittsburgh, PA, 2010

Market shares are shown based on area volume.

Giant Eagle	35.0%
Wal-Mart	15.0
Other	50.0

Source: *MMR*, June 20, 2011, p. 33.

★ 2847 ★
Grocery Stores
SIC: 5411; NAICS: 44511

Top Grocery Stores in Providence, RI, 2011

Market shares are shown in percent.

Stop & Shop	38.8%
Shaw's	16.1
BJ's	6.2
Wal-Mart Supercenter	5.3
Price Rite	4.3
Other	29.3

Source: *Supermarket News*, April 25, 2011, p. NA, from Metro Market Studies.

★ 2848 ★
Grocery Stores
SIC: 5411; NAICS: 44511

Top Grocery Stores in Raleigh-Cary, NC, 2010

Market shares are shown based on area volume.

Food Lion	24.0%
Wal-Mart	19.0
Harris Teeter	18.0
Kroger	8.0
Other	31.0

Source: *MMR*, June 20, 2011, p. 33.

★ 2849 ★
Grocery Stores
SIC: 5411; NAICS: 44511

Top Grocery Stores in Russia, 2010

Market shares are shown in percent.

Pyaterochka (XS Group)	12.5%
Perekriostok (XS Group)	4.3
Dixie	2.9
Kopeyka	1.2
Monetka	1.2
Sedmoi Kontinent	1.2
Other	76.7

Source: "Russian Federation Retail Foods." [online] from http://gain.fas.usda.gov [September 2, 2011], from Euromonitor.

★ 2850 ★
Grocery Stores
SIC: 5411; NAICS: 44511

Top Grocery Stores in St. Louis, MO, 2010

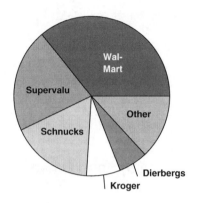

Market shares are shown in percent.

Wal-Mart	36.0%
Supervalu	21.0
Schnucks	17.0
Kroger	7.0
Dierbergs	6.0
Other	13.0

Source: *The Packer*, August 8, 2011, p. C8, from *Shelby Report*.

★ 2851 ★
Grocery Stores
SIC: 5411; NAICS: 44511

Top Grocery Stores in St. Petersburg-Tampa-Clearwater, FL, 2010

Market shares are shown based on area volume.

Publix	43.0%
Wal-Mart	16.0
Sweet Bay	14.0
Winn-Dixie	7.0
Other	20.0

Source: *MMR*, June 20, 2011, p. 33.

★ 2852 ★
Grocery Stores
SIC: 5411; NAICS: 44511

Top Grocery Stores in Salt Lake City, UT, 2010

Market shares are shown based on area volume.

Smiths Food & Drug	22.0%
Wal-Mart	18.0

Continued on next page.

★ 2852 ★

[Continued]

Grocery Stores

SIC: 5411; NAICS: 44511

Top Grocery Stores in Salt Lake City, UT, 2010

Market shares are shown based on area volume.

Associated/Fresh Markets	15.0%
Harmon's	11.0
Costco	10.0
Other	24.0

Source: *MMR*, June 20, 2011, p. 33.

★ 2853 ★

Grocery Stores

SIC: 5411; NAICS: 44511

Top Grocery Stores in San Francisco-Oakland-Fremont, CA, 2010

Market shares are shown based on area volume.

Safeway	29.0%
Costco	15.0
Lucky Stores	14.0
Trader Joe's	7.0
Other	35.0

Source: *MMR*, June 20, 2011, p. 33.

★ 2854 ★

Grocery Stores

SIC: 5411; NAICS: 44511

Top Grocery Stores in Seattle-Tacoma-Bellevue, WA, 2010

Market shares are shown based on area volume.

Safeway	22.0%
Quality Food Centers	15.0
Costco	12.0
Fred Meyer	10.0
Albertsons	8.0
Other	33.0

Source: *MMR*, June 20, 2011, p. 33.

★ 2855 ★

Grocery Stores

SIC: 5411; NAICS: 44511

Top Grocery Stores in South Africa, 2009

Market shares are shown in percent.

ShopRite Holdings	41.6%
Pick n Pay Retail Group	34.6

Spar Group	20.4%
Other	3.5

Source: "South Africa 2010 Annual Retail Food Sector." [online] from http://gain.fas.usda.gov [Published January 5, 2011], from Euromonitor.

★ 2856 ★

Grocery Stores

SIC: 5411; NAICS: 44511

Top Grocery Stores in South Florida, 2010

Market shares are shown in percent.

Publix	50.0%
Winn-Dixie	11.0
Other	39.0

Source: *Palm Beach Post*, February 12, 2011, p. NA.

★ 2857 ★

Grocery Stores

SIC: 5411; NAICS: 44511

Top Grocery Stores in the Caribbean, 2010

Companies are ranked by sales in millions of dollars.

Wal-Mart	$ 1,250
Kmart	420
A. Cordero Badillo (Food Price)	330
J.F. Montalvo Cash & Carry	250
Almacenes Pitusa	220
Supermercados Nacionel	175
SuperPlus Food Stores	125
Supermercados Pola	120
City Market	55
Super Value	50
Solomon's Hypermarket	30

Source: *Caribbean Food & Drink Report*, July 2011, p. 78, from Business Monitor International.

★ 2858 ★

Grocery Stores

SIC: 5411; NAICS: 44511

Top Grocery Stores in the Czech Republic, 2010

Market shares are shown in percent.

Lidl & Schwartz	22.0%
Rewe (incl. Tengelmann's Stores)	17.5
Ahold	10.0
Tesco	8.0

Continued on next page.

★ 2858 ★

[Continued]

Grocery Stores

SIC: 5411; NAICS: 44511

Top Grocery Stores in the Czech Republic, 2010

Market shares are shown in percent.

COP Jednote	7.3%
Other	35.2

Source: *Czech Republic Food & Drink Report*, July 2011, p. 29, from Business Monitor International.

★ 2859 ★

Grocery Stores

SIC: 5411; NAICS: 44511

Top Grocery Stores in the United Kingdom, 2011

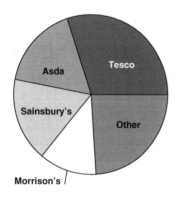

Market shares are shown for the 12 weeks ended December 25, 2011.

Tesco	30.1%
Asda	17.2
Sainsbury's	16.7
Morrison's	12.2
Other	23.7

Source: *Financial Times*, January 13, 2012, p. 15, from Kantar Worldpanel.

★ 2860 ★

Grocery Stores

SIC: 5411; NAICS: 44511

Top Grocery Stores in Tunisia, 2010

Market shares are shown in percent.

UTIC Group	34.9%
Mabrouk Group	33.3

Magasin Generale	30.6%
Other	1.0

Source: "Tunisia Retail Foods." [online] from http://gain.fas. usda.gov [Published December 26, 2011], from AgTunis.

★ 2861 ★

Grocery Stores

SIC: 5411; NAICS: 44511

Top Grocery Stores in Virginia Beach-Norfolk-Newport News, VA-NC, 2010

Market shares are shown based on area volume.

Food Lion	26.0%
Farm Fresh	20.0
Wal-Mart	18.0
Other	36.0

Source: *MMR*, June 20, 2011, p. 33.

★ 2862 ★

Grocery Stores

SIC: 5411; NAICS: 44511

Top Grocery Stores in Washington-Arlington-Alexandria, D.C.-VA-MD-WV, 2010

Market shares are shown based on area volume.

Giant Food	30.0%
Safeway	16.0
Costco	9.0
Shoppers	7.0
Other	38.0

Source: *MMR*, June 20, 2011, p. 33.

★ 2863 ★

Grocery Stores

SIC: 5411; NAICS: 44511

Top Grocery Stores in Worcester, MA, 2010

Market shares are shown based on area volume.

Stop & Shop	17.0%
Shaw's	13.0
Hannaford	12.0
Price Chopper	11.0
Wal-Mart	10.0

Source: *MMR*, June 20, 2011, p. 33.

★ 2864 ★

Organic Food Retailing

SIC: 5411; NAICS: 44511

Sales of Organic Food and Beverages in China, 2007

In 2007, more then 2,500 organic enterprises produced and sold organic products for domestic consumption and export. A total of 3.6 million hectares were used in organic production. Wild plants claimed the most acreage, followed by livestock, aquaculture and crops (tea, grains and produce).

Supermarkets/hypermarkets	37.0%
Small grocery retailers	30.0
Non-store retailing	3.0
Other store-based retailers	30.0

Source: "China's - People's Republic of Organics Report." [online] from http://gain.fas.usda.gov [Published October 26, 2010], from Euromonitor.

★ 2865 ★

Fish Markets

SIC: 5421; NAICS: 44522

Fish and Seafood Markets, 2007

Data show the percent of industry sales held by the largest 4, 8, 20 and 50 firms in the sector. There are approximately 2,063 firms operating in the industry generating employment for 10,012 people.

4 largest firms	4.1%
8 largest firms	7.0
20 largest firms	14.3
50 largest firms	25.6

Source: "2007 Economic Census." [online] from http://www.census.gov/econ/concentration.html [Accessed August 12, 2011], from U.S. Bureau of the Census.

★ 2866 ★

Farmers Markets

SIC: 5431; NAICS: 44523

Farmers Markets by State, 2011

According to the U.S. Department of Agriculture, more than 1,000 farmers markets opened over the previous year. Growth was strongest in Alaska, up 46%, and Texas, up 38%. A total of 7,175 were believed to be in operation during the year.

	Markets	Share
California	729	10.01%
New York	520	7.14
Michigan	349	4.79
Illinois	305	4.19

	Markets	Share
Ohio	278	3.82%
Pennsylvania	266	3.65
Massachusetts	255	3.50
Iowa	237	3.25
Wisconsin	231	3.17
North Carolina	217	2.98
Other	3,898	53.51

Source: *The Packer*, August 15, 2011, p. 1, from U.S. Department of Agriculture.

★ 2867 ★

Fruit and Vegetable Markets

SIC: 5431; NAICS: 44523

Fruit and Vegetable Markets, 2007

Data show the percent of industry sales held by the largest 4, 8, 20 and 50 firms in the sector. There are approximately 2,938 firms operating in the industry generating employment for 19,444 people.

4 largest firms	6.9%
8 largest firms	9.9
20 largest firms	15.9
50 largest firms	26.3

Source: "2007 Economic Census." [online] from http://www.census.gov/econ/concentration.html [Accessed August 12, 2011], from U.S. Bureau of the Census.

★ 2868 ★

Chocolate Retailing

SIC: 5441; NAICS: 445292

Premium Chocolate Sales, 2010

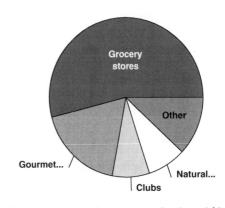

Premium chocolate sales generated sales of $2.2 billion.

Grocery stores	54.0%
Gourmet/specialty stores	18.0
Clubs	8.0

Continued on next page.

★ 2868 ★

[Continued]

Chocolate Retailing

SIC: 5441; NAICS: 445292

Premium Chocolate Sales, 2010

Premium chocolate sales generated sales of $2.2 billion.

Natural food stores 8.0%
Other 12.0

Source: *The Manufacturing Confectioner*, June 2011, p. 14, from Mintel.

★ 2869 ★

Bakeries

SIC: 5461; NAICS: 311811

Commercial Bakeries, 2010

Total shipments were valued at $25.61 billion. "NSK" stands for Not Specified by Kind.

	($ 000)	Share
Bread (white, wheat, rye, etc.), including frozen	$ 11,839,999	46.24%
Rolls, bread-type (including muffins, bagels, and croissants)	6,370,781	24.88
Soft cakes, excluding frozen . .	2,769,531	10.82
Commercial bakeries, nsk, total .	1,742,033	6.80
Pies (fruit, cream, and custard), excluding frozen	307,417	1.20
Other sweet goods, excluding frozen	2,578,073	10.07

Source: "Annual Survey of Manufactures." [online] from http://www.census.gov/manufacturing/asm/index.html [Accessed January 18, 2012], from U.S. Department of Commerce.

★ 2870 ★

Bread Retailing

SIC: 5461; NAICS: 311811

Bread Market Shares, 2010

The industry was valued at $36.5 billion.

Supermarkets 64.1%
Foodservice and hospitality markets 10.7
Convenience stores 10.3
Direct sales 7.5
Specialty stores 4.8
Exports 2.6

Source: "Specialty Foods Manufacturing: A Sectoral Analysis." [online] from http://www.cdtech.org/wp-content/uploads/2011/02/UCLA-Specialty-Foods-Sector-Analysis.pdf [Published Fall 2010], from IBISWorld.

SIC 55 - Automotive Dealers and Service Stations

★ 2871 ★
Auto Dealerships
SIC: 5511; NAICS: 44111

Top Auto Dealerships, 2011

Companies are ranked by new vehicle sales.

AutoNation Inc.	224,034
Penske Automotive Group Inc.	154,829
Sonic Automotive Inc.	114,132
Group 1 Automotive Inc.	102,022
Van Tuyl Group	96,139
Hendrick Automotive Group	69,676
Asbury Automotive Group	68,770
Staluppi Auto Group	54,225
Lithia Motors Inc.	44,537
Larry H. Miller Group of Cos.	30,865

Source: *Automotive News*, March 19, 2012, p. 14, from Automotive News Data Center.

★ 2872 ★
Used Car Retailing
SIC: 5521; NAICS: 44112

Top Sellers of Used Cars, 2011

The industry sold an all time high of 1,742,147 certified used cars and trucks. GM Certified includes Buick, Chevrolet, GMC, Pontiac and Saturn. Chrysler includes Chrysler, Dodge and Jeep.

Toyota Division	331,805
GM Certified	285,957
Honda Division	228,506
Chrysler Group	114,852
Ford Division	108,761

Source: *Automotive News*, January 23, 2012, p. 24, from Automotive News Data Center.

★ 2873 ★
Used Car Retailing
SIC: 5521; NAICS: 44112

Top Used Car Dealer Chains, 2011

There were a total of 119,450 businesses operating in the United States during the year. They generated revenues of $69.8 billion. Used vehicles claimed 37.2% of the total, parts and service 29.5%, finance and insurance 27.6% and other products 5.7%.

CarMax Inc.	12.8%
America's Car-Mart	0.5
Other	86.7

Source: "Used Car Dealers in the U.S." [online] from http://www.ibisworld.com [Published December 2011], from IBISWorld.

★ 2874 ★
Used Car Retailing
SIC: 5521; NAICS: 44112

Top Used Car Retailers, 2011

Companies are ranked by sales of used cars.

CarMax Inc.	396,181
AutoNation	171,094
Penske Automotive	129,652
Sonic Automotive	102,874
Van Tuyl Group	74,460

Source: *Automotive News*, March 26, 2012, p. 23, from Automotive News Data Center.

★ 2875 ★
Auto Parts Stores
SIC: 5531; NAICS: 44131

Top Auto Parts Chains, 2010

Companies are ranked by store count.

Autozone	4,404
O'Reilly Auto Parts	3,570
Advance Auto Parts	3,563
General Parts Inc.	1,500
Genuine Parts Co.	1,000
Pep Boys	612
Fisher APW	364

Continued on next page.

★ 2875 ★
[Continued]
Auto Parts Stores
SIC: 5531; NAICS: 44131

Top Auto Parts Chains, 2010

Companies are ranked by store count.

Auto Plus/Uni-Select	268
Replacement Parts Inc.	160
BWP Distributors Inc.	125

Source: *Counterman*, February 2011, p. 48.

★ 2876 ★
Tire Retailing
SIC: 5531; NAICS: 44132

Retail Tire Sales, 2011

Data refer to sales conducted offline. An estimated 21% of shoppers buy tires online.

National tire/service centers	49.0%
Local tire stores	19.0
Retail stores	10.0
Warehouse stores	10.0
Auto dealerships	7.0
Other	5.0

Source: *Tire Business*, April 9, 2012, p. 17, from *Google Inc. Complete Vehicle Tire Shopper Study.*

★ 2877 ★
Tire Retailing
SIC: 5531; NAICS: 44132

Top Tire Dealerships, 2010

Companies are ranked by retail sales in millions of dollars.

Discount Tire Co.	$ 3,310.0
Tire Kingdom	2,250.0
Les Schwab Tire Centers	1,242.9
Pep Boys - Manny, Moe & Jack	1,050.0
Kal Tire	410.0
Monro Muffler Brake	309.8
Best One Tire & Service	210.0
Belle Tire Distributors	200.0
Fountain Tire	189.3
Dunlap & Kyle	125.3

Source: *Tire Business*, October 24, 2011, p. 21.

★ 2878 ★
Gas Stations
SIC: 5541; NAICS: 44719

Top Gas Station Firms, 2011

The industry generated revenues of $106 billion in 2011.

Royal Dutch/Shell Group	12.2%
BP PLC	10.0
Chevron	7.3
Marathon Petroleum Co.	5.4
Other	65.1

Source: "Gas Stations in the U.S." [online] from http://www.ibisworld.com [Published October 2011], from IBISWorld.

★ 2879 ★
Gas Stations
SIC: 5541; NAICS: 44719

Top Refinery-Branded Gas Stations, 2010

Companies are ranked by number of outlets.

CITGO Petroleum Corp.	6,500
Sunoco Inc.	4,711
Marathon Petroleum Co.	4,613
Valero Energy Corp.	4,000
Sinclair Oil Co.	2,600
Speedway SuperAmerica L.L.C.	1,603
CHS (Cenex)	1,600
Hess	1,357
Getty Petroleum	1,000
Alon USA	900

Source: *National Petroleum News*, MarketFacts 2010, p. NA.

★ 2880 ★
Boat Dealers
SIC: 5551; NAICS: 441222

Boat Dealers, 2007

Data show the percent of industry sales held by the largest 4, 8, 20 and 50 firms in the sector. There are approximately 5,735 firms operating in the industry generating employment for 44,258 people.

4 largest firms	15.5%
8 largest firms	18.1
20 largest firms	21.9
50 largest firms	27.8

Source: "2007 Economic Census." [online] from http://www.census.gov/econ/concentration.html [Accessed August 12, 2011], from U.S. Bureau of the Census.

★ 2881 ★

Motorcycle and Powersports Dealers

SIC: 5571; NAICS: 441221

Motorcycle and Powersports Dealers, 2011

Data show the players in the industry by type of business.

New and used unit sales - single location . . .	45.8%
Service	23.6
Used unit sales only	7.0
Accessory/apparel shop	4.7
New and used powersports dealers - multiple locations	3.8
Other	15.0

Source: *MPN - Motorcycle & Powersports News*, February 2012, p. 30.

SIC 56 - Apparel and Accessory Stores

★ 2882 ★

Apparel Retailing

SIC: 5611; NAICS: 44811

Men's Apparel Sales, 2011

The industry generated revenues of $104.6 billion.

Clothing/footwear retailers	53.2%
Department stores	23.5
Hypermarkets, supermarkets and discounters	15.7
Discount/general merchandise retailers . . .	5.9
Other	1.8

Source: *Datamonitor Industry Market Research*, February 2, 2012, p. NA, from Datamonitor.

★ 2883 ★

Apparel Retailing

SIC: 5611; NAICS: 44811

Men's Specialty Clothing Market, 2010

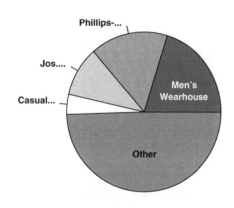

The men's clothing store industry generates approximately $9 billion in annual sales. Suits and formalwear claimed 31.9% of the market, shirts and T-shirts 23.3% and casual slacks 13.6% and other sectors 31.2%.

Men's Wearhouse	20.2%
Phillips-Van Heusen Corp.	16.0
Jos. A. Bank Clothiers Inc.	10.3
Casual Male	4.4
Other	49.1

Source: *Atlanta Business Chronicle*, August 26, 2011, p. NA, from IBISWorld.

★ 2884 ★

Apparel Retailing

SIC: 5611; NAICS: 44811

Top Men's Suit Retailers, 2007

Market shares are shown in percent. In 2011, men's suit sales rose 23% over 2010, part of a trend in increased sales in men's dress apparel, with sales of men's dress shirts up 14% and men's sports coats up 20%.

Men's Wearhouse	18.0%
Macy's	8.0
J.C. Penney	6.0
Nordstrom	5.0
Burlington Coat Factory	3.0
Dollar General	3.0
Jos. A. Bank Clothiers Inc.	3.0
Marshalls	3.0
Wal-Mart	3.0
Other	48.0

Source: "Men's Wearhouse." [online] from http://www.cfaso-ciety.org/memphis/Linked%20Files/Men%27s%20Wearhouse-Written.pdf [Published April 3, 2008], from NPD Fashion-world.

★ 2885 ★

Apparel Retailing

SIC: 5621; NAICS: 44812

Top Women's Clothing Stores, 2011

The industry generated revenues of $40.6 billion in 2011. T-shirts, knit and woven shirts, blouses and sweaters claimed 32% of the total, pants, jeans, shorts and skirts 24%, dresses 18% and other sectors 27%.

Ann Taylor Stores Inc.	5.2%
Charming Shoppes Inc.	5.1
Other	89.7

Source: "Women's Clothing Stores in the U.S." [online] from http://www.ibisworld.com [Published August 2011], from IBISWorld.

★ 2886 ★
Apparel Retailing
SIC: 5621; NAICS: 44819

Women's Jean Sales, 2010-2011

Women's jeans sales generated sales of $8.6 billion for the 12 months ended September 30, up 3.2% over the same period a year earlier. This gives jeans approximately 10% of the sportswear market.

	2010	2011
Specialty stores	39.4%	42.4%
Department stores	14.8	13.4
National chains	13.2	12.6
Mass merchants	13.8	12.4
Off-price retailers	9.8	9.6
Direct mail/e-tail pureplays	4.3	4.4
Other	4.7	5.2

Source: *WWD*, November 9, 2011, p. 2B, from NPD Group Inc.

★ 2887 ★
Apparel Retailing
SIC: 5632; NAICS: 44819

Largest Luxury Handbag and Accessory Stores in China, 2010

Companies are ranked by number of retail stores.

Bally	56
Burberry	53
Coach	43
Gucci	39
Louis Vuitton	34
Lance	28
Botega Veneta	21
Hermes	20
Marc Jacobs	19

Source: "Overview of Global and China Luxury Markets." [online] from http://www.research.hsbc.com [Published December 9, 2011], from Bank of America Merrill Lynch.

★ 2888 ★
Apparel Retailing
SIC: 5632; NAICS: 44819

Low-Cost Wedding Dress Sales, 2010

David's Bridal claims 20-30% of the overall $2.0 billion wedding dress retail market. It claims an estimated 50% of the $600-and-under wedding dress market.

David's Bridal	50.0%
Other	50.0

Source: "The Wal-Mart of Weddings." [online] from http://www.msnbc.msn.com/id/31324765/ns/business-us_business/ [Published June 15, 2011].

★ 2889 ★
Apparel Retailing
SIC: 5632; NAICS: 44815

Retail Handbag Sales, 2011

Total retail sales were $8.5 billion.

Specialty stores	30.0%
Department stores	18.0
Mass merchants	10.0
National chains	9.0
Internet pureplays	5.0
Home shopping	3.0
Other	25.0

Source: *Accessories Magazine*, Annual 2012, p. 18, from NPD Group Consumer Tracking Service.

★ 2890 ★
Apparel Retailing
SIC: 5632; NAICS: 44819

Retail Lingerie Sales, 2011

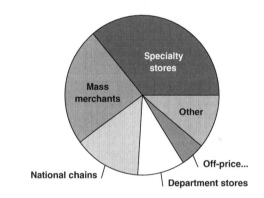

Market shares are shown in percent.

Specialty stores	36.0%
Mass merchants	24.0
National chains	14.0
Department stores	10.0
Off-price retailers	5.0
Other	11.0

Source: "MaidenForm Company Overview." [online] from http://solutions.standardandpoors.com/SP/stkscreener [Published March 27, 2012], from NPD Group Inc.

★ 2891 ★

Apparel Retailing

SIC: 5632; NAICS: 44815

Women's Hosiery Sales, 2011

Total sales were $2.7 billion.

Mass merchants	35.0%
Specialty stores	17.0
Off-price/factory outlet/warehouse clubs	13.0
Department stores	12.0
National chains	11.0
Other	10.2

Source: *Accessories Magazine*, Annual 2012, p. 28, from NPD Group Consumer Tracking Service.

★ 2892 ★

Apparel Retailing

SIC: 5641; NAICS: 44813

Retail Children's Apparel Sales in China, 2009

Market shares are shown in percent.

Department stores	40.1%
Independent stores	34.5
Wholesalers	16.5
Online stores	5.8
Catalogs	0.8
Child and maternity specialty stores	0.4
Other	1.9

Source: "A Rising Children's Products Developer and Retailer." [online] from http://www.bocomgroup.com/mediafiles/documents/p2_5823_en.pdf [Published March 7, 2011], from Frost & Sullivan.

★ 2893 ★

Apparel Retailing

SIC: 5641; NAICS: 44813

Top Children's and Infants' Clothing Stores, 2011

The industry generated revenues of $9.7 billion in 2011.

Toys R Us	33.0%
Children's Place Retail Stores Inc.	14.8
Gymboree Corp.	11.8
Dressbarn Inc.	10.5
Carter's Inc.	9.6
Other	20.3

Source: "Children's and Infants' Clothing Stores in the U.S." [online] from http://www.ibisworld.com [Published September 2011], from IBISWorld.

★ 2894 ★

Apparel Retailing

SIC: 5641; NAICS: 45112

Top Childrenswear Retailers, 2011

The retail industry was valued at $54.3 billion in 2011.

Clothing and footwear retailers	64.3%
Hypermarkets, supermarkets and discounters	14.2
Department stores	13.6
Discount/general merchandise retailers	7.7
Other	0.2

Source: *Datamonitor Industry Market Research*, February 6, 2012, p. NA, from Datamonitor.

★ 2895 ★

Apparel Retailing

SIC: 5651; NAICS: 44814

Retail Apparel Sales, 2011

Market shares are shown for May 2010-April 2011.

Specialty stores	32.5%
Mass merchants	19.3
Department stores	13.4
National chains	13.0
Off-price retailers	9.5
Direct mail/e-tail pure plays	5.4
Factory outlets	2.1
Other	4.7

Source: *WWD*, July 13, 2011, p. NA, from NPD Group Inc.

★ 2896 ★

Apparel Retailing

SIC: 5651; NAICS: 44814

Top Apparel Retailers, 2008

The industry is projected to climb from $297 billion in 2008 to $328 billion in 2014. Women's wear claimed 51% of the total, men's apparel 32% and children's apparel 16%.

Wal-Mart	11.0%
Macy's	8.0
Federated	7.0
J.C. Penney's	5.0
Kohl's	5.0
Target	5.0
TJX Companies	5.0
The Gap	4.0
Limited Brands	4.0
Other	46.0

Source: "Global Apparel and Textile Report." [online] from http://www.docin.com [Published September 10, 2010], from company reports.

★ 2897 ★

Apparel Retailing

SIC: 5651; NAICS: 44814

Top Apparel Retailers, 2010

Firms are ranked by retail sales in billions of dollars.

TJX Companies	$ 14.82
The Gap	11.71
Ross Stores	7.86
Limited Brands	5.50
Burlington Coat Factory	3.66
Foot Locker	3.57
Abercrombie & Fitch	2.84
Dressbarn Inc.	2.72
American Eagle Outfitters	2.67
Aeropostale	2.28
Collective Brands	2.28
Ann Taylor	1.98

Source: *Stores*, July 2011, p. NA, from Kantar Retail.

★ 2898 ★

Apparel Retailing

SIC: 5651; NAICS: 44814

Top Clothing and Footwear Retailers in China, 2009

Market shares are shown based on retail sales.

Belle International Holdings Ltd.	8.7%
Li Ning Company Ltd.	3.2
Anta (China) Co. Ltd.	2.3
Prime Success International Group Ltd.	2.3
Metersbonwe Group	2.1
361 Degrees International Ltd.	1.5
Other	79.9

Source: "Clothing and Footwear Specialist Retailers - China." [online] from http://www.scribd.com [Published January 2010], from Euromonitor.

★ 2899 ★

Apparel Retailing

SIC: 5651; NAICS: 44814

Top Family Clothing Stores, 2011

The industry generated revenues of $85.8 billion in 2011.

TJX Companies	17.2%
The Gap	15.3
Ross Stores	9.4
Abercrombie & Fitch	4.0
Other	54.1

Source: "Family Clothing Stores in the U.S." [online] from http://www.ibisworld.com [Published August 2011], from IBISWorld.

★ 2900 ★

Shoe Retailing

SIC: 5661; NAICS: 44821

Children's and Juveniles' Shoe Stores, 2007

Data show the percent of industry sales held by the largest 4, 8, 20 and 50 firms in the sector. There are approximately 1,088 firms operating in the industry generating employment for 6,874 people.

4 largest firms	78.2%
8 largest firms	81.2
20 largest firms	85.1
50 largest firms	89.6

Source: "2007 Economic Census." [online] from http://www.census.gov/econ/concentration.html [Accessed August 12, 2011], from U.S. Bureau of the Census.

★ 2901 ★

Shoe Retailing

SIC: 5661; NAICS: 44821

Shoe Retailing by Channel, 2011

Market shares are shown in percent.

Athletic specialty/sporting goods	18.0%
Mass merchandisers	12.0
Shoe stores	12.0
Department stores	11.0
Shoe chains	10.0
National chains	8.0
Off-price chains	6.0
Internet	5.0
Other	15.0

Source: "World Footwear Market and Perspectives for Leather." [online] from http://www.tyche.com.tw [Published December 9, 2011].

★ 2902 ★

Shoe Retailing

SIC: 5661; NAICS: 44821

Sports Footwear Sales, 2010

Market shares are shown in percent.

Sporting goods stores	19.7%
Discount stores	19.5
Athletic/footwear stores	13.7
Online/Internet	12.9
Department stores	10.9
Family footwear stores	7.7

Continued on next page.

★ 2902 ★

[Continued]

Shoe Retailing

SIC: 5661; NAICS: 44821

Sports Footwear Sales, 2010

Market shares are shown in percent.

Factory outlet stores	6.6%
Other	9.0

Source: ''Where They Buy.'' [online] from http://mobile.rab. com/ibresult.cfm?id60 [Accessed December 1, 2011], from National Sporting Goods Association.

★ 2903 ★

Shoe Retailing

SIC: 5661; NAICS: 44821

Top Shoe Store Chains, 2011

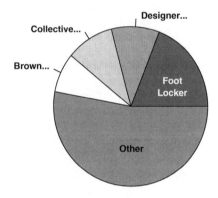

There were a total of 10,362 businesses operating in the United States during the year. They generated revenues of $20 billion. Collective Brands owns Payless and Stride Rite.

Foot Locker	18.7%
Designer Shoe Warehouse	10.5
Collective Brands	9.6
Brown Shoe Company	8.4
Other	52.8

Source: ''Shoe Stores in the U.S.'' [online] from http://www. ibisworld.com [Published August 2011], from IBISWorld.

SIC 57 - Furniture and Homefurnishings Stores

★ 2904 ★

Furniture Stores

SIC: 5712; NAICS: 44211

Top Furniture Stores, 2010

Companies are ranked by estimated furniture, bedding and accessory sales in millions of dollars.

Ashley Furniture HomeStores	$ 2,394.0
IKEA	2,095.0
Pier 1 Imports	1,937.4
Rooms To Go	1,410.0
Williams-Sonoma	1,250.0
Berkshire Hathaway furniture division	1,145.7
American Signature	1,013.9
Raymour & Flanigan	972.3
Sleepy's	765.0
La-Z-Boy Furniture Galleries	739.6
Crate & Barrel	717.6
Ethan Allen	657.2
Haverty's	620.3
Bob's Discount Furniture	584.6
Select Comfort	546.7
Art Van	430.0

Source: *Furniture Today*, November 15, 2011, p. 5.

★ 2905 ★

Office Furniture Retailing

SIC: 5712; NAICS: 44211

Office Furniture Sales, 2010

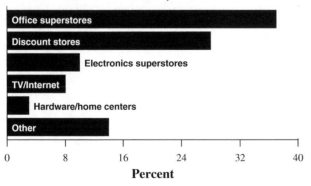

Percent

Market shares are shown by channel.

Office superstores	37.0%
Discount stores	28.0
Electronics superstores	10.0
TV/Internet	8.0%
Hardware/home centers	3.0
Other	14.0

Source: *HomeWorld Business*, June 13, 2011, p. 2, from *HomeWorld Business* estimates.

★ 2906 ★

Flooring

SIC: 5713; NAICS: 44221

Retail Flooring Sales, 2002, 2007 and 2010

Market shares are shown in percent.

	2002	2007	2010
Floor covering stores	58.6%	47.4%	42.8%
Home centers	19.5	25.5	29.6
Hard surface flooring and other building material stores	10.6	13.6	13.6
Furniture stores	3.2	2.1	1.8
Department stores	2.5	1.8	1.6
Other	5.6	9.6	10.6

Source: *Floor Covering Weekly*, July 18, 2011, p. 4, from Catalina Research and U.S. Department of Commerce.

★ 2907 ★

Flooring

SIC: 5713; NAICS: 44221

Retail Rug Sales, 2010

Total retail sales were $3.5 billion.

	($ bil.)	Share
Discount department stores	$ 1.25	44.80%
Direct-to-consumer	0.60	21.51
Mid-price chains	0.30	10.75
Home improvement centers	0.27	9.68
Specialty chains	0.19	6.81
Carpet/floor covering stores	0.18	6.45

Source: *Home Textiles Today*, January 30, 2012, p. 39, from *Home Textiles Today* market research.

★ 2908 ★
Flooring
SIC: 5713; NAICS: 44221

Top Specialty Flooring Retailers, 2011

Companies are ranked by sales in millions of dollars.

Lumber Liquidators	$ 681.6
Empire Home Services dba Empire Carpets	578.0
Floor & Decor	264.9
ABC Carpet & Home	149.5
Redi Carpet	135.0
Rite Rug	110.0
Avalon Carpet Tile and Flooring	82.0
Great Floors	80.0
Nebraska Furniture Market	79.9
Carpet Exchange/GSO Investments	63.2

Source: *Floor Covering Weekly*, May 7, 2012, p. 4.

★ 2909 ★
Bedding Stores
SIC: 5719; NAICS: 442299

Top Bedding Stores, 2010

Companies are ranked by estimated bedding sales in millions of dollars.

Sleepy's	$ 725.0
Mattress Firm	543.6
Select Comfort	475.0
Sam's Club	325.0
The Sleep Train	282.0
Macy's Inc.	266.0
Ashley Furniture HomeStores	265.0
America's Mattress	224.1
Berkshire Hathaway furniture division	196.0
Mattress Giant	185.0

Source: *Furniture Today*, November 15, 2011, p. 44, from *Furniture Today* market research.

★ 2910 ★
Bedding Stores
SIC: 5719; NAICS: 442299

Where We Purchase Bedding, 2008-2010

Market shares are shown in percent.

	2008	2009	2010
Bedding specialty stores	41.0%	42.0%	43.0%
Furniture stores	39.0	39.0	38.0
Department stores	6.0	5.0	5.0
Direct-to-consumer	5.0	5.0	5.0

	2008	2009	2010
Warehouse clubs	4.0%	5.0%	5.0%
Other	5.0	4.0	4.0

Source: *Furniture Today*, September 26, 2011, p. 16, from *Furniture Today* market research.

★ 2911 ★
Homefurnishings
SIC: 5719; NAICS: 442299

Leading Houseware Retailers, 2010

Companies are ranked by houseware sales in millions of dollars.

Wal-Mart	$ 20,375
Costco	9,850
Target	8,200
Sam's Club	4,325
Bed Bath & Beyond	3,825
Williams-Sonoma	2,710
Walgreens	2,280
Home Depot	2,235
Kmart	2,155
Dollar General	1,730
Kohl's	1,710
Sears	1,580
Kroger	1,470
Lowe's	1,350
Macy's	1,175

Source: *HomeWorld Business*, September 19, 2011, p. NA, from *HomeWorld Business* estimates.

★ 2912 ★
Homefurnishings
SIC: 5719; NAICS: 442299

Leading Houseware Retailers (Online Only), 2010

Firms are ranked by sales in millions of dollars. Some data is estimated.

Amazon	$ 32,200.0
Overstock.com	1,100.0
CSN Stores	380.0
Hayneedle	265.0
Cymax Stores	90.0
Furniture.com	75.0
ivgStores	34.9
Stacks and Stacks	25.0
One Way Furniture	17.5
Everything Furniture	14.9
FurnitureBuzz	14.9
Max Furniture	14.9

Continued on next page.

★ 2912 ★

[Continued]

Homefurnishings

SIC: 5719; NAICS: 442299

Leading Houseware Retailers (Online Only), 2010

Firms are ranked by sales in millions of dollars. Some data is estimated.

iFurn.com	$ 11.0
GreatPricedFurniture.com	9.9
Wholesale Furniture Brokers	9.9

Source: *Furniture Today*, July 18, 2011, p. 14.

★ 2913 ★

Homefurnishings

SIC: 5719; NAICS: 442299

Leading Houseware Textile Retailers, 2010

Market shares are shown based on home textile sales. Discount stores and supercenters claimed 41% of all home textile sales, specialty stores 26%, department stores 21%, direct-to-consumer 4%, dollar stores 3%, warehouse clubs 2%, home improvement centers 1% and other channels 2%.

	($ mil.)	Share
Wal-Mart	$ 3,575	14.3%
Bed Bath & Beyond	3,535	14.1
Target	2,550	10.2
J.C. Penney	2,275	9.1
Kohl's	1,275	5.1
Kmart	841	3.4
Macy's	820	3.3
T.J. Maxx/Marshalls	690	2.8
Williams-Sonoma	535	2.1
Ross Stores	480	1.9
Family Dollar	453	1.8
Big Lots	424	1.7

Source: *Home Textiles Today*, January 30, 2012, p. 12, from *Home Textiles Today* market research.

★ 2914 ★

Homefurnishings

SIC: 5719; NAICS: 442299

Retail Cutlery Sales, 2009-2010

Total sales were valued at $621.9 million.

Discount stores	29.0%
Gourmet stores	24.0
Housewares specialty stores	22.2
Department stores	15.4

Internet	6.2%
Other	3.2

Source: *HomeWorld Business*, January 2011, p. 142, from *HomeWorld Business* research.

★ 2915 ★

Homefurnishings

SIC: 5719; NAICS: 442299

Retail Sales of Housewares, 2010

Figures include metal bakeware and cookware, cutlery, kitchen tools, scales, clocks, plastic storage and small appliances.

Mass merchants and clubs	54.0%
Supermarkets and drug stores	11.0
Internet	10.0
Specialty stores	10.0
Department stores	7.0
Catalogs	1.0
Other	3.0

Source: *HFN*, February 2011, p. 18, from *HFN State of the Industry Report*.

★ 2916 ★

Homefurnishings

SIC: 5719; NAICS: 442299

Retail Sales of Tabletop Products, 2010

Figures include dinnerware, glassware, crystal and flatware.

Mass merchants and clubs	44.0%
Specialty stores	28.0
Department stores	14.0
Online	10.0
Catalogs	3.0
Other	1.0

Source: *HFN*, February 2011, p. 21, from *HFN State of the Industry Report*.

★ 2917 ★

Homefurnishings

SIC: 5719; NAICS: 442299

Retail Sales of Textiles, 2010

Figures include bagged bed ensembles, mattress pads, sheets, comforters, towels, pillows, curtains, drapes and kitchen textiles.

Mass merchants and clubs	51.0%
Specialty stores	20.0
Department stores	13.0
Catalogs	7.0

Continued on next page.

★ 2917 ★

[Continued]

Homefurnishings

SIC: 5719; NAICS: 442299

Retail Sales of Textiles, 2010

Figures include bagged bed ensembles, mattress pads, sheets, comforters, towels, pillows, curtains, drapes and kitchen textiles.

Internet	7.0%
Other	2.0

Source: *HFN*, February 2011, p. 25, from *HFN State of the Industry Report*.

★ 2918 ★

Appliance Retailing

SIC: 5722; NAICS: 443111

Retail Blender Sales, 2010

Total sales were 17.9 million units in 2010, valued at $576.1 million. Push-button units claimed 67% of the market, touch-pad units claimed 23% and dial units 10%.

Discount stores	45.0%
Specialty stores	20.0
Department stores	14.0
Warehouse clubs	9.0
Other	12.0

Source: *HomeWorld Business*, January 2011, p. 40, from *HomeWorld Business* research.

★ 2919 ★

Appliance Retailing

SIC: 5722; NAICS: 443111

Retail Drip Coffeemaker Sales, 2010

A total of 18.5 million units were sold in 2010, valued at $481.4 million.

Discount stores	63.0%
Department stores	11.0

Specialty stores	10.0%
Warehouse clubs	6.0
Other	10.0

Source: *HomeWorld Business*, January 2011, p. 10, from *HomeWorld Business* research.

★ 2920 ★

Appliance Retailing

SIC: 5722; NAICS: 443111

Retail Home Appliance Sales, 2009-2010

In spite of the depressed market, the top 100 retailers generated sales of $24.3 billion, a surprising 5.5% boost over sales in 2009. Sears was the top retailer of 2010 based on sales, followed by Lowe's, Home Depot, Best Buy and then Wal-Mart.

	2009	2010
Home improvement stores	38.4%	37.4%
Mass merchandisers	36.2	35.0
Electronics/appliance stores multi-region	10.0	10.2
Electronics/appliance stores regional .	8.2	8.3
Appliance-only stores	2.7	2.6
Home furnishings stores	3.5	2.4
Electronics/appliance stores one market	2.0	1.9

Source: *Twice*, June 20, 2011, p. 22, from *Twice* market research.

★ 2921 ★

Appliance Retailing

SIC: 5722; NAICS: 443111

Retail Sales of Sewing Machines, 2010

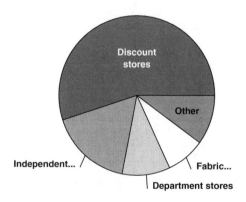

Data show 3.0 million units sold in 2010, valued at $945 million. Sales have fallen steadily since the $1.05 billion generated in 2007.

Discount stores	55.0%
Independent dealers	17.0

Continued on next page.

★ **2921** ★

[Continued]

Appliance Retailing

SIC: 5722; NAICS: 443111

Retail Sales of Sewing Machines, 2010

Data show 3.0 million units sold in 2010, valued at $945 million. Sales have fallen steadily since the $1.05 billion generated in 2007.

Department stores	10.0%
Fabric and craft stores	8.0
Other	10.0

Source: *HomeWorld Business*, January 2011, p. 10, from *HomeWorld Business* research.

★ **2922** ★

Appliance Retailing

SIC: 5722; NAICS: 443111

Retail Toaster Sales, 2010

A total of 14.8 million units were sold in 2010, valued at $249.38 million.

Discount stores	55.0%
Specialty stores	12.0
Department stores	11.0
Warehouse clubs	7.0
Other	14.0

Source: *HomeWorld Business*, January 2011, p. 60, from *HomeWorld Business* research.

★ **2923** ★

Appliance Retailing

SIC: 5722; NAICS: 443111

Retail Vacuum Cleaner Sales, 2010

A total of 19.3 million upright vacuum cleaners were sold in 2010, valued at $2.4 billion.

Discount stores	41.0%
Department stores	15.0
Electronics specialty stores	11.0

Warehouse club	8.0%
Home centers/hardware stores	4.0
Independent dealers	4.0
Direct sales	3.0
Other	10.0

Source: *HomeWorld Business*, January 2011, p. 108, from *HomeWorld Business* research.

★ **2924** ★

Car Audio Retailing

SIC: 5731; NAICS: 443112

Car Audio Entertainment Purchases, 2010

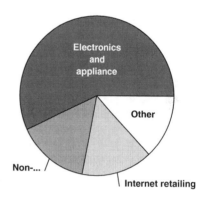

Market shares are shown in percent.

Electronics and appliance stores	56.9%
Non-store retailing	15.3
Internet retailing	15.1
Other	12.7

Source: "Car Audio Internet Sales Figures." [online] from http://satelliteradioplayground.com/2012/03/14/car-audio-internet-sales-figures/#more-17266 [Published March 14, 2012], from Euromonitor.

★ **2925** ★

Electronics Retailing

SIC: 5731; NAICS: 443112

Top Consumer Electronics Retailers, 2010

Companies are ranked by consumer electronics sales in billions of dollars.

Best Buy	$ 35.62
Dell Inc.	35.58
Hewlett-Packard Co.	30.49
Wal-Mart	26.00
CDW	9.06
Amazon	9.00
Apple Computer Retail Stores	8.71

Continued on next page.

★ 2925 ★

[Continued]

Electronics Retailing

SIC: 5731; NAICS: 443112

Top Consumer Electronics Retailers, 2010

Companies are ranked by consumer electronics sales in billions of dollars.

Staples	$ 7.76
GameStop	7.08
Target	6.89
Costco	5.70
Best Buy Canada	5.45
Sam's Club	4.89
RadioShack	4.44

Source: *Dealerscope*, March 2011, p. NA.

★ 2926 ★

App Stores

SIC: 5734; NAICS: 44312

Top App Stores, 2010

Market shares are shown based on revenues of $4.27 billion.

Apple App Store	82.5%
RIM Blackberry App World	7.6
Google Android	5.0
Nokia Ovi Store	4.9

Source: "External Influences Reshape the Semiconductor Industry." [online] from http://www.eciaonline.org [Published October 2011], from *IHS Screen Digest Mobile Media Research*.

★ 2927 ★

Computer Retailing

SIC: 5734; NAICS: 44312

Top Computer Retailers, 2011

The industry was valued at $19.7 billion. Laptops generated 35% of these revenues, desktop computers 32%, printers, scanners and related supplies 11%, computer peripherals 10%, software 8% and storage devices 4%. The source estimates that the industry will see further declines, falling 1.8% annually from 2011 through 2016 to $17.9 billion. The market has been affected by increased competition and falling prices. Computer stores are concentrated in the Western and Southeast regions of the country.

Best Buy	32.2%
Apple Inc.	17.4
Fry's Electronics Inc.	9.6

RadioShack	4.5%
Other	36.3

Source: "Computer Stores in the U.S." [online] from http://www.scribd.com [Published January 2011], from IBISWorld.

★ 2928 ★

Computer Retailing

SIC: 5734; NAICS: 44312

Where We Purchased Computers, 2009-2010

The top 25 firms generated sales of $44.3 billion in 2010, a 12.1% increase over 2009. Best Buy was the top retailer based on sales, followed by Apple, Wal-Mart, Dell and then Newegg.com.

	2009	2010
Electronics/appliance stores	28.4%	31.4%
Consumer direct	21.9	22.5
Electronics-only stores	14.1	18.2
Mass merchandisers	12.5	14.0
Home office stores	7.0	7.9
Computer stores	2.4	3.2
Other	3.2	3.4

Source: *Twice*, June 6, 2011, p. 1, from *TWICE's Top 25 Retailer Report*.

★ 2929 ★

DVD Retailing

SIC: 5735; NAICS: 45122

Top DVD Retailers, 2011

Market shares are shown in percent.

Wal-Mart	40.5%
Target	14.5
Best Buy	11.0
Amazon	8.5

Continued on next page.

★ 2929 ★
[Continued]
DVD Retailing
SIC: 5735; NAICS: 45122

Top DVD Retailers, 2011

Market shares are shown in percent.

Costco	4.0%
Other	21.5

Source: *Wall Street Journal*, March 19, 2012, p. C8, from IHS Screen Digest.

★ 2930 ★
Music Retailing
SIC: 5735; NAICS: 45122

Top Music Retailers, 2010-2011

Market shares are estimated based on Billboard's interviews with key distribution executives in the major, independent and digital sectors, which represent about 90% of U.S. recorded music revenues. Billboard asked executives to supply account-by-account market share based on net purchases. Each merchandiser share was weighted accordingly by each distributor share. Data supplied by digital and independent distributors are extrapolated to account for these channels.

	2010	2011
iTunes	32.98%	38.23%
Anderson	19.34	17.86
Amazon	6.88	7.93
Alliance Entertainment	5.66	5.97
Target	7.79	5.45
Trans World Entertainment	3.47	1.97
Rhapsody	1.94	1.88
Super D	1.57	1.60
Vevo	0.41	1.15
Microsoft	0.55	1.09
Verizon	1.78	1.05
YouTube	0.41	0.77
Hastings Entertainment	1.05	0.75
Other	15.87	14.30

Source: *Billboard*, May 12, 2012, p. 6, from *Billboard* research.

★ 2931 ★
Musical Instrument Stores
SIC: 5736; NAICS: 45114

Music Stores by State, 2011

The number of storefronts climbed from 7,993 in 2010 to 8,084 in 2011, making it the first time since 2004 that the number of storefronts exceeded 8,000.

	Stores	Share
California	1,040	12.86%
New York	497	6.15
Texas	454	5.62
Florida	408	5.05
Pennsylvania	373	4.61
Illinois	342	4.23
Ohio	323	4.00
Georgia	246	3.04
Michigan	234	2.89
North Carolina	231	2.86
New Jersey	216	2.67
Massachusetts	205	2.54
Other	3,515	43.48

Source: *Musical Merchandise Review*, July 2011, p. 42.

★ 2932 ★
Musical Instrument Stores
SIC: 5736; NAICS: 45114

Top Musical Product Retailers, 2010

Companies are ranked by estimated revenues in millions of dollars.

Guitar Center Inc.	$ 2,000.0
Sam Ash Music Corp.	410.0
Sweetwater	200.0
American Musical Supply	175.0
Full Compass Systems Ltd.	105.0
Best Buy	75.0
Washington Music Center	70.5
B&H Photo & Video	60.0
J.W. Peter	59.0
Schmitt Music Company	44.0
Unique Squared	40.0
West L.A. Music	36.0
West Music Co.	30.2

Source: *Music Trades*, August 2011, p. 62.

SIC 58 - Eating and Drinking Places

★ 2933 ★
Coffee and Snack Shops
SIC: 5812; NAICS: 722213

Leading Coffee Chains, 2010

Companies are ranked by number of outlets.

Starbucks	11,158
Dunkin' Donuts	6,900
Caribou Coffee	539
Peet's Coffee & Tea	193
Dutch Bros.	156
Biggby Coffee	118
The Coffee Beanery	100
Scooters Coffeehouse	89

Source: "America's Fastest-Growing Coffee Chains." [online] from http://www.cnbc.com/id/44344031/America_s_Fastest_Growing_Coffee_Chains [Published December 15, 2009], from Technomic.

★ 2934 ★
Coffee and Snack Shops
SIC: 5812; NAICS: 722213

Top Coffee and Snack Shops, 2010

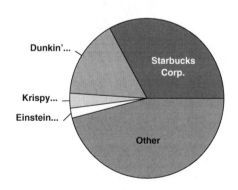

The industry was valued at $26.5 billion. Coffee shops claimed 25% of the market, donut shops 18%, ice cream shops 16%, bagel shops 15%, frozen yogurt shops 6%, cookie shops 2% and other snack shops 18%. There are an estimated 48,857 establishments employing 479,856 people.

Starbucks Corp.	32.6%
Dunkin' Brands Inc.	16.1

Krispy Kreme Doughnut	3.0%
Einstein Noah Restaurant Group	2.5
Other	45.8

Source: "Coffee & Snack Shops in the U.S." [online] from http://www.ibisworld.com [Published February 2011], from IBISWorld.

★ 2935 ★
Foodservice
SIC: 5812; NAICS: 72231

Foodservice Industry, 2010

Market shares are shown based on type.

Fast food	37.0%
Full-service restaurants	33.0
Cafés and bars	10.0
Pizza foodservice	9.0
Street stalls and kiosks	6.0
Delivery and takeaway	5.0

Source: "Food and Beverage in the United States." [online] from http://www.nzte.govt.nz [Published May 2012], from Euromonitor.

★ 2936 ★
Foodservice
SIC: 5812; NAICS: 72231

Top Catering Firms in the Asia-Pacific Region, 2010

Market shares are shown in percent.

LSG Sky Chefs	26.6%
Gategroup	13.9
TFK Corp. (Japan Airlines)	8.6
Quantus Catering	7.7
SATS	4.9
Cathay Pacific Catering Services	4.4
Other	33.9

Source: "Cathay Pacific Catering Services." [online] from http://www.scribd.com [Accessed December 1, 2011], from company reports and Deutsche Bank.

★ 2937 ★

Foodservice

SIC: 5812; NAICS: 722211

Top Chain Foodservice Brands in Mexico, 2010

Brands are ranked by number of outlets.

OXXO	8,275
7-Eleven	1,070
Extra	950
Hawaiian Paradise	747
Heladerias Holanda	600
Subway	495
Domino's Pizza	426
The Italian Coffee Company	397
McDonalds	390
Burger King	385

Source: "Mexico Food Service - Hotel Restaurant." [online] from http://www.gain.usda.gov [Published December 28, 2011], from Euromonitor.

★ 2938 ★

Foodservice

SIC: 5812; NAICS: 72231

Top Consumer Foodservice Firms in Spain, 2009

There were 247,331 consumer foodservice chains in the country. Cafes and bars claimed 69% of the total, full-service restaurants 28%, fast-food outlets 1.9% and other outlets 1.1%. Market shares are shown based on value.

McDonald's	19.3%
TelePizza S.A.	9.8
Burger King Holdings Inc.	7.7
Heineken N.V.	5.4
Agrolimen S.A.	5.2
Zena Group	5.0
Comess Group SL	4.9
Vips Group	4.4
Rodilla Sanchez S.L.	3.2
Other	35.1

Source: "Foodservice Profile Spain." [online] from http://publications.gc.ca/collections/collection_2011 [Published June 2011], from Euromonitor.

★ 2939 ★

Foodservice

SIC: 5812; NAICS: 72231

Top Foodservice Contractors, 2011

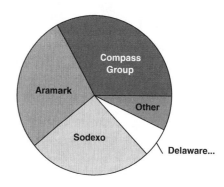

Market shares are shown in percent.

Compass Group	32.8%
Aramark	28.3
Sodexo	25.6
Delaware North	6.5
Other	6.8

Source: "Highly Concentrated: Companies That Dominate Their Industries." [online] from http://www.ibisworld.com [Published February 2012], from IBISWorld.

★ 2940 ★

Foodservice

SIC: 5812; NAICS: 72231

Top Foodservice Operators in the United Kingdom, 2010

Market shares are shown based on banner sales.

Punch Taverns	5.90%
McDonald's	3.53
Mitchells & Butlers	2.82
JD Wetherspoon	1.56
Whitbread	1.56
Yum! Brands	1.50
Greggs	1.03
Subway	0.97
Domino's Pizza	0.67
Other	80.56

Source: "The United Kingdom - A Diverse Foodservice Sector." [online] from http://www.gov.mb.ca [Published May 2011], from Planet Retail.

★ 2941 ★
Restaurants
SIC: 5812; NAICS: 722212

Cafeterias, Grill Buffets and Buffet Sales, 2007

Data show the percent of industry sales held by the largest 4, 8, 20 and 50 firms in the sector.

4 largest firms	35.6%
8 largest firms	43.7
20 largest firms	52.0
50 largest firms	58.0

Source: "2007 Economic Census." [online] from http://www.census.gov/econ/concentration.html [Accessed August 12, 2011], from U.S. Bureau of the Census.

★ 2942 ★
Restaurants
SIC: 5812; NAICS: 72211

Full-Service Restaurant Industry, 2010

Consumer households claimed 85% of the market, while corporations claimed the remaining 15%.

Casual dining	39.4%
Asian	19.7
Traditional American	12.1
Pizza	10.2
European	9.7
Latin American	7.6
Middle Eastern	1.3

Source: "Full-Service Restaurants." [online] from http://www.pacificedc.org/./Restaurant%20Industry%20Snapshot.pdf [Accessed September 1, 2011], from IBISWorld.

★ 2943 ★
Restaurants
SIC: 5812; NAICS: 722212

Mobile Food Shops, 2007

Data show the percent of industry sales held by the largest 4, 8, 20 and 50 firms in the sector. According to IBISWorld, mobile food preparation businesses increased 15% over five years to make up 37% of the $1.4 billion of U.S. street vending revenues in 2011. Approximately 55% of mobile food vendors operate on street corners, 15% industrial or construction sites and 20% other locations.

4 largest firms	7.9%
8 largest firms	12.8

20 largest firms	23.5%
50 largest firms	35.5

Source: "2007 Economic Census." [online] from http://www.census.gov/econ/concentration.html [Accessed August 12, 2011], from U.S. Bureau of the Census.

★ 2944 ★
Restaurants
SIC: 5812; NAICS: 722211

Restaurant Industry Sales, 2011

The industry was valued at $604 billion. There are 960,000 restaurants in the United States offering employment to 12.8 million people.

	($ bil.)	Share
Eating places	$ 404.5	66.52%
Retail, vending, recreation and mobile	57.2	9.41
Managed services	42.1	6.92
Lodging place restaurants	28.7	4.72
Bars and taverns	18.3	3.01
Other	57.3	9.42

Source: "Restaurant by the Numbers." [online] from http://www.restaurant.org/pdfs/research/2011forecast_pfb.pdf [Accessed September 1, 2011], from National Restaurant Association.

★ 2945 ★
Restaurants
SIC: 5812; NAICS: 722211

Top Asian Restaurant Chains, 2010

The Asian category is relatively untapped at the national level, with only 1.7% of sales of the top 500 restaurant firms coming from Asian foods. Panda Express has 45.7% of the market.

Panda Express	$ 1,400.0
Pei Wei	310.0
Leeann Chin's	46.7

Source: *Advertising Age*, May 15, 2011, p. NA, from Technomic.

★ 2946 ★
Restaurants
SIC: 5812; NAICS: 72211

Top Bakery Cafe Chains, 2010

Firms are ranked by systemwide sales in millions of dollars.

Tim Horton's	$ 443.0
Einstein's Bros. Bagels	413.0

Continued on next page.

★ 2946 ★

[Continued]

Restaurants

SIC: 5812; NAICS: 72211

Top Bakery Cafe Chains, 2010

Firms are ranked by systemwide sales in millions of dollars.

Au Bon Pain	$ 301.8
Corner Bakery Cafe	247.0
Bruegger's Bagel Bakery	203.4

Source: *Nation's Restaurant News*, June 27, 2011, p. 64, from *Nation's Restaurant News* research.

★ 2947 ★

Restaurants

SIC: 5812; NAICS: 722211

Top Burger Restaurants, 2009-2011

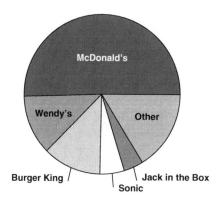

Market shares are shown in percent.

	2009	2010	2011
McDonald's	48.2%	48.8%	49.6%
Wendy's	13.0	12.6	12.3
Burger King	13.9	13.1	12.2
Sonic	5.9	5.5	5.3
Jack in the Box	4.8	4.5	4.4
Other	14.2	15.5	16.2

Source: *Advertising Age*, May 28, 2012, p. 2, from Technomic.

★ 2948 ★

Restaurants

SIC: 5812; NAICS: 722211

Top Casual Chain Restaurants, 2010

Companies are ranked by systemwide sales in millions of dollars.

Applebee's Neighborhood Grill & Bar	$ 4,319.5
Chili's Grill & Bar	3,785.0
Olive Garden	3,493.0

Red Lobster	$ 2,420.0
Outback Steakhouse	2,256.0
T.G.I. Friday's	1,794.0
Buffalo Wild Wings Grill & Bar	1,703.0
The Cheesecake Factory	1,448.9
Ruby Tuesday	1,439.0
Texas Roadhouse	1,250.0

Source: *Nation's Restaurant News*, June 27, 2011, p. 52, from *Nation's Restaurant News* research.

★ 2949 ★

Restaurants

SIC: 5812; NAICS: 72211

Top Casual Dining Wing Chains, 2010

Companies are ranked by sales in millions of dollars.

Buffalo Wild Wings Grill & Bar	$ 1,700.0
Hooters	888.0
Quaker Steak & Lube	109.2
Wow Café & Wingery	82.4
Buffalo Wings & Rings	62.0
Hurricane Grill & Wings	47.0
Wild Wing Café	40.2
Ker's Winghouse Bar & Grill	40.0

Source: *Meatingplace*, June 2011, p. 68, from Technomic.

★ 2950 ★

Restaurants

SIC: 5812; NAICS: 722211

Top Chicken Restaurants, 2010

Companies are ranked by systemwide sales in millions of dollars. Market shares are estimated.

	($ mil.)	Share
KFC	$ 4,700.0	35.20%
Chick-fil-A	3,582.8	26.84
Popeyes	1,635.0	12.25
Church's Chicken	872.7	6.54
Zaxby's	777.6	5.82
Bojangles	712.8	5.34
El Pollo Loco	557.0	4.17
Boston Market	513.0	3.84

Source: *QSR Magazine*, August 2011, p. NA.

★ 2951 ★
Restaurants
SIC: 5812; NAICS: 72211

Top Family Chains, 2010

Firms are ranked by systemwide sales in millions of dollars.

International House of Pancakes	$ 2,573.0
Denny's	2,186.0
Cracker Barrel Old Country Store	1,911.7
Bob Evans Restaurants	970.0
Waffle House	946.0
Steak-N-Shake	764.0
Perkins Restaurant and Bakery	716.0

Source: *Nation's Restaurant News*, June 27, 2011, p. 64, from *Nation's Restaurant News* research.

★ 2952 ★
Restaurants
SIC: 5812; NAICS: 722211

Top Fast Food Restaurant Firms Worldwide, 2010

The industry generated revenues of $321 billion in 2010. Sandwiches, including hamburgers, claimed 15.4% of the total, chicken-based take-out foods 7.2%, pizza style meals 6.8% and others 70.6%.

McDonald's	7.2%
Burger King	6.8
Yum! Brands Inc.	3.5
Wendy's/Arby's Group Inc..	1.0
Domino's	0.5
Doctor's Associates (Subway)	0.2
Other	86.8

Source: "Global Fast Food Restaurants." [online] from http://www.docin.com/p-80016932.html [Published April 2010], from IBISWorld.

★ 2953 ★
Restaurants
SIC: 5812; NAICS: 722213

Top Frozen Yogurt Shops, 2011

The industry was valued at $723 million.

TCBY	18.0%
Pinkberry	16.0
Reed Mango	14.0
Yogurtland	8.0
Other	44.0

Source: *Advertising Age*, May 14, 2012, p. 6, from IBISWorld.

★ 2954 ★
Restaurants
SIC: 5812; NAICS: 722213

Top Ice Cream Shops, 2008

Market shares are shown based on revenues.

Dairy Queen	40.1%
Baskin-Robbins	9.9
Cold Stone Creamery	6.8
Braum's Ice Cream & Dairy Stores	4.9
Ben & Jerry's	2.5
Freshens Smoothies & Frozen Treats	2.5
Other	33.3

Source: *Patriot Ledger*, June 27, 2009, p. NA.

★ 2955 ★
Restaurants
SIC: 5812; NAICS: 722211

Top Mexican QSR Restaurants, 2010

Firms are ranked by systemwide sales in millions of dollars. Taco Bell controls 53% of the Mexican fast-food market. QSR stands for quick service.

Taco Bell	$ 6,900
Chipotle	1,840
Del Taco	579
Qdoba	480

Source: *QSR Magazine*, August 2011, p. NA, from Technomic.

★ 2956 ★
Restaurants
SIC: 5812; NAICS: 722211

Top Pizza Firms, 2011

Firms are ranked by sales in millions of dollars.

Pizza Hut	$ 11,000.0
Domino's Pizza	6,700.0
Papa John's International	2,390.1
Little Caesars Pizza	1,345.0
California Pizza Kitchen	710.0
Papa Murphy's Take 'N Bake Pizza	653.3
Sbarro	620.0
CiCi's Pizza	560.0
Chuck E. Cheese's	436.0
Round Table Pizza	410.0
Godafather's Pizza	309.0
Old Chicago/Rock Bottom Restaurant	300.0
Hungry Howie's Pizza	278.0

Source: *Pizza Today*, November 2011, p. 54, from *2011 Directory of Chain Restaurant Operations*.

★ 2957 ★
Restaurants
SIC: 5812; NAICS: 722211

Top Quick-Service Restaurants, 2010

Chains are ranked by systemwide sales in billions of dollars.

McDonald's	$ 32.39
Subway	10.60
Burger King	8.60
Wendy's	8.34
Starbucks	7.56
Taco Bell	6.90
Dunkin' Donuts	6.00
Pizza Hut	5.40
KFC	4.70
Sonic	3.61
Chick-fil-A	3.58
Domino's Pizza	3.30
Panera Bread	3.10
Arby's	3.01
Jack in the Box	2.93

Source: *QSR Magazine*, August 31, 2011, p. NA.

★ 2958 ★
Restaurants
SIC: 5812; NAICS: 722211

Top Quick-Service Restaurants in China, 2010

Market shares are projected.

Yum! Brands Inc.	5.2%
McDonald's	2.0
Ting Hsin International	1.2
Hua Lai Shi Catering Management and Service	0.5
Shigemitsu Industry	0.4
Other	90.4

Source: *Wall Street Journal*, February 29, 2012, p. B7, from Euromonitor.

★ 2959 ★
Restaurants
SIC: 5812; NAICS: 722211

Top Seafood QSR Restaurants, 2010

Firms are ranked by systemwide sales in millions of dollars. Long John Silver's controls 37% of the market. QSR stands for quick service.

Long John Silver's	$ 700.0
Captain D's	436.2

Source: *QSR Magazine*, August 2011, p. NA, from Technomic.

★ 2960 ★
Drinking Places
SIC: 5813; NAICS: 72241

Drinking Places (Alcoholic Beverages), 2007

Data show the percent of industry sales held by the largest 4, 8, 20 and 50 firms in the sector.

4 largest firms	2.1%
8 largest firms	3.0
20 largest firms	4.5
50 largest firms	6.7

Source: "2007 Economic Census." [online] from http://www.census.gov/econ/concentration.html [Accessed August 12, 2011], from U.S. Bureau of the Census.

★ 2961 ★
Nightclubs
SIC: 5813; NAICS: 72241

Top Nightclubs and Bars, 2010

Concept names are shown estimated revenues in millions of dollars. The top 100 generated estimated revenues of $1.3 billion. LIV is located in Miami Beach. The other clubs are all in Las Vegas. In the survey, nearly half identify their operation as a nightclub, with 67.3% of them described as dance clubs, 11.9% as lounges and 10.4% as live music venues. On the bar front, from the 29.1% who identify as bars, 26.3% are described as sports bars and 25.1% are categorized as traditional bars/taverns.

TAO	$ 60
XS Nightclub	60
Haze Nightclub	35
LAX Nightclub	35
Pure Nightclub	35
The Bank Nightclub	25
Lavo	25
LIV	25
Tryst Nightclub	25
Vanity Nightclub	25

Source: *Nightclub & Bar*, March 7, 2011, p. NA, from *Nightclub & Bar* research and Technomic.

SIC 59 - Miscellaneous Retail

★ 2962 ★

Analgesics

SIC: 5912; NAICS: 44611

Where We Purchase Cough and Cold Remedies, 2010

Sales are shown by channel.

Drug stores	29.0%
Supermarkets	23.0
Supercenters	22.0
Club stores	10.0
Mass merchandisers	10.0
Dollar stores	3.0
Other	3.0

Source: "An Insider's Guide to Retail Success 2011-2012." [online] from http://www.rx-edge.com/research%20pdfs/OTC_Health%5B1%5D.pdf [Accessed May 1, 2012], from Nielsen Homescan Consumer Facts.

★ 2963 ★

Analgesics

SIC: 5912; NAICS: 44611

Where We Purchase Pain Remedies, 2010

Sales are shown by channel.

Supercenters	25.0%
Supermarkets	23.0
Drug stores	22.0
Club stores	12.0
Mass merchandisers	10.0
Dollar stores	4.0
Other	4.0

Source: "An Insider's Guide to Retail Success 2011-2012." [online] from http://www.rx-edge.com/research%20pdfs/OTC_Health%5B1%5D.pdf [Accessed May 1, 2012], from Nielsen Homescan Consumer Facts.

★ 2964 ★

Drug Stores

SIC: 5912; NAICS: 44611

Top Drug Stores, 2010

Companies are ranked by sales in billions of dollars.

Walgreens	$ 46.7
CVS	39.8
Wal-Mart	21.4
Rite Aid	17.1
Kroger	6.9
Health Mart	6.7
Shoppers Drug Mart	5.0
Target	4.4
Katz Group	4.1
Safeway	4.0
Jean Coutu Group	2.4
Supervalu	2.3
Ahold USA	2.0

Source: *Chain Drug Review*, August 29, 2011, p. 47.

★ 2965 ★

Drug Stores

SIC: 5912; NAICS: 44611

Top Drug Stores in Atlanta-Sandy Springs-Marietta, GA, 2010

Market shares are shown based on area volume.

CVS	26.0%
Walgreens	25.0
Wal-Mart	11.0
Kroger	10.0
Other	28.0

Source: *Chain Drug Review*, October 24, 2011, p. NA.

★ 2966 ★

Drug Stores

SIC: 5912; NAICS: 44611

Top Drug Stores in Baton Rouge, LA, 2010

Market shares are shown based on area volume.

Walgreens	36.0%
CVS	20.0
Wal-Mart	19.0
Other	25.0

Source: *Chain Drug Review*, October 24, 2011, p. NA.

★ 2967 ★

Drug Stores

SIC: 5912; NAICS: 44611

Top Drug Stores in Birmingham-Hoover, AL, 2010

Market shares are shown based on area volume.

CVS	30.0%
Walgreens	25.0
Wal-Mart	18.0
Other	27.0

Source: *Chain Drug Review*, October 24, 2011, p. NA.

★ 2968 ★

Drug Stores

SIC: 5912; NAICS: 44611

Top Drug Stores in Boston-Cambridge-Quincy, MA-NH, 2010

Market shares are shown based on area volume.

CVS	48.0%
Walgreens	25.0
Rite Aid	11.0
Other	16.0

Source: *Chain Drug Review*, October 24, 2011, p. NA.

★ 2969 ★

Drug Stores

SIC: 5912; NAICS: 44611

Top Drug Stores in Chicago-Naperville-Joliet, IL-IN-WI, 2010

Market shares are shown based on area volume.

Walgreens	53.0%
Jewel-Osco	17.0
CVS	14.0
Other	16.0

Source: *Chain Drug Review*, October 24, 2011, p. NA.

★ 2970 ★

Drug Stores

SIC: 5912; NAICS: 44611

Top Drug Stores in Cleveland-Elyria-Mentor, OH, 2010

Market shares are shown based on area volume.

Walgreens	22.0%
CVS	21.0
Marc's	17.0
Other	40.0

Source: *Chain Drug Review*, October 24, 2011, p. NA.

★ 2971 ★

Drug Stores

SIC: 5912; NAICS: 44611

Top Drug Stores in Columbia, SC, 2010

Market shares are shown based on area volume.

CVS	30.0%
Walgreens	25.0
Wal-Mart	13.0
Other	32.0

Source: *Chain Drug Review*, October 24, 2011, p. NA.

★ 2972 ★

Drug Stores

SIC: 5912; NAICS: 44611

Top Drug Stores in Columbus, OH, 2010

Market shares are shown based on area volume.

CVS	31.0%
Walgreens	23.0
Kroger	14.0
Other	32.0

Source: *Chain Drug Review*, October 24, 2011, p. NA.

★ 2973 ★

Drug Stores

SIC: 5912; NAICS: 44611

Top Drug Stores in Denver-Aurora, CO, 2010

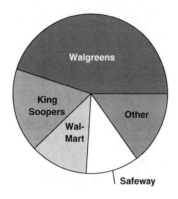

Market shares are shown based on area volume.

Walgreens	45.0%
King Soopers	17.0
Wal-Mart	12.0
Safeway	11.0
Other	15.0

Source: *Chain Drug Review*, October 24, 2011, p. NA.

★ 2974 ★

Drug Stores

SIC: 5912; NAICS: 44611

Top Drug Stores in Des Moines-West Des Moines, IA, 2010

Market shares are shown based on area volume.

Walgreens	48.0%
Wal-Mart	13.0
Medicap	11.0
Hy-Vee	10.0
Other	18.0

Source: *Chain Drug Review*, October 24, 2011, p. NA.

★ 2975 ★

Drug Stores

SIC: 5912; NAICS: 44611

Top Drug Stores in Detroit-Warren-Livonia, MI, 2010

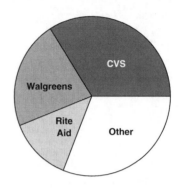

Market shares are shown based on area volume.

CVS	34.0%
Walgreens	22.0
Rite Aid	13.0
Other	31.0

Source: *Chain Drug Review*, October 24, 2011, p. NA.

★ 2976 ★

Drug Stores

SIC: 5912; NAICS: 44611

Top Drug Stores in Houston-Sugar Land-Baytown, TX, 2010

Market shares are shown based on area volume.

Walgreens	45.0%
CVS	26.0
Wal-Mart	11.0
Other	18.0

Source: *Chain Drug Review*, October 24, 2011, p. NA.

★ 2977 ★

Drug Stores

SIC: 5912; NAICS: 44611

Top Drug Stores in Kansas City, MO, 2010

Market shares are shown based on area volume.

CVS	33.0%
Walgreens	30.0
Wal-Mart	14.0
Other	23.0

Source: *Chain Drug Review*, October 24, 2011, p. NA.

★ 2978 ★
Drug Stores
SIC: 5912; NAICS: 44611
Top Drug Stores in Knoxville, TN, 2010

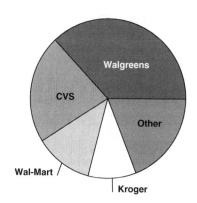

Market shares are shown based on area volume.

Walgreens	37.0%
CVS	22.0
Wal-Mart	12.0
Kroger	10.0
Other	19.0

Source: *Chain Drug Review*, October 24, 2011, p. NA.

★ 2979 ★
Drug Stores
SIC: 5912; NAICS: 44611
Top Drug Stores in Los Angeles-Long Beach-Santa Ana, CA, 2010

Market shares are shown based on area volume.

CVS	40.0%
Rite Aid	20.0
Walgreens	19.0
Other	21.0

Source: *Chain Drug Review*, October 24, 2011, p. NA.

★ 2980 ★
Drug Stores
SIC: 5912; NAICS: 44611
Top Drug Stores in Oklahoma City, OK, 2010

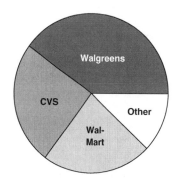

Market shares are shown based on area volume.

Walgreens	40.0%
CVS	25.0
Wal-Mart	23.0
Other	12.0

Source: *Chain Drug Review*, October 24, 2011, p. NA.

★ 2981 ★
Drug Stores
SIC: 5912; NAICS: 44611
Top Drug Stores in Orlando-Kissimmee, FL, 2010

Market shares are shown based on area volume.

Walgreens	45.0%
CVS	21.0
Publix	11.0
Wal-Mart	10.0
Other	13.0

Source: *Chain Drug Review*, October 24, 2011, p. NA.

★ 2982 ★
Drug Stores
SIC: 5912; NAICS: 44611
Top Drug Stores in Phoenix-Mesa-Scottsdale, AZ, 2010

Market shares are shown based on area volume.

Walgreens	45.0%
CVS	17.0
Wal-Mart	11.0
Other	27.0

Source: *Chain Drug Review*, October 24, 2011, p. NA.

★ 2983 ★

Drug Stores

SIC: 5912; NAICS: 44611

Top Drug Stores in Pittsburgh, PA, 2010

Market shares are shown based on area volume.

Rite Aid	35.0%
Walgreens	15.0
CVS	14.0
Giant Eagle	13.0
Wal-Mart	10.0

Source: *Chain Drug Review*, October 24, 2011, p. NA.

★ 2984 ★

Drug Stores

SIC: 5912; NAICS: 44611

Top Drug Stores in Providence-New Bedford-Rall River, RI, 2010

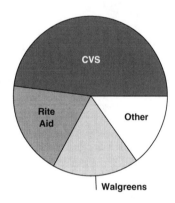

Market shares are shown based on area volume.

CVS	48.0%
Rite Aid	19.0
Walgreens	18.0
Other	15.0

Source: *Chain Drug Review*, October 24, 2011, p. NA.

★ 2985 ★

Drug Stores

SIC: 5912; NAICS: 44611

Top Drug Stores in Richmond, VA, 2010

Market shares are shown based on area volume.

CVS	34.0%
Walgreens	22.0
Rite Aid	13.0
Other	31.0

Source: *Chain Drug Review*, October 24, 2011, p. NA.

★ 2986 ★

Health Food Stores

SIC: 5912; NAICS: 44611

Leading Health Food Stores, 2011

The industry generated revenues of $15.6 billion. Sports supplements claimed 45% of the market, Vitamins, minerals and herbal supplements claimed 30% of the market and other sectors 25%.

GNC	8.0%
Vitamin Shoppe	5.0
Bodybuilding	1.0
NBTY	1.0
Other	15.0

Source: "GNC Holdings." [online] from http://uoinvestment-group.org/wp-content/uploads/2012/02/GNC.pdf [Published March 2, 2012], from IBISWorld.

★ 2987 ★

Pharmacy Benefit Managers

SIC: 5912; NAICS: 44611

Top Pharmacy Benefit Managers, 2011

SXC and Catalyst show the projected market share after merger.

Express Scripts	31.0%
CVS Caremark	17.3
Argus Health Systems	11.3
SXC/Catalyst	8.0
Other	32.4

Source: *Investor's Business Daily*, May 21, 2012, p. A8, from AISHealth.com and Atlantic Information Services Inc.

★ 2988 ★

Prescription Dispensing

SIC: 5912; NAICS: 44611

Leading Pharmacies by Prescription Revenues, 2011

In April 2012, the government approved the merger of Medco and Express Solutions.

	($ bil.)	Share
CVS Caremark	$ 56.6	20.7%
Walgreen	45.1	16.5
Medco Health Solutions/Express Scripts	39.7	14.6
Wal-Mart	17.4	6.4
Rite Aid	17.1	6.3

Source: *Wall Street Journal*, April 8, 2012, p. B1, from Pembroke Consulting.

★ 2989 ★

Prescription Dispensing

SIC: 5912; NAICS: 44611

Prescription Dispensing Industry, 2011

Sales are shown in billions of dollars.

	($ bil.)	Share
Chain stores	$ 112.6	34.09%
Mail service	55.1	16.68
Clinics	38.4	11.63
Independent	38.4	11.63
Non-federal hospitals	38.4	11.63
Food stores	21.5	6.51
Long-term care	15.2	4.60
Federal facilities	4.2	1.27
Home health care	2.8	0.85
HMOs	2.7	0.82
Other	1.0	0.30

Source: *Pharmaceutical Executive*, May 2012, p. 25.

★ 2990 ★

Vitamins and Supplements

SIC: 5912; NAICS: 44611

Retail Vitamin and Supplement Sales, 2010

The industry generated sales of $12 billion, up 8% over the same period from the previous year. The jump has been driven by an increase in the number of consumers and the size of their average expenditure. Market shares are shown based on sales at supermarkets, drug stores and mass merchandisers (excluding Wal-Mart) for the 52 weeks ended May 15, 2011.

Discounters	19.5%
Warehouse clubs	17.9
Drug stores	16.2
Online/catalog retailers	15.3
Vitamin specialty retailers	11.5
Food	9.5
Health food stores	7.2
Other	2.9

Source: *MMR*, July 11, 2011, p. 34, from SymphonyIRI Group Inc.

★ 2991 ★

Beer, Wine, and Liquor Stores

SIC: 5921; NAICS: 44531

Beer, Wine, and Liquor Stores, 2007

Data show the percent of industry sales held by the largest 4, 8, 20 and 50 firms in the sector. There are approximately 31,485 firms operating in the industry generating employment for 141,255 people.

4 largest firms	8.8%
8 largest firms	13.3
20 largest firms	18.6
50 largest firms	22.3

Source: "2007 Economic Census." [online] from http://www.census.gov/econ/concentration.html [Accessed August 12, 2011], from U.S. Bureau of the Census.

★ 2992 ★

Pawnshops

SIC: 5932; NAICS: 45331

Top Pawnshop Chains, 2011

Firms are ranked by sales in millions of dollars. According to the source, there are approximately 11,000 U.S. pawnshops, concentrated in the Southeast and Southwest. They constituted a $14.5 billion market in 2011. Revenues are forecast to grow to $19.88 billion by 2016.

Cash America	$ 1,540
EZCorp.	869
First Cash Financial	521

Source: "U.S. Pawnshops Industry Sails Through the Recession." [online] from http://www.prweb.com [Press release May 22, 2012], from Marketdata Enterprises.

★ 2993 ★

Used Merchandise Stores

SIC: 5932; NAICS: 45331

Top Used Merchandise Retailers, 2010

The industry generated revenues of $12.9 billion. A total of 66,886 businesses operate in the sector. Women's wear claimed 19% of sales, children's products 16%, furniture 14%, kitchenware and home furnishings 10% and other sectors 20%.

Goodwill Industries International	15.3%
Winmark Corp.	5.1
Salvation Army National Corp.	4.5
Other	75.1

Source: "Industry at a Glance." [online] from http://www.maricopa-sbdc.com/Research%20Reports [Published September 2010], from IBISWorld.

★ 2994 ★
Used Merchandise Stores
SIC: 5932; NAICS: 45331

Top Used Merchandise Retailers in Australia, 2009

Market shares are shown in percent.

CCV	6.1%
St. Vincent de Paul	5.0
Salvation Army	4.3
Smith Family	1.0
Other	83.6

Source: "Company Initiation." [online] from http://www.cashconverters.com/Files/Download/816 [Published February 2010], from IBISWorld.

★ 2995 ★
Bicycle Retailing
SIC: 5941; NAICS: 45111

Bicycle Sales by Channel, 2010

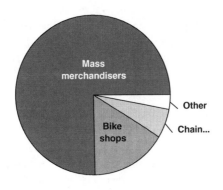

The industry sold 19.8 million units.

Mass merchandisers	75.5%
Bike shops	15.5
Chain sporting goods	6.0
Other	2.9

Source: *Bicycle Retailer & Industry News*, July 1, 2011, p. 1, from Gluskin Townley Group.

★ 2996 ★
Sporting Goods Stores
SIC: 5941; NAICS: 45111

Top Sporting Goods Chains, 2011

There were a total of 36,528 businesses operating in the United States during the year. They generated revenues of $39.8 billion. Equipment claimed 46% of the total, athletic footwear 34% and athletic apparel 20%.

Dick's Sporting Goods	13.6%
Foot Locker Inc.	10.3

Sports Authority Inc.	8.6%
Other	67.3

Source: "Sporting Goods and Stores in the U.S." [online] from http://www.ibisworld.com [Published January 2012], from IBISWorld.

★ 2997 ★
Sporting Goods Stores
SIC: 5941; NAICS: 45111

Top Sporting Goods Chains in the United Kingdom, 2011

Market shares are shown based on outlets.

Independents	37.8%
Sports Direct	18.7
JD Sports	16.8
Blacks Leisure	12.2
JJB Sports	9.8
Cotsworld Outdoor	2.0
Sweaty Betty	1.0
Snow + Rock	0.9
North Face	0.5
Decathalon	0.4

Source: *Marketing*, November 30, 2011, p. 32, from Mintel.

★ 2998 ★
Book Retailing
SIC: 5942; NAICS: 451211

Retail Book Sales, 2010-2011

Market shares are shown for the second quarter of 2011. Print paperback's share fell from 58.3% to 51%. Print hardcover's share fell from 33.3% to 28.6%. E-books grew from 3.2% to 13.7% of the total. Audio books grew from 1.2% to 1.6%.

	2010	2011
E-commerce	27.6%	37.0%
Trade and large chains	30.6	27.3
Trade/nontraditional book stores	5.1	7.4
Mass merchandisers	5.7	5.2
Trade/independent book stores	4.5	5.0
Trade/Christian book stores	2.4	2.9
Book clubs	5.6	2.8
Warehouse clubs	2.8	2.3
Other	15.7	10.1

Source: *Publishers Weekly*, October 14, 2011, p. NA, from Bowker.

★ **2999** ★

Book Retailing

SIC: 5942; NAICS: 451211

Top Book Retailers, 2009-2010

Market shares are shown in percent. Borders declared bankruptcy in August 2011.

	2009	2010
Barnes & Noble	22.5%	23.0%
Borders	14.0	13.1
Amazon	12.5	15.1
Wal-Mart	7.0	5.8
Warehouse clubs	3.6	4.0
Independents	3.4	3.5
Books-A-Million	2.8	2.7
Supermarkets and grocery stores	2.0	1.7
Target	2.0	1.9
Other	30.3	29.2

Source: *Publishers Weekly*, March 21, 2011, p. NA, from Bowker Pubtrack Consumer.

★ **3000** ★

College Book Stores

SIC: 5942; NAICS: 451211

College Book Stores, 2007

Data show the percent of industry sales held by the largest 4, 8, 20 and 50 firms in the sector. There are approximately 2,180 firms operating in the industry generating employment for 27,905 people.

4 largest firms	74.9%
8 largest firms	78.0
20 largest firms	83.6
50 largest firms	90.2

Source: "2007 Economic Census." [online] from http://www.census.gov/econ/concentration.html [Accessed August 12, 2011], from U.S. Bureau of the Census.

★ **3001** ★

E-Books

SIC: 5942; NAICS: 451211

Leading E-Book Retailers, 2012

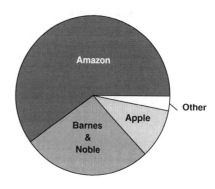

Some analysts believed that the arrival of the iPad would wipe out e-readers such as Amazon's Kindle. This has not happened. The Kindle has become a strong enough brand to withstand new entrants into the market. However, industry leader Amazon does seem to be trying to adapt to the markets changing offerings. In 2011, the Kindle released the Kindle Fire, an e-reader with a color screen and functionality similar to tablet computers. Barnes & Noble produces the Nook.

Amazon	60.0%
Barnes & Noble	27.0
Apple	10.0
Other	3.0

Source: *Wall Street Journal*, May 1, 2012, p. B6, from Albert N. Greco Institute for Publishing Research.

★ **3002** ★

Textbooks

SIC: 5942; NAICS: 451211

Where Students Purchase Textbooks, 2009

Market shares are shown based on units.

Campus bookstores	41.0%
Online stores	26.0
Campus bookstore web sites	18.0
Student to student web sites	1.0
Other stores	7.0
Other student alumni	4.0
Other	3.0

Source: "Assessing Campus Store Performance." [online] from http://www.nacas.org/Content/NavigationMenu/Education2 [Published November 8, 2011], from National Association of College Bookstores.

★ 3003 ★
Greeting Cards

SIC: 5943; NAICS: 45321

Retail Greeting Card Sales, 2011

Sales at food stores, drug stores and mass merchandisers (excluding Wal-Mart) reached $7.1 billion.

Mass merchandisers	40.0%
Food stores	33.0
Drug stores	27.0

Source: *Non-Foods Management*, Annual 2011-2012, p. 168, from SymphonyIRI Group Inc.

★ 3004 ★
Jewelry Retailing

SIC: 5944; NAICS: 339911

Jewelry Industry in Hong Kong and Macau, 2010

Market shares are shown based on retail value.

Chow Tai Fook	20.1%
Chow Sang Sang	8.7
Luk Fook	7.3
MaBelle	3.9
Cartier	2.8
Tiffany & Co.	2.2
King Fook	2.0
Seng Feng	1.6
Chow Sang Sang	1.5
Qeelin	1.5
Other	48.4

Source: "Riding the Luxury Boom." [online] from http://www.clsa.com [Published December 21, 2011], from Frost & Sullivan.

★ 3005 ★
Jewelry Retailing

SIC: 5944; NAICS: 44831

Largest Jewelry and Watch Retailers, 2010

Firms are ranked by estimated jewelry and watch sales in millions of dollars. Zale's data is for North America.

Wal-Mart	$ 2,800.0
Sterling Jewelers Inc.	2,744.2
Zale Corp.	1,616.3
Tiffany & Co.	1,574.5
Macy's Inc.	1,500.0
QVC	1,015.0
Sears Holding Corp.	860.0
J.C. Penney Co.	710.0
Costco	500.0
Target	465.0

Neiman Marcus Group	$ 406.0
Jewelry Television	400.0
Helzberg Diamonds	380.0
Cartier	360.0
Fred Meyer Jewelers	350.0

Source: *National Jeweler*, May 2011, p. NA.

★ 3006 ★
Jewelry Retailing

SIC: 5944; NAICS: 44831

Top Gold Jewelry Retailers in China, 2010

Market shares are shown in percent.

Chow Tai Fook	6.25%
Lao Fengxiang	4.10
Yuyuan	3.68
LF	1.91
Ming	1.61
Chow Sang Sang	0.96
TSL Jewellery	0.40
CHJ	0.33
Other	80.76

Source: "Global Luxury Goods." [online] from http://www.research.hsbc.com [Published September 2, 2011], from China gold association.

★ 3007 ★
Jewelry Retailing

SIC: 5944; NAICS: 44831

Women's Costume and Fashion Jewlery Sales, 2011

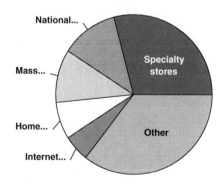

Total retail sales were $10.4 billion.

Specialty stores	27.0%
National chains	11.0
Mass merchandisers	10.0
Home shopping	7.0

Continued on next page.

★ 3007 ★

[Continued]

Jewelry Retailing

SIC: 5944; NAICS: 44831

Women's Costume and Fashion Jewlery Sales, 2011

Total retail sales were $10.4 billion.

Internet pureplays 5.0%
Other 33.0

Source: *Accessories Magazine*, Annual 2012, p. 28, from NPD Group Consumer Tracking Service.

★ 3008 ★

Software Retailing

SIC: 5945; NAICS: 45112

Top Retailers of Game Software, 2011

The retail industry was valued at $13.2 billion in 2011.

Electricals and electronics retailers 41.6%
Music, video, books and stationery retailers . . 20.7
Hypermarkets, supermarkets and discounters . 18.3
Discount stores and general merchandise . . . 12.4
Other 7.0

Source: *Datamonitor Industry Market Research*, February 3, 2012, p. NA, from Datamonitor.

★ 3009 ★

Toys and Games Retailing

SIC: 5945; NAICS: 45112

Top Toy and Game Retailers Worldwide, 2011

The retail industry was valued at $78 billion in 2011.

Specialist stores 48.7%
Hypermarkets, supermarkets and discounters . 22.7
Department stores 11.6
Discount, variety and general retailers 9.3
Other 7.7

Source: *Datamonitor Industry Market Research*, January 31, 2012, p. NA, from Datamonitor.

★ 3010 ★

Camcorder and Digicam Retailing

SIC: 5946; NAICS: 44313

Where We Purchase Camcorders and Digicams, 2010

The top 25 firms generated sales of $9.3 billion in 2010. Best Buy was the top retailer, followed by Amazon, Wal-Mart, Costco and then RadioShack.

Electronics/appliance stores 33.5%
Mass merchandisers 21.4

Consumer direct 19.2%
Warehouse clubs 8.8
Camera specialty stores 7.9
Other 9.2

Source: *Twice*, June 20, 2011, p. 35, from *Twice* market research.

★ 3011 ★

Camera Stores

SIC: 5946; NAICS: 44313

Camera Store Industry, 2011

The industry generated revenues of $3.6 billion in 2011. The market is highly competitive, as warehouse clubs, department stores and superstores have moved into the retail camera market. Ritz Camera & Image is the major camera store chain with a 13.5% share. "Other" includes video cameras, gaming consoles and repair services.

Photographic equipment and supplies 73.2%
Computer hardware software and supplies . . 11.3
Audio equipment 8.3
Other 7.2

Source: "Camera Stores in the U.S." [online] from http://www.ibisworld.com [Published March 2011], from IBISWorld.

★ 3012 ★

Gift, Card and Novelty Stores

SIC: 5947; NAICS: 45322

Top-Selling Sectors at Gift and Novelty Stores, 2010

The industry includes about 30,000 stores with combined annual revenues of about $18 billion. Major companies include Hallmark, Spencer Gifts, and Disney Stores. The industry is fragmented with the top 50 companies accounting for about 30 percent of sales.

Souvenirs and novelty items 25.0%
Seasonal items 12.0

Continued on next page.

★ 3012 ★

[Continued]

Gift, Card and Novelty Stores

SIC: 5947; NAICS: 45322

Top-Selling Sectors at Gift and Novelty Stores, 2010

The industry includes about 30,000 stores with combined annual revenues of about $18 billion. Major companies include Hallmark, Spencer Gifts, and Disney Stores. The industry is fragmented with the top 50 companies accounting for about 30 percent of sales.

Greeting cards	10.0%
Giftware	5.0
Other	48.0

Source: "Gift, Novelty & Souvenir Stores Industry Profile." [online] from http://www.firstresearch.com/industry-research/ Gift-Novelty-and-Souvenir-Stores.html [Published May 7, 2012], from First Research.

★ 3013 ★

Gift, Card and Novelty Stores

SIC: 5948; NAICS: 44832

Top Gift Shop and Card Stores, 2011

The industry generated revenues of $15.3 billion in 2011. Souvenirs claimed 28% of the market, cards 21%, collectibles 16% and other sectors 35%. AmScan owns Party America and Party City. Market shares are estimated.

Amscan Holdings	7.5%
Kirklands	3.0
Things Remembered	2.0
Hallmark Gold Crown	1.0
Spencer Gifts	1.0
Other	85.5

Source: "Gift Shops & Card Stores in the U.S." [online] from http://www.ibisworld.com [Published October 2011], from IBISWorld.

★ 3014 ★

Handbag, Luggage and Accessory Stores

SIC: 5948; NAICS: 44832

Top Handbag, Luggage and Accessory Stores, 2011

The industry generated revenues of $17.4 billion in 2011. Handbags claimed 28.5% of the total, jewelry and watches 17.5%, travel and sports bags 16.2%, men's accessories 10.2% and other sectors 27.6%. Genesco Inc. owns Hat World, Hat Shack, Hat Zone, Lids and Lids Kids.

Coach Inc.	33.5%
Claire's Stores Inc.	10.3

LVMH	7.8%
Genesco Inc.	6.3
Other	42.1

Source: "Handbag, Luggage & Accessory Stores in the U.S." [online] from http://www.ibisworld.com [Published September 2011], from IBISWorld.

★ 3015 ★

Arts, Crafts and Sewing Stores

SIC: 5949; NAICS: 45113

Top Arts, Crafts and Sewing Product Stores, 2011

The industry generated sales of $4.4 billion. There are 17,333 businesses operating in the sector providing employment to 62,258 people. With the expected recovery of the economy, consumers will have more of their income to spend on fabric, arts and craft products. However, the major chains will find increased competition from e-commerce and auction sites.

Michaels	19.5%
Jo-Ann Stores	10.2
Hobby Lobby	9.6
Other	60.7

Source: *Atlanta Business Chronicle*, July 15, 2011, p. NA, from IBISWorld.

★ 3016 ★

Catalog Retailing

SIC: 5961; NAICS: 454111, 454112

Top Catalog Retailers, 2010

Companies are ranked by direct sales in billions of dollars.

Dell	$ 52.1
Thermo Fisher Scientific	10.7
IBM	10.4
Staples	9.8
CDW Corp.	8.8
Henry Schein	7.5
Wesco International	5.0
United Stationers	4.8
OfficeMax	3.7
Hewlett-Packard Co.	3.6

Source: *Multichannel Merchant*, August 2011, p. NA.

★ 3017 ★
Home Shopping
SIC: 5961; NAICS: 454111, 454112

Leading E-Retailers/Television Retailers, 2010

Companies are ranked by sales in millions of dollars.

QVC	$ 821
HSN	802
Amazon	615
Overstock.com	77
CSN Stores	67

Source: *HomeWorld Business*, September 19, 2011, p. 28, from *HomeWorld Business* estimates.

★ 3018 ★
Home Shopping
SIC: 5961; NAICS: 454111, 454112

Top Home Shopping Firms in China, 2008

The Chinese home television market was valued at 11.3 billion renminbi in 2008, representing 0.21% of total retail sales.

Acorn International	17.0%
HappiGo	13.0
Oriental CJ	12.0
China Seven Star	9.0
Best One	5.0
CCTV Home Shopping	4.0
Other	40.0

Source: "Great Potential in Chinese TV Shopping Market." [online] from http://www.docin.com/p-218033753.html [Published April 1, 2009], from Analysys International.

★ 3019 ★
Vending Machines
SIC: 5962; NAICS: 45421

Top Vending Machine Operators, 2011

There were a total of 29,174 businesses operating in the United States during the year. They generated revenues of $7.2 billion. Drinks claimed 40.4% of the total, food 39.8%, toys 1% and other sectors 18.8%.

Compass Group PLC	11.4%
Aramark Corp.	11.3
Other	77.3

Source: "Vending Machine Operators in the U.S." [online] from http://www.ibisworld.com [Published August 2011], from IBISWorld.

★ 3020 ★
Vending Machines
SIC: 5962; NAICS: 45421

Vending Machine Sales, 2007 and 2010

Data show the location of vending machines. Industry revenues were $19.25 billion. In 2010, cold beverages claimed 31% of sales, manual foodservice 28%, candy, snacks and confections 21%, office coffee services 6.3% and other sectors 14.5%.

	2007	2010
Offices	19.5%	28.5%
Manufacturing	36.2	26.8
Retail sites	8.0	9.1
Hospitals and nursing care	6.2	8.8
Universities and colleges	12.6	5.9
Hotels and motels	3.6	4.7
Other	23.9	16.2

Source: *Automatic Merchandiser*, June-July 2011, p. 19.

★ 3021 ★
Direct Selling
SIC: 5963; NAICS: 45439

Top Direct Selling Firms Worldwide, 2010

Firms are ranked by revenues in billions of dollars.

Avon Products Inc.	$ 10.9
Amway	9.2
Natura Cosmeticos S.A.	3.0
Vorwerk & Co. KG	2.9
Herbalife Ltd.	2.7
Mary Kay Inc.	2.5
Tupperware Brands Corp.	2.3
Oriflame Cosmeticos S.A.	2.2
Forever Living Products	1.7
Nu Skin Enterprises Inc.	1.5

Source: *Direct Selling News*, June 2, 2011, p. NA.

★ 3022 ★
Propane Retailing
SIC: 5983; NAICS: 454311

Top Propane Retailers, 2011

Firms are ranked by retail sales of millions of gallons.

AmeriGas Propane	874.2
Ferrellgas	823.5
Heritage Propane	539.0
Inergy L.P.	326.8
Suburban Propane Partners L.P.	298.9
Growmark Inc.	214.9
CHS	204.0

Continued on next page.

★ 3022 ★

[Continued]

Propane Retailing

SIC: 5983; NAICS: 454311

Top Propane Retailers, 2011

Firms are ranked by retail sales of millions of gallons.

NGL Energy Partners L.P.	110.0
MFA Oil Co.	89.6
Blossman Gas Inc.	76.5
United Propane Gas	73.5
Southern States Co-Op	64.0

Source: *LP Gas*, February 2012, p. 29.

★ 3023 ★

Florists

SIC: 5992; NAICS: 45311

Leading Online Flower Shops, 2012

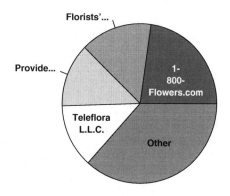

There are more than 3,500 businesses in the market, generating revenues of $2.1 billion. Flower sales claimed 63.5% of the total, gift baskets and other deliveries 19%, plants 10.5% and floral network services 7%. Provide Commerce owns Pro Flowers.

1-800-Flowers.com Inc.	23.2%
Florists' Transworld Deliveries Inc. (FTD)	14.8
Provide Commerce	12.6
Teleflora L.L.C.	12.6
Other	36.8

Source: ''Online Flower Shops.'' [online] from http://www.ibisworld.com [Published February 2012], from IBISWorld.

★ 3024 ★

Tobacco Retailing

SIC: 5993; NAICS: 453991

Top Tobacco Retailers, 2011

Shares are shown based on the 2,144 chains held by the top 50 firms.

	Units	Share
Smoker Friendly International	760	35.45%
Admiral Discount Tobacco	173	8.07
Tobacco Central (Low Bob's)	129	6.02
Tobacco Superstores Inc.	85	3.96
Discount Smoke Shops	48	2.24
Smokers Choice	48	2.24
Cheap Tobacco	42	1.96
Brookshire Brothers (Tobacco Barn)	41	1.91
Kwik Trip (Tobacco Outlet Plus)	39	1.82
NBS Inc.	39	1.82
Other	740	34.51

Source: *Tobacco Outlet Business*, January/February 2012, p. 34.

★ 3025 ★

Magazines

SIC: 5994; NAICS: 451212

Magazine Sales by Channel, 2011

Market shares are shown for the first half of the year.

Supermarkets	33.4%
Supercenters	14.1
Book stores	11.5
Drug stores	11.0
Transportation terminals	7.3
Mass merchandisers	7.2
Convenience stores	5.3
Other	10.2

Source: *Supermarket News*, September 5, 2011, p. NA, from MagNetData.net.

★ 3026 ★
Magazines
SIC: 5994; NAICS: 451212

Top Magazine Distributors, 2010

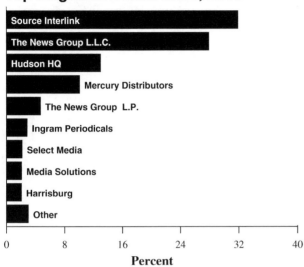

0   8   16   24   32   40
Percent

Market shares are shown for issues dated January 1-September 30, 2010.

Source Interlink	31.92%
The News Group L.L.C.	27.92
Hudson HQ	12.96
Mercury Distributors	10.06
The News Group L.P.	4.68
Ingram Periodicals	2.86
Select Media	2.18
Media Solutions	2.10
Harrisburg	2.08
Other	3.02

Source: "Update: Source Interlink Stats, Initiatives." [online] from http://ipdahome.org [Published April 25, 2011], from Source Interlink.

★ 3027 ★
Optical Goods Stores
SIC: 5995; NAICS: 44613

Top Optical Goods Retailers, 2010

Firms are ranked by sales in millions of dollars. Shares are shown based on the top 40 firms.

	($ mil.)	Share
Luxottica Retail	$ 2,470.0	33.91%
Wal-Mart Stores	1,375.5	18.88
HVHC Retail Group	698.1	9.58
National Vision	595.0	8.17
Costco Wholesale	577.0	7.92
Refac Optical Group	239.7	3.29
Eyemart Express	162.0	2.22
Cohen's Fashion Optical	128.0	1.76

	($ mil.)	Share
For Eyes/Insight Optical Manufacturing	$ 105.0	1.44%
Shopko Stores	85.0	1.17
Texas State Optical	80.9	1.11
Eyecarecenter	67.7	0.93
Other	700.3	9.61

Source: *Vision Monday*, May 16, 2011, p. NA.

★ 3028 ★
Sunglasses Stores
SIC: 5995; NAICS: 44613

Top Retailers of Sunglasses, 2011

There were 834 businesses in the industry generating employment for nearly 11,400 people and revenues of $1 billion. The top two companies hold more than 80% of the market revenues, up from 53.6% they held in 2007. Luxottica's share of revenues has grown significantly over the past five years, primarily due to its mix of high-end designer and house sunglasses brands. Luxottica's brands include Sunglass Hut, ILORI and Optical Shop of Aspen. Safilo's share is estimated. Its brands include Giorgio Armani, Boss and Pierre Cardin.

Luxottica	77.6%
Safilo	3.0
Other	19.4

Source: *PR Web*, May 14, 2012, p. NA, from IBISWorld.

★ 3029 ★
Sunglasses Stores
SIC: 5995; NAICS: 44613

Women's Sunglasses Sales, 2011

Total sales were $1.7 billion.

Specialty stores	35.0%
Mass merchandisers	17.0
Department stores	11.0

Continued on next page.

★ 3029 ★

[Continued]

Sunglasses Stores

SIC: 5995; NAICS: 44613

Women's Sunglasses Sales, 2011

Total sales were $1.7 billion.

Off-price/factory outlets/warehouse clubs. . .	7.0%
National chains	5.0
Other	26.0

Source: *Accessories Magazine*, Annual 2012, p. 36, from NPD Group Consumer Tracking Service.

★ 3030 ★

Cosmetics, Beauty Supplies, and Perfume Stores

SIC: 5999; NAICS: 44612

Cosmetics, Beauty Supplies, and Perfume Stores, 2007

Data show the percent of industry sales held by the largest 4, 8, 20 and 50 firms in the sector. There are approximately 13,584 firms operating in the industry generating employment for 86,278 people. Major players include Limited Brands, Sally Beauty Holdings Inc. and Ulta Salon, Cosmetics and Fragrance Inc. According to IBISWorld, the industry saw revenues of $13 billion in 2011.

4 largest firms	54.2%
8 largest firms	64.3
20 largest firms	70.9
50 largest firms	73.7

Source: "2007 Economic Census." [online] from http://www.census.gov/econ/concentration.html [Accessed August 12, 2011], from U.S. Bureau of the Census.

★ 3031 ★

Juvenile Product Retailing

SIC: 5999; NAICS: 453998

Retail Sales of Juvenile Products, 2010

The industry was valued at $17.8 billion in 2010. Toys (age 1-5) claimed 44% of the total, furniture 17%, strollers 14%, car seats 12% and other products 13%.

Mass merchandisers	43.0%
Specialty stores	30.0
Online	19.0
Department stores	5.0
Other	3.0

Source: "Juvenile Products." [online] from http://www.capstonellc.com [Published Fourth Quarter 2011], from Packaged Facts.

★ 3032 ★

Pet Groomers

SIC: 5999; NAICS: 45391

Pet Groomers by State, 2010

There were 30,106 groomers operating in the United States in 2010. Total grooming spending was $1.42 billion.

California	9.26%
Florida	7.02
Texas	6.34
Pennsylvania	4.89
New York	4.41
Ohio	4.29
Illinois	4.06
Michigan	3.80
Other	55.93

Source: *eGroomer Journal*, July/August 2011, p. 6.

★ 3033 ★

Pet Stores

SIC: 5999; NAICS: 45391

Top Pet Stores, 2010

The industry generated revenues of $14.6 billion. Pet food claimed 58% of the total, pet supplies 27.3%, pet services 10.2% and live animals 4.5%. Pet Food Express has less than 1% of the market.

PetSmart Inc.	41.8%
PETCO Animal Supplies Inc.	20.2
Pet Supplies Press	3.6
Pet Supermarket Inc.	1.6
Pet Food Express	1.0
Other	31.8

Source: "Pet Stores in the U.S." [online] from http://www.ibisworld.com [Published October 2011], from IBISWorld.

SIC 60 - Depository Institutions

★ 3034 ★
Banking
SIC: 6021; NAICS: 52211

Top Banks in Alabama, 2011

Market shares are shown based on deposits as of June 30, 2011.

Regions Bank	26.20%
Compass Bank	10.10
Wells Fargo Bank NA	10.01
Branch Banking & Trust Co.	5.39
Synovus Bank	4.38
RBC Bank USA	4.04
Servisfirst Bank	2.12
Banktrust	2.02
Superior Bank NA	1.50
Other	33.24

Source: "Deposit Market Share Report." [online] from http://www.2fdic.gov [Published October 1, 2011], from Federal Deposit Insurance Corp.

★ 3035 ★
Banking
SIC: 6021; NAICS: 52211

Top Banks in Alaska, 2011

Market shares are shown based on deposits as of June 30, 2011.

Wells Fargo Bank NA	50.61%
First National Bank of Alaska	19.10
Keybank NA	9.81
Northrim Bank	9.57
Other	10.91

Source: "Deposit Market Share Report." [online] from http://www.2fdic.gov [Published October 1, 2011], from Federal Deposit Insurance Corp.

★ 3036 ★
Banking
SIC: 6021; NAICS: 52211

Top Banks in Arizona, 2011

Market shares are shown based on deposits as of June 30, 2011.

Wells Fargo Bank NA	26.1%
J.P. Morgan Chase Bank NA	23.5
Bank of the America NA	19.3
Compass Bank	4.7
National Bank of Arizona	4.4
Other	22.0

Source: "Deposit Market Share Report." [online] from http://www.2fdic.gov [Published October 1, 2011], from Federal Deposit Insurance Corp.

★ 3037 ★
Banking
SIC: 6021; NAICS: 52211

Top Banks in Arkansas, 2011

Market shares are shown based on deposits as of June 30, 2011.

Arvest Bank	10.73%
Regions Bank	8.15
Bank of America NA	6.44
First Security Bank	5.85
Liberty Bank of Arkansas	3.86
Bancorpsouth Bank	3.57
Centennial Bank	3.33
Bank of the Ozarks	3.11
Simmons First National Bank	2.53
Other	52.43

Source: "Deposit Market Share Report." [online] from http://www.2fdic.gov [Published October 1, 2011], from Federal Deposit Insurance Corp.

★ 3038 ★

Banking

SIC: 6021; NAICS: 52211

Top Banks in California, 2011

Market shares are shown based on deposits as of June 30, 2011.

Bank of America NA	25.60%
Wells Fargo Bank NA	19.44
J.P. Morgan Chase Bank NA	7.34
Union Bank NA	6.04
Citibank	5.12
US Bank NA	3.49
Bank of the West	2.93
City National Bank	2.00
Onewest Bank FSB	1.77
Other	26.27

Source: "Deposit Market Share Report." [online] from http://www.2fdic.gov [Published October 1, 2011], from Federal Deposit Insurance Corp.

★ 3039 ★

Banking

SIC: 6021; NAICS: 52211

Top Banks in Colorado, 2011

Market shares are shown based on deposits as of June 30, 2011.

Wells Fargo Bank NA	25.11%
Firstbank	10.01
J.P. Morgan Chase Bank NA	9.22
US Bank NA	8.80
Bank of the West	3.67
Keybank NA	2.14
Alpine Bank	2.01
Compass Bank	2.00
Vectra Bank Colorado NA	1.90
Other	35.14

Source: "Deposit Market Share Report." [online] from http://www.2fdic.gov [Published October 1, 2011], from Federal Deposit Insurance Corp.

★ 3040 ★

Banking

SIC: 6021; NAICS: 52211

Top Banks in Connecticut, 2011

Market shares are shown based on deposits as of June 30, 2011.

Bank of America NA	23.91%
Webster Bank NA	11.42
Peoples United Bank	9.96
Wells Fargo Bank NA	7.89

TD Bank NA	5.38%
First Niagara Bank NA	4.83
J.P. Morgan Chase Bank NA	3.99
Citibank NA	2.79
Liberty Bank	2.67
Other	27.16

Source: "Deposit Market Share Report." [online] from http://www.2fdic.gov [Published October 1, 2011], from Federal Deposit Insurance Corp.

★ 3041 ★

Banking

SIC: 6021; NAICS: 52211

Top Banks in Delaware, 2011

Market shares are shown based on deposits as of June 30, 2011.

FIA Card Services NA	28.32%
ING Bank FSB	25.39
TD Bank NA	13.34
Discover Bank	10.93
Chase Bank USA NA	7.93
HSBC Bank USA NA	3.23
Manufacturers & Traders Trading Co.	2.30
Barclays Bank Delaware	2.17
Aurora Bank FSB	1.03
Other	5.36

Source: "Deposit Market Share Report." [online] from http://www.2fdic.gov [Published October 1, 2011], from Federal Deposit Insurance Corp.

★ 3042 ★

Banking

SIC: 6021; NAICS: 52211

Top Banks in Florida, 2011

Market shares are shown based on deposits as of June 30, 2011.

Bank of America NA	19.07%
Wells Fargo Bank NA	15.84
Suntrust Bank	10.42
Regions Bank	4.68
Branch Banking & Trust Co.	3.07
J.P. Morgan Chase Bank NA	2.92
Citibank NA	2.69
Everbank	2.42
Fifth Third Bank	1.96
Other	36.93

Source: "Deposit Market Share Report." [online] from http://www.2fdic.gov [Published October 1, 2011], from Federal Deposit Insurance Corp.

★ 3043 ★
Banking
SIC: 6021; NAICS: 52211

Top Banks in Georgia, 2011

Market shares are shown based on deposits as of June 30, 2011.

Suntrust Bank	18.74%
Wells Fargo Bank NA	15.30
Bank of America NA	12.19
Synovus Bank	7.22
Branch Banking & Trust Co.	5.62
Regions Bank	3.33
United Community Bank	2.74
RBC Bank USA	1.58
State Bank & Trust Co.	1.29
Other	31.99

Source: "Deposit Market Share Report." [online] from http://www.2fdic.gov [Published October 1, 2011], from Federal Deposit Insurance Corp.

★ 3044 ★
Banking
SIC: 6021; NAICS: 52211

Top Banks in Hawaii, 2011

Market shares are shown based on deposits as of June 30, 2011.

First Hawaiian Bank	35.76%
Bank of Hawaii	30.85
American Savings Bank FSB	13.54
Central Pacific Bank	10.84
Other	9.01

Source: "Deposit Market Share Report." [online] from http://www.2fdic.gov [Published October 1, 2011], from Federal Deposit Insurance Corp.

★ 3045 ★
Banking
SIC: 6021; NAICS: 52211

Top Banks in Idaho, 2011

Market shares are shown based on deposits as of June 30, 2011.

Wells Fargo Bank NA	23.09%
US Bank NA	15.41
Zions First National Bank	6.51
Bank of America NA	5.96
Keybank NA	5.43
DL Evans Bank	4.03
Bank of Commerce	3.40
Mountain West Bank	3.34

Panhandle State Bank	3.28%
Other	39.55

Source: "Deposit Market Share Report." [online] from http://www.2fdic.gov [Published October 1, 2011], from Federal Deposit Insurance Corp.

★ 3046 ★
Banking
SIC: 6021; NAICS: 52211

Top Banks in Illinois, 2011

Market shares are shown based on deposits as of June 30, 2011.

J.P. Morgan Chase Bank NA	15.55%
Harris NA	8.98
Bank of America NA	6.93
Northern Trust Co.	5.08
PNC Bank NA	3.91
State Farm Bank FSB	2.66
Citibank NA	2.55
Private Bank & Trust Co.	2.36
Fifth Third Bank	2.16
Other	49.82

Source: "Deposit Market Share Report." [online] from http://www.2fdic.gov [Published October 1, 2011], from Federal Deposit Insurance Corp.

★ 3047 ★
Banking
SIC: 6021; NAICS: 52211

Top Banks in Indiana, 2011

Market shares are shown based on deposits as of June 30, 2011.

J.P. Morgan Chase Bank NA	12.84%
PNC Bank NA	10.53
Fifth Third Bank	6.61
Old National Bank	4.67
1st Source Bank	3.38
First Merchants Bank NA	2.97
Wells Fargo Bank NA	2.85
Keybank NA	2.61
Regions Bank	2.45
Other	51.09

Source: "Deposit Market Share Report." [online] from http://www.2fdic.gov [Published October 1, 2011], from Federal Deposit Insurance Corp.

★ 3048 ★
Banking
SIC: 6021; NAICS: 52211
Top Banks in Iowa, 2011

Market shares are shown based on deposits as of June 30, 2011.

Wells Fargo Bank NA	8.68%
US Bank NA	6.40
Bank of America NA	5.06
Principal Bank	3.12
Bankers Trust Co.	2.28
Hills Bank & Trust Co.	2.12
Midwestone Bank	1.80
Great Western Bank	1.69
Bank of the West	1.43
First American Bank	1.43
Other	65.99

Source: "Deposit Market Share Report." [online] from http://www.2fdic.gov [Published October 1, 2011], from Federal Deposit Insurance Corp.

★ 3049 ★
Banking
SIC: 6021; NAICS: 52211
Top Banks in Kansas, 2011

Market shares are shown based on deposits as of June 30, 2011.

Bank of America NA	8.03%
Capitol Federal Savings Bank	7.66
InTrust Bank NA	4.69
Commerce Bank	4.67
US Bank NA	2.78
Emprise Bank	2.13
Fidelity Bank	1.79
Wells Fargo Bank NA	1.73
Other	66.52

Source: "Deposit Market Share Report." [online] from http://www.2fdic.gov [Published October 1, 2011], from Federal Deposit Insurance Corp.

★ 3050 ★
Banking
SIC: 6021; NAICS: 52211
Top Banks in Kentucky, 2011

Market shares are shown based on deposits as of June 30, 2011.

PNC Bank NA	9.32%
Fifth Third Bank	7.13
J.P. Morgan Chase Bank NA	6.52
Branch Banking & Trust Co.	5.62

US Bank NA	4.95%
Community Trust Bank Inc.	3.42
Republic Bank & Trust Co.	2.50
Central Trust & Bank Co.	2.33
PBI Bank	2.10
Other	56.11

Source: "Deposit Market Share Report." [online] from http://www.2fdic.gov [Published October 1, 2011], from Federal Deposit Insurance Corp.

★ 3051 ★
Banking
SIC: 6021; NAICS: 52211
Top Banks in Louisiana, 2011

Market shares are shown based on deposits as of June 30, 2011.

Capital One NA	20.90%
J.P. Morgan Chase Bank NA	16.35
Whitney Bank	10.20
Regions Bank	8.43
Iberiabank	5.96
First NBC Bank	1.60
Community Trust Bank	1.36
First Guaranty Bank	1.21
Bancorpsouth Bank	1.13
Other	32.86

Source: "Deposit Market Share Report." [online] from http://www.2fdic.gov [Published October 1, 2011], from Federal Deposit Insurance Corp.

★ 3052 ★
Banking
SIC: 6021; NAICS: 52211
Top Banks in Maine, 2011

Market shares are shown based on deposits as of June 30, 2011.

TD Bank USA NA	29.38%
TD Bank NA	11.24
Keybank NA	8.01
Bangor Savings Bank	5.97
Bank of America NA	5.49
Camden National Bank	5.10
First National Bank NA	3.26
Other	31.55

Source: "Deposit Market Share Report." [online] from http://www.2fdic.gov [Published October 1, 2011], from Federal Deposit Insurance Corp.

★ 3053 ★

Banking

SIC: 6021; NAICS: 52211

Top Banks in Maryland, 2011

Market shares are shown based on deposits as of June 30, 2011.

Bank of America NA	20.47%
Manufacturers & Traders Trading Co.	14.91
PNC Bank NA	9.15
Capital One NA	8.27
Wells Fargo Bank NA	7.12
Suntrust Bank	7.07
Branch Banking & Trust Co.	5.69
Sandy Spring Bank	2.11
Susquehanna Bank	1.74
Other	23.47

Source: "Deposit Market Share Report." [online] from http://www.2fdic.gov [Published October 1, 2011], from Federal Deposit Insurance Corp.

★ 3054 ★

Banking

SIC: 6021; NAICS: 52211

Top Banks in Massachusetts, 2011

Market shares are shown based on deposits as of June 30, 2011.

Bank of America NA	22.81%
State Street Bank & Trust Co.	12.37
RBS Citizens NA	12.30
Sovereign Bank	6.66
TD Bank NA	4.24
Bank of New York Mellon	3.06
Eastern Bank	2.67
Rockland Trust Co.	1.65
Middlesex Savings Bank	1.50
Other	32.74

Source: "Deposit Market Share Report." [online] from http://www.2fdic.gov [Published October 1, 2011], from Federal Deposit Insurance Corp.

★ 3055 ★

Banking

SIC: 6021; NAICS: 52211

Top Banks in Michigan, 2011

Market shares are shown based on deposits as of June 30, 2011.

J.P. Morgan Chase Bank NA	16.23%
Comerica Bank	13.80
PNC Bank NA	9.55
Bank of America NA	9.06

Fifth Third Bank	8.29%
Huntington National Bank	4.51
Flagstar Bank FSB	4.43
Citizens Bank	3.82
RBS Citizens National Bank	2.95
Other	27.36

Source: "Deposit Market Share Report." [online] from http://www.2fdic.gov [Published October 1, 2011], from Federal Deposit Insurance Corp.

★ 3056 ★

Banking

SIC: 6021; NAICS: 52211

Top Banks in Minnesota, 2011

Market shares are shown based on deposits as of June 30, 2011.

Wells Fargo Bank NA	30.6%
US Bank National NA	25.1
TCF National Bank	3.2
Ameriprise Bank FSB	2.9
M&I Marshall & Ilsley Bank	1.7
Bremer Bank NA	1.5
Other	35.0

Source: "Deposit Market Share Report." [online] from http://www.2fdic.gov [Published October 1, 2011], from Federal Deposit Insurance Corp.

★ 3057 ★

Banking

SIC: 6021; NAICS: 52211

Top Banks in Mississippi, 2011

Market shares are shown based on deposits as of June 30, 2011.

Regions Bank	15.58%
Trustmark National Bank	13.78
Bancorpsouth Bank	10.90
Hancock Bank	6.43
Bankplus	3.69
Renasant Bank	3.52
Merchants & Farmers Bank	2.59
Citizens National Bank of Meridian	2.05
Other	41.46

Source: "Deposit Market Share Report." [online] from http://www.2fdic.gov [Published October 1, 2011], from Federal Deposit Insurance Corp.

★ 3058 ★
Banking
SIC: 6021; NAICS: 52211

Top Banks in Missouri, 2011

Market shares are shown based on deposits as of June 30, 2011.

US Bank NA	11.11%
Bank of America NA	9.56
Commerce Bank	8.71
Scottrade Bank	5.54
UMB Bank NA	5.47
M&I Marshall & Ilsley Bank	2.21
Regions Bank	1.81
Enterprise Bank & Trust	1.51
Other	54.08

Source: "Deposit Market Share Report." [online] from http://www.2fdic.gov [Published October 1, 2011], from Federal Deposit Insurance Corp.

★ 3059 ★
Banking
SIC: 6021; NAICS: 52211

Top Banks in Montana, 2011

Market shares are shown based on deposits as of June 30, 2011.

First Interstate Bank	15.92%
Wells Fargo Bank	10.95
US Bank NA	10.33
Stockman Bank of Montana	8.19
Glacier Bank	4.35
First Security Bank Missoula	3.92
Western Security Bank	3.20
Mountain West Bank NA	3.16
First Security Bank	2.63
Other	47.35

Source: "Deposit Market Share Report." [online] from http://www.2fdic.gov [Published October 1, 2011], from Federal Deposit Insurance Corp.

★ 3060 ★
Banking
SIC: 6021; NAICS: 52211

Top Banks in Nebraska, 2011

Market shares are shown based on deposits as of June 30, 2011.

First National Bank of Omaha	13.45%
Wells Fargo Bank NA	9.31
Mutual of Omaha Bank	5.56
US Bank NA	5.33
Great Western Bank	5.16

Pinnacle Bank	5.15%
Union Bank & Trust Co.	4.06
Bank of the West	2.92
American National Bank	2.20
Other	46.86

Source: "Deposit Market Share Report." [online] from http://www.2fdic.gov [Published October 1, 2011], from Federal Deposit Insurance Corp.

★ 3061 ★
Banking
SIC: 6021; NAICS: 52211

Top Banks in Nevada, 2011

Market shares are shown based on deposits as of June 30, 2011.

Citibank NA	64.08%
Charles Schwab Bank	19.40
Wells Fargo Bank NA	4.95
Bank of America NA	4.14
Other	7.43

Source: "Deposit Market Share Report." [online] from http://www.2fdic.gov [Published October 1, 2011], from Federal Deposit Insurance Corp.

★ 3062 ★
Banking
SIC: 6021; NAICS: 52211

Top Banks in New Hampshire, 2011

Market shares are shown based on deposits as of June 30, 2011.

RBS Citizens NA	25.03%
TD Bank NA	19.07
Bank of America NA	17.73
Peoples United Bank	4.74
Laconia Savings Bank	3.21
Sovereign Bank	3.08
Lake Sunapee Bank FSB	2.35
Northway Bank	2.19
Other	22.60

Source: "Deposit Market Share Report." [online] from http://www.2fdic.gov [Published October 1, 2011], from Federal Deposit Insurance Corp.

★ 3063 ★
Banking
SIC: 6021; NAICS: 52211
Top Banks in New Jersey, 2011

Market shares are shown based on deposits as of June 30, 2011.

Bank of America NA	15.92%
Wells Fargo Bank NA	11.26
TD Bank NA	10.85
Hudson City Savings Bank	8.00
PNC Bank NA	7.62
J.P. Morgan Chase Bank NA	4.65
Sovereign Bank	3.35
Valley National Bank	3.17
Investors Savings Bank	2.65
Other	32.53

Source: "Deposit Market Share Report." [online] from http://www.2fdic.gov [Published October 1, 2011], from Federal Deposit Insurance Corp.

★ 3064 ★
Banking
SIC: 6021; NAICS: 52211
Top Banks in New Mexico, 2011

Market shares are shown based on deposits as of June 30, 2011.

Wells Fargo Bank NA	24.44%
Bank of America NA	14.85
US Bank NA	5.88
Los Alamos National Bank	5.14
Bank of the West	4.90
BOKF NA	4.79
New Mexico Bank & Trust	2.57
Compass Bank	2.48
First National Bank of Santa Fe	2.41
Other	32.54

Source: "Deposit Market Share Report." [online] from http://www.2fdic.gov [Published October 1, 2011], from Federal Deposit Insurance Corp.

★ 3065 ★
Banking
SIC: 6021; NAICS: 52211
Top Banks in New York, 2011

Market shares are shown based on deposits as of June 30, 2011.

J.P. Morgan Chase Bank NA	35.49%
Bank of New York Mellon	9.33
HSBC Bank USA NA	7.00
Bank of America	6.65
Citibank NA	6.53%
Capital One NA	3.64
Manufacturers & Traders Trading Co.	2.44
TD Bank NA	2.06
Deutsche Bank Trading Co. Americas	1.95
Other	24.91

Source: "Deposit Market Share Report." [online] from http://www.2fdic.gov [Published October 1, 2011], from Federal Deposit Insurance Corp.

★ 3066 ★
Banking
SIC: 6021; NAICS: 52211
Top Banks in North Carolina, 2011

Market shares are shown based on deposits as of June 30, 2011.

Bank of America NA	47.38%
Wells Fargo Bank NA	13.64
Branch Banking & Trust Co.	12.34
First-Citizens Bank & Trust Co.	4.31
RBC Bank USA	3.61
Suntrust Bank	2.57
First Bank	0.85
Fifth Third Bank	0.74
Other	14.56

Source: "Deposit Market Share Report." [online] from http://www.2fdic.gov [Published October 1, 2011], from Federal Deposit Insurance Corp.

★ 3067 ★
Banking
SIC: 6021; NAICS: 52211
Top Banks in North Dakota, 2011

Market shares are shown based on deposits as of June 30, 2011.

Wells Fargo Bank NA	9.45%
State Bank & Trust	6.84
US Bank NA	6.36
Gate City Bank	5.60
Bremer Bank NA	4.98
First International Banking & Trust	4.01
Alerus Financial NA	3.54
Starion Financial	3.08
American Bank Center	2.73
Other	53.41

Source: "Deposit Market Share Report." [online] from http://www.2fdic.gov [Published October 1, 2011], from Federal Deposit Insurance Corp.

★ 3068 ★
Banking
SIC: 6021; NAICS: 52211
Top Banks in Ohio, 2011

Market shares are shown based on deposits as of June 30, 2011.

Fifth Third Bank	13.57%
Huntington National Bank	11.45
US Bank NA	11.29
PNC Bank NA	10.61
J.P. Morgan Chase Bank NA	8.50
Keybank NA	8.09
FirstMerit Bank NA	3.49
RBS Citizens NA	2.98
Third FS&LA of Cleveland	2.64
Other	27.38

Source: "Deposit Market Share Report." [online] from http://www.2fdic.gov [Published October 1, 2011], from Federal Deposit Insurance Corp.

★ 3069 ★
Banking
SIC: 6021; NAICS: 52211
Top Banks in Oklahoma, 2011

Market shares are shown based on deposits as of June 30, 2011.

BOKF NA	12.96%
MDFirst Bank	7.61
Bancfirst	6.57
Arvest Bank	5.11
Bank of America NA	4.97
J.P. Morgan Chase Bank NA	4.45
Stillwater NB&T Co.	2.38
RCB Bank	2.15
International Bank of Commerce	2.10
Other	51.70

Source: "Deposit Market Share Report." [online] from http://www.2fdic.gov [Published October 1, 2011], from Federal Deposit Insurance Corp.

★ 3070 ★
Banking
SIC: 6021; NAICS: 52211
Top Banks in Oregon, 2011

Market shares are shown based on deposits as of June 30, 2011.

US Bank NA	17.97%
Bank of America NA	15.39
Umpqua Bank	14.58
J.P. Morgan Chase Bank NA	7.69

Bank of America Oregon NA	5.82%
Keybank NA	5.53
Sterling Savings Bank	2.98
West Coast Bank	2.82
Washington FS&LA	2.15
Other	22.07

Source: "Deposit Market Share Report." [online] from http://www.2fdic.gov [Published October 1, 2011], from Federal Deposit Insurance Corp.

★ 3071 ★
Banking
SIC: 6021; NAICS: 52211
Top Banks in Pennsylvania, 2011

Market shares are shown based on deposits as of June 30, 2011.

PNC Bank NA	20.73%
Wells Fargo Bank of PA	12.03
Citizens Bank of PA	8.22
Sovereign Bank	3.68
TD Bank NA	3.66
Manufacturers & Traders Trading Co.	2.82
Bank of America NA	2.75
First National Bank of Pennsylvania	2.37
Other	43.65

Source: "Deposit Market Share Report." [online] from http://www.2fdic.gov [Published October 1, 2011], from Federal Deposit Insurance Corp.

★ 3072 ★
Banking
SIC: 6021; NAICS: 52211
Top Banks in Puerto Rico, 2011

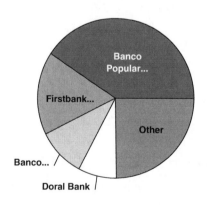

Market shares are shown based on deposits as of June 30, 2011.

Banco Popular de Puerto Rico	40.92%
Firstbank of Puerto Rico	16.60

Continued on next page.

★ 3072 ★

[Continued]

Banking

SIC: 6021; NAICS: 52211

Top Banks in Puerto Rico, 2011

Market shares are shown based on deposits as of June 30, 2011.

Banco Santander Puerto Rico	10.18%
Doral Bank	8.34
Other	24.96

Source: "Deposit Market Share Report." [online] from http://www.2fdic.gov [Published October 1, 2011], from Federal Deposit Insurance Corp.

★ 3073 ★

Banking

SIC: 6021; NAICS: 52211

Top Banks in Rhode Island, 2011

Market shares are shown based on deposits as of June 30, 2011.

Bank of America Rhode Island NA	32.92%
RBS Citizens NA	22.98
Bank of America NA	15.22
Metlife Bank NA	9.48
Sovereign Bank	4.61
Other	14.79

Source: "Deposit Market Share Report." [online] from http://www.2fdic.gov [Published October 1, 2011], from Federal Deposit Insurance Corp.

★ 3074 ★

Banking

SIC: 6021; NAICS: 52211

Top Banks in South Carolina, 2011

Market shares are shown based on deposits as of June 30, 2011.

Wells Fargo Bank NA	17.69%
Bank of America NA	13.32
Branch Banking & Trust Co.	9.82
First Citizens B&T Co. Inc.	8.96
TD Bank NA	4.88
Synovus Bank	4.00
First FS&LA of Charleston	3.11
SCBT NA	3.02
Suntrust Bank	3.01
Other	32.19

Source: "Deposit Market Share Report." [online] from http://www.2fdic.gov [Published October 1, 2011], from Federal Deposit Insurance Corp.

★ 3075 ★

Banking

SIC: 6021; NAICS: 52211

Top Banks in South Dakota, 2011

Market shares are shown based on deposits as of June 30, 2011.

Wells Fargo Bank	78.96%
Great Western Bank	1.58
Dacotah Bank	1.39
First Premier Bank	1.17
Citibank South Dakota NA	1.05
Other	15.85

Source: "Deposit Market Share Report." [online] from http://www.2fdic.gov [Published October 1, 2011], from Federal Deposit Insurance Corp.

★ 3076 ★

Banking

SIC: 6021; NAICS: 52211

Top Banks in Tennessee, 2011

Market shares are shown based on deposits as of June 30, 2011.

Regions Bank	14.88%
First Tennessee Bank NA	13.43
Suntrust Bank	9.59
Bank of America NA	6.99
Pinnacle National Bank	3.28
Branch Banking & Trust Co.	2.36
U.S. Bank NA	1.74
Greenbank	1.59
First Bank	1.48
Other	44.66

Source: "Deposit Market Share Report." [online] from http://www.2fdic.gov [Published October 1, 2011], from Federal Deposit Insurance Corp.

★ 3077 ★

Banking

SIC: 6021; NAICS: 52211

Top Banks in Texas, 2011

Market shares are shown based on deposits as of June 30, 2011.

J.P. Morgan Chase Bank NA	17.66%
Bank of America NA	14.28
Wells Fargo Bank NA	9.42
USAA Federal Savings Bank	8.06
Compass Bank	4.78
Wells Fargo Bank Central NA	3.07
Frost National Bank	2.79

Continued on next page.

★ 3077 ★

[Continued]

Banking

SIC: 6021; NAICS: 52211

Top Banks in Texas, 2011

Market shares are shown based on deposits as of June 30, 2011.

Capital One NA	1.67%
Amegy Bank NA	1.56
Other	36.71

Source: "Deposit Market Share Report." [online] from http://www.2fdic.gov [Published October 1, 2011], from Federal Deposit Insurance Corp.

★ 3078 ★

Banking

SIC: 6021; NAICS: 52211

Top Banks in Utah, 2011

Market shares are shown based on deposits as of June 30, 2011.

Morgan Stanley Bank NA	19.93%
Ally Bank	13.09
Goldman Sachs Bank USA	10.83
USB Bank USA	9.38
American Express Bank FSB	7.12
Wells Fargo Bank NW NA	5.38
GE Money Bank	5.24
J.P. Morgan Chase Bank NA	3.98
Zions First National Bank	3.81
Other	21.24

Source: "Deposit Market Share Report." [online] from http://www.2fdic.gov [Published October 1, 2011], from Federal Deposit Insurance Corp.

★ 3079 ★

Banking

SIC: 6021; NAICS: 52211

Top Banks in Vermont, 2011

Market shares are shown based on deposits as of June 30, 2011.

Peoples United Bank	22.61%
TD Bank NA	21.29
Merchants Bank	10.11
RBS Citizens NA	7.21
Keybank NA	6.47
Northfield Savings Bank	4.68
Community National Bank	3.82
Union Bank	3.32

Passumpsic Savings Bank	3.00%
Other	17.49

Source: "Deposit Market Share Report." [online] from http://www.2fdic.gov [Published October 1, 2011], from Federal Deposit Insurance Corp.

★ 3080 ★

Banking

SIC: 6021; NAICS: 52211

Top Banks in Virginia, 2011

Market shares are shown based on deposits as of June 30, 2011.

Capital One Bank USA NA	16.23%
E*Trade Bank	13.80
Wells Fargo Bank NA	11.95
Bank of America NA	9.54
Branch Banking & Trust Co.	8.92
Suntrust Bank	7.30
Capital One NA	5.89
Union First Market Bank	1.37
Carter Bank & Trust	1.27
Other	23.73

Source: "Deposit Market Share Report." [online] from http://www.2fdic.gov [Published October 1, 2011], from Federal Deposit Insurance Corp.

★ 3081 ★

Banking

SIC: 6021; NAICS: 52211

Top Banks in Washington, 2011

Market shares are shown based on deposits as of June 30, 2011.

Bank of America NA	21.7%
Wells Fargo Bank NA	10.4
U.S. Bank NA	9.7
J.P. Morgan Chase Bank NA	8.7
Keybank NA	7.4
Washington FS&LA	4.0
Sterling Savings Bank	2.9
Columbia State Bank	2.6
Washington Trust Bank	2.5
Other	30.0

Source: "Deposit Market Share Report." [online] from http://www.2fdic.gov [Published October 1, 2011], from Federal Deposit Insurance Corp.

★ 3082 ★

Banking

SIC: 6021; NAICS: 52211

Top Banks in Washington D.C., 2011

Market shares are shown based on deposits as of June 30, 2011.

Wells Fargo Bank NA	22.33%
Bank of America NA	19.36
PNC Bank NA	11.82
Suntrust Bank	11.48
HSBC Bank USA NA	7.21
Other	27.80

Source: "Deposit Market Share Report." [online] from http://www.2fdic.gov [Published October 1, 2011], from Federal Deposit Insurance Corp.

★ 3083 ★

Banking

SIC: 6021; NAICS: 52211

Top Banks in West Virginia, 2011

Market shares are shown based on deposits as of June 30, 2011.

Branch Banking & Trust Co.	17.47%
United Bank	9.87
Westbanco Bank Inc.	7.59
City National Bank of West Virginia	6.80
Huntington National Bank	6.35
J.P. Morgan Chase Bank NA	5.52
First Community Bank	3.04
Summit Community Bank Inc.	2.68
Central Bank Inc.	2.16
Other	38.52

Source: "Deposit Market Share Report." [online] from http://www.2fdic.gov [Published October 1, 2011], from Federal Deposit Insurance Corp.

★ 3084 ★

Banking

SIC: 6021; NAICS: 52211

Top Banks in Wisconsin, 2011

Market shares are shown based on deposits as of June 30, 2011.

U.S. Bank NA	16.95%
M&I Marshall & Ilsley Bank	16.91
Associated Bank NA	7.81
J.P. Morgan Chase Bank NA	5.44
Wells Fargo Bank NA	2.91
Johnson Bank	2.38
Anchor Bank FSB	2.06
Bank Mutual	1.56

North Shore Bank FSB	1.05%
Other	42.93

Source: "Deposit Market Share Report." [online] from http://www.2fdic.gov [Published October 1, 2011], from Federal Deposit Insurance Corp.

★ 3085 ★

Banking

SIC: 6021; NAICS: 52211

Top Banks in Wyoming, 2011

Market shares are shown based on deposits as of June 30, 2011.

First Interstate Bank	17.40%
Wells Fargo Bank NA	16.33
Bank of the West	6.77
Bank of Jackson Hole	3.93
Hilltop National Bank	3.89
Pinnacle Bank Wyoming	3.78
1st Bank	3.42
American National Bank	3.42
First National Bank of Gillette	3.07
Other	37.99

Source: "Deposit Market Share Report." [online] from http://www.2fdic.gov [Published October 1, 2011], from Federal Deposit Insurance Corp.

★ 3086 ★

Banking

SIC: 6021; NAICS: 52211

Top Private Banking Firms Worldwide, 2010

Firms are ranked by assets under management in billions of dollars.

Bank of America NA	$ 1,945
Morgan Stanley	1,628
UBS	1,560
Wells Fargo Bank NA	1,398
Credit Suisse	865
Royal Bank of Canada	435
HSBC	390
Deutsche Bank	369
BNP Paribas	340
J.P. Morgan Chase Bank NA	284

Source: *Financial Times*, November 21, 2011, p. NA, from Capgemini, Merrill Lynch and Scorpio Partnership.

★ 3087 ★
Credit Unions
SIC: 6061; NAICS: 52213

Top Credit Unions, 2010

Credit unions are ranked by assets in billions of dollars.

Navy Federal Credit Union	$ 39.6
State Employees Credit Union	19.6
Pentagon Federal Credit Union	14.0
Boeing Employees Credit Union	8.6
Schoolsfirst Federal Credit Union	8.0
The Golden 1 Credit Union	7.6
Alliant Credit Union	7.0
Security Service Federal Credit Union	5.5
Suncoast Schools Federal Credit Union	5.4
American Airlines Federal Credit Union	5.1
Star One Credit Union	5.1

Source: "Largest 100 U.S. Credit Unions by Assets." [online] from http://www.creditunionsonline.com [Accessed December 1, 2011].

★ 3088 ★
Financial Transactions
SIC: 6099; NAICS: 52232

Financial Transaction Processing and Clearing, 2007

Data show the percent of industry sales held by the largest 4, 8, 20 and 50 firms in the sector. There are approximately 5,761 firms operating in the industry generating employment for 142,212 people.

4 largest firms	33.1%
8 largest firms	48.7
20 largest firms	71.3
50 largest firms	85.8

Source: "2007 Economic Census." [online] from http://www.census.gov/econ/concentration.html [Accessed August 12, 2011], from U.S. Bureau of the Census.

★ 3089 ★
Prepaid Cards
SIC: 6099; NAICS: 52232

Top Prepaid Card Issuing Banks, 2009

Firms are ranked by purchase volume in billions of dollars. Payroll cards claimed 33% of the prepaid sector, general purpose 29%, gifts and incentives 12% each, government 10% and health care 4%.

J.P. Morgan Chase Bank NA	$ 8.99
H&R Block	8.93
Comerica	5.28
MetaBank	5.03
The Bancorp Bank	3.24
GE Money	$ 3.19
Citi	2.25
U.S. Bank NA	1.96
Synovus/Columbus	1.80

Source: "Prepaid Card Industry." [online] from http://cfile6.uf.tistory.com/attach/160797314C8ED681034F19 [Published August 29, 2010], from *Nilson Report* and Credit Suisse.

SIC 61 - Nondepository Institutions

★ 3090 ★

Credit Cards

SIC: 6141; NAICS: 52221

Credit Card Market, 2010

Market shares are shown in percent.

Visa	57.0%
MasterCard	25.0
American Express	15.0
Discover	3.0

Source: "The Role of Interchange Fees on Debit and Credit Card Transactions." [online] from http://www.richmondfed. org/publications/research/economic_brief/2011 [Published May 2011], from *Nilson Report.*

★ 3091 ★

Credit Cards

SIC: 6141; NAICS: 52221

Top Credit Card Marketers, 2010

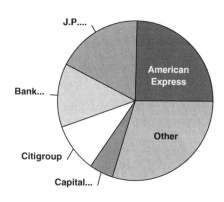

Market shares are shown based on general purpose volume.

American Express	24.6%
J.P. Morgan Chase Bank	17.7
Bank of America	12.7
Citigroup	10.3
Capital One Financial Corp.	5.3
Other	29.5

Source: *Advertising Age,* June 20, 2011, p. 10, from *Nilson Report.*

★ 3092 ★

Debit Cards

SIC: 6141; NAICS: 522298

Market for PIN-Based Debit Transactions, 2010

The Federal Reserve proposed in December 2010 to cap interchange fees at 12 cents per transaction. At the time, card processing networks charged merchants an average of 1 percent of the purchase price, regardless of cost, and passed that money to banks that issue cards. The average debit interchange fee in 2009 was 44 cents per transaction, or 1.14 percent of the purchase price, according to a draft of the proposed rules. The loss in fees may be offset in other ways.

Visa	50.0%
First Data	20.0
Other	30.0

Source: "KKR-Controlled First Data May Escape Harm From Lower Fees, Analyst Says." [online] from http://www. bloomberg.com [Published December 23, 2010], from Credit Suisse.

★ 3093 ★

Debit Cards

SIC: 6141; NAICS: 52221

Top Debit Card Issuers, 2010

Market shares are shown based on $1.09 trillion in purchasing volume.

Bank of America NA	22.5%
Wells Fargo Bank NA	18.0
J.P. Morgan Chase Bank	14.8
U.S. Bancorp	3.8
PNC Bank NA	3.5
Citigroup	2.5
Regions	2.5
Suntrust Bank	2.3
Other	30.0

Source: *Wall Street Journal,* October 28, 2011, p. C1, from *Nilson Report.*

★ 3094 ★
Debit Cards

SIC: 6141; NAICS: 522298

Top PIN Debit Networks, 2007

Market shares are shown in percent.

Interlink	37.0%
Star	29.0
Pulse	11.0
NYCE	8.0
Other	15.0

Source: "Debit Networks Market Share Report." [online] from http://3dmerchant.com/blog/credit-card-processing-rates/debit-networks-market-share [Accessed March 2, 2012], from Federal Reserve.

★ 3095 ★
Auto Loans

SIC: 6159; NAICS: 522298

Top Auto Finance Providers, 2011

Market shares are shown for the third quarter of 2011.

Ally	5.2%
Toyota	4.3
Chase	3.4
Honda	3.3
Wells Fargo Bank NA	3.3
Other	80.5

Source: "Ally Financial Inc." [online] from http://phx.corporate-ir.net [Published November 2, 2011], from Experian Automotive.

★ 3096 ★
Auto Loans

SIC: 6159; NAICS: 52222

Top New Car Loan Providers, 2011

Market shares are shown for the second quarter of 2011.

Ally	12.05%
Honda	8.70
Ford Motor Co.	8.35
Toyota	8.13
Chase	6.50
Nissan Infiniti	4.26
Bank of America NA	3.96
Wells Fargo Bank NA	3.46
Hyundai	3.35
Other	41.24

Source: "After the Storm." [online] from http://www.vscac.com/uploads/VSCAC/Gray_Presentation.pdf [Accessed April 1, 2012], from Experian Automotive.

★ 3097 ★
Auto Loans

SIC: 6159; NAICS: 52222

Top Used Car Loan Providers, 2011

Market shares are shown for the second quarter of 2011.

Wells Fargo Bank NA	7.17%
Ally	3.90
Chase	3.71
Capital One	3.31
Toyota	2.89
Santander	1.88
Bank of America NA	1.80
Credit Acceptance	1.56
Americredit	1.37
Other	72.41

Source: "After the Storm." [online] from http://www.vscac.com/uploads/VSCAC/Gray_Presentation.pdf [Accessed April 1, 2012], from Experian Automotive.

★ 3098 ★
Farm Loans

SIC: 6159; NAICS: 522292

Farm Real Estate Market, 2000, 2007 and 2010

Market shares are shown in percent.

	2000	2007	2010
Farm Credit System	35.0%	41.5%	45.0%
Other	65.0	58.5	55.0

Source: "Farmers Bet on Rates as MetLife Battles Rural Lenders." [online] from http://www.bloomberg.com [Published January 20, 2012], from U.S. Department of Agriculture.

★ 3099 ★
Student Loans

SIC: 6159; NAICS: 522298

Top Providers of Federal Student Loans, 2010

Companies are ranked by loan value in millions of dollars. In October 2011, the Federal Reserve Bank reported that student loan debt crossed the $100 billion mark for the first time and total loans will exceed $1 trillion for the first time in 2011. This means Americans now owe more on their student loans than on their credit cards.

Sallie Mae Corp.	$ 148,649
Nelnet	24,514
Wells Fargo Bank NA	20,722
Brazos Group	12,080

Continued on next page.

★ 3099 ★

[Continued]

Student Loans

SIC: 6159; NAICS: 522298

Top Providers of Federal Student Loans, 2010

Companies are ranked by loan value in millions of dollars. In October 2011, the Federal Reserve Bank reported that student loan debt crossed the $100 billion mark for the first time and total loans will exceed $1 trillion for the first time in 2011. This means Americans now owe more on their student loans than on their credit cards.

J.P. Morgan Chase Bank	$ 9,616
Pennsylvania Higher Education Assistant Authority (PHEAA)	9,575
College Loan Corp.	8,669
CIT	8,317
PNC Bank	7,549
Goal Financial	6,881

Source: "SLM Corporation." [online] from http://www.sallie-mae.com [Accessed October 1, 2011], from U.S. Department of Education.

★ 3100 ★

Mortgage Loans

SIC: 6162; NAICS: 522292

Top Jumbo Loan Arrangers, 2011

Jumbo loans exceed the Fannie Mae/Freddie Mac loan limit of $625,000.

Chase Iselin	11.14%
Wells Fargo & Co.	10.66
Bank of America	9.68
PHH Mortgage	8.81
CitiMortgage Inc.	8.03
Union Bank	5.41
U.S. Bank Home Mortgage	4.45
Astoria FS&LA	2.83
Other	38.99

Source: *National Mortgage News*, April 16, 2012, p. 10, from *National Mortgage News/Quarterly Data Report.*

★ 3101 ★

Mortgage Loans

SIC: 6162; NAICS: 522292

Top Mortgage Banks in Australia, 2009

Market shares are shown in percent.

Commonwealth Bank of Australia	22.7%
Westpac	16.5
National Australia Bank	13.3
Australia and New Zealand Banking Group	12.7%
Other	34.8

Source: "Australian Mortgage Industry." [online] from http://www.aventree.com/pdf/austalian_mortgage_industry_vol11.pdf [April 10, 2010], from Australian Prudential Regulation Authority, Reserve Bank of Australia and J.P. Morgan estimates.

★ 3102 ★

Mortgage Loans

SIC: 6162; NAICS: 522292

Top Mortgage Firms in San Diego, CA, 2010

Companies are ranked by value of loans originated in millions of dollars.

BlueFi Lending Corp.	$ 465.7
Residential Wholesale Mortgage Inc.	462.4
Integrity First Financial Group	350.0
San Diego Funding	190.2
Avalon Mortgage Corp.	150.9
Pacific Southwest Realty Services	140.0
Southwestern Mortgage Co.	76.1
California Mortgage Consultants	69.0
Senior American Funding	50.8

Source: *San Diego Business Journal*, August 15, 2011, p. 22, from company reports.

★ 3103 ★

Mortgage Loans

SIC: 6162; NAICS: 522292

Top Mortgage Firms in Utah, 2010

Market shares are shown based on dollar volume.

Wells Fargo & Co.	15.26%
Provident Funding Associates	7.40
Bank of America Fork	6.87
America First Credit Union	5.49
J.P. Morgan Chase Bank	4.78
Zions First National Bank	3.53
Castle & Cooke Mortgage L.L.C.	2.84
Other	54.23

Source: *Utah Business*, May 2011, p. 86, from *Mortgage Data Web Market Share Report.*

★ 3104 ★
Mortgage Loans
SIC: 6162; NAICS: 522292

Top Residential Correspondent Lenders, 2011

Market shares are shown for the second quarter of 2011. Correspondent volume represents ''already funded'' loans purchased from another originator.

Wells Fargo & Co.	21.80%
Bank of America	18.00
Chase	10.83
Ally/ResCap (GMAC)	8.99
CitiMortgage Inc.	4.54
Flagstar Bank	2.33
Other	33.51

Source: *National Mortgage News*, September 19, 2011, p. 6, from *National Mortgage News/Quarterly Data Report*.

★ 3105 ★
Mortgage Loans
SIC: 6162; NAICS: 522292

Top Residential Interest-Only Lenders, 2011

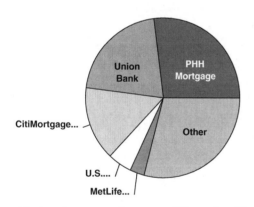

Market shares are shown as of December 31, 2011.

PHH Mortgage	27.44%
Union Bank	21.37
CitiMortgage Inc.	14.73
U.S. Bank Home Mortgage	4.57
MetLife Home Loans	2.78
Other	29.11

Source: *National Mortgage News*, April 2, 2012, p. 2, from *National Mortgage News/Quarterly Data Report*.

★ 3106 ★
Mortgage Loans
SIC: 6162; NAICS: 522292

Top Residential Originators, 2011

Market shares are shown for the second quarter of 2011.

Wells Fargo & Co.	22.62%
Bank of America	14.27
Chase	12.40
Ally/ResCap (GMAC)	4.25
CitiMortgage Inc.	4.21
PHH Mortgage	3.36
Other	38.89

Source: *National Mortgage News*, September 19, 2011, p. 6, from *National Mortgage News/Quarterly Data Report*.

★ 3107 ★
Mortgage Loans
SIC: 6162; NAICS: 522292

Top Residential Retail Lenders, 2011

Market shares are shown for the first half of 2011.

Wells Fargo & Co.	24.10%
Bank of America	13.83
Chase	12.70
PHH Mortgage	4.61
CitiMortgage Inc.	3.94
Quicken Loans Inc.	2.97
U.S. Bank Home Mortgage	2.24
Other	55.61

Source: *National Mortgage News*, October 10, 2011, p. 6, from *National Mortgage News/Quarterly Data Report*.

★ 3108 ★
Mortgage Loans
SIC: 6162; NAICS: 522292

Top Residential Second Lien Servicers, 2011

Market shares are shown based on the fourth quarter of 2011.

Wells Fargo & Co.	25.00%
Bank of America	14.03
PHH Mortgage	5.69
TD Banknorth	5.23
Chase	5.12
Other	54.93

Source: *National Mortgage News*, April 2, 2012, p. 2, from *National Mortgage News/Quarterly Data Report*.

★ **3109** ★

Mortgage Loans

SIC: 6162; NAICS: 522292

Top Residential Servicers, 2011

Market shares are shown for the second quarter of 2011.

Bank of America	21.54%
Wells Fargo & Co.	19.37
Chase	13.06
CitiMortgage Inc.	6.14
Ally/ResCap (GMAC)	4.13
PHH Mortgage	1.75
Other	34.01

Source: *National Mortgage News*, September 19, 2011, p. 6, from *National Mortgage News/Quarterly Data Report.*

★ **3110** ★

Mortgage Loans

SIC: 6162; NAICS: 522292

Top Residential Wholesale Lenders, 2011

Market shares are shown for the first half of 2011. Wholesaling involves the table funding of mortgages through loan brokers.

Provident Funding Associates	11.50%
Wells Fargo & Co.	11.24
U.S. Bank Home Mortgage	8.20
ING Bank FSB	6.39
CBC National Bank	4.43
Flagstar Bank	4.19
MetLife Home Loans	3.78
Union Bank	3.69
Fifth Third Mortgage	3.63
Other	42.95

Source: *National Mortgage News*, October 10, 2011, p. 6, from *National Mortgage News/Quarterly Data Report.*

★ **3111** ★

Mortgage Loans

SIC: 6162; NAICS: 522292

Top Subprime Servicers, 2011

Market shares are shown based on a number of loans serviced.

Chase	20.99%
Ocwen Loan Servicing	19.94
American Home Mortgage Servicing	12.70
Wells Fargo & Co.	7.19

Bank of America	5.76%
Other	33.42

Source: *National Mortgage News*, April 2, 2012, p. 2, from *National Mortgage News/Quarterly Data Report.*

★ **3112** ★

Mortgage Loans

SIC: 6162; NAICS: 522292

Top Subservicers, 2011

Market shares are shown as of December 31, 2011.

Cenlar	17.12%
Dovenmuehle Mortgage	13.50
Nationstar	10.43
Bank of America	7.91
PHH Mortgage	6.31
Other	44.73

Source: *National Mortgage News*, April 2, 2012, p. 2, from *National Mortgage News/Quarterly Data Report.*

★ **3113** ★

Mortgage Loans

SIC: 6162; NAICS: 522292

Who Owns Home Loans, 2011

Approximately one million homes are expected to be eligible for reductions in mortgage principal under a proposed legal settlement between state and federal governments and five large banks (Bank of America Corp., J.P. Morgan Chase & Co., Wells Fargo & Co., Citigroup Inc. and Ally Financial Inc. (formerly GMAC)).

Fannie Mae	28.1%
Banks not in settlement	24.8
Freddie Mac	17.6
FHA and VAA	11.3
Investors	10.9
Five banks in settlement	7.3

Source: *USA TODAY*, February 10, 2012, p. B1, from *Inside Mortgage Finance.*

★ 3114 ★
Reverse Mortgages
SIC: 6162; NAICS: 522292

Top Reverse-Mortgage Lenders, 2010

Reverse mortgages allow people age 62 and older to tap the equity in their homes without having to make payments. Bank of America and Wells Fargo announced plans during the first half of 2011 to leave this business, which has come under increased pressures. Shares are shown based on number of loans for the 12 months ended April 2011.

Wells Fargo & Co.	26.2%
Bank of America	17.4
MetLife	15.3
Urban Financial	7.9
Generation Mortgage	7.2
Genworth Financial	6.4
One Reverse Mortgage	5.1
Financial Freedom	2.4
Security One Lending	2.0
Sun West Mortgage	1.5
Other	8.6

Source: *New York Times*, June 18, 2011, p. B1, from Reverse Market Insights.

★ 3115 ★
Multifamily Lending
SIC: 6163; NAICS: 52231

Multifamily Lending Market, 2009 and 2011

Multifamily housing is enjoying strong rental growth, rising values and increasing occupancy rates. This has prompted some nontraditional funding sources such as life insurance companies to move into the sector. Government sponsored enterprises claimed 75-80% of the market in 2009, but by 2011 their share had dropped to approximately 50%. The total value of outstanding multifamily mortgage debt was placed at $802.2 billion for the first quarter of 2011.

	2009	2011
Government sponsored enterprises	80.0%	50.0%
Insurance companies	1.0	9.0
Other	19.0	41.0

Source: *National Real Estate Investor*, November 9, 2011, p. NA, from Real Capital Analytics.

SIC 62 - Security and Commodity Brokers

★ 3116 ★
Investment Banking
SIC: 6211; NAICS: 52311

Bond Market in China, 2010

Data show amounts outstanding by type of investor.

Commercial banks	67.9%
Insurers	9.5
Fund managers	7.1
Individuals	1.1
Other	14.4

Source: *Financial Times*, November 3, 2011, p. 23, from China Bonds and Dealogic.

★ 3117 ★
Investment Banking
SIC: 6211; NAICS: 52311

Corporate Loan Market Worldwide, 2011

Market shares are shown for the third quarter of 2011.

United States	37.0%
Europe	36.0
Asia-Pacific	18.0
Canada	8.0

Source: *Wall Street Journal*, November 23, 2011, p. NA, from Thomson Reuters.

★ 3118 ★
Investment Banking
SIC: 6211; NAICS: 52311

Private Equity, Hedge Funds and Investment Vehicles, 2011

The industry generated revenues of $46.6 billion. Revenues declined 10.6% per year on average from 2006 to 2011. The industry is composed of financial vehicles that pool investor funds for investment in traditional and alternative assets. The number of establishments in this industry is forecast to increase from 14,868 in 2010 to 15,990 in 2015.

Hedge funds	57.0%
Private equity funds	36.6

Closed-end funds and investment trusts . . .	4.4%
Structured investment vehicles	2.0

Source: "Private Equity, Hedge Funds and Investment Vehicles in the U.S." [online] from http://www.ibisworld.com [Published March 2011], from IBISWorld.

★ 3119 ★
Investment Banking
SIC: 6211; NAICS: 52311

Top Currency Dealers Worldwide, 2011

Market shares are shown in percent.

Deutsche Bank	15.65%
Barclays Capital	10.76
UBS	10.60
Citigroup	8.86
J.P. Morgan Chase & Co.	6.44
HSBC	6.27
RBS	6.20
Credit Suisse	4.80
Goldman Sachs	4.13
Other	26.29

Source: *Wall Street Journal*, May 10, 2012, p. C4, from *Euromoney*.

★ 3120 ★
Investment Banking
SIC: 6211; NAICS: 52311

Top ECM Managers Worldwide, 2011

Market shares are shown for year-to-date August 2011.

Goldman Sachs	9.3%
Morgan Stanley	7.8
Bank of America Merrill Lynch	7.3
J.P. Morgan Chase & Co.	7.0
Credit Suisse	6.2
Deutsche Bank	6.1
Citi	5.7
UBS	5.1

Source: *Euroweek*, August 12, 2011, p. NA.

★ 3121 ★
Investment Banking
SIC: 6211; NAICS: 52311

Top ETF Fund Managers, 2011

Market shares are shown for June 2011.

BlackRock (iShares)	43.3%
State Street Global	22.7
Vanguard	16.0
InvescoPowerShares	4.0
ProFunds	2.5
Van Eck	2.1
Other	9.4

Source: "U.S. ETF Market Update." [online] from http://www.sionline.com [Published July 27, 2011], from Strategic Insight Simfund MF.

★ 3122 ★
Investment Banking
SIC: 6211; NAICS: 52311

Top Healthcare Financing Firms, 2010

Market shares are shown based on value of underwritten loans.

J.P. Morgan Chase & Co.	21.9%
Bank of America Merrill Lynch	20.7
Citigroup	12.1
Goldman Sachs	5.6
Deutsche Bank	5.0
U.S. Bancorp	4.9
Credit Suisse	4.6
Wells Fargo Securities	3.4
Other	11.8

Source: *Modern Healthcare*, November 21, 2011, p. 34, from Dealogic.

★ 3123 ★
Investment Banking
SIC: 6211; NAICS: 52311

Top Issuers of Mortgage Securities, 2003-2008

The largest issuers to Fannie Mae and Freddie Mac are ranked by value of securities in billions of dollars.

Countrywide Financial	$ 160.2
Ameriquest Mortgage	112.3
Lehman Brothers	61.3
Washington Mutual	61.0
New Century	48.0
Option One	48.0
Credit Suisse	39.0
GMAC-RFC	37.4

Bank of America Merrill Lynch	$ 29.0
Bear Stearns	28.2

Source: *Financial Times*, September 6, 2011, p. 18, from *Inside Mortgage Finance* and Bloomberg.

★ 3124 ★
Investment Banking
SIC: 6211; NAICS: 52311

Top M&A Financial Advisors Worldwide, 2011

Market shares are shown based on value of deals for the year through September 28, 2011.

Goldman Sachs	24.5%
Morgan Stanley	21.5
J.P. Morgan Chase & Co.	21.3
Citigroup	18.4
Credit Suisse	18.4
Bank of America Merrill Lynch	16.1
Deutsche Bank	12.7
Barclays Capital	11.8
UBS	10.0
Lazard	9.8

Source: *New York Times*, September 29, 2011, p. F11, from Thomson Reuters.

★ 3125 ★
IPOs
SIC: 6211; NAICS: 52311

Largest Initial Public Offerings as of May 2012

Companies are ranked by value of proceeds in billions of dollars. Date of IPO is shown in parentheses and figures have been adjusted for inflation.

General Motors (Nov. 2010)	$ 24.1
Visa (March 2008)	21.1
Facebook (May 2012)	16.0
AT&T Wireless Group (April 2000) . . .	14.2
Kraft Foods (June 2001)	11.2
UPS (Nov. 1999)	7.4
CIT Group (July 2002)	6.2
Conoco (Oct. 1998)	6.2
Travelers Property (March 2002)	5.5
Agere Systems (March 2001)	5.4

Source: *New York Times*, May 17, 2012, p. B10, from Thomson Reuters.

★ 3126 ★
Commodity Contracts
SIC: 6221; NAICS: 52314

Commodity Contracts Brokerages, 2007

Data show the percent of industry sales held by the largest 4, 8, 20 and 50 firms in the sector. There are approximately 1,379 firms operating in the industry generating employment for 11,553 people.

4 largest firms	46.9%
8 largest firms	58.2
20 largest firms	71.0
50 largest firms	81.4

Source: "2007 Economic Census." [online] from http://www.census.gov/econ/concentration.html [Accessed August 12, 2011], from U.S. Bureau of the Census.

★ 3127 ★
Commodity Contracts
SIC: 6221; NAICS: 52313

Commodity Contracts Dealing, 2007

Data show the percent of industry sales held by the largest 4, 8, 20 and 50 firms in the sector. There are approximately 951 firms operating in the industry generating employment for 8,231 people.

4 largest firms	43.4%
8 largest firms	57.7
20 largest firms	75.5
50 largest firms	89.8

Source: "2007 Economic Census." [online] from http://www.census.gov/econ/concentration.html [Accessed August 12, 2011], from U.S. Bureau of the Census.

★ 3128 ★
Inter-Dealer Brokers
SIC: 6231; NAICS: 52321

Top Inter-Dealer Brokers Worldwide, 2010

Market shares are shown based on revenues from over-the-counter credit instruments.

Tullett Prebon	25.0%
bgc	20.0
ICAP	19.0
GFI	15.0
Tradition	14.0
Creditex	7.0

Source: *Financial Times*, February 17, 2012, p. 15, from TABB Group and BIS.

★ 3129 ★
Stock Exchanges
SIC: 6231; NAICS: 52321

Largest Stock Exchanges Worldwide, 2010

Companies are ranked by market capitalization in trillions of dollars as of June 2011. BM&FBOVESPA refers to the merger of the Sao Paulo Stock Exchange (Bovespa) and the Brazilian Mercantile and Futures Exchange (BM&F).

New York Stock Exchange Euronet	$ 13.79
Nasdaq	4.06
London Stock Exchange	3.84
Tokyo Stock Exchange	3.65
NYSE Euronext	3.24
Shanghai Stock Exchange	2.80
Hong Kong Exchange	2.71
TMX Group	2.23
Deutsche Borse	1.62
BM&FBOVESPA	1.55

Source: "World's 10 Largest Stock Exchanges." [online] from http://www.rediff.com/business/slide-show/slide-show-1-largest-stock-exchanges/20111104.htm [Published November 2011].

★ 3130 ★
Financial Information
SIC: 6282; NAICS: 52392, 52393

Leading Financial Data Firms Worldwide, 2010

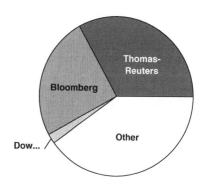

The industry was valued at $23.7 billion in 2010. It is expected to grow just 2% in 2011.

Thomas-Reuters	33.2%
Bloomberg	25.1
Dow Jones	1.6
Other	40.1

Source: *Wall Street Journal*, November 14, 2011, p. B8, from Burton-Taylor International Consulting.

★ 3131 ★
Online Brokers
SIC: 6282; NAICS: 52392, 52393
Top Online Brokers, 2010

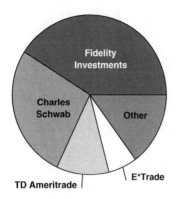

The total market was valued at $2.5 trillion as of December 31, 2010.

Fidelity Investments	41.0%
Charles Schwab	27.0
TD Ameritrade	11.0
E*Trade	6.0
Other	15.0

Source: *Forbes*, July 25, 2011, p. NA, from company reports and Aite Group.

SIC 63 - Insurance Carriers

★ 3132 ★
Insurance
SIC: 6300; NAICS: 524113, 524114, 524126
Largest Insurers Worldwide, 2009

Companies are ranked by non-banking assets in millions of dollars.

Japan Post Insurance Co. Ltd.	$ 1,095.6
AXA S.A.	962.8
American International Group Inc.	847.5
Allianz Societas Europaea	807.3
Assicurazioni Generali S.p.A.	607.4
Aviva PLC	564.0
MetLife Inc.	539.3
Prudential Financial Inc.	480.0
Legal & General Group PLC	473.1
Nippon Life Insurance Co.	472.8

Source: *Best's Review*, November 2011, p. S45, from A.M. Best & Co.

★ 3133 ★
Insurance
SIC: 6300; NAICS: 524113, 524114, 524126
Top Insurance Groups, 2010

Companies are ranked by net premiums written in billions of dollars.

State Farm IL Group	$ 50.80
Allstate Insurance Group	24.79
Liberty Mutual Insurance Group	21.48
Berkshire Hathaway Insurance Group	21.35
Travelers Group	20.59
Chartis/American International Group	19.71
Zurich Insurance Group	18.52
Nationwide Group	14.48
Progressive Group	14.47
USAA Group	10.67
Hartford Fire & Casualty Group	9.68
Chubb & Son Group	8.92
CNA Insurance Group	6.18

Source: *National Underwriter*, July 25, 2011, p. 15.

★ 3134 ★
Insurance
SIC: 6311; NAICS: 524113, 524128, 52413
Top Insurers in Australia, 2010

Companies are ranked by value of gross written premiums in millions of dollars.

Vero	$ 2,463
QBE	2,445
Insurance Australia Ltd.	2,237
Allianz	2,095
IMA	1,742
CGU	1,664
AAMI	1,344
Gio General	1,293
Suncorp Metway	1,027
Zurich	820

Source: "Country Profile Australia." [online] from http://www.lloyds.com/The-Market/Tools-and-Resources/Research/Market-Intelligence-Toolkit/Country-Profiles [Published July 2011], from Australia regulators.

★ 3135 ★
Insurance
SIC: 6311; NAICS: 524113, 524128, 52413
Top Insurers in Canada, 2010

Companies are ranked by value of gross written premiums in billions of dollars.

Lloyd's	$ 1,498
Aviva	878
Chartis	877
Intact	834
AXA	697
Zurich	690
Northbridge	682
Co-operators	635
RSA	538
Economical	440

Source: "Country Profile Canada." [online] from http://www.lloyds.com/The-Market/Tools-and-Resources/Research/Market-Intelligence-Toolkit/Country-Profiles [Published May 2011], from Canada regulators.

★ 3136 ★
Insurance
SIC: 6311; NAICS: 524113, 524128, 52413
Top Insurers in China, 2009

Market shares are shown based on gross written premiums.

PICC	38.7%
Pingan	14.6
CPIC	12.8
China United	4.9
China Continent P&C	3.3
China Life P&C	2.7
Other	21.9

Source: "Country Profile China." [online] from http://www.lloyds.com/Lloyds/Offices/Asia/China-in-Chinese/~/media/Files/The Market/Tools and resources/New Market Intelligence/Country Profiles [Published July 2011], from CIRC.

★ 3137 ★
Insurance
SIC: 6311; NAICS: 524113, 524128, 52413
Top Insurers in Denmark, 2010

Market shares are shown based on directly written premiums.

TrggVesta	21.0%
Topdanmark	18.0
Codan	14.0
Alm Brand	10.0
if...	5.0
Other	32.0

Source: "Country Profile Denmark." [online] from http://www.lloyds.com [Published May 2011], from company reports.

★ 3138 ★
Insurance
SIC: 6311; NAICS: 524113, 524128, 52413
Top Insurers in Finland, 2010

Market shares are shown based on gross written premiums.

if...	24.0%
Pohjola	24.0
Tapiola	20.0
Fennia	10.0
Other	22.0

Source: "Country Profile Finland." [online] from http://www.lloyds.com/The-Market/Tools-and-Resources/Research/Market-Intelligence-Toolkit/Country-Profiles [Published May 2011], from company reports.

★ 3139 ★
Insurance
SIC: 6311; NAICS: 524113, 524128, 52413
Top Insurers in Germany, 2009

Market shares are shown based on gross written premiums.

Allianz	9.0%
AXA	3.0
R+V	2.6
HDI	2.5
PSV	2.5
Alliance (Corporate)	2.4
Zurich	2.0

Source: "Country Profile Germany." [online] from http://www.lloyds.com/The-Market/Tools-and-Resources/Research/Market-Intelligence-Toolkit/Country-Profiles [Published April 2011], from *Versicherungswirtschaft*.

★ 3140 ★
Insurance
SIC: 6311; NAICS: 524113, 524128, 52413
Top Insurers in Greece, 2010

Companies are ranked by value of gross written premiums in millions of dollars.

Ethniki	$ 460
Interamerican Property	203
Agrotiki	182
Intersaonika General	169
Aspis Pronia	152
Commercial Value	151
Idrogios General	147
General Union	142
Grupoama Phoenix	139
AXA	130

Source: "Country Profile Greece." [online] from http://www.lloyds.com/The-Market/Tools-and-Resources/Research/Market-Intelligence-Toolkit/Country-Profiles [Published April 2011], from Greece regulators.

★ 3141 ★
Insurance
SIC: 6311; NAICS: 524113, 524128, 52413
Top Insurers in Hong Kong, 2010

Companies are ranked by value of gross written premiums in millions of dollars.

HSBC	$ 267
Zurich	222
BOC	201
A&H	189

Continued on next page.

★ 3141 ★

[Continued]

Insurance

SIC: 6311; NAICS: 524113, 524128, 52413

Top Insurers in Hong Kong, 2010

Companies are ranked by value of gross written premiums in millions of dollars.

Bupa	$ 164
QBE	125
Asia Insurance	123
Lloyd's	120
Hong Kong Mortgage	111
MISC	110

Source: "Country Profile Hong Kong." [online] from http://www.lloyds.com/The-Market/Tools-and-Resources/Research/Market-Intelligence-Toolkit/Country-Profiles [Published May 2011], from Insurance Information Institute.

★ 3142 ★

Insurance

SIC: 6311; NAICS: 524113, 524128, 52413

Top Insurers in Israel, 2010

Companies are ranked by value of gross written premiums in millions of dollars.

Harel	$ 947.2
Clal	708.6
The Phoenix	653.1
Menora Mivtachim	505.5
Migdal	426.6
Ayalon	333.1
I.D.I.	215.1
I.L.D.	189.4
Eliahu	187.0
AIG (Chartis)	155.0
Clal health	151.7

Source: "Country Profile Israel." [online] from http://www.lloyds.com/The-Market/Tools-and-Resources/Research/Market-Intelligence-Toolkit/Country-Profiles [Published April 2011], from Israel regulators.

★ 3143 ★

Insurance

SIC: 6311; NAICS: 524113, 524128, 52413

Top Insurers in Italy, 2010

Market shares are shown based on gross written premiums.

Generali	21.5%
Gruppo Fondiara SAI	19.8
UGF Assicurazioni	12.2
Allianz	11.1

Reale Mutua	5.5%
Cattloica	4.5
Other	25.4

Source: "Country Profile Italy." [online] from http://www.lloyds.com/The-Market/Tools-and-Resources/Research/Market-Intelligence-Toolkit/Country-Profiles [Published September 2011], from CIRC.

★ 3144 ★

Insurance

SIC: 6311; NAICS: 524113, 524128, 52413

Top Insurers in Norway, 2011

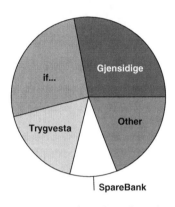

Market shares are shown based on directly written premiums.

Gjensidige	28.0%
if...	26.0
Trygvesta	17.0
SpareBank	10.0
Other	19.0

Source: "Country Profile Norway." [online] from http://www.lloyds.com [Published May 2011], from company reports.

★ 3145 ★

Insurance

SIC: 6311; NAICS: 524113, 524128, 52413

Top Insurers in Portugal, 2010

Companies are ranked by value of gross written premiums in millions of dollars.

Fidelidade-Mundial	$ 975
Imperio Bonança	521
AXA Insurance	464
Tranquilidade	435
Allianz	390
Zurich	388
Lusitania Seguros	308
Occidental Seguros	281

Continued on next page.

★ 3145 ★

[Continued]

Insurance

SIC: 6311; NAICS: 524113, 524128, 52413

Top Insurers in Portugal, 2010

Companies are ranked by value of gross written premiums in millions of dollars.

Açoreana	$ 249
Liberty Mutual	228

Source: "Country Profile Portugal." [online] from http://www.lloyds.com/The-Market/Tools-and-Resources/Research/Market-Intelligence-Toolkit/Country-Profiles [Published July 2011], from Portuguese regulators.

★ 3146 ★

Insurance

SIC: 6311; NAICS: 524113, 524128, 52413

Top Insurers in Spain, 2010

Companies are ranked by value of gross written premiums in millions of dollars.

Mapfre	5.2%
Grupo Axa	2.4
Allianz	2.0
Grupo Caixa	1.9
Grupo Catalana Occidente	1.5
Generali	1.4
Grupo Mutua Madrileña	1.3
Zurich	1.3
Caser	1.1
Santas	1.1
Other	80.8

Source: "Country Profile Spain." [online] from http://www.lloyds.com/The-Market/Tools-and-Resources/Research/Market-Intelligence-Toolkit/Country-Profiles [Published May 2011], from Spanish regulatory commission.

★ 3147 ★

Insurance

SIC: 6311; NAICS: 524113, 524128, 52413

Top Insurers in Sweden, 2010

Market shares are shown based on directly written premiums.

Länsförsäkringar	30.0%
if...	19.0
Other	51.0

Source: "Country Profile Sweden." [online] from http://www.lloyds.com [Published May 2011], from company reports.

★ 3148 ★

Life Insurance

SIC: 6311; NAICS: 524113

Top Credit Life Insurers, 2010

Credit life is term life insurance that pays the balance due on a loan or line of credit directly to the lender in the event the borrower dies. Companies are ranked by issuances in billions of dollars.

Cuna Mutual Group	$ 170,262
Citi Assurance Services Group	70,434
Amer Enterprise Group	70,369
Assurant Inc. Group	70,135
Life of the South Group	69,913
Independence Holding Co. Group	69,756

Source: *Insurance Facts and Stats*, Annual 2010, p. 31, from A.M. Best & Co.

★ 3149 ★

Life Insurance

SIC: 6311; NAICS: 524113

Top Life Insurers, 2010

Market shares are shown based on directly written premiums.

Metropolitan Group	7.76%
American International Group	6.54
Northwestern Mutual Group	5.92
New York Life Group	5.70
Prudential of America Group	4.82
Lincoln National Group	3.89
John Hancock Group	3.55
Aegon US Holding Group	3.09
Other	58.73

Source: "Life and Fraternal Insurance Industry." [online] from http://www.naics.org [Published March 28, 2011], from National Association of Insurance Commissioners.

★ 3150 ★

Life Insurance

SIC: 6311; NAICS: 524113

Top Term Life Insurers, 2010

Term life insurance provides protection for a specified period of time. It pays a benefit only if the insured's death occurs during the coverage period. It can be considered a pure protection product and an entry-level life insurance product. Companies are ranked by issuances in billions of dollars.

Metropolitan Life & Affiliated Cos.	$ 70,192
Prudential of America Group	70,189
Primerica Group	70,183

Continued on next page.

★ 3150 ★

[Continued]

Life Insurance

SIC: 6311; NAICS: 524113

Top Term Life Insurers, 2010

Term life insurance provides protection for a specified period of time. It pays a benefit only if the insured's death occurs during the coverage period. It can be considered a pure protection product and an entry-level life insurance product. Companies are ranked by issuances in billions of dollars.

ING USA Life Group	$ 70,153
State Farm Life Group	70,126
New York Life Group	69,714
Northwestern Mutual Group	69,515

Source: *Insurance Facts and Stats*, Annual 2010, p. 31, from A.M. Best & Co.

★ 3151 ★

Health Insurance

SIC: 6321; NAICS: 524114

Top Accident and Health Insurers in Michigan, 2010

Market shares are shown in percent.

Blue Cross Blue Shield of Michigan	29.48%
Blue Care Network of Michigan	10.51
Health Alliance Plan of Michigan	7.76
Priority Health	7.44
Meridian Health Plan of Michigan	3.93
Molina Healthcare of Michigan Inc.	3.63
Other	37.25

Source: *D Business*, May-June 2012, p. 40, from Michigan Office of Financial and Insurance Regulation.

★ 3152 ★

Health Insurance

SIC: 6321; NAICS: 524114

Top Accident and Health Insurers in Missouri, 2011

Market shares are shown in percent.

Healthy Alliance Life Insurance Company . .	23.24%
UnitedHealthcare	14.70
Coventry Health	10.26
Blue Cross and Blue Shield of Kansas City .	9.74
Other	42.06

Source: "Missouri Department of Insurance." [online] from http://insurance.mo.gov [Accessed May 14, 2012], from Missouri Department of Insurance.

★ 3153 ★

Health Insurance

SIC: 6321; NAICS: 524114

Top Health Insurers, 2010

Companies are ranked by revenues generated from health, life and statutory filings in billions of dollars.

	($ bil.)	Share
UnitedHealthCare	$ 80.0	12.55%
WellPoint	53.7	8.37
Kaiser Foundation	51.3	8.00
Humana Inc.	29.1	4.54
Aetna	25.2	3.94
Health Care Service Corp.	20.1	3.14
Aflac	15.8	2.47
Highmark	13.7	2.13
Cigna Corp.	11.7	1.80
Health Net	11.2	1.75
Coventry Health	10.8	1.67
MetLife	10.3	1.60
Blue Shield of California	9.7	1.52
EmblemHealth	9.5	1.50
Blue Cross and Blue Shield of Michigan	9.0	1.40

Source: *Modern Healthcare*, June 27, 2011, p. 32, from Weiss Ratings.

★ 3154 ★

Health Insurance

SIC: 6321; NAICS: 524113

Top Health Insurers in Colorado, 2010

Market shares are shown based on deposits.

Kaiser Foundation Health Plan of Colorado . .	24.2%
Anthem Blue Cross and Blue Shield	12.5
United Healthcare Insurance Colorado	10.9
Pacificare of Colorado Inc.	7.3
Humana Inc.	3.0
Other	42.1

Source: "Annual Report of the Commissioner of Insurance." [online] from http://www.dora.state.co.us/insurance/legi/2012/legiHealthCostReport021612R.pdf [Published February 2012], from *Colorado Insurance Statistical Report*.

★ 3155 ★
Health Insurance
SIC: 6321; NAICS: 524114

Top Health Insurers in Washington (Individual Market), 2010

Market shares are shown in percent.

Regence	41.2%
Premera	32.0
Group Health	20.6
Kaiser Permanente	1.4
Other	2.4

Source: "Consolidation & Competition in Health Insurance & Provider Markets." [online] from http://www.academyhealth. org/files/2011/monday/flye.pdf [Published June 13, 2011], from Washington State Office of the Insurance Commissioner.

★ 3156 ★
Health Insurance
SIC: 6324; NAICS: 524114

Top Medicare Advantage Enrollment Firms, 2011

A total of 11.9 million people were enrolled in Medicare Advantage.

UnitedHealthcare	18.0%
Blue Cross Blue Shield	17.0
Humana Inc.	16.0
Kaiser Permanente	8.0
Aetna	3.0
Other	37.0

Source: "Medicare Advantage Enrollment Market Update." [online] from http://www.kff.org/medicare/upload/8228.pdf [Published September 2011], from MPR/Kaiser Family Foundation.

★ 3157 ★
Health Insurance
SIC: 6324; NAICS: 524114

Top Medicare Advantage Enrollment Firms in Arizona, 2011

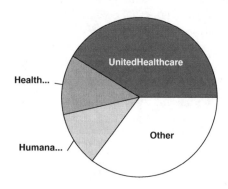

Market shares are shown based on enrollment in Medicare Advantage.

UnitedHealthcare	41.0%
Health Net Inc.	12.0
Humana Inc.	11.0
Other	35.0

Source: "Medicare Advantage Enrollment Market Update." [online] from http://www.kff.org/medicare/upload/8228.pdf [Published September 2011], from MPR/Kaiser Family Foundation.

★ 3158 ★
Health Insurance
SIC: 6324; NAICS: 524114

Top Medicare Advantage Enrollment Firms in California, 2011

Market shares are shown based on enrollment in Medicare Advantage.

Kaiser Foundation	45.0%
UnitedHealthcare	18.0
Health Net Inc.	7.0
Other	30.0

Source: "Medicare Advantage Enrollment Market Update." [online] from http://www.kff.org/medicare/upload/8228.pdf [Published September 2011], from MPR/Kaiser Family Foundation.

★ **3159** ★
Health Insurance
SIC: 6324; NAICS: 524114

Top Medicare Advantage Enrollment Firms in Florida, 2011

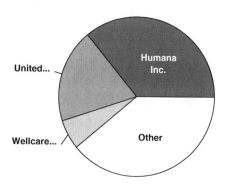

Market shares are shown based on enrollment in Medicare Advantage.

Humana Inc.	36.0%
UnitedHealthcare	19.0
Wellcare Health Plans Inc.	6.0
Other	39.0

Source: "Medicare Advantage Enrollment Market Update." [online] from http://www.kff.org/medicare/upload/8228.pdf [Published September 2011], from MPR/Kaiser Family Foundation.

★ **3160** ★
Health Insurance
SIC: 6324; NAICS: 524114

Top Medicare Advantage Enrollment Firms in Louisiana, 2011

Market shares are shown based on enrollment in Medicare Advantage.

Humana Inc.	58.0%
New Orleans Reg. Physician Hospital Organization Inc.	29.0
Vantage Health Plan Inc.	4.0
Other	9.0

Source: "Medicare Advantage Enrollment Market Update." [online] from http://www.kff.org/medicare/upload/8228.pdf [Published September 2011], from MPR/Kaiser Family Foundation.

★ **3161** ★
Health Insurance
SIC: 6324; NAICS: 524114

Top Medicare Advantage Enrollment Firms in Michigan, 2011

Market shares are shown based on enrollment in Medicare Advantage.

Blue Cross Blue Shield of Michigan	56.0%
Spectrum Health System	14.0
Health Alliance Plan	11.0
Other	19.0

Source: "Medicare Advantage Enrollment Market Update." [online] from http://www.kff.org/medicare/upload/8228.pdf [Published September 2011], from MPR/Kaiser Family Foundation.

★ **3162** ★
Health Insurance
SIC: 6324; NAICS: 524114

Top Medicare Advantage Enrollment Firms in New York, 2011

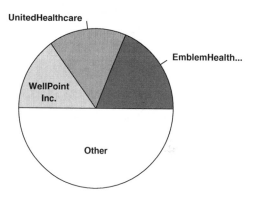

Market shares are shown based on enrollment in Medicare Advantage.

EmblemHealth Inc.	15.0%
UnitedHealthcare	13.0
WellPoint Inc.	12.0
Other	40.0

Source: "Medicare Advantage Enrollment Market Update." [online] from http://www.kff.org/medicare/upload/8228.pdf [Published September 2011], from MPR/Kaiser Family Foundation.

★ 3163 ★
Health Insurance
SIC: 6324; NAICS: 524114

Top Medicare Advantage Enrollment Firms in North Carolina, 2011

Market shares are shown based on enrollment in Medicare Advantage.

UnitedHealthcare	37.0%
BlueCross and Blue Shield of North Carolina	23.0
Humana Inc.	12.0
Other	28.0

Source: "Medicare Advantage Enrollment Market Update." [online] from http://www.kff.org/medicare/upload/8228.pdf [Published September 2011], from MPR/Kaiser Family Foundation.

★ 3164 ★
Health Insurance
SIC: 6324; NAICS: 524114

Top Medicare Advantage Enrollment Firms in Ohio, 2011

Market shares are shown based on enrollment in Medicare Advantage.

Humana Inc.	27.0%
WellPoint Inc.	25.0
Aetna Inc.	15.0
Other	33.0

Source: "Medicare Advantage Enrollment Market Update." [online] from http://www.kff.org/medicare/upload/8228.pdf [Published September 2011], from MPR/Kaiser Family Foundation.

★ 3165 ★
Health Insurance
SIC: 6324; NAICS: 524114

Top Medicare Advantage Enrollment Firms in Pennsylvania, 2011

Market shares are shown based on enrollment in Medicare Advantage.

Highmark Inc.	34.0%
Aetna Inc.	11.0
University of Pittsburgh Medical Center	11.0
Other	44.0

Source: "Medicare Advantage Enrollment Market Update." [online] from http://www.kff.org/medicare/upload/8228.pdf [Published September 2011], from MPR/Kaiser Family Foundation.

★ 3166 ★
Health Insurance
SIC: 6324; NAICS: 524114

Top Medicare Advantage Enrollment Firms in South Carolina, 2011

Market shares are shown based on enrollment in Medicare Advantage.

Humana Inc.	33.0%
XLHealth Corp.	21.0
BlueCross BlueShield of South Carolina	17.0
Other	29.0

Source: "Medicare Advantage Enrollment Market Update." [online] from http://www.kff.org/medicare/upload/8228.pdf [Published September 2011], from MPR/Kaiser Family Foundation.

★ 3167 ★
Health Insurance
SIC: 6324; NAICS: 524114

Top Medicare Advantage Enrollment Firms in Tennessee, 2011

Market shares are shown based on enrollment in Medicare Advantage.

Humana Inc.	33.0%
HealthSpring Inc.	27.0
UnitedHealthcare	21.0
Other	19.0

Source: "Medicare Advantage Enrollment Market Update." [online] from http://www.kff.org/medicare/upload/8228.pdf [Published September 2011], from MPR/Kaiser Family Foundation.

★ 3168 ★
Health Insurance
SIC: 6324; NAICS: 524114

Top Medicare Advantage Enrollment Firms in Wisconsin, 2011

Market shares are shown based on enrollment in Medicare Advantage.

UnitedHealthcare	26.0%
Humana Inc.	20.0
Affinity Health System	15.0
Other	39.0

Source: "Medicare Advantage Enrollment Market Update." [online] from http://www.kff.org/medicare/upload/8228.pdf [Published September 2011], from MPR/Kaiser Family Foundation.

★ 3169 ★
Aircraft Insurance
SIC: 6331; NAICS: 524126

Top Aircraft Insurance Providers, 2010

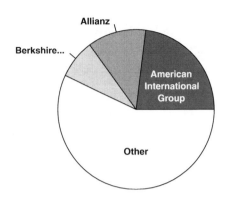

Market shares are shown in percent.

American International Group	23.0%
Allianz	12.0
Berkshire Hathaway	8.0
Other	57.0

Source: *National Underwriter*, August 8, 2011, p. 13.

★ 3170 ★
Allied Line Insurance
SIC: 6331; NAICS: 524126

Top Allied Line Insurers in California, 2010

Market shares are shown based on directly written premiums.

Newport Insurance Co.	17.72%
Meritplan Insurance Co.	9.42
Factory Mutual Insurance Co.	8.57
American Security Insurance Co.	7.44
Travelers Property Casualty Co. of America .	5.00
Fire Insurance Exchange	4.93
Safeco Insurance Co. of America	4.14
Other	42.78

Source: ''2010 California P&C Market Share Report.'' [online] from http://www.insurance.ca.gov [Accessed December 1, 2011], from NAICS Database.

★ 3171 ★
Auto Insurance
SIC: 6331; NAICS: 524126

Top Auto Insurers in Florida, 2010

Market shares are shown in percent.

State Farm Group	20.8%
Berkshire Hathaway (Geico)	16.2

Allstate Insurance Group	13.9%
Progressive Insurance Group	10.9
USAA Group	5.6
Other	67.4

Source: *A.M. Best Newswire*, February 7, 2012, p. NA, from BestLink.

★ 3172 ★
Auto Insurance
SIC: 6331; NAICS: 524126

Top Auto Insurers in Massachusetts, 2010

Market shares are shown for the private sector.

Mapfre North American Group	28.2%
Safety Group	11.1
Liberty Mutual Insurance Cos.	11.0
Arbella Insurance Group	8.9
Plymouth Rock Cos.	5.8
Other	35.0

Source: *A.M. Best Newswire*, March 9, 2012, p. NA, from BestLink.

★ 3173 ★
Auto Insurance
SIC: 6331; NAICS: 524126

Top Auto Insurers in Michigan, 2010

Market shares are shown in percent.

State Farm Group	19.85%
Auto Club Group	16.38
Auto-Owners Insurance Group	9.58
Progressive Insurance Group	9.37
Other	44.82

Source: *A.M. Best Newswire*, October 14, 2011, p. NA, from A.M. Best & Co.

★ 3174 ★
Auto Insurance
SIC: 6331; NAICS: 524126

Top Auto Insurers in New Jersey, 2010

Market shares are shown in percent.

Berkshire Hathaway Insurance Group	14.85%
Allstate Insurance Group	14.24
NJM Insurance Group	13.11
Palisades Group	10.46
State Farm Group	9.72
Other	35.62

Source: *A.M. Best Newswire*, January 31, 2012, p. NA, from A.M. Best & Co.

★ 3175 ★
Auto Insurance
SIC: 6331; NAICS: 524126

Top Auto Insurers in New York, 2010

Market shares are shown for the private sector.

Berkshire Hathaway (Geico)	24.05%
Allstate Insurance Group	18.66
State Farm Group	12.12
Liberty Mutual	6.17
Progressive Insurance Group	5.83
Other	33.17

Source: *A.M. Best Newswire*, December 21, 2011, p. NA, from BestLink.

★ 3176 ★
Auto Insurance
SIC: 6331; NAICS: 524126

Top Auto Insurers in Ohio, 2010

Market shares are shown based on directly premiums written for the commercial sector.

Cincinnati Financial Group	8.9%
Westfield Group	7.2
Travelers Group	6.8
Liberty Mutual Group	5.3
Nationwide Group	5.3
Other	66.5

Source: "Ohio: 2010 Property and Casualty Insurance Market Share Report." [online] from http://www.insurance.ohio.gov [Accessed December 1, 2011], from Ohio Department of Insurance.

★ 3177 ★
Auto Insurance
SIC: 6331; NAICS: 524126

Top Auto Insurers in Pennsylvania, 2010

Market shares are shown for the private sector.

State Farm Group	19.2%
Allstate Insurance Group	13.5
Erie Insurance Group	13.4
Nationwide Group	10.8
Progressive Insurance Group	7.8
Other	35.3

Source: *A.M. Best Newswire*, March 5, 2012, p. NA, from BestLink.

★ 3178 ★
Auto Insurance
SIC: 6331; NAICS: 524126

Top Auto Insurers in South Carolina, 2010

Market shares are shown for the private sector.

State Farm Group	24.74%
Allstate Insurance Group	15.73
Nationwide Group	9.74
Berkshire Hathaway (Geico)	8.63
USAA Group	6.27
Other	34.89

Source: *A.M. Best Newswire*, February 13, 2012, p. NA, from BestLink.

★ 3179 ★
Auto Insurance
SIC: 6331; NAICS: 524126

Top Auto Insurers in Washington, 2010

Market shares are shown in percent.

State Farm Group	15.0%
Farmers Insurance Group	11.0
Liberty Mutual Insurance Cos.	10.3
Allstate Insurance Group	9.9
Progressive Insurance Group	7.5
Other	46.3

Source: *A.M. Best Newswire*, February 8, 2012, p. NA, from BestLink.

★ 3180 ★
Auto Insurance
SIC: 6331; NAICS: 524126

Top Auto Liability Insurers, 2010

Market shares are shown based on directly written premiums.

State Farm Group	15.7%
Allstate Insurance Group	8.7
Progressive Insurance Group	8.0
Berkshire Hathaway (Geico)	7.8
Farmers Insurance Group	5.4
Liberty Mutual Insurance Group	4.9
Nationwide Group	4.3
USAA Group	3.4
Travelers Group	3.2
Hartford Insurance Group	1.8
Other	32.8

Source: *Best's Review*, October 2011, p. 45, from A.M. Best & Co.

★ 3181 ★
Auto Insurance
SIC: 6331; NAICS: 524126

Top Auto Physical Damage Insurers, 2010

Market shares are shown based on directly written premiums.

State Farm Group	17.0%
Allstate Insurance Group	10.4
Berkshire Hathaway (Geico)	7.6
Progressive Insurance Group	7.0
Farmers Insurance Group	5.7
Liberty Mutual Insurance Co.	4.7
USAA Group	4.6
Nationwide Group	4.2
Travelers Group	2.4
American Family Insurance Group	2.0
Other	34.4

Source: *Best's Review*, October 2011, p. 45, from A.M. Best & Co.

★ 3182 ★
Auto Insurance
SIC: 6331; NAICS: 524126

Top Commercial Auto Insurers, 2010

Market shares are shown based on directly written premiums.

Travelers Group	8.8%
Liberty Mutual Insurance Group	6.8
Progressive Insurance Group	6.3
Zurich Financial Services N.A. Group	5.4
American International Group	4.2
Nationwide Group	3.9
Old Republic Insurance Group	3.2
Auto-Owners Insurance Group	2.3
Hartford Insurance Group	2.3
Great American P&C Insurance Group	2.0
State Farm Group	2.0
Other	44.8

Source: *Best's Review*, October 2011, p. 45, from A.M. Best & Co.

★ 3183 ★
Burglary Insurance
SIC: 6331; NAICS: 524126

Top Burglary and Theft Insurers, 2010

Burglary and theft insurance is provided in standard homeowner and business multiple peril policies. Companies are ranked by issuances in billions of dollars.

Travelers Group	$ 18,674
Zurich Financial Services	18,549
American International Group	18,540
Nationwide Group	5,987
Hanover Insurance Group Property & Casualty Cos.	4,861

Source: *Insurance Facts and Stats*, Annual 2010, p. 21, from A.M. Best & Co.

★ 3184 ★
Commercial Line Insurance
SIC: 6331; NAICS: 524126

Top Commercial Line Insurers in Ohio, 2010

Market shares are shown based on directly written premiums.

Cincinnati Financial Group	7.9%
American International Group	7.6
Travelers Group	5.9
Liberty Mutual Group	5.7
Westfield Group	4.9
Other	68.0

Source: "Ohio: 2010 Property and Casualty Insurance Market Share Report." [online] from http://www.insurance.ohio.gov [Accessed December 1, 2011], from Ohio Department of Insurance.

★ 3185 ★
Earthquake Insurance
SIC: 6331; NAICS: 524126

Top Earthquake Insurers, 2010

Earthquakes are not covered by standard homeowners policies so must be purchased separately. Companies are ranked by issuances in billions of dollars.

GeoVera U.S. Insurance Group	$ 25,045
Travelers Group	18,674
Endurance Specialty Group	18,620
Zurich Financial Services	18,549
American International Group	18,540
California Earthquake Authority	12,534

Source: *Insurance Facts and Stats*, Annual 2010, p. 31, from A.M. Best & Co.

★ 3186 ★

Earthquake Insurance

SIC: 6331; NAICS: 524126

Top Earthquake Malpractice Insurers in California, 2010

Market shares are shown based on directly written premiums.

California Earthquake Authority	49.47%
Geovera Insurance Co.	7.47
Chartis Property Casualty Co.	4.33
State Farm General	4.09
Other	35.04

Source: "2010 California P&C Market Share Report." [online] from http://www.insurance.ca.gov [Accessed December 1, 2011], from NAICS Database.

★ 3187 ★

Excess and Surplus Insurance

SIC: 6331; NAICS: 524126

Top Excess and Surplus Insurers, 2011

Market shares are shown in percent.

American International Group	23.2%
Nationwide Mutual Group	5.3
Zurich Financial Services	4.6
W.R. Berkley Corp.	4.1
ACE Ltd.	3.7
Markel Corp.	3.3
Other	56.8

Source: *National Underwriter*, May 7, 2012, p. NA, from SNL Financial.

★ 3188 ★

Fire and Allied Insurance

SIC: 6331; NAICS: 524126

Top Fire and Allied Insurers in Ohio, 2010

Market shares are shown based on directly written premiums.

Assurant Inc. Group	10.9%
American International Group	9.4
FM Global Group	8.7
Zurich Insurance Group	7.5
Travelers Group	5.1
Other	58.4

Source: "Ohio: 2010 Property and Casualty Insurance Market Share Report." [online] from http://www.insurance.ohio.gov [Accessed December 1, 2011], from Ohio Department of Insurance.

★ 3189 ★

Fire and Allied Insurance

SIC: 6331; NAICS: 524126

Top Fire Insurers in California, 2010

Market shares are shown based on directly written premiums.

American Security Insurance Co.	13.24%
Newport Insurance Co.	11.57
Metriplan Insurance	5.82
Travelers Property Casualty	3.10
Factory Mutual Insurance Co.	3.02
ACA Insurance Co.	2.93
Other	60.32

Source: "2010 California P&C Market Share Report." [online] from http://www.insurance.ca.gov [Accessed December 1, 2011], from NAICS Database.

★ 3190 ★

Flood Insurance

SIC: 6331; NAICS: 524126

Top Federal Flood Insurers, 2010

Floods are not covered by standard homeowners policies so must be purchased separately. Companies are ranked by issuances in billions of dollars.

Travelers Group	$ 18,674
Fidelity National Group	18,606
Assurant Property & Casualty Group . . .	18,523
Nationwide Group	5,987
USAA Group	4,080

Source: *Insurance Facts and Stats*, Annual 2010, p. 21, from A.M. Best & Co.

★ 3191 ★

Flood Insurance

SIC: 6331; NAICS: 524126

Top Flood Insurers in California, 2010

Market shares are shown based on directly written premiums.

Fidelity National Group	17.12%
Fire Insurance Exchange	16.78
State Farm Fire & Casualty Co.	10.61
Allstate Insurance Co.	10.18
American Bankers Insurance Co. of Florida .	5.55
Other	39.76

Source: "2010 California P&C Market Share Report." [online] from http://www.insurance.ca.gov [Accessed December 1, 2011], from NAICS Database.

★ 3192 ★
Homeowners Insurance
SIC: 6331; NAICS: 524126

Top Homeowners Insurers, 2010

Shares are shown based on directly written premiums for the multiple peril market.

State Farm	21.88%
Allstate Insurance Group	9.59
Zurich Insurance Group	6.57
Liberty Mutual Group	5.21
Travelers Group	4.60
USAA Group	4.43
Nationwide Corp. Group	3.95
Chubb & Son Inc. Group	2.46
American Family Insurance Group	2.12
Other	39.19

Source: "Property and Casualty Insurance Industry." [online] from http://www.naics.org [Published March 28, 2011], from National Association of Insurance Commissioners.

★ 3193 ★
Homeowners Insurance
SIC: 6331; NAICS: 524126

Top Homeowners Insurers in Alabama, 2010

Market shares are shown in percent.

State Farm Group	28.2%
Alfa Insurance Group	17.7
Allstate Insurance Group	10.1
Farmers Insurance Group	8.0
Travelers Group	6.0
Other	30.0

Source: *A.M. Best Newswire*, January 24, 2012, p. NA, from A.M. Best & Co.

★ 3194 ★
Homeowners Insurance
SIC: 6331; NAICS: 524126

Top Homeowners Insurers in Arkansas, 2010

Market shares are shown in percent.

State Farm Group	24.0%
Farm Bureau Mutual Insurance Co. of Arkansas Inc.	19.0
Allstate Insurance Group	9.4
Farmers Insurance Group	8.2
Other	39.4

Source: *A.M. Best Newswire*, December 13, 2011, p. NA, from A.M. Best & Co.

★ 3195 ★
Homeowners Insurance
SIC: 6331; NAICS: 524126

Top Homeowners Insurers in California, 2010

Market shares are shown in percent.

State Farm Group	22.0%
Farmers Insurance Group	17.0
Allstate Insurance Group	9.2
California State Auto Group	6.5
Liberty Mutual Insurance Cos.	5.1

Source: *A.M. Best Newswire*, December 3, 2011, p. NA, from A.M. Best & Co.

★ 3196 ★
Homeowners Insurance
SIC: 6331; NAICS: 524126

Top Homeowners Insurers in Florida, 2010

Market shares are shown in percent.

Citizens Property Insurance Corp.	16.06%
State Farm Group	13.61
Universal Insurance Holdings Group	8.38
USAA Group	4.87
St. Johns Insurance Co. Inc.	3.44
Other	43.64

Source: *A.M. Best Newswire*, September 20, 2011, p. NA, from A.M. Best & Co.

★ 3197 ★
Homeowners Insurance
SIC: 6331; NAICS: 524126

Top Homeowners Insurers in Illinois, 2010

Market shares are shown in percent.

State Farm Group	30.4%
Allstate Insurance Group	11.2
Countrywide Financial	7.8
Farmers Insurance Group	5.1
American Family Insurance Group	4.9
Other	40.6

Source: *A.M. Best Newswire*, December 8, 2011, p. NA, from A.M. Best & Co.

★ 3198 ★
Homeowners Insurance
SIC: 6331; NAICS: 524126

Top Homeowners Insurers in Louisiana, 2010

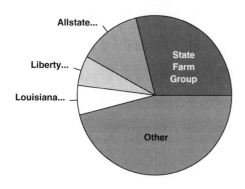

Market shares are shown in percent.

State Farm Group	28.6%
Allstate Insurance Group	13.4
Liberty Mutual Insurance Cos.	6.5
Louisiana Farm Bureau Mutual Insurance Co.	5.8
Other	45.6

Source: *A.M. Best Newswire*, December 13, 2011, p. NA, from BestLink.

★ 3199 ★
Homeowners Insurance
SIC: 6331; NAICS: 524126

Top Homeowners Insurers in Mississippi, 2010

Market shares are shown in percent.

State Farm Group	25.49%
Southern Farm Bureau Casualty Group	16.37
Allstate Insurance Group	11.79
Nationwide Group	9.12
Farmers Insurance Group	6.04
Other	31.19

Source: *A.M. Best Newswire*, March 5, 2012, p. NA, from BestLink.

★ 3200 ★
Homeowners Insurance
SIC: 6331; NAICS: 524126

Top Homeowners Insurers in Missouri, 2010

Market shares are shown in percent.

State Farm Group	27.80%
American Family Insurance Group	16.69
Farmers Insurance Group	7.24
Shelter Insurance Cos.	6.05
Liberty Mutual Insurance Cos.	5.10
Other	37.12

Source: *A.M. Best Newswire*, September 20, 2011, p. NA, from A.M. Best & Co.

★ 3201 ★
Homeowners Insurance
SIC: 6331; NAICS: 524126

Top Homeowners Insurers in North Carolina, 2010

Market shares are shown for fire and multiple peril lines.

State Farm Group	14.21%
North Carolina Farm Bureau Insurance Group	13.49
Nationwide Group	11.36
Allstate Insurance Group	6.27
Travelers Group	4.46

Source: *A.M. Best Newswire*, December 12, 2011, p. NA, from BestLink.

★ 3202 ★
Homeowners Insurance
SIC: 6331; NAICS: 524126

Top Homeowners Insurers in Ohio, 2010

Market shares are shown based on directly written premiums.

State Farm Group	23.6%
Allstate Insurance Group	10.5
Nationwide Group	10.0
Grange Mutual	5.5
Liberty Mutual Group	5.1
Other	45.3

Source: "Ohio: 2010 Property and Casualty Insurance Market Share Report." [online] from http://www.insurance.ohio.gov [Accessed December 1, 2011], from Ohio Department of Insurance.

★ 3203 ★
Homeowners Insurance
SIC: 6331; NAICS: 524126

Top Homeowners Insurers in Rhode Island, 2010

Market shares are shown in percent.

Allstate Insurance Group	15.42%
Amica Mutual Group	11.98
Liberty Mutual Insurance Cos.	9.82
Nationwide Group	7.81
MetLife Auto & Home Group	5.82
Other	49.15

Source: *A.M. Best Newswire*, September 22, 2011, p. NA, from A.M. Best & Co.

★ 3204 ★
Homeowners Insurance
SIC: 6331; NAICS: 524126

Top Homeowners Insurers in South Carolina, 2010

Market shares are shown in percent.

Travelers Group	36.04%
Nationwide Group	20.67
ACE INA Group	19.36
State Farm Group	12.02
Other	21.91

Source: *A.M. Best Newswire*, November 16, 2011, p. NA, from BestLink.

★ 3205 ★
Homeowners Insurance
SIC: 6331; NAICS: 524126

Top Homeowners Insurers in Texas, 2010

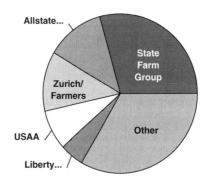

Market shares are shown in percent.

State Farm Group	28.9%
Allstate Insurance Group	12.5
Zurich/Farmers	12.4
USAA	7.7
Liberty Mutual Insurance Co.	5.2
Other	33.3

Source: *National Underwriter*, September 19, 2011, p. 10, from Highline Data and Moody's.

★ 3206 ★
Homeowners Insurance
SIC: 6331; NAICS: 524126

Top Homeowners Insurers in Wisconsin, 2010

Market shares are shown in percent.

American Family Insurance Group	22.9%
State Farm Group	17.0
Allstate Insurance Group	4.2
Farmers Insurance Group	3.9
Other	52.0

Source: *A.M. Best Newswire*, December 13, 2011, p. NA, from BestLink.

★ 3207 ★
Homeowners Insurance
SIC: 6331; NAICS: 524126

Top Homeowners Insurers in Wyoming, 2010

Market shares are shown in percent.

State Farm Group	24.7%
Farmers Insurance Group	18.9
Mountain West Insurance Group	12.4
Liberty Mutual	9.1
Other	35.9

Source: *A.M. Best Newswire*, December 13, 2011, p. NA, from BestLink.

★ 3208 ★
Liability Insurance
SIC: 6331; NAICS: 524126

Top Multiperil Liability Insurers in Georgia, 2009

Market shares are shown in percent.

Travelers Group	10.3%
Auto-Owners Insurance Group	8.6
Liberty Mutual Insurance Cos.	5.9
State Farm Group	5.2
Nationwide Group	4.7
Other	55.3

Source: *A.M. Best Newswire*, March 11, 2011, p. NA, from A.M. Best & Co.

★ 3209 ★
Malpractice Insurance
SIC: 6331; NAICS: 524126

Top Medical Liability Insurers, 2010

Market shares are shown based on directly written premiums.

MLMIC Group	7.21%
Berkshire Hathaway Group	6.86
Doctors Co. Group	6.59
ProAssurance Corp. Group	5.32
CNA Insurance Group	4.88
American International Group	4.42
Physicians Reciprocal Insurers	3.70
Promutual Group	3.63
Ismie Group	2.91
Other	54.58

Source: "Property and Casualty Insurance Industry." [online] from http://www.naics.org [Published March 28, 2011], from National Association of Insurance Commissioners.

★ 3210 ★
Malpractice Insurance
SIC: 6331; NAICS: 524126

Top Medical Malpractice Insurers in California, 2010

Market shares are shown based on directly written premiums.

Doctors Co. Group	38.05%
Norcal Mutual Insurance Co.	27.00
Medical Insurance Exchange of California	6.32
Medical Protective Co.	5.35
National Union Fire Insurance Co. of Pittsburgh	3.18
Other	20.90

Source: "2010 California P&C Market Share Report." [online] from http://www.insurance.ca.gov [Accessed December 1, 2011], from NAICS Database.

★ 3211 ★
Malpractice Insurance
SIC: 6331; NAICS: 524126

Top Medical Professional Liability Insurers in Ohio, 2010

Market shares are shown based on directly written premiums.

Doctors Co. Group	21.6%
Berkshire Hathaway Group	19.9
ProAssurance Corp. Group	16.5
CNA Insurance Group	4.8
Preferred Professional Insurance Cos.	4.6
Other	32.6

Source: "Ohio: 2010 Property and Casualty Insurance Market Share Report." [online] from http://www.insurance.ohio.gov [Accessed December 1, 2011], from Ohio Department of Insurance.

★ 3212 ★
Marine Insurance
SIC: 6331; NAICS: 524126

Top Inland Marine Insurers, 2010

Companies are ranked by issuances in billions of dollars.

Travelers Group	$ 18,674
Zurich Financial Services	18,549
American International Group	18,540
Assurant Insurance Group	18,523
Allianz of America	18,429

Source: *Insurance Facts and Stats*, Annual 2010, p. 31, from A.M. Best & Co.

★ **3213** ★

Marine Insurance

SIC: 6331; NAICS: 524126

Top Inland Marine Insurers in California, 2010

Market shares are shown based on directly written premiums.

Liberty Mutual Insurance Co.	17.02%
Factory Mutual Insurance Co.	12.29
State Farm General	4.10
Firemans Fund Insurance Co.	3.47
Affiliated Fm Insurance Co.	3.18
Other	69.94

Source: "2010 California P&C Market Share Report." [online] from http://www.insurance.ca.gov [Accessed December 1, 2011], from NAICS Database.

★ **3214** ★

Marine Insurance

SIC: 6331; NAICS: 524126

Top Ocean Marine Insurers, 2010

Market shares are shown in percent.

Travelers Group	9.8%
American International Group	9.7
Allianz of America	7.1
CNA Insurance Cos.	7.1
Starr Cos.	6.9
Other	59.4

Source: *A.M. Best Newswire*, February 6, 2012, p. NA, from BestLink.

★ **3215** ★

Marine Insurance

SIC: 6331; NAICS: 524126

Top Ocean Marine Insurers in California, 2010

Market shares are shown based on directly written premiums.

AGCS Marine Insurance Co.	9.82%
National Union Fire Insurance Co. of Pittsburgh	7.95
St. Paul Fire & Marine Insurance	7.09
Continental Insurance Co.	6.93
Starr Individual & Liability Co.	6.21
Navigators Insurance Co.	5.44
Federal Insurance Co.	4.08
Other	52.48

Source: "2010 California P&C Market Share Report." [online] from http://www.insurance.ca.gov [Accessed December 1, 2011], from NAICS Database.

★ **3216** ★

Multiperil Insurance

SIC: 6331; NAICS: 524126

Top Commercial Multiperil Insurers in Maryland, 2010

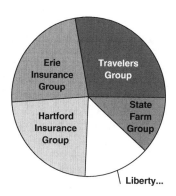

Market shares are shown in percent.

Travelers Group	11.7%
Erie Insurance Group	9.5
Hartford Insurance Group	9.5
Liberty Mutual Insurance Cos.	5.8
State Farm Group	5.4

Source: *A.M. Best Newswire*, January 31, 2012, p. NA, from A.M. Best & Co.

★ **3217** ★

Multiperil Insurance

SIC: 6331; NAICS: 524126

Top Commercial Multiperil Insurers in Texas, 2010

Market shares are shown in percent.

Hartford Insurance	8.8%
Travelers Group	8.7
Liberty Mutual Insurance Cos.	7.3
Nationwide Group	6.0
Zurich Financial Services North America	5.8
Other	63.4

Source: *A.M. Best Newswire*, January 31, 2012, p. NA, from A.M. Best & Co.

★ 3218 ★
Multiperil Insurance
SIC: 6331; NAICS: 524126

Top Homeowners Multiperil Insurers in Louisiana, 2010

Market shares are shown in percent.

State Farm Group	28.63%
Allstate Insurance Group	13.41
Liberty Mutual Insurance Cos.	6.52
Louisiana Farm Bureau Mutual Insurance Co.	5.79
Louisiana Citizens Property Insurance Corp. .	5.29
Other	40.36

Source: *A.M. Best Newswire*, February 9, 2012, p. NA, from BestLink.

★ 3219 ★
Multiperil Insurance
SIC: 6331; NAICS: 524126

Top Multiperil Insurers in Virginia, 2010

Market shares are shown in percent.

Travelers Group	10.6%
Erie Insurance Group	8.4
Hartford Insurance Group	7.2
Nationwide Group	6.6
Cincinnati Insurance Cos.	4.9
Other	62.3

Source: *A.M. Best Newswire*, February 7, 2012, p. NA, from BestLink.

★ 3220 ★
Multiple Peril Insurance
SIC: 6331; NAICS: 524126

Top Farmowners Multiple Peril Insurers, 2010

Policies are similar to homeowners insurance protecting farmowners against a number of named perils and liabilities. Companies are ranked by issuances in billions of dollars.

Travelers Group	$ 18,674
QBE Americas Group	18,173
Tennessee Farmers Insurance Cos.	18,154
Nationwide Group	5,987
Farm Bureau Property & Casualty Group . .	4,233
United Farm Bureau of Indiana Group . . .	4,232

Source: *Insurance Facts and Stats*, Annual 2010, p. 31, from A.M. Best & Co.

★ 3221 ★
Personal Line Insurance
SIC: 6331; NAICS: 524126

Top Personal Line Insurers in Iowa, 2010

Market shares are shown in percent.

State Farm Group	23.0%
Nationwide Group	13.0
Progressive Group	10.0
Iowa Farm Bureau	7.5
American Family Insurance Group	7.2
Grinnell Mutual	3.3
Other	36.0

Source: *National Underwriter*, April 18, 2011, p. 13, from Highline Data.

★ 3222 ★
Property Insurance
SIC: 6331; NAICS: 524126

Top Property and Casualty Insurers, 2010

Market shares are shown based on directly written premiums.

State Farm Group	10.88%
Zurich Insurance Group	5.70
Allstate Insurance Group	5.37
American International Group	5.28
Liberty Mutual Group	5.26
Travelers Group	4.48
Berkshire Hathaway	3.44
Nationwide Group	3.09
Progressive Group	3.09
Other	53.41

Source: "Property and Casualty Insurance Industry." [online] from http://www.naics.org [Published March 28, 2011], from National Association of Insurance Commissioners.

★ 3223 ★
Property Insurance
SIC: 6331; NAICS: 524126

Top Property Insurance Firms in China, 2010

The top domestic firms are ranked by premium in billions of renminbi for the first nine months of the year. The top foreign insurance firms were AIG (787.3 million), Mitsui Sumitomo (313.1 million) and Tokio Marine & Nichido Fire (303.8 million).

PICC	¥ 118.3
Ping An	45.4

Continued on next page.

★ 3223 ★

[Continued]

Property Insurance

SIC: 6331; NAICS: 524126

Top Property Insurance Firms in China, 2010

The top domestic firms are ranked by premium in billions of renminbi for the first nine months of the year. The top foreign insurance firms were AIG (787.3 million), Mitsui Sumitomo (313.1 million) and Tokio Marine & Nichido Fire (303.8 million).

China Pacific	¥ 39.0
China United Property	15.1
China Continent	10.3
China Life P&C	8.2
Sunshine P&C	8.0
Tianan	6.7
Sinosure	6.5

Source: *China Insurance Report*, July 2011, p. 42, from Business Monitor International.

★ 3224 ★

Property Insurance

SIC: 6331; NAICS: 524126

Top Property Insurers in Florida, 2011

Market shares are shown based on personal and commercial residential policies.

Citizens Property Insurance Corp.	21.1%
State Farm Florida	9.7
Universal Property & Casualty Insurance Co.	9.5
St. Johns Insurance Company Inc.	2.8
United Services Automobile Assn.	2.4
Castle Key Insurance Co.	2.2
Castle Key Indemnity Co.	2.1
ASI Insurance Corp.	2.0
Security First Insurance Co.	2.0
Other	36.2

Source: "Top 25 Policies in Force." [online] from http://www.floir.com/siteDocuments/QUASRngQuarterlyRpts [Published June 22, 2011], from Florida Office of Insurance Regulation.

★ 3225 ★

Workers Compensation Insurance

SIC: 6331; NAICS: 524126

Top Workers Compensation Insurers, 2010

Market shares are shown based on directly written premiums.

Liberty Mutual Group	10.29%
American International Group	9.07

Travelers Group	7.12%
Hartford Fire & Casualty Group	6.68
Zurich Insurance Group	6.12
State Insurance Fund	3.31
State Compensation Insurance Fund	2.88
ACE Ltd. Group	2.69
Old Republic Group	2.15
Other	49.69

Source: "Property and Casualty Insurance Industry." [online] from http://www.naics.org [Published March 28, 2011], from National Association of Insurance Commissioners.

★ 3226 ★

Workers Compensation Insurance

SIC: 6331; NAICS: 524126

Top Workers Compensation Insurers in California, 2010

Market shares are shown in percent.

California State Compensation Insurance Fund	16.04%
Travelers Group	7.74
American International Group	6.55
Hartford Insurance Group	6.37
Zurich Financial Group	5.91
Other	57.39

Source: *A.M. Best Newswire*, October 10, 2011, p. NA, from A.M. Best & Co.

★ 3227 ★

Workers Compensation Insurance

SIC: 6331; NAICS: 524126

Top Workers Compensation Insurers in Michigan, 2010

Market shares are shown in percent.

Accidental Fund Group	19.47%
Liberty Mutual Insurance Cos.	9.02
Travelers Group	6.39
Hartford Insurance Group	6.37
Amerisure Cos.	4.89
Other	53.86

Source: *A.M. Best Newswire*, December 8, 2011, p. NA, from BestLink.

★ 3228 ★
Workers Compensation Insurance
SIC: 6331; NAICS: 524126

Top Workers Compensation Insurers in Missouri, 2010

Market shares are shown in percent.

Missouri Employers Mutual	16.14%
Liberty Mutual Insurance Cos.	11.18
Travelers Group	10.50
American International Group	7.98
Hartford Insurance Group	6.66
Other	47.54

Source: *A.M. Best Newswire*, February 29, 2012, p. NA, from BestLink.

★ 3229 ★
Workers Compensation Insurance
SIC: 6331; NAICS: 524126

Worker's Compensation Insurance Market by State, 2010

States are ranked by premiums in billions of dollars.

California	$ 7.10
New York	3.62
Illinois	2.25
Texas	1.92
New Jersey	1.63
Florida	1.56
Wisconsin	1.47
North Carolina	1.06
Georgia	0.95

Source: *National Underwriter*, August 22, 2011, p. 26, from NAIC annual statement database.

★ 3230 ★
Liability Insurance
SIC: 6351; NAICS: 524126

Top Commercial Liability Insurers in Florida, 2010

Market shares are shown in percent.

Travelers Group	10.5%
Erie Insurance Group	9.9
Liberty Mutual Insurance Cos.	8.8
Hartford Insurance Group	8.3
State Farm Group	5.1
Other	57.4

Source: *A.M. Best Newswire*, February 9, 2012, p. NA, from BestLink.

★ 3231 ★
Liability Insurance
SIC: 6351; NAICS: 524126

Top General Liability Insurers in Ohio, 2010

Market shares are shown based on directly written premiums.

American International Group	18.3%
Cincinnati Financial Group	7.3
Chubb & Son Inc. Group	6.5
Travelers Group	5.0
Zurich Insurance Group	4.5
Other	58.4

Source: "Ohio: 2010 Property and Casualty Insurance Market Share Report." [online] from http://www.insurance.ohio.gov [Accessed December 1, 2011], from Ohio Department of Insurance.

★ 3232 ★
Liability Insurance
SIC: 6351; NAICS: 524126

Top Liability Insurers, 2010

Liability insurance coverage protects against legal liability resulting from negligence, carelessness or a failure to act causing property damage or personal injury to others. Companies are ranked by issuances in billions of dollars.

Travelers Group	$ 18,674
Zurich Financial Services	18,549
American International Group	18,540
ACE INA Group	18,498
XL America Group	18,130
Nationwide Group	5,987

Source: *Insurance Facts and Stats*, Annual 2010, p. 31, from A.M. Best & Co.

★ 3233 ★
Liability Insurance
SIC: 6351; NAICS: 524126

Top Professional Liability Insurers, 2010

Market shares are shown based on directly written premiums.

MLMIC Group	7.27%
Berkshire Hathaway Insurance Group	6.83
Doctors Co. Group	6.64
ProAssurance Group	5.36
CNA Insurance Cos.	4.74
American International Group	4.45

Continued on next page.

★ 3233 ★

[Continued]

Liability Insurance

SIC: 6351; NAICS: 524126

Top Professional Liability Insurers, 2010

Market shares are shown based on directly written premiums.

Physicians Reciprocal Insurers	3.72%
Coverys	3.66
ISMIE Mutual Insurance Co.	2.93
Other	54.40

Source: *Modern Healthcare*, February 6, 2012, p. 32, from A.M. Best & Co.

★ 3234 ★

Mortgage Guaranty Insurance

SIC: 6351; NAICS: 524126

Top Mortgage Guaranty Insurers, 2011

Also known as private mortgage insurance (PMI), mortgage guaranty insurance covers the lender originating the mortgage in event that the mortgage holder defaults on the loan.

MGIC Investment Corp.	24.57%
American International Group	16.57
Radian Group Inc.	16.57
Genworth Financial inc.	13.64
PMI Group Inc.	12.44
Other	16.21

Source: *National Underwriter*, April 30, 2012, p. NA, from SNL Financial.

★ 3235 ★

Mortgage Guaranty Insurance

SIC: 6351; NAICS: 524126

Top Mortgage Guaranty Insurers in California, 2010

Market shares are shown based on directly written premiums.

Radian Guaranty Inc.	24.85%
Mortgage Guaranty Insurance Co.	17.15
PMI Mortgage Insurance Co.	13.53
Triad Guaranty Insurance Co.	13.53
Other	30.94

Source: "2010 California P&C Market Share Report." [online] from http://www.insurance.ca.gov [Accessed December 1, 2011], from NAICS Database.

★ 3236 ★

Title Insurance

SIC: 6361; NAICS: 524127

Top Title Insurers, 2011

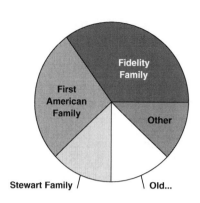

Market shares are shown based on premiums written for the first six months of the year.

Fidelity Family	35.05%
First American Family	26.90
Stewart Family	13.24
Old Republic Family	13.10
Other	11.71

Source: "Industry Financial Data." [online] from http://www.alta.org/industry/financial.cfm [Accessed November 1, 2011], from American Land Title Association.

★ 3237 ★

Pensions

SIC: 6371; NAICS: 52511

Top Pension Funds Worldwide, 2010

Public sector bonds claimed 39% of the total, sovereign funds 29%, corporations 19% and the private sector 13%.

Government Pension Investment (Japan)	$ 1,432,122
Government Pension Fund (Global)	550,858
ABP (Netherlands)	318,807
National Pension (Korea)	289,418
Federal Retirement Thrift (United States)	264,013
California Public Employee (United States)	214,387
Local Government Officials	189,633
Canada Pension	149,142
Employees Provident Fund (Malaysia)	145,570
Central Provident Fund (Singapore)	144,844

Source: *Pensions & Investments*, February 2011, p. NA, from Towers Perrin.

★ 3238 ★
Claims Adjusting
SIC: 6411; NAICS: 524291

Claims Adjusting, 2007

Data show the percent of industry sales held by the largest 4, 8, 20 and 50 firms in the sector. There are approximately 5,724 firms operating in the industry generating employment for 54,142 people.

4 largest firms	46.7%
8 largest firms	55.7
20 largest firms	61.4
50 largest firms	68.4

Source: ''2007 Economic Census.'' [online] from http://www.census.gov/econ/concentration.html [Accessed August 12, 2011], from U.S. Bureau of the Census.

★ 3239 ★
Reinsurance Industry
SIC: 6411; NAICS: 52421

Top Reinsurance Firms Worldwide, 2010

Market shares are shown based on $203 billion in gross written premiums.

Munich Re	15.0%
Swiss Re	12.0
Berkshire Hathaway	7.0
Hannover Re	7.0
Lloyd's	6.0
Reinsurance Group of America	4.0
SCOR	4.0
Allianz	3.0
Everest Re	2.0
Partner Re	2.0
Other	36.0

Source: *Financial Stability Review*, September 2011, p. NA, from A.M. Best & Co.

SIC 65 - Real Estate

★ 3240 ★
Building Leasing
SIC: 6512; NAICS: 53112

Lessors of Manufacturing and Industrial Buildings, 2007

Data show the percent of industry sales held by the largest 4, 8, 20 and 50 firms in the sector. There are approximately 4,245 firms operating in the industry generating employment for 16,266 people.

4 largest firms	37.4%
8 largest firms	46.4
20 largest firms	57.2
50 largest firms	65.6

Source: "2007 Economic Census." [online] from http://www.census.gov/econ/concentration.html [Accessed August 12, 2011], from U.S. Bureau of the Census.

★ 3241 ★
Building Leasing
SIC: 6512; NAICS: 53112

Lessors of Miniwarehouses and Self-Storage Units, 2007

Data show the percent of industry sales held by the largest 4, 8, 20 and 50 firms in the sector. There are approximately 14,168 firms operating in the industry generating employment for 38,000 people.

4 largest firms	34.4%
8 largest firms	38.8
20 largest firms	43.0
50 largest firms	46.9

Source: "2007 Economic Census." [online] from http://www.census.gov/econ/concentration.html [Accessed August 12, 2011], from U.S. Bureau of the Census.

★ 3242 ★
Building Leasing
SIC: 6512; NAICS: 53112

Lessors of Nonresidential Buildings (except Miniwarehouses), 2007

Data show the percent of industry sales held by the largest 4, 8, 20 and 50 firms in the sector. There are approximately 35,021 firms operating in the industry generating employment for 180,540 people.

4 largest firms	14.3%
8 largest firms	21.0
20 largest firms	32.5
50 largest firms	47.1

Source: "2007 Economic Census." [online] from http://www.census.gov/econ/concentration.html [Accessed August 12, 2011], from U.S. Bureau of the Census.

★ 3243 ★
Building Leasing
SIC: 6512; NAICS: 53112

Lessors of Professional and Other Office Buildings, 2007

Data show the percent of industry sales held by the largest 4, 8, 20 and 50 firms in the sector. There are approximately 16,382 firms operating in the industry generating employment for 78,523 people.

4 largest firms	18.9%
8 largest firms	27.9
20 largest firms	41.1
50 largest firms	55.2

Source: "2007 Economic Census." [online] from http://www.census.gov/econ/concentration.html [Accessed August 12, 2011], from U.S. Bureau of the Census.

★ 3244 ★

Real Estate

SIC: 6512; NAICS: 53112

Leading Managers of Retail Real Estate, 2010

Companies are ranked by gross leasable area managed in millions of square feet.

Simon Property Group	262.0
CB Richard Ellis Group	200.0
General Growth Properties	166.4
Developers Diversified Realty	121.0
Kimco Realty	113.0
Centro Properties Group	96.0
Jones Lang LaSalle Americas	92.2
CBL & Associates Properties	84.1
Inland Real Estate Group of Cos.	83.7
Macerich	72.5

Source: *Retail Traffic*, May 11, 2011, p. NA.

★ 3245 ★

Real Estate

SIC: 6512; NAICS: 53112

Leading Owners of Retail Real Estate, 2010

Companies are ranked by gross leasable area in millions of square feet.

Simon Property Group	251.0
General Growth Properties	164.1
Developers Diversified Realty	121.0
Kimco Realty	112.9
Centro Properties Group	96.0
Inland Real Estate Group of Cos.	83.1
CBL & Associates Properties	82.1
Macerich	72.5
Westfield	63.0
Weingarten Realty	54.2

Source: *Retail Traffic*, May 11, 2011, p. NA.

★ 3246 ★

Shopping Center Leasing

SIC: 6512; NAICS: 53112

Lessors of Shopping Centers and Retail Stores, 2007

Data show the percent of industry sales held by the largest 4, 8, 20 and 50 firms in the sector. There are approximately 10,228 firms operating in the industry generating employment for 61,392 people.

4 largest firms	32.9%
8 largest firms	42.6
20 largest firms	56.4%
50 largest firms	66.4

Source: "2007 Economic Census." [online] from http://www.census.gov/econ/concentration.html [Accessed August 12, 2011], from U.S. Bureau of the Census.

★ 3247 ★

Apartments

SIC: 6513; NAICS: 53111

Top Apartment Managers, 2011

Companies are ranked by units managed as of January 1, 2011.

Greystar Real Estate Partners L.L.C.	187,360
Riverstone Residential Group	162,182
Pinnacle Family of Companies	151,367
Lincoln Property Company	133,425
Equity Residential	129,604
AIMCO	117,119
WinnCompanies	84,817
Archstone	81,613
Camden Property Trust	63,498
Bell Partners Inc.	60,182

Source: *Units*, May 2011, p. 58, from National Multi-Housing Council.

★ 3248 ★

Apartments

SIC: 6513; NAICS: 53111

Top Apartment Owners, 2011

Companies are ranked by number of apartments with ownership interest as of January 1, 2011.

Boston Capital	158,947
Centerline Capital Group	152,600
Boston Financial Investment Management L.P.	145,545
SunAmerica Affordable Housing Partners Inc.	141,113
Equity Residential	129,604
PNC Tax Credit Capital	123,462
AIMCO	110,946
National Equity Fund Inc.	107,138
Enterprise Community Investment Inc.	96,195
The Richman Group Affordable Housing Corp.	94,925

Source: *National Real Estate Investor*, April 2011, p. 4, from National Multi-Housing Council.

★ 3249 ★
Building Leasing
SIC: 6514; NAICS: 53111

Lessors of Dwellings Other Than Apartment Buildings, 2007

Data show the percent of industry sales held by the largest 4, 8, 20 and 50 firms in the sector. There are approximately 14,481 firms operating in the industry generating employment for 41,153 people.

4 largest firms	7.2%
8 largest firms	9.7
20 largest firms	12.4
50 largest firms	16.6

Source: "2007 Economic Census." [online] from http://www.census.gov/econ/concentration.html [Accessed August 12, 2011], from U.S. Bureau of the Census.

★ 3250 ★
Building Leasing
SIC: 6514; NAICS: 53111

Lessors of Residential Buildings and Dwellings, 2007

Data show the percent of industry sales held by the largest 4, 8, 20 and 50 firms in the sector. There are approximately 62,876 firms operating in the industry generating employment for 289,990 people.

4 largest firms	11.0%
8 largest firms	15.7
20 largest firms	21.2
50 largest firms	27.7

Source: "2007 Economic Census." [online] from http://www.census.gov/econ/concentration.html [Accessed August 12, 2011], from U.S. Bureau of the Census.

★ 3251 ★
Manufactured Home Leasing
SIC: 6515; NAICS: 53119

Lessors of Manufactured (Mobile) Home Sites, 2007

Data show the percent of industry sales held by the largest 4, 8, 20 and 50 firms in the sector. There are approximately 6,921 firms operating in the industry generating employment for 25,375 people.

4 largest firms	19.1%
8 largest firms	23.2
20 largest firms	28.0
50 largest firms	33.4

Source: "2007 Economic Census." [online] from http://www.census.gov/econ/concentration.html [Accessed August 12, 2011], from U.S. Bureau of the Census.

★ 3252 ★
Real Estate
SIC: 6531; NAICS: 53121

Top Real Estate Firms in Boulder, CO, 2010

Market shares are shown based on number of properties sold during the first half of the year.

RE/MAX	13.0%
Century 21	5.5
Baird & Warner	5.1
Prudential	4.9
Real Living	3.2
Keller Williams	3.1
Other	65.2

Source: "RE/MAX Network Reports First Half 2010 Market Share." [online] from http://www.theboulderrealestatesite.com [Published August 2, 2011].

★ 3253 ★
Real Estate
SIC: 6531; NAICS: 53121

Top Real Estate Firms in Chicago, IL, 2010

Market shares are shown based on number of properties sold.

RE/MAX	18.3%
Coldwell Banker	13.9
Century 21	5.3
Baird & Warner	5.2
Prudential	4.8
Keller Williams	3.2
Real Living	3.2
Other	46.1

Source: "RE/MAX Again Was No. 1 in Home Sales Across Metro Chicago Real Estate Market." [online] from http://www.illinois.realestaterama.com [Published February 8, 2011], from Midwest Real Estate Data L.L.C.

★ 3254 ★
Real Estate
SIC: 6531; NAICS: 53121

Top Real Estate Firms in Northern Indiana, 2011

Market shares are shown based on number of properties sold for the month of September 2011.

RE/MAX	26.7%
Coldwell Banker	16.7
Baird & Warner	9.5
Century 21	9.5

Continued on next page.

★ 3254 ★

[Continued]

Real Estate

SIC: 6531; NAICS: 53121

Top Real Estate Firms in Northern Indiana, 2011

Market shares are shown based on number of properties sold for the month of September 2011.

Keller Williams	5.9%
Prudential	5.9
Other	25.8

Source: "Market Share Sold 9/1/11-9/30/11." [online] from http://www.gowithcb.com/storage/Northwest.pdf [Published October 4, 2011], from Midwest Real Estate Data L.L.C. and Greater Northwest Indiana Association of Realtors.

★ 3255 ★

Real Estate

SIC: 6531; NAICS: 531311

Top Real Estate Firms in Sarasota, FL, 2011

Market shares are shown based on number of properties sold for the 12 months ended March 2011.

Michael Saunders and Company	23.1%
Coldwell Banker Real Estate	13.6
RE/MAX Alliance Group	9.8
Signature Sotheby's	5.6
Other	47.9

Source: "Top Sarasota Real Estate Brokers." [online] from http://www.luxurysarasotarealestate.com [Published March 28, 2011], from Trendgraphix.com.

★ 3256 ★

Real Estate

SIC: 6531; NAICS: 531311

Top Real Estate Firms in Twin City Region, Ontario, Canada, 2011

Market shares are shown based on number of properties sold from January 1-July 31, 2011.

RE/MAX Twin City Inc..	26.1%
RE/MAX Solid Gold Realty Ltd..	8.2
Coldwell Banker Peter Berringer	7.8
Peak Realty Inc..	6.1
RE/MAX Real Estate Centre	4.9
Other	46.9

Source: "RE/Max Twin CIty Takes 26.1% of Market Share." [online] from http://www.johnsummers1.com [Published July 2011], from Kitchener Waterloo Association of Realtors.

★ 3257 ★

Real Estate

SIC: 6531; NAICS: 531311

Top Real Estate Management and Development Firms Worldwide, 2011

The industry generated revenues of $479.3 billion.

Mitsubishi Estate Co.	2.6%
Sumitomo Realty & Development Co. ltd. . .	1.9
Mitsui Fudoshan	1.8
CB Richard Ellis Group	1.2
Other	92.4

Source: *Datamonitor Industry Market Research*, May 1, 2012, p. NA, from Datamonitor.

★ 3258 ★

Vacation Homes

SIC: 6531; NAICS: 53139

Vacation Home Sales, 2010

There were 7.9 million vacation homes and 41.6 million investment units in the United States. The median vacation-home price was $150,000 in 2010, down 11.2 percent from $169,000 in 2009. The typical vacation home buyer in 2010 was 49 years old, had a median household income of $99,500 and purchased a property that was a median distance of 375 miles from his or her primary residence.

South	36.0%
West	27.0
Northeast	19.0
Midwest	15.0

Source: "Vacation- and Investment-Home Shares Hold Even in 2010." [online] from http://www.realtor.org [Published March 30, 2011], from U.S. Bureau of the Census.

★ 3259 ★

Title Abstract and Settlement Offices

SIC: 6541; NAICS: 541191

Title Abstract and Settlement Offices, 2007

Data show the percent of industry sales held by the largest 4, 8, 20 and 50 firms in the sector. There are approximately 12,460 firms operating in the industry generating employment for 77,310 people.

4 largest firms	19.9%
8 largest firms	24.3

Continued on next page.

★ 3259 ★

[Continued]

Title Abstract and Settlement Offices

SIC: 6541; NAICS: 541191

Title Abstract and Settlement Offices, 2007

Data show the percent of industry sales held by the largest 4, 8, 20 and 50 firms in the sector. There are approximately 12,460 firms operating in the industry generating employment for 77,310 people.

20 largest firms	30.3%
50 largest firms	37.5

Source: ''2007 Economic Census.'' [online] from http://www. census.gov/econ/concentration.html [Accessed August 12, 2011], from U.S. Bureau of the Census.

★ 3260 ★

Cemeteries

SIC: 6553; NAICS: 81222

Top For-Profit Cemetery Owners, 2010

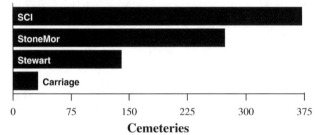

Cemeteries

Companies are ranked by number of cemeteries. There were 9,600 for-profit cemeteries in the United States in 2010 and 13,000 municipal, military, religious and non-profit cemeteries.

SCI	372
StoneMor	273
Stewart	140
Carriage	32

Source: ''StoneMor Bank of America Leveraged Finance Conference.'' [online] from http://www.stonemor.com [Published December 2011].

SIC 67 - Holding and Other Investment Offices

★ 3261 ★
Bank Holding Companies
SIC: 6712; NAICS: 551111

Top Bank Holding Companies, 2011

Institutions are ranked by assets in millions of dollars.

J.P. Morgan Chase & Co.	$ 2,265.7
Bank of America Corp.	2,136.5
Citigroup Inc.	1,873.8
Wells Fargo & Co.	1,313.8
Goldman Sachs Group Inc.	923.7
MetLife Inc.	799.6
Morgan Stanley	749.8
Taunus Corp.	354.7
U.S. Bancorp	340.1
HSBC North American Holdings Inc.	331.4

Source: "Top 50 Bank Holding Companies." [online] from http://www.ffiec.gov [Accessed March 1, 2012], from Federal Reserve System.

★ 3262 ★
Trust, Fiduciary, and Custody Activities
SIC: 6726; NAICS: 52599

Trust, Fiduciary, and Custody Activities, 2007

Data show the percent of industry sales held by the largest 4, 8, 20 and 50 firms in the sector. There are approximately 2,512 firms operating in the industry generating employment for 44,295 people.

4 largest firms	35.2%
8 largest firms	53.9
20 largest firms	72.3
50 largest firms	82.0

Source: "2007 Economic Census." [online] from http://www.census.gov/econ/concentration.html [Accessed August 12, 2011], from U.S. Bureau of the Census.

★ 3263 ★
Franchises
SIC: 6794; NAICS: 53311

Largest Franchise Systems Worldwide, 2010

Franchises are ranked by worldwide sales in millions of dollars.

McDonald's	$ 77,380
7-Eleven	63,000
KFC	19,400
Subway	15,200
Ace Hardware	12,500
Circle K	10,726
Pizza Hut	10,200
Wendy's	9,100
Marriott Hotels, Resorts & Suites	8,000
Hertz	7,600
Hilton Hotels & Resorts	7,000
Health Mart	6,920
RE/MAX	6,625

Source: *Franchise Times*, October 2011, p. 4.

★ 3264 ★
Patents
SIC: 6794; NAICS: 53311

Top U.S. Patent Receivers, 2011

Companies are ranked by patents received during 2011.

Hon Hai Precision Industry Co. Ltd.	11,514
IBM	6,180
Samsung	4,894
Canon	2,821
Panasonic	2,559
Toshiba	2,483
Microsoft	2,311
Sony	2,286
Seiko Epson	1,533
Hitachi	1,465

Source: "Performance and Accountability Report of Fiscal Year 2011." [online] from http://www.uspto.gov/about/strat-plan/ar/2011/index.jsp [Accessed February 20, 2012], from U.S. Patent and Trade Office.

★ 3265 ★
Real Estate Investment Trusts
SIC: 6798; NAICS: 53111

Real Estate Investment Trust Industry, 2011

The industry consists of 178 businesses which generated $54.3 billion in revenues.

Equity REITs - other commercial property . .	54.2%
Equity REITs - retail properties	23.1
Equity REITs - residential properties	15.2
Mortgage REITs	6.1
Hybrid REITs	1.4

Source: ''Analysis of the Real Estate Investment Trust (REIT) Industry.'' [online] from http://scholarsarchive.jwu.edu/mba_student/6 [Published January 9, 2012], from IBISWorld.

SIC 70 - Hotels and Other Lodging Places

★ 3266 ★
Bed and Breakfasts
SIC: 7011; NAICS: 721191
Bed and Breakfasts, 2007

According to the Census, this industry comprises "establishments primarily engaged in providing short-term lodging in facilities known as bed-and-breakfast inns. These establishments provide short-term lodging in private homes or small buildings converted for this purpose. Bed-and-breakfast inns are characterized by a highly personalized service and inclusion of a full breakfast in a room rate." Data show the percent of industry sales held by the largest 4, 8, 20 and 50 firms in the sector.

4 largest firms	3.8%
8 largest firms	5.5
20 largest firms	9.4
50 largest firms	15.5

Source: "2007 Economic Census." [online] from http://www.census.gov/econ/concentration.html [Accessed August 12, 2011], from U.S. Bureau of the Census.

★ 3267 ★
Bed and Breakfasts
SIC: 7011; NAICS: 721191
Bed and Breakfasts Industry, 2010

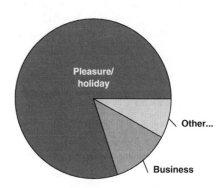

The Census defines this industry as establishments "primarily engaged in providing short-term lodging in facilities known as bed-and-breakfast inns. These establishments provide short-term lodging in private homes or small buildings converted for this purpose. Bed-and-breakfast inns are characterized by a highly personalized service and inclusion of a full breakfast in a room rate." A total of 4,140 businesses operated in this industry, generating revenues of $1.5 billion.

Pleasure/holiday short break	80.0%
Business	12.0
Other, including meetings	8.0

Source: "Market Analysis." [online] from http://victoriabunte.com/files/marketanalysis.pdf [Accessed April 1, 2012], from IBISWorld.

★ 3268 ★
Hotels
SIC: 7011; NAICS: 72112
Casino Hotels, 2007

Data show the percent of industry sales held by the largest 4, 8, 20 and 50 firms in the sector. There are approximately 307 firms operating in the industry generating employment for 433,606 people.

4 largest firms	41.4%
8 largest firms	51.6

Continued on next page.

★ 3268 ★

[Continued]

Hotels

SIC: 7011; NAICS: 72112

Casino Hotels, 2007

Data show the percent of industry sales held by the largest 4, 8, 20 and 50 firms in the sector. There are approximately 307 firms operating in the industry generating employment for 433,606 people.

20 largest firms	69.4%
50 largest firms	86.1

Source: ''2007 Economic Census.'' [online] from http://www.census.gov/econ/concentration.html [Accessed August 12, 2011], from U.S. Bureau of the Census.

★ 3269 ★

Hotels

SIC: 7011; NAICS: 72111

Top Budget Hotels in China, 2010

Market shares are shown in percent.

Home Inns	16.58%
7 Days Inn	10.53
Jin Jiang	9.93
Hanting Inn	9.23
Motel 168	7.68
GreenTree Inn	5.31
Super 8	3.22
Vienna	1.66
Other	35.86

Source: ''Industry Overview.'' [online] from http://www.hkgem.com/listing/prelist/ELEGEND-20110622-10.pdf [Accessed October 1, 2011], from Inntie.

★ 3270 ★

Hotels

SIC: 7011; NAICS: 72111

Top Hotel Companies, 2011

The industry generated revenues of $121.7 billion. Business travelers claimed 28.5% of the market, vacation travelers 25.7%, conference travelers 25% and personal or family travelers 20.8%.

Marriott International Inc.	6.7%
Hilton Hotels	5.0
Starwood Hotels and Resorts	3.5
Wyndham Worldwide	2.5
Other	80.5

Source: ''Hotel Industry.'' [online] from http://faculty.cit.cornell.edu/jl2545/4160/presentation/Hotel%20Pricing-1.pptx [Published April 14, 2011], from IBISWorld.

★ 3271 ★

Hotels

SIC: 7011; NAICS: 72111

Top Hotel Management Companies, 2010

Companies are ranked by guestrooms under third-party management.

Westmont Hospitality Group	52,308
Interstate Hotels & Resorts	46,470
Hotel Equities Group	42,361
White Lodging Services Group	19,612
GF Management	17,204
IPG Hospitality	16,975
Ocean Hospitalities	13,675
Crescent Hotels & Resorts	13,642
Pyramid Hotel Group	13,613
Sage Hospitality	13,584

Source: *Hotel & Motel Management*, March 2011, p. 16.

★ 3272 ★

Rooming and Boarding Houses

SIC: 7021; NAICS: 72131

Rooming and Boarding Houses by State, 2010

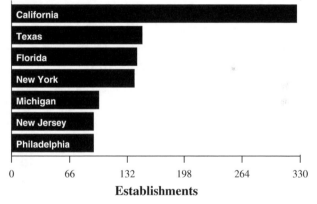

According to the Census, these are establishments primarily engaged ''in operating rooming and boarding houses and similar facilities, such as fraternity houses, sorority houses, off-campus dormitories, residential clubs, and workers' camps. These establishments provide temporary or longer-term accommodations which, for the period of occupancy, may serve as a principal residence. These establishments also may provide complementary services, such as housekeeping, meals, and laundry services.''

California	326
Texas	149
Florida	143

Continued on next page.

★ 3272 ★
[Continued]
Rooming and Boarding Houses
SIC: 7021; NAICS: 72131

Rooming and Boarding Houses by State, 2010

According to the Census, these are establishments primarily engaged "in operating rooming and boarding houses and similar facilities, such as fraternity houses, sorority houses, off-campus dormitories, residential clubs, and workers' camps. These establishments provide temporary or longer-term accommodations which, for the period of occupancy, may serve as a principal residence. These establishments also may provide complementary services, such as housekeeping, meals, and laundry services."

New York	140
Michigan	99
New Jersey	93
Philadelphia	93

Source: "Rooming and Boarding Houses." [online] from http://business.highbeam.com [Accessed April 1, 2012], from Dun & Bradstreet.

★ 3273 ★
Recreational and Vacation Camps
SIC: 7032; NAICS: 721214

Recreational and Vacation Camps (except Campgrounds), 2007

Data show the percent of industry sales held by the largest 4, 8, 20 and 50 firms in the sector. There are approximately 3,065 firms operating in the industry generating employment for 19,860 people.

4 largest firms	5.0%
8 largest firms	7.6
20 largest firms	13.2
50 largest firms	20.7

Source: "2007 Economic Census." [online] from http://www.census.gov/econ/concentration.html [Accessed August 12, 2011], from U.S. Bureau of the Census.

★ 3274 ★
RV Parks
SIC: 7033; NAICS: 721211

RV Park Revenues, 2009-2013

The number of RVs in use is on the rise, with 8% of all vehicle-owning households owning an RV. Ten percent of RV owners use the vehicle as their primary residence. Revenues are shown in millions of dollars. The number of establishments is projected to increase from 12,804 to 13,543. Employment will increase from 41,865 to 44,150.

2013	$ 4,711
2012	4,587
2011	4,501
2010	4,434
2009	4,404

Source: "RV Parks." [online] from http://www.kitsapeda.org/pdfs/RV%20Park%20Industry%20Snapshot.pdf [Published May 2011], from IBISWorld.

SIC 72 - Personal Services

★ 3275 ★
Laundromats and Drycleaners
SIC: 7211; NAICS: 81232

Non-Coin-Operated Laundromat and Drycleaning Services, 2010

The industry was valued at $9.2 billion. Dry cleaning services claimed 75.7%, laundry services 19%, garment alteration 2.1%, garment and textile restoration and repair 0.8% and other products 2.4%. Consumers reacted to the recent recession by cutting their spending. This meant fewer trips to the laundromat and wearing clothes longer that need to be drycleaned. Revenues in this sector fell approximately 1% annually. EnviroStar Inc. owns DryClean USA one of the largest franchise systems in the United States.

Martin Franchises Inc.	1.3%
EnviroStar Inc.	0.7
U.S. Dry Cleaning Services Corp.	0.3
Widmer's Cleaners	0.2
Zoots Corp.	0.1
Other	97.1

Source: "Non-Coin-Operated Laundromats and Dry Cleaners in the U.S." [online] from http://www.scribd.com [Published March 2011], from IBISWorld.

★ 3276 ★
Laundry and Garment Services
SIC: 7212; NAICS: 81232

Garment Pressing and Agents For Laundries, 2007

Data show the percent of industry sales held by the largest 4, 8, 20 and 50 firms in the sector. There are approximately 3,829 firms operating in the industry generating employment for 12,083 people.

4 largest firms	7.6%
8 largest firms	10.5
20 largest firms	16.0
50 largest firms	24.1

Source: "2007 Economic Census." [online] from http://www.census.gov/econ/concentration.html [Accessed August 12, 2011], from U.S. Bureau of the Census.

★ 3277 ★
Industrial Laundries and Linen Suppliers
SIC: 7213; NAICS: 812331

Top Industrial Laundry and Linen Suppliers, 2011

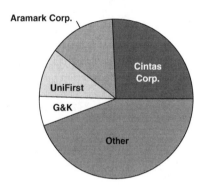

The industry generated revenues of $11.1 billion in 2011. The industry will benefit from rebounding employment in the foodservice and hospitality sectors. Increased traffic in hospitals will mean more outsourcing of linens to be cleaned. Uniform rental and cleaning claimed 34.8% of the market, followed by linen rental and cleaning with 22.6%, linen supply garments rental and cleaning with 18%.

Cintas Corp.	25.6%
Aramark Corp.	13.6
UniFirst	9.8
G&K	5.9
Other	45.1

Source: "Industrial Laundry & Linen Supply in the U.S." [online] from http://www.ibisworld.com [Published October 2011], from IBISWorld.

★ 3278 ★
Commercial Laundries
SIC: 7215; NAICS: 81231

Top Commercial Laundry Operators, 2011

The industry generated revenues of $4.2 billion in 2010. A total of 21,747 establishments operated in this sector providing employment to more than 49,800 people. Figure for PWS Inc. is estimated.

CoinMach Corp.	13.2%
Mac-Gray Corp.	7.7
PWS Inc.	2.9
Other	76.2

Source: "Laundromats in the U.S." [online] from http://www.ibisworld.com [Published March 2011], from IBISWorld.

★ 3279 ★
Laundry Routes
SIC: 7215; NAICS: 81231

Coin-Operated Laundry Routes, 2007

Data show the percent of industry sales held by the largest 4, 8, 20 and 50 firms in the sector. There are approximately 346 firms operating in the industry generating employment for 5,040 people.

4 largest firms	64.4%
8 largest firms	76.4
20 largest firms	87.4
50 largest firms	95.5

Source: "2007 Economic Census." [online] from http://www.census.gov/econ/concentration.html [Accessed August 12, 2011], from U.S. Bureau of the Census.

★ 3280 ★
Carpet Cleaning Services
SIC: 7217; NAICS: 56174

Top Carpet Cleaning Firms, 2011

The industry generated revenues of $3.8 billion in 2011. Residential carpet and upholstery claimed 58.3% of the total, commercial carpet and upholstery cleaning 22.5%, damage restoration cleaning 9.1% and other sectors 10.1%.

Chem-Dry	6.7%
Stanley Steemer Intl.	4.9
ServiceMaster Co.	3.2
DuraClean	3.0
Coit Services Inc.	2.2
Other	80.0

Source: "Carpet Cleaning Services in the U.S." [online] from http://www.ibisworld.com [Published October 2011], from IBISWorld.

★ 3281 ★
Industrial Laundries
SIC: 7218; NAICS: 812332

Industrial Launderers, 2007

Data show the percent of industry sales held by the largest 4, 8, 20 and 50 firms in the sector. There are approximately 1,489 firms operating in the industry generating employment for 75,843 people.

4 largest firms	71.6%
8 largest firms	77.3
20 largest firms	83.3
50 largest firms	88.3

Source: "2007 Economic Census." [online] from http://www.census.gov/econ/concentration.html [Accessed August 12, 2011], from U.S. Bureau of the Census.

★ 3282 ★
Photography
SIC: 7221; NAICS: 541921

Top Photography Firms, 2011

The industry generated revenues of $8.8 billion. Wedding photos claimed 28.3% of the total, commercial photography 25.6%, school portraits 11.2%, passports 0.5% and other sectors 34.3%. Lifetouch Inc. owns Studio at Target and J.C. Penney Portraits. CPI Corp. owns Sears Portraits.

Lifetouch Inc.	17.6%
CPI Corp.	6.5
Olan Mills	2.6
Other	74.3

Source: "Photography in the U.S." [online] from http://www.ibisworld.com [Published August 2011], from IBISWorld.

★ 3283 ★
Hair and Nail Salons
SIC: 7231; NAICS: 812112, 812113

Top Hair and Nail Salon Operators, 2010

The industry generated revenues of $41.1 billion in 2010. Hair cutting claimed 46.8% of the total, hair coloring 20.4%, nail care 10.4%, skin care 5%. Regis Corp. owns Supercuts and a number of other hair cutting chains.

Regis Corp.	5.0%
J.C. Penney	1.5
Ratner Companies	1.3
Other	92.2

Source: "Hair and Nail Salons in the U.S." [online] from http://www.ibisworld.com [Published September 2011], from IBISWorld.

★ 3284 ★
Shoe and Leather Goods Repair
SIC: 7251; NAICS: 81143

Number of Firms in Shoe and Leather Goods Repair, 2000-2008

This market covers companies that repair footwear and other leather or leather-like goods, such as handbags and briefcases. They exclude companies primarily engaged in the retailing of such items. The market generated revenues of $326 million in 2011, according to IBIS-World. The economic downturn has brought a slight boost to this market as consumers try to extend the life of shoes and leather goods that they normally would just replace.

2000	1,674
2001	1,505
2002	1,381
2003	1,269
2004	1,209
2005	1,156
2006	1,095
2007	1,060
2008	990

Source: "Statistics of U.S. Businesses, 2008." [online] from http://www.census.gov [Accessed May 1, 2012], from U.S. Bureau of the Census.

★ 3285 ★
Funeral Services
SIC: 7261; NAICS: 81221

Top Funeral Service Providers, 2011

Companies are ranked by revenues in millions of dollars.

Service International Corp.	$ 2,316
Stewart	513
Arbor Memorial	264
StoneMor	226
Carriage	191

Source: "Service Corp. International." [online] from http://phx.corporate-ir.net [Published March 2012], from company reports.

★ 3286 ★
Tax Preparation
SIC: 7291; NAICS: 541213

Leading Tax Preparers, 2010

Companies are ranked by tax revenues in millions of dollars.

H&R Block	$ 2,979.9
PricewaterhouseCoopers	2,410.2
Deloitte & Touche	$ 2,296.9
Ernst & Young	2,272.0
KPMG	1,271.1
RSM/McGladrey & Pullen	475.5
Grant Thornton	304.0
Liberty Tax Services	291.6
Ryan	216.5
Jackson Hewitt	213.8

Source: *Accounting Today*, Annual 2011, p. 100.

★ 3287 ★
Tax Preparation
SIC: 7291; NAICS: 541213

Top Tax Return Firms, 2011

The industry generated revenues of $8.9 billion.

H&R Block	32.8%
Jackson Hewitt	2.1
Other	65.1

Source: "Tax Preparation Services in the U.S." [online] from http://www.ibisworld.com [Published August 2011], from IBISWorld.

★ 3288 ★
Dating Services
SIC: 7299; NAICS: 81299

Leading Dating Service Chains, 2011

Total spending on matchmaking and dating services was $2.14 billion in 2011. There are approximately 250 physical offices run by off-line dating service chains where one sees the client in person. Some of these services typically charge $2,000-6,000 and are able to verify a person's appearance, weight, age, etc. - an advantage over dating websites. Online dating web sites generated revenues of $1.33 billion and 53% of total industry revenues. Match.com was the leader with revenues of $480 million, eHarmony had $270 million and Friendfinder $233 million. An estimated 1,800 matchmakers are believed to be operating in the United States.

	Offices	Share
It's Just Lunch	150	59.76%
eLove	56	22.31
Great Expectations	32	12.75
Matchmakers International	13	5.18

Source: "U.S. Dating Services Market Worth $2.1 Billion." [online] from http://www.prweb.com [Press release February 7, 2012], from Marketdata Enterprises.

★ 3289 ★
Hair Loss and Treatment
SIC: 7299; NAICS: 812199

Top Hair Loss Treatment and Removal Firms, 2010

The industry generated revenues of $621 million in 2010. A total of 4,936 businesses operated in this sector providing employment to 7,110 people. Regis Corp. acquired Hair Club for Men and Women in 2005.

Regis Corp.	23.5%
Advanced Laser Clinics	4.9
American Laser Center	3.7
Other	67.9

Source: "Hair Loss Treatment & Removal in the U.S." [online] from http://www.ibisworld.com [Published September 2010], from IBISWorld.

★ 3290 ★
Weight Loss Services
SIC: 7299; NAICS: 812191

Top Weight Loss Service Firms, 2011

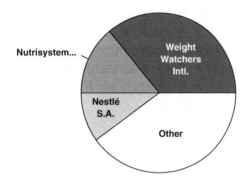

The industry generated revenues of $3.3 billion in 2011. Nestlé S.A. owns Jenny Craig.

Weight Watchers Intl.	36.3%
Nutrisystem Inc.	13.7
Nestlé S.A.	9.9
Other	40.1

Source: "Weight Loss Services in the U.S." [online] from http://www.ibisworld.com [Published October 2011], from IBISWorld.

SIC 73 - Business Services

★ 3291 ★
Advertising
SIC: 7311; NAICS: 54181
Advertising Market in China, 2010

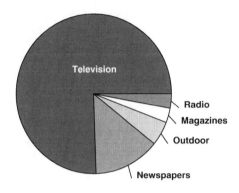

Total spending was placed at $89.5 billion.

Television	77.0%
Newspapers	14.0
Outdoor	5.0
Magazines	3.0
Radio	3.0

Source: *Wall Street Journal*, November 29, 2011, p. B4, from CRT Media Intelligence.

★ 3292 ★
Advertising
SIC: 7311; NAICS: 54181
Top Advertisers, 2011

Companies are ranked by spending in millions of dollars.

Procter & Gamble Co.	$ 2,949.1
AT&T Inc.	1,924.6
General Motors Corp.	1,784.1
Verizon Communications	1,636.9
Comcast Corp.	1,577.2
L'Oréal S.A.	1,343.5
Time Warner Inc.	1,279.4
Pfizer Inc.	1,203.5

Chrysler Group L.L.C.	$ 1,193.0
News Corp.	1,170.5

Source: *Business Wire*, March 12, 2012, p. NA, from Kantar Media.

★ 3293 ★
Advertising
SIC: 7311; NAICS: 54181
Top Advertisers in Australia, 2011

Companies are ranked by spending in millions of dollars for the first six months of the year. Television claimed 37.5% of the advertising market, newspapers 30.8%, magazines 9.4% and other sectors 22.3%.

Westfarmers Limited	$ 93.8
Commonwealth Government	76.5
Woolworths Limited	69.9
Harvey Norman Holdings	66.2
Commonwealth Bank	38.7
NSW Government	38.4
Victorian Government	38.1
Unilever Group	37.1
Telstra Corp. Limited	35.7
Queensland Government	34.0

Source: *AdNews*, p. 32, from Nielsen Company.

★ 3294 ★
Advertising
SIC: 7311; NAICS: 54181
Top Advertising Agencies, 2010

Firms are ranked by revenues in millions of dollars.

McCann Erickson Worldwide	$ 457
BBDO Worldwide	450
JWT	356
Young & Rubicam	304
DDB Worldwide	264
TBWA Worldwide	260
Leo Burnett Worldwide/Arc	255
DraftFCB	239

Continued on next page.

★ 3294 ★

[Continued]

Advertising

SIC: 7311; NAICS: 54181

Top Advertising Agencies, 2010

Firms are ranked by revenues in millions of dollars.

Saatchi & Saatchi	$ 214
Grey	191

Source: *Advertising Age*, April 25, 2011, p. 30, from AdAge DataCenter.

★ 3295 ★

Advertising

SIC: 7311; NAICS: 54181

Top Advertising Agencies Worldwide, 2010

Firms are ranked by revenues in millions of dollars.

Dentsu	$ 2,494
McCann Erickson Worldwide	1,438
BBDO Worldwide	1,210
DDB Worldwide	1,149
JWT	1,149
TBWA Worldwide	1,082
Hakuhodo	1,028
Publicis	1,023
Young & Rubicam	987
Leo Burnett Worldwide/Arc	877

Source: *Advertising Age*, April 25, 2011, p. 30, from AdAge DataCenter.

★ 3296 ★

Advertising

SIC: 7312; NAICS: 54185

Top Outdoor Advertising Firms, 2011

There were a total of 2,115 businesses in the industry, generating revenues of $6.7 billion. CC Media owns Clear Channel.

CC Media Holdings Inc.	18.2%
Lamar Advertising Company	17.0
CBS Corp.	16.0
Other	48.8

Source: "Billboard & Outdoor Advertisers." [online] from http://www.ibisworld.com [Published November 2011], from IBISWorld.

★ 3297 ★

Advertising

SIC: 7312; NAICS: 54185

Top Outdoor Advertising Firms in the United Kingdom, 2010

The market consists of roadside, transportation (buses, taxis, airports) and retail/leisure/POS (supermarkets, gas stations, malls). Market shares are shown based on revenues.

JCDecaux	30.0-40.0%
Clear Channel U.K.	25.0-35.0
CBS Outdoor	20.0-30.0
Other	0.0-25.0

Source: "Outdoor Advertising." [online] from http://www.oft.gov.uk/shared_oft/market-studies/oft1304.pdf [Published February 2012].

★ 3298 ★

Advertising

SIC: 7313; NAICS: 54184

Cinema Advertising Spending Worldwide, 2011-2015

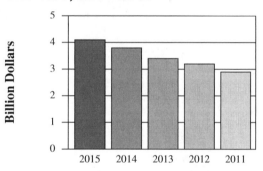

Spending is projected in billions of dollars.

2015	$ 4.1
2014	3.8
2013	3.4
2012	3.2
2011	2.9

Source: "2011 Advertising Forecast." [online] from http://www.magnaglobal.com [Accessed May 1, 2012], from Magna-Global.

★ **3299** ★

Advertising

SIC: 7313; NAICS: 54184

Internet Advertising Spending, 2009-2015

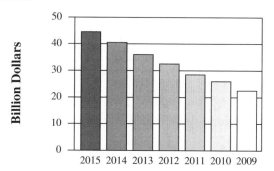

Spending is shown in billions of dollars. Data include banner ads, search ads, rich media, video, sponsorships, embedded email ads and mobile spending.

2015	$ 44.5
2014	40.5
2013	36.0
2012	32.6
2011	28.5
2010	25.8
2009	22.7

Source: *Electronic Retailer*, May 2011, p. 16, from eMarketer.

★ **3300** ★

Advertising

SIC: 7313; NAICS: 54184

Internet Advertising Spending Worldwide, 2011-2015

Spending is projected in billions of dollars.

2015	$ 106.6
2014	96.4
2012	87.0
2013	78.5
2011	70.9

Source: "2011 Advertising Forecast." [online] from http://www.magnaglobal.com [Accessed May 1, 2012], from MagnaGlobal.

★ **3301** ★

Advertising

SIC: 7313; NAICS: 54184

Magazine Advertising Spending Worldwide, 2011-2015

Spending is projected in billions of dollars.

2013	$ 35.9
2014	35.9

2015	$ 35.9
2011	35.8
2012	35.7

Source: "2011 Advertising Forecast." [online] from http://www.magnaglobal.com [Accessed May 1, 2012], from MagnaGlobal.

★ **3302** ★

Advertising

SIC: 7313; NAICS: 54184

Mobile Advertising Worldwide, 2011 and 2015

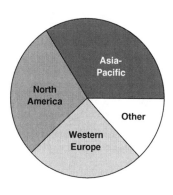

The industry is forecast to climb from $3.31 billion to $20.61 billion in 2015.

	2011	2015
Asia-Pacific and Japan	49.2%	33.6%
North America	21.2	28.1
Western Europe	17.2	24.9
Other	12.4	13.4

Source: *Investor's Business Daily*, June 29, 2011, p. A4, from Gartner Inc.

★ **3303** ★

Advertising

SIC: 7313; NAICS: 54184

Newspaper Advertising Spending Worldwide, 2011-2015

Spending is projected in billions of dollars.

2015	$ 85.2
2014	83.6
2013	82.2
2012	81.2
2011	80.1

Source: "2011 Advertising Forecast." [online] from http://www.magnaglobal.com [Accessed May 1, 2012], from MagnaGlobal.

★ 3304 ★
Advertising
SIC: 7313; NAICS: 54184

Radio Advertising Spending Worldwide, 2011-2015

Spending is projected in billions of dollars.

2015	$ 34.5
2014	33.0
2013	31.7
2012	30.6
2011	29.5

Source: "2011 Advertising Forecast." [online] from http://www.magnaglobal.com [Accessed May 1, 2012], from MagnaGlobal.

★ 3305 ★
Advertising
SIC: 7313; NAICS: 54184

Television Advertising Spending Worldwide, 2011-2015

Spending is projected in millions of dollars.

2015	$ 224.1
2014	211.2
2013	194.5
2012	183.8
2011	169.1

Source: "2011 Advertising Forecast." [online] from http://www.magnaglobal.com [Accessed May 1, 2012], from MagnaGlobal.

★ 3306 ★
Advertising
SIC: 7313; NAICS: 54181

Top Display Ad Publishers, 2010-2012

Companies are ranked by revenues in millions of dollars.

	2010	2011	2012
Facebook	$ 1,209	$ 2,187	$ 2,871
Yahoo!	1,426	1,620	1,855
Google	855	1,149	1,819
Microsoft	508	602	711
AOL	473	522	581

Source: *USA TODAY*, September 8, 2011, p. 2B, from eMarketer.

★ 3307 ★
Advertising
SIC: 7313; NAICS: 54184

Top Internet Advertisers, 2011

Companies are ranked by spending in millions of dollars.

IAC/Interactive Corp.	$ 316.2
Experian Group Ltd.	277.8
General Motors Corp.	270.8
AT&T Inc.	245.7
Progressive Corp.	239.7
Verizon Communications Inc.	230.3
Comcast Corp.	203.7
Capital One Financial Corp.	203.4
Amazon	199.8
eBay Inc.	173.2

Source: *Business Wire*, March 12, 2012, p. NA, from Kantar Media.

★ 3308 ★
Advertising
SIC: 7313; NAICS: 54181

Top Internet Advertisers Worldwide, 2008-2010

Market shares are shown in percent.

	2008	2009	2010
Google	42.5%	41.9%	44.1%
Yahoo!	11.7	9.6	8.3
AOL	4.2	2.2	1.5
Microsoft	4.2	4.0	4.0
Facebook	0.6	1.4	3.1
Other	37.8	40.9	39.0

Source: *USA TODAY*, January 26, 2012, p. 2B, from Zenith-Optimedia.

★ 3309 ★
Advertising
SIC: 7313; NAICS: 54184
Top Mobile Display Advertisers, 2011

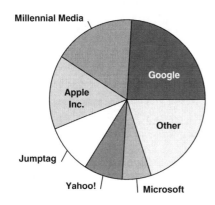

Shares are shown based on a $630 million market.

Google	24.0%
Millennial Media	17.0
Apple Inc.	15.0
Jumptag	10.0
Yahoo!	8.0
Microsoft	6.0
Other	20.0

Source: *Wall Street Journal*, December 13, 2011, p. B1, from
International Data Corp.

★ 3310 ★
Advertising
SIC: 7313; NAICS: 54181
Top Super Bowl Advertisers, 2002-2011

Companies are ranked by spending in millions of dollars. The top 5 spent 37% of the $1.72 billion on advertising during this period.

Anheuser-Busch InBev	$ 239
PepsiCo	174
General Motors Corp.	83
Walt Disney	74
Coca-Cola Co.	67

Source: *Financial Times*, February 4, 2012, p. 8, from Kantar
Media.

★ 3311 ★
Advertising
SIC: 7313; NAICS: 54184
Top Television Advertisers, 2011

Companies are ranked by spending in millions of dollars.

Procter & Gamble Co.	$ 1,718.7
AT&T Inc.	1,332.6
General Motors Corp.	1,112.2
Verizon Communications	1,064.1
Chrysler Group L.L.C.	890.4
General Mills Inc.	842.4
Comcast Corp.	840.3
Ford Motor Co.	781.0
Toyota Motor Corp.	767.4
Time Warner Inc.	766.2

Source: *Business Wire*, March 12, 2012, p. NA, from Kantar
Media.

★ 3312 ★
Advertising
SIC: 7319; NAICS: 54187
Advertising Material Distribution Services, 2007

Data show the percent of industry sales held by the largest 4, 8, 20 and 50 firms in the sector. There are approximately 931 firms operating in the industry generating employment for 14,946 people.

4 largest firms	27.2%
8 largest firms	39.9
20 largest firms	58.5
50 largest firms	76.2

Source: "2007 Economic Census." [online] from http://www.
census.gov/econ/concentration.html [Accessed August 12,
2011], from U.S. Bureau of the Census.

★ 3313 ★
Sign Painting and Lettering Shops
SIC: 7319; NAICS: 54189
Sign Painting and Lettering Shops, 2007

Data show the percent of industry sales held by the largest 4, 8, 20 and 50 firms in the sector. There are approximately 2,605 firms operating in the industry generating employment for 11,676 people.

4 largest firms	11.1%
8 largest firms	14.3

Continued on next page.

★ 3313 ★

[Continued]

Sign Painting and Lettering Shops

SIC: 7319; NAICS: 54189

Sign Painting and Lettering Shops, 2007

Data show the percent of industry sales held by the largest 4, 8, 20 and 50 firms in the sector. There are approximately 2,605 firms operating in the industry generating employment for 11,676 people.

20 largest firms	19.6%
50 largest firms	28.1

Source: "2007 Economic Census." [online] from http://www.census.gov/econ/concentration.html [Accessed August 12, 2011], from U.S. Bureau of the Census.

★ 3314 ★

Collection Services

SIC: 7322; NAICS: 56144

Collection Industry by State, 2010

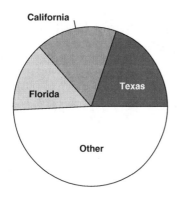

California

Florida

Texas

Other

Data show share of total receivables. Revenues fell from $12.9 billion in 2007 to $11.9 billion in 2010. The industry lost 864 debt collection agencies, with total agencies falling to 9,871.

Texas	13.7%
California	11.6
Florida	9.7
Other	35.0

Source: *Houston Business Journal*, September 2, 2011, p. NA, from IBISWorld.

★ 3315 ★

Debt Collection Agencies

SIC: 7322; NAICS: 56144

Top Debt Collection Agencies, 2010

The industry generated revenues of $11.7 billion in 2010. Market shares for Asset Acceptance Capital Corp. and Portfolio Recovery Associates Inc. are estimated. There were 8,950 establishments providing employment to 137,754 people.

NCO Group Inc.	11.3%
GC Services	3.8
Asset Acceptance Capital Corp.	2.0
Portfolio Recovery Associates Inc.	1.9
Other	81.0

Source: "Debt Collection Agencies in the U.S." [online] from http://www.ibisworld.com [Published June 2011], from IBIS-World.

★ 3316 ★

Credit Reporting Agencies

SIC: 7323; NAICS: 56145

Leading Credit Rating Firms, 2011

Companies are ranked by number of ratings. The top three firms came under fire for offering triple-A ratings on complex mortgage backed securities that ultimately imploded. This collapse helped fuel the economic crisis that followed.

	Ratings	Share
Standard & Poor's	1,190,500	42.27%
Moody's	1,039,187	36.90
Fitch	505,024	17.93
DBRS	42,584	1.51
Kroll	17,624	0.63
Morningstar	8,322	0.30
A.M. Best	7,159	0.25
Other	6,199	0.22

Source: *Wall Street Journal*, September 17, 2011, p. C8, from U.S. Securities and Exchange Commission.

★ 3317 ★

Direct Marketing

SIC: 7331; NAICS: 54186

Top Direct Marketing Firms, 2010

Firms are ranked by revenues in millions of dollars.

Wunderman	$ 943
Acxiom Corp.	785

Continued on next page.

★ 3317 ★

[Continued]

Direct Marketing

SIC: 7331; NAICS: 54186

Top Direct Marketing Firms, 2010

Firms are ranked by revenues in millions of dollars.

Rapp	$ 644
DraftFCB	552
OgilvyOne Worldwide	522
Epsilon	454
MRM Worldwide	278
Merkle	254
Rosetta	218
JWT	155

Source: *Advertising Age*, April 25, 2011, p. 30, from AdAge DataCenter.

★ 3318 ★

Promotional Industry

SIC: 7331; NAICS: 51114

Top Promotions Firms, 2010

The top 100 U.S. promotion agencies indicates that brand clients are beginning to loosen up budget spending, with 34 agencies reporting 2-year revenue losses in 2010, compared to 44 in 2009. Firms are ranked by net revenues in millions of dollars.

DraftFCB	$ 644.0
Digitas	502.0
Wunderman	446.0
Aspen Marketing Services	284.9
BDA	253.3
Integrated Marketing Services	236.0
Momentum Worldwide	189.0
Euro RSCG Worldwide	185.0
Marketstar Corporation	148.0
The Integer Group	145.0

Source: *Promo Magazine*, Annual 2011, p. NA.

★ 3319 ★

Quick Printing

SIC: 7334; NAICS: 561439

Top Quick Printing Firms, 2010

Firms are ranked by sales in millions of dollars. The top 100 generated sales of $532.1 million.

	($ mil.)	Share
CCI/CoakleyTech	$ 34.72	6.53%
Balmar/HBP Inc.	32.00	6.01
ColorNet/RockVille Printing & Graphics	15.30	2.88
ASAP Printing Corp.	14.79	2.78
Frank Gumpert Printing of Annapolis	11.80	2.22
Econoprint	11.45	2.15
Landmark Print	10.86	2.04
Western Graphics	10.68	2.01
Hatteras Inc.	10.15	1.91
Copy Central	9.56	1.80
Other	370.79	69.68

Source: *Quick Printing*, June 2011, p. NA.

★ 3320 ★

Commercial Photography

SIC: 7335; NAICS: 541922

Commercial Photography, 2007

Data show the percent of industry sales held by the largest 4, 8, 20 and 50 firms in the sector. There are approximately 3,870 firms operating in the industry generating employment for 12,453 people.

4 largest firms	4.2%
8 largest firms	6.6
20 largest firms	11.9
50 largest firms	20.6

Source: "2007 Economic Census." [online] from http://www.census.gov/econ/concentration.html [Accessed August 12, 2011], from U.S. Bureau of the Census.

★ 3321 ★
Graphic Design
SIC: 7336; NAICS: 54143

Graphic Design Industry Worldwide, 2011

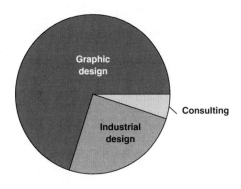

Graphic designers handle the design and production of printed materials, packaging, advertising, signs and logos. The industry is expected to generate revenues of $41.4 billion in 2011. Data show the sources of revenues. Fast-moving consumer goods makers claimed 30% of the market, advertising agencies 25%, consumer durable goods makers 20%, publishers 15%, and other segments 10%. Schawk Inc. was the market leader with a 1.1% share. IDEO and SGS Industries each claimed less than 1% of the market.

Graphic design 70.0%
Industrial design 25.0
Consulting 5.0

Source: "Global Graphic Designers." [online] from http://www.docin.com/p-320645709.html [Published December 2011], from IBISWorld.

★ 3322 ★
Court Reporting Services
SIC: 7338; NAICS: 561492

Court Reporting and Stenotype Services, 2007

Data show the percent of industry sales held by the largest 4, 8, 20 and 50 firms in the sector. There are approximately 3,463 firms operating in the industry generating employment for 14,106 people. The industry is estimated to be worth $3.0 billion, by one estimate.

4 largest firms 19.7%
8 largest firms 27.5
20 largest firms 34.9
50 largest firms 43.4

Source: "2007 Economic Census." [online] from http://www.census.gov/econ/concentration.html [Accessed August 12, 2011], from U.S. Bureau of the Census.

★ 3323 ★
Pest Control
SIC: 7342; NAICS: 56172

Top Commercial Pest Removal Firms, 2010

Firms are ranked by revenues in millions of dollars.

Rollins . . . . $ 477.5
Massey Services 127.7
ISS Hicare Pvt. 96.0
Western Exterminator Co. 41.9
Landscape Concepts Management 30.6
Cook's Pest Control 26.5
Truly Nolen of America 21.4
Plunkett's Pest Control 21.1
Assured Environments 20.8
Arrow Exterminators (Atlanta) 18.5

Source: *Pest Management Professional*, December 2011, p. S4.

★ 3324 ★
Pest Control
SIC: 7342; NAICS: 56172

Top Pest Control Firms, 2010

Firms are ranked by revenues in millions of dollars.

Terminix International . . . . $ 1,200.0
Rollins 1,136.8
Ecolab 327.7
Rentokil/Ehrlich-Presto-X 233.1
Massey Services 129.0
Cook's Pest Control 106.4
The Steritech Group 104.4
Arrow Exterminators 103.0
Terminix Service 101.5
Clark Pest Control 100.5

Source: *Pest Control Technology*, May 2011, p. NA.

★ 3325 ★
Pest Control
SIC: 7342; NAICS: 56172

Top Rodent Removal Firms, 2010

Firms are ranked by revenues in millions of dollars.

ISS Hicare Pvt. . . . . $ 54.4
Dodson Bros. Exterminating Co. 10.0
Poulin's Pest Control 5.8
Assured Environments 5.2
Sprague Pest Solutions 4.3
EFS Services Saudi 3.0
Critter Control 2.6

Continued on next page.

★ 3325 ★

[Continued]

Pest Control

SIC: 7342; NAICS: 56172

Top Rodent Removal Firms, 2010

Firms are ranked by revenues in millions of dollars.

Catseye Pest Control	$ 2.2
ABC Home & Commercial Services (TX)	1.8

Source: *Pest Management Professional*, December 2011, p. S4.

★ 3326 ★

Pest Control

SIC: 7342; NAICS: 56172

Top Termite/Wood-Destroying Insect Removal Firms, 2010

Firms are ranked by revenues in millions of dollars.

ISS Hicare Pvt.	$ 32.0
Florida Pest Control & Chemical Co.	24.5
Dodson Bros. Exterminating Co.	12.2
TerminixCo.	9.6
Palmetto Exterminators	6.4
Your Way Fumigation	6.3
Bug Out Service	5.5
Lloyd's Pest Control	5.0
Killingsworth Environmental of the Carolinas	4.9
Fischer Environmental Services	4.7

Source: *Pest Management Professional*, December 2011, p. S4.

★ 3327 ★

Building Exterior Cleaning

SIC: 7349; NAICS: 56179

Cleaning Building Exteriors (except Sandblasting), 2007

Data show the percent of industry sales held by the largest 4, 8, 20 and 50 firms in the sector. There are approximately 1,264 firms operating in the industry generating employment for 4,587 people.

4 largest firms	13.2%
8 largest firms	18.7
20 largest firms	27.4
50 largest firms	39.9

Source: "2007 Economic Census." [online] from http://www.census.gov/econ/concentration.html [Accessed August 12, 2011], from U.S. Bureau of the Census.

★ 3328 ★

Janitorial Services

SIC: 7349; NAICS: 56179

Contract Cleaning Services, 2011

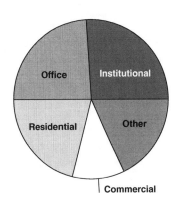

The industry was valued at $56.7 billion. The source notes that the increasing number of households and businesses will be a boost to the market. Demographics should also play a role. The number of seniors is growing, a segment of the population that typically has trouble with household cleaning and upkeep. But some of these changes should help the consumer, as businesses are expected to offer competitive services and pricing.

Institutional	26.0%
Office	24.0
Residential	21.0
Commercial	11.0
Other	18.0

Source: "Contract Cleaning Services." [online] from http://www.freedoniagroup.com [Published May 2012], from Freedonia Group.

★ 3329 ★

Janitorial Services

SIC: 7349; NAICS: 56179

Top Janitorial Firms, 2011

The industry generated revenues of $40.6 billion in 2011. Standard commercial cleaning claimed 59.3% of the total, residential cleaning claimed 7.7%, damage restoration 4.7%, exterior windows 1.9%. ServiceMaster and Jani-King's shares are estimated.

ABM Industries Inc.	6.0%
UGL Limited	2.3
Jani-King International Inc.	0.8
ServiceMaster	0.3
Other	90.6

Source: "Janitorial Services in the U.S." [online] from http://www.ibisworld.com [Published September 2011], from IBIS-World.

★ 3330 ★

Heavy Equipment Rental

SIC: 7350; NAICS: 53249

Leading Equipment Rental Firms, 2010

Firms are ranked by rental volume in millions of dollars.

United Rentals	$ 1,834.0
RSC Equipment Rental	1,060.3
Sunbelt Rentals	1,029.9
Hertz Equipment Rental Corp.	858.0
Home Depot Rentals	525.0
Aggreko	288.0
Ahern Rentals	246.8
Maxim Crane Rental Corp.	245.0
Finning	221.1
NES Rentals	208.0

Source: *Rental Equipment Register*, May 2011, p. 22.

★ 3331 ★

Heavy Equipment Rental

SIC: 7350; NAICS: 53249

Leading Equipment Rental Firms Worldwide, 2011

Firms are ranked by turnover in millions of euros.

Aggreko	€ 1,433
United Rentals	1,368
Ashtead Group	951
RSC Equipment Rental	921
Algeco Scotsman	810
Coates Hire Ltd.	802
Hertz Equipment Rental Corp.	798
Loxam	703
Nishio Rental All Co.	635
Nikken Corp.	616

Source: *International Rental News*, June 2011, p. 19.

★ 3332 ★

Heavy Equipment Rental

SIC: 7350; NAICS: 53249

Top Rental Firms in North America, 2010

Market shares are shown in percent.

United Rentals	6.0%
RSC Equipment	4.2
Hertz	3.6
Sunbelt Rentals	3.5
Home Depot	1.8
AMECO	1.5
Williams Scotsman	1.4

Mobile Mini	1.1%
Ahern Rentals	1.0
Classic Party Rentals	0.9
Other	75.0

Source: *International Rental News*, September-October 2011, p. 13.

★ 3333 ★

Home Health Care Equipment Rental

SIC: 7352; NAICS: 532291

Home Health Equipment Rental, 2007

Data show the percent of industry sales held by the largest 4, 8, 20 and 50 firms in the sector. There are approximately 3,762 firms operating in the industry generating employment for 33,001 people.

4 largest firms	66.6%
8 largest firms	75.4
20 largest firms	80.1
50 largest firms	85.0

Source: ''2007 Economic Census.'' [online] from http://www.census.gov/econ/concentration.html [Accessed August 12, 2011], from U.S. Bureau of the Census.

★ 3334 ★

Medical Equipment Rental and Leasing

SIC: 7352; NAICS: 532291

Medical Equipment Rental & Leasing, Except Home Health Equipment, 2007

Data show the percent of industry sales held by the largest 4, 8, 20 and 50 firms in the sector. There are approximately 1,507 firms operating in the industry generating employment for 16,456 people.

4 largest firms	52.7%
8 largest firms	62.2
20 largest firms	70.9
50 largest firms	77.8

Source: ''2007 Economic Census.'' [online] from http://www.census.gov/econ/concentration.html [Accessed August 12, 2011], from U.S. Bureau of the Census.

★ 3335 ★
Container Leasing
SIC: 7353; NAICS: 532412

Top Container Lessors Worldwide, 2011

Companies are ranked by dry freight standard and special containers leased in thousands of twenty-foot equivalent units as of mid-2011.

	(000)	Share
Textainer	2,440	17.90%
Triton	1,925	14.12
Florens	1,710	12.54
TAL	1,605	11.77
GESeaCo	990	7.26
CAL International	885	6.49
SeaCube Container	875	6.42
Cronos Group	707	5.19
Gold Container	515	3.78
Dong Fang	480	3.52
Other	1,503	11.02

Source: "Textainer." [online] from http://files.shareholder. com [Published November 2011], from Andrew Foxcroft Container Data.

★ 3336 ★
Furniture Rental
SIC: 7359; NAICS: 532299

Top Furniture Rental Firms, 2011

Companies are ranked by number of stores.

	Stores	Share
Rent-A-Center/ColorTyme	3,843	44.69%
Aarons	1,858	21.60
Buddy's Home Furnishings	110	1.28
Bestway	90	1.05
Premier Rental	63	0.73
Rent One	53	0.62
Baber's	52	0.60
American Rentals	50	0.58
Other	2,481	28.85

Source: "Investor Presentation Second Quarter 2011." [online] from http://phx.corporate-ir.net [Accessed February 20, 2012], from Association of Progressive Rental Organizations.

★ 3337 ★
Office Machinery Rental and Leasing
SIC: 7359; NAICS: 53242

Office Machinery and Equipment Rental and Leasing, 2007

Data show the percent of industry sales held by the largest 4, 8, 20 and 50 firms in the sector. There are approximately 826 firms operating in the industry generating employment for 6,041 people.

4 largest firms	30.6%
8 largest firms	41.6
20 largest firms	56.1
50 largest firms	73.6

Source: "2007 Economic Census." [online] from http://www. census.gov/econ/concentration.html [Accessed August 12, 2011], from U.S. Bureau of the Census.

★ 3338 ★
Portable Toilet Rental
SIC: 7359; NAICS: 562991

Portable Toilet Rental, 2007

Data show the percent of industry sales held by the largest 4, 8, 20 and 50 firms in the sector. There are approximately 995 firms operating in the industry generating employment for 9,994 people. The Portable Sanitation Association estimates the portable sanitation industry at $1.5 billion.

4 largest firms	27.4%
8 largest firms	33.0
20 largest firms	42.0
50 largest firms	54.1

Source: "2007 Economic Census." [online] from http://www. census.gov/econ/concentration.html [Accessed August 12, 2011], from U.S. Bureau of the Census.

★ 3339 ★
Railroad Car Rental and Leasing
SIC: 7359; NAICS: 53249

Railroad Car Rental and Leasing, 2007

Data show the percent of industry sales held by the largest 4, 8, 20 and 50 firms in the sector. There are approximately 128 firms operating in the industry generating employment for 1,878 people.

4 largest firms	70.8%
8 largest firms	83.0
20 largest firms	95.4
50 largest firms	99.6

Source: "2007 Economic Census." [online] from http://www. census.gov/econ/concentration.html [Accessed August 12, 2011], from U.S. Bureau of the Census.

★ 3340 ★

Vessel Rental and Leasing

SIC: 7359; NAICS: 532411

Commercial Vessel Rental and Leasing Without Crew, 2007

Data show the percent of industry sales held by the largest 4, 8, 20 and 50 firms in the sector. There are approximately 139 firms operating in the industry generating employment for 1,024 people.

4 largest firms	55.0%
8 largest firms	68.4
20 largest firms	82.8
50 largest firms	94.3

Source: "2007 Economic Census." [online] from http://www.census.gov/econ/concentration.html [Accessed August 12, 2011], from U.S. Bureau of the Census.

★ 3341 ★

Staffing Industry

SIC: 7363; NAICS: 56132, 56133

Top Engineering/Design Staffing Firms, 2009

Companies are ranked by staffing revenues in millions of dollars.

	($ mil.)	Share
Adecco (includes MPS)	$ 625	11.0%
Aerotek (Allegis)	593	11.0
Volt Information Sciences	334	6.0
Advantage Resourcing	300	5.0
PDS Technical Services	253	5.0
Kelly Services	229	4.0
System One Holdings	210	4.0
CDI	153	3.0
Belcan	141	3.0

Source: "Engineering/Design Staffing Growth Update." [online] from http://www.staffingindustry.com [Published April 26, 2011], from Staffing Industry Analysts.

★ 3342 ★

Staffing Industry

SIC: 7363; NAICS: 56132, 56133

Top Staffing Firms in Europe, 2009

Companies are ranked by sales in millions of dollars. Europe represented 53% of the global market for recruitment process outsourcing. Industrial needs claimed 50% of the market, office and clerical needs 23%, IT 12% and other sectors 15%.

Randstad Holding	$ 14,043
Adecco	13,450
ManpowerGroup	$ 10,998
USG People	4,083
Hays	3,662
Impellam	1,460
Groupe CRIT	1,284
Synergie	1,261
Trenkwalder	1,075
Kelly Services	1,015

Source: "What's Hot in Europe?" [online] from http://www.staffingindustry.com [Accessed November 1, 2011], from Staffing Industry Analysts.

★ 3343 ★

Staffing Industry

SIC: 7363; NAICS: 56132, 56133

Top Staffing Firms Worldwide, 2010

Firms are ranked by staffing revenues in billions of dollars.

Adecco	$ 24.0
ManpowerGroup	18.8
Randstad Holding	18.7
Allegis Group	6.4
Kelly Services	4.9
Recruit Staffing and Staff Service	4.5
Hays	4.1
USG People	4.1
Robert Half International	2.7
Temp Holdings	2.3

Source: "2011 List of Largest Staffing Firms." [online] from http://www.jacksonhealthcare.com/media/183638/sialargest-global2011.pdf [Published August 3, 2011], from Staffing Industry Analysts.

★ 3344 ★

Software

SIC: 7372; NAICS: 334611, 51121

Infrastructure Spending on Software in China, 2014

Spending is projected by sector.

Enterprise resource planning	32.0%
Office suites	18.0
Supply chain management	7.0
Digital content creation	5.0
Enterprise content management	5.0
Customer relationship management	4.0
E-mail and calendaring	4.0
Other	26.0

Source: "Global Technology: Software." [online] from http://www.kingdee.com/news/12344.html [Published August 22, 2010], from Gartner Inc. and Goldman Sachs.

★ 3345 ★
Software
SIC: 7372; NAICS: 334611, 51121

Software Industry Worldwide, 2010

The industry generated total revenues of $265.4 billion in 2010.

General business productivity and home use	24.0%
Network and database management	22.3
Cross-industry and vertical application	20.9
Operating system software	17.6
Other	14.9

Source: *Datamonitor Industry Market Research*, November 21, 2011, p. NA, from Datamonitor.

★ 3346 ★
Software
SIC: 7372; NAICS: 334611, 51121

Top BI, Analytics and PM Providers Worldwide, 2011

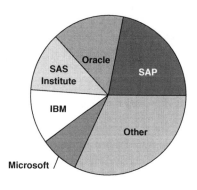

The industry for business intelligence, analytics and performance management software generated revenues of $12.2 billion in 2011.

	($ bil.)	Share
SAP	$ 2.88	22.2%
Oracle	1.90	14.6
SAS Institute	1.54	11.9
IBM	1.47	11.3
Microsoft	1.05	8.1
Other	4.16	32.0

Source: "Gartner Reports Billions More for BI." [online] from http://www.information-management.com/news [Published April 2, 2012], from Gartner Inc.

★ 3347 ★
Software
SIC: 7372; NAICS: 334611, 51121

Top Data Protection Software Makers, 2010

Market shares are shown based on volume.

Symantec/Veritas	37.9%
IBM	32.2
CA Technologies	9.5
Other	20.4

Source: *CRN*, March 23, 2011, p. NA, from NPD Group Inc.

★ 3348 ★
Software
SIC: 7372; NAICS: 334611, 51121

Top Design, Editing and Rendering Software Firms, 2011

The industry generated revenues of $23.9 billion. AEC (Architecture, Engineering and Construction) design claimed 25% of the total, general CAD (Computer Aided Design) 24%, interior design 21% and other sectors 20%.

Autodesk Inc.	8.6%
Adobe Systems Inc.	8.2
Dassault Systems	6.9
Other	82.3

Source: "Design, Editing and Rendering Software Publishing in the U.S." [online] from http://www.ibisworld.com [Published July 2011], from IBISWorld.

★ 3349 ★
Software
SIC: 7372; NAICS: 334611, 51121

Top ERP Firms in China, 2009

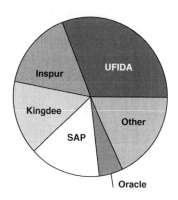

ERP stands for Enterprise Resource Planning.

UFIDA	31.0%
Inspur	16.0

Continued on next page.

★ 3349 ★

[Continued]

Software

SIC: 7372; NAICS: 334611, 51121

Top ERP Firms in China, 2009

ERP stands for Enterprise Resource Planning.

Kingdee	15.0%
SAP	15.0
Oracle	5.0
Other	18.0

Source: "Global Technology: Software." [online] from http://www.kingdee.com/news/12344.html [Published August 22, 2010], from Gartner Inc. and Goldman Sachs.

★ 3350 ★

Software

SIC: 7372; NAICS: 334611, 51121

Top Firewall Makers, 2010

Market shares are shown based on volume.

Check Point	53.5%
SonicWall	13.5
Symantec	11.8
Other	21.2

Source: *CRN*, March 23, 2011, p. NA, from NPD Group Inc.

★ 3351 ★

Software

SIC: 7372; NAICS: 334611, 51121

Top Human Capital Management Software Firms, 2010

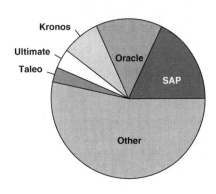

Market shares are shown in percent.

SAP	17.6%
Oracle	13.5
Kronos	8.2
Ultimate	3.5

Taleo	3.3%
Other	53.9

Source: *Investor's Business Daily*, December 30, 2011, p. A9, from International Data Corp. and Thomson Reuters.

★ 3352 ★

Software

SIC: 7372; NAICS: 334611, 51121

Top Operating Systems, 2011 and 2012

Figures are in millions of users.

	Oct. 2011	Dec. 2012
Firefox	9.4	13.8
Internet Explorer	3.4	5.5
Chrome and other	2.3	8.8

Source: *USA TODAY*, December 30, 2011, p. 2B, from Abine.

★ 3353 ★

Software

SIC: 7372; NAICS: 334611, 51121

Top Operating Systems Worldwide for Smartphones, 2010 and 2015

Market shares are shown in percent.

	2010	2015
Google Android	22.7%	48.8%
Microsoft	4.2	19.5
Apple iOS	15.7	17.2
RIM Blackberry	16.0	11.1
Nokia Symbian	37.6	0.1
Other	3.8	3.3

Source: *Investor's Business Daily*, April 11, 2011, p. A4, from Gartner Inc.

★ 3354 ★

Software

SIC: 7372; NAICS: 334611, 51121

Top Operating Systems Worldwide for Tablet PCs, 2011 and 2015

Market shares are estimated.

	2011	2015
Apple iOS	73.4%	45.6%
Google Android	17.3	35.7
RIM's QNX	4.7	8.0
Other	4.6	10.7

Source: *Investor's Business Daily*, September 23, 2011, p. A4, from Gartner Inc.

★ 3355 ★
Software
SIC: 7372; NAICS: 334611, 51121

Top Providers of IPTV Middleware, 2010

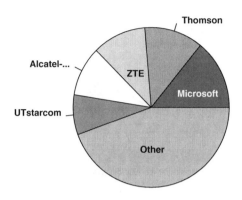

Market shares are estimated in percent. IPTV stands for Internet Protocol Television.

Microsoft	14.1%
Thomson	12.0
ZTE	11.2
Alcatel-Lucent	10.5
UTstarcom	8.3
Other	43.9

Source: "Global IPTV Equipment Market and Provider Competition Analysis." [online] from http://www.frostchina.com [Published July 2009], from Frost & Sullivan.

★ 3356 ★
Software
SIC: 7372; NAICS: 334611, 51121

Top Relational Database Makers, 2010

Market shares are shown based on volume.

Microsoft	45.5%
IBM	26.3
Oracle	24.9
Other	3.3

Source: *CRN*, March 23, 2011, p. NA, from NPD Group Inc.

★ 3357 ★
Software
SIC: 7372; NAICS: 334611, 51121

Top SaaS Firms in China, 2009

SaaS stands for Software as a Service.

UPIDA Wecoo	21.0%
Kingdee Younshang	17.0
Eabax	14.0

Xtools	9.0%
Other	39.0

Source: "Global Technology: Software." [online] from http://www.kingdee.com/news/12344.html [Published August 22, 2010], from Gartner Inc. and Goldman Sachs.

★ 3358 ★
Software
SIC: 7372; NAICS: 334611, 51121

Top Security Software Firms, 2011

Market shares are shown in percent.

Norton	32.0%
McAfee	27.0
AVG	16.0
Windows Live One Care Security Suite	9.0
Avast	8.0
Other	8.0

Source: "McAfee and Norton Still Rule the Market for Security Software." [online] from http://www.npdfashionworld.com [Published September 7, 2011], from NPD Group Inc.

★ 3359 ★
Software
SIC: 7372; NAICS: 334611, 51121

Top Simulation Software Firms Worldwide, 2010

Market shares are shown in percent.

Ansys	24.0%
MSN Software	10.0
Other	66.0

Source: *Investor's Business Daily*, December 7, 2011, p. A5, from Goldman Sachs.

★ 3360 ★
Software
SIC: 7372; NAICS: 334611, 51121

Top Software Firms Worldwide, 2010

Companies are ranked by revenues in millions of dollars.

Microsoft	$ 54,270
IBM	22,485
Oracle	20,958
SAP	12,558
Ericsson	7,274
Hewlett-Packard	6,669
Symantec	5,636
Nintendo	5,456

Continued on next page.

★ 3360 ★
[Continued]
Software
SIC: 7372; NAICS: 334611, 51121

Top Software Firms Worldwide, 2010

Companies are ranked by revenues in millions of dollars.

EMC	$ 4,356
Activision Blizzard	4,279
Nokia Siemens Networks	4,229
Computer Associates	4,136

Source: "Global Software Top 100." [online] from http://www.softwaretop100.org [Published August 23, 2011].

★ 3361 ★
Software
SIC: 7372; NAICS: 334611, 51121

Top Supply Chain Management Firms Worldwide, 2011

Companies are ranked by revenues in millions of dollars.

	($ mil.)	Share
SAP	$ 1,542	19.9%
Oracle	1,306	16.9
JDA Software	390	5.0
Ariba	367	4.7
Manhattan Associates	142	1.8
Other	3,995	51.7

Source: "Gartner Says Worldwide Supply Chain Management Software Market Grew 12.3 Percent." [online] from http://www.gartner.com [Press release May 16, 2012], from Gartner Inc.

★ 3362 ★
Video Game Software
SIC: 7372; NAICS: 334611, 51121

Best-Selling Computer Game Genres, 2010

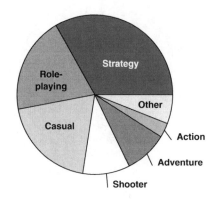

Market shares are shown based on unit sales.

Strategy	33.6%
Role-playing	20.3
Casual	19.5
Shooter	9.7
Adventure	8.7
Action	2.7
Other	5.5

Source: "2011 Essential Facts - About the Computer and Video Game Industry." [online] from http://www.esafacts.org [Accessed December 1, 2011], from NPD Group Retail Tracking Service.

★ 3363 ★
Video Game Software
SIC: 7372; NAICS: 334611, 51121

Best-Selling Video Game Genres, 2010

Market shares are shown based on unit sales.

Action	21.7%
Sports games	16.3
Shooter	15.9
Family entertainment	9.1
Role-playing	7.7
Adventure	7.5
Racing	5.8
Casual	5.2
Fighting	3.0

Source: "2011 Essential Facts - About the Computer and Video Game Industry." [online] from http://www.esafacts.org [Accessed December 1, 2011], from NPD Group Retail Tracking Service.

★ **3364** ★

Video Game Software

SIC: 7372; NAICS: 334611, 51121

Best-Selling Video Games Worldwide, 2011

Titles are ranked by sales in millions of units.

Call of Duty: Modern Warfare 3 (Xbox 360) .	12.77
Call of Duty: Modern Warfare 3 (PS3) . . .	10.10
Kinect Adventures! (Xbox 360)	8.08
Pokemon Black/White Version (DS)	7.83
Just Dance 3 (Wii)	6.77
Wii Sports Resort	6.33
Wii Sports	6.14
Mario Kart Wii	5.43
Super Mario 3D Land (3DS)	5.34
Gears of War 3 (Xbox 360)	5.12
Battlefield 3 (Xbox 360)	5.02

Source: "Global Yearly Chart." [online] from http://www.vg-chartz.com/yearly/2011/Global [Accessed February 6, 2012], from VGChartz.

★ **3365** ★

Video Game Software

SIC: 7372; NAICS: 334611, 51121

Top Video Game Publishers in Europe, 2010

Market shares are shown based on value. The United Kingdom claimed 25%, Germany 20%, France 18% and other countries 37%.

Electronic Arts	17.5%
Nintendo	17.1
Activision Blizzard	14.5
Ubisoft	9.0
Sony Computer Entertainment	6.9
Take-Two	5.8
Microsoft	3.7
Sega	3.6
Konami	2.9
Square Enix	2.6
Other	16.4

Source: *MCV*, June 3, 2011, p. 62, from GfK.

★ **3366** ★

Video Game Software

SIC: 7372; NAICS: 334611, 51121

Top Video Game Software Publishers, 2011

Action titles claimed 22%, sports and shooter titles claimed 16% of revenues each, role-playing titles 8% and other titles 38%.

Activision Blizzard	9.0%
Electronic Arts Inc.	7.0
Nintendo	7.0
Microsoft	6.0
Other	71.0

Source: "Activision Blizzard." [online] from http://tippie.uiowa.edu/krause/fall_2011/atvi_f11.pdf [Published November 14, 2011], from IBISWorld.

★ **3367** ★

Video Game Software

SIC: 7372; NAICS: 334611, 51121

Top Video Game Software Publishers in Japan, 2010

Market shares are shown in percent.

Nintendo	18.7%
Namco Bandai	12.1
Capcom	11.0
Square-Enix	10.7
Konami	8.4
Pokemon	8.4
Sega	5.1
SCE	3.6
Level Five	2.9
Tecmo Koei Games	2.9
Other	16.2

Source: "Capcom Annual Report 2011." [online] from http://capcom.co.jp/ir/english/data/pdf/annual/2011/annual_2011_09.pdf [Published September 2011], from Enterbrain.

★ **3368** ★

Networks

SIC: 7373; NAICS: 541512

Top SAN Makers, 2010

Market shares are shown in percent. SAN stands for storage area network.

Hewlett-Packard Co.	37.4%
IBM	22.4
QLogic	8.0
Other	32.2

Source: *CRN*, March 23, 2011, p. NA, from NPD Group Inc.

★ 3369 ★

Servers

SIC: 7373; NAICS: 541512

Top Blade Server Makers, 2010

Market shares are shown in percent.

IBM	65.0%
Hewlett-Packard Co.	34.5
Other	10.5

Source: *CRN*, March 23, 2011, p. NA, from NPD Group Inc.

★ 3370 ★

Servers

SIC: 7373; NAICS: 541512

Top Server Makers Worldwide, 2011

Market shares are shown based on third quarter revenues.

IBM	41.8%
Hewlett-Packard Co.	25.5
Dell	13.9
Oracle	5.1
Lenovo	3.2
Other	10.6

Source: "Asia Pacific Server Market Continued Double Digit Growth in Third Quarter of 2011, Says Gartner." [online] from http://www.gartner.com [Press release November 29, 2011], from Gartner Inc.

★ 3371 ★

Data Processing and Hosting

SIC: 7374; NAICS: 51821

Data Processing, Hosting, and Related Services, 2007

Data show the percent of industry sales held by the largest 4, 8, 20 and 50 firms in the sector. There are approximately 17,129 firms operating in the industry generating employment for 393,741 people.

4 largest firms	25.8%
8 largest firms	31.2
20 largest firms	40.9
50 largest firms	51.5

Source: "2007 Economic Census." [online] from http://www.census.gov/econ/concentration.html [Accessed August 12, 2011], from U.S. Bureau of the Census.

★ 3372 ★

Data Processing and Outsourcing

SIC: 7374; NAICS: 51821

Top Data Processors/Outsourcing Service Providers Worldwide, 2010

The global market was valued at $601.1 billion.

IBM	3.7%
Hewlett-Packard Co.	3.3
First Data Corp.	1.7
Accenture	1.5
Other	89.8

Source: *Datamonitor Industry Market Research*, June 13, 2011, p. NA, from Datamonitor.

★ 3373 ★

Business Processing Outsourcing

SIC: 7375; NAICS: 51711, 517919

Leading Providers Worldwide of Finance & Accounting BPO Services, 2003-2011

Market shares are shown based on total contract value from 2003 through 2011.

Accenture	26.0%
IBM	20.0
Genpact	10.0
Capgemini	9.0
Hewlett-Packard Co.	5.0
Steria	5.0
Xerox (ACS)	5.0
Wipro	4.0
EXL Service	3.0
TCS	3.0
Other	10.0

Source: "The F&A BPO Market Landscape in 2011." [online] from http://www.accenture.com [Published April 2011], from HFS Research.

★ 3374 ★

Information Technology

SIC: 7375; NAICS: 51711, 517919

Leading IT Outsourcing Firms Worldwide, 2011

Firms are ranked by revenues in millions of dollars.

	($ mil.)	Share
IBM	$ 26,923	10.9%
Hewlett-Packard Co.	15,107	6.1
Fujitsu	10,981	4.5
CSC	10,374	4.2

Continued on next page.

★ 3374 ★

[Continued]

Information Technology

SIC: 7375; NAICS: 51711, 517919

Leading IT Outsourcing Firms Worldwide, 2011

Firms are ranked by revenues in millions of dollars.

	($ mil.)	Share
Accenture	$ 6,530	2.6%
Other	176,640	71.7

Source: "Gartner Says Worldwide IT Outsourcing Market Grew 7.8 Percent in 2011." [online] from http://www.gartner.com [Press release May 21, 2012], from Gartner Inc.

★ 3375 ★

Information Technology

SIC: 7375; NAICS: 51711, 517919

Top IT Consulting Firms Worldwide, 2010

The industry generated revenues of $792.9 billion.

IBM	7.1%
Hewlett-Packard Co.	4.5
Fujitsu	3.0
Acenture	2.8
CSC	2.0
Other	80.6

Source: "Gartner Says Worldwide IT Services Revenue Returned to Growth in 2010." [online] from http://www.gartner.com [Press release May 4, 2011], from Gartner Inc.

★ 3376 ★

Computer Facilities Management Services

SIC: 7376; NAICS: 541513

Computer Facilities Management Services, 2007

Data show the percent of industry sales held by the largest 4, 8, 20 and 50 firms in the sector. There are approximately 5,047 firms operating in the industry generating employment for 132,523 people.

4 largest firms	63.5%
8 largest firms	67.9
20 largest firms	75.1
50 largest firms	81.7

Source: "2007 Economic Census." [online] from http://www.census.gov/econ/concentration.html [Accessed August 12, 2011], from U.S. Bureau of the Census.

★ 3377 ★

Computer Rental and Leasing

SIC: 7377; NAICS: 53242

Computer Rental and Leasing, 2007

Data show the percent of industry sales held by the largest 4, 8, 20 and 50 firms in the sector. There are approximately 448 firms operating in the industry generating employment for 3,401 people.

4 largest firms	41.1%
8 largest firms	54.9
20 largest firms	70.0
50 largest firms	86.1

Source: "2007 Economic Census." [online] from http://www.census.gov/econ/concentration.html [Accessed August 12, 2011], from U.S. Bureau of the Census.

★ 3378 ★

Computer and Office Machine Repair

SIC: 7378; NAICS: 811212

Computer and Office Machine Repair and Maintenance, 2007

Data show the percent of industry sales held by the largest 4, 8, 20 and 50 firms in the sector. There are approximately 5,241 firms operating in the industry generating employment for 50,140 people.

4 largest firms	34.2%
8 largest firms	41.3
20 largest firms	52.7
50 largest firms	62.8

Source: "2007 Economic Census." [online] from http://www.census.gov/econ/concentration.html [Accessed August 12, 2011], from U.S. Bureau of the Census.

★ 3379 ★

Computer Repair and Maintenance

SIC: 7378; NAICS: 811212

Largest Computer Repair Franchises, 2011

Companies are ranked by number of outlets. The industry consists of 12,300 businesses and provides employment to 47,000 employees.

Fast-Teks On-Site Computer Services	264
Computer Troubleshooters	194
CMIT Solutions	124
Geeks on Call	123
Friendly Computers	75

Continued on next page.

★ 3379 ★

[Continued]

Computer Repair and Maintenance

SIC: 7378; NAICS: 811212

Largest Computer Repair Franchises, 2011

Companies are ranked by number of outlets. The industry consists of 12,300 businesses and provides employment to 47,000 employees.

Computer Medics of America	58
TeamLogic IT	41

Source: "Computer Service and Repair." [online] from http://ads.eztouse.com/BooksOnline/Profiles/Computer-Service-and-Repair-Snapshot.pdf [Accessed May 1, 2012], from *Entrepreneur*.

★ 3380 ★

Computer Systems Design

SIC: 7379; NAICS: 541512

Computer Systems Design Services, 2007

Data show the percent of industry sales held by the largest 4, 8, 20 and 50 firms in the sector. There are approximately 46,687 firms operating in the industry generating employment for 518,508 people.

4 largest firms	32.4%
8 largest firms	41.9
20 largest firms	51.6
50 largest firms	59.3

Source: "2007 Economic Census." [online] from http://www.census.gov/econ/concentration.html [Accessed August 12, 2011], from U.S. Bureau of the Census.

★ 3381 ★

Secured Logistics

SIC: 7381; NAICS: 561611, 561612, 561613

Top Secured Logistic Providers Worldwide, 2010

The industry was valued at $14 billion.

Brink's	21.0%
G4S	14.0
Loomis	11.0
Prosegur	9.0
Gada	4.0
Other	41.0

Source: "Brink's Company." [online] from http://edg1.vcall.com/irwebsites/brinks/May_2011_IR_Presentation.pdf [Published May 2011], from internal estimates.

★ 3382 ★

Security Industry

SIC: 7382; NAICS: 561621

Security Market Worldwide, 2004 and 2019

The market is forecast to grow from 57 billion euros in 2004 to 155 billion euros in 2019.

	2004	2019
North America	36.0%	28.0%
Western Europe	31.0	24.0
Asia	15.0	23.0
Latin America	8.0	11.0
Africa and Middle East	7.0	9.0
Eastern Europe	3.0	5.0

Source: "Nick Buckles." [online] from http://www.g4s.com [Published September 2011], from Freedonia Group and Frost & Sullivan.

★ 3383 ★

Security Industry

SIC: 7382; NAICS: 561621

Top Providers of Manned Security Worldwide, 2010

Market shares are shown in percent.

Securitas	12.0%
G4S	9.0
Prosegur	3.0
Allied Security	2.0
ISS	2.0
Secom	1.0
UTC	1.0
Other	70.0

Source: "Nick Buckles." [online] from http://www.g4s.com [Published September 2011], from G4s estimates and market data.

★ 3384 ★

Security Industry

SIC: 7382; NAICS: 561621

Top Security Alarm Companies, 2010

Firms are ranked by monthly recurring revenues as of December 31, 2010.

ADT	$ 290.7
Protection 1	25.2
Monotronics International	24.4
Vivint Inc.	20.6
Stanley Convergent Security Solutions	18.7
Slomins Inc.	13.0
Vector Security Inc.	9.6

Continued on next page.

★ **3384** ★

[Continued]

Security Industry

SIC: 7382; NAICS: 561621

Top Security Alarm Companies, 2010

Firms are ranked by monthly recurring revenues as of December 31, 2010.

Guardian Protection Services	$ 8.0
ASG Security	6.0
Bay Alarm Company	5.8

Source: *Security Distributing & Marketing*, May 2011, p. 41.

★ **3385** ★

Security Industry

SIC: 7382; NAICS: 561621

Top Security Firms in the United States and Canada, 2011

The market for residential and small business security services was placed at $12.5 billion.

ADT	25.0%
Protection One	4.0
Monitronics	3.0
Vivint	2.0
Other	66.0

Source: "Tyco ADT." [online] from http://phx.corporate-ir.net [Published April 10, 0212], from ADT analysis and IMS Research.

★ **3386** ★

News Syndicates

SIC: 7383; NAICS: 51911

Top News Syndicates, 2010

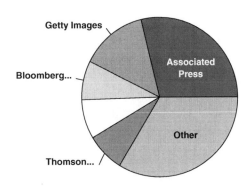

The industry generated revenues of $2.4 billion. News reporting text claimed 50% of the total, photographs and graphics 30%, video 19% and audio 1%.

Associated Press	29.0%
Getty Images	14.0

Bloomberg L.P.	8.5%
News Corp.	8.0
Thomson Reuters Corp.	8.0
Other	33.5

Source: "News Syndicates in the U.S." [online] from http://www.ibisworld.com [Published November 2010], from IBIS-World.

★ **3387** ★

Photofinishing

SIC: 7384; NAICS: 812921

Photofinishing Market, 2011

Companies are ranked by unit share of printed photos across all photo printing outlets, which include store and self-service kiosks and online sectors. Shutterfly and Snapfish are leaders in the sector of photos printed online and then mailed home with market shares of 32% and 30%, respectively.

Walgreens	23.5%
Wal-Mart	20.7
Snapfish	10.3
CVS	9.0
Shutterfly	9.0
Costco	4.8
Target	3.4
Rite Aid	2.2
Kodak	2.0
Sams Wholesale	1.6
Other	13.5

Source: *Twice*, May 7, 2012, p. 14, from *TraQline Photo Behavior Report*.

★ **3388** ★

Audio Production Studios

SIC: 7389; NAICS: 51224

Top Audio Production Studios, 2011

There were a total of 4,955 businesses in the United States. They generated revenues of $735.4 million. Album production claimed 20% of the total, original music 16%, audio post-production 15%, demos 13% and mastering services 11%. Companies all have less than 3% market shares.

Manhattan Sound Recording Studios	3.0%
Paramount Recording Studios	3.0
Sterling Sound Inc.	3.0
Other	91.0

Source: "Audio Production Studios in the U.S." [online] from http://www.ibisworld.com [Published July 2011], from IBIS-World.

★ 3389 ★
Building Inspection Services
SIC: 7389; NAICS: 54135

Building Inspection Services, 2007

Data show the percent of industry sales held by the largest 4, 8, 20 and 50 firms in the sector. There are approximately 5,764 firms operating in the industry generating employment for 16,291 people.

4 largest firms	19.5%
8 largest firms	22.5
20 largest firms	28.1
50 largest firms	36.8

Source: ''2007 Economic Census.'' [online] from http://www.census.gov/econ/concentration.html [Accessed August 12, 2011], from U.S. Bureau of the Census.

★ 3390 ★
Business Coaching
SIC: 7389; NAICS: 561499

Business Coaching Industry, 2011

This industry includes firms that offer short courses and seminars for management and professional development. Training is provided through public courses or through employers' training programs, and the courses can be customized or modified. Instruction may be provided at the training facilities of the establishment or client, educational institutions, the workplace or the home. The industry generated revenues of $8.8 billion in 2011. Professional development training claimed 60% of the total, management training 23%, quality assurance 10% and business coaching 7%.

The Washington Post Co.	3.6%
Frankin Covey	1.1
Center for Creative Leadership	0.9
Other	94.4

Source: ''Business Coaching in the U.S.'' [online] from http://www.ibisworld.com [Published October 2011], from IBIS-World.

★ 3391 ★
Carsharing
SIC: 7389; NAICS: 561599

Top Carsharing Firms in North America, 2009

There are an estimated 398,500 members in the United States and 55,000 in Canada.

Zipcar	74.0%
PhillyCarShare	8.0
Communato	4.0
City CarShare	3.0
Connect by Hertz	2.0%
I-Go Car Sharing	2.0
Other	7.0

Source: ''Sustainable and Innovative Personal Transport Solutions.'' [online] from http://xa.yimg.com/kq/groups/1088789/1632531212/name/F%26S_M4FA_European+Carsharing_Key+Findings.pdf [Published January 2010], from Frost & Sullivan.

★ 3392 ★
Convention and Visitors Bureaus
SIC: 7389; NAICS: 561591

Convention and Visitor Bureaus, 2007

Data show the percent of industry sales held by the largest 4, 8, 20 and 50 firms in the sector. There are approximately 1,322 firms operating in the industry generating employment for 11,956 people.

4 largest firms	13.2%
8 largest firms	18.7
20 largest firms	30.5
50 largest firms	48.4

Source: ''2007 Economic Census.'' [online] from http://www.census.gov/econ/concentration.html [Accessed August 12, 2011], from U.S. Bureau of the Census.

★ 3393 ★
Document Preparation
SIC: 7389; NAICS: 56141

Document Preparation Services, 2007

Data show the percent of industry sales held by the largest 4, 8, 20 and 50 firms in the sector. There are approximately 5,208 firms operating in the industry generating employment for 46,781 people.

4 largest firms	22.3%
8 largest firms	27.9
20 largest firms	35.0
50 largest firms	43.3

Source: ''2007 Economic Census.'' [online] from http://www.census.gov/econ/concentration.html [Accessed August 12, 2011], from U.S. Bureau of the Census.

★ 3394 ★

Document Preparation

SIC: 7389; NAICS: 56141

Top Document Preparation Firms, 2011

The industry generated revenues of $4.2 billion in 2011. Transcription and stenographic services claimed 55% of revenues, typing, word processing and desktop publishing 30% and document editing and proofreading 15%.

MedQuist L.L.C.	9.0%
Nuance Communications Inc.	8.2
Other	82.8

Source: "Document Preparation Services in the U.S." [online] from http://www.ibisworld.com [Published June 2011], from IBISWorld.

★ 3395 ★

Garment Repair and Alterations

SIC: 7389; NAICS: 81299

Garment Repair and Alteration Services, 2007

Data show the percent of industry sales held by the largest 4, 8, 20 and 50 firms in the sector. There are approximately 2,245 firms operating in the industry generating employment for 6,713 people.

4 largest firms	5.3%
8 largest firms	8.7
20 largest firms	15.3
50 largest firms	23.3

Source: "2007 Economic Census." [online] from http://www.census.gov/econ/concentration.html [Accessed August 12, 2011], from U.S. Bureau of the Census.

★ 3396 ★

Language Services

SIC: 7389; NAICS: 54193

Top Language Service Providers Worldwide, 2011

Data show the top providers of translation, localization and interpreting services ranked by revenues in millions of dollars. North America claimed 49.2% of demand, Western Europe 21.1%, Northern Europe 12.7% and other regions 17%.

Mission Essential Personnel	$ 588.0
HP ACG	460.0
Global Linguist Solutions	435.0
Lionbridge Technologies	405.2
TransPerfect/Translations.com	252.4
SDL	245.0
L-3 Linguist Operations & Technical Support	167.0
STAR Group	$ 145.0
euroscript International S.A.	124.1
ManpowerGroup	101.0

Source: "Top 50 Language Service Providers." [online] from http://www.commonserviceadvisory.com [Published May 31, 2011], from Common Sense Advisory.

★ 3397 ★

Meteorological Services

SIC: 7389; NAICS: 54199

Meteorological Services (Weather Forecasting), 2007

Data show the percent of industry sales held by the largest 4, 8, 20 and 50 firms in the sector. There are approximately 157 firms operating in the industry generating employment for 2,601 people. Major players include Accuweather, National Oceanic and Atmospheric Administration and Weather Underground.

4 largest firms	62.0%
8 largest firms	74.9
20 largest firms	88.3
50 largest firms	97.3

Source: "2007 Economic Census." [online] from http://www.census.gov/econ/concentration.html [Accessed August 12, 2011], from U.S. Bureau of the Census.

★ 3398 ★

Planning and Development Organizations

SIC: 7389; NAICS: 56199

Economic or Industrial Planning or Development Organizations, 2007

Data show the percent of industry sales held by the largest 4, 8, 20 and 50 firms in the sector. There are approximately 2,894 firms operating in the industry generating employment for 17,283 people.

4 largest firms	24.7%
8 largest firms	28.5
20 largest firms	35.4
50 largest firms	45.6

Source: "2007 Economic Census." [online] from http://www.census.gov/econ/concentration.html [Accessed August 12, 2011], from U.S. Bureau of the Census.

★ 3399 ★
Repossession Services
SIC: 7389; NAICS: 561491

Repossession Services, 2007

Data show the percent of industry sales held by the largest 4, 8, 20 and 50 firms in the sector. There are approximately 965 firms operating in the industry generating employment for 6,212 people.

4 largest firms	10.0%
8 largest firms	15.9
20 largest firms	27.6
50 largest firms	40.7

Source: ''2007 Economic Census.'' [online] from http://www.census.gov/econ/concentration.html [Accessed August 12, 2011], from U.S. Bureau of the Census.

★ 3400 ★
Special Events Industry
SIC: 7389; NAICS: 56192

Top Special Event Companies, 2011

Companies are ranked by forecast annual revenues from special events in millions of dollars. TBA Global generated sales of $60-70 million. Index generated sales of $72-75 million. The industry generated revenues of $1.7 billion. Shares are shown based on this total.

	($ mil.)	Share
George P. Johnson Experience Marketing	$ 250.0	14.71%
Universal WorldEvents	130.0	7.65
Vok Dams Gruppe	120.0	7.06
Pico Global Services	90.0	5.29
Premier Global Sports	80.0	4.71
Index	75.0	4.41
AMCI	70.0	4.12
TBA Global	70.0	4.12
Imagination Group	65.6	3.86
Hartmann Studios	61.0	3.59
Hagen Invent	44.5	2.62
InVision	32.0	1.88
Switch	29.9	1.76
Uniplan	28.5	1.68
Global Events	21.0	1.24
Other	532.5	31.32

Source: *Special Events Magazine*, September-October 2011, p. 17.

★ 3401 ★
Telemarketers and Call Centers
SIC: 7389; NAICS: 561422

Top Telemarketing and Call Center Firms, 2011

The industry generated revenues of $18.4 billion in 2011. Telemarketing claimed 64.3% of the total, customer service 23.1%, debt collection 4.0%, fundraising 1.8% and other sectors 6.8%.

Convergys Corp.	10.7%
West Corp.	6.4
Sitel Corp.	2.5
Teletech Holdings	2.3
Other	78.1

Source: ''Telemarketing and Call Center Services in the U.S.'' [online] from http://www.ibisworld.com [Published August 2011], from IBISWorld.

★ 3402 ★
Timeshares
SIC: 7389; NAICS: 561599

Timeshare Resorts by Region, 2011

There are a total of 1,548 timeshare properties available in the United States, valued at $6.4 billion.

Florida	23.0%
Mountain	18.0
Northeast	11.0
Pacific	9.0
South Central	9.0
California	8.0
Midwest	8.0
South Atlantic	8.0
South Carolina	7.0

Source: *USA TODAY*, May 2, 2012, p. B1, from American Resort Development Association.

★ **3403** ★

Timeshares

SIC: 7389; NAICS: 561599

Vacation Timeshare Sales, 2006-2010

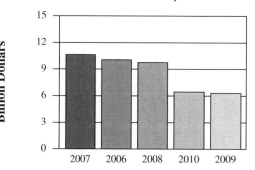

Sales are shown in billions of dollars. Developers intentionally scaled back sales efforts during the economic crisis.

2007	$ 10.6
2006	10.0
2008	9.7
2010	6.4
2009	6.3

Source: "Timeshare Datashare." [online] from http://www.arda.org [Accessed December 1, 2011], from *2011 State of the Vacation Timeshare Industry.*

★ **3404** ★

Trade Shows and Event Planning

SIC: 7389; NAICS: 56192

Largest Trade Shows, 2010

Data show the largest trade shows of 2010, ranked by thousands of net square feet. Las Vegas was the top site for conventions, hosting 60 (24%) of the top 250. Orlando hosted 25 (10%) and Chicago was third with 23 conventions, or 8% of the total. Two show management companies tied for the top spot, with Reed Exhibitions and Nielsen Business Media managing 11 shows each, giving them each a 4.4% share of the source's top 250 trade shows.

2010 International CES - Consumer Electronics Association	1,442.0
IMTS 2010 - International Manufacturing Technology Show	1,137.5
Pack Expo International/Process Expo/CPP Expo	1,054.5
Winter 2010 Las Vegas Market (Gift + Home)	1,005.9
International Woodworking Machinery and Furniture Supply Assn.	813.0
RECon - The Global Real Estate Convention .	800.0
WSAW - World Shoe Association	758.0
MAGIC Marketplace	753.1

48th Annual National RC Trade Show . . .	752.1
National Business Aviation Association . .	17.4

Source: "Top 250 U.S. Trade Shows." [online] from http://www.tsnn.com/datasite [Accessed October 1, 2011], from Trade Show News Network.

★ **3405** ★

Trade Shows and Event Planning

SIC: 7389; NAICS: 56192

Top Trade Show and Event Planning Firms, 2011

The industry generated revenues of $12.5 billion in 2011.

Freeman Companies	10.2%
Viad Corp.	8.2
United Business Media PLC	1.8
Other	79.8

Source: "Trade Show and Event Planning in the U.S." [online] from http://www.ibisworld.com [Published November 2011], from IBISWorld.

★ **3406** ★

Trading Stamp Services

SIC: 7389; NAICS: 561499

Trading Stamp Services, 2007

Trading stamps were first distributed by retailers in the 1890s and became popular through the twentieth century. The stamps could be redeemed for housewares, toys and other items by the stamp companies that distributed them. Trading stamps were eventually replaced by retailer loyalty cards. S&H Green Stamps, the most popular company in the sector, filed for bankruptcy in 1996 and re-emerged in the customer loyalty market in 2001. Data show the percent of industry sales held by the largest 4, 8, 20 and 50 firms in the sector. There are approximately 57 firms operating in the industry generating employment for 521 people.

4 largest firms	82.0%
8 largest firms	90.5
20 largest firms	96.3
50 largest firms	99.9

Source: "2007 Economic Census." [online] from http://www.census.gov/econ/concentration.html [Accessed August 12, 2011], from U.S. Bureau of the Census.

SIC 75 - Auto Repair, Services, and Parking

★ 3407 ★
Truck Rental
SIC: 7513; NAICS: 53212

Truck Rental Industry, 2010

Market shares are shown in percent.

U-Haul	50.0%
Other	50.0

Source: "Inside Wall Street: U-Haul Ahead of its Industry." [online] from http://money.msn.com/top-stocks/post.aspx?post0731d6c7-811b-4e05-9d79-8f06ad44fbc0 [Published February 21, 2012].

★ 3408 ★
Auto Rental
SIC: 7514; NAICS: 532111

Top Auto Rental Firms, 2011

Companies are ranked by number of cars in service. Enterprise includes Alamo Rent A Car, Enterprise Rent A Car and National Car Rental. Hertz includes Advantage Rent-A-Car.

	Cars	Share
Enterprise Holdings	920,861	53.81%
Hertz	320,000	18.70
Avis Budget Group	285,000	16.65
Dollar Thrifty Automotive Group	118,000	6.90
U-Save Auto Rental System Inc.	11,500	0.67
Fox Rent A Car	11,000	0.64
Payless Car Rental Systems Inc.	10,000	0.58
ACE Rent A Car	9,000	0.53
Zipcar	7,400	0.43
Independents	5,500	0.32
Rent-A-Wreck of America	5,500	0.32
Triangle Rent-A-Car	4,200	0.25
Affordable/Sensible	3,300	0.19

Source: *Auto Rental News*, Fact Book 2012, p. 6.

★ 3409 ★
Fleet Management
SIC: 7515; NAICS: 532112

Top Fleet Management Firms, 2011

Companies are ranked by total funded and managed vehicles. Funded is defined as any vehicle acquired either through self funds, a bank line, securitization or syndication.

GE Capital Fleet Services	762,490
ARI	610,000
PHH Arval	481,000
LeasePlan USA	385,000
Wheels	300,000
Enterprise	261,261
Donlen	152,000
Emkay	83,000
Mike Albert Fleet Solutions	38,000
Sutton Leasing	18,000

Source: *Automotive Fleet*, Fact Book 2011, p. 44.

★ 3410 ★
Vehicle Leasing
SIC: 7515; NAICS: 532112

Vehicle Leasing Industry, 2012

Data are as of March 31, 2012.

Light duty trucks	54.0%
Cars	19.0
Medium duty trucks	13.0
Heavy duty trucks	7.0
Equipment	3.0
Trailers	3.0
Forklifts	2.0

Source: "PHH Corporation Investor Presentation." [online] from http://phx.corporate-ir.ne [Published May 7, 2012].

★ 3411 ★

Parking Lots and Garages

SIC: 7521; NAICS: 81293

Top Parking Lot and Garage Operators, 2011

The industry generated revenues of $8.2 billion in 2011. Rising gas prices have meant that more people are looking into mass transit and similar options to save money, which means fewer people spending money on parking and garages. Many airport garages are reportedly operating at under capacity. Many analysts expect consolidation in the industry to take place.

Central Parking Corp.	15.8%
Standard Parking Corp.	9.3
ABM Industries Inc.	6.0
Ace Parking Management	4.9
Other	64.0

Source: "Parking Lots & Garages in the U.S." [online] from http://www.ibisworld.com [Published August 2011], from IBISWorld.

★ 3412 ★

Automotive Repair

SIC: 7530; NAICS: 811112, 811113

Leading Automotive Repair/Service Franchises, 2011

Companies are ranked by number of locations.

Midas	2,291
NOVUS Glass	1,696
Meineke Car Care Centers	955
AAMCO Transmissions and Total Car Care	865
Line-X Franchise Development Corp.	480
Maaco Franchising	463
Tuffy Associates Corp./Car-X Associates Corp.	382
Ziebart	376
Precision Tune Auto Care	339
Superglass Windshield Repair	272
Colors on Parade	202
Mr. Transmissions/Transmissions USA	103

Source: *Entrepreneur*, January 2012, p. 148.

★ 3413 ★

Automotive Repair

SIC: 7532; NAICS: 811121

Market Shares of MLOs, 2010

MLO stands for multiple-location collision repair operators. There are 56 such MLOs that generate revenues of $20 or more and they process 10.8% of the $31.0 billion in collision repair revenues generated nationally. There were 37,700 independent and dealer operated collision repair firms operating in the United States in 2010, down from a high of 80,000 in 1980. Caliber Collision, AutoNation and ABRA were the top three multiple location operators.

Southeast	25.2%
Southwest	23.1
West	22.9
Midwest	22.7
Northeast	6.1

Source: *Collision Week*, October 7, 2011, p. NA, from Romans Group.

★ 3414 ★

Automotive Repair

SIC: 7533; NAICS: 811112

Automotive Exhaust System Repair, 2007

Data show the percent of industry sales held by the largest 4, 8, 20 and 50 firms in the sector. There are approximately 2,756 firms operating in the industry generating employment for 9,002 people.

4 largest firms	4.8%
8 largest firms	6.4
20 largest firms	9.8
50 largest firms	15.4

Source: "2007 Economic Census." [online] from http://www.census.gov/econ/concentration.html [Accessed August 12, 2011], from U.S. Bureau of the Census.

★ 3415 ★

Tire Retreading

SIC: 7534; NAICS: 326212

Top Tire Retreaders in North America, 2010

Companies are ranked by millions of pounds of rubber used in medium and heavy truck tires.

Wingfoot Commercial Tire Systems L.L.C.	39.40
Bridgestone Bandag Tire Solutions L.L.C.	21.74
Southern Tire Market L.L.C.	20.00
Snider Tire Inc.	15.00

Continued on next page.

★ 3415 ★

[Continued]

Tire Retreading

SIC: 7534; NAICS: 326212

Top Tire Retreaders in North America, 2010

Companies are ranked by millions of pounds of rubber used in medium and heavy truck tires.

Best One Tire & Service	14.26
Tire Centers L.L.C.	14.00
Les Schwab Tire Centers	10.50
Kal Tire	10.00
Pomp's Tire & Auto Service	9.50
Purcell Tire & Auto Service Inc.	9.50

Source: *Tire Business*, February 13, 2012, p. 9, from *Tire Business* estimates.

★ 3416 ★

Automotive Repair

SIC: 7536; NAICS: 811122

Automotive Glass Replacement Shops, 2007

Data show the percent of industry sales held by the largest 4, 8, 20 and 50 firms in the sector. There are approximately 6,978 firms operating in the industry generating employment for 31,025 people.

4 largest firms	26.0%
8 largest firms	29.7
20 largest firms	34.9
50 largest firms	41.1

Source: "2007 Economic Census." [online] from http://www.census.gov/econ/concentration.html [Accessed August 12, 2011], from U.S. Bureau of the Census.

★ 3417 ★

Automotive Repair

SIC: 7537; NAICS: 811113

Automotive Transmission Repair, 2007

Data show the percent of industry sales held by the largest 4, 8, 20 and 50 firms in the sector. There are approximately 6,158 firms operating in the industry generating employment for 24,834 people.

4 largest firms	4.1%
8 largest firms	5.4
20 largest firms	7.9
50 largest firms	11.8

Source: "2007 Economic Census." [online] from http://www.census.gov/econ/concentration.html [Accessed August 12, 2011], from U.S. Bureau of the Census.

★ 3418 ★

Automotive Repair

SIC: 7538; NAICS: 811111

Brake, Front End, and Wheel Alignment, 2007

Data show the percent of industry sales held by the largest 4, 8, 20 and 50 firms in the sector. There are approximately 2,352 firms operating in the industry generating employment for 10,693 people.

4 largest firms	18.1%
8 largest firms	21.2
20 largest firms	26.3
50 largest firms	33.8

Source: "2007 Economic Census." [online] from http://www.census.gov/econ/concentration.html [Accessed August 12, 2011], from U.S. Bureau of the Census.

★ 3419 ★

Automotive Repair

SIC: 7538; NAICS: 811111

Carburetor Repair, 2007

Data show the percent of industry sales held by the largest 4, 8, 20 and 50 firms in the sector. There are approximately 261 firms operating in the industry generating employment for 1,109 people.

4 largest firms	14.2%
8 largest firms	21.8
20 largest firms	36.4
50 largest firms	61.9

Source: "2007 Economic Census." [online] from http://www.census.gov/econ/concentration.html [Accessed August 12, 2011], from U.S. Bureau of the Census.

★ 3420 ★

Car Washes

SIC: 7542; NAICS: 811192

Top Car Wash Chains, 2010

Companies are ranked by number of locations. Shares are shown based on the top 40 firms.

	Units	Share
Wash Depot	84	9.14%
Mister Car Wash	69	7.51
Autobell Car Wash	63	6.86
Mike's Express Car Wash	63	6.86
AutoWorld Car Wash	37	4.03
Delta Sonic	28	3.05
Original $2 Car Wash	28	3.05
Terrible Herbst	28	3.05
Drive Clean L.L.C.	27	2.94

Continued on next page.

★ 3420 ★

[Continued]

Car Washes

SIC: 7542; NAICS: 811192

Top Car Wash Chains, 2010

Companies are ranked by number of locations. Shares are shown based on the top 40 firms.

	Units	Share
Goo Goo Car Wash	27	2.94%
Other	465	50.60

Source: *Professional Carwashing & Detailing*, September 2011, p. NA.

★ 3421 ★

Motor Vehicle Towing

SIC: 7549; NAICS: 48841

Motor Vehicle Towing, 2007

Data show the percent of industry sales held by the largest 4, 8, 20 and 50 firms in the sector. There are approximately 8,165 firms operating in the industry generating employment for 55,598 people.

4 largest firms	6.3%
8 largest firms	8.7
20 largest firms	11.5
50 largest firms	15.4

Source: ''2007 Economic Census.'' [online] from http://www.census.gov/econ/concentration.html [Accessed August 12, 2011], from U.S. Bureau of the Census.

★ 3422 ★

Oil Change Industry

SIC: 7549; NAICS: 811191

Leading Fast-Lube Shops, 2010

Companies are ranked by number of outlets. Shares are shown based on the top 31 firms.

	Units	Share
Jiffy Lube	1,963	29.41%
Valvoline Instant Oil Change	872	13.07
Pennzoil 10-Minute Oil Change . . .	750	11.24
Kwik Kar	390	5.84
Havoline Xpress Lube	350	5.24
Valvoline Express Care	342	5.12
Mobil 1 Lube Express	330	4.94
ConocoPhillips Lube Shop	186	2.79
Express Oil Change & Service Center .	186	2.79
Grease Monkey	186	2.79
Other	1,119	16.77

Source: *National Oil & Lube News*, February 2011, p. 20.

SIC 76 - Miscellaneous Repair Services

★ 3423 ★
Appliance Repair
SIC: 7629; NAICS: 811412

Appliance Repair and Maintenance, 2007

Data show the percent of industry sales held by the largest 4, 8, 20 and 50 firms in the sector. There are approximately 4,504 firms operating in the industry generating employment for 23,834 people.

4 largest firms	NA
8 largest firms	42.6%
20 largest firms	45.9
50 largest firms	50.3

Source: "2007 Economic Census." [online] from http://www.census.gov/econ/concentration.html [Accessed August 12, 2011], from U.S. Bureau of the Census.

★ 3424 ★
Consumer Electronics Repair and Maintenance
SIC: 7629; NAICS: 811211

Consumer Electronics Repair and Maintenance Services, 2007

Data show the percent of industry sales held by the largest 4, 8, 20 and 50 firms in the sector. There are approximately 2,419 firms operating in the industry generating employment for 17,612 people.

4 largest firms	28.6%
8 largest firms	35.2
20 largest firms	44.1
50 largest firms	54.0

Source: "2007 Economic Census." [online] from http://www.census.gov/econ/concentration.html [Accessed August 12, 2011], from U.S. Bureau of the Census.

★ 3425 ★
Medical Equipment Maintenance
SIC: 7629; NAICS: 811219

Leading Clinical/Diagnostic Equipment Maintenance Operations, 2009-2010

Firms are ranked by number of national healthcare clients.

	2009	2010
HSS	491	596
Crest Services	461	515
Modern Biomedical & Imaging	298	317
ABM Industries	216	231

Source: *Modern Healthcare's By the Numbers*, Annual 2011-2012, p. 36, from *Modern Healthcare's 2011 Outsourcing Survey.*

★ 3426 ★
Watch, Clock and Jewelry Repair
SIC: 7631; NAICS: 81149

Watch, Clock and Jewelry Repair, 2007

Data show the percent of industry sales held by the largest 4, 8, 20 and 50 firms in the sector. There are approximately 1,372 firms operating in the industry generating employment for 5,772 people.

4 largest firms	17.5%
8 largest firms	22.5
20 largest firms	31.3
50 largest firms	41.3

Source: "2007 Economic Census." [online] from http://www.census.gov/econ/concentration.html [Accessed August 12, 2011], from U.S. Bureau of the Census.

★ **3427** ★

Consumer Electronics Repair and Maintenance

SIC: 7641; NAICS: 81142

Number of Firms in Consumer Electronics Repair and Maintenance, 2000-2008

The market generated revenues of $21 billion in 2012, according to IBISWorld. It is one of the few that benefit from economic downturn. While it might be tempting to simply replace many broken consumer electronics, the economic downturn means consumers are more willing to stretch the life of such items. As well, some items such as flat screen televisions cost less to fix than replace.

2000	3,894
2001	3,545
2002	3,410
2003	3,100
2004	2,888
2005	2,661
2006	2,445
2007	2,326
2008	2,162

Source: "Statistics of U.S. Businesses, 2008." [online] from http://www.census.gov [Accessed May 1, 2012], from U.S. Bureau of the Census.

★ **3428** ★

Furniture Upholstery and Repair

SIC: 7641; NAICS: 81142

Number of Firms in Reupholstery and Furniture Repair, 2000-2008

This market refers to companies that reupholster, repair and refinish furniture. The market generated revenues of $2 billion in 2011, according to IBISWorld. It saw a decline of 5.8% annually from 2006-2011, largely because of the recession, which prompted consumers to postpone unnecessary spending.

2000	6,150
2001	5,964
2002	5,940
2003	5,436
2004	5,383
2005	5,212
2006	4,967
2007	4,792
2008	4,413

Source: "Statistics of U.S. Businesses, 2008." [online] from http://www.census.gov [Accessed May 1, 2012], from U.S. Bureau of the Census.

★ **3429** ★

Boat Repair Services

SIC: 7699; NAICS: 81149

Boat Repair, 2007

Data show the percent of industry sales held by the largest 4, 8, 20 and 50 firms in the sector. There are approximately 2,704 firms operating in the industry generating employment for 10,531 people.

4 largest firms	6.7%
8 largest firms	9.6
20 largest firms	15.5
50 largest firms	25.0

Source: "2007 Economic Census." [online] from http://www.census.gov/econ/concentration.html [Accessed August 12, 2011], from U.S. Bureau of the Census.

★ **3430** ★

Communication Equipment Repair

SIC: 7699; NAICS: 81131

Communication Equipment Repair and Maintenance, 2007

Data show the percent of industry sales held by the largest 4, 8, 20 and 50 firms in the sector. There are approximately 1,746 firms operating in the industry generating employment for 20,729 people.

4 largest firms	31.1%
8 largest firms	38.4
20 largest firms	47.8
50 largest firms	59.2

Source: "2007 Economic Census." [online] from http://www.census.gov/econ/concentration.html [Accessed August 12, 2011], from U.S. Bureau of the Census.

★ **3431** ★

Home Repair Industry

SIC: 7699; NAICS: 811411

Leading Home Repair Franchises, 2011

A study by the Joint Center for Housing Studies at Harvard University and the Commerce Department placed total remodeling spending in the United States at $279 billion in 2011. Various sources have estimated the percentage of revenues that would be claimed by the professional handyman industry. Companies are ranked by number of locations.

Mr. Handyman International L.L.C.	269
Handyman Connection	120
Handyman Matters Franchise Inc.	113
House Doctors	105
Case Handyman and Remodeling Services L.L.C.	50

Continued on next page.

★ 3431 ★

[Continued]

Home Repair Industry

SIC: 7699; NAICS: 811411

Leading Home Repair Franchises, 2011

A study by the Joint Center for Housing Studies at Harvard University and the Commerce Department placed total remodeling spending in the United States at $279 billion in 2011. Various sources have estimated the percentage of revenues that would be claimed by the professional handyman industry. Companies are ranked by number of locations.

Andy OnCall	48
Yellow Van Handyman	43
HandyPro Handyman Services Inc.	12
Servistar	7
Handyman-Network Franchise Systems L.L.C.	5

Source: *Entrepreneur*, January 2012, p. NA.

★ 3432 ★

Locksmiths

SIC: 7699; NAICS: 561622

Locksmiths, 2007

Data show the percent of industry sales held by the largest 4, 8, 20 and 50 firms in the sector. There are approximately 3,818 firms operating in the industry generating employment for 15,774 people.

4 largest firms	5.9%
8 largest firms	8.3
20 largest firms	13.1
50 largest firms	20.5

Source: "2007 Economic Census." [online] from http://www.census.gov/econ/concentration.html [Accessed August 12, 2011], from U.S. Bureau of the Census.

★ 3433 ★

Machinery Repair and Maintenance

SIC: 7699; NAICS: 81131

Commercial Machinery Repair and Maintenance, 2007

Data show the percent of industry sales held by the largest 4, 8, 20 and 50 firms in the sector. There are approximately 22,749 firms operating in the industry generating employment for 181,534 people.

4 largest firms	6.2%
8 largest firms	9.6

20 largest firms	15.9%
50 largest firms	22.7

Source: "2007 Economic Census." [online] from http://www.census.gov/econ/concentration.html [Accessed August 12, 2011], from U.S. Bureau of the Census.

★ 3434 ★

Septic Tank Services

SIC: 7699; NAICS: 562991

Cesspool and Septic Tank Cleaning Services, 2007

Data show the percent of industry sales held by the largest 4, 8, 20 and 50 firms in the sector. There are approximately 2,331 firms operating in the industry generating employment for 11,936 people.

4 largest firms	6.4%
8 largest firms	10.4
20 largest firms	16.8
50 largest firms	25.8

Source: "2007 Economic Census." [online] from http://www.census.gov/econ/concentration.html [Accessed August 12, 2011], from U.S. Bureau of the Census.

SIC 78 - Motion Pictures

★ 3435 ★
Motion Pictures
SIC: 7812; NAICS: 51211

Largest Motion Picture Markets Worldwide, 2010

There were approximately 5,669 films produced global-ly. Of the top 10 countries, only the United Kingdom, Japan and Germany did not see an increase in the num-ber of films produced. Total film box office was $31.8 billion.

	($ mil.)	Share
United States	$ 9,609.0	30.22%
Japan	2,514.7	7.91
France	1,779.0	5.59
United Kingdom	1,554.8	4.89
China	1,506.7	4.74
India	1,358.2	4.27
Germany	1,220.5	3.84
Australia	1,041.4	3.27
Russia	1,016.5	3.20
Canada	999.7	3.14
Spain	878.3	2.76
Brazil	713.9	2.24
Other	7,607.3	23.92

Source: *Screen Digest*, August 2011, p. 237.

★ 3436 ★
Motion Pictures
SIC: 7812; NAICS: 51211

Top 3-D Film Makers, 2010

Box office revenues from 3-D in North America nearly doubled to $2.17 billion in 2010, equivalent to nearly 21% of the total box office. 3-D film prices are higher than regular films, but even premium pricing did not off-set a decline a nearly percent

Disney	30.6%
20th Century Fox	20.1
DWA	18.1
Warner Brothers	10.1
Paramount	8.1
Universal	5.9
Lionsgate	2.8
Sony Pictures	2.3

Weinstein Company	1.1%
Imax (Warner)	0.9

Source: *Screen Digest*, January 2011, p. 8.

★ 3437 ★
Motion Pictures
SIC: 7812; NAICS: 51211

Top Films, 2011

Films are ranked by box office gross in millions of dol-lars.

Harry Potter and the Deathly Hallows Part 2	$ 381.0
Transformers: Dark of the Moon	352.3
The Twilight Saga: Breaking Dawn Part 1	275.4
The Hangover Part II	254.4
Pirates of the Caribbean: On Stranger Tides	241.0
Fast Five	209.8
Cars 2	191.4
Thor	181.0
Rise of the Planet of the Apes	176.7
Captain America: The First Avenger	176.6
The Help	169.4
Bridesmaids	169.1
Kung Fu Panda 2	165.2
X-Men: First Class	146.4
Puss in Boots	145.5

Source: *Entertainment Weekly*, January 27, 2012, p. 60, from Box Office Mojo.

★ 3438 ★
Television Shows
SIC: 7812; NAICS: 51211

Popular Late-Night Programs, 2011

Data show average audience share, age 2 and up, from December 27, 2010-July 31, 2011.

Nightline	4.0
The Tonight Show with Jay Leno	3.9
Late Show with David Letterman	3.4
The Daily Show	2.0
The Colbert Report	1.4
Conan	1.1

Source: *Wall Street Journal*, August 18, 2011, p. B1, from Nielsen Company.

★ 3439 ★
Television Shows
SIC: 7812; NAICS: 51211
Top Talk Shows, 2011

The top syndicated and network television shows are ranked by average millions of viewers for season-to-date.

Dr. Phil	4.0
The Dr. Oz Show	3.7
The View	3.7
Live With Regis and Kelly	3.4
Maury	3.2
The Ellen Degeneres Show	3.0
The Jerry Springer Show	2.1
Today: Kathie Lee & Hoda	2.1
The Chew	2.0
Rachel Ray	2.0
The Talk	2.0

Source: *Entertainment Weekly*, December 9, 2011, p. 17.

★ 3440 ★
Audio and Video Media Reproduction
SIC: 7819; NAICS: 512191
Audio and Video Media Reproduction, 2007

Data show the percent of industry sales held by the largest 4, 8, 20 and 50 firms in the sector. There are approximately 470 firms operating in the industry generating employment for 20,111 people.

4 largest companies	43.6%
8 largest companies	61.3
20 largest companies	77.8
50 largest companies	88.0

Source: "2007 Economic Census." [online] from http://www.census.gov/econ/concentration.html [Accessed August 12, 2011], from U.S. Bureau of the Census.

★ 3441 ★
Film Distribution
SIC: 7822; NAICS: 51212
Top Film Distributors, 2011

Market shares are shown in percent.

Paramount	19.2%
Warner Bros.	17.9
Sony/Columbia	12.5
Buena Vista	12.2
Universal	10.2
20th Century Fox	9.6
Summit Entertainment	4.0
Weinstein Company	2.9
Relativity	2.2%
Lionsgate	1.8
Fox Searchlight	1.5
FilmDistrict	1.2
Focus Features	1.2
Other	4.1

Source: "Studio Market Share." [online] from http://boxofficemojo.com [Accessed April 1, 2012].

★ 3442 ★
Sound Recording Studios
SIC: 7822; NAICS: 51212
Sound Recording Studios, 2007

Data show the percent of industry sales held by the largest 4, 8, 20 and 50 firms in the sector. There are approximately 1,722 firms operating in the industry generating employment for 6,566 people.

4 largest firms	9.8%
8 largest firms	15.1
20 largest firms	23.5
50 largest firms	36.3

Source: "2007 Economic Census." [online] from http://www.census.gov/econ/concentration.html [Accessed August 12, 2011], from U.S. Bureau of the Census.

★ 3443 ★
Motion Pictures
SIC: 7832; NAICS: 512131

Movie Theater Industry, 2011

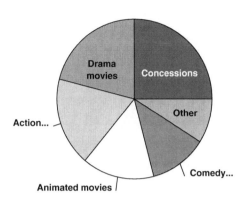

The industry was valued at $12.6 billion in 2011. Data show the sources of revenues. Competition is high, with consumers favoring facilities that offer the best viewing experience, such as a digital picture and stadium seating. Some theaters offer bargain priced matinees to further attract customers. A total of 1,850 businesses are believed to be operating in this sector, offering employment to 118,186 people.

Concessions	25.0%
Drama movies	21.0
Action and adventure movies	18.0
Animated movies	15.4
Comedy movies	12.0
Other	8.6

Source: "Movie Theaters in the U.S." [online] from http://www.ibisworld.com [Published June 2011], from IBISWorld.

★ 3444 ★
Movie Theaters
SIC: 7832; NAICS: 512131

Largest Theater Circuits in Latin America, 2010

There are an estimated 7,897 screens at 1,052 sites in Central and South America.

Cinepolis (Mexico)	2,065
Cinemex (Mexico)	1,678
Cinemark (Brazil)	438
Cinemark (Mexico)	296
CineCo (Cine Columbia)	221
Kinoplex (Brazil)	213
Cines Unidos (Venezuela)	190

UCI (Brazil)	153
Cinex (Venezuela)	144

Source: *Screen Digest*, November 2011, p. 32, from IHS Screen Digest.

★ 3445 ★
Movie Theaters
SIC: 7832; NAICS: 512131

Top Theater Chains, 2010

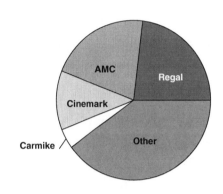

Market shares are shown in percent.

Regal	23.0%
AMC	21.0
Cinemark	12.0
Carmike	4.0
Other	40.0

Source: "Cineplex Entertainment." [online] from http://cineplexgalaxy.disclosureplus.com/SiteResources [Published March 8, 2011].

★ 3446 ★
Drive-In Theaters
SIC: 7833; NAICS: 512132

Drive-In Theaters by Year, 2002-2008

The first drive-in theater is believed to have opened in 1933. The number of establishments have been on a slow decline, now at roughly half of the 597 theaters that existed as recently as 1995.

2007	268
2002	265
2008	249
2003	244
2006	241
2004	238
2005	237

Source: "Statistics of U.S. Businesses, 2008." [online] from http://www.census.gov [Accessed May 1, 2012].

★ 3447 ★
Movie Theaters
SIC: 7833; NAICS: 512132

Drive-in Motion Picture Theaters, 2007

Data show the percent of industry sales held by the largest 4, 8, 20 and 50 firms in the sector. There are approximately 254 firms operating in the industry generating employment for 1,546 people.

4 largest firms	23.0%
8 largest firms	30.7
20 largest firms	44.0
50 largest firms	64.9

Source: "2007 Economic Census." [online] from http://www.census.gov/econ/concentration.html [Accessed August 12, 2011], from U.S. Bureau of the Census.

★ 3448 ★
Home Video industry
SIC: 7841; NAICS: 53223

DVD Rental Market, 2009-2010

Market shares are shown in percent. Coinstar owns Redbox.

	2009	2010
Netflix	25.7%	34.8%
Blockbuster (traditional)	22.8	19.9
Coinstar	11.9	18.9
Other traditional	28.2	16.1
Other subscription	8.6	7.2
Other kiosk	2.7	3.1

Source: *Screen Digest*, January 2011, p. 3, from IHS Screen Digest.

★ 3449 ★
Online Movies
SIC: 7841; NAICS: 53223

Online Movie Market, 2011

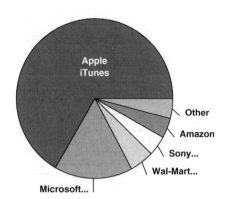

Market shares are shown based on sales and rentals for the first half of the year.

Apple iTunes	65.8%
Microsoft Zune Video Marketplace	16.2
Wal-Mart Vudu	5.3
Sony PlayStation Store	4.4
Amazon	4.2
Other	4.1

Source: *Home Media Retailing*, August 22, 2011, p. A5, from IHS iSuppli.

SIC 79 - Amusement and Recreation Services

★ 3450 ★

Art, Drama, and Music Schools

SIC: 7911; NAICS: 61161

Art, Drama, and Music Schools, 2007

Data show the percent of industry sales held by the largest 4, 8, 20 and 50 firms in the sector. There are approximately 3,600 firms operating in the industry generating employment for 27,439 people.

4 largest firms	7.6%
8 largest firms	11.4
20 largest firms	19.4
50 largest firms	30.7

Source: "2007 Economic Census." [online] from http://www.census.gov/econ/concentration.html [Accessed August 12, 2011], from U.S. Bureau of the Census.

★ 3451 ★

Dance Schools

SIC: 7911; NAICS: 61161

Dance Schools (including Children's and Professionals'), 2007

Data show the percent of industry sales held by the largest 4, 8, 20 and 50 firms in the sector. There are approximately 7,878 firms operating in the industry generating employment for 46,696 people.

4 largest firms	2.0%
8 largest firms	3.4
20 largest firms	6.1
50 largest firms	10.2

Source: "2007 Economic Census." [online] from http://www.census.gov/econ/concentration.html [Accessed August 12, 2011], from U.S. Bureau of the Census.

★ 3452 ★

Agents

SIC: 7922; NAICS: 71141

Agents and Managers For Public Figures, 2007

Data show the percent of industry sales held by the largest 4, 8, 20 and 50 firms in the sector. There are approximately 3,534 firms operating in the industry generating employment for 18,676 people.

4 largest firms	16.8%
8 largest firms	24.3
20 largest firms	32.5
50 largest firms	43.3

Source: "2007 Economic Census." [online] from http://www.census.gov/econ/concentration.html [Accessed August 12, 2011], from U.S. Bureau of the Census.

★ 3453 ★

Concerts

SIC: 7922; NAICS: 71151

Top Concert Tours in North America, 2011

Tours are ranked by gross revenues in millions of dollars.

U2	$ 156.0
Taylor Swift	97.7
Kenny Chesney	84.6
Lady Gaga	63.7
Bon Jovi	57.1
Elton John	51.8
Sade	48.6
Kanye West/Jay-Z	48.3
Lil Wayne	44.4
Celine Dion	41.2

Source: *USA TODAY*, January 19, 2012, p. D1, from Pollstar.

★ 3454 ★
Orchestras and Chamber Music Groups
SIC: 7922; NAICS: 71111

Sales of Symphony Orchestras and Chamber Music Groups, 2007

Data show the percent of industry sales held by the largest 4, 8, 20 and 50 firms in the sector.

4 largest firms	20.1%
8 largest firms	30.9
20 largest firms	51.7
50 largest firms	70.3

Source: "2007 Economic Census." [online] from http://www.census.gov/econ/concentration.html [Accessed August 12, 2011], from U.S. Bureau of the Census.

★ 3455 ★
Performing Arts Companies
SIC: 7922; NAICS: 71111, 71112

Sales of Performing Arts Companies, 2007

Data show the percent of industry sales held by the largest 4, 8, 20 and 50 firms in the sector.

4 largest firms	10.7%
8 largest firms	13.7
20 largest firms	19.7
50 largest firms	29.6

Source: "2007 Economic Census." [online] from http://www.census.gov/econ/concentration.html [Accessed August 12, 2011], from U.S. Bureau of the Census.

★ 3456 ★
Talent Agents
SIC: 7922; NAICS: 71131, 71132

Largest Talent Agencies in Los Angeles, CA, 2010

Companies are ranked by number of agents.

Creative Artists Agency	315
WME Entertainment	250
United Talent Agency	108
International Creative Management Inc.	101
APA Talent & Literary Agency	68
Paradigm	60
Gersh Agency	49
Diverse Talent Group	45
Innovative Artists Talent	38
Abrams Artists Agency	32

Source: *Los Angeles Business Journal*, December 27, 2010, p. 96.

★ 3457 ★
Theatrical Entertainment
SIC: 7922; NAICS: 71111

Sales of Theater Companies, 2007

Data show the percent of industry sales held by the largest 4, 8, 20 and 50 firms in the sector.

4 largest firms	14.1%
8 largest firms	19.0
20 largest firms	30.0
50 largest firms	44.8

Source: "2007 Economic Census." [online] from http://www.census.gov/econ/concentration.html [Accessed August 12, 2011], from U.S. Bureau of the Census.

★ 3458 ★
Theatrical Entertainment
SIC: 7922; NAICS: 71111

Top Broadway Shows, 2010-2011

Shows are ranked by box office in millions of dollars. Broadway and road shows generated $1.6 billion in box office during the season. A total of 42 plays, musicals and special attractions took place on Broadway during the season.

Wicked	$ 86.0
The Lion King	79.8
Jersey Boys	55.7
Billy Elliot	53.0
The Addams Family	50.9
Mary Poppins	47.6
The Phantom of the Opera	44.1
Mamma Mia!	43.2
Promises, Promises	34.3
American Idiot	33.4
Spider-Man: Turn off the Dark	30.0

Source: *Variety*, June 6, 2011, p. 30.

★ 3459 ★
Bowling Alleys
SIC: 7933; NAICS: 71395

Top Bowling Alley Operators, 2011

The industry generated revenues of $3.1 billion in 2011. More than 3,900 establishments were operating in the sector and provided employment to 77,211 people.

AMF Bowling World	13.5%
Brunswick	10.2
Other	76.3

Source: "Bowling Alleys in the U.S." [online] from http://www.ibisworld.com [Published October 2011], from IBISWorld.

★ 3460 ★
Celebrity and Sports Agents
SIC: 7941; NAICS: 71141

Celebrity and Sports Agent Revenues, 2009

The industry generated revenues of $6.4 billion. Performers includes stage and screen actors, singers and models. California has 30.2% of all establishments. IMG is the major player with 19% of the market. Other major players include Creative Artists Agency and International Creative Management Inc.

Performers	45.0%
Professional athletes and sporting organizations	35.0
Publishing authors and writers	15.0
Other public figures	5.0

Source: "Celebrity & Sports Agents in the U.S." [online] from http://www.scribd.com [Published November 2009], from IBISWorld.

★ 3461 ★
Sports
SIC: 7941; NAICS: 711211

Popular Sports and Activities, 2008-2010

Data show the millions of participants age 6 and over for selected activities and sports.

	2008	2009	2010
Walking for fitness	111.6	110.0	114.0
Bowling	58.6	57.2	55.8
Treadmill	49.3	51.4	53.1
Running/jogging	41.1	43.8	49.4
Billiards/pool	49.0	43.0	39.3
Fishing (freshwater)	40.3	40.9	38.8
Weight/resistance machines .	38.3	39.7	38.6
Free weight dumbells . . .	34.3	35.7	37.3
Elliptical motion trainer . . .	25.2	26.5	28.1
Free weights, barbells . . .	26.1	27.0	27.3
Aerobics, low impact	24.1	25.6	27.1
Golf	28.5	27.1	26.1
Yoga	17.7	20.1	21.8
Aerobics, high impact . . .	12.2	13.2	15.8
Camping (RV)	16.5	17.4	15.8
Soccer, outdoor	14.2	13.6	14.0
Aerobics, step	10.3	10.7	11.2
Aquatic exercise	9.2	8.6	9.2

Source: "Sports, Fitness & Recreational Activities Topline Participation Report." [online] from http://www.aahperd.org [Accessed September 1, 2011], from Sporting Goods Manufacturers Association.

★ 3462 ★
Sports
SIC: 7941; NAICS: 711211

Popular Team Sports, 2008-2010

Data show the millions of participants age 6 and over for selected activities and sports.

	2008	2009	2010
Basketball	26.2	24.0	26.3
Baseball	15.0	13.8	14.5
Soccer, outdoor	14.2	13.6	14.0
Softball, slow-pitch	9.8	8.5	8.4
Football, touch	10.4	8.9	8.3
Volleyball, court	8.1	7.2	7.3
Football, tackle	7.6	6.7	6.9
Football, flag	7.3	6.5	6.7
Volleyball, beach	4.1	4.4	5.0
Soccer, indoor	4.7	4.9	4.9
Gymnastics	3.8	4.0	4.8
Ultimate frisbee	4.8	4.3	4.7
Volleyball, grass	5.0	4.8	4.5
Paintball	4.8	4.5	3.6

Source: "Sports, Fitness & Recreational Activities Topline Participation Report." [online] from http://www.aahperd.org [Accessed September 1, 2011], from Sporting Goods Manufacturers Association.

★ 3463 ★
Sports
SIC: 7941; NAICS: 711211

Sales of Baseball Clubs, 2007

Data show the percent of industry sales held by the largest 4, 8, 20 and 50 firms in the sector.

4 largest firms	21.4%
8 largest firms	36.6
20 largest firms	72.8
50 largest firms	95.1

Source: "2007 Economic Census." [online] from http://www. census.gov/econ/concentration.html [Accessed August 12, 2011], from U.S. Bureau of the Census.

★ 3464 ★
Sports
SIC: 7941; NAICS: 711211

Sales of Football Clubs, 2007

Data show the percent of industry sales held by the largest 4, 8, 20 and 50 firms in the sector.

4 largest firms	16.7%
8 largest firms	30.3

Continued on next page.

★ 3464 ★
[Continued]
Sports
SIC: 7941; NAICS: 711211
Sales of Football Clubs, 2007

Data show the percent of industry sales held by the largest 4, 8, 20 and 50 firms in the sector.

20 largest firms 66.8%
50 largest firms 99.8

Source: ''2007 Economic Census.'' [online] from http://www.census.gov/econ/concentration.html [Accessed August 12, 2011], from U.S. Bureau of the Census.

★ 3465 ★
Sports
SIC: 7941; NAICS: 71132
Sales of Promoters of Performing Arts, Sports, and Similar Events, 2007

Data show the percent of industry sales held by the largest 4, 8, 20 and 50 firms in the sector.

4 largest firms 25.5%
8 largest firms 34.1
20 largest firms 41.7
50 largest firms 50.3

Source: ''2007 Economic Census.'' [online] from http://www.census.gov/econ/concentration.html [Accessed August 12, 2011], from U.S. Bureau of the Census.

★ 3466 ★
Sports
SIC: 7941; NAICS: 711211
Top Sports for High School Boys, 2010-2011

Data show number of participants.

Football 1,100,000
Track and field, indoor 579,302
Basketball 545,844
Baseball 471,025
Soccer 398,351

Source: *USA TODAY*, May 4, 2012, p. A1, from National Federation of State High School Associations.

★ 3467 ★
Sports
SIC: 7941; NAICS: 711211
Top Sports for High School Girls, 2010-2011

Data show number of participants.

Track and field (indoor) 475,265
Basketball 438,933
Volleyball 409,332
Softball 373,535
Cross country 204,653

Source: *USA TODAY*, May 4, 2012, p. A1, from National Federation of State High School Associations.

★ 3468 ★
Racetracks
SIC: 7948; NAICS: 711212
Leading Nations for Horse Races, 2011

A total of 154,307 races were held during the year.

	Races	Share
United States	46,220	29.95%
Australia	19,281	12.50
Japan	17,563	11.38
Great Britain	6,309	4.09
Argentina	5,528	3.58
Chile	5,172	3.35
France	4,778	3.10
Brazil	4,555	2.95
Canada	4,539	2.94
Turkey	3,920	2.54
South Africa	3,880	2.51
Other	32,562	21.10

Source: ''Thoroughbred Racing and Breeding Worldwide 2010.'' [online] from http://www.jockeyclub.com/factbook.asp?section17 [Accessed May 1, 2012], from International Federation of Horseracing Authorities.

★ 3469 ★
Racetracks
SIC: 7948; NAICS: 711212
Sales of Auto Racetracks, 2007

Data show the percent of industry sales held by the largest 4, 8, 20 and 50 firms in the sector.

4 largest firms 39.1%
8 largest firms 56.3

Continued on next page.

★ 3469 ★

[Continued]

Racetracks

SIC: 7948; NAICS: 711212

Sales of Auto Racetracks, 2007

Data show the percent of industry sales held by the largest 4, 8, 20 and 50 firms in the sector.

20 largest firms	79.7%
50 largest firms	95.7

Source: "2007 Economic Census." [online] from http://www.census.gov/econ/concentration.html [Accessed August 12, 2011], from U.S. Bureau of the Census.

★ 3470 ★

Racetracks

SIC: 7948; NAICS: 711212

Sales of Dog Racetracks, 2007

Data show the percent of industry sales held by the largest 4, 8, 20 and 50 firms in the sector.

4 largest firms	65.5%
8 largest firms	77.7
20 largest firms	93.4
50 largest firms	100.0

Source: "2007 Economic Census." [online] from http://www.census.gov/econ/concentration.html [Accessed August 12, 2011], from U.S. Bureau of the Census.

★ 3471 ★

Gyms

SIC: 7991; NAICS: 71394

Gym Revenues, 2005-2010

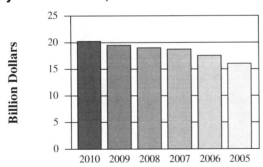

Revenues are in billions of dollars.

2010	$ 20.3
2009	19.5
2008	19.1
2007	18.7

2006	$ 17.6
2005	15.9

Source: "Health, Nutrition & Fitness Report." [online] from https://www.acg.org/assets/10/documents/Health__Nutrition_&_Fitness_Report.pdf [Published Spring 2012], from International Health, Racquet & Sportsclub Association.

★ 3472 ★

Gyms

SIC: 7991; NAICS: 71394

Largest Gym Companies, 2010

Companies are ranked by number of members.

24 Hour Fitness USA Inc.	3,800,000
Bally Total Fitness	3,500,000
Gold's Gym International Inc.	3,500,000
Planet Fitness	2,348,270
Curves International Inc.	1,900,000
McFit GmbH	975,000
Virgin Active	975,000
Anytime Fitness	940,000
Konami Sports & Life Co. Ltd.	801,000
GoodLife Fitness Clubs	670,533
Life Time Fitness Inc.	612,556

Source: *Club Business International*, July 2011, p. 41, from International Health, Racquet & Sportsclub Association.

★ 3473 ★

Gyms

SIC: 7991; NAICS: 71394

Largest Health Clubs in the United Kingdom, 2010

Companies are ranked by membership.

David Lloyd/Next Gen./Harbour Club . . .	450,000
Virgin Active/Esporta	419,000
Fitness First	400,000
DW Sports Fitness	250,000
LA Fitness	215,000
Bannatyne's Health Club	180,000
Nuffield Health Fitness & Wellbeing . . .	150,000

Source: *Marketing*, August 3, 2011, p. 30, from Mintel.

★ 3474 ★
Golf Courses
SIC: 7992; NAICS: 71391

Golf Course Industry, 2011

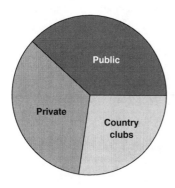

The industry is expected to bring in revenues of $21.6 billion from its 11,427 operating businesses. Approximately 75% of all golfers are male. Participation rates correlate to income level. Those making between $25,000 and $60,000 see rates at 8-20%. Those with incomes above $150,000 see participation rates of 30%. Professional and management workers claimed 38% of all participants, blue collar workers 25%, clerical and sales workers 16%, retired workers 15% and other workers 6%.

Public	38.5%
Private	34.1
Country clubs	27.4

Source: "Golf Courses Industry Snapshot." [online] from http://www.kitsapeda.org [Published February 2011], from IBISWorld.

★ 3475 ★
Golf Courses
SIC: 7992; NAICS: 71391

Largest Golf Management Companies Worldwide, 2011

The world's largest management companies operate 1,653 18-hole equivalent golf courses.

Troon Golf	209.5
Pacific Golf Management	157.5
Accordia Golf	138.0
Billy Casper Golf	131.0
ClubCorp	128.0
American Golf	109.0
KemperSports	107.0
Eagle Golf	77.0

Century Golf Partners/Arnold Palmer Golf Management	65.0
Marriott Golf	62.5

Source: *Golf Inc.*, Summer 2011, p. 28.

★ 3476 ★
Miniature Golf Courses
SIC: 7992; NAICS: 71391

Miniature Golf Courses, 2007

Data show the percent of industry sales held by the largest 4, 8, 20 and 50 firms in the sector. There are approximately 1,135 firms operating in the industry generating employment for 5,609 people.

4 largest firms	5.9%
8 largest firms	9.6
20 largest firms	17.1
50 largest firms	28.9

Source: "2007 Economic Census." [online] from http://www.census.gov/econ/concentration.html [Accessed August 12, 2011], from U.S. Bureau of the Census.

★ 3477 ★
Arcade, Food and Entertainment Complexes
SIC: 7993; NAICS: 71312

Arcade Industry in Japan, 2005-2010

Figures are in billions of yen.

2007	¥ 702.9
2006	682.5
2008	678.1
2005	649.2
2009	573.1
2010	504.3

Source: "Capcom Annual Report 2011." [online] from http://capcom.co.jp/ir/english/data/pdf/annual/2011/annual_2011_09.pdf [Published September 2011], from JAMMA's Survey of the Amusement Industry.

★ 3478 ★
Arcade, Food and Entertainment Complexes
SIC: 7993; NAICS: 71312

Leading Arcade, Food and Entertainment Complexes, 2010

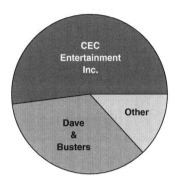

The industry generated revenues of $1.5 billion. Video games claimed 36.5% of this total, food and beverage sales 24%, venue hiring fees 5%, pinball machines 3.8%. CEC Entertainment owns Chuck E Cheeses.

CEC Entertainment Inc.	52.2%
Dave & Busters Holdings Inc.	35.0
Other	12.8

Source: "Arcade, Food and Entertainment Complexes in the U.S." [online] from http://www.ibisworld.com [Published November 2011], from IBISWorld.

★ 3479 ★
Slot Machines
SIC: 7993; NAICS: 71312

Top Slot Machine Makers, 2010

The top three firms are ranked by revenues in millions of dollars. They control approximately two-thirds of the market. Commercial casinos claim 50.6% of the slot machine market, tribal casinos 39.5% and non-casinos 9.9%.

IGT	$ 2,000
WMS Industries Inc.	783
Bally Technologies	758

Source: "Slot Machines - U.S." [online] from http://www.freedoniagroup.com [Published November 2011], from Freedonia Group.

★ 3480 ★
Amusement Parks
SIC: 7996; NAICS: 71311

Top Amusement Park/Theme Park Chains Worldwide, 2010

Parks are ranked by attendance in millions of visitors.

Magic Kingdom at Walt Disney World	16.97
Disneyland	15.98
Tokyo Disneyland	14.45
Tokyo Disneysea	12.66
Epcot at Walt Disney World	10.82
Disneyland Park at Disneyland Paris	10.50
Disney's Animal Kingdom at Walt Disney World	9.68
Disney's Hollywood Studios at Walt Disney World	9.60
Universal Studios Japan	8.16
Everland	6.88

Source: "2010 Theme Index." [online] from http://www.tea.org [Accessed August 1, 2010], from Themed Entertainment Association.

★ 3481 ★
Amusement Parks
SIC: 7996; NAICS: 71311

Top Amusement Park/Theme Park Companies Worldwide, 2010

Chains are ranked by attendance in millions of visitors.

Walt Disney Attractions	120.6
Merlin Entertainments Group	41.0
Universal Studios Recreation Group	26.3
Parques Reunidos	25.8
Six Flags Inc.	24.3
Cedar Fair Entertainment Company	22.8
Bisch Entertainment	22.4
OCT Parks China	19.3
Herschend Entertainment	9.6
Compaigne Des Alpes	9.0

Source: "2010 Theme Index." [online] from http://www.tea.org [Accessed August 1, 2010], from Themed Entertainment Association.

★ 3482 ★
Sports
SIC: 7997; NAICS: 71394

Top MLB Teams, 2011

Teams are ranked by average attendance.

Chicago Cubs	36,718
New York Yankees	36,563

Continued on next page.

★ 3482 ★

[Continued]

Sports

SIC: 7997; NAICS: 71394

Top MLB Teams, 2011

Teams are ranked by average attendance.

San Francisco Giants	36,300
Philadelphia Phillies	36,202
Milwaukee Brewers	35,150
Los Angeles Dodgers	34,717
St. Louis Cardinals	34,045
Texas Rangers	33,533
Boston Red Sox	33,043
Detroit Tigers	30,197

Source: "MLB Attendance Report 2012." [online] from http://espn.go.com/mlb/attendance [Accessed May 1, 2012], from Major League Baseball.

★ 3483 ★

Sports

SIC: 7997; NAICS: 71394

Top NBA Teams, 2011

Sports are ranked by average attendance.

Chicago Bulls	20,075
Miami Heat	19,667
New York Knicks	19,085
Dallas Mavericks	19,023
Los Angeles Lakers	19,015
Portland Trail Blazers	18,830
Los Angeles Clippers	18,781
Boston Celtics	18,456
Utah Jazz	18,118
Orlando Magic	18,028

Source: "NBA Attendance Report - 2012." [online] from http://espn.go.com/nba/attendance [Accessed May 1, 2012], from National Basketball Association.

★ 3484 ★

Sports

SIC: 7997; NAICS: 71399

Top NCAA Division 1 Football Teams, 2011

Data show average attendance.

University of Michigan	112,179
Ohio State	105,231
Alabama Crimson Tide	101,821
Penn State Nittany Lions	101,427
Texas Longhorns	100,524
Tennessee Volunteers	94,642
LSU Tigers	92,868

Georgia Bulldogs	92,613
Texas A&M	87,183

Source: "2011 National College Football Attendance." [online] from http://fs.ncaa.org/Docs/stats/football_records/Attendance/2011.pdf [Accessed May 1, 2012].

★ 3485 ★

Sports

SIC: 7997; NAICS: 71394

Top NFL Teams, 2011

Data show average attendance at home and road games.

Dallas Cowboys	78,685
New York Giants	77,009
New York Jets	74,212
Washington Redskins	73,784
Philadelphia Eagles	70,573
Green Bay Packers	70,188
Denver Broncos	69,350
Kansas City Chiefs	69,200
New Orleans Saints	69,120
Carolina Panthers	68,661

Source: "NFL Attendance - 2011." [online] from http://espn.go.com/nfl/attendance [Accessed May 1, 2012], from National Football League.

★ 3486 ★

Sports

SIC: 7997; NAICS: 71394

Top NHL Teams, 2011

Teams are ranked by average attendance.

Chicago Blackhawks	19,557
Montreal Canadiens	19,482
Detroit Red Wings	18,884
Philadelphia Flyers	18,837
Toronto Maple Leafs	18,658
Ottawa Rangers	18,342
Vancouver Canucks	18,285
Pittsburgh Penguins	18,223
Calgary Flames	18,158
St. Louis Blues	18,039

Source: "NHL Attendance Report 2012." [online] from http://espn.go.com/nba/attendance [Accessed May 1, 2012], from National Hockey League.

★ **3487** ★
Casinos
SIC: 7999; NAICS: 71321

Casino Spending by State, 2009-2010

Revenues are shown in millions of dollars. Las Vegas is the largest market with spending of $5.77 billion.

	2009	2010	Share
Nevada	$ 10,390.00	$ 10,400.00	30.06%
New Jersey	3,940.00	3,570.00	10.32
Pennsylvania . . .	1,970.00	2,490.00	7.20
Mississippi	2,470.00	2,390.00	6.91
Louisiana	2,460.00	2,370.00	6.85
Missouri	1,730.00	1,790.00	5.17
Michigan	1,340.00	1,380.00	3.99
Illinois	1,430.00	1,370.00	3.96
Iowa	1,380.00	1,370.00	3.96
New York	1,020.00	1,090.00	3.15
West Virginia . . .	905.59	877.65	2.54
Colorado	734.59	759.61	2.20
Delaware	564.24	571.38	1.65
Florida	216.74	329.12	0.95

Source: ''AGA Survey of Casino Entertainment.'' [online] from http://www.americangaming.org [Accessed September 1, 2010], from state gaming regulatory agencies.

★ **3488** ★
Casinos
SIC: 7999; NAICS: 71321

Casinos (except Casino Hotels), 2007

Data show the percent of industry sales held by the largest 4, 8, 20 and 50 firms in the sector. There are approximately 300 firms operating in the industry generating employment for 111,240 people.

4 largest firms	15.9%
8 largest firms	27.0
20 largest firms	50.1
50 largest firms	75.6

Source: ''2007 Economic Census.'' [online] from http://www. census.gov/econ/concentration.html [Accessed August 12, 2011], from U.S. Bureau of the Census.

★ **3489** ★
Casinos
SIC: 7999; NAICS: 71321

Top Casino Firms in Macau, 2011

Market shares are shown based on revenues for June 2011.

SJM	29.0%
Venetian Macau	16.0

Galaxy Casino	15.0%
Wynn Resorts	15.0
Melco Crown	14.0
MGM Grand Paradise	11.0

Source: *Financial Times*, September 22, 2011, p. 18, from GBGC.

★ **3490** ★
Casinos
SIC: 7999; NAICS: 71321

Top Casinos in Detroit, MI, 2011

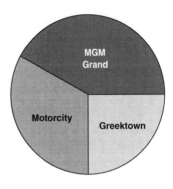

In March 2012, another casino was looking to open in the Detroit area. This move is not supported by the governor or by the casinos already established in the area. Casinos are ranked by revenues in millions of dollars.

	($ mil.)	Share
MGM Grand	$ 600	42.11%
Motorcity	472	33.12
Greektown	353	24.77

Source: *D Business*, March-April 2012, p. 37, from Michigan Gaming Control Board.

★ **3491** ★
Casinos
SIC: 7999; NAICS: 71321

Top Non-Hotel Casinos, 2011

The industry generated revenues of $15.5 billion. On-premises gaming (riverboat and barge casinos) claimed 69.3% of revenues, off-tracking betting (riverboat and barge casinos) 14.7%, cruise casinos 7.0% and other sectors 9%.

Penn National Gaming Inc.	15.4%
Caesars Entertainment Corp.	6.1

Continued on next page.

[Continued]
Casinos
SIC: 7999; NAICS: 71321

Top Non-Hotel Casinos, 2011

The industry generated revenues of $15.5 billion. On-premises gaming (riverboat and barge casinos) claimed 69.3% of revenues, off-tracking betting (riverboat and barge casinos) 14.7%, cruise casinos 7.0% and other sectors 9%.

Isle of Capri Casinos Inc.	6.1%
Other	72.4

Source: "Non-Hotel Casinos in the U.S." [online] from http://www/ibisworld.com [Published August 2011], from IBIS-World.

★ 3492 ★
Concessions
SIC: 7999; NAICS: 71399

Concession Operators of Amusement Devices and Rides, 2007

Data show the percent of industry sales held by the largest 4, 8, 20 and 50 firms in the sector. There are approximately 587 firms operating in the industry generating employment for 4,059 people.

4 largest firms	21.6%
8 largest firms	29.6
20 largest firms	41.8
50 largest firms	57.3

Source: "2007 Economic Census." [online] from http://www.census.gov/econ/concentration.html [Accessed August 12, 2011], from U.S. Bureau of the Census.

★ 3493 ★
Gambling
SIC: 7999; NAICS: 71321

Gambling Industry, 2004-2009

Figures are in billions of dollars.

2007	$ 92.3
2008	91.6
2006	90.9
2009	88.2
2005	84.7
2004	78.6

Source: "Market Overview 2011 Global Gaming Bulletin." [online] from http://www.ey.com [Accessed February 20, 2012], from American Gaming Association.

★ 3494 ★
Gambling
SIC: 7999; NAICS: 71321

Gambling Market in France, 2009-2010

The French gaming market is dominated by the state-owned La Francaise des Jeux (FDJ), the national lottery, and the Pari Mutuel Urbain (PMU), which focuses on horse racing and sports betting. The casino market is very concentrated with 60% of gross gaming revenues claimed by Groupe Lucien Barriere and Partouche.

	2009	2010
La Francaise des Jeux	$ 4,924	$ 5,027
Pari Mutuel Urbain	3,137	3,188
Casinos	3,127	3,064
New online operators	0	381

Source: "Market Overview 2011 Global Gaming Bulletin." [online] from http://www.ey.com [Accessed February 20, 2012], from various company websites.

★ 3495 ★
Gambling
SIC: 7999; NAICS: 71321

Gambling Market in Germany, 2010

The industry was valued at $13.7 billion.

Gaming machines	38.0%
National lottery	37.0
Betting	19.0
Casinos	6.0

Source: "Market Overview 2011 Global Gaming Bulletin." [online] from http://www.ey.com [Accessed February 20, 2012], from FERI, DeSIA, DLTB and VDAI, Goldmedia, Ifo-Institute.

★ 3496 ★
Gambling
SIC: 7999; NAICS: 71321

Government-Owned Gambling Market in Canada, 2009-2010

Canada's gaming industry operates exclusively under the control of the provincial and territorial governments. Casino style gambling is available in all provinces except for New Brunswick, Price Edward Island and Newfoundland and Labrador. Total revenues exceed $16 billion annually.

Casinos	41.0%
E GM	31.0
Lotteries	24.0

Continued on next page.

★ 3496 ★

[Continued]

Gambling

SIC: 7999; NAICS: 71321

Government-Owned Gambling Market in Canada, 2009-2010

Canada's gaming industry operates exclusively under the control of the provincial and territorial governments. Casino style gambling is available in all provinces except for New Brunswick, Price Edward Island and Newfoundland and Labrador. Total revenues exceed $16 billion annually.

Bingo	2.0%
Horse racing	2.0

Source: "Market Overview 2011 Global Gaming Bulletin." [online] from http://www.ey.com [Accessed February 20, 2012], from *Canadian Gambling Digest, 2009-2010.*

★ 3497 ★

Online Ticketing

SIC: 7999; NAICS: 71131

Top Online Event Ticket Firms, 2012

There are a total of 265 businesses in the industry, generating $3.2 billion in revenues. Concert online ticket sales claimed 52.3% of the total, sporting event online ticket sales 21.1%, theater and opera ticket sales 14.3% and fairs and pageants 12.3%.

Live Nation Entertainment Inc.	33.0%
eBay Inc. (Stubhub.com)	20.9
Other	46.1

Source: "Online Event Ticket Sales in the U.S." [online] from http://www.ibisworld.com [Published February 2012], from IBISWorld.

★ 3498 ★

Skating Rinks

SIC: 7999; NAICS: 71399

Roller Skating Rinks, 2007

Data show the percent of industry sales held by the largest 4, 8, 20 and 50 firms in the sector. There are approximately 1,302 firms operating in the industry generating employment for 13,587 people.

4 largest firms	5.7%
8 largest firms	8.2
20 largest firms	13.1
50 largest firms	22.3

Source: "2007 Economic Census." [online] from http://www.census.gov/econ/concentration.html [Accessed August 12, 2011], from U.S. Bureau of the Census.

★ 3499 ★

Ski and Snowboard Resorts

SIC: 7999; NAICS: 71392

Leading Ski and Snowboard Resort Firms, 2010

The industry generated revenues of $2.4 billion. Lift tickets generated 50.5% of revenues, food and beverage sales 12.3%, snowsports instruction 8.9%, Season pass sales 7.3%, merchandise sales 5.9% and equipment rental 5.6%. Market shares are estimated.

Vail Resorts Inc.	24.0%
Booth Creek Ski Holdings Inc.	4.8
Boyne USA Resorts	4.1
Aspen Skiing Company	2.0
Crested Butte Mountain Resort Inc.	1.5
Other	63.6

Source: "Ski & Snowboard Resorts in the U.S." [online] from http://www.ibisworld.com [Published December 2010], from IBISWorld.

★ 3500 ★

Sports and Recreation Instruction

SIC: 7999; NAICS: 61162

Sports and Recreation Instruction, 2007

Data show the percent of industry sales held by the largest 4, 8, 20 and 50 firms in the sector. There are approximately 12,292 firms operating in the industry generating employment for 80,085 people.

4 largest firms	4.0%
8 largest firms	5.3
20 largest firms	7.9
50 largest firms	12.4

Source: "2007 Economic Census." [online] from http://www.census.gov/econ/concentration.html [Accessed August 12, 2011], from U.S. Bureau of the Census.

★ 3501 ★
Sports and Recreation Instruction
SIC: 7999; NAICS: 61162

Sports Coaching Industry, 2008

The industry was valued at $5.2 billion in 2009. Those 13-18 years of age represented 45% of the users of coaching services, those over 18 years of age 30% and those under 13 years of age 25%.

Recreational sports instruction	50.0%
Intensive sports instruction	30.0
Sports camps	20.0

Source: ''Sports Coaching in the U.S.'' [online] from http://www.maricopa-sbdc.com/Research%20Reports [Published August 18, 2008], from IBISWorld.

★ 3502 ★

Doctors

SIC: 8011; NAICS: 621111

Leading Specialties for Doctors, 2011

There were a total of 985,000 physicians in the United States in 2011. Specialty doctors claimed 67% of the total, with primary care doctors claiming the remaining 33%.

Internal medicine	13.0%
Pediatrics	6.0
Anesthesiology	4.0
Obstetrics and gynecology	4.0
Dermatology and cosmetic surgery	3.0
Emergency medicine	3.0
General surgery	3.0
Other	31.0

Source: "Primer: Physicians." [online] from http://americanactionforum.org [Published September 2011], from IBISWorld.

★ 3503 ★

Doctors

SIC: 8011; NAICS: 621111

Number of Physician Offices, 2000-2008

According to the Census, this industry comprises establishments of health practitioners "having the degree of M.D. (Doctor of medicine) or D.O. (Doctor of osteopathy) primarily engaged in the independent practice of general or specialized medicine (e.g., anesthesiology, oncology, ophthalmology, psychiatry) or surgery. These practitioners operate private or group practices in their own offices (e.g., centers, clinics) or in the facilities of others, such as hospitals or HMO medical centers." An estimated 2.1 million people were employed in this industry in 2008.

2008	192,312
2007	191,961
2006	190,876
2005	189,562
2004	187,558
2003	184,261
2002	179,583

2001	177,127
2000	174,006

Source: "Statistics of U.S. Business." [online] from http://www.census.gov [Accessed May 1, 2012], from U.S. Department of Commerce.

★ 3504 ★

Dentists

SIC: 8021; NAICS: 62121

Dental Practice Revenues, 2011

There were approximately 154,000 practices in the United States, generating revenues of $107.6 billion. Revenues are expected to climb to $130 billion by 2016, boosted by favorable demographics and new technology.

Examinations	20.0%
Radiographs	20.0
Caries treatment	18.0
Cleanings	18.0
Oral surgery	8.5
Fluoride/sealant applications	8.0
Periodontal treatments	4.5
Prosthodontics/orthodontics	3.0

Source: "Industry Perspective." [online] from http://www.burkhartdental.com/sites/default/files/files/news/dental_offices_9_2011.pdf [Accessed April 1, 2012], from IBISWorld.

★ 3505 ★

Dentists

SIC: 8021; NAICS: 62121

Number of Dentist Offices, 2000-2008

According to the Census, this industry comprises establishments of health practitioners "having the degree of D.M.D. (Doctor of Dental Medicine), D.D.S. (Doctor of Dental Surgery), or D.D.Sc. (Doctor of Dental Science) primarily engaged in the independent practice of general or specialized dentistry or dental surgery." A total of 835,884 people were employed in this industry in 2008.

2008	121,686
2007	120,676

Continued on next page.

★ 3505 ★

[Continued]

Dentists

SIC: 8021; NAICS: 62121

Number of Dentist Offices, 2000-2008

According to the Census, this industry comprises establishments of health practitioners "having the degree of D.M.D. (Doctor of Dental Medicine), D.D.S. (Doctor of Dental Surgery), or D.D.Sc. (Doctor of Dental Science) primarily engaged in the independent practice of general or specialized dentistry or dental surgery." A total of 835,884 people were employed in this industry in 2008.

2006	119,471
2005	118,163
2004	116,559
2003	114,768
2002	113,128
2001	112,802
2000	112,373

Source: "Statistics of U.S. Business." [online] from http://www.census.gov [Accessed May 1, 2012], from U.S. Department of Commerce.

★ 3506 ★

Chiropractors

SIC: 8041; NAICS: 62131

Leading Services Provided by Chiropractors, 2010

There were a total of 56,524 practices in the United States, which generated revenues of $12.5 billion.

Manual manipulation for back pain	25.0%
Extremity manipulating and adjusting	20.0
Rehabilitation	20.0
Non-manual procedures for back pain	15.0
Manual manipulation for neck pain	11.0
Non-manual procedures for neck pain	9.0

Source: "Chiropractor Marketing Report." [online] from http://thrivehive.com/pdf/ThriveHive_The_Chiropractor_Marketing_Report.pdf [Accessed April 1, 2012], from IBISWorld.

★ 3507 ★

Chiropractors

SIC: 8041; NAICS: 62131

Number of Chiropractor Offices, 2000-2008

According to the Census, this industry comprises establishments of health practitioners "having the degree of D.C. (Doctor of chiropractic) primarily engaged in the independent practice of chiropractic. These practitioners provide diagnostic and therapeutic treatment of neuromusculoskeletal and related disorders through the manipulation and adjustment of the spinal column and extremities, and operate private or group practices in their own offices (e.g., centers, clinics) or in the facilities of others, such as hospitals or HMO medical centers." A total of 122,685 people were employed in this industry in 2008.

2007	37,401
2008	37,059
2006	36,907
2005	36,775
2004	36,005
2003	35,085
2002	33,738
2001	32,682
2000	31,807

Source: "Statistics of U.S. Business." [online] from http://www.census.gov [Accessed May 1, 2012], from U.S. Department of Commerce.

★ 3508 ★

Optometrists

SIC: 8042; NAICS: 62132

Number of Optometrists Offices, 2000-2008

According to the Census, this industry comprises "establishments of health practitioners having the degree of O.D. (Doctor of optometry) primarily engaged in the independent practice of optometry. These practitioners provide eye examinations to determine visual acuity or the presence of vision problems and to prescribe eyeglasses, contact lenses, and eye exercises. They operate private or group practices in their own offices (e.g., centers, clinics) or in the facilities of others, such as hospitals or HMO medical centers, and may also provide the same service as opticians, such as selling and fitting prescription eyeglasses and contact lenses." A total of 107,377 people were employed in this industry in 2008.

2008	18,698
2007	18,495
2006	18,204

Continued on next page.

★ 3508 ★

[Continued]

Optometrists

SIC: 8042; NAICS: 62132

Number of Optometrists Offices, 2000-2008

According to the Census, this industry comprises "establishments of health practitioners having the degree of O.D. (Doctor of optometry) primarily engaged in the independent practice of optometry. These practitioners provide eye examinations to determine visual acuity or the presence of vision problems and to prescribe eyeglasses, contact lenses, and eye exercises. They operate private or group practices in their own offices (e.g., centers, clinics) or in the facilities of others, such as hospitals or HMO medical centers, and may also provide the same service as opticians, such as selling and fitting prescription eyeglasses and contact lenses." A total of 107,377 people were employed in this industry in 2008.

2005	18,008
2004	17,674
2003	17,272
2002	17,127
2001	16,582
2000	16,499

Source: "Statistics of U.S. Business." [online] from http://www.census.gov [Accessed May 1, 2012], from U.S. Department of Commerce.

★ 3509 ★

Optometrists

SIC: 8042; NAICS: 62132

Sources of Optometrist Revenues, 2010

The industry is shown based on sector. Growth in the Optometrists industry persisted through the economic recession, mainly due to resilient demand from the aging population and eye diseases associated with diabetes and computer use. During the five years to 2012, revenue is expected to increase at an annualized rate of 2.9% to $14.0 billion.

Prescription eyewear	43.0%
Eye exams	22.0
Medical eye exams	17.0
Contact lenses	16.0
Other	2.0

Source: "Assessing Optometric Practice Performance." [online] from http://www.sunburstoptics.com/document_center/Practice_Management_Tools/Key_Metrics_2011.pdf [Accessed May 1, 2012], from Jobson Optical.

★ 3510 ★

Podiatrists

SIC: 8043; NAICS: 621391

Number of Podiatrist Offices, 2000-2008

According to the Census, this industry comprises establishments of health practitioners "having the degree of D.P.M. (Doctor of Podiatric Medicine) primarily engaged in the independent practice of podiatry. These practitioners diagnose and treat diseases and deformities of the foot and operate private or group practices in their own offices (e.g., centers, clinics) or in the facilities of others, such as hospitals or HMO medical centers." There were 36,867 people employed in this industry in 2008.

2005	8,177
2006	8,172
2007	8,163
2004	8,135
2008	8,113
2003	8,106
2002	7,912
2000	7,902
2001	7,883

Source: "Statistics of U.S. Business." [online] from http://www.census.gov [Accessed May 1, 2012], from U.S. Department of Commerce.

★ 3511 ★

Podiatrists

SIC: 8043; NAICS: 621391

Top Sources of Revenues for Podiatrists, 2010

There were a total of 12,412 businesses operating in the industry, generating revenues of $4.4 billion. Demand for services is expected to grow with the aging of the population as well as from the increase in diabetes, obesity and other diseases.

Patient care - musculoskeletal and connective tissue	34.0%
Patient care - skin and subcutaneous care	23.0
Patient care - injuries and adverse effects	8.0
Other	35.0

Source: "Podiatrists in the U.S." [online] from http://www.physiciansbusinessacademy.com/wp-content/uploads/2011/04/Podiatrists-in-the-US-Industry-Report.pdf [Published June 2010], from IBISWorld.

★ 3512 ★
Nursing Care
SIC: 8051; NAICS: 62311

Top Nursing Care Firms, 2010

There are approximately 16,000 Medicare nursing homes in the United States with 1.7 million beds and 1.6 million residents. Approximately half of all Americans over 65 years of age will be admitted to a nursing home at least once. One out of four over the age of 85 currently reside there. The average annual cost of a private room in a nursing home is $77,000.

HCR ManorCare	3.0%
Kindred Healthcare	1.9
Golden Living	1.7
Life Care Centers of America	1.5
Genesis Healthcare	1.1
Other	90.8

Source: "Long-Term Care Market." [online] from http://www.docin.com [Published March 2012], from Kalorama Information.

★ 3513 ★
Hospice Care
SIC: 8052; NAICS: 623311

Top Hospice Care Firms, 2010

The hospice industry began in the United States in 1974 with the opening of the first hospice in Connecticut. In 2011, there were more than 35,000 Medicare-approved facilities. They cared for more than 1.2 million people.

Vitas Healthcare	6.6%
Gentiva	4.4
HCR ManorCare	1.9
Sunrise	1.5
Golden Living	1.3
Other	84.3

Source: "Long-Term Care Market." [online] from http://www.docin.com [Published March 2012], from Kalorama Information.

★ 3514 ★
Hospitals
SIC: 8060; NAICS: 62211

Largest Catholic Health Care Systems, 2010

Hospitals are ranked by number of acute-care beds.

Ascension Health	12,579
Catholic Health Initiatives	7,855
Catholic Healthcare West	7,658
Providence Health & Services	7,000
Catholic Health East	6,272

Trinity Health	5,546
Christus Health	5,236
Catholic Health Partners	4,289
Sisters of Mercy Health System	3,603
SSM Health Care	2,936

Source: *Modern Healthcare*, June 6, 2011, p. 29, from *Modern Healthcare's 2011 Hospital Systems Survey.*

★ 3515 ★
Hospitals
SIC: 8060; NAICS: 62211

Largest For-Profit Health Care Systems, 2010

Hospitals are ranked by number of acute-care beds.

HCA	41,472
Community Health Systems	19,372
Tenet Healthcare Corp.	13,428
Health Management Associates	8,864
LifePoint Hospitals	5,915
Universal Health Services	5,689
Vanguard Health Systems	4,135
Iasis Healthcare	2,877
Prime Healthcare Services	2,365
Capella Healthcare	1,507

Source: *Modern Healthcare*, September 5, 2011, p. 40, from *Modern Healthcare's 2011 Hospital Systems Survey.*

★ 3516 ★
Hospitals
SIC: 8060; NAICS: 62211

Largest Health Care Systems, 2010

Hospitals are ranked by number of acute-care beds.

U.S. Department of Veteran Affairs	17,300
Carolinas HealthCare System	2,772
Jackson Health System	1,724
LSU Health System	1,496
Broward Health	1,378
Lee Memorial Health System	1,258
WellStar Health System	1,143
Huntsville Hospital	1,040
Harris County Hospital District	789
West Tennessee Healthcare	764

Source: *Modern Healthcare*, June 6, 2011, p. 29, from *Modern Healthcare's 2011 Hospital Systems Survey.*

★ 3517 ★

Hospitals

SIC: 8060; NAICS: 62211

Largest Hospitals, 2010

Hospitals are ranked by number of staffed beds.

New York-Presbyterian Hospital	2,249
Florida Hospital	2,084
Central Texas Veterans Healthcare System	1,852
Jackson Health System	1,765
Clarian Health Partners	1,534
Montefiore Medical Center	1,490
UPMC Presbyterian	1,487
Methodist Hospital	1,452
Orlando Regional Medical Center	1,437
Veterans Affairs Greater Los Angeles Health Care System	1,327

Source: *Modern Healthcare*, April 18, 2011, p. 34, from American Hospital Association.

★ 3518 ★

Behavioral Health

SIC: 8063; NAICS: 62221

Leading Behavioral Health Providers, 2010

Companies are ranked by net patient revenues in millions of dollars.

Universal Health Services	$ 1,757.2
Devereux	362.6
Aurora Behavioral Health Care	121.1
Sheppard Pratt Health Systems	109.1
Partners HealthCare	94.1
Texas Department of State Health Services	67.4
Alexian Brothers Health System	58.1
SharpHealthCare	57.4
HCA	54.8
EMHS	48.9

Source: *Modern Healthcare*, February 20, 2012, p. 34, from Billian's HealthData.

★ 3519 ★

Rehabilitation Hospitals

SIC: 8069; NAICS: 62231

Largest Rehabilitation Providers, 2010

Companies are ranked by number of staffed beds.

Select Medical Holdings Corp.	492
Vibra Healthcare	336
Carolinas Rehabilitation	172
Good Shepherd Rehabilitation Network	164
Brooks Rehabilitation	157
UPMC Community Provider Services	157

National Rehabilitation Hospital	137
Keman Orthopaedics and Rehabilitation	104

Source: *Modern Healthcare*, December 12, 2011, p. 33, from *Modern Healthcare's 2011 Post-Acute-Care Survey*.

★ 3520 ★

Rehabilitation Hospitals

SIC: 8069; NAICS: 62231

Top Rehabilitation Hospitals in Detroit, MI, 2011

Market shares are shown based on inpatient rehabs for the first six months of the year.

Henry Ford Hospital	19.7%
St. John Providence Health System	14.0
Detroit Medical Center, Beaumont Health System, Oakwood Healthcare	9.3
Other	57.0

Source: *Crain's Detroit Business*, January 22, 2012, p. NA, from Michigan Inpatient Database.

★ 3521 ★

Dental Laboratories

SIC: 8072; NAICS: 339116

Dental Laboratories, 2007

Data show the percent of industry sales held by the largest 4, 8, 20 and 50 firms in the sector. There are approximately 7,051 firms operating in the industry generating employment for 52,617 people.

4 largest companies	18.0%
8 largest companies	23.9
20 largest companies	29.3
50 largest companies	36.2

Source: "2007 Economic Census." [online] from http://www.census.gov/econ/concentration.html [Accessed August 12, 2011], from U.S. Bureau of the Census.

★ 3522 ★

Home Health Care

SIC: 8082; NAICS: 62161

Top Home Health Care Firms, 2010

Home health care has become an attractive option to seniors who need assistance but not full-time nursing care. Most users have cardiac or respiratory issues or suffer from mental health problems or diabetes.

Apria Healthcare Group	2.6%
Lincare	2.2
Amedisys	1.8

Continued on next page.

★ 3522 ★

[Continued]

Home Health Care

SIC: 8082; NAICS: 62161

Top Home Health Care Firms, 2010

Home health care has become an attractive option to seniors who need assistance but not full-time nursing care. Most users have cardiac or respiratory issues or suffer from mental health problems or diabetes.

Gentiva	1.1%
Manor Care	0.4
Other	91.9

Source: "Long-Term Care Market." [online] from http://www. docin.com [Published March 2012], from Kalorama Information.

★ 3523 ★

Dialysis Industry

SIC: 8092; NAICS: 621492

Top Dialysis Providers, 2010

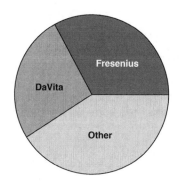

Market shares are shown in percent.

Fresenius	33.0%
DaVita	26.0
Other	41.0

Source: *Los Angeles Times*, November 18, 2011, p. NA.

★ 3524 ★

Dialysis Industry

SIC: 8092; NAICS: 621492

Top Dialysis Providers in China, 2009

Market shares are estimated.

Fresenius	40.0%
Nipro	10.0

Gambro	8.0%
Other	42.0

Source: "China Healthcare Sector." [online] from http://download.bioon.com.cn/upload/201105/17235814_9161.pdf [Published December 3, 2010], from Citi Investment Research.

★ 3525 ★

Outpatient Mental Health & Substance Abuse Centers

SIC: 8093; NAICS: 62142

Outpatient Mental Health and Substance Abuse Centers, 2007

Data show the percent of industry sales held by the largest 4, 8, 20 and 50 firms in the sector. There are approximately 8,848 firms operating in the industry generating employment for 193,583 people.

4 largest firms	3.7%
8 largest firms	5.8
20 largest firms	9.7
50 largest firms	17.3

Source: "2007 Economic Census." [online] from http://www. census.gov/econ/concentration.html [Accessed August 12, 2011], from U.S. Bureau of the Census.

★ 3526 ★

Blood and Organ Banks

SIC: 8099; NAICS: 621991

Top Blood and Organ Banks, 2011

Market shares are estimated based on $10.5 billion in revenues. There are 329 businesses operating in this sector providing employment to 83,746 people.

American Red Cross	22.0%
Musculoskeletal Transplant Foundation Inc.	3.0
Community Blood Center & Community Tissue Services	2.5
CSL Ltd.	2.5
Other	70.0

Source: "Blood and Organ Banks in the U.S." [online] from http://www.ibisworld.com [Published November 2011], from IBISWorld.

★ 3527 ★
Emergency Department Contractors
SIC: 8099; NAICS: 621999

Leading Emergency Department Contractors, 2010

Firms are ranked by number of national healthcare clients.

EmCare	393
TeamHealth	296
Schumacher Group	163
Hospital Physician Partners	112
Emergency Consultants	108
CEP America	72
Emergency Medicine Physicians	61
Premier Health Care Services	39
Emergency Physicians Medical Group	37
Emergency Service Partners	22

Source: *Modern Healthcare's By the Numbers*, Annual 2011-2012, p. 38, from *Modern Healthcare's 2011 Outsourcing Survey*.

★ 3528 ★
Family Planning Centers
SIC: 8099; NAICS: 62141

Number of Family Planning Centers, 2000-2008

According to the Census, this industry comprises establishments "with medical staff primarily engaged in providing a range of family planning services on an outpatient basis, such as contraceptive services, genetic and prenatal counseling, voluntary sterilization, and therapeutic and medically induced termination of pregnancy." A total of 21,550 people were employed in this industry in 2008.

2008	1,409
2007	1,382
2006	1,165
2005	1,141
2004	1,095
2002	1,090
2003	1,073
2001	1,013
2000	992

Source: "Statistics of U.S. Business." [online] from http://www.census.gov [Accessed May 1, 2012], from U.S. Department of Commerce.

★ 3529 ★
Medical Case Management
SIC: 8099; NAICS: 621999

Medical Case Management, 2007

Data show the percent of industry sales held by the largest 4, 8, 20 and 50 firms in the sector. There are approximately 1,940 firms operating in the industry generating employment for 42,986 people.

4 largest firms	28.4%
8 largest firms	40.9
20 largest firms	55.3
50 largest firms	70.5

Source: "2007 Economic Census." [online] from http://www.census.gov/econ/concentration.html [Accessed August 12, 2011], from U.S. Bureau of the Census.

★ 3530 ★

Legal Services

SIC: 8111; NAICS: 54111

Legal Aid Societies and Similar Legal Services, 2007

Data show the percent of industry sales held by the largest 4, 8, 20 and 50 firms in the sector. There are approximately 2,236 firms operating in the industry generating employment for 27,374 people.

4 largest firms	14.0%
8 largest firms	18.2
20 largest firms	26.7
50 largest firms	40.2

Source: ''2007 Economic Census.'' [online] from http://www.census.gov/econ/concentration.html [Accessed August 12, 2011], from U.S. Bureau of the Census.

★ 3531 ★

Legal Services

SIC: 8111; NAICS: 54111

Top Legal Firms, 2010

Firms are ranked by revenues in millions of dollars.

Baker & McKenzie (verein)	$ 2.10
Skadden	2.10
DLA Piper (verin)	1.96
Latham & Watkins	1.93
Hogan Lovells (verein)	1.66
Kirkland & Ellis	1.63
Jones Day	1.62
Sidley Austin	1.34
White & Case	1.28
Greenberg & Traurig	1.24

Source: *American Lawyer*, April 2011, p. NA.

SIC 82 - Educational Services

★ 3532 ★
Education
SIC: 8211; NAICS: 61111

Education Sector, 2011

There are 100,136 public schools operating in the United States, according to the source. Revenues have increased in the education sector, due largely to the Obama administration's American Recovery and Reinvestment Act. Public schools continue to face many challenges, with increased class sizes, budget issues, teacher layoffs and threats from alternatives such as charter schools. An estimated 50 million students are believed to be in elementary and secondary schools.

Regular education	89.9%
Alternative education	6.6
Special education	2.2
Vocation education	1.3

Source: "Public Schools in the U.S." [online] from http://www.ibisworld.com [Published February 2011], from IBISWorld.

★ 3533 ★
Fine Arts Schools
SIC: 8211; NAICS: 61111

Top Fine Arts Schools, 2011

During the recession, reduced consumer incomes and business sentiment hurt enrollment and revenue at fine art schools. While the recovering economy should also benefit fine arts schools, the schools are emphasizing corporate and philanthropic donations. The schools generated revenues of $3.7 billion. Combined schools claimed 52%, music schools 40%, visual art schools 5%, dance studios 2% and theater schools 1%.

Art Institute of Chicago	4.6%
Carnegie Mellon	4.4
Juillard School	1.8
New England Conservatory	0.5
Other	88.7

Source: "Fine Art Schools in the U.S." [online] from http://www.ibisworld.com [Published July 2011], from IBISWorld.

★ 3534 ★
Schools
SIC: 8211; NAICS: 61111

Charter School Enrollment, 2010-2011

Data show the places with the highest percentages of charter school enrollment.

New Orleans, LA	70.0%
Washington D.C.	39.0
Detroit, MI	37.0
Kansas City, MO	35.0
Flint, MI	32.0
Gary, IN	30.0
St. Louis, MO	29.0
Dayton, OH	27.0
Youngstown, OH	24.0
Albany, NY	23.0
Cleveland, OH	23.0
Toledo, OH	23.0

Source: "NAPCS Report: Charter School Market Share Climbs." [online] from http://www.charterschoolcenter.org [Published Ocotber 17, 2011], from National Alliance for Public Charter Schools.

★ 3535 ★
Schools
SIC: 8211; NAICS: 61111

Largest School Districts, 2009-2010

Schools are ranked by enrollment.

New York City, NY	1,038,741
Los Angeles Unified, CA	670,746
Chicago, IL	407,157
Miami-Dade County	345,804
Clark County, NV	307,059
Broward County, FL	256,137
Houston, TX	202,773
Hillsborough County, FL	193,265
Hawaii	180,196
Orange County, FL	173,259

Source: *American School & University*, September 2011, p. NA.

★ 3536 ★
Colleges and Universities
SIC: 8221; NAICS: 61131

Largest Colleges and Universities, 2009-2010

Institutions are ranked by enrollment.

University of Phoenix	380,232
Kaplan University	71,011
Arizona State University	68,064
Miami Dade College	59,120
Ohio State University	55,014
Houston Community College	54,942
Strayer University	54,325
University of Central Florida	53,401
University of Texas at Austin	51,659
University of Minnesota	50,995

Source: *American School & University*, September 2011, p. NA.

★ 3537 ★
For-Profit Education
SIC: 8221; NAICS: 61131

For-Profit Education Enrollment, 2011

For-profit college saw their enrollments plunge in 2011. One reason is that these colleges have pulled back on recruitment because of high student loan default rates. Another reason is that some critics have questioned the value of a degree that costs considerably more than what is available at local community colleges. Although they enroll about 12% of all post-secondary students, for-profit education companies receive 25% of federal aid for such students. The aid represents up to 90% of revenues for some companies.

University of Phoenix	398,400
Corinthian Colleges	102,450
Kaplan Higher Education	78,534
DeVry University	64,317

Source: *Wall Street Journal*, August 23, 2011, p. B1, from company reports.

★ 3538 ★
Libraries
SIC: 8231; NAICS: 51912

Largest Libraries, 2009

Libraries are ranked by millions of volumes.

Library of Congress	33.5
Boston Public Library	24.0
New York Public Library	16.6
Harvard University	16.5
University of Illinois Urbana-Champaign . . .	12.7

Yale University	12.5
University of California - Berkeley	11.0
Columbia University	10.4
University of Texas - Austin	9.8
University of Michigan	9.5

Source: "Nation's Largest Libraries." [online] from http://www.ala.org [Accessed December 1, 2011], from American Library Association.

★ 3539 ★
Libraries
SIC: 8231; NAICS: 51912

Largest Patent Libraries, 2010

The Patent and Trademark Resource Center Program is a USPTO designation for libraries to provide public access to patent and trademark documents. The program dates back to 1871, when it was created by federal statute. All participating libraries hold at least 20 years of U.S. patents. Libraries are ranked by millions of visitors.

Boston Public Library	24.0
New York Public Library	16.6
University of Texas at Austin Library	9.8
University of Michigan Library	9.5
Public Library of Cincinnati and Hamilton County	8.9

Source: "Top 5: Largest Patent Resource Libraries." [online] from http://info.articleonepartners.com [Published October 28, 2011].

★ 3540 ★
Libraries
SIC: 8231; NAICS: 51912

Libraries by Type, 2009

There are an estimated 122,105 libraries of various kinds in the United States.

	Types	Share
School	99,180	81.23%
Public	9,225	7.55
Special	8,476	6.94
Academic	3,827	3.13
Government	1,113	0.91
Armed Forces	284	0.23

Source: "Number of Libraries in the United States." [online] from http://www.ala.org [Accessed November 1, 2011], from American Library Association.

★ 3541 ★
Apprenticeship Training
SIC: 8299; NAICS: 611512

Apprenticeship Training, 2007

Data show the percent of industry sales held by the largest 4, 8, 20 and 50 firms in the sector. There are approximately 1,496 firms operating in the industry generating employment for 14,745 people.

4 largest firms	10.2%
8 largest firms	15.4
20 largest firms	27.1
50 largest firms	42.3

Source: "2007 Economic Census." [online] from http://www.census.gov/econ/concentration.html [Accessed August 12, 2011], from U.S. Bureau of the Census.

★ 3542 ★
Educational Services
SIC: 8299; NAICS: 611691

Leading Children's Educational Service Franchises, 2011

Companies are ranked by number of locations.

Goddard Systems Inc.	386
Huntington Learning Centers	280
Tutor Doctor	268

Source: *Entrepreneur*, January 2012, p. 148.

★ 3543 ★
Language Instruction
SIC: 8299; NAICS: 61163

Language Instruction Industry, 2010

The industry generated revenues of $1.0 billion in 2010. Foreign language instruction claimed 75% of the total, English instruction claimed 20% and sign language 5%. A total of 10,382 establishments were operating in 2010.

Benesse Corp.	14.6%
Rosetta Stone Inc.	3.6
Global English Corp.	2.6
Other	79.2

Source: "Language Instruction in the U.S." [online] from http://www.ibisworld.com [Published August 2010], from IBISWorld.

★ 3544 ★
Test Preparation
SIC: 8299; NAICS: 61171

SAT Prep Market in China, 2010

In 2009-2010, China surpassed South Korea to become America's largest source of foreign undergraduates, with 39,921 Chinese students attending U.S. colleges and universities. New Oriental is one of the leaders in prepping these students for U.S. colleges. In addition to its 90% share of the SAT prep market, it controls three-quarters of the TOEFL (Test of English as a Second Language) market.

New Oriental	90.0%
Other	10.0

Source: *BusinessWeek*, May 5, 2011, p. NA.

SIC 83 - Social Services

★ 3545 ★
Community Food Services
SIC: 8322; NAICS: 62421

Community Food Services, 2007

Data show the percent of industry sales held by the largest 4, 8, 20 and 50 firms in the sector. There are approximately 4,215 firms operating in the industry generating employment for 32,048 people.

4 largest firms	7.2%
8 largest firms	11.7
20 largest firms	21.9
50 largest firms	38.8

Source: ''2007 Economic Census.'' [online] from http://www.census.gov/econ/concentration.html [Accessed August 12, 2011], from U.S. Bureau of the Census.

★ 3546 ★
Job Training and Career Counseling
SIC: 8331; NAICS: 62431

Job Training and Career Counseling, 2011

The industry generated revenues of $13.1 billion. Services for adults claimed 45% of the total, services for youth 30% and services for the disabled 25%. Nonprofits and government agencies represent 85.3% of the businesses operating in this industry. Market shares are estimated.

Raytheon Company	10.8%
ResCare	2.6
Other	86.6

Source: ''Job Training & Career Counseling in the U.S.'' [online] from http://www.ibisworld.com [Published April 2011], from IBISWorld.

★ 3547 ★
Vocational Rehabilitation Services
SIC: 8331; NAICS: 62431

Vocational Rehabilitation Services, 2007

Data show the percent of industry sales held by the largest 4, 8, 20 and 50 firms in the sector. There are approximately 7,631 firms operating in the industry generating employment for 303,713 people.

4 largest firms	5.6%
8 largest firms	8.8
20 largest firms	16.2
50 largest firms	25.7

Source: ''2007 Economic Census.'' [online] from http://www.census.gov/econ/concentration.html [Accessed August 12, 2011], from U.S. Bureau of the Census.

★ 3548 ★
Child Care
SIC: 8351; NAICS: 62441

Top For-Profit Child Care Organizations in North America, 2010

Organizations are ranked by capacity.

KinderCare Learning Centers	218,300
Learning Care Group Inc.	156,110
Bright Horizons Family Solutions	80,000
Nobel Learning Communities Inc.	28,500
Child Development Schools	22,874
Phoenix Children's Academy	21,000
The Sunshine House	20,023
Minnieland Private Day School Inc.	13,184
New Horizon Academy	13,032
CCLC Inc.	12,343
Children of America	9,000
Brightside Academy Inc.	7,840
Crème de la Crème	7,000
Children's Choice Learning Centers Inc.	6,902

Source: *Exchange*, January-February 2011, p. 30.

★ **3549** ★
Acute Care
SIC: 8361; NAICS: 623312
Top Post Acute-Care Firms, 2010

Firms are ranked by net revenues in millions of dollars.

Kindred Healthcare	$ 4,359.7
Golden Living	2,725.0
Genesis Healthcare	2,500.0
Select Medical Holdings Corp.	2,390.3
Brookdale Senior Living	2,213.3
Sun Healthcare Group	1,906.9
Amedisys	1,634.3
Sunrise Senior Living	1,406.7
Extendicare Health Services	1,347.6
Meridian Health	1,324.0

Source: *Modern Healthcare*, September 12, 2011, p. 32, from *Modern Healthcare's 2011 Post-Acute-Care Survey.*

★ **3550** ★
Adult Living Facilities
SIC: 8361; NAICS: 62399
Adult Living Facilities, 2010

The industry consisted of 20,278 establishments that provided employment to 659,887 people. It generated revenues of $37.8 billion.

Assisted living facilties	41.0%
Independent living facilities	37.0
Continuing care retirement communities	22.0

Source: "Adult Family Homes." [online] from http://www.pacificedc.org/./Adult%20Family%20Homes%20Snapshot.pdf [Published November 2010], from IBISWorld.

★ **3551** ★
Senior Living Services
SIC: 8361; NAICS: 623312
Largest Senior Living Providers, 2011

Companies are ranked by resident capacity as of January 1, 2011.

Emeritus Senior Living	51,725
Brookdale Senior Living	47,986
Holiday Retirement	36,863
Sunrise Senior Living	33,983
Life Care Services L.L.C.	25,963
Horizon Bay Retirement Communities	15,332
Atria Senior Living	14,249
Capital Senior Living	10,780
Five Star Senior Living	10,489
Assisted Living Concepts	9,305

Source: *Assisted Living Executive*, May/June 2011, p. 16.

★ **3552** ★
Charities
SIC: 8399; NAICS: 813311, 813312
Largest Charities, 2010

Organizations are ranked by revenues in billions of dollars.

YMCA of the USA	$ 5.91
Catholic Charities USA	4.66
United Way	4.22
Goodwill Industries International	4.04
American Red Cross	3.58
The Salvation Army	3.34
Habitat for Humanity International	1.54
Boys & Girls Clubs of America	1.49
Easter Seals	1.35
Boy Scouts of America	1.21

Source: *NonProfit Times*, November 1, 2011, p. 1.

★ **3553** ★
Charities
SIC: 8399; NAICS: 813311, 813312
Largest Health Care Foundations, 2009

Foundations are ranked by total awarded endowment in millions of dollars.

Bill & Melinda Gates Foundation	$ 1,689.9
Robert Wood Johnson Foundation	272.9
Susan Thompson Buffet Foundation	247.3
California Endowment	55.5
Community Foundation for Greater Atlanta	52.2
Doris Duke Charitable Foundation	52.1
Lincy Foundation	52.1
Robert W. Woodruff Foundation	51.3
Harold Simmons Foundation	51.2
Starr Foundation	50.7

Source: *Modern Healthcare*, October 17, 2011, p. 33, from Foundation Center.

★ **3554** ★
Charities
SIC: 8399; NAICS: 813311, 813312
Where Donations Went, 2010

A total of $290.9 billion was donated during the year.

	($ bil.)	Share
Religion	$ 100.63	34.59%
Education	41.67	14.33
Gifts to grantmaking foundations	33.00	11.34
Human services	26.49	9.11
Public society benefit	24.24	8.33
Health	22.83	7.85

Continued on next page.

★ 3554 ★

[Continued]

Charities

SIC: 8399; NAICS: 813311, 813312

Where Donations Went, 2010

A total of $290.9 billion was donated during the year.

	($ bil.)	Share
International affairs	$ 15.77	5.42%
Arts, culture and humanities . . .	13.28	4.57
Other	12.98	4.46

Source: *USA TODAY*, November 29, 2011, p. 8D, from *Giving USA*.

★ 3555 ★
Auction Houses
SIC: 8412; NAICS: 71211
Top Auction House Firms Worldwide, 2010

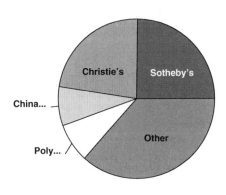

Market shares are shown based on lot sold. Paintings claimed 44.3% of lots sold, drawings 21.8%, prints 20.6%, sculpture 6.8%.

Sotheby's	25.0%
Christie's	23.0
China Guardian	8.0
Poly International	8.0
Other	37.0

Source: "Art Market Trends 2011." [online] from http://www.artmarket.com [Accessed April 1, 2012].

★ 3556 ★
Historical Sites
SIC: 8412; NAICS: 71212
Historical Sites, 2007

Data show the percent of industry sales held by the largest 4, 8, 20 and 50 firms in the sector. There are approximately 1,191 firms operating in the industry generating employment for 10,286 people.

4 largest firms	18.7%
8 largest firms	25.6
20 largest firms	37.7%
50 largest firms	55.7

Source: "2007 Economic Census." [online] from http://www.census.gov/econ/concentration.html [Accessed August 12, 2011], from U.S. Bureau of the Census.

★ 3557 ★
Museums
SIC: 8412; NAICS: 71211
Leading Art Museums Worldwide, 2011

Museums are ranked by millions of visitors.

Louvre (Paris)	8.88
Metropolitan Museum of Art (New York)	6.00
British Museum (London)	5.84
National Gallery (London)	5.25
Tate Modern (London)	4.80
National Gallery of Art (Washington D.C.)	4.39
National Palace Museum (Taipei)	3.84
Centre Pompidou (Paris)	3.61
National Museum of Korea (Seoul)	3.23
Musée D'Orsary (Paris)	3.15

Source: *Art Newspaper*, April 2012, p. 35.

★ 3558 ★
National Parks
SIC: 8422; NAICS: 71219
Top National Parks, 2011

Parks are ranked by millions of visitors.

Great Smoky Mountains National Park	9.00
Grand Canyon National Park	4.29
Yosemite National Park	3.95
Yellowstone National Park	3.39
Rock Mountain National Park	3.17
Olympic National Park	2.96
Zion National Park	2.82
Grand Teton National Park	2.58
Arcadia National Park	2.37
Cuyahoga Valley National Park	2.16

Source: "Ranking the National Parks by Visitation in 2011." [online] from http://www.nationalparkstraveler.com [Published March 8, 2012], from National Park Service.

★ 3559 ★
Tourist Attractions
SIC: 8422; NAICS: 71213

Top Tourist Attractions Worldwide, 2010

Data show the most-visited tourist attractions based on a survey of readers. Tourist attractions are defined as "cultural and historical sites, natural landmarks and officially designated spaces." This eliminates certain sites such as the Mall of America, which boasted 40 million visitors.

Times Square	39.2
Central Park, New York	38.0
Union Station, Washington D.C.	37.0
Las Vegas Strip	29.5
Niagara Falls	22.5
Grand Central Terminal, Manhattan	21.6
Faneuil Hall Marketplace, Boston	18.0
Walt Disney World's Magic Kingdom, Orlando	17.0
Disneyland Park, Anaheim CA	16.0
Grand Bazaar, Istanbul	15.0

Source: *USA TODAY*, September 30, 2011, p. 4D, from *Travel & Leisure*.

SIC 86 - Membership Organizations

★ 3560 ★
Business Associations
SIC: 8611; NAICS: 81391

Business Associations, 2007

Data show the percent of industry sales held by the largest 4, 8, 20 and 50 firms in the sector. There are approximately 17,028 firms operating in the industry generating employment for 116,055 people.

4 largest firms	5.4%
8 largest firms	9.1
20 largest firms	14.9
50 largest firms	23.5

Source: "2007 Economic Census." [online] from http://www.census.gov/econ/concentration.html [Accessed August 12, 2011], from U.S. Bureau of the Census.

★ 3561 ★
Unions
SIC: 8631; NAICS: 81393

Largest Unions, 2008

Unions are ranked by membership. Approximately 14.8 million workers are members of the United States in 2011, or 11.8% of workers. Men had higher membership rates than women (12.4% compared to 11.2%). California had the most union members, 2.4 million.

National Education Association of the United States	2,731,419
Service Employees International Union	1,505,100
American Federation of State, County and Municipal Employees	1,459,511
International Brotherhood of Teamsters	1,396,174
United Food and Commercial Workers International Union	1,311,548
American Federation of Teachers	828,512
United Steelworkers of America	754,978
International Brotherhood of Electrical Workers	704,798
Laborers' International Union of North America	669,772

Source: "National Labor Organizations." [online] from http://www.infoplease.com [Accessed March 19, 2012], from U.S. Department of Labor.

★ 3562 ★
Civic Organizations
SIC: 8641; NAICS: 81341

Civic and Social Organizations, 2007

Data show the percent of industry sales held by the largest 4, 8, 20 and 50 firms in the sector. There are approximately 25,870 firms operating in the industry generating employment for 188,072 people.

4 largest firms	3.0%
8 largest firms	4.7
20 largest firms	7.5
50 largest firms	11.6

Source: "2007 Economic Census." [online] from http://www.census.gov/econ/concentration.html [Accessed August 12, 2011], from U.S. Bureau of the Census.

★ 3563 ★
Twitter
SIC: 8641; NAICS: 81341

Twitter Users with the Most Followers, 2012

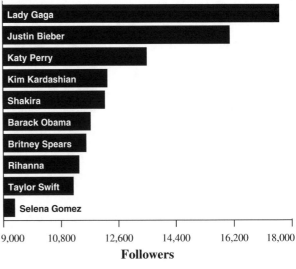

Data show number of followers as of January 4, 2012.

Lady Gaga	17,618
Justin Bieber	16,074
Katy Perry	13,487

Continued on next page.

★ 3563 ★
[Continued]
Twitter
SIC: 8641; NAICS: 81341

Twitter Users with the Most Followers, 2012

Data show number of followers as of January 4, 2012.

Kim Kardashian	12,260
Shakira	12,180
Barack Obama	11,715
Britney Spears	11,574
Rihanna	11,358
Taylor Swift	11,178
Selena Gomez	9,350

Source: *Junior Scholastic*, January 30, 2012, p. 29, from Twitaholic.com.

★ 3564 ★
Lobbying Groups
SIC: 8651; NAICS: 81394

Largest Lobbying Groups, 2011

There were 12,654 lobbyists in the United States in 2011. Total spending was $3.3 billion. Groups are ranked by spending in millions of dollars.

Patton Boggs L.P.	$ 47.6
Akin, Gump et al	37.9
Podesta Group	27.2
Van Scoyoc Associates	24.8
Brownstein, Hyatt et al	22.0
Ogilvy Government Relations	20.0
Cassidy & Associates	19.8
Holland & Knight	18.8
K&L Gates	18.7
Williams & Jensen	17.9

Source: "Top Lobbying Groups." [online] from http://www.opensecrets.org [Accessed April 3, 2012], from Center for Responsive Politics.

★ 3565 ★
Political Action Committees
SIC: 8651; NAICS: 81394

Top Political Action Committees, 2011

The largest political action committees are ranked by fundraising totals in millions of dollars.

American Crossroads (Karl-Rove founded Republican group)	$ 18.36
Restore Our Future (pro-Mitt Romney group)	17.94
Make Us Great Again (pro-Rick Perry group)	5.48
Priorities USA Action (pro-President Obama group)	4.40
American Bridge 21st Century (Democratic group)	$ 3.72
AFL-CIO Workers' Voice PAC (Democratic group)	3.70
House Majority PAC (Democratic group)	3.02
FreedomWorks for America (Republican group)	2.69
Our Destiny PAC (pro-John Huntsman group)	2.68
Majority PAC (Democratic group)	2.52

Source: *USA TODAY*, February 2, 2012, p. 7A, from USA TODAY analysis of Federal Action Committee data.

★ 3566 ★
Churches
SIC: 8661; NAICS: 81311

Largest Gigachurches, 2011

Gigachurches are churches with weekly attendance of more than 10,000.

Lakewood Church (TX)	43,500
North Point Community Church (GA)	27,429
LifeChurch.tv (OK)	26,776
Willow Creek Community Church (IL)	24,377
Without Walls International (FL)	23,900
Southeast Christian Church (KY)	20,801
West Angeles Church of God in Christ (CA)	20,000
Saddleback Church (CA)	19,742
Woodlands Church (TX)	18,386
Central Christian Church (NV)	18,223

Source: *Outreach Magazine*, September 2011, p. NA.

★ 3567 ★
Religion
SIC: 8661; NAICS: 81311

Religious Denominations, 1990 and 2008

Data show percent of U.S. population based on a survey of 113,713 people.

	1990	2008
Catholic	26.2%	25.1%
Baptist	19.3	15.8
Methodist	8.0	5.0
Lutheran	5.2	3.8
Presbyterian	2.8	2.1
Jewish	1.8	1.2
Episcopal, Anglican	1.7	1.1

Source: *USA TODAY*, April 6, 2012, p. 2A, from *American Religious Identification Survey*.

★ 3568 ★

Automobile Clubs

SIC: 8699; NAICS: 561599

Automobile Clubs, 2007

Data show the percent of industry sales held by the largest 4, 8, 20 and 50 firms in the sector. There are approximately 819 firms operating in the industry generating employment for 22,332 people.

4 largest firms	46.3%
8 largest firms	60.6
20 largest firms	83.0
50 largest firms	96.9

Source: "2007 Economic Census." [online] from http://www.census.gov/econ/concentration.html [Accessed August 12, 2011], from U.S. Bureau of the Census.

SIC 87 - Engineering and Management Services

★ 3569 ★
Design Industry
SIC: 8711; NAICS: 54133

Top Design Firms, 2010

Companies are ranked by sales in millions of dollars.

CH2M Hill	$ 3,602.7
Fluor Corp.	3,127.4
Tetra Tech Inc.	2,200.0
Parsons Brinckerhoff	1,561.4
HDR	1,500.3
Stantec Inc.	1,470.0
Hawkins Design Group Inc.	1,458.3
CDM	740.0
Burns & McDonnell	684.5
Sargent & Lundy L.L.C.	504.0

Source: *EC&M*, May 23, 2011, p. NA.

★ 3570 ★
Engineering Services
SIC: 8711; NAICS: 54133

Engineering Industry, 2010

The industry generated revenues of $172.8 billion and employs approximately 995,000 people. Most establishments are small and the number of such operations has been relatively flat during the economic downturn of 2008-2010.

Industrial and manufacturing plant and process projects	17.0%
Transportation projects	15.5
Commercial public and institutional projects	13.5
Municipal utility projects	12.0
Miscellaneous federal government projects	10.0
Project management services	10.0
Residential building projects	7.5

Source: "Engineering Services in the U.S." [online] from http://www.slideshare.net [Published November 2010], from IBISWorld.

★ 3571 ★
Green Design
SIC: 8711; NAICS: 54133

Top Green Design Firms, 2010

Firms are ranked by green design revenues in millions of dollars.

URS Corp.	$ 333.2
Gensler	321.5
Aecom Technology Corp.	192.5
Perkins + Will	171.5
HOK	158.2
Tetra Tech Inc.	158.0
CH2M Hill	140.6
HDR	122.4
NBBJ	109.4
HKS Inc.	100.0

Source: *ENR*, July 4, 2011, p. 60.

★ 3572 ★
Architectural Services
SIC: 8712; NAICS: 54131

Market Sectors of the Architectural Services Industry, 2011

There were an estimated 98,312 architecture firms operating in 2011. Revenues are projected to increase from $40.2 billion in 2011 to $49.9 billion in 2016. Approximately half of industry establishments are sole proprietors or partnerships that have no employees. The market is driven by factors such as overall construction demand and competition from building construction firms that offer design services.

Basic design services	61.5%
Construction phase services	14.5
Expanded design services	11.5
Operation, maintenance and other services	7.0
Drafting services	5.5

Source: "Architectural Services in the U.S." [online] from http://www.aia-mn.org/_assets/pdf/IBIS_Arch_1-11-10.pdf [Published July 2011], from IBISWorld.

★ 3573 ★
Architectural Services
SIC: 8712; NAICS: 54131

Top Architectural Firms, 2011

Firms are ranked by architectural revenues in millions of dollars.

AECOM Technology	$ 666.4
Gensler	656.8
Perkins + Will	400.3
HDR	336.9
HDK	334.1
URS Corp.	282.8
NBBJ	193.8
HKS Inc.	190.5
RTKL	176.0
Skidmore Ownings & Merrill L.L.P.	169.9

Source: *Architectural Record*, July 2011, p. NA, from Mc-Graw-Hill.

★ 3574 ★
Accounting Services
SIC: 8721; NAICS: 541214

Accounting Industry Product and Segments, 2010

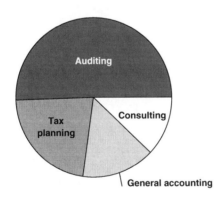

The industry was valued at $75 billion. Deloitte & Touche claimed 15.8% of the market, Ernst & Young 11.4%, PricewaterhouseCoopers 9.6%, KPMG 6.7%, H&R Block 4.0% and other firms 52.5%.

Auditing	50.0%
Tax planning and preparation services	22.5
General accounting	15.0
Consulting	12.5

Source: *Crain's Chicago Business*, October 18, 2010, p. 24, from IBISWorld.

★ 3575 ★
Accounting Services
SIC: 8721; NAICS: 541214

Top Accounting Service Firms, 2010

Companies are ranked by revenues in millions of dollars.

Deloitte & Touche	$ 10,938.0
PricewaterhouseCoopers	8,034.0
Ernst & Young	7,100.0
KPMG	4,889.0
RSM/McGladrey & Pullen	1,378.8
Grant Thornton	1,085.7
BDO USA	585.0
CBIZ/Mayer Hoffman McCann	575.3
Crowe Horwath	481.0
BKD L.L.P.	391.0

Source: *Accounting Today*, May 2011, p. NA.

★ 3576 ★
Payroll Services
SIC: 8721; NAICS: 541214

Top Payroll Firms, 2011

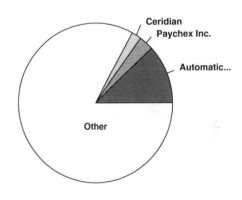

The industry generated revenues of $46.2 billion.

Automatic Data Processing Inc.	11.9%
Paychex Inc.	3.2
Ceridian	1.5
Other	83.4

Source: "Payroll & Bookkeeping Services in the U.S." [online] from http://www.ibisworld.com [Published July 2011], from IBISWorld.

★ 3577 ★
Contract Research Organizations
SIC: 8732; NAICS: 54172

Leading Contract Research Organizations Worldwide, 2009

A contract research organization provides research, clinical testing and other services on a contract basis for the pharmaceutical and biotechnology industries.

Quintiles	10.0%
Covance	8.0
Pharmaceutical Product Development Inc. (PPD)	6.0
CRL	5.0
PRXL	5.0
ICLR	4.0
Other	62.0

Source: "ICON PLC." [online] from http://www.jefferies.com [Published September 2011], from Thomson Reuters and company reports.

★ 3578 ★
Lab Testing
SIC: 8732; NAICS: 54172

Lab Testing Industry, 2010

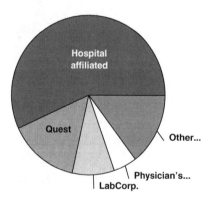

The industry was valued at $55 billion.

Hospital affiliated	58.0%
Quest	15.0
LabCorp.	9.0
Physician's office	5.0
Other independent	15.0

Source: "Americas: Medical Technology: Life Science Tools & Diagnostics." [online] from http://www.genomicslawreport.com [Published February 23, 2011], from Goldman Sachs.

★ 3579 ★
Marketing Research
SIC: 8732; NAICS: 54172

Marketing Research and Public Opinion Polling, 2007

Data show the percent of industry sales held by the largest 4, 8, 20 and 50 firms in the sector. There are approximately 5,823 firms operating in the industry generating employment for 117,822 people.

4 largest firms	22.9%
8 largest firms	31.2
20 largest firms	44.2
50 largest firms	55.6

Source: "2007 Economic Census." [online] from http://www.census.gov/econ/concentration.html [Accessed August 12, 2011], from U.S. Bureau of the Census.

★ 3580 ★
Marketing Research
SIC: 8732; NAICS: 54172

Top Marketing Research Firms, 2010

Firms are ranked by revenues in millions of dollars.

The Nielsen Co.	$ 2,407.0
Kantar	914.7
IMS Health Inc.	801.0
SymphonyIRI Group Inc.	457.0
Westat Inc.	455.3
Arbitron Inc.	390.4
Ipsos	379.6
GfK USA	290.0
Synovate	235.8
The NPD Group Inc.	173.7
ICF International Inc.	153.2
J.D. Power and Associates	147.3
comScore Inc.	142.0

Source: *Marketing News*, June 30, 2011, p. NA, from *Honomichl Top 50*.

★ 3581 ★
Promotional Auditing
SIC: 8732; NAICS: 54172

Top Promotional Auditing Firms, 2010

In 2011, the Federal Trade Commission announced that Healthcare Technology Holdings, Inc., the parent company of market research firm IMS Health Inc., has agreed to sell two product lines of rival SDI Health L.L.C. as a condition of allowing it to proceed with its acquisition of SDI.

SDI	68.0%
IMS Health	30.0
Cegedim	2.0

Source: "FTC Requires Parent of Market Research Firm IMS Health to Sell Two Product Lines Before Acquiring Rival SDI Health." [online] from http://www.ftc.gov/opa/2011/10/ims_shtm [Published October 28, 2011].

★ 3582 ★
Research & Development
SIC: 8732; NAICS: 54172

R&D Industry in Japan, 2010

The Japanese government spent $195.6 billion on research and development from April 2009 to March 2010. Businesses spent 69.5% of the total, universities and colleges 20.6% and non-profits and public institutions 9.9%.

Life sciences	15.6%
Information and communications	15.5
Environment	6.0
Energy	5.6
Compounds and materials	4.2
Space exploration	1.4
Nano technology	1.1
Oceanic development	0.6
Other	50.0

Source: "Japan: Analytical Instruments Industry." [online] from http://www.export.gov [Published October 2011], from Japanese Statistics Bureau.

★ 3583 ★
Research & Development
SIC: 8732; NAICS: 54172

R&D Spending Worldwide, 2009 and 2011

Total spending is expected to reach $1.2 trillion in 2011.

	2009	2011
United States	34.7%	34.0%
Europe	24.1	23.2

	2009	2011
Japan	12.6%	12.1%
China	11.2	12.9
India	2.5	3.0

Source: *R&D Magazine*, December 2010, p. 3, from Battelle.

★ 3584 ★
Research & Development
SIC: 8732; NAICS: 541711

Research & Development In Biotechnology, 2007

Data show the percent of industry sales held by the largest 4, 8, 20 and 50 firms in the sector. There are approximately 2,483 firms operating in the industry generating employment for 99,325 people.

4 largest firms	35.8%
8 largest firms	43.5
20 largest firms	53.3
50 largest firms	66.4

Source: "2007 Economic Census." [online] from http://www.census.gov/econ/concentration.html [Accessed August 12, 2011], from U.S. Bureau of the Census.

★ 3585 ★
Research & Development
SIC: 8732; NAICS: 541712

Research & Development In The Physical & Engineering Sciences, 2007

Data show the percent of industry sales held by the largest 4, 8, 20 and 50 firms in the sector. There are approximately 6,978 firms operating in the industry generating employment for 389,741 people.

4 largest firms	33.8%
8 largest firms	45.1
20 largest firms	60.4
50 largest firms	72.1

Source: "2007 Economic Census." [online] from http://www.census.gov/econ/concentration.html [Accessed August 12, 2011], from U.S. Bureau of the Census.

★ 3586 ★
Research & Development
SIC: 8732; NAICS: 54172

Research & Development In The Social Sciences and Humanities, 2007

Data show the percent of industry sales held by the largest 4, 8, 20 and 50 firms in the sector. There are approximately 1,712 firms operating in the industry generating employment for 31,519 people.

4 largest firms	31.6%
8 largest firms	40.9
20 largest firms	56.1
50 largest firms	69.8

Source: "2007 Economic Census." [online] from http://www.census.gov/econ/concentration.html [Accessed August 12, 2011], from U.S. Bureau of the Census.

★ 3587 ★
Life Sciences
SIC: 8733; NAICS: 541711

Top Life Science Tool/Service Firms Worldwide, 2011

The industry consists of companies involved in drug discovery, development and production continuum by providing analytical tools, instruments, consumables and supplies. Total revenues were $20.3 billion.

Quintiles Transnational Corp.	16.3%
Covance Inc.	11.0
Pharmaceutical Product Development Inc. . .	8.0
ICON PLC	6.4
Other	58.3

Source: *Datamonitor Industry Market Research*, May 1, 2012, p. NA, from Datamonitor.

★ 3588 ★
Consulting Services
SIC: 8742; NAICS: 541611

Administrative Management Consulting Services, 2007

Data show the percent of industry sales held by the largest 4, 8, 20 and 50 firms in the sector. There are approximately 61,583 firms operating in the industry generating employment for 351,829 people.

4 largest firms	19.0%
8 largest firms	25.2
20 largest firms	32.6
50 largest firms	38.6

Source: "2007 Economic Census." [online] from http://www.census.gov/econ/concentration.html [Accessed August 12, 2011], from U.S. Bureau of the Census.

★ 3589 ★
Employment Services
SIC: 8742; NAICS: 541611

Top Human Resource and Employment Firms Worldwide, 2011

The industry generated revenues of $513.2 billion in 2011. Temporary placement claimed 67% of revenues, permanent staffing 22%, employment leasing 5% and other sectors, such as payroll services, the remaining 6%.

Adecco S.A.	4.7%
Manpower Inc.	3.6
Randstad Holdings	3.6
Kelly Services	0.9
USG People	0.8
Other	86.4

Source: "Global HR & Recruitment Services." [online] from http://www.docin.com/p-320645711.html [Published August 2011], from IBISWorld.

★ 3590 ★
Executive Search Industry
SIC: 8742; NAICS: 561312

Executive Search Industry Worldwide, 2010

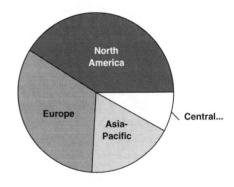

Market shares are shown for the third quarter 2010.

North America	41.0%
Europe	33.0
Asia-Pacific	18.0
Central and South America	8.0

Source: "Executive Search in Transition." [online] from https://members.aesc.org/eweb/upload/Executive%20Search%20in%20Transition%202010.pdf [Accessed October 1, 2011], from Association of Executive Search Consultants.

★ 3591 ★

Executive Search Industry

SIC: 8742; NAICS: 561312

Leading Healthcare Search Firms, 2010

Firms are ranked by number of U.S. placements for senior-level (V.P. and above) executives.

B.E. Smith	323
Korn/Ferry International	320
Witt/Kieffer	249
Reaction Search International	203
Cejka Search	202
Russell Reynolds Associates	153
Solomon Page Group Healthcare	145
Quick Leonard Kieffer International	137
Grant Cooper Healthcare	135
Diversified Search Odgers Berndtson	115

Source: *Modern Healthcare's By the Numbers*, Annual 2011-2012, p. 10, from *Modern Healthcare's 2011 Executive Search Firms Survey*.

★ 3592 ★

Healthcare Management Consulting

SIC: 8742; NAICS: 541611

Largest Healthcare Management Consulting Firms, 2010

Firms are ranked by provider revenues in millions of dollars.

Deloitte Consulting	$ 372.0
Advisory Board Co.	276.4
Huron Healthcare	261.7
Dell Services	196.9
Navigant Consulting	151.9
ACS	125.9
Quorum Health Resources	115.0
Ernst & Young	102.0
FTI Consulting	98.2
GE Healthcare	95.0

Source: *Modern Healthcare*, August 29, 2011, p. 34, from *Modern Healthcare's 2011 Healthcare Management Consultant Firms*.

★ 3593 ★

Public Relations Industry

SIC: 8743; NAICS: 54182

Top Public Relations Firms, 2011

Firms are ranked by revenues in millions of dollars.

Edelman	$ 383.4
Waggener Edstrom Worldwide	100.5
APCO Worldwide	72.9
WCG	44.4

ICF International	$ 40.6
MWW Group	38.6
Ruder Finn	37.7
ICR	32.7
DKC	27.4
Finn Partners	23.0

Source: *PR Week*, May 2012, p. NA.

★ 3594 ★

Public Relations Industry

SIC: 8743; NAICS: 54182

Top Public Relations Firms Worldwide, 2010

Firms are ranked by revenues in millions of dollars.

Edelman	$ 532
Fleishman-Hillard	500
Burson-Marsteller	450
Weber Shandwick	450
MSL Group	405
Ketchum	360
Ogilvy Public Relations Worldwide	255
FD	193
Brunswick	175
Hill & Knowlton	39

Source: *Advertising Age*, April 25, 2011, p. 30, from AdAge DataCenter.

★ 3595 ★

Prisons

SIC: 9221; NAICS: 92212

Top Private Prison Providers, 2011

Companies are ranked by bed capacity. GEO Group was formerly known as Wackenhut. The 1990s saw a rapid growth in the prison privatization at the start of the decade followed by a cooling off period. The industry saw industry capacity grow 36% annually from 1992 to 1998. From 1999 to 2006, growth declined to just 4% a year. There are approximately 1.6 million prisoners in federal and state correctional facilities.

	Capacity	Share
Corrections Corporation of America	90,277	44.3%
GEO Group	63,366	31.1
Management & Training Corporation	25,295	12.4
Community Education Centers	9,243	4.5
LaSalle Southwest Corrections	7,680	3.8
Louisiana Corrections Services Inc.	4,738	2.3
Emerald Companies	3,416	1.7

Source: *Prison Legal News*, October 2011, p. 4, from company reports.

★ 3596 ★

U.S. Department of Education

SIC: 9411; NAICS: 92311

U.S. Department of Education Discretionary Funding, 2011

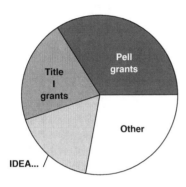

Nearly all federal education programs are funded through the appropriations process, but a few, such as student loans, are funded through mandatory spending. Total discretionary spending was $68.3 billion. Most education funding in the United States is provided by state and local governments. For elementary and secondary education, federal spending accounts for between 9-10% of total funding.

Pell grants	33.6%
Title I grants	21.2
IDEA grants to states	16.8
Other	28.4

Source: "U.S. Department of Education Budget." [online] from http://febp.newamerica.net/background-analysis/education-federal-budget [Published March 22, 2012], from U.S. Department of Education.

★ 3597 ★

Government Spending

SIC: 9431; NAICS: 92312

Spending by U.S. Department of Health and Human Services, 2011

Total outlay spending was $911 billion.

Medicare	51.0%
Medicaid	33.0

Discretionary programs	10.0%
Children's Entitlement Programs (includes CHIP)	3.0
Temporary Aid for Needy Families	2.3
Other mandatory programs	0.4

Source: "FY 2011 President's Budget for HHS." [online] from http://dhhs.gov/asfr/ob/docbudget/2011budgetinbrief.pdf [Accessed April 1, 2012], from U.S. Department of Health and Human Services.

★ 3598 ★

Dog Parks

SIC: 9532; NAICS: 92512

Leading Cities for Dog Parks, 2010

Dog parks are the fastest-growing segment of city parks. There are 5.7 dog parks for every 100,000 residents in Portland. The push for parks mirrors the changing society. According to the Census, there are now more households with dogs (43 million) than kids (38 million).

Portland, OR	32
San Francisco, CA	27
Las Vegas, NV	23
Albuquerque, NM	12
Norfolk, VA	12
Tampa, FL	8
Arlington, VA	7
Madison, WI	7
Henderson, NV	6
St. Petersburg, FL	6

Source: *USA TODAY*, December 8, 2011, p. A1, from Trust for Public Land.

★ 3599 ★
Federal Contracting
SIC: 9611; NAICS: 92611

Federal Professional Services, 2009

The federal professional services market was valued at $280 billion in 2009. Professional, administrative and management support claimed 34%, facilities-related services 22%, research and development 21% and other segments 23%.

Department of Defense	58.0%
Department of Energy	10.0
NASA	6.0
DHS	4.0
HHS	4.0
GSA	3.0
Other	15.0

Source: ''Government Contractors.'' [online] from http://www.capstonellc.com/research/industryreports [Published Third Quarter 2011], from Center for Strategic and International Studies.

★ 3600 ★

Defense

SIC: 9711; NAICS: 92811

Top Nations by Defense Spending, 2010-2015

Countries are ranked by spending in billions of dollars.

United States	$ 2,354
China	561
United Kingdom	198
Russia	183
Japan	146
India	114
France	111
Brazil	110
Germany	86
Australia	78
South Korea	73
Israel	62

Source: *Financial Times*, October 13, 2011, p. 18, from IHS Jane's.

★ 3601 ★

Government Contracting

SIC: 9711; NAICS: 92811

Top Contractors to the Department of Homeland Security, 2010

Countries are ranked by value of contracts in millions of dollars.

IBM	$ 560.3
Lockheed Martin Corp.	422.7
Unisys Corp.	398.5
Science Applications International Corp. . .	376.2
Computer Sciences Corp.	343.1
Bollinger Shipyards Inc.	323.9
L-3 Communications Corp.	269.8
The Boeing Company	215.2
General Dynamics	213.0
Booz Allen Hamilton Inc.	197.9

Source: *Homeland Security Today*, April 2011, p. 24.

SOURCE INDEX

This index is divided into *secondary sources* and *primary sources*. Secondary sources are the publications which quote market share data from a primary source. Primary sources are either the publications from which a particular market share is taken when no other source has been quoted or are the sources cited by a secondary source. Numbers following the sources are entry numbers, arranged sequentially; the first number refers to the first appearance of the source in *Market Share Reporter*. All told, 1,974 organizations are listed. Roman numerals indicate volume number.

Secondary Sources

"$3.8 Billion Water System Markets 2011." [online] from http://www.pumps-processes.com/magazine/news_en/doc5571x.asp [Published January 8, 2011], I-1925

"$59 Billion Valve Market in 2015 with 7 Percent Annual Growth Rate in Asia." [online] from http://home.mcilvainecompany.com [Published June 2011], I-1800

"2006-2010 Flavor & Fragrance Industry Leaders." [online] from http://www.leffingwell.com/top_10.htm [Published May 19, 2011], I-1527

"2007 Economic Census." [online] from http://www.census.gov/econ/concentration.html [Accessed August 12, 2011], I-410, 641, 773, 991, 993-995, 998, 1006-1008, 1012, 1039, 1041-1043, 1046, 1056, 1064, 1082, 1088, 1097, 1117, 1124, 1126, 1150, 1153, 1155, 1157, 1163, 1231, 1238, 1240-1242, 1252, 1290, 1408, 1521, 1533, 1536, 1538, 1582, 1584, 1617, 1622, 1626-1627, 1652, 1693-1694, 1733, 1739, 1742-1743, 1746, 1760, 1770, 1774-1775, 1787, 1791-1793, 1797, 1799, 1804, 1812, 1815, 1862, 1871, 1878, 1906, 1977, 1990, II-1994, 2110, 2232-2234, 2322, 2331, 2403, 2425, 2429, 2431, 2435, 2457, 2467-2470, 2507, 2523, 2533-2534, 2537, 2565, 2570-2571, 2623, 2689, 2722-2726, 2731-2733, 2735-2736, 2738-2747, 2750-2753, 2755-2756, 2758-2762, 2764-2781, 2865, 2867, 2880, 2900, 2941, 2943, 2960, 2991, 3000, 3030, 3088, 3126-3127, 3238, 3240-3243, 3246, 3249-3251, 3259, 3262, 3266, 3268, 3273, 3276, 3279, 3281, 3312-3313, 3320, 3322, 3327, 3333-3334, 3337-3340, 3371, 3376-3378, 3380, 3389, 3392-3393, 3395, 3397-3399, 3406, 3414, 3416-3419, 3421, 3423-3424, 3426, 3429-3430, 3432-3434, 3440, 3442, 3447, 3450-3452, 3454-3455, 3457, 3463-3465, 3469-3470, 3476, 3488, 3492, 3498, 3500, 3521, 3525, 3529-3530, 3541, 3545, 3547, 3556, 3560, 3562, 3568, 3579, 3584-3586, 3588

"2010 California P&C Market Share Report." [online] from http://www.insurance.ca.gov [Accessed December 1, 2011], II-3170, 3186, 3189, 3191, 3210, 3213, 3215, 3235

"2010 Coal Producer Survey." [online] from http://www.nma.org/pdf/members/coal_producer_survey2010.pdf [Published May 2011], I-185

"2010 DuPont Global Automotive Color Popularity Report." [online] from http://www2.dupont.com [Published December 7, 2010], I-1518

2010 EFT Data Book - A Supplement to ATM & Debit News, II-2685

"2010 Ingredients Market Overview." [online] from http://newhope360.com [Published November 19, 2010], I-1298

"2010 International Trade Statistics Yearbook." [online] from http://comtrade.un.org/pb/CommodityPagesNew.aspx?y=2010 [Accessed April 1, 2012], I-135, 694, 928, 997, 1108, 1748, 1777, 1786, 1807, 1816, 1887-1888, 1900, 1972, II-2085, 2104, 2416

"2010 Theme Index." [online] from http://www.tea.org [Accessed August 1, 2010], II-3480-3481

"2010 USAF Dental Laboratory Equipment/Product Survey." [online] from http://airforcemedicine.afms.mil [Published June 2011], II-2395-2400

"2010 Worldwide Digital Camera Market Shares by Vendor." [online] from http://nikonrumors.com [Published April 15, 2011], II-2415

2011-2012 Nonfoods Handbook - A Supplement to Grocery Headquarters, I-450, 466, 468, 510-511, 984-985, 987-988, 1161, 1178, 1181-1182, 1300, 1305, 1307, 1316, 1344, 1393-1394, 1426, 1432, 1448, 1456, 1458, 1470, 1500, 1547, 1621, 1752, II-2056-2057, 2166, 2168, 2174, 2473, 2483, 2485, 2491

"2011 Advertising Forecast." [online] from http://www.magnaglobal.com [Accessed May 1, 2012], II-3298, 3300-3301, 3303-3305

2011 Consumer Perishables Hand-book - A Supplement to Grocery Headquarters, I-76-78, 97-98, 101, 349-350, 365, 374, 376, 602, 925

"2011 Energy Conference." [online] from http://www.howardweil. com [Accessed February 10, 2012], I-211-212, 222

"2011 Essential Facts - About the Computer and Video Game Industry." [online] from http://www.esa-facts.org [Accessed December 1, 2011], II-3362-3363

"2011 Full Year Best-Selling Car Brands and Manufacturers in Switzerland." [online] from http:// cars.european-traveler.com/tag/ 2011 [Published January 5, 2012], II-2206

"2011 Full Year Best-Selling Car Brands and Marques in the U.K." [online] from http://cars.european-traveler.com/tag/2011/ [Published January 7, 2012], II-2209

"2011 Full Year Best-Selling Car Models in Japan." [online] from http://cars.european-traveler.com/ tag/2011 [Published January 11, 2012], II-2204

"2011 Full Year Top-Selling Car Brands and Manufacturers in Germany." [online] from http://cars.european-traveler.com/germany [Published January 3, 2012], II-2201

"2011 General Aviation Statistical Databook & Industry Outlook." [online] from http://www.gama.org [Accessed April 19, 2012], II-2266

"2011 Interim Results." [online] from http://www.todayir.com/web-casting/yingde_gases_11ir/ppt.pdf [Accessed October 1, 2011], I-1262

"2011 International Book Market Overview." [online] from http:// www.slideshare.net [Accessed February 20, 2012], I-1214

"2011 List of Largest Staffing Firms." [online] from http://www. jacksonhealthcare.com/media/ 183638/sialargestglobal2011.pdf [Published August 3, 2011], II-3343

"2011 Mid-Year Review of North American HDPE Pipe Market." [online] from http://plasticmarket-data.com [Published August 2011], I-1628

"2011 State of the Hearth Industry Report." [online] from http://www. hpba.org [Accessed December 21, 2011], I-1979

"2011 Top Line Data." [online] from http://www.imshealth.com [Published February 23, 2012], I-1335-1336, 1338

"2011 TV Shipments Fall After Six Consecutive Years of Growth." [online] from http://www.display-search.com [Published March 14, 2012], II-2081

"2011 Year End Review and Forecast." [online] from http://www.aia-aerospace.org/assets/YE_Analysis. pdf [Accessed January 2, 2012], II-2306

"The 2012 Metal Paste Market to Grow into a $3 Billion Business." [online] from http://www.solarenergy.com [Published October 24, 2011], I-1550

"2012 PV Glass Market to Grow into a $2.28 Billion Industry." [online] from http://www.solarnenergy. com [Press release November 3, 2011], I-1661-1662

"4Q2011 and 2011 YE Sales Review." [online] from http://magnet-data.net/IntheNews/Feb242012. htm [Published February 24, 2012], I-1209

"6th Annual Value Investing Congress." [online] from http://value-hunteruk.files.wordpress.com/ 2011/03 [Published October 13, 2010], I-1663

"7 And I Holdings Corporate Outline 2011." [online] from http:// www.7andi.com/en/ir/pdf/corpo-rate/2011_all.pdf [Accessed September 1, 2011], II-2793, 2798, 2804

"7th Annual Global Consumer Conference." [online] from http:// natura.infoinvest.com.br [Published June 2010], I-1483-1485

"802.11n-Enables Wi-Fi Networking Equipment Unit Shipments Increase 17%, Q2'11 over Q1'11." [online] from http://instat-com [Press release September 27, 2011], II-2118

"A Growing Differentiated Polyester Yarn Manufacturer." [online] from http://hk.gtja.com/gtja_Report/Report [Published July 25, 2011], I-1005

"A Rising Children's Products Developer and Retailer." [online] from http://www.bocomgroup.com/ mediafiles/documents/p2_5823_en. pdf [Published March 7, 2011], I-1026, II-2892

"A Softer Consumer Faces Inflation." [online] from http://www. docint.com [Published March 20, 2008], I-481, 916, 918

"A User Guide to Commodities." [online] from http://www.etc.db. com [Published May 2011], I-52-53, 56-57, 60-61, 63-64, 66-67, 113-114, 156, 161, 165-166, 168, 170-171, 176, 178-180, 184, 642-643, 721, 723, 736-737, 847-848, 1286, 1288, 1704, 1718-1719, 1722

"A123 Investor Presentation." [online] from http://files.shareholder. com [Published August 2011], II-2169-2170

"AbitibiBowater Inc." [online] from http://research-ca.bmocapital-markets.com [Published February 4, 2011], I-1136

"Abrasive and Sand Paper Manufacturing." [online] from http://www. ibisworld.com [Published July 2011], I-1690

Accessories Magazine, I-1053, 1058, 1060, 1640, 1650, II-2889, 2891, 3007, 3029

"Activated Carbon." [online] from http://www.freedoniagroup.com [Published January 2011], I-1265

"Active & Intelligent Packaging." [online] from http://www.freedoniagroup.com [Published June 2011], I-35

"Activision Blizzard." [online] from http://tippie.uiowa.edu/krause/fall_2011/atvi_f11.pdf [Published November 14, 2011], II-3366

"Adhesives and Sealants." [online] from http://lowes.retailforward.com [Published August 2011], I-1549

Adhesives Magazine, I-1544

AdNews, II-3293

"Adult Family Homes." [online] from http://www.pacificedc.org/.../Adult%20Family%20Homes%20Snapshot.pdf [Published November 2010], II-3550

"Adult Stem Cell Fact Sheet." [online] from http://clients.criticalimpact.com/user/24825/files/StemCell_Fact_Sheet2012.pdf [Accessed March 1, 2012], I-1358

"Advanced Ceramics." [online] from http://www.freedoniagroup.com [Published September 2011], I-1680

Advertising Age, I-560, 783, 834, 1202-1203, 1207, 1749, 1918, 1929, II-2627, 2632, 2692, 2694, 2945, 2947, 2953, 3091, 3294-3295, 3317, 3594

"AEO2012 Early Release Overview." [online] from http://www.eia.gov/forecasts/aeo/er/pdf/0383er%282012%29.pdf [Accessed May 1, 2012], I-187, II-2705-2706

"Aerospace and Defense." [online] from http://bizavnews.ru/images/bizavweek/JPMorgan_Investment_Research_02.2012.pdf [Published February 16, 2012], II-2271-2272

"Aerospace Global Report 2010." [online] from http://www.imap.com/imap/media/resources/Aerospace_8_1FED752787A1E.pdf [Accessed September 1, 2011], II-2276-2277

"After the Storm." [online] from http://www.vscac.com/uploads/VSCAC/Gray_Presentation.pdf [Accessed April 1, 2012], II-3096-3097

"AGA Survey of Casino Entertainment." [online] from http://www. americangaming.org [Accessed September 1, 2010], II-3487

"Agribusiness Chartbook." [online] from http://www.docin.com [Published July 7, 2010], I-646

"Agricultural Equipment Manufacturing." [online] from http://tippie.uiowa.edu/henry/reports11/ag_equipment.pdf [Published February 9, 2011], I-1831

"Agrimarine." [online] from http://www.agrimarine.com [Accessed May 1, 2012], I-133

"Alcoholic Drinks - Azerbaijan." [online] from http://www.scribd.com [Published December 2010], I-751

Algeria Petrochemicals Report, I-1526

"All-in-One Laser Printer Sales Climb." [online] from http://www.channelmea.com [Published September 11, 2011], I-1962-1964

"Ally Financial Inc." [online] from http://phx.corporate-ir.net [Published November 2, 2011], II-3095

"Alphaliner - Top 100." [online] from http://www.alphaliner.com/top100/index.php [Accessed September 8, 2011], II-2527

"Alternative Sweeteners." [online] from http://www.freedoniagroup.com [Published December 2011], I-1523

A.M. Best Newswire, II-3171-3175, 3177-3179, 3193-3201, 3203-3204, 3206-3208, 3214, 3216-3219, 3226-3228, 3230

"Ambition 2015 Objective." [online] from http://www.airliquide.com [Published December 2010], II-2161

"Americas: Medical Technology: Life Science Tools & Diagnostics." [online] from http://www.genomicslawreport.com [Published February 23, 2011], I-1356, II-3578

"America's Fastest-Growing Coffee Chains." [online] from http://www.cnbc.com/id/44344031/America_s_Fastest_Growing_Coffee_Chains [Published December 15, 2009], II-2933

America's Intelligence Wire, II-2624

"America's Top Tower Companies." [online] from http://www.wirelessestimator.com [Accessed April 17, 2012], II-2112

"An Insider's Guide to Retail Success 2011-2012." [online] from http://www.rx-edge.com/research%20pdfs/OTC_Health%5B1%5D.pdf [Accessed May 1, 2012], II-2806, 2962-2963

"An Introduction to Praxair." [online] from http://www.praxair.com [Accessed April 1, 2012], I-1261

"Analysis of the Real Estate Investment Trust (REIT) Industry." [online] from http://scholarsarchive.jwu.edu/mba_student/6 [Published January 9, 2012], II-3265

"ANCOA Study of the Antimony Market." [online] from http://www.ancoa.com.au/RoskillCRT.pdf [Published October 17, 2011], I-174

"Angel Broking." [online] from http://web.angelbackoffice.com/research/archives/fundamental/company_reports [Published April 18, 2011], I-633

"Annual Report 2010." [online] from http://www.rengo.co.jp/financial/img/pdf/2010_english.pdf [Accessed February 14, 2012], I-1148

"Annual Report of the Commissioner of Insurance." [online] from http://www.dora.state.co.us/insurance/legi/2012/legiHealthCostReport021612R.pdf [Published February 2012], II-3154

"Annual Survey of Manufactures." [online] from http://www.census.gov/manufacturing/asm/index.html [Accessed January 18, 2012], I-347, 381, 411, 735, 902, 992, 996, 999, 1009, 1014, 1055, 1061-1062, 1065, 1089, 1098, 1110, 1119, 1125, 1144, 1156, 1162, 1164-1165, 1230, 1239, 1243, 1253, 1263, 1269, 1351, 1519, 1528, 1537, 1545, 1583, 1618, 1635, 1688, 1695, 1702-1703, 1708, 1732, 1734, 1737, 1740, 1744, 1747, 1758, 1771, 1776, 1778, 1783, 1790, 1803, 1806, 1808,

1825, 1863, 1869, 1874-1875, 1902, 1911, 1971, 1978, 1980, 1987-1989, II-1999, 2012, 2017, 2059, 2176, 2265, 2278-2279, 2285, 2318, 2394, 2412, 2426, 2432, 2471-2472, 2869

"Apparel Knitting Mills in the U.S." [online] from http://www. ibisworld.com [Published December 2010], I-990

"Apple Retakes Top Mobile PC Market Share Position from Hewlett-Packard in Q2 '11." [online] from http://www.displaysearch. com [Press release August 18, 2011], I-1938

"Appliance Market Research Report." [online] from http://www.appliancemagazine.com [Published January 2010], I-1985, II-2019-2021, 2024, 2027-2028, 2040, 2042, 2044

"APVMA RIS Review." [online] from http://www.animalhealthalliance.org.au [Published November 2008], I-1542

"Arcade, Food and Entertainment Complexes in the U.S." [online] from http://www.ibisworld.com [Published November 2011], II-3478

Architectural Record, II-3573

"Architectural Services in the U.S." [online] from http://www.aia-mn. org/_assets/pdf/IBIS_Arch_1-11-10.pdf [Published July 2011], II-3572

Argentina Autos Report, II-2197

Argentina Telecommunications Report, II-2577, 2634

"Around the World, Around the World." [online] from http://www. luxesf.com/wp-content/uploads/ 2011/10 [Published October 2011], I-26, II-2567

"Aseptic Packaging." [online] from http://www.freedoniagroup.com [Published December 2011], I-31

"The Asia/Pacific PC Market Grew 11% in 2011." [online] from http://www.idc.com [Published January 25, 2012], I-1944

"Asia Pacific Server Market Continued Double Digit Growth in

Third Quarter of 2011, Says Gartner." [online] from http://www.gartner.com [Press release November 29, 2011], II-3370

AsiaPulse News, II-2077

"Asics Sustainability Reporting." [online] from http://actionlearning. mit.edu/files/slab_files/Projects/ 2011/Asics%20report.pdf [Published May 12, 2011], I-1031-1032, 1613-1614

"Assa Abloy/Cardo Regulation Merger Procedure." [online] from http://ec.europa.eu [Published March 9, 2011], I-1772

"Assessing Campus Store Performance." [online] from http://www. nacas.org/Content/Navigation-Menu/Education2 [Published November 8, 2011], II-3002

"Assessing Optometric Practice Performance." [online] from http:// www.sunburstoptics.com/document_center/Practice_Management_Tools/Key_Metrics_2011. pdf [Accessed May 1, 2012], II-3509

"AT&T Leads U.S. Biz ISP Market." [online] from http://www.marketingcharts.com/direct/att-leads-us-biz-isp-market-20081/comscore-biz-isp-sharejpg [Accessed June 1, 2012], II-2638

Atlanta Business Chronicle, II-2883, 3015

Atlantic, I-1970

"Audio Production Studios in the U.S." [online] from http://www. ibisworld.com [Published July 2011], II-3388

Australia Telecommunications Report, II-2578, 2635

"Australian Mortgage Industry." [online] from http://www.aventree. com/pdf/austalian_mortgage_industry_vol11.pdf [April 10, 2010], II-3101

"Austria - Consumer Goods." [online] from http://www.bene.com [Published October 2011], I-1122

"Austria Food and Drink Market." [online] from http://www.fft.com [Published July 2011], I-306

Automotive News, II-2178, 2180, 2185, 2213, 2219, 2871-2872, 2874

Bahrain Telecommunications Report, II-2579

"Baked Goods." [online] from http://wenku.baidu.com/view/ f1ea02573c1ec5da50e270e4.html [Published September 2010], I-611

Baking Management, I-610, 613-614, 935

"Baking Mixes and Prepared Foods in the U.S." [online] from http://www.ibisworld.com [Published June 2011], I-898

Baltimore Business Journal, I-247

Bangladesh Telecommunications Report, II-2580

"Baofeng Modern." [online] from http://chinabaofeng.todayir.com/attachment/201107281217442_tc. pdf [Published June 3, 2011], I-1639

"Baotou Rare Earth." [online] from http://doc.research-and-analytics.csfb.com [Published April 13, 2011], I-181

Barron's, II-2443

"Batteries." [online] from http:// www.freedoniagroup.com [Published September 2011], II-2163

"Bearings." [online] from http:// www.freedoniagroup.com [Published September 2009], I-1904

"Beer Statistics News." [online] from http://www.beerinsights.com [Accessed May 1, 2012], I-756

"Behold: The ClimaCool Seduction, Brought to You by Adidas." [online] from http://www.oregonlive.com [Published March 28, 2012], I-1615

"Being the Best at What We do Everyday." [online] from http://www. mcbride.co.uk/media/57754/annualreport2011.pdf [Accessed December 1, 2011], I-1360, 1371

"Belgium and Luxembourg Food and Drink Market." [online] from http://www.fft.com [Published July 2011], I-307

Belgium Telecommunications Report, II-2581

Best's Review, II-3132, 3180-3182

Beverage Dynamics, I-782, 791

Beverage Industry, I-434, 438, 492, 499, 768, 772, 784, 796, 805, 809-810, 812, 815, 830, 851, 860, 915, 932

Beverage Spectrum, I-485, 829

Beverage World, I-769, 814

"Bicycle Manufacturing in China." [online] from http://www.docin. com/p-313015406.html [Published September 2011], II-2298

Bicycle Retailer & Industry News, II-2297, 2299, 2995

Billboard, II-2930

"Billboard & Outdoor Advertisers." [online] from http://www.ibisworld.com [Published November 2011], II-3296

"Billboard and Sign Manufacturing in the U.S." [online] from http://www.ibisworld.com [Published August 2011], II-2478

"Biotechnology 2011." [online] from http://www.ibef.org/download/Biotechnology50112.pdf [Published November 2011], I-1353

"Blind and Shade Manufacturing in the U.S." [online] from http://www.ibisworld.com [Published April 2011], I-1063

"Blood and Organ Banks in the U.S." [online] from http://www.ibisworld.com [Published November 2011], II-3526

"Blood Products and Blood Testing Markets." [online] from http://www.docin.com [Published February 2011], II-2359

"Blount." [online] from http://uoinvestmentgroup.org/wp-content/uploads/2011/02/BLOUNT.pdf [Published February 2011], I-1882

"Bodywear Market in the EU." [online] from http://www.cbi.eu/marketinfo/cbi/?action=showDetails&id=3957 [Published July 2009], I-1020

"Book Publishing in the U.S." [online] from http://www.ibisworld.com [Published January 2012], I-1217

Bottled Water Reporter, I-799, 801

"Bowling Alleys in the U.S." [online] from http://www.ibisworld.com [Published October 2011], II-3459

"BP Oil Spill: Cleanup Stocks to Watch." [online] from http://www.thestreet.com/story/10783927.html [Published June 15, 2010], II-2728

"Brand Loyalty - Is it Dead?" [online] from http://www.farm-equipment.com [Published December 23, 2010], I-1832

"Bridge and Tunnel Construction in the U.S." [online] from http://www.ibisworld.com [Published August 2011], I-278

"Brink's Company." [online] from http://edg1.vcall.com/irwebsites/brinks/May_2011_IR_Presentation.pdf [Published May 2011], II-3381

"British American Tobacco." [online] from http://global.tobaccofreekids.org [Published August 2010], I-957, 964

Broadcasting & Cable, II-2697

"BTM Says Vestas Loses Market Share but Stays in Top Spot." [online] from http://www.rechargenews.com [Published March 27, 2012], I-1824

"Bulgaria Food and Drink Market." [online] from http://www.fft.com [Published July 2011], I-308

Bulgaria Telecommunications Report, II-2584

"Business Coaching in the U.S." [online] from http://www.ibisworld.com [Published October 2011], II-3390

Business Economics, II-1998

Business Wire, II-2131, 2134, 2358, 3292, 3307, 3311

BusinessWeek, I-567, 759, 845, II-2014

Cabinetmaker + FDM, I-1092

"Cabinets." [online] from http://www.freedoniagroup.com [Published August 2010], I-1091

"Caltex Australia Limited." [online] from http://afr.com/rw/2009-2014/AFR/2011/05/09 [Published May 2011], II-2797

"Camcorders in Canada." [online] from http://www.scribd.com [Published September 2011], II-2070

"Camera Stores in the U.S." [online] from http://www.ibisworld.com [Published March 2011], II-3011

"Campaign Briefing Document." [online] from http://www.10campaign.com/static/faq.pdf [Published September 19, 2011], I-722

"Canada & U.S. Top 20 Lumber Producers." [online] from http://www.woodmarkets.com [Published March 20, 2012], I-1095

"Canada Food and Drink Market." [online] from http://www.fft.com [Published July 2011], I-309

"Canada Retail Food Sector Report." [online] from http://gain.fas.usda.gov [Published March 9, 2012], II-2789

Candy Industry, I-877

"Canned Products Markets in Western Europe." [online] from http://www.fft.com [Published July 2010], I-455

"Capcom Annual Report 2011." [online] from http://capcom.co.jp/ir/english/data/pdf/annual/2011/annual_2011_09.pdf [Published September 2011], II-3367, 3477

"Car Audio Internet Sales Figures." [online] from http://satelliteradioplayground.com/2012/03/14/car-audio-internet-sales-figures/#more-17266 [Published March 14, 2012], II-2924

"Car Sales Israel 2011." [online] from http://raycee1234.blogspot.com/2012/01/car-sales-israel-2010.html [Published January 21, 2012], II-2191

"Car Sales Lebanon 2010." [online] from http://raycee1234.blogspot.com/2012/01/car-sales-lebanon-2010.html [Published January 21, 2012], II-2192

"Car Sales Turkey 2011." [online] from http://raycee1234.blogspot.com/2012/01/car-sales-lebanon-2010.html [Published January 21, 2012], II-2195

"Carbo Ceramics." [online] from http://www.freeman.tulane.edu/bur-kenroad/pdf/CRR.pdf [Published November 16, 2011], I-221

"Cargo Traffic 2010 Final." [online] from http://www.airports.org [Published August 1, 2011], II-2561

Caribbean Food & Drink Report, II-2857

"Carpet Cleaning Services in the U.S." [online] from http://www.ibisworld.com [Published October 2011], II-3280

"Carpets & Rugs." [online] from http://www.freedoniagroup.com [Published January 2012], I-1000

"Carrier Shares." [online] from http://www.transtats.bts.gov [Accessed February 10, 2012], II-2542-2547, 2549-2556

"Carters Third Quarter Business Update." [online] from http://phx.corporate-ir.net [Published October 27, 2011], I-1021

"Cathay Pacific Catering Services." [online] from http://www.scribd.com [Accessed December 1, 2011], II-2936

"Celebrity & Sports Agents in the U.S." [online] from http://www.scribd.com [Published November 2009], II-3460

"Cement Manufacturing in the U.S." [online] from http://www.ibisworld.com [Published August 2011], I-1669

Center Store - A Supplement to Grocery Headquarters, I-422, 449, 487-488, 517-518, 520, 554, 578, 582, 584, 634, 865, 875-876, 878, 895, 923-924, 1185

Central America Telecommunications Report, II-2582, 2591, 2594-2595, 2611

"CHA Announces 2010 Craft Industry Statistics." [online] from http://craftandhobby.wordpress.com/2011/04/06/cha-announces-2010-craft-industry-statistics [Published April 6, 2011], II-2459

Chain Drug Review, I-1, 1168, 1180, 1310, 1326, 1350, 1355, 1357, 1382, 1425, 1441, 1453, 1489-1490, 1499, 1502, II-2030, 2372-2373, 2375

"Challenges for the PV Equipment Supply Chain in 2011." [online] from http://www.pv-tech.org [Published May 17, 2011], I-1764

Channel Insider, I-1926

"Charter: An Introduction." [online] from http://www.investis.com/chtr_int/docs/intro_to_chrtr_apr11.pdf [Published April 2011], I-1883

"Cheaper Than the Best, Better Than the Rest." [online] from http://www.einhell.com/download/researchstudy/2010-04-19_en.pdf [Published April 2010], I-1880

"Chemical Monthly - March 2010." [online] from http://www.docstoc.com [Published March 26, 2010], I-1254, 1277-1278, 1281

Chemical Week, I-1531

Chemical Weekly, I-1413

"Children's and Infants' Clothing Stores in the U.S." [online] from http://www.ibisworld.com [Published September 2011], II-2893

Chile Mining Report, I-153, 162

Chile Telecommunications Report, II-2586, 2636

"China Beverage Market 2009-2010." [online] from http://wenku.baidu.com [Published April 2010], I-497, 797

China Chemical Reporter, I-32

"China Consumer Staples." [online] from http://search.deutsche-bank.de [Published November 19, 2010], I-798, 819, 1449, 1480, 1488, 1501, 1505, II-2484

"China Fishery Public Annual." [online] from http://gain.fas.usda.gov [Published January 31, 2011], I-144

China Food & Drink Report, I-310

"China Gerui Investor Presentation." [online] from http://www.geruigroup.com [Published May 2011], I-1711

"China Healthcare Sector." [online] from http://doc.research-and-analytics.csfb.com [Published May 31, 2011], II-2353

"China Healthcare Sector." [online] from http://download.bioon.com. cn/upload/201105/17235814_9161.pdf [Published December 3, 2010], II-2352, 2366, 2383, 2386, 3524

"China in 2015." [online] from http://wpc.186f.edgecastcdn.net [Published January 1, 2011], I-183, 1668, 1698, 1716, 1720, II-2587, 2625

China Insurance Report, II-3223

"China Planting Seed Annual." [online] from http://gain.fas.usda.gov [Published January 28, 2011], I-50

"China's Apparel Market, 2010." [online] from http://www.lifung-group.com [Published October 2010], I-1022, 1027, 1036, 1040, 1045, 1049

"China's Cosmetics Market, 2010." [online] from http://www.lifung-group.com/eng/knowledge/research/industry_series17.pdf [Published January 2011], I-1438, 1454, 1503

"China's Local Champions." [online] from http://www.booz.com [Accessed November 1, 2011], I-1363, 1372, 1400

"China's - People's Republic of Organics Report." [online] from http://gain.fas.usda.gov [Published October 26, 2010], II-2864

"Chinese Ceramic Raw Material Market Trends and Trade." [online] from http://www.roskill.com [Published March 28, 2012], I-1678, 1683, 1761

"Chinese Demand Fuels Swiss Watch Success." [online] from http://www.thelocal.ch/1875/20111128 [Published November 28, 2011], II-2424

"Chinese PV Equipment Suppliers Grab Further Market Share Gains." [online] from http://www.solarbuzz.com/node/3590 [Published January 17, 2012], I-1767

"Chiropractor Marketing Report." [online] from http://thrivehive.com/pdf/ThriveHive_The_Chiropractor_Marketing_Report.pdf [Accessed April 1, 2012], II-3506

"Cigarette Manufacturing in China." [online] from http://www.docin.com/p-313022643.html [Published November 2011], I-958

"Cigars - China." [online] from http://www.docin.com/p-79627361.html [Published August 2010], I-970

"Citi: Big Changes are Coming to the Women's Underwear Market." [online] from http://mobile.businessinsider.com/citi-womens-lingerie-market-2012-4?op=1 [Published April 13, 2012], I-1050

"Class 1 Railroad Statistics." [online] from http://www.aar.org [Published June 17, 2011], II-2499

"Clay Brick and Block Manufacturing in the U.S." [online] from http://www.ibisworld.com [Published June 2011], I-1677

"Clearwater Paper Corporation." [online] from http://files.shareholder.com [Published March 16, 2011], I-1140

"Clothing and Footwear Specialist Retailers - China." [online] from http://www.scribd.com [Published January 2010], II-2898

Club Business International, II-3472

"Codelco." [online] from http://www.codelco.cl [Published January 2012], I-1717

"Codelco Update." [online] from http://www.codelco.cl [Published July 2011], I-152, 177

"Coffee and Ready-to-Drink Coffee in the United States." [online] from http://www.docin.com/p-299329891.html [Published December 2011], I-853-855, 857-858

"Coffee & Snack Shops in the U.S." [online] from http://www.ibisworld.com [Published February 2011], II-2934

"Coffee Market of China." [online] from http://wenku.baidu.com [Published January 2011], I-850

"College Publishing Market Forecast 2011-2012." [online] from http://www.docin.com/p- 284322476.html [Accessed March 1, 2012], I-1227

Collision Week, II-3413

Colombia Telecommunications Report, II-2588

"Colour Cosmetics." [online] from http://wenku.baidu.com/view/869cf3ff04a1b0717fd5dd77.html [Published May 2010], I-1420

"Commercial Vehicle Outlook Conference 2011." [online] from http://www.hdma.org [Accessed September 1, 2011], II-2223, 2227

"Community Network Game Project." [online] from http://www.fines-cluster.eu [Published March 15, 2012], II-2677

"Company Initiation." [online] from http://www.cashconverters.com/Files/Download/816 [Published February 2010], II-2994

"Compass Minerals Investor Day." [online] from http://phx.corporate-ir.net [Published September 22, 2011], I-1567-1569

"Compressors." [online] from http://www.bostonstrategies.com/clientlogin/rawmaterials/CompressorsMay.pdf [Published April 2010], I-1907

"Computer Service and Repair." [online] from http://ads.eztouse.com/BooksOnline/Profiles/Computer-Service-and-Repair-Snapshot.pdf [Accessed May 1, 2012], II-3379

"Computer Stores in the U.S." [online] from http://www.scribd.com [Published January 2011], II-2927

"comScore Media Metrix Ranks Top 50 U.S. Web Properties for April 2012." [online] from http://www.comscore.com [Press release May 24, 2012], II-2663, 2665

"comScore Media Metrix Ranks Top 50 U.S. Web Properties for February 2012." [online] from http://www.comscore.com [Press release March 21, 2012], II-2660, 2662

"Concrete Pipe & Block Manufacturing in the U.S." [online] from http://www.ibisworld.com [Published September 2011], I-1684

"Consolidation & Competition in Health Insurance & Provider Markets." [online] from http://www.

academyhealth.org/files/2011/monday/flye.pdf [Published June 13, 2011], II-3155

"Construction Equipment Industry in China." [online] from http://www.lectura.de/files/2011_01_lectura_messenger_conexpo_screen.pdf [Accessed November 1, 2011], I-1838

"Construction Materials." [online] from http://finance.sauder.ubc.ca/~carlsonm/bafi521/ppt/jpmMaterials.pdf [Published April 5, 2011], I-215, 1670

"Consumer Trends Salty Snack Food in the United States." [online] from http://publications.gc.ca [Published April 2011], I-861

"Consumer Trends Wine, Beer and Spirits in Hong Kong." [online] from http://www.ats.agr.gc.ca [Published June 2011], I-777, 787

"Contact Lenses." [online] from http://www.clspectrum.com/articleviewer.aspx?articleid=106550 [Published January 1, 2012], II-2405

"Continental Fact Book Fiscal Year 2010." [online] from http://www.conti-online.com [Accessed September 1, 2011], I-1599, II-2224-2225, 2235-2240, 2244, 2247-2248, 2252-2253, 2255-2256, 2260-2262

"Continuous Development and Renewal at Kone." [online] from http://www.kone.com [Published May 19, 2011], I-1857

"Contract Cleaning Services." [online] from http://www.freedoniagroup.com [Published May 2012], II-3328

Convenience Store News, II-2796

"Cooking Oils in Taiwan." [online] from [online] from http://www.ats.agr.gc.ca [Published June 2011], I-742

"Cooper Investor Presentation." [online] from http://files.shareholder.com/downloads [Published December 8, 2011], II-2406

"Corporate Groups of Top 50 Regional Airlines." [online] from http://www.raa.org/Portals/0/IndustryStats/RAAChartsApr2011.pdf [Published April 2011], II-2559

"Cosmetic & Beauty Products Manufacturing in the U.S." [online] from http://colgate-palmolive.wikispaces.com [Published November 2011], I-1476, 1487

Cosmetics Business, I-1416, 1418-1419

"Cotton Farming in the U.S." [online] from http://www.ibisworld.com [Published December 2010], I-137

"Coughing up More for Capex." [online] from https://cimbequityresearch.cimb.com [Published February 29, 2012], I-945

"Countertops." [online] from http://www.freedoniagroup.com [Published September 2011], I-1085

"Countries by Commodity." [online] from http://faostat.fao.org [Accessed February 28, 2012], I-70, 82, 87, 103, 105, 110, 927

"Country Profile Australia." [online] from http://www.lloyds.com/The-Market/Tools-and-Resources/Research/Market-Intelligence-Toolkit/Country-Profiles [Published July 2011], II-3134

"Country Profile Canada." [online] from http://www.lloyds.com/The-Market/Tools-and-Resources/Research/Market-Intelligence-Toolkit/Country-Profiles [Published May 2011], II-3135

"Country Profile China." [online] from http://www.lloyds.com/Lloyds/Offices/Asia/China-in-Chinese/~/media/Files/The Market/Tools and resources/New Market Intelligence/Country Profiles [Published July 2011], II-3136

"Country Profile Denmark." [online] from http://www.lloyds.com [Published May 2011], II-3137

"Country Profile Finland." [online] from http://www.lloyds.com/The-Market/Tools-and-Resources/Research/Market-Intelligence-Toolkit/Country-Profiles [Published May 2011], II-3138

"Country Profile Germany." [online] from http://www.lloyds.com/The-

Market/Tools-and-Resources/Research/Market-Intelligence-Toolkit/Country-Profiles [Published April 2011], II-3139

"Country Profile Greece." [online] from http://www.lloyds.com/The-Market/Tools-and-Resources/Research/Market-Intelligence-Toolkit/Country-Profiles [Published April 2011], II-3140

"Country Profile Hong Kong." [online] from http://www.lloyds.com/The-Market/Tools-and-Resources/Research/Market-Intelligence-Toolkit/Country-Profiles [Published May 2011], II-3141

"Country Profile Israel." [online] from http://www.lloyds.com/The-Market/Tools-and-Resources/Research/Market-Intelligence-Toolkit/Country-Profiles [Published April 2011], II-3142

"Country Profile Italy." [online] from http://www.lloyds.com/The-Market/Tools-and-Resources/Research/Market-Intelligence-Toolkit/Country-Profiles [Published September 2011], II-3143

"Country Profile Norway." [online] from http://www.lloyds.com [Published May 2011], II-3144

"Country Profile Portugal." [online] from http://www.lloyds.com/The-Market/Tools-and-Resources/Research/Market-Intelligence-Toolkit/Country-Profiles [Published July 2011], II-3145

"Country Profile Spain." [online] from http://www.lloyds.com/The-Market/Tools-and-Resources/Research/Market-Intelligence-Toolkit/Country-Profiles [Published May 2011], II-3146

"Country Profile Sweden." [online] from http://www.lloyds.com [Published May 2011], II-3147

Crain's Chicago Business, II-3574

Crain's Detroit Business, II-3520

"Credit Suisse Business Services Conference." [online] from http://www.dp-dhl.com [Published December 6, 2011], II-2516-2519

CRN, I-1936, 1948, 1952, 1954, 1958, 1965, 1968, II-2005, 2083-

2084, 2111, 2119-2120, 3347, 3350, 3356, 3368-3369

Croatia Telecommunications Report, II-2589

"Crop Production." [online] from http://usda.mannlib.cornell.edu [Published November 9, 2011], I-55, 59, 65, 71-72, 74, 91

"Crop Production." [online] from http://usda.mannlib.cornell.edu [Published October 12, 2011], I-69

"CRTC: Broadband and Wireless Gaining Momentum in Canada." [online] from http://www.thetelecomblog.com [Published July 29, 2011], II-2585

"Crude Oil Processing and Petroleum Product Processing in China." [online] from http://www.docin.com/p-313048912.html [Published December 2011], I-1580

CSP, I-369, 505, 605, 635, 705, 771, 774, 808, 827, 882, 955, 965-967, 969, 972, 1563-1564, 1592

"Current Industrial Reports." [online] from http://www.census.gov/manufacturing/cir/index.html [Accessed August 15, 2011], I-1509, 1666, 1706-1707, 1709-1710, 1780, 1802, 1809-1810, 1829-1830, 1897-1898, 1903, 1981-1983, II-2001-2003, 2023, 2031, 2113, 2125, 2135, 2327, 2329, 2335, 2338

Czech Republic Food & Drink Report, II-2858

Czech Republic Telecommunications Report, II-2618

D Business, II-3151, 3490

"Dairy Alternative Beverages in the U.S." [online] from http://www.docin.com [Published January 2012], I-425

Dairy Foods, I-386, 421, 424, 484, 495, 498

Datamonitor Industry Market Research, I-38, 334-335, 453, 456, 662-677, 750, 786, 826, 937-944, 946-951, 975-981, 1199, 1247, 1249-1250, 1385, 1430, 1471, 1504, 1821, 1852, 1923, II-2143-2145, 2157, 2159, 2203, 2205, 2207-2208, 2303, 2307-2316, 2441-2442, 2449, 2621, 2707-2716,

2748, 2803, 2882, 2894, 3008-3009, 3257, 3345, 3372, 3587

"DD's Coffee Club." [online] from http://www.ddifo.org/pdfs/Coffee%20Trends.pdf [Published April 19, 2011], I-852

"The Deal 2010 - P&G's Acquisition of Reckitt Benckiser." [online] from http://www.slideshare.net [Accessed May 1, 2012], I-1171, 1486, II-2475

"The Deal Case Study." [online] from http://www.scribd.com [Published October 2010], I-1364-1369, 1409-1412, 1557, 1559-1562, 1574-1579

Dealernews, II-2326

"Debit Networks Market Share Report." [online] from http://3dmerchant.com/blog/credit-card-processing-rates/debit-networks-market-share [Accessed March 2, 2012], II-3094

"Debt Collection Agencies in the U.S." [online] from http://www.ibisworld.com [Published June 2011], II-3315

"December 2011 Dashboard: Sales Still Climbing." [online] from http://www.hybridcars.com [Published January 9, 2012], II-2214, 2217-2218

"Decorative Laminates." [online] from http://www.freedoniagroup.com [Published February 2012], I-1625

"Del Monte Foods Investor Fact Sheet." [online] from http://phx.corporate-ir.net [Published September 2011], I-452, 457, 476-477, 580-581, 583, 589

"Denmark Food and Drink Market." [online] from http://www.fft.com [Published July 2011], I-311

"Dentsply Acquires Astra Tech for $1.8B." [online] from http://www.drbicuspid.com [Published June 22, 2011], II-2401

"Deposit Market Share Report." [online] from http://www.2fdic.gov [Published October 1, 2011], II-3034-3085

"Design, Editing and Rendering Software Publishing in the U.S."

[online] from http://www.ibisworld.com [Published July 2011], II-3348

"Despite Strong CEE Performance, EMEA PC Shipments." [online] from http://www.idc.com [Published January 19, 2012], I-1940

"Detailed Assessment of the Market Potential and Demand for an EU ETV Scheme." [online] from http://ec.europa.eu [Published June 2011], I-1921

Detroit Free Press, II-2196

"Deutsche Bank European TMT Conference." [online] from http://www.equitystory.com [Published September 7, 2011], II-2127, 2138, 2142

"Development and Application of a Value Chain Research." [online] from http://repository.lib.ncsu.edu/ir/bitstream/1840.16/6190/1/etd.pdf [Accessed December 1, 2011], I-982-983, 1004, 1019, 1025

"Diamond Announces Top-Selling Comic Books and Graphic Novels for Year 2011." [online] from http://www.diamondcomics.com/Home/1/1/3/597?articleID=116973 [Published January 10, 2012], I-1206

"Diamond Foods Platform for Future Growth." [online] from http://phx.corporate-ir.net [Published September 7, 2011], I-883-884

"Digital Textbooks Reaching the Tipping Point in U.S. Higher Education." [online] from http://info.xplana.com/report/pdf/Xplana_Whitepaper_2011.pdf [Published March 2011], I-1225

"DisplaySearch Raises 2011 China PC Shipment Forecast." [online] from http://wwww.displaysearch.com [Press release November 14, 2011], I-1935

"Disposable Medical Supplies." [online] from http://www.freedoniagroup.com [Published March 2012], II-2387

"Document Preparation Services in the U.S." [online] from http://www.ibisworld.com [Published June 2011], II-3394

"Domestic Airlines in the U.S." [online] from http://www.ibisworld.com [Published December 2010], II-2539

"Domestic Dairy Semen Sales." [online] from http://www.naab-css.org/sales/table32.html [Accessed May 18, 2012], I-139

Door and Window Manufacturer, I-244

Drinks International, I-780-781, 790, 793-794

"Drivers of Consolidation in the Seed Industry and its Consequences for Innovation." [online] from http://www.cogem.net [Published January 14, 2011], I-51

Drug Store News, I-10, 458, 469, 478, 503, 507-509, 523, 657, 739, 831-833, 835-836, 879, 897, 1299, 1301, 1320-1321, 1362, 1380, 1387-1388, 1390, 1395-1397, 1399, 1402, 1404, 1406-1407, 1428, 1440, 1445-1446, 1473, 1506, 1511, 1753, II-2039, 2367, 2371, 2456, 2460-2462, 2465

DrugStore Management, I-1177, 1297, 1308, 1314, 1322, 1329, 1422-1423, 1447, 1457, 1491, II-2032, 2374, 2414, 2489, 2494

"Drywall Contractors in the U.S." [online] from http://lowes.retailforward.com [Published December 2010], I-288

"Eagle Industry Financial Result." [online] from http://www.ekk.co.jp/.../Financial_Result_Fiscal_Year_ending_March_2011.pdf [Published May 20, 2011], I-1620

Earth Imaging Journal, II-2106

"Eastern Asia Will Account for 30 Percent of Industrial Pump Market in 2011." [online] from http://impeller.net/magazine/news_en/doc5509x.asp [Published June 22, 2011], I-1899

"Economic Outlook - What it Means to the Chemical Industry." [online] from http://www.ccfei.net/UpFile/Conference/201104211607067968873.pdf [Published April 2011], I-1522, 1530

Editor & Publisher, I-1201, 1204

EE Times, II-2128

Egypt Telecommunications Report, II-2590

"Electric Transmission & Distribution Equipment." [online] from http://www.freedoniagroup.com [Published May 2011], II-1993

"Electrical." [online] from http://www.bostonstrategies.com/client-login/rawmaterials/ElectricalFeb.pdf [Published January 2010], II-2007

Electronic Retailer, II-3299

"Energy Drinks, Ready-to-Drink Teas and Sports Beverages Grew Aggressively; Carbonated Soft Drinks Stumbled Yet Again." [online] from http://www.beverage-marketing.com [Press release March 20, 2012], I-752

"Engineering/Design Staffing Growth Update." [online] from http://www.staffingindustry.com [Published April 26, 2011], II-3341

"Engineering Services in the U.S." [online] from http://www.slideshare.net [Published November 2010], II-3570

ENR, I-243, 281, 283-285, 287, 291, 295, 297, 1837

Entertainment Weekly, II-3437

"Equine Market Analysis." [online] from http://www.tranzon.com/otherdocs/Seminole_equine_market.pdf [Accessed April 1, 2012], I-131

"Estimated Value of the Domestic Seed Market in Selected Countries." [online] from http://www.worldseed.org [Accessed April 1, 2012], I-49

"Ethylene and Polyethylene Global Overview." [online] from http://spi.files.cms-plus.com/about/fbf [Published May 2011], I-1275, 1279

"EU Market for Protective Gloves." [online] from http://www.cbi.eu/marketinfo/cbi/?action=showDetails&id=768 [Published July 2008], I-1057

"EU Market in Denim Jeans." [online] from http://www.cbi.eu [Published January 2009], I-1023

"Eurasia Drilling Company." [online] from http://www.eurasiadrilling.com/files/EDC_Presentation_2011_Interim_Period_Results.pdf [Published September 2011], I-201

Eurofresh Distribution, I-104

"The European Optical Market 2010-2011." [online] from http://www.swv4u.com/173.html?file=tl_files/references/2011...pdf [Accessed May 1, 2012], II-2411

"Excavation Contractors in the U.S." [online] from http://lowes.retailforward.com [Published April 2011], I-296

"Excipients." [online] from http://www.freedoniagroup.com [Published May 2011], I-1348

"Executive Search in Transition." [online] from https://members.aesc.org/eweb/upload/Executive%20Search%20in%20Transition%202010.pdf [Accessed October 1, 2011], II-3590

"Explosives Manufacturing in the U.S." [online] from http://www.ibisworld.com [Published September 2011], I-1551

"Explosives Trace Detection." [online] from http://www.homelandsecurityresearch.com [Accessed April 1, 2012], II-2339

"External Influences Reshape the Semiconductor Industry." [online] from http://www.eciaonline.org [Published October 2011], II-2926

"Facts and Figures 2011." [online] from http://www.cefic.org [Accessed April 1, 2012], I-1246

"Family Clothing Stores in the U.S." [online] from http://www.ibisworld.com [Published August 2011], II-2899

"The F&A BPO Market Landscape in 2011." [online] from http://www.accenture.com [Published April 2011], II-3373

"Farm Product Storage & Warehousing in the U.S." [online] from http://www.ibisworld.com [Published August 2011], II-2520

"Farmers Bet on Rates as MetLife Battles Rural Lenders." [online]

from http://www.bloomberg.com [Published January 20, 2012], II-3098

"Farms, Land in Farms, and Livestock Operations 2011 Summary." [online] from http://usda01.library.cornell.edu/usda/current/FarmLandIn/FarmLandIn-02-17-2012.pdf [Published February 2012], I-136

"Fats and Salad/Cooking Oils in the U.S. Market." [online] from http://www.scribd.com [Published October 2011], I-514, 734, 738, 741, 744-745

"Faurecia 2011-2015 Targeting Profitable Growth." [online] from http://www.faurecia.com [Published November 7, 2011], I-1127-1128, II-2242-2243, 2249

Feedstuffs, I-357, 380, 1330, 1524, II-2810

"Fertilizer Manufacturing in the U.S." [online] from http://www.ibisworld.com [Published April 2011], I-1534

"Filters." [online] from http://www.freedoniagroup.com [Published June 2011], I-1916

Finance & Commerce, II-2476

Financial Stability Review, II-3239

Financial Times, I-24-25, 148, 151, 194, 197, 234, 748, 900, 1205, 1332, 1738, II-2091-2092, 2199, 2220, 2267, 2423, 2497, 2541, 2548, 2557-2558, 2575, 2626, 2671-2672, 2703, 2859, 3086, 3116, 3123, 3128, 3310, 3489, 3600

"Fine Art Schools in the U.S." [online] from http://www.ibisworld.com [Published July 2011], II-3533

"Fine Grain, High Density Graphite." [online] from http://www.bis.doc.gov [Published April 2010], II-2011

"Finland Food and Drink Market." [online] from http://www.fft.com [Published July 2011], I-312

"First Half 2011 LSA Market Report." [online] from http://www.bydanjohnson.com [Published July 21, 2011], II-2268

"First Solar and Suntech Led 2011's Module Manufacturer Rankings, says Lux Research Report." [online] from http://www.pv-tech.org [Published March 14, 2012], I-1769

Flexible Packaging, I-29, 39

Floor Covering Weekly, I-14, II-2480, 2906

"Floriculture Crops 2010 Summary." [online] from http://usda.mannlib.cornell.edu [Published April 2011], I-107

"Flour Milling in the U.S." [online] from http://www.ibisworld.com [Published July 2011], I-555

"Flow Chemistry Technologies." [online] from http://www.i-micronews.com/upload/Rapports/Yole_Flow_Chemistry_Technologies_Sample_March_2012_.pdf [Accessed June 1, 2012], I-1891

"Flower Foods." [online] from http://research-us.bmocapitalmarkets.com [Published April 29, 2011], I-607, 629

"Food and Beverage in Japan." [online] from http://www.nzte.govt.nz [Published March 2012], I-318

"Food and Beverage in the United States." [online] from http://www.nzte.govt.nz [Published May 2012], II-2935

"Food and Beverage Industry in Germany." [online] from http://www.gtai.com [Accessed November 1, 2011], I-302

Food & Beverage Packaging, I-33

Food Business News, I-301, 909-910

"Food Containers: Rigid & Flexible." [online] from http://www.freedoniagroup.com [Published April 2011], I-1745

Food Engineering, I-331

"Foodservice Disposables." [online] from http://www.freedoniagroup.com [Published August 2011], I-1152

"Foodservice Profile Spain." [online] from http://publications.gc.ca/collections/collection_2011 [Published June 2011], II-2938

"Footwear Market in the EU." [online] from http://www.ipex.jccm.es/www/download/GuiasyObservatorios/gscalzado/gscalzado/docs/footwear_cbi.pdf [Published May 2010], I-1610

Forbes, II-3131

Fort Worth Star-Telegram, II-2492

Fortune, I-1030,

"France Food and Drink Market." [online] from http://www.fft.com [Published July 2011], I-313

France Telecommunications Report, II-2592-2593

"Freight Rail Transportation in China." [online] from http://www.docin.com [Published September 2011], II-2498

"Frost & Sullivan's Study on Potential Market for Carbon Nanomaterials Applications." [online] from http://www.frost.com [Published February 28, 2011], II-2010

Frozen & Dairy Buyer, I-126, 348, 375, 382, 393, 407-409, 416-417, 419, 436-437, 464, 483, 486, 524, 527-528, 531-532, 540, 542-544, 547-551, 570-571, 599, 606, 616, 621, 840, 844

"Full-Service Restaurants." [online] from http://www.pacificedc.org/.../Restaurant%20Industry%20Snapshot.pdf [Accessed September 1, 2011], II-2942

Furniture Today, I-1120, II-2909-2910

"FY 2011 President's Budget for HHS." [online] from http://dhhs.gov/asfr/ob/docbudget/2011budgetinbrief.pdf [Accessed April 1, 2012], II-3597

"Galaxy Surfactants." [online] from http://www.spacapital.com [Published May 13, 2011], I-1477

"Gartner Reports Billions More for BI." [online] from http://www.information-management.com/news [Published April 2, 2012], II-3346

"Gartner Says Apple Became the Top Semiconductor Customer in 2011." [online] from http://www.gartner.com [Press release January 24, 2012], II-2147

"Gartner Says India PC Market Grew 13 Percent In The Third Quarter of 2011." [online] from http://www.gartner.com [Published November 10, 2011], I-1943

"Gartner Says India Printer Copier and Multifunctional Product Market Grew 2.4 Percent in The Third Quarter of 2011." [online] from http://www.gartner.com [Press release December 15, 2011], I-1966

"Gartner Says Western European PC Shipments Fell 16 Percent." [online] from http://www.gartner.com [Press release February 7, 2012], I-1941-1942, 1945

"Gartner Says Worldwide External Controller-Based Disk Storage Market." [online] from http://www.gartner.com [Press release September 8, 2011], I-1951

"Gartner Says Worldwide IT Outsourcing Market Grew 7.8 Percent in 2011." [online] from http://www.gartner.com [Press release May 21, 2012], II-3374

"Gartner Says Worldwide IT Services Revenue Returned to Growth in 2010." [online] from http://www.gartner.com [Press release May 4, 2011], II-3375

"Gartner Says Worldwide Supply Chain Management Software Market Grew 12.3 Percent." [online] from http://www.gartner.com [Press release May 16, 2012], II-3361

"Gas Stations in the U.S." [online] from http://www.ibisworld.com [Published October 2011], II-2878

"GE Energy/Converteam." [online] from http://ec.europa.eu [Published July 25, 2011], I-1819, II-2008

Gear Technology, I-1913

"General Aviation Airplane Shipment Report." [online] from http://www.gama.org [Published April 19, 2012], II-2270

"General Electric Company." [online] from http://www.docstoc.com [Published June 20, 2010], II-2006, 2053, 2158, 2269, 2274, 2296, 2363, 2693, 2749

"General Mills." [online] from http://www.generalmills.com [Accessed August 1, 2011], I-442-444

"German Corporate Conference Jungheinrich." [online] from http:// cheuvreux-gcc.com/sites/default/ files/pdf/presentation/Jungheinrich. pdf [Published January 19, 2011], I-1868

"Germany Food and Drink Market." [online] from http://www.fft. com [Published July 2011], I-314

"Gfk: Growth from Knowledge." [online] from http://www.gfk.com [Published September 28, 2011], II-2061

"Gift, Novelty & Souvenir Stores Industry Profile." [online] from http://www.firstresearch.com/industry-research/Gift-Novelty-and-Souvenir-Stores.html [Published May 7, 2012], II-3012

"Gift Shops & Card Stores in the U.S." [online] from http://www. ibisworld.com [Published October 2011], II-3013

"Gildan Activewear Reports Record Second Quarter Sales and Earnings." [online] from http:// www.istockanalyst.com [Published May 11, 2011], I-1037

"Global Airport Operations." [online] from http://retail.ibisworld. com [Published January 10, 2011], II-2562

"Global Apparel and Textile Report." [online] from http://www. docin.com [Published September 10, 2010], II-2896

"Global Auto Report." [online] from http://www.scotiacapital.com/ English/bns_econ/bns_auto.pdf [Published November 29, 2011], II-2198

"Global Biotechnology." [online] from http://www.scribd.com [Published January 1, 2011], I-1354

"Global Candy and Chocolate Manufacturing." [online] from http:// www.docin.com/p-317611146. html [Published August 2011], I-658

"Global Cardboard Container Manufacturing." [online] from http:// www.docin.com/p-83941330.html [Published March 22, 2010], I-1147

Global Cement, I-1671

"Global Commercial Printing." [online] from http://www.docin.com [Published September 2011], I-1236

Global Cosmetic Industry, I-1437

"Global Fast Food Restaurants." [online] from http://www.docin. com/p-80016932.html [Published April 2010], II-2952

"Global Forest Resource Assessment, 2010." [online] from http:// www.fao.org/docrep/014/am859e/ am859e08.pdf [Published in November 2011], I-141

"Global Graphic Designers." [online] from http://www.docin.com/p-320645709.html [Published December 2011], II-3321

"Global Handbag and Purse Manufacturing." [online] from http:// www.docin.com/p-320063080. html [Published July 2011], I-1651

"Global Heroin Market." [online] from http://www.unodc.org/documents/data-and-analysis/DR2011/ The_opium-heroin_market.pdf [Accessed September 1, 2011], I-1333

"Global High Speed Rail Market on the Fast Track for Business Development." [online] from http:// www.docstoc.com [Published April 13, 2011], II-2294

"Global HR & Recruitment Services." [online] from http://www.docin.com/p-320645711.html [Published August 2011], II-3589

"Global IPTV Equipment Market and Provider Competition Analysis." [online] from http://www. frostchina.com [Published July 2009], II-2698, 3355

"Global Luxury Goods." [online] from http://www.research.hsbc. com [Published September 2, 2011], II-3006

"Global Magazine Publishing." [online] from http://www.docin.com/p-320063081.html [Published August 2011], I-1208

"Global Office Furniture Industry Trends." [online] from http://www. rightplace.org [Published March 16, 2011], I-1121, 1123

"Global Oil and Gas Market." [online] from http://www.hkexnews.hk [Published December 14, 2011], I-205, 209, 1514, 1712-1714

"Global Packaged Confectionery Trends." [online] from http://publications.gc.ca [Published May 2011], I-659

"Global Pathfinder Report - Baby Food." [online] from http://www. ats.agr.gc.ca [Published July 2011], I-446

"Global Solar PV Installs of 2011." [online] from http://www.electroiq. com/articles/pvw/2011/11/global-solar-pv-installs-of-2011.html [Published November 11, 2011], I-1766

"Global Sugar Manufacturing." [online] from http://www.docin.com/p-317611151.html [Published June 2011], I-644

"Global Technology: Software." [online] from http://www.kingdee. com/news/12344.html [Published August 22, 2010], II-3344, 3349, 3357

"Global Themes Strategy." [online] from http://fa.morganstanley-individual.com/public/project files/20f58b5f-3d4e-40d8-99f9-6914f6c73980.pdf [Published October 17, 2011], I-46

"Global Yearly Chart." [online] from http://www.vgchartz.com/ yearly/2011/Global [Accessed February 6, 2012], II-3364

Globalization and Health, I-338-344, 818, 820, 822-825

"Globe Specialty Metals." [online] from http://files.shareholder.com [Published September 2011], I-1728

"Gluten-Free Packaged Foods." [online] from http://publications.gc.ca/ collections/collection_2011/agr/

A74-1-16-2011-eng.pdf [Published July 2011], I-333, 612

"GNC Holdings." [online] from http://uoinvestmentgroup.org/wp-content/uploads/2012/02/GNC.pdf [Published March 2, 2012], II-2986

"Golf Courses Industry Snapshot." [online] from http://www.kitsapeda.org [Published February 2011], II-3474

"Google's Market Share by Country." [online] from http://visualeconomics.creditloan.com/2010-02-03-planet-google-from-philosophies-to-market-shares [Accessed December 1, 2011], II-2647

"Government Contractors." [online] from http://www.capstonellc.com/research/industryreports [Published Third Quarter 2011], II-3599

Government Fleet, II-2187

"The Great Leap Forward." [online] from http://www.scribd.com [Published July 8, 2010], I-384, 412, 423, 454, 521, 732, 892, 922, 1176, 1179, 1186, 1192, 1317, 1389, 1392, 1401, 1421, 1424, 1427, 1461, 1472, 1558

"Great Potential in Chinese TV Shopping Market." [online] from http://www.docin.com/p-21803 3753.html [Published April 1, 2009], II-3018

Greece Autos Report, II-2300

"Greece Food and Drink Market." [online] from http://www.fft.com [Published July 2011], I-315

"Greece Retail Foods 2011." [online] from http://gain.fas.usda.gov [Published December 16, 2011], II-2829

"Green Building Materials." [online] from http://www.freedoniagroup.com [Published April 2011], I-3

"Green Housing Cleaning Products in the U.S." [online] from http://www.docint.com [Published June 2010], I-1391

Grocer, I-462, 530, 559, 576, 579, 653, 1318

Grocery Headquarters, I-73, 79-80, 84, 88, 92, 364, 372, 388, 394-396, 402-404, 415, 418, 426, 440, 459-460, 463, 471-475, 489-491, 493-494, 519, 525-526, 572-573, 577, 590-591, 609, 730, 804, 837, 856, 889-890, 893-894, 920-921, 936, 1183, 1194, 1374, 1469, II-2820

"Group Presentation for Investors." [online] from http://www.bicworld.com [Published August 2011], II-2458

"GSK Vaccines in 2011." [online] from http://www.gsk.com [Accessed December 1, 2011], I-1359

"Guns and Ammunition Manufacturing in the U.S." [online] from http://www.ibisworld.com [Published October 2011], I-1794

"Gym and Exercise Equipment Manufacturing in the U.S." [online] from http://www.ibisworld.com [Published July 2011], II-2446

"Hair and Nail Salons in the U.S." [online] from http://www.ibisworld.com [Published September 2011], II-3283

"Hair Loss Treatment & Removal in the U.S." [online] from http://www.ibisworld.com [Published September 2010], II-3289

"Handbag, Luggage & Accessory Stores in the U.S." [online] from http://www.ibisworld.com [Published September 2011], II-3014

"Hard Surface Flooring." [online] from http://www.freedoniagroup.com [Published July 2011], II-2482

"Hardware Stores in the U.S." [online] from http://lowes.retailforward.com/RichMedia/RfMedia_634643927934460627.pdf [Published February 2012], II-2785

"Health, Nutrition & Fitness Report." [online] from https://www.acg.org/assets/10/documents/Health__Nutrition_&_Fitness_Report.pdf [Published Spring 2012], I-336, 813, 1296, II-2445, 3471

"Healthcare Equipment & Supplies Global Report 2012." [online] from http://www.clearwatercf.com [Accessed October 1, 2011], II-2347

"Heavy Industrial Facilities Construction in the U.S." [online] from http://www.ibisworld.com [Published December 2011], I-279

"Heineken-APB China." [online] from http://www.heinekeninternational.com/content/live/FMC2011/4.%20Malcolm_Tan.pdf [Published December 8, 2011], I-754

"Hershey Facts." [online] from http://www.thehersheycompany.com/assets/pdfs/hersheycompany/FactBook-October-2011.pdf [Published October 2011], I-661, 717, 724

HFN, II-2915-2917

"Highly Concentrated: Companies That Dominate Their Industries." [online] from http://www.ibisworld.com [Published February 2012], I-1191, II-2939

"Hiwin." [online] from https://mm.jpmorgan.com [Published March 12, 2011], II-2334

"HMS Group." [online] from http://grouphms.com/upload/research_reports [Published July 11, 2011], I-1896

Home Channel News, I-8, 17, 22, 1755-1756, 1762, 1835, 1879, II-2016

Home Media Retailing, I-11, II-3449

"Home Organization in the U.S." [online] from http://www.packagedfacts.com [Published November 2011], I-19

"Home Organization Products." [online] from http://www.freedoniagroup.com [Published June 2011], I-18

Home Textiles Today, I-1066-1079, II-2907, 2913

HomeWorld Business, I-2, 1116, 1118, 1789, II-2033-2038, 2041, 2430, 2786, 2905, 2911, 2914, 2918-2919, 2921-2923, 3017

Hong Kong Telecommunications Report, II-2596

"Horse Breed Registration Figures." [online] from http://www.jockeyclub.com/factbook.asp?section=16 [Accessed April 1, 2012], I-132

"Hotel Industry." [online] from http://faculty.cit.cornell.edu/jl2545/4160/presentation/Hotel%20Pricing-1.pptx [Published April 14, 2011], II-3270

Household & Personal Products Industry, I-1196, 1373, 1376, 1386, 1403, 1405, 1494, 1566

"Household Floor Care Appliances - U.S." [online] from http://www.freedoniagroup.com [Published September 2011], II-2043

"Household Refrigerator and Freezer Manufacturing in China." [online] from http://www.docin.com/p-80616558.html [Published December 2009], II-2025

Houston Business Journal, II-3314

Hungary Food and Drink Report, I-761, 821

Hungary Telecommunications Report, II-2597

"Hunting and Trapping in the U.S." [online] from http://www.ibisworld.com [Published April 2011], I-147

"HVAC Equipment." [online] from http://www.freedoniagroup.com [Published November 2011], I-1986

"IARW Global Top 25 List." [online] from http://www.gcca.org [Published May 2012], II-2521

"Ice Business Heats Up in Summer." [online] from http://www.wnyc.org [Published July 13, 2011], I-887

"ICON PLC." [online] from http://www.jefferies.com [Published September 2011], II-3577

IDEX Magazine, II-2428

"Implantable Cardioverter Defibrillators and Cardiac Resynchronization." [online] from http://www.free-press-release.com/news/print-1321006002.html [Published November 11, 2011], II-2360

"India as an MRO Destination: Myth or Reality." [online] from http://www.slideshare.net [Published September 21, 2011], II-2273

"India Capital Goods Sector." [online] from http://doc.research-and-analytics.csfb.com [Published March 31, 2011], II-2000

"Indian Two-Wheeler Industry." [online] from http://www.icra.in/Files/ticker/Indian%202W%20Industry.pdf [Published November 2011], II-2304

"Indorama Ventures." [online] from http://www.dcs-digital.com/setweb/downloads/2554q1/20110518_ivl.pdf [Published May 18, 2011], I-1283

"Industrial Gases." [online] from http://www.docstoc.com/docs/29548811/CS-Industrial-Gases-Primer [Published February 25, 2009], I-1255, 1258-1260

"Industrial Laundry & Linen Supply in the U.S." [online] from http://www.ibisworld.com [Published October 2011], II-3277

"Industrial Power Transmission Equipment." [online] from http://www.bostonstrategy.com [Published January 2012], I-1805

"Industrial Sectors Market Characterization." [online] from http://www.calmac.org/publications/Final_Cement_Industrial_Market_Characterization_Report.pdf [Published February 2012], I-1676

"Industry at a Glance." [online] from http://www.maricopa-sbdc.com/Research%20Reports [Published September 2010], II-2993

"Industry Financial Data." [online] from http://www.alta.org/industry/financial.cfm [Accessed November 1, 2011], II-3236

"Industry Information - Synthetic Wood." [online] from http://www.wchservices.com [Accessed May 1, 2012], I-1100

"Industry Overview." [online] from http://corpsv.etnet.com.hk/data/documents/ipo/LTN20110505013/114_e.pdf [Accessed September 1, 2011], I-1292

"Industry Overview." [online] from http://corpsv.etnet.com.hk/data/documents/ipo/LTN20110516025/113_e.pdf [Accessed September 1, 2011], I-12, 1084, II-2481

"Industry Overview." [online] from http://iis.aastocks.com/20110616/001223928-11.PDF [Accessed September 1, 2011], I-1645-1647

"Industry Overview." [online] from http://iis.aastocks.com/20110630/001231091-10.PDF [Accessed September 1, 2011], II-2245-2246, 2250

"Industry Overview." [online] from http://webapps.dpworld.com [Accessed November 1, 2011], II-2536

"Industry Overview." [online] from http://www.haitian.com/files/industry_overview.pdf [Accessed February 20, 2012], I-1892

"Industry Overview." [online] from http://www.hkexnews.hk/list-edco/listconews/sehk [Published September 2011], I-933

"Industry Overview." [online] from http://www.hkexnews.hk/listedco/listconews/sehk/2011/1202/01293_1217327/E113.pdf [Accessed December 1, 2011], II-2188, 2212

"Industry Overview." [online] from http://www.hkexnews.hk/listedco/listconews/sehk/20110912/.../E113.pdf [Accessed October 1, 2011], I-1642

"Industry Overview." [online] from http://www.hkexnews.hk/listedco/listconews/sehk/2012/0410 [Published April 2012], I-1811

"Industry Overview." [online] from http://www.hkexnews.hk/reports/prelist/EHOSAI-20110610-09.pdf [Published June 10, 2011], I-1033-1034, 1047

"Industry Overview." [online] from http://www.hkgem.com [Accessed December 1, 2011], I-1481

"Industry Overview." [online] from http://www.hkgem.com/listing/prelist/ECSNHC-20110729-10.pdf [Accessed October 1, 2011], I-1779

"Industry Overview." [online] from http://www.hkgem.com/listing/prelist/ELEGEND-20110622-10.pdf [Accessed October 1, 2011], II-3269

"Industry Overview." [online] from http://www.hkgem.com/listing/prelist/EWPSHICL-20110902-10.pdf [Accessed October 1, 2010], I-1839, 1841-1843, 1866

"Industry Overview." [online] from http://www.hkgem.com/reports [Accessed December 1, 2011], I-1861

"Industry Overview." [online] from http://www.hkgem.com/reports/prelist/Documents/EWPGRAFF-20120518-10.pdf [Accessed June 1, 2012], I-27

"Industry Perspective." [online] from http://www.burkhartdental.com/sites/default/files/files/news/dental_offices_9_2011.pdf [Accessed April 1, 2012], II-3504

"Industry Statistics & Trends." [online] from http://www.americanpetproducts.org/press_Industrytrends.asp [Accessed December 1, 2011], I-40

"Infant, Toddler and Preschool Furnishings Toys, Accessories in the U.S." [online] from http://www.packagedfacts.com [Published November 2010], II-2438

Instore Buyer, I-631, 899, 919

"Insulation." [online] from http://www.freedoniagroup.com [Published March 2012], I-1691

Insurance Facts and Stats, II-3148, 3150, 3183, 3185, 3190, 3212, 3220, 3232

"Intel Reasserts Semiconductor Market Leadership in 2011." [online] from http://www.isuppli.com [Published December 1, 2011], II-2146

"International Copper Association." [online] from http://industrial-energy.lbl.gov/files/industrial-energy [Published September 11, 2011], II-2009

"Internet Service Providers." [online] from http://www.docin.com/p-320610766.html [Published May 2011], II-2641

"Investment in Exploration-Production and Refining." [online] from http://www.ifpenergiesnouvelles.com [Published October 2011], I-203-204, 208

"Investor Overview." [online] from http://www.fishercoachworks.com/pdf/investor_overview_web.pdf [Published January 2010], II-2221

"Investor Presentation Second Quarter 2011." [online] from http://phx.corporate-ir.net [Accessed February 20, 2012], II-3336

Investor's Business Daily, I-1510, 1513, 1893, 1895, 1933, 1937, 1950, 1956, 1959-1960, II-2075-2076, 2082, 2094, 2099, 2116-2117, 2132-2133, 2141, 2231, 2332, 2668, 2675-2676, 2679, 2987, 3302, 3351, 3353-3354, 3359

Iran Telecommunications Report, II-2599

"Ireland Food and Drink Market." [online] from http://www.fft.com [Published July 2011], I-316

Ireland Telecommunications Report, II-2600, 2639

"Is There a Danger of Oversupplying in Iron Ore Market?" [online] from http://www.docstoc.com [Published March 25, 2011], I-149

"Italy: Toiletries and Cosmetics." [online] from http://www.export.gov [Published September 2011], I-1417

"Italy Food and Drink Market." [online] from http://www.fft.com [Published July 2011], I-317

"J&J's Heart Stent Sales, Market Share Declining." [online] from http://seadev.bonnint.net/category/money_news_articles [Published June 15, 2011], II-2351

"Janitorial Equipment and Supplies." [online] from http://www.freedoniagroup.com [Published August 2011], I-20

"Janitorial Services in the U.S." [online] from http://www.ibisworld.com [Published September 2011], II-3329

"Japan: Analytical Instruments Industry." [online] from http://www.export.gov [Published October 2011], II-3582

"Japan: Contemporary Women's Wear Market." [online] from http://

www.export.gov [Published September 2011], I-1018

"Japan: Food Processing Equipment." [online] from http://www.export.gov [Published May 2011], I-303

"Japan: Generics Market." [online] from http://www.export.gov [Published November 2011], I-1346

"Japan: Pet Products Industry." [online] from http://www.export.gov [Published November 2011], II-2493

Japan Telecommunications Report, II-2601, 2637

"Japanese Watch & Clock Industry in 2011." [online] from http://www.jcwa.or.jp/eng/statistics/industry_11.html [Accessed April 30, 2012], II-2421-2422

"JCI/CRH Merger Procedure." [online] from http://ec.europa.eu [Published January 14, 2011], I-1129, II-2259

"Job Training & Career Counseling in the U.S." [online] from http://www.ibisworld.com [Published April 2011], II-3546

"John Deere Committed to Those Linked to the Land." [online] from http://www.deere.com [Published December 2011], I-241

Jordan Telecommunications Report, II-2602

"JT International." [online] from http://www.jt.com/investors/results/tobaccobusiness/pdf/20110208tobacco_E.pdf [Published February 8, 2011], I-953-954

"JT International Western Europe Region." [online] from http://www.jti.com [Published September 19, 2011], I-959-962

Junior Scholastic, II-3563

"Juvenile Products." [online] from http://www.capstonellc.com [Published Fourth Quarter 2011], II-2486, 3031

"K8e." [online] from http://www.slideshare.net/Ken_ruck/k8e [Accessed June 1, 2012], I-1222, 1224

"Kardex Group Investor Handbook." [online] from http://www.dynamicsgroup.ch [Published April 2011], I-1858

"Key Pick: Akzo Nobel." [online] from http://www.morganstanley.com/views/perspectives/ChinaBlue-Paper_EU.pdf [Published October 29, 2010], I-1512

Kids Today, I-1109

"Kitchen Furniture Market." [online] from http://www.vararesearch.de [Accessed April 1, 2012], I-1112

"KKR-Controlled First Data May Escape Harm From Lower Fees, Analyst Says." [online] from http://www.bloomberg.com [Published December 23, 2010], II-3092

"Korea Tops Global Lithium-Ion Battery Market in 2nd Quarter." [online] from http://www.korea.net [Published September 7, 2011], II-2172

"Labels." [online] from http://www.freedoniagroup.com [Published August 2011], I-1237

"Lamps." [online] from http://www.freedoniagroup.com [Published August 2011], II-2047-2048

"Landscaping Products." [online] from http://www.freedoniagroup.com [Published June 2011], I-21

"Language Instruction in the U.S." [online] from http://www.ibisworld.com [Published August 2010], II-3543

"Large Diameter Pipe." [online] from http://www.freedoniagroup.com [Published April 2011], I-41

Laser Focus World, II-2129

Latin Trade, II-2574

"Laundromats in the U.S." [online] from http://www.ibisworld.com [Published March 2011], II-3278

"Lawn & Garden Consumables." [online] from http://www.freedoniagroup.com [Published May 2012], I-1540

"Lawn and Garden Products Services in the U.S. 9th Edition." [online] from http://www.packagedfacts.com [Published December 2011], I-1757, 1834

"Lawn Mowers." [online] from http://ads.eztouse.com/BooksOnline/Profiles/Lawn-Mowers-Snapshot.pdf [Accessed December 1, 2011], I-1833

"Leading Fiber Innovation." [online] from http://www.lenzing.com [Published August 2011], I-1293

"Leather Tanning & Finishing in the U.S." [online] from http://www.ibisworld.com [Published August 2011], I-1636

"LED Industry." [online] from http://www.docstoc.com [Published March 28, 2011], II-2162

"LED Lighting." [online] from http://www.research.hsbc.com [Published December 13, 2011], II-2049

"Lego Toys With Hasbro's U.S. Games Monopoly." [online] from http://www.toydirectory.com [Published August 2010], II-2439

"Levi Strauss Case Study." [online] from http://essays24.com/print/Levi039S-Case-Study/50811.html [Accessed September 1, 2011], I-1024

"LIB Materials Industry." [online] from http://gold-estate.com/content/Lithium/LiB12611.pdf [Published January 26, 2011], II-2171

"Life and Fraternal Insurance Industry." [online] from http://www.naics.org [Published March 28, 2011], II-3149

"Lighting." [online] from http://www.havells.com/Admin/Forms/Brochures [Published March 2011], I-1909, II-2054, 2058

"Lighting the Way." [online] from http://img.ledsmagazine.com/pdf/LightingtheWay.pdf [Accessed May 1, 2012], II-2050-2051

"Lime Manufacturing in the U.S." [online] from http://www.ibisworld.com [Published August 2011], I-1685

"Livestock and Poultry: World Markets and Trade." [online] from http://www.fas.usda.gov [Published April 2012], I-115-116, 119-120, 123-124, 127-128, 377, 379

"Livestock Slaughter." [online] from http://www.usda.gov [Published April 2011], I-352

"Location Analysis." [online] from http://www.warehouseclubfocus.com/warehouse_club_industry/2011_selling_bjs_location_analysis.pdf [Accessed September 1, 2011], II-2807-2809

"Logging." [online] from http://www.pacificedc.org/.../Industry%20Snapshot%20-%20Timber.pdf [Published January 2011], I-1083

Logistics Management, II-2512-2513

"Long-Term Care Market." [online] from http://www.docin.com [Published March 2012], II-3512-3513, 3522

"Louisiana-Pacific Corporation." [online] from http://phx.corporate-ir.net [Published September 13, 2011], I-1107

Lube Report, I-1586-1589, 1594

"Lumber & Building Material Stores in the U.S." [online] from http://lowes.retailforward.com [Published February 2011], II-2783

"Machine Tools in China." [online] from http://www.freedoniagroup.com [Published August 2011], I-1876

"Magic Holdings." [online] from http://www.cinda.com.hk/attachment/201112011751521_en.pdf [Published November 30, 2011], I-1497

"Maidenform CL King's 9th Annual." [online] from http://phx.corporate-ir.net [Published September 14, 2011], I-1048

"MaidenForm Company Overview." [online] from http://solutions.standardandpoors.com/SP/stk-screener [Published March 27, 2012], II-2890

"Malaysia Full Year 2011." [online] from http://bestsellingcarsblog.com/2012/02/13/malaysia-full-year-2011-perodua-myvi-and-proton-saga-rule/ [Published February 13, 2012], II-2193

Malaysia Palm Oil Fortune, I-746

Malaysia Telecommunications Report, II-2603

"Man Wah." [online] from http://www.dbpower.com.hk/columns/reports/cinda/en/201003181844201_en.pdf [Published March 18, 2010], I-1113-1114

"Mango Category Retailer Toolkit." [online] from http://www.mango.org [Published October 1, 2011], I-95

The Manufacturing Confectioner, I-648-649, 651-652, 656, 678-685, 687-693, 695-697, 699-704, 706-715, 718-720, 725-727, 862-863, 866-867, 871-872, II-2795, 2868

"Marinas in the U.S." [online] from http://www.ibisworld.com [Published August 2011], II-2538

"Marine Harvest." [online] from http://hugin.info/209/R/1522721/458927.pdf [Published June 9, 2011], I-143

"Marine Market in the United States." [online] from http://www.nzte.govt.nz [Published June 2011], II-2281, 2288, 2293

"Market Analysis." [online] from http://victoriabunte.com/files/marketanalysis.pdf [Accessed April 1, 2012], II-3267

"Market Assessment and Forecast." [online] from http://www.bostonstrategies.com [Published December 2009], I-1619, 1674, 1682

"Market Assessment and Forecast." [online] from http://www.bostonstrategies.com [Published June 2010], I-1848-1849

"Market Assessment and Forecast." [online] from http://www.bostonstrategies.com [Published March 2010], I-1901

"Market Assessment and Forecast." [online] from http://www.bostonstrategies.com [Published May 2009], I-1924

"Market for Home Care Products." [online] from http://www.docin.com [Published December 2010], II-2355-2357, 2376-2377

"Market Overview 2011 Global Gaming Bulletin." [online] from http://www.ey.com [Accessed February 20, 2012], II-3493-3496

"Market Research Estimates Thermal Management Revenues at $11 Billion by 2016." [online] from http://www.tmcnet.com [Published February 24, 2012], I-1910

"Market Share Sold 9/1/11-9/30/11." [online] from http://www.go-withcb.com/storage/Northwest.pdf [Published October 4, 2011], II-3254

"Market Shares of Consumer Payment Systems." [online] from http://www.nilsonreport.com [Published December 2011], I-9

Marketing, I-390, 447, 482, 553, 568, 637, 776, 785, 800, 888, 1361, 1398, 1478, 1495, II-2997, 3473

Marketing News, II-3580

"Marketshare Chart." [online] from http://www.kingston.com/company/marketshare.asp [Published May 2011], II-2137

"Masonry in the U.S." [online] from http://lowes.retailforward.com [Published October 2011], I-286

"McAfee and Norton Still Rule the Market for Security Software." [online] from http://www.npdfashionworld.com [Published September 7, 2011], II-3358

MCV, II-3365

"Measuring, Testing & Navigational Instrument Manufacturing in the U.S." [online] from http://www.ibisworld.com [Published November 2009], II-2333

"Meat, Poultry & Seafood Packaging." [online] from http://www.freedoniagroup.com [Published April 2011], I-36

Meatingplace, II-2949

"Medical Beds and Medical Chairs." [online] from http://www.docin.com [Published February 2009], I-1130

"Medical Device Makers in China." [online] from http://www.docin.com [Published June 2011], II-2362

Medical Marketing & Media, I-1331

Medical Product Outsourcing, II-2388

Medical Textiles, I-1011

"Medicare Advantage Enrollment Market Update." [online] from http://www.kff.org/medicare/upload/8228.pdf [Published September 2011], II-3156-3168

"Medicated Skin Care." [online] from http://wenku.baidu.com/view/dc30ff19a8114431b90dd845.html [February 2011], I-1319

"Medicated Skin Care." [online] from http://wenku.baidu.com/view/dc30ff19a8114431b90dd845.html [Published February 2011], I-1492

"Men's and Boy's Apparel Manufacturing in the U.S." [online] from http://www.ibisworld.com [Published September 2011], I-1038

"Men's Wearhouse." [online] from http://www.cfasociety.org/memphis/Linked%20Files/Men%27s%20WearhouseWritten.pdf [Published April 3, 2008], II-2884

"Metal Powders." [online] from http://www.freedoniagroup.com [Published October 2011], I-1814

Metalworking Insiders Report, I-1872-1873

"Mexico: Market Concentration in Selected Agricultural and Food Subsectors." [online] from http://gain.fas.usda.gov [Published May 25, 2011], I-356, 378, 385, 401, 413, 448, 467, 506, 522, 557, 561, 569, 574, 594, 604, 650, 733, 763, 778, 788, 803, 891, II-2791, 2799, 2805, 2837

"Mexico Food Service - Hotel Restaurant." [online] from http://www.gain.usda.gov [Published December 28, 2011], II-2937

Mexico Telecommunications Report, II-2605

"Microcontroller Solutions Group." [online] from http://phx.corporate-ir.net [Published June 2011], II-2139

Middle East Economic Digest, I-1953

"Mill Rolls Industry Research Report." [online] from http://www.bostonstrategies.com [Published May 2008], I-1696

Milling & Baking News, I-304, 562, 617, 619, 626, 639, 896

"Mineral Commodity Summaries." [online] from http://minerals.usgs.gov/minerals/pubs/mcs/2012/mcs2012.pdf [Accessed January 23, 2012], I-150, 154-155, 157, 159, 163-164, 167, 169, 175, 182, 213, 216-218, 224-226, 228-232, 235-237, 239-240, 1266-1268, 1273, 1570, 1572, 1675, 1686, 1689, 1699-1700, 1705, 1721, 1723-1726, 1729, 1735-1736

"Missouri Department of Insurance." [online] from http://insurance.mo.gov [Accessed May 14, 2012], II-3152

"MLB Attendance Report 2012." [online] from http://espn.go.com/mlb/attendance [Accessed May 1, 2012], II-3482

MMR, I-373, 397-399, 406, 435, 539, 552, 620, 740, 743, 806, 1158, 1160, 1170, 1173, 1309, 1312, 1327, 1375, 1377, 1383, 1431, 1439, 1444, 1450, 1452, 1462-1463, 1466-1468, 1543, 1548, 1633, 1731, 1754, II-2370, 2455, 2464, 2466, 2474, 2487-2488, 2990

"Mobile Payments 2012." [online] from http://www.mobeyforum.org [Accessed May 1, 2012], II-2684

Model Railroad News, II-2437

Modern Baking, I-600, 623

Modern Brewery Age, I-770

Modern Healthcare, I-1927, II-3122, 3153, 3233, 3514-3519, 3549, 3553, 3592

Modern Healthcare's By the Numbers, II-3425, 3527, 3591

Modern Materials Handling, I-1867

"Modern Media." [online] from http://www.dbpower.com.hk/columns/reports/cinda/en/201105270932081_en.pdf [Published May 27, 2011], I-1212

"Mohawk Industries Investor Presentation." [online] from http://www.scribd.com [Published November 2011], I-1002

"Molson Coors Expands: What It Means for Aluminum Sheet, Cans." [online] from http://www.agmetalminer.cm/2012/04/05 [Published April 5, 2012], I-760

Montreal Gazette, II-2275

"Morningstar Research Conference." [online] from http://phx.corporate-ir.net/External.File?item...t=1 [Accessed May 1, 2012], I-1341

"Morocco September 2011." [online] from http://bestsellingcarsblog.com/2011/11/03/morocco-september-2011-renault-kangoo-reclaims-leadership [Published November 3, 2011], II-2194

"Motorcycle Brief." [online] from http://www.export.gov [Published June 2011], II-2302

"Motorcycle Sales Statistics." [online] from http://www.webbikeworld.com/motorcycle-news/statistics/motorcycle-sales-statistics.htm [Accessed January 1, 2012], II-2305

"Motorcycles and Motor Scooters." [online] from http://www.profile-america.com/images/Motorcycles%20and%20Motor%20Scooters.pdf [Accessed May 1, 2012], II-2301

"Movie Theaters in the U.S." [online] from http://www.ibisworld.com [Published June 2011], II-3443

MR Magazine, I-1015

"Multimodal Freight Transportation Within the Great Lakes-Saint Lawrence Basin." [online] from http://www.duffphelps.com [Published February 7, 2012], II-2530

"Municipal Building Construction in the U.S." [online] from http://www.ibisworld.com [Published December 2011], I-271

"NAPCS Report: Charter School Market Share Climbs." [online] from http://www.charterschoolcenter.org [Published Ocotber 17, 2011], II-3534

"NASF Corporate Finance Seminar." [online] from http://hugin.info/143208/R/1592588/500884.pdf [Published March 8, 2012], I-145

"National Labor Organizations." [online] from http://www.infoplease.com [Accessed March 19, 2012], II-3561

National Mortgage News, II-3100, 3104-3112

National Provisioner, I-361, 363, 366-367, 370

National Real Estate Investor, II-3115, 3248

National Underwriter, II-3187, 3205, 3221, 3229, 3234

"Nation's Largest Libraries." [online] from http://www.ala.org [Accessed December 1, 2011], II-3538

Nation's Restaurant News, II-2946, 2948, 2951

Natural Foods Merchandiser, I-929, 1303

"Nature's Own Investor Presentation." [online] from http://www.flowersfoods.com [Published June 2011], I-618

"NBA Attendance Report - 2012." [online] from http://espn.go.com/nba/attendance [Accessed May 1, 2012], II-3483

"Netherlands Food and Drink Market." [online] from http://www.fft.com [Published July 2011], I-329

"New Registrations in Europe." [online] from http://www.acea.be [Accessed January 16, 2012], II-2200

"New Textile Machinery Shipments Surge in 2011." [online] from http://ei.wtin.com/article/rNVQMxCk2Q/2012/05/16 [Published May 16, 2012], I-1884

"New Vehicle Sales Top the Million Mark in 2011." [online] from http://www.fcau.com.au [Published January 5, 2012], II-2189

New York Post, I-512

New York Times, I-502, 515, 1159, 1174, 1328, 1378, 1768, 1949, II-2136, 2369, 2540, 2667, 2669-2670, 2674, 3114, 3124-3125

"Newpark Resources." [online] from http://files.newpark.com/np/presentations/NR%20Investor%20Presentation%20Nov%202011.pdf [Published November 2011], I-1850

"News Syndicates in the U.S." [online] from http://www.ibiorld.com [Published November 2010], II-3386

"NFL Attendance - 2011." [online] from http://espn.go.com/nfl/attendance [Accessed May 1, 2012], II-3485

"NHL Attendance Report 2012." [online] from http://espn.go.com/nba/attendance [Accessed May 1, 2012], II-3486

"Nick Buckles." [online] from http://www.g4s.com [Published September 2011], II-3382-3383

"Nielsen Company and Billboard's 2011 Music Industry Report." [online] from http://www.businesswire.com [Published January 5, 2012], II-2088-2090

Nightclub & Bar, II-2961

"No Surprise: U.S. is 75% of Global E-Reader Market." [online] from http://publishingperspectives.com [Published January 11, 2011], II-2074

"NOAA: U.S. Domestic Seafood Landings and Values Increase in 2010." [online] from http://www.noaanews.noaa.gov/stories2011/20110907_usfisheriesreport.html [Published September 7, 2011], I-146

"Non-Coin-Operated Laundromats and Dry Cleaners in the U.S." [online] from http://www.scribd.com [Published March 2011], II-3275

Non-Foods Management, I-698, 1166, 1302, 1306, 1311, 1313, 1315, 1323-1324, 1349, 1381, 1415, 1429, 1433-1436, 1451, 1459-1460, 1464, 1474, 1496, 1498, 1565, 1750, II-2177, 2417, 2463, 2490, 3003

"Non-Hotel Casinos in the U.S." [online] from http://www/ibisworld.com [Published August 2011], II-3491

"Non-Lethal Weapons Market." [online] from http://www.homelandsecurityresearch.com [Accessed April 1, 2012], I-1796

"Nonresidential Prefabricated Building Systems." [online] from http://www.freedoniagroup.com [Published September 2011], I-1781

Nonwovens Industry, I-1169

"Norbord Leverage Finance Conference." [online] from http://www.norbord.com/documents/BAML_HY_Conference_Dec1_2011.pdf [Published December 1, 2011], I-1106

"North Face Inc: Market Segmentation and Target Market Selection." [online] from http://www.docstoc.com/docs/84899987/The-North-Face_-Inc [Published March 21, 2007], II-2450

"Norway Food and Drink Market." [online] from http://www.fft.com [Published July 2011], I-321

Norway Telecommunications Report, II-2608

"Nova Scotia's Ocean Technologies." [online] from http://www.cggc.duke.edu/pdfs/2012-03-05_Nova%20Scotia%20OTReport.pdf [Published March 5, 2012], II-2282, 2291, 2343-2344, 2346

"Number of Libraries in the United States." [online] from http://www.ala.org [Accessed November 1, 2011], II-3540

"NVC Lighting Holding Ltd." [online] from http://www.research.hsbc.com [Published July 9, 2010], II-2052

"NYK Fact Book 2011." [online] from http://www.nyk.com [Accessed April 28, 2011], II-2529, 2560, 2573

"Nyrstar and the Outlook for the Zinc Industry." [online] from http://www.nyrstar.com/investors/fr/Documents/Fran%C3%A7ais/2011-05-12a.pdf [Published May 12, 2011], I-158

"Office Stationery Manufacturing in the U.S." [online] from http://www.ibisworld.com [Published May 2011], I-1197

"Office Stationery Wholesalers in the U.S." [online] from http://www.ibisworld.com [Published December 2011], II-2763

Official Board Markets, I-30, 1096

"Offshore Drillers." [online] from http://www.docstoc.com [Published May 24, 2010], I-1851

"Ohio: 2010 Property and Casualty Insurance Market Share Report." [online] from http://www.insurance.ohio.gov [Accessed December 1, 2011], II-3176, 3184, 3188, 3202, 3211, 3231

"Oil & Gas Drilling in China." [online] from http://www.docin.com/p-314858991.html [Published May 2011], I-202

"Oil & Gas Pipeline Construction in the U.S." [online] from http://www.ibisworld.com [Published September 2011], I-280

Oil Daily, I-199

"Oil Services & Equipment Digest." [online] from http://www.floatingpath.com/wp-content/uploads/2012/06/oil-services-and-equipment.pdf [Published June 6, 2012], I-206-207, 210, 1847, 1855

"Oils and Fats in China." [online] from http://wenku.baidu.com [Published October 2011], I-731

Oman Telecommunications Report, II-2609

"Online Dieting Represents a $910 Million Market." [online] from http://www.prweb.com/releases/2011/01/prweb4961684.htm [Published January 6, 2011], II-2659

"Online Event Ticket Sales in the U.S." [online] from http://www.ibisworld.com [Published February 2012], II-3497

"Online Flower Shops." [online] from http://www.ibisworld.com [Published February 2012], II-3023

"Onward Packs." [online] from http://mcguireexperience.com/2012/AR/OnwardPacks.pdf [Accessed June 1, 2012], I-1080

"Operating and Monitoring Solutions." [online] from http://www.frost.com [Published June 2011], I-1919

Optician, II-2404

Oregonian, II-2843

"Outdoor Furniture & Grills." [online] from http://www.freedoniagroup.com [Published January 2012], I-28

"Overview of Global and China Luxury Markets." [online] from http://www.research.hsbc.com [Published December 9, 2011], II-2887

"Overview of the U.S. Tuna Market." [online] from http://www.info-fish.org/ptf/3rdPTF2011/Day%202/21.%20Michael%20McGowan.pdf [Published September 6-7, 2011], I-838, 842

"Packaged Food Sales in Saudi Arabia." [online] from http://www.ats.agr.gc.ca [Published January 2011], I-324

Packaging Digest, I-1912

The Packer, I-81, 85, 96, II-2813, 2850, 2866

"Paint Manufacturing in Australia." [online] from http://www.disb2b.com [Published June 2011], I-1516

Pakistan Telecommunications Report, II-2610, 2640

"Pan-European Strategic Decisions Conference." [online] from http://www.wolterskluwer.com [Published September 21, 2010], I-1232-1234

"Panacea or Bitter Pill?" [online] from http://www.bakerinstitute.org [Published November 11, 2011], I-1337

"Pandora." [online] from http://phx.corporate-ir.net [Published November 10, 2011], II-2687

"Parking Lots & Garages in the U.S." [online] from http://www.ibisworld.com [Published August 2011], II-3411

"Passenger Traffic 2010 Final." [online] from http://www.airports.org [Published August 1, 2011], II-2563

"Payroll & Bookkeeping Services in the U.S." [online] from http://www.ibisworld.com [Published July 2011], II-3576

"PC Market Stumbles on HDD Storage While U.S. Market Sees Worst Annual Growth Since 2001." [online] from http://www.idc.com [Published January 11, 2012], I-1939, 1946

Pensions & Investments, II-3237

"People Screening Technologies." [online] from http://www.home-landsecurityresearch.com [Accessed April 1, 2012], II-2340, 2342

"PepsiCo Not Poised to Split: Analyst." [online] from http://www.the-street.com/print/story/11232109.html [Published August 26, 2011], I-885

"Performance and Accountability Report of Fiscal Year 2011." [online] from http://www.uspto.gov/about/stratplan/ar/2011/index.jsp [Accessed February 20, 2012], II-3264

Peru Telecommunications Report, II-2612

"Pet Food in Canada." [online] from http://www.ats.agr.gc.ca [Published July 2011], I-585

"Pet Food in Mexico." [online] from http://www.ats.agr.gc.ca [Published December 2010], I-586

"Pet Food in Morocco." [online] from http://www.ats.agr.gc.ca [Published January 2011], I-587

Pet Product News, I-575

"Pet Stores in the U.S." [online] from http://www.ibisworld.com [Published October 2011], II-3033

"Petrochemicals." [online] from http://www.morganstanley.com/views/perspectives/preparingfor_supercycle.pdf [Published October 18, 2010], I-1276, 1525, 1529

Pharmaceutical Executive, I-1339, 1345

"Philip Morris." [online] from http://uoinvestmentgroup.org/wp-content/uploads/2011 [Published November 30, 2011], I-952

"Philip Morris in the Philippines." [online] from http://global.tobaccofreekids.org [Published April 2009], I-963

"Philips - Building Global Category Leadership." [online] from http://www.newscenter.philips.com [Accessed April 1, 2012], II-2018

"Photography in the U.S." [online] from http://www.ibisworld.com [Published August 2011], II-3282

"Pinsent Mason Water Yearbook 2011-2012." [online] from http://wateryearbook.pinsentmasons.com [Accessed April 1, 2012], II-2721

Pit & Quarry, I-214

Pizza Today, II-2956

"Plant and Flower Growing." [online] from http://www.ibisworld.com [Published August 2011], I-108

"Plumbing Fixtures & Fittings." [online] from http://www.freedoniagroup.com [Published September 2011], I-1763

"Podiatrists in the U.S." [online] from http://www.physiciansbusinessacademy.com/wp-content/uploads/2011/04/Podiatrists-in-the-US-Industry-Report.pdf [Published June 2010], II-3511

"Poland Food and Drink Market." [online] from http://www.fft.com [Published July 2011], I-322

"Polk Forecasts Global New Vehicle Auto Sales to Reach 77.7M in 2012." [online] from http://www.greencarcongress.com [Published January 3, 2012], II-2211

"Portugal Food and Drink Market." [online] from http://www.fft.com [Published July 2011], I-323

"Portuguese Cosmetics and Toiletries Market." [online] from http://www.export.gov [Published October 2011], I-1479

The Post-Standard, I-6

"Poured Concrete Contractors in the U.S." [online] from http://lowes.retailforward.com [Published February 2011], I-292

"Power Tool Batteries." [online] from http://www.elsevierdirect.com/brochures/ecps/PDFs/Power-Tools_Batteries.pdf [Accessed September 1, 2011], II-2173

"PPG Industries Investor Presentation." [online] from http://www.ppg.com [Accessed November 1, 2011], I-1508

PR Newswire, II-2402

PR Web, I-16, II-3028

"Prefabricated Housing - U.S." [online] from http://www.freedoniagroup.com [Published January 2012], I-1099

"Prepaid Card Industry." [online] from http://cfile6.uf.tistory.com/attach/160797314C8ED681034F19 [Published August 29, 2010], II-3089

Prepared Foods, I-332, 420, 513

"Presentation to Analysts/Investors Johnson Matthey Group." [online] from http://www.matthey.com [Published February 2, 2011], I-1347

"Primer: Physicians." [online] from http://americanactionforum.org [Published September 2011], II-3502

"Prince Frog." [online] from http://www.dbpower.com.hk/columns/reports/cinda/en/1259_HK_29_11_2011.pdf [Published November 29, 2011], I-1465, 1482, 1493

Prison Legal News, II-3595

"Private Equity, Hedge Funds and Investment Vehicles in the U.S." [online] from http://www.ibisworld.com [Published March 2011], II-3118

Private Label Buyer, I-1187

"Procter & Gamble." [online] from http://www.trinity.edu/smf/inc/reports/fl2011/pg.pdf [Published November 8, 2011], I-1195, 1455, 1475, II-2167

Produce Retailer, I-75, 83, 102, 109

"Production, Supply and Distribution." [online] from http://www.fas.usda.gov [Published December 2011], I-54, 58, 62, 68, 89-90, 93-94, 99-100, 353-354, 387, 389, 400, 405, 432-433, 645

Professional Builder, I-249

Professional Deck Builder, I-1101

Progressive Grocer, I-686, 917, II-2175

"Promising EU Export Markets for Parts in Agricultural Machinery." [online] from http://www.cbi.eu [Accessed April 1, 2012], I-1828

"Property and Casualty Insurance Industry." [online] from http://

www.naics.org [Published March 28, 2011], II-3192, 3209, 3222, 3225

"Public Schools in the U.S." [online] from http://www.ibisworld.com [Published February 2011], II-3532

Publishers Weekly, I-1215, 1220, 1223, II-2998-2999

"Publishing Market Shows Steady Title Growth in 2011 Fueled Largely by Self-Publishing Sector." [online] from http://www.bowker.com/en-US/aboutus/press_room [Press release June 5, 2012], I-1219

Pulp & Paper International, I-1149

"Putting America's Waterways to Work." [online] from http://www.kirbycorp.com/documents/2011_Sept13.pdf [Published September 2011], II-2528

"PVC and Chlor-Alkali In a Vibrant Region." [online] from http://www.ptq.pemex.com/productosyservicios/eventosdescargas/Documents [Published June 2011], I-1282

"Q2 Investor Kits." [online] from http://www.swedishmatch.com [Published June 2011], I-973

QSR Magazine, II-2955, 2959

"Quarterly Hogs and Pigs." [online] from http://www.usda.gov [Published September 28, 2011], I-117

Quick Frozen Foods International, I-537

Radio Ink, II-2691

R&D Magazine, II-3583

"Ranking the National Parks by Visitation in 2011." [online] from http://www.nationalparkstraveler.com [Published March 8, 2012], II-3558

"Raw Material of Iron Oxide Will Continue to Rally." [online] from http://www.tpychemical.com/NewShow.aspx?id=49,0 [Published June 9, 2011], I-1264

"RE/MAX Again Was No. 1 in Home Sales Across Metro Chicago Real Estate Market." [online] from

http://www.illinois.realestaterama.com [Published February 8, 2011], II-3253

"RE/Max Twin CIty Takes 26.1% of Market Share." [online] from http://www.johnsummers1.com [Published July 2011], II-3256

Redbook - A Supplement to Baking & Snack, I-597-598

"Refractories as a Bauxite Market - Current Status and Future Prospects." [online] from http://www.roskill.com [Accessed April 1, 2012], I-1681

Refrigerated & Frozen Foods, II-2811

Refrigerated & Frozen Foods Retailer, I-427, 445, 545-546

"Regulation Merger Procedure." [online] from http://ec.europa.eu [Published July 18, 2011], II-2251, 2254

"Regulation Merger Procedure." [online] from http://ec.europa.eu [Published June 6, 2011], I-1379

"Renewable Energy Outlook Europe." [online] from http://wenku.baidu.com/view/d9a321c658f5f61fb736664e.html [Published January 10, 2010], I-1785

The Republic, I-470

Research Alert, I-601

Research Studies - Freedonia Group, I-1284

"Restaurant by the Numbers." [online] from http://www.restaurant.org/pdfs/research/2011forecast_pfb.pdf [Accessed September 1, 2011], II-2944

"Revolutionizing the Timing Market Silicon Replaces Quartz." [online] from http://www.i-micronews.com/upload/.../Microtech-SiTime%20June%202010.pdf [Published June 2010], II-2148

"RFID: Prospects for Europe." [online] from http://ftp.jrc.es/EURdoc/JRC58486.pdf [Accessed February 20, 2012], II-2122

"Riding the Luxury Boom." [online] from http://www.clsa.com [Published December 21, 2011], II-2427, 3004

"The Rise of Greek." [online] from http://www.msnbcmedia.msn.com [Published March 12, 2011], I-439

"Road/Highway Construction in the U.S." [online] from http://www.ibisworld.com [Published December 2011], I-277

"RockTenn Company." [online] from http://research-ca.bmocapitalmarkets.com [Published January 22, 2012], I-1142, 1145

"The Role of Interchange Fees on Debit and Credit Card Transactions." [online] from http://www.richmondfed.org/publications/research/economic_brief/2011 [Published May 2011], II-3090

"Roofing." [online] from http://www.freedoniagroup.com [Published November 2011], I-1585

"Roofing Contractors in the U.S." [online] from http://lowes.retailforward.com [Published March 2011], I-289

"Rooming and Boarding Houses." [online] from http://business.highbeam.com [Accessed April 1, 2012], II-3272

Running Insight, I-986

"Rural/Metro Corporation." [online] from http://files.shareholder.com/downloads/RURL/2Q11_Investor__Presentation.pdf [Accessed February 20, 2012], II-2500

"Russian Federation Pet Food Market Brief." [online] from http://static.globaltrade.net/files/pdf/20110528180505646.pdf [Published April 21, 2011], I-588

"Russian Federation Retail Foods." [online] from http://gain.fas.usda.gov [September 2, 2011], II-2800, 2849

"Russian Organic Market Taking Root." [online] from http://gain.fas.usda.gov [Published April 27, 2011], I-337

RV Business, II-2263-2264, 2319-2320

"RV Parks." [online] from http://www.kitsapeda.org/pdfs/RV%20Park%20Industry%20Snapshot.pdf [Published May 2011], II-3274

"Safety and Security." [online] from http://www.bostonstrategies.com/clientlogin/rawmaterials/Safety090724.pdf [Published July 2009], I-1854, II-2114-2115, 2379

"Salon Hair Care." [online] from http://www.klinegroup.com/reports/brochures/y357l/factsheeteurope.pdf [Accessed October 1, 2011], I-1443

"Samsonite." [online] from http://www.research.hsbc.com [Published July 27, 2011], I-1644, 1648-1649

"Samsung SDI." [online] from https://mm.jpmorgan.com [Published April 6, 2011], II-2153-2155, 2165

San Diego Business Journal, II-3102

San Francisco Chronicle, I-747

"Sand and Gravel Mining in the U.S." [online] from http://www.ibisworld.com [Published September 2011], I-219

"Sateri Build by Cellulose." [online] from https://doc.research-and-analytics.csfb.com [Published January 18, 2011], I-1133, 1291, 1294

Saudi Arabia Telecommunications Report, II-2613

"Schneider Electric." [online] from http://www.research.hsbc.com [Published September 23, 2010], II-2004

Screen Digest, II-2108, 3444, 3448

"Screw, Nut & Bolt Manufacturing in the U.S." [online] from http://www.ibisworld.com [Published June 2011], I-1782

Seafood Business, I-843

"Sealed Air's Acquisition of Diversey." [online] from http://phx.corporate-ir.net [Published June 2011], I-1370

"Search Engine Market Share." [online] from http://www.chandlernguyen.com/2011 [Accessed December 1, 2011], II-2644, 2646, 2648, 2651, 2655

"Sector Capsule: RTD Coffee China." [online] from http://www.docin.com/p-156050911.html [Published February 4, 2011], I-859

"Sector Capsule Analgesics - China." [online] from http://www.docin.com/p-156050185.html [Published February 18, 2011], I-1340

"Sector Capsule Chocolate Confectionery - China." [online] from http://www.docin.com/p-86276941.html [Published January 14, 2010], I-716

"Sector Capsule Emergency Contraception." [online] from http://www.docin.com/p-156050192.html [Published February 18, 2011], I-1343

"Sector Capsule - Frozen Processed Food China." [online] from http://www.docin.com/p-86278832.html [Published September 14, 2010], I-538

"Sector Capsule - Fruit/Vegetable Juice." [online] from http://www.docin.com/p-156050917.html [Published February 4, 2011], I-496

"Sector Capsule - Sports and Energy Drinks." [online] from http://www.docin.com/p-156050912.html [Published February 4, 2011], I-828

"Seizing China's MedTech Opportunities." [online] from http://www.medcitynews.com/wordpress/wp-content/uploads/China-MedTech.pdf [Published January 6, 2012], II-2348, 2350, 2354, 2364-2365

Serbia Food & Drink Report, I-764

Seri Quarterly, II-1991-1992,

"Service Corp. International." [online] from http://phx.corporate-ir.net [Published March 2012], II-3285

"Shale Gas." [online] from http://www.freedoniagroup.com [Published August 2011], I-198

"Sheep and Goats." [online] from http://www.usda.gov [Published January 28, 2011], I-121

"Sherwin-Williams Company." [online] from http://investors.sherwin-williams.com [Published Second Quarter 2011], II-2784

"Ship Building in the U.S." [online] from http://www.ibisworld.com [Published July 2011], II-2284

"Ship Building Market Monitoring." [online] from http://www.cesa.eu [Published September 2011], II-2283

"Shipments of Payment Cards Worldwide 2010." [online] from http://www.nilsonreport.com [Published October 2011], II-2121

"Shoe Stores in the U.S." [online] from http://www.ibisworld.com [Published August 2011], II-2903

"Sidoti & Company." [online] from http://www.lancastercolony.com/_admin/_includes/_uploads/Sidoti_AllSlides_11_10_11.pdf [Published November 10, 2011], I-428, 516, 622, 624, 627

"Sightseeing Transportation in the U.S." [online] from http://www.ibisworld.com [Published August 2011], II-2504

"Simba Information´s 2011 National Textbook Adoption Scorecard and 2012 Outlook." [online] from http://www.docin.com/p-326729915.html [Accessed March 1, 2012], I-1228

Singapore Food & Drink Report, I-766

Singapore Telecommunications Report, II-2614

"Ski & Snowboard Resorts in the U.S." [online] from http://www.ibisworld.com [Published December 2010], II-3499

"Sleep Apnea Diagnostic Systems." [online] from http://www.marketshare.com [Published December 19, 2011], II-2368

"SLM Corporation." [online] from http://www.salliemae.com [Accessed October 1, 2011], II-3099

"Slot Machines - U.S." [online] from http://www.freedoniagroup.com [Published November 2011], II-3479

"Slovakia Food and Drink Market." [online] from http://www.fft.com [Published July 2011], I-325

Slovakia Food & Drink Report, I-765

"Smart Balance." [online] from http://research-us.bmocapitalmar

kets.com [Published December 21, 2011], I-391-392

"Smart Meters." [online] from http://www.freedoniagroup.com [Published February 2012], II-2336

"Smart Technologies." [online] from http://abea-4cueer.client.shareholder.com [Published January 11, 2011], II-2495-2496

"Smartphone Market Hits All-Time Quarterly High." [online] from http://www.idc.com [Press release February 6, 2012], II-2100

Snack Food & Wholesale Bakery, I-596, 603, 608, 625, 628, 640, 873, 886

Snack World, I-504, 638, 729, 864, 868, 870, 874, 880-881, 901

"Snowmobiles." [online] from http://www.mediacenteronline.com [Accessed November 1, 2011], II-2325

"Snyder's-Lance." [online] from http://research-us.bmocapitalmarkets.com [Published December 21, 2011], I-869

"Soap & Cleaning Compound Manufacturing in the U.S." [online] from http://www.ibisworld.com [Published September 2011], I-1384

Solitaire International, I-233

Sosland Publishing Corporate Profiles - Milling & Baking News Supplement, I-362, 368, 371, 414, 441, 465, 500, 533-536, 541, 558, 636, 728, 795, 802, 811, 849

Soundings, II-2289-2290, 2292, 2324

"South Africa 2010 Annual Retail Food Sector." [online] from http://gain.fas.usda.gov [Published January 5, 2011], II-2855

Southern Africa Telecommunications Report, II-2576, 2583, 2604, 2606-2607

"Spain Food and Drink Market." [online] from http://www.fft.com [Published July 2011], I-326

Spain Telecommunications Report, II-2615

"Specialty Foods Manufacturing: A Sectoral Analysis." [online] from http://www.cdtech.org/wp-content/uploads/2011/02/UCLA-Specialty-

Foods-Sector-Analysis.pdf [Published Fall 2010], I-451, 654, II-2870

"Specialty Surfactant." [online] from http://www.freedoniagroup.com [Published February 2006], I-1414

"Spectrum Brands Presentation to Chicago Investors." [online] from http://phx.corporate-ir.net/External.File?item...t=1 [Published March 21, 2012], I-1541

"Sporting Goods and Stores in the U.S." [online] from http://www.ibisworld.com [Published January 2012], II-2996

"Sporting Goods Sales by Product Category." [online] from http://www.statab.com [Accessed April 1, 2012], I-1616, II-2452

"Sports, Fitness & Recreational Activities Topline Participation Report." [online] from http://www.aahperd.org [Accessed September 1, 2011], II-3461-3462

"Sports Coaching in the U.S." [online] from http://www.maricopa-sbdc.com/Research%20Reports [Published August 18, 2008], II-3501

"Sports Equipment Manufacturing in China." [online] from http://www.docin.com [Published September 2011], II-2453

Sports Insight, I-1029

SportsBusiness Journal, I-1607, II-2690

Spray, Technology and Marketing, I-1554-1556

"Standoff Person-Borne and Vehicle-Borne Explosives & Weapon Detection." [online] from http://www.homelandsecurityresearch.com [Accessed April 1, 2012], II-2341

"Stanley Black & Decker 2011 Investor Day." [online] from http://phx.corporate-ir.net [Accessed August 1, 2011], I-45

"State of the Blogosphere 2010 Introduction." [online] from http://www.technorati.com [Accessed August 1, 2010], II-2629

"The State of the Running Shoe Market." [online] from http://www.runblogger.com/2012/02/state-of-running-shoe-market-december.html [Published February 8, 2012], I-1611

"The State of World Fisheries and Aquaculture." [online] from http://www.fao.org/docrep/013/i1820e/i1820e01.pdf [Accessed April 1, 2012], I-134

StateWays, I-792

"Stationery, Office and School Supplies Market in the EU." [online] from http://www.scribd.com [Published December 2009], I-1198

"Statistics of U.S. Business." [online] from http://www.census.gov [Accessed May 1, 2012], II-3503, 3505, 3507-3508, 3510, 3528

"Statistics of U.S. Businesses, 2008." [online] from http://www.census.gov [Accessed May 1, 2012], II-3284, 3427-3428

"Steel Framing in the U.S." [online] from http://lowes.retailforward.com [Published September 2011], I-294

"Steel Primer." [online] from http://www.steeldistributors.org/portals/0/NewsAndViews/Q1_2011/Steel_Primer.pdf [Published January 18, 2011], I-1697

"Steve Madden." [online] from http://phx.corporate-ir.net [Accessed March 22, 2012], I-1641, 1643

"Stevia Market Share to Explode in 2011, Says Report." [online] from http://www.foodnavigator-usa.com/On-your-radar/Natural-sweeteners [Published September 1, 2010], I-647

Stores, II-2790, 2897

"Strategic Analysis of the Global Market for Low-Cost Chassis Systems." [online] from http://www.hqpec.com [Published March 2009], II-2210

"Strategy for Success." [online] from http://www.airproducts.com [Published September 2011], I-1256

"Strawberry Category Review." [online] from http://www.calstrawberry.com/fileData/docs/Strawber-

ryCategoryReviewSept2011.pdf [Published September 2011], I-86

"Stretch & Shrink Film." [online] from http://www.freedoniagroup.com [Published December 2011], I-1624

"STX OSV." [online] from http://www.remisiers.org/cms_images/STX-OSV-1101111.pdf [Published January 11, 2011], I-1846, 1853

Supermarket News, I-300, 429, 431, 753, 908, 1304, II-2164, 2788, 2814-2815, 2827, 2839, 2847, 3025

"Supply Chain Management in Electronics Industry." [online] from http://www.sematech.org [Accessed October 1, 2011], II-2149-2152

"Surgical Drapes, Gowns and Gloves Market in Europe." [online] from http://www.sicherheitimop.at/documents/SurgicalDrapesEurope-FSDec2009.pdf [Published December 2009], II-2391-2393

"Sustainable and Innovative Personal Transport Solutions." [online] from http://xa.yimg.com/kq/groups/1088789/1632531212/name/F%26S_M4FA_European+Carsharing_Key+Findings.pdf [Published January 2010], II-3391

"Sweden Food and Drink Market." [online] from http://www.fft.com [Published July 2011], I-327

"Switzerland Food and Drink Market." [online] from http://www.fft.com [Published July 2011], I-328

Switzerland Telecommunications Report, II-2616

"SymphonyIRI Frozen Food Pulse." [online] from http://www.scribd.com [Accessed December 1, 2011], I-529

"Synthetic Lubricants & Functional Fluids." [online] from http://www.freedoniagroup.com [Published February 2012], I-1593

Talkers Magazine, II-2688

"Tank & Armored Vehicle Manufacturing in the U.S." [online] from http://www.ibisworld.com [Published August 2011], II-2323

"Tax Preparation Services in the U.S." [online] from http://www.

ibisworld.com [Published August 2011], II-3287

"Tea and Ready-to-Drink Tea in the U.S." [online] from http://www.docin.com/p-270881394.html [Published October 2011], I-931, 934

"Telecom Sector." [online] from http://web.angelbackoffice.com/research/archives/fundamental/company_reports [Published June 17, 2011], II-2598

"Telemarketing and Call Center Services in the U.S." [online] from http://www.ibisworld.com [Published August 2011], II-3401

"Ten Years of Innovation." [online] from http://www.crunchpak.com [Accessed October 1, 2011], I-912

"Tenfu." [online] from http://doc.research-and-analytics.csfb.com [Published November 7, 2011], I-930, 1667

"Tennant Corp." [online] from http://phx.corporate-ir.net [Published January 2011], II-2045

"Textainer." [online] from http://files.shareholder.com [Published November 2011], II-3335

Thailand Telecommunications Report, II-2617

"Thermoplastics Market Review." [online from [online] from http://www.apurchasingd.com/files/CMAI%20-%20Paul%20Blanchard%20-%20Emerging%20Market%20Supply%20Demand.pdf [Published May 2011], I-1280

"Thoroughbred Racing and Breeding Worldwide 2010." [online] from http://www.jockeyclub.com/factbook.asp?section=17 [Accessed May 1, 2012], II-3468

"Tibet 500 Water Resources." [online] from http://iis.aastocks.com/20110630/001231141-8.PDF [Published June 2011], I-807

"Timeshare Datashare." [online] from http://www.arda.org [Accessed December 1, 2011], II-3403

"Tire and Rubber Industry." [online] from https://mm.jpmorgan.com [Published January 5, 2011], I-1289, 1595

Tire Business, I-1605, II-2734, 2876, 3415

Tire Review, I-1597, 1600

"Toll Roads and Weighing Stations in the U.S." [online] from http://www.ibisworld.com [Published September 2011], II-2572

"Top 10 U.S. Utilities by DSM Investment." [online] from http://smartgridresearch.org/wp-content/uploads/sgi_reports [Published March 2011], II-2720

"Top 100 City Destinations Ranking." [online] from http://blog.euromonitor.com/2012/01 [Published January 2012], II-2566

"Top 20 U.S. Yellow Pages Markets 2011-2015." [online] from http://www.docin.com/p-274428671.html [Accessed June 1, 2012], I-1235

"Top 25 Cable Programming Networks." [online] from http://www.ncta.com/Stats/TopMSOs.aspx [Accessed September 1, 2011], II-2695

"Top 25 Consumer Magazines." [online] from http://accessabc.wordpress.com/2011/08/09/the-top-25-consumer-magazines-from-june-2011-fas-fax [Published August 9, 2011], I-1210-1211

"Top 25 Multichannel Video Programming Distributors." [online] from http://www.ncta.com/Stats/TopMSOs.aspx [Accessed September 1, 2011], II-2701

"Top 25 Policies in Force." [online] from http://www.floir.com/siteDocuments/QUASRngQuarterlyRpts [Published June 22, 2011], II-3224

"Top 250 U.S. Trade Shows." [online] from http://www.tsnn.com/datasite [Accessed October 1, 2011], II-3404

"Top 50 Bank Holding Companies." [online] from http://www.ffiec.gov [Accessed March 1, 2012], II-3261

"Top 50 Language Service Providers." [online] from http://www.commonserviceadvisory.com [Published May 31, 2011], II-3396

"Top 50 World Container Ports." [online] from http://www.world-shipping.org/about-the-industry/global-trade/top-50-world-container-ports [Accessed June 1, 2012], II-2535

"Top 500 Statistics." [online] from http://i..top500.org/stats [Published November 2011], I-1931

"Top Fishing Equipment Brands for 2011." [online] from http://www.southwickassociates.com [Press release February 27, 2012], II-2451

"Top Lobbying Groups." [online] from http://www.opensecrets.org [Accessed April 3, 2012], II-3564

"Top Sarasota Real Estate Brokers." [online] from http://www.luxurysarasotarealestate.com [Published March 28, 2011], II-3255

"Top Steel Producers." [online] from http://www.worldsteel.org [Accessed October 1, 2011], I-1701

"The Top Ten Tin Producers of 2011." [online] from http://en.smn.cn/news/industrial-news [Published February 23, 2012], I-1730

"Top Tissue Hersteller in Europa 2010." [online] from http://www.lebensmittelzeitung.net [Accessed September 1, 2011], I-1139

"Top U.S. Postal Service Suppliers." [online] from http://www.huschblackwell.com [Accessed April 1, 2012], II-2525

Total Telecom, II-2683

Touch Panel, II-2160

"Tour Operators in the U.S." [online] from http://www.ibisworld.com [Published November 2011], II-2569

"Toy Markets in the World Annual 2010." [online] from http://www.toyassociation.org/AM/PDFs/Trends/ToyMarkets11.pdf [Published October 17, 2011], II-2440

"Trade Show and Event Planning in the U.S." [online] from http://www.ibisworld.com [Published November 2011], II-3405

"TreeHouse Foods." [online] from http://research-us.bmocapital

markets.com [Published April 29, 2011], I-480, 565, 904-907

"Trends in the Marketing of Fresh-Produce and Fresh-Cut Products." [online] from http://ucce.ucdavis.edu/files/datastore/234-2115.pdf [Published September 13, 2011], I-913-914, 926

"Triton/Compo Merger Procedure." [online] from http://ec.europa.eu [Published September 23, 2011], I-1535, 1539

"Tunisia Retail Foods." [online] from http://gain.fas.usda.gov [Published December 26, 2011], II-2860

"Turbines." [online] from http://www.bostonstrategies.com/clientlogin/rawmaterials/Turbines-10FEB27.pdf [Published February 2010], I-1822-1823

Turkey Telecommunications Report, II-2619

"TV, DVD and Video Equipment Manufacturing in China." [online] from http://www.docin.com [Published August 2011], II-2073

Twice, I-4-5, 1947, 1957, 1967, II-2062-2069, 2078-2080, 2096-2097, 2101-2103, 2105, 2107, 2109, 2123, 2328, 2418, 2920, 2928, 3010, 3387

"TXC Corp." [online] from https://mm.jpmorgan.com [Published September 1, 2010], II-2130

"Tyco ADT." [online] from http://phx.corporate-ir.net [Published April 10, 0212], II-3385

"Ülker Investor Presentation." [online] from http://www.ulkerbiskuvi.com.tr/documents/Ulker/pdf/ULKER_TI_IR_Presentation_1Q2011.pdf [Published First Quarter 2011], I-632

"Under Armour Signs Kemba Walker." [online] from http://www.cnbc.com/id/43645176/Under_Armour_Signs_Kemba_Walker [Published July 5, 2011], I-1608

"The United Kingdom - A Diverse Foodservice Sector." [online] from http://www.gov.mb.ca [Published May 2011], II-2940

United Kingdom Autos Report, II-2222, 2226

"United Kingdom Food and Drink Market." [online] from http://www. fft.com [Published July 2011], I-330

"U.S. Autos & Auto Parts." [online] from http://www.ceres.org [Published March 14, 2011], II-2179

"U.S. Autos and Auto Parts." [online] from http://www.ceres.org/resources/reports/electric-vehicles-report [Published February 23, 2011], II-2215

"United States Book Market." [online] from http://www.buchmesse. de/pdf/buchmesse/buchmarkt_usa. pdf [Accessed February 20, 2012], I-1216

"U.S. Dating Services Market Worth $2.1 Billion." [online] from http:// www.prweb.com [Press release February 7, 2012], II-3288

"U.S. Department of Education Budget." [online] from http://febp. newamerica.net/background-analysis/education-federal-budget [Published March 22, 2012], II-3596

"U.S. ETF Market Update." [online] from http://www.sionline.com [Published July 27, 2011], II-3121

"U.S. Eyewear Market." [online] from http://www.packagedfacts. com [Published June 2009], II-2408-2410

"The U.S. Hardwood Industry." [online] from http://www.woodcomponents.org/app/portal/mm/Judd_ Johnson.pdf [Accessed April 1, 2012], I-1093

"U.S. Ladder Market Trends." [online] from http://lowes.retailforward.com/RichMedia/RfMedia_ 633555554132514459.pdf [Published August 2006], I-1813

"U.S. Mink: State of the Industry." [online] from http://www.furcommission.com/us-mink-state-of-the-industry-2011 [Published December 13, 2011], I-130, 1054

"U.S. Pawnshops Industry Sails Through the Recession." [online] from http://www.prweb.com [Press release May 22, 2012], II-2992

"U.S. Rice Domestic Usage Report." [online] from http://www. usarice.org [Accessed October 1, 2011], I-563-564, 566

"United States Telecommunications Report Second Quarter 2012." [online] from http://www. docin.com [Accessed June 1, 2012], II-2622, 2633, 2699

"U.S. Textile and Apparel Trade Policy Update." [online] from http://www.usaita.com/pdf_files/ 2011-Conference-Glas.pdf [Published November 8, 2011], I-974

Units, II-3247

"Update: Source Interlink Stats, Initiatives." [online] from http://ipdahome.org [Published April 25, 2011], II-3026

"Uranium Metal Prospects." [online] from http://www.scribd.com [Published April 18, 2011], I-172-173

USA TODAY, I-7, 190, 630, 1245, 1928, 1930, 1934, II-2087, 2098, 2657, 2661, 2673, 2704, 2719, 3113, 3306, 3308, 3352, 3402, 3453, 3466-3467, 3554, 3559, 3565, 3567, 3598

"Used Car Dealers in the U.S." [online] from http://www.ibisworld. com [Published December 2011], II-2873

"USG Creating Our Own Recovery." [online] from http://phx. corporate-ir.net [Published March 2012], I-1687

"USPS Financial Future." [online] from https://ribbs.usps.gov/webinar/CustomerWebinar.pdf [Published October 5, 2011], II-2524

Utah Business, II-3103

"Vacation- and Investment-Home Shares Hold Even in 2010." [online] from http://www.realtor.org [Published March 30, 2011], II-3258

"Vacon - the AC Drives Company." [online] from http://www.vacon.com [Published August 31, 2011], II-1996

"Valinger Innovation - Powder Technology." [online] from http:// www.valinge.se [Published September 14, 2011], I-13

"Vehicle Electrification and Other Lithium End Users." [online] from http://www.roskill.com [Published January 23, 2012], I-1271

"Vending Machine Operators in the U.S." [online] from http://www. ibisworld.com [Published August 2011], II-3019

Venezuela Telecommunications Report, II-2620

"Veterinary Services in the U.S." [online] from http://www.ibisworld. com [Published August 2011], I-138

"Vinda - Growth of a Baby Panda." [online] from http://www.docin.com [Published July 21, 2011], I-1172, 1175, 1184, 1193

"Vitamins and Dietary Supplements in Hong Kong, China." [online] from http://www.scribd.com [Published July 2010], I-1325

"Voice Over Internet Protocol Providers in the U.S." [online] from http://www.ibisworld.com [Published June 2010], II-2682

"Vulcan." [online] from http:// www.merit.gr/phocadownload/ userupload/21232f297a/TITAN% 20VALUATION%20REPORT% 20may%2011.pdf [Published May 2011], I-1672

"Wacker Chemie." [online] from http://www.research.hsbc.com [Published September 29, 2011], I-1727

"Wall Coverings." [online] from http://www.freedoniagroup.com [Published July 2011], I-48

Wall Street Journal, I-160, 461, 501, 749, 757-758, 767, 789, 903, 1016, 1334, 1342, 1352, 1612, 1751, 1932, 1961, II-2015, 2093, 2140, 2378, 2413, 2628, 2630-2631, 2658, 2666, 2678, 2680, 2929, 2958, 2988, 3001, 3093, 3117, 3119, 3130, 3291, 3309, 3316, 3438, 3537

"Wärtsilä Corporation Interim Report January-June 2011." [online] from http://www.wartsila.com [Published July 20, 2011], I-1817-1818

"Water & Waterwater Pipe." [online] from http://www.freedoniagroup.com [Published February 2012], I-42

"Water Supply & Irrigation Systems in the U.S." [online] from http://www.ibisworld.com [Published February 2012], II-2730

"Water Well Drilling in the U.S." [online] from http://lowes.retailforward.com [Published September 2011], I-293

"Weight Loss Services in the U.S." [online] from http://www.ibisworld.com [Published October 2011], II-3290

"What the Specialty Paper Market Will Look Like in 2015." [online] from http://www.convertingquarterly.com [Published September 18, 2011], I-1135

"What's for Dinner 2011." [online] from http://www.docin.com [Published March 2011], I-358, 839

"What's Hot in Europe?" [online] from http://www.staffingindustry.com [Accessed November 1, 2011], II-3342

"Where They Buy." [online] from http://mobile.rab.com/ibresult.cfm?id=60 [Accessed December 1, 2011], II-2902

Window & Door, I-1090

Wines & Vines, I-775

"Women's and Girl's Apparel Manufacturing in the U.S." [online] from http://www.ibisworld.com [Published August 2011], I-1044

"Women's Clothing Stores in the U.S." [online] from http://www.ibisworld.com [Published August 2011], II-2885

"Wood & Competitive Decking." [online] from http://lowes.retailforward.com [Published April 2009], I-1102-1103

"Woodworking Machinery Manufacturing in the U.S." [online] from http://www.ibisworld.com [Published June 2011], I-1885

"World Bioplastics." [online] from http://www.freedoniagroup.com [Published November 2011], I-1274

"World Bulk Packaging." [online] from http://www.freedoniagroup.com [Published May 2011], I-34

"World Caps & Closures." [online] from http://www.freedoniagroup.com [Published January 2011], I-1788

"World Disposable Medical Supplies." [online] from http://www.freedoniagroup.com [Published December 2010], II-2390

"World Electric Vehicle Market Exceeds One Million Units This Year." [online] from http://www.solarenergy.com [Press release November 11, 2011], II-2216

"World Elevators." [online] from http://www.freedoniagroup.com [Published January 2012], I-1856

"World Fertilizers." [online] from http://www.freedoniagroup.com [Published April 2011], I-1532

"World Filters." [online] from http://www.freedoniagroup.com [Published March 2012], I-1917

"World Foodservice Disposables." [online] from http://www.freedoniagroup.com [Published December 2011], I-1151

"World Fuel Cells." [online] from http://www.freedoniagroup.com [Published June 2011], I-1765

"World Gears." [online] from http://www.freedoniagroup.com [Published April 2010], I-1914

"World Geosynthetics." [online] from http://www.freedoniagroup.com [Published December 2011], I-238

World Grain, I-556

"World Industrial Valves." [online] from http://www.freedoniagroup.com [Published November 2011], I-1801

"World Insulation." [online] from http://www.freedoniagroup.com [Published February 2011], I-1692

"The World is Our Market." [online] from http://www.homag.com [Published November 11, 2011], I-1886

"World Kaolin." [online] from http://www.freedoniagroup.com [Published February 2012], I-223

"World Lubricants." [online] from http://www.freedoniagroup.com [Published July 2011], I-1591

"World Major Household Appliances." [online] from http://www.freedoniagroup.com [Published November 2011], II-2013

"World Market of Consumer Technics." [online] from http://www1.messe-berlin.de/vip8_1/website/Internet/Internet/www.ifa-gpc [Accessed November 1, 2011], II-2060

"World Membrane Separation Technologies." [online] from http://www.freedoniagroup.com [Published June 2011], I-1920

"World Mining Equipment." [online] from http://www.freedoniagroup.com [Published January 2012], I-1844

"World Nutraceutical Ingredients." [online] from http://www.freedoniagroup.com [Published November 2011], I-1295

"World PCB Production." [online] from http://www.tpca.org.tw/download.aspx?dlfn=TPCAShow_Market.pdf [Accessed February 14, 2012], II-2124

"World Pharmaceutical Packaging." [online] from http://www.freedoniagroup.com [Published May 2011], I-37

"World Plastic Pipe." [online] from http://www.freedoniagroup.com [Published May 2011], I-1629

"World Power Lawn & Garden Equipment." [online] from http://www.freedoniagroup.com [Published August 2011], I-1836

"World Power Tools." [online] from http://www.freedoniagroup.com [Published May 2011], I-1881

"World Residential Countertops." [online] from http://www.freedoniagroup.com [Published January 2010], I-1087

"World Robotics 2011." [online] from http://www.worldrobotics.org/uploads/media/2011_Executive_Summary.pdf [Accessed November 1, 2011], I-1922

"World Salt." [online] from http://www.freedoniagroup.com [Published February 2012], I-1571

"World Tires." [online] from http://www.freedoniagroup.com [Published February 2012], I-1596

"Worldwide Mobile Phone Market Maintains Its Growth Trajectory in the Fourth Quarter." [online] from http://www.idc.com [Press release February 1, 2012], II-2095

"Worldwide Purpose-Built Backup Appliance 2011-2015." [online] from http://www.emc.com [Published May 2011], I-1955

"Worldwide Smart Meter Market Continues to Grow With First Quarter 2011." [online] from http://www.waterefficiency.net/the-latest/smart-meter-market.aspx [Published June 14, 2011], II-2337

"Woven Outerwear Market in the EU." [online] from http://www.cbi.eu [Published October 2009], I-989

"Wuhan Investor Presentation." [online] from http://wuhangeneral.com/images/9-16-2010%20WUHN%20Investor%20Presentation.pdf [Published September 2010], I-1908

WWD, II-2886, 2895

Your Convenience Manager, I-655

"ZF/Hansen Merger Procedure." [online] from http://ec.europa.eu [Published September 30, 2011], I-1784

Primary Sources

2010 CHA U.S. Attitude & Usage Study, II-2459

2010 DuPont Global Automotive Color Popularity Report, I-1518

2010 EFT Data Book - A Supplement to ATM & Debit News, I-1969

"2011 Airgas Annual Report." [online] from http://www.slideshare.net [Accessed October 1, 2011], I-1257

2011 China Statistics Yearbook Table, I-144

2011 Directory of Chain Restaurant Operations, II-2956

"2011 National College Football Attendance." [online] from http://fs.ncaa.org/Docs/stats/football_records/Attendance/2011.pdf [Accessed May 1, 2012], II-3484

2011 State of the Vacation Timeshare Industry, II-3403

Abine, II-3352

"About Us." [online] from http://www.aaglobal.com [Accessed February 20, 2012], I-1974

"About Us." [online] from http://www.vanstone.com/about-us [Accessed April 1, 2012], I-1859

Access International, I-1860

Accounting Today, II-3286, 3575

Acimail, I-1886

ACNielsen, I-852, 953-954, 959-961, II-2789

ACNielsen ScanTrack, II-2797

ACT Research, I-1837

AdAge DataCenter, I-1203, 1207, II-2692, 2694, 3294-3295, 3317, 3594

ADT analysis, II-3385

Advertising Red Book, 2004, I-1024

Aerospace Industries Association, II-2306

Africa News Service, I-762

AgTunis, II-2860

Airline Business, II-2280

Airport Coordination Limited, II-2548

Airports Council International, II-2561, 2563

AISHealth.com, II-2987

Aite Group, II-3131

Albert N. Greco Institute for Publishing Research, II-3001

Alphaliner, II-2527

A.M. Best & Co., II-3132, 3148, 3150, 3173-3174, 3180-3183, 3185, 3190, 3193-3197, 3200, 3203, 3208, 3212, 3216-3217, 3220, 3226, 3232-3233, 3239

The AME Group, I-184

American Association of Railroads, II-2497, 2499

American Gaming Association, II-3493

"American Greetings." [online] from http://www.slideshare.net/jasonbgass/american-greetings-8697423 [Published May 4, 2011], I-1244

American Hospital Association, II-3517

American Iron and Steel Institute, I-1697

American Land Title Association, II-3236

American Lawyer, II-3531

American Library Association, II-3538, 3540

American Religious Identification Survey, II-3567

American Resort Development Association, II-3402

American School & University, II-3535-3536

Analysys International, II-2658, 2680, 3018

Andrew Foxcroft Container Data, II-3335

Angel Research, I-633, II-2598

Annual Directory of Chains and Groups, II-2820

"Anticipated Acquisition by Assa Abloy." [online] from http://www.oft.gov.uk/shared_oft/mergers_ea02/2011/Assa_Abloy.pdf [Published March 8, 2011], I-1773

Apparel Magazine, I-1017, 1638

APPA's 2011-2012 National Pet Owners Survey, I-40

AppData, II-2678

Appliance estimates, I-1985, II-2019-2021, 2024, 2027-2028, 2040, 2042, 2044

"Arab Potash Annual Report." [online] from http://www.arabpotash.com/_potash/App_Upload/PDF/2010annualenglish.pdf [Accessed February 27, 2012], I-227

Aranca Research, I-1353

Arbitron, II-2688, 2690

ARCEP, II-2592

"Art Market Trends 2011." [online] from http://www.artmarket.com [Accessed April 1, 2012], II-3555

Art Newspaper, II-3557

Ascend, II-2267

Asociation de Fabricacion de Auto-motores de Argentina, II-2197

Assisted Living Executive, II-3551

Association of American Publishers, I-1215

Association of Contact Lens Manufacturers, II-2404

Association of Executive Search Consultants, II-3590

Association of International Automobile Manufacturers of Canada, II-2198

Association of Progressive Rental Organizations, II-3336

Atlantic Information Services Inc., II-2987

Audit Bureau of Circulations, I-1205, 1210-1211

Australian Prudential Regulation Authority, II-3101

Auto Rental News, II-3408

Auto Schweiz, II-2206

Autodata, II-2196,

Automatic Merchandiser, I-846, II-3020

Automobil Industrie, II-2258

Automotive Fleet, II-3409

Automotive News, II-2241

Automotive News Data Center, II-2178, 2180, 2185, 2213, 2871-2872, 2874

Avery Dennison, II-2476

Avicenne, II-2173

AWA Specialty Paper Industry Conference, I-1135

Bain & Company, I-24-25, 27

Bangladesh Telecommunications and Regulatory Commission, II-2580

Bank of America Merrill Lynch, II-2887

Bank Vontobel, II-2424

Barclays Capital, I-1522, 1530, II-2806

"Barclays/Investcorp/N&V Global Vending." [online] from http://ec.europa.eu [Published October 31, 2008], I-1975-1976

Battelle, II-3583

Baum & Associates, II-2179, 2214-2215, 2217-2218

BCC Research, I-1910

BDSI, I-656

Beer Marketer's Insights, I-756

BestLink, II-3171-3172, 3175, 3177-3179, 3198-3199, 3201, 3204, 3206-3207, 3214, 3218-3219, 3227-3228, 3230

Beverage Digest, I-816-817

Beverage Information Group, I-782, 791-792

Beverage Marketing Corp., I-752, 799, 801, 814

BIA/Kelsey, I-1203, II-2691,

Billboard, II-2930

Billian's HealthData, II-3518,

"Binder + Co." [online] from http://www.binder-co.com/downloads/Analyse_Research/August2011 [Published August 30, 2011], I-1845, 1894

"Birla/Columbian Chemicals." [online] from http://ec.europa.eu [Published June 15, 2011], I-1553

BIS - Bureau of Industry and Statistics, II-3128

Bloomberg, II-2703, 3123

Bloomberg New Energy Finance, II-2704

Bloomberg News, II-2658

Blount, I-1882

BMO Capital Markets, I-233, 391-392, 480, 565, 607, 629, 869, 904-907, 1136

Boeing, II-2267

Book Business, I-1229

Book Industry Study Group, I-1215

BookStats, I-1216

Booz & Company, I-1363, 1372, 1400

Boston Biomedical Research, I-1356

Boston Strategies International, I-1619, 1674, 1682, 1696, 1805, 1822-1823, 1848-1849, 1854, 1901, 1907, 1924, II-2007, 2114-2115, 2379

Bowker, I-1219-1220, II-2998

Bowker Pubtrack Consumer, II-2999

Box Office Mojo, II-3437

BP Statistical Review of World Energy, I-186, 188-189, 191-193, II-2717-2718

Branchendienst, I-1139

Brewers Association, I-769

British Aerosol Manufacturers Association, I-1556

Brook Hunt, I-156, 158, 176, 1719, 1722, 1738

BTM Consult, I-1785, 1824

Builder, I-248, 250-267

Building Design and Construction, I-269-270, 272-274

Bulgaria Food & Drink Report, II-2819

Burkenroad Reports, I-221

Burton-Taylor International Consulting, II-3130

Business and Institutional Furniture Manufacturers Association, I-1121, 1123

Business Monitor International, I-153, 162, 310, 318, 761, 764-766, 821, 1526, II-2576-2578, 2580-2582, 2584, 2586, 2588-2597, 2599-2600, 2602-2620, 2622, 2633-2637, 2639-2640, 2699, 2857-2858, 3223

BusinessWeek, II-3544

BVE, I-302

Cabinetmaker + FDM, I-1111

"Cable and Satellite TV Industry." [online] from https://faculty.cit.cornell.edu/jl2545/4160/presentation/2012presentation [Accessed May 1, 2012], II-2696, 2702

Canadian Gambling Digest, 2009-2010, II-3496

Canadian Grocer, II-2820

Candy Industry, I-660

Caobisco, I-693, 695, 715, 718

Capgemini, II-3086

Capstone Research Inc., I-1037

"Car Audio Market - The Lack of Voice." [online] from http://weihua.articlesbase.com [Published July 13, 2010], II-2071

Cargo Systems, I-1864

Carlos Richer estimates, I-1169

Catalina Research, I-14, 1813, II-2480, 2906

Cattle Buyers Weekly, I-357

"Cavalier Corp." [online] from http://www.cfasociety.org.nz/Documents/New%20Zealand%20Report.pdf [Published February 6, 2011], I-1001

CBGGC Ocean Technology Database, II-2343-2344, 2346

CDU TEK, I-201

Cefic Chemdata International, I-1246

Cegedim Strategic Data, I-1342

Cellular Telecommunications Industry Association, II-2685
Cellulose Gap, I-1293
Center for Responsive Politics, II-3564
Center for Strategic and International Studies, II-3599
Ceresana Research, I-1264
Chain Drug Review, II-2964-2985
Chain Store Guide, II-2784
Chemical & Engineering News, I-1251
Chemical Market Associates Inc., I-1005, 1275, 1279-1280, 1282, 1289, 1292, 1525, 1529, 1595
China Bonds, II-3116
China Chemical Reporter, I-220,
China Construction Machinery Business Outline, I-1841-1843, 1861, 1866
China gold association, II-3006
China International Seed Summit, I-50
China National Commercial Information Centre, I-1022, 1027, 1036, 1040, 1045, 1049
"Christie has 50% Share of DLP Cinema Market." [online] from http://www.installationeurope.com [Published December 14, 2011], II-2407
CIBC World Markets, II-2820
"The Cigars are Kept Leading the World Market." [online] from http://www.cubaheadlines.com 2012/03/02/34702/the_cigars_are_kept_leading_the_world_market.html [Published March 2, 2012], I-968
CIMB Research, I-945, 1846, 1853
CINDRA International, I-1113-1114
"Cineplex Entertainment." [online] from http://cineplexgalaxy.disclosureplus.com/SiteResources [Published March 8, 2011], II-3445
CIRA, II-2215
CIRC, II-3136, 3143
CIRL, I-1212
Citi Investment Research, I-852, 1050, II-2348, 2350, 2352, 2354, 2364-2366, 2383, 2386, 3524
Citigroup, II-2231, 2806
Clarkson's *Tanker Register 2011*, II-2529

Clearwater, II-2276-2277
"Cliffs Natural Resources." [online] from http://uoinvestment-group.org/wp-content/uploads/2011/05/Final-CLF.pdf [Published May 20, 2011], I-1715
Clothesource, I-1291
CNCIC - China National Chemical Information Center, I-1438, 1454, 1503
Cobalt Development Inc., I-168
Cocoa Barometer 2010, I-722
Codelco, I-152, 1717
Colorado Insurance Statistical Report, II-3154
Common Sense Advisory, II-3396
Community of European Shipyards Associations, II-2283
companiesandmarkets.com, II-2358
"Competitors." [online] from http://www.sca.com [Accessed February 20, 2012], I-1138, 1146, 1167, 1188-1190
comScore, II-2094, 2638, 2644, 2646-2648, 2651, 2655, 2660-2663, 2665, 2668-2669, 2673, 2676
Consumer Electronics Association, II-2060-2061
Consumer Reports, I-1664
Consumer Specialty Products Association, I-1554
Context, I-1962-1964
Continental estimates, I-1599, II-2224-2225, 2235-2240, 2244, 2247-2248, 2252-2253, 2255-2256, 2260-2262
Counterman, II-2875
CPCS Transcom Limited, II-2530
Crain's Chicago Business, II-2642
Credit Suisse estimates, I-181, 183, 646, 1133, 1171, 1254, 1259, 1277-1278, 1281, 1294, 1486, 1668, 1697-1698, 1716, 1720, II-2475, 2587, 2625, 3089, 3092
CropLife, II-2787
CRT Media Intelligence, II-3291
CRTC - Canadian Radio Television Telecommunications, II-2585
CRU, I-1704, 1728
CSIL, I-1122
CSM Worldwide, I-1129, II-2259

CTR Facial Masks Industry Report, I-1497
D Business, I-242
Daily Star, I-1590
Dairy Foods, I-383
Dairy Management Inc., I-753
databank.com.lb, II-2192
Datamonitor, I-38, 334-335, 453, 456, 632, 659, 662-677, 750, 786, 813, 826, 861, 937-944, 946-951, 975-981, 1199, 1247, 1249-1250, 1385, 1430, 1471, 1479, 1821, 1852, 1923, II-2143-2145, 2157, 2159, 2203, 2205, 2207-2208, 2303, 2307-2316, 2347, 2441-2442, 2449, 2621, 2707-2716, 2748, 2803, 2882, 2894, 3008-3009, 3257, 3345, 3372, 3587
De Beers, I-234
Dealerscope, II-2925
Dealogic, II-3116, 3122
Deere analysis, I-241
Demolition & Recycling International, I-298
Deutsche Bank, I-148, 151, 166, 178-180, 384, 412, 423, 454, 521, 732, 798, 819, 892, 922, 1142, 1145, 1176, 1179, 1186, 1192, 1317, 1389, 1392, 1401, 1421, 1424, 1427, 1449, 1461, 1472, 1480, 1488, 1501, 1505, 1558, 1749, 1918, II-2484, 2936
Deutsche Securities, II-2171
Diamond Comics, I-1206
Direct Selling News, II-3021
"DirecTV PanAmericana." [online] from http://files.shareholder.com [Published December 2, 2010], II-2700
DisplaySearch, I-1935, 1937-1938, II-2075-2076, 2081, 2161
Distilled Spirits Council, I-747
Diversey Management estimates, I-1370
Dr. Pepper Snapple Group, I-827
Drewry Shipping Consultants, II-2536
"DSM at a Glance." [online] from http://www.dsm.com [Published February 2011], I-911
Ducker Worldwide, I-1090
Dun & Bradstreet, II-3272

"E Ink Holdings Inc." [online] from https://mm.jpmorgan.com [Published January 19, 2011], II-2156

EagleBurgmann, I-1620

Easy Analytic Software Inc., I-1109

EC&M, II-3569

Economics of Basic Cable Networks, II-2695

Educational Market Research, I-1222, 1224

Egg Industry, I-125

eGroomer Journal, II-3032

Eileen Hao Consultancy, I-1678

eMarketer, I-1929, II-2632, 3299, 3306

Enders Analysis, II-2092

Energy Information Administration, I-190, 194, 197

Engine Yearbook, I-1820

ENR, I-275, II-3571

ENR's Top 600 Specialty Contractors, I-281, 283-285, 287, 291, 295, 297

Enterbrain, II-3367

Entertainment Weekly, II-3439,

Entrepreneur, II-3379, 3412, 3431, 3542

ESAB A.B., I-1883

Euroconsult, II-2106

Eurocopter, II-2276-2277

Eurofresh Distribution, I-106

Euromoney, II-3119,

Euromonitor, I-324, 333, 337-344, 356, 378, 384-385, 401, 412-413, 423, 442-444, 446, 448, 454, 461, 467, 496-497, 506, 521-522, 538, 557, 561, 569, 574-575, 585-587, 594, 604, 611-612, 633, 650, 716, 731-733, 742, 749, 751, 754, 757-760, 763, 767, 777-778, 780-781, 787-788, 790, 793-794, 797-798, 803, 807, 818-820, 822-825, 828, 850, 859, 861, 883-884, 891-892, 900, 922, 930, 933, 957, 963-964, 970, 989, 1019-1020, 1023, 1025, 1172, 1175-1176, 1179, 1184, 1186, 1192-1193, 1317, 1319, 1325, 1340, 1343, 1360, 1363-1369, 1371-1372, 1379, 1389, 1392, 1400-1401, 1409-1412, 1416, 1418-1421, 1424, 1427, 1437, 1449, 1461, 1472, 1480-1481, 1483-1485, 1488, 1492, 1501, 1505, 1557-1562, 1574-

1579, 1610, 1642, 1663, 1667, 1751, II-2018, 2070, 2188, 2212, 2484, 2566-2567, 2626, 2791, 2799-2800, 2805, 2829, 2837, 2849, 2855, 2864, 2898, 2924, 2935, 2937-2938, 2958

European Automobile Manufacturers Association, II-2200

"European Diesel Powerboat Market Large, But Fragmented." [online] from http://powerproductsperspectives.com [Published February 23, 2011], I-1826

Eurostat, I-989, 1020, 1023, 1057, 1198, 1828

Euroweek, II-3120

Exchange, II-3548

Experian Automotive, II-3095-3097

Experian Hitwise, II-2657, 2667, 2670

FAOSTAT, I-70, 82, 87, 103, 105, 110, 927

FAS-FAX, I-1204

FEA 2011 Capacity Report, I-1107

Federal Aviation Administration, II-2268

Federal Communications Commission, I-1201

Federal Deposit Insurance Corp., II-3034-3085

Federal Reserve, II-3094, 3261

Feed International, I-592-593

Feedstuffs, I-595

FERI, II-3495,

First Research, II-3012

Flexible Packaging Association, I-39

Floor Covering Weekly, II-2737, 2908

Floor Focus, I-15, 1002-1003

Florida Office of Insurance Regulation, II-3224

Fondazione Altagamma, I-24

Food Additives and Ingredients Association, I-910

Food and Agriculture Organization, I-133, 141

Food for Thought, I-306-309, 311-317, 321-323, 325-330, 455, 537

Food Processing, I-305

Foodservice Equipment & Supplies, II-2754

Forbes, I-1051

Forrester Research, I-1928, II-2627

Foundation Center, II-3553

Fountain Agricounsel L.L.C., I-1330

"France Full Year 2011." [online] from http://bestsellingcarsblog.com [Published January 21, 2012], II-2190

France Télécom, II-2583

Franchise Times, II-3263

Freedonia Group, I-3, 13, 18, 20-21, 28-32, 34-37, 41-42, 48, 198, 214, 223, 238, 1000, 1011, 1085, 1087, 1091, 1096, 1099-1100, 1102-1103, 1151-1152, 1237, 1265, 1274, 1284, 1295, 1348, 1414, 1510, 1513, 1523, 1531-1532, 1540, 1549, 1571, 1585-1586, 1591, 1593, 1596, 1624-1625, 1629, 1680, 1691-1692, 1711, 1745, 1763, 1765, 1781, 1788, 1801, 1814, 1833, 1836, 1844, 1856, 1858, 1876, 1880-1881, 1892, 1904, 1913-1914, 1916-1917, 1920, 1986, II-1993, 1998, 2013, 2043, 2047-2048, 2052, 2163, 2221, 2282, 2336, 2387, 2390, 2482, 3328, 3382, 3479

"Fresenius Annual Report 2010." [online] from http://annualreport2010.fresenius.com [Accessed April 13, 2012], II-2349

FreshLook Marketing, I-81, 85-86

Frost & Sullivan, I-12, 1026, 1033-1034, 1047, 1057, 1084, 1465, 1482, 1493, 1639, 1644-1649, 1896, 1919, II-2004, 2009-2010, 2049, 2210, 2245-2246, 2250, 2294, 2391-2393, 2427, 2481, 2698, 2892, 3004, 3355, 3382, 3391

"FTC Requires Parent of Market Research Firm IMS Health to Sell Two Product Lines Before Acquiring Rival SDI Health." [online] from http://www/ftc.gov/opa/2011/10/ims_shtm [Published October 28, 2011], II-3581

Fuji Keizai, I-1346

"Full Focus: GameStop and the Digital Future." [online] from http://www.nintendojo.com [Published April 23, 2011], II-2681

Furniture Today, I-1115, 1120, II-2904, 2909-2910, 2912

Futuresource Consulting, II-2495-2496

G4s, II-3383

Gardner Publications, I-1872-1873

Gartner Inc., I-1893, 1895, 1927, 1930, 1934, 1941-1943, 1945, 1951, 1966, II-2098, 2128, 2147, 2679, 3302, 3344, 3346, 3349, 3353-3354, 3357, 3361, 3370, 3374-3375

GBGC - Global Betting and Gaming Consultancy, II-3489

General Aviation Manufacturers Association, II-2266, 2270

"Germany: The Industrial Chemicals Market." [online] from http://www.export.gov [Published December 2011], I-1248

Gestamp's internal estimates, II-2251, 2254

GfK, II-2018, 2060-2061, 3365

GFMS Ltd., I-166

Girl Scouts of America, I-630

Giving USA, II-3554

Glad Products data, I-1159

Global Cement, I-1673, 1890

Global Food Markets, I-331

"Global Software Top 100." [online] from http://www.softwaretop-100.org [Published August 23, 2011], II-3360

Global Water Intelligence, I-1921

GlobalData, II-2360, 2368

Gluskin Townley Group, II-2995

Goldman Sachs, I-1356, II-3344, 3349, 3357, 3359, 3578

Golf Inc., II-3475

Google Inc. Complete Vehicle Tire Shopper Study, II-2876

"Google's Market Share by Country." [online] from http://visualeconomics.creditloan.com/2010-02-03-planet-google-from-philosophies-to-market-shares [Accessed December 1, 2011], II-2645, 2649-2650, 2652-2654, 2656

GP Bullhound, II-2671-2672

"Great Lakes Growing Through Opportunities." [online] from http://www.faqs.org/sec-filings/110914/Great-Lakes-Dredge-and-Dock-

CORP_8-K [Published September 14, 2011], I-282

Greater Northwest Indiana Association of Realtors, II-3254

Greece regulators, II-3140

"Group Presentation for Investors." [online] from http://www.bicworld.com [Published August 2011], I-43-44

GTM Research, I-1768, II-2719

Gypsum Association, I-1687

Hallmark Cards, I-1245

Hanley Wood Market Intelligence, I-247

Harris Consulting, I-1779

Hauck und Aufhäuser, I-1122

The Headliner, I-1086

Hearth, Patio & Barbecue Association, I-1979

Heavy Duty Trucking Association, II-2223, 2227

Hesnes Shipping AS, *Car Carrier Market 2010*, II-2573

HFN State of the Industry Report, II-2915-2917

HFS Research, II-3373

Highline Data, II-3205, 3221

Hoard's Dairyman, I-430

Hobby Manufacturers Association, II-2437

Home Channel News, II-2782

Home Textiles Today market research, I-1066-1079, II-2907, 2913

Homeland Security Research, I-1796, II-2339-2342

Homeland Security Today, II-3601

HomeWorld Business, I-2, 1116, 1118, 1789, II-2033-2038, 2041, 2430, 2786, 2905, 2911, 2914, 2918-2919, 2921-2923, 3017

Honomichl Top 50, II-3580

Hoover's, II-2343-2344, 2346

Hotel & Motel Management, II-3271

HSBC, I-26, 1727

http://www.lavieeco.com, II-2194

http://www.motortrader.com.my, II-2193

"Hyundai Heavy Industries." [online] from http://www.hhiir.com/upload/presentation/Woori%20conference.pdf [Published March 28, 2011], II-2287

IBISWorld, I-6-7, 16, 108, 131, 137-138, 147, 202, 219, 271, 277-280, 286, 288-289, 292-294, 296, 451, 555, 644, 654, 658, 815, 885, 898, 908, 952, 958, 982-983, 990, 1004, 1038, 1044, 1063, 1080, 1083, 1147, 1191, 1197, 1208, 1217, 1236, 1354, 1384, 1476, 1487, 1516, 1534, 1542, 1551, 1580, 1636, 1651, 1669, 1676-1677, 1684-1685, 1690, 1782, 1794, 1811, 1831, 1885, II-2006, 2014, 2025, 2053, 2073, 2158, 2269, 2274, 2281, 2284, 2288, 2293, 2296, 2298, 2323, 2333, 2362-2363, 2446, 2453, 2478, 2498, 2504, 2520, 2538-2539, 2562, 2569, 2572, 2641, 2682, 2693, 2728, 2730, 2749, 2763, 2783, 2785, 2870, 2873, 2878, 2883, 2885, 2893, 2899, 2903, 2927, 2934, 2939, 2942, 2952-2953, 2986, 2993-2994, 2996, 3011, 3013-3015, 3019, 3023, 3028, 3033, 3118, 3265, 3267, 3270, 3274-3275, 3277-3278, 3280, 3282-3283, 3287, 3289-3290, 3296, 3314-3315, 3321, 3329, 3348, 3366, 3386, 3388, 3390, 3394, 3401, 3405, 3411, 3443, 3459-3460, 3474, 3478, 3491, 3497, 3499, 3501-3502, 3504, 3506, 3511, 3526, 3532-3533, 3543, 3546, 3550, 3570, 3572, 3574, 3576, 3589

ICRA Ltd., I-1909, II-2054, 2304

IDC's Worldwide Quarterly Smart Meter Tracker, II-2337

IdTechEX, II-2122

IE Market Research, II-2684

IESG analysis, I-1817-1818

IFP, I-203-204

IFP Energies Nouvelles, I-208

IHS Automotive, II-2219

IHS Global insight, I-241

IHS iSuppli, I-1933, 1949, II-2082, 2139-2141, 2146, 3449

IHS Jane's, II-3600

IHS Screen Digest, I-11, II-2108, 2929, 3444, 3448

IHS Screen Digest Mobile Media Research, II-2926

Imperial Capital L.L.C., I-45

IMS Health, I-1331, 1335-1336, 1338-1339, 1341-1342, 1345, 1347, 1352, II-2353

IMS Research, I-1766, 1819, II-1996, 2008, 2160, 3385

In-Stat, II-2118

Inc., II-2420

Indec, II-2634

Indianapolis Business Journal, II-2479

Industrial Minerals, I-1683, 1761

Industrial Truck Association, I-1867

Informa Economics, II-2528

Information Resources Inc., I-391-392, 428, 480-481, 516, 565, 607, 618, 622, 624, 627, 629, 869, 904-907, 916, 918, II-2175

Information Resources Inc. Info-Scan, I-427, 638, 729, 864, 868, 874

InfoTek, I-1589

"Ingenico Oddo MidCap Forum." [online] from http://www.ingenico.com [Published January 2011], I-1973

Ink World, I-1552

Inmar, I-10

Inntie, II-3269

Inside Mortgage Finance, II-3113, 3123

Inside Self-Storage, II-2522

"Inside Wall Street: U-Haul Ahead of its Industry." [online] from http://money.msn.com/top-stocks/post.aspx?post=0731d6c7-811b-4e05-9d79-8f06ad44fbc0 [Published February 21, 2012], II-3407

Instrument Business Outlook, II-2330

Insurance Information Institute, II-3141

International Air Travel Association, II-2560

International Association of Refrigerated Warehouses, II-2521

International Cocoa Organization, I-721, 723

International Coffee Organization, I-847-848

International Confectionery Association, I-693, 695, 715, 718

International Construction, I-276, 1840

International Data Corp., I-1932, 1939-1940, 1944, 1946, 1950, 1953, 1955-1956, 1959-1961, II-1991-1992, 2074, 2095, 2099-2100, 2131, 2133-2134, 2413, 3309, 3351

International Data Corp. Japan, II-2415

International Federation of Horse-racing Authorities, II-3468

International Federation of Robotics, I-1922

International Food Information Council, I-910

International Fur Trade Federation, I-1054

International Health, Racquet & Sportsclub Association, II-3471-3472

International Kiwi Fruit Organization, I-104

International Narcotics Control Board, I-1347

International Packaged Ice Association, I-887

International Rental News, II-3331-3332

International Rubber Study Group, I-1286, 1288

International Seed Federation, I-49, 51

International Snowmobile Association, II-2325

International Telecommunication Union, II-2574

International Textile Manufacturers Federation, I-1884

International Tin Research Institute, I-1730

International Trade Commission, I-1768

International Wine & Spirits Research, I-789

"Investor Kit January-March 2010." [online] from http://www.swed-ishmatch.com [Accessed March 2, 2012], I-971

Investor's Business Daily, I-1028

iResearch, II-2666

IRI Infoscan, I-910

Israel regulators, II-3142

Israel Vehicle Importers Association, II-2191

iSuppli, II-2136-2137, 2149-2152

Italian Association of Cosmetic Industries Annual Report 2010, I-1417

It's Academic, II-2492

Jack Link's, I-369

JAMMA's Survey of the Amusement Industry, II-3477

Japan Automobile Dealers Association, II-2204

Japan Automobile Manufacturers Association, II-2305

Japan Tobacco Inc., I-953-954

Japanese Statistics Bureau, II-3582

Japanese Watch & Clock Association, II-2421-2422

"JCI/CRH Merger Procedure." [online] from http://ec.europa.eu [Published January 14, 2011], II-2257

J.D. Power, II-2231

Jefferies & Co., II-2351

Jobson Optical, II-3509,

Jockey Club, I-132

Johnson & Johnson, II-2351

Joint Center for Housing Studies, I-244

Jon Northup analysis of IMS Health data, I-1337

Journal of Commerce, II-2506

J.P. Morgan, I-149, 215, 1232-1233, 1364-1369, 1409-1412, 1557, 1559-1562, 1574-1579, 1670, 1851, 1950, II-2130, 2153-2155, 2162, 2165, 2271-2272, 2334, 3101

Kaiyuan Circulation Research Report Q4 2010, I-1212

Kalorama Information, I-1130, II-2355-2357, 2359, 2376-2377, 3512-3513, 3522

Kantar Media, II-3292, 3307, 3310-3311

Kantar Retail, II-2790, 2806, 2897

Kantar Worldpanel, I-530, II-2859

Kepler Capital Markets, II-2423

KeyBanc Capital Markets, I-1256, II-2015

Kitchener Waterloo Association of Realtors, II-3256

Kline & Co., I-1413, 1443, 1477, 1587-1588, 1594

Kone estimates, I-1857

Kontali, I-143, 145

Kopenhagen Fur Auctions, I-130

KPMG, I-1332, II-2291

Kraftfahrt-Bundesamt, II-2201

Kusumgar, Nerlfi & Growney Inc., I-1544

Land Report, I-142

Landscape Management, I-140,

"Largest 100 U.S. Credit Unions by Assets." [online] from http://www.creditunionsonline.com [Accessed December 1, 2011], II-3087

Latin Business Chronicle, II-2574

Le Journal Moto du Net, II-2302

Leatherhead Food Research, I-331-332, 909

Leffingwell & Associates, I-1527

Leisure Trends Group, I-986, 1029

"Libbey Inc. 2010 Annual Report." [online] from http://www.libbey.com [Accessed February 20, 2012], I-1665

License Magazine, I-23

Limousine, Charter & Tour, II-2501

"Lithium Info." [online] from http://www.lithiumamericas.com/about-us/lithium-info [Accessed April 2, 2012], I-1272

LMC Automotive, II-2199

Los Angeles Business Journal, II-3456

Los Angeles Times, II-3523,

"Louisiana-Pacific Corporation." [online] from http://phx.corporate-ir.net [Published September 13, 2011], I-47, 1104

LP Gas, II-3022

Lutz Muller, II-2439

Lux Research, I-1769

Macleans, II-2436

MagnaGlobal, II-2697, 3298, 3300-3301, 3303-3305

MagNetData.net, I-1209, II-3025

Major League Baseball, II-3482

Malaysia Food & Drink Report, I-319

Manfredi & Associates, I-1837,

Marine Log, I-1798

"Marine Products Corporation." [online] from http://www.freeman.tulane.edu [Published March 15, 2011], II-2286

Market Intelligence, II-2516-2519

"Market Share." [online] from http://www.cruisemarketwatch.com/blog1/market-share-2 [Accessed September 16, 2011], II-2531-2532

Marketdata Enterprises, II-2659, 2992, 3288

Marketresearch.com, II-2388

MarketsandMarkets, I-910, II-2402

Marketsmith.com, II-2231

"Maruti Suzuki: Will it Sustain Leadership?" [online] from http://www.inin.co.in [Accessed April 1, 2012], II-2202

Maxim Group, II-2332

McCoy Power Report, I-1817-1818

McGraw-Hill, II-3573

McIlvaine Company, I-1800, 1899, 1925

McKinsey Global, I-25, II-2050-2051

McLane Co., I-955, 965-967

Meating Place, I-351

Medical Product Outsourcing, II-2361

Merrill Lynch, II-3086

"Metal Management Services." [online] from http://www.metalmanagementservices.com/content.do?method=longhai [Accessed May 1, 2012], I-1759

Metalworking Insiders Report, I-1877

Metro Magazine, II-2502-2503,

Metro Market Studies, II-2814-2815, 2827, 2839, 2847

Mexico Food & Drink Report, I-320

Michigan Gaming Control Board, II-3490

Michigan Inpatient Database, II-3520

Michigan Office of Financial and Insurance Regulation, II-3151

Midwest Real Estate Data L.L.C., II-3253-3254

Millicom International Center, II-2604, 2606-2607

MinCom, II-2588

Ministry of Economy, Trade and Industry, I-1148, II-2793, 2798, 2804

Ministry of Land, Infrastructure, Transport and Tourism, II-2558

Mintel, I-390, 447, 482, 513, 553, 568, 637, 776, 785, 800, 888, 1318, 1361, 1398, 1478, 1495, 1610, II-2868, 2997, 3473

Missouri Department of Insurance, II-3152

MMR, II-2816-2818, 2821-2824, 2826, 2828, 2830-2831, 2833-2836, 2838, 2840-2841, 2844-2846, 2848, 2851-2854, 2861-2863

Modern Brewery Age, I-755

Modern Casting, I-1741

Modern Healthcare's 2011 Executive Search Firms Survey, II-3591

Modern Healthcare's 2011 Healthcare Management Consultant Firms, II-3592

Modern Healthcare's 2011 Hospital Systems Survey, II-3514-3516

Modern Healthcare's 2011 Outsourcing Survey, II-3425, 3527

Modern Healthcare's 2011 Post-Acute-Care Survey, II-3519, 3549

Modern Materials Handling, I-1870

Modern Tire Dealer, I-1601-1603

"Mohawk Industries." [online] from http://phx.corporate-ir.net [Published August 2011], I-1679

Moody's, II-3205

Morgan Stanley Research, I-1276, 1512

Mortgage Data Web Market Share Report, II-3103

Motorcycle Industry Council, II-2301

MPA International, I-1198

MPN - Motorcycle & Powersports News, II-2881

MPR/Kaiser Family Foundation, II-3156-3168

MR Magazine, I-1035

MTN, II-2583

Multichannel Merchant, II-3016

Multifamily Executive, I-268

Music & Copyright, II-2091-2092

Music Trades, II-2433-2434, 2932

Musical Merchandise Review, II-2931

"Mystic Tan HD." [online] from http://www.the palmstanning resort. com [Accessed May 1, 2012], I-1507

NAICS Database, II-3170, 3186, 3189, 3191, 3210, 3213, 3215, 3235

National Alliance for Public Charter Schools, II-3534

National Association of Animal Breeders, I-139

National Association of College Bookstores, II-3002

National Association of Convenience Stores, II-2795

National Association of Insurance Commissioners, II-3149, 3192, 3209, 3222, 3225, 3229

National Basketball Association, II-3483

National Bureau of Economic Research, I-46

National Cable & Telecommunications Association, II-2633, 2699

National Cattlemen, I-111-112

National Federation of State High School Associations, II-3466-3467

National Football League, II-3485

National Hockey League, II-3486

National Jeweler, II-3005

National Kitchen and Bath Association, I-1092

National Mining Association, I-185

National Mortgage News/Quarterly Data Report, II-3100, 3104-3112

National Multi-Housing Council, II-3247-3248

National Oceanic and Atmospheric Administration, I-146

National Oil & Lube News, II-3422

National Park Service, II-3558

National Petroleum News, II-2879

National Pork Board, I-380

National Provisioner, I-355, 359

National Restaurant Association, II-2944

National Sporting Goods Association, I-1616, II-2452, 2902

National Telecommunications Commission, II-2617

National Trade Sources and Research, I-1610

National Underwriter, II-3133, 3169

Nation's Restaurant News research, II-2946, 2948, 2951

Nerlfi & Grownley, I-1508

NERSC/Lawrence Berkeley National Laboratory, I-1931

NetJets, II-2275

New York Times, II-2664

Nielsen Company, I-10, 73, 304, 369, 439, 452, 457, 462, 476-477, 580-581, 583, 589, 603, 655, 661, 717, 724, 827, 838, 842, 913-914, 926, 936, 972-973, 1214, II-2089, 2166, 2168, 2174, 2674, 3293, 3438

Nielsen Convenience Industry Store Count, II-2795

Nielsen/Crunch Pak Database, I-912

Nielsen Homescan Consumer Facts, II-2962-2963

Nielsen SoundScan, II-2087-2088, 2090

Nielsen TDLinx, II-2796

NielsenWire, II-2675

Nightclub & Bar research, II-2961

Nikkan Keizai Tsushinsha, I-303

Nilson Report, I-9, II-2121, 3089-3091, 3093

"NKT Annual Report 2011-2015." [online] from http://www.nkt.dk [Accessed September 1, 2011], I-1915

Nomura Research, II-2378

NonProfit Times, II-3552

Nonwovens Industry, I-1010, 1013

NPD Fashionworld, I-1021, II-2884

NPD Group Consumer Tracking Service, I-1053, 1058, 1060, 1640, 1650, II-2889, 2891, 3007, 3029

NPD Group Inc., I-4-5, 8, 17, 22, 420, 1015, 1048, 1755-1756, 1762, 1835, 1879, 1936, 1947-1948, 1952, 1954, 1957-1958, 1965, 1967-1968, 1970, II-2005, 2016, 2062-2069, 2077-2080, 2083-2084, 2096-2097, 2101-2103, 2105, 2107, 2109, 2111, 2119-2120, 2123, 2328, 2418, 2440, 2886, 2890, 2895, 3347, 3350, 3356, 3358, 3368-3369

NPD Group Retail Tracking Service, I-1641, 1643, II-3362-3363

NPD Solarbuzz, I-1767

"NSG and the Flat Glass Industry 2011." [online] from http://www. nsg.com [Accessed February 20, 2012], I-1653-1660

N.T. Information, II-2124

Nutrition Business Journal, I-336, 1296

"NYK Fact Book 2011." [online] from http://www.nyk.com [Accessed April 28, 2011], II-2526

OAG, II-2559

ODD, II-2195

ODS-Petrodata, I-203-204, 208

Off-Highway Research, I-1832, 1838

Office of Apparel and Textiles, I-974

Ohio Department of Insurance, II-3176, 3184, 3188, 3202, 3211, 3231

Oil & Gas Journal, I-195-196, 200, 1581

Oil World, I-746

OneStore Research, I-1671

Oppenheimer & Co., II-2666

Orr & Boss and Kusumgar, I-1508

"Osram/Siteco Lighting." [online] from http://ec.europa.eu [Published June 22, 2011], II-2055

"Outdoor Advertising." [online] from http://www.oft.gov.uk/shared_ oft/market-studies/oft1304.pdf [Published February 2012], II-3297

Outreach Magazine, II-3566

Outside, I-1059,

"Overview of the Retail Dollar Store Market." [online] from http:// www.ats.agr.gc.ca/amr/4356-eng. pdf [Published May 2011], II-2801

Ovum, I-1926

Packaged Facts, I-19, 358, 425, 514, 647, 734, 738, 741, 744-745, 1391, 1757, 1834, II-2408-2410, 2438, 2486, 3031

Packaging Machinery Manufacturers Institute, I-1912

The Packer, II-2825, 2832, 2842

Paint & Coatings Industry, I-1517

Palm Beach Post, II-2856

PaperAge, I-1143

Patriot Ledger, II-2954,

PCI Fibres, I-1133, 1294

Pearl Driver Technologies, I-1358,

Pembroke Consulting, II-2988

Perishables Group, I-73, 75-80, 83-
84, 88, 92, 95, 97-98, 101-102,
109, 349-350, 365, 374, 376, 396,
600-602, 623, 631, 837, 843, 899,
912, 919, 925
Perishables Group FreshFacts,
I-603
Pest Control Technology, II-3324
Pest Management Professional,
II-3323, 3325-3326
Pew Research Center's Internet &
American Life Project, I-1223
Pharmaceutical Executive,
II-2989
"PHH Corporation Investor Presen-
tation." [online] from http://phx.
corporate-ir.ne [Published May 7,
2012], II-3410
Pinsent Mason, II-2721
Pipeline & Gas Journal, II-2564
Planet Retail, I-1016, II-2940,
Plastics News, I-1623, 1632, 1634
Point Topic, II-2683
Polk & Co., II-2211, 2220
Pollstar, II-3453,
Pool & Spa News, I-299
"Pool Corp." [online] from http://
www.zacks.com/ZER/zer_get_pdf.
php?r=Z869569&t=POOL&
id=21365 [Published May 2012],
II-2757
Portland Cement Association, I-243,
1672
Portugal Telecom, II-2576
Portuguese regulators, II-3145
"Power Products Market Informa-
tion." [online] from http://www02.
abb.com [Published November 4,
2011], II-1995, 1997
Power Products Marketing, II-2326
Powergrid, II-2000
PR Newswire, I-1630
PR Week, II-3593
Prime Consulting, I-431
Principia Partners, I-1101
Professional Builder, I-246
*Professional Builder's 2011 Hous-
ing Giants Report*, I-249
*Professional Carwashing & Detail-
ing*, II-3420
Promo Magazine, II-3318
"PSI and Meritor Channel." [on-
line] from http://www.bigtrucktv.

com/channel.aspx?mtis_adv [Ac-
cessed October 1, 2011], I-1905
Publishers Weekly, I-1200, 1218,
1221
Pulp & Paper International, I-1137
QSR Magazine, II-2950, 2957
Quick Printing, II-3319
Railway Age, II-2295
Rauch Guide, II-2784,
RBC Capital Markets, I-172-173,
II-2116-2117
"RE/MAX Network Reports First
Half 2010 Market Share." [online]
from http://www.theboulderreales-
tatesite.com [Published August 2,
2011], II-3252
Real Capital Analytics, II-3115
"Recticel Strategy Update." [on-
line] from http://www.scribd.com
[Published November 30, 2010],
I-1631
RedTech Advisors, II-2631
Refrigerated & Frozen Foods,
I-345-346, 360, 479, 615
Refrigerated Transporter, II-2510
"Regulation Merger Procedure."
[online] from http://ec.europa.eu
[Published May 8, 2011], I-1865
Remodeling Magazine, I-245
Renewable Fuels Association,
I-1524
Rental Equipment Register,
II-3330
Reserve Bank of Australia, II-3101
Retail Traffic, II-3244-3245
Reverse Market Insights, II-3114
RigLogix, I-1851
RISI, I-1136, 1149
Robert W. Baird, I-1950, II-2401,
2405
RockTenn Presentation, I-1142, 1145
Roland Berger, I-1127-1128,
II-2169-2170, 2242-2243, 2249
Romans Group, II-3413
Roofing Contractor, I-290
Roskill Information Services,
I-174, 1271, 1569, 1681, 1683,
1761
RS Platou, I-1846, 1853
Rubber & Plastics News, I-1285,
1287, 1520
Rubber Manufacturers Association,
II-2734
Running Insight, I-1052

SABMiller, I-748,
SAI Report, I-1262,
St. Louis Post-Dispatch, II-2448
"Sales Charts of the Top 10 Best-
Selling Cars of 2011 and Decem-
ber 2011, by Class." [online] from
http://www.examiner.com [Ac-
cessed March 20, 2012], II-2181-
2184, 2186
"Sappi." [online] from http://www.
sappi.com [Published February 11,
2011], I-1154
"Sawn Softwood Production 2011."
[online] from http://www.infra.fr
[Published December 16, 2011],
I-1094
SBA-CCI, I-1283
School Bus Fleet, II-2505
Scorpio Partnership, II-3086
Screen Digest, II-3435-3436
Seafood Business, I-841
"Search Engine Market Share." [on-
line] from http://www.statowl.com/
search_engine_market_share.php
[Accessed June 1, 2012], II-2643
Secondary Search, II-2273
Security Distributing & Marketing,
II-3384
See Change Strategy L.L.C., I-1334
Semiconductor Industry Associa-
tion, II-2132
Senken Shimbun, I-1018
"Sewing Machine Brands." [on-
line] from http://www.consumerep-
orts.org [Accessed October 1,
2011], II-2046
SGB Golf, I-1609
Shelby Report, II-2813, 2843, 2850
Shooting Industry, I-1795
SIGET, II-2591, 2594-2595,
Signs of the Times, II-2477
Simba Information, I-1227-1228,
1235
"Singulus Optical Disc and Solar."
[online] from http://www.singulus.
com [Published January 2011],
I-1889
S.J. Consulting Group Inc., II-2512-
2513
SNL Financial, II-3187, 3234,
SNL Kagan, II-2695, 2701
Snow Magazine, II-2729
Society of Indian Automobile Man-
ufacturers, II-2304

Society of Motor Manufacturers and Traders, II-2209, 2222, 2226

Solar & Energy, I-1550, 1661-1662, II-2216

Solar Energy Industries Association, II-2719

Solarbuzz, I-1764

Source Interlink, II-3026

Southwick Associates, II-2451

Spanish regulatory commission, II-3146

Spears & Associates, I-206-207, 210-212, 222, 1847, 1850, 1855

Spears Report, I-205, 209, 1514, 1712-1714

Special Events Magazine, II-3400

SPINSscan, I-929, 1298, 1303,

Spiritus Consulting, I-1261

Sporting Goods Intelligence, I-1030-1032, 1613-1614

Sporting Goods Manufacturers Association, II-2445, 3461-3462

SportsOneSource, I-1607-1608, 1611-1612, 1615

"Spotlight on Decorative Paints." [online] from http://www.akzonobel.com [Published December 1, 2011], I-1515

"SQM." [online] from http://www.sqm.com [Published May 2011], I-1270

SRI Consulting, I-1255, 1258, 1260, 1276

Staffing Industry Analysts, II-3341-3343

Statistical Surveys Inc., II-2263-2264, 2289-2290, 2292, 2319-2320, 2324

Statistics Canada, II-2789

"Statistics of U.S. Businesses, 2008." [online] from http://www.census.gov [Accessed May 1, 2012], II-3446

Stitches, I-1081

"StoneMor Bank of America Leveraged Finance Conference." [online] from http://www.stonemor.com [Published December 2011], II-3260

Stores, II-2792

Strategic Insight Simfund MF, II-3121

Strategies Unlimited, II-2129

Strategy Analytics, II-2127, 2138, 2142, 2677

Strategy With Vision, II-2411

"Stryker Fact Book 2010-2011." [online] from http://hx.corporate-ir.net [Accessed October 1, 2011], I-1131-1132, II-2380-2382, 2384-2385, 2389

"Studio Market Share." [online] from http://boxofficemojo.com [Accessed April 1, 2012], II-3441

Subtel, II-2636

Successful Farming, I-118

"Sun Art Retail Group." [online] from http://pg.jrj.com.cn/acc/Res%5CHK_ES%5CSTOCK%5C2011%5C8%5C18%5CF5468742-06ce-442f-a166-2763fd9f5bde.pdf [Published August 18, 2011], II-2794

Supermarket News, II-2812

Swedish Match, I-972,

SymphonyIRI Group Inc., I-1, 126, 300-301, 348, 358, 361-364, 366-368, 370-373, 375, 382, 386, 388, 390, 393-395, 397-399, 402-404, 406-409, 414-419, 421-422, 424-426, 429, 434-438, 440-441, 445, 449-450, 458-460, 463-466, 468-475, 478, 483-495, 498-505, 507-512, 514-515, 517-520, 523-529, 531-536, 539-552, 554, 558-560, 562, 570-573, 576-579, 582, 584, 590-591, 596-599, 605-606, 608-610, 613-614, 616-617, 619-621, 625-626, 628, 634-636, 639-640, 648-649, 651-653, 657, 661, 678-692, 696-714, 717, 719-720, 724-728, 730, 734, 738-741, 743-745, 768, 770-772, 774-775, 783-784, 795-796, 800, 802, 804-806, 808-812, 829-836, 839-840, 844-845, 849, 851, 853-858, 860, 862-863, 865-867, 870-873, 875-882, 886, 889-890, 893-897, 901, 903, 915, 917, 920-921, 923-924, 931-932, 934-935, 969, 984-985, 987-988, 1158, 1160-1161, 1166, 1168, 1170, 1173-1174, 1177-1178, 1180-1183, 1185, 1187, 1194-1196, 1297, 1299-1302, 1304-1316, 1320-1324, 1326-1329, 1344, 1349-1350, 1355, 1357, 1362, 1373-1378, 1380-1383, 1386-1388,

1390, 1393-1397, 1399, 1402-1407, 1415, 1422-1423, 1425-1426, 1428-1429, 1431-1436, 1439-1441, 1444-1448, 1450-1453, 1455-1460, 1462-1464, 1466-1470, 1473-1475, 1478, 1489-1491, 1494, 1496, 1498-1500, 1502, 1504, 1506, 1511, 1543, 1547-1548, 1563-1566, 1592, 1621, 1633, 1731, 1749-1750, 1752-1754, 1918, II-2030, 2032, 2039, 2056-2057, 2164, 2167, 2177, 2367, 2369-2375, 2414, 2417, 2438, 2455-2456, 2460-2466, 2473-2474, 2483, 2485-2491, 2494, 2788, 2811, 2990, 3003

Systems Contractor News, II-2419

T-Index 2015 study by Translated, II-2624

TABB Group, II-3128

Talkers Magazine research, II-2688

"Tattoo Manufacturing." [online] from http:.//www.tattoosales.com/aboutus.aspx [Accessed December 1, 2011], I-1573

Teal Group, II-2271-2272

Techno Systems Research, II-2172

Technomic, II-2933, 2945, 2947, 2949, 2955, 2959, 2961

Technorati, II-2629

Telecommunications Carrier Association, II-2601

"Tembec Investor Presentation." [online] from http://tembec.com/sites/default/files/en/Investors/Presentations [Published March 17, 2011], I-1134

Texas Education Agency, I-1228

Texas Railroad Commission, I-199

Thai Aerosol Association, I-1555

Themed Entertainment Association, II-3480-3481

Thomson Reuters, I-1895, II-3117, 3124-3125, 3351, 3577

Thomson Reuters Datastream, I-148, 151, 748, II-2557, 2575, 2626

Tire Business, I-1604-1606, II-2877, 3415

Tire Review, I-1597-1598, 1600

Tissue World, I-1141

Tobacco Outlet Business, II-3024

Today's Trucking, II-2228-2230

"Top 5: Largest Patent Resource Libraries." [online] from http://info. articleonepartners.com [Published October 28, 2011], II-3539

Towers Perrin, II-3237

Townsend Solutions estimates, I-1628

Toy Industry Association, II-2443

Trade Show News Network, II-3404

Trailer/Body Builders, II-2321

Transport Topics, II-2508-2509, 2511, 2514-2515

TraQline Photo Behavior Report, II-3387

Travel & Leisure, II-3559,

Travel Weekly, II-2568

Trendgraphix.com, II-3255

TriAthlete Magazine, II-2447,

Triton Digital, II-2687,

Trust for Public Land, II-3598,

TV Veopar Journal, I-1984, II-2022, 2026, 2029, 2072, 2086

Twice market research, II-2920, 3010

Twice's Top 25 Retailer Report, II-2928

Twitaholic.com, II-3563

UBS, II-2575

UN Comtrade, I-135, 694, 928, 997, 1108, 1748, 1777, 1786, 1807, 1816, 1887-1888, 1900, 1972, II-2085, 2104, 2416

United Industries, I-1541

United Nations Environmental Programme, II-2704

United Nations Office on Drugs and Crime, I-1333

U.S. Bureau of the Census, I-39, 410, 641, 773, 991, 993-995, 998, 1006-1008, 1012, 1039, 1041-1043, 1046, 1056, 1064, 1082, 1088, 1097, 1117, 1124, 1126, 1150, 1153, 1155, 1157, 1163, 1231, 1238, 1240-1242, 1252, 1290, 1408, 1509, 1521, 1533, 1536, 1538, 1582, 1584, 1617, 1622, 1626-1627, 1652, 1666, 1693-1694, 1706-1707, 1709-1710, 1733, 1739, 1742-1743, 1746, 1760, 1770, 1774-1775, 1780, 1787, 1791-1793, 1797, 1799, 1802, 1804, 1809-1810, 1812, 1815, 1829-1830, 1862, 1871, 1878, 1897-1898, 1903, 1906,

1977, 1981-1983, 1990, II-1994, 2001-2003, 2023, 2031, 2110, 2113, 2125, 2135, 2232-2234, 2322, 2327, 2329, 2331, 2335, 2338, 2403, 2425, 2428-2429, 2431, 2435, 2457, 2467-2470, 2500, 2507, 2523, 2533-2534, 2537, 2565, 2570-2571, 2623, 2689, 2722-2726, 2731-2733, 2735-2736, 2738-2747, 2750-2753, 2755-2756, 2758-2762, 2764-2781, 2865, 2867, 2880, 2900, 2941, 2943, 2960, 2991, 3000, 3030, 3088, 3126-3127, 3238, 3240-3243, 3246, 3249-3251, 3258-3259, 3262, 3266, 3268, 3273, 3276, 3279, 3281, 3284, 3312-3313, 3320, 3322, 3327, 3333-3334, 3337-3340, 3371, 3376-3378, 3380, 3389, 3392-3393, 3395, 3397-3399, 3406, 3414, 3416-3419, 3421, 3423-3424, 3426-3430, 3432-3434, 3440, 3442, 3447, 3450-3452, 3454-3455, 3457, 3463-3465, 3469-3470, 3476, 3488, 3492, 3498, 3500, 3521, 3525, 3529-3530, 3541, 3545, 3547, 3556, 3560, 3562, 3568, 3579, 3584-3586, 3588

U.S. Bureau of Transportation, II-2541

U.S. Department of Agriculture, I-52-69, 71-72, 74, 89-91, 93-94, 96, 99-100, 107, 113-117, 119-121, 123-124, 127-128, 136, 352-354, 377, 379, 387, 389, 400, 405, 432-433, 642-643, 645, 736-737, II-2866, 3098

U.S. Department of Commerce, I-14, 347, 381, 411, 735, 902, 992, 996, 999, 1009, 1014, 1055, 1061-1062, 1065, 1089, 1098, 1110, 1119, 1125, 1144, 1156, 1162, 1164-1165, 1230, 1239, 1243, 1253, 1263, 1269, 1351, 1519, 1528, 1537, 1545, 1583, 1618, 1635, 1688, 1695, 1702-1703, 1708, 1732, 1734, 1737, 1740, 1744, 1747, 1758, 1771, 1776, 1778, 1783, 1790, 1803, 1806, 1808, 1825, 1863, 1869, 1874-1875, 1902, 1911, 1971, 1978, 1980, 1987-1989, II-1999, 2012, 2017, 2059, 2176, 2265, 2278-2279, 2285, 2297, 2299, 2318,

2394, 2412, 2426, 2432, 2471-2472, 2480, 2869, 2906, 3503, 3505, 3507-3508, 3510, 3528

U.S. Department of Education, II-3099, 3596

U.S. Department of Energy, II-2720

U.S. Department of Health and Human Services, II-3597

U.S. Department of Labor, II-3561

U.S. Department of Transportation, II-2542-2547, 2549-2556

U.S. Energy Information Administration, I-187, II-2705-2706

U.S. Food and Agriculture Organization, I-134

U.S. General Services Administration, II-2187

U.S. Geological Survey, U.S. Department of the Interior, I-150, 154-155, 157, 159, 163-164, 167, 169, 175, 182, 213, 216-218, 224-226, 228-232, 235-237, 239-240, 1266-1268, 1273, 1570, 1572, 1675, 1686, 1689, 1699-1700, 1705, 1721, 1723-1726, 1729, 1735-1736

U.S. Patent and Trade Office, II-3264

U.S. Postal Service, II-2524-2525

U.S. Securities and Exchange Commission, II-3316

University of Mannheim, I-1931

University of Tennessee, I-1931

USA Rice Federation, I-563-564, 566-567

"USA Technologies Company Overview." [online] from http://www.usatech.com/company_info/dl/USAT_company_overview.pdf [Published January 2012], II-2686

USA TODAY analysis of Federal Action Committee data, II-3565

"USA Yearly Chart." [online] from http://www.vgchartz.com/yearly/2011/USA [Accessed March 20, 2012], II-2444

USAF Dental Equipment & Consultation Service, II-2395-2400

Utsunomiya, I-556

Ux Consulting, I-171-173

Vacon estimates, II-1996

Välinge, I-13

Value Retail News, II-2802

Vara Research, I-1112

Variety, II-3458

VDAI, II-3495

VDMA, I-1886

Versicherungswirtschaft, II-3139

VFACTS, II-2189

VFC Corp., II-2450

VGChartz, II-3364

Vision Monday, II-3027

Vlad VneshService, I-588

VRL Publishing, I-1234

"The Wal-Mart of Weddings." [online] from http://www.msnbc.msn.com/id/31324765/ns/business-us_business/ [Published June 15, 2011], II-2888

Wall Street Journal, I-956, 1546, II-2454

Warehouse Club research, II-2807-2809

Washington State Office of the Insurance Commissioner, II-3155

Washington Technology, II-2317

Waste Age, II-2727

Watt Poultry, I-122, 129,

Weiss Ratings, II-3153

Willard Bishop, II-2810

Wine Business Monthly, I-779

Wolf Trahan & Co., II-2540

Wolters Kluwer, I-1232-1234, 1331

Wood Components, I-1093

Wood Mackenzie, I-156, 176, 1719, 1722, 1738

Wood Markets, I-1095, 1105

World Association of Newspapers, I-1202

World Bureau of Metal Statistics, I-161, 165, 170, 1718

"World Footwear Market and Perspectives for Leather." [online] from http://www.tyche.com.tw [Published December 9, 2011], I-1637, II-2901

World Gold Council, I-160-161, 165

World Industrial Trucks Statistics, I-1868

"World Leader in Reproduction Biotechnology." [online] from http://www.ofi-pecapital.com/uk/imv_technologies.php [Accessed May 1, 2012], I-1827

World Nuclear Association, I-172-173

World Oil, II-2345

"World PCB Production." [online] from http://www.tpca.org.tw/download.aspx?dlfn=TPCAShow_Market.pdf [Accessed February 14, 2012], II-2126

World Shipping Council, II-2535

World Steel Association, I-1701

"World's 10 Largest Stock Exchanges." [online] from http://www.rediff.com/business/slide-show/slide-show-1-largest-stock-exchanges/20111104.htm [Published November 2011], II-3129

WWD, I-1442

Xplana, I-1225

"The Xplanation." [online] from http://blog.xplana.com [Published August 5, 2011], I-1213, 1226

Yamaha Motor, II-2300

Yano Research Institute, II-2493

Yengst Associates, I-1839

Yole Developpement, I-1891, II-2148

ZenithOptimedia, II-3308

ZookNIC Internet Intelligence, II-2630

PLACE NAMES INDEX

This index shows countries, political entities, states, and provinces, regions within countries, parks, airports, and cities. For items in the index that refer to a large number of entries, a subject subheading is provided to make it as easy as possible to access entries of interest. The numbers that follow the place name, or one of its subheadings, are entry numbers; they are arranged sequentially so that the first mention of a place is listed first. The Roman numerals indicate the volume number. This index provides references for 422 places.

Africa, I-173, 446, 593, 645, 1333, 1712, 1800, 1857, 1899, 1940, II-2009, 2273, 2516

Africa and the Middle East, I-32, 1011, 1284, 1913

Alabama, I-65, 91, II-2178, 2816, 2967, 3034, 3193

Alaska, I-146, 190, II-3035

Albany, NY, II-3534

Albuquerque, NM, II-3598

Alexandria, VA, II-2862

Algeria, I-53, 61, 105, 188-189, 231, 848

Americas, I-1683, II-2132, 2496, 2518

Anchorage, AK, II-2561

Angola, I-237, II-2576

Antalya, II-2566

Arcadia National Park, ME, II-3558

Argentina
  Agriculture - Crops, I-49, 52, 56, 60, 63, 70, 82
  Agriculture - Livestock, I-113-116, 124
  Chemicals and Allied Products, I-1273
  Communications, II-2574, 2577, 2634, 2644
  Food and Kindred Products, I-353-354, 400, 405, 433
  Instruments and Related, II-2339
  Motion Pictures, II-3468
  Transportation Equipment, II-2197
  Wholesale Trade - Durables, II-2700

Arizona, I-65, 121, 262, II-2554, 2719, 2845, 2982, 3036, 3157

Arkansas, I-55, II-3037, 3194

Arlington, TX, I-252, II-2823

Arlington, VA, II-3598

Asia, I-1031, 1289, 1515, 1595, 1613, 1644-1645, 1712, 1800, 1839, 1884, II-2300

Asia-Pacific, I-24, 30, 32
  Apparel and Textile Products, I-1011
  Chemicals and Allied Products, I-1284, 1295, 1531
  Communications, II-2629
  Electric/Gas/Sanitary Services, II-2683
  Electronic/Electric Equip., II-2013, 2132
  Food and Kindred Products, I-446, 593
  Furniture Stores, II-2936
  Industry Machinery/Equip., I-1913, 1917, 1926, 1944
  Nat. Security and Interntl. Affairs, II-3590
  Nonmetallic Minerals, I-214
  Paper and Allied Products, I-1135
  Real Estate, II-3302
  Transportation Equipment, II-2267, 2273
  Trucking and Warehousing, II-2496
  Water Transportation, II-2519

Atlanta, GA, II-2563, 2813, 2965

Aurora, CO, I-253, II-2824, 2973

Australasia, I-446

Australia
  Agriculture - Crops, I-52, 54, 66, 68
  Agriculture - Livestock, I-114-116
  Business Services, II-3435
  Chemicals and Allied Products, I-1266, 1273, 1333, 1516, 1542
  Coal Mining, I-173
  Communications, II-2578, 2635
  Depository Institutions, II-3101

Fabricated Metal Products, I-1766

Food and Kindred Products, I-354, 405, 575, 642, 748, 757

General Building Contractors, I-230, 235-236, 240

General Merchandise Stores, II-2797

Industry Machinery/Equip., I-1873

Instruments and Related, II-2339

Insurance Agents and Brokers, II-3293

Metal Mining, I-145, 148, 150, 154, 157, 159, 163

Misc. Manufacturing Industries, II-2440

Miscellaneous Retail, II-2994

Motion Pictures, II-3468

Nat. Security and Interntl. Affairs, II-3600

Nonmetallic Minerals, I-200, 217

Oil and Gas Extraction, I-184, 186

Petroleum and Coal Products, I-1572

Primary Metal Industries, I-1689, 1721, 1736

Security and Commodity Brokers, II-3134

Tobacco Products, I-938

Transportation Equipment, II-2189, 2216

Transportation Services, II-2567

Austria, I-306, 989, 1094, 1409, 1689, 1828, II-2018

Azerbaijan, I-751

Bahamas, I-1572

Bahrain, I-1416, 1721, II-2579

Bakersfield, CA, II-2814

Baltimore, MD, I-247, II-2815

Bangkok, Thailand, II-2566

Bangladesh, I-57-58, 67, 736, 927, 974, 1884, II-2580
Baton Rouge, LA, II-2966
Baytown, TX, I-255, II-2976
Beijing, China, II-2563
Belarus, I-119-120, 228
Belgium
  Apparel and Textile Products, I-989, 1020
  Chemicals and Allied Products, I-1268
  Communications, II-2581
  Food and Kindred Products, I-307, 694, 718
  Lumber and Wood Products, I-1057
  Metal Mining, I-165
  Primary Metal Industries, I-1748
  Printing and Publishing, I-1198
Belize, II-2582
Bellevue, WA, I-266, II-2854
Birmingham, AL, II-2816, 2967
Bloomington, MN, I-260
Bolivia, I-157, 159
Boston, MA, II-2817, 2968
Botswana, I-235, 237, II-2583
Boulder, CO, II-3252
Brazil
  Agricultural Services, I-127-128
  Agriculture - Crops, I-49, 53, 56, 63, 66, 68, 70, 82, 89-90, 93-94, 103, 106
  Agriculture - Livestock, I-113-116, 119-120, 123-124
  Apparel and Textile Products, I-1016
  Business Services, II-3435
  Chemicals and Allied Products, I-1266, 1268, 1273, 1339
  Communications, II-2574, 2624, 2632, 2645
  Electronic/Electric Equip., II-2018, 2099
  Food and Kindred Products, I-353-354, 377, 379, 400, 432-433, 575, 592, 642, 645, 659, 693, 695, 715, 718, 721, 723, 737, 754, 801, 818, 847
  General Building Contractors, I-230, 239, 241
  Industry Machinery/Equip., I-1872-1873
  Instruments and Related, II-2339
  Metal Mining, I-143, 148, 150, 163

Misc. Manufacturing Industries, II-2440
Motion Pictures, II-3468
Nat. Security and Interntl. Affairs, II-3600
Oil and Gas Extraction, I-191-192
Petroleum and Coal Products, I-1572
Primary Metal Industries, I-1689, 1700, 1718, 1721, 1736
Printing and Publishing, I-1169, 1202
Stone/Clay/Glass Products, I-1637, 1675, 1686
Tobacco Products, I-939
Transportation Equipment, II-2211-2212, 2223, 2227
Wholesale Trade - Durables, II-2704, 2717
Bridgeport, CT, II-2818
Broomfield, CO, I-253
Broward County, FL, II-3535
Bulgaria, I-308, II-2416, 2584, 2819
Burkina, I-66
Burma, I-58
Busan, South Korea, II-2535
California
  Agriculture - Crops, I-55, 71, 86, 107
  Agriculture - Livestock, I-121
  Business Services, II-3402
  Depository Institutions, II-3102
  Fishing, Hunting, and Trapping, I-136
  Food and Kindred Products, I-352
  Food Stores, II-2814, 2828, 2836, 2853, 2866
  Furniture Stores, II-2931
  General Building Contractors, I-249
  General Merchandise Stores, II-2795
  Heavy Construction, I-258
  Insurance Carriers, II-3158, 3170, 3186, 3189, 3191, 3195, 3210, 3213, 3215, 3226, 3229, 3235, 3272
  Metal Mining, I-146
  Misc. Repair Services, II-3456
  Miscellaneous Retail, II-2979, 3032, 3038
  Nat. Security and Interntl. Affairs, II-3598
  Oil and Gas Extraction, I-190

Real Estate, II-3314
Social Services, II-3559
Wholesale Trade - Durables, II-2719
Cambodia, I-56, 974
Cambridge, MA, I-248, II-2817, 2968
Camden, NJ, II-2844
Cameron, LA, I-146
Cameroon, I-723
Canada
  Agricultural Services, I-127-128
  Agriculture - Crops, I-49, 52, 54, 60, 63, 87, 110
  Agriculture - Livestock, I-115, 119-120
  Amusement and Recreation, II-3496
  Business Services, II-3385, 3435
  Coal Mining, I-173
  Communications, II-2585, 2629, 2646
  Electronic/Electric Equip., II-2070
  Fabricated Metal Products, I-1766
  Fishing, Hunting, and Trapping, I-130
  Food and Kindred Products, I-309, 354, 379, 387, 400, 432, 442, 575, 585, 655, 694, 758, 848
  Food Stores, II-2820
  General Building Contractors, I-228, 237, 239
  General Merchandise Stores, II-2789
  Instruments and Related, II-2326
  Insurance Carriers, II-3256
  Metal Mining, I-145, 150, 154, 157, 159, 163
  Misc. Manufacturing Industries, II-2416, 2440
  Motion Pictures, II-3468
  Nonmetallic Minerals, I-200
  Oil and Gas Extraction, I-188, 191-194
  Paper and Allied Products, I-1094
  Petroleum and Coal Products, I-1572
  Primary Metal Industries, I-1689, 1721, 1724, 1736
  Security and Commodity Brokers, II-3135
  Stone/Clay/Glass Products, I-1656
  Textile Mill Products, I-976

Transportation Equipment, II-2198, 2299

Wholesale Trade - Durables, II-2704, 2717-2718

Canada & Mexico, I-1284

Caribbean, II-2857

Carmel, IN, I-256

Central African Republic, I-237

Central and Eastern Europe, II-2231

Central and South America, I-32, 1011, 1284, 1899, 1913, II-2231, 3590

Central Europe, I-1595, 1922

Central Park, New York, II-3559

Charlotte, NC, I-250

Charlotte Douglas International, NC, II-2542

Chicago, IL, II-2563, 2821, 2969, 3253, 3535

Chicago O'Hare International, IL, II-2543

Chile, I-90, 100, 104, 134, 145, 153-154, 162, 228, 957, 1273, 1483, II-2574, 2586, 2636, 2647, 3468

China, I-12, 24, 26

Agricultural Services, I-127-128

Agriculture - Crops, I-49-50, 54, 56, 63-64, 67-68, 70, 82, 89-90, 93-94, 99-100, 103-104, 106, 110

Agriculture - Livestock, I-113-116, 119-120, 123-124

Apparel and Accessory Stores, II-2887, 2892, 2898

Apparel and Textile Products, I-997, 1016, 1022, 1026-1027, 1033-1034, 1036

Business Services, II-3349, 3357, 3435

Chemicals and Allied Products, I-1212, 1246-1247, 1262, 1264, 1266, 1268, 1273, 1286, 1317, 1319, 1326, 1332-1333, 1340, 1343, 1363, 1372, 1389, 1392, 1400-1401, 1413, 1420-1421, 1424, 1427, 1438, 1449, 1454, 1461, 1465, 1472, 1480, 1482, 1488, 1492-1493, 1497, 1501, 1503, 1505, 1512, 1514, 1526, 1529, 1558

Communications, II-2587, 2624-2625, 2631-2632, 2658

Eating and Drinking Places, II-2958

Electric/Gas/Sanitary Services, II-2666, 2680

Electronic/Electric Equip., II-2011, 2018, 2025, 2060, 2071, 2073, 2085, 2099, 2104, 2124

Engineering/Management Services, II-3583

Fabricated Metal Products, I-1759, 1761, 1766, 1777, 1807, 1811

Fishing, Hunting, and Trapping, I-130, 134-135

Food and Kindred Products, I-310, 339, 353-354, 377, 379, 384, 412, 423, 432-433, 454, 496-497, 521, 538, 611, 643, 645, 659, 662, 694, 716, 731-732, 736, 754, 759, 797-798, 801, 807, 819, 828, 850, 859, 892

Food Stores, II-2864

General Building Contractors, I-220, 226, 228, 230-231, 233, 235-236, 239-241

General Merchandise Stores, II-2794

Health Services, II-3524

Industry Machinery/Equip., I-1838-1839, 1841-1843, 1857, 1866, 1872-1873, 1876, 1888, 1900, 1908, 1922, 1935, 1972

Instruments and Related, II-2339, 2341-2342, 2348, 2350, 2352-2354, 2362, 2364-2366, 2383, 2386

Insurance Carriers, II-3223, 3269, 3291

Legal Services, II-3544

Local and Passenger Transit, II-2481, 2484

Lumber and Wood Products, I-1040, 1045, 1047, 1049

Metal Mining, I-143-144, 150-151, 154, 157, 159-160, 163, 165

Misc. Manufacturing Industries, II-2440, 2453

Miscellaneous Retail, II-3006, 3018

Nat. Security and Interntl. Affairs, II-3600

Nondepository Institutions, II-3116

Nonmetallic Minerals, I-202, 205

Oil and Gas Extraction, I-183-184, 186, 188, 191-192

Paper and Allied Products, I-1084, 1105, 1114

Personal Services, II-3344

Petroleum and Coal Products, I-1572, 1580

Primary Metal Industries, I-1689, 1698, 1700, 1704, 1711-1713, 1716, 1718, 1720-1721, 1724, 1727, 1736, 1748

Printing and Publishing, I-1169, 1172, 1175-1176, 1179, 1184, 1186, 1192-1193, 1202

Rubber and Misc. Plastics, I-1596, 1604

Security and Commodity Brokers, II-3136

Stone/Clay/Glass Products, I-1637, 1639, 1642, 1653, 1659, 1667-1668, 1671, 1675, 1678, 1683, 1686

Textile Mill Products, I-958, 970, 974, 977

Tobacco Products, I-922, 927-928, 930

Transportation by Air, II-2535

Transportation Equipment, II-2188, 2199, 2211-2212, 2216, 2223, 2227, 2231, 2245-2246, 2250, 2283, 2287, 2298-2300, 2308

Transportation Services, II-2563

Trucking and Warehousing, II-2498

Wholesale Trade - Durables, II-2704, 2707

Chna, I-25

C.I.S., I-130, 148, 1899, II-2273

Clark County, NV, II-3535

Clearwater, FL, I-267

Cleveland, OH, II-2822, 2970, 3534

Colombia, I-61, 103, 115-116, 184, 194, 642, 737, 847, II-2574, 2588, 2648, 2700

Colorado, I-121, 253, 352, II-2545, 2563, 2719, 2824, 2973, 3039, 3154, 3252, 3487

Columbia, SC, I-251, II-2971

Columbus, OH, II-2972

Community of European Shipyards, II-2283

Congo, I-154, 235, 237

Connecticut, II-2818, 3040

Cordova, AK, I-146

Costa Rica, I-106

Croatia, II-2589

Cuba, I-1736

Cuyahoga Valley National Park, OH, II-3558

Czech Republic, I-676, 1828, II-2618, 2704, 2858

Dallas, TX, I-252, II-2823

Dallas/Ft. Worth, TX, II-2563

Dallas/Ft. Worth International Airport, TX, II-2544

Davidson, TN, II-2840

Dayton, OH, II-3534

Delaware, II-2844, 3041, 3487

Denmark, I-130, 311, 663, 1094, 1379, 1559, 1574, 1828, II-3137

Denver, CO, I-253, II-2563, 2824, 2973

Denver International Airport, CO, II-2545

Des Moines, IA, II-2825, 2974

Detroit, MI, I-242, 254, II-2826, 2975, 3490, 3520, 3534

Detroit Metro Wayne County Airport, MI, II-2546

Disneyland, CA, II-3480, 3559

Disney's Animal Kingdom, FL, II-3480

Disney's Hollywood Studios, CA, II-3480

Dominican Republic, II-2574

Dubai, United Arab Emirates, II-2535, 2561

Dutch Harbor-Unalaska, AK, I-146

East Asia, I-172, 1899, II-2009, 2122

Eastern Europe, I-32, 446, 760, 1011, 1284, 1880, 1899, 1913, 1922, II-2009, 2516, 2683

Ecuador, I-103, 723, 737, II-2574

Egypt, I-53, 61, 64, 105, 188, 240, 340, 746, 820, 1675, II-2590

El Salvador, I-974, II-2574, 2591

Elyria, OH, II-2822, 2970

Empire-Venice, LA, I-146

Epcot at Walt Disney World, FL, II-3480

EU-27, I-52-53, 57, 60-61, 64, 89-90, 93-94, 99-100, 113-116, 119-120, 123-124, 127-128, 353-354, 377, 379, 387, 389, 400, 405, 433, 642-643, 645, 736, 848, 1246, II-2283

Europe, I-26
   Apparel and Textile Products, I-989, 1032
   Business Services, II-3365
   Chemicals and Allied Products, I-1286, 1413

Electronic/Electric Equip., II-2060, 2117, 2122, 2124, 2132

Engineering/Management Services, II-3583

Fabricated Metal Products, I-1761, 1800

Food and Kindred Products, I-529, 593

General Building Contractors, I-233

Industry Machinery/Equip., I-1826, 1828, 1839, 1940

Instruments and Related, II-2391-2393

Lumber and Wood Products, I-1057

Nat. Security and Interntl. Affairs, II-3590

Paper and Allied Products, I-1105-1106, 1122, 1135, 1138, 1146

Personal Services, II-3342

Primary Metal Industries, I-1704, 1712

Printing and Publishing, I-1188, 1190, 1198

Rubber and Misc. Plastics, I-1599, 1614

Stone/Clay/Glass Products, I-1644, 1647, 1654, 1659, 1683

Transportation Equipment, II-2200, 2211, 2216, 2258, 2267, 2273, 2300

Wholesale Trade - Durables, II-2708

Europe, Middle East and Africa, I-1857, 1926, 1940, II-2496

European Economic Area, I-1129, 1539, 1553, 1784, 1975-1976, II-2055, 2251, 2254, 2257, 2259

European Union, I-143, 1020, 1023, 1637, II-2341-2342, 2629

Everland, South Korea, II-3480

Fall River, RI, II-2984

Faneuil Hall Marketplace, MA, II-3559

Far East, I-205, 1712

Fargo, ND, II-2827

Faroe Islands, I-145

Finland, I-130, 217, 312, 1094, 1777, II-2649, 3138

Flint, MI, II-3534

Florida
   Agriculture - Crops, I-72, 91, 107
   Amusement and Recreation, II-3487

Business Services, II-3402

Depository Institutions, II-3042

Food Stores, II-2838, 2851, 2856

Furniture Stores, II-2931

General Merchandise Stores, II-2795

Heavy Construction, I-259

Insurance Carriers, II-3159, 3171, 3196, 3224, 3229-3230, 3255, 3272

Miscellaneous Retail, II-3032

Nat. Security and Interntl. Affairs, II-3598

Real Estate, II-3314

Social Services, II-3559

Special Trade Contractors, I-267

Stone/Clay/Glass Products, I-1672

Fort Lauderdale, FL, I-259, II-2838

Fort Worth, TX, I-252, II-2823

France
   Agriculture - Crops, I-49, 54, 104
   Apparel and Textile Products, I-989, 997, 1020, 1023
   Business Services, II-3435
   Communications, II-2592
   Electronic/Electric Equip., II-2018, 2144
   Fabricated Metal Products, I-1766, 1807
   Food and Kindred Products, I-313, 575, 659, 664, 693, 695, 715, 718, 801
   General Building Contractors, I-226, 240-241
   Industry Machinery/Equip., I-1816, 1828, 1873, 1888, 1900, 1941
   Instruments and Related, II-2339
   Lumber and Wood Products, I-1057
   Misc. Manufacturing Industries, II-2440
   Motion Pictures, II-3468
   Nat. Security and Interntl. Affairs, II-3600
   Nonmetallic Minerals, I-217
   Paper and Allied Products, I-1094
   Printing and Publishing, I-1169, 1198, 1202
   Tobacco Products, I-940
   Transportation Equipment, II-2190, 2212, 2302, 2309
   Transportation Services, II-2561, 2563
   Wholesale Trade - Durables, II-2704, 2709, 2718

Frankfurt, Germany, II-2561, 2563
Fremont, CA, II-2853
Fresno, CA, II-2828
Fujian, China, I-144
Gary, IN, II-3534
Gastonia, NC, I-250
Georgia, I-65, 91, II-2547, 2563, 2795, 2813, 2931, 2965, 3043, 3208, 3229
Germany
  Agriculture - Crops, I-49, 54, 87
  Amusement and Recreation, II-3495
  Apparel and Textile Products, I-989, 997, 1020, 1023
  Business Services, II-3435
  Chemicals and Allied Products, I-1248, 1410, 1526
  Communications, II-2593, 2632, 2650
  Electric/Gas/Sanitary Services, II-2671
  Electronic/Electric Equip., II-2018
  Fabricated Metal Products, I-1766, 1777, 1807
  Fishing, Hunting, and Trapping, I-135
  Food and Kindred Products, I-302, 314, 575, 656, 659, 665, 693-695, 715, 718, 721, 754, 801
  General Building Contractors, I-228, 241
  Industry Machinery/Equip., I-1816, 1828, 1872-1873, 1888, 1900, 1922, 1942, 1962, 1972
  Instruments and Related, II-2310, 2339
  Lumber and Wood Products, I-1057
  Metal Mining, I-151, 160, 165
  Misc. Manufacturing Industries, II-2440
  Nat. Security and Interntl. Affairs, II-3600
  Nonmetallic Minerals, I-217
  Oil and Gas Extraction, I-186, 191
  Petroleum and Coal Products, I-1572, 1575
  Primary Metal Industries, I-1689, 1718, 1748
  Printing and Publishing, I-1198, 1202
  Security and Commodity Brokers, II-3139

Stone/Clay/Glass Products, I-1675, 1686
  Transportation Equipment, II-2201, 2212
  Transportation Services, II-2561, 2563
  Wholesale Trade - Durables, II-2704, 2710, 2718
Ghana, I-163, 237, 721, 723
Glendale, AZ, I-262
Grand Bazaar, Istanbul, II-3559
Grand Canyon National Park, AZ, II-3558
Grand Central Terminal, Manhattan, II-3559
Grand Teton National Park, WY, II-3558
Great Britain, II-3468
Great Lakes region, I-86, II-2530
Great Smoky Mountains National Park, TN, II-3558
Greece, I-66, 104-105, 315, 1020, II-2829, 3140
Guangdong, China, I-144
Guangxi, China, I-144
Guangzhou Harbor, China, II-2535
Guatemala, I-103, 642, 847, 928, II-2574, 2594
Guinea, I-237, 1266
Hartsfield-Jackson Atlanta International, GA, II-2547
Hawaii, I-72, 107, II-2830, 3044, 3535
Heathrow Airport, United Kingdom, II-2548
Henderson, NV, II-3598
Hillsborough County, FL, II-3535
Honduras, I-737, 847, 974, II-2574, 2595
Hong Kong, I-24, 143, 777, 787, 997, 1325, 1748, 1972, II-2104, 2535, 2561, 2566-2567, 2596, 2651, 2717-2718, 3004, 3141
Honolulu, HI, II-2830
Hoover, AL, II-2816, 2967
Houston, TX, I-255, II-2976, 3535
Hubei, China, I-144
Hungary, I-666, 761, 821, 1816, 1828, II-2085, 2597
Idaho, I-71, 121, II-3045
Illinois, I-117, 136, 263, 352, II-2178, 2543, 2795, 2821, 2866, 2931, 3032, 3046, 3197, 3229, 3253, 3487

Incheon, Korea, II-2561
India, I-24
  Agriculture - Crops, I-49, 56, 58, 60, 66, 68, 70, 82, 99-100, 103, 106
  Agriculture - Livestock, I-113-116, 124
  Apparel and Textile Products, I-1016
  Business Services, II-3435
  Chemicals and Allied Products, I-1249, 1266, 1286, 1333, 1341, 1353, 1477, 1526
  Communications, II-2598, 2632
  Electronic/Electric Equip., II-2000, 2018, 2022, 2026, 2029, 2072, 2086, 2099
  Engineering/Management Services, II-3583
  Fabricated Metal Products, I-1766
  Fishing, Hunting, and Trapping, I-134-135
  Food and Kindred Products, I-341, 353-354, 387, 389, 432-433, 633, 645, 667, 736, 749, 822, 847
  General Building Contractors, I-231, 233, 236, 239, 241
  Industry Machinery/Equip., I-1872, 1884, 1909, 1943, 1966, 1984
  Instruments and Related, II-2311, 2339, 2341-2342
  Metal Mining, I-148, 150, 157, 159-160, 165
  Misc. Manufacturing Industries, II-2416, 2440
  Nat. Security and Interntl. Affairs, II-3600
  Oil and Gas Extraction, I-186, 191
  Petroleum and Coal Products, I-1572
  Primary Metal Industries, I-1700, 1718, 1721, 1724
  Printing and Publishing, I-1202
  Rubber and Misc. Plastics, I-1587, 1590, 1595
  Stone/Clay/Glass Products, I-1637, 1686
  Textile Mill Products, I-974
  Tobacco Products, I-927-928, 942
  Transportation Equipment, II-2202, 2212, 2223, 2227, 2231, 2304
  Transportation Services, II-2557
  Wholesale Trade - Durables, II-2704, 2711

Indiana, I-59, 117, 256, 352, 1699, 1735, II-2178, 2821, 2831, 3047, 3254, 3534

Indianapolis, IN, I-256, II-2831

Indonesia
  Agriculture - Crops, I-53, 57-58, 64, 67, 70, 103, 106, 110
  Fishing, Hunting, and Trapping, I-134
  Food and Kindred Products, I-643, 721, 723, 736-737, 801, 847
  Industry Machinery/Equip., I-1884
  Metal Mining, I-154, 163
  Oil and Gas Extraction, I-184, 188
  Primary Metal Industries, I-1736
  Printing and Publishing, I-1169
  Stone/Clay/Glass Products, I-1637
  Textile Mill Products, I-974
  Tobacco Products, I-927-928

Intracoastal City, LA, I-146

Iowa, I-59, 117, 121, 352, II-2825, 2866, 2974, 3048, 3221, 3487

Iran, I-57, 61, 104, 150, 188-189, 191-193, 200, 231, 240, 928, 1333, 1526, 1675, II-2599

Iraq, I-57, 192-194

Ireland, I-110, 145, 157, 159, 316, 668, 959, II-2018, 2600, 2639

Israel, I-228, 230, II-2191, 2339, 3142, 3600

Istanbul, Turkey, II-2566

Italy
  Agriculture - Crops, I-49, 70, 104-105, 110
  Apparel and Textile Products, I-989, 997, 1020, 1023
  Chemicals and Allied Products, I-1364, 1417
  Communications, II-2652
  Fabricated Metal Products, I-1766, 1777, 1807
  Fishing, Hunting, and Trapping, I-135
  Food and Kindred Products, I-317, 575, 659, 669, 693, 695, 715, 718, 801
  General Building Contractors, I-226, 240-241
  Industry Machinery/Equip., I-1828, 1872-1873, 1888, 1900, 1922, 1963

Instruments and Related, II-2312, 2339
Lumber and Wood Products, I-1057
Metal Mining, I-165
Misc. Manufacturing Industries, II-2416
Nonmetallic Minerals, I-217
Paper and Allied Products, I-1108
Primary Metal Industries, I-1718
Printing and Publishing, I-1198
Security and Commodity Brokers, II-3143
Stone/Clay/Glass Products, I-1686
Textile Mill Products, I-960, 978
Tobacco Products, I-943
Transportation Equipment, II-2203, 2212, 2293, 2299
Wholesale Trade - Durables, II-2704

Ivory Coast, I-721, 723, 737

Jamaica, I-1266

Japan, I-24, 26, 1857
  Agriculture - Crops, I-49, 53, 61, 64, 104
  Agriculture - Livestock, I-119-120, 123
  Apparel and Textile Products, I-1005, 1010, 1016, 1018
  Business Services, II-3435
  Chemicals and Allied Products, I-1246, 1268, 1286, 1342, 1413, 1526
  Communications, II-2601, 2624, 2632, 2637
  Electronic/Electric Equip., II-2018, 2060, 2094, 2124, 2132, 2145
  Engineering/Management Services, II-3582-3583
  Fabricated Metal Products, I-1766, 1777, 1807
  Fishing, Hunting, and Trapping, I-134
  Food and Kindred Products, I-303, 318, 353, 377, 379, 432, 556, 575, 659, 693, 695, 715, 848
  General Building Contractors, I-226, 233, 240-241
  General Merchandise Stores, II-2793, 2798
  Industry Machinery/Equip., I-1816, 1872-1873, 1880, 1900, 1922, 1972
  Instruments and Related, II-2313, 2339, 2341-2342

Local and Passenger Transit, II-2493
Metal Mining, I-143, 151, 165
Misc. Manufacturing Industries, II-2421, 2440
Motion Pictures, II-3468, 3477
Nat. Security and Interntl. Affairs, II-3600
Oil and Gas Extraction, I-191
Paper and Allied Products, I-1148
Primary Metal Industries, I-1700, 1704, 1718, 1724
Printing and Publishing, I-1169, 1202
Real Estate, II-3302
Stone/Clay/Glass Products, I-1637, 1644, 1655, 1659, 1675, 1686
Tobacco Products, I-927, 944
Transportation Equipment, II-2204, 2211-2212, 2216, 2223, 2283, 2300, 2305
Transportation Services, II-2558, 2561, 2563, 2567
Wholesale Trade - Durables, II-2712, 2717-2718

Jiangsu, China, I-144

John F. Kennedy International, NY, II-2549

Joliet, IL, II-2821, 2969

Jordan, I-228, 230, II-2602

Kansas, I-59, 121, 136, 352, II-2178, 3049

Kansas City, MO, II-2832, 2977, 3534

Kazakhstan, I-52, 54, 154, 159, 173, 184, 186, 193, 231, 1266, 1724

Kentucky, I-69, 136, 1735, II-2178, 2561, 3050

Kenya, I-82, 762

Knoxville, TN, II-2833, 2978

Kodiak, AK, I-146

Korea, I-104, 226, 927, 997, 1268, 1637, 1675, 1700, 1724, 1777, 1872-1873, 1922, II-2216, 2223, 2339

Kuala Lumpur, II-2566

Kuwait, I-193, 200

LaGuardia Airport, NY, II-2550

Lancaster, PA, II-2834

Las Vegas, NV, I-257, II-2835, 3559, 3598

Latin America, I-446, 593, 1246, 1644, 1880, II-2009, 2267, 2574, 2683, 3444

Lebanon, II-2192

Liaoning, China, I-144

Libya, I-193

Lithuania, I-87

Livonia, MI, I-254, II-2826, 2975

London, England, II-2563, 2566

Long Beach, CA, I-258, II-2836, 2979

Long Island, NY, I-261

Los Angeles, CA, I-146, 258, II-2563, 2836, 2979, 3456, 3535

Louisiana, I-55, 72, 146, II-2966, 3051, 3160, 3198, 3218, 3487

Louisville, KY, II-2561

Luxembourg, I-307

Macau, I-24, II-2566-2567, 3004, 3489

Madison, WI, II-3598

Magic Kingdom at Walt Disney World, FL, II-3480

Maine, II-3052

Malawi, I-70

Malaysia, I-61, 226, 319, 643, 721, 736-737, 848, 945, II-2085, 2104, 2193, 2339, 2567, 2603

Mali, I-66

Marietta, GA, II-2965

Maryland, I-247, II-2815, 2844, 2862, 3053, 3216

Massachusetts, I-146, 248, II-2817, 2863, 2866, 2931, 2968, 3054, 3172, 3559

Mauritius, II-2604

McCarran International, NV, II-2552

Memphis, TN, II-2561

Mentor, OH, II-2822, 2970

Mesa, AZ, I-262, II-2845, 2982

Mexico

Agricultural Services, I-127-128

Agriculture - Crops, I-61, 64, 67-68, 82, 93-94, 103

Agriculture - Livestock, I-113-116, 119-120, 123-124

Chemicals and Allied Products, I-1484

Communications, II-2574, 2605, 2629

Electronic/Electric Equip., II-2077, 2085, 2104

Fabricated Metal Products, I-1761

Food and Kindred Products, I-320, 342, 353-354, 356, 377-378, 385, 387, 389, 400-401, 413, 432-433, 448, 467, 506, 522, 557, 561, 569, 574, 586, 594, 604, 642, 645, 650, 670, 694, 733, 763, 778, 788, 801, 803, 823, 847, 891

Food Stores, II-2805, 2837

Furniture Stores, II-2937

General Building Contractors, I-226, 231, 239

General Merchandise Stores, II-2791, 2799

Industry Machinery/Equip., I-1816

Instruments and Related, II-2314, 2339

Metal Mining, I-154, 157, 159

Nonmetallic Minerals, I-200

Oil and Gas Extraction, I-188, 191-192, 194

Primary Metal Industries, I-1724, 1748

Printing and Publishing, I-1169

Stone/Clay/Glass Products, I-1637, 1686

Textile Mill Products, I-974

Tobacco Products, I-946

Miami, FL, I-259, II-2838, 3535

Miami Beach, FL, II-2838

Michigan

Agriculture - Crops, I-59, 71, 96, 107

Amusement and Recreation, II-3487, 3490

Depository Institutions, II-3055

Electronic/Electric Equip., II-2178

Food Stores, II-2826, 2866

Furniture Stores, II-2931

General Building Contractors, I-242, 254

General Merchandise Stores, II-2795

Health Services, II-3520, 3534

Insurance Carriers, II-3161, 3173, 3227, 3272

Miscellaneous Retail, II-2975, 3032

Primary Metal Industries, I-1699

Security and Commodity Brokers, II-3151

Transportation by Air, II-2546

Middle East, I-205, 446, 593, 1529, 1712, 1857, 1899, 1940, II-2060, 2267, 2273, 2341-2342, 2516

Middle East and North Africa, I-1683, 1761

Midwestern United States, I-1109, II-3402

Minneapolis, MN, I-260, II-2839

Minnesota, I-59, 71, 117, 260, 352, II-2839, 3056

Mississippi, I-55, 65, 91, II-3057, 3199, 3487

Missouri, I-55, 65, 117, 136, 263, II-2178, 2832, 2850, 2977, 3058, 3152, 3200, 3228, 3487, 3534

Montana, II-3059

Morocco, I-53, 105, 230-231, 587, 1108, II-2194

Mountain states, United States, II-3402

Mozambique, I-135, II-2606

Murfreesboro, TN, II-2840

Myanmar, I-82, 134

Namibia, I-237, II-2607

Naperville, IL, II-2821, 2969

Nashville, TN, II-2840

Nebraska, I-59, 117, 352, II-2842, 3060

Nepal, I-927

Netherlands

Agriculture - Crops, I-87, 110

Apparel and Textile Products, I-989, 1020, 1023

Communications, II-2656

Electronic/Electric Equip., II-2085

Fishing, Hunting, and Trapping, I-130

Food and Kindred Products, I-329, 694-695, 721

Industry Machinery/Equip., I-1828, 1888, 1972

Lumber and Wood Products, I-1057

Oil and Gas Extraction, I-188

Primary Metal Industries, I-1724

Printing and Publishing, I-1198

Textile Mill Products, I-979

Transportation by Air, II-2535

Transportation Equipment, II-2208, 2293

Nevada, I-257, II-2719, 2835, 3061, 3487, 3598

New Barunfels, TX, I-265

New Bedford, MA, I-146, II-2984

New Caledonia, I-1736

New Hampshire, I-248, II-2817, 3062

New Jersey, I-261, II-2719, 2844, 2931, 3063, 3174, 3229, 3272, 3487

New Mexico, II-2719, 3064, 3598

New Orleans, LA, II-3534

New York
　Agriculture - Crops, I-96
　Amusement and Recreation, II-3487
　Depository Institutions, II-3065
　Food Stores, II-2866
　Furniture Stores, II-2931
　General Merchandise Stores, II-2795
　Insurance Carriers, II-3162, 3175, 3229, 3272
　Miscellaneous Retail, II-3032
　Pipelines, II-2550
　Social Services, II-3559
　Special Trade Contractors, I-261
　Transportation by Air, II-2549
　Wholesale Trade - Durables, II-2719

New York City, NY, II-2566, 3535

New Zealand, I-87, 104, 116, 389, 433, 1001

Newport News, VA, II-2861

Niagara Falls, II-3559

Nigeria, I-53, 57, 106, 189, 192-194, 643, 723, 736-737, 927

Ningbo-Zhoushan, China, II-2535

Norfolk, VA, II-2861, 3598

North America, I-11, 30, 32
　Apparel and Textile Products, I-1011
　Business Services, II-3391, 3415
　Chemicals and Allied Products, I-1254, 1277-1278, 1281-1282, 1285, 1295, 1442, 1520, 1529, 1531, 1552
　Coal Mining, I-172
　Educational Services, II-3548
　Electric/Gas/Sanitary Services, II-2683
　Electronic/Electric Equip., II-2009, 2013, 2018, 2060, 2122
　Food and Kindred Products, I-345-346, 360, 446, 479, 593, 615, 841
　Food Stores, II-2806
　General Merchandise Stores, II-2784
　Industry Machinery/Equip., I-1832, 1839, 1857, 1880, 1905, 1913, 1917, 1922, 1926

Instruments and Related, II-2321, 2326

Leather and Leather Products, I-1628

Nat. Security and Interntl. Affairs, II-3590

Nonmetallic Minerals, I-205, 214

Paper and Allied Products, I-1104-1105, 1107, 1132, 1135, 1140

Personal Services, II-3332

Petroleum and Coal Products, I-1568

Primary Metal Industries, I-1712, 1715

Printing and Publishing, I-1189

Real Estate, II-3302

Rubber and Misc. Plastics, I-1594-1596, 1601, 1605

Stone/Clay/Glass Products, I-1644, 1648, 1659

Textile Mill Products, I-971

Transportation Equipment, II-2223-2224, 2227, 2231, 2236-2237, 2239, 2241, 2247, 2252, 2267, 2273, 2295, 2300

Trucking and Warehousing, II-2499, 2502

Water Transportation, II-2531

North Asia, II-2009

North Carolina, I-65, 69, 91, 107, 117, 136, 250, 352, 1735, II-2542, 2719, 2795, 2848, 2861, 2866, 2931, 3066, 3201, 3229

North Central United States, II-2807

North Dakota, I-71, 190, II-2827, 3067

North Korea, I-239

Northeastern United States, I-86, 1109, II-3402

Northern Europe, I-1333

Norwalk, CT, II-2818

Norway, I-145, 321, 947, 1365, 1560, II-2205, 2608, 2717, 3144

Oakland, CA, II-2853

Ohio
　Agriculture - Crops, I-59, 107
　Agriculture - Livestock, I-117
　Depository Institutions, II-3068
　Electronic/Electric Equip., II-2178
　Fishing, Hunting, and Trapping, I-136
　Food Stores, II-2822, 2866
　Furniture Stores, II-2931

General Merchandise Stores, II-2795
　Health Services, II-3534
　Insurance Carriers, II-3164, 3176, 3184, 3188, 3202, 3211
　Miscellaneous Retail, II-2970, 2972, 3032
　Primary Metal Industries, I-1699

Oklahoma, I-91, 117, 136, 190, II-2841, 2980, 3069

Oklahoma City, OK, II-2841, 2980

Olympic National Park, WA, II-3558

Omaha, NE, II-2842

Oman, I-1418, II-2609

Ontario, Canada, II-3256

Orange County, FL, II-3535

Oregon, I-121, II-3070, 3598

Pakistan, I-56, 67-68, 70, 113-114, 353-354, 645, 736, 974, 1572, II-2610, 2640

Panama, II-2611

Papua New Guinea, I-723, 737

Paradise, NV, I-257, II-2835

Paraguay, I-60, 63

Paris, France, II-2561, 2563, 2566

Pennsylvania
　Agriculture - Crops, I-107
　Amusement and Recreation, II-3487
　Depository Institutions, II-3071
　Fishing, Hunting, and Trapping, I-136
　Food Stores, II-2834, 2844, 2846, 2866
　Furniture Stores, II-2931
　Insurance Carriers, II-3165, 3177
　Miscellaneous Retail, II-2983, 3032
　Primary Metal Industries, I-1699, 1735
　Special Trade Contractors, I-261
　Wholesale Trade - Durables, II-2719

Peru, I-134, 154, 157, 159, 163, 230, 847, 1485, II-2574, 2612

Philadelphia, PA, II-2844, 3272

Philadelphia International, PA, II-2553

Philippines, I-57-58, 103, 106, 134, 379, 848, 927, 963, 1736, II-2283

Phoenix, AZ, I-262, II-2845, 2982

Phoenix Sky Harbor, AZ, II-2554

Pittsburgh, PA, II-2846, 2983

Plain States, United States, I-86

Poland
  Agriculture - Crops, I-87, 110
  Apparel and Textile Products,
    I-989, 1020
  Communications, II-2653
  Electronic/Electric Equip., II-2085
  Fabricated Metal Products, I-1777
  Fishing, Hunting, and Trapping,
    I-130
  Food and Kindred Products, I-322,
    671, 715, 718
  General Building Contractors,
    I-226
  Industry Machinery/Equip., I-1828
  Primary Metal Industries, I-1724,
    1748
  Printing and Publishing, I-1198
Pompano Beach, FL, I-259
Port Hueneme-Oxnard-Ventura, CA,
  I-146
Portland, OR, II-3598
Portugal, I-105, 323, 1108, 1273,
  1479, II-2104, 3145
Providence, RI, II-2847, 2984
Puerto Rico, I-1554, II-2700, 3072
Qatar, I-189, 1526
Qingdao, China, II-2535
Quincy, MA, I-248, II-2817, 2968
Raleigh-Cary, NC, II-2848
Reedville, VA, I-146
Rhode Island, II-2847, 2984, 3073,
  3203
Richmond, VA, II-2985
Rock Hill, SC, I-250
Rock Mountain National Park, CO,
  II-3558
Romania, I-87, 239, II-2654
Rotterdam, Netherlands, II-2535
Russia
  Agricultural Services, I-127-128
  Agriculture - Crops, I-49, 52, 54,
    87
  Agriculture - Livestock, I-113-114,
    116, 119, 123-124
  Business Services, II-3435
  Chemicals and Allied Products,
    I-1266, 1333, 1411-1412, 1561
  Coal Mining, I-173
  Communications, II-2632
  Electric/Gas/Sanitary Services,
    II-2672
  Electronic/Electric Equip., II-2018
  Fishing, Hunting, and Trapping,
    I-134

Food and Kindred Products, I-337,
  353-354, 377, 379, 387, 389, 405,
  432-433, 575, 588, 643, 645, 659,
  754, 848
Food Stores, II-2849
General Building Contractors,
  I-228, 231, 235, 237, 241
General Merchandise Stores,
  II-2800
Industry Machinery/Equip., I-1872
Metal Mining, I-143, 150, 154,
  157, 163
Nat. Security and Interntl. Affairs,
  II-3600
Nonmetallic Minerals, I-201, 205
Oil and Gas Extraction, I-184, 186,
  188-189, 191-194
Paper and Allied Products, I-1094
Petroleum and Coal Products,
  I-1576
Primary Metal Industries, I-1700,
  1712, 1718, 1721, 1736
Printing and Publishing, I-1169
Rubber and Misc. Plastics, I-1589
Stone/Clay/Glass Products, I-1657,
  1673, 1675, 1686
Textile Mill Products, I-953
Tobacco Products, I-948
Transportation Equipment, II-2212,
  2223, 2227
Wholesale Trade - Durables,
  II-2714, 2717-2718
St. Louis, MO, I-263, II-2850, 3534
St. Paul, MN, I-260
St. Petersburg, FL, I-267, II-2851,
  3598
Salt Lake City, UT, I-264, II-2852
Salt Lake City International, UT,
  II-2555
San Antonio, TX, I-265
San Diego, CA, II-3102
San Francisco, CA, II-2853, 3598
Sandy Springs, GA, II-2965
Santa Ana, CA, I-258, II-2836, 2979
Sarasota, FL, II-3255
Saudi Arabia, I-57, 188-189, 192-
  194, 200, 324, 1419, 1526, 1675,
  II-2339, 2613
Scottsdale, AZ, II-2845, 2982
Seattle, WA, I-266, II-2854
Serbia, I-60, 764
Shandong, China, I-144
Shanghai, China, II-2535, 2561
Shenzhen, China, II-2535

Sierra Leone, I-237
Singapore, I-24, 949, 1526, 1972,
  II-2339, 2535, 2566-2567, 2614
Slovakia, I-325, 765, II-2085
South Africa
  Agricultural Services, I-127-128
  Agriculture - Crops, I-60, 63
  Food and Kindred Products, I-343,
    642, 672, 824
  Food Stores, II-2855
  General Building Contractors,
    I-230, 235, 237
  Instruments and Related, II-2315
  Metal Mining, I-150, 157, 163
  Motion Pictures, II-3468
  Oil and Gas Extraction, I-184, 186
South America, I-172, 205, 1105,
  1135, 1659, 1712, 1761, 1857,
  II-2060, 2273, 2629, 3590
South Atlantic region, United
  States, II-3402
South Carolina, I-65, 91, 250-251,
  II-2971, 3074, 3166, 3178, 3204,
  3402
South Central states, United States,
  I-86, II-3402
South Dakota, I-59, II-3075
South Korea, I-24
  Agriculture - Crops, I-53, 61, 64,
    67
  Agriculture - Livestock, I-119-120
  Chemicals and Allied Products,
    I-1526
  Communications, II-2628, 2655
  Electronic/Electric Equip., II-2124
  Food and Kindred Products, I-643,
    673, 848
  Metal Mining, I-143, 151, 165
  Nat. Security and Interntl. Affairs,
    II-3600
  Oil and Gas Extraction, I-191
  Primary Metal Industries, I-1718
  Printing and Publishing, I-1202
  Textile Mill Products, I-950
  Transportation by Air, II-2535
  Transportation Equipment, II-2283
  Transportation Services, II-2567
  Wholesale Trade - Durables,
    II-2718
Southeast Asia, I-1595, 1659, 1761
Southeastern United States, II-2809
Southern Asia, I-172, II-2009, 2683
Southern United States, I-618
Soviet Union, I-1659

Spain
  Agriculture - Crops, I-105, 110
  Apparel and Textile Products,
    I-989, 1020, 1023
  Business Services, II-3435
  Chemicals and Allied Products,
    I-1366, 1535, 1562
  Communications, II-2615
  Food and Kindred Products, I-326,
    674, 693-695, 715, 718, 801
  Furniture Stores, II-2938
  General Building Contractors,
    I-226, 240
  Industry Machinery/Equip., I-1873,
    1964
  Instruments and Related, II-2339
  Lumber and Wood Products,
    I-1057
  Nonmetallic Minerals, I-217
  Paper and Allied Products, I-1108
  Petroleum and Coal Products,
    I-1577
  Printing and Publishing, I-1198
  Security and Commodity Brokers,
    II-3146
  Textile Mill Products, I-951, 961
  Wholesale Trade - Durables,
    II-2704
Sri Lanka, I-239
Stamford, CT, II-2818
Sugar Land, TX, I-255, II-2976
Suriname, I-1266
Sweden, I-87, 130, 157, 327, 675,
  989, 1094, 1198, 1772, II-2717,
  3147
Switzerland, I-160, 328, 718, 848,
  1367, 1578, 1873, 1888, II-2018,
  2206, 2616
Syria, I-105
Tacoma, WA, I-266, II-2854
Taiwan, I-24, 61, 64, 67, 143, 742,
  1637, 1718, 1872-1873, 1922,
  II-2124, 2207, 2299
Tajikistan, I-66
Tampa, FL, I-267, II-2851, 3598
Tanzania, I-82, 103
Tennessee, I-65, 69, 136, II-2561,
  2833, 2840, 2978, 3076, 3167
Texas
  Agriculture - Crops, I-55, 65, 72,
    91
  Agriculture - Livestock, I-121
  Chemicals and Allied Products,
    I-1228

Depository Institutions, II-3077
Electronic/Electric Equip., II-2178
Fishing, Hunting, and Trapping,
  I-136
Food and Kindred Products, I-352
Food Stores, II-2823
Furniture Stores, II-2931
General Building Contractors,
  I-252
General Merchandise Stores,
  II-2795
Heavy Construction, I-255
Insurance Carriers, II-3205, 3217,
  3229, 3272
Miscellaneous Retail, II-2976, 3032
Oil and Gas Extraction, I-190
Real Estate, II-3314
Special Trade Contractors, I-265
Transportation by Air, II-2544
Transportation Services, II-2563
Wholesale Trade - Durables,
  II-2719
Thailand, I-24
  Agriculture - Crops, I-56, 58, 64,
    67, 106
  Chemicals and Allied Products,
    I-1555
  Communications, II-2617
  Electronic/Electric Equip., II-2104
  Food and Kindred Products, I-642,
    645, 736-737, 801
  General Building Contractors,
    I-240
  Industry Machinery/Equip., I-1922
  Metal Mining, I-160, 165
  Misc. Manufacturing Industries,
    II-2416
  Printing and Publishing, I-1202
  Stone/Clay/Glass Products, I-1637,
    1675
  Tobacco Products, I-927
  Transportation Services, II-2567
Times Square, NY, II-3559
Tobago, II-2700
Tokyo, Japan, II-2561, 2563
Tokyo Disneyland, China, II-3480
Tokyo Disneysea, China, II-3480
Toledo, OH, II-3534
Trinidad, II-2700
Tunisia, I-105, 230, II-2860
Turkey
  Agriculture - Crops, I-52, 67-68,
    89-90, 99-100, 105
  Agriculture - Livestock, I-124

Chemicals and Allied Products,
  I-1369
Communications, II-2619
Food and Kindred Products, I-825
General Building Contractors,
  I-226, 231, 240
Industry Machinery/Equip., I-1872,
  1884
Instruments and Related, II-2339
Metal Mining, I-160
Motion Pictures, II-3468
Nonmetallic Minerals, I-217
Printing and Publishing, I-1169
Social Services, II-3559
Stone/Clay/Glass Products, I-1686
Textile Mill Products, I-954
Transportation Equipment, II-2195,
  2293
Turkmenistan, I-66, 68, 189
Twin Cities, Ontario, II-3256
Uganda, I-82, 847
Ukraine, I-52, 54, 60, 63, 119-120,
  143, 150, 186, 239, 432, 659,
  1686, 1700, II-2718
Union Station, Washington D.C.,
  II-3559
United Arab Emirates, I-192-193,
  642-643, 1721, II-2339
United Kingdom, I-165
  Agriculture - Crops, I-110
  Apparel and Textile Products,
    I-989, 1016, 1020, 1023
  Business Services, II-3435
  Chemicals and Allied Products,
    I-1318, 1361, 1368, 1398, 1437,
    1478, 1495, 1556
  Communications, II-2632
  Eating and Drinking Places,
    II-2940
  Electronic/Electric Equip., II-2018,
    2099
  Fabricated Metal Products, I-1766,
    1773, 1807
  Food and Kindred Products, I-330,
    447, 462, 482, 530, 553, 559, 568,
    575-576, 579, 637, 653, 659, 677,
    693, 695, 715, 718, 776, 785,
    800, 888
  Food Stores, II-2859
  General Building Contractors,
    I-241
  Industry Machinery/Equip., I-1816,
    1828, 1900, 1945

Instruments and Related, II-2339, 2404

Lumber and Wood Products, I-1057

Metal Mining, I-145

Misc. Manufacturing Industries, II-2416, 2440

Miscellaneous Retail, II-2997

Motion Pictures, II-3473

Nat. Security and Interntl. Affairs, II-3600

Nonmetallic Minerals, I-217

Oil and Gas Extraction, I-188

Petroleum and Coal Products, I-1579

Printing and Publishing, I-1169, 1198, 1202, 1205

Real Estate, II-3297

Rubber and Misc. Plastics, I-1609

Textile Mill Products, I-980

Transportation by Air, II-2548

Transportation Equipment, II-2209, 2212, 2222, 2226

Transportation Services, II-2563

Wholesale Trade - Durables, II-2715

United States, I-1-5, 7, 9, 15-22, 26, 28-29, 31, 33, 35-36, 39-44, 241

Agricultural Services, I-126-128

Agriculture - Crops, I-47-49, 52, 54-56, 59-60, 63, 65-66, 68-72, 75-80, 82-85, 87-89, 91-102, 104, 107-108, 110

Agriculture - Livestock, I-112-125

Amusement and Recreation, II-3482-3488, 3491-3493, 3497-3509, 3511-3516

Apparel and Accessory Stores, II-2884-2886, 2888-2890, 2893-2897, 2900-2903

Apparel and Textile Products, I-984-985, 987-988, 990-1000, 1002-1004, 1006-1009, 1012, 1014-1017, 1021, 1024-1025, 1028-1030, 1035, 1037-1038

Auto Repair/Services/Parking, II-3441-3442, 3445-3452, 3454

Automotive Dealers, II-2876-2883

Building Materials, II-2766-2778

Business Services, II-3347-3348, 3350-3351, 3356, 3358, 3362, 3366, 3368-3369, 3371, 3376-3380, 3384-3385, 3387-3389,

3392-3395, 3397-3401, 3403-3410, 3414, 3416-3424, 3426-3437, 3440

Chemicals and Allied Products, I-1207, 1210-1211, 1213-1224, 1226-1227, 1229-1231, 1235, 1237-1245, 1252-1253, 1255, 1257-1258, 1260, 1263, 1265, 1267, 1269, 1284, 1286, 1290, 1296-1302, 1304-1306, 1308-1314, 1321-1324, 1327, 1330-1331, 1333, 1335-1338, 1344-1345, 1348-1351, 1355, 1357-1358, 1362, 1373-1375, 1377-1378, 1380-1384, 1386-1388, 1390-1391, 1393-1397, 1399, 1402-1404, 1406-1408, 1413-1415, 1422-1423, 1425-1426, 1428-1429, 1431-1436, 1439-1441, 1444-1445, 1447-1448, 1450-1453, 1455-1457, 1459-1460, 1462-1464, 1466-1471, 1473-1476, 1487, 1489-1491, 1494, 1496, 1498-1500, 1502, 1504, 1506-1507, 1509-1511, 1513, 1519, 1521, 1523-1524, 1526, 1528, 1533, 1536-1538, 1540, 1543-1545, 1547-1549, 1551, 1554, 1557, 1563

Communications, II-2570-2572, 2575, 2622-2624, 2626-2627, 2629, 2632-2633, 2638, 2642-2643, 2657, 2659-2663

Depository Institutions, II-3087-3100

Eating and Drinking Places, II-2939, 2941-2944, 2946-2949, 2951, 2953-2957, 2959-2961

Educational Services, II-3545-3547, 3549-3554

Electric/Gas/Sanitary Services, II-2664-2665, 2667-2668, 2674-2675, 2679, 2681-2682, 2685-2686

Electronic/Electric Equip., II-1994, 1998-1999, 2001-2003, 2005-2006, 2010, 2012, 2014, 2016-2017, 2019-2021, 2023-2024, 2027-2028, 2030-2044, 2046-2048, 2053, 2056-2057, 2059, 2062-2066, 2068-2069, 2078-2080, 2082-2085, 2087-2090, 2093, 2096, 2099, 2101-2105, 2107, 2109-2113, 2116, 2119-

2120, 2124-2125, 2135, 2143, 2156, 2158, 2163-2164, 2166-2168, 2174-2183

Engineering/Management Services, II-3570-3572, 3574-3576, 3578, 3580-3581, 3583-3584

Fabricated Metal Products, I-1749-1750, 1752-1758, 1760-1763, 1766, 1768, 1770-1771, 1774-1778, 1780-1783, 1787, 1790-1797, 1799-1800, 1802-1804, 1806-1810, 1812

Fishing, Hunting, and Trapping, I-130-132, 134, 136-137

Food and Kindred Products, I-274, 277-278, 280-297, 299-301, 304-305, 333-334, 336, 338, 347-355, 357-359, 361-367, 369-377, 379-383, 386-389, 391-400, 402-411, 414-422, 424-430, 432-441, 445, 449-453, 457-460, 463-466, 468-473, 475-478, 480-481, 483-495, 498-505, 508-511, 513-520, 523-528, 531-533, 535, 537, 540-552, 554-555, 558, 560, 562-567, 570-573, 575, 577-578, 580, 582-584, 590-591, 595-603, 605-609, 612-614, 616-631, 634-636, 638-641, 643, 645-649, 651-652, 654, 657, 659, 661, 679-680, 682-713, 715, 718-719, 721, 724-725, 727, 729-730, 734-736, 738-741, 743, 745, 747, 750, 752-756, 768-775, 779, 783-784, 786, 791-792, 795-796, 801-802, 804-806, 808-817, 827, 829-830, 832-840, 842-846, 848-849, 851-858, 860-865, 868-874, 876-882, 885-887, 889-890, 893-899, 901-908, 912-920

Food Stores, II-2809, 2812, 2865-2875

Forestry, I-129

Furniture and Fixtures, I-1066-1068, 1070-1074, 1076-1082

Furniture Stores, II-2904-2917, 2919-2935

General Building Contractors, I-219, 221, 224-226, 230-231, 233, 236, 240, 243-246

General Merchandise Stores, II-2779-2783, 2785-2788, 2790, 2792, 2795-2796, 2802

Health Services, II-3517-3519, 3521-3523, 3525-3527, 3529-3532, 3537-3538, 3540-3541, 3543

Hotels and Lodging Places, II-3322-3328

Industry Machinery/Equip., I-1813-1816, 1825, 1829-1831, 1833-1834, 1837, 1858-1860, 1862-1863, 1869, 1871-1875, 1878-1879, 1885, 1888, 1897-1898, 1900, 1902-1904, 1906, 1911-1912, 1916, 1928-1929, 1932, 1936-1937, 1947-1948, 1952, 1954, 1956-1959, 1965, 1967-1968, 1970-1972, 1974, 1977-1983, 1985-1990, II-1993

Instruments and Related, II-2317-2320, 2322-2331, 2333, 2335-2336, 2338-2342, 2355-2357, 2363, 2367, 2369-2372, 2374-2377, 2387, 2394-2400, 2403, 2405

Insurance Agents and Brokers, II-3294

Insurance Carriers, II-3156, 3169, 3180-3183, 3185, 3187, 3190, 3192, 3209, 3212, 3214, 3220, 3222, 3225, 3229, 3232, 3234, 3236, 3238, 3240-3247, 3249-3251, 3258-3262, 3265-3268, 3270-3276, 3278-3290, 3292

Justice/Public Order/Safety, II-3585

Leather and Leather Products, I-1630, 1632-1635

Local and Passenger Transit, II-2482-2483, 2485-2492, 2494

Lumber and Wood Products, I-1039, 1041-1044, 1046, 1048, 1050-1053, 1055-1056, 1058-1065

Membership Organizations, II-3565-3569

Metal Mining, I-138-140, 142-143, 145, 147, 151, 154-155, 157, 159-160, 163-165

Misc. Manufacturing Industries, II-2408, 2412-2414, 2416-2418, 2420, 2425-2426, 2428-2441, 2443-2447, 2450-2452, 2455-2457, 2459-2469, 2471-2478

Misc. Repair Services, II-3455, 3457-3459

Miscellaneous Retail, II-2962-2964, 2986-2993, 2996, 2998-3000, 3002-3003, 3005, 3007-3008, 3010-3016, 3020, 3022-3033

Motion Pictures, II-3460, 3462-3472, 3474, 3476, 3478-3479

Museums/Botanical/Gardens, II-3560-3562, 3564

Nat. Security and Interntl. Affairs, II-3586, 3588, 3591-3593, 3595-3597, 3599-3600

Nondepository Institutions, II-3105-3115, 3118, 3121-3122

Nonmetallic Minerals, I-199-200, 211-212, 215-218

Oil and Gas Extraction, I-175, 182, 184-186, 188-194

Paper and Allied Products, I-1083, 1085, 1088-1089, 1091-1097, 1099-1103, 1108-1111, 1113, 1116-1121, 1124-1126, 1130, 1142, 1144-1145, 1150, 1152-1157

Personal Services, II-3329-3330, 3333-3334, 3337-3341

Petroleum and Coal Products, I-1564-1566, 1570, 1572

Primary Metal Industries, I-1688-1691, 1693-1695, 1697, 1699-1700, 1702-1710, 1718, 1721, 1723-1724, 1729, 1731-1735, 1737, 1739-1748

Printing and Publishing, I-1158-1166, 1168-1171, 1173-1174, 1177-1178, 1180-1183, 1185, 1187, 1191, 1194-1197, 1199, 1201-1203, 1206

Railroad Transportation, II-2479-2480

Real Estate, II-3296, 3299, 3306-3307, 3309-3316, 3318-3320

Rubber and Misc. Plastics, I-1582-1585, 1588, 1592-1593, 1597-1598, 1600, 1602-1603, 1607-1608, 1611-1612, 1615-1618, 1621-1627

Security and Commodity Brokers, II-3123, 3125-3127, 3131, 3133, 3148-3150, 3153

Social Services, II-3556, 3558

Special Trade Contractors, I-268-273

Stone/Clay/Glass Products, I-1636-1638, 1640-1641, 1643, 1650, 1652, 1656, 1664-1666, 1669-1670, 1675-1677, 1679-1680, 1684-1687

Textile Mill Products, I-955-956, 965-967, 972-975, 982-983

Tobacco Products, I-923-926, 931-932, 934-937, 941

Transportation by Air, II-2533-2534, 2537-2541

Transportation Equipment, II-2184-2187, 2196, 2211-2220, 2228-2230, 2232-2234, 2263-2265, 2268-2269, 2274-2275, 2278-2279, 2281, 2285-2286, 2289-2290, 2292-2293, 2296-2297, 2299, 2301, 2303, 2306-2307

Transportation Services, II-2559, 2564-2565, 2567-2569

Trucking and Warehousing, II-2500-2501, 2503-2505, 2507-2514

Water Transportation, II-2520, 2523-2525, 2528, 2530

Wholesale Trade - Durables, II-2688-2696, 2699, 2701-2705, 2717-2727, 2729-2739

Wholesale Trade - Nondurables, II-2740-2747, 2749-2765

Universal Studios Japan, II-3480

Uruguay, I-56, 63

Utah, I-264, II-2555, 2852, 3078, 3103

Uzbekistan, I-66, 68, 135, 163, 188

Venezuela, I-189, 192-194, 964, II-2574, 2620, 2700, 2717

Vermont, II-3079

Vietnam, I-56, 58, 67, 160, 184, 231, 377, 379, 766, 847, 928, 974, 1637, 1675, II-2283, 2567

Virginia, I-69, 91, 146, II-2795, 2861-2862, 2985, 3080, 3219, 3598

Virginia Beach, VA, II-2861

Walt Disney World's Magic Kingdom, FL, II-3559

Warren, MI, I-254, II-2826, 2975

Washington, I-96, 107, 266, II-2854, 3081, 3155, 3179

Washington D.C., II-2862, 3082, 3534

Washington Dulles Airport, II-2556

West Virginia, II-2862, 3083, 3487

Western and Central Europe, I-172, 1333

Western Asia, I-1899

Western Europe, I-11, 30, 32
  Apparel and Textile Products, I-1011
  Chemicals and Allied Products, I-1259, 1284, 1295, 1529, 1531
  Electric/Gas/Sanitary Services, II-2683
  Electronic/Electric Equip., II-2009, 2013
  Food and Kindred Products, I-446, 455
  Industry Machinery/Equip., I-1880, 1899, 1917, 1926
  Nonmetallic Minerals, I-214
  Real Estate, II-3302
  Rubber and Misc. Plastics, I-1595-1596
  Transportation Equipment, II-2223, 2227, 2231

Western United States, I-86

Wisconsin, I-59, 136, 260, II-2821, 2866, 3084, 3168, 3206, 3229, 3598

Worcester, MA, II-2863

World, I-23, 26-27, 30, 32, 34, 37-38, 45
  Agricultural Services, I-127-128
  Agriculture - Crops, I-46, 49, 51-54, 56-58, 60-61, 63-64, 66-67, 70, 82, 87, 89-90, 93-94, 99-100, 103-106
  Agriculture - Livestock, I-114-115, 119-120, 123-124
  Amusement and Recreation, II-3481
  Apparel and Textile Products, I-997, 1016, 1019
  Business Services, II-3345, 3353-3355, 3359-3361, 3364, 3370, 3372-3375, 3381, 3396, 3435
  Chemicals and Allied Products, I-1208, 1232, 1234, 1236, 1246, 1250-1251, 1256, 1261, 1266, 1270-1276, 1279-1280, 1283-1284, 1291-1295, 1333, 1347, 1352, 1354, 1356, 1370, 1385, 1413, 1430, 1486, 1508, 1517-1518, 1522, 1525-1527, 1529-1532, 1546, 1550
  Coal Mining, I-170-173

Communications, II-2573, 2621, 2624, 2629-2630, 2632, 2641

Depository Institutions, II-3086

Educational Services, II-3555

Electric/Gas/Sanitary Services, II-2677, 2684

Electronic/Electric Equip., II-1995-1997, 2004, 2007-2009, 2013, 2015, 2018, 2045, 2050-2051, 2054, 2058, 2060-2061, 2074-2076, 2081, 2085, 2091-2092, 2098-2100, 2104, 2106, 2108, 2114-2115, 2118, 2121-2122, 2124, 2126-2134, 2136-2142, 2146-2155, 2157, 2159-2160, 2162, 2165, 2169-2173

Engineering/Management Services, II-3577, 3583

Fabricated Metal Products, I-1751, 1761, 1764-1767, 1769, 1777, 1779, 1785, 1788, 1798, 1800-1801, 1805, 1807

Fishing, Hunting, and Trapping, I-133, 135

Food and Kindred Products, I-276, 298, 331-332, 335, 344, 354, 377, 379, 387, 389, 400, 405, 432-433, 446, 456, 461, 575, 593, 632, 642-645, 659-660, 694, 715, 718, 721-723, 736-737, 754, 767, 780, 789-790, 793-794, 801, 826, 847-848, 883-884, 900, 909, 911

General Building Contractors, I-222-223, 226-228, 230-231, 233-237, 239, 241

General Merchandise Stores, II-2803

Industry Machinery/Equip., I-1816-1824, 1827, 1836, 1840, 1844-1857, 1861, 1864-1865, 1867-1868, 1870, 1872-1873, 1877, 1880-1884, 1886, 1888-1896, 1899-1901, 1907, 1910, 1913-1915, 1917, 1919-1927, 1930-1931, 1933-1934, 1938, 1946, 1949, 1951, 1955, 1960-1961, 1969, 1972-1973, II-1992

Instruments and Related, II-2316, 2332, 2334, 2337, 2341-2347, 2349, 2351, 2358-2361, 2368, 2378-2382, 2384-2385, 2388-2390, 2401-2402

Insurance Agents and Brokers, II-3295

Insurance Carriers, II-3237, 3239, 3257, 3264

Investment Offices, II-3321

Leather and Leather Products, I-1629, 1631

Metal Mining, I-143, 145, 148-152, 154, 156, 158-161, 163, 165-166, 168

Misc. Manufacturing Industries, II-2406-2407, 2409-2410, 2415-2416, 2422-2424, 2440, 2442, 2449, 2454, 2458

Miscellaneous Retail, II-3009, 3021

Motion Pictures, II-3468, 3480

Nat. Security and Interntl. Affairs, II-3589-3590, 3594

Nondepository Institutions, II-3119-3120

Nonmetallic Minerals, I-196, 200, 203-210, 214, 217

Oil and Gas Extraction, I-176-181, 184, 188-189, 191-193

Paper and Allied Products, I-1087, 1090, 1094, 1105, 1108, 1123, 1127-1128, 1131, 1133-1134, 1136-1137, 1141, 1143, 1147, 1151

Personal Services, II-3331, 3335, 3343

Petroleum and Coal Products, I-1567, 1571-1572

Primary Metal Industries, I-1689, 1692, 1696, 1701, 1704, 1712, 1714, 1717-1719, 1721-1722, 1724-1725, 1727, 1730, 1736, 1738, 1748

Printing and Publishing, I-1167, 1169, 1200, 1202

Real Estate, II-3298, 3300-3305, 3308, 3317

Rubber and Misc. Plastics, I-1581, 1591, 1595-1596, 1606, 1619-1620

Security and Commodity Brokers, II-3124, 3128-3130, 3132

Social Services, II-3557

Stone/Clay/Glass Products, I-1637, 1644, 1649, 1659-1663, 1674-1675, 1681-1683, 1686

Textile Mill Products, I-952, 981

Tobacco Products, I-927-928

Transportation by Air, II-2536

Transportation Equipment, II-2210-2212, 2216, 2221, 2223, 2225,

2227, 2231, 2235, 2238, 2242-
  2243, 2248-2249, 2253, 2255-
  2256, 2260, 2262, 2266, 2271,
  2273, 2276-2277, 2280, 2282,
  2291, 2293, 2300
Transportation Services, II-2560-
  2563, 2566-2567
Trucking and Warehousing,
  II-2496, 2506
Water Transportation, II-2521,
  2526-2527, 2529, 2532
Wholesale Trade - Durables,
  II-2698, 2716-2718
Wholesale Trade - Nondurables,
  II-2748
Wyoming, I-71, 121, II-3085, 3207
Yellowstone National Park, WY,
  II-3558
Yosemite National Park, CA, II-3558
Youngstown, OH, II-3534
Zambia, I-154
Zhejiang, China, I-144
Zimbabwe, I-70, 1273
Zion National Park, UT, II-3558

PRODUCTS, SERVICES, NAMES, AND ISSUES INDEX

This index shows, in alphabetical order, references to products, services, personal names, and issues covered in *Market Share Reporter, 23rd Edition*. More than 2,290 terms are included. Terms include subjects not readily categorized as products and services, including such subjects as aerospace and churches. The numbers that follow each term refer to entry numbers and are arranged sequentially so that the first mention is listed first. Roman numerals indicate volume number.

3-D technology, II-2077-2078, 3436
Ab machines, II-2445
Abrasives, I-1688-1690
Açai juice, I-1298
Access controls, I-45
Access equipment, I-1860
Accounting services, II-3574-3575
Acetic acid, I-1522
Acids, I-1269
Acidulants, I-909
Acne treatments, I-1491-1492
Acoustical instruments, II-2343
Acrylics, I-1291, 1544
Activated carbon, I-1265
Active Pharmaceutical Ingredients, I-1347
Actuators, II-2235-2236
Acute care, II-3549
Acyclic chemicals, I-1528
Addressing machines, I-1971
Adele, II-2088
Adhesives and sealants, I-1544-1547
Adult incontinence products, I-1166-1167
Adult living facilities, II-3550
Advanced ceramics, I-1680
Advertising, I-1239, II-3291-3312
Aerial work platforms, I-1863
Aerobics, I-1616, II-3461
Aeronautical, nautical and navigational instruments, II-2327
Aeronautical services, II-2265, 2278
Aerosols, I-1554-1556
Aerospace and defense, I-1508, II-2306-2317
Agents, II-3452, 3460
Aggregate, I-214-215
Agricultural products, I-1528, 1539
Agricultural retailing, II-2787
Air bags, II-2239-2240

Air care, I-1557-1562
Air cargo, II-2560-2561
Air conditioners, I-1980-1981, 1984, 1986
Air fresheners, I-1556
Air purification equipment, I-1977-1978
Aircraft, I-1783, II-2265-2272, 2278, 2755
Aircraft insurance, II-3169
Aircraft maintenance, repair and overhaul, II-2265, 2273-2274
Aircraft parts, II-2278-2280
Airlines, II-2539-2550, 2552-2559
Airports, II-2562-2563
Alarm monitoring, I-45
Alcoholic beverages, I-302-303, 747-751, 754, 756-762, 764-772, 775-782, 784-794
Alcohols, I-1528
Alkalies and chlorine, I-1252-1254, II-2163
Allergy treatments, I-1314-1316
Allied line insurance, II-3170
Alloys, I-182
Aloe vera, I-485
Alpha olefins, I-1525
Alternative energy industry, II-2213
Alternators, II-2176
Alumina, I-1719
Aluminum, I-1090, 1720-1723, 1732-1734, 1741, 1744, 1814
Aluminum foil, I-1731-1732
Aluminum plates, I-1732
Aluminum sheet, plate and foil, I-1732
Ambulance services, II-2500
Ambulatory aids, II-2355, 2376
Amino acids, I-1303
Ammonia, I-1390

Ammunition, I-785, 1794-1795
Amusement parks, II-3480-3481
Analgesics, I-1304-1329, 1332, 1336, II-2962-2963
Analytical and life science instruments, II-2329-2330
Animal health, I-1330
Animal slaughtering, I-347
Anodes, II-2153
Antacids, I-1306-1308
Anti-diarrhea tablets, I-1309
Anti-inflammatories, I-1358
Anti-itch products, I-1310
Anti-smoking products, I-1311-1312
Anti-ulcerants, I-1336
Antidepressants, I-1336
Antifreeze, I-1563
Antigens, I-1351
Antimony, I-174-175
Antioxidants, I-909
Antiperspirants, I-1431-1432
Antipsychotics, I-1336
Antiseptics, II-2373
Apartments, II-3247-3248
App stores, II-2926
Apparel, I-27, 975-981, 1009, 1015-1027, 1033-1047, 1049, 1052, 1061, II-2627, 2766
Apparel, children's, I-1021-1022, 1025-1026, II-2893-2894
Apparel, girl's, I-1046
Apparel, men's, I-25, 1038-1043, II-2883-2884
Apparel, women's, I-25, 1044-1046, 1050, 1058, II-2885-2886, 2890
Apparel accessories, I-1055, 1061
Apparel retailing, II-2882-2888, 2890, 2892-2899
Apparel wholesalers, II-2767
Appetizers, I-346, 546

Apples, I-83, 85, 96-97, 99-100, 484, 486, 912

Appliance repair, II-3423

Appliance retailing, II-2918-2923, 3010

Appliances, I-1716, 1735, II-2013-2015, 2019-2020, 2023-2024, 2028, 2033-2040, 2042, 2749, 2920

Apprenticeship training, II-3541

Aprons, I-1067

Aquaculture, I-133-134

Aquatic exercise, II-3461

Arcade, food and entertainment complexes, II-3477-3478

Archery, II-2452

Architectural services, II-3572-3573

Argon, I-1255

Armored transportation, I-45

Armored vehicles and tank parts, II-2322-2323

Art, I-27, II-2781, 3554

Art, drama and music schools, II-3450

Artichokes, I-75

Artificial insemination, I-139, 1827

Artificial lifts, I-1847

Artificial sweeteners, I-1523

Arts, crafts and sewing stores, II-2921, 3015

Arts and crafts, I-1511, II-2459

Asbestos, I-232

Asparagus, I-75, 81

Asphalt, I-1582-1583, 1838, 1841

Asphalt shingles, I-1583

Assisted living facilties, II-3550

Auction houses, II-3555

Audio and video media reproduction, II-3440

Audio equipment, I-1215, II-2059, 2068, 3011

Audio production studios, II-3388

Auto dealerships, II-2871, 2876

Auto insurance, II-3171-3182

Auto loans, II-3095-3097

Auto parts, I-1508, II-2176, 2233-2262, 2627

Auto parts stores, II-2875

Auto rental, II-3408

Autocatalysts, I-180

Autoimmune diseases, I-1336

Automated teller machines, I-1969

Automated test equipment, I-1893

Automated tire inflation systems, I-1905

Automobile and motorcycle wholesalers, II-2731

Automobile clubs, II-3568

Automotive ceilings, I-1010

Automotive electronics, II-2176

Automotive glass replacement, II-3416

Automotive interiors, II-2243-2244

Automotive markets, I-1248, 1554, 1556, 1697, 1919, II-2138

Automotive repair, II-3412, 3414, 3417-3419

Automotive seating, I-1127-1129

Automotive treatments, I-1564

Autonomous underwater vehicles, II-2344

Autos, I-1698, 1716, 1720, II-2178-2214

Avocados, I-83, 85, 101

Baby care, I-1, 1168, 1377, 1415, II-2483-2486

Baby food, I-1, 446-450, 487-488

Baby oil, I-1

Baby powder, I-1

Back pain, II-3506

Backhoes, I-1837

Backpacks, I-1080

Bacon, I-361-362

Bagels, I-596-599, 603

Bags, I-22, 1162-1164

Baked beans, I-470

Bakeries, II-2869

Bakery products, I-302, 332, 600-609, 611-617, 640

Bakeware, I-2, 1664

Baking chocolate, I-706-707

Baking mixes and prepared food, I-898

Ball bearings, I-1902

Ballasts and control gear, II-2049

Bananas, I-83, 85, 103

Bandages, II-2369, 2371

Bank holding companies, II-3261

Banking, II-3034-3086

Bar joists, I-1771

Barack Obama, II-3563

Barbecue sauces, I-469, 513

Barbells, II-3461

Barite, I-231

Barrels, I-1747

Bars, I-1708, 1734, 1771, II-2935

Baseball, II-2452, 3462, 3466, 3482

Basketball, I-1608, 1616, II-3462, 3466-3467, 3483

Bath accessories, I-1066, 1068, 1380, 1482

Bathing suits, I-1020, 1047

Bathroom safety supplies, II-2376

Bathrooms, I-244

Batteries, I-5, 239, II-2163-2175

Battery separators, II-2154

Bauxite, I-176, 1266

Beans, I-81, 471, 478

Bearings, I-1902-1904

Bed and breakfasts, II-3266-3267

Bedding, I-1120, II-2910

Bedding stores, II-2909-2910

Bedspreads, I-1065

Beef, I-113-114, 347, 349, 352-353, 365, 369

Beer, I-300, 563, 748, 754-772, 1663, II-2778, 2991

Behavioral health, II-3518

Belts, I-1015, 1055, 1060

Bench lathes, II-2395

Bentonite, I-224

Berries, I-83

Betting, II-3495

Beverages, I-35, 300, 302, 334-335, 752-753, 1663, 1912

Beverageware, I-1665

Bicycles, II-2297-2299, 2995

Bicycling, II-3461

Bike shops, II-2995

Billboards, II-2478

Billiards, II-3461

Bins, I-17, 22

Biological products, I-1351-1352

Biometrics, I-45

Bioplastics, I-1274

Biotechnology, I-1353-1354

Birds, I-40

Biscuits, I-621, 656

Blackberries, I-84-85

Blankets, I-1070

Bleach, I-1385

Blenders, II-2037, 2040, 2918

Blinds and shades, I-1062-1063

Blood, I-1351

Blood and organ banks, II-3526

Blood pressure kits, I-1355

Blouses, I-992

Blow molding, I-1275, 1632

Blowers, I-1908

Blowout preventers, I-1851

Blu-ray DVD replication machines, I-1889

Blu-ray players, II-2062

Blueberries, I-84-85, 87

Boarding houses, II-3272

Boat repair, II-2538, 3429

Boats, II-2285-2292, 2538, 2880

Body scrubbers, II-2487

Bodywear, I-1020

Boilers, I-1775-1777

Bologna, I-365

Bolts, I-1782-1783

Bon Jovi, II-3453

Bonds, II-3116

Book clubs, II-2998

Book printing, I-1229-1230

Book retailing, II-2998-2999, 3025

Books, I-1199, 1213-1222, 1230,
    II-2627

Boomboxes, II-2064

Boosters, II-1999

Boring machines, I-1874

Boron, I-1267

Bottled tea, I-795-798

Bottled water, I-300, 753, 799-808

Bottles, I-1276

Bottling machinery, I-1911

Bouillon, I-902

Bourbon, I-784

Bowling, II-3461

Bowling alleys, I-1125, II-3459

Bowls, I-1173

Boxes, I-1147-1149, 1153

BPO services, II-3373

Brads, I-1707, 1808

Brakes, I-239, II-2247-2248, 2252-
    2253

Brandy, I-749, 788

Bras, I-1048

Bread, I-300-301, 334-335, 530, 603,
    618-622, II-2869-2870

Breakfast, I-540

Breakfast bars, I-648-649

Breath fresheners, I-651-652, 1464

Bricks, I-225

Bridge and tunnel construction, I-278

Britney Spears, II-3563

Broadband services, II-2633

Broadwoven fabrics, I-999

Broccoli, I-75, 81

Broilers, I-122-124

Brooms, II-2472-2473

Broth, I-452

Brownies, I-601, 607

Browning/cooking sprays, I-738

Bruno Mars, II-2088

Brushes, II-2472

Bubble bath, I-1380

Buckles, II-2471

Buffets, II-2941

Building inspection services, II-3389

Building leasing, II-3240-3243,
    3249-3250

Building materials, I-3, 183, 1669

Buildings, I-243, 271, 289, 1723,
    II-3327

Buns and rolls, I-623-626

Burglary insurance, II-3183

Burnout ovens, II-2396

Buses, II-2221-2223, 2502, 2732

Business associations, II-3560

Business processing outsourcing,
    II-3373

Butter, I-386-395, 734

Buttermilk, I-435

Buttons, II-2471

c-si cell equipment, I-1764

Cabbage, I-75, 81

Cabinets, I-17, 19, 1091-1093

Cable television, I-11, 1915, II-2694,
    2696

Cables, I-1276, 1737, 1740, 1808-
    1811

Cadmium, I-1724

Cafés and bars, II-2935

Cafeterias, I-1125, II-2941

Cakes, I-603

Calcium, I-1298

Calculators, I-1970

Call centers, II-3401

Camcorder and digicam retailing,
    II-3010

Camcorders, II-2063, 2070

Camera stores, II-3010-3011

Cameras, II-2413-2414

Camping, II-2452, 3461

Campus bookstores, II-3002

Can openers, II-2040

Candles, II-2488

Candy, I-16, 301, 655, 662-665,
    667-677, 680, 682-683, 686-692,
    694-697, 709-719

Canes, II-2377

Canned food, I-451-458, 470-478,
    II-2769

Cans, I-1729, 1744

Cantaloupes, I-85, 102

Capacitors, II-2150-2152

Caps, I-992, 1053

Caps and closures, I-1788

Car audio, II-2071, 2924

Car transportation, II-2573

Car washes, II-3420

Caramel apples, I-657

Caramel corn, I-880

Carbon black, I-1553

Carbon nanotubes, II-2010

Carbon paper and inked ribbons,
    II-2468, 2763

Carburetors, I-1987, II-3419

Card making, II-2459

Card stores, II-3012-3013

Cardiovascular machines, II-2446

Cardiovascular treatments, I-1331

Cards, I-16

Carpet cleaning services, II-3280

Carpets and rugs, I-12-13, 1000-
    1003

Carrots, I-81

Carsharing, II-3391

Casinos, II-3487-3491, 3495

Caskets, II-2479

Castings, I-1741

Cat food, I-577, 581-582, 589

Catalogs, I-1239, II-2892, 2915-
    2917, 3016

Catalysts, I-181-182

Catering, II-2936

Catfish, I-837

Cathodes, I-1546, II-2155

Cats, I-40

Cattle, I-115-116, 592

Cauliflower, I-75

Caulk, I-1545, 1549

Caulking compounds, I-1545

Caustic soda, I-1253

CD players, II-2065, 2067

CD-R, II-2177

CDs, I-11

Ceiling contracting, I-285

Celebrity and sports agents,
    II-3460

Celery, I-81

Celine Dion, II-3453

Cellphone chargers, I-5

Cellular phone accessories, I-4-5

Cellular phones, II-2061, 2093-2095,
    2171

Cellulose, I-1691

Cement, I-225, 1583, 1668-1675

Cemeteries, II-3260

Ceramic tiles, I-1678-1679

Ceramics, I-2, 13, 175, 182, 1271

Cereal, I-300-301, 558-562

Cereal bars, I-648-650

Chain saws, I-1755

Chair pads, I-1067

Chalk, II-2460

Chamber music groups, II-3454

Charcoal, I-1565

Charities, II-3552-3554

Cheese, I-300, 396-407

Cheesecakes, I-606

Chemical catalytic preparations, I-1269

Chemical manufacturing machinery, I-1989

Chemicals, I-175, 180, 198, 229, 1148, 1246-1251, 1256, 1258-1260, 1356, 1528, 1587, 1735, 1896, 1912, II-2497

Cherries, I-85

Chewing tobacco, I-938-944, 947-950

Chickens, I-374-375, 381

Child and maternity specialty stores, II-2892

Child care, II-3548

Children's Entitlement Programs, II-3597

Chili, I-532

China, II-2736

Chip cards, II-2127

Chiropractors, II-3506-3507

Chlorine, I-1252-1254, II-2163

Chocolate, I-301, 632, 655-656, 706-720, II-2868

Chow mein, I-458

Chris Brown, II-2088

Christmas, I-6, 1245

Christmas trees, I-6-7

Churches, II-3566

Cider, I-484, 783

Cigarettes, I-300, 936-944, 946-951, 953-967

Cigars, I-936, 938-944, 947-950, 968-971

Circuit breakers, II-2001

Civic organizations, II-3562

Claims adjusting, II-3238

Clay, I-225

Clay bricks and blocks, I-1677

Cleaning products, I-1386-1400

Clock repair, II-3426

Clocks, II-2421

Closets, I-8

Closures, I-1787-1788

Cloud computing, I-1926-1928

Club stores, II-2788, 2811, 2962-2963

Coal, I-183-186, 1260, II-2497, 2705, 2745

Coated fabrics, I-1008-1009

Coated paper, I-1154-1157

Coatings, I-1275, 1508-1518, 1554, 1747, II-2785

Coats, I-1043

Cobalt, I-168-169

Cocoa, I-721-723

Coconuts, I-95

Cod, I-837

Coffee, I-302, 845-858, II-2773

Coffee and snack shops, II-2933-2934

Coffee creamers, I-409

Coffee drinks, I-859-860

Coffeecakes, I-614

Coffeemakers, II-2037-2038, 2040, 2919

Cognac, I-749, 781

Coils, II-1994

Cold remedies, I-655, 1314-1316, 1318, II-2962

Collard greens, I-80

Collection services, II-3314

College book stores, II-3000

Colleges, II-3020

Colleges and universities, II-3536

Colored pencils, II-2461

Comforters, I-1079

Comic books, I-1206

Commercial line insurance, II-3184

Commercial photography, II-3320

Commercial screen printing, I-1243

Commercial vehicles, II-2224-2226

Commodity contracts, II-3126-3127

Communications equipment wholesalers, II-2746

Community food services, II-3545

Compactors, I-1837

Completion services, I-206

Composite wood, I-1100

Compressors, I-1906-1907, 1980-1981, II-2245

Computer-aided design, II-3348

Computer data storage, I-1948-1954

Computer facilities management services, II-3376

Computer leasing, II-3377

Computer peripherals, I-1956, II-2742-2743

Computer printers, I-1957-1966

Computer rental and leasing, II-3377

Computer repair, II-3378-3379

Computer retailing, II-2927-2928

Computer systems design, II-3380

Computers, I-1213, 1927, 1929-1946, II-2061, 2131, 2627, 2741

Concert tickets, II-3497

Concerts, II-3453

Concessions, II-3492

Concrete, I-3, 218, 1669, 1676, 1684

Concrete contracting, I-292

Condensed products, I-410-411

Condensers, II-2246

Condiments, I-512, 521-522

Condoms, I-1621

Confectionery products, I-302-303, 653-697

Construction, I-155, 218, 241, 243, 289, 294, 1549, 1669, 1697-1698, 1716, 1720, 1729, II-1995, 2010, 3572

Construction equipment, I-1837-1843

Consulting, intelligence and investigations, I-45

Consulting services, II-3588

Consumer electronics, II-2059-2073, 2075, 2077-2086, 3424, 3427

Consumer spending, I-9

Contact lenses, II-2404-2406, 2412

Container leasing, II-3335

Containerboard, I-1142-1143

Containers, I-19, 1096-1097, 1697

Continuing care retirement communities, II-3550

Contraception, I-1343-1344

Contract research organizations, II-3577

Contractors, I-242, 275-276

Control gear, II-2012, 2049

Convenience stores, II-2788-2789, 2795-2800, 2811, 2870, 3025

Convention and visitors bureaus, II-3392

Converters, I-1912

Conveyors, I-1858-1859

Cookies, I-301, 570, 603, 630-637

Cooking, I-1213

Cooking and salad oils, I-739-741

Cooking equipment, II-2016-2022

Cookware, I-1789

Copper, I-151-155, 1716-1718, 1740-1741, 1743

Copper wire, I-1739-1740

Cordage, I-1014, 1808

Cork, I-1108, II-2480

Corn, I-50, 59-62, 81

Corn flour, I-574

Corn oil, I-746

Correctional products, II-2458, 2462

Cosmetic storage, I-1633

Cosmetics, I-25, 1148, 1416-1430, 1476, II-3030

Costumes, I-16, 1025, 1061

Cottage cheese, I-424

Cotton, I-50, 65-68, 137, 1291

Cotton balls, II-2370

Cotton linters, I-735

Cottonseed, I-137, 735

Cough and cold remedies, I-655, 1318, II-2962

Cough syrup, I-698

Countertops, I-1085-1087

Couplings, I-1803, 1805

Coupons, I-10, II-2657-2658

Court reporting services, II-3322

Crackers, I-301, 638-639

Craft stores, II-3015

Cranberries, I-508

Cranberry juices, I-489, 495

Cranes, I-1861-1866, 1869

Craniomaxillofacial implants, II-2385

Crating, I-1618, II-2571

Crawler dozers, I-1838

Crayons, II-2463

Cream cheese, I-408

Credit cards, II-3090-3091

Credit reporting agencies, II-3316

Credit unions, II-3087

Cribs, I-1109

Crocheting, II-2459

Cross-industry and vertical application, II-3345

Cross training, I-1616

Croutons, I-627

Crowns and closures, I-1787

Cruise lines, II-2531-2532

Crushed stone, I-216

Crutches, II-2377

Crystals, II-2130

CT scans, II-2354, 2402

Cucumbers, I-81

Cupcakes, I-607

Curtain wall contracting, I-295

Custodial equipment wholesalers, II-2753

Custody activities, II-3262

Customer relationship management, II-3344

Cutlery, I-1748, II-2429, 2914

Cyclic crude, I-1519

Cyclic intermediates, I-1519

Cylinders, I-1778

Dairy alternatives, I-411, 425

Dairy foods, I-302, 332, 334-335, 383-385, 411, II-2770-2771

Dance schools, II-3451

Dandruff treatments, I-1444

Danishes, I-614

Data processing, II-3371-3372

Data protection, II-3347

Data storage, II-2129

Database management, II-3345

Dates, I-95

Dating services, II-3288

Debit cards, II-3092-3093

Debit networks, II-3094

Debt collection agencies, II-3315

Decking, I-1100-1103

Decorated apparel, I-1081

Decorations, I-6, 16

Deep foundation work, I-296

Deep fryers, II-2037

Defense, I-1508, II-2306-2317, 3600

Defibrillators, II-2360

Degreasers, I-1396

Dehumidifiers, I-1980, 1985

Dehydrated food, I-412, 902

Demolition work, I-298

Dental care, I-1358, 1466, 1469, II-2030, 2394, 2401

Dental equipment, II-2394-2400

Dental laboratories, II-3521

Dentists, II-3504-3505

Denture care, I-1467-1468, 1471

Deodorants, I-1431-1432, 1476, 1478-1479, 1556

Department stores, II-2792-2793, 2882, 2886, 2889-2892, 2894-2895, 2901-2902, 2906, 2910, 2914-2917, 2921-2923, 3009, 3029, 3031

Depilatories, I-1445

Design industry, II-3569

Design services, II-3572

Dessert bars, I-601

Desserts, I-899

Development organizations, II-3398

Diabetes, I-1336, 1356, 1358

Diagnostic imaging, II-2402

Diagnostics, I-1356

Dialysis industry, II-2349, 3523-3524

Diamonds, I-233-235

Diapers, I-1, 1169-1172

Dickies, I-1055

Diesel injection systems, II-2260

Diet foods, I-900

Diets, I-1303

Digestive aids, I-1303

Digital cameras, II-2171, 2415

Digital content creation, II-3344

Digital video recorders, II-2697

Dimension stone, I-213

Dining rooms, I-1110

Dinnerware, I-1635

Dip mixes, I-901

Dips, I-426-428

Direct marketing, II-2870, 2886, 2895, 2910, 2923, 3317

Direct selling, II-3021

Directories, I-1231, 1239

Disaster repairs, I-244

Discount stores, II-2794, 2882, 2894, 2902, 2905, 2914, 2921-2923, 2990, 3008-3009

Discretionary programs, II-3597

Dishcloths, I-1067

Dishwashers, II-2042

Dishwashing detergents, I-1360-1369

Disinfectants, I-1386

Disposable plates and bowls, I-1173

Diving, II-2452

Doctors, II-3502-3503, 3506, 3511

Document preparation, II-3393-3394

Dog food, I-575, 578, 580, 583-584, 590-591, II-2494

Dog parks, II-3598

Dogs, I-40

Dollar stores, II-2788, 2801, 2811, 2962-2963

Dolls, II-2435-2436, 2441-2442

Donuts, I-603, 608-609, 616

Doors, I-1772-1773

Dough, I-529, 570-571

Downhole tools, I-1848

Drafting services, II-3572

Drain cleaners, I-1386

Drama schools, II-3450

DRAMs, II-2136-2137

Drawing, II-2459

Dredging, I-282

Products, Services, Names, and Issues Index

Dresses, I-1044, 1046

Dried and dehydrated food, I-902

Drill pipe, I-1712-1714

Drilling equipment, I-198, 1874

Drilling mud, I-224

Drilling services, I-198

Drills, I-1849, 1879

Drinking places, II-2960

Drinks, I-300-331, 563, 897, 1148-
1150, 1258-1259, 1896, 1919,
II-1998, 2459, 2497, 2538

Drive-in theaters, II-3446

Driver assistance systems, II-2237-
2238

Driveways, I-277, 292

Drug delivery products, II-2387

Drug stores, II-2788-2789, 2962-
2985, 2990, 3003, 3025

Drugs, I-35, 37, 1148, 1248, 1331-
1347, 1896, 1912, II-2764-2765

Drums, I-1747

Dry, condensed and evaporated
products, I-410-412

Dry packaged dinners, I-903-907

Drycleaners, II-3275

Dryers, II-2027

Drying racks, I-22

Drywall contracting, I-288

Ducts, I-1780

Dust collection equipment, I-1978

Dusters, II-2472

Duvets, I-1079

DVD players, II-2062, 2072-2073

DVD rental, II-3448

DVD retailing, II-2929

Dyes, I-1263

E-Books, I-1215, 1223, II-3001

E-Cards, II-2660

E-mail, II-3344

E-Reader displays, II-2156

E-Readers, I-1929, II-2074, 2160

Ear care, I-1433

Earthquake insurance, II-3185-3186

Easter, I-1245

Edgers, I-1833-1834

Editing services, II-3394

Education, I-243, II-3532, 3542,
3554

Eggnog, I-435

Eggplant, I-75

Eggs, I-125-126

Electric components, II-2159

Electric vehicles, II-2215-2217

Electric waxers, II-2397

Electrical contracting, I-284

Electricity, I-1587, 1776, 1896,
II-1997, 1999, 2705-2716

Electronic commerce, II-2624-2628,
2669-2670, 2892, 2990, 2998, 3023

Electronic ink, II-2160

Electronic music products, II-2433

Electronics, I-155, 1148, 1248,
1255-1256, 1258, 1723, 1725,
1729, 1735, II-2006, 2010, 2055,
2157-2158, 2176, 2747-2748, 2924,
2928, 3008

Electronics retailing, II-2905, 2920,
2923, 2925, 2928, 3010

Electroplating and polishing, I-1791

Elevators and escalators, I-1856-
1857

Elliptical machines, II-2445

Elliptical motion trainers, II-3461

Elton John, II-3453

Embroidery, I-995, 997

Embroidery shops, I-1082

Emergency department contractors,
II-3527

Eminem, II-2088

Emissions control, II-2249

Employment services, II-3589

Emulsifiers, I-909

Enamels and glazes, I-1267

Endoscopy, II-2389

Energy, I-1256, II-2703-2704, 3582

Energy drinks, I-810-811, 828

Energy shots, I-812

Engineered stone, I-1085

Engineered wood products, I-1104

Engineering services, II-3570

Engines, I-1816-1820, 1825-1826,
II-2176

English muffins, I-628-629

Engraving, I-1793

Enterprise content management,
II-3344

Enterprise resource planning,
II-3344, 3349

Entertainment, I-11, II-3363

Entertainment complexes, II-3477-
3478

Envelopes, II-2763

Enzymes, I-909

Epoxy, I-1544

Equines, I-40, 131-132

Equipment, I-1697, 1833-1836

Escalators, I-1856-1857

Espresso machines, II-2037

Ethanol, I-1524

Ethnic food, I-513, 566, 908

Ethylbenzene, I-1525

Ethylene, I-1525-1526

Ethylene dichloride, I-1525

Ethylene oxide, I-1525

Ethylene vinyl acetate, I-1544

Evaporated products, I-410-411

Evaporators, II-2250

Event planning, II-3404-3405

Excavation and foundation work,
I-296-297

Excavators, I-1837, 1842

Excess and surplus insurance,
II-3187

Exchange traded funds, II-3121

Excimer lithography, II-2129

Excipients, I-1348

Executive search industry, II-3590-
3591

Exercise, II-2452

Exercise equipment, II-2445-2446

Expanded design services,
II-3572

Explosives, I-1551

Explosives trace detection, II-2339

Express delivery services, II-2516-
2519

Extruded products, I-1734

Eye care, I-1434

Eye mascara, I-1422-1423

Eyewear, II-2408-2410

Fabric mills, I-982-983

Fabric softeners, I-1401-1403

Fabric stores, II-2921

Fabrics, I-975-981, 999, 1009

Facial care market, I-1478-1479,
1496, 1498

Facial tissue, I-1174-1175, 1187

Factory outlet stores, II-2895, 2902

Family planning centers, II-3528

Fans, I-1909, II-2035

Farm loans, II-3098

Farm machinery, I-1828-1832

Farm supplies, II-2785

Farm warehousing and storage,
II-2520

Farmers markets, II-2866

Farms, I-136

Fast-food industry, II-2935, 2946-
2948, 2950, 2952, 2955, 2959

Fasteners, I-1783, II-2471

Father's Day, I-1245

Fats and oils, I-302-303, 332, 731-734, 736-737, 742

Fatty acids, I-1528

Faucets, I-1762

Federal contracting, II-3599

Feed industry, I-592-594

Feedlots, I-111

Feldspar, I-226

Feminine hygiene products, I-1176-1180

Fencing, I-1100, 1706, 1808

Ferroalloys, I-1703

Ferrochrome, I-1704

Ferrosilicon, I-1703

Fertilizers, I-1531-1534, 1536-1538, 1540, 1834

Fiber optics, I-1725

Fiberglass, I-1090, 1691, II-2480

Fibers, I-1004, 1290-1294

Fiduciary activities, II-3262

Field bean wholesalers, II-2774

Fighting, II-3363

Figs, I-95

Film, I-1292, II-2417

Film projectors, II-2407

Filters, I-1916-1918

Financial services, I-1239, 1927, II-3088, 3130, 3373

Fine arts schools, II-3533

Fire and allied insurance, II-3188-3189

Fire detection equipment, II-2115

Fire safety equipment, II-2114, 2762

Firewalls, II-3350

First aid products, II-2369, 2371-2374

Fish markets, II-2865

Fish oil, I-1298-1299

Fishing, I-143-146, II-2451-2452, 3461

Fishing lines, II-2451

Fitness, II-2449

Fitnesswear, I-1033

Fittings, I-1803, 1806

Fixtures, II-2049

Flakes, I-1708

Flame retardants, I-175

Flanges, I-1806

Flat panel displays, II-2161

Flatware, II-2430

Flavor enhancers, I-909

Flavor oil mixtures, I-1528

Flavorings and fragrances, I-909, 1527

Flax, I-1298

Fleet management, II-3409

Flexographic printing, I-1241

Flood insurance, II-3190-3191

Floor care equipment, II-2043-2045

Floor cleaners, I-1389

Floor covering stores, II-2906

Floor coverings, I-3

Flooring, I-12-15, 1084, 1089, 1093, II-2480-2482, 2737, 2906, 2908

Florist and nursery supplies, II-2779

Florists, II-3023

Flounder, I-837

Flour, I-303, 555-557

Flowers and plants, I-107-108, II-2627, 2662

Fluid power, I-1988

Folding campers, II-2319

Food additives, I-909

Food and drinks, I-300-331, 412, 563, 897, 902, 1148-1150, 1258-1259, 1896, 1919, II-1998, 2459, 2497, 2538

Food complexes, II-3477-3478

Food machinery, I-1888

Food preservatives, I-910

Food processors, I-566, 1248, II-2040

Food specialties, I-911

Food supplements, I-1303

Foodservice, I-431, 566, II-2754, 2870, 2935, 2937-2940

Foodservice disposables, I-1151-1152

Foot care, I-1435-1436

Foot control parts (automotive), II-2251

Football, II-3462, 3464, 3466, 3484-3485

Footpaths, I-292

Footwear, I-25, 1607-1616, 1635, 1637, 1641-1643, II-2882, 2894, 2902

Footwear retailing, II-2902

For-profit education, II-3537

Forestry, I-141

Forgings, I-1694-1695

Forklifts, I-1837

Formalwear, II-2883

Foundation, I-1425-1426

Foundation contracting, I-286

Foundation work, I-296-297

Foundries, I-224, 1742, 1989, II-2128

Fractional jet industry, II-2275

Fragrances, I-909, 1416, 1418-1419, 1437-1441, 1477-1479, 1527

Franchises, II-3263

Free weights, II-2445-2446, 3461

Fretted instruments, II-2433

Frisbee, II-3462

Frozen desserts, I-413-419, 529

Frozen dinners, I-300, 533-536

Frozen foods, I-345-346, 524, 529-551, 599, 624

Frozen pies, I-640

Frozen pizza, I-554

Frozen vegetables, I-525-529

Fruit, I-83-90, 92-106, 302, 334-335, 457, 479, 484, 537, 902, 913, 1148, II-2772

Fruit and vegetable markets, II-2867

Fruit drink mixes, I-915

Fuel, I-1580, II-2530, 2538

Fuel cells, I-1765

Functional foods, I-332, 813

Funeral services, II-3285

Fungicides, I-1534

Fur, I-1054

Furnaces, I-1980, 1985

Furniture, I-1093, 1109-1118, 1124-1125, 1635

Furniture rental, II-3336

Furniture stores, II-2904, 2906, 2910

Furniture upholstery and repair, II-3428

Furniture wholesalers, II-2735

Gambling, II-3493, 3495-3496

Games, I-11, II-2435-2436, 2438-2443, 2758, 3495

Garages, I-17, II-3411

Garbage, trash and leaf bags, I-1158-1159

Garden equipment, I-1833-1836

Garden supplies, I-1540, II-2785

Garlic spreads, I-832

Garment repair and alterations, II-3395

Garment services, II-3276, 3395

Garment textile manufacturing industries, I-137

Garnets, I-236

Gas and fire detection equipment, II-2115

Gas cans, I-1630

Gas cylinders, I-1778

Gas equipment, I-1847-1852, 1855

Gas extraction, I-1258-1259

Gas pipeline construction, I-280
Gas stations, II-2789, 2878-2879
Gas wells, I-201-204
Gaskets, packing and sealing devices, I-1617-1619
Gasoline, I-1580, II-2703
Gasoline injection systems, II-2261
Gates, I-1808
Gearboxes, I-1784-1785
Gears, I-1913-1914
Gemstones, I-237, II-2428
Gene sequencing tools, II-2332
Generators, II-2007-2008, 2176
Generics (drugs), I-1345
Geophysics, I-208
Geosynthetics, I-238
Germanium, I-1725
Gift, card and novelty stores, II-3012-3013
Gift cards, I-6
Gift wrapping, I-1156
Gifts, I-6, 1015, II-2662, 3012, 3554
Gin, I-782
Ginger, I-927
Glass, I-2, 180, 229, 1267, 1271, 1653-1662, II-2033
Glass cleaners, I-1386, 1390
Glass containers, I-1663
Glass polishing and ceramics, I-182
Glassware, I-1666
Glazes, I-503, 1267
Glazing and curtain wall contracting, I-295
Glee cast, II-2088
Gloves and mittens, I-992, 1056-1058, II-2392
Glucosamine/chondroitin, I-1298-1299
Glues, I-1545, 1548
Gluten-free products, I-333, 612
Goats, I-121
Gold, I-160-164
Golf, I-1609, 1616, II-2449, 3461
Golf courses, II-3474, 3476
Gourmet stores, II-2914
Government, I-269, 1927, II-3597, 3601
Grain and field bean wholesalers, II-2774
Granite, I-213, 216
Granola bars, I-699-700
Grapefruit, I-92, 484
Grapes, I-83, 85, 88-90
Graphic design, II-3321

Graphite, I-239, II-2011
Gravel, I-217-219
Gravy mixes, I-916
Gray iron, I-1741
Greases, I-1271
Great Lakes transportation, II-2530
Green beans, I-472-473
Green design, II-3571
Green products, I-1391
Greeting cards, I-6, 1244-1245, II-3003, 3012
Grills, I-28
Grocery stores, II-2627, 2788-2789, 2810-2863, 3003
Grocery wholesalers, II-2768
Grounds equipment, I-1833
Growing media, I-1540
Guards, I-45
Guided missile and space vehicle parts, II-2318
Gum, I-655, 724-728
Gummed products, I-1156
Guns and ammunition, I-785, 1794-1795
Gym and exercise equipment, II-2445-2446
Gymnastics, II-3462
Gyms, I-1616, II-2445, 3471-3473
Gypsum, I-240
Haddock, I-837
Hair accessories, II-2489
Hair and nail salons, II-3283
Hair care, I-1416-1419, 1442-1456, 1476-1477, 1479, 1556
Hair dryers, II-2037
Hair loss, I-1319, II-3289
Halibut, I-837
Halloween, I-16
Halogen, II-2047
Ham, I-347, 365, 370-373
Hamburgers, II-2947
Hammers, I-1756
Hampers, I-22
Hand care, I-1479, 1499-1501
Hand mixers, II-2040
Hand sanitizers, I-1381
Hand tools, I-1757-1758
Handbag, luggage and accessory stores, II-3014
Handbags and purses, I-1650-1652, II-2889
Handheld entrees, I-541
Handpieces, high-speed, II-2398
Handyman services, II-3431

Hardware, I-1910, 1912, II-2785
Hardware stores, II-2785-2786, 2905
Hardwood, I-1089, 1093
Hashbrowns, I-544
Hats and caps, I-992, 1053
Haulers, I-1837
HDPE (High-Density Polyethylene), I-1277, 1628
Head rests, II-2257
Headsets, II-2096-2097
Health care, I-1213, 1256, II-3122, 3554, 3592
Health food stores, II-2986, 2990
Health foods, I-303
Health insurance, II-3151-3168
Health publishing, I-1232
Hearing implants, II-2378
Hearths, I-1979
Heat exchangers, I-1776
Heat/ice packs, II-2374
Heat pumps, I-1980, 1985
Heat transfer equipment, I-1980
Heating and cooling, I-1806, 1980-1986, II-2031
Heavy equipment rental, II-3330-3332
Heavy industrial facility construction, I-279
Hedge trimmers, I-1834
Helicopters, II-2276-2277, 2279
Hemorroidal remedies, I-1320
Hens, I-381
Herbicides, I-1534-1535
Hides, skins and pelts, I-347, II-2776
High-density polyethylene (HDPE), I-1277, 1628
High-fructose corn syrup, I-646
Highway construction, I-277
Highways and streets, I-243, 292, 1569
Hinges, II-2254
Historical sites, II-3556
HIV antivirals, I-1336
Hobbies, II-2437
Hockey, II-3486
Hogs, I-117-120
Hoists, I-1863
Home care beds, II-2376
Home centers, II-2906, 2923
Home health care, II-3333, 3522
Home improvement stores, II-2782, 2920
Home office stores, II-2928

Home organization products, I-17-19
Home repair industry, II-3431
Home shopping, II-2889, 3007, 3017-3018
Home video industry, II-3448
Homefurnishings, I-137, 1064-1079, II-2911-2913, 2915-2917, 2920
Homeland security, I-45, II-2340
Homeowners insurance, II-3192-3207
Honey, I-506, 929
Hoses, I-1803
Hosiery, I-984-985, 1050, II-2891
Hospice care, II-3513
Hospitals, I-243, II-3020, 3514-3517
Hot dogs, I-363-364, 625
Hotels and motels, I-243, 270, II-3020, 3268-3271
Housewares, II-2627, 2914
Human Machine Interfaces, I-1919, II-2256
Humidifiers, II-2039
Hunting, I-147, II-2452
Hybrid cars, II-2218
Hydration belts, II-2447
Hydrocolloids, I-909
Hydroelectric power, II-2703, 2717
Hydrostatic transmission parts, I-1988
Hypermarkets, II-2794, 2882, 2894, 3008-3009
Ice, I-887
Ice cream, I-300, 411, 420-423, 529, 537, 656
Ice pops, I-418-419
Ignition wiring harnesses, II-2176
Immunoassay, I-1356
Incinerators, II-2722
Independent living facilities, II-3550
Indium, I-1268
Inductors, II-1994
Industrial controls, II-2012
Industrial feed, I-595
Industrial filaments, I-1292
Industrial gases, I-1255-1262
Industrial laundries, II-3277, 3281
Industrial machinery, I-1635, 1735, 1821, 1989
Industrial trucks, I-1869
Infant formula, I-1, 459-461
Information security, I-45
Information technology, I-1716, II-3374-3375
Infotainment, II-2255

Infrared optics, I-1725
Infrastructure, I-1668
Injection molding, I-1275, 1277, 1280, 1634
Ink, I-1552
Inked ribbons, II-2468, 2763
Inorganic acids, I-1269
Inorganic aluminum compounds, I-1269
Inorganic chemicals, I-1269
Inorganic dyes and pigments, I-1263
Insect bite treatments, I-1321
Insect repellents, I-1566
Insecticides, I-1534, 1556
Institutional cleaning, I-1370
Instruments, II-2327, 2329-2330, 2333
Insulation, I-1691-1692
Insulin, II-2353
Insurance, II-3132-3147, 3187-3189
Inter-dealer brokers, II-3128
Interface materials, I-1910
Internet, II-2625-2627, 2629-2632, 2642-2677, 2889, 2901-2902, 2914-2917, 2924, 3007, 3031, 3299-3300, 3307-3309
Internet Protocol Television, II-2698, 3355
Internet service providers, II-2633-2641
Internet sites, II-2675
Investment banking, II-3117-3120, 3122-3124
Iodine, I-1270
IPOs, II-3125
Iron, I-150, 1264, 1695, 1708, 1741, 1814
Iron ore, I-148-149, 224, 1715
Irons, II-2037, 2040
Irradiation apparatus, II-2403
Isocyanates, I-1520
Jackets, I-990
Jams and jellies, I-480-482, 506
Janitorial equipment, I-20
Janitorial services, II-3328-3329
Jeans, I-1023-1024, II-2886
Jellies, I-480-482, 506
Jets, II-2266, 2272
Jewelry, I-25, 180, 1015, II-2425-2426, 2428, 2431, 2459, 2469, 2761
Jewelry materials and lapidary work, II-2432
Jewelry repair, II-3426

Jewelry retailing, II-2432, 3004-3007
Job training, II-3546
Jogging, I-1616
Juices, I-300, 483-501, 753
Justin Bieber, II-3563
Juvenile product retailing, II-3031
Kale, I-80
Kanye West/Jay-Z, II-3453
Kaolin, I-223
Katy Perry, II-2088, 3563
Kenny Chesney, II-3453
Ketchup, I-502, 512
Kettles, II-2033
Keyboards, II-2433
Kilns, I-1890
Kim Kardashian, II-3563
Kiosks, II-2935
Kitchen cleaners, I-1392
Kitchen textiles, I-1067, 1074
Kitchens, I-244, 1110
Kitchenware, I-1635
Kiwi, I-95, 104
Knitting mills, I-989-996
Knives, II-2451
Lab testing, II-3578
Labels, I-1237, 1239, 1243
Laboratory instruments, II-2331-2332
Lace, embroidery and ribbons, I-995, 997
Lacquers, I-1556
Ladders, I-1702, 1813
Lady Gaga, II-2088, 3453, 3563
Lamb, I-347, 352
Laminates, I-13, 1085, 1625, II-2482
Lamp ballasts, II-1999
Lamps, II-2047-2048
Land improvement, I-296
Land ownership, I-142
Landfills, II-2723
Landing nets, II-2451
Landscaping, I-21, 140
Language services, II-3396, 3543
Lapidary work, II-2432
Laptops, I-1929, 1937, II-2061, 2171
Lard, I-347-348
Lasers, II-2129
Lathes, I-1874, 1885
Laundromats, II-3275, 3278
Laundry aids, I-1391, 1404-1407
Laundry and garment services, II-3276
Laundry detergents, I-1371-1375

Laundry equipment, II-2027-2029
Laundry rooms, I-22
Laundry routes, II-3279
Lawn, garden and farm supplies, II-2785
Lawn and garden consumables, I-1540
Lawn and garden equipment, I-1833-1836
Lawn mowers, I-1833-1834
Laxatives, I-1322-1323
Lead, I-156-157
Leaf bags, I-1158-1159
Leaf blowers, I-1834-1835
Leather goods, I-25, 27, 1015, 1115
Leather goods repair, II-3284
Leather tanning and finishing, I-1636
Legal & regulatory publishing, I-1233, 1239
Legal services, II-3530-3531
Lemonade, I-484, 498
Lemons, I-85, 92
Length adjusters, II-2259
Lens shutters, II-2418
Lenses, II-2411
Letter machines, I-1971
Lettering shops, II-3313
Lettuce, I-81
Liability insurance, II-3208, 3230-3233
Libraries, II-3538-3540
Lice treatments, I-1324
Licensed merchandise, I-23
Licorice, I-682-683
Lids, I-1744
Life insurance, II-3148-3150
Life science instruments, II-2329-2330
Life sciences, II-3582, 3587
Lift trucks, I-1867
Light bulbs, II-2056-2057
Light vehicles, II-2219-2220
Lighter fluid, I-936
Lighters, I-936, II-2490-2491
Lighting, I-1255, 1698, II-2049-2055, 2058
Lil Wayne, II-2088, 3453
Lime, I-1685-1686
Lime removal, I-1386, 1393-1394
Limes, I-85, 92
Limestone, I-213, 216
Limousine services, II-2501

Linear low-density polyethylene (LLDPE), I-1278
Linear motion technology, II-2334
Linens, II-2738
Liners, I-1162, 1164
Lingerie, I-1048-1051, II-2890
Linoleum, II-2480
Lip care, I-1427, 1457-1459
Lipid regulators, I-1336
Lipstick, I-1429
Liquor, I-748, 780-794, 1663
Lithium, I-1271-1273, II-2163
Lithium iron batteries, I-1271
Lithographic printing, I-1238-1239
LLDPE (Linear Low-Density Poly-ethylene), I-1278
LMFAO, II-2088
LNG tankers, II-2526
Lobbying groups, II-3564
Locker accessories, II-2492
Lockers, I-1126
Locksmiths, II-3432
Logging, I-1083
Logistics, II-2506
Lotteries, II-3495
Low-voltage products, II-1995-1996
Lubricants, I-239, 1580, 1586-1593
Luggage, I-1644-1649, II-3014
Luggage stores, II-3014
Lumber, II-2739, 2783, 2785
Lunch meat, I-365-368
Luxury goods, I-24-27
Luxury vinyl tile, II-2480
Macaroni, I-895, 902
Macaroni & cheese, I-905
Machine shops, I-1990
Machine tools, I-1871-1877
Machinery, I-1549, 1698, 1702, 1720, 1723, II-2530, 3433
Machining centers, I-1874
Magazines, I-1138, 1199, 1205, 1207-1212, 1239, II-3025-3026, 3301
Magnesium, I-1741
Magnet wires, I-1737, 1740
Magnets, I-181-182
Mailing machines, I-1971
Makeup, I-1417, 1477-1479
Malpractice insurance, II-3209-3211
Malt, I-773
Malt beverages, I-774
Managed services, II-2944
Manganese, I-1705
Mangos, I-95

Manufactured home leasing, II-3251
Marble, I-213
Margarines, spreads and butter, I-391-395
Marinades, I-503-504
Marinas, II-2538
Marine insurance, II-3212-3215
Marine machinery wholesalers, II-2756
Markers, II-2458, 2466-2467, 2763
Marketing research, II-3580
Marshmallows, I-684-685
Masonry contracting, I-286-287
Mass merchandisers, I-1215, II-2788-2789, 2811, 2886, 2889-2891, 2895, 2901, 2915-2917, 2920, 2928, 2962-2963, 2995, 2998, 3003, 3007, 3010, 3025, 3029, 3031
Massagers, II-2037
Massively multiplayer online role-playing games, II-2677
Materials handling equipment, I-1868, 1870, II-2751
Materials recovery, II-2724
Maternity specialty stores, II-2892
Mattresses, I-1119
Mayonnaise, I-512, 734
Mayonnaise and sandwich spreads, I-514
Meal replacements and supplement powders, I-1303
Measuring, testing and navigational instruments, II-2333
Meat, I-36, 302, 332, 335, 347, 349-360, 371-372, 374, 376-380, 382, 529-530, 537, 542
Meat sauces and marinades, I-503
Meat snacks, I-369
Meat substitutes, I-543
Medicaid, II-3597
Medical beds, I-1130
Medical case management, II-3529
Medical products, I-1332, II-2347-2368, 2375-2378, 3334, 3425
Medicare, II-3597
Medium-density fiberboard, I-1105
Melatonin, I-1299
Melons, I-85, 102
Membrane technologies, I-1920-1921
Memory cards, II-2123
Memory crafts, II-2459
Metal alloys, I-181

Metal cans, I-1744-1745

Metal coating and engraving, I-1793

Metal containers, I-1746-1747

Metal products, I-1260, 1702, 1735, 1771

Metal sales offices wholesalers, II-2744

Metal stampings, I-1774

Metal tanks, I-1778

Metallurgical applications and alloys, I-182

Metals, I-1255-1256, 1259-1260, 1587, 1919, II-1995

Metalworking, I-1594, 1821, 1874-1875

Meteorological services, II-3397

Meters and test devices, II-2335, 2338

Mexican foods, I-504, 907, 917

Micro reaction technology, I-1891

Microbiology, I-1356

Microblogging, II-2631

Microprocessors, II-2131, 2134, 2139

Microturbines, I-1822

Microwaves, II-2021-2022

Microwaveware, I-1635

Middleware, II-3355

Military markets, II-2281-2282

Milk, I-300, 303, 411, 429-437, 753

Milkshakes, I-438

Mill products, I-302, 1696

Milling machines, I-1874

Millwork, I-1088-1089, 1093

Mineral wool, I-1691

Mining equipment, I-1844

Miniwarehouses, II-3241

Mink, I-130

Mints, I-701-702

Missiles, II-2318

Mittens, I-992, 1056-1058, II-2392

Mobile advertising, II-3302, 3309

Mobile financial services, II-2684-2685

Mobile straddle carriers, I-1869

Model railroading, II-2437

Moist towelettes, I-1181-1182

Moldings, I-1089

Molds, I-1878

Molybdenum, I-177

Monorail systems, I-1863

Mops, II-2472

Mortgage guaranty insurance, II-3234-3235

Mortgage loans, II-3100-3113, 3115, 3265

Motels, I-243, 270, II-3020, 3268-3271

Mother's Day, I-1245

Motion pictures, II-2627, 3435-3437, 3441, 3443, 3449

Motor coaches, II-2221

Motor graders, I-1837

Motor oil, I-1592

Motor vehicle towing, II-3421

Motorboats, II-2285

Motorcoaches, II-2503

Motorcycles, II-2300-2305, 2731, 2881

Motorhomes, II-2263-2264

Motors, I-1988, II-2009

Moulding and trim, I-1100

Mouthwash, I-1469-1471

Movie theaters, I-11, II-3298, 3444-3445, 3447

MRIs, II-2364, 2402

Muffins, I-602-603, 613

Mufflers, I-992

Multifamily construction, I-268

Multiperil insurance, II-3216-3220

Multivitamins, I-1298

Muscle support devices, II-2375

Museums, II-3557

Mushrooms, I-81, 109-110

Music, II-2087-2092, 2433, 2679

Music retailing, II-2930, 3008

Music schools, II-3450

Musical instrument stores, II-2931-2932

Musical instruments, II-2433-2434

Musicians, II-3454

Mustard, I-512, 515

Mustard greens, I-80

Mutton, I-347, 352

Nail care, I-1460-1461

Nail salons, II-3283

Nailers, I-1879

Nails, staples, tacks, spikes and brads, I-1707, 1808

NAND, II-2141

Nano technology, II-3582

Nasal care, I-1326, 1462-1463

National parks, II-3558

Natural gas, I-187-189, 195-196, 1896, II-1995, 2705

Natural gas liquids, I-200

Natural stone, I-1085

Nautical instruments, II-2327

Navigational instruments, II-2327, 2333

Nebulizers, II-2356

Neckwear, I-1015, 1041, 1055

Nectarines, I-85

Needles, II-2471

Nerve repair, I-1358

Netbooks, I-1929

Network and database management, II-3345

Networking equipment, II-2116-2120

Networks, II-3368

News syndicates, II-3386

Newspapers, I-1199, 1201-1204, II-3303

Newsprint, I-1136

Nickel, I-170, 1735-1737

Nightclubs, II-2961

Nightwear, I-993

Nitrogen, I-1258-1259

Non-lethal weapons, I-1796

Nonferrous metals, I-1737

Nonwoven fabrics, I-1011-1013, II-2387

Noodles, I-889-890, 894, 902

Notebooks, I-1937, II-2133

Novelty items, II-3012

Novelty stores, II-3012-3013

Nuclear energy, I-1776, II-2703, 2705, 2718

Nuclear medicine, II-2402

Nursery supplies, II-2779

Nursing care, I-1, II-3512

Nutraceuticals, I-1295

Nutrition bars, I-703-705

Nuts, I-91, 729-730, 861, 1782-1783

Nylon, I-1291

Oatmeal, I-562

Oceanic development, II-3582

Off-price retailers, II-2886, 2890-2891, 2895, 2901, 3029

Office equipment wholesalers, II-2740

Office furniture, I-1121-1123, II-2905

Office machinery, I-1971-1972, II-3337

Office supply stores, II-2905

Oil, I-190-194, II-2705

Oil and gas, I-195-196, 1896, II-1995

Products, Services, Names, and Issues Index

Oil and gas equipment, I-1847-1852, 1854-1855
Oil and gas extraction, I-1258-1259
Oil and gas pipeline construction, I-280
Oil and gas wells, I-201-204
Oil change industry, II-3422
Oil Country Tubular Goods, I-209
Oil field services, I-205-212
Oils, I-302-303, 332, 731-734, 736-737, 739-742
Oilseeds, I-735
Olive oil, I-734, 743-744
Olives, I-105
Oncologics, I-1336
Onion rings, I-548
Onions, I-81, 85
Online brokers, II-3131
Online dating, II-2666
Online gaming, II-2677-2678
Online ticketing, II-3497
Online video, II-2680
Operating room equipment, I-1131
Operating systems, II-3345, 3352-3354
Ophthalmic goods, II-2412
Opiates, I-1347
Optical goods stores, II-3027
Optics, II-2452
Optometrists, II-3508-3509
Oral care, I-1327, 1417, 1464-1478
Oral surgery, II-3504
Orange juice, I-484, 499-500
Oranges, I-85, 92-94
Orchestras and chamber music groups, II-3454
Ordnance, I-1797
Organ banks, II-3526
Organic foods, I-83, 334-337, II-2864
Oriented strand board, I-1106-1107
Original design manufacturing, II-1992
Orthopedic appliances, I-1358, II-2380-2386
Oscillators, II-2130
Outdoor gear, II-2450
Outerwear, I-991-992
Outpatient mental health & substance abuse centers, II-3525
Oven cleaners, I-1386, 1396
Ovens, II-2017, 2037
Ovenware, I-1635
Oxygen, I-1260

Oxygen concentrators, II-2357
Packaged food, I-338-344
Packaging, I-29-39, 1152, 1508, 1635, 1702, 1723, 1812, 1919
Packaging, active, I-35
Packaging, aseptic, I-31-32
Packaging, assembly equipment, I-1893
Packaging, green, I-30
Packaging, intelligent, I-35
Packaging machinery, I-1911-1912
Packing and crating, I-1618, II-2571
Packing devices, I-1617-1619
Packing machinery, I-1911
Pads, II-2472
Paint stores, II-2784
Paintball, II-3462
Painting contracting, I-283
Paints and coatings, I-1508-1518, 1554, 1556, 1747, II-2785
Palladium, I-178
Pallets, I-1093
Palm oil, I-736, 746
Pamphlets, I-1230
Pans, I-1790
Panties, I-1048, 1050
Pants, I-1038, 1042, II-2883
Pantyhose, I-984-985
Pantyliners, I-1176
Papayas, I-95
Paper, I-1135-1137, 1139-1141, 1156, II-2763
Paper bags, I-1164
Paper napkins, I-1187
Paper towels, I-1183-1187
Paperboard, I-1144-1146
Parking brakes, II-2258
Parking lots and garages, II-3411
Partitions, I-1126
Passports, II-3282
Pasta, I-301, 888-896
Pasta sauces, I-519-520
Pastes, I-656, 1708
Pastries, I-537, 614
Patents, II-3264
Patient handling equipment, I-1132
Patient monitoring, II-2365-2366
Pawnshops, II-2992
Pay television, II-2695, 2699-2701
Payment cards, II-2121
Payment terminals, I-1973
Payroll services, II-3576

Pbied and vbied equipment, II-2341
PC cameras, I-1967
PC servers, II-2134
Peaches, I-85
Peanut butter, I-918
Peanuts, I-91
Pears, I-83, 85, 98
Pedals, II-2251
Pegboard assemblies, I-17
Pelts, I-347, II-2776
Pencils, II-2457, 2464-2465, 2763
Pens, II-2454-2458, 2763
Pensions, II-3237
People screening technologies, II-2342
Pepper, I-833-834
Peppers, I-78
Performance apparel, I-1028-1029
Performing arts companies, II-3455
Perfume, I-27, 1476
Periodontal treatments, II-3504
Peripheral vascular devices, II-2358
Perms, I-1443
Personal care products, I-1417, 1439, 1476-1489, 1554, 1912, II-2627
Personal digital assistants, I-1947
Personal line insurance, II-3221
Personal massagers, II-2036
Personal watercraft, II-2324
Pest control, II-3323-3326
Pesticides, I-1528, 1540-1542
Pet food, I-563, 575-591
Pet groomers, II-3032
Pet products, II-2493-2494
Pet stores, II-3033
Petrochemicals, I-1521
Petroleum jelly, I-1
Petroleum refining, I-1258-1260, 1580-1581, II-2777
Pets, I-40
Pharmacy benefit managers, II-2987
Phosphate rock, I-230
Phosphatic fertilizers, I-1537
Phosphoric acid, I-1269, 1537
Phosphors, I-181
Photo sharing, II-2667
Photofinishing, II-3387
Photographic equipment and supplies, II-3011
Photography, II-3282
Photovoltaics, I-1766-1767
Pianos, II-2433
Pierogi, I-549

Pies, I-600, 603, 640, II-2869
Pigments, I-1263
Pigs, I-592
Pillowcases, I-1065
Pillows, I-1071-1072, 1076
Pineapple juices, I-493-494
Pineapples, I-106
Pins, II-2471
Pipe, I-41-42, 1275-1276, 1806
Pipe fittings, I-1806
Pipeline construction, I-280
Pipelines, II-2564-2565
Pistons, I-1987, II-2266
Pitches, I-1583
Pizza, I-530, 537, 552-554, 571, 919, II-2935, 2942
Pizza dough, I-572-573
Pizza kits, I-920
Planning and development organizations, II-3398
Plants, I-107-108, II-2627, 2662
Plasma, II-2359
Plaster contracting, I-285
Plastic bags, I-1162
Plastic film and sheet, I-1275-1276, 1622-1624, II-2416
Plastic pipe, I-1627-1629
Plastic plates, sheets and shapes, I-1626
Plastic products, I-1635
Plasticizers, I-1528
Plastics, I-1275-1282, 1626, 1635, 1691, 1821, II-2033
Plastics machinery, I-1892
Plate work, I-1792
Plates, I-1173
Platform supply vessels, I-1853
Platinum, I-179-180, 1726
Plumbing products, I-1682, 1762-1763, 1806
Podiatrists, II-3510-3511
Polishes, I-181, 1408, 1556
Political action committees, II-3565
Polychloroprene, I-1544
Polyester, I-1283, 1291-1292
Polyethylene, I-1275, 1279, 1525
Polymerization catalysts, I-1725
Polypropylene, I-1280-1281
Polyurethane foam, I-1631
Polyvinyl acetate, I-1544
Polyvinyl chloride, I-1276, 1282
Pomegranates, I-95
Popcorn, I-861, 870, 873, 880
Popcorn makers, II-2034

Pork, I-347, 352, 376-380
Pork rinds, I-874
Portable navigation devices, II-2328
Portable toilet rental, II-3338
Portraits, II-3282
Ports, II-2535
Postal service, II-2524-2525
Pot pies, I-550
Potash, I-227-228
Potassium compounds, I-1269
Potassium sulfate, I-1567
Potato chips, I-861, 869, 875-876
Potatoes, I-73, 81, 529-530, 537, 544
Potholders, I-1067
Pots, I-1790
Pouches, I-1162, 1164
Poultry, I-36, 360, 374, 381, 530, 592, II-2775
Powder metallurgy, I-1815
Powdered drinks, II-2773
Power tools, I-1879-1881, II-2171
Power toothbrushes, II-2032
Power transmissions, II-2232
Poyurethane, I-1544
Precipitated silica, I-220
Prefabricated buildings, I-1099, 1781
Pregnancy tests, I-1357
Prepaid cards, II-3089
Prepared foods, I-334-335, 898
Prescription dispensing, II-2988-2989
Preservatives, I-909
Pressure pumping services, I-198
Pressure-sensitive products, I-1156
Pretzels, I-545, 861, 877-878
Print-on-demand services, I-1219
Printed circuit boards, I-1989, II-2124-2126
Printing, I-1236, 1239-1240, 1243
Prisons, II-3595
Probiotics, I-1298-1299
Profiles and tubes, I-1276
Project management services, II-3570
Projectors, II-2419
Promotional industry, II-3318
Promotional products, I-43-44
Proofreading services, II-3394
Propane retailing, II-3022
Propellers, II-2279
Property improvement, I-244
Property insurance, II-3222-3224
Proppants, I-221-222

Prosthodontics/orthodontics, II-3504
Public relations industry, II-3593-3594
Publishing, I-1199-1200
Pulp, I-1133-1134
Pumping services, I-210
Pumps, I-1896-1901, 1982, 1988
Purpose-built backup appliances, I-1955
Purses, I-1650-1652, II-2889
Puzzles, II-2439
PVC flooring, I-12
Quick printing, II-3319
Racetracks, II-3468-3470
Racing, II-3363
Radio broadcasting, II-2687-2691, 3304
Radio controlled products, II-2437
Radiographs, II-3504
Radios, II-2104
Railroad car rental and leasing, II-3339
Railroad equipment, II-2294-2295
Railroads, II-1995, 2497-2499
Railway ties, I-1093
Raincoats, I-1061
Raisins, I-509
Rakes, I-1757
Ranges, II-2017, 2019-2020
Rare earth, I-181-182
Raspberries, I-84-85
Razor blades, I-1749-1752
Ready meals, I-530, 537, 922
Real estate, I-1668, II-2668, 3244-3245, 3252-3257
Real estate investment trusts, II-3265
Recording produsts, II-2433
Recreation instruction, II-3500-3501
Recreational and vacation camps, II-3273
Recyclable material wholesalers, II-2759-2760
Refractories, I-286, 1681, 1693
Refrigerated and frozen foods, I-345-346
Refrigeration equipment, I-1980, II-2750
Refrigerators, I-1980, II-2023-2026, 2037
Regulators, II-2176
Rehabilitation hospitals, II-3519-3520
Reinsurance industry, II-3239
REITs, II-3265

Relational databases, II-3356
Relays and controls, II-2012
Religion, I-243, 1213, 1223, 1230, II-3554, 3567
Remodeling, I-244-245
Remote controllers, II-2105
Remotely operated vehicles, II-2345-2346
Renewable energy, II-2705
Repackers, I-566
Repossession services, II-3399
Reptiles, I-40
Research & development, II-2318, 3582-3586
Residential construction, I-14, 246-267, 292, II-3570
Resins, I-1292, 1545
Resorts, II-3499
Respirators, II-2379
Respiratory agents, I-1336
Restaurants, I-1125, II-2935, 2941-2959
Retailing, I-273, 566, 1149, 1927, II-2788-2791, 2876, 2944, 3020
Reverse mortgages, II-3114
RFID tags and scanning, I-45, II-2122
Ribbons, I-995, 997, II-2468, 2763
Rice, I-50, 55-58, 563-569, 1286, 1288
Rice cakes, I-879
Rihanna, II-2088, 3563
Rings, I-1987
Rivets, I-1783
Road and highway construction, I-277
Robes, I-990
Robotics, I-1922-1923
Rodent removal, II-3325
Rods, I-1734
Role-playing games, II-3362-3363
Roller bearings, I-1902
Rollers, II-2472
Rolls, I-603, 621, 623-626, II-2869
Roofing, I-3, 290, 1583, 1585
Roofing contracting, I-289
Rooming and boarding houses, II-3272
Rope, cordage and twine, I-1014, 1808
Routers, II-2120
Rowing machines, II-2445
Rubber, I-1009, 1061, 1284-1285, 1287, 1289, II-2480

Rugs, I-12-13, 1000-1003, 1066, II-2907
Rum, I-749, 784-785, 788, 790
Running, I-1029, 1611, 1615, II-3461
Runways, I-277
Rust removal, I-1393-1394
RV parks, II-3274
Sade, II-3453
Sake, I-563
Salad dressing mixes, I-923-924
Salad dressings, I-516-518, 521-522
Salad oils, I-739-741
Salads, I-925-926
Salami, I-365
Salmon, I-145, 837-838
Salon care, I-1443
Salsa, I-504, 512
Salt, I-835, 1568-1572
Sand and gravel, I-217-219
Sanders, I-1879
Sandstone, I-213, 216
Sanitary napkins, I-1177
Sanitary paper products, I-1174-1175, 1183-1192, 1195, 1912
Sanitaryware, I-1760-1761
Sapphire ingots, II-2162
Satellite broadcasting, II-2702
Satellite equipment, II-2103
Satellites, II-2106
Sauces, I-513, 520-523
Sausage and ham, I-347, 370-373
Saw blades, I-1759
Saw chains, I-1882
Saws, I-1885
Scales, II-2037
Scanners, I-1968
Scarfs, I-1055
School buses, II-2221, 2505
Schools, I-274, 431, 1125, 1224, II-2433, 3450, 3534-3535
Scissors, I-1753-1754
Scooters, II-2301, 2377
Scrapbooking and memory crafts, II-2459
Screen printing, I-1242-1243
Screen protectors, I-5
Screening equipment, I-1845
Screws, I-1783
Seafood, I-36, 40, 529, 537, 837-844
Sealants, I-1544-1547
Sealants and caulk, I-1549
Sealing devices, I-1617-1619
Seals, I-1618, 1620

Search engines, II-2645-2653, 2655-2656
Seasonal items, II-3012
Seasonings, I-303, 833-836
Seat structures, I-1129
Secured logistics, II-3381
Security industry, I-45, II-2244, 3382-3385
Security software, II-3358
Seeds, I-49-51, 729, 1540
Seedstock, I-112
Selena Gomez, II-3563
Self storage industry, II-2522, 3241
Semiconductor equipment, I-1893
Semiconductors, II-2132-2133, 2135-2138, 2140-2147
Senior living services, II-3551
Septic tank services, II-3434
Servers, II-3369-3370
Serviceware, I-1152
Set-top decoder boxes, II-2107-2108
Settlement offices, II-3259
Sewer systems, I-243
Sewing machines, II-2046, 2921
Sewing stores, II-3015
Shades, I-1062-1063
Shakira, II-3563
Shale gas, I-197-199
Shampoo, I-1443-1444, 1453-1455, 1478, 1482
Shampooers, II-2043-2044
Shapewear, I-1048, 1050-1051
Shaving products, I-1478, 1490, 1556
Sheeps and goats, I-121
Sheet metal contracting, I-291
Sheets, I-1065
Shelf-stable dinners, I-906-907
Shelving, I-17, 19, 1126
Shingles, I-1584
Ship building, II-2281-2284
Ship repair, II-2281
Shipping, I-46, II-2527
Shipping containers, I-1747, 1779
Shirts, I-992, 1038-1040
Shoe and leather goods repair, II-3284
Shoe retailing, II-2900-2901, 2903
Shopping centers, II-3246
Shops, II-2933-2934, 3313
Shortening, I-745
Shorts, I-990
Shovels, I-1757

Showcases, partitions, shelving and lockers, I-1126

Shower curtains, I-1066, 1075

Shrimp, I-844

Shrink wrap, I-431, 1624

Shuttles, II-2221

Side dishes, I-346

Siding, I-47, 1583

Sightseeing, II-2504, 2533

Sign and transportation reflective materials, II-2476

Sign painting and lettering shops, II-3313

Signs, II-2477-2478

Silicon, I-1728

Silicon alloys, I-1703

Silicon metal, I-1727

Silicon timing industry, II-2148

Silicon wafers, II-2149

Silicone, I-2

Silk, I-135

Silver, I-165-167

Silverware, II-2430

Skating rinks, II-3498

Ski and snowboard resorts, II-3499

Ski machines, II-2445

Skiing, II-2452

Skin care, I-1416, 1418-1419, 1476-1477, 1479, 1491-1503

Skins, I-347, II-2776

Skirts, I-990, 1044

Slate, I-213

Sleep apnea, II-2368

Slide fasteners, II-2471

Slippers, I-1638-1640

Slot machines, II-3479

Slow cookers, II-2037

Small animals, I-40

Small game, I-381

Smart cards, I-45

Smart meters, II-2336-2337

Smartphones, II-2061, 2098-2100, 3353

Smokeless tobacco, I-972

Smoking accessories, I-936

Smoking tobacco, I-936

Smoothies, I-484, 505

Snack bars, I-648-650

Snack cakes, I-616

Snack shops, II-2933-2934

Snacks, I-300-301, 546, 656, 729, 861-886

Snow blowers, I-1834

Snow removal contractors, II-2729

Snowboard resorts, II-3499

Snowmobiles, II-2325

Snuff, I-973

Soap, I-1, 229, 1267, 1377-1384, 1478-1479

Soccer, II-3461-3462, 3466

Socks, I-986-988, 1015, 1020, 1050

Soda ash, I-229

Sodium compounds, I-1269

Sodium hydroxide, I-1253

Sofas, I-1113

Soft cakes, II-2869

Soft drinks, I-303, 753, 814-827

Softball, II-3462, 3467

Software, I-1910, II-3011, 3344-3361

Software retailing, II-3008

Softwood, I-1094-1095

Solar cell metal paste, I-1550

Solar panels, I-1768-1769

Solar power, II-2719

Solid-state voice recorders, II-2109

Solid surfaces, I-1085

Sound recording studios, II-3442

Soup, I-300-301, 462-468, 510-511, 537, 902

Souvenirs and novelty items, II-3012

Soy, I-434, 1298

Soy sauces, I-523

Soya products, I-332

Soybeans, I-63-64

Space exploration, II-3582

Space vehicle parts, II-2318

Spaghetti, I-895

Spark plugs, II-2176

Spas, I-299

Speakers, II-2059, 2066

Special events industry, II-3400

Specialty stores, II-2789, 2870, 2886, 2889-2891, 2895, 2915-2917, 2922, 3007, 3029, 3031

Spices, I-303, 928

Spikes, I-1707, 1808

Spinach, I-80

Spinal implants, II-2383

Sport utility vehicles, II-2182

Sporting goods, II-2448-2453, 2901, 2995

Sporting goods stores, II-2902, 2996-2997

Sports, I-753, 1303, II-2449, 3363, 3461-3464, 3466-3467, 3482-3486

Sports agents, II-3460

Sports and recreation instruction, II-3500-3501

Sports bras, I-1052

Sports camps, II-3501

Sports drinks, I-828-830

Sports promoters, II-3465

Sportswear, I-1028-1034, 1052, II-2902

Spray tanning, I-1507

Spreaders, I-1757

Spreads, I-391-395, 506, 734

Springs, I-1804

Squash, I-528

Stackers, I-1869

Staffing industry, II-3341-3343

Stain removers, I-1409-1412

Stainless steel, II-2033

Stairwork, I-1089

Staples, I-1707, 1808

Starters, II-2176

Stationery, I-1197-1198, II-2763

Steak sauces, I-503

Steam condensers, I-1776

Steel, I-183, 294, 1697-1701, 1708-1711, 1741, 1744, 1747

Steering, II-2234

Stem cells, I-1358

Stents, II-2351-2352

Stereos, II-2069

Stock exchanges, II-3129

Stomach pain remedies, I-1304

Stone contracting, I-286

Stone fruit, I-83

Storage, I-19, II-2520

Storage area networks, II-3368

Strawberries, I-84-86

Streets, I-243, 292, 1569

Structural metal, I-1770-1771

Student loans, II-3099

Stuffing, I-551

Styrene, I-1529, 1544

Subsea trees, I-211

Substrates, I-1910

Subway cars, II-2296

Sugar, I-641-645, 656

Sugar cane, I-929

Sugar substitutes, I-647

Sugarbeets, I-71

Sugarcane, I-72

Suits, I-1036, 1043, II-2883-2884

Sulfuric acid, I-1269

Sump pumps, I-1897

Sun care, I-1476, 1504-1507

Sunbeam oil, I-746

Sunflower oil, I-746

Sunglasses, I-1015, II-2409, 3029

Sunglasses stores, II-3028

Super Bowl, II-3310

Supercenters, II-2788, 2803-2804, 2811, 2962-2963, 3025

Supercomputing, I-1931

Supermarkets, I-654, II-2794, 2811, 2813-2817, 2819-2820, 2822, 2825-2826, 2828-2829, 2832, 2835-2838, 2840-2844, 2846, 2849-2851, 2853, 2855, 2857-2858, 2860-2861, 2863, 2870, 2882, 2894, 2915, 2962-2963, 3008-3009, 3025

Superphosphates, I-1537

Superyachts, II-2293

Supplements, I-1296-1299, 1303, II-2990

Supplies, II-2785

Supply chain management, II-3344

Surfactants, I-1413-1414

Surgical supplies, II-2387-2393

Surplus insurance, II-3187

Sweaters, I-992

Sweet potatoes, I-81

Sweeteners, I-909, 929

Swimming pools, I-299, II-2757

Switchgear, II-2002-2003

Swordfish, I-837

Syrup, I-929

Systems integration, I-45

T-shirts, I-990, 1020, 1027, II-2883

Tablets, I-1929, 1932-1934, II-2061, 3354

Tableware, I-1635, 1683

Tackle boxes, II-2451

Tacks, I-1707, 1808

Taco sauce, I-504

Talent agents, II-3456

Talk shows, II-2664

Tampons, I-1180

T&D equipment, II-1993, 1998

Tangerines, I-92

Tank barges, II-2528

Tank parts, II-2322-2323

Tank sets, I-1066

Tanker fleets, II-2529

Tanks, I-1778

Tanning, I-1636

Tape, I-1160-1161, II-2369

Tar, I-1519, 1583

Taverns, II-2944

Tax & accounting publishing, I-1234

Tax preparation, II-3286-3287

Taylor Swift, II-3453, 3563

Tea, I-930-934, II-2773

Teaching machines, II-2113

Teaware, I-1667

Telecommunications equipment, II-2111

Telemarketers and call centers, II-3401

Telephone services, II-2622-2623

Telephones, II-2101-2102

Television broadcasting, II-2692-2693

Television receivers, II-2059

Television shows, II-3438-3439

Televisions, II-2061, 2073, 2075-2086, 3305, 3311

Temporary Aid for Needy Families, II-3597

Temporary tattoos, I-1573

Tennis, I-1616, II-2452

Tequila, I-788, 791

Terminal operators, II-2536

Termite removal, II-3326

Test devices, II-2335, 2338

Test of English as a Second Language, II-3544

Test preparation, II-3544

Testing instruments, II-2333

Textbooks, I-1225-1228, 1230, II-3002

Textile finishing, I-998-999

Textile machinery, I-1884

Textiles, I-974-981, 998, 1292

Theatrical entertainment, II-3457-3458

Thermal management, I-1910

Thermometers, II-2367

Thread, yarn and fibers, I-1004-1005

Throws, I-1078

Ticketing, II-2674

Ties, I-1041

Tilapia, I-837

Tile cleaners, I-1386-1387

Tiles, I-12

Timber, I-1093

Timeshares, II-3402-3403

Tin, I-1729-1730

Tinware, I-1744

Tire retailing, II-2876

Tires, I-1595-1606, II-2734, 2876-2877, 3415

Tissue paper, I-1139-1141, 1189-1190

Titanium, I-1737

Titanium dioxide, I-1263

Title abstract and settlement offices, II-3259

Title insurance, II-3236

Toaster ovens, II-2037, 2040

Toasters, II-2037, 2040, 2922

Tobacco, I-69-70, 936-952, 954, 960, 965, II-2780, 3024

Tofu, I-416

Toilet bowl cleaners, I-1386, 1399-1400

Toilet tissue, I-1187, 1193-1195

Toiletries, I-1477

Toll roads, I-277, II-2572

Tomatillos, I-95

Tomatoes, I-79, 81, 476

Toning products, I-1612

Tooth whiteners, I-1474

Toothbrushes, II-2474-2475

Toothpaste, I-1471, 1475

Tortilla chips, I-861, 886

Tortillas, I-935

Totes and bins, I-17

Tour operators, II-2569

Tourism, II-2566

Tourist attractions, II-3559

Towels, I-1065-1066, 1069

Towing, II-2537

Toxoids, I-1351

Toys and games, II-2435-2436, 2438-2443, 2758

Toys and games retailing, II-3009

Track and field, II-3467

Tractors, I-1832, 1834, 1837, 1869

Trade shows and event planning, II-3404-3405

Trading stamp services, II-3406

Trail mixes, I-871-872

Trailers, I-1869

Train, subway and transit cars, II-2296

Trainers and teaching machines, II-2113

Training pants, I-1

Transcription services, II-3394

Transducers, II-1994

Transformers, II-1999-2000

Transit buses, II-2221

Transit cars, II-2296

Transit displays, II-2478

Transmissions, II-2262, 2733, 3417

Transportation, I-155, 175, 1723, 1729, 1735, II-2010, 2570, 3025, 3570

Transportation reflective materials, II-2476

Traprock, I-216

Trash bags, I-1158-1159

Trauma products, II-2385-2386

Travel, II-2567-2568, 2675

Travel trailers, II-2320-2321

Treadmills, II-2445, 3461

Trim, I-1100

Trimmers and edgers, I-1833

Trout, I-837

Truck rental, II-3407

Trucking, II-2507-2515

Trucks, I-1837, 1868-1869, II-2227-2231

Trust, fiduciary, and custody activities, II-3262

Tub cleaners, I-1386-1387

Tubes, I-1276, 1702, 1732, 1734, 1803

Tug supply vessels, I-1846

Tuna, I-837-838, 842

Tunnel construction, I-278

Turbines, I-1822-1824

Turboprops, II-2266

Turf and grounds equipment, I-1833

Turkeys, I-127-129, 365, 381-382

Turnip greens, I-80

Twine, I-1014, 1808

Twitter, II-3563

U2, II-3453

Ultrasound equipment, II-2348, 2402

Underwear, I-990, 1020, 1034, 1038

Uniforms, I-1025, 1061

Uninterruptible power, II-2004-2005

Unions, II-3561

Universities, II-3020, 3536

Upholstery, I-1636

Uranium, I-171-173

Used car retailing, II-2872-2874

Used merchandise stores, II-2993-2994

Utensils, pots and pans, I-1790

Utilities, I-1919, II-1995, 1997, 2720, 3570

Utility contracting, I-281

Utility vehicles, II-2326

Vacation camps, II-3273

Vacation homes, II-3258

Vaccines, I-1351, 1359

Vacuum cleaners, II-2041, 2043-2044, 2923

Vacuum sealers, II-2037

Vaginal treatments, I-1329

Valentine's Day, I-1245

Valves, I-1798-1803, 1806-1807, 1987, II-2752

Vans, II-2186

Vaporizers, II-2039

Vbied equipment, II-2341

Veal, I-347, 353-354, 359

Vegetable markets, II-2867

Vegetable oils, I-735, 746

Vegetables, I-75-82, 301, 474-475, 477, 530, 537, 902, 914

Vegetarian products, I-530

Vehicle leasing, II-3410

Velvet, I-1115

Vending machines, I-1974-1976, II-3019-3020

Vertical application, II-3345

Vessel leasing, II-3340

Vessel rental and leasing, II-3340

Vestments, I-1061

Veterinary services, I-138

Video equipment, I-11, II-2059

Video game consoles, II-2444

Video game digital distribution, II-2681

Video game software, II-2627, 3362-3367

Video media reproduction, II-3440

Video-on-demand, II-3449

Video surveillance, I-45

Vinyl, I-1090, II-2482

Vinyl acetate, I-1525

Vinyl acetate ethylene copolymer, I-1544

Vinyl acetate monomer, I-1530

Vinyl composite tile, II-2480

Visitors bureaus, II-3392

Vitamins, I-1300-1303, II-2990

Vitamins and supplements, II-2990

Vocational rehabilitation services, II-3547

Vodka, I-749, 784-785, 792-793

Voice over internet protocol, II-2682-2683

Volleyball, II-3462, 3467

Wafer fab equipment, I-1893

Waffle irons, II-2040

Waffles, I-547

Walkers, II-2377

Walking, I-1616, II-3461

Walking sticks, II-2377

Wall contracting, I-285

Wallboard, I-1687

Wallcoverings, I-48, 1156

Warehouse clubs, I-566, II-1998, 2789, 2805-2809, 2876, 2891, 2910, 2922-2923, 2990, 2998, 3010

Warehousing, I-1868, II-2521, 2523

Washcloths, I-1065

Washers, I-1783

Washing machines, II-2028

Waste disposal, II-2725-2727

Waste glass processing, I-1894

Waste treatment and disposal, II-2726-2727

Watch, clock and jewelry repair, II-3426

Watches, I-25, II-2422-2424, 2428

Water, I-243, 809, 1896, 1925, II-2721, 2730

Water heaters, I-1983

Water softeners, I-1543, 1574-1579

Water transportation, II-2534

Water treatment equipment, I-1924

Water well drilling, I-293

Watermelons, I-102

Waterproof-breathable fabrics, I-1059

Waxes and polishes, I-1556

Wearable-cams, II-2420

Wedding dresses, II-2888

Weddings, II-2459

Weight control products, I-1349-1350

Weight loss services, II-3290

Weight machines, II-2446, 3461

Welding, I-1255, 1883

Wells, I-201-204

Wheat, I-50, 52-54

Wheelbarrows, I-1757

Wheelchairs, II-2376

Whiskey, I-749, 784, 788, 794

Whiteboards, II-2495-2496

Winches, I-1863

Windows, I-3, 1090, 1100

Wine, I-300, 748, 775-779, 1663

Winter, II-2449

Wipes, I-1, 1196

Wire and cable, I-1808, 1811

Wire bonding equipment, I-1895

Wireless payments, II-2686

Wireless services, II-2574-2621

Wireless towers, II-2112

Wirelines, I-1855

Wires and cables, I-1276, 1737, 1740, 1809-1810

Wood, I-12-13, 1089-1090, 1821, II-2482

Woodworking machinery, I-1885-1886, II-2459

Word processing, II-3394

Workers compensation insurance, II-3225-3229

Worktops, I-17

World Wide Web, II-2625-2627, 2630-2631, 2642-2657, 2660-2672, 2674-2677, 2680, 2687, 3299-3300, 3307-3309

Wound care, II-2387-2388

Wrenches, I-1879

Writing instruments, II-2457-2458

X-rays, II-2402

Yard trimmers, I-1834

Yarn, I-975-981, 1004, 1006-1007, 1009

Yellow pages publishing, I-1235

Yoga, II-3461

Yogurt, I-300, 416, 439-445

Zinc, I-158-159, 1738, 1741, 1814

Zippers, II-2471

Zucchini, I-528

COMPANY INDEX

The more than 6,570 companies and institutions in this book are indexed here in alphabetical order. Numbers following the terms are entry numbers. They are arranged sequentially; the first entry number refers to the first mention of the company in *Market Share Reporter, 23rd Edition*. Although most organizations appear only once, some entities are referred to under abbreviations in the sources and these have not always been expanded. Roman numerals indicate volume numbers.

1-800-Flowers.com Inc., II-3023
1888 Mills, I-1069, 1073-1074
1st Source Bank, II-3047, 3085
20th Century Fox, II-3436, 3441
24 Hour Fitness USA Inc., II-3472
3 Day Blinds, I-1063
361 Degrees International Ltd., II-2898
3M, I-20, 44, 1155, 1157, 1161, 1514, 1547, 1690, 1854, II-2379, 2462, 2473
3MAE, II-2476
4 Imprint US, I-43
44 Farms, I-112
7 Days Inn, II-3269
7-Eleven Inc., II-2796-2797, 2812, 2937, 3263
84 Lumber Co., II-2782-2783
8ta, II-2613
99 bil Corp., II-2625
99 Cents Only, II-2801
+movil, II-2611
A. Cordero Badillo, II-2857
A-Data Technology, II-2137
A Vogel Oy, I-337
A123 Systems, II-2169-2170, 2173
AAA Travel, II-2568
AAMCO Transmissions and Total Car Care, II-3412
AAMI Australia, II-3134
A&A Global Industries, I-1974
A&E Television Networks, II-2694
A&H, II-3141
A&R Logistics, II-2511
AAR Corp., II-2274
Aarons, II-3336
AB Electrolux, II-2749
AB Foods L.L.C., I-357
AbaciCard, II-2121
ABB Ltd., I-1819, II-1993, 1996, 2006, 2008, 2157, 2159

ABB Robotics, I-1923
Abbey Carpet & Floor, II-2782
Abbott Laboratories, I-1337, 1341, II-2351, 2355, 2358, 2361
Abbott Nutrition, I-460-461
ABC Carpet & Home, II-2908
ABC Group Inc., I-1632
ABC Home & Commercial Services, II-3325
Abdul-Kadir Al Muhaidib & Sons Group, I-324
Abengoa Bioenergy Corp., I-1524
Abercrombie & Fitch, I-1019, II-2897, 2899
ABF Freight System, I-911, II-2512
ABK, II-2800
ABM Industries Inc., II-3329, 3411, 3425
ABP (Netherlands), II-3237
Abrams Artists Agency, II-3456
ABS Global, I-139
Abu Dhabi National Oil Co., I-195-196
ACA Insurance Co., II-3189
Academy Express, II-2503
Accelerated Genetics Inc., I-139
Accenture, II-2525, 3372-3374
Access HD, II-2080
Accidental Fund Group, II-3227
Accuweather, II-3397
Ace Hardware, II-2786, 3263
ACE INA Group, II-3204, 3232
ACE Ltd., II-3187, 3225
Ace Luggage, I-1649
Ace Parking Management, II-3411
Ace Products USA, II-2491
ACE Rent A Car, II-3408
Aceites Borges Pont S.A., I-742
Aceites Grasas y Derivados S.A. de C.V., I-733

Aceites Industriales El Zapote S.A. de C.V., I-733
Acenture, II-3375
Acer Group, I-1932, 1935, 1937-1946
ACH Foods Cos., I-741, 834
Ache, I-1339
ACIPCO, I-42
ACME, II-2162
Acme Markets, II-2844
Açoreana, II-3145
Acorn International, II-3018
Acos Villares S.A., I-1696
Acoustic Engineering Co. of Florida, I-285
ACS Groupe, I-276
ACS (healthcare), II-3592
Actavis, I-1345
Actia, II-2225
Activision Blizzard, II-3360, 3365-3366
Acxiom Corp., II-3317
AD Technologies, I-1628
Adams Pool Solutions, I-299
Adecco, II-3341-3343, 3589
Adi Pet Inc., I-578
Adidas Group, I-1022, 1030-1032, 1613-1615
ADM, I-331, 555, 595, 646, 722, 898, 1524, II-2520
Admiral Discount Tobacco, II-3024
Adobe Systems Inc., II-3348
ADT, II-3384-3385
Advance Auto Parts, II-2875
Advance Publications, I-1203, 1207-1208
Advanced Drainage Systems, I-41-42, 1628
Advanced Laser Clinics, II-3289
Advanced Shipping Manager, II-2669

AdvancePierre Foods, I-345
Advantage Resourcing, II-3341
Adventures in Advertising, I-43
Advics, II-2235-2236, 2247-2248, 2252-2253
Advisory Board Co., II-3592
AECOM Technology Corp., I-269, II-3571, 3573
Aegon US Holding Group, II-3149
Aeolus Tyre Co. Ltd., I-1604
AEP Industries Inc., I-1623-1624
Aer Lingus, II-2548
Aéroports de Paris, II-2562
Aeropostale, II-2897
Aeropuertos Españoles y Navegación Aérea, II-2562
Aerotek (Allegis), II-3341
AERT, I-1103
Aetna Inc., II-3153, 3156, 3164-3165
Affiliated Farm Insurance Co., II-3213
Affiliated Midwest, II-2825, 2842
Affinia Group, I-1916
Affinity Health System, II-3168
Affordable/Sensible, II-3408
AFL-CIO Workers' Voice PAC, II-3565
Aflac, II-3153
Ag Processing Inc., II-2520
AGC, I-1654-1658, 1660-1662
AGCO Corp., I-1831-1832
AGCS Marine Insurance Co., II-3215
Agere Systems, II-3125
Aggreko, II-3330-3331
Agilent Technologies, II-2330
Agio International, I-28
Agrium, I-227, 1532
Agrium U.S. Rental, II-2787
Agro Farma Inc., I-441
Agrolimen S.A., II-2938
Agropur Cooperative, I-309, 383
Agrotiki, II-3140
AgustaWestland, II-2276-2277
Ahern Rentals, I-1860, II-3330, 3332
Ahlstrom, I-1013
Ahold USA, II-2812, 2858, 2964
Ahrend Group, I-1122
AIA S.p.A., I-317
Aidells Sausage Co., I-372
AIMCO, II-3247-3248
Aimer, I-1049
Ainsworth, I-1107
Air France, II-2560

Air India, II-2557
Air Liquide, I-1257, 1261-1262
Air Products & Chemicals, I-1261
Aircel, II-2598
Airgas, I-1257
AirGas, I-1261
AirSep, II-2357
Airtel Bangladesh, II-2580
AirTran, II-2547, 2550
AIS Wireless, II-2617
Aisin Seiki, I-1914, II-2262
Ajab, I-1772
Ajay Glass & Mirror Co. Inc., I-295
Ajinmoto General Foods Inc., I-318
Akebono, II-2235, 2252-2253
Aker RGI, I-321
Aker Solutions, I-211
AKERS National Roll Co., I-1696
Akin, Gump et al, II-3564
Akzo Nobel N.V., I-1414, 1510, 1512-1513, 1515-1517, 1571, II-2784
Al Doha Co. for Processing & Distribution, I-340
Alabama Crimson Tide, II-3484
Alabama Power Co., II-2720
Alamance Foods, I-418
Alba, I-1722
Albany Door Systems, I-1772
Albert D. Seeno Construction/ Discovery Builders, I-249
Alberto Culver Co., I-1448
Albertsons, II-2814, 2823, 2835-2836, 2843, 2854
Alcatel-Lucent, II-3355
Alcoa Inc., I-176, 1719, 1722, 1782
Alerus Financial NA, II-3067
Alexander McQueen, I-1651
Alexandria Carbon Black, I-1553
Alexian Brothers Health System, II-3518
Alfa-Beta Vassilopoulos S.A., II-2829
Alfa Insurance Group, II-3193
Alfa Laval, I-1924
Algeco Scotsman, II-3331
Alimentation Couche-Tard, II-2796
Alipay, II-2625
Aliph, II-2096
Alkem, I-1341
All Nippon Airways, II-2558
Allan Candy Company Ltd., I-683
Allegis Group, II-3343
Allendale Pharmaceuticals, I-1344

Allens Inc., I-473, 475, 479
Alliance (Corporate), II-3139
Alliance Entertainment, II-2930
Alliance Residential Co., I-268
Alliance Resource Partners, I-185
Alliant Credit Union, II-3087
Alliant Techsystems Inc., I-1794
Allianz of America, II-3214
Allianz S.E., II-3134, 3139, 3143, 3145, 3169, 3239
Allianz Societas Europaea, II-3132
Allied Security, II-3383
Allied System Holdings, II-2515
Allied West Paper Co., I-1185
Allstate Insurance Group, II-3133, 3171, 3174-3175, 3177-3181, 3191-3195, 3197-3199, 3201-3203, 3205-3206, 3218, 3222
Allure Home Creation, I-1068
Allure Home Fashions, I-1075
Allure Home Improvements, I-245
Ally Bank, II-3078, 3095-3097
Ally/ResCap (GMAC), II-3104, 3106, 3109
Alm Brand, II-3137
Almacenes Pitusa, II-2857
Almarai Co. Ltd., I-324
ALNO Gruppe, I-1112
Alok Industries U.S., I-1070, 1073, 1079
Alon USA, II-2879
Alpek, I-1283
Alpha Natural Resources L.L.C., I-185
Alpine Bank, II-3039
Alpla Inc., I-1632
Alrosa, I-234
Alsay Inc., I-293
Alstom, I-1817, 1821, 1823, II-2296
Altia Group, I-312
Altour International, II-2568
Altria Group Inc., I-937, 952, 956, 971, 973, 1805
Alumina Limited, I-176, 1719
Alva/Amco Pharmaceutical Co. Inc., I-1435
Alyeska Pipeline Service Co., II-2564
A.M. Best, II-3316
Amada, I-1877
Amanco Mexico, I-1628
Amazon, I-1933, II-2074, 2663, 2912, 2925, 2929-2930, 2999, 3001, 3010, 3017, 3307, 3449

Ambassador, I-1235

AMC Theaters, II-3445

AMCI (special events), II-3400

AMCOL Intl., I-219

Amcor Ltd., I-37-38, 1632

AMD, II-2131, 2133-2134, 2146

AMECO, II-3332

Amedisys, II-3522, 3549

Amegy Bank NA, II-3077

AMEPA A.C., I-594

Amer Enterprise Group, II-3148

Amerex, II-2114

America First Credit Union, II-3103

Americal Corp., I-985, 988

American Airlines, II-2540-2544, 2549-2550, 2552-2556

American Airlines Federal Credit Union, II-3087

American and Efird, I-1004

American Apparel Inc., I-990, 1044, 1081

American Bank Center, II-3067

American Bankers Insurance Co. of Florida, II-3191

American Bridge 21st Century, II-3565

American Commercial Lines L.L.C., II-2528

American Crossroads, II-3565

American Eagle, II-2543-2544, 2549, 2559

American Eagle Outfitters, I-1017, II-2897

American Electric Power Company, II-2713

American Express, II-2568, 3090-3091

American Express Bank, II-3078

American Family Insurance Group, II-3181, 3192, 3197, 3200, 3206, 3221

American Federation of State, County and Municipal Employees, II-3561

American Federation of Teachers, II-3561

American Foods Group L.L.C., I-357

American Greetings, I-1244

American Home Mortgage Servicing, II-3111

American Importing Co. Inc., I-872

American International Group, II-3132, 3142, 3149, 3169, 3182-

3185, 3187-3188, 3209, 3214, 3222, 3225-3226, 3228, 3232-3234

American Italian Pasta Co., I-890, 896

American Laser Center, II-3289

American Licorice Co., I-683, 697

American Media, I-1207

American Media Inc., I-1209

American Musical Supply, II-2932

American National Bank, II-3060, 3085

American Red Cross, II-3526, 3552

American Rentals, II-3336

American River Transportation Co., II-2528

American Rock Salt, I-1569

American Safety Razor, I-1752

American Savings Bank FSB, II-3044

American Seafoods Group L.L.C., I-345, 841

American Security Insurance Co., II-3170, 3189

American Signature, II-2904

American Standard, I-1682, 1763, 1985

American States Water Corp., II-2721, 2730

American Sugar Refining, I-644

American Tombow, II-2462

American Tourister, I-1645

American Tours International L.L.C., II-2569

American Tower, II-2112

American Water Works, II-2721, 2730

American Woodwark, I-1091

Americana Group, I-324, 340

America's Car-Mart, II-2873

America's Mattress, II-2909

Americold Logistics L.L.C. and China Merchants Americold, II-2521

Americredit, II-3097

Amerifit Nutrition, I-1305, 1307

AmeriGas Propane, II-3022

Ameriphone, II-2101

Ameriprise Bank FSB, II-3056

Ameriquest Mortgage, II-3123

Amerisure Cos., II-3227

AMF, I-306

AMF Bowling World, II-3459

AMG, I-1728

Amgen Inc., I-1338, 1354

Amica Mutual Group, II-3203

Amore Pacific Cosmetics (Shanghai) Co. Ltd., I-1420

Amperex, II-2165

AMR, II-2500

Amscan Holdings, II-3013

Amtrak, II-2295

Amway, I-900, 1317, 1325, 1363, 1369, 1411, 1420, 1424, 1480, 1488, II-3021

Amy's Kitchen Inc., I-466, 468, 536, 541

Anchor Bank FSB, II-3084

Anchor Hocking, I-1664

And 1, I-1608

Andersen Corp., I-1111

Anderson, II-2930

Anderson Trucking Service, II-2508

The Andersons, I-1524

Andre Post Inc., I-924

Andy OnCall, II-3431

Anecop, I-326

Angelicoussis Group, II-2529

Anglo Platinum, I-178-179

AngloGold Ashanti, I-161

Anheuser-Busch InBev, I-33, 305, 307, 309, 331, 750, 756-760, 767, 818, II-3310

Anhui Conch, I-1671

Anhui Liugong, I-1866

Ann, I-1026

Ann Taylor Stores Inc., II-2885, 2897

Annabelle Candy Co. Inc., I-692

Annie Chun's, I-511

Annie's Inc., I-679

Ansaldo, I-1819, 1823

Ansell Health, I-1621, II-2392

Ansteel, I-1701

Anta (China) Co. Ltd., II-2898

Anthem Blue Cross and Blue Shield, II-3154

Anthony & Sylvan Pools, I-299

Antler, I-1647

Anytime Fitness, II-3472

Anzob, I-174

AOC, I-1935

AOL, II-2643, 2663, 2676, 3306, 3308

Aone, II-2169

Aoyang, I-1293

APA Talent & Literary Agency, II-3456

Apacer Technology, II-2137
Apatar, I-1587
Apatinska Pivara, I-764
APB (VBL), I-766
APC, I-227, II-2005
APCI, I-1262
APCO Worldwide, II-3593
APL, II-2527
APM-Maersk, II-2527
APM Terminals, II-2536
Apollo Distributing Co., II-2737
Apotex, I-1345
Apothecus, I-1344
Apple & Eve, I-489
Apple App Store, II-2926
Apple Computer Retail Stores,
    II-2925, 2927
Apple Inc., I-1932-1933, 1935-1939,
    1941, 1945, II-2095, 2100, 2116,
    2147, 2663, 2928, 3001, 3309
Applebee's Neighborhood Grill &
    Bar, II-2948
Applica (Windmere/Black & Deck-
    er), II-2040
Applied Materials, I-1767
Appro, I-1931
Apria Healthcare Group, II-3522
AptarGroup Inc., I-1634, 1788
Aqua America, II-2721, 2730
Aquarius Platinum, I-178-179
Aramark Corp., II-2939, 3277
Arbella Insurance Group, II-3172
Arbitron Inc., II-3580
Arbor Homes, I-256
Arbor Memorial Services Inc.,
    II-3285
Arby's, II-2957
ArcelorMittal, I-1701, 1715
Arch Coal Inc., I-185
Architectural Glass & Aluminum Co.
    Inc., I-295
Archstone, II-3247
Arcor Group, I-660
Arctic Cat, II-2325
Arctic Glacier, I-887
Arctic Snow & Ice Control, II-2729
Areva, I-171, II-2000
Argus Health Systems, II-2987
ARI, II-3409
Ariba, II-3361
Aristed Construction Co., I-242
AriZona Beverage Co., I-934
Arizona State University, II-3536
Arjo Huntleigh, I-1130

Arkema, I-1274
Arla Foods, I-311-312, 327, 390
Arlee Home Fashions, I-1071
Arma Food Industries, I-340
Armadillo Homes, I-265
Armour-Eckrich Meats L.L.C.,
    I-368, 371-372, 745
Armour Star, I-745
Armstrong, I-15, II-2482
ARMZ, I-171
Arnest, I-1561
Arpin Van Lines, II-2514
Arrow Exterminators, II-3323-3324
Arrow Stage Lines, II-2503
Art Institute of Chicago, II-3533
Art Van, II-2904
Arvato Print US, I-1229
Arvest Bank, II-3037, 3069
Aryzta Food North America, I-615
Asahi Breweries Ltd., I-318
Asahi Kasei, I-1921, II-2154
ASAP Printing Corp., II-3319
Asbury Automotive Group, II-2871
The Ascena Retail Group, I-1017
Ascension Health, II-3514
Asda, I-462, II-2859
ASG Security, II-3384
Ash City, I-44, 1081
Ashland, I-1593, 1924
Ashley Furniture HomeStores,
    II-2904, 2909
Ashley Furniture Industries Inc.,
    I-1111
Ashtead Group, I-1860, II-3331
ASI Insurance Corp., II-3224
Asia Insurance, II-3141
Asia Pulp & Paper, I-1141, 1192
Asics, I-1031, 1611, 1613-1615
Ask, II-2643, 2646
ASM International, I-1895
Aspen Contracting Inc., I-290
Aspen Marketing Services,
    II-3318
Aspen Skiing Company, II-3499
Aspire Design, I-245
Aspis Pronia, II-3140
Asset Acceptance Capital Corp.,
    II-3315
Assicurazioni Generali S.p.A.,
    II-3132
Assisted Living Concepts, II-3551
Associated Bank NA, II-3084
Associated British Foods, I-644, 733
Associated/Fresh Markets, II-2852

Associated Milk Producers Inc.,
    I-430
Associated Press, II-3386
Assurant Inc. Group, II-3148, 3188
Assurant Property & Casualty
    Group, II-3190
Assured Environments, II-3323,
    3325
Astellas, I-1342
Astoria FS&LA, II-3100
AstraZeneca, I-1337-1338
ASUS, I-1935, 1940, 1942, 1944,
    1946
AT&T, I-1235, II-2101-2102, 2575,
    2622, 2633, 2638, 2641, 2685,
    2698-2699, 2701, 3125, 3292,
    3307, 3311
AT&T Towers, II-2112
Atkins Nutritional Inc., I-700, 704
Atkinson Candy Co., I-692
Atlantic Express Transportation
    Corp., II-2505
Atlantic S.A., II-2829
Atlantic Southeast, II-2547, 2559
Atlas Copco, I-1844, 1907
Atlas Elektronik, II-2343
Atlas World Group, II-2514
Atmei, II-2139
Atria, I-312, 327
Atria Senior Living, II-3551
Au Bon Pain, II-2946
Audi, II-2201, 2206, 2209
August Storck A.G., I-660
Aunt Millie's Bakeries, I-619
Aurora Bank FSB, II-3041
Aurora Behavioral Health Care,
    II-3518
Aurora Casket Co., II-2479
Aurora Products Inc., I-872
AUS, I-1941
Australia and New Zealand Banking
    Group, II-3101
Authentic Specialty Foods Inc.,
    I-917
AuthorHouse, I-1219
Auto Club Group, II-3173
Auto-Owners Insurance Group,
    II-3173, 3182, 3208
Auto Plus/Uni-Select, II-2875
Autobell Car Wash, II-3420
Autodesk Inc., II-3348
Autoliv, II-2237-2239
Automatic Data Processing Inc.,
    II-3576

Automotive Components Holdings L.L.C., I-1634
AutoNation Inc., II-2871, 2874
AutoWorld Car Wash, II-3420
Autozone, II-2875
AV Cell Group, I-1133
Avalon Carpet Tile and Flooring, II-2908
Avalon Mortgage Corp., II-3102
AvalonBay Communities, I-249, 268
Avalotis Corp., I-283
Avastin, I-1352
Avatar Press Inc., I-1206
Avaya, II-2111
Avea, II-2619
Aventine Renewable Energy L.L.C., I-1524
Avery Dennison, I-1155, 1157, 1237, 1547
Avgol, I-1013
AVI Ltd., I-343
Avid Pro Audio, II-2434
Avis Budget Group, II-3408
Aviva PLC, II-3132, 3135
AVM, II-2117
AVMC Management Systems, I-118
Avnet, II-2748
Avon Products, I-1420, 1424, 1480, 1486, 1501, II-3021
AWG, II-2832
AXA Insurance, II-3135, 3139-3140, 3145
Axa S.A., II-3132
Axion Technology, II-2080
Axis Wake Research, II-2292
Ayalon, II-3142
Azek, I-1101, 1103
Azeri Brewery, I-751
Azimut Benetti Group, II-2291
Azkoyen, I-1976
B. Braun, II-2361, 2390
Baber's, II-3336
Bacardi & Co. Ltd., I-777-778, 786, 788-789
Bach Homes, I-264
Bachman Co., I-865, 878
BAE Systems PLC, II-2307, 2314, 2316, 2323
Bagels Forever, I-598
BAIC, II-2199
Baidu, II-2651
Baihe, II-2666
Bailey Nurseries Inc., I-108

Baird & Warner, II-3252-3254
Baixiang, I-412
Baja, I-1909
Bajaj Auto, II-2304
Baker & McKenzie, II-3531
Baker Concrete Construction, I-292
Baker Hughes Intl., I-206-207, 210, 1847-1850, 1852, 1855, 1924
Bakertriangle, I-285
Baki Sherab Zavodu, I-751
Baldor Electric Co., II-2006, 2395, 2399
Balfour Beatty U.S., I-270, 272, 274
Bali, I-1050
Ball Corp., I-38, 1745
Ball's, II-2832
Bally, II-2887
Bally Ribbon Mills, I-983
Bally Technologies, II-3479
Bally Total Fitness, II-3472
Balmar/HBP Inc., II-3319
The Bama Companies, I-615
Bancfirst, II-3069
Banco Popular de Puerto Rico, II-3072
Banco Santander Puerto Rico, II-3072
The Bancorp Bank, II-3089
Bancorpsouth Bank, II-3037, 3051, 3057
B&G Foods, I-481
B&H Photo & Video, II-2932
Bangkit, II-2462
Banglalink, II-2580
Bangor Savings Bank, II-3052
Bank Mutual, II-3084
The Bank Nightclub, II-2961
Bank of America NA, II-3037-3038, 3040, 3042-3043, 3045-3046, 3048-3049, 3052-3055, 3058, 3061-3066, 3069-3071, 3073-3074, 3076-3077, 3080-3082, 3086, 3091, 3093, 3096-3097, 3100, 3103-3104, 3106-3109, 3111-3112, 3114, 3120, 3122-3124, 3261
Bank of Commerce, II-3045
Bank of Hawaii, II-3044
Bank of Jackson Hole, II-3085
Bank of New York Mellon, II-3054, 3065
Bank of the America NA, II-3036
Bank of the Ozarks, II-3037
Bank of the West, II-3038-3039, 3048, 3060, 3064, 3085

Bankers Trust Co., II-3048
Bankplus, II-3057
Banktrust, II-3034
Bannatyne's Health Club, II-3473
Baosheng Group, I-1811
Baosteel, I-1701
Bar-S Foods Co., I-362, 364, 368
Barbara's Bakery, I-560
Barclays Bank Delaware, II-3041
Barclays Capital, II-3119, 3124
Barco, II-2407
Bardwell Linens, I-1077
Bargreen-Ellingson Inc., II-2754
Barilla, I-314, 317, 892, 896
Barnes & Noble, I-1933, II-2074, 2999, 3001
Barrick Gold, I-161
Barry Callebaut, I-722
Bartlett Tree Experts, I-140
Barton Malow Co., I-242, 274
BASE, II-2581
BASF, I-223, 1251, 1274, 1414, 1517, 1924
Bashas', II-2845
Basic Packaging, I-1394
Baskin-Robbins, II-2954
Bass Energy Company, I-212
Bass Shoe Outlet, II-2802
Batelco, II-2579
Batz, II-2251
Bauer Publishing Group, I-1207, 1209
Bausch & Lomb, II-2405-2406
Bawang, I-1449
Baxter International, II-2349, 2359, 2361, 2363
Bay Alarm Company, II-3384
Bay Valley Foods L.L.C., I-488
Bayer, I-51, 1251, 1326, 1534, 1541
Bayer Animal Health, I-1330
Bayer Consumer Health Division, I-1305
Bayer CropScience, I-1542
Bayliner, II-2290
BBA Aviation PLC, II-2274
BBDO Worldwide, II-3294-3295
BCD Travel, II-2568
BD, II-2390
BDA, I-43, II-3318
BDO USA, II-3575
B.E. Smith, II-3591
The Beachwood Organization, I-261
Beacon Power, II-2491
Beam, I-789

Bear Creek Country Kitchens, I-511
Bear Naked, I-560
Bear Stearns, II-3123
Beaulieu, I-15, 1002
Beaumont Health System, II-3520
Beauty China Holdings Ltd., I-1420-1421, 1461
Beaver Brook, I-174
The Beaver Excavating Co., I-297
Beaver Manufacturing Co., I-1520
Beaver Street Fisheries, I-841
Beazer Homes, I-246-247, 256, 258, 267
Bechtel Group Inc., I-275-276, 278-280
BeckRidge Hunting Preserrve, I-147
Becton Dickinson, I-31, 37, II-2330, 2361
Bed Bath & Beyond, II-2911, 2913
Beech-Nut Corp., I-450, 488
Beelen Sloopwerken BV, I-298
Beemiller, I-1795
Behr, II-2250
Beiersdorf, I-1379, 1458, 1480, 1486, 1500-1501, 1505
Beijing Huiyuan Beverage & Food Group Corp., I-496
Beijing Libeier, II-2386
Beijing No. Machine Tool, I-1876
Beijing Novartis, I-1326
Beijing Railway Administration, II-2498
Beijing XinCheng Sci-Tech Development Inc., II-2011
Beijing Yanjing Brewer, I-767
Beijing ZizhuPharm Co. Ltd., I-1343
Beijning Novartis Pharma Ltd., I-1340
Beingmate, I-1026
Bekins Holding Corp., II-2514
Belaruskali, I-227
Belcan, II-3341
Belcorp, I-1485
The Beldon Group, I-290
Belize Telemedia, II-2582
Belk, II-2792
Belkin, II-2116
Bell, II-2276-2277, 2585
Bell Partners Inc., II-3247
Bell Trans, II-2501
Belle International Holdings Ltd., I-1642, II-2898
Belle Tire Distributors, II-2877
Bellisio Foods Inc., I-345, 536

Bell's Brewery Inc., I-769
Belo Corp., II-2692
Bemis Co. Inc., I-36, 1623
Ben & Jerry's, I-422, II-2954
Bene Group, I-1122
Benesse Corp., II-3543
Benjamin Moore, II-2784
Beretta U.S.A., I-1795
Bergelectric Corp., I-284
Bergland Rottaler, I-306
Berkel & Co. Contractors Inc., I-297
Berkshire Hathaway, I-990, 1025, 1070, 1078
Berkshire Hathaway furniture division, II-2904, 2909
Berkshire Hathaway Insurance Group, II-3133, 3169, 3171, 3174-3175, 3178, 3180-3181, 3209, 3211, 3222, 3233, 3239
Bernecken's Nursery Inc., I-108
Berry Plastics Corp., I-1623-1624, 1634
Bertelsmann, I-1200, 1208
Besam, I-1773
Best Buy, II-2790, 2920, 2925, 2927-2929, 2932, 3010
BEST Contracting Services Inc., I-290
Best One Tire & Service, II-2877, 3018, 3415
Best Sweet Inc., I-697
Bestway, II-3336
bgc, II-3128
Bharti, II-2598
BHP Billiton, I-149, 152, 156, 166, 168, 170-171, 176, 234, 1717, 1719, 1722
Bianchi, I-1976
BiblioBazaar, I-1219
BIC Corp., I-1752, II-2456, 2458, 2462, 2465, 2491
BIC Graphic US + Norwood Promotional Products, I-44
BIC S.A., I-1751
Bien Air, II-2398
Biesse, I-1886
Big Lots, II-2913
Big Red, I-817
Big Rock, I-758
Biggby Coffee, II-2933
Bill & Melinda Gates Foundation, II-3553
Billabong, I-1031

Billion Fujian, I-1005
Bimbo Bakeries USA, I-597, 607, 609, 618-619, 626, 629, 636, 649
Bimbo S.A. de C.V., I-342
Bing, II-2643
Biocon, I-1353
BioFuel Energy, I-1524
Biolab, I-1394
Biomet, II-2381-2382, 2385
BioSpringer, I-911
Birds Eye Foods Inc., I-526, 535-536, 917
Birla, I-1294
Bisch Entertainment, II-3481
Bissell, II-2044
Bivitec, I-1845, 1894
BJ's, II-2806-2807, 2809, 2847
BKD L.L.P., II-3575
Black & Decker Corp., I-1885
BlackRock (iShares), II-3121
Blacks Leisure, II-2997
Blacksmith Brands Inc., I-698
Blandford Homes, I-262
Blariex Labs, I-1344
Blessey Marine Services, II-2528
Blistex, I-1458
Blitz USA, I-1630
Blockbuster, II-3448
Blommer, I-722
Bloom Energy, I-1765
Bloomberg L.P., II-3130, 3386
Blossman Gas Inc., II-3022
Blount, I-1882
Blue Bell Creameries Inc., I-414, 422
Blue Care Network of Michigan, II-3151
Blue Coat Systems, II-2119
Blue Cross and Blue Shield of Kansas City, II-3152
Blue Cross Blue Shield, II-3156
Blue Cross Blue Shield of Michigan, II-3151, 3153, 3161
Blue Diamond Growers, I-730
Blue Haven Pools & Spas, I-299
Blue Microphone, II-2097
Blue Moon, I-1400
Blue Shield of California, II-3153
BlueAnt Wireless, II-2096
BlueCross and Blue Shield of North Carolina, II-3163
BlueCross Blue Shield of South Carolina, II-3166
BlueFi Lending Corp., II-3102

BlueScope, I-1781

BM&FBOVESPA, II-3129

BMI, II-2548

BMW, II-2196, 2200-2201, 2206, 2209

BNA, I-1233

BNP Paribas, II-3086

BNSF Railway, II-2499

Bob Evans Farms Inc., I-371

Bob Evans Restaurants, II-2951

Bob's Discount Furniture, II-2904

BOC, II-3141

Bodek & Rhodes, I-44, 1081

Boehringer Ingelheim Pharmaceuticals, I-1307

Boehringer Ingelheim Vetmedica, I-1330

Boeing, II-2269, 2274, 2277, 2307-2308, 2310-2317, 3601

Boeing Employees Credit Union, II-3087

The Boelter Companies, II-2754

Bohler, I-1883

Boiron-Borneman Inc., I-698

Boise Cascade, I-1104

Boisha, I-1026

Bojangles, II-2950

BOKF NA, II-3064, 3069

Bollinger Shipyards Inc., II-3601

Bolton, I-455

Bombardier, II-2272, 2296, 2324-2325

Bon-Ton, II-2792

Bonduelle, I-455, 479

Bongrain, I-313

Bonnie Bell Inc., I-1460

Books-A-Million, II-2999

Boom! Studios, I-1206

Booth Creek Ski Holdings Inc., II-3499

Booz Allen Hamilton Inc., II-2317, 3601

Boppy Co., II-2485

Boral Ltd., I-1677

Border Bros. & Co., I-44

Borders, II-2999

Borealis/Borouge, I-1279-1280

Borregaard, I-1133

BorSod, I-761

Bosch, I-1784-1785, 1881, II-2015, 2225, 2235-2236, 2238-2239, 2244, 2247-2248, 2252-2253, 2255, 2260, 2262

Bose, II-2096

Boss, II-3028

Boston Beer Co., I-756, 769

Boston Capital, II-3248

Boston Celtics, II-3483

Boston Financial Investment Management L.P., II-3248

Boston Public Library, II-3538-3539

Boston Red Sox, II-3482

Boston Scientific Corp., II-2351, 2358, 2360-2361, 2389

Botega Veneta, II-2887

Boulevard Brewing Co., I-769

Bouygues, I-275-276, II-2592

BOWA Builders, I-245

Boy Scouts of America, II-3552

Boyne USA Resorts, II-3499

Boys & Girls Clubs of America, II-3552

BP Castrol Industrial, I-1594

BP North America, II-2796

BP PLC, I-195, 1522, 1581, 1588, 1590-1591, 1593, II-2797, 2878

BPI, II-2737

B.R. Funsten & Co., II-2737

Brady Corp., II-2478

Brady (SPC), I-1854

Branch Banking & Trust Co., II-3034, 3042-3043, 3050, 3053, 3066, 3074, 3076, 3080, 3083

Brandenburg Industrial Services Co., I-298

Brano, II-2251

Braskem Group, I-1274, 1279-1280

Brassler, II-2398

Brau Union (Heineken), I-761

Braum's Ice Cream & Dairy Stores, II-2954

Brazos Group, II-3099

Bremer Bank NA, II-3056, 3067

Brent Scarborough & Co., I-281

Brentwood Originals, I-1071

Breyers Yogurt Co., I-441

Brick Brewing, I-758

Brickman Group, I-140, II-2729

Bric's, I-1647

Bridge Terminal Transport, II-2509

Bridgestone Americas Inc., I-1287

Bridgestone Bandag Tire Solutions L.L.C., II-3415

Bridgestone Corp., I-1285, 1289, 1606

Bridgestone/Firestone, I-1599, 1605

Bright Food Group Co. Ltd., I-339

Bright Horizons Family Solutions, II-3548

Bright House Networks L.L.C., II-2701

BrightFood, I-384, 454, 922

Brightside Academy Inc., II-3548

Brink's, II-3381

Bristol-Myers Squibb, I-1326

Britannia Industries Ltd., I-341

British American Tobacco PLC, I-938-941, 943-950, 952, 957, 959-964

Broadcom, II-2146

The Brock Group, I-283

Broder Bros. Co., I-1081

Bronco Wine Company, I-779

Brookbinder Foods, I-466

Brookdale Senior Living, II-3549, 3551

Brookfield Homes, I-258

Brooks Rehabilitation, II-3519

Brookshire Brothers (Tobacco Barn), II-3024

Brookstone, II-2786

Brose, I-1127, II-2259

Brother, I-1956, 1959-1964, II-2046

Broward Health, II-3516

Brown-Forman Corp., I-787

Brown Jordan, I-28

Brown Shoe Company, II-2903

Brownstein, Hyatt et al, II-3564

Bruegger's Bagel Bakery, II-2946

Bruker, II-2330

Brunswick Marine Group, II-2288-2289, 2291, 3459, 3594

Brush HMA, II-2008

Brynwood Partners, I-704

BSH, II-2042

BSNL, II-2598

B.T. Mancini Co. Inc., I-291

BTC, II-2583

BTR New Materials, II-2153

Buckeye, I-1013, 1133-1134

Buckeye Feed Mills, I-586

Buddy's Home Furnishings, II-3336

Buena Vista, II-3441

Buffalo, II-2117

Buffalo Dental, II-2395

Buffalo Wild Wings Grill & Bar, II-2948-2949

Buffalo Wings & Rings, II-2949

Bug Out Service, II-3326

Bull, I-1931

Bumble Bee Foods, I-841

Bunge Ltd., II-2520

Bupa, II-3141

Burberry Group, I-1651, II-2887

Burckhardt, I-1907

Burger King, II-2937-2938, 2947, 2952, 2957

Burlington Coat Factory, II-2884, 2897

Burlington (Conoco), I-199

Burns & McDonnell, I-269, II-3569

Burson-Marsteller, II-3594

Burton's Foods, I-637

Burts Bees, I-1458

Bush Brothers, I-470

Bushmaster Firearms, I-1795

Butler Home Products Co., II-2473

Butterball L.L.C., I-129

Buzz Unicem, I-1670

BWP Distributors Inc., II-2875

C.A. Lindman Cos., I-287

CA Technologies, II-3347

Cablevision, II-2634, 2696, 2699-2701

Cabot Creamery, I-402, 1553

Cadbury PLC, I-340-344, 661, 724

Cadum, I-1562

Caesars Entertainment Corp., II-3491

Cafection, I-846

Cafejo, I-846

CAL International, II-3335

Cal-Maine Foods Inc., I-125, 898

Calbee, I-884

Calgary Flames, II-3486

Calgon Carbon, I-1265

Calico Laboratories Inc., I-1460

California Dairies Inc., I-430

California Drywall Co., I-285

California Earthquake Authority, II-3185-3186

California Endowment, II-3553

California Mortgage Consultants, II-3102

California Pizza Kitchen, II-2956

California Pools, I-299

California Public Employee, II-3237

California State Auto Group, II-3195

California State Compensation Insurance Fund, II-3226

California Water Service Corp., II-2721, 2730

Calsonic Kansei, II-2246, 2249

Caltex, I-1590, II-2797

Cam-West Development, I-266

Camden National Bank, II-3052

Camden Property Trust, II-3247

Cameco, I-171

Camelbak Products L.L.C., I-1080

Cameron, I-211, 1801, 1851

Camino Real Foods Inc., I-541

Campari Milano SpA David, I-777

The Campbell Companies, I-290

Campbell Ewald, II-2525

Campbell Soup Co., I-338, 452, 466-468, 491, 520

Campofrio Foods, I-313, 322-323, 326

Canada Bread, Frozen Bakery, I-615

Canada Pension, II-3237

Canada Safeway, II-2820

Canadian National Railway, II-2499

Canadian Pacific, II-2499

Canadian Solar, I-1769

Canal Barge Company Inc., II-2528

C&A, I-1019

C&S Wholesale Grocers, II-2812

Candyrific, I-690

Canon, I-1956, 1959-1964, 1966, 1968, II-2413, 2415, 3264

Cape Cod Potato Chip, I-876

Capella Healthcare, II-3515

Capgemini, II-3373

Capital One Financial Corp., II-3091, 3307

Capital One NA, II-3051, 3053, 3065, 3077, 3080, 3097

Capital Senior Living, II-3551

Capitol Federal Savings Bank, II-3049

Capstone, I-1822

Captain D's, II-2959

CARBO, I-222

Cardinal Health, I-1656, II-2355, 2361, 2391, 2393

CareFusion Corp., II-2368

Cargill, I-118, 351, 358, 555, 646, 722, 911, 1348, 1568-1569, 1571, II-2520

Cargill Animal Nutrition, I-595

Cargill Meat Solutions, I-357

Cargill North America Meats, I-360

Cargill Value Added Meats, I-129

Cargolux, II-2560

Cargotec/Kalmar, I-1864

Caribou Coffee, II-2933

Carl Buddig & Co., I-368

Carl Zeiss, II-2410

Carlisle Companies Inc., I-1287, 1585

Carlisle Development Group, I-268

Carlsberg, I-33, 311-312, 319, 321, 328, 751, 760, 764, 766-767

Carlson Wagonlit Travel, II-2568

Carma Labs, I-1458

CarMax Inc., II-2873-2874

Carmeuse Lime Inc., I-1685

Carmike, II-3445

Carnegie Mellon, II-3533

Carnival, II-2531-2532

Carolina Panthers, II-3485

Carolina Skiff, II-2290

Carolinas HealthCare System, II-3516

Carolinas Rehabilitation, II-3519

Carpenter, I-1072-1073, 1631

Carpet Exchange/GSO Investments, II-2908

Carrefour S.A., II-2794, 2803, 2829

Carriage, II-3260, 3285

Carrizo Oil & Gas, I-199

Carr's, I-639

Carter Bank & Trust, II-3080

Carter's Inc., I-1021, 1025, II-2893

Carter's Outlets, II-2802

The Carthage System, I-118

Cartier, II-3004-3005

Cartiera Lucchese Group, I-1139

Casa Ley S.A. de C.V., II-2805, 2837

Cascades, I-1140

Case Design/Remodeling, I-245

Case Handyman and Remodeling Services L.L.C., II-3431

Case IH, I-1832

Casella Waste Systems Inc., II-2727

Casey's General Stores Inc., II-2796

Cash America, II-2992

Casio, II-2415

Cassens Transport, II-2515

Cassidy & Associates, II-3564

Castle & Cooke Cold Storage, II-2521

Castle & Cooke Mortgage L.L.C., II-3103

Castle Key Indemnity Co., II-3224

Castle Key Insurance Co., II-3224

Castrol, I-1590

Casual Male, II-2883

Catan, II-2439

Caterpillar, I-1818, 1826, 1831, 1840, 1842, 1844, II-2007

Cathay Pacific Airways, II-2560

Cathay Pacific Catering Services, II-2936
Catholic Charities USA, II-3552
Catholic Health East, II-3514
Catholic Health Initiatives, II-3514
Catholic Health Partners, II-3514
Catholic Healthcare West, II-3514
Catoca, I-234
Catseye Pest Control, II-3325
Cattloica, II-3143
Cavalier, I-1001
Cavendish Farms Corp., I-346
Caviness Beef Packers Ltd., I-355
CB Richard Ellis Group, II-3244, 3257
CBA Bulgaria, II-2819
CBC National Bank, II-3110
CBIZ/Mayer Hoffman McCann, II-3575
CBL & Associates Properties, II-3244-3245
CBO Glass Inc., I-295
CBS Corp., II-2687, 2692-2694, 3296
CBS Outdoor, II-3297
CBS Radio, II-2691
CC Media Holdings Inc., II-3296
CCA Global Partners, II-2782
CCCS, II-2573
CCI/CoakleyTech, II-3319
CCL Industries, I-1237
CCLC Inc., II-3548
CCTV Home Shopping, II-3018
CCV, II-2994
CDI, II-3341
CDM, II-3569
CDW Corp., II-2925, 3016
Ce De Candy Inc., I-690
Cebeco, I-329
CEC Entertainment Inc., II-3478
Ceceab, I-587
Cecel Concrete Construction, I-292
Cedar Fair Entertainment Company, II-3481
Cedar's Mediterranean Foods, I-427
Cederroth, I-1379
Cegedim, II-3581
Cejka Search, II-3591
Celanese, I-1522, 1530
Celcom, II-2603
Celgard, II-2154
Cell C, II-2613
Ceme, I-1975

Cemex, I-215, 1670, 1672, 1674, 1676
Cengage Learning, I-1200, 1217, 1227-1228
Cenlar, II-3112
Cenova, II-2729
Centare Foods Inc., I-427
Centennial Bank, II-3037
Center Fresh Egg Group, I-125
Centerline Capital Group, II-3248
Centerline Homes, I-259
CentiMark Corp., I-290
Central Bank Inc., II-3083
Central Christian Church, II-3566
Central Garden & Pet, I-21, 1330, 1541
Central Glass Co., I-1655
Central Pacific Bank, II-3044
Central Parking Corp., II-3411
Central Provident Fund, II-3237
Central Texas Veterans Healthcare System, II-3517
Central Trust & Bank Co., II-3050
Centrica PLC, II-2715
Centro Properties Group, II-3244-3245
Centrotherm, I-1764, 1767
Century 21, II-3252-3254
Century Communities, I-253
CenturyLink, II-2622, 2633, 2638
Cenveo Inc., I-1197
CEP America, II-3527
Ceradyne, I-1680
Cereal Partners Worldwide S.A., I-561, 604
Cerestar, I-646
Ceridian, II-3576
CertainTeed, I-1585
CEVA Logistics, II-2506
CF Industries, I-1532
C.F. Sauer, I-514
CFE (Comision Federal de Electricided), II-2713
CFM International, II-2280
CFMI, I-1820
CGG Veritas, I-208
CGU Insurance, II-3134
C.H. Robinson Worldwide, II-2506
CH2M Hill Companies, II-2721, 3569, 3571
Chalco, I-176, 1719, 1722
Challenge Dairy Products, I-388
Challenger, II-2271
Chang'an, II-2199

Changlin, I-1841
Changzhou Xinhuachang International Containers, I-1779
Charles Schwab Bank, II-3061, 3131
Charming Shoppes Inc., II-2885
Charms Inc., I-681
Charter Communications, II-2633, 2696, 2699, 2701
Chartis, II-3133, 3135, 3186
Chase, II-3041, 3095-3097, 3100, 3104, 3106-3109, 3111
Chattem Inc., I-1316, 1435, 1470, 1500
Chattow Limited, I-690
Cheap Tobacco, II-3024
Check Point, II-3350
The Cheesecake Factory, II-2948
The Chef in Black, I-924
Chem-Dry, II-3280
Chemetall, I-1272
Chemfine, I-1539
Chemical Lime Company, I-1685
Chemtool, I-1594
ChemTrix, I-1891
Chengdu Rongguang Carbon, II-2011
Cherokee Group, I-23
Chesapeake Energy, I-199
Chesebrough-Pond's USA, I-1500
Chevron Corp., I-1581, 1591, 1593, II-2796, 2878
Chevron Phillips, I-1277-1279
CHF Industries, I-1073
Chiaus, I-1172
Chicago Blackhawks, II-3486
Chicago Bulls, II-3483
Chicago Cubs, II-3482
Chicago Transit Authority, II-2502
Chick-fil-A, II-2950, 2957
Child Development Schools, II-3548
Children of America, II-3548
Children's Choice Learning Centers Inc., II-3548
Children's Place Retail Stores Inc., II-2893
Chili's Grill & Bar, II-2948
China Airlines, II-2560
China Carbon Graphite Group, II-2011
China Communications Construction Group, I-276
China Continent, II-3136, 3223
China Foods Ltd., I-310

China Gerui Advanced Materials
　Group, I-1711
China Guardian, II-3555
China International Marine Contain-
　ers, I-1779
China JDC, I-177
China Lians, I-1629
China Life P&C, II-3136, 3223
China Metallurgical Group, I-276
China Mobile, II-2587, 2596, 2621
China Molybdenum, I-177
China National Offshore Oil Corp.,
　I-202, 732, 1580
China National Petroleum Corp.,
　I-202, 1289, 1580-1581
China National Salt Industry, I-1571
China National Tobacco Corp., I-952
China Pacific, II-3223
China Railway Construction Corp.,
　I-276
China Railway Group, I-276
China Resources Breweries, I-310
China Resources Enterprise Ltd.,
　I-759, 767
China Seven Star, II-3018
China Shipping Group, II-2529
China Southern Glass Holding Co.
　Ltd., I-1653
China Southern Power Grid, II-2707,
　2716
China State Construction & Engi-
　neering, I-276
China Telecom, II-2587, 2698
China Tin Group, I-174
China Tobacco Anhui Industry
　Group, I-970
China Tobacco Chuanyu Industry
　Group, I-970
China Tobacco Hubei, I-958, 970
China Tobacco Hunan Industrial Co.
　Ltd., I-958
China Unicom, II-2587
China United, II-3136, 3223
Chinburg Builders, I-248
Chipotle, II-2955
Chiquita, I-306, 479, 913
CHJ, II-3006
Chloride Power, II-2004
Chobani, I-439
Chocoladerfabriken Lindt & Sprüng-
　li, I-660
Chow Sang Sang, II-3004, 3006
Chow Tai Fook, II-3004, 3006
Christian Dior, I-1420, 1651

Christie, II-2407
Christie's, II-3555
Christus Health, II-3514
Chrysler Group L.L.C., II-2196,
　2198, 2872, 3292, 3311
CHS, II-2879, 3022
Chubb & Son Inc. Group, II-3133,
　3192
Chubu Electric Power Company,
　II-2712
Chuck E. Cheese's, II-2956
Chuquicamata (Codelco), I-153
Church & Dwight Co., I-1373-1374,
　1432, 1621
Church's Chicken, II-2950
Ciba Vision, II-2405-2406, 2410
Cichin, I-1853
CiCi's Pizza, II-2956
Cigna Corp., II-3153
Cimos, II-2251, 2254
Cincinnati Financial Group,
　II-3176, 3184
Cincinnati Insurance Cos., II-3219
CineCo (Cine Columbia), II-3444
Cinemark, II-3445
Cines Unidos, II-3444
Cinex (Venezuela), II-3444
Cintar Landscape Management,
　II-2729
Cintas Corp., I-43, II-3277
Cipla, I-1341
Circle K, II-2796, 2798, 3263
Cisco Systems, II-2111, 2119-2120
CIT, II-3099, 3125
Citadel, II-2687
CITGO Petroleum Corp., II-2796,
　2879
Citi, II-3089, 3120
Citi Assurance Services Group,
　II-3148
Citibank NA, II-3038, 3040, 3042,
　3046, 3061, 3065, 3075
Citigroup, II-3091, 3093, 3119,
　3122, 3124, 3261
CitiMortgage Inc., II-3100, 3104-
　3107, 3109
Citizens Bank, II-3055
Citizens Bank of Pennsylvania,
　II-3071
Citizens National Bank of Meridian,
　II-3057
Citizens Property Insurance Corp.,
　II-3196, 3224
Citrus World Inc., I-500

City CarShare, II-3391
City Market, II-2857
City National Bank, II-3038
City National Bank of West Virginia,
　II-3083
Citycell, II-2580
C.J. Hughes Construction Co. Inc.,
　I-281
Claire's Stores Inc., II-3014
Clal, II-3142
CLARCOR, I-1916
Clarian Health Partners, II-3517
Clarion, II-2255
Clarity, II-2101-2102
Clark Associates, II-2754
Clark Builders Group, I-268
Clark Group, I-272
Clark Pest Control, II-3324
Claro, II-2577, 2586, 2591, 2594-
　2595, 2611-2612
Classic Party Rentals, II-3332
Clean Harbors, II-2727
Clear Channel, II-2687, 2691
Clear Channel U.K., II-3297
Clearview Homes, I-254
Clearwater, I-1145
Clif Bar & Co., I-679, 700, 704-705
Cliffs Natural Resources, I-1715
Cloetta Fazer A.B., I-663, 675
Clorox Co., I-518, 924, 1385, 1918,
　II-2473
Cloud Peak Energy Inc., I-185
Clougherty Packaging Co. Inc., I-371
Clover Ltd., I-343
Cloverdale/Rodda, II-2784
Club Car, II-2326
CMA CGM Group, II-2527, 2536
CMC, II-2207
CMH Space Flooring, II-2737
CMIT Solutions, II-3379
CMPC S.A., I-1141
CNA Insurance, II-3133, 3209, 3211,
　3214, 3233
CNBM, I-1671
CNH Global N.V., I-1831
CNP, I-307
CNT (Telsur), II-2636
Coach Inc., I-1651, II-2503, 2887,
　3014
Coast Mountain Bus Co., II-2502
Coates Hire Ltd., II-3331
Coborn's/Little Duke's, II-2827
Coby, II-2080

Coca-Cola Co., I-33, 305, 307-308, 311, 314-315, 320-321, 326, 329, 331, 496, 795, 798, 802-804, 811, 817-826, 934, II-3310

Cochlear, II-2378

Coctree, I-1026

Codan, II-3137

Codelco, I-152-153, 177, 1717

Cody Pools Inc., I-299

COFCO, I-716

The Coffee Beanery, II-2933

Cogent, II-2638

Cohen's Fashion Optical, II-3027

CoinMach Corp., II-3278

Coinstar, II-3448

Coit Services Inc., II-3280

Cold Stone Creamery, II-2954

Coldwell Banker, II-3253-3254

Coldwell Banker Peter Berringer, II-3256

Coldwell Banker Real Estate, II-3255

Coldwell Consumer Health, I-1344

Coles Express, II-2797

Colgate-Palmolive Co., I-586, 1373, 1379, 1384-1385, 1401, 1432, 1471-1472, 1475, 1484, 1486-1487, II-2475

Collahuasi (Anglo American/Xstrata), I-153

Collective Brands, II-2897, 2903

The College Board, I-1228

College Loan Corp., II-3099

Collegiate Licensing Co., I-23

Colomer USA, I-1456

ColorNet/RockVille Printing & Graphics, II-3319

Colors on Parade, II-3412

Colt's Manufacturing, I-1795

Columbia, I-1035, II-2450

Columbia Petro, I-1587

Columbia State Bank, II-3081

Columbia University, II-3538

Columbian, I-1553

Comair, II-2546

Combe Inc., I-1435-1436

Comcast Corp., II-2633, 2638, 2641, 2682, 2692, 2694, 2696, 2699, 2701, 3292, 3307, 3311

Comcel, II-2588

Comerica Bank, II-3055, 3089

Comess Group SL, II-2938

Comex/Pro Paint Inc., II-2784

Comfort Solutions, I-1120

Commerce Bank, II-3049, 3058

Commercial Contracting Group, I-242

Commercial Value, II-3140

Commonwealth Bank, II-3293

Commonwealth Bank of Australia, II-3101

Commonwealth Edison Co., II-2720

Commonwealth Government, II-3293

Commonwealth Worldwide Chauffered Transportation, II-2501

Communato, II-3391

Community Blood Center & Community Tissue Services, II-3526

Community Coffee Co. Inc., I-849, 858

Community Education Centers, II-3595

Community Foundation for Greater Atlanta, II-3553

Community Health Systems, II-3515

Community National Bank, II-3079

Community Trust Bank Inc., II-3050-3051

Compagnie de Saint-Gobain, I-1690

Compaigne Des Alpes, II-3481

Compal, II-1992

Compañia Arrocera Covadonga S.A. de C.V., I-569

Compass Bank, II-3034, 3036, 3039, 3064, 3077

Compass Group, II-2939

Compass Minerals, I-1567-1569, 1571

Complete Production Services, I-212

Computer Associates, II-3360

Computer Medics of America, II-3379

Computer Sciences Corp., II-3601

Computer Troubleshooters, II-3379

comScore Inc., II-3580

Con-Way Freight, II-2512

CONAFAB, I-594

ConAgra Foods Inc., I-305, 338, 345-346, 351, 364, 391-392, 395, 453, 456, 468, 470, 476, 520, 535-536, 555, 734, 741, 880, 884, 906, 918

Concord Confections Inc., I-725

Concord Foods, I-924

Condé Nast Publications Group, I-1209

Conmed, I-1131

Connect by Hertz, II-3391

Connecticut (DOT/N.Y. MTA), II-2295

Connex United Processor's Group, I-587

ConocoPhillips Inc., I-1581, II-2796, 3125

ConocoPhillips Lube Shop, II-3422

Conros Corp., I-1161

Conservas La Costeña S.A. de C.V., I-342, 506, 522, 917

Conserverie Morbihannaise, I-587

Conso International Corp., I-983

CONSOL Energy Inc., I-185

Consolidated Container Co. L.L.C., I-1632

Consolidated Edison Co.-NY Inc., II-2720

Consolidated Fastfrate Inc., II-2509

Consolidated Murchison, I-174

Consorzio Granlatte, I-317

Constellation Wines, I-779

Contains Group, II-2508

Contech, I-41

Contessa Premium Foods, I-535

Continental, I-1285, 1287, 1599, 1606, II-2224-2225, 2235-2239, 2244, 2247-2248, 2252-2253, 2255-2256, 2260, 2262

Continental Automotive Systems, II-2241

Continental Express Inc., II-2510

Continental Insurance Co., II-3215

Continental Tire, I-1605

Continentale Nutrition S.A., I-587

Contour Designs, I-4

Controladora Comercial Mexicana S.A. de C.V., II-2791, 2805, 2837

Convergys Corp., II-3401

Converse, I-1608

Converteam, II-1996, 2008

Cook-Illinois Corp., II-2505

Cook's Pest Control, II-3323-3324

Cookson Group, I-1677, 1680

Coop de Québec, I-309

Coop Schweiz, I-328

Cooper-Standard Automotive, I-1285, 1287

Cooper Tire & Rubber Co., I-1287, 1605-1606

Cooper Vision, II-2406, 2410

Cooperative Resources International, I-139

Coopers Brewery, I-757

CooperVision, II-2405

CoorsTek, I-1680

COP Jednote, II-2858

Copaxone, I-1352

Copy Central, II-3319

Cordis Corp., II-2358

CORE Construction Group, I-274

Corfuerte S.A. de C.V., I-522

Corman, I-1178

Corn Products International, I-646, 1523

Corner Bakery Cafe, II-2946

Correct Craft, II-2292

Corrections Corporation of America, II-3595

Corsair Memory, II-2137

Corsicana, I-1120

Cortelco Kellogg, II-2101

Cosco, I-1813, II-2527, 2536

Coship, II-2108

COSL, I-203

Costco, II-2626, 2790, 2806-2807, 2809, 2812, 2814-2815, 2818, 2820-2821, 2824, 2826, 2828, 2830, 2834, 2836, 2838, 2843, 2845, 2852-2854, 2862, 2911, 2925, 2929, 3005, 3010, 3027, 3387

Cotsworld Outdoor, II-2997

Cott Corp., I-817, 826

Cotton Buds Co., I-1182

Couer d'Alene, I-166

Countrywide Financial, II-3123, 3197

Coupang, II-2628

Courier Corp., I-1229

Covalent, II-2149

Covance Inc., II-3577, 3587

Covanta Energy Corp., II-2727

Coventry Health, II-3152-3153

Coveright, I-1625

Coverteam, I-1819

Coverys, II-3233

Covidien, I-1131, 1347, II-2361, 2363, 2389-2390

Cox Communications, II-2633, 2638, 2701

Cox Enterprises Inc., I-1203, II-2682, 2696

Cox Radio Inc., II-2691

CPI Corp., II-2121, 3282

CPIC, II-3136

C.R. England, II-2513

Cracker Barrel Old Country Store, II-2951

Crane, I-48, 846, 1801, 1976

Crate & Barrel, II-2904

Cray Inc., I-1931

Crayola, I-1547, II-2458

CRC, I-1671

CRE, II-2794

CreateSpace, I-1219

Creative Artists Agency, II-3456, 3460

Creative Bath Products, I-1068, 1075

Creative Labs, II-2097

Credit Acceptance, II-3097

Credit Suisse, II-3086, 3119-3120, 3122-3124

Creditex, II-3128

Creekstone Farms Premium Beef, I-355

Crème de la Crème, II-3548

Cremonini, I-317

Crescent Hotels & Resorts, II-3271

Crest Foods, II-2841

Crest Services, II-3425

Crested Butte Mountain Resort Inc., II-3499

Crete Carrier Corp., II-2513

CRH PLC, I-21, 215, 219, 1676, 1684, 1781, II-2257, 2259

Critter Control, II-3325

CRL, II-3577

Crompton Greaves, I-1909

Cronos Group, II-3335

Croscill Home, I-1068

Crosley, II-2101

Cross Plus, I-1018

Crossville, I-1679

Crosswinds Communities, I-254

Crowe Horwath, II-3575

Crown, I-1745, 1788

Crown Castle, II-2112

Crown Corr Inc., I-291

Crown Equipment Corp., I-1867

Crown Imports, I-756

Crown Luggage, I-1645-1646

CRST International, II-2513

Crucial Technology, II-2137

Crunch Pak, I-913

Crystal Farms, I-403-404

Crystal Geyser Water Co., I-795, 802

C's lshishara, II-2493

CSAV Group, II-2527, 2573

CSC, II-3374-3375

CSC Naturals and Organics, I-466, 468

CSCL, II-2527

CSG Holding, I-1661

CSL Ltd., II-3526

CSL New World Mobility, II-2596

CSL Plasma, II-2359

CSM Bakery Supplies North America, I-615

CSN Stores, II-2912, 3017

CSS Industries, I-1244

CSX Transportation, II-2499

CTT, I-168

Cub Food, II-2839

Cuddy Group, I-298

Cuisinart, II-2040

Cummins Inc., I-1826, 1916, II-2007-2008, 2241

Cumulus Media, II-2691

Cuna Mutual Group, II-3148

Curimbaba, I-222

Curvation Hosiery, I-985

Curves International Inc., II-3472

CVC Capital, I-308

CVS, II-2964-2972, 2975-2985, 3387

CVS Caremark, II-2626, 2790, 2987-2988

Cyber Acoustics, II-2097

Cybex International, II-2445

Cymax Stores, II-2912

D-Link, II-2116-2118, 2120

Dacotah Bank, II-3075

Dadida, I-1022

Dad's Products Co., I-582, 584

Dahn Corp., II-2522

Dai-Ichi Seiko, I-1895

Dai Nippon Printing Co. Ltd., I-1236

Daifuku Co. Ltd., I-1870

Daihatsu, II-2204

Daiichi Sankyo, I-1342

Daimler Chrysler, II-2196, 2200

Dairen Chemical, I-1530

Dairy Crest, I-390

Dairy Farmers of America Inc., I-403, 430

Dairy Mart, II-2796

Dairy Queen, II-2954

Dairybelle Pty. Ltd., I-343

Dairylea Cooperative Inc., I-430

Daito-Osin Healthcare Manufacturing Co. Ltd., II-2453

Daiwa House, I-276

Dakota Growers Pasta Co., I-896
Daktronics Inc., II-2478
Dal-Tile, I-48, II-2782
Dale and Thomas Popcorn, I-880
Dalian Machine Tool Group, I-1876-1877
Dallas Cowboys, II-3485
Dallas Mavericks, II-3483
Dana Holding Corp., II-2241
Danaher, II-2330
Danfoss, II-1996
Danisco, I-911
Danish Crown, I-311, 314
Dannon Co., I-441
Danone, I-307, 310, 313, 439, 442-444, 461, 823, 922
Dapai, I-1646
Dare Foods Ltd., I-639
Dark Horse Comics, I-1206
Darrell Lea, I-683
Dart Container, I-1151-1152
Dassault Systems, II-2272, 3348
Datev, I-1233
Daum, II-2655
Dauphin, I-1122
Dav El Chauffered Transportation, II-2501
Dave & Busters Holdings Inc., II-3478
The Davey Tree Expert Co., I-140
David Lloyd/Next Gen./Harbour Club, II-3473
David's Bridal, II-2888
DaVita, II-3523
Davy Roll Company, I-1696
Dawn Food Products Inc., I-615
Daybreak Foods, I-125
DaYi, I-930
DB Schenker Logistics, II-2506
DBRS, II-3316
DC Comics, I-1206
DCI Cheese/Fairmount Food Group, I-427
DDB Worldwide, II-3294-3295
De Beers, I-234
De Cecco, I-888, 892
De Rigo, II-2409
Dean Foods Co., I-305, 383
DeBruycker Charolais, I-112
Decathalon, II-2997
DeCoster Egg Farms & Affiliates, I-125
Dee Brown Inc., I-286-287
Dee Cramer Inc., I-291

Deep Ocean Engineering, II-2346
Deere & Co., I-1831-1832, 1836, 1840, II-2326
Del Monte Foods, I-418, 452-453, 456-457, 473, 475-477, 578, 582, 584, 591, 913
Del Sol Food Co., I-518
Del Taco, II-2955
Delaware North, II-2939
Delaware River Port Authority of Pennsylvania and New Jersey, II-2572
Delhaize America, II-2812
Dell Inc., I-1931, 1935, 1937-1946, 1951, 1955, II-2147, 2925, 2928, 3016, 3370
Dell Services, II-3592
Deloitte & Touche, II-3286, 3574-3575
Deloitte Consulting, II-3592
Delphi, II-2238, 2241, 2244-2246, 2250, 2260, 2262
Delsey, I-1647, 1649
Delta Air Lines, II-2540-2542, 2544-2547, 2549-2550, 2552-2555, 2559
Delta Maxi, II-2819
Delta Rice SAE, I-340
Delta Sonic, II-3420
Demag, I-1865
Demaria Building Company Inc., I-242
Demet's Candy Company, I-713, 867
DeMoulas/Market Basket, II-2817
Denny's, II-2951
Denso, II-2237-2239, 2241, 2244-2246, 2250, 2255-2256, 2260, 2262
Dentsply, II-2396, 2401
Dentsu, II-3295
Denver Broncos, II-3485
Depai, I-1645
Derivados de Leche La Esmeralda S.A. de C.V., I-401
Dermatic, I-1870
Derrel's Mini Storage Inc., II-2522
Desan Trading, I-337
Descente, I-1031
Deschutes Brewery, I-769
Designer Shoe Warehouse, II-2903
Desoto Mills, I-988
Detecsa, I-298
Detroit Medical Center, II-3520
Detroit Red Wings, II-3486
Detroit Salt, I-1569
Detroit Tigers, II-3482

Deutsche Bank, II-3086, 3119-3120, 3122, 3124, 3129
Deutsche Bank Trading Co. Americas, II-3065
Developers Diversified Realty, II-3244-3245
Developus, I-1456
Devereux, II-3518
Devilbiss, II-2356-2357
Devon Energy, I-199
Devrian Global Industries, II-2465
Dewson Construction Co., I-245
DexOne, I-1235
DFM, II-2199
DFV Wines, I-779
DHL, II-2506, 2516-2519, 2669
Diageo PLC, I-33, 316, 330, 779, 786-789
The Dial Corp., I-1374, 1432
Diamond Foods Inc., I-730, 872, 884
Diamond Offshore, I-203
Diamond Vogel, II-2784
Dickies, I-1035
Dick's Sporting Goods, II-2996
Diebold Inc., I-1969
Dierbergs, II-2850
DiGi, II-2603
Digicel El Salvador, II-2591
Digicel Honduras, II-2595
Digicel Panama, II-2611
Digitas, II-3318
Digitel, II-2620
Digrans S.A. de C.V., I-569
Dimantis Masoutis S.A., II-2829
Dimeo Construction Co., I-248
Diplomat, I-1645
DirecTV, II-2699-2702
Discera, II-2148
Discount Beverage Outlet, II-2796
Discount Smoke Shops, II-3024
Discount Tire Co., II-2877
Discover, II-3090
Discover Bank, II-3041
Discovery Communications, II-2694
Discovery Foods, I-536
DISH Network, II-2699, 2701-2702
Disney Consumer Products, I-23
Disney Cruise Line, II-2531-2532
Divatex, I-1073, 1079
Diverse Talent Group, II-3456
Diversey, I-1370
Diversified Drilling Corp., I-293
Diversified Search Odgers Berndtson, II-3591

The Dixie Group, I-15, 1002, II-2849

Dixon Ticonderoga, II-2465

DKC, II-3593

DL Evans Bank, II-3045

DLA Piper, II-3531

Do-It-Best, II-2786

Doane Pet Care Enterprises Inc., I-587

Doctor's Associates, II-2952

Doctors Co. Group, II-3209-3211, 3233

Dodson Bros. Exterminating Co., II-3325-3326

Doe Run, I-156

DoggyMan, II-2493

Dogswell L.L.C., I-578

Dole Foods Co., I-457, 479, 914, 926

Dollar General, II-2801, 2884, 2911

Dollar Thrifty Automotive Group, II-3408

Dollar Tree, II-2801

Domino's Pizza, II-2937, 2940, 2952, 2956-2957

Domoclean, I-1574

Domsjô, I-1133

Don Juan, I-282

Don Quijote Food, II-2830

Donaldson Co., I-1916

Dong Fang, II-3335

Dongguan Hsu Fu-Chin Food Co. Ltd., I-611

Dongguan Huaja Food Co. Ltd., I-611

Dongguan Humen Ri Long, I-892

Donlen, II-3409

Dons International, I-985

Doosan, I-1840, 1842, 1864

Doral Bank, II-3072

Dorel Industries, II-2486

Dorel Juvenile Group, II-2485

Doris Duke Charitable Foundation, II-3553

Dorma, I-1773

Double Coin Holdings Ltd., I-1604

Douglass Colony Group, I-290

Dovenmuehle Mortgage, II-3112

Dow Chemical, I-51, 1251, 1254, 1277-1279, 1348, 1530, 1924

Dow Corning, I-1549

Dow Jones, II-3130

Downlite, I-1076, 1078

DP Master, I-1713

DP World, II-2536

DPMS, I-1795

D.R. Horton, I-246, 249-253, 255, 257, 259-262, 264-267

Dr. Krauss & Dr. Beckmann, I-1409-1410

Dr. Pepper Snapple Group, I-795, 811, 817, 826, 934

Draeger, II-2366, 2379

DraftFCB, II-3294, 3317-3318

Dream Products L.L.C., I-815

The Drees Co., I-256

Dreher (SABMiller), I-761

Dressbarn Inc., II-2893, 2897

Dresser Rand, I-1907

Dreyer's Grand Ice Cream Holdings, I-414, 422

Dri-Pak, I-1579

Drive Clean L.L.C., II-3420

Drydock World, I-1846

DS Smith, I-1146

DSE Healthcare Solutions, I-1305

DSIC, I-1846

DSM, I-911

DSV, II-2506

DTAC, II-2617

Dubal, I-1722

Duke Energy Carolinas L.L.C., II-2720

Duluxgroup Limited, I-1516

Dun Edwards, II-2784

Duni AB, I-1559

Dunkin & Bush Inc., I-283

Dunkin' Brands Inc., II-2934

Dunkin' Donuts, II-2933, 2957

Dunlap & Kyle, II-2877

DuPont, I-51, 1013, 1087, 1251, 1514, 1517, 1530, 1534, 1550, 1552, 1623

DuraClean, II-3280

Duramed Pharmaceuticals, I-1344

Düring, I-1578

Dutch Bros., II-2933

Dutch Lady Milk Industries, I-319

DW Sports Fitness, II-3473

DWA, II-3436

Dymo, I-1161

Dynamite Entertainment, I-1206

Dyno Nobel, I-1551

Dyson, II-2044

E Ink Holdings, II-2156, 2160

E-One, II-2173

E-Plus, II-2593

E*Trade, II-3080, 3131

EAB, I-1772

Eabax, II-3357

EADS, II-2307-2316

Eagelmoss Publications Ltd., I-1206

Eagle Materials, I-1687

EagleBurgmann, I-1620

E&J Gallo Winery, I-778-779

Earthbound Farm, I-926

East African Breweries Ltd., I-762

East Hope, I-1722

Easter Seals, II-3552

Eastern Bank, II-3054

Eastern Shipbuilding, I-1853

Easton Coach Co., II-2503

Eastpak, I-1080, 1647

Eastwood Homes, I-250

Eat Smart, I-914

Eaton Corp., II-1993, 2004-2006, 2158

Ebara, I-1901

eBay Inc., II-2671, 3307, 3497

Eberspächer, II-2249

ECA S.A., II-2344, 2346

Echostar, II-2108

Ecolab Inc., I-1370, 1384, II-3324

Economical, II-3135

Econoprint, II-3319

Ecover, I-1368

EDC, I-201

Edelman, II-3593-3594

EdF Energy, II-2708-2709, 2715

Edrington Group, I-787

Education Media and Publishing Group Ltd., I-1217

Edward Don & Co., II-2754

Efes, I-764

Efko, I-306

EFS Services Saudi, II-3325

Egger, I-1106

Ehrfeld, I-1891

Eiffage, I-276

Eight O'Clock Coffee Co., I-849, 854, 858

Einstein Noah Restaurant Group, II-2934

Einstein's Bros. Bagels, II-2946

eircom, II-2639

El Pollo Loco, II-2950

El Tenienta (Codelco), I-153

Elanco Animal Health, I-1330

ELCOT, II-2086

Electrolux, I-20, 1985, II-2014-2015, 2019-2020, 2024, 2027, 2042, 2044

Electronic Arts, II-2678, 3365-3366

Eli Lilly, II-2353
Eliahu, II-3142
Elkay Manufacturing, I-1091
Elkem/Blue Star, I-1728
Ella's Kitchen, I-450
Ellery Homestyles, I-1078
Elmer's Products, I-1547
Elosa S.A., I-744
eLove, II-3288
Elpida, II-2136
Elrene Home Fashions, I-1074, 1077
Elsai, I-1342
Elseter, II-2336
Elsevier Science, I-1227
EM Vinto, I-1730
Embla Systems, II-2368
EmblemHealth Inc., II-3153, 3162
Embotelladoras Arca, I-320
Embraer, II-2271-2272
Embryform, I-1049
EMC, I-1951, 1953-1955, II-2000, 3360
EmCare, II-3527
Emcor Group Inc., I-284
Emerald Companies, II-3595
Emergency Consultants, II-3527
Emergency Medicine Physicians, II-3527
Emergency Physicians Medical Group, II-3527
Emergency Service Partners, II-3527
Emeritus Senior Living, II-3551
Emerson Electric, I-18, 1801, 1805, II-2004, 2008, 2158
EMHS, II-3518
EMI Music, II-2090-2092
Emirates Airline, II-2560
EMJ Corporation, I-273
Emkay, II-3409
Emmis Communications, II-2691
Empire CLS Worldwide, II-2501
Empire Home Services dba Empire Carpets, II-2908
Employees Provident Fund (Malaysia), II-3237
Emprise Bank, II-3049
EMS Pharma, I-1339
Emtel, II-2604
Enbrel, I-1352
Enbridge Energy L.P., II-2564
EnBW AG, II-2710
Encana, I-199
Enclos Corp., I-295

Encore Sales, II-2462
Endurance Specialty Group, II-3185
Enel S.p.A, II-2337, 2708
Ener-G Foods Inc., I-333, 612
Enercon, I-1824
Energizer Holdings, I-1504, 1751-1752, II-2057, 2167, 2486
Engine Alliance, II-2280
Englander, I-1120
The Engle Burman Group, I-261
Enjoy Life Foods L.L.C., I-333, 612
Ennis, I-44
Ennis (Alstyle Apparel), I-1081
Enpro, I-1619
ENSCO International Inc., I-203
Ensign Resource Services, I-204
Entel, II-2586, 2636
Entercom, II-2687, 2691
Enterprise, II-3409
Enterprise Bank & Trust, II-3058
Enterprise Community Investment Inc., II-3248
Enterprise Crude Pipeline L.L.C., II-2564
Enterprise Holdings, II-3408
Enterprise Investors, I-322
Enterprise Products Partners, II-2528
Enterprise Transportation Co., II-2511
EnviroStar Inc., II-3275
EOG Resources, I-199
E.ON, II-2708-2710, 2715
Eos Getranke GmBH, I-337
Epsilon, II-3317
Epson, I-1956, 1959-1964, 1966, II-2130
Equistar, I-1277-1278
Equity Residential, II-3247-3248
Eramet, I-168, 170
Ericsson, II-3360
Erie Insurance Group, II-3177, 3216, 3219, 3230
Ernst & Young, II-3286, 3574-3575, 3592
E.S. Wagner Co., I-297
ESAB, I-1883
Escondida (BHP/Rio tinto), I-153
ESI, II-2096
Essex Homes, I-251
Essilor, II-2410-2411
Estée Lauder Companies Inc., I-1430, 1486
Estes Express Lines, II-2512

Esther Price Candies Corp., I-720
Estridge Cos., I-256
ESW, I-1696
ETA, II-2423
Etam, I-1045
Ethan Allen, II-2904
Ethniki, II-3140
Etisalat Misr, II-2590
EUKOR, II-2573
Euro Pro (Fantom), II-2044
Euro RSCG Worldwide, II-3318
Eurocement, I-1673
Eurocopter, II-2276-2277
Eurofarma, I-1339
Eurogate, II-2536
euroscript International S.A., II-3396
Eurovia (VBU) GmbH, I-298
Evans Network of Cos., II-2509
Everbank, II-3042
Everbeauty, I-1172
Everest Re, II-3239
Everett Smith Group Ltd., I-1636
Evergreen, I-1145, II-2536
Evergreen Line, II-2527
Everything Furniture, II-2912
Evialis S.A., I-586
Eviant, II-2080
Evonik, I-1553
Ex-Cell Home Fashions, I-1068, 1075
Excel Corp., I-380
ExecuCar, II-2501
EXL Service, II-3373
Expedia Inc., II-2568
Expeditors International, II-2506
Experian Group Ltd., II-3307
Express Mail Services, II-2669
Express Oil Change & Service Center, II-3422
Express Ranches, I-112
Express Scripts, II-2987
ExpressJet, II-2543, 2556, 2559
Extendicare Health Services, II-3549
Exterran, I-1907
Extra, II-2937
Extra Space Storage, II-2522
Extraordinary Vacations Group Inc., II-2569
ExxonMobil Corp., I-1251, 1277-1281, 1581, 1588-1589, 1591, 1593-1594, II-2796
ExxonMobil Pipeline Co., II-2564
Eyecarecenter, II-3027

Eyemart Express, II-3027

EZCorp., II-2992

F. Gaviña & Sons, I-854, 858

Fabrica de Harinas Elizondo, I-557

Fabrica De Jabon La Corona S.A. de C.C., I-733

Facebook, II-2663, 2671, 2676, 2678, 3125, 3306, 3308

Factory Brand Shoes, II-2802

Factory Mutual Insurance Co., II-3170, 3189, 3213

Fage, I-315, 439, 441

Falconer, II-2271

FalconStor, I-1955

Familia (Equest), II-2819

Family Dairies USA, I-430

Family Dollar, II-2801, 2913

FamilyMart, II-2798

Famous Footwear, II-2802

Fannie Mae, II-3113

Fannie May Candy, I-720

FANUC Ltd., I-1923

Far East Holdings Group Co. Ltd., I-1811

Far Eastern Textile, I-1283

Faragello Group, I-340

Farbest Foods Inc., I-129

Fareway, II-2825

Farley's & Sathers Candy, I-681, 688, 690, 692, 697, 702

Farm Bureau Mutual Insurance Co. of Arkansas Inc., II-3194

Farm Bureau Property & Casualty Group, II-3220

Farm Credit System, II-3098

Farm Fresh, II-2861

Farmers Insurance Group, II-3179-3181, 3193-3195, 3197, 3199-3200, 3206-3207

Farmland Foods Inc., I-362

Fast-Teks On-Site Computer Services, II-3379

Fastenal, II-2782

Faurecia, I-1127-1128, II-2241-2243, 2249

Fazer Konfektyr, I-312, 327

FCX, I-1717

FD, II-3594

FD Thomas Inc., I-283

Fedders, I-1985

Federal Express, II-2560

Federal Housing Authority, II-3113

Federal Insurance Co., II-3215

Federal Retirement Thrift, II-3237

Federated, II-2896

FedEx, II-2516-2519, 2525, 2669

FedEx Freight, II-2512

Feit Electric Co., II-2057

Female Health Company, I-1344

Fennia, II-3138

Ferno-Washington, I-1132

Ferolito, Vultaggio & Sons, I-795

Ferrandino & Son, II-2729

Ferrara Pan Candy Co. Inc., I-679, 681, 692

Ferrellgas, II-3022

Ferrero China Ltd., I-716

Ferrero Group, I-344, 660

Ferrero S.p.A., I-317, 658, 664-665

Ferrero USA Inc., I-652, 692, 711, 720

Ferretti Group, II-2291

Ferro, I-1550

FerroAtlantica, I-1728

Ferrocarril Mexicano, II-2499

Fewer Musical Instruments, II-2434

FGC (RAO UESR), II-2708, 2714, 2716

FIA Card Services NA, II-3041

Fiat, II-2197, 2203

Fiberton, I-1101

Fiberweb (BBA), I-1013

Ficosa, II-2251

Fidelidade-Mundial, II-3145

Fidelity Bank, II-3049

Fidelity Family, II-3236

Fidelity Investments, II-3131

Fidelity National Group, II-3190-3191

FieldStone Communities, I-264-265

Fifth Third Bank, II-3042, 3046-3047, 3050, 3055, 3066, 3068

Fifth Third Mortgage, II-3110

Fila, I-1031, 1608, 1613

FilmDistrict, II-3441

Filterfresh, I-846

Financial Freedom, II-3114

Fineline, II-2292

Fing'rs, I-1460

Finmeccanica, II-2307, 2309-2313

Finn Partners, II-3593

Finning, II-3330

Fire Insurance Exchange, II-3170, 3191

Firemans Fund Insurance Co., II-3213

Firestone, I-1585

Firmenich, I-1527

Firs, I-1036

First Alert/Powermate, II-2057

First American Bank, II-3048

First American Family, II-3236

First Bank, II-3066, 3076

First Cash Financial, II-2992

First Citizens Bank & Trust Co., II-3066, 3074

First Community Bank, II-3083

First Data, II-3092, 3372

First FS&LA of Charleston, II-3074

First Guaranty Bank, II-3051

First Hawaiian Bank, II-3044

First International Banking & Trust, II-3067

First Interstate Bank, II-3059, 3085

First Juice, I-488

First Merchants Bank NA, II-3047

First National Bank, II-3052

First National Bank of Alaska, II-3035

First National Bank of Gillette, II-3085

First National Bank of Omaha, II-3060

First National Bank of Pennsylvania, II-3071

First National Bank of Santa Fe, II-3064

First NBC Bank, II-3051

First Niagara Bank NA, II-3040

First Premier Bank, II-3075

First Quality Products, I-1013, 1167

First Security Bank, II-3037, 3059

First Security Bank Missoula, II-3059

First Solar, I-1769

First Student Inc., II-2505

First Tennessee Bank NA, II-3076

First Texas Homes, I-252

Firstbank, II-3039

Firstbank of Puerto Rico, II-3072

FirstGroup America, II-2503

FirstMerit Bank NA, II-3068

FirstService, I-18

Fischer & Frichtel, I-263

Fischer Environmental Services, II-3326

Fisher APW, II-2875

Fisher Development, I-261

Fisher Price, II-2485

Fisker, II-2215

Fitch, II-3316

Fitness First, II-3473

Five Star Senior Living, II-3551

Fives Group, I-1870

FL Smidth, I-1890

Flagstar Bank, II-3055, 3104, 3110

Flat Glass, I-1661

Fleishman-Hillard, II-3594

Fletcher Building Ltd., I-1087

Flex 'n Gale, II-2254

FlexJet, II-2275

Flight Centre Ltd., II-2569

Flint Group, I-1552

Flint Hills Resources, I-1278, 1524

Flintco, I-270

Floor & Decor, II-2908

Florens, II-3335

Florida Bottling Co., I-494

Florida Hospital, II-3517

Florida Marine, II-2528

Florida Pest Control & Chemical Co., II-3326

Florida Power & Light Co., II-2720

Florida Tile/Panaria, I-1679

Florida Turbine, I-1822

Florim, I-1679

Florists' Transworld Deliveries Inc. (FTD), II-3023

FlorStar Sales, II-2737

Flowers Foods Bakeries Group, I-607, 618-619, 626, 629

Flowserve, I-1620, 1801, 1901

Fluidotech, I-1975

Fluor Corp., I-269, 275-276, 279-280, II-3569

Flyte Tyme Worldwide Transportation, II-2501

FM Global Group, II-3188

FMC Corp., I-1272, 1348

FMC Technologies, I-211

FMG, I-149

Foamex, I-1631

Foamline, I-1631

Focus Features, II-3441

Fomento de Construccion y Contratas S.A., I-275

Fomento Economico Mexicano S.A. de C.V. (FEMSA), II-2791, 2799

Fongbu HiTek, II-2128

Fonterra Co-operative Group, I-742

Food City, II-2833

Food Directions Inc., I-333, 896

Food Land, II-2830

Food Lion, II-2815, 2848, 2861

Food So Inc., I-742

Foodliner Inc./Quest Logistics, II-2511

Foot Locker, II-2897, 2903, 2996

For Eyes/Insight Optical Manufacturing, II-3027

Ford Motor Co., I-1914, II-2196-2198, 2200-2201, 2203, 2205-2209, 2215, 2228-2229, 2872, 3096, 3311

Foreign Candy Co. Inc., I-683

Foremost Farms USA, I-430

Forest River, II-2264, 2319-2320

Forever Living Products, II-3021

Formica, I-1086, 1625

Formosa Chemicals & Fibre Corp., I-1283, 1293-1294

Formosa Plastics, I-1251

ForRent.com, II-2668

Fort Dearborn, I-1237

Fortune Brands Inc., I-786, 788

Fortune Tobacco Corp., I-963

Forward Foods L.L.C., I-705

Foshan Haitian, I-521

Foster Farms, I-122, 129, 351

Foster Poultry Farms, I-541

Foster's Group Ltd., I-757, 777

Foulds Inc., I-890, 896

Fountain Tire, II-2877

Four Winns, II-2289

Fox Rent A Car, II-3408

Fox Searchlight, II-3441

Foxconn, II-2126

FPC USA, I-1254, 1277-1278, 1281-1282

FPL Food L.L.C., I-355

FRAM Group, I-1593

France Telecom, II-2698

Franco Manufacturing, I-1074

Francopia, I-1347

Frank Gumpert Printing of Annapolis, II-3319

Fraser & Neave, I-319

Fred Meyer, II-2843, 2854, 3005

Freddie Mac, II-3113

Fredriksen Group, II-2529

Fred's, II-2801

Free, II-2698

Freedom Group, I-1794

FreedomWorks for America, II-3565

Freeman Companies, II-3405

Freeport-McMoRan Copper & Gold Inc., I-152, 161, 177

Freescale, II-2138-2139

Freightliner, II-2228-2230

Freixenet S.A., I-778

Fremont Farms of Iowa, I-125

Fresenius, II-2349, 3523-3524

Fresh Express, I-914, 926

Freshco Ltd., I-500

Freshens Smoothies & Frozen Treats, II-2954

Fresnillo, I-166

Freudenberg, I-1013, 1285, 1619

Freudenberg Household Products, II-2473

Friendly Computers, II-3379

Friendly Corp., I-422

Friesland-Campina, I-307, 329

Frito-Lay, I-865, 867, 869, 872, 874, 876, 878, 880, 885

Frog Street, I-1228

Frontier, II-2545, 2622

Frontier Natural Products Co-op, I-924

Frost National Bank, II-3077

Frozen Food Express Industries, II-2510

Fruit of the Loom, I-1050

Fry's Electronics Inc., II-2845, 2927

FTI Consulting, II-3592

Fu Yao Group, I-1653

Fuchs, I-1594

FuelBelt, II-2447

FuelCell Energy, I-1765

Fugro, I-208

Fuji, II-1996, 2413, 2415

Fuji Pharma Co. Ltd., I-1346

Fujian Fuma Food Co. Ltd., I-611

Fujian Jinlun Fiebr, I-1005

Fujian Mawei, I-1853

Fujitsu, I-1951, 1968, II-2094, 3374-3375

Fulida Group, I-1293-1294

Full Compass Systems Ltd., II-2932

Fulton Homes, I-262

Furniture Brands International, I-1111

Furniture Transportation Group, II-2514

FurnitureBuzz, II-2912

Furniture.com, II-2912

Furukawa Electric, II-2157, 2159

Futaba, II-2249

Future Pipe, I-1629

Fyffes, I-322

G4S, II-3381, 3383

GA/Heathgate, I-171

Company Index

Gada, II-3381
GAFMC, I-1585
Galaxy Casino, II-3489
Galderma Laboratories, I-1500
The Gambrinus Co., I-769
Gambro, II-2349, 3524
Gamesa, I-1824
GameStop, II-2925
Gamma USA Inc., I-295
Gammastamp, II-2254
Gammon, II-2000
Ganaderos Productores de Leche
  Pura S.A. de C.V., I-342, 385, 401
G&D, II-2121
G&K Services, II-3277
Ganedan Biotech, I-1307
Gannett Co., I-1203, II-2692
Gaomi Chemical Fibre, I-1294
The Gap Inc., I-1017, 1019, II-2802,
  2896-2897, 2899
Garbett Homes, I-264
Garden Fresh Salsa Co, I-427
Garden Highway, I-913
Gardiner Angus Ranch, I-112
Gardner Denver, I-1907
Garnier, I-1448, 1456
Gasa, I-311
Gate City Bank, II-3067
Gategroup, II-2936
GC Services, II-3315
GdF-Suez, II-2709
GE Capital Fleet Services, II-3409
GE Healthcare, II-2361-2362, 2366,
  3592
GE Money Bank, II-3078, 3089
GE Plastics, I-1155, 1157
GE Water, I-1921
GEA Westfalia, I-1924
Geberit, I-1682
Gécamines, I-168
Geeks on Call, II-3379
Geiger, I-43
Gejiu-Zi-Li, I-1730
Gemalto, II-2121
General Books L.L.C., I-1219
General Cable, I-1915
General Dynamics Corp., II-2274,
  2284, 2317, 2323, 2343, 3601
General Electric Co., I-1817, 1819-
  1820, 1823-1824, 1907, 1920,
  1924, II-1993, 2006, 2014-2015,
  2019-2020, 2024, 2027-2028, 2042,
  2048, 2053-2054, 2057-2058, 2097,
  2101, 2115, 2158, 2269, 2274,

2280, 2296, 2330, 2336-2337,
  2348, 2350, 2354, 2363-2365,
  2693, 2749
General Growth Properties, II-3244-
  3245
General Mills Inc., I-305, 338, 344,
  423, 439, 441, 468, 477, 479, 535,
  554-555, 560, 573, 615, 649-650,
  660, 679, 700, 704-705, 885, 907,
  917, II-3311
General Motors Corp., I-23, 1914,
  II-2196-2198, 2200, 2215, 3125,
  3292, 3307, 3310-3311
General Nutrition Centers Inc.,
  I-1325, II-2986
General Parts Inc., II-2875
General Smontaggi S.p.A., I-298
General Union, II-3140
Generali, II-3143
Generation Mortgage, II-3114
Genesco Inc., II-3014
Genesis Healthcare, II-3512, 3549
Genmar Group, II-2288, 2291
Genpact, II-3373
Gensler, II-3571, 3573
Gentex, II-2237
Gentiva, II-3513, 3522
Genuine Parts Co., II-2875
Genuine Parts Company Inc., II-2763
Genworth Financial, II-3114, 3234
Genzyme, II-2380
GEO Group, II-3595
Geokinetics, I-208
GeoPro Mining, I-174
George Krapf Jr. & Sons Inc.,
  II-2505
George P. Johnson Experience Mar-
  keting, II-3400
Georgia Bulldogs, II-3484
Georgia Gulf, I-1282
Georgia-Pacific, I-48, 1095, 1107,
  1139-1143, 1145, 1152, 1185,
  1188-1191, 1687
Georgia Power Co., II-2720
Geovera Insurance Co., II-3186
GeoVera U.S. Insurance Group,
  II-3185
Gepa Fair Handelshaus, I-337
Gerber Products Co., I-460
Gerdau, I-1701
Gerresheim, I-37
Gersh Agency, II-3456
GESeaCo, II-3335
Gestamp, II-2251, 2254

Getty Images, II-3386
Getty Petroleum, II-2879
GF Management, II-3271
GFI, II-3128
GfK USA, II-3580
Ghirardelli Chocolate Co., I-661,
  707, 711, 717, 720
Giant, II-2834, 2844
Giant (China) Co. Ltd., II-2298
Giant Eagle, II-2822, 2846, 2983
Giant Food, II-2815, 2862
Gibson Enterprises, II-2491
Gibson Guitar Corp., II-2434
Gilbane Building Co., I-272, 274
Gilbane Inc., I-271
Gildan, I-1037
Gildemaster, I-1877
Gilsa Dairy Products, I-441
Gio General, II-3134
Giorgio Armani, I-1035, II-3028
Girdear, I-1045
Giroux Glass Inc., I-295
GITI Tire Pte. Ltd., I-1604
Givaudan, I-1527
Gjensidige, II-3144
GL Homes, I-259
Glaceau Water Co. Inc., I-802, 804
Glacier Bank, II-3059
Glad Products Co., I-1623
Glam Media, II-2663
Glanbia, I-316
Glastron, II-2289
GlaxoSmithKline, I-341, 728, 1305,
  1307, 1325-1326, 1337-1338,
  1340-1341, 1359, 1458, 1470
Glencore, I-156, 158, 1738
Global Closures, I-1788
Global English Corp., II-3543
Global Events, II-3400
Global Linguist Solutions, II-3396
Global Protection, I-1621
Global Tower Partners, II-2112
GlobalFoundries, II-2128
Globe Electric Co., II-2057
Globe Specialty Metals, I-1728
Globul, II-2584
Globus, II-2384
Glovis, II-2573
Glutino Importations, I-878
Glutino USA, I-333, 612
GMAC, II-3123
Goal Financial, II-3099
Godfather's Pizza, II-2956
Godfrey Hirst, I-1001

Godfrey Phillips India Ltd., I-942

Godiva Chocolatier, I-711, 720

Godrej, II-2022, 2026, 2029

Gold Container, II-3335

Gold Fields, I-161

Gold Toe Brands, I-988

Goldbug, II-2485

Goldcorp, I-161, 166

The Golden 1 Credit Union, II-3087

Golden Flake Snack Foods, I-865, 874

Golden Living, II-3512-3513, 3549

Golden Temple of Oregon Inc., I-931

Goldlion, I-1027, 1040

Goldman Sachs, II-3078, 3119-3120, 3122, 3124, 3261

Gold's Gym International Inc., II-3472

Goldway, II-2365

Goldwind, I-1824

Gontermann-Peipers Gmbh, I-1696

Goo Goo Car Wash, II-3420

Good Earth Tea, I-931

Good Humor/Breyer's, I-414, 422

Good Shepherd Rehabilitation Network, II-3519

GoodLife Fitness Clubs, II-3472

Goodman, I-1985-1986

Goodwill Industries International, II-2993, 3552

Goodyear/Dunlop, I-1605

Goodyear/Sumitomo, I-1599

Goodyear Tire & Rubber Co., I-1287, 1606

Google, II-2643-2656, 2663, 2671, 2676, 2926, 3306, 3308-3309

GoPro, II-2420

Gore-Tex, I-1059

The Gorilla Glue Co., I-1161, 1547

Gotec, I-1975

Gourmet Express L.L.C., I-535

Government of Guinea, I-176

Government Pension Fund, II-3237

Government Pension Investment, II-3237

Goya Foods Inc., I-917

Graco, II-2485

Graebel Cos., II-2514

Graham Packaging Co. L.P., I-35, 1632

Grameenphone, II-2580

Grammar, II-2257

Grange Mutual, II-3202

Granite Construction, I-277

Granite Rock Construction, I-248

Grant Cooper Healthcare, II-3591

Grant Thornton, II-3286, 3575

Grasim, I-1293

Gray Line, II-2504

Grease Monkey, II-3422

Great American P&C Insurance Group, II-3182

Great Dane Limited Partnership, II-2321

Great Expectations, II-3288

Great Floors, II-2908

Great Lakes Dredge & Dock, I-282

Great Southern Homes, I-251

Great Western Bank, II-3048, 3060, 3075

Greater Dayton Building and Remodeling, I-245

Greater Omaha Packing Co. Inc., I-355, 357

GreatPricedFurniture.com, II-2912

Greatwide Logistics Services, II-2508

Greektown Casino, II-3490

Green Bay Packers, II-3485

Green Giant, I-473, 475, 526

Green Mountain Coffee Co., I-852, 854, 857-858, 931

Green Plains Renewable Energy, I-1524

Greenbank, II-3076

Greenberg & Traurig, II-3531

Greenery International, I-329

Greenline, I-914

GreenTree Inn, II-3269

Greenwood Industries Inc., I-291

Greenwood Mills, I-982

Greenwood Packing Plant, I-368

Greggs, II-2940

Greif Brothers Corp., I-1746

Greif Inc., I-34

Grey, II-3294

Greystar Real Estate Partners L.L.C., II-3247

Griffin Land & Nurseries Inc., I-108

Griffin Technology, I-4

Grifols, II-2359

Grimaldi, II-2573

Grimmway, I-914

Grinnell Mutual, II-3221

Groendyke Transport, II-2511

Group 1 Automotive Inc., II-2871

Group Builders Inc., I-285

Group Health, II-3155

Group II Communication, I-43

Group Michelin, I-1606

Groupe CRIT, II-3342

Groupe Danone, I-324, 326, 344, 384-385, 803, 807

Groupe Pernod Ricard, I-778

Groupon, II-2628

Growmark Inc., II-2787, 3022

Gruma Corp., I-320, 574, 874, 907

Grundfos, I-1901

Grupo ALTEX S.A. de C.V., I-557

Grupo Bafar, I-378

Grupo Bimbo S.A. de C.V., I-320, 506, 586, 604, 650

Grupo Cuervo S.A. de C.V., I-788

Grupo DESC S.A. de C.V., I-733

Grupo Embotelladoras Unidas, I-320

Grupo FEMSA, I-320

Grupo Ferrovial S.A., II-2562

Grupo Fuertes, I-326

Grupo GUSI, I-356

Grupo Herdez S.A. de C.V., I-522

Grupo Industrial Lala S.A. de C.V., I-385, 401

Grupo Kowi S.A. de C.V., I-378

Grupo La Moderna S.A. de C.V., I-320, 557, 891

Grupo Mexico, I-177

Grupo Minsa SAB de C.V., I-574

Grupo Modelo S.A. de C.V., I-320, 758, 763, II-2799

Grupo Planeta, I-1200

Grupo Porcicola Mexicano (Keken), I-378

Grupo SIS, I-315

Grupo S.O.S., I-744

Grupo Sumoi, I-323

Grupo VIZ, I-356

Grupoama Phoenix, II-3140

Gruppo Fondiara SAI, II-3143

GS Yuasa, II-2169

GSE Holdings, I-238

GTAT, I-1767

GTC Industries Ltd., I-942

Guangdang Jianlibao Group, I-828

Guangdong Kaiping Chunhui, I-1005

Guangdong Kelon Electrical Holdings Co. Ltd., II-2025

Guangdong Tandem Industries Co. Ltd., II-2298

Guangdong Vinda, I-1186

Guangwei Group Co. Ltd., II-2453

Guangxi China Tin, I-1730

Guangzhou, I-798

Guangzhou Blue Moon, I-1389, 1392, 1401

Guangzhou Railway Group, II-2498

Guardian, I-1654, 1656-1658, 1660

Guardian Protection Services, II-3384

Gucci, I-1651, II-2887

Guess?, I-1017

Guilford Mills, I-982

Guillin Tianhe Pharma, I-1326

Guinness Anchor, I-319

Guitar Center Inc., II-2932

Guittard Chocolate Co., I-707

Guizhou Tyre Co. Ltd., I-1604

Gujarat Co-operative Milk Marketing Federation Ltd., I-341

Gujin, I-1049

Gulfstream, II-2271-2272

Gutterplan's Bakery, I-573

Gwaltney of Smithfield Ltd., I-362

Gymboree Corp., II-2893

Habanos S.A., I-968

Habeco, I-766

Habitat for Humanity International, I-254, II-3552

Hachette, I-1218, 1221-1222

Hagen Invent, II-3400

Haier Group, II-2015, 2079-2080

The Hain Celestial Group, I-333, 450, 488, 931, 934

Hair Club for Men and Women, II-3289

Hako, II-2045

Hakuhodo, II-3295

Halliburton, I-206-208, 210, 1848-1850, 1852, 1855, II-2277, 2573

Hallmark, I-1244, II-3012-3013

HALO, I-43

Halperns' Steak and Seafood Co., I-359

Halwani Bros. Co., I-324

Hamilton Beach, II-2040

Hamlet Homes, I-264

The Hammer Corporation, I-697

Hampton Affiliates, I-1095

Hanaro Telecom, II-2698

Hancock Bank, II-3057

Handan, II-2108

H&E Equipment Services, I-1860

H&R 1871, I-1795

H&R Block, II-3089, 3286-3287, 3574

Handyman Connection, II-3431

Handyman Matters Franchise Inc., II-3431

Handyman-Network Franchise Systems L.L.C., II-3431

HandyPro Handyman Services Inc., II-3431

Hanes Hosiery, I-985

Hanesbrands Inc., I-985, 988, 990, 1004, 1035, 1038, 1044, 1050

Hangshou Wahaha Group, I-339

Hangzhou Mary Kay Cosmetics, I-1420

Hangzhou Metal Rolling Plant, I-1711

Hangzhou Wahaha Group, I-496

Hangzhou Zhongce Rubber Co. Ltd., I-1604, 1606

Hanjin Shipping, II-2527

Hankook Tire Co. Ltd., I-1605-1606

Hannaford, II-2863

Hannover Re, II-3239

Hanover Insurance Group Property & Casualty Cos., II-3183

Han's Technologies, II-2721

Hansen, I-1784-1785

Hansen Beverage Co., I-811

Hansen Natural, I-494

Hansen Specialty, I-911

Hanson Pipe, I-41-42

Hanson PLC, I-1676

Hanting Inn, II-3269

Hanwha Solar One, I-1769

Hapag-Lloyd, II-2527

HappiGo, II-3018

Harbin, II-2225

Harbin Pharma, I-1317

Hardin Construction, I-270

Hardwood Companies Inc., I-1042

Harel, II-3142

Haribo GmbH & Co., I-660

Harkins Builders, I-268

Harlan Bakeries Inc., I-615

Harlequin, I-1218, 1221

Harley Davidson, II-2303

Harman, II-2255

Harman Professional, II-2434

Harmon's, II-2852

Harmony Gold, I-161

Harmony Homes, I-257

Harold Simmons Foundation, II-3553

HarperCollins, I-1218, 1221-1222

Harpoon Brewery Inc., I-769

Harris County Hospital District, II-3516

Harris National Assn., II-3046

Harris Ranch Beef Co., I-355

Harris Teeter, II-2848

Harrisburg, II-3026

Hartford Fire & Casualty Group, II-3133, 3225

Hartford Insurance Group, II-3180, 3182, 3216-3217, 3219, 3226-3228, 3230

Hartman Walsh Painting Co., I-283

Hartmann Group, II-2391, 2393

Hartmann Studios, II-3400

Hartz Mountain Corp., I-578

Harvard University, II-3538

Harvest Land Co-Op, II-2787

Harvey Norman Holdings, II-3293

Harworth Europe, I-1122

Hasbro, I-23, II-2439, 2443

Hastings Entertainment, II-2930

Hat Shack, II-3014

Hat World, II-3014

Hat Zone, II-3014

Hatfield Quality Meats Inc., I-371, 380

Hatteras Inc., II-3319

Havells, I-1909

Haverty's, II-2904

Havoline Xpress Lube, II-3422

Havyard, I-1846

Hawaiian Paradise, II-2937

Hawker, II-2271

Hawkins Design Group Inc., II-3569

Haworth Inc., I-1111, 1121, 1123

Hayneedle, II-2912

Hays, II-3342-3343

Hayward Baker Inc., I-297

Haze Nightclub, II-2961

HCA, II-3515, 3518

HCL, I-1943

HCR ManorCare, II-3512-3513

HDI, II-3139

HDK, II-3573

HDR Architecture Inc., I-269, II-3569, 3571, 3573

H.E. Butt Grocery Co., II-2812, 2837

The Headblade Co., I-1752

Health Alliance Plan, II-3161

Health Alliance Plan of Michigan, II-3151

Health Care Products, I-698

Health Care Service Corp., II-3153

Health Management Associates, II-3515

Health Mart, II-2964, 3263

Health Net Inc., II-3153, 3157-3158

Health Valley Natural Foods, I-468

HealthSpring Inc., II-3167

Healthy Alliance Life Insurance Company, II-3152

Hearst Communication Inc., I-1209

Hearst Corp., I-1203, 1207-1208, II-2692

Hebei Dachang, I-1711

Hebei Iron & Steel Group, I-1711

Hebel Hua Long, I-412

Hefel Melling Co. Ltd., II-2025

HeidelbergCement, I-21, 215, 219, 1670, 1674, 1684

Heijongjiang Emperial Spring Drinks Co. Ltd., I-807

Hein & Lehmann, I-1845

Heineken, I-33, 306, 308, 315-316, 322-323, 325-326, 329-330, 756, 758, 760, 763-765, 767, II-2938

Heinen's, II-2822

Heinrich Bauer Zeitschreflen Verlag, I-1208

Heladerias Holanda, II-2937

Held A.G., I-1367, 1578

Helen of Troy, I-1432

Helena Chemical Company, II-2787

Helene Curtis, I-1432, 1448, 1500

Hella, II-2224, 2237-2238, 2244

Hellenic Q Foods, I-315

Helmerich & Payne, I-204

Helong, I-1293

Helzberg Diamonds, II-3005

Henan Lingrui, I-1326

Henan Synear Food Holdings Ltd., I-538

Henan Xinfel Electric Co. Ltd., II-2025

Hendrick Automotive Group, II-2871

Hengan, I-1026, 1141, 1172, 1176, 1179, 1186, 1192

Hengyi, I-1283

Henkel, I-1161, 1364, 1367, 1369, 1384, 1409-1410, 1486, 1557, 1574, 1594, II-2484

Henkels & McCoy Inc., I-281

Hennes & Mauritz (H&M), I-1019

Henry Ford Hospital, II-3520

Henry RAC Holding Corp., I-1795

Henry Schein, II-3016

Henry Walken Homes, I-264

Hensel Phelps Construction, I-272

Heraeus, I-1550

Herbalife Ltd., I-900, II-3021

Herbruck's Poultry Ranch, I-125

Herceptin, I-1352

Heristo, I-314, 455

Heritage Propane, II-3022

Herman Lepsee, I-1560

Herman Miller, I-1111, 1121, 1123

Hermes Inc., I-1651, II-2887

Hero MotoCorp, II-2304

Herr Foods, I-865, 867, 876, 878

Herschend Entertainment, II-3481

The Hershey Company, I-338, 652, 681, 683, 688, 692, 697, 707, 711, 713, 717, 720, 724-725, 727-728

Hershey Foods Corp., I-660-661

Hertz, II-3408

Hertz Equipment Rental Corp., I-1860, II-3263, 3330-3332

Hess Corp., II-2796, 2879

Hess Print Solutions, I-1229

Hewlett-Packard Co., I-1931, 1935-1946, 1951-1956, 1958-1966, 1968, II-2147, 2317, 2925, 3016, 3360, 3368-3370, 3372-3375

High Liner Foods, I-345, 841

High Performance Beverage, I-811

Highland Homes, I-252

Highland Mills, I-985

Highmark Inc., II-3153, 3165

Higman Barge Lines Inc., II-2528

Hill & Knowlton, II-3594

Hill Mechanical Group, I-291

Hill-Rom, I-1130, 1132

Hillandale Farms of Pennsylvania, I-125

Hillenbrand, II-2479

Hills Bank & Trust Co., II-3048

Hilltop National Bank, II-3085

Hilong, I-209, 1514, 1713

Hilton Hotels, II-3263, 3270

Hindustan Zinc, I-156, 158, 1738

Hino USA, II-2228-2229

Hipp GmbH & Co. Vertrieb KG, I-337

Hisense Group, II-2073

History Maker Homes, I-252

Hitachi, I-1842, 1931, 1951, II-2169, 2237-2238, 3264

Hitachi Chemical, II-2153

Hitachi Construction Equipment, I-1840

Hitachi Sumitomo Heavy Industries, I-1861

Hiwin, II-2334

H.J. Heinz Co., I-346, 455-456, 470, 511, 520, 535-536, 916

HKS Inc., II-3571, 3573

HKScan, I-312, 327

HL Corp., II-2298

HMH, I-1228

HMO, II-2989

HNI Corp., I-1111, 1121, 1123

Hoar Construction, I-273

Hobby Lobby, II-3015

Hochschild Mining, I-166

Hochtief A.G., I-275-276

Hoffman Corporation, I-273

Hogan Lovells, II-3531

HOK, I-269, II-3571

Holcim Inc., I-1670, 1674, 1676

Holiday Retirement, II-3551

Holland & Knight, II-3564

Hollander Home Fashions, I-1073, 1076

Holmen, I-1138

Holmes Homes, I-264

Homag, I-1886

Home City Ice, I-887

Home Depot, II-2626, 2782, 2790, 2911, 2920, 3332

Home Depot Rentals, II-3330

Home Fashions International, I-1071

Home Inns, II-3269

Home Products Intl., I-18

Home Run Inn, I-554

Home2US Communications, II-2702

Homeland, II-2841

Homes.com, II-2668

Homestat Farm Ltd., I-466

Homewear Linens/Sam Hedaya, I-1077

Hon Hai Precision Industry Co. Ltd., II-3264

Honda, II-2196, 2198, 2204, 2215, 2237-2238, 2303-2305, 2324, 2872, 3095-3096

Honest Tea Inc., I-795

Honeywell, II-2115

Hong Kong Exchange, II-3129

Hong Kong Mortgage, II-3141

Hongguo International Holdings Ltd., I-1642

Hongshi, I-1671

Hongta Group, I-958

Hongyun Honghe Group, I-958

Hooters, II-2949
Horizon Air, II-2559
Horizon Bay Retirement Communities, II-3551
Hörmann, I-1772
Hormel Foods Corp., I-351, 358, 360, 362, 368, 380, 453, 906, 917
Hornbacher's/Supervalu, II-2827
Hosiery Mills Industry, I-988
Hosonic, II-2130
Hospira, I-1345
Hospital Physician Partners, II-3527
Hostess Brands Inc., I-607, 609, 617-619, 626
Hostmann-Steinberg, I-1552
Hotel Equities Group, II-3271
Houghton, I-1594
Houghton Mifflin Harcourt, I-1224
House Doctors, II-3431
House Majority PAC, II-3565
House of Raeford Farms Inc., I-122, 129
Houston Community College, II-3536
Hovnanian Enterprises, I-246, 249, 252, 255, 261
Howden Engineering, I-1908
Hoya, II-2410
HP ACG, II-3396
HP Hood L.L.C., I-383
Hradok, I-325
HSBC Bank, II-3041, 3065, 3082, 3086, 3119, 3141
HSBC North American Holdings Inc., II-3261
Hsikwangshan Twinkling Star, I-174
HSN, II-3017
HSS, II-3425
HTC, II-2100
Hua Lai Shi Catering Management and Service, II-2958
Huaxin, I-1671
Hub Group, II-2509
Hubbard Radio, II-2691
Huber Corp., I-1107, 1348
Hubert Co., II-2754
Hudson City Savings Bank, II-3063
Hudson HQ, II-3026
Hudson Industries, I-1072
Hugo Boss, I-1035
Hulu, II-2676
Humana Inc., II-3153-3154, 3156-3157, 3159-3160, 3163-3164, 3166-3168

Humax, II-2108
Humira, I-1352
Hunan Chenzhou Mining, I-174
Hungry Howie's Pizza, II-2956
Hunter-Douglas N.V., I-1063
Huntington Chase Homes & Development, I-263
Huntington Ingalls Industries Inc., II-2284
Huntington National Bank, II-3055, 3068, 3083
Huntsville Hospital, II-3516
Huron Healthcare, II-3592
Hurricane Boats, II-2290
Hurricane Builders, I-251
Hurricane Grill & Wings, II-2949
Husqvarna, I-1836
Hutchinson 3G HK Ltd., II-2596
Hutchinson 3G Ireland, II-2600
Hutchinson North America, I-1287
Hutchinson Port Holdings, II-2536
Hutchinson S.A., I-1285
HVHC Retail Group, II-3027
Hy-Vee, II-2825, 2832, 2842, 2974
Hydril, I-1851
Hydro Aluminum, I-1722
Hydro-Quebec Distribution, II-2713
Hydrospace, II-2324
Hyflux, I-1921
Hyland's, I-1305
Hynix, II-2136, 2141, 2146
Hypercom, I-1973
Hyperion, I-1218
Hyundai, I-1864, II-2196, 2198, 2202, 2210, 2321, 3096
Hyundai Heavy Industries, I-1842, II-2008, 2287
I-Go Car Sharing, II-3391
IAC Group, I-1634
IAC/Interactive Corp., II-3307
IAE, I-1820, II-2280
IAG, II-2548
Iasis Healthcare, II-3515
IBC, I-1120
Iberiabank, II-3051
Ibiden, II-2126
IBM, I-1931, 1948, 1951, 1953, 1955, II-2128, 2525, 3016, 3264, 3346-3347, 3356, 3360, 3368-3370, 3372-3375, 3601
IBP, I-358
ICAP, II-3128
ICF International Inc., II-3580, 3593

ICI AkzoNobel Decorative Paints US, II-2782
ICL, I-227
ICLR, II-3577
ICON PLC, II-3587
Iconix Brand Goup, I-23
ICR, II-3593
Idea, II-2598
Idea Village, I-1547
IDEO, II-3321
Idex, I-1901, II-2114
IDEXX Laboratories, I-138, 1330
I.D.I., II-3142
Idrogios General, II-3140
IDW Publishing, I-1206
if..., II-3137-3138, 3144, 3147
IFB, II-2022, 2029
IFE, I-1845
IFF, I-1527
iFurn.com, II-2912
IGT, II-3479
IKEA, II-2904
I.L.D., II-3142
Illinois Central School Bus Co., II-2505
Illinois Tool Works Inc., I-34, 1634, 1782, 1883
Illumina, II-2330, 2332
illycaffe North America, I-858
ILORI, II-3028
IMA (Insurance Manufacturers Association), II-3134
Image Comics, I-1206
Imagination Group, II-3400
Imagine Foods Inc., I-468
Imax (Warner), II-3436
Imerys S.A., I-223
IMG, II-3460
IMM, I-1891
Impala, I-178-179
Impellam, II-3342
Imperial Tobacco Group PLC, I-938, 940-941, 946, 951-952, 959-961, 971
Imperio Bonança, II-3145
IMS Health Inc., II-3580-3581
IMV Technologies, I-1827
Incase Designs, I-4
Independence Holding Co. Group, II-3148
Indian Oil, I-1587
Indiana Packers, I-380
IndiGo, II-2557
INDITEX, I-1019

Indo Bharat, I-1293

Indorama Ventures, I-1283

Industrial Lala S.A. de C.V., I-342

Industrias Bachoco, I-320

Industrie Cartarie Tronchetti, I-1139

Ineos, I-1251, 1277, 1279, 1281, 1530

Inergy Automotive Systems L.L.C., I-1632

Inergy L.P., II-3022

Infineon Technologies, II-2127, 2138-2139, 2142, 2146

Infinity, I-1752

ING Bank FSB, II-3041, 3110

ING USA Life Group, II-3150

Ingersoll-Rand, I-1773, 1822, 1986

Ingram Barge Co., II-2528

Ingram Micro, II-2748

Ingram Periodicals, II-3026

Inland Real Estate Group of Cos., II-3244-3245

Inn Maid Products, I-890

Inner Mongolia Mengniu Dairy Industry Group Co Ltd., I-339, 384

Inner Mongolia Mengniu Milk, I-384, 423

Inner Mongolia Yili Industrial Group Co. Ltd., I-339, 423

Innovative Artists Talent, II-3456

Innovative Beverage Group, I-815

Innovia, I-1274

Inoac, I-1631

Insight Communications Co., II-2701

Insight Pharmaceuticals, I-1305

Inspur, II-3349

Insurance Australia Ltd., II-3134

Intact, II-3135

The Integer Group, II-3318

Integra, I-201

Integrated Electrical Services Inc., I-284

Integrated Marketing Services, II-3318

Integrity First Financial Group, II-3102

Intel, I-1954, II-2131, 2133-2134, 2143-2146

IntelCav, II-2121

Intelfon (RED), II-2591

Intelligrated, I-1870

Inteplast Group, I-1623

Interamerican Corp., I-896

Interamerican Property, II-3140

Interceramic, I-1679

Interface, I-15, 1002-1003

Interlake Mecalux, I-1870

Interlink, II-3094

International, I-1142, II-2228-2230

International Automotive Components, II-2243

International Bank of Commerce, II-3069

International Beauty, I-1460

International Brotherhood of Electrical Workers, II-3561

International Brotherhood of Teamsters, II-3561

International Business Publications USA, I-1219

International Cobalt Co. Inc., I-168

International Creative Management Inc., II-3456, 3460

International Foodsource L.L.C., I-863, 872

International House of Pancakes, II-2951

International Paper Company, I-36, 38, 1137, 1143, 1145, 1147

International Specialty Products, I-1348

Intersaonika General, II-3140

InterSnack, I-884

Interstate Hotels & Resorts, II-3271

Intratech, II-2396

InTrust Bank National Assn, II-3049

Intuit, I-1234

Invacare, I-1130, II-2356-2357, 2376

Invensys, I-1975

Inventec, II-1992

InvescoPowerShares, II-3121

Investors Savings Bank, II-3063

InVision, II-3400

Inway Musical Instruments, II-2434

INX International, I-1552

Iowa Farm Bureau, II-3221

Iowa Select Farms, I-118

IPG Hospitality, II-3271

IPSd.Sign, II-2400

Ipsos, II-3580

iQiyi, II-2680

Iraq National Oil Co., I-195-196

IrisOhyama, II-2493

iRobot Corp., II-2344

Irving, I-1140

ISE America, I-125, II-2254

Isetan Mitsukoshi, II-2793

iShip, II-2669

Isle of Capri Casinos Inc., II-3491

Ismie Group, II-3209

ISMIE Mutual Insurance Co., II-3233

ISS, II-3383

ISS Ground Control, I-140

ISS Hicare Pvt., II-3323, 3325-3326

Italcementi, I-1670, 1674

Italgru, I-1865

The Italian Coffee Company, II-2937

Itautec Inc., I-1969

ITC Limited, I-942

ITG, I-982

Itokin, I-1018

Itron Inc., II-2336-2337

It's Just Lunch, II-3288

ITT, I-1801, 1901

iTunes, II-2930, 3449

ITW, I-1087

ivgStores, II-2912

Ivory, I-1026

Ivory Homes, I-264

IVRCL, II-2000

J. Front Retailing, II-2793

Jabra, II-2096

Jack Cooper Transport, II-2515

Jack in the Box, II-2947, 2957

Jackson Family Wines, I-779

Jackson Health System, II-3516-3517

Jackson Hewitt, II-3286-3287

Jacobs Engineering Group Inc., I-269, 279-280

Jacuzzi, I-1763

Jakks Pacific, II-2456

Jam Industries, II-2434

J&J Snack Foods Corp., I-346, 414

Jani-King International Inc., II-3329

Jansport Inc., I-1080

Japan Airlines, II-2558

Japan Post Insurance Co. Ltd., II-3132

Japan Synthetic Rubber Corp., I-1289

Japan Tobacco Inc., I-943-945, 948-949, 951-952, 959-963

Japan Vilene, I-1010

Jarden Corp., II-2040

Jarden Home Brands, II-2491

Jayco, II-2319-2320

J.B. Hunt Intermodal, II-2509

J.B. Hunt Transport Services, II-2513

JBS USA, I-305, 331, 351, 357, 360, 380

J.C. Penney, II-2792, 2884, 2896, 2913, 3005, 3283

J.C. Penney Portraits, II-3282

JCDecaux, II-3297

J.D. Heiskell & Co., I-595

J.D. Power and Associates, II-3580

JD Sports, II-2997

JD Wetherspoon, II-2940

JDA Software, II-3361

JE Dunn Construction Group, I-272, 274

Jean Coutu Group, II-2964

Jeanswest, I-1027

Jel Sert Co., I-418

Jelenko, II-2396, 2398

Jelmar, I-1394

Jelrus, II-2396

Jennie-O Turkey Store, I-129, 371

Jensen, II-2080

Jerome Russell Cosmetics, I-1456

Jerry's Foods, II-2839

Jet Airways, II-2557

JetBlue, II-2549, 2556

Jewel, II-2821, 2969

Jewelry Television, II-3005

J.F. Montalvo Cash & Carry, II-2857

JFE Chemical, I-1701, II-2153

J.H. Routh, I-380

Jiangnan Cable, I-1811

Jiangsu Aoyang, I-1294

Jiangsu Huaxi Group, I-1711

Jiangsu Shagang, I-1701

Jiangsu Sopo, I-1522

Jiangsu Xinxin, I-922

Jiayuan, II-2666

Jidong, I-1671

Jieshi Carbon Material Co., II-2011

Jiffy Lube, II-3422

Jimmy Sanders Inc., II-2787

Jin Jiang, II-3269

Jinchuan, I-170

JinJing Group, I-1661

Jinko Solar, I-1769

Jinxing (Fujian) Fiber Textile Industrial, I-1005

J.J. Haines & Co., II-2737

JJB Sports, II-2997

JM Eagle, I-41-42, 1628-1629

J.M. Smucker Co., I-481, 506, 541, 734, 741, 745, 849, 852, 854, 857-858, 918

Jo-Ann Stores, II-3015

Jockey International, I-1050

Johanna Foods Inc., I-441, 500

John Christner Trucking L.L.C., II-2510

John Crane, I-1620

John Deere, I-1840

John Frieda, I-1448, 1456

John Hancock Group, II-3149

John Morrell & Co., I-368, 745

The John Ritzenthaler Co., I-1074

John Wiley & Sons, I-1227

Johnny Trading, II-2493

Johns Manville, I-1013, 1692

Johnson & Johnson Co., I-652, 1131, 1176, 1178-1179, 1307, 1317, 1326, 1337-1338, 1470-1471, 1500-1501, 1504, II-2352, 2361, 2363, 2380-2385, 2389-2390, 2405-2406, 2410, 2484

Johnson Bank, II-3084

Johnson Controls Inc., I-1127-1128, 1986, II-2170, 2241, 2243, 2256-2257, 2259

Johnson Health Ted (Shanghai) Co. Ltd., II-2453

Johnson Matthey, I-1347

Johnsonville Sausage L.L.C., I-371-372

The Jones Co. of Tennessee, I-263

Jones Day, II-3531

Jones Group, I-1017

Jones Lang LaSalle Americas, II-3244

Jos. A. Bank Clothiers Inc., II-2883-2884

Joseph Enterprises, II-2456

Joseph's Fine Foods Inc., I-427

Jotun, I-1517

Joy Global, I-1844

J.P. Morgan Chase & Co., II-3091, 3119-3120, 3122, 3124, 3261

J.P. Morgan Chase Bank NA, II-3036, 3038-3040, 3042, 3046-3047, 3050-3051, 3055, 3063, 3065, 3068-3070, 3077-3078, 3081, 3083-3084, 3086, 3089, 3093, 3099, 3103

J.R. Simplot Co., I-346, II-2787

JSL Foods Co., I-894

JTEKT, I-1877, 1904

Juanitas Foods, I-917

Juhayna Dairy Corp., I-820

Juhayna Food Industries, I-340

Juillard School, II-3533

Jumptag, II-3309

Jungheinrich Lift Truck Corp., I-1867

Just Born Inc., I-688

Just My Size, I-1050

Just Wireless, I-4, II-2096

Justin & Dave's, I-924

Justrite, I-1854

Jusung Engineering, I-1764

JVC, II-2070

JW Medical, II-2352

J.W. Peter, II-2932

JWT, II-3294-3295, 3317

"K" Line, II-2526, 2573

K2, II-2450

K2 Industrial Services Inc., I-283

Kabat-Toustova, I-325

Kaiser Foundation, II-3153-3154, 3158

Kaiser Permanente, II-3155-3156

Kal Tire, II-2877, 3415

Kalitta Air L.L.C., II-2525

Kalpataru Power, II-2000

Kameda, I-884

KaMin L.L.C., I-223

K&L Gates, II-3564

K+S, I-227, 1567-1569, 1571

Kanghui Medical, II-2386

Kansai Electric Power Company, II-2712

Kansai Paint Co. Ltd., I-1517

Kansas City Chiefs, II-3485

Kansas City Southern, II-2499

Kansas City Southern de México, II-2499

Kantar, II-3580

Kao Brands, I-1373, 1432, 1500

Kao Corp., I-1486

Kaplan University, II-3536

Karas & Karas Glass Co. Inc., I-295

Karcher, II-2045

Kardex Remstar, I-1870

Karl Storz, II-2389

Karnataka Cooperative Milk Producers Federation Ltd., I-341

Kar's Nut, I-872

Katz Group, II-2964

KaVo, II-2395-2396, 2398-2399

Kawasaki, I-1821, II-2305, 2326

Kayser-Roth Corp., I-985, 988

KazAtomProm, I-171

KB Home, I-246, 249-251, 253, 255, 257-258, 262, 265

KB PCB Group, II-2126

KBR Inc., I-279, II-2317
KCI, I-1132
KDAC, II-2235
KDS, II-2130
KEC, II-2000
Keebler Co., I-636, 639, 867
Keihin, II-2239, 2262
Keiper, II-2257, 2259
Keith Zars Pools Ltd., I-299
Kel-Tec CNC, I-1795
Keller Williams, II-3252-3254
Keller's Creamery, I-388
Kellogg Co., I-305, 338, 342, 344, 536, 560-561, 604, 636, 639, 649-650, 679, 700, 704-705, 900
Kellwood Company, I-1025, 1044, 1046
Kelly-Moore, II-2784
Kelly Services, II-3341-3343, 3589
Keltbray, I-298
Keman Orthopaedics and Rehabilitation, II-3519
KEMET, II-2152
Kemps L.L.C., I-414, 422
Kenan Advantage Group, II-2511
Kendall/Hunt, I-1227
Kenneth Cole Productions, I-1035
Kenny's Candy Co., I-683
Ken's Foods, I-518
Kensington, I-1218
Kent Feeds, I-595
Kenworth, II-2228-2230
Kerr, II-2397
Kerry Group, I-316, 330
KerryBS, I-911
Ker's Winghouse Bar & Grill, II-2949
Kesko, I-312
Kessinger Publishing L.L.C., I-1219
Ketchum, II-3594
Kettle Foods, I-869, 876
Keurig, I-846
Key Energy Services Inc., I-212
Key Land Homes, I-260
Keybank NA, II-3035, 3039, 3045, 3047, 3052, 3068, 3070, 3079, 3081
Keystone Foods L.L.C., I-351, 360
KFC, II-2950, 2957, 3263
KGHM, I-166
KHD, I-1890
Khiton, I-1561
KHS&S Contractors, I-285, 288

KI Furniture, I-1121, 1123
Kia Motors, II-2196
Kid Brands, II-2438
Kids II, II-2438
Kiewit Corp., I-277-278
Kiewit Mining Group Inc., I-185
Kigili, I-1369, 1576
Kikkoman Corp., I-318
Killingsworth Environmental of the Carolinas, II-3326
Kimball, I-1121, 1123
Kimberly-Clark Corp., I-1013, 1139-1141, 1167, 1171-1172, 1176, 1178-1179, 1182, 1185, 1188-1192, 1195, 1486, II-2390
Kimco Realty, II-3244-3245
KinderCare Learning Centers, II-3548
Kindred Healthcare, II-3512, 3549
Kinetic Concepts, I-1130
Kinetics, I-291
King County DOT/Metro Transit, II-2502
King Fook, II-3004
The King of Shaves Co., I-1752
King Ranch, I-147
King Soopers, II-2824, 2973
Kingdee, II-3349, 3357
Kingfisher, II-2557
Kingmax Semiconductor, II-2137
Kingsdown, I-1120
Kingston Technology, II-2137
Kinnarps, I-1122
Kinoplex, II-3444
Kinross Gold, I-161
Kion Group, I-1867
Kirby Corp., II-2528
Kirin Brewing Co., I-318, 757
Kirin Holdings Co. Ltd., I-33, 767
Kirkland & Ellis, II-3531
Kirklands, II-3013
Kisko Products, I-418
Kiss Products Inc., I-1460
Kisscat Co. Ltd., I-1642
Kitz, I-1801
Kjustendil, I-308
Kleven Maritime, I-1846, 1853
KLLM Transport Services L.L.C., II-2510
Kloosbeheer B.V., II-2521
Kmart, II-2857, 2911, 2913
Knauf, I-1692
Knight Transportation, II-2513
Knoll, I-1121, 1123

Kobayashi, I-1558
Kobelco, I-1842, 1861, 1907
Koch Farms Inc., I-122
Koch Industries Inc., I-1147, 1195
Kochu Shokuhin, I-318
Kodak, I-1959, 1961, II-2413, 2415, 3387
Kohler, I-1682, 1763
Kohl's, II-2792, 2896, 2911, 2913
Komatsu, I-1767, 1840, 1842, 1844, 1877
Komatsu Utility Co., I-1867
Konami Corp., II-3365
Konami Sports & Life Co. Ltd., II-3472
Kone, I-1856
Konecranes, I-1864
Kongsber Maritime, II-2343
Kongsberg Defense Systems, II-2344
Kongsberg Hydroid Inc., II-2344
Kongsberg Maritime AS, II-2344
Koninklijke Philips Electronics N.V., II-2053
Konka Group Co. Ltd., II-2073
Kopeyka, II-2849
Korea Electric Power Corp., II-2716
Korea Telecom, II-2698
Korea Tobacco & Ginseng Corp., I-950
Korea Zinc Group, I-1738
Korean Air, II-2560
Korn/Ferry International, II-3591
Koryo, II-2022
Kovach Inc., I-291
KPMG, II-3286, 3574-3575
KPN Telecom, II-2698
Kraft Foods Inc., I-129, 305-309, 311, 313, 316-317, 321-322, 324-328, 330-331, 338, 344, 346, 362, 364, 368, 383, 402-404, 427, 514, 518, 598, 636-637, 639, 649, 652, 658, 660, 663-668, 671-672, 674-676, 685, 688, 697, 700, 707, 711, 725, 727-728, 730, 734, 802, 846, 849-850, 852, 854, 857, 863, 867, 872, 884-885, 904-905, 924, 934, II-3125
Kraus-Anderson Construction, I-274
Kremechug, I-1553
Krispy Kreme Doughnut, I-609, II-2934

Kroger, II-2626, 2790, 2812-2813, 2823, 2826, 2831-2833, 2840, 2842, 2848, 2850, 2911, 2964-2965, 2972, 2978

Kroll, II-3316

Kronos, II-3351

Kronospan, I-1106

Kronoswiss, I-1106

Krosaki, I-1681

Kroy, I-1102

Kruger, I-1140-1141

Krups, II-2040

Kruse, I-1411

KSB, I-1901

KTR, I-1805

Kubota Corp., I-1831, II-2326

Kuehne & Nagel, II-2506

Kuka Industrial Robots, I-1923

Kulicke & Soffa, I-1895

Kumho Group, I-1289

Kumho Tire Co. Ltd., I-1606

Kuok Oils & Grains Pte Ltd., I-339, 732

Kuozui, II-2207

Kureha Corp., I-1546

Kurita, I-1924

Küster, II-2258

Kuwait Petroleum Corp., I-196

Kvartal, II-2800

KWH Pipe Canada Ltd., I-1628

Kwik Kar, II-3422

Kwik Trip (Tobacco Outlet Plus), II-3024

KWS, I-51

Kyocera, I-1680, II-2151-2152, 2162

Kyocera Kinseki, II-2130

Kyushu Electric Power Company, II-2712

L-3 Communications Corp., II-2317, 3601

L-3 Linguist Operations & Technical Support, II-3396

La Brea Bakery, I-619

LA Fitness, II-3473

La Maderileña S.a. de C.V., I-778

La Preferida Inc., I-917

La-Z-Boy Furniture Galleries, II-2904

La-Z-Boy Inc., I-1111

LabCorp., II-3578

Laborers' International Union of North America, II-3561

Laclede, I-1344

Laconia Savings Bank, II-3062

Lactalis, I-313, 317, 323, 402

Lactogal, I-323

Lady Americana, I-1120

Lafarge, I-215, 1670, 1674, 1684, 1687

Lagardère Publishing/ Hachette Livre, I-1200

Lagunitas Brewing Co., I-769

Laiteries Réunies, I-328

Lake Sunapee Bank FSB, II-3062

Lakeshore Engineering Services, I-242

Lakeside Foods Inc., I-479

Lakewood Church, II-3566

Lam Soon, I-1389, 1392

Lamar Advertising Company, II-3296

Lamers Bus Lines Inc., II-2505

Lancaster Colony Corp., I-615

Lance, II-2887

Land O'Frost Inc., I-368

Land O'Lakes, I-383, 388, 391-392, 395, 430, 500, 595, 734

L&F, II-2155

L&H Packing Surelan Foods, I-355

Landis + Gyr, II-2337

Landmark Print, II-3319

Landscape Concepts Management, II-3323

Landstar System, II-2508

Lane Construction Corp., I-277

Langaard, I-947

Langer Juice Co., I-489, 494

Länsförsäkringar, II-3147

Lantmännen, I-311

Lantus, I-1352

Lao Fengxiang, II-3006

Larry H. Miller Group of Cos., II-2871

LaSalle Southwest Corrections, II-3595

Latham & Watkins, II-3531

Laufen, I-1679

Laura's Lean Beef, I-358

Lavazza, I-846

Lavendon, I-1860

Lavo, II-2961

Lawson, II-2798

LAX Nightclub, II-2961

Layne Christensen, I-293

Layton Construction, I-270

Lazard, II-3124

LDC, I-313

LDK Solar, I-1769

Le Pages Inc., I-1161

Leachman Cattle of Colorado, I-112

Leaf International B.V., I-675

Lear Corp., I-1128, II-2241, 2244, 2259

Learjet, II-2271

Learning Care Group Inc., II-3548

Learning Cuve Brands, II-2485

LeasePlan USA, II-3409

Lee & Man Paper, I-1143

Lee Enterprises, I-1203

Lee Homes, I-258

Lee Kum Kee, I-521, 1317

Lee Memorial Health System, II-3516

Leeann Chin's, II-2945

Lefebvre, I-1234

Legal & General Group PLC, II-3132

L'eggs Hanes Bali Playtex, II-2802

L'eggs Products, I-985

Lego, II-2439

Lehigh Phoenix, I-1229

Lehman Brothers, II-3123

Lennar Corp., I-246-247, 249-250, 252, 255, 257-261, 265, 267

Lennox, I-1986

Lenovo, I-1935-1938, 1940, 1942-1944, 1946, II-2147, 3370

Lenzing, I-1133, 1293-1294

Leo Burnett Worldwide, II-2607, 3294-3295

Leon Hup Holdings, I-319

Leone Construction Co., I-254

Leprino Foods Co., I-383

Lepu, II-2352

Les Schwab Tire Centers, II-2877, 3415

Level 3, II-2638

Lever Brothers Co., I-1432, 1448

Levi Strauss and Co., I-1017, 1035, 1039, 1042, 1046

Lewis Bakeries Inc., I-619

Lexmark, I-1956, 1958, 1965

LF, II-3006

LG Chemicals, II-2165, 2169, 2172-2173

LG Electronics, I-1984-1985, II-2014-2015, 2021-2022, 2026, 2029, 2072, 2077-2078, 2081-2082, 2086, 2095-2096, 2147

LG Group, I-1289

LG Siltron, II-2149

Li Ning Company Ltd., I-1651, II-2898

Liaoning Fuwa Heavy Industry Machinery Co. Ltd., I-1861

Libbey Inc., I-1665

Liberté, I-442

Liberty Bank, II-3040

Liberty Bank of Arkansas, II-3037

Liberty Media Corp., II-2694

Liberty Mutual, II-3133, 3145, 3172, 3175-3176, 3179-3182, 3184, 3192, 3195, 3198, 3200, 3202-3203, 3205, 3207-3208, 3213, 3216-3218, 3222, 3225, 3227-3228, 3230

Liberty Tax Services, II-3286

The Libman Co., II-2473

Library of Congress, II-3538

Liby, I-1363, 1372

Lidestri Foods, I-520

Lidl & Schwartz, II-2858

Lidl Hellas & Co. E.E., II-2829

Lids, II-3014

Lids Kids, II-3014

Liebherr, I-1840, 1861, 1864-1865

Life Care Centers of America, II-3512

Life Care Services L.L.C., II-3551

Life Fitness, II-2445

Life of the South Group, II-3148

Life Sciences, II-2332

Life Technologies, II-2330

Life Time Fitness Inc., II-3472

LifeChurch.tv, II-3566

LifePoint Hospitals, II-3515

Lifetouch Inc., II-3282

Lilly, I-1337-1338

Limagrain, I-51

Limited Brands, I-1017, 1019, II-2896-2897, 3030

Lincare, II-3522

Lincoln Electric, I-1883

Lincoln National Group, II-3149

Lincoln Property Company, II-3247

Lincy Foundation, II-3553

Linde, I-1257, 1261-1262

Lindt & Sprüngli A.G., I-661, 711, 717, 720

Line-X Franchise Development Corp., II-3412

Linksys, II-2116-2118

Lion, I-1373

Lion Capital, I-312

Lion Shoji, II-2493

Lionbridge Technologies, II-3396

Lionsgate, II-3436, 3441

Lipinski Snow Services, II-2729

Lipton, I-934

Literary Licensing L.L.C., I-1219

Lithia Motors Inc., II-2871

Little Busy Bodies, I-1182

Little Caesars Pizza, II-2956

Little Debbie, I-617

Little Giant, I-1813

Little Things Factory, I-1891

Liugong, I-1841

LIV, II-2961

Live Nation Entertainment Inc., II-3497

Liz Claiborne Inc., I-1019, 1046

L.L. Bean Inc., I-1080, II-2450

Lloyd's, II-3135, 3141, 3239

Lloyd's Pest Control, II-3326

Loblaw Cos. Ltd., II-2812, 2820

Local Government Officials, II-3237

LocalEdge, I-1235

LOCAP L.L.C., II-2564

LockerMate, II-2492

Lockheed Martin CA, II-2343

Lockheed Martin Corp., II-2269, 2310, 2312, 2314-2317, 3601

Loctite Corp., I-1547

Loftex, I-1069

Lofthouse Foods, I-636

Logitech, II-2097

Lombardo Homes, I-254

London Stock Exchange, II-3129

Lone Star Transportation, II-2508

Long Bright, I-1713

Long Fong Group, I-538

Long John Silver's, II-2959

Long Lake Ltd., I-255

Longhai Duoling Saw Blade Co. Ltd., I-1759

Longview Fibre, I-1746

Lonkey, I-1400

Lonking, I-1841

Lonmin, I-178-179

Lonza, I-1539

Look's Gourmet Food Co., I-466

Loomis, II-3381

L'Oréal, I-1420-1421, 1424, 1426-1427, 1430, 1448, 1455-1456, 1461, 1480, 1483, 1486-1488, 1505, II-3292

Lorillard Inc., I-937, 956

Los Alamos National Bank, II-3064

Los Angeles Clippers, II-3483

Los Angeles Dodgers, II-3482

Los Angeles (LACMTA), II-2295

Los Angeles Lakers, II-3483

Los Pelambres (Antofagasta), I-153

Lotte Group, I-662

Louis Cruise Line, II-2532

Louis Vuitton, II-2887

Louisiana Citizens Property Insurance Corp., II-3218

Louisiana Corrections Services Inc., II-3595

Louisiana Farm Bureau Mutual Insurance Co., II-3198, 3218

Louisiana-Pacific, I-1107

Louisville Bedding, I-1076

Louisville Ladder, I-1813

Lousiana-Pacific, I-1104

Lovenox, I-1352

Low & Bonar, I-238

Lowe's, II-2782, 2790, 2911, 2920

Loxam, II-3331

Loyalty Travel Agency, II-2568

LSG Sky Chefs, II-2936

LSU Health System, II-3516

LSU Tigers, II-3484

Lucas World Inc., I-690

Lucky Country Inc., I-683

Lucky Stores, II-2853

Lufthansa, II-2548, 2560

Luk Fook, II-3004

LukOil, I-1589

Lumber Liquidators, II-2908

Luobupo, I-1567

Luotong, I-1841

Lusacell, II-2605

Lusitania Seguros, II-3145

Luxottica, II-2409-2410, 3027-3028

LVI Services, I-298

LVMH, I-777, 787, 1421, 1424, 1651, II-3014

LyondellBasell, I-1251, 1279-1281

M. Aron Corp., I-1041

M/I Homes, I-246, 250, 256, 267

M1, II-2614

MA Labs, II-2137

Maaco Franchising, II-3412

MaBelle, II-3004

Mabrouk Group, II-2860

Mabthera, I-1352

Mac-Gray Corp., II-3278

Macerich, II-3244-3245

Mack, II-2230

Macmillan, I-1218, 1221, 1227

Macquarie Infrastructure L.L.C., II-2572

Mac's Snacks, I-874

Macy's, II-2790, 2792, 2884, 2896, 2909, 2911, 2913, 3005

Maersk Container Industry, I-1779

Magasin Generale, II-2860

Magna International Inc., I-1128, 1634, II-2241, 2243

Magnavox, II-2079

Magnesitas, I-1681

Magnetti Marelli, II-2251, 2255

Magnit, II-2800

Magnolia, II-2800

Magnum, II-2242

Mahindra and Mahindra, II-2202

Mahyco, I-1353

Maidenform, I-1050

Mail Contractors of America Inc., II-2525

Majestic Drug Co., I-1621

Major League Baseball, I-23, II-3482

Majority PAC, II-3565

Make Us Great Again, II-3565

Makita, I-1881

Malaysia Smelting Corp., I-1730

Malco Products, I-1394

Malcolm Drilling Co. Inc., I-297

Malibu, II-2292

Malt-O-Meal Co., I-560

MAN, I-1818, 1821, 1826, 1907

MANAC, II-2321

Management & Training Corporation, II-3595

M&G, I-1283

M&I Marshall & Ilsley Bank, II-3056, 3058, 3084

Mando, II-2235-2236, 2248, 2252-
2253

Mane S.A., I-1527

Manhattan Associates, II-3361

Manhattan Sound Recording Studios, II-3388

Maniform, I-1049

Manischewitz Co., I-466

Manitowoc Co., I-1861

Manitowoc Milk Producers Cooperative, I-430

Mankattan Food Co. Ltd., I-611

Mankind, I-1341

Mannington, I-15, 1002, II-2482

Mann's, I-914

Manor Care, II-3522

Manpower Inc., II-3589

ManpowerGroup, II-3342-3343, 3396

Manson, I-282

Manual Woodworkers, I-1078

Manufacturers & Traders Trading Co., II-3041, 3053, 3065, 3071

Mapfre North American Group, II-3172

Maple Leaf, I-309, 597

Maples Rugs, I-1073

Marathon Oil Corp., II-2528, 2796

Marathon Petroleum Co., II-2879

Marathon Petroleum Corp., II-2878

Marathon Pipe Line L.L.C., II-2564

Marazzi, I-15, 1679

Marc Jacobs, II-2887

Marcal Paper Mills, I-1140, 1185

Marcho Farms/Provimi Foods, I-359

Marchon, II-2409

Marc's, II-2970

Mariani Packing Co. Inc., I-863

Marine Harvest USA, I-841

Marine Products Corp., II-2288-2289

The Mark Travel Corp., II-2569

Markel Corp., II-3187

Marketstar Corporation, II-3318

Marks and Spencer PLC, I-1019

Marlin Firearms, I-1795

Marquez Brothers International, I-917

Marriott Hotels, Resorts & Suites, II-3263

Marriott International Inc., II-3270

Marrokal Design & Remodeling, I-245

Marry5, II-2666

Mars Drinks, I-846

Mars Inc., I-305-306, 314, 316, 323-
324, 330-331, 338-339, 344, 414, 455, 578, 582, 584, 586-588, 658, 660-662, 664-666, 668, 671, 674, 676, 688, 700, 705, 711, 713, 716-
717, 724, 878, 888

Mars Petcare U.S., I-591

Marsh, II-2831

Marshalls, II-2884

Martec Handels, I-1412

Marten Transport Ltd., II-2510

Martin Franchises Inc., II-3275

Martin Marietta, I-215, 219, 1685

Martin's Famous Pastry Shoppe Inc., I-626

Maruti Suzuki, II-2202

Marvel Comics, I-1206

Marvel Entertainment, I-23

Mary Kay, I-1421, 1461, II-3021

Maryland (MARC), II-2295

The Maschhoffs, I-118

Masco Corp., I-288, 1091, 1111, 1510, 1682, 1763

Mascom, II-2583

Mason Distributors, I-1300

Massey Energy Company, I-185

Massey Services Inc., I-140, II-3323-3324

Massimo Zanetti USA, I-849, 854

Mastec Inc., I-281, 297

Master Chem, I-1594

MasterBrand Cabinets Inc., I-1111

MasterBrands, I-1091

MasterCard, II-3090

MasterCraft, II-2292

Masterra Doral, I-259

Matchmakers International, II-3288

Mathson, I-1257

Matrix Essentials, I-1448

Matrix Fitness, II-2445

Matt Brewing Co., I-769

Mattamy Homes, I-260

Mattel Inc., I-23, II-2436, 2438-
2439, 2443, 2486

Matthews International, II-2479

Mattress Firm, II-2909

Mattress Giant, II-2909

Mauser A.G., I-34

Maverick USA, II-2508

Max Furniture, II-2912

Maxim Crane Rental Corp., II-3330

Maxima, II-2819

Maxis Communications, II-2603

Maxxis International/Cheng Shin Rubber, I-1606

May Trucking Co., II-2510

Maybelline, I-1426

Mayer Labs, I-1344, 1621

Mayfield Dairy Farms, I-422

Maytex Mills, I-1075

Mazak, I-1876

Mazda, II-2196, 2198, 2204

M.B. Sports, II-2292

M.C. Dean Inc., I-284

McBride, I-1576

McBride & Son Homes, I-263

McCain Foods USA, I-346

McCall Foods, I-475

McCann Erickson Worldwide, II-3294-3295

McCarthy Holdings, I-274

McClatchy Co., I-1203

McCormick & Co. Inc., I-506, 522, 834, 916

McDonald's, II-2937-2938, 2940, 2947, 2952, 2957-2958, 3263

Mcel, II-2606

McFit GmbH, II-3472

McGee Brothers Co. Inc., I-287

McGee Group, I-298

McGraw-Hill, I-1217, 1224, 1228

McGraw-Hill Education, I-1200, 1227

McGree Brothers Co. Inc., I-286

MCI, II-2599

McKee Foods Corp., I-609, 617, 636, 649, 700

McKelvey Homes, I-263

McKinnery Drilling Co., I-297

McNeil Consumer Products, I-1305, 1307, 1316

MCP, I-646

McShane Construction Co., I-268

MDFirst Bank, II-3069

MDHI, II-2276

M.D.C. Holdings/Richmond American Homes, I-253, 257, 262, 264

Mead Johnson Nutrition Co., I-448, 460-461

Meadow Buffalo, I-358

MeadWestvaco Corp., I-37, 1145, 1155, 1197, 1265

Mears Transportation, II-2503

Mechanical Inc., I-291

Med-El, II-2378

Medco Health Solutions/Express Scripts, II-2988

Media Solutions, II-3026

Mediacom Communications Corp., II-2701

MediaNews Group, I-1203

Medical Insurance Exchange of California, II-3210

Medical Management Inc., I-138

Medical Protective Co., II-3210

Medicap, II-2974

Mediterranean Farms S.A., I-333

Mediterranean Shipping Co., II-2527

Medley, I-1339

Medline, I-1130

MedQuist L.L.C., II-3394

Medtronic Inc., I-1131, II-2351, 2358, 2360-2361, 2363, 2380-2381, 2383-2384

Mega Brands, I-1547, II-2456, 2465

Meijer Inc., II-2812, 2826, 2831

Meiji Co., I-660

Meiji Dairies Corp., I-318

Meiji Seika Kaisha, I-318, 1346

Meineke Car Care Centers, II-3412

Melco Crown, II-3489

Melitta USA, I-854

MEMC, II-2149

Menards, II-2782

Mengniu Dairy Industry, I-310

Menora Mivtachim, II-3142

Men's Wearhouse, I-1017, 1043, II-2883-2884

Mentholatum Co., I-1458

The Meow Mix Co., I-582

Mercedes-Benz, II-2197, 2201, 2206, 2209

Mercer Transportation, II-2508

Merchants & Farmers Bank, II-3057

Merchants Bank, II-3079

Merck & Co., I-1307, 1316, 1337-1338, 1342, 1359, 1504

Merck Animal Health, I-1330

Merck KGaA, I-1354, II-2330

Mercury Distributors, II-3026

Meredith Corp., I-1207, 1209

Merial Ltd., I-1330

Meridian Health, II-3151, 3549

Meritage Homes Corp., I-246, 252-253, 255, 262, 265

Meritplan Insurance Co., II-3170

Merkle, II-3317

Merlin Entertainments Group, II-3481

Merrell, I-1611

Merrick & Co., I-269

Mesa Airlines, II-2542, 2554, 2556, 2559

Mesaba Airlines, II-2546, 2555, 2559

Messer, I-1262

Met-Rx Substrate Technology, I-704

MetaBank, II-3089

Metallo Chimique, I-1730

Metalworking Lubricants, I-1594

Meteor, II-2600

Metersbonwe Group, II-2898

Methodist Hospital, II-3517

MetLife Auto & Home Group, II-3203

MetLife Bank NA, II-3073

MetLife Home Loans, II-3105, 3110

MetLife Inc., II-3114, 3132, 3153, 3261

Metriplan Insurance, II-3189

Metro, II-2502, 2820

Metro A.G., II-2803

Metro Cars, II-2501

Metro Group, II-2819

Metro S.A., II-2829

Metropolitan Group, II-3149

Metropolitan Life & Affiliated Cos., II-3150

Metsä Tissue, I-1139

Mey Icki Sanayi ve Ticaret AS, I-751

Meyer Burger, I-1767

MFA Inc., II-2787

MFA Oil Co., II-3022

MGA Entertainment, II-2436

MGIC Investment Corp., II-3234

MGM Grand, II-3489-3490

MGM Mirage, I-257

MHI, I-1817, 1823

Miami Dade College, II-3536

Miami Heat, II-3483

Michael Foods, I-125

Michael Saunders and Company, II-3255

The Michaels Organization, I-268

Michaels Stores, II-3015

Michelin North America Inc., I-1287, 1599

Michelin/Uniroyal Goodrich, I-1605

Microchip, II-2139

Micron Technology, II-2141, 2146

Microsoft, II-2097, 2352, 2646, 2663, 2671, 2676, 2930, 3264, 3306, 3308-3309, 3346, 3355-3356, 3360, 3365-3366, 3449

Midas, II-3412

Middlesex Savings Bank, II-3054

Midwest Drywall Co. Inc., I-285

Midwest Poultry Services, I-125

Midwestone Bank, II-3048

Migdal, II-3142

Migros, I-328

Mike Albert Fleet Solutions, II-3409

Mike's Express Car Wash, II-3420

Milacron, I-1594

Millard, II-2521

Millennial Media, II-3309

Millennium, I-1522, 1530

Miller & Long Company Inc., I-292

Miller Pipeline Corp., I-281

MillerCoors, I-305, 756

Millie and More, I-1178

Milliken & Company Inc., I-982, 1003

Millipore, I-1920

Milwaukee Brewers, II-3482

Mindray, II-2365-2366

Minera Volcan, I-158, 166

Ming, II-3006

Minghong, I-930

Mingyang, I-1824

Minimax, II-2114

Ministop, II-2798

Minks Custom Homes, I-260

Minmetals, I-156

Minnieland Private Day School Inc., II-3548

Minnmetals, I-158

Minsur, I-1730

Minto Group, I-259

The Minute Maid Co., I-500

MISC, II-2526, 2529, 3141

Mission Essential Personnel, II-3396

Mission Foods, I-874

Missouri Employers Mutual, II-3228

Mister Car Wash, II-3420

Mitchells & Butlers, II-2940

Mitsubishi, I-1856, II-2007, 2142, 2196, 2204, 2458

Mitsubishi Caterpillar Forklift, I-1867

Mitsubishi Chemical Corp., I-1251, 1289, II-2153

Mitsubishi Electric, II-1996, 2004

Mitsubishi Estate Co., II-3257

Mitsubishi Fuso, II-2228-2229

Mitsubishi Heavy Industries Ltd., I-1821, II-2308, 2311, 2313

Mitsubishi Tanabe, I-1342

Mitsui, I-1864

Mitsui Engineering & Shipbuilding, II-2346

Mitsui Fudoshan, II-3257

Mitsui O.S.K. Lines, II-2526, 2529, 2573

Mizuno, I-1031, 1613

MJC Cos., I-254

MLMIC Group, II-3209, 3233

MMC Corp., I-291

MMR Group Inc., I-284

Moark L.L.C., I-125

Mobil, I-1590, II-2797

Mobil 1 Lube Express, II-3422

Mobile Mini, II-3332

Mobilink, II-2610

Mobilitie, II-2112

Mobiltel, II-2584

Mobinil, II-2590

Mobis, II-2241, 2248

Mobistar, II-2581

Modelo, I-767

Modern Biomedical & Imaging, II-3425

Modern Retail, II-2072

Moen, I-1763

Mogensen, I-1845, 1894

Mohawk, I-15, 1002-1003, 1073, 1677, 1679, II-2482

Moitz Embroidery Works Inc., I-983

Molina Healthcare of Michigan Inc., II-3151

Molinera de Mexico S.A. de C.V., I-557

Molino E. PastifFLLI De Cecco, I-896

Molnlycke Health Care, II-2391-2393

Molson Coors, I-309, 330, 750, 758, 767

Momentive Performance Materials, I-1549

Momentum Worldwide, II-3318

Mondi, I-1143, 1146

Monetka, II-2849

Monitronics, II-3385

Monocrystal, II-2162

Monotronics International, II-3384

Monro Muffler Brake, II-2877

Monsanto, I-51, 1354, 1534

Monster Beverage Co., I-817

Montagut, I-1027

Montblanc, II-2454

Montefiore Medical Center, II-3517

Monterey Gourmet Foods, I-894

Montreal (AMT), II-2295

Montreal Canadiens, II-3486

Montreal Urban Transit, II-2502

Moody's, II-3316

Moosehead, I-758

Mordovcement, I-1673

Morgan Corp., I-297

Morgan Stanley, II-3078, 3086, 3120, 3124, 3261

Mori Seiki, I-1877

Morningstar, II-3316

Morpho, II-2121

Morrison's, II-2859

Mortenson Construction, I-272

Mortgage Guaranty Insurance Co., II-3235

Morton Salt, I-1394

Mosaic, I-227, 1532

Mossberg/Maverick Arms, I-1795

Motel 168, II-3269

Motorcity Casino, II-3490

Motorola, I-1932, II-2096, 2102, 2108

Mountain States Rosen L.L.C., I-359

Mountain West Bank, II-3045, 3059

Mountain West Insurance Group, II-3207

Mountaire Farms Inc., I-122

Move Inc. sites, II-2668

Moventas, I-1784-1785

Movicel, II-2576

Movilnet, II-2620

Movistar, II-2577, 2586, 2588, 2591, 2594, 2611-2612, 2620

Mr. Handyman International L.L.C., II-3431

Mr. Roof, I-290

Mr. Transmissions/Transmissions USA, II-3412

MRB Snacks & Associates, I-874

MRM Worldwide, II-3317

MSA, II-2379

MSC, II-2536

MSC Cruises, II-2531-2532

MSD, I-1339

MSL Group, II-3594

MSN Real Estate, II-2668

MT Irancell, II-2599

MTA New York City Transit, II-2502

MTC, II-2607

MTD Products, I-1836

MTML, II-2604

MTN, II-2613

Müller, I-443-444

Multiglass, I-1658

Multimatic, II-2254

Multisorb, I-35

Munchkin Bottling, II-2438

Munchkin Inc., II-2485-2486

The Mungo Cos., I-251

Munich Re, II-3239

Murata, I-1680, II-2151

Murata Machinery Ltd., I-1870

Murray Biscuit Co., I-636

Murray Franklyn Cos., I-266

Musculoskeletal Transplant Foundation Inc., II-3526

Music Express, II-2501

Mutual of Omaha Bank, II-3060

MVNOs, II-2592, 2609

MWW Group, II-3593

My Bella Flor Co., I-1178

Mybaby, I-1026

Mylan, I-1345-1346

Mylykoski, I-1138

MYR Group Inc., I-284

Nabors Industries Ltd., I-204, 212

NACCO Industries, I-1867

Nafine, I-1363, 1372

Nalco, I-176, 1924

Namiki, II-2162

Nan Tong, I-1289

N&W, I-1976

Nanya PCB, II-2126

Nasdaq, II-3129

Nash Finch, II-2842

Nathan's Famous, I-364

National, I-1687

National Aeronautics and Space Administration, II-2187

National Australia Bank, II-3101

National Bank of Arizona, II-3036

National Basketball Assn., II-3483

National Beef Packing Co. L.L.C., I-351, 357, 360

National Beverage, I-817

National Construction Enterprises Inc., I-285

National Dairy Development Board, I-341

National Distributors (Cyprus) Ltd., II-2819

National Education Association of the United States, II-3561

National Envelope Corp., I-1197

National Equity Fund Inc., II-3248

National Express Corp., II-2505

National Football League, I-23, II-3485

National Golden Tissue, I-1185

National Grape Coop, I-481

National Hockey League, II-3486

National Iranian Oil Co., I-195-196

National Oceanic and Atmospheric Administration, II-3397

National Oil Corp., I-196

National Oilwell Varco Inc., I-1848-1849, 1851, 1901

National Pen Corp., I-43

National Pension (Korea), II-3237

National Rehabilitation Hospital, II-3519

National Thermal Power Corp., II-2711

National Union Fire Insurance Co. of Pittsburgh, II-3210, 3215

National Veterinary Associates, I-138

National Vision, II-3027

Nations Roof L.L.C., I-290

Nationstar, II-3112

Nationwide Group, II-3133, 3176-3178, 3180-3183, 3187, 3190, 3192, 3199, 3201-3204, 3208, 3217, 3219-3222, 3232

Natracare, I-1178

Natura Cosmeticos S.A., II-3021

Natural Food Holdings, I-359

Natural Waters of Viti Ltd., I-802

Naturally Fresh, I-924

Nature Inc. (Happy Baby), I-450

Nature's Bounty, I-1300

Nature's Path Foods, I-560

NatureWork, I-1274

NAUE, I-238

Nautic Global Group, II-2289

Nautic Star, II-2289

Nautilus Hyosung America Inc., I-1969

Naver, II-2655

Navigant Consulting, II-3592

Navigators Insurance Co., II-3215

Navoi, I-171

Navoi MMC, I-161

Navy Federal Credit Union, II-3087

Nawras Telecom, II-2609

NayaTel, II-2640

NBBJ, II-3571, 3573

NBS Inc., II-3024

NBTY, II-2986

NCI Building Systems, I-1781

NCO Group Inc., II-3315

NCR Corp., I-1969

NDK, II-2130

Nebraska Beef Ltd., I-357

Nebraska Furniture Market, II-2908

NEC, II-2094, 2152, 2407

Neil Kelly Co., I-245

Neiman Marcus Group, II-2792, 3005

Nelnet, II-3099

Neo Epoch, I-259

Neo Quimica, I-1339

Nephew, II-2380

NES Rentals, I-1860, II-3330

Nestlé China Ltd., I-310, 716, 859

Nestlé Healthcare Nutrition, I-450, 460, 488

Nestlé Malaysia, I-319

Nestlé Purina PetCare Co., I-578, 582, 584, 591

Nestlé S.A., I-33, 305, 307-309, 313-317, 321-331, 338-344, 385, 413, 423, 443-444, 448, 455, 461, 521, 586-588, 637, 658, 660-661, 666-668, 671-672, 674, 676, 690, 807, 821, 850, 888, II-3290

Nestlé USA Inc., I-345, 383, 491, 535-536, 541, 554, 681, 683, 697, 705, 707, 711, 717, 894

Nestlé Waters North America, I-802, 804

NetApp, I-1951, 1953

NetCom, II-2608

Netflix, II-3448

Netgear, II-2116-2118, 2120

Netjets, II-2275

Neucei, I-1133

Neuf Cegetel, II-2698

Neulasta, I-1352

Neutrogena Corp., I-1426

Neuville Industries, I-988

Nevin, II-2399

New Balance, I-1611, 1613, 1615

New Belgium Brewing Co., I-769

New Boliden, I-158, 1738

New Century, II-3123

New England Coffee Co., I-854

New England Conservatory, II-3533

New Holland, I-1832

New Horizon Academy, II-3548

New Jersey Transit Corp., II-2502

New Mexico Bank & Trust, II-3064

New Oriental, II-3544

New Orleans (NORTA), II-2295

New Orleans Reg. Physician Hospital Organization Inc., II-3160

New Orleans Saints, II-3485

New Page, I-1154

New Pig, I-1854

New Sun Nutrition Co., I-811

New World Pasta, I-890, 896

New York Giants, II-3485

New York Jets, II-3485

New York Knicks, II-3483

New York Life Group, II-3149-3150

New York Lighter Co., II-2491

New York/New Jersey (PATH), II-2295

New York (NYC Transit), II-2295

New York-Presbyterian Hospital, II-3517

New York Public Library, II-3538-3539

New York State Thruway Authority, II-2572

New York Stock Exchange Euronet, II-3129

New York Times Co., I-1203

New York Yankees, II-3482

Newcrest Mining, I-161

Newegg.com, II-2928

Newell Rubbermaid Inc., I-18, 20, 1063, 1634, II-2456, 2458, 2465, 2486

Newman's Own, I-518, 520

Newmont Mining, I-161

Newpark Resources Inc., I-1850, II-2727

Newport Insurance Co., II-3170, 3189

Newport/Layton Home, I-1071

News Corp., I-1203, II-2692-2694, 3292, 3386

The News Group, II-3026

Nexans, I-1915

Next PLC, I-1019

Nextel, II-2577, 2605, 2612, 2685

Nexxus Products Co., I-1448

Ney, II-2396, 2398

NGL Energy Partners L.P., II-3022

Nibco Inc., I-1628

Nice Group, I-1363, 1372-1373

Nice-Pak Products, I-1182

Nichi-Iko Pharmaceutical Co. ltd., I-1346

Nichia, II-2155

Nichicon, II-2150

Nichirei Logistics, Euofrigo, Frigo Logistics. HIWA Rotterdam, II-2521

Nichols Farms, I-112

Nichols Partnership, I-253

Nicholson Construction Co., I-297

Nick A. Panicholas & Sons, I-858

Nickelodeon Consumer Products, I-23

Nielsen Business Media, II-3404

The Nielsen Co., II-3580

Nigerian National Petroleum Corp., I-196

Nihon Kohden, II-2366

Nike, I-988, 1017, 1030-1032, 1035, 1608, 1611, 1613-1615

Nikken Corp., I-1860, II-3331

Nikon, II-2413, 2415

Nilfisk Advance, II-2045

Nine Dragons Paper Holdings, I-1137, 1143

Nine West Outlet, II-2802

Nintendo, II-3360, 3365-3366

NIOC, II-2529

Nippon Carbon, II-2153

Nippon Chemi-con, II-2150

Nippon Chemiphar Co. Ltd., I-1346

Nippon Kayaku Co. Ltd., I-1346

Nippon Life Insurance Co., II-3132

Nippon Meat Packers, I-318

Nippon Mektron, II-2126

Nippon Paint Co., I-1512, 1515, 1517

Nippon Paper, I-1137

Nippon Seiki, II-2256

Nippon Steel, I-1701

Nippon Suisan USA, I-345, 841

Nippon Telegraph & Telephone Corp., II-2641

Nippon Zeon, I-1289

Nippun, I-556

Nipro, I-1346, II-3524

Nishio Rental All Co., II-3331

Nissan, II-2196, 2198, 2204, 2209, 2215, 2228-2229, 3096

Nissan Forklift Corp., I-1867

Nisshin, I-556

Nissin Foods Holdings Co. Ltd., I-891

Nissin Kogyo, II-2247-2248

Nitro, II-2290

Nitto Denko, I-1920

Nitto-Fuji, I-556

Nizchecansk, I-1553

NJM Insurance Group, II-3174

N.K. Hurst Co., I-511

NKMZ, I-1696

NKT, I-20

N.M.C.C., II-2573

Nobel Biocare, II-2401

Nobel Learning Communities Inc., II-3548

Nobilia, I-1112

Nobilium, II-2399

Noble Drilling, I-203

NOK Inc., I-1285

Nokia, II-2095, 2100, 2147, 3360

Nokia Ovi Store, II-2926

Nolte, I-1112

Nomura, I-455

Nonnis Food Co., I-639

Nont X-Flow, I-1921

Norampac, I-1142

Noranco, I-1347

Norbord, I-1106-1107

Norcal Mutual Insurance Co., II-3210

Norcraft, I-1091

Nord Contor, I-314

Nordstrom, I-1017, II-2792, 2884

Norfolk, I-282

Norfolk Southern, II-2499

Norilsk, I-178-179

Norit America, I-1265

Normandy Builders, I-245

NORPAC Foods Inc., I-479

Norse Skog, I-1138

Norson, I-378

North American Coal Corporation, I-185

North American Coatings L.L.C., I-283

North American Philips Light, II-2057

North American Shipbuilding, I-1853

North Carolina Farm Bureau Insurance Group, II-3201

North Face, I-1080, II-2450, 2997

North Pacific Canners, I-526

North Point Community Church, II-3566

North Shore Bank FSB, II-3084

Northam, I-179

Northbridge, II-3135

Northern Foods, I-637

Northern Trust Co., II-3046

Northfield Savings Bank, II-3079

Northland Residential Corp., I-248

Northrim Bank, II-3035

Northrop Grumman, II-2317, 2525

Northway Bank, II-3062

The Northwest Company, I-1078

Northwest Dairy Association, I-430

Northwest Natural Products, I-1300

Northwestern Mutual Group, II-3149-3150

Nortura, I-321

Norwegian Cruise Line, II-2531-2532

NOV Grant Prideco, I-1713-1714

NOV Tuboscope, I-209

Novamont, I-1274

Novartis, I-1337-1339, 1342, 1345, 1359

Novartis Animal Health, I-1330

Novartis Consumer Health, I-698, 1305, 1307, 1316, 1435

Novo Nordisk, I-1353, II-2353

Novoroscement, I-1673

Novozymes, I-911

NOVUS Glass, II-3412

The NPD Group Inc., II-3580

NRF Distributors, II-2737

The NRP Group, I-268

NSG Group, I-1654-1658, 1660-1662

NSK, I-1904, II-2334, 2398

NSW Government, II-3293

NTC, II-2640

NTC Marketing, I-494

NTN Corp., I-1904

Nu Skin Enterprises Inc., I-1325, II-3021

Nuance Communications Inc., II-3394

Nucor Corp., I-1701, 1781-1782

Nufarm, I-1542

Nuffield Health Fitness & Wellbeing, II-3473

Numark Industries, II-2434

Nuprecon/CST Holdings L.L.C., I-298

NutraSweet, I-1523

Nutrisa S.A., I-413

Nutrisystem Inc., II-3290

Nuvasive, II-2384

Nuziveedu Seeds, I-1353

NV Homes, I-247

NVR, I-246-247, 250-251

NXP, II-2127, 2138

NYCE, II-3094

NYK Line, II-2526, 2529, 2573

Nypro Inc., I-1634

Nyrstar, I-1738

NYSE Euronext, II-3129

O2, II-2593, 2621

O2 Ireland, II-2600

Oakwood Healthcare, II-3520

Oakwood Homes, I-253

OAO Rosneft, I-195-196

OB Cos - Simply Self Storage, II-2522

Oberthur, II-2121

Occidental Seguros, II-3145

Ocean Hospitalities, II-3271

Ocean Spray Cranberries Inc., I-489, 872

Oceaneering International Inc., II-2346

OceanServer Technology Inc., II-2344

Ochirly, I-1045

OCT Parks China, II-3481

Octapharma, II-2359

Ocwen Loan Servicing, II-3111

Ode (Defond), I-1975

Odom's Tennessee Pride Sausage Inc., I-371

Odwalla Inc., I-500, 649

Oerlikon, I-1767

Oetker, I-314

OfficeMax, I-1161, II-3016

Officine, I-238

Ogilvy Government Relations, II-3564

Ogilvy Public Relations Worldwide, II-3594

OgilvyOne Worldwide, II-3317

O'Grae, I-337

Ohio State University, II-3484, 3536

Ohio Turnpike Commission, II-2572

Ohio Valley Flooring, II-2737

Oiwas, I-1646

Oji Paper, I-1137, 1143

Okuma, I-1877

Olab, I-1975

Olan Mills, II-3282

Old Castle, I-1672

Old Chicago/Rock Bottom Restaurant, II-2956

Old Dominion Foods Inc., I-692

Old Dominion Freight Line, II-2512

Old Dutch Foods Inc., I-865, 876

Old Herrold Ferm, I-325

Old National Bank, II-3047

Old North State Masonry L.L.C., I-287

Old Orchard Brands, I-491

Old Republic Family, II-3236

Old Republic Group, II-3182, 3225

Old World, I-1593

Olin, I-1254

Olive Garden, II-2948

Olivet, I-1648

Olympus, II-2389, 2415

OM Group Inc., I-168

Oman Mobile, II-2609

Omat, I-1822

Omega 900, II-2400

Omega World Travel, II-2568

OMNOVA Solutions, I-48

Omron, II-2244, 2356

Omsk, I-1553

On-Cor Frozen Foods L.L.C., I-535

One Reverse Mortgage, II-3114

One Way Furniture, II-2912

Onecare, II-2473

O'Neil Industries/W.E. O'Neil, I-273

Onewest Bank FSB, II-3038

Onida, II-2022, 2072, 2086

Onkyo, II-2065

ONLY, I-1045

Onward Kashiyama Co. Ltd., I-1018

Onyx Corp., I-1460

Ooma Inc., II-2102

Opel, II-2201, 2206

Optical Shop of Aspen, II-3028

Option One, II-3123

Optus Mobile, II-2578

Optus (On-net), II-2635

Oracle, I-1951, 1955, II-3346, 3349, 3351, 3356, 3360-3361, 3370

Orange, II-2583, 2592, 2602, 2604, 2615-2616

Orbitz Worldwide, II-2568

Orchard Supply Hardware, II-2786

Orchard Valley Harvest Inc., I-863

Orchid Island Juice Co., I-500

Orchids Paper Products Co., I-1185

Oreck, II-2044

O'Reilly Auto Parts, II-2875

Organic Girl, I-926

Organica, I-1631

Organizacion Soriana S.A. de C.V., II-2791, 2805, 2837

Orica Ltd., I-1551

Orient, I-1909

Oriental CJ, II-3018

Oriental Weavers, I-1073

Oriflame Cosmeticos S.A., II-3021

Original $2 Car Wash, II-3420

Orion (China) Co. Ltd., I-611

Orkla, I-321, 327, 455

Orlando Magic, II-3483

Orlando Regional Medical Center, II-3517

Orval Kent Foods Co., I-346

Oscar Mayer, I-345, 351, 360, II-2072

OshKosh, I-1021

OSI Group L.L.C., I-351, 360

Osram, II-2048, 2054-2055, 2057
Otis Elevator, I-1856
Otsuka, I-900, 1010, 1342
Otsuka Sims (Guangdong) Beverage
  Co. Ltd., I-828
Ottawa Rangers, II-3486
Otter Products, I-4
Otto Baum Co. Inc., I-287
Otto Marine, I-1846
Our Destiny PAC, II-3565
Outback Steakhouse, II-2948
Overseas Shipholding, II-2529
Overstock.com, II-2912, 3017
Overwaitea Food Group, II-2820
Owens Corning, I-1585, 1692
Owens Country Sausage Inc., I-874
Oxford Industries, I-1043
Oxford University Press, I-1227
OXXO, II-2937
Oxy Vinyls LP, I-1282
OxyChem, I-1254
Pabco, I-1687
Pabst, I-756
Pace, II-2108, 2118
Pace Suburban Bus, II-2502
Paceco Esp, I-1864
Pacer International, II-2509
Paceshave Corp., I-1752
Pacific Coast Feather, I-1073, 1076
Pacific Foods of Oregon, I-466, 468
Pacific Gas & Electric Co., II-2720
Pacific Metals, I-170
Pacific Southwest Realty Services,
  II-3102
Pacific Western Transportation,
  II-2503
Pacific World Products, I-1460
Pacificare of Colorado Inc., II-3154
Packaging Corp., I-1142
Paclantic, I-1022
Paddock Pools and Spas, I-299
Paladin, I-171
Palermo Villa Inc., I-554
Palisades Group, II-3174
Pall, I-1920
Palmer Candy Co., I-867
Palmetto Exterminators, II-3326
Paloma, I-1986
Pamir Tianquan Co. Ltd., I-807
Pan American Silver, I-166
Panacea Biotec, I-1353
Panalpina, II-2506
Panasonic, I-1765, II-2044, 2079,
  2081, 2094, 2101-2102, 2147,

2150, 2169-2170, 2172-2173, 2255,
  2415, 2749, 3264
Panda Choc-Finfoods, I-683
Panda Express, II-2945
Pandigital, II-2074
Pandora, II-2687
Panera Bread, II-2957
Panhandle State Bank, II-3045
Panolam, I-1625
The Pantry Inc., II-2796
Papa John's International, II-2956
Papa Murphy's Take 'N Bake Pizza,
  II-2956
Papa-yannis, I-315
Paradigm, II-3456
Paramount, II-3436, 3441
Paramount Farms, I-730
Paramount Recording Studios,
  II-3388
Parkdale Mills, I-1004
Parke Bisleri Ltd., I-822
Parker, II-2454
Parker Hannifin Corp., I-1285, 1287,
  1619, 1916
ParkWhiz, II-2642
Parle Products Pvt Ltd., I-341
Parmalat Group, I-309, 317, 323,
  343, 442
Parques Reunidos, II-3481
Parsons Brinckerhoff, I-269, II-3569
Parsons Corp., I-278
Partner Logistics, II-2521
Partner Re, II-3239
Partners HealthCare, II-3518
Party America, II-3013
Party City, II-3013
Passumpsic Savings Bank, II-3079
Pasta Foods, I-888
Pasta Zara, I-892
Pat Salmon & Sons Inc., II-2525
Patagonia, II-2450
Patrick Industries, I-48
Patriot Coal Corp., I-185
Patterson-UTI Energy Inc., I-204
Patton Boggs L.P., II-3564
Pavel Vais, I-325
Pavestone, I-21
Paychex Inc., II-3576
Payless, II-2903
Payless Car Rental Systems Inc.,
  II-3408
Payne Family Homes, I-263
PBI Bank, II-3050
PCCW, II-2698

PCCW Mobile, II-2596
PDS Technical Services, II-3341
Peabody Energy Corp., I-185
Peak Realty Inc., II-3256
Pearson Candy Co., I-692, 1200,
  1222, 1224, 1227-1228
Pearson PLC, I-1217
Peavey Electronics Corp., II-2434
Peco Foods Inc., I-122
Peerless Clothing, I-1035
Peet's Coffee & Tea Inc., I-849, 854,
  858, II-2933
Pegatron, II-1992
Peguform, II-2242
Pei Wei, II-2945
Pella Corp., I-1111
Pendleton Woolen Mills, I-1070
Penguin USA, I-1218, 1221
Penn National Gaming Inc.,
  II-3491
Penn State Nittany Lions, II-3484
Pennfield Corp., I-595
Pennsylvania Higher Education As-
  sistant Authority (PHEAA), II-3099
Penny Press/Dell, I-1209
Pennzoil 10-Minute Oil Change,
  II-3422
Penske Automotive Group Inc.,
  II-2871, 2874
Pentagon Federal Credit Union,
  II-3087
Pentair, I-1901
Pentax, II-2415
Pentel, II-2456, 2458, 2462, 2465
People's Food, I-454
Peoples United Bank, II-3040, 3062,
  3079
Pep Boys, II-2875, 2877
Pepperidge Farm, I-597, 618-619,
  636, 639
Pepsi Lipton Tea Partnership N.A.,
  I-795
PepsiCo, I-33, 305, 309-310, 315,
  329-331, 338, 340, 342-344, 561,
  604, 650, 802-804, 811, 817-826,
  828, 884, II-3310
Perdue Farms Inc., I-122, 129, 351,
  360
Perekriostok (XS Group), II-2849
Perfect, II-2121
Perfect Fit Industries, I-1076
Perfection Learning, I-1228
Perfetti Van Melle, I-660, 667, 702,
  727-728

Performance Contracting Group Inc., I-285

Performance Pipe, I-1628

Pericom, II-2130

PerkinElmer, II-2330

Perkins + Will, II-3571, 3573

Perkins Restaurant and Bakery, II-2951

Permanis Sdn Bhd, I-319

Pernod Ricard, I-311, 316, 322, 327, 330, 777, 787-789

Perry Homes, I-255

Pescanova, I-326

Pet Food Express, II-3033

Pet Supermarket Inc., II-3033

Pet Supplies Press, II-3033

PETCO Animal Supplies Inc., II-3033

Peter Pan Bus Lines, II-2503

Peterbilt, II-2228-2230

Petermann Ltd., II-2505

PetersDean Inc., I-290

Petra Foods, I-722

PetroChina, I-195, 1279-1280, 1591

Petroleo Brasiliero S.A., I-195

Petroleos de Venezuela S.A., I-195-196, 1581

Petroleos Mexicanos, I-195

Petroleum Geo-Service, I-208

PetSmart Inc., II-3033

Peugeot, II-2206, 2209

Pez Candy, I-690

PF Clearwater Paper, I-1140

PFC Wild Products, I-1460

Pfizer Animal Health, I-1330

Pfizer Inc., I-448, 461, 1305, 1316, 1337-1339, 1342, 1345, 1359, 1458, II-3292

Pfleiderer, I-15

PGI, I-1013

Pharmaceutical Product Development Inc., II-3577, 3587

Pharmavite Corp., I-1300

PHH Arval, II-3409

PHH Mortgage, II-3100, 3105-3109, 3112

Philadelphia Eagles, II-3485

Philadelphia Flyers, II-3486

Philadelphia Phillies, II-3482

Philip Morris International Inc., I-938-941, 943-946, 948-952, 959-963

Philips, I-1935, II-2055, 2072, 2080, 2348, 2350, 2354, 2356-2357

Philips Healthcare, II-2361, 2364-2366

Philips Lighting Co., II-2048, 2054, 2057-2058

Philips Respironics, II-2368

Phillips-Van Heusen Corp., I-23, 1035, 1038-1039, II-2883

PhillyCarShare, II-3391

Phoenix, II-2224

Phoenix Brands, I-1394

Phoenix Children's Academy, II-3548

The Phoenix, II-3142

Physicians Reciprocal Insurers, II-3209, 3233

PICC, II-3136, 3223

Pick n Pay Retail Group, II-2855

Pico Global Services, II-3400

The Pictsweet Co., I-479

Pier 1 Imports, II-2904

Pierre Cardin, I-1027, 1040, II-3028

Pike Electric Corp., I-284

Pilgrim's Pride Corp., I-122, 360

Piller, II-2004

Pillsbury USA, I-346

Pilot, II-2456, 2458

Ping An, II-3223

Pingan, II-3136

Pinkberry, II-2953

Pinnacle Airlines Corp., II-2546-2547, 2559

Pinnacle Bank, II-3060, 3085

Pinnacle Family of Companies, I-268, II-3247

Pinnacle Foods Corp., I-345, 479, 536, 554, 598, 745

Pinnacle National Bank, II-3076

Pioneer, II-2065

Pioneer Food Group Ltd., I-343

The Pipestone System, I-118

Pirelli & C S.p.A., I-1599, 1606

Pittsburgh Penguins, II-3486

Pivovary Topvar (SABMiller), I-765

Pizza Hut, II-2956-2957, 3263

Plains Pipeline L.P., II-2564

Planet Fitness, II-3472

Plantronics, II-2096-2097, 2101-2102

Plastic Omnium, II-2242

Plastics Corp., I-1628

Plastipak Packaging Inc., I-1632

Platinum Pools, I-299

Platinum Storage Group, II-2522

Playboy Inc., I-1027

Playtex Products Inc., I-1050, 1182, II-2485

Plodo-vitovo, I-308

Plovdiv, I-308

Plum Organics, I-450

Plumrose USA, I-362

Plunkett's Pest Control, II-3323

Plymouth Rock Cos., II-3172

PMI Group Inc., II-3234

PMI Mortgage Insurance Co., II-3235

PNC Bank NA, II-3046-3047, 3050, 3053, 3055, 3063, 3068, 3071, 3082, 3093, 3099

PNC Tax Credit Capital, II-3248

Podesta Group, II-3564

POET Biorefining, I-1524

Pohjola, II-3138

Polaris Industries, II-2325-2326

Polo Ralph Lauren, I-1017, 1035

Poly International, II-3555

Polycom, II-2111

Polyconcept North America, I-44

Polygon Northwest Co., I-266

Polymetal, I-166

PolyPipe Inc., I-1628

Polysius, I-1890

Pompeian, I-744

Pomp's Tire & Auto Service, II-3415

Pons Quimicas, I-1577

Pool Corp., II-2757

Popeyes, II-2950

Portfolio Recovery Associates Inc., II-3315

Portland Trail Blazers, II-3483

POSCO, I-1701

Post Cereals, I-560, 649

Potash Corp., I-227, 1532

Poulin's Pest Control, II-3325

Power Bar Inc., I-704

Powerchip Technology, II-2128, 2141

Powermat USA, I-4

PPG Industries, I-1254, 1510, 1513, 1516-1517, 1656, 1662, II-2784

PPR S.A., I-1651

PQI, II-2137

Praderas Huasteca, I-356

Prairie Farms Dairy, I-383, 414, 500

Pratt & Whitney, I-1820, II-2280

Pratt Paper, I-1142

Praxair, I-1257, 1261-1262

Precision Castparts Corp., I-1782

Precision Drilling Corp., I-204

Company Index

Precision Tune Auto Care, II-3412
Precision Walls Inc., I-285
Preferred Freezer Services, II-2521
Preferred Professional Insurance
  Cos., II-3211
Premera, II-3155
Premier Foods, I-316, 330
Premier Global Sports, II-3400
Premier Health Care Services,
  II-3527
Premier Pools and Spas, I-299
Premier Rental, II-3336
President Enterprises China Invest-
  ment, I-496, 859
Pressman, II-2439
Pressure Systems International,
  I-1905
Prestage Farms, I-118
Prestige Brands Holdings, I-698
Pretty Women L.L.C., I-1460
Price Chopper, II-2863
Price Rite, II-2847
Priceline.com, II-2568
PricewaterhouseCoopers, II-3286,
  3574-3575
Pride International Inc., I-203
Pride Transport Inc., II-2510
Prido, I-1772
Prime Healthcare Services, II-3515
Prime Inc., II-2513
Prime Success International Group
  Ltd., II-2898
Prime Tanning Co. Inc., I-1636
Primerica Group, II-3150
Princes, I-888
Princess Yachts Intl. Ltd., II-2291
Principal Bank, II-3048
Printpack Inc., I-1623
Priorities USA Action, II-3565
Priority Health, II-3151
Private Bank & Trust Co., II-3046
PRM International Inc., I-1517
Pro Flowers, II-3023
Pro Foot Footcare Products, I-1436
Pro Source, I-705
ProAssurance Corp. Group, II-3209,
  3211, 3233
ProBuild Holdings Inc., II-2782-
  2783
The Procaccianti Group, I-248
Procesdora De Alimentos Cale, I-679
Procter & Gamble Co., I-578, 582,
  584, 586, 591, 698, 876, 884, 1140-
  1141, 1171-1172, 1176, 1178-1179,

1182, 1185, 1191-1192, 1195,
  1307, 1316, 1364, 1366, 1368,
  1372-1374, 1384, 1410, 1414,
  1426, 1430, 1432, 1448-1449,
  1455-1456, 1470-1472, 1475,
  1483-1488, 1557, 1751-1752, 1918,
  II-2167, 2473, 2475, 3292, 3311
Productos Valle Verde S.A. de C.V.,
  I-569
Professional Property Manintenance,
  II-2729
Profill Holdings (TSC Apparel and
  WearMagic), I-1081
Proforma, I-43
ProFunds, II-3121
Progold, I-646
Progress Energy Florida Inc., II-2720
Progressive Insurance Group,
  II-3133, 3171, 3173, 3175, 3177,
  3179-3182, 3221-3222, 3307
Progressive Waste Solutions Ltd.,
  II-2727
Project/Major, II-2526
Promo in Motion Inc., I-679, 863
Promotions Unlimited, II-2462
Promutual Group, II-3209
Prosegur, II-3381, 3383
Protection 1, II-3384
Protection One, II-3385
Provide Commerce, II-3023
Providence Health & Services,
  II-3514
Provident Funding Associates,
  II-3103, 3110
Proximus, II-2581
Prudential, II-3132, 3149-3150,
  3252-3254
PRXL, II-3577
PSA, II-2197, 2200, 2203, 2205,
  2208, 2536
PSV, II-3139
PT Timah, I-1730
Public Library of Cincinnati and
  Hamilton County, II-3539
Public Storage Inc., II-2522
Publicis, II-3295
Publix, II-2790, 2812-2813, 2816,
  2838, 2840, 2851, 2856, 2981
Pulse, II-3094
Pulte/Del Webb/Centex, I-248, 250,
  252-257, 259-263, 265-267
Pulte Group, I-246, 249
Puma, I-1031-1032, 1613-1614
Punch Taverns, II-2940

Purcell Tire & Auto Service Inc.,
  II-3415
Pure Nightclub, II-2961
PWS Inc., II-3278
Pyaterochka (XS Group), II-2849
Pyramid Hotel Group, II-3271
Pyrsmian, I-1915
Qatar Petroleum Corp., I-196
QBE, II-3134, 3141, 3220
Qdoba, II-2955
Qeelin, II-3004
QGTC, II-2526
Qiansiniao, I-1481
Qinchuan, I-1876
Qingdao Doublestar Industrial Co.
  Ltd., I-1604
Qingdao Haier Co. Ltd., II-2025
Qingdao Laoshan Spring Co. Ltd.,
  I-807
Qinman, I-1040
QLogic, II-3368
QNPL, I-168
QST Industries Inc., I-983
Quad/Graphics Inc., I-1236
Quaker Chemical, I-1594
Quaker Oats Company, I-560, 649,
  700, 802
Quaker Steak & Lube, II-2949
Qualcomm, II-2146
Quality Distribution Inc., II-2511
Quality Food Centers, II-2854
Quality Liquid Feeds, I-595
Quanta Services Inc., I-281, 284,
  II-1992
Quantum, I-1948, 1955
Quantus Catering, II-2936
QuebecorWorld Inc., I-1229
Queensland Government, II-3293
Queensland Nickel, I-170
Quest, II-3578
Quick Leonard Kieffer International,
  II-3591
Quicken Loans Inc., II-3107
Quickie Manufacturing Corp.,
  II-2473
Quicksilver, I-1032
Quicksilver Resources, I-199
Quinoa Corp., I-333
Quintiles, I-1353, II-3577, 3587
Quorum Health Resources,
  II-3592
Quzi, I-1481
QVC, II-3005, 3017
R B Pamplin, I-982

R. Twining, I-931, 934

Raasi Seeds, I-1353

Rabenhorst GmbH, I-337

Radian Group Inc., II-3234

Radian Guaranty Inc., II-3235

Radio One Inc., II-2691

RadioShack, II-2925, 2927, 3010

Rainbow, I-23

Rainbow Foods, II-2839

Rakon, II-2130

Ralcorp Frozen Bakery Products, I-615

Ralphs, II-2836

Ramaxel Technology, II-2137

Ranbaxy, I-1341

Randa, I-1035

R+L Carriers, II-2512

Random House, I-1218, 1221-1222

Randstad Holding, II-3342-3343, 3589

R+V, II-3139

Range Resources, I-199

Ranger, II-2290

RAO Norilsk, I-170

Rapp, II-3317

Rapunzel Naturkost A.G., I-337

Ratner Companies, II-3283

Ratos, I-321

Raymond Geddes & Co., II-2465

Raymour & Flanigan, II-2904

Rayonier, I-1133-1134

Rays New York, I-598

Raytheon Co., II-2317

Raytheon Systems, II-2343

Razer, II-2097

RBC Bank USA, II-3034, 3043, 3066

RBS Citizens NA, II-3054-3055, 3062, 3068, 3073, 3079, 3119

R.C. Bigelow Inc., I-931, 934

RC2 Corp., II-2486

RCA, II-2079, 2101-2102

RCB Bank, II-3069

RDA Holding Co., I-1207

RE/MAX, II-3252-3256, 3263

Reaction Search International, II-3591

Reader's Digest, I-1209

Ready Pac Produce Inc., I-479, 913, 926

Real Living, II-3252-3253

Reale Mutua, II-3143

Reckitt Benckiser, I-698, 1316, 1344, 1364-1369, 1373, 1394, 1409-1412, 1486, 1557, 1559, 1562, 1574-1579, 1621

Recology Inc., II-2727

Record, I-1773

Recruit Staffing and Staff Service, II-3343

Recticel, I-1631

Red Bull, I-811, 817, 828

Red Co. Foods Inc., I-931

Red Diamond, I-934

Red Gold, I-476

Red Lobster, II-2948

Redbox, II-3448

Reddy Ice, I-887

Redi Carpet, II-2908

Redwing, II-2395

Reebok, I-1608, 1612, 1615, II-2802

Reed Elsevier, I-1200, 1208, 1232-1233

Reed Exhibitions, II-3404

Reed Mango, II-2953

Refac Optical Group, II-3027

Regal, II-2289, 3445

Regence, II-3155

Regency Corp., I-1343

Regions Bank, II-3034, 3037, 3042-3043, 3047, 3051, 3057-3058, 3076, 3093

Regis Corp., II-3283, 3289

Rehau, II-2242

Reily Foods, I-854

Reinsurance Group of America, II-3239

Related Cos., I-268

The Related Group, I-248, 259

Relativity, II-3441

The Relaxing Co. Inc., I-815

Reliance, I-1283

Reliance Energy Limited, II-2711

Reliance Industries, I-1280

Reliance Life Sciences, I-1353

Relly Foods Inc., I-931, 934

Rembrandt Enterprises, I-125

Remicade, I-1352

Remington Arms, I-1795

Rémy Conintreau Group, I-787

Renasant Bank, II-3057

Renault, II-2197, 2201, 2206, 2208, 2210

Renesas, II-2127, 2138-2139, 2146

Renfert, II-2397

Renfro Hosiery Mills, I-988

Renrenle, II-2794

Rent-A-Center/ColorTyme, II-3336

Rent-A-Wreck of America, II-3408

Rent One, II-3336

Rentokil/Ehrlich-Presto-X, II-3324

Replacement Parts Inc., II-2875

Republic Bank & Trust Co., II-3050

Republic Holdings, II-2559

Republic Services Inc., II-2727

Research in Motion, I-1932, II-2100

Reser's Fine Foods, I-346

Residential Wholesale Mortgage Inc., II-3102

Restonic, I-1120

Restore Our Future, II-3565

Revlon, I-1420, 1426-1427, 1432, 1456, 1460-1461, 1487

Rewe AG, II-2819, 2858

Rexam, I-1634, 1788

Rexnord, I-1805

Reynolds American Inc., I-937, 956, 963, 973

Reynolds Group, I-31, 36, 1151-1152, 1788

Reynolds (Lane), I-971

RG Barry, I-1638

Rhapsody, II-2930

Rhea, I-1976

RHI, I-1681

Rhodes, I-1347

Rhodia, I-1414

Rice University, I-1228

Rich Products Consumer Brands, I-346

Rich Products Inc., I-615

Richemont, II-2424

The Richman Group Affordable Housing Corp., II-3248

Riddell, II-2448

Ridley Inc., I-595

Riello UPS, II-2004

RIM Blackberry App World, II-2926

Rimowa, I-1647, 1649

Rinker, I-41-42

Rio Tinto, I-149, 152, 171, 176, 234, 1717, 1719, 1722

Rite Aid, II-2790, 2964, 2968, 2975, 2979, 2983-2985, 2988, 3387

Rite Rug, II-2908

Ritter GmbH & Co. KG, Alfred, I-337

Ritz Camera & Image, II-3011

Riverband Ranches, I-112

River's End Trading Co., I-1081

Riverstone Residential Group, II-3247

RIWAL, I-1860

RJ Technology, II-2080

RoadLink, II-2509

Robert Bosch L.L.C., II-2241

Robert Half International, II-3343

Robert Talbott Inc., I-1041

Robert W. Woodruff Foundation, II-3553

Robert Wood Johnson Foundation, II-3553

Roberts American Gourmet, I-865

Roberts Hawaii, II-2503

Robi, II-2580

Roche, I-1337-1338, 1342, 1354, II-2332

Rockland Trust Co., II-3054

Rockline, I-1182

Rockstar International, I-811, 817

RockTenn, I-1142-1143

Rockwell Automation Inc., II-1996, 2006

Rockwool International, I-1692

Rodale, I-1207

Rodenburg, I-1274

Rodilla Sanchez S.L., II-2938

Rogers, II-2585

Rogers Family, I-858

Rolex, II-2423-2424

Rollins, II-3323-3324

Rolls-Royce, I-1820, II-2280, 2315

Romon, I-1036

Roncelli Inc., I-242

Rooms To Go, II-2904

Roquette, I-1348, 1523

Rose Acre Farms, I-125

Rosendin Electric Inc., I-284

RosEnergoAtom OAO, II-2714

Rosetta Stone Inc., II-3317, 3543

Rosneft, I-1589

Ross Stores, II-2897, 2899, 2913

Roth & Rau, I-1764

Rottlund Homes, I-260

Round Table Pizza, II-2956

Rouse, I-1040

Rowland Coffee Roasters, I-849

Royal Bafokeng, I-178-179

Royal Bank of Canada, II-3086

Royal Carribean, II-2531-2532

Royal Dutch/Shell Group, I-1251, 1581, II-2878

Royal Highway Tours, II-2503

Royal Outdoor Products, I-1102

Royal Philip, I-21

Royal Ten Cate, I-238

Royal Unibrew, I-311, 327

Royale Linens/Yununs, I-1079

RPM International, I-1549

R.R. Donnelley & Sons, I-1236-1237

RSA, II-3135

RSC Equipment Rental, I-1860, II-3330-3332

RSI Home Products, I-1091

RSM/McGladrey & Pullen, II-3286, 3575

RTKL, II-3573

Ruan Transport Corp., II-2511

Rubicon, II-2162

Ruby Tuesday, II-2948

Rubycon, II-2150

Ruchi Group, I-341

Ruder Finn, II-3593

Ruiz Food Products Inc., I-541

Ruiz Foods Inc., I-345

Rukpke Consolidated Companies Inc., II-2727

Rural/Metro, II-2500

RusHydro, II-2714

Russell Reynolds Associates, II-3591

Russell Stover Candies Inc., I-661, 713, 717, 720

R.W. Knudsen Family, I-489

RWE, II-2710, 2715

Ryan, II-3286

Ryan Construction U.S., I-273

Ryan Homes, I-247

The Ryland Group, I-246

Ryland Homes, I-247, 256-257, 260, 265, 267

SA Cisco, II-2108

Saab Seaeye Ltd., II-2346

Saarioinen, I-312

Saatchi & Saatchi, II-3294

Sabeco, I-766

SABIC, I-1251, 1279-1280

SABMiller, I-33, 322, 325, 750, 757-758, 760, 767

Sabormex S.A. de C.V., I-506

Sabra Dipping Co. L.L.C., I-427

SABS, II-2235-2236

Saddleback Church, II-3566

Saeco USA, I-846

Safeco Insurance Co. of America, II-3170

Safety Group, II-3172

Safeway, II-2790, 2812, 2814-2815, 2821, 2823-2824, 2830, 2836, 2843, 2845, 2853-2854, 2862, 2964, 2973

Safilo, II-2409-2410, 3028

SAFRAN, II-2309

Sage, I-1234

Sage Hospitality, II-3271

Sage Products, I-1182

Saia Motor Freight Line, II-2512

SAIC, II-2199

SAICA, I-1146

Saiichi Sankyo, I-1345

Sainsbury's, I-462, II-2859

Saint Angelo, I-1036

Saint-Gobain, I-222, 1653-1654, 1660-1662, 1687, 1692

St. John Providence Health System, II-3520

St. Johns Insurance, II-3196, 3224

St. Jude Medical, II-2360-2361

St. Louis Blues, II-3486

St. Louis Cardinals, II-3482

St. Paul Fire & Marine Insurance, II-3215

St. Vincent de Paul, II-2994

Saipem S.p.A., I-204, 275

Sak Construction L.L.C., I-281

Sakata, I-51

Salem Communications Corp., II-2691

Sallie Mae Corp., II-3099

Sally Beauty Holdings Inc., II-3030

Salova S.P.A., I-744

Salsa Tamazula S.A. de C.V., I-522

Salt Lake City (UTA), II-2295

Salter Labs, II-2356

Saltigo, I-1539

Salton, II-2040

Salvation Army, II-2993-2994, 3552

Sam Ash Music Corp., II-2932

Sam Kane Beef Processors Inc., I-355, 357

Samas Group, I-1123

Sam's Club, II-2626, 2806-2807, 2809, 2827, 2909, 2911, 2925, 3387

Samsonite, I-1645-1649

Samsung, I-1933, 1935, 1960, 1962-1964, 1966, 1984, II-2015, 2021-2022, 2026, 2029, 2072, 2077-2079, 2081-2084, 2086, 2095-2096,

2100, 2108, 2127, 2136, 2139, 2141, 2143-2144, 2146-2147, 2172, 2415, 3264
Samy Worldwide, I-1456
San Diego Funding, II-3102
San Francisco Giants, II-3482
Sanchez S.A. de C.V., I-1552
Sanden, II-2245
Sanderson Farms Inc., I-122
S&H Green Stamps, II-3406
S&P Co., I-758
Sandpoint Cattle Co., I-112
S+S, I-1894
S&S Activewear, I-44, 1081
Sandvik, I-1690, 1844
Sandy Spring Bank, II-3053
Sanei International Co. Ltd., I-1018
Sanex, I-1379
Sanford Ink, II-2462
SanMar, I-44, 1081
Sanofi-Aventis, I-1337, 1339, 1345, 1359, II-2353
Sanrio, I-23, II-2456, 2465
Sansui, II-2079
Santander, II-3097
Sany, I-1840-1843, 1861, 1866
Sanyo, II-2152, 2172
SAP, II-3346, 3349, 3351, 3360-3361
Sapphire Tech, II-2162
Sappi, I-1133, 1137, 1154
Sapporo, I-758
Sapporo Holdings, I-318
Saputo Inc., I-309, 383
Sara Lee, I-129, 326, 329, 1389, 1559-1562
Sara Lee Food & Beverage, I-351, 364, 368, 371-372, 541, 597, 618-619, 626, 629, 857
Sara Lee Household, I-1436
Sara Lee North American Retail & Foodservice, I-360, 615
Sares-Regis Group, I-249
Sargent & Lundy L.L.C., II-3569
Sargento Foods Co., I-403-404
Sarris Candies Inc., I-867
SAS Institute, II-2548, 3346
Sateri, I-1133, 1293
Sateri Jiangxi, I-1294
SATS, II-2936
Satum Nordic, I-322
Saturday Knight Ltd., I-1068, 1075
Saucony, I-1611
Sauder, I-18

Saudi Arabian Oil Co., I-195-196
Saudi Aramco, I-1581
Saudi Dairy & Foodstuff Co. Ltd., I-324
Savage Arms, I-1795
Save Mart, II-2814, 2828
Savola Group, I-324, 340
Sawai Pharmaceutical Co. Ltd., I-1346
SB Foot Tanning Co., I-1636
SB Global Foods Inc., I-685
SB LiMotive, II-2169
SBA Communications, II-2112
Sbarro, II-2956
SBS, I-1122
S.C. Johnson & Son, I-1384, 1389, 1392, 1400, 1411-1412, 1541, 1557-1562, 1576, II-2473
SCA, I-1137-1141, 1146, 1167, 1188-1190
Scania, II-2200
SCBT NA, II-3074
SCF Group, II-2529
Schaefer Holding International GmbH, I-1870
Schaeffler, I-1904
Schawk Inc., II-3321
Schenik, I-328
Schering-Plough, I-1435-1436
Schiff/Weider Nutrition Internet, I-1300
Schilling Robotics, II-2345
Schindler, I-1856
Schirm, I-1539
Schlumberger, I-206-210, 1847-1848, 1850, 1852, 1855
Schmid, I-1767
Schmidgall, I-1409, 1412
Schmitt Music Company, II-2932
Schneider Electric S.A., II-1993, 2004, 2006, 2157-2159
Schneider National, II-2513
Schneider National Bulk Carriers, II-2511
Schneider Toshiba, II-1996
Schnitzer West, I-266
Schnucks, II-2850
Scholastic, I-1200, 1217, 1224, 1228
Scholle, I-31
School Specialty, I-1224
Schoolsfirst Federal Credit Union, II-3087
Schreiber Foods, I-383
Schüeller, I-1112

Schumacher Group, II-3527
Schutt Sports, II-2448
The Schwan Food Company, I-345, 554, 615
Schwarz, II-2819
SCI, II-3260
Science Applications International Corp., I-269, II-2317, 3601
SCM Group, I-1885-1886
Scooters Coffeehouse, II-2933
SCOR, II-3239
Scottrade Bank, II-3058
Scotts Lawn Service, I-140
Scott's Miracle Gro, I-1541
Scripps Network Interactive, II-2694
Scripto Tokai, II-2491
SDC Homes, I-266
SDI, II-2165, 2173, 3581
SDL, II-3396
Sea Ray, II-2290
Seaboard Foods, I-118, 380
SeaBotix Inc., II-2346
SeaCube Container, II-3335
SeaDrill, I-203
Seagate, I-1949-1950, 1952
Sealed Air, I-35-36, 1623
Sealy, I-1120
Seamap U.K., II-2343
Sears Holding, II-2790, 2792, 2911, 2920, 3005
Sears Portraits, II-3282
Seattle's Best L.L.C., I-849
Seaway Crude Pipeline Co., II-2564
Secom, II-3383
Securitas, II-3383
Security First Insurance Co., II-3224
Security One Lending, II-3114
Security Service Federal Credit Union, II-3087
Sedmoi Kontinent, II-2849
Sedus Group, I-1122
Seedorff Masonry Inc., I-287
Sega, II-3365
Seidio, I-4
Seiko Epson, II-3264
Sekisui House, I-276
Select Comfort, I-1120, II-2904, 2909
Select Media, II-3026
Select Medical Holdings Corp., II-3519, 3549
Select Milk Producers Inc., I-430
Select Sires Inc., I-139
Sellita, II-2423

Selon, I-1036

SEMCO, II-2126

Sempac Systems, I-1157

Sempermed, II-2392

Seneca Foods Corp., I-473

Seng Feng, II-3004

Senior American Funding, II-3102

Sennheiser, II-2097

Sensient Flavors, I-1527

Sensus USA, II-2336-2337

Sepaton, I-1955

Sercel Underwater Acoustics Division, II-2343

Serebryakov, I-1673

Serta, I-1120

Serum Institute of India, I-1353

Servaas Labs, I-1394

Service Employees International Union, II-3561

Service International Corp., II-3285

ServiceMaster Co., II-3280, 3329

Servisfirst Bank, II-3034

Servistar, II-3431

Seven & I Holdings Co. Ltd., II-2799

Seven-Eleven Japan, II-2798

Seventh Generation, I-1185

Severstal, I-1701

SFR, II-2592

SFX, I-1283

SGI, I-1931

SGK, I-201

SGS Industries, II-3321

Shandong Helon, I-1294

Shandong JingaWei, I-1326

Shandong Linglong Rubber Co. Ltd., I-1604

Shandong Liuhe Groupo, I-538

Shandong Luhua, I-732

Shandong Shengtai Tyre Co. Ltd., I-1604

Shandong Weigao, II-2383

Shandong Zhucheng Foreign Trade Co. Ltd., I-538

Shandongh Weigao, II-2386

Shanghai Blower Works, I-1908

Shanghai Carbon Co., II-2011

Shanghai Fosum, II-2353

Shanghai Golden Monkey Food Co., I-716

Shanghai Huayin, I-1449

Shanghai Jahwa United, I-1480, 1501

Shanghai Logistics Equipment, I-1779

Shanghai Machine Tool & Tool Group, I-1876

Shanghai Railway Administration, II-2498

Shanghai Stock Exchange, II-3129

Shanghai Suntory-Maling Foods Co. Ltd., I-859

Shanghai Tobacco (Group) Corp., I-958

Shanghai Uni-Charm, I-1176, 1179

Shanghai Wujing, I-1522

Shanghair Liangyou, I-732

Shanghair White Cat, I-1392

Shanshui, I-1671

Shantui, I-1841

Shanxi Blower, I-1908

Shapell Homes, I-258

Sharp, I-1769, II-2021, 2078, 2081, 2084, 2094

Sharper Image, II-2080

SharpHealthCare, II-3518

Shasta Industries, I-299

Shaw Industries, I-15, 1002-1003, II-2482

Shaw Living, I-1073

Shaw's, II-2817, 2847, 2863

Shea Homes, I-249, 258, 262

Sheffield Forgemasters, I-1696

Shell, I-1588-1591, 1593

Shell Oil Products US/Motiva Enterprises, II-2796

Shell Pipeline Company L.P., II-2564

Shelter Insurance Cos., II-3200

Shensi Yanchang Petroleum Group, I-1580

Shenyang Group, I-1877, 1908

Shenyang Huacheng Antimony, I-174

Shenyang No. 1 Pharma Fty, I-1343

Shenyang Railway Administration, II-2498

Shenzhen A-Best, II-2794

Shenzhen Mindray Bio-Medical Electronics Co. Ltd., II-2362

Sheppard Pratt Health Systems, II-3518

Sherwin-Williams Co., I-1510, 1513, 1517, II-2782, 2784

Shigemitsu Industry, II-2958

Shijiazhuang Sanlu, I-384

Shimadzu, II-2330

Shimano Group, II-2298

Shin-Etsu, II-2149

Shinagawa, I-1681

Shinema, I-1026

Shineway Group, I-339, 454

Shinkawa, I-1895

Shinko Denki, II-2126

SHINTECH, I-1282

Shinva Medical Instrument Co. Ltd., II-2362

Shiseido, I-1420-1421, 1424, 1427, 1461, 1488, 1505

Shofu, II-2398

Shopko Stores, II-3027

Shoppers Drug Mart, II-2815, 2862, 2964

ShopRite Holdings, II-2818, 2855

Shore Inc., II-2434

Showa, I-556

Showyu, I-1481

Shumaker Homes, I-251

Shutterfly, II-3387

Siam Tin Food Product SCO Ltd., I-588

Sibirskiycement, I-1673

Sichuan Changhong Electronics Corp., II-2073

Sidenor, I-1696

Sidley Austin, II-3531

Siegwerk, I-1552

Sielaff, I-1976

Siemens, I-1785, 1805, 1817, 1819, 1823-1824, 1907, 1921, 1924, II-1993, 1996, 2006, 2008, 2053, 2102, 2115, 2157, 2159, 2348, 2350, 2354

Siemens Electric S.A., II-2000

Siemens Healthcare, II-2361, 2364

Siemens Ltd. China Medical Solutions Group, II-2362

Sierra Nevada Brewing Co., I-769

Sierra-Pacific Industries, I-1095

SIG SAUER, I-1795

Sigma-Aldrich, II-2330

Sigma Alimentos S.A. de C.V., I-342, 385, 401

Sigma Plastics Group, I-1623-1624

Signature Brands L.L.C., I-880

Signature Sotheby's, II-3255

Sikorsky, II-2276-2277

Silgan Plastics Corp., I-1632, 1745

Silohuette, II-2409

Siltronic, II-2149

SilverLining Interiors, I-245

Silvinit, I-227

Similasan Corp., I-698

Simmons, I-1120

Simmons First National Bank, II-3037

Simon & Schuster, I-1218, 1221-1222

Simon Property Group, II-3244-3245

Sinclair Broadcast Group, II-2692

Sinclair Oil Co., II-2879

Singamas Container Holdings, I-1779

Singapore Airlines, II-2560

Singer, II-2046

Singer Equipment Co., II-2754

SingTel Mobile, II-2614

Singulus Technologies, I-1889

Sino-Pacific, I-1853

Sinochem Corp., I-1580

Sinoma, I-1671, 1890

Sinomax, I-1072

Sinopec, I-1251, 1279-1280, 1283, 1289, 1581, 1591

Sinosteel Xingtai Machinery & Mill Roll Co. Ltd., I-1696

Sinosure, II-3223

Sinovel, I-1824

Sirva Inc., II-2514

Sisecam, I-1654

Sisters of Mercy Health System, II-3514

Sitel Corp., II-3401

SiTime, II-2148

Sitz Angus Ranch, I-112

Six Flags Inc., II-3481

SJM, II-3489

SJW Corp., II-2721

SK Energy, II-2154

Sk Group, I-1514

SK Merch, II-2462

Skadden, II-3531

Skanska A.B., I-271-272, 274-276

Skanska USA Building Inc., I-242

Skechers, I-1612, 1614

SKF Group, I-1619, 1904

Skidmore Ownings & Merrill L.L.P., II-3573

Skier's Choice, II-2292

Sklavenitis S&S S.A., II-2829

Skoda, II-2201, 2206

Skymark, II-2558

SkyWest, II-2543, 2545, 2555, 2559

Skyworth Group, II-2073, 2108

Slacker, II-2687

Slaveneft, I-201

Sleep Innovations, I-1072-1073

Sleep Studio, I-1072

The Sleep Train, II-2909

Sleepy's, II-2904, 2909

Slim Fast Foods Co., I-704

Slomins Inc., II-3384

Small Planet Foods, I-468, 560, 649, 700

Smart, II-2582

Smart Balance, I-391-392, 395, 734, 741

Smart Modular Technologies, II-2137

Smart Technologies, II-2496

SmarTone, II-2596

Smartply, I-1106

SMD Ltd., II-2346

SMIC, II-2128

Smith & Nephew, II-2381-2382, 2385, 2389

Smith & Wesson, I-1794-1795

Smith Family, II-2994

Smith Hosiery, I-985

Smith Oil Company, I-1849

Smithfield Foods Inc., I-118, 305, 351, 360, 380

Smithfield Packaging Co., I-362

Smith's Food & Drug, II-2835, 2852

Smiths Medical, II-2355

Smoker Friendly International, II-3024

Smokers Choice, II-3024

Smurfit Kappa Group, I-1137, 1143, 1146

Smurfit-Stone Container, I-36, 1137, 1147

The Snack Factory Inc., I-639

Snak Club Inc., I-863, 872

Snapfish, II-3387

SNCF Geodis, II-2506

Snider Tire Inc., II-3415

Snow + Rock, II-2997

Snow's/Doxsee Inc., I-466

Snyder's-Lance Inc., I-692, 865, 867, 869, 876, 878, 880, 884

Sobeys, II-2812, 2820

Socomec, II-2004

Socopa Vlandes, I-313

Sodexo, II-2939

Sofidel, I-1139, 1141, 1190

Soft Sheen Carson, I-1456

Sogo & Seibu, II-2793

Sohy TV, II-2680

Solaris Paper Mills, I-1185

SolarWorld, I-1769

Solo Cup, I-1151-1152

Solomon Page Group Healthcare, II-3591

Solomon's Hypermarket, II-2857

Sonae, I-1106

Sonic, II-2947, 2957

Sonic Automotive Inc., II-2871, 2874

SonicWall, II-2119, 3350

Sonora Agropecuaria, I-378

Sonova, II-2378

Sony, II-2065, 2070, 2072, 2074, 2077-2079, 2081-2082, 2084, 2090-2092, 2146-2147, 2165, 2172-2173, 2413, 2415, 2749, 3264, 3365, 3436, 3441

Sony PlayStation Store, II-3449

Soprod, II-2423

SOS Corporacion Alimentaria, I-733

Sotheby's, II-3555

Souhait, I-1022

SoundBuilt Homes, I-266

Source Interlink, I-1207, 1209, II-3026

South Beach Beverage Co., I-795, 802

South Korean lines, II-2526

Southeast Christian Church, II-3566

Southeastern Container Co. L.L.C., I-1632

Southern California Edison Co., II-2720

Southern Company, II-2713

Southern Farm Bureau Casualty Group, II-3199

Southern Refrigerated Transport Inc., II-2510

Southern States Cooperative Inc., I-595, II-2787, 3022

Southern Tire Market L.L.C., II-3415

Southfield, I-745

Southwest, II-2540-2541, 2545, 2552-2555

SouthWest Water Company, II-2721

Southwestern Mortgage Co., II-3102

Souza Cruz, I-939

Sovereign Bank, II-3054, 3062-3063, 3071, 3073

Sovran Self Storage Inc., II-2522

Soyuzplodimport ZAO, I-787

SP-MSD, I-1359

Spangler Candy Co., I-681

Spanx, I-1050

Spar Group, II-2855

Sparboe Companies Inc., I-898

Sparboe Summit Farms, I-125

SpareBank, II-3144

Spartan Foods, I-573

Spartech Corp., I-1623

Spawn Lab's Impulse, II-2681

Specialized Transportation Inc., II-2514

Speck Products, I-4

Spectrum Health System, II-3161

Speedway SuperAmerica L.L.C., II-2879

Spencer Gifts, II-3012-3013

Spencer N Enterprises, I-1071

Sperian, II-2379

Sphinx, I-1073

SpiceJet, II-2557

Spira Interes, I-311

Spirit, II-2546

Sports Authority Inc., II-2996

Sports Direct, II-2997

Sprague Pest Solutions, II-3325

Spring Air, I-1120

Springer Science, I-1232

Springs Global, I-1073, 1079

Springs Window Fashions, I-1063

Sprint, II-2575, 2638, 2685

Spyder Active Sports Inc., II-2450

SQM, I-227, 1270, 1272, 1567

Square Enix, II-3365

SRG Global Inc., I-1634

SSA Marine, II-2536

SSK, I-201

SSM Health Care, II-3514

Stacks and Stacks, II-2912

Stacy's Pita Chip Co., I-639

Stada, I-1345

Stafford-Smith Inc., II-2754

Stagecoach, II-2504

Staley, I-646

Staluppi Auto Group, II-2871

Stampede Meat Inc., I-355

Stamps.com, II-2669

Standard & Poor's, II-3316

Standard Drywall Inc., I-285

Standard Foods Corp., I-742

Standard Pacific Corp., I-249

Standard Pacific Homes, I-250, 258, 267

Standard Parking Corp., II-3411

Stanley Black & Decker, I-1881

Stanley Convergent Security Solutions, II-3384

Stanley Steemer Intl., II-3280

Stantec Inc., II-3569

Staples, II-2925, 3016

Staples Promo Products, I-43

Star, II-3094

STAR Group, II-3396

Star One Credit Union, II-3087

Star Trac, II-2445

StarBev, I-760

Starbucks Coffee Co., I-33, 849, 852, 854, 858, II-2933-2934, 2957

Starcraft Marine, II-2289

StarFlyer, II-2558

StarHub, II-2614

Starion Financial, II-3067

StarKist, I-841

Staropram en Slovakia (InBev), I-765

Starr Cos., II-3214

Starr Foundation, II-3553

Starr Individual & Liability Co., II-3215

Starwood Hotels and Resorts, II-3270

Stash Tea Co., I-931

State Bank & Trust, II-3043, 3067

State Compensation Insurance Fund, II-3225

State Employees Credit Union, II-3087

State Farm Group, II-3046, 3133, 3150, 3171, 3173-3175, 3177-3182, 3186, 3191-3202, 3204-3208, 3213, 3216, 3218, 3221-3222, 3224, 3230

State Grid Corp. of China, II-2707, 2716

State Insurance Fund, II-3225

State Street Bank & Trust Co., II-3054

State Street Global, II-3121

Staton Corporate & Casual, I-44, 1081

Ste. Michelle Wine Estates, I-779

Steak-N-Shake, II-2951

Steel Series, II-2097

Steelcase, I-1111, 1121-1123

Stella McCartney, I-1651

Stepan Company, I-1414

Steria, II-3373

Stericycle Inc., II-2727

Sterilite, I-18

The Steritech Group, II-3324

Sterling, I-1522

Sterling Jewelers Inc., II-3005

Sterling Savings Bank, II-3070, 3081

Sterling Sound Inc., II-3388

Sterlite Tech, II-2000

Stevens Transport Inc., II-2510

Stew Leonard's, II-2818

Stewart, II-3260, 3285

Stewart Family, II-3236

Stillwater, I-178-179, II-3069

STMicroelectronics, II-2127, 2138, 2142, 2144-2146

Stock Building Supply Inc., II-2783

Stock USA L.P., I-681, 697

Stockman Bank of Montana, II-3059

Stone Group, I-1317

Stone Peak/Fiandre, I-1679

StoneMor, II-3260, 3285

Stoneridge, II-2224-2225

Stonyfield Farm Inc., I-441

Stop & Shop, II-2817-2818, 2847, 2863

Stora Enso, I-1137-1138

StorageMart, II-2522

Stoughton Trailers, II-2321

Strabag S.E., I-275

Strategic Equipment & Supply Co., II-2754

Straumann, II-2401

Strayer University, II-3536

Streamlite, II-2669

Stretch Island Fruit Inc., I-679

Strick Corp., II-2321

Stride Rite, II-2903

Structure Tone, I-270, 272-273

Stryker Corp., I-1130-1132, II-2361, 2381-2385, 2389

Student Transportation Inc., II-2505

Studio at Target, II-3282

Sturm, Ruger & Company, I-1794-1795

STX OSV, I-1846, 1853

Subaru, II-2196, 2204

Suburban Propane Partners L.P., II-3022

Subway, II-2937, 2940, 2957, 3263

Süd-Chemie Inc., I-35

Suddath Cos., II-2514

Suddenlink Communications, II-2701

Südzuker A.G., I-644

Suez, I-1924

Suffolk Construction, I-270, 274

Suli Group, I-1811

Sulzer, I-1901

SUMCO, II-2149

Sumitomo, I-156, 158, 166, 168

Sumitomo Metal Mining, I-170

Sumitomo Realty & Development Co. ltd., II-3257

Sumitomo Rubber Industries Ltd., I-1606

Summer Infant Products, II-2485

Summit Brands, I-1394

Summit Community Bank Inc., II-3083

Summit Entertainment, II-3441

Sun, I-1341, 1931, 1948

Sun Art, II-2794

Sun Chemical, I-1552

Sun Healthcare Group, II-3549

Sun Maid Growers, I-863

Sun Mart/Nash Finch, II-2827

Sun Products, I-1373-1374

Sun-Rype Products Ltd., I-679

Sun Valley Masonry Inc., I-287

Sun West Mortgage, II-3114

SunAmerica Affordable Housing Partners Inc., II-3248

Sunbeam, I-1070

Sunbelt Rentals, II-3330, 3332

Suncare, II-2376

Suncoast Schools Federal Credit Union, II-3087

Suncorp Metway, II-3134

Suncrest Farms Inc., I-874

Sundown Vitamins, I-1300

Sunglass Hut, II-3028

Sunoco Inc., I-1281, II-2796, 2879

Sunoco Pipeline L.P., II-2564

Sunrise, I-1130, II-2616, 3513

Sunrise Senior Living, II-3549, 3551

Sunseeker International Ltd., II-2291

The Sunshine House, II-3548

Sunshine P&C, II-3223

Suntech Power, I-1768-1769

Suntrust Bank, II-3042-3043, 3053, 3066, 3074, 3076, 3080, 3082, 3093

Super 8, II-3269

Super D, II-2930

Super Target, II-2825

Super Value, II-2857

Superglass Windshield Repair, II-3412

Superior Air Handling, I-291

Superior Bank National Assn., II-3034

Superior Bulk Logistics, II-2511

Superior Foods Inc., I-479

Superior Quality Foods, I-511

SuperMedia, I-1235

Supermercados Nacionel, II-2857

Supermercados Organizados S.A. de C.V., II-2837

Supermercados Pola, II-2857

SuperPlus Food Stores, II-2857

Supervalu, II-2790, 2812, 2850, 2964

Surehold, I-1547

SurgutNG, I-201

Susan Thompson Buffet Foundation, II-3553

Susquehanna Bank, II-3053

Sutton Leasing, II-3409

Suzlon, I-1824

Suzuki Group, II-2204, 2210, 2303, 2305

SVDO, II-2258

Svenska, I-1151

Swannee, I-1672

Swanson & Youngdale Inc., I-283

Swatch, II-2424

Sweaty Betty, II-2997

Swedish Match, I-947, 971, 973

Sweet Bay, II-2851

Sweet Leaf Tea Inc., I-795

Sweetwater, II-2932

Swift Galey, I-982

Swift Transportation, II-2513

Swinterton Builders, I-270

Swire Cold Storage, II-2521

Swisher, I-971, 973

Swiss Re, II-3239

Swisscom, II-2616

Swisslog AG, I-1870

Switch, II-3400

SXC/Catalyst, II-2987

Sylvania, II-2048, 2054, 2057-2058, 2079

Symantec, II-3347, 3350, 3360

Symbol, I-1120

SymphonyIRI Group Inc., II-3580

Symrise, I-1527

Synergie, II-3342

Syngenta A.G., I-51, 1354

Syngenta CropProtection, I-1542

Synovate, II-3580

Synovus Bank, II-3034, 3043, 3074, 3089

Synthes Inc., II-2380-2381, 2383-2386

Syrris, I-1891

Sysco Corp., I-351

System One Holdings, II-3341

T. Hasegawa, I-1527

T. Marzetti Co., I-427, 518

T-Mobile, II-2112, 2575, 2589, 2593, 2597, 2618, 2621, 2685

Taco Bell, II-2955, 2957

Tadano Ltd., I-1861

Tahoe, II-2290

Tai Sun Enterprise Co. Ltd., I-742

Taishan Sports Industry Group Co. Ltd., II-2453

Taisho Yakuhin Co. Ltd., I-1346

Taiwan Glass Industry Corp., I-1653

Taiwan Sugar Corp., I-742

Taiwan Synthetic Rubber Corp., I-1289

Taiyo Nippon Sanso, I-1261

Taiyo-yuden, II-2151

Taiyuan Railway Administration, II-2498

Takashimaya, II-2793

Take-Two, II-3365

Takeda, I-1342

Takesago, I-1527

TAL, II-3335

Talecris, II-2359

Taleo, II-3351

Talison, I-1272

Taliya, II-2599

Tamil Nadu Cooperative Milk Producers Federation Ltd., I-341

Tandus, I-1003

Tandy Brands, I-1041

Tangshan, I-1293-1294

TAO, II-2961

Tapiola, II-3138

Target, II-2626, 2790, 2839, 2896, 2911, 2913, 2925, 2929-2930, 2964, 2999, 3005, 3387

Tarkett, I-15, II-2482

Tarrytown Baker, I-573

TASA, II-2634

Tasty Baking, I-617

Tata Motors, II-2202

Tata Power Company Ltd., II-2000, 2711

Tata Steel, I-1701

Tate & Lyle, I-898, 1523

Tauck Inc., II-2569

Taunus Corp., II-3261

Tauris, I-325

Taylor Fresh Foods Inc., I-479

Taylor Morrison, I-246, 262, 267

Taylor Provisions Co., I-371

Taylor Specialty Books, I-1229

Tazo Inc., I-934

TBA Global, II-3400

TBWA Worldwide, II-3294-3295

TCBY, II-2953

TCF National Bank, II-3056

TCL Corp., II-2073

TCM Corp., I-1867

TCS, II-3373

TD Ameritrade, II-3131

TD Bank NA, II-3040-3041, 3052, 3054, 3062-3063, 3065, 3071, 3074, 3079

TD Banknorth, II-3108

TDK, II-2151

Team Fishel, I-281

TeamHealth, II-3527

TeamLogic IT, II-3379

Tech Data Corp., II-2748

Technical Consumer Products, II-2057

Technicolor, II-2108

Technip, I-275

Techno Coatings Inc., I-283

Techtronic, I-1881

Teck, I-156, 158

TECO, I-1819

Tecta America, I-290

Teekay Corporation, II-2529

Teekay Shipping, II-2526

Tegucel Sulacel, II-2595

Telcel, II-2605

Tele2, II-2589

Telecom Argentina, II-2634

Telecom Namibia, II-2607

Telecom Personal, II-2577

Teledyne Gavia ehf, II-2344

Teledyne Technologies Inc., II-2343

Teledyne Webb Research, II-2344

Teleflora L.L.C., II-3023

Telefónica, II-2700

Telefónica Chile, II-2636

Telefonica Moviles, II-2615

Telefónica O2, II-2618

Telenor, II-2597, 2608, 2610

TelePizza S.A., II-2938

Teletalk, II-2580

Teletech Holdings, II-3401

Telmex, II-2700

Telstra, II-2578, 2635, 3293

Telus, II-2585

Tembec, I-1133-1134

Temp Holdings, II-3343

Temple, I-1687

Temple-Inland, I-1142

Tempur-Pedic, I-1120

Tenaris, I-1714

Tenet Healthcare Corp., II-3515

Tenfu, I-930

Tennant, I-20, II-2045

Tenneco, II-2249

Tennessee Farmers, II-2787, 3220

Tennessee Volunteers, II-3484

Tenpay, II-2625

Ter Beke, I-307

Terex Corp., I-1840, 1861, 1865

Terje Hoili AS, I-1365

Terminix International, II-3324

Terminix Service, II-3324

TerminixCo., II-3326

Terrena, I-313

Terrible Herbst, II-3420

Tesco, I-462, II-2794, 2803, 2858-2859

Tessenderlo Group, I-1567

Tetley, I-931

Tetra Pak, I-31

Tetra Tech Inc., II-3569, 3571

Teva, I-1337-1338, 1345

TEW, II-2130

Texas A&M, II-3484

Texas Department of State Health Services, II-3518

Texas Instruments, I-1970, II-2143-2144, 2146

Texas Longhorns, II-3484

Texas Rangers, II-3482

Texas Roadhouse, II-2948

Texas State Optical, II-3027

Textainer, II-3335

TFK Corp., II-2936

T.G.I. Friday's, II-2948

TGS-NOPEC, I-208

Thai Rayon, I-1293

Thai Union International, I-841

Thaisarco, I-1730

Thales, II-2309

Thales Underwater System, II-2343

Therapedic, I-1120

Thermal Industries, I-1102

Thermo Fisher Scientific, II-2330, 3016

Things Remembered, II-3013

Third FS&LA of Cleveland, II-3068

THK, II-2334

Thoma-Sea, I-1853

Thomas Industrial Coatings Inc., I-283

Thomson Reuters, I-1200, 1232-1234, II-3130, 3355, 3386

Thor Industries, II-2263-2264, 2320

ThyssenKrupp, I-1856

Tianan, II-3223

Tianjin Fujita Group Co. Ltd., II-2298

Tianjing Yumeljing, II-2484

Tianui, I-1671

Tibet 5100 Water Resources Holdings Ltd., I-807

Tibet Cheezheng Tibetan Medicine Co. Ltd., I-1326, 1340

Ticket Monster, II-2628

Tiemahrung Deuerer GmbH, I-588

Tiffany & Co., II-3004-3005

Tiffin Motorhomes Inc., II-2263

Tige, II-2292

Tiger Brands Ltd., I-343, 672, 824

Tigo, II-2588

Tigo El Salvador, II-2591

Tigo Guatemala, II-2594

Tigo Honduras, II-2595

Tillamook County Creamery, I-388, 402, 404

Tim Horton's, II-2946

Timber Ridge Homes, I-261

Timberland, I-1080

TimberTech, I-1101, 1103

Time Warner, I-1207-1209, II-2633, 2638, 2641, 2682, 2694, 2696, 2699, 2701, 3292, 3311

Times, II-2830

Timken, I-1904

Timpte Inc., II-2321

Tine, I-321

Ting Hsin International Group, I-339, 412, 496, 611, II-2958

Tingyi, I-310, 798

Tiny Grass, I-1481

Tire Centers L.L.C., II-3415

Tire Kingdom, II-2877

Titan, I-1672

TJX Companies, II-2896-2897, 2899, 2913

TKMF, II-2251, 2254

TMC, II-2508

TMEIC, I-1819

TMM (Movistar), II-2605

TMX Group, II-3129

TNK-BP, I-1589

TNT, II-2516-2517, 2519

TOA Group, I-1515

Tobacco Central (Low Bob's), II-3024

Tobacco Superstores Inc., II-3024

Toda Kogyo, II-2155

Tognum, II-2007

Tokai Rubber Industries Ltd., I-1285

Tokyo Electric Power Company, II-2712

Tokyo Stock Exchange, II-3129

Tolko, I-1107

Toll Brothers, I-246, 254, 261

Tomkins P.L.C., I-1285, 1287

TOMS Group A.B., I-663

Tonen, II-2154

Tongjun, I-1283

Tootsie Roll Industries, I-681, 690, 711

Topdanmark, II-3137

Toppan, II-2121

Toppan Printing Co. Ltd., I-1236

The Topps Company Inc., I-690

Toray, I-1920

Torishima, I-1901

Toro, I-1836

Toronto Maple Leafs, II-3486

Toronto Transit Commission, II-2502

Toshiba, I-1765, 1939, 1945, 1950, II-2004, 2078-2079, 2082, 2141-2143, 2145-2147, 2336, 2354, 2361, 3264

Total, I-1251, 1280-1281, 1581, 1590

TOTO, I-1682

Towa Pharmaceutical Co. Ltd., I-1346

Tower Glass Inc., I-295

TowerCo, II-2112

TowerJazz, II-2128

Town and Country Living, I-1074, 1077

Toyo Ink America, I-1552

Toyo Suisan Kiasha Ltd., I-891

Toyo Tire & Rubber Co. Ltd., I-1605-1606

Toyota, I-1867, II-2196-2198, 2204-2205, 2209-2210, 2215, 2872, 3095-3097, 3311

Toys R Us, II-2893

TP-LINK, II-2118

Tracker Marine, II-2289

Tractor Supply, II-2782

Trader Joe's, II-2853

Tradewinds Beverage Co., I-795

Traditional Baking, I-636

Trailer Bridge Inc., II-2509

Trailways Transportation Systems, II-2504

Tranax Technologies Inc., I-1969

Tranquilidade, II-3145

Trans World Entertainment, II-2930

Transasia, I-1353

Transcontinental, I-1229

TransForce Inc., II-2508

Transocean Inc., I-203

TransPerfect/Translations.com, II-3396

Transtyle Transportation, II-2501

Trauson, II-2386

Travel and Transport, II-2568

Travel Leaders Group, II-2568

Travelong, II-2568

Travelers Group, II-3125, 3133, 3170, 3176, 3180-3185, 3188-3190, 3192-3193, 3201, 3204, 3208, 3214, 3216-3217, 3219-3220, 3222, 3225-3228, 3230, 3232

Treasury Wine Estates, I-779

Trek, I-1103

Trelleborg, I-1285, 1619

Trenkwalder, II-3342

Trevicos, I-297

Trex, I-1101

TrggVesta, II-3137

Tri-Marine International, I-841

Tri-Pak Industries, I-1161

Tri-West LTD, II-2737

Triad Guaranty Insurance Co., II-3235

Triangle Group Co. Ltd., I-1604, 1606

Triangle Rent-A-Car, II-3408

Tribe Mediterranean Foods, I-427

Tribune Co., I-1203, II-2692

Trident Seafoods, I-841, 1069

Tridonic/Zumtobel, II-2055

Trimac Group, II-2511

TriMark USA Inc., II-2754

TRIMEX S.A. de C.V., I-557

Trina Solar, I-1768-1769

Trinchero Family Estates, I-779

Trinity Health, II-3514

Trinity Industries Inc., I-1746, II-2296

Tripod, II-2126

Tripp Lite, II-2005

Tristar Worldwide Chauffeur Services, II-2501

Triton, II-3335

Triton Systems of Delaware Inc., I-1969

Triumph Foods, I-118, 380

Tropicana Dole Beverages, I-500

The True Green Cos., II-2729

True Homes, I-250

True North Services, II-2729

True Value, II-2786

TrueMove, II-2617

TruGreen Lawncare and Landcare, I-140

Truland Group of Cos., I-284

Trulia, II-2668

Truly Nolen of America, II-3323

Trumpf, I-1877

Trustmark National Bank, II-3057

TRW, II-2235-2236, 2239, 2241, 2247-2248, 2252-2253, 2258

Trygvesta, II-3144

Tryst Nightclub, II-2961

Tsingtao Brewery Company Ltd., I-310, 759, 767

TSL Jewellery, II-3006

TSMC, II-2128

TTI Floor Care North America, II-2044

TTM Technologies, II-2126

Tudou, II-2680

Tuffy Associates Corp./Car-X Associates Corp., II-3412

Tullett Prebon, II-3128

Tumi Inc., I-1645-1646, 1648-1649

Tupperware Brands Corp., II-3021

Turbec, I-1822

Turkcell, II-2619

Turkey Creek Pork Skins Inc., I-874

Turkey Hill Dairy, I-422, 934

Turner Construction Co., I-242

The Turner Corporation, I-270-274

Tuscany Development, I-254

Tutor Perini Corporation, I-270

TVS, II-2304

TW Telecom, II-2638

TXC, II-2130

Tyco, I-1801, II-2114-2115, 2379

Tyndale, I-1218

Tyson Foods Inc., I-122, 305, 331, 351, 357, 360, 362, 380

U:fon, II-2618

U-Haul International Inc., II-2522, 3407

U-Save Auto Rental System Inc., II-3408

U-Store-It Trust Inc., II-2522

UB Group, I-789

Ube Industries, II-2154

Ubisoft, II-3365

UBM, I-1232

UBS, II-3086, 3119-3120, 3124

UC Rusal, I-176, 1719, 1722

UCI (Brazil), II-3444

UFIDA, II-3349

Ufone, II-2610

UGF Assicurazioni, II-3143

UGL Limited, II-3329

Ukralkali, I-227

Uline.com, II-2669

Ulta Salon, Cosmetics and Fragrance Inc., II-3030

Ultimate, II-3351

Ultra Diamond Outlet, II-2802

Ultrafem, I-1178

UMB Bank National Assn., II-3058

UMC, II-2128

Umicore, I-168, II-2155

Umniah, II-2602

Umpqua Bank, II-3070

UNA, I-594

Uncle Dan's Inc., I-924

Under Armour, I-1028, 1030, 1608

Uni-President Enterprises Corp., I-412, 742, 798

Unicer, I-323

Unicharm, I-1167, 1172, II-2493

Uniden, II-2101-2102

Unifi Inc., I-983, 1004

UniFirst, II-3277

UniGroup Inc., II-2514

Unilever, I-306-308, 313-317, 319, 321-323, 325, 327-329, 331, 338, 342-344, 390-392, 395, 413, 423, 455, 467, 514, 522, 733-734, 900, 916, 918, 1364-1367, 1372-1373, 1379, 1384-1385, 1401, 1432, 1449, 1455, 1472, 1483-1488, 1501, 1575, II-3293

Unilever Bestfoods North America, I-414, 511, 518, 520, 535, 931

Unimicron Group, II-2126

Union Bank, II-3038, 3060, 3079, 3100, 3105, 3110

Union del Niquel, I-170

Union Electric Steel, I-1696

Union First Market Bank, II-3080

Union Pacific, II-2499

Unionpay, II-2625

Uniplan, II-3400

Unique Squared, II-2932

Unisys Corp., II-3601

United Airlines, II-2525, 2540, 2543-2545, 2549-2550, 2552, 2556

United Bank, II-3083

United Biscuits, I-637

United Business Media PLC, II-3405

United Community Bank, II-3043

United Confections, I-660

United Continental, II-2541

United Farm Bureau of Indiana Group, II-3220

United Food and Commercial Workers International Union, II-3561

United Foods, I-526

United Healthcare Insurance, II-3154

United Industries, I-1541

United Power, I-1824

United Propane Gas, II-3022

United Rentals, I-1860, II-3330-3332

United Road, II-2515

United Salt, I-1568

United Services Automobile Assn., II-3224

United States Bakery, I-619

U.S. Bancorp, II-3093, 3122, 3261

U.S. Bank Home Mortgage, II-3100, 3105, 3107, 3110

U.S. Bank NA, II-3076, 3081, 3084, 3089

United States Cellular Co., II-2112

U.S. Chemicals, I-1854

U.S. Department of Agriculture, II-2187

U.S. Department of Energy, II-2187

U.S. Department of Health and Human Services, II-2187

U.S. Department of Homeland Security, II-2187

U.S. Department of Justice, II-2187

U.S. Department of State, II-2187

U.S. Department of the Interior, II-2187

U.S. Department of Transportation, II-2187

U.S. Department of Veteran Affairs, II-3516

U.S. Department of Veterans Affairs, II-2187

U.S. Dry Cleaning Services Corp., II-3275

United States Lime & Minerals Inc., I-1685

U.S. Nutrition, I-705, 1300

U.S. Postal Service, I-1161, II-2669

U.S. Salt, I-1568

U.S. Steel Corp., I-1715

U.S. Tile, I-1679

U.S. Xpress Enterprises, II-2513

United Stationers Inc., II-2763, 3016

United Steelworkers of America, II-3561

United Subcontractors, I-288

United Talent Agency, II-3456

United Technologies Corp., I-1986, II-2269, 2274

United Vision Logistics, II-2508

United Way, II-3552

UnitedHealthcare, II-3152-3153, 3156-3159, 3162-3163, 3167-3168

Unitel, II-2576

Universal, II-3436, 3441

Universal Health Services, II-3515, 3518

Universal Insurance Holdings Group, II-3196

Universal Music Group, II-2090-2091

Universal Music Publishing, II-2092

Universal Property & Casualty Insurance Co., II-3224

Universal Razor Industries, I-1752

Universal Shipbuilding, I-1853

Universal Studios Recreation Group, II-3481

Universal Truckload Services, II-2509

Universal WorldEvents, II-3400

University of California - Berkeley, II-3538

University of Central Florida, II-3536

University of Illinois Urbana-Champaign, II-3538

University of Michigan, II-3484, 3538-3539

University of Minnesota, II-3536

University of Phoenix, II-3536

University of Pittsburgh Medical Center, II-3165

University of Texas at Austin, II-3536, 3538-3539

Univision, II-2691-2692
UPC, II-2639
UPIDA Wecoo, II-3357
UPM, I-1137-1138
UPMC Community Provider Services, II-3519
UPMC Presbyterian, II-3517
UPS, II-2506, 2512, 2516-2519, 2560, 2669, 3125
Upsher-Smith Labs, I-1300
Uranium One, I-171
Urban Financial, II-3114
Urban Outfitters, I-1017
URS Corp., I-269, II-3571, 3573
US 1 Industries, II-2509
US Airways, II-2541-2542, 2544, 2547, 2550, 2552-2554
US Bank NA, II-3038-3039, 3045, 3048-3050, 3056, 3058-3060, 3064, 3067-3068, 3070
USA Technologies, II-2686
USAA Federal Savings Bank, II-3077
USAA Group, II-3133, 3171, 3178, 3180-3181, 3190, 3192, 3196, 3205
USANA Hong Kong Ltd., I-1325
USB Bank USA, II-3078
USG People, I-1687, II-3342-3343, 3589
USM, I-140, 1122, II-2729
Utah Jazz, II-3483
UTC, I-1765, 1907, 1985, II-2114-2115, 3383
UTIC Group, II-2860
Utilities Inc., II-2721
Utility Trailer Manufacturing, II-2321
UTstarcom, II-3355
Utz Quality Foods, I-865, 867, 869, 874, 876, 878
Vacon, II-1996
Vail Resorts Inc., II-3499
Valco, II-2250
Vale, I-149, 168, 170, 176, 178-179, 223, 1719
Valence, II-2170
Valeo, II-2237-2238, 2245-2246, 2256
Valero Energy Corp., I-1581, II-2796, 2879
Valero Renewable Fuels, I-1524
Valio, I-312
Vallarta Supermarkets, II-2814
Valley, I-1235

Valley Fine Foods Co., I-894
Valley National Bank, II-3063
Valleycrest Companies, II-2729
ValleyCrest Landscape Cos., I-140
Vallourec, I-1714
The Valspar Corp., I-1513, 1517
Valve's Steam, II-2681
Valvoline, I-1588
Valvoline Express Care, II-3422
Valvoline Instant Oil Change, II-3422
Van Eck, II-3121
Van Heusen, II-2802
Van Holding Ltd., II-2819
Van Scoyoc Associates, II-3564
Van Stone Conveyor Inc., I-1859
Van Tuyl Group, II-2871, 2874
Vancouver Canucks, II-3486
Vanderlande Industries, I-1870
Vanguard, II-3121
Vanguard Health Systems, II-3515
Vanguard International, II-2128
Vanguard National Trailer Corp., II-2321
Vanity Fair, I-1050
Vanity Nightclub, II-2961
Vantage Health Plan Inc., II-3160
Varel, I-1849
Varian Medical Systems Inc., II-2158
Vattenfall, II-2710
Vauxhall, II-2209
VCA Anatech, I-138
VDM Verlag, I-1219
VE Global Solutions, I-846
Vector Security Inc., II-3384
Vectra Bank Colorado NA, II-3039
Vedanta, I-158
Venetian Macau, II-3489
Ventron, II-2130
Ventura Foods, I-741
Veolia, I-1924
Veolia Environmental Services, North America Corp., II-2727
Verifone, I-1973
Verizon, II-2112, 2575, 2622, 2633, 2638, 2685, 2696, 2698-2699, 2701, 2930, 3292, 3307, 3311
Vermejo Park Ranch, I-147
Vermillion Ranches, I-112
Vero, II-3134
VERO MODA, I-1045
Veropoulos Bros S.A., II-2829
VersaCold, II-2521
Versatile, II-2121

Verso, I-1154
Vestas, I-1824
Vesuvius, I-1681
Vetco, I-211
Veterans Affairs Greater Los Angeles Health Care System, II-3517
Vevo, II-2676, 2930
VF Corp., I-1017, 1019, 1032, 1035, 1038, 1042, 1044, 1080, 1614, 1648-1649
VHA (wireless broadband), II-2635
Vi-Jon Labs, I-1182
Via Technologies, II-2133
Viacom Digital, II-2676, 2694
Viad Corp., II-3405
Vibra Healthcare, II-3519
Vibram, I-1611
Victoria Carpets, I-1001
Victorian Government, II-3293
Victorinox, I-1645-1646
Vid Group, II-2086
Videocon Group, II-2022, 2026, 2029, 2072
VideoRay L.L.C., II-2346
Vienna, II-3269
Viewsonic, II-2083
Viña Concha y Toro S.A., I-778
Vinci, I-275-276
Vinda Group, I-1192
Vinicola LA Cetto S.A. de C.V., I-778
Vinus Vita, I-328
Vion, I-314, 329
Viore, II-2080
VIP Industries, I-1645
Vipnet, II-2589
Vips Group, II-2938
Virbac S.A., I-1330
Virgin Active, II-3472-3473
Virgin Atlantic, II-2548
Virgin Mobile, II-2613
Virginia Electric & Power Co., II-2720
Virginia Poultry Growers Cooperative, I-129
Visa, II-3090, 3092, 3125
Vishay, I-1680, II-2142, 2152
Vista, II-2784
Vista Higher Learning, I-1227
Visteon, II-2243, 2245-2246, 2250, 2256, 2262
Vita, I-1631
Vita Green Health Products Co. Ltd., I-1325

Vitamin Shoppe, II-2986
Vitas Healthcare, II-3513
Viterra, I-595
Vitra International A.G., I-1122
VIVA, II-2579
Vivacom, II-2584
Vivartia, I-308, 315
Vivint Inc., II-3384-3385
Vivitar, II-2415
Viz Media, I-1206
Vizio, II-2082-2083
VLAM, I-307
VLG, I-306
Vodacom, II-2606, 2613
Vodafone, II-2578, 2590, 2593,
    2597-2598, 2600, 2615, 2618-2619,
    2621, 2639
Vogue International, I-1448
Vok Dams Gruppe, II-3400
Volgograd, I-1553
Volkswagen, I-1914, II-2196-2201,
    2203, 2205-2206, 2208-2210
Volt Information Sciences, II-3341
Voltas, I-1984
Volva Penta, I-1826
Volvo, I-1840, 1842, II-2196, 2230
Vonage Holdings Corp., II-2682
Vorwerk & Co. KG, II-3021
Votorantim, I-1738
Vtech, II-2102
VTR, II-2636, 2700
Vulcan Materials, I-215, 219, 1672,
    1676
W S Packaging, I-1237
W.A. Chester L.L.C., I-281
Wabash National Corp., II-2321
Wabco, II-2224-2225
Wacoal, I-1049-1050
Waffle House, II-2951
Waggener Edstrom Worldwide,
    II-3593
The Waggoners Trucking, II-2515
Wahaha-Danone, I-798
Wal-Mart, II-2626, 2788, 2790-2791,
    2794, 2803, 2805, 2811-2813,
    2816, 2820, 2822-2827, 2831-2835,
    2837-2838, 2840-2843, 2845-2848,
    2850-2852, 2857, 2861, 2863,
    2884, 2896, 2911, 2913, 2920,
    2925, 2928-2929, 2964-2967, 2971,
    2973-2974, 2976-2978, 2980-2983,
    2988, 2999, 3005, 3010, 3027,
    3387, 3449
Walbridge, I-242

Walgreens, II-2626, 2790, 2911,
    2964-2985, 2988, 3387
Wallenius Wilhelmsen Line, II-2573
Walsh Construction Co., I-242
Walsh Group, I-277
The Walsh Group, I-272
Walsworth Publishing, I-1229
Walt Disney Co., II-3012
Walt Disney Co., II-2079, 2692-
    2694, 3310, 3436, 3481
Walters & Wolf, I-295
Wanda Group Company, I-1811
W&O, I-1798
W&W Glass L.L.C., I-295
Want Want Group, I-339, 662, 884
Warnaco Group Inc., I-1035, 1039
Warner, I-1050
Warner Bros., I-23, II-3436, 3441
Warner Chappell, II-2092
Warner Music Group, II-2090-2091
Wärtsilä, I-1817-1818, II-2007
Wasco Inc., I-287
Wash Depot, II-3420
Washington Area Metropolitan Tran-
    sit Authority, II-2502
Washington FS&LA, II-3070, 3081
Washington Mills Electro Minerals
    Company, I-1690
Washington Music Center, II-2932
Washington Mutual, II-3123
Washington Redskins, II-3485
Washington Trust Bank, II-3081
Wasserstrom Co., II-2754
Waste Connections, II-2727
Waste Industries USA Inc., II-2727
Waste Management, II-2727
Waterman, II-2454
Waters, II-2330
Watson Pharmaceuticals, I-1344-
    1345
Wattyl Limited, I-1516
Wausau Paper, I-1140
Wavin, I-1629
Wawa, II-2844
Wayne Farms L.L.C., I-122
W.C. Bradley, I-28
WCG, II-3593
WD, II-2117
WDC Exploration & Wells, I-293
We Make Price, II-2628
WE Transport, II-2505
Weather Underground, II-3397
Weatherford Intl., I-206, 210, 1847-
    1848, 1852, 1855

Webcrafters Inc., I-1229
Weber Shandwick, II-3594
Weber-Stephens, I-28
Webster Bank National Assn.,
    II-3040
Weed Man, I-140
Weeks, I-282
WEG, I-1819, II-2008
Wei Chuan, I-742
Weight Watchers Intl., II-3290
Weingarten Realty, II-3245
Weinstein Company, II-3436, 3441
Weiqiao Textile Group, I-1719
Weir, I-1901
Weis Builders, I-273
Weis Markets, II-2834
The Weitz Company, I-273
WEL Companies Inc., II-2510
Welch Foods Inc., I-491
Wellcare Health Plans Inc., II-3159
WellPoint Inc., II-3153, 3162, 3164
Wells' Dairy, I-414, 422
Wells Fargo & Co., II-3099-3100,
    3103-3104, 3106-3111, 3114, 3261
Wells Fargo Bank NA, II-3034-3036,
    3038-3040, 3042-3043, 3045,
    3047-3049, 3053, 3056, 3059-3061,
    3063-3064, 3066-3067, 3071,
    3074-3075, 3077-3078, 3080-3082,
    3084-3086, 3093, 3095-3097
Wells Fargo Securities, II-3122
WellStar Health System, II-3516
Welspun USA, I-1069, 1073, 1079
Wendy's, II-2947, 2952, 2957, 3263
Wenner Media, I-1207, 1209
WEPA, I-1139, 1141
Werner, I-1813
Werner Enterprises, II-2513
Wesco International, II-3016
Wescon, I-248
Wessanene NV, Koninklije, I-337
West Angeles Church of God in
    Christ, II-3566
West Coast Bank, II-3070
West Corp., II-3401
West Fraser, I-1095
West L.A. Music, II-2932
West Mining, I-156
West Music Co., II-2932
West Pharmaceutical Services, I-31,
    37
West Tennessee Healthcare, II-3516
West Valley Construction Co. Inc.,
    I-281

Westat Inc., II-3580

Westbanco Bank Inc., II-3083

Westco Products Group, II-2491

Westech, I-1102

Western Bagel, I-597

Western Construction Group,
   I-286-287

Western Digital, I-1949-1950, 1952

Western Exterminator Co.,
   II-3323

Western Graphics, II-3319

Western National Group, I-268

Western Presidio/Evenflo Co. Inc.,
   II-2486

Western Security Bank, II-3059

Western Star, II-2230

Westfarmers Limited, II-3293

Westfield Group, II-3176, 3184,
   3245

Westlake, I-1278

Westmont Hospitality Group, II-3271

Westomatic, I-1976

Weston Foods, I-615

Westpac, II-3101

WestPoint Home, I-1069-1070, 1073

Westport Homes, I-256

Westways Feed Products, I-595

Weyco, I-1104

Weyerhaeuser, I-266, 1095, 1107

WFT, I-201

Wheaton Van Lines, II-2514

Wheeler Bros. Inc., II-2525

Wheels, II-3409

WHEMCO, I-1696

Whink Products Co., I-1394

Whip Mix, II-2396-2397

Whirlpool, I-18, 1985, II-2014-2015,
   2019-2020, 2022, 2024, 2026-2029,
   2040, 2042

Whitbread, II-2940

White & Case, II-3531

White Castle System Inc., I-541

White Cat, I-1363, 1400

White Energy, I-1524

White Lodging Services Group,
   II-3271

White Oak Exotic Hunting Preserve,
   I-147

The Whiting-Turner Contracting Co.,
   I-273

Whitman's Chocolates, I-713, 720

Whitney Bank, II-3051

Whittaker Homes, I-263

Wholesale Furniture Brokers,
   II-2912

W.I. Gore and Associates Inc.,
   I-1043

Widmer's Cleaners, II-3275

Wikimedia Foundation sites, II-2663

Wikoff Color, I-1552

Wilbur-Ellis Company, II-2787

Wild Wing Café, II-2949

Wilks Masonry Corp., I-287

William Lyon Homes, I-258

William M. Bird & Co., II-2737

William Wrigley Jr. Co., I-652, 661,
   681, 688, 697, 702, 717, 724-725,
   727-728

Williams, I-199

Williams & Jensen, II-3564

Williams Scotsman, II-3332

Williams-Sonoma, II-2904, 2911,
   2913

Willow Creek Community Church,
   II-3566

Wilo, I-1901

Wilson Trailer Co., II-2321

Wilsonart, I-1086, 1625

WinCo, II-2828

Wincor Nixdorf A.G., I-1969

Windham Weavers (Natco Home),
   I-1077

Windmill Consumer Products,
   I-1300

Windsor Foods Inc., I-345-346, 541

Windstream, II-2622

The Wine Group, I-779

Winergy, I-1784

Wingfoot Commercial Tire Systems
   L.L.C., II-3415

Winmark Corp., II-2993

Winn-Dixie, II-2838, 2851, 2856

WinnCompanies, II-3247

Winnebago, II-2263-2264

Wipro, II-3373

Wisconsin, II-2542, 2553

Wise Foods, I-865, 876, 880

Wistron, II-1992

Without Walls International, II-3566

Witt/Kieffer, II-3591

WME Entertainment, II-3456

WMS Industries Inc., II-3479

Wolters Kluwer, I-1200, 1232-1234

Wood-Mizer Products inc., I-1885

Wood Partners, I-268

Woodlands Church, II-3566

Woodside Homes, I-260

Woolworths Limited, II-3293

Workman/Algonquin, I-1221

World Co. Ltd., I-1018

World Finer Foods Inc., I-896

World Kitchen, I-1664

World Wire Series, I-139

Worldcall, II-2640

World's Finest Chocolate Inc., I-720

Worldtex Inc. (Regal Manufacturing), I-983

Worldwide Sports Nutrition, I-704

Wow Café & Wingery, II-2949

W.R. Berkley Corp., II-3187

Wrid Telecom, II-2610

Wright Brand Foods Inc., I-362

Wuchang, I-1846

Wuhan General, I-1908

Wunderman, II-3317-3318

W.W. Norton, I-1227

Wyeth Labs Inc., I-698

Wyndham Worldwide, II-3270

Wynn Resorts, II-3489

Xayal Brewery Azerbaijan, I-751

XCMG, I-1840-1841, 1861, 1866

Xentris, I-4

Xerox, I-1958, 1965, II-3373

XGMA, I-1841

Xiamen Dongfeng, I-1326

Xiamen Yinlu, I-922

Xi'An Aircraft International Corp.,
   II-2308

Xi'an Kaimi, I-1392, 1401

Xianju Pharmaceutical Co. Ltd.,
   I-1343

Xinfa Aluminum Electrical, I-1719

Xingyuan Tyre Co. Ltd., I-1604

Xinxiang Bailu, I-1294

Xinyi Glass, I-1661-1662

Xinyl Holdings Ltd., I-1653

Xinzhonghua, I-1026

Xiushentong, I-1481

XL America Group, II-3232

XL Four Star Beef, I-357

XLHealth Corp., II-3166

Xlibris Corp., I-1219

xpress, II-2602

XS Nightclub, II-2961

Xstrata A.G., I-152, 156, 158, 168,
   170, 178-179, 1717

XTO (Exxon Mobil), I-199

Xtools, II-3357

Xuzhou Carbon Co., II-2011

Xyience Xtreme Science, I-811

Yaduo, I-1022

Yahoo!, II-2643, 2646, 2651, 2655, 2663, 2668, 2676, 3306, 3308-3309
Yakuit, I-444
Yale University, II-3538
Yamaha, II-2065, 2290, 2303, 2305, 2324, 2434
Yamahisa, II-2493
Yamazaki Baking Co. Ltd., I-318
Yamazaki Mazak, I-1877
Yankuang Cathay, I-1522
Yanmar, I-1826
Yara, I-1532
Yara Soumi OY, I-1567
Yaroslav, I-1553
Yaskawa Electric Corp., I-1923, II-1996
The Yates Companies, I-270
Yazaki, II-2225, 2256
Yee Lee Corporation, I-319
Yellow Van Handyman, II-3431
Yellowbook, I-1235
Yeo Hiap Seng, I-319
Yildiz Holding A.S., I-660, 825
Yili Industrial Group Company Ltd., I-310
Yingde Gases, I-1262
Yingli Green Energy, I-1768-1769
Yixiu, I-1026
YMCA of the USA, II-3552
Yogurtland, II-2953
Yoigo, II-2615
Yokohama Rubber Co. Ltd., I-1605-1606
Yoplait, I-441-444
Youku, II-2680
Young & Rubicam, II-3294-3295
Young Electric Sign Company, II-2478
Youngor, I-1036, 1040, 1651
Your Way Fumigation, II-3326
YouTube, II-2930
YRC National, II-2512
YRC Regional, II-2512
YTO, I-1841
Yuen Foong Yu Paper, I-1186
Yuengling, I-756
Yuhua Glass, I-1661
Yulon Motor Co. Ltd., II-2207
Yum! Brands Inc., II-2940, 2952, 2958
Yunnan Baiyao Group, I-1326, 1340
Yunnan Chengfeng, I-1730
Yunnan Tin, I-1730
Yurun Food Group, I-310

Yuyuan, II-3006
Yves Saint Lauren, I-1651
Zagg, I-4
Zain, II-2579, 2602
Zale Corp., II-3005
Zaner-Block, I-1228
Zanet, I-852
Zaxby's, II-2950
Zebra Pen, II-2456, 2458, 2465
Zegna (Ermengildo Zegna Group), I-1035
Zena Group, II-2938
ZF, II-2251
ZFF, I-1914
Zhang iy uan, I-930
Zhenai, II-2666
Zhengzhou Sanquan Food Co. Ltd., I-538
Zhongjin Lingnan Metals, I-156
Zhongshan Aerstar Fine, I-1558
Zhongshan Worldmark Sporting Goods Co. Ltd., II-2453
Zhuhai YatHing, I-892
Ziebart, II-3412
Zimmer, I-1131, II-2381-2382, 2385
Zions First National Bank, II-3045, 3078, 3103
Zipcar, II-3391, 3408
Zippon Manufacturing Co., II-2491
ZMV, I-328
Zoneperfect Nutrition Co., I-704
Zong, II-2610
Zoomlion, I-1840, 1843, 1861, 1866
Zoots Corp., II-3275
ZTE, II-2095, 3355
Zumtobel, II-2058
Zurich Financial Services, II-3182-3183, 3185, 3187, 3217, 3226, 3232
Zurich Insurance Group, II-3133-3135, 3139, 3141, 3145, 3188, 3192, 3205, 3222, 3225
Zydus Cadila, I-1341
Zynga, II-2678

BRANDS INDEX

This index shows 3,130 brands—including names of periodicals, television programs, popular movies, and other "brand-equivalent" names. Each brand name is followed by one or more numerals; these are entry numbers; they are arranged sequentially, with the first mention of the brand shown first. Roman numerals indicate volume number.

1-2-3 Vegetable Oil, I-740
1-800-Flowers.com, II-2662
123Greetings.com, II-2660
14 Day Cleanse, I-1349
2000 Flushes, I-1399
21, Adele, II-2087
24qun, II-2658
3M Nexcare, II-2371
4 Grain, I-126
5 Hour Energy, I-812
5 Hour Energy Extra Strength, I-812
5100 Tibet Glacial Spring Water, I-807
55tuan, II-2658
8th Continent, I-434
8th Continent Soymilk, I-425
9 Lives, I-581, 589
A1 Steak House, I-503
AARP Bulletin, I-1210
AARP the Magazine, I-1210
Abilify, I-1335
Abreva, I-1457
Absolut, I-784, 792
Accent, I-835
Access, II-2107
Access HD, II-2080
Ace, II-2374-2375
ACE Tekzone, II-2375
Acme, I-839, 1754
Acoustic Research, II-2105
Act II, I-870
Act II Butter Lovers, I-870
Acura TL, II-2185
The Addams Family, II-3458
Adidas, I-1034, 1607, 1613-1615
Adidas Moves, I-1440
Advair Diskus, I-1335
Advanced Listerine, I-1469
Affresh, I-1396
Affy Tapple, I-657
Africa's Best, I-1450
Afrin, I-1462

Afrin No Drip, I-1462
After Bite, I-1321
After Bite Kids, I-1321
After Bite Xtra, I-1321
Aidells, I-370
Aimer, I-1034
Ainsley Harriott, I-462
Airborne, I-1301
Ajax, I-1362, 1387
Al Fresco, I-370
Alberto Consort, I-1451
Alberto VO5, I-1447
Alcon Opti Free Express, I-1434
Alcon Opti Free Replenish, I-1434
Alcon Systane, I-1434
Alcon Systane Ultra, I-1434
Alexander Dennis, II-2222
Alexander McQueen, I-1651
Alexia, I-544
Alexia Artisan Bread, I-621
Aliph, II-2096
Alka Seltzer Plus, I-1315
All, I-1375
All Hershey's Products, I-714
All Pro, I-987
Allegro, I-503
Allens, I-472, 474
Alli, I-1349
Almay Intense 1 Color, I-1422
Almond Breeze, I-425
Aloe King, I-485
Aloe Life, I-485
Aloe Organics, I-485
Alpine, II-2067, 2328
Alpine Lace, I-398
Alpo, I-585, 590
Altoids, I-651
Altoids Smalls, I-651
Always, I-1177
Always Fresh, I-1177
Always Infinity, I-1177
Always Tender, I-358

Amazon, II-2663
AmazonLocal, II-2657
Ambi, I-1494
American Beauty, I-889, 895
American Crew, I-1452
American Express, II-3090
American Greetings Interactive, II-2660
American Idiot, II-3458
American Legend, II-2268
American Standard, I-1763
AmericanGreetings.com, II-2662
Ameriphone, II-2101
Amiodipine beysylate, I-1331
Amlactin, I-1499
Amore, I-832
Amp, I-810
Amport, I-508
Amy's, I-550
Anbesol, I-1327
And 1, I-1608
A & D Baby, I-1415
Andros, I-482
Angel Soft, I-1194
Annabelle Big Hunk, I-691
Annie Chuns, I-897
Annie Chuns Noodle Express, I-897
Annie Chuns Rice Express, I-897
Answer, I-1357
Antler, I-1647
Anxi Tiekuanyin, I-1667
AOL, II-2643, 2663, 2676
Apex, II-2107
Apple, II-2068, 2095, 2100, 2663
Apple IOS, II-3354
Applied Nutrition, I-1349
Aqua Star, I-844
Aquafina, I-805
Aquafresh Whitetrays, I-1474
Aquanet, I-1451
Aquaphor Baby Advanced Therapy, I-1415

Arena, I-1047
ARIS, I-1114
Aristrocrat, I-792
Arizona, I-796
Arizona Arnold Palmer, I-796
Arm & Hammer, I-1375
Arm & Hammer Clean Shower, I-1395
Arm & Hammer Essentials, I-1391
Arm & Hammer Fresh & Soft, I-1402
Arm & Hammer Spinbrush PC, II-2032
Arm & Hammer Whitening Booster, I-1474
Armour, I-542
Arnold, I-620
Arrowhead, I-805-806, 809
Art Advantage, I-1511
Artskills, I-1511
Ashley Furniture, I-1113
Asian Gourmet, I-739
Asics, I-1613-1615
Ask, II-2643, 2646
Astroglide, I-1489
AT&T, II-2101-2102
Atkinson's Chick 'O Stick, I-691
Atlanta Cheesecake, I-606
Audi, II-2181, 2185, 2206
Aunt Jemima, I-531, 547
Aupres, I-1503
Auro, I-1433
Auro Dri, I-1433
Aurora, I-508
Aussie Instant Freeze, I-1451
Avast, II-3358
Aveeno Active Natural Ultimate Clean, I-1498
Aveeno Active Naturals, I-1310, 1447
Aveeno Active Naturals Daily Moisturizing, I-1499
Aveeno Active Naturals Positively Radiant, I-1498
Aveeno Baby, I-1377
Aveeno Clear Complex, I-1491
Aveeno Daily Moisturizing, I-1499
AVG, II-3358
Axe, I-1439
Axe Detailer, II-2487
Axe Dry, I-1431
Axion Technology, II-2080
Axis Communications, I-1967
Azteca, I-935

Bab O, I-1387
Baby Orajel, I-1327
Bacardi, I-784, 790
Bacardi Breezer, I-785
Bacardi Silver, I-774
Bacardi Superior, I-785
Bachman Jax, I-864
Bachman's, I-877
Bactine, II-2373
Badia, I-833, 836
Bagel Bites, I-546
Bagpiper, I-794
Baidu, II-2631
Bailey's, I-409
Baked Cheetos, I-864
Baked Lay's, I-875
Baked Tostitos Scoops, I-886
Baken Ets, I-874
Bakers, I-579
Baker's Joy, I-738
Ball Park, I-363
Ballantine's, I-794
Balmex Baby, I-1415
Ban, I-1431
Banana Boat Sport Performance, I-1506
Banana Boat UltraMist Sport Performance, I-1506
Band-Aid, II-2369, 2371
Band-Aid Comfort Flex, II-2371
Band-Aid Tough Strips, II-2371
Bangli Cuo Chuang Wang, I-1492
Banquet, I-534, 550, 640
Baofeng, I-1639
Bar-S, I-361, 363, 367, 370
Barbara's Bakery, I-560
Barbasol, I-1490
Barber Foods, I-375
Barbie, II-2436
Barcel Takis, I-886
Barefoot, I-775
Barilla, I-895
Barilla Plus, I-895
Barkeepers Friend, I-1387
Basic, I-955, 965
Basics, I-1633
Baskin Robbins, I-696
Basto, I-1642
Batchelors, I-462
Bath Essentials, II-2487
Battlefield 3, II-3364
Bausch & Lomb Renu, I-1434
Bausch & Lomb Renu Fresh, I-1434
Bawang, I-1454

Baxters, I-462
Bazaar, I-1212
BD, II-2367
Be Koool, II-2374
Bear Creek Country Kitchens, I-510
Bear Naked, I-560
Bed Buddy, II-2374
Beechnut Stage 2, I-449
Beggin', I-580
Beijing Wuy utai Tea, I-1667
Belenkaya, I-793
BelGioioso, I-397, 408
Belkin, II-2068
Belle, I-1642
Bellywashers, I-490
Ben & Jerry's, I-421
Ben & Jerry's Lighten Up, I-416
Benadryl, I-1310, 1314-1315
Benefiber, I-1322
Beneful, I-583, 585, 590
Berkley Trilene, II-2451
Berkline, I-1113
Berlinger California Collection, I-775
Bertolli, I-519, 533, 743
Bertolli Meal Soups, I-464
Best Foods, I-512, 514
Best Home Furnishing, I-1113
Best of the West, I-1565
Better Homes and Gardens, I-1210
Better Than Bouillon, I-510
Betty Crocker, II-2488
Betty Crocker Fruit by the Foot, I-678
Betty Crocker Fruit Gushers, I-678
Betty Crocker Fruit Roll Ups, I-678
Betty Crocker Hamburger Helper, I-903
Betty Crocker Scooby Doo, I-678
Betty Crocker Tuna Helper, I-903
Betty Crocker Whole Grain Helper, I-903
BeyondtheRack.com, II-2661
BFGoodrich, I-1600-1603
BIC, II-2464, 2490
BIC Cristal, II-2455
BIC Limited Edition, II-2490
BIC Luminere, II-2490
BIC Mark It, II-2466
BIC Matic Grip, II-2464
BIC Soleil, I-1750
BIC Sure Start, II-2490
BIC Velocity, II-2455, 2464
Big Sexy Hair, I-1451

Big Tex, I-493
Bigelow, I-932
The Biggest Loser Club, II-2659
Billy Elliot, II-3458
Bimbo, I-613-614
Binaca, I-1464
Binaca Blast, I-1464
Binaca Fast Blast, I-1464
Bing, II-2643
Bing Maps, II-2675
Biore, I-1496
Biotene, I-1473
Biotene Oral Balance, I-1473
Birds Eye, I-525, 528
Birds Eye C&W, I-528
Birds Eye Farm Fresh, I-525
Birds Eye Southland, I-528
Birds Eye Steamfresh, I-525
Birds Eye Steamfresh Premium
  Selects, I-527
Birds Eye Voila, I-533
Birritella's, I-572
BKT, I-1598
Black Flag, I-1541
Black Opal, I-1494
Blairex Simply Saline, I-1462
BleedArrest, II-2372
Blistex, I-1457
Blitz, I-1630
Bloomspot, II-2657
Blossom Hill, I-776
Bltl's, I-1639
Blue Bell, I-415, 421
Blue Bird, I-608, 614
Blue Bonnet, I-394
Blue Diamond, I-729
Blue Diamond Almond Breeze, I-434
BlueAnt Wireless, II-2096
BMW, II-2192, 2206, 2302
BMW 3 series, II-2181, 2185
BMW 335d, II-2214
BMW X5, II-2214
Boar's Head, I-366
Bob Evans, I-373, 540
Bob's Red Mill, I-562
Bobs Sweet Stripes, I-701
Boca, I-543
Bod Man, I-1439-1440
Body Benefits, II-2487
Body Image Body, II-2487
Bolthouse Bom Dia, I-483
Bolthouse Farms, I-483
Bombay Sapphire, I-785
Bon Ami, I-1387

Bon Appetit, I-605
Boost, I-1350
Boots, I-1495
Boppy, II-2483
Boral, I-955
Borax 20 Mule Team, I-1407
Borden, I-406-407, 435, 437
Born Free, I-126
Born This Way, Lady Gaga, II-2087
Bosch Siemens, II-2015
Bose, II-2066, 2068, 2096
BOSS, I-1438
Boss, II-2067
Bossa Nova, I-483
Boston Chowda, I-464
Boston Market, I-550
Botticelli, I-743
Boudreaux's Butt Paste Baby, I-1415
Bounce, I-1402-1403
Bounty, I-1183
Bounty Basic, I-1183
Bounty Extra Soft, I-1183
Bowers & Wilkins, II-2066
Brach's Maple Nut Goodies, I-691
Bratz, II-2436
Braun Oral-B Precision Clean,
  II-2030
Braun Thermoscan, II-2367
Brawny, I-1183
Brawny Pick A Size, I-1183
Breaking Dawn, Stephenie Meyer,
  I-1220
Breakstone's, I-386, 424
Breakstone's Cottage Doubles, I-424
Breath Savers, I-651
Breath Savers 3 Hour, I-651
Breathe Right, I-1463
Breathe Right Near Clear, I-1463
Breeze, I-1193
Breyers, I-421
Bric's, I-1647
Bridesmaids, II-3437
Bridgestone, I-1600-1603
Bridgford, I-366
Brita, I-1918
Britannia, I-633
Britney Spears Fantasy, I-1441
Brooks, I-471
Brother, I-1957, II-2046
Bryan, I-363
BSH, II-2042
Bubba Burger, I-542
Bud Light, I-755, 771
Buddig, I-367

Budweiser, I-755, 771
Bug Juice, I-492
Bugles, I-868
Buitoni, I-893
Buitoni Riserva, I-893
Bullseye, I-469
Bumble Bee, I-842
Burberry, I-1438
Burnett's, I-792
Burt Bees Lip Shimmer, I-1429
Burt's Bees, I-1457
Burts Bees Radiance, I-1498
Busch, I-755
Busch Light, I-755
Bush's Best, I-471
Butchers, I-579
Butterball, I-361, 382
Butterfly Bakery, I-613
Buxton, I-800
BuyWithMe, II-2657
C-Span, II-2695
C2F Pro Art, I-1511
Cabela, II-2451
Cabin Fever, Jeff Kinney, I-1220
Caboodles, I-1633
Cabot, I-386
Cabot Vermont, I-397
Cadbury, I-653
Cadbury Dairy Milk, I-653
Cadbury India, I-633
Cadillac CTS, II-2181, 2185
Cadillac Escalade, II-2182
Cafe Valley, I-613
Cake Mate, II-2488
Cal Maine Sunup, I-126
Calavo, I-426
Calbee, I-883
Caldrea/Mrs. Meyer's, I-1391
Calico, II-2490
California Pizza Kitchen, I-552
Calise & Sons Bakery, I-571
Call of Duty: Modern Warfare 3,
  II-3364
Calmol 4, I-1320
Camel, I-966
Camelbak, I-1080
Campbell's, I-462-463, 465
Campbell's Chunky Healthy Re-
  quest, I-465
Campbell's Chunky Soup, I-465
Campbell's Healthy Request,
  I-463
Campbell's Light, I-463
Campbell's Select Harvest, I-465

Campbell's Select Harvest Healthy
  Request, I-465
Campbell's Soup at Hand, I-465
Campbell's SpongeBob Squarepants,
  I-463
Campfire, I-684
Candie's, I-23
C&S, I-1175, 1193
Canilla, I-567
Canon, II-2063, 2070, 2415
Capatriti, I-743
Cape Cod, I-875
Cape Gourmet, I-840, 844
Captain America: The First Avenger,
  II-3437
Captain Morgan, I-784, 790
Carapelli, I-743
Cardini's, I-627
Carefree to Go, I-1177
Caress Dailk Silk, I-1383
Carlo Rossi, I-775
Carmex, I-1457
Carolina Pride, I-367
Cars 2, II-3437
Carter's, I-1021
Carvel, I-417
Cascade Ice, I-808-809
Cascadian Farm, I-524, 528, 699
Casio, II-2415
Castrol GTX, I-1592
Cat Chow, I-581, 585
Catching Fire, Suzanne Collins,
  I-1214, 1220
Catnapper, I-1113
C.banner, I-1642
CBS News, II-2665
Cedar's Mediterrenean, I-393
Celebration Foods Oreo, I-417
Celestial Seasonings, I-932
Censea, I-844
Centrum, I-1301
Centrum Silver, I-1301
CEP, I-986
CeraVe, I-1499
Certs, I-651
Cesar, I-579, 590
Cessna, II-2268
Cetaphil, I-1383, 1496, 1498-1499
Cetaphil Facial Cleansers, I-1502
Challenge Butter, I-386
Champion, I-509
Champion Raisels, I-509
Chanel, I-1438
Chao Mein, I-458

Chapstick, I-1457
Chapstick Classic, I-1457
Char-Broil, I-28
Charlie Rose, II-2664
Charmin Basic, I-1194
Charmin Fresh Mates, I-1181
Charmin Ultra Soft, I-1194
Charmin Ultra Strong, I-1194
Charms Blow Pop, I-680
Charms Super Blow Pop, I-680
Chateau Ste. Michelle, I-775
Chatham Village, I-627
Cheer Brightclean, I-1375
Cheerios, I-558-559
Cheers, I-1113-1114
Cheetos, I-864, 883
Cheetos 100-Cal Pack, I-864
Cheetos Mighty Zingers, I-864
Cheetos Natural, I-864
Chelsea Lately, II-2664
Chengda, I-1639
Chesapeake Bay Candle, II-2488
Chester's, I-864, 881-882
Chevrolet, II-2192, 2195
Chevrolet Cruze, II-2180, 2183
Chevrolet Express, II-2186
Chevrolet Impala, II-2184
Chevrolet Malibu, II-2184
Chevrolet Silverado, II-2180
Chevrolet Volt, II-2217
Chevron Supreme, I-1592
The Chew, II-3439
Chex Mix, I-881-882
Chi Chi's, I-504
Chicago Town, I-553
Chicago Tribune, I-1204
Chicken of the Sea, I-842
Chigarid, I-1321
Chiggerex, I-1321
Children's Advil, I-1313
Children's Motrin, I-1313
Children's Tylenol, I-1313
China Boy, I-458
Chinet, I-1173
Chinet Classic White, I-1173
Chips Ahoy!, I-635
Chiquita, I-912-913
Chobani, I-440
Chock Full O'Nuts, I-851
Christian Dior, I-1438, 1651
Christmas, Michael Bublé, II-2087
Chrysler Town & Country, II-2186
Chug, I-438
Chung's, I-546

Ciba Vision Clear Care, I-1434
Cif, I-1398
Cillit Bang, I-1398
Cinch 2 in 1, I-1390
Cinnabon, I-860
Cinnamon Toast Crunch, I-558
Citracel, I-1297
Citroen Berlingo, II-2194
Citroen C3, II-2190
Citrucel, I-1322
Citrus World Donald Duck, I-499
Claim Jumper, I-640
Clairol Herbal Essences, I-1452
Clairol Herbal Essences Hello Hy-
  dration, I-1453
Clairol Nice 'n Easy, I-1446
Clarion, II-2067, 2328
Claritin, I-1315
Claritin D, I-1315
Clarity, II-2101-2102
Clarks England, I-1643
Classico Signature Recipes, I-519
Classico Traditional Favorites, I-519
Clear Eyes, I-1434
Clearasil Ultra, I-1491
Clearblue Easy, I-1357
Clearskin, I-1492
Clif, I-703
Clif Builder's, I-703
Clif Luna, I-703
Clorox, I-1395, 1399
Clorox Cloth, I-1196
Clorox Green Works, I-1390-1391
Clorox Green Works Cloth, I-1196
Clos du Bois, I-775
Closetmaid, I-19
Cloverdale, I-366
Cloverhill, I-614
CLR, I-1393
Cnice, I-1465
CNN, II-2695
CNN Network, II-2665
Coach, I-1643, 1651
Coby, II-2064, 2080, 2109
Coco Pops, I-559
Coffee People, I-856
Coke, I-752, 816
Colace, I-1323
Colavita, I-743
The Colbert Report, II-2664, 3438
Cole's, I-621-622
Colgate, I-1465
Colgate 360, II-2032, 2474
Colgate Extra Clean, II-2474

Colgate Max White, II-2474

Colgate Octagon, I-1405

Colgate Wave, II-2474

Colgate Wisp, II-2474

Columbia, II-2450

Combos, I-877

Comet, I-1387

Comfort Scanner, II-2367

Community, I-860

Conair, II-2489

Conair Styling Essentials, II-2489

Conan, II-2664, 3438

Concord, I-923

Conferreria Raffaello, I-691

Connoisseurs, I-1397

Contents, I-1633

Contessa, I-790

Continental, I-1601

Contour Designs, I-4

Converse, I-1608

Cooked Perfect, I-542

Cooper, I-1602-1603

Coors Light, I-755, 771

Copenhagen, I-972

Coppertone Sport, I-1506

CopperTop, II-2168

Coralite, II-2370

Corn Flakes, I-559

Corona Extra, I-755, 772

Corona Light, I-772

Cortaid, I-1310

Cortelco Kellogg, II-2101

Cortizone 10, I-1310

Cortizone 10 Plus, I-1310

Cosco Scenera, II-2483

Cosmo, I-1212

Cosmopolitan, I-1211

Country Fresh, I-912

Country Time, I-915

Courvoisier, I-781

CoverGirl & Olay Simply Ageless, I-1425

CoverGirl Clean, I-1425

CoverGirl Continuous Color, I-1429

CoverGirl Lash Blast, I-1423

CoverGirl Lash Blast Fusion, I-1423

CoverGirl LipPerfection, I-1428

CoverGirl Liquid Blast, I-1422

CoverGirl Outlast, I-1429

CoverGirl Outlast Topcoat, I-1459

CoverGirl Perfect Point Plus, I-1422

CoverGirl Smoothwear, I-1459

Cowboy, I-1565

Cra-Z-Art, I-1633, II-2463

Cracker Jack, I-873, 880

Crane, II-2039

Crayola, I-1511, 1548, II-2460-2461, 2463, 2466

Crayola Beginnings, II-2463

Crayola Color, II-2466

Crayola Color Wonder, II-2466

Crayola Glow, II-2460

Crayola Pip Squeaks, II-2461, 2466

Crayola Sidewalk, II-2460

Crayola Telescoping Tower, II-2463

Crayola Twist Slick Stix, II-2463

Crayola Twistables, II-2461, 2463

Cream of Wheat, I-562

Creamette, I-889, 895

Creative Snaks, I-862

Crest 3D Whitening Whitestrip, I-1474

Crest 3D Whitening Whitestrip Advanced SL, I-1474

Crest Glide, I-1466

Crest Glide Comfort Plus, I-1466

Crest Glide Deep Clean, I-1466

Crest Pro-Health, I-1469

Crest Spoonbrush Pro White, II-2032

Crestor, I-1331, 1335

Crisco, I-738, 740, 743, 745

Crispin, I-783

Crocs, I-1639

Crosley, II-2069, 2101

Crossville, I-1679

Crown Royal, I-784

Crunch 'n Munch, I-873, 880

Crunch Pak, I-912-913

Crunchy Nut, I-559

Cruz, I-935

Cryo Max, II-2374

Crystal Farms, I-126, 386, 397, 406-407

Crystal Geyser, I-806, 809

Crystal Light, I-915

Crystal Light On The Go, I-915

CubCrafters, II-2268

Culligan, I-1543

Curve For Men, I-1440

Cutter Bite MD, I-1321

Cutter Skinsations, I-1566

Cymbalta, I-1335

Czech Sport Aircraft, II-2268

Czysta de Luxe, I-793

D-Link, I-1967

Da Fei Xin, I-1319

Dacia, II-2195

Dacia Duster, II-2194

Dacia Logan, II-2194

Dacia Sandero, II-2194

Daf Trucks, II-2226

Daihatsu, II-2204

Daily Mail, I-1205

The Daily Show, II-2664, 3438

Daily Telegraph, I-1205

Daisy, I-424

Dale's, I-503

The Dallas Morning News, I-1204

Dane-Elec, II-2123

Dannon Activia, I-440

Dannon Activia Light, I-440

Dannon Light & Fit, I-440

Danone, I-442-444

Darigold, I-386, 435

Darrell Lea, I-682, 686

Das Dutchman Essenhaus, I-889

Dasani, I-752, 805

Daum, II-2655

David, I-729

Davidoff Cool Water, I-1440

Dawn, I-1362

Dawn Plus Hand Renewal, I-1362

DaYi, I-933

DC Shoes, I-1607

DCP, I-832

De Cecco, I-895

De La Rosa, I-684

DealChicken.com, II-2657

Dealfind, II-2657

Dean's, I-424, 426, 435-436

Dean's Choco Riffic, I-438

Debrox, I-1433

Decathalon, I-1033

Deco Art Crafters Acrylic, I-1511

Deepwoods Off, I-1566

Deer Park, I-805-806

Definitive, II-2066

Degree Men, I-1431

Del Monte, I-474, 509, 913

Del Monte Fresh Cut, I-472

Del Monte Fresh Cut Specialties, I-472

Del Monte Fruit Chillers, I-419

Del Monte Specialties, I-474

Delicare, I-1404

Delicious Fresh Pierogi, I-549

Delimex, I-546

Delkin Devices, II-2123

Delsey, I-1647

Delta Creamcoat, I-1511

Demet's Turtles, I-712

Denon, II-2062, 2065

Dentaburst, I-1473
Dentek, II-2030
Dentyne Ice, I-726
Depend, I-1166
Depend Boost, I-1166
Der, II-2481
Deschutes, I-768
Desitin Baby, I-1415
Desitin Creamy Baby, I-1415
Destined, P.C. and Kristin Cast,
 I-1220
Dettol, I-1398
Dexatrim Max Complex 7, I-1349
Di Giorno, I-406, 552
Dial, I-1378, 1381-1382
Dial Complete, I-1382
Diamond Crystal, I-835, 1543
Diary of a Wimpy Kid: Cabin Fever,
 Jeff Kinney, I-1214
Didatuan, II-2658
Diet Coke, I-816
Diet Dr. Pepper, I-816
Diet Mountain Dew, I-816
Diet Pepsi, I-816
Diet Snapple, I-796
Digital Stream, II-2107
Dimetapp, I-1314
Dingo, II-2494
Dingo Bone, II-2494
Dingo Dynostix, II-2494
Dingo Goof Balls, II-2494
Dingo Meat in the Middle, II-2494
Diovan, I-1331
Diovan HCT, I-1331
DirecTV, II-2103, 2105
Discover, II-3090
Discovery, II-2695
Dishwasher Magic, I-1396
Disney, II-2064, 2079
Disney Garden, I-912
Dixie, I-1173
Dixie Ultra, I-1173
Dixon, II-2461
Dixon Ticonderoga, II-2464
Doctor Li, I-1497
Dodge Grand Caravan, II-2186
Dodge Ram, II-2180
Dog Chow, I-583, 585
Dolce & Gabbana Light Blue, I-1441
Dole, I-483, 509, 524
Don Jose, I-438
Don Marcos, I-935
Donatos, I-920
Donut House Collection, I-856

Doral, I-965
Doritos, I-883, 886
Dos Equis Lager Especial, I-772
Doubleshot, I-860
Doubleshot Light, I-860
Dove, I-709, 712, 1378, 1383, 1431,
 1451
Dove Go Fresh Cool, I-1383
Dove Men + Care, I-1383, II-2487
Dove Nourishing Care, I-1383
Downy, I-1402-1403
Downy Free and Sensitive, I-1403
Downy Simple Pleasures, I-1402-
 1403
Downy Unstoppables, I-1407
Dr. Fred Summit, I-1494
Dr. Fresh Infectiguard, I-1381
Dr. Katz TheraBreath, I-1473
Dr. Miracles, I-1450
Dr. Oetker, I-553
The Dr. Oz Show, II-3439
Dr. Pepper, I-752
Dr. Phil, II-3439
Dr. Teal's, I-1380
Drake, I-614
Drakkar Noir, I-1440
Drano, I-1388
Drano Dual Force, I-1388
Drano Max, I-1388
Drano Snake Plus, I-1388
Dreher, I-780
Dreyer's/Edy's, I-415
Dreyer's/Edy's Fun Flavors, I-421
Dreyer's/Edy's Grand, I-421
Dreyer's/Edy's Slowchurned,
 I-416, 421
Drogheria & Alimentari, I-833
Dry Cleaners Secret, I-1406
Dryel, I-1405-1406
Dual Audio, II-2067
Duck, I-1160
Duck Tape, I-1160
Dulcolax, I-1323
Dulcolax Balance, I-1322
Dunkin' Donuts, I-851, 853
Dunlop, I-1600
Durable Foil, I-1731
Duracell, II-2166, 2174
Duracell Easytab, II-2175
Duracell Ultra + Pix, II-2168
Dynasty, I-739
Earthbound Farm Organic, I-509
Earth's Best Tots, I-487
Eastpak, I-1080, 1647

Easy Off, I-1396
Easy Off Fume Free Max, I-1396
Easy Spirit, I-1643
Echo Falls, I-776, 839
Eckrich, I-363, 370
Ecover, I-1404
Edge, I-1490
eDiets.com, II-2659
Edi's, I-621
Edward's, I-640
Edward's Singles, I-640
Efferdent, I-1468
Efferdent Plus, I-1468
Eggland's Best, I-126
Eight Horse Tea Group, I-1667
Eight O'Clock, I-851
El Guapo, I-836
El Jimador, I-791
El Monterey, I-539, 546
Electra, II-2297
Electrolux, II-2014-2015, 2019-
 2020, 2024, 2027, 2042
Eli's, I-606
Elizabeth Taylor's White Diamonds,
 I-1441
Ella's Kitchen, I-447
Elle, I-1212
The Ellen Degeneres Show, II-3439
Elmer's, I-1511, 1548
Elmer's Glue-All, I-1548
Elmer's Squeeze N Brush, I-1511
Emerald, I-729, 871
Emerald Breakfast On The Go, I-871
Emerson, II-2064
Emmi, I-860
Emperial Spring, I-807
Enbrel, I-1335
Energizer, II-2166, 2174-2175
Energizer Lithium, II-2168
Energizer Max, II-2168
Energy, II-2066
Enfamil Gentlease, I-459
Enfamil Premium, I-459
Ensure, I-1350
Entenmann's, I-608, 614
Entenmann's Little Bites, I-613
Entenmann's Softees, I-608
e.p.t., I-1357
Equal, I-647
Era, I-1375
ESI, II-2096
ESPN, II-2695
ESPN2, II-2695
Estée Lauder, I-1503

Ester C, I-1302
Esther Price, I-719
Etnies, I-1607
Eucerin, I-1499
Eucerin Aquaphor, I-1499
Eucerin Plus, I-1499
Evektor, II-2268
Evenflo, II-2483
Eventbrite, II-2674
Eventful, II-2674
Evenue.net, II-2674
Everfresh, I-493
Eversave.com, II-2657
Everyday by L'eggs, I-984
Everyday Essentials, II-2488
Evian, I-800, 807
Eviant, II-2080
Evite.com, II-2660
Evolution, I-483
Evoraplus, I-1473
Ex Lax, I-1323
Excel, I-358
Expedia, II-2675
Exquisita, I-935
Eye-Fi, II-2123
Facebook, II-2663, 2676
Fage Total, I-440
Fairy, I-1361
Faith Hill Parfums, I-1441
Falken, I-1600
Family Circle, I-1210-1211
Family Finest Take N Bake, I-920
Famous Dave's, I-469
Fancy Feast, I-577, 589
Fannie May, I-719
FanSnap, II-2674
Fanta, I-816
Farm Rich, I-546
Farmer John, I-361, 363, 373
Farmland, I-361
Farrell, I-1114
Fast Five, II-3437
The Father's Table, I-606
Febreze, II-2488
Felix, I-576
Fels Naptha, I-1405-1406
Femina, I-1212
Ferrara Pan Boston Baked Beans,
   I-691
Ferrera Pan Lemonhead, I-680
Ferrero Collection, I-719
Ferrero Rocher, I-719
Fiat, II-2195-2196
Fiat Punto, II-2194

Fiber Choice, I-1323
Fiber One, I-703
Fila, I-1608, 1613
Filippo Berio, I-743
Financial Times, I-1205
Finish, I-1361
Firestone, I-1598, 1600, 1602-1603
First, I-1211
First Aid Only, II-2372
First Cape, I-776
First Response, I-1357
First Years, II-2483
Fisher Price, II-2483
Fishin', I-840
Fiskers, I-1754
Fixodent, I-1467
Fixodent Advanced Whitening,
   I-1468
Fixodent Food Seal, I-1467
Fixodent Free, I-1467
Fixodent Original, I-1467
Fixodent Plus Scope, I-1468
Fla-Vor-Ice, I-419
Flander, I-542
Flash, I-1398
Fleet, I-1322-1323
Fleet Enema Extra, I-1322
Fleet Pedia Lax, I-1322
Flexsteel, I-1113
Flickr, II-2667
Flight Design, II-2268
Flintstones, I-1301
Flip Video, II-2070
Flipz, I-866
Florida Tile, I-1679
Florida's Natural, I-499
Florim, I-1679
Folgers, I-851, 853, 855
Folgers Gourmet Selections, I-856
Food Network, II-2695
FootJoy, I-1609
Ford, II-2189, 2191, 2195-2196,
   2206
Ford E-Series, II-2186
Ford Escape, II-2180, 2218
Ford F-series, II-2180
Ford Focus, II-2183, 2194
Ford Fusion, II-2180, 2184, 2218
Ford Transit Connect, II-2186
Formula Shell, I-1592
ForRent.com, II-2668
Fortune, I-731, 893
Foster Farms, I-363, 382, 539, 546
Four Loko, I-774

Fourseas, I-731
Fox News, II-2695
Frabill, II-2451
Francesco Rinaldi, I-519
Franklin Furniture, I-1113
Franzia box, I-775
Frappuccino, I-860
French Meadow Bakery, I-570
French's, I-512, 515
Freschetta, I-552
Fresh Frozen, I-527-528
Fresh Gourmet, I-627
Friendship, I-424
Frigo Cheese Heads, I-399
Friskies, I-577, 581, 585, 589
Frito-Lay, I-871, 901
Fritos, I-868, 883, 901
Fritos Flavor Twists, I-868
Fritos Scoops, I-868
Fritos Singles, I-868
Frizz Ease, I-1452
Frog Prince, I-1465, 1493
Froot Loops, I-558
Frosted Flakes, I-558
Frosted Mini-Wheats, I-558
Frosties, I-559
Fruit Full Island, I-739
Fruit of the Earth, I-485
Fruit of the Loom, I-987
FTD.com, II-2662
Ftuan, II-2658
Fuji, II-2177, 2415
Fuji Quicksnap Flash, II-2414
Fuji Super HQ, II-2417
Fuji Superia Xtra, II-2417
Fujifilm, II-2177, 2417
Full Throttle, I-810
Fun Pops, I-419
Funyuns, I-881-882
Futuro, II-2375
Futuro Infinity, II-2375
Futuro Sport, II-2375
Fuze Slenderize, I-492
Fynex, I-1639
G2, I-829
G2 Perform, I-830
Gain, I-1362, 1375, 1402-1403
Galaxy, I-653
Gallo, I-568, 776
Gallo Family Vineyards, I-775
Game Informer Magazine, I-1210
GaoPeng, II-2658
Garden, I-611
Garden Fresh, I-393

Brands Index

Garden Highway, I-913
Gardenburger, I-543
Gardetto's, I-881-882
Garelick Farms, I-436-437
Garmin, II-2328
Garnier, I-1495
Garnier Fructis S&S, I-1447
Garnier Fructis Style Full Control, I-1451
Garnier Nutrisse, I-1446
Gas X, I-1306, 1308
Gatorade, I-752, 829-830
Gatorade Cool Blue, I-829
Gatorade Frost, I-829
Gatorade G2, I-829
Gatorade Perform, I-829-830
Gatorade Recover, I-829
Gaviscon, I-1306
GE, II-2056
GE Energy Smart, II-2056
GE Longer Life, II-2056
GE Reveal, II-2056
GE Soft White, II-2056
Gears of War 3, II-3364
General Electric, II-2014-2015, 2019-2020, 2024, 2027, 2042, 2101, 2105
General Motors, II-2191
Genune Black and White, I-1494
Georges, I-485
Geratherm, II-2367
Gerber, I-449, 487
Gerber First Foods, I-449
Gerber Good Start Gentle, I-459
Gerber Good Start Gentle Plus, I-459
Gerber Graduates, I-449
Gerber Graduates Fruit Splashes, I-487
Gerber Graduates Smart Sips, I-487
Gerber Harvest Juice, I-487
Gerber Second Foods, I-449
Gerber Tender Harvest, I-487
Gerber Third Foods, I-449
Germ X, I-1381
Gifts.com, II-2662
Gillette, I-1749
Gillette Custom Plus, I-1750
Gillette Foamy, I-1490
Gillette Fusion Hydra Gel, I-1490
Gillette Good News, I-1750
Gillette Good News Plus, I-1750
Gillette Mach3, I-1750
Gillette Sensor 3, I-1750
Gillette Series, I-1490

Gilt.com, II-2661
Giovanni Rana, I-893
Glaceau, I-805
Glaceau Smartwater, I-805
Glad, I-1158-1159
Glad Force Flex, I-1158
Glad Force Flex Odor Shield, I-1158
Glad Odor Shield, I-1158
Glade, II-2488
Glade 2 in 1, II-2488
Gladiator GarageWorks, I-19
Glam Media, II-2663
Glass Plus, I-1390
Glen's, I-785
Glorious!, I-462
Glory Foods, I-472
Glyoxide, I-1327
Go-Cat, I-576
Gold Bond, I-1310
Gold Bond Ultimate, I-1381, 1499
Gold Leaf, I-375
Gold Meadow Bakery Fiber One, I-628
Gold N Plump, I-375
Gold Star Chili, I-532
Goldbug Eddie Bauer, II-2483
Golden Flake, I-874
Golden Gourmet, I-549
Golden Grahams Treats, I-648
Golden Peak, I-796
Goldstar Events, II-2674
Good & Plenty, I-682, 686
Good Housekeeping, I-1210
Good Seasons, I-923
Goodfella's, I-553
Goody, II-2489
Goody Ouchless, II-2489
Goodyear, I-1598, 1600-1603
Google, II-2643, 2646-2647, 2649-2653, 2655-2656, 2663, 2672, 2675-2676, 3354
GoPro, II-2063
Gordon's, I-785
Gordo's, I-426
Gorilla Glue, I-1548
Gorlla Tape, I-1160
Gorton's, I-840, 844
got2b glued, I-1452
Gourmet, I-576
Gourmet Garden, I-832
Goya, I-471, 503, 524, 527, 743
GPX, II-2064, 2069
Graco Nautilus, II-2483
Grand Prix, I-967

GrandMa's, I-635
Great American, I-840, 844
Great Fish, I-840
Great Range, I-358
Great Wall, I-970
Green Giant, I-472, 474
Green Giant Kitchen Sliced, I-472
Green Giant Mexicorn, I-474
Green Giant Simply Steam, I-525
Green Mountain, I-856
Greenies, I-580
Gregory's, I-570
Grey Goose, I-792-793
Grey Poupon, I-515
Griffin Technology, I-4, II-2068
Grizzly, I-972
Groupon, II-2657-2658
GSKCHL, I-633
The Guardian, I-1205
Gucci, I-1651
Guerrero, I-874
Guess, I-1641
Gulden's, I-515
Gumout, I-1564
Guttenplan's, I-571-572
Gwaltney, I-361, 363
Gwaltney Great Dogs, I-363
Häagen-Dazs, I-415-416, 421
Habitrol, I-1312
Haier, II-2015, 2079-2080
Haishi, I-731
HalfOffDepot.com, II-2657
Halle by Halle Berry, I-1441
Halls Refresh, I-696
Handi Foil, I-1731
Handi Foil Bake America, I-1731
Handi Foil Cook 'n Carry, I-1731
Handi Foil Ultimates, I-1731
Handycam, II-2070
Hanes, I-984, 987
Hanes Premium, I-987
The Hangover Part II, II-3437
Hankook, I-1601, 1603
Hanover, I-471-472
Hansen's, I-493
Hapi, I-523, 897
Happy Apples, I-657
Hardys, I-776
Haribi Gold Bears, I-687
Haribo, I-653
Haro, II-2297
Harry Potter and the Deathly Hallows Part 2, II-3437
Harson, I-1642

Hartz, II-2494

Hartz American BFHD, II-2494

Hartz Americas Prime, II-2494

Hatfield, I-373

Hautelook.com, II-2661

Havana Club, I-790

Havoline, I-1592

Hawaiian Punch, I-492

Head & Shoulders, I-1454

Head & Shoulders Classic, I-1444

Head & Shoulders Classic Clean 2, I-1444

Head & Shoulders Dry Scalp, I-1444

Head & Shoulders Hair Endurance, I-1444

Head & Shoulders Ocean Lift, I-1444

Head & Shoulders Refresh, I-1444

Head & Shoulders Smooth & Silky 2, I-1444

Healthy Choice, I-465, 534

Healthy Choice Cafe Steamers, I-534

Hearttex, I-1175, 1184, 1193

Heatwave, I-1047

Heaven is for Real, Todd Burpo, I-1214

Hebrew National, I-363, 366

Hefty, I-1158-1159, 1173

Hefty Cinch Sak, I-1158

Hefty Deluxe, I-1173

Hefty Everyday, I-1173

Hefty EZ Foil, I-1731

Hefty EZ Foil EZ Elegance, I-1731

Hefty Gripper, I-1158

Heineken, I-755, 772

Heinz, I-447, 462, 502, 512, 916

Hellmann's, I-512, 514

Heluva Good, I-426

Hengren, I-1639

Hennessy, I-781

Hermes, I-1651

Herr's, I-866, 877

Hershey's, I-438, 708-709, 712, 714

Hershey's Cookies 'N Creme, I-708

Hershey's Kisses, I-709

Hershey's Nuggets, I-709

Hershey's Pot of Gold, I-719

Hewlett-Packard, I-1947, 1957, 1967

HGTV, II-2695

Hibiclens, II-2373

Hidden Valley, I-901, 923

Hidden Valley Ranch, I-517, 901, 923

Highland Spring, I-800

Higueral, I-366

Hiland, I-437

Hillandale Farms, I-126

Hills, I-583

Hill's Science Diet, I-585

Hillshire Farm, I-370

Hillshire Farm Deli Select, I-367

HiPP Organic, I-447

Hogs Heaven, I-874

Holden, II-2189

Hollywood, I-740

Hollywood Beauty, I-1494

Holmes, II-2039

Home Pride, I-620

HoMedics, I-1355

HoMedics Thera P, I-1355

Homes.com, II-2668

Homestyle Two-Bite, I-614

Honda, II-2189, 2191, 2204, 2302

Honda Accord, II-2180, 2184

Honda City, II-2193

Honda Civic, II-2183

Honda CR-Z, II-2218

Honda Insights, II-2218

Honda Odyssey, II-2186

Honey Bee, I-780

Honey Bunches of Oats, I-558

Honey Nut Cheerios, I-558

Honeysuckle White, I-382

Honeywell, II-2039

Honeywell Easy Care, II-2039

Hood, I-424, 435-437

Hood Country Creamer, I-409

Hood Lactaid, I-436-437

Horizon Organic, I-436-437

Hormel, I-361

Hormel Black Label, I-361

Hormel Natural Choice, I-367

Hornsby's, I-783

Hosa, I-1033-1034, 1047

Hostess, I-605, 608, 613-614

Hostess Donettes, I-608

Hostess Smartbakes, I-613

Hostess Sweet Sixteen, I-608

Hostess Zingers, I-605

Hot Pockets, I-539-540

Hot Shot Outdoor, I-1566

Hotel Bar, I-386

House of Cazadores, I-791

House of Pasta, I-571

House of Tsang, I-739

Howes Lubricator, I-1564

HPMG News, II-2665

Hu Ji Hun, I-731

Hualong, I-1639

Huggies Little Movers, I-1170

Huggies Little Snugglers, I-1170

Huggies Natural Care, I-1168

Huggies Overnites, I-1170

Huggies Snug & Dry, I-1170

Huggies Soft Skin, I-1168

Hui Yuan, I-497

Hulu, II-2676

Humira, I-1335

Hunagbao, I-1639

Hungry Man, I-534

Hunter-Douglas, I-1063

Hunt's, I-469, 502, 512, 519

Hydroxycut Advanced, I-1349

Hygienix, I-1193

Hyland's, I-1327, 1433

Hyundai, II-2189, 2191-2192, 2195

Hyundai Elantra, II-2183

Hyundai Genesis, II-2185

Hyundai Sonata, II-2184, 2218

I Can't Believe It's Not Butter, I-394

I Can't Believe It's Not Butter Light, I-394

Iams, I-581, 583, 585

IBP, I-358

Ice Breakers, I-651

Ice Breakers Frost, I-651

Ice Crops, I-1464

Idea Village, I-1548

Ideeli.com, II-2661

iHealth, I-1355

iHome, I-1967, II-2068

Illy Issimo, I-860

Imation, II-2177

Imodium, I-1309

Imodium A-D, I-1309

Imperial, I-394

Imperial Blue, I-794

In Touch Weekly, I-1211

Incase Designs, I-4

Infant's Advil, I-1313

Infant's Motrin, I-1313

Infiniti, II-2196

Infiniti G, II-2181, 2185

Infiniti QX, II-2182

Inheritance, Christopher Paolini, I-1214, 1220

Inn Maid, I-889

Innovative Technology, II-2069

Innovera, II-2177

Instagram, II-2667

InStyle, I-1441

Interceramic, I-1679

International Delight, I-409
International Delight Coffee House Inspirations, I-409
iPhone, II-2093
Iris Bus, II-2222
Iron Chef, I-523
Italian Rose, I-832
ITC, I-633
It's Academic Ultimate, I-1754
It's All Good Garden, I-543
Ivory, I-1378, 1383
Jabiru USA, II-2268
Jabra, II-2096
Jack Daniel's, I-469, 794
Jack Daniel's Tennessee whiskey, I-784
Jack Link's, I-369
Jacks Original, I-552
Jacob's Creek, I-776
Jacuzzi, I-1763
Jagermeister, I-784
James Skinner, I-614
J&D's, I-923
Jaret Swedish Fish, I-687
Jaru, II-2460
Jasco, II-2105
Java Monster, I-810
Jayone, I-485
Jay's O-Ke-Doke, I-873, 880
Jean Nate, I-1441
Jeep, II-2196
Jell-O Temptations, I-606, 616
Jennie-O, I-363, 366, 370, 382
Jennie-O Turkey Store, I-373
Jensen, II-2064, 2067, 2080
Jeremiah Weed, I-774
Jergens Natural Glow, I-1499
Jergens Ultra Healing, I-1499
The Jerry Springer Show, II-3439
Jersey Boys, II-3458
Jerzees, I-987
Jessica Simpson, I-1641, 1643
Jif, I-918
Jillian Michaels, I-1349, II-2659
Jim Beam, I-784
Jimmy Dean, I-373, 531, 540
Jimmy Dean Breakfast Bowls, I-531
Jimmy Dean D Lights, I-540
Jinlongyu, I-731
Joan of Arc, I-471
Jobst, II-2375
John Morrell, I-361, 363, 366
John Morrell Snow Cap, I-348
Johnnie Walker, I-794

Johnson & Johnson, II-2372
Johnson & Johnson 1st Aid to Go, II-2372
Johnson & Johnson Reach, I-1466
Johnson & Johnson Safe Travels, II-2372
Johnson's, I-1377
Johnson's Baby, I-1493
Johnson's Bedtime Bath, I-1377
Johnson's Clean & Clear Advance, I-1491
Johnson's Clean & Clear Morning Burst, I-1496
Johnson's First Touch, I-1377
Johnson's Head-to-Toe, I-1377
Johnson's Moisture Care, I-1377
Johnsonville, I-370, 373
Jolly Rancher, I-680, 696
Jon Donaire, I-417
Jones, I-366
Joose, I-774
Jordana Easyliner, I-1428
Jose Cuervo, I-784, 791
José Olè, I-546
Joseph Campione, I-621
Joseph's, I-393
Jovan Musk for Women, I-1441
Joy, I-1362
Juarez, I-791
Junior Johnson, I-874
Junshan, I-933
Just Born Mike & Ike, I-687
Just Dance 3, II-3364
Just for Me, I-1450
Just My Size, I-984
Just Wireless, I-4, II-2096
JVC, II-2063-2064, 2067, 2069-2070
K-Byte Reptron, I-1947
K-Lite, I-1543
K-Y, I-1489
K-Y Intense, I-1489
K-Y Liquid, I-1489
K-Y Silk E, I-1329
K-Y Warming Jelly, I-1489
K-Y Yours + Mine, I-1489
K2, II-2450
Kaboom, I-1395
Kaboom Foam Tastic, I-1395
Kadoya, I-739
Kahn's, I-366
Kame, I-739, 897
Kank-A, I-1327
Kank-A Softbrush, I-1327
Kashi, I-547

Kashi TLC, I-648, 699
Kasia's, I-549
Kawasaki, II-2302
K.C. Masterpiece, I-469, 503
Keebler Club, I-638
Keebler Fudge Shoppe Right Bites, I-866
Keebler Townhouse, I-638
Keller's, I-386
Kellogg's, I-560
Kellogg's Eggo, I-531, 547
Kellogg's Eggo Minis, I-547
Kellogg's Eggo Nutri Grain, I-547
Kellogg's Eggo Thick & Fluffy, I-547
Kellogg's Fiber Plus, I-699
Kellogg's Nutri Grain Bars, I-648
Kellogg's Nutri Grain Eggo, I-547
Kellogg's Rice Krispies Treats, I-648
Kellogg's Special K Bar, I-648
Kellogg's Special K Fruit Crisps, I-648
Kellogg's Special K Protein, I-703
Kellogg's Yogos, I-862
Kemp's, I-416, 424, 435
Kemps Select, I-435-436
Kendall-Jackson Vintners Reserve, I-775
Kenny's, I-616
Ken's Steak House, I-503, 517
Kenwood, II-2067, 2328
Kern's Aguas Frescas, I-438
Kettle, I-875
Kettle Cuisine, I-464
Keurig Caribou Coffee, I-856
Kgbdeals, II-2657
Khlibniy Dar, I-793
Khortytsa, I-793
Kia, II-2191-2192
Kiddle 'n Bits, I-583
Kikkoman, I-523
Kim & Scott's Gourmet Pretzels, I-545
Kindle, II-3001
Kinect Adventures!, II-3364
Kingsford, I-1565
Kingsford BBQ Bag, I-1565
Kingsford Competition, I-1565
Kingsford Matchlight, I-1565
Kingston Technology, II-2123
Kinnikinnick Foods, I-571
Kisscat, I-1642
Kit Kat, I-653, 708-709, 714
Kit 'n Kaboodle, I-581

Kitchen of India, I-897
Kleencut, I-1754
Kleenex, I-1174-1175, 1193
Kleenex Cottonelle, I-1181, 1194
Kleenex Cottonelle Fresh, I-1181
Kleenex Cottonelle Soothing Clean, I-1181
Kleenex Cottonelle Ultra, I-1194
Kleenex Viva, I-1183
Klipsch, II-2066
Klondike, I-415
Knorr, I-462-463, 510, 916
Knudsen, I-424
Kodak, I-1967, II-2063, 2070, 2123, 2177, 2415
Kodak Advantix, II-2417
Kodak Fun Saver, II-2414
Kodak Gold, II-2417
Kodak Gold Max, II-2417
Kodak Max Sport, II-2414
Kodak Max Zoom, II-2414
Kodak Power Flash, II-2414
Kodak Ultra, II-2417
Kodak Ultra Max, II-2417
Kodiak, I-972
Kohler, I-1763
Konsyl, I-1322
Kontos, I-572
Kool, I-966
Kool Aid, I-915
Kool Aid Bursts, I-492
Kool Aid Singles Mio, I-915
Kool Aid Twists, I-915
Kotex, I-1177
Kotex Security, I-1180
Kraft, I-393, 397-399, 406, 408, 426, 469, 512, 517
Kraft Bagel-fuls, I-599
Kraft Big Slice, I-398
Kraft Cheez Whiz, I-901
Kraft Cracker Barrel, I-397
Kraft Deli Deluxe, I-407
Kraft Deli Fresh, I-398
Kraft Free, I-517
Kraft Jet Puffed, I-684
Kraft Jet Puffed Funmallows, I-684
Kraft Mayo, I-512
Kraft Mayonnaise, I-514
Kraft Miracle Whip, I-512
Kraft Pasta Salad, I-923
Kraft Philadelphia, I-406, 408
Kraft Philadelphia Flavors, I-408
Kraft Polly O, I-399
Kraft Singles, I-407

Kraft Snackables, I-399
Kraft South Beach Living, I-648
Kraft Velveeta, I-407
Kraft Velveeta Cheezy Skillets, I-903
Krazy Glue, I-1548
Krispy Kreme, I-608
Kristall, I-793
Kuka, I-1114
Kumala, I-776
Kumho, I-1600
Kung Fu Panda 2, II-3437
La Choy, I-458, 523, 897
La Costena, I-478
La Crème, I-409
La Croix, I-809
La Preferida, I-478
La-Z-Boy, I-1113
Labatt Blue, I-772
Labatt Blue Light, I-772
Lakewood, I-493
Lakewood Organic, I-485, 493
Lance, I-691, 873
Lancôme, I-1438, 1503
Land O'Frost Premium, I-367
Land O'Lakes, I-126, 386, 394, 398
L&M, I-955, 965
Lane, I-1113
Langers, I-486, 490, 493
Larabar, I-648
Lashou, II-2658
Late Night with Jimmy Fallon, II-2664
Late Show with David Letterman, II-2664, 3438
Laufen, I-1679
Laughing Cow Mini Babybel, I-397
Laura's Meats, I-358
Lawry's, I-503, 832, 835
Lay's, I-875, 883, 901
Lay's Natural, I-875
Le Saunda, I-1642
Le Sueur, I-474
Lean Pockets, I-539
Lee Kum Kee, I-523
L'eggs Sheer Energy, I-984
L'eggs Silken Mist, I-984
Lenders, I-599
Lender's Big N Crusty, I-599
Lever 2000, I-1383
Lexar Media, II-2123
Lexmark, I-1957
Lexus CT 200h, II-2218
Lexus ES, II-2181, 2185
Lexus GX, II-2182

Lexus IS, II-2185
Lexus RX400, II-2218
LG Electronics, II-2014-2015, 2021, 2062, 2078, 2081-2082, 2095-2096
Libbey, I-1665
Libby's, I-472, 474, 493
Lice Freee, I-1324
Lice Ice, I-1324
Licemd, I-1324
Life Savers, I-680, 696, 701
Life Savers Gummies, I-687
Lifehouse, I-657
Lifesource, I-1355
Lifeway Kefir, I-434
Liggett Select, I-955
Light N Fluffy, I-889
Lightlife Smart Dogs, I-543
Lilly of the Desert, I-485
Lime A Way, I-1393
Lime Out Extra, I-1393
Lincoln, II-2196
Lincoln MKZ Hybrid, II-2218
Lindeman's, I-776
Lindt Lindor, I-709, 719
Lindt Petits Desserts, I-719
Linksys Group, I-1967
The Lion King, II-3458
Lipitor, I-1331, 1335
Lipton, I-796, 916, 932
Lipton Brisk, I-492, 796
Lipton Cold Brew, I-932
Lipton Cup A Soup, I-510
Lipton Diet, I-796
Lipton Pureleaf, I-796
Lipton Recipe Secrets, I-510
Lipton Soup Secrets, I-510
Liquid Plumr, I-1388
Liquid Plumr Foaming Pipe Snake, I-1388
Liquid Plumr Penetrex, I-1388
Lisinopril, I-1331
Listerine, I-1469
Listerine Pocketmist, I-1464
Listerine Pocketpaks, I-651
Listerine Total Care, I-1469
Listerine Whitening, I-1474
Litehouse, I-428, 516
Little Debbie, I-605, 608, 613-614, 634-635
Little Debbie Nutty Bar, I-634
Little Fevers, I-1313
Little Tummys, I-1306
Live With Regis and Kelly, II-3439
Living Social, II-2657

Livingston Cellars, I-775
Lixiang Tea Group, I-1667
L.L. Bean, I-1080, II-2450
Loctite, I-1548
Lofthouse, I-634
Logitech, I-1967, II-2105
Loloka, I-1639
Lomographic, II-2418
London Fog, I-23
Long Trail, I-768
Longhorn, I-972
Longo's, I-572
L'Oréal, I-1503
L'Oréal Colour Riche,
  I-1428-1429
L'Oréal Dermo Expertise Advanced
  RevitaLift Facial Anti-Aging,
  I-1502
L'Oréal Double Extend, I-1423
L'Oréal Excellence, I-1446
L'Oréal Extreme Volume Collagen,
  I-1423
L'Oréal Infallible, I-1422, 1428
L'Oréal Lineur Intense, I-1422
L'Oréal Paris, I-1495
L'Oréal Pencil Perfect, I-1422
L'Oréal Superior Preference, I-1446
L'Oréal True Match, I-1425
L'Oréal True Match Naturale, I-1459
L'Oréal Voluminous, I-1423
Loriva, I-739
Lornamead, I-1324
Los Angeles Times, I-1204
Lotrimin AF, I-1310
Lou Ana, I-740
Louis Kemp Crab Delight, I-839
Louis Rich Oscar Mayer, I-361, 367
Lovenox, I-1331
Lubriderm Daily Moisture, I-1499
Lucarelli, I-572
Lucks, I-471
Lucky Charms, I-558
Lucky Country, I-686
Luhun, I-731
Lundberg, I-879
Lundy's, I-348
Luntan, I-933
Luster's Pink Smooth, I-1450
Luster's S-Curl, I-1450
Luvs, I-1170
Luvs Ultra Leakguards, I-1170
Luzianne, I-932
Lynn Wilson, I-935
Lysol, I-1395, 1399

Lysol Cling, I-1399
Lysol Cloth, I-1196
Lysol Complete Clean, I-1395
Lysol Dual Action Cloth, I-1196
Lysol Healthy Touch, I-1382
Lysol Power, I-1399
LYY, I-1034
Maalox Advanced, I-1306
Maalox Multi Symptom, I-1306
Mac's (Mac's Snacks), I-874
Madden Girl, I-1641
Magellan, II-2328
Magic, I-1497
Magic Hat, I-768
Magnavox, II-2079, 2107
Magner's, I-783
Magnum, I-415
Mahatma, I-567
Maidenform, I-1051
Mail.ru Group, II-2672
Malt-O-Meal, I-560, 562
Maltesers, I-653
Mama Lucia, I-542
Mama Mary's, I-572
Mama Rosa, I-920
Mamma Bella, I-621
Mamma Mia!, II-3458
MAN, II-2226
Manco, I-1160
Mandi, I-1319
M&M's, I-708-709, 714
Manischewitz, I-889
Mankattan, I-611
Mansion House, I-780
Manzuo, II-2658
MapQuest, II-2675
Marazzi, I-1679
Margaret Holmes, I-474
Margaritaville, I-791
Mariani, I-508, 862
Marie Callender's, I-533-534, 550,
  640
Marie's, I-428, 516
Mario Kart Wii, II-3364
Marlboro, I-966
Mars, I-653
Martell, I-781
Mary Poppins, II-3458
Marzetti, I-428, 516, 627, 657
Masco, I-1763
Master Kong, I-497, 797
MasterCard, II-3090
Mata Piojos, I-1324
Matador, I-369

Matchlight, I-1565
Maury, II-3439
Maverick, I-967
Maxell, II-2177
Maxwell House, I-850-851, 853, 855
Maxwell House International, I-855
May Flower, I-1175, 1184
Maybelline Color Sensational,
  I-1428-1429
Maybelline Define-A-Lash, I-1423
Maybelline Define-A-Line, I-1422
Maybelline Great Lash, I-1423
Maybelline Lash Stiletto, I-1423
Maybelline Last Drama, I-1422
Maybelline Superstay Lip Color,
  I-1429
Maybelline Unstop, I-1422
Maybelline Virtual Express Colla-
  gen, I-1423
Maybelline Volum Express Falsies,
  I-1423
Mazda, II-2189, 2191-2192, 2204
Mazola, I-740
Mazola Corn Plus, I-740
Mazola Vegetable Plus, I-740
McAfee, II-3358
McCain, I-553
McCann's, I-562
McCormick, I-832-833, 835-836
McCormick Gourmet Collection,
  I-833, 836
McCormick Grill Mates, I-836
McCormick Spice Classics, I-833
McDowell's No. 1, I-780, 794
McDowell's No. 1 Celebration,
  I-790
Mederma, II-2373
Medifast, II-2659
Mega T, I-1349
Meituan, II-2658
Melitta, I-853
Memorex, II-2062, 2064, 2177
Mennen Speed Stick, I-1431
Mentos, I-701
Meow Mix, I-581
Mercedes-Benz, II-2196, 2206, 2226
Mercedes-Benz C-Class, II-2181,
  2185
Mercedes-Benz GL, II-2182
Mercedes-Benz GL320, II-2214
Mercedes-Benz ML320, II-2214
Mercury, II-2196
Metamucil, I-1322-1323

Method, I-1382, 1387, 1390-1391, 1397

MexAmerica, I-935

Michelin, I-1598, 1600-1603

Michelob Ultra Light, I-755

Microlife, I-1355

Microsoft, I-1967, II-2646, 2663, 2676

Mike-sell's, I-868

Mike's Hard, I-774

Milani Easyliner, I-1428

Milk-Bone, I-580

Milky Way, I-708-709, 714

Miller High Life, I-755

Miller Lite, I-755, 771

Millstone, I-853, 856

Mint Asure, I-1464

Minute Maid, I-497, 499

Minute Maid Premium, I-498-499

Minute Maid Premium Kids Plus, I-499

Mio, II-2328

Miracle Whip, I-514

Mirage, II-2066

Miralax, I-1322

Mission, I-874, 886, 901, 907, 935

Misty, I-955, 965

Mitsubishi, II-2189, 2191-2192, 2204

Mitsubishi i, II-2217

Mizuno, I-1613

Mocha Mix, I-409

Mockingjay, Suzanne Collins, I-1214, 1220

Modella, I-1633

Modelo Especial, I-772

Modern Weekly, I-1212

Moen, I-1763

Mohawk, I-1679

Monistat 1, I-1329

Monistat 1 Day, I-1329

Monistat 3, I-1329

Monistat 7, I-1329

Monster, II-2068

Monster Energy, I-810

Monster Energy XXL, I-810

Monster Hitman, I-812

Monster Mega Energy, I-810

Montego, I-967

Monterey Pasta, I-893

Montezuma Tequila, I-791

Montilla, I-790

Moran, I-542

Moran's, I-358

Morningstar Farms, I-375, 543

Morningstar Farms Grillers, I-543

Morningstar Farms Grillers Prime, I-543

Morton, I-1543

Morton Crystal, I-1543

Morton McCormick, I-835

Morton Season All, I-835

Morton System Saver, I-1543

Morton's, I-835

Motions, I-1450

Motorola, II-2096, 2102

Mott's Fresh Apples, I-912

Mountain Dew, I-752, 816

Mouth Note, I-1473

Move Inc. sites, II-2668

Moving Comfort, I-1052

Mr. Bubble, I-1380

Mr. Clean Magic Eraser Duo Cloth, I-1196

Mr. Muscle, I-1398

Mrs. Cubbison's, I-627

Mrs. Dash, I-836

Mrs. Meyes Clean Day, I-1387

Mrs. Paul's, I-840

Mrs. Smith's, I-640

Mrs. T's, I-549

MSN Real Estate, II-2668

MSNBC Network, II-2665

MTC, II-2695

Mucinex, I-1315

Mucinex DM, I-1315

Mueller Sport Care, II-2375

Mueller's, I-889, 895

Mug Shot, I-462

Multi-Mile, I-1602

Munchies, I-881-882

Munchkin, II-2483

Murine, I-1433

Murine Eargate, I-1433

My Kinda Party, Jason Aldean, II-2087

MyFunCards.com, II-2660

Mylanta, I-1306

Mylanta Supreme, I-1306

Mylicon, I-1306

Mystic Tan, I-1507

Nabisco 100 Calorie Packs, I-862, 866

Nabisco Chips Ahoy, I-634

Nabisco Honey Maid, I-638

Nabisco Newtons, I-634

Nabisco Oreo, I-634-635

Nabisco Oreo Double Stuff, I-634

Nabisco Premium, I-638

Nabisco Ritz, I-638, 866

Nabisco Triscuit, I-638

Nabisco Wheat Thins, I-638

Nads, I-1445

Nair, I-1445

Naked, I-505

Naked Energy, I-505

Naked Protein Zone, I-505

Naked Superfood, I-505

Nathan, I-363

National, I-987

National Enquirer, I-1211

National Geographic, I-1210

Natural Light, I-755

Naturally Fresh, I-516, 923

Nature, II-2481

Nature Made, I-1297, 1302

Nature Valley, I-699

Nature Valley Chewy Trail Mix, I-699

Nature Valley Sweet & Salty Nut, I-699

Nature's Bounty, I-1297, 1302

Nature's Bounty Q Sorb, I-1297

Nature's Own, I-620, 1543

Nature's Path Foods, I-560

Nature's Way, I-1302

Natuzzi, I-1113

Naver, II-2655

Neese's, I-366

NeilMed Nasaflo, I-1462

NeilMed Sinus Rinse, I-1462

Nemiroff, I-793

Neosporin, II-2373

Neosporin Lip Health, I-1459

Neosporin Neo To Go, II-2373

Nescafé, I-850

Nescafé Clasico, I-855

Nestea, I-796

Nestlé Butterfinger, I-714

Nestlé Coffee Mate, I-409

Nestlé Coffee Mate Carb Select, I-409

Nestlé Drumstick, I-415

Nestlé Juicy Juice, I-490

Nestlé Nesquik, I-435, 438

Nestlé Pure Life, I-752, 805

Netease, II-2631

Neutrogena, I-1496

Neutrogena Acne Stress Control, I-1491

Neutrogena Deep Clean, I-1496

Neutrogena Healthy Defense, I-1498

Neutrogena Moisture, I-1498
Neutrogena Oil Free Acne Wash,
  I-1491, 1502
Neutrogena Rapid Clear, I-1491
Neutrogena T Gel, I-1444
Neutrogena Trip Moist, I-1447
Neutrogena Ultra Sheer, I-1506
New Balance, I-1613, 1615
New Belgium, I-768
New Covent Garden, I-462
New England, I-853
New York, I-621
New York Brand and Mamma Bella,
  I-622
New York Color Lippin Large,
  I-1459
New York Daily News, I-1204
New York Post, I-1204
The New York Times, I-1204
Newcastle Brown Ale, I-772
Newman's Own, I-509, 517, 519
Newman's Own Lighten Up, I-517
Newman's Own Organics, I-856
Newport, I-966
Newsday, I-1204
Nexium, I-1335
Nexxus Humectress, I-1447
Nick Jr. Dora The Explorer, II-2463
Nickelodeon, II-2695
Nicoderm CQ, I-1312
Nicorette, I-1311
Nightline, II-2664, 3438
Nike, I-1034, 1607-1608, 1613-1615
Nikon, II-2415, 2418
Nine West, I-1643
Nintendo 3DS, II-2444
Nintendo DS, II-2444
Nintendo Wii, II-2444
Nioxin, I-1442
Nips, I-680, 696
Nissan, II-2189, 2192, 2195, 2204
Nissan Altima, II-2180, 2184
Nissan Grand Livinia, II-2193
Nissan Leaf, II-2217
Nissan Maxima, II-2181
Nitro 2 Go, I-812
Nivea Body, I-1499
Nivea Visage, I-1495
Nix, I-1324
Nizoral, I-1444
No Nonsense, I-984, 987
No Nonsense Complete Comfort,
  I-987
No Nonsense Essential Basics, I-984

No Nonsense Great Shapes Figure
  Enhancement, I-984
No Yolks, I-889
Noble, I-483
Nokia, II-2095
Nook, II-3001
North Face, I-1080, II-2450
Norton, II-3358
NOS, I-810
Nursery, I-806
Nutricia, I-447
Nutrisystem, II-2659
Nuts About Florida, I-508
O, The Oprah Magazine, I-1211
Oasis, I-1473
o.b., I-1180
o.b. Pro Comfort, I-1180
Ocean Eclipse, I-840
Ocean Spray, I-508
Ocean Spray Craisins, I-508, 871
Ocean Spray Cranberry/Cocktail,
  I-495
Ocean Spray Light, I-495
Odom's Tennessee Pride, I-540
Odwalla, I-499, 648
Odwalla Protein Monster, I-434
Odwalla Superfood, I-505
Off Active, I-1566
Off Outdoor, I-1566
Office Max, I-1160
Officer's Choice, I-794
Oil of Olay, I-1495
Olay, I-1497, 1503
Olay Active Hydrating, I-1498
Olay Age Defying Facial Anti-
  Aging, I-1502
Olay Body Ultra, I-1383
Olay Complete, I-1498
Olay Complete Facial Moisturizers,
  I-1502
Olay Daily Facials, I-1496
Olay Professional Pro-X Facial Anti-
  Aging, I-1502
Olay Regenerist, I-1496
Olay Regenerist Facial Anti-Aging,
  I-1502
Olay Regenerist Micro Sculpting
  Facial Anti-Aging, I-1502
Old Admiral, I-780
Old Cask, I-790
Old Dominion, I-691
Old El Paso, I-478, 907
Old Orchard, I-486, 490
Old Port Rum, I-790

Old Spice, I-1439
Old Spice High Endurance, I-1431
Old Spice Red Zone, I-1431, 1439
Old Tavern, I-794
Olympus, II-2109, 2415, 2418
Omni Party, II-2460
Omron, I-1355
On-Cor Traditionals, I-533
On the Border, I-886
On the Go, I-984
One Arm Bandit, I-1160
OneKingsLane.com, II-2661
Onkyo, II-2065
Ooma, II-2102
Opel, II-2195, 2206
Open Pit, I-469
Optare, II-2222
Orajel, I-1327, 1473
Oral-B Advantage 3D White, II-2474
Oral-B Complete Advantage, II-2474
Oral-B Crossaction Power Max,
  II-2032
Oral-B Crossaction Pro Health,
  II-2474
Oral-B Dual Action, II-2030
Oral-B Indicator, II-2474
Oral-B Pro Health, II-2032
Oral-B Pulsar, II-2032
Oral-B Satinfloss, I-1466
Oral-B Slide Pro Health, I-1466
Oral-B Super Floss, I-1466
Orbit, I-726
Orbit White, I-726
Orchard Valley, I-862
Ore-Ida, I-544
Ore-Ida Golden Crinkles, I-544
Ore-Ida Tater Tots, I-544
Oreo, I-634-635
Organic Root Stimulator, I-1450
Organic Slo Delicious, I-416
Organic Valley, I-436-437
Organix, I-447, 1447
Original, I-797
Original Choice, I-794
The Original Superman, I-464
Orion, I-611
Oroweat, I-620, 628
Ortega, I-504
Orville Redenbacher, I-870
Orville Redenbacher Smart Pop,
  I-870
Orville Redenbacher's Poppycock,
  I-873, 880
Orvis, II-2451

Oscar Mayer, I-361, 363, 366-367
Oscar Mayer Deli Fresh, I-367
OshKosh, I-1021
Osteo Bi Flex, I-1297
Otis Spunkmeyer, I-570, 613
Otter Products, I-4
Our Certified, I-358
Owens, I-373
Owens Country Creek, I-874
Own the Night, Lady Antebellum, II-2087
Oxi Clean, I-1407
Oxi Clean Max Force, I-1407
Ozarka, I-806
Pace, I-504, 512
Painters Cocoa Butter Formula, I-1499
Pall Mall, I-955, 965
Palm, I-1947
Palmers Cocoa Butter Formula, I-1494
Palmers Skin Success, I-1494
Palmolive, I-1362, 1391
PAM, I-738
Pampers, I-1168
Pampers Baby Dry, I-1170
Pampers Baby Fresh, I-1168
Pampers Cruisers, I-1170
Pampers Cruisers Dry Max, I-1170
Pampers Kandoo, I-1181
Pampers Stages Sensitive, I-1168
Pampers Swaddlers New Baby, I-1170
Panasonic, I-1967, II-2062-2063, 2069-2070, 2079, 2081, 2101-2102, 2415
Panda, I-682, 686
Pantene Pro-V, I-1454
Pantene Pro-V Classic Care, I-1453
Pantene Pro-V Color, I-1447
Pantene Pro-V Color Preserve, I-1453
Pantene Pro-V Curly, I-1452
Pantene Pro-V Fine, I-1447, 1453
Pantene Pro-V Medium Thick, I-1447, 1453
Paper Mate, II-2464
Paper Mate & Write, II-2455, 2464
Paper Mate Clearpoint, II-2464
Paper Mate Comfort, II-2464
Paper Mate Flair, II-2455
Paper Mate Profile, II-2455
Paper Mate Write Bros., II-2464

Parkay, I-394
Parle, I-633
Pasta Prima, I-893
Patagonia, II-2450
Patron, I-791
Pay Day, I-691
Peak, I-1563
Pearson's Salted Nut Roll, I-691
Pedia Sure, I-1350
Pediacare, I-1313
Pedigree, I-579-580, 583, 585, 590
Peds, I-987
Peet's, I-853
Penn Dutch Farms, I-126
Pennsylvania Dutch, I-889
Pennzoil, I-1592
Penrose, I-369
Pentax, II-2415
People, I-1210-1211
People Stylewatch, I-1211
Pepcid AC, I-1308
Pepcid Complete, I-1308
Pepe Lopez, I-791
Pepito, I-935
Pepperidge Farm, I-596, 620-622, 634
Pepperidge Farm Goldfish, I-638
Pepperidge Farm Milano, I-634
Pepperidge Farm Mini, I-596
Pepsi, I-752, 816
Pepto-Bismol, I-1328
Perdue, I-375, 382
Perdue Perfect Portions, I-375
Perfect Purity, I-1381
Perfectly Clear, I-800
Perodua Alza, II-2193
Perodua Myvi, II-2193
Perodua Viva, II-2193
Perrier, I-807-809
Peter Pan, I-918
Peter Paul Almond Joy, I-708
Peugeot, II-2192, 2206
Peugeot 206, II-2194
Peugeot 207, II-2190
Peugeot 3008, II-2190
Peugeot 308, II-2190
Peugeot Partner, II-2194
P.F. Chang's Home Menu, I-533
The Phantom of the Opera, II-3458
Pharos, I-1947
Philips Duramax, II-2056
Philips Norelco, I-1753

Phillips, I-464, 839, 1323, 1328, II-2062, 2064, 2068-2069, 2080, 2105, 2109
Phillips Colon Health, I-1323
Philly Gourmet, I-542
Photobucket, II-2667
Physician Formula Plump Potion, I-1459
Piaoxue, I-933
Picasa Web Albums, II-2667
Pictsweet, I-525, 527-528
Pictsweet All Natural, I-527
Pictsweet Deluxe Steamables, I-525
Pieryoga, I-1033
Pilgrim's Pride, I-375
Pillsbury, I-572, 613, 616, 621
Pillsbury Sweet Moments, I-616
Pilot Easy Touch, II-2455
Pilot G2, II-2455
Pilot Precise V5, II-2455
Pinata, I-935
Pinnacle, I-792
Pioneer, II-2065, 2067, 2071, 2328
Pirate's Booty, I-881
Pirates of the Caribbean: On Stranger Tides, II-3437
Pirelli, I-1601
PlainVille Farms, I-382
Plano, II-2451
Planters, I-729, 871, 883
Planters Nutrition, I-729, 871
Plantronics, II-2096, 2101-2102
Plavix, I-1331, 1335
Playskool, II-2461
PlayStation 3, II-2444
PlayStation Portable, II-2444
Playtex Diaper Genie Li Elite, II-2483
Playtex Gentle Glide, I-1180
Playtex Sport, I-1180
Pledge cloth, I-1196
Plumrose, I-361
Plus White, I-1474
PNY Electronics, II-2123
Poise, I-1166
Pokemon Black/White Version, II-3364
Poland Spring, I-752, 805-806, 808-809
Polaner, I-481
Polar, I-1563
Polaroid, II-2418
Polident, I-1468

Polident Overnight, I-1468
Polk, II-2066
Polysporin, II-2373
POM Wonderful, I-483
Pompeian, I-743
PomX, I-860
Ponds, I-1498
Pop Ice, I-419
Pop Secret, I-870
Pop Secret Homestyle, I-870
Popcorn, Indiana, I-873, 880
Popcorn Expressions, I-873, 880
Popov Vodka, I-792
Poppy's Pierogies, I-549
Popsicle, I-415
Porsche Cayenne, II-2182
Post Cereals, I-560
Power Bar Performance, I-703
Power Bar Protein Plus, I-703
Power Dekor, II-2481
Power Service, I-1564
Power Stick, I-1439
Power Striker, II-2490
Power X EZ Scrub, I-1387
Powerade, I-829
Powerade ION4, I-829
Powerade Zero, I-829
Powermat USA, I-4
Prairie Farms, I-424, 435-437
Prang Fun Pro, I-1511
Praters, I-551
Pravastatin, I-1331
Precious Stringsters, I-399
Precise, II-2374
Prego, I-519
Premier Foods, I-482
Premio, I-370
Preparation H, I-1320
Preparation H Totables, I-1320
President, I-397, 497, 797
Prestige, I-1428
Prevacid 24Hr, I-1308
Prevail, I-1166
Priceline, II-2675
Prilosec OTC, I-1308
Primatene Mist, I-1462
Primo, I-806
Pringles, I-883
Pringles Super Stack, I-875
Pro Brand, II-2103
ProFlowers.com, II-2662
Progresso, I-465
Progresso Light, I-465
Promises, Promises, II-3458

Pronto Plus, I-1324
Propel, I-830
Propel Calcium, I-830
Protec, II-2039
Proton Persona, II-2193
Proton Saga, II-2193
Puffs, I-1174
Puma, I-1613-1614
Pup-Peroni, I-580
Pur, I-1918
Pure Digital, II-2063
Pure Life, I-800
Pure Protein, I-703
Purell, I-1381
Purex, I-1375
Purex Complete 3-in-1, I-1405-1406
Purina One, I-583, 585
Puss in Boots, II-3437
Pyat Ozer, I-793
Pyle, II-2067
Pyramid, I-768, 955
Pyrex, I-1664
Q-Tips, II-2370
Q-Tips Precision Cloud, II-2370
Quaker, I-560, 562, 879
Quaker Chewy, I-699
Quaker Chewy Dipps, I-699
Quaker Dinosaur Eggs, I-562
Quaker Mini Delights, I-879
Quaker Quakes, I-879
Quaker Simple Harvest, I-562
Quaker Tortillaz, I-868
Quaker True Delights, I-879
Quaker Wheat Control, I-562
Quality Street, I-653
Quantum OraMoist, I-1473
Queen Ann, I-719
Queen Helene, I-1494
Quilted Northern Soft & Strong, I-1194
Quilted Northern Ultra Plush, I-1194
Quit Nits, I-1324
Rachel Ray, II-3439
Ragu, I-519
Ragu Old World Style, I-519
Raid, I-1541
Raid Outdoor, I-1566
Raid Yard Guard, I-1566
Rain X, I-1390
Raleigh, II-2297
Ram, II-2196
Rampage, I-1641
Ranch Style, I-471
Range Rover, II-2182

Range Rover Sport, II-2182
Rapela, II-2451
Rayli Fashion, I-1212
Rayli Her Style, I-1212
Rayovac, II-2166, 2174
Ray's New York Bagels, I-599
Razz, II-2487
RCA, II-2064, 2069, 2079, 2101-2103, 2105, 2107, 2109
Reader's Digest, I-1210
Ready Pac, I-912-913
Reames, I-464
Red Baron, I-552
Red Bird, I-701
Red Bull, I-810, 812
Red Door, I-1441
Red Seal, I-972
Red Square, I-785
Red Vines, I-682, 686, 696
Redhook, I-768
Reebok, I-1608, 1615
Reed's, II-2488
Reese's, I-708-709, 712, 714
Reese's Pieces, I-687
Rejoice, I-1454
Rembrandt, I-1474
Remicade, I-1335
Remington, I-1753
Remos, II-2268
Rémy Martin, I-781
Renault, II-2192, 2195, 2206
Renault Clio, II-2190
Renault Kangoo, II-2194
Renault Mégane, II-2190
Renault Scénic, II-2190
Renault Twingo, II-2190
Reno's, I-920
Rephresh, I-1329
Rephresh Brilliant, I-1180
Replens, I-1329
Report, I-1641
Request, I-485
Reser's Stonemill Kitchens, I-426
Resolve, I-1407
Revlon, II-2489
Revlon Age Defying, I-1425
Revlon ColorSilk, I-1446
Revlon Colorstay, I-1422, 1425, 1428
Revlon Colorstay OT, I-1429
Revlon Colorstay S&S, I-1429
Revlon Colorstay Ultra, I-1429
Revlon Moon Drops, I-1459
Revlon Super Lustrous, I-1429

Rhodes, I-624
Rice-A-Roni, I-565, 567
Rice Dream, I-425, 438
Rice Krispies, I-558-559
Richard's, I-551
Richard's Krazy Cajun, I-551
Rid, I-1324
Rid X, I-1399
Rimmel Exaggerate, I-1428
Rimowa, I-1647
RIM's QNX, II-3354
Ring Relief, I-1433
Rips, I-682, 686
Rise of the Planet of the Apes,
   II-3437
RJ Technology, II-2080
Robert's American Gourmet Smart
   Puffs, I-864
Robinsons Fruit Shoot, I-800
Robitussin, I-1314
Robitussin CF, I-1314
Rockstar, I-810
Rockstar Recovery, I-810
Rodrick Rules, Jeff Kinney, I-1220
Rold Gold, I-866, 877
Rold Gold Natural, I-877
Rolls-Royce, II-2196
Ronzoni, I-895
Ronzoni Healthy Harvest, I-895
Rosarita, I-478
Rose Acre, I-126
Rose Art, I-1511, 1548, II-2460-
   2461, 2463
Rosen, II-2328
Rosina, I-542
Rotella T, I-1592
Royal Oak, I-1565
Royal Stag, I-794
Rubykist, I-493
RueLALA.com, II-2661
Ruffles, I-875, 883
Rugby, I-1311
Russell Stover, I-712, 719
Russian Standard, I-785
R.W. Knudsen Family, I-493
Sabila, I-485
Sabra, I-393
Sabrett, I-363
Saco Dolci Frutta, I-901
Safety 1st, II-2039, 2483
Safety 1st Hospital's Choice, II-2372
St. Ives Fresh Skin, I-1496
St. Ives Natural Clear, I-1491
Sal de Uvas Picot, I-1306

Sally Hansen, I-1445
Sally Hansen Demand 12 Hour,
   I-1459
Sally Hansen Depilatories, I-1502
Sally Hansen Lip Inflation, I-1459
Sally Hansen Lip Inflation Exterior,
   I-1459
Salon Grafix, I-1451
Samsonite, I-1647-1649
Samsung, I-1957, II-2015, 2021,
   2062-2063, 2070, 2078-2079,
   2081-2083, 2095-2096, 2415
Samuel Adams, I-768
San Giorgio, I-895
San J, I-523
San Jose Mercury News, I-1204
San Marco, I-553
San Pellegrino, I-800, 808-809
S&D, II-2373
SanDisk, II-2068, 2123
S&W, I-471
Sanford Expo, II-2466
Sanford Expo 2, II-2466
Sanford Sharpie, II-2455, 2466
Sanford Sharpie Accent, II-2466
Sanford Sharpie Rt, II-2466
Sani Hands for Kids, I-1381
Sansui, II-2079
Santitas, I-886
Sanyo, II-2063
Sara Lee, I-596, 620, 628, 640
Sara Lee Fresh Ideas, I-367
Sara Lee Soft & Smooth, I-596
Sargento, I-398-399, 406
Sargento Artisan Blends, I-406
Sargento Chefstyle, I-406
Sargento Deli Style, I-398
Sarris, I-866
Sathers, I-701
Sauza, I-791
Savoie's, I-551
Sazon Goya, I-836
Scania, II-2222, 2226
Schick, I-1749
Schick Quattro for Women, I-1750
Schick Slim Twin, I-1750
Schick Xtreme3 Comfort Plus,
   I-1750
Schiff, I-1302
Schreiber Weight Watchers, I-399
Scientific Angler, II-2451
Scope, I-1464
Scotch, I-1160, 1548, 1754
Scotch Blue, I-1160

Scotch Long Mask, I-1160
Scotch Magic, I-1160
Scott, I-1183, 1194
Scott Naturals, I-1181, 1183
Scripto Aim N Flame II, II-2490
Scripto Wind Resistant, II-2490
Scrubbing Bubbles, I-1395, 1399
Scrubbing Bubbles Fresh Blush,
   I-1399
Scunci, II-2489
Scunci Effortless Beauty, II-2489
Scunci No Damage, II-2489
Scunci No Slip Grip, II-2489
Sea Best, I-840, 844
Sea Bond, I-1467
SeaMazz, I-844
SeaPak, I-844
Seattle's Best, I-851, 853, 860
Secret, I-1431
Secret Clinical Strength, I-1431
Secret Scent Expressions, I-1431
Seidio, I-4
Self, I-1212
Selsun Blue, I-1444
Seneca, I-486
Senokot S, I-1323
Senseo, I-856
Serenity, I-1166
Serenity Dri Active Plus, I-1166
Serenity Tena, I-1166
Serenity Tena Odorsorb, I-1166
Seroquel, I-1335
Sesame Street, I-1380
Setton Farms, I-508
Seventh Generation, I-1391
Shady Brook Farms, I-370, 382
Shakespeare, II-2451
Sharp, II-2021, 2062, 2069, 2078,
   2081
Sharper Image, II-2080
Sheba, I-576
Shedds Country Crock, I-394
Shedds Country Crock Plus, I-394
Shell Zone, I-1563
Shimano, II-2451
Shiner, I-768
Shout, I-1407
Shout Color Catcher, I-1407
Shreddies, I-559
Shunfeng Cuo Chuang Wang, I-1492
Shutterfly, II-2667
Si Bi Shen, I-1319
Siemens, II-2102
Sierra Nevada, I-768

Brands Index

Sigh No More, Mumford & Sons, II-2087

Silk, I-409, 434

Silk Light, I-434

Silk Lite Soymilk, I-425

Silk Plus, I-434

Silk Plus Soymilk, I-425

Silk Pure Almond, I-425, 434

Silk Pure Coconut, I-425

Silk Soymilk, I-425

Silver Swan, I-523

Similac Advance, I-459

Similac Advance Early Shield, I-459

Similac Sensitive, I-459

Similasan, I-1433

Simple, I-1495

Simply Asian, I-897

Simply Lemonade, I-498

Simply Limeade Refrigerated Lemonade, I-498

Simply Orange, I-499

Simply Organic, I-923

Simvastatin, I-1331

Sina, II-2631

Singer, I-1754, II-2046

Singulair, I-1335

Sinoway, I-1497

Sister Schubert's, I-621, 624

Skechers, I-1641

Sketchers, I-1614

The Skinny Cow, I-415

Skintastic, I-1566

Skintimate Signature Scents, I-1490

Skintimate Skintherapy, I-1490

Skippy, I-918

Skittles, I-687

Skoal, I-972

Skoda, II-2206

Skullcandy, II-2068

Skyline Chili, I-532

Skyy, I-792

Slek, I-1454

Slim-Fast, I-900

Slim-Fast Optima On-the-Go, I-1350

Slim Jim, I-369

Slimquick, I-1349

Slimquick Ultra, I-1349

Small Planet Foods, I-560

Smart Balance, I-394

Smart Balance Omega, I-740

Smart ED, II-2217

Smart Food, I-880

Smartfood, I-873

Smirnoff, I-784, 792-793

Smirnoff Ice, I-774, 785

Smirnoff Premium Mixed Drinks, I-774

Smirnoff Red Label, I-785

Smithfield, I-361

Smuckers, I-480-481, 918

Smuckers Uncrustables, I-539

Snak Club, I-862, 871

Snapfish, II-2667

Snapple, I-492, 796

Snickers, I-708, 714

Snuggle, I-1402-1403

Snuggle Exhilarations, I-1403

Snuggle With Febreze, I-1402

Snyder's of Hanover, I-866, 877

Snyder's of Hanover 100-Calorie Pack, I-877

SoBe Lifewater, I-805

Socket Communications, I-1947

Soft & Beautiful, I-1450

Soft Scrub, I-1387

Soft Scrub Total, I-1395

SoftSheen-Carson, I-1450

Softsoap, I-1382

Softsoap Aquarium Series, I-1382

Softsoap Kitchen Fresh Hands, I-1382

Sohu, II-2631

Solo, I-1173

Solo Italia, I-616

Solo Sologrips, I-1173

SomeEcards.com, II-2660

Sonance, II-2066

Sonicare, II-2030, 2032

Sonicare Essence, II-2032

Sonicare Flexcare, II-2032

Sonicare Proresults, II-2030

Sony, II-2062-2069, 2071, 2078-2079, 2081-2082, 2105, 2109, 2123, 2177, 2328, 2415

Sorrento Stringsters, I-399

Soup Supreme, I-464

The Soup, II-2664

Sour Patch Kids, I-687

Southern Tsunami, I-523

Spangler Dum Dum Pops, I-680

Sparkle, I-1183, 1390

Sparkling Ice, I-809

Sparks, I-774

Special K Original, I-559

Special K Red Berries, I-559

Specialized, II-2297

Speck Products, I-4

Spectrum Naturals, I-740

Speedo, I-1047

Spenda, I-647

Spice Islands, I-833, 836

Spice World, I-836

Spider-Man: Turn off the Dark, II-3458

Spike TV, II-2695

Sport Aid, II-2375

Sprayway, I-1390

Sprite, I-752, 816

Spyder, II-2450

Staccato, I-1642

Stacker2, I-812

Stacker2 6 Hour Power, I-812

Stacy's Pita Chips, I-638

ST&SAT, I-1642

Staples, II-2177, 2463

Star, I-743

Starbucks, I-616, 851, 853, 856

Starbucks Via, I-855

Starburst, I-687

StarKist, I-842

Stash, I-932

State Fair, I-539

Stayfree, I-1177

Steak Umm, I-542

Stefano's, I-571, 920

Stella, I-406

Stella Artois, I-772

Stella McCartney, I-1651

Stetson, I-1440

Steve Jobs, Walter Isaacson, I-1214

Steve Madden, I-1641, 1643

Stiefel Panoxyl, I-1491

Stingese Max2, I-1321

Stolichnaya, I-792

Stone Peak, I-1679

Stonyfield Farm, I-436, 440

Stouffer's, I-533-534, 550, 552

Stouffer's Corner Bistro, I-464, 539

Stouffer's Easy Express Skillets, I-533

Stouffer's Lean Cuisine Cafe Cuisine, I-534

Stouffer's Lean Cuisine One Dish Favorite, I-534

Stouffer's Lean Cuisine Simple Favorites, I-534

Stowells, I-776

STP, I-1564

Stride, I-726

Strike King, II-2451

Strongbow, I-783

Stubbs, I-469, 503

StubHub, II-2674
Suave, I-1451
Suave Naturals, I-1453
Suavitel, I-1403
Subaru, II-2189, 2204
Sugardale, I-361
Sun Luck, I-458, 739
Sun Maid, I-508-509, 862
Sun Maid Baking Raisins, I-509
Sun Maid Mini Snacks, I-509
Sun of Italy, I-572
Sun Soft, I-1543
Sun Vista, I-471
Sunbeam, I-620
Sunbelt, I-699
SunChips, I-881
Sundown Naturals, I-1302
Sunmark, I-1355
Sunrana, I-1492
Sunshine, I-638
Sunshine Cheez-It, I-881
Sunstar G-U-M Go Betweens,
  II-2030
Sunyoga, I-1033
Super Mario 3D Land, II-3364
Super Poligrip, I-1467
Super Poligrip Extra Care, I-1467
Super Poligrip Free, I-1467
Super Pretzel, I-545
Super Pretzel Pretzelfils, I-545
Super Pretzel Softstix, I-545
Sure Soft, I-1543
Surehold, I-1548
Surya Foods & Agro Pvt. Ltd., I-633
Sushi Chef, I-739
Sutter Home, I-775
Suzuki, II-2191, 2204, 2302
Svenhards, I-614
Swanson, I-550
Swanson Flavor Boost, I-463
Sweet Baby Ray's, I-469
Sweet Breath, I-1464
Sweet Martha's, I-570
Sweet 'N Low, I-647
Sweetarts, I-689
Swim Ear, I-1433
Swiss Beauty, II-2370
Swisspers, II-2370
Swisspers Supreme, II-2370
Sylvania, II-2056, 2079
Sylvania Double Life, II-2056
Sylvania Super Saver, II-2056
T. Marzetti, I-426
Taaka, I-792

Tabatchnick, I-464
Taco Bell Home Originals, I-478
Take Care, Drake, II-2087
The Talk, II-3439
Tampax, I-1180
Tampax Compak Pearl, I-1180
Tampax Pearl, I-1180
Tampico, I-492
Tamxicos, I-935
Tanduay, I-790
Tang, I-915
Tarn X, I-1397
A Taste of Thai, I-897
Tastee Choice, I-844
Taster's Choice, I-855
Tastykake, I-605
Tata, I-1642
Taylor, I-373
Tayoi, I-1497
Tazo, I-932
TBS, II-2695
TDK, II-2177
Tecate, I-772
Tecnam, II-2268
Teenmix, I-1642
Temptations, I-577
Tena, I-1166
Tencent, II-2631
Tenfu, I-933, 1667
Tennessee Pride, I-540
Terra, I-881
Tetley, I-932
Texas Toast, I-627
T.G.I. Friday's, I-375, 533, 546
Tha Carter IV, Lil Wayne, II-2087
Thai Kitchen, I-897
The Help, Kathryn Stockett, I-1214,
  II-3437
The Hunger Games, Suzanne Col-
  lins, I-1214, 1220
The Son of Neptune, Rick Riordan,
  I-1220
The Throne of Fire, Rick Riordan,
  I-1220
The Ugly Truth, Jeff Kinney,
  I-1220
Therabreath Plus, I-1464
Theraflu, I-1314-1315
Therma Med, II-2374
Thermacare, II-2374
Thermalon, II-2374
Thermipaq, II-2374
Thomas, I-596, 628
Thomas Bagel Thins, I-596

Thomas Better Start, I-628
Thomas Hearty Grains, I-596, 628
Thomas Toaster Cakes, I-628
Thor, II-3437
Three Musketeers, I-708, 714
Tiantan, I-1114
Tic Tac, I-651
Ticketmaster, II-2674
Tickets, II-2674
TicketsNow, II-2674
Ticonderoga, II-2464
Tide, I-1375, 1396, 1407
Tide To Go, I-1407
Tide with Febreze, I-1375
Tiki Outdoor, I-1566
Tilda, I-568
Tilex, I-1395
Tilex Fresh Shower, I-1395
Tillamook, I-386, 397-398, 406
Tilt, I-774
Timber Wolf, I-972
Timberland, I-1080
Time, I-1210
The Times, I-1205
Tiseo, I-571
Titan, I-1598
Titanium, I-1754
TIVO, II-2105
TLC, II-2695
TNT, II-2695
Today: Kathie Lee & Hoda, II-3439
Tofurky, I-543
Tombstone, I-552
TomTom, II-2328
The Tonight Show with Jay Leno,
  II-2664, 3438
Tony's, I-552
Tootsie Roll Child's Play, I-689
Tootsie Roll Pops, I-680
Top Flo, I-1543
Topo Chico, I-808-809
Topps Baby Bottle Pop, I-689
Topps Juicy Drop Pop, I-689
Topps Push Pop, I-689
Topps Ring Pop, I-689
Toshiba, II-2062, 2078-2079, 2082
Tostitos, I-504, 512, 883, 886, 901
Tostitos Scoops, I-886
Totino's Party Pizza, I-552
Totino's Pizza Rolls, I-546
Toyota, II-2189, 2191-2192, 2195,
  2204
Toyota Camry, II-2180, 2184
Toyota Corolla/Matrix, II-2180, 2183

Toyota Exora, II-2193
Toyota Hilux, II-2193
Toyota Prius, II-2183, 2218
Toyota Sienna, II-2186
Toyota Vios, II-2193
Trans-Ocean, I-839
Transcend, II-2123
Transformers: Dark of the Moon, II-3437
Tree Ripe, I-499
Tree Top, I-486
Trek, II-2297
TRENDnet, I-1967
Tresemme Tres Two, I-1451
Triaminic, I-1313-1314
Tride Mediterrenean, I-393
Trident, I-726
Trident Layers, I-726
Trident White, I-726
TripAdvisor, II-2675
Tropicana, I-752
Tropicana Pure Premium, I-483, 499
Truform, II-2375
Trulia, II-2668
Tucks, I-1320
Tucks Take Alongs, I-1320
Tully's Coffee, I-856
Tum-E Yummies, I-492
Tums, I-1308
Tums Ultra, I-1308
Turbo Snake, I-1388
Turkey Creek Snacks, I-874
Turkey Hill, I-416, 421
Tuscan Dairy Farms, I-437
Tweezerman, I-1753
The Twilight Saga: Breaking Dawn Part I, II-3437
Twinings, I-932
Twinlab, I-1302
Twisted Tea Hard Iced Tea, I-774
TwitPic, II-2667
Twix, I-708, 714
Twizzlers, I-682
Twizzlers Nibs, I-682
Twizzlers Pull N Peel, I-682, 686
Ty Ling, I-739
Tylenol, I-1313
Tylenol Cold, I-1314
Tyson, I-361, 375
U by Kotex Click, I-1180
U+, I-1212
Udi's, I-571
UGG, I-1643
Ultra Glow, I-1494

Unbroken, Laura Hillenbrand, I-1214
Uncle Ben's, I-567-568
Uncle Dan's, I-923
Under Armour, I-1028, 1608
Under the Mistletoe, Justin Bieber, II-2087
Uni Ball Signo 207, II-2455
Uniden, II-2101-2102
Universal Remote Controller, II-2105
University Medical Acne Free, I-1491
Uno, I-920
US Weekly, I-1211
USA Network, II-2695
USA (tobacco), I-955
USA TODAY, I-1204, II-2665
Utz, I-866, 874-875, 877, 901
V-8, I-501
V-8 Splash, I-492
V-8 V-Fusion, I-490
Vagistat 1, I-1329
Valued Naturals, I-508, 862
Valvoline, I-1588
Van de Kamp's, I-840
Vanity Fair, I-1173
Van's, I-547, 1607
Veet, I-1445
Veet Supreme Essence, I-1445
Veetee, I-568
Veg All, I-474
Vevo, II-2676
VH Essentials, I-1329
Viacom Digital, II-2676
Vicks, II-2039, 2367
Vicks Comfort Flex, II-2367
Vicks Dayquil, I-1314
Vicks Nyquil, I-1314
Vicks Sinex Vapospray, I-1462
Vicks Speed Read, II-2367
The View, II-3439
Viewsonic, II-2083
Village Candle, II-2488
Village Naturals Bath Shoppe, I-1380
Vinda, I-1175, 1184, 1193
Viore, II-2080
Visa, II-3090
Visine Original, I-1434
Vita, I-839
Vital 4U Scream Energy, I-812
Viva La Juicy, I-1441
Vivitar, II-2063, 2415, 2418
Vizio, II-2062, 2082-2083
vKontakte, II-2672

Vogue, I-1212
Vohringer, II-2481
Volkswagen, II-2189, 2191, 2195, 2206
Volkswagen Golf, II-2214
Volkswagen Jetta, II-2183, 2214
Volkswagen Passat, II-2214
Volkswagen Polo, II-2190
Volkswagen Touareg, II-2214
Volvic, I-800
Volvo Bus, II-2222
Volvo Trucks, II-2226
VPX Redline Power Rush, I-812
Vtech, II-2102
Waggin' Train, I-580
Waggin' Train Meat Blast, II-2494
Wahaha, I-497, 797
Wahl, I-1753
Walkers, I-883
The Wall Street Journal, I-1204
Wanchai Ferry, I-533
Wang Guan, I-970
Warren, I-1592
The Washington Post, I-1204
Watch the Throne, Jay-Z and Kanye West, II-2087
Waterpik, II-2030
Wavy Lay's, I-875
The Weather Channel, II-2695
Weber grill, I-28
Weetabix, I-559
Wei-Pac, I-458
Weight Watchers, I-415, 613
Weight Watchers Smart Ones, I-417, 534
Weight Watchers Smart Ones Morning Express, I-540
Weightwatchers.com, II-2659
Weiman Cook Top, I-1396
Weiman's, I-1397
Welch's, I-481, 490, 678
Welch's Fruit 'N Yogurt, I-862
Wells' Blue Bunny, I-416, 421
Wenner, I-572
Werther's Original, I-680, 696
Wesson, I-740
Westcott, I-1754
Westcott Microban, I-1754
Westcott Value, I-1754
Western, I-1565
Wet 'n Wild, I-1428
Wet Ones, I-1181
Whink, I-1393
Whink Lime Buster, I-1393

Whirlpool, I-19, II-2014-2015, 2019-2020, 2024, 2027, 2042
Whiskas, I-576, 585
Whisker Lickins, I-577
White Castle, I-539
White Rain Classic Care, I-1451
Whitman's Sampler, I-712, 719
Wholly Guacamole, I-426
Wicked, II-3458
Widmer, I-768
Wii Sports, II-3364
Wii Sports Resort, II-3364
Wikimedia Foundation sites, II-2663
Wiley Wallaby, I-686
Wilkin & Sons, I-482
Willow Tree, I-550
Winalot, I-579
Windex, I-1390
Windex Cloth, I-1196
Windows Live One Care Security Suite, II-3358
Winston, I-966
Winx Club, I-23
Wise, I-873, 880
Wise Cheese Doodles, I-864
Wise Dipsy Doodles, I-868
Wishbone, I-517
Wisk, I-1375
Witch & Wizard, James Patterson, Garbielle Charbonnet, I-1220
WKD, I-785
Wolf Blass, I-776
Woman's Day, I-1210
Woman's World, I-1211
Wonder, I-620
Wonderful, I-729
Wonderful Pistachios, I-729
Wong Lo Kat, I-797
Wonka Kazoozles, I-682
Wonka Laffy Taffy, I-687
Wonka Mix Ups, I-689
Wonka Nerds, I-689
Wonka Sweetarts, I-689
Woodbridge by R. Mondavi, I-775
Woodchuck, I-783
Woolite, I-1404
Woolite Complete, I-1404
Woot.com, II-2661
The Works, I-1393, 1399
World Harbors, I-503
Worlds Best, I-606
Worth, I-967
Wright, I-361
Wrights, I-1397

Wrigley's, I-653
Wrigley's 5, I-726
Wrigley's Eclipse, I-651, 726
Wrigley's Extra, I-726
Wu Yutai, I-933
Wyder's, I-783
Wyler's Mrs. Grass, I-510
Wyman's, I-524
X-Men: First Class, II-3437
Xbox 360, II-2444
Xenadrine Ultra, I-1349
Xentris, I-4
Xerox, I-1957
Xiangyi, I-933
Xiaoxiang, I-933
Xin Fu Man Ling, I-1492
Xtra, I-1375, 1388
Yahoo!, II-2643, 2646, 2655, 2663, 2665, 2668, 2675-2676
Yamaha, II-2065-2066, 2069, 2302
Yamasa, I-523
Yandex, II-2672
YangZi Flooring, II-2481
Yaoli, I-1639
Yellow Box, I-1641
Yellow Tail, I-775
Yokohama, I-1600, 1602-1603
Yoo Hoo, I-438
Yoplait, I-442-444
Yoplait Go-Gurt, I-440
Yoplait Light, I-440
Yoplait Original, I-440
York Peppermint Patty, I-712
Yuan Bao, I-731
Yuban, I-851
Yucatan, I-426
Yumejing, I-1493
Yves Saint Lauren, I-1651
Zacky Farms, I-382
Zagg, I-4
Zantac 150, I-1308
Zegerid OTC, I-1308
Zelenaya Marka, I-793
Zephyrhills, I-806
Zerex, I-1563
Zest, I-1383
Zhuyeqing, I-933
Zicam, I-1462
Zico, I-490
Zoke, I-1033, 1047
Zone Perfect, I-703
Zoom, II-2451
Zote, I-1405-1406
ZTE, II-2095

Zud, I-1393
Zulily.com, II-2661
Zvents, II-2674
Zyrtec, I-1315

APPENDIX I - INDUSTRIAL CLASSIFICATIONS

SIC COVERAGE

This appendix lists the Standard Industrial Classification Codes (SICs) included in *Market Share Reporter*. A volume and page number are shown following each SIC category; the page shown indicates the first occurrence of an SIC. NEC stands for not elsewhere classified.

Agricultural Production - Crops

0110 Cash grains, p. I-14
0111 Wheat, p. I-15
0112 Rice, p. I-15
0115 Corn, p. I-16
0116 Soybeans, p. I-17
0131 Cotton, p. I-18
0132 Tobacco, p. I-19
0133 Sugarcane and sugar beets, p. I-19
0134 Irish potatoes, p. I-20
0161 Vegetables and melons, p. I-20
0171 Berry crops, p. I-22
0172 Grapes, p. I-23
0173 Tree nuts, p. I-24
0174 Citrus fruits, p. I-24
0175 Deciduous tree fruits, p. I-25
0179 Fruits and tree nuts, nec, p. I-26
0181 Ornamental nursery products, p. I-27
0182 Food crops grown under cover, p. I-28

Agricultural Production - Livestock

0211 Beef cattle feedlots, p. I-29
0212 Beef cattle, except feedlots, p. I-29
0213 Hogs, p. I-30
0214 Sheep and goats, p. I-31
0251 Broiler, fryer, and roaster chickens, p. I-31
0252 Chicken eggs, p. I-32
0253 Turkeys and turkey eggs, p. I-32
0271 Fur-bearing animals and rabbits, p. I-33
0272 Horses and other equines, p. I-33
0273 Animal aquaculture, p. I-34
0279 Animal specialties, nec, p. I-34
0291 General farms, primarily animal, p. I-34

Agricultural Services

0722 Crop harvesting, p. I-35
0742 Veterinary services, specialties, p. I-35
0752 Animal specialty services, p. I-35
0782 Lawn and garden services, p. I-35

Forestry

0811 Timber tracts, p. I-36

Fishing, Hunting, & Trapping

0912 Finfish, p. I-37
0971 Hunting, trapping, game propagation, p. I-38

Metal Mining

1011 Iron ores, p. I-39
1021 Copper ores, p. I-39
1031 Lead and zinc ores, p. I-40
1041 Gold ores, p. I-41
1044 Silver ores, p. I-42
1061 Ferroalloy ores, except vanadium, p. I-43
1094 Uranium-radium-vanadium ores, p. I-44
1099 Metal ores, nec, p. I-45

Coal Mining

1220 Bituminous coal and lignite mining, p. I-48

Oil & Gas Extraction

1311 Crude petroleum and natural gas, p. I-50
1321 Natural gas liquids, p. I-53
1381 Drilling oil and gas wells, p. I-53
1389 Oil and gas field services, nec, p. I-55

Nonmetallic Minerals, Except Fuels

1411 Dimension stone, p. I-57
1420 Crushed and broken stone, p. I-57
1442 Construction sand and gravel, p. I-58
1446 Industrial sand, p. I-58
1455 Kaolin and ball clay, p. I-59
1459 Clay and related minerals, nec, p. I-59
1474 Potash, soda, and borate minerals, p. I-60
1475 Phosphate rock, p. I-60
1479 Chemical and fertilizer mining, nec, p. I-61
1499 Miscellaneous nonmetallic minerals, p. I-61

General Building Contractors

1500   General building contractors, p. I-64
1521   Single-family housing construction, p. I-64
1522   Residential construction, nec, p. I-69
1542   Nonresidential construction, nec, p. I-69

Heavy Construction, Ex. Building

1600   Heavy construction, ex. building, p. I-71
1611   Highway and street construction, p. I-71
1622   Bridge, tunnel, & elevated highway, p. I-71
1623   Water, sewer, and utility lines, p. I-72
1629   Heavy construction, nec, p. I-72

Special Trade Contractors

1721   Painting and paper hanging, p. I-73
1731   Electrical work, p. I-73
1741   Masonry and other stonework, p. I-73
1742   Plastering, drywall, and insulation, p. I-74
1761   Roofing, siding, and sheet metal work, p. I-74
1771   Concrete work, p. I-75
1781   Water well drilling, p. I-75
1791   Structural steel erection, p. I-75
1793   Glass and glazing work, p. I-75
1794   Excavation work, p. I-76
1795   Wrecking and demolition work, p. I-76
1799   Special trade contractors, nec, p. I-76

Food & Kindred Products

2000   Food and kindred products, p. I-77
2011   Meat packing plants, p. I-88
2013   Sausages and other prepared meats, p. I-91
2015   Poultry slaughtering and processing, p. I-95
2020   Dairy products, p. I-97
2021   Creamery butter, p. I-97
2022   Cheese, natural and processed, p. I-99
2023   Dry, condensed, evaporated products, p. I-102
2024   Ice cream and frozen desserts, p. I-103
2026   Fluid milk, p. I-105
2032   Canned specialties, p. I-111
2033   Canned fruits and vegetables, p. I-116
2034   Dehydrated fruits, vegetables, soups, p. I-125
2035   Pickles, sauces, and salad dressings, p. I-126
2037   Frozen fruits and vegetables, p. I-129
2038   Frozen specialties, nec, p. I-130
2041   Flour and other grain mill products, p. I-136
2043   Cereal breakfast foods, p. I-136
2044   Rice milling, p. I-137
2045   Prepared flour mixes and doughs, p. I-139
2046   Wet corn milling, p. I-140
2047   Dog and cat food, p. I-140
2048   Prepared feeds, nec, p. I-144

2051   Bread, cake, and related products, p. I-144
2052   Cookies and crackers, p. I-152
2053   Frozen bakery products, except bread, p. I-155
2061   Raw cane sugar, p. I-155
2062   Cane sugar refining, p. I-156
2064   Candy & other confectionery products, p. I-156
2066   Chocolate and cocoa products, p. I-170
2067   Chewing gum, p. I-174
2068   Salted and roasted nuts and seeds, p. I-175
2070   Fats and oils, p. I-176
2074   Cottonseed oil mills, p. I-177
2076   Vegetable oil mills, nec, p. I-177
2079   Edible fats and oils, nec, p. I-178
2080   Beverages, p. I-180
2082   Malt beverages, p. I-181
2083   Malt, p. I-185
2084   Wines, brandy, and brandy spirits, p. I-185
2085   Distilled and blended liquors, p. I-187
2086   Bottled and canned soft drinks, p. I-190
2087   Flavoring extracts and syrups, nec, p. I-198
2091   Canned and cured fish and seafoods, p. I-199
2092   Fresh or frozen prepared fish, p. I-200
2095   Roasted coffee, p. I-201
2096   Potato chips and similar snacks, p. I-205
2097   Manufactured ice, p. I-211
2098   Macaroni and spaghetti, p. I-211
2099   Food preparations, nec, p. I-213

Tobacco Products

2100   Tobacco products, p. I-224
2111   Cigarettes, p. I-227
2121   Cigars, p. I-230
2131   Chewing and smoking tobacco, p. I-231

Textile Mill Products

2200   Textile mill products, p. I-232
2211   Broadwoven fabric mills, cotton, p. I-232
2241   Narrow fabric mills, p. I-233
2251   Women's hosiery, except socks, p. I-234
2252   Hosiery, nec, p. I-234
2253   Knit outerwear mills, p. I-235
2254   Knit underwear mills, p. I-236
2257   Weft knit fabric mills, p. I-236
2258   Lace & warp knit fabric mills, p. I-236
2261   Finishing plants, cotton, p. I-237
2273   Carpets and rugs, p. I-237
2281   Yarn spinning mills, p. I-238
2282   Throwing and winding mills, p. I-239
2295   Coated fabrics, not rubberized, p. I-239
2297   Nonwoven fabrics, p. I-239
2298   Cordage and twine, p. I-240

Apparel & Other Textile Products

2300 Apparel and other textile products, p. I-241
2311 Men's and boys' suits and coats, p. I-245
2320 Men's and boys' furnishings, p. I-245
2321 Men's and boys' shirts, p. I-246
2323 Men's and boys' neckwear, p. I-246
2325 Men's and boys' trousers and slacks, p. I-246
2330 Women's and misses' outerwear, p. I-247
2331 Women's & misses' blouses & shirts, p. I-247
2335 Women's, juniors', & misses' dresses, p. I-247
2339 Women's and misses' outerwear, nec, p. I-247
2341 Women's and children's underwear, p. I-248
2342 Bras, girdles, and allied garments, p. I-248
2353 Hats, caps, and millinery, p. I-249
2371 Fur goods, p. I-249
2381 Fabric dress and work gloves, p. I-249
2385 Waterproof outerwear, p. I-250
2387 Apparel belts, p. I-250
2389 Apparel and accessories, nec, p. I-250
2391 Curtains and draperies, p. I-250
2392 Housefurnishings, nec, p. I-251
2393 Textile bags, p. I-254
2395 Pleating and stitching, p. I-254
2397 Schiffli machine embroideries, p. I-254

Lumber & Wood Products

2411 Logging, p. I-255
2426 Hardwood dimension & flooring mills, p. I-255
2431 Millwork, p. I-255
2434 Wood kitchen cabinets, p. I-256
2435 Hardwood veneer and plywood, p. I-257
2436 Softwood veneer and plywood, p. I-257
2448 Wood pallets and skids, p. I-258
2451 Mobile homes, p. I-258
2493 Reconstituted wood products, p. I-259
2499 Wood products, nec, p. I-260

Furniture & Fixtures

2511 Wood household furniture, p. I-261
2512 Upholstered household furniture, p. I-262
2514 Metal household furniture, p. I-262
2515 Mattresses and bedsprings, p. I-263
2520 Office furniture, p. I-264
2531 Public building & related furniture, p. I-265
2541 Wood partitions and fixtures, p. I-265
2599 Furniture and fixtures, nec, p. I-265

Paper & Allied Products

2611 Pulp mills, p. I-267
2621 Paper mills, p. I-267
2631 Paperboard mills, p. I-269

2652 Setup paperboard boxes, p. I-270
2653 Corrugated and solid fiber boxes, p. I-270
2656 Sanitary food containers, p. I-270
2657 Folding paperboard boxes, p. I-271
2671 Paper coated & laminated, packaging, p. I-271
2672 Paper coated and laminated, nec, p. I-271
2673 Bags: plastics, laminated, & coated, p. I-273
2674 Bags: uncoated paper & multiwall, p. I-273
2675 Die-cut paper and board, p. I-274
2676 Sanitary paper products, p. I-274
2678 Stationery products, p. I-281

Printing & Publishing

2700 Printing and publishing, p. I-282
2711 Newspapers, p. I-282
2721 Periodicals, p. I-283
2731 Book publishing, p. I-285
2732 Book printing, p. I-289
2741 Miscellaneous publishing, p. I-289
2750 Commercial printing, p. I-290
2752 Commercial printing, lithographic, p. I-290
2754 Commercial printing, gravure, p. I-291
2759 Commercial printing, nec, p. I-291
2771 Greeting cards, p. I-292

Chemicals & Allied Products

2800 Chemicals and allied products, p. I-293
2812 Alkalies and chlorine, p. I-294
2813 Industrial gases, p. I-295
2816 Inorganic pigments, p. I-296
2819 Industrial inorganic chemicals, nec, p. I-297
2821 Plastics materials and resins, p. I-299
2822 Synthetic rubber, p. I-301
2823 Cellulosic manmade fibers, p. I-303
2833 Medicinals and botanicals, p. I-304
2834 Pharmaceutical preparations, p. I-306
2836 Biological products exc. diagnostic, p. I-316
2841 Soap and other detergents, p. I-318
2842 Polishes and sanitation goods, p. I-324
2843 Surface active agents, p. I-330
2844 Toilet preparations, p. I-331
2851 Paints and allied products, p. I-350
2865 Cyclic crudes and intermediates, p. I-352
2869 Industrial organic chemicals, nec, p. I-353
2873 Nitrogenous fertilizers, p. I-355
2874 Phosphatic fertilizers, p. I-357
2875 Fertilizers, mixing only, p. I-357
2879 Agricultural chemicals, nec, p. I-357
2891 Adhesives and sealants, p. I-358
2892 Explosives, p. I-360
2893 Printing ink, p. I-360
2895 Carbon black, p. I-361
2899 Chemical preparations, nec, p. I-361

Appendix I - Industrial Classifications

Petroleum & Coal Products

2911 Petroleum refining, p. I-367
2951 Asphalt paving mixtures and blocks, p. I-367
2952 Asphalt felts and coatings, p. I-368
2992 Lubricating oils and greases, p. I-368

Rubber & Misc. Plastics Products

3011 Tires and inner tubes, p. I-371
3021 Rubber and plastics footwear, p. I-373
3053 Gaskets, packing and sealing devices, p. I-375
3069 Fabricated rubber products, nec, p. I-376
3081 Unsupported plastics film & sheet, p. I-376
3083 Laminated plastics plate & sheet, p. I-377
3084 Plastics pipe, p. I-378
3085 Plastics bottles, p. I-378
3086 Plastics foam products, p. I-378
3089 Plastics products, nec, p. I-379

Leather & Leather Products

3111 Leather tanning and finishing, p. I-381
3131 Footwear cut stock, p. I-381
3142 House slippers, p. I-381
3144 Women's footwear, except athletic, p. I-382
3161 Luggage, p. I-382
3171 Women's handbags and purses, p. I-384

Stone, Clay, & Glass Products

3211 Flat glass, p. I-385
3221 Glass containers, p. I-387
3229 Pressed and blown glass, nec, p. I-387
3241 Cement, hydraulic, p. I-388
3250 Structural clay products, p. I-390
3253 Ceramic wall and floor tile, p. I-390
3255 Clay refractories, p. I-390
3261 Vitreous plumbing fixtures, p. I-391
3262 Vitreous china table & kitchenware, p. I-391
3271 Concrete block and brick, p. I-391
3274 Lime, p. I-391
3275 Gypsum products, p. I-392
3291 Abrasive products, p. I-392
3292 Asbestos products, p. I-393
3297 Nonclay refractories, p. I-393

Primary Metal Industries

3312 Blast furnaces and steel mills, p. I-394
3313 Electrometallurgical products, p. I-396
3315 Steel wire and related products, p. I-396
3316 Cold finishing of steel shapes, p. I-397
3317 Steel pipe and tubes, p. I-397
3321 Gray and ductile iron foundries, p. I-398

3331 Primary copper, p. I-398
3334 Primary aluminum, p. I-399
3339 Primary nonferrous metals, nec, p. I-400
3353 Aluminum sheet, plate, and foil, p. I-402
3354 Aluminum extruded products, p. I-402
3356 Nonferrous rolling and drawing, nec, p. I-403
3357 Nonferrous wiredrawing & insulating, p. I-404
3360 Nonferrous foundries (castings), p. I-404
3363 Aluminum die-castings, p. I-404
3366 Copper foundries, p. I-404

Fabricated Metal Products

3411 Metal cans, p. I-405
3412 Metal barrels, drums, and pails, p. I-405
3421 Cutlery, p. I-406
3423 Hand and edge tools, nec, p. I-407
3425 Saw blades and handsaws, p. I-408
3431 Metal sanitary ware, p. I-408
3432 Plumbing fixture fittings and trim, p. I-409
3433 Heating equipment, except electric, p. I-409
3441 Fabricated structural metal, p. I-411
3442 Metal doors, sash, and trim, p. I-411
3443 Fabricated plate work (boiler shops), p. I-412
3444 Sheet metalwork, p. I-413
3448 Prefabricated metal buildings, p. I-413
3451 Screw machine products, p. I-413
3452 Bolts, nuts, rivets, and washers, p. I-414
3462 Iron and steel forgings, p. I-414
3463 Nonferrous forgings, p. I-414
3466 Crowns and closures, p. I-415
3469 Metal stampings, nec, p. I-415
3471 Plating and polishing, p. I-416
3479 Metal coating and allied services, p. I-416
3482 Small arms ammunition, p. I-416
3489 Ordnance and accessories, nec, p. I-417
3491 Industrial valves, p. I-417
3492 Fluid power valves & hose fittings, p. I-418
3493 Steel springs, except wire, p. I-419
3494 Valves and pipe fittings, nec, p. I-419
3496 Misc. fabricated wire products, p. I-420
3497 Metal foil and leaf, p. I-421
3499 Fabricated metal products, nec, p. I-421

Industrial Machinery & Equipment

3511 Turbines and turbine generator sets, p. I-422
3519 Internal combustion engines, nec, p. I-424
3523 Farm machinery and equipment, p. I-424
3524 Lawn and garden equipment, p. I-425
3531 Construction machinery, p. I-426
3532 Mining machinery, p. I-428
3533 Oil and gas field machinery, p. I-428
3534 Elevators and moving stairways, p. I-431
3535 Conveyors and conveying equipment, p. I-431

3536 Hoists, cranes, and monorails, p. I-431

3537 Industrial trucks and tractors, p. I-433

3541 Machine tools, metal cutting types, p. I-434

3544 Special dies, tools, jigs & fixtures, p. I-436

3546 Power-driven handtools, p. I-436

3548 Welding apparatus, p. I-437

3552 Textile machinery, p. I-437

3553 Woodworking machinery, p. I-437

3554 Paper industries machinery, p. I-438

3556 Food products machinery, p. I-438

3559 Special industry machinery, nec, p. I-438

3561 Pumps and pumping equipment, p. I-440

3562 Ball and roller bearings, p. I-441

3563 Air and gas compressors, p. I-442

3564 Blowers and fans, p. I-442

3565 Packaging machinery, p. I-443

3566 Speed changers, drives, and gears, p. I-444

3569 General industrial machinery, nec, p. I-444

3571 Electronic computers, p. I-447

3572 Computer storage devices, p. I-452

3577 Computer peripheral equipment, nec, p. I-453

3578 Calculating and accounting equipment, p. I-456

3581 Automatic vending machines, p. I-457

3585 Refrigeration and heating equipment, p. I-457

3592 Carburetors, pistons, rings, valves, p. I-460

3594 Fluid power pumps and motors, p. I-460

3599 Industrial machinery, nec, p. I-460

Electronic & Other Electric Equipment

3600 Electronic & other electric equipment, p. II-461

3612 Transformers, except electronic, p. II-461

3613 Switchgear and switchboard apparatus, p. II-463

3621 Motors and generators, p. II-464

3624 Carbon and graphite products, p. II-465

3625 Relays and industrial controls, p. II-465

3630 Household appliances, p. II-465

3631 Household cooking equipment, p. II-466

3632 Household refrigerators and freezers, p. II-468

3633 Household laundry equipment, p. II-468

3634 Electric housewares and fans, p. II-469

3635 Household vacuum cleaners, p. II-471

3639 Household appliances, nec, p. II-471

3641 Electric lamps, p. II-472

3643 Current-carrying wiring devices, p. II-474

3645 Residential lighting fixtures, p. II-475

3651 Household audio and video equipment, p. II-475

3652 Prerecorded records and tapes, p. II-480

3661 Telephone and telegraph apparatus, p. II-481

3663 Radio & TV communications equipment, p. II-483

3669 Communications equipment, nec, p. II-485

3672 Printed circuit boards, p. II-487

3674 Semiconductors and related devices, p. II-488

3675 Electronic capacitors, p. II-493

3679 Electronic components, nec, p. II-494

3691 Storage batteries, p. II-496

3694 Engine electrical equipment, p. II-499

3695 Magnetic and optical recording media, p. II-499

Transportation Equipment

3711 Motor vehicles and car bodies, p. II-500

3713 Truck and bus bodies, p. II-509

3714 Motor vehicle parts and accessories, p. II-511

3716 Motor homes, p. II-517

3721 Aircraft, p. II-518

3724 Aircraft engines and engine parts, p. II-521

3731 Ship building and repairing, p. II-522

3732 Boat building and repairing, p. II-522

3743 Railroad equipment, p. II-524

3751 Motorcycles, bicycles, and parts, p. II-525

3761 Guided missiles and space vehicles, p. II-527

3769 Space vehicle equipment, nec, p. II-529

3792 Travel trailers and campers, p. II-530

3795 Tanks and tank components, p. II-530

3799 Transportation equipment, nec, p. II-531

Instruments & Related Products

3812 Search and navigation equipment, p. II-532

3821 Laboratory apparatus and furniture, p. II-532

3824 Fluid meters and counting devices, p. II-533

3825 Instruments to measure electricity, p. II-534

3826 Analytical instruments, p. II-534

3829 Measuring & controlling devices, nec, p. II-535

3841 Surgical and medical instruments, p. II-536

3842 Surgical appliances and supplies, p. II-541

3843 Dental equipment and supplies, p. II-547

3844 X-ray apparatus and tubes, p. II-548

3851 Ophthalmic goods, p. II-548

3861 Photographic equipment and supplies, p. II-550

3873 Watches, clocks, watchcases & parts, p. II-552

Miscellaneous Manufacturing Industries

3911 Jewelry, precious metal, p. II-554

3914 Silverware and plated ware, p. II-555

3915 Jewelers' materials & lapidary work, p. II-555

3931 Musical instruments, p. II-555

3942 Dolls and stuffed toys, p. II-556

3944 Games, toys, and children's vehicles, p. II-556

3949 Sporting and athletic goods, nec, p. II-558

3951 Pens and mechanical pencils, p. II-560

3952 Lead pencils and art goods, p. II-561

3953 Marking devices, p. II-563

3955 Carbon paper and inked ribbons, p. II-564

3961 Costume jewelry, p. II-564

3965 Fasteners, buttons, needles, & pins, p. II-564

3991 Brooms and brushes, p. II-564

3993 Signs and advertising specialities, p. II-565
3995 Burial caskets, p. II-566
3996 Hard surface floor coverings, nec, p. II-566
3999 Manufacturing industries, nec, p. II-567

Railroad Transportation

4011 Railroads, line-haul operating, p. II-570

Local & Interurban Passenger Transit

4119 Local passenger transportation, nec, p. II-571
4141 Local bus charter service, p. II-571
4151 School buses, p. II-572

Trucking & Warehousing

4210 Trucking & courier services, ex. air, p. II-573
4212 Local trucking, without storage, p. II-573
4214 Local trucking with storage, p. II-574
4215 Courier services, except by air, p. II-575
4221 Farm product warehousing and storage, p. II-576
4222 Refrigerated warehousing and storage, p. II-576
4225 General warehousing and storage, p. II-576
4226 Special warehousing and storage, nec, p. II-576

U.S. Postal Service

4311 U.S. Postal Service, p. II-577

Water Transportation

4412 Deep sea foreign trans. of freight, p. II-578
4424 Deep sea domestic trans. of freight, p. II-578
4432 Freight trans. on the great lakes, p. II-579
4481 Deep sea passenger trans., ex. ferry, p. II-579
4489 Water passenger transportation, nec, p. II-579
4491 Marine cargo handling, p. II-580
4492 Towing and tugboat service, p. II-580
4493 Marinas, p. II-580

Transportation By Air

4512 Air transportation, scheduled, p. II-581
4513 Air courier services, p. II-585
4581 Airports, flying fields, & services, p. II-585

Pipelines, Except Natural Gas

4612 Crude petroleum pipelines, p. II-587

Transportation Services

4720 Passenger transportation arrangement, p. II-588
4724 Travel agencies, p. II-588
4725 Tour operators, p. II-588
4731 Freight transportation arrangement, p. II-589

4783 Packing and crating, p. II-589
4785 Inspection & fixed facilities, p. II-589
4789 Transportation services, nec, p. II-589

Communication

4812 Radiotelephone communications, p. II-590
4813 Telephone communications, exc. radio, p. II-598
4822 Telegraph & other communications, p. II-598
4832 Radio broadcasting stations, p. II-611
4833 Television broadcasting stations, p. II-612
4841 Cable and other pay TV services, p. II-612

Electric, Gas, & Sanitary Services

4900 Electric, gas, and sanitary services, p. II-615
4911 Electric services, p. II-615
4931 Electric and other services combined, p. II-618
4941 Water supply, p. II-618
4953 Refuse systems, p. II-618
4959 Sanitary services, nec, p. II-620
4971 Irrigation systems, p. II-620

Wholesale Trade - Durable Goods

5012 Automobiles and other motor vehicles, p. II-621
5013 Motor vehicle supplies and new parts, p. II-621
5014 Tires and tubes, p. II-621
5021 Furniture, p. II-622
5023 Homefurnishings, p. II-622
5031 Lumber, plywood, and millwork, p. II-622
5044 Office equipment, p. II-623
5045 Computers, peripherals & software, p. II-623
5051 Metals service centers and offices, p. II-623
5052 Coal and other minerals and ores, p. II-624
5063 Electrical apparatus and equipment, p. II-624
5064 Electrical appliances, TV & radios, p. II-624
5078 Refrigeration equipment and supplies, p. II-624
5084 Industrial machinery and equipment, p. II-625
5085 Industrial supplies, p. II-625
5087 Service establishment equipment, p. II-625
5088 Transportation equipment & supplies, p. II-625
5091 Sporting & recreational goods, p. II-626
5092 Toys and hobby goods and supplies, p. II-626
5093 Scrap and waste materials, p. II-626
5094 Jewelry & precious stones, p. II-627
5099 Durable goods, nec, p. II-627

Wholesale Trade - Nondurable Goods

5112 Stationery and office supplies, p. II-628
5122 Drugs, proprietaries, and sundries, p. II-628
5131 Piece goods & notions, p. II-629
5136 Men's and boys' clothing, p. II-629
5141 Groceries, general line, p. II-629

5142 Packaged frozen foods, p. II-629

5143 Dairy products, exc. dried or canned, p. II-629

5148 Fresh fruits and vegetables, p. II-630

5149 Groceries and related products, nec, p. II-630

5153 Grain and field beans, p. II-630

5154 Livestock, p. II-630

5159 Farm-product raw materials, nec, p. II-630

5172 Petroleum products, nec, p. II-631

5181 Beer and ale, p. II-631

5193 Flowers & florists' supplies, p. II-631

5194 Tobacco and tobacco products, p. II-631

5199 Nondurable goods, nec, p. II-631

Building Materials & Garden Supplies

5211 Lumber and other building materials, p. II-632

5231 Paint, glass, and wallpaper stores, p. II-632

5251 Hardware stores, p. II-632

5261 Retail nurseries and garden stores, p. II-633

General Merchandise Stores

5300 General merchandise stores, p. II-634

5311 Department stores, p. II-635

5331 Variety stores, p. II-635

Food Stores

5411 Grocery stores, p. II-639

5421 Meat and fish markets, p. II-649

5431 Fruit and vegetable markets, p. II-649

5441 Candy, nut, and confectionery stores, p. II-649

5461 Retail bakeries, p. II-650

Automotive Dealers & Service Stations

5511 New and used car dealers, p. II-651

5521 Used car dealers, p. II-651

5531 Auto and home supply stores, p. II-651

5541 Gasoline service stations, p. II-652

5551 Boat dealers, p. II-652

5571 Motorcycle dealers, p. II-653

Apparel & Accessory Stores

5611 Men's & boys' clothing stores, p. II-654

5621 Women's clothing stores, p. II-654

5632 Women's accessory & specialty stores, p. II-655

5641 Children's and infants' wear stores, p. II-656

5651 Family clothing stores, p. II-656

5661 Shoe stores, p. II-657

Furniture & Homefurnishings Stores

5712 Furniture stores, p. II-659

5713 Floor covering stores, p. II-659

5719 Misc. homefurnishings stores, p. II-660

5722 Household appliance stores, p. II-662

5731 Radio, TV, & electronic stores, p. II-663

5734 Computer and software stores, p. II-664

5735 Record & prerecorded tape stores, p. II-664

5736 Musical instrument stores, p. II-665

Eating & Drinking Places

5812 Eating places, p. II-666

5813 Drinking places, p. II-671

Miscellaneous Retail

5912 Drug stores and proprietary stores, p. II-672

5921 Liquor stores, p. II-677

5932 Used merchandise stores, p. II-677

5941 Sporting goods and bicycle shops, p. II-678

5942 Book stores, p. II-678

5943 Stationery stores, p. II-680

5944 Jewelry stores, p. II-680

5945 Hobby, toy, and game shops, p. II-681

5946 Camera & photographic supply stores, p. II-681

5947 Gift, novelty, and souvenir shops, p. II-681

5948 Luggage and leather goods stores, p. II-682

5949 Sewing, needlework, and piece goods, p. II-682

5961 Catalog and mail-order houses, p. II-682

5962 Merchandising machine operators, p. II-683

5963 Direct selling establishments, p. II-683

5983 Fuel oil dealers, p. II-683

5992 Florists, p. II-684

5993 Tobacco stores and stands, p. II-684

5994 News dealers and newsstands, p. II-684

5995 Optical goods stores, p. II-685

5999 Miscellaneous retail stores, nec, p. II-686

Depository Institutions

6021 National commercial banks, p. II-687

6061 Federal credit unions, p. II-698

6099 Functions related to deposit banking, p. II-698

Nondepository Institutions

6141 Personal credit institutions, p. II-699

6159 Misc. business credit institutions, p. II-700

6162 Mortgage bankers and correspondents, p. II-701

6163 Loan brokers, p. II-704

Security & Commodity Brokers

6211 Security brokers and dealers, p. II-705

6221 Commodity contracts brokers, dealers, p. II-707

6231 Security and commodity exchanges, p. II-707

6282 Investment advice, p. II-707

Appendix I - Industrial Classifications

Insurance Carriers

6300 Insurance carriers, p. II-709

6311 Life insurance, p. II-709

6321 Accident and health insurance, p. II-713

6324 Hospital and medical service plans, p. II-714

6331 Fire, marine, and casualty insurance, p. II-717

6351 Surety insurance, p. II-728

6361 Title insurance, p. II-729

6371 Pension, health, and welfare funds, p. II-729

Insurance Agents, Brokers, & Service

6411 Insurance agents, brokers, & service, p. II-730

Real Estate

6512 Nonresidential building operators, p. II-731

6513 Apartment building operators, p. II-732

6514 Dwelling operators, exc. apartments, p. II-733

6515 Mobile home site operators, p. II-733

6531 Real estate agents and managers, p. II-733

6541 Title abstract offices, p. II-734

6553 Cemetery subdividers and developers, p. II-735

Holding & Other Investment Offices

6712 Bank holding companies, p. II-736

6726 Investment offices, nec, p. II-736

6794 Patent owners and lessors, p. II-736

6798 Real estate investment trusts, p. II-737

Hotels & Other Lodging Places

7011 Hotels and motels, p. II-738

7021 Rooming and boarding houses, p. II-739

7032 Sporting and recreational camps, p. II-740

7033 Trailer parks and campsites, p. II-740

Personal Services

7211 Power laundries, family & commercial, p. II-741

7212 Garment pressing & cleaners' agents, p. II-741

7213 Linen supply, p. II-741

7215 Coin-operated laundries and cleaning, p. II-742

7217 Carpet and upholstery cleaning, p. II-742

7218 Industrial launderers, p. II-742

7221 Photographic studios, portrait, p. II-742

7231 Beauty shops, p. II-742

7251 Shoe repair and shoeshine parlors, p. II-743

7261 Funeral service and crematories, p. II-743

7291 Tax return preparation services, p. II-743

7299 Miscellaneous personal services, nec, p. II-743

Business Services

7311 Advertising agencies, p. II-745

7312 Outdoor advertising services, p. II-746

7313 Radio, TV, publisher representatives, p. II-746

7319 Advertising, nec, p. II-749

7322 Adjustment & collection services, p. II-750

7323 Credit reporting services, p. II-750

7331 Direct mail advertising services, p. II-750

7334 Photocopying & duplicating services, p. II-751

7335 Commercial photography, p. II-751

7336 Commercial art and graphic design, p. II-752

7338 Secretarial & court reporting, p. II-752

7342 Disinfecting & pest control services, p. II-752

7349 Building maintenance services, nec, p. II-753

7350 Misc. equipment rental & leasing, p. II-754

7352 Medical equipment rental, p. II-754

7353 Heavy construction equipment rental, p. II-755

7359 Equipment rental & leasing, nec, p. II-755

7363 Help supply services, p. II-756

7372 Prepackaged software, p. II-756

7373 Computer integrated systems design, p. II-761

7374 Data processing and preparation, p. II-762

7375 Information retrieval services, p. II-762

7376 Computer facilities management, p. II-763

7377 Computer rental & leasing, p. II-763

7378 Computer maintenance & repair, p. II-763

7379 Computer related services, nec, p. II-764

7381 Detective & armored car services, p. II-764

7382 Security systems services, p. II-764

7383 News syndicates, p. II-765

7384 Photofinishing laboratories, p. II-765

7389 Business services, nec, p. II-765

Auto Repair, Services, & Parking

7513 Truck rental and leasing, no drivers, p. II-770

7514 Passenger car rental, p. II-770

7515 Passenger car leasing, p. II-770

7521 Automobile parking, p. II-771

7530 Automotive repair shops, p. II-771

7532 Top & body repair & paint shops, p. II-771

7533 Auto exhaust system repair shops, p. II-771

7534 Tire retreading and repair shops, p. II-771

7536 Automotive glass replacement shops, p. II-772

7537 Automotive transmission repair shops, p. II-772

7538 General automotive repair shops, p. II-772

7542 Carwashes, p. II-772

7549 Automotive services, nec, p. II-773

Miscellaneous Repair Services

7629 Electrical repair shops, nec, p. II-774

7631 Watch, clock, and jewelry repair, p. II-774

7641 Reupholstery and furniture repair, p. II-775
7699 Repair services, nec, p. II-775

Motion Pictures

7812 Motion picture & video production, p. II-777
7819 Services allied to motion pictures, p. II-778
7822 Motion picture and tape distribution, p. II-778
7832 Motion picture theaters, ex drive-in, p. II-779
7833 Drive-in motion picture theaters, p. II-779
7841 Video tape rental, p. II-780

Amusement & Recreation Services

7911 Dance studios, schools, and halls, p. II-781
7922 Theatrical producers and services, p. II-781
7933 Bowling centers, p. II-782
7941 Sports clubs, managers, & promoters, p. II-783
7948 Racing, including track operation, p. II-784
7991 Physical fitness facilities, p. II-785
7992 Public golf courses, p. II-786
7993 Coin-operated amusement devices, p. II-786
7996 Amusement parks, p. II-787
7997 Membership sports & recreation clubs, p. II-787
7999 Amusement and recreation, nec, p. II-789

Health Services

8011 Offices & clinics of medical doctors, p. II-793
8021 Offices and clinics of dentists, p. II-793
8041 Offices and clinics of chiropractors, p. II-794
8042 Offices and clinics of optometrists, p. II-794
8043 Offices and clinics of podiatrists, p. II-795
8051 Skilled nursing care facilities, p. II-796
8052 Intermediate care facilities, p. II-796
8060 Hospitals, p. II-796
8063 Psychiatric hospitals, p. II-797
8069 Specialty hospitals exc. psychiatric, p. II-797
8072 Dental laboratories, p. II-797
8082 Home health care services, p. II-797
8092 Kidney dialysis centers, p. II-798
8093 Specialty outpatient clinics, nec, p. II-798
8099 Health and allied services, nec, p. II-798

Legal Services

8111 Legal services, p. II-800

Educational Services

8211 Elementary and secondary schools, p. II-801
8221 Colleges and universities, p. II-802
8231 Libraries, p. II-802
8299 Schools & educational services, nec, p. II-803

Social Services

8322 Individual and family services, p. II-804
8331 Job training and related services, p. II-804
8351 Child day care services, p. II-804
8361 Residential care, p. II-805
8399 Social services, nec, p. II-805

Museums, Botanical, Zoological Gardens

8412 Museums and art galleries, p. II-807
8422 Botanical and zoological gardens, p. II-807

Membership Organizations

8611 Business associations, p. II-809
8631 Labor organizations, p. II-809
8641 Civic and social associations, p. II-809
8651 Political organizations, p. II-810
8661 Religious organizations, p. II-810
8699 Membership organizations, nec, p. II-811

Engineering & Management Services

8711 Engineering services, p. II-812
8712 Architectural services, p. II-812
8721 Accounting, auditing, & bookkeeping, p. II-813
8732 Commercial nonphysical research, p. II-814
8733 Noncommercial research organizations, p. II-816
8742 Management consulting services, p. II-816
8743 Public relations services, p. II-817

Justice, Public Order, & Safety

9221 Police protection, p. II-818

Administration of Human Resources

9411 Admin. of educational programs, p. II-819
9431 Admin. of public health programs, p. II-819

Environmental Quality & Housing

9532 Urban and community development, p. II-820

Administration of Economic Programs

9611 Admin. of general economic programs, p. II-821

National Security & Intl. Affairs

9711 National security, p. II-822

Appendix I - Industrial Classifications

APPENDIX I - INDUSTRIAL CLASSIFICATIONS

NAICS COVERAGE

This appendix lists the North American Industrial Classification System codes (NAICS) included in *Market Share Reporter*. A volume and page number are shown following each NAICS category; the page shown indicates the first occurrence of a NAICS.

Crop Production

111110 Soybeans, p. I-17
111140 Wheat, p. I-14
111150 Corn, p. I-14
111160 Rice, p. I-14
111211 Potatoes, p. I-20
111219 Other vegetables & melons, p. I-20
111310 Orange groves, p. I-24
111320 Citrus (exc orange) groves, p. I-24
111331 Apple orchards, p. I-25
111332 Grape vineyards, p. I-23
111333 Strawberries, p. I-22
111334 Berries (exc strawberries), p. I-22
111335 Tree nuts, p. I-24
111336 Fruit & tree nut combination, p. I-26
111339 Other noncitrus fruits, p. I-25
111411 Mushroom production, p. I-28
111421 Nursery & tree production, p. I-27
111422 Floriculture production, p. I-27
111910 Tobacco, p. I-19
111920 Cotton, p. I-18
111930 Sugarcane, p. I-20
111991 Sugar beets, p. I-19

Animal Production

112111 Beef cattle ranching & farming, p. I-29
112112 Cattle feedlots, p. I-29
112210 Hogs & pigs, p. I-30
112310 Chicken eggs, p. I-32
112320 Broilers & other chicken production, p. I-31
112330 Turkey production, p. I-32
112410 Sheep farming, p. I-31
112420 Goat farming, p. I-31
112511 Finfish farming & fish hatcheries, p. I-34
112512 Shellfish farming, p. I-34
112519 Other aquaculture, p. I-34
112920 Horses & other equine production, p. I-33
112930 Fur-bearing animal production, p. I-33
112990 All other animal production, p. I-34

Forestry and Logging

113110 Timber tract operations, p. I-36
113310 Logging, p. I-255

Fishing, Hunting & Trapping

114111 Finfish fishing, p. I-37
114210 Hunting & trapping, p. I-38

Agriculture & Forestry Support Activities

115113 Crop harvesting, primarily machine, p. I-35
115210 Animal production support activities, p. I-35

Oil & Gas Extraction

211111 Crude petroleum & natural gas, p. I-50
211112 Natural gas liquid, p. I-53

Mining (except Oil & Gas)

212111 Bituminous coal & lignite mining, p. I-48
212112 Bituminous coal underground mining, p. I-48
212210 Iron ore, p. I-39
212221 Gold ore, p. I-41
212222 Silver ore, p. I-42
212231 Lead ore & zinc ore, p. I-40
212234 Copper ore & nickel ore, p. I-39
212291 Uranium-radium-vanadium ore, p. I-44
212299 All other metal ore mining, p. I-43
212311 Dimension stone, p. I-57
212312 Crushed & broken limestone, p. I-57
212313 Crushed & broken granite, p. I-57
212319 Other crushed & broken stone, p. I-57
212321 Construction sand & gravel, p. I-58
212322 Industrial sand, p. I-58
212324 Kaolin & ball clay, p. I-59
212325 Clay/ceramic/refractory minerals, p. I-59
212391 Potash/soda/borite mineral mining, p. I-60
212392 Phosphate rock, p. I-60

212393 Other chemical/fertilizer minerals, p. I-61
212399 Other nonmetallic minerals, p. I-61

Mining Support Activities

213111 Drilling oil & gas wells, p. I-53
213112 Oil & gas operation support, p. I-54

Utilities

221111 Hydroelectric power generation, p. II-615
221112 Fossil fuel electric pwr generation, p. II-615
221113 Nuclear electric power generation, p. II-615
221310 Water supply & irrigation systems, p. II-618

Building Construction

236115 New single-family housing (exc operative),
   p. I-65
236116 New multifamily housing (exc operative),
   p. I-69
236118 Residential remodelers, p. I-64
236210 Industrial building construction, p. I-64
236220 Commercial & institutional building construction, p. I-64

Heavy & Civil Engineering Construction

237110 Water & sewer line & related structures, p. I-71
237120 Oil & gas pipeline & related structures, p. I-71
237310 Highway, street, & bridge construction, p. I-71

Specialty Trade Contractors

238110 Poured concrete foundation & structure contractors, p. I-75
238120 Structural steel & precast concrete contractors,
   p. I-75
238140 Masonry contractors, p. I-73
238150 Glass & glazing contractors, p. I-75
238160 Roofing contractors, p. I-74
238210 Electrical contractors, p. I-73
238310 Drywall & insulation contractors, p. I-74
238320 Painting & wall covering contractors, p. I-73
238390 Other building finishing contractors, p. I-74
238910 Site preparation contractors, p. I-72
238990 All other specialty trade contractors, p. I-76

Food Manufacturing

311111 Dog & cat food manufacturing, p. I-140
311119 Other animal food manufacturing, p. I-144
311211 Flour milling, p. I-77
311212 Rice milling, p. I-77

311213 Malt manufacturing, p. I-185
311221 Wet corn milling, p. I-77
311223 Other oilseed processing, p. I-177
311225 Fats & oils refining & blending, p. I-84
311230 Breakfast cereal manufacturing, p. I-136
311311 Sugarcane mills, p. I-155
311312 Cane sugar refining, p. I-156
311320 Chocolate/confectionery mfg, p. I-170
311330 Confectionery mfg, from chocolate, p. I-156
311340 Nonchocolate confectionery mfg, p. I-156
311411 Frozen fruit/juice/vegetable mfg, p. I-78
311412 Frozen specialty food mfg, p. I-84
311421 Fruit & vegetable canning, p. I-87
311422 Specialty canning, p. I-77
311423 Dried & dehydrated food mfg, p. I-125
311511 Fluid milk manufacturing, p. I-97
311512 Creamery butter manufacturing, p. I-97
311513 Cheese manufacturing, p. I-97
311514 Dry/condensed/evaporated dairy mfg, p. I-102
311520 Ice cream & frozen dessert mfg, p. I-103
311611 Animal (exc poultry) slaughtering, p. I-88
311612 Meat processed from carcasses, p. I-91
311615 Poultry processing, p. I-77
311711 Seafood canning, p. I-81
311712 Fresh & frozen seafood processing, p. I-200
311811 Retail bakeries, p. II-650
311812 Commercial bakeries, p. I-78
311813 Frozen cakes/other pastries mfg, p. I-155
311821 Cookie & cracker manufacturing, p. I-85
311822 Flour mixes & dough manufacturing, p. I-139
311823 Dry pasta manufacturing, p. I-85
311830 Tortilla manufacturing, p. I-222
311911 Roasted nuts & peanut butter mfg, p. I-175
311919 Other snack food manufacturing, p. I-205
311920 Coffee & tea manufacturing, p. I-181
311941 Mayonnaise/dressing/other sauce, p. I-126
311942 Spice & extract manufacturing, p. I-198
311991 Perishable prepared food mfg, p. I-88
311999 Other food manufacturing, p. I-214

Beverage & Tobacco Product Manufacturing

312111 Soft drink manufacturing, p. I-77
312112 Bottled water manufacturing, p. I-77
312113 Ice manufacturing, p. I-211
312120 Breweries, p. I-81
312130 Wineries, p. I-180
312140 Distilleries, p. I-180
312210 Tobacco stemming & redrying, p. I-224
312221 Cigarette manufacturing, p. I-224
312229 Other tobacco product manufacturing, p. I-224

Textile Mills

313111 Yarn spinning mills, p. I-238
313112 Yarn texturizing & twisting mills, p. I-239
313210 Broadwoven fabric mills, p. I-232
313221 Narrow fabric mills, p. I-233
313222 Schiffli machine embroidery, p. I-254
313230 Nonwoven fabric mills, p. I-239
313241 Weft knit fabric mills, p. I-236
313249 Other knit fabric & lace mills, p. I-236
313311 Broadwoven fabric finishing mills, p. I-237
313312 Fabric finishing mills, p. I-236
313320 Fabric coating mills, p. I-239

Textile Product Mills

314110 Carpet & rug mills, p. I-237
314121 Curtain & drapery mills, p. I-250
314129 Other household textile prod mills, p. I-251
314911 Textile bag mills, p. I-254
314991 Rope, cordage, & twine mills, p. I-240
314999 Other textile product mills, p. I-245

Apparel Manufacturing

315111 Sheer hosiery mills, p. I-234
315119 Other hosiery & sock mills, p. I-234
315191 Outerwear knitting mills, p. I-235
315211 Men's & boys' apparel contractors, p. I-241
315212 Women's/girls'/infants' apparel, p. I-241
315221 Men's & boys' underwear mfg, p. I-241
315222 Men's & boys' suit/overcoat mfg, p. I-243
315223 Men's & boys' shirt (exc work) mfg, p. I-245
315224 Men's & boys' trouser/jean mfg, p. I-242
315231 Women's/girls' loungewear mfg, p. I-242
315232 Women's/girls' blouse/shirt mfg, p. I-247
315233 Women's/girls' dress mfg, p. I-247
315234 Women's/girls' suit/coat/skirt mfg, p. I-243
315239 Women's/girls' other outerwear mfg, p. I-242
315292 Fur & leather apparel manufacturing, p. I-249
315299 All other apparel manufacturing, p. I-250
315991 Hat, cap, & millinery manufacturing, p. I-241
315992 Glove & mitten manufacturing, p. I-241
315993 Men's & boys' neckwear mfg, p. I-241
315999 Other apparel manufacturing, p. I-247

Leather & Allied Product Manufacturing

316110 Leather & hide tanning & finishing, p. I-381
316211 Rubber & plastics footwear mfg, p. I-373
316212 House slipper manufacturing, p. I-381
316214 Women's footwear (exc athletic) mfg, p. I-382
316991 Luggage manufacturing, p. I-382

316992 Women's handbag & purse mfg, p. I-384
316999 All other leather good mfg, p. I-381

Wood Product Manufacturing

321211 Hardwood veneer & plywood mfg, p. I-257
321212 Softwood veneer & plywood mfg, p. I-257
321219 Reconstituted wood product mfg, p. I-259
321911 Wood window & door manufacturing, p. I-256
321918 Other millwork (including flooring), p. I-255
321920 Wood container & pallet mfg, p. I-258
321991 Manufactured (mobile) home mfg, p. I-258
321999 Other wood product manufacturing, p. I-260

Paper Manufacturing

322110 Pulp mills, p. I-267
322121 Paper (except newsprint) mills, p. I-267
322130 Paperboard mills, p. I-269
322211 Corrugated & solid fiber box mfg, p. I-270
322212 Folding paperboard box mfg, p. I-271
322215 Nonfolding sanitary food cont mfg, p. I-270
322222 Coated & laminated paper mfg, p. I-271
322223 Plastics/foil/coated paper bag mfg, p. I-273
322225 Laminated aluminum foil mfg, p. I-421
322231 Die-cut paper/paperboard supplies, p. I-274
322233 Stationery & related product mfg, p. I-281
322291 Sanitary paper product mfg, p. I-274

Printing & Related Support Activities

323110 Commercial lithographic printing, p. I-290
323111 Commercial gravure printing, p. I-291
323112 Commercial flexographic printing, p. I-291
323113 Commercial screen printing, p. I-291
323117 Books printing, p. I-289

Petroleum & Coal Products Manufacturing

324110 Petroleum refineries, p. I-367
324121 Asphalt paving mixture & block mfg, p. I-367
324122 Asphalt shingle & coating materials, p. I-368
324191 Petroleum lubricating oil & grease, p. I-368

Chemical Manufacturing

325110 Petrochemical manufacturing, p. I-353
325120 Industrial gas manufacturing, p. I-295
325131 Inorganic dye & pigment mfg, p. I-296
325132 Synthetic organic dye & pigment mfg, p. I-293
325181 Alkalies and chlorine manufacturing, p. I-294
325182 Carbon black manufacturing, p. I-361
325188 Other basic inorganic chemical mfg, p. I-293
325192 Cyclic crude & intermediate mfg, p. I-352

325193 Ethyl alcohol manufacturing, p. I-353
325199 Other basic organic chemical mfg, p. I-354
325211 Plastics material & resin mfg, p. I-299
325212 Synthetic rubber manufacturing, p. I-301
325221 Cellulosic organic fiber mfg, p. I-303
325311 Nitrogenous fertilizer mfg, p. I-355
325312 Phosphatic fertilizer manufacturing, p. I-357
325314 Fertilizer (mixing only) mfg, p. I-357
325320 Pesticide, other ag chemicals, p. I-357
325411 Medicinal and botanical mfg, p. I-304
325412 Pharmaceutical preparation mfg, p. I-306
325414 Biological product manufacturing, p. I-316
325510 Paint & coating mfg, p. I-350
325520 Adhesive manufacturing, p. I-358
325611 Soap & other detergent mfg, p. I-318
325612 Polish & other sanitation good mfg, p. I-324
325613 Surface active agent manufacturing, p. I-330
325620 Toilet preparation manufacturing, p. I-331
325910 Printing ink manufacturing, p. I-360
325920 Explosives manufacturing, p. I-360
325992 Photographic film/paper/plate mfg, p. II-551
325998 All other chemical product mfg, p. I-298

Plastics & Rubber Products Manufacturing

326111 Plastics bag manufacturing, p. I-273
326112 Plastics film/sheet (incl laminated) mfg, p. I-271
326113 Unlaminated plastics film/sheet (exc packaging),
  p. I-376
326121 Unlaminated plastics profile shape, p. I-379
326122 Plastics pipe & pipe fitting mfg, p. I-378
326130 Laminated plastics plate/sheet mfg, p. I-377
326150 Urethane & other foam products, p. I-378
326160 Plastics bottle manufacturing, p. I-378
326192 Resilient floor covering mfg, p. II-566
326199 Other plastics product mfg, p. I-379
326211 Tire manufacturing (exc retreading), p. I-371
326212 Tire retreading, p. II-771
326299 All other rubber product mfg, p. I-376

Nonmetallic Mineral Product Manufacturing

327111 China & earthenware bathroom items, p. I-391
327112 Other pottery product manufacturing, p. I-391
327122 Ceramic wall & floor tile mfg, p. I-390
327124 Clay refractory manufacturing, p. I-390
327125 Nonclay refractory manufacturing, p. I-393
327211 Flat glass manufacturing, p. I-385
327212 Other pressed & blown glass, p. I-387
327213 Glass container manufacturing, p. I-387
327310 Cement manufacturing, p. I-388
327331 Concrete block and brick mfg, p. I-391
327410 Lime manufacturing, p. I-391
327420 Gypsum product manufacturing, p. I-392

327910 Abrasive product manufacturing, p. I-392
327999 Other nonmetallic mineral products, p. I-393

Primary Metal Manufacturing

331111 Iron and steel mills, p. I-394
331112 Electrometallurgical ferroalloy, p. I-396
331210 Iron & steel pipe & tube mfg, p. I-397
331221 Rolled steel shape manufacturing, p. I-397
331222 Steel wire drawing, p. I-396
331311 Alumina refining, p. I-297
331312 Primary aluminum production, p. I-399
331315 Aluminum sheet, plate, and foil mfg, p. I-402
331316 Aluminum extruded product mfg, p. I-402
331411 Primary smelting/refining of copper, p. I-398
331419 Primary smelt/refine, nonferrous, p. I-400
331422 Copper wire drawing, p. I-404
331491 Nonferrous roll/draw/extrude, p. I-403
331511 Iron foundries, p. I-398
331521 Aluminum die-casting foundries, p. I-404
331525 Copper foundries (exc die-casting), p. I-404

Fabricated Metal Product Manufacturing

332111 Iron and steel forging, p. I-414
332112 Nonferrous forging, p. I-414
332115 Crown and closure manufacturing, p. I-415
332117 Powder metallurgy part mfg, p. I-421
332211 Cutlery & flatware mfg, p. I-406
332212 Hand and edge tool manufacturing, p. I-407
332213 Saw blade and handsaw manufacturing, p. I-408
332214 Kitchen utensil, pot, & pan mfg, p. I-415
332311 Prefabricated metal bldg/components, p. I-413
332312 Fabricated structural metal mfg, p. I-411
332313 Plate work manufacturing, p. I-413
332321 Metal window & door mfg, p. I-411
332322 Sheet metal work manufacturing, p. I-413
332410 Power boiler & heat exchanger mfg, p. I-412
332420 Metal tank (heavy gauge) mfg, p. I-413
332431 Metal can manufacturing, p. I-405
332439 Other metal container manufacturing, p. I-405
332611 Spring (heavy gauge) manufacturing, p. I-419
332618 Other fabricated wire product mfg, p. I-420
332710 Machine shops, p. I-460
332721 Precision turned product mfg, p. I-413
332722 Bolt/nut/screw/rivet/washer mfg, p. I-414
332812 Metal coating/engraving services, p. I-416
332813 Plating/polishing/anodizing, p. I-416
332911 Industrial valve manufacturing, p. I-417
332912 Fluid power valve & hose fittings, p. I-418
332913 Plumbing fixture fitting/trim mfg, p. I-409
332919 Other metal valve/pipe fitting mfg, p. I-419
332991 Ball and roller bearing mfg, p. I-441
332992 Small arms ammunition manufacturing, p. I-416

332995 Other ordnance & accessories mfg, p. I-417
332998 Enameled iron/metal sanitary ware, p. I-408
332999 Other fabricated metal product mfg, p. I-419

Machinery Manufacturing

333111 Farm machinery & equipment mfg, p. I-424
333112 Lawn & garden equipment mfg, p. I-425
333120 Construction machinery mfg, p. I-426
333131 Mining machinery & equipment mfg, p. I-428
333132 Oil & gas field machinery & equip, p. I-428
333210 Sawmill & woodwoking machinery mfg, p. I-437
333220 Plastics/rubber industry machinery, p. I-439
333291 Paper industry machinery mfg, p. I-438
333292 Textile machinery manufacturing, p. I-437
333294 Food product machinery mfg, p. I-438
333295 Semiconductor machinery mfg, p. I-439
333298 Other industrial machinery mfg, p. I-439
333311 Automatic vending machine mfg, p. I-457
333313 Office machinery manufacturing, p. I-456
333315 Photograph/photocopy equip mfg, p. II-550
333319 Other commercial/service machinery, p. I-438
333412 Industrial/commercial fan & blower, p. I-442
333414 Heating equip manufacturing, p. I-409
333415 Ac/heating equip & commercial refrig, p. I-457
333511 Industrial mold manufacturing, p. I-436
333512 Machine tools (metal cutting types), p. I-434
333611 Turbine & turbine generator mfg, p. I-422
333612 Speed changer/high-speed drive mfg, p. I-444
333618 Other engine equipment mfg, p. I-424
333911 Pump & pumping equipment mfg, p. I-440
333912 Air and gas compressor mfg, p. I-442
333921 Elevator & moving stairway mfg, p. I-431
333922 Conveyor & conveying equipment mfg, p. I-431
333923 Overhead crane/hoist/monorail, p. I-431
333924 Industrial truck/tractor/stacker, p. I-433
333991 Power-driven handtool manufacturing, p. I-436
333992 Welding & soldering equipment mfg, p. I-437
333993 Packaging machinery manufacturing, p. I-443
333994 Industrial process furnace/oven mfg, p. II-532
333996 Fluid power pump & motor mfg, p. I-460
333999 Other general purpose machinery mfg, p. I-266

Computer & Electronic Product Manufacturing

334111 Electronic computer manufacturing, p. I-447
334112 Computer storage device mfg, p. I-452
334119 Other computer peripheral equip mfg, p. I-453
334210 Telephone apparatus manufacturing, p. II-481
334220 Radio/tv/wireless equipment mfg, p. II-483
334290 Other communications equip. mfg, p. II-485
334310 Audio and video equipment mfg, p. II-461
334412 Bare printed circuit board mfg, p. II-487

334413 Semiconductor & related device mfg, p. II-488
334414 Electronic capacitor manufacturing, p. II-493
334416 Electronic coil/inductor mfg, p. II-461
334417 Electronic connector manufacturing, p. II-461
334419 Other electronic component mfg, p. II-494
334510 Electromedical/electrotheraputic apparatus, p. II-543
334511 Search/detection/navigation system, p. II-532
334514 Totalizing fuel meter/count device, p. II-533
334515 Electricity measuring/testing mfg, p. II-534
334516 Analytical laboratory instrument, p. II-534
334517 Irradiation apparatus manufacturing, p. II-548
334518 Watch, clock, and part mfg, p. II-552
334519 Other measuring, controlling device, p. II-535
334611 Software reproducing, p. II-756
334612 Cd/tape/record reproducing, p. II-480
334613 Magnetic/optical recording media, p. II-499

Electrical Equip, Appliance & Component Mfg

335110 Electric lamp bulb & part mfg, p. II-472
335121 Res electric light fixture mfg, p. II-475
335211 Electric housewares/household fan, p. II-469
335212 Household vacuum cleaner mfg, p. II-465
335221 Household cooking appliance mfg, p. II-465
335222 Household refrigerator/freezer mfg, p. II-465
335224 Household laundry equipment mfg, p. II-466
335228 Other major household appliance mfg, p. II-471
335311 Pwr/distribution/spclty transformer, p. II-461
335312 Motor & generator mfg, p. II-464
335313 Switchgear & switchboard apparatus, p. II-463
335314 Relay & industrial control mfg, p. II-465
335911 Storage battery manufacturing, p. II-496
335929 Other communication/energy wire mfg, p. I-420
335931 Current-carrying wiring device mfg, p. II-474
335991 Carbon and graphite product mfg, p. II-465

Transportation Equipment Manufacturing

336111 Automobile manufacturing, p. II-500
336112 Light truck/utility vehicle mfg, p. II-508
336211 Motor vehicle body manufacturing, p. II-509
336213 Motor home manufacturing, p. II-517
336214 Travel trailer & camper mfg, p. II-530
336311 Carburetor/piston/piston ring/valve, p. I-460
336312 Gasoline engine & engine parts mfg, p. II-511
336322 Other motor vehicle electric equip, p. II-499
336330 Motor vehicle steering/suspension, p. II-511
336340 Motor vehicle brake system mfg, p. II-514
336350 Motor vehicle transmission mfg, p. II-511
336399 Other motor vehicle parts mfg, p. II-513
336411 Aircraft manufacturing, p. II-518
336412 Aircraft engine & engine parts mfg, p. II-521
336414 Guided missile & space vehicle mfg, p. II-527

336419 Other missile/space vehicle parts, p. II-529
336510 Railroad rolling stock mfg, p. II-524
336611 Ship building and repairing, p. II-522
336612 Boat building, p. II-522
336991 Motorcycle/bicycle/parts mfg, p. II-525
336992 Military armored vehicle/component, p. II-530
336999 Other transporation equipment mfg, p. II-531

Furniture & Related Product Manufacturing

337110 Wood kitchen cabinet & countertop, p. I-256
337121 Upholstered household furniture mfg, p. I-262
337122 Nonupholstered wood furniture, p. I-261
337124 Metal household furniture mfg, p. I-262
337127 Institutional furniture mfg, p. I-265
337214 Office furniture (exc wood) mfg, p. I-264
337215 Showcase/partition/shelving/locker, p. I-265
337910 Mattress manufacturing, p. I-263

Miscellaneous Manufacturing

339112 Surgical & medical instrument mfg, p. II-536
339113 Surgical appliance & supplies mfg, p. II-541
339114 Dental equipment & supplies mfg, p. II-547
339115 Ophthalmic goods manufacturing, p. II-548
339116 Dental laboratories, p. II-797
339911 Jewelry (exc costume) mfg, p. II-554
339913 Jewelers' material & lapidary work, p. II-555
339914 Costume jewelry & novelty mfg, p. II-564
339920 Sporting & athletic goods mfg, p. II-558
339931 Doll and stuffed toy manufacturing, p. II-556
339932 Game/toy/children's vehicle mfg, p. II-556
339941 Pen and mechanical pencil mfg, p. II-560
339942 Lead pencil & art good mfg, p. II-561
339943 Marking device manufacturing, p. II-563
339944 Carbon paper & inked ribbon mfg, p. II-564
339950 Sign manufacturing, p. II-565
339991 Gasket/packing/sealing device mfg, p. I-375
339992 Musical instrument manufacturing, p. II-555
339993 Fastener/button/needle/pin mfg, p. II-564
339994 Broom, brush, and mop mfg, p. II-564
339995 Burial casket manufacturing, p. II-566
339999 All other miscellaneous mfg, p. II-567

Merchant Wholesalers, Durable Goods

423110 Automobile & other motor vehicles, p. II-621
423120 Motor vehicle supplies & new parts, p. II-621
423130 Tire & tube merchant wholesalers, p. II-621
423210 Furniture merchant wholesalers, p. II-622
423220 Home furnishing merchant wholesalers, p. II-622
423310 Lumber/plywood/millwork/wood panel, p. II-622

423420 Office equipment merchant wholesalers, p. II-623
423430 Computer/peripheral equipment/software, p. II-623
423510 Metal service centers & other metal wholesalers, p. II-623
423520 Coal & other mineral & ore merchant wholesalers, p. II-624
423610 Electrical equipment & wiring supplies & related, p. II-624
423620 Electrical appliance, television, & radio set, p. II-624
423740 Refrigeration equipment & supplies, p. II-624
423830 Industrial machinery & equipment, p. II-625
423840 Industrial supplies merchant wholesalers, p. II-625
423850 Service establishment equipment & supplies, p. II-625
423860 Transportation equip & supply (exc motor vehicle), p. II-625
423910 Sporting & recreational goods & supplies, p. II-626
423920 Toy & hobby goods & supplies, p. II-626
423930 Recyclable material merchant wholesalers, p. II-626
423940 Jewelry/watch/precious stone/precious metal, p. II-627
423990 Other misc durable goods merchant wholesalers, p. II-627

Merchant Wholesalers, Nondurable Goods

424120 Stationery & office supplies, p. II-628
424210 Drugs & druggists' sundries, p. II-628
424320 Men's & boys' clothing & furnishings, p. II-629
424410 General line grocery merchant wholesalers, p. II-629
424420 Packaged frozen food merchant wholesalers, p. II-629
424430 Dairy product (exc dried or canned), p. II-629
424480 Fresh fruit & vegetable merchant wholesalers, p. II-630
424490 Other grocery & related products, p. II-630
424510 Grain & field bean merchant wholesalers, p. II-630
424520 Livestock merchant wholesalers, p. II-630
424590 Other farm product raw material, p. II-630
424720 Petroleum & products (exc bulk station & terminal), p. II-631
424810 Beer & ale merchant wholesalers, p. II-631
424930 Flowers, nursery stock, & florists' supplies, p. II-631

424940 Tobacco & tobacco products, p. II-631

424990 Other misc nondurable goods merchant wholesalers, p. II-631

Wholesale Electronic Markets, Agents, & Brokers

425120 Wholesale trade agents and brokers, p. II-629

Motor Vehicle & Parts Dealers

441110 New car dealers, p. II-651

441120 Used car dealers, p. II-651

441221 Motorcycle, atv, & personal watercraft dealers, p. II-653

441222 Boat dealers, p. II-652

441310 Automotive parts/accessories stores, p. II-651

441320 Tire dealers, p. II-652

Furniture & Home Furnishings Stores

442110 Furniture stores, p. II-659

442210 Floor covering stores, p. II-659

442299 All other home furnishings stores, p. II-660

Electronics & Appliance Stores

443111 Household appliance stores, p. II-662

443112 Radio/tv/other electronics stores, p. II-663

443120 Computer and software stores, p. II-664

443130 Camera/photographic supply stores, p. II-681

Bldg Material & Garden Equip & Supp Dealers

444110 Home centers, p. II-632

444120 Paint and wallpaper stores, p. II-632

444130 Hardware stores, p. II-632

444190 Other building material dealers, p. II-632

444220 Nursery and garden centers, p. II-633

Food & Beverage Stores

445110 Supermarkets & other grocery stores, p. II-639

445220 Fish and seafood markets, p. II-649

445230 Fruit and vegetable markets, p. II-649

445292 Confectionery and nut stores, p. II-649

445310 Beer, wine, and liquor stores, p. II-677

Health & Personal Care Stores

446110 Pharmacies and drug stores, p. II-672

446120 Cosmetics & perfume stores, p. II-686

446130 Optical goods stores, p. II-685

Gasoline Stations

447190 Other gasoline stations, p. II-652

Clothing & Clothing Accessories Stores

448110 Men's clothing stores, p. II-654

448120 Women's clothing stores, p. II-654

448130 Children's/infants' clothing stores, p. II-656

448140 Family clothing stores, p. II-656

448150 Clothing accessories stores, p. II-655

448190 Other clothing stores, p. II-655

448210 Shoe stores, p. II-657

448310 Jewelry stores, p. II-680

448320 Luggage and leather goods stores, p. II-682

Sporting Goods, Hobby, Book, & Music Stores

451110 Sporting goods stores, p. II-678

451120 Hobby, toy, and game stores, p. II-656

451130 Sewing/needlework/piece goods stores, p. II-682

451140 Musical instrument/supplies stores, p. II-665

451211 Book stores, p. II-678

451212 News dealers and newsstands, p. II-684

451220 Prerecorded tape/cd/record stores, p. II-664

General Merchandise Stores

452111 Department stores (exc discount), p. II-634

452112 Discount department stores, p. II-634

452910 Warehouse clubs and superstores, p. II-634

452990 All other gen merchandise stores, p. II-635

Miscellaneous Store Retailers

453110 Florists, p. II-684

453210 Office supplies & stationery stores, p. II-680

453220 Gift, novelty, and souvenir stores, p. II-681

453310 Used merchandise stores, p. II-677

453910 Pet and pet supplies stores, p. II-686

453991 Tobacco stores, p. II-684

453998 Other stores (exc tobacco stores), p. II-686

Nonstore Retailers

454111 Electronic shopping, p. II-682

454112 Electronic auctions, p. II-682

454210 Vending machine operators, p. II-683

454311 Heating oil dealers, p. II-683

454390 Other direct selling establishments, p. II-683

Air Transportation

481111 Scheduled passenger air transport, p. II-581

Appendix I - Industrial Classifications

Rail Transportation

482111 Line-haul railroads, p. II-570

Water Transportation

483111 Deep sea freight transportation, p. II-578
483112 Deep sea passenger transportation, p. II-579
483113 Coastal/great lakes freight transport, p. II-578
483114 Coastal/great lakes passenger transport, p. II-579
483212 Inland water passenger transport, p. II-579

Truck Transportation

484110 General freight trucking, local, p. II-573
484121 Gen freight truck/long-distance, p. II-573
484122 Freight/long-distance/<truckload, p. II-573
484220 Special freight trucking, local, p. II-573

Transit & Ground Passenger Transportation

485320 Limousine service, p. II-571
485410 School & employee bus transport, p. II-572
485510 Charter bus industry, p. II-571

Pipeline Transportation

486110 Pipeline transport of crude oil, p. II-587

Scenic & Sightseeing Transportation

487210 Scenic/sightseeing transport, water, p. II-579

Transportation Support Activities

488111 Air traffic control, p. II-585
488310 Port and harbor operations, p. II-580
488330 Navigational services to shipping, p. II-580
488410 Motor vehicle towing, p. II-773
488490 Road transport support activities, p. II-589
488510 Freight transportation arrangement, p. II-589
488991 Packing and crating, p. II-589
488999 Other transport support activities, p. II-589

Postal Service

491110 Postal service, p. II-577

Couriers & Messengers

492110 Couriers & express delivery services, p. II-575
492210 Local messengers/local delivery, p. II-575

Warehousing & Storage

493110 General warehousing and storage, p. II-576
493120 Refrigerated warehousing storage, p. II-576
493130 Farm product warehousing storage, p. II-576
493190 Other warehousing and storage, p. II-576

Publishing Industries (exc Internet)

511110 Newspaper publishers, p. I-282
511120 Periodical publishers, p. I-282
511130 Book publishers, p. I-282
511140 Directory & mailing list publishers, p. I-289
511191 Greeting card publishers, p. I-292
511210 Software publishers, p. II-756

Motion Picture & Sound Recording Industries

512110 Motion picture & video production, p. II-777
512120 Motion picture & video distribution, p. II-778
512131 Motion picture theaters, p. II-779
512132 Drive-in motion picture theaters, p. II-779
512191 Teleproduction/other postproduction, p. II-778
512220 Integrated record prod/distribution, p. II-480
512240 Sound recording studios, p. II-765

Broadcasting (except Internet)

515111 Radio networks, p. II-611
515112 Radio stations, p. II-611
515120 Television broadcasting, p. II-612
515210 Cable & other subscription programming,
   p. II-612

Telecommunications

517110 Wired telecommunications carriers, p. II-598
517210 Wireless telecommunications (exc satellite),
   p. II-590
517911 Telecommunications resellers, p. II-590
517919 All other telecommunications, p. II-762

Data Processing, Hosting, and Related Services

518210 Data processing, hosting, and related services,
   p. II-762

Other Information Services

519110 News syndicates, p. II-765
519120 Libraries and archives, p. II-802

Credit Intermediation Activities

522110 Commercial banking, p. II-687
522130 Credit unions, p. II-698
522210 Credit card issuing, p. II-699
522220 Sales financing, p. II-700
522292 Real estate credit, p. II-700
522298 Nondepository credit intermediation, p. II-699
522310 Mortgage/nonmortgage loan brokers, p. II-704
522320 Financial transaction processing, p. II-698

Security, Commodity Contracts & Like Activity

523110 Investment banking & securities, p. II-705
523130 Commodity contracts dealing, p. II-707
523140 Commodity contracts brokerage, p. II-707
523210 Securities and commodity exchanges, p. II-707
523920 Portfolio management, p. II-707
523930 Investment advice, p. II-707

Insurance Carriers & Related Activities

524113 Direct life insurance carriers, p. II-710
524114 Direct health/medical ins carriers, p. II-709
524126 Direct property/casualty insurance, p. II-709
524127 Direct title insurance carriers, p. II-729
524128 Other direct insurance carriers, p. II-709
524130 Reinsurance carriers, p. II-709
524210 Insurance agencies and brokerages, p. II-730
524291 Claims adjusting, p. II-730

Funds, Trusts & Other Financial Vehicles

525110 Pension funds, p. II-729
525990 Other financial vehicles, p. II-736

Real Estate

531110 Lessors residential bldgs/dwellings, p. II-732
531120 Lessors nonresidential buildings, p. II-731
531190 Other real estate lessors, p. II-733
531210 Real estate agents/brokers offices, p. II-733
531311 Residential property managers, p. II-734
531390 Other real estate related activity, p. II-734

Rental & Leasing Services

532111 Passenger car rental, p. II-770
532112 Passenger car leasing, p. II-770
532120 Truck/utility trailer/rv rent/lease, p. II-770
532230 Video tape and disc rental, p. II-780
532291 Home health equipment rental, p. II-754
532299 All other consumer goods rental, p. II-755
532411 Commercial transport equip leasing, p. II-756

532412 Heavy machinery rental & leasing, p. II-755
532420 Office equipment rental & leasing, p. II-755
532490 Other com/industrial equip rental, p. II-754

Lessors of Nonfinancial Intangible Asset

533110 Intangible asset lessors (exc copyrighted works),
    p. II-736

Professional, Scientific & Technical Services

541110 Offices of lawyers, p. II-800
541191 Title abstract/settlement offices, p. II-734
541213 Tax preparation services, p. II-743
541214 Payroll services, p. II-813
541310 Architectural services, p. II-812
541330 Engineering services, p. II-812
541350 Building inspection services, p. II-766
541430 Graphic design services, p. II-752
541512 Computer systems design services, p. II-761
541513 Computer facilities management, p. II-763
541611 Admin & general management services,
    p. II-816
541711 Biotechnology R&D, p. II-527
541712 Physical/engineering/life sciences R&D
    p. II-527
541720 Social science & humanities R&D, p. II-814
541810 Advertising agencies, p. II-745
541820 Public relations agencies, p. II-817
541840 Media representatives, p. II-746
541850 Display advertising, p. II-746
541860 Direct mail advertising, p. II-750
541870 Ad material distribution services, p. II-749
541890 Other advertising services, p. II-749
541921 Photography studios, portrait, p. II-742
541922 Commercial photography, p. II-751
541930 Translation/interpretation services, p. II-767
541940 Veterinary services, p. I-35
541990 Professional/science/tech services, p. II-767

Management Companies & Enterprises

551111 Offices of bank holding companies, p. II-736

Administrative & Support Services

561312 Executive search services, p. II-816
561320 Temporary help services, p. II-756
561330 Employee leasing services, p. II-756
561410 Document preparation services, p. II-766
561422 Telemarketing bureaus, p. II-768
561439 Other business service centers, p. II-751
561440 Collection agencies, p. II-750
561450 Credit bureaus, p. II-750

Appendix I - Industrial Classifications

561491 Repossession services, p. II-768
561492 Court reporting/stenotype services, p. II-752
561499 All other business support services, p. II-766
561510 Travel agencies, p. II-588
561520 Tour operators, p. II-588
561591 Convention and visitors bureaus, p. II-766
561599 Other travel arrangement services, p. II-766
561611 Investigation services, p. II-764
561612 Security guards and patrol services, p. II-764
561613 Armored car services, p. II-764
561621 Security services (exc locksmiths), p. II-764
561622 Locksmiths, p. II-776
561720 Janitorial services, p. II-752
561730 Landscaping services, p. I-35
561740 Carpet/upholstery cleaning services, p. II-742
561790 Other building & dwelling services, p. II-620
561920 Convention/trade show organizers, p. II-768
561990 All other support services, p. II-767

Waste Management & Remediation Services

562211 Hazardous waste treatment/disposal, p. II-618
562212 Solid waste landfill, p. II-618
562910 Remediation services, p. II-620
562920 Materials recovery facilities, p. II-619
562991 Septic tank and related services, p. II-755

Educational Services

611110 Elementary and secondary schools, p. II-801
611310 College/university/prof schools, p. II-802
611512 Flight training, p. II-803
611610 Fine arts schools, p. II-781
611620 Sports and recreation instruction, p. II-791
611630 Language schools, p. II-803
611691 Exam preparation and tutoring, p. II-803
611710 Educational support services, p. II-803

Ambulatory Health Care Services

621111 Physician offices (exc mental health), p. II-793
621210 Offices of dentists, p. II-793
621310 Offices of chiropractors, p. II-794
621320 Offices of optometrists, p. II-794
621391 Offices of podiatrists, p. II-795
621410 Family planning centers, p. II-799
621420 Outpatient mental health centers, p. II-798
621492 Kidney dialysis centers, p. II-798
621610 Home health care services, p. II-797
621910 Ambulance services, p. II-571
621991 Blood and organ banks, p. II-798
621999 Ambulatory health care services, p. II-799

Hospitals

622110 General medical/surgical hospitals, p. II-796
622210 Psychiatric/substance abuse hospitals, p. II-797
622310 Specialty hospitals, p. II-797

Nursing & Residential Care Facilities

623110 Nursing care facilities, p. II-796
623311 Continuing care retirement community, p. II-796
623312 Homes for the elderly, p. II-805
623990 Other residential care facilities, p. II-805

Social Assistance

624210 Community food services, p. II-804
624310 Vocational rehabilitation services, p. II-804
624410 Child day care services, p. II-804

Perform Arts, Spectator Sports & Related

711110 Theater companies & dinner theaters, p. II-782
711120 Dance companies, p. II-782
711211 Sports teams and clubs, p. II-783
711212 Racetracks, p. II-784
711310 Arts/sports promoters w/facilities, p. II-782
711320 Arts/sports promoters wo/facilities, p. II-782
711410 Agents & managers for public figures, p. II-781
711510 Independent artists/writers/performers, p. II-781

Museums, Historical Sites & Like Institutions

712110 Museums, p. II-807
712120 Historical sites, p. II-807
712130 Zoos and botanical gardens, p. II-808
712190 Nature parks/similar institutions, p. II-807

Amusement, Gambling, & Recreation Industries

713110 Amusement and theme parks, p. II-787
713120 Amusement arcades, p. II-786
713210 Casinos (except casino hotels), p. II-789
713910 Golf courses and country clubs, p. II-786
713920 Skiing facilities, p. II-791
713930 Marinas, p. II-580
713940 Fitness/recreational sports centers, p. II-785
713950 Bowling centers, p. II-782
713990 Amusement/recreation industries, p. II-788

Accomodation

721110 Hotels (exc casino) & motels, p. II-739
721120 Casino hotels, p. II-738
721191 Bed-and-breakfast inns, p. II-738

721211 RV parks & campgrounds, p. II-740
721214 Recreational & vacation camps, p. II-740
721310 Rooming and boarding houses, p. II-739

Food Services & Drinking Places

722110 Full-service restaurants, p. II-668
722211 Limited-service restaurants, p. II-667
722212 Cafeterias & buffets, p. II-668
722213 Snack & nonalcoholic beverage bars, p. II-666
722310 Food service contractors, p. II-666
722410 Drinking places (alcoholic beverages), p. II-671

Repair & Maintenance

811111 General automotive repair, p. II-772
811112 Automotive exhaust system repair, p. II-771
811113 Automotive transmission repair, p. II-771
811121 Auto body/interior repair/maintain, p. II-771
811122 Auto glass replacement shops, p. II-772
811191 Auto oil change & lube shops, p. II-773
811192 Car washes, p. II-772
811211 Consumer electronics repair, p. II-774
811212 Office machine repair & maintain, p. II-763
811219 Other electronic equip repair, p. II-774
811310 Commercial mach repair & maintain, p. II-775
811411 Home/garden equip repair & maintain, p. II-775
811412 Appliance repair & maintenance, p. II-774
811420 Reupholstery and furniture repair, p. II-775
811430 Footwear & leather goods repair, p. II-743
811490 Personal & household goods repair, p. II-774

Personal & Laundry Services

812112 Beauty salons, p. II-742
812113 Nail salons, p. II-742
812191 Diet and weight reducing centers, p. II-744
812199 Other personal care services, p. II-744
812210 Funeral homes & services, p. II-743
812220 Cemeteries and crematories, p. II-735
812310 Coin-operated laundries, p. II-742
812320 Dry cleaning & laundry services, p. II-741
812331 Linen supply, p. II-741
812332 Industrial launderers, p. II-742
812921 Photofinishing laboratories (exc one-hour),
  p. II-765
812930 Parking lots and garages, p. II-771
812990 All other personal services, p. II-743

Religious/Grantmaking/Prof/Like Organizations

813110 Religious organizations, p. II-810
813311 Human rights organizations, p. II-805
813312 Environ/conserve/wildlife org, p. II-805
813410 Civic and social organizations, p. II-809
813910 Business associations, p. II-809
813930 Labor unions/similar organizations, p. II-809
813940 Political organizations, p. II-810

Justice, Public Order & Safety Activities

922120 Police protection, p. II-818

Administration of Human Resource Programs

923110 Admin of education programs, p. II-819
923120 Admin of public health programs, p. II-819

Administration of Housing & Community Development

925120 Urban planning & development admin, p. II-820

Administration of Economic Programs

926110 General economic program admin, p. II-821

National Security & International Affairs

928110 National security, p. II-822

Appendix I - Industrial Classifications

APPENDIX I - INDUSTRIAL CLASSIFICATIONS

ISIC COVERAGE

This appendix lists the International Standard Industrial Classification Codes (ISICs). Entries in the body of the book are arranged according to the Standard Industrial Classification (SIC) system of the U.S. Department of Commerce. Products may be located using either the SIC Coverage listing beginning on page 967 or the Products, Services, Names, and Issues Index beginning on page 877.

0110 Growing of crops; market gardening; horticulture
0111 Growing of cereals and other crops nec
0112 Growing of vegetables, horticultural specialties and nursery products
0113 Growing of fruits, nuts, beverage and spice crops
0120 Farming of animals
0121 Farming of cattle, sheep, goats, horses, asses, mules and hinnies; dairy farming
0122 Other animal farming; production of animal products nec
0130 Growing of crops combined with farming of animals (mixed farming)
0140 Agricultural and animal husbandry service activities, except veterinary activities
0150 Hunting, trapping and game propagation including related service activities
0200 Forestry, logging, and related service activities
0500 Fishing, operation of fish hatcheries and fish farms; service activities incidental to fishing
1010 Mining and agglomeration of hard coal
1020 Mining and agglomeration of lignite
1030 Extraction and agglomeration of peat
1110 Extraction of crude petroleum and natural gas
1120 Service activities incidental to oil and gas extraction excluding surveying
1200 Mining of uranium and thorium ores
1310 Mining of iron ores
1320 Mining of non-ferrous metal ores, except uranium and thorium ores
1410 Quarrying of stone, sand and clay
1420 Mining and quarrying, nec
1421 Mining of chemical and fertilizer minerals
1422 Extraction of salt
1429 Other mining and quarrying nec
1510 Production, processing, and preservation of meat, fish, fruit, vegetables, oils and fats
1511 Production, processing and preserving of meat and meat products
1512 Processing and preserving of fish and fish products

1513 Processing and preserving of fruits and vegetables
1514 Manufacture of vegetable and animal oils and fats
1520 Manufacture of dairy products
1530 Manufacture of grain mill products, starches and starch products, and prepared animal feeds
1531 Manufacture of grain mill products
1532 Manufacture of starches and starch products
1533 Manufacture of prepared animal feeds
1540 Manufacture of other food products
1541 Manufacture of bakery products
1542 Manufacture of sugar
1543 Manufacture of cocoa, chocolate, and sugar confectionery
1544 Manufacture of macaroni, noodles, couscous and similar farinaceous products
1549 Manufacture of other food products nec
1550 Manufacture of beverages
1551 Distilling, rectifying and blending of spirits; ethyl alcohol production from fermented materials
1552 Manufacture of wines
1553 Manufacture of malt liquors and malt
1554 Manufacture of soft drinks; production of mineral waters
1600 Manufacture of tobacco products
1710 Spinning, weaving and finishing of textiles
1711 Preparation and spinning of textile fibers; weaving of textiles
1712 Finishing of textiles
1720 Manufacture of other textiles
1721 Manufacture of made-up textile articles, except apparel
1722 Manufacture of carpets and rugs
1723 Manufacture of cordage, rope, twine and netting
1729 Manufacture of other textiles nec
1730 Manufacture of knitted and crocheted fabrics and articles
1810 Manufacture of wearing apparel, except fur apparel

1820	Dressing and dyeing of fur; manufacture of articles of fur	2422	Manufacture of paints, varnishes, and similar coatings, printing ink and mastics
1910	Tanning and dressing of leather; manufacture of luggage, handbags, saddlery and harness	2423	Manufacture of pharmaceuticals, medicinal chemicals, and botanical products
1911	Tanning and dressing of leather	2424	Manufacture of soap and detergents, cleaning and polishing preparations, perfumes and toilet preparations
1912	Manufacture of luggage, handbags and the like, saddlery and harness		
1920	Manufacture of footwear	2429	Manufacture of other chemical products nec
2010	Sawmilling and planning of wood	2430	Manufacture of man-made fibers
2020	Manufacture of products of wood, cork, straw and plaiting materials	2510	Manufacture of rubber products
		2511	Manufacture of rubber tires and tubes; retreading and rebuilding of rubber tires
2021	Manufacture of veneer sheets; manufacture of plywood, laminboard, particle board and other panels and boards	2519	Manufacture of other rubber products
		2520	Manufacture of plastic products
		2610	Manufacture of glass and glass products
2022	Manufacture of builders' carpentry and joinery	2690	Manufacture of non-metallic minerals products nec
2023	Manufacture of wood containers	2691	Manufacture of non-structural non-refractory ceramic ware
2029	Manufacture of other products of wood; manufacture of articles of cork, straw and plaiting materials		
		2692	Manufacture of refractory ceramic products
		2693	Manufacture of structural non-refractory clay and ceramic products
2101	Manufacture of pulp, paper, and paperboard		
2102	Manufacture of corrugated paper and paperboard and of containers of paper and paperboard	2694	Manufacture of cement, lime and plaster
		2695	Manufacture of articles of concrete, cement and plaster
2109	Manufacture of other articles of paper and paperboard	2696	Cutting, shaping, and finishing of stone
		2699	Manufacture of other non-metallic mineral products nec
2210	Publishing		
2211	Publishing of books, brochures, musical books, and other publications	2710	Manufacture of basic iron and steel
		2720	Manufacture of basic precious and non-ferrous metals
2212	Publishing of newspapers, journals, and periodicals		
		2730	Casting of metals
2213	Publishing of recorded media	2731	Casting of iron and steel
2219	Other publishing	2732	Casting of non-ferrous metals
2220	Printing and service activities related to printing	2810	Manufacture of structural metal products, tanks, reservoirs and steam generators
2221	Printing		
2222	Service activities related to printing	2811	Manufacture of structural metal products
2230	Reproduction of recorded media	2812	Manufacture of tanks, reservoirs and containers of metals
2310	Manufacture of coke oven products		
2320	Manufacturer of refined petroleum products	2813	Manufacture of steam generators, except central heating hot water boilers
2330	Processing of nuclear fuel		
2410	Manufacture of basic chemicals	2890	Manufacture of other fabricated metal products; metal working service activities
2411	Manufacture of basic chemicals, except fertilizers and nitrogen compounds		
		2891	Forging, pressing, stamping and roll-forming of metal; powder metallurgy
2412	Manufacture of fertilizers and nitrogen compounds		
		2892	Treatment and coating of metals; general mechanical engineering on a fee or contract basis
2413	Manufacture of plastics in primary forms and of synthetic rubber		
		2893	Manufacture of cutlery, hand tools, and general hardware
2420	Manufacture of other chemical products		
2421	Manufacture of pesticides and other agro-chemical products	2899	Manufacture of other fabricated metal products nec
		2910	Manufacture of general purpose machinery
		2911	Manufacture of engines and turbines, except aircraft, vehicle and cycle engines

2912	Manufacture of pumps, compressors, taps, and valves	3320	Manufacture of optical instruments and photographic equipment
2913	Manufacture of bearings, gears, gearing and driving elements	3330	Manufacture of watches and clocks
2914	Manufacture of ovens, furnaces and furnace burners	3410	Manufacture of motor vehicles
2915	Manufacture of lifting and handling equipment	3420	Manufacture of bodies (coachwork) for motor vehicles; manufacture of trailers and semi-trailers
2919	Manufacture of other general purpose machinery	3430	Manufacture of parts and accessories for motor vehicles and their engines
2920	Manufacture of special purpose machinery	3510	Building and repairing of ships and boats
2921	Manufacture of agricultural and forestry machinery	3511	Building and repairing of ships
2922	Manufacture of machine-tools	3512	Building and repairing of pleasure and sporting boats
2923	Manufacture of machinery for metallurgy	3520	Manufacture of railway and tramway locomotives and rolling stock
2924	Manufacture of machinery for mining, quarrying and construction	3530	Manufacture of aircraft and spacecraft
2925	Manufacture of machinery for food, beverage, and tobacco processing	3590	Manufacture of transport equipment nec
2926	Manufacture of machinery for textile, apparel and leather production	3591	Manufacture of motorcycles
2927	Manufacture of weapons and ammunition	3592	Manufacture of bicycles and invalid carriages
2929	Manufacture of other special purpose machinery	3599	Manufacture of other transport equipment nec
2930	Manufacture of domestic appliances nec	3610	Manufacture of furniture
3000	Manufacture of office, accounting, and computing machinery	3690	Manufacturing nec
3110	Manufacture of electric motors, generators and transformers	3691	Manufacture of jewelry and related articles
		3692	Manufacture of musical instruments
3120	Manufacture of electricity distribution and control apparatus	3693	Manufacture of sports goods
		3694	Manufacture of games and toys
3130	Manufacture of insulated wire and cable	3699	Other manufacturing nec
3140	Manufacture of accumulators, primary cells, and primary batteries	3710	Recycling of metal waste and scrap
		3720	Recycling of non-metal waste and scrap
3150	Manufacture of electric lamps and lighting equipment	4010	Production, collection, and distribution of electricity
3190	Manufacture of other electrical equipment nec	4020	Manufacture of gas; distribution of gaseous fuels through mains
3210	Manufacture of electronic valves and tubes and other electronic components	4030	Steam and hot water supply
		4100	Collection, purification, and distribution of water
3220	Manufacture of television and radio transmitters and apparatus for line telephony and line telegraphy	4510	Site preparation
		4520	Building of complete constructions or parts thereof; civil engineering
3230	Manufacture of television and radio receivers, sound or video recording or reproducing apparatus, and associated goods	4530	Building installation
		4540	Building completion
		4550	Renting of construction or demolition equipment with operator
3310	Manufacture of medical appliances and instruments and appliances for measuring, checking, testing, navigating, and other purposes, except optical instruments	5010	Sale of motor vehicles
		5020	Maintenance and repair of motor vehicles
		5030	Sale of motor vehicle parts and accessories
		5040	Sale, maintenance and repair of motorcycles and related parts and accessories
3311	Manufacture of medical and surgical equipment and orthopedic appliances	5050	Retail sale of automotive fuel
		5110	Wholesale on a fee or contract basis
3312	Manufacture of instruments and appliances for measuring, checking, testing, navigating, and other purposes, except industrial process control equipment	5120	Wholesale of agricultural raw materials, live animals, food, beverages and tobacco
		5121	Wholesale of agricultural raw materials and live animals
3313	Manufacture of industrial process control equipment	5122	Wholesale of food, beverages, and tobacco
		5130	Wholesale of household goods

Appendix I - Industrial Classifications

5131	Wholesale of textiles, clothing, and footwear
5139	Wholesale of other household goods
5140	Wholesale of non-agricultural intermediate products, waste and scrap
5141	Wholesale of solid, liquid and gaseous fuels and related products
5142	Wholesale of metals and metal ores
5143	Wholesale of construction materials, hardware, plumbing and heating equipment and supplies
5149	Wholesale of other intermediate products, waste and scrap
5150	Wholesale of machinery, equipment, and supplies
5190	Other wholesale
5210	Non-specialized retail trade in stores
5211	Retail sale in non-specialized stores with food, beverages, or tobacco predominating
5219	Other retail sale in non-specialized stores
5220	Retail sale of food, beverages, and tobacco in specialized stores
5230	Other retail trade of new goods in specialized stores
5231	Retail sale of pharmaceutical and medical goods, cosmetic and toilet articles
5232	Retail sale of textiles, clothing, footwear, and leather goods
5233	Retail sale of household appliances, articles, and equipment
5234	Retail sale of hardware, paints and glass
5239	Other retail sale in specialized stores
5240	Retail sale of second-hand goods in stores
5250	Retail trade not in stores
5251	Retail sale via mail-order houses
5252	Retail sale via stalls and markets
5259	Other non-store retail sale
5260	Repair of personal and household goods
5510	Hotels; camping sites and other provision of short-stay accommodation
5520	Restaurants, bars and canteens
6010	Transport via railways
6020	Other land transport
6021	Other scheduled passenger land transport
6022	Other non-scheduled passenger land transport
6023	Freight transport by road
6030	Transport via pipelines
6110	Sea and coastal water transport
6120	Inland water transport
6210	Scheduled air transport
6220	Non-scheduled air transport
6300	Supporting and auxiliary transport activities; activities of travel agencies
6301	Cargo handling
6302	Storage and warehousing
6303	Other supporting transport activities

6304	Activities of travel agencies and tour operators; tourist assistance activities nec
6309	Activities of other transport agencies
6410	Post and courier activities
6411	National post activities
6412	Courier activities other than national post activities
6420	Telecommunications
6510	Monetary intermediation
6511	Central banking
6519	Other monetary intermediation
6559	Other financial intermediation nec
6590	Other financial leasing
6591	Financial leasing
6592	Other credit granting
6600	Insurance and pension funding, except compulsory social security
6601	Life insurance
6602	Pension funding
6603	Non-life insurance
6710	Activities auxiliary to financial intermediation, except insurance and pension funding
6711	Administration of financial markets
6712	Security dealing activities
6719	Activities auxiliary to financial intermediation nec
6720	Activities auxiliary to insurance and pension funding
7010	Real estate activities with own or leased property
7020	Real estate activities on a fee or contract basis
7110	Renting of transport equipment
7111	Renting of land transport equipment
7112	Renting of water transport equipment
7113	Renting of air transport equipment
7120	Renting of other machinery and equipment
7121	Renting of agricultural machinery and equipment
7122	Renting of construction and civil engineering machinery and equipment
7123	Renting of office machinery and equipment (including computers)
7129	Renting of other machinery and equipment nec
7130	Renting of personal and household goods nec
7210	Hardware consultancy
7220	Software consultancy and supply
7230	Data processing
7240	Database activities
7250	Maintenance and repair of office, accounting and computing machinery
7290	Other computer related activities
7310	Research and experimental development on natural sciences and engineering (NSE)

7320   Research and experimental development on social sciences and humanities (SSH)

7410   Legal, accounting, bookkeeping, and auditing activities; tax consultancy; market research and public opinion polling; business and management consultancy

7411   Legal activities

7412   Accounting, book-keeping and auditing activities; tax consultancy

7413   Market research and public opinion polling

7414   Business and management consultancy activities

7420   Architectural, engineering and other technical activities

7421   Architectural and engineering activities and related technical consultancy

7422   Technical testing and analysis

7430   Advertising

7490   Business activities nec

7491   Labor recruitment and provision of personnel

7492   Investigation and security activities

7493   Building-cleaning activities

7494   Photographic activities

7495   Packaging activities

7499   Other business activities nec

7510   Administration of the State and the economic and social policy of the community

7511   General (overall) public service activities

7512   Regulation of the activities of agencies that provide health care, education, cultural service, and other social services, excluding social security

7513   Regulation of and contribution to more efficient operation of business

7514   Ancillary service activities for the Government as a whole

7520   Provision of services to the community as a whole

7521   Foreign affairs

7522   Defense activities

7523   Public order and safety activities

7530   Compulsory social security activities

8010   Primary education

8020   Secondary education

8021   General secondary education

8022   Technical and vocational secondary education

8030   Higher education

8090   Adult and other education

8510   Human health activities

8511   Hospital activities

8512   Medical and dental practice activities

8519   Other human health activities

8520   Veterinary activities

8530   Social work activities

8531   Social work with accommodation

8532   Social work without accommodation

9000   Sewage and refuse disposal, sanitation, and similar activities

9110   Activities of business, employers and professional organizations

9111   Activities of business and employers' organizations

9112   Activities of professional organizations

9120   Activities of trade unions

9190   Activities of other membership organizations

9191   Activities of religious organizations

9192   Activities of political organizations

9199   Activities of other membership organizations nec

9210   Motion picture, radio, television and other entertainment activities

9211   Motion picture and video production and distribution

9212   Motion picture projection

9213   Radio and television activities

9214   Dramatic arts, music, and other arts activities

9219   Other entertainment activities nec

9220   News agencies activities

9230   Library, archives, museums and other cultural activities

9231   Library and archives activities

9232   Museums activities and preservation of historical sites and buildings

9233   Botanical and zoological gardens and nature reserves activities

9240   Sporting and other recreational activities

9241   Sporting activities

9249   Other recreational activities

9300   Other service activities

9301   Washing and (dry-) cleaning of textile and fur products

9302   Hairdressing and other beauty treatment

9303   Funeral and related activities

9309   Other service activities nec

9500   Private households with employed persons

9900   Extra-territorial organizations and bodies

Appendix I - Industrial Classifications

APPENDIX I - INDUSTRIAL CLASSIFICATIONS
HARMONIZED CODE COVERAGE

This appendix lists the Harmonized Code Classifications (HCs). Entries in the body of the book are arranged according to the Standard Industrial Classification (SIC) system of the U.S. Department of Commerce. Products may be located using either the SIC Coverage listing beginning on page 967 or the Products, Services, Names, and Issues Index beginning on page 877.

01 Live animals

02 Meat and edible meat offal

03 Fish and crustaceans, mollusks and other aquatic invertebrates

04 Dairy produce; birds' eggs; natural honey, edible products of animal origin, not elsewhere specified or included

05 Products of animal origin, not elsewhere specified or included

06 Live trees and other plants; bulbs, roots, and the like; cut flowers and ornamental foliage

07 Edible vegetables and certain roots and tubers

08 Edible fruits and nuts; peel of citrus fruits or melons

09 Coffee, tea, mate, and spices

10 Cereals

11 Products of the milling industry; malt; starches; insulin; wheat gluten

12 Oil seeds and oleaginous fruits; miscellaneous grains, seeds, and fruits; industrial or medicinal plants; straw and fodder

13 Lac; gums, resins and other vegetable saps and extract

14 Vegetable plaiting materials; vegetable products not elsewhere specified or included

15 Animal or vegetable fats and oils and their cleavage products; prepared edible fats; animal or vegetable waxes

16 Preparation of meat, of fish, or of crustaceans, mollusks, or other aquatic invertebrates

17 Sugars and sugar confectionery

18 Cocoa and cocoa preparations

19 Preparations of cereals, flour, starch or milk; bakers' wares

20 Preparations of vegetables, fruits, nuts, or other parts of plants

21 Miscellaneous edible preparations

22 Beverages, spirits, and vinegar

23 Residues and waste from the food industries; prepared animal feed

24 Tobacco and manufactured tobacco substitutes

25 Salt; sulfur; earths and stone; plastering materials, lime and cement

26 Ores, slag, and ash

27 Mineral fuels, mineral oils and products of their distillation; bituminous substances; mineral waxes

28 Inorganic chemicals; organic or inorganic compounds of precious metals, of rare-earth metals, of radioactive elements, or of isotopes

29 Organic chemicals

30 Pharmaceutical products

31 Fertilizers

32 Tanning or dyeing extracts; tannins and their derivatives; dyes, pigments, and other coloring matter; paints and varnishes; putty and other mastics; inks

33 Essential oils and resinoids; perfumery, cosmetic or toilet preparations

34 Soaps; organic surface-active agents; washing preparations; lubricating preparations; artificial waxes; prepared waxes; polishing or scouring preparations; candles and similar articles; modeling pastes; "dental waxes," and dental preparations with a basis of plaster

35 Albuminoidal substances; modified starches; glues; enzymes

36 Explosives; pyrotechnic products; matches; pyrotechnic alloys; certain combustible preparations

37 Photographic or cinematographic goods

38 Miscellaneous chemical products

39 Plastics and articles thereof

40 Rubber and articles thereof

41 Raw hides and skins (other than furskins) and leather

42 Articles of leather; saddlery and harness; travel goods, handbags and similar containers; articles of animal gut (other than silkworm gut)

43 Furskins and artificial fur; manufactures thereof

44 Wood and articles of wood; wood charcoal

45 Cork and articles of cork

46 Manufacturers of stray, of esparto or of other plaiting materials; basketware and wickerwork

47 Pulp of wood or of other fibrous cellulosic material; waste and scrap of paper or paperboard

48 Paper and paperboard; articles of paper pulp, of paper, or of paperboard

49 Printed books, newspapers, pictures, and other products of the printing industry; manuscripts, typescripts, and plans

50 Silk

51 Wool; fine or coarse animal hair; horsehair yarn and woven fabric

52 Cotton

53 Other vegetable textile fibers; paper yarn and woven fabrics of paper yarn

54 Man-made filaments

55 Man-made staple fibers

56 Wadding, felt and nonwovens; special yarns; twine, cordage, ropes and cables and articles thereof

57 Carpets and other textile floor coverings

58 Special woven fabrics; tufted textile fabrics; lace; tapestries; trimmings; embroidery

59 Impregnated, coated, covered or laminated textile fabrics; textile articles of a kind suitable for industrial use

60 Knitted or crocheted fabrics

61 Articles of apparel and clothing accessories, knitted or crocheted

62 Articles of apparel and clothing accessories, not knitted or crocheted

63 Other made-up textile articles; needle craft sets; worn clothing and worn textile articles; rags

64 Footwear, gaiters and the like; parts of such articles

65 Headgear and parts thereof

66 Umbrellas, sun umbrellas, walking sticks, seatsticks, whips, riding crops and parts thereof

67 Prepared feathers and down and articles made of feathers or of down; artificial flowers; articles of human hair

68 Articles of stone, plaster, cement, asbestos, mica or similar materials

69 Ceramic products

70 Glass and glassware

71 Natural or cultured pearls, precious or semiprecious stones, precious metals; metals clad with precious metal, and articles thereof; imitation jewelry; coin

72 Iron and steel

73 Articles of iron or steel

74 Copper and articles thereof

75 Nickel and articles thereof

76 Aluminum and articles thereof

77 Reserved for possible future use

78 Lead and articles thereof

79 Zinc and articles thereof

80 Tin and articles thereof

81 Other base metals; cermets; articles thereof

82 Tools, implements, cutlery, spoons and forks, of base metal; parts thereof of base metal

83 Miscellaneous articles of base metal

84 Nuclear reactors, boilers, machinery and mechanical appliances; parts thereof

85 Electrical machinery and equipment and parts thereof; sound recorders and reproducers, television image and sound recorders and reproducers, and parts and accessories of such articles

86 Railway or tramway locomotives, rolling stock and parts thereof; railway or tramway track fixtures and fittings and parts thereof; mechanical (including electromechanical) traffic signalling equipment of all kinds

87 Vehicles, other than railway or tramway rolling stock, and parts and accessories thereof

88 Aircraft, spacecraft, and parts thereof

89 Ships, boats, and floating structures

90 Optical, photographic, cinematographic, measuring, checking, precision, medical or surgical instruments and apparatus; parts and accessories thereof

91 Clocks and watches and parts thereof

92 Musical instruments; parts and accessories of such articles

93 Arms and ammunition; parts and accessories thereof

94 Furniture; bedding, mattresses, mattress supports, cushions and similar stuffed furnishings; lamps and lighting fittings, not elsewhere specified or included; illuminated signs; illuminated nameplates and the like; prefabricated buildings

95 Toys, games, and sports equipment; parts and accessories thereof

96 Miscellaneous manufactured articles

97 Works of art, collectors' pieces and antiques

APPENDIX II

Annotated Source List

The following listing provides the names, publishers, addresses, telephone and fax numbers (if available), and frequency of publication for the primary sources used in *Market Share Reporter*.

2010 EFT Data Book - A Supplement to ATM & Debit News, PaymentsSource, One State Street Plaza, 27th Floor, New York, NY 10004, *Telephone*: (212) 803-8200, *Fax*: (212) 843-9600, *Published*: annual, *Price*: $995 one year.

2011-2012 Nonfoods Handbook - A Supplement to Grocery Headquarters, Grocery Headquarters Magazine, Macfadden Communications Group, 333 Seventh Ave. 11th Floor, New York, N.Y. 10001, *Telephone*: (646) 274-3525, *Published*: annual, *Price*: free to qualified subscribers.

2011 Consumer Perishables Handbook - A Supplement to Grocery Headquarters, Grocery Headquarters Magazine, Macfadden Communications Group, 333 Seventh Ave. 11th Floor, New York, N.Y. 10001, *Telephone*: (646) 274-3525, *Published*: annual, *Price*: free to subscribers.

Adhesives Magazine, Adhesives and Sealants Industry, 2401 W. Big Beaver Rd., Suite 700, Troy, MI 48084, *Telephone*: (281) 256-8492, *Fax*: (248) 283-6543, *Published*: monthly, *Price*: free to qualified subscribers.

AdNews, Yaffa Publishing Group, 17-21 Bellevue Street, Surry Hills NSW, 2010 Australia, *Telephone*: 02 9281 2333, *Fax*: 02 9281 2750, *Published*: monthly, *Price*: $110 one year.

Advertising Age, Crain Communications, Inc., 711 Third Avenue, New York, NY 10017-4036, *Telephone*: (212) 210-0100, *Fax*: (212) 210-0200, *Published*: weekly, *Price*: $99 per year.

Africa News Service, 922 M Street, Se #920-922, Washington, D.C. 20003-3615, *Telephone*: (202) 546-0777, *Published*: real-time.

Algeria Petrochemicals Report, Business Monitor International, Senator House, 85 Queen Victoria Street, London EC4V 4AB, United Kingdom, *Telephone*: +44 (0) 20 7248 0468, *Fax*: +44 (0) 20 7248 0467, *Published*: monthly.

A.M. Best Newswire, A.M. Best Co. Inc., Ambest Rd., Oldwick, NJ 08858, *Telephone*: (908) 439-2200, *Published*: real-time.

America's Intelligence Wire, FT Publications Inc., 14 East 60th Street, New York, NY 21002, *Telephone*: (212) 752-4500, *Fax*: (212) 319-0704, *Published*: real-time.

Architectural Record, Two Penn Plaza, 9th Floor, New York, NY 10121-2298, *Telephone*: (212) 904-2594, *Fax*: (212) 904-4256, *Published*: monthly, *Price*: $49 one year.

Argentina Autos Report, Business Monitor International, Senator House, 85 Queen Victoria Street, London EC4V 4AB, United Kingdom, *Telephone*: +44 (0) 20 7248 0468, *Fax*: +44 (0) 20 7248 0467, *Published*: monthly.

Argentina Telecommunications Report, Business Monitor International, Senator House, 85 Queen Victoria Street, London EC4V 4AB, United Kingdom, *Telephone*: +44 (0) 20 7248 0468, *Fax*: +44 (0) 20 7248 0467, *Published*: monthly.

AsiaPulse News, P.O. Box 3411, Rhodes Waterside, Rhodes NSW 2138, Australia, *Telephone*: +61 2 9322 8634, *Fax*: + 61 2 9322 8639, *Published*: real-time.

Atlanta Business Chronicle, American City Business Journals, Inc., 1801 Peachtree Street, Suite 150, Atlanta, GA 30309, *Telephone*: (404) 249-1000, *Fax*: (404) 249-1048, *Published*: weekly, *Price*: $87 one year.

Atlantic, Atlantic Media Company, 600 New Hampshire Ave., NW, Washington, D.C. 20008, *Telephone*: (202) 266-6000, *Fax*: (202) 266-6001, *Published*: 10 issues, *Price*: $14.90 one year.

Australia Telecommunications Report, Business Monitor International, Senator House, 85 Queen Victoria Street, London EC4V 4AB, United Kingdom, *Telephone*: +44 (0) 20 7248 0468, *Fax*: +44 (0) 20 7248 0467, *Published*: monthly.

Automotive News, Crain Communications Inc., 1155 Gratiot Avenue, Detroit, MI 48207-2997, *Telephone*: (313) 446-6031, *Fax*: (313) 446-8030, *Published*: weekly, *Price*: $149 one year.

Bahrain Telecommunications Report, Business Monitor International, Senator House, 85 Queen Victoria Street, London EC4V 4AB, United Kingdom, *Telephone*: +44 (0) 20 7248 0468, *Fax*: +44 (0) 20 7248 0467, *Published*: monthly.

Baking Management, Penton Media Inc., 330 N. Wabash, Ste. 2300, Chicago, IL 60611, *Telephone*: (312) 840-8449, *Fax*: (913) 514-3937, *Published*: monthly, *Price*: free to qualified subscribers.

Baltimore Business Journal, 111 Market Place, Suite 720, Baltimore, MD 21202, *Telephone*: (410) 576-1161, *Published*: weekly, *Price*: $93 one year.

Bangladesh Telecommunications Report, Business Monitor International, Senator House, 85 Queen Victoria Street, London EC4V 4AB, United Kingdom, *Telephone*: +44 (0) 20 7248 0468, *Fax*: +44 (0) 20 7248 0467, *Published*: monthly.

Barron's, 1211 Ave. of the Americas, New York, NY 10036, *Telephone*: (800)-DOWJONES, *Published*: weekly, *Price*: $99 one year.

Belgium Telecommunications Report, Business Monitor International, Senator House, 85 Queen Victoria Street, London EC4V 4AB, United Kingdom, *Telephone*: +44 (0) 20 7248 0468, *Fax*: +44 (0) 20 7248 0467, *Published*: monthly.

Best's Review, A.M. Best Co. Inc., Ambest Rd., Oldwick, NJ 08858, *Telephone*: (908) 439-2200, *Published*: monthly, *Price*: $60 one year.

Beverage Dynamics, Adams Beverage Group, 17 High Street, 2nd Floor, Norwalk, CT 06851, *Telephone*: (203) 855-8499, *Fax*: (203) 855-9446, *Published*: bimonthly, *Price*: free to qualified subscribers.

Beverage Industry, Stagnito Communications, 155 Pfingsten Road, Suite 205, Deerfield, IL 60015, *Telephone*: (847) 205-5660, *Fax*: (847) 205-5680, *Published*: monthly, *Price*: free to qualified subscribers.

Beverage Spectrum, 44 Pleasant St., Suite 110, Watertown, MA 02472, *Telephone*: (617) 715-9670, *Fax*: (617) 876-1279, *Published*: 7x/year, *Price*: free to qualified subscribers.

Beverage World, VNU Business Publications USA, Inc., 770 Broadway, New York, NY 10003, *Telephone*: (847) 763-9050, *Fax*: (847) 763-9037, *Published*: monthly, *Price*: $179 one year.

Bicycle Retailer & Industry News, VNU Business Publications USA, Inc., 25431 Cabot Road, Suite 204, Laguna Hills, CA 92653, *Telephone*: (949) 206-1677, *Fax*: (949) 206-1675, *Published*: monthly, *Price*: $65 one year.

Billboard, VNU Business Publications USA, Inc., 770 Broadway, New York, NY 10003, *Telephone*: (847) 763-9050, *Fax*: (847) 763-9037, *Published*: weekly, *Price*: $24.95 one year.

Book Business, North American Publishing Company, 1500 Spring Garden Street - 12th Floor, Philadelphia PA 19130, *Telephone*: (888) 889-9491, *Published*: monthly, *Price*: free.

Bottled Water Reporter, International Bottled Water Association, 1700 Diagonal Road Suite 650, Alexandria, VA 22314, *Telephone*: (703) 683-5213, *Published*: monthly, *Price*: free to qualified subscribers.

Broadcasting & Cable, Reed Business Information, 360 Park Avenue South, New York, NY 10010, *Telephone*: (646) 746-6400, *Published*: monthly, *Price*: $199.99.

Bulgaria Telecommunications Report, Business Monitor International, Senator House, 85 Queen Victoria Street, London EC4V 4AB, United Kingdom, *Telephone*: +44 (0) 20 7248 0468, *Fax*: +44 (0) 20 7248 0467, *Published*: monthly.

Business Economics, National Association for Business Economics, 1233 20th Street NW #505, Washington D.C. 20036, *Telephone*: (202) 463-6223, *Fax*: (202) 463-6239, *Published*: 4x/year, *Price*: $269 one year.

Business Wire, 44 Montgomery Street, 39th Floor, San Francisco, CA 94104, *Telephone*: (415) 986-4422, *Published*: real-time.

BusinessWeek, 1221 Avenue of The Americas, 43rd fl., New York, NY 10020, *Telephone*: (212) 512-2511, *Published*: weekly, *Price*: $46 for 46 issues.

Cabinetmaker+ FDM, CCI Media, 2240 Country Club Pkwy. SE, Cedar Rapids, IA 52403, *Telephone*: (448) 807-3540, *Published*: monthly, *Price*: free to qualified subscribers.

Candy Industry, Stagnito Communications, 155 Pfingsten Road, Suite 205, Deerfield, IL 60015, *Telephone*: (847) 205-5660 Ext. 4039, *Fax*: (847) 205-5680, *Published*: monthly, *Price*: free to qualified subscribers.

Caribbean Food & Drink Report, Business Monitor International, Senator House, 85 Queen Victoria Street, London EC4V 4AB, United Kingdom, *Telephone*: +44 (0) 20 7248 0468, *Fax*: +44 (0) 20 7248 0467, *Published*: monthly.

Center Store - A Supplement to Grocery Headquarters, Macfadden Grocery Headquarters, 333 Seventh Ave., 11th Floor, New York, NY 10001, *Telephone*: (212) 979-4800, *Fax*: (646) 674-0102, *Published*: annual, *Price*: free to qualified subscribers.

Central America Telecommunications Report, Business Monitor International, Mermaid House, 2 Puddle Dock, London EC4V 3DS, United Kingdom, *Telephone*: +44 (0) 20 7248 0468, *Fax*: +44 (0) 20 7248 0467, *Published*: monthly.

Chain Drug Review, Racher Press, 220 5th Ave, New York, NY 10001, *Telephone*: (212) 213-6000, *Fax*: (212) 725-3961, *Published*: 21x/yr., *Price*: free to qualified subscribers.

Channel Insider, T in Canada.ca Inc. 24-4 Vata Court Aurora, ON, L4G 4B6, *Telephone*: (905) 727-3875, *Fax*: (905) 727-4428, *Published*: 10x/year.

Chemical Week, Chemical Week Associates, 110 William Street, New York, NY 10038, *Telephone*: (212) 621-4900, *Fax*: (212) 621-4800, *Published*: weekly, except four combination issues (total of 49 issues), *Price*: $159 per year in the U.S.; $180 per year in Canada.

Chemical Weekly, 602, 6th Floor, B-Wing, Godrej Coliseum, K.J. Somaiya Hospital Road, Sion (East), Mumbai 400 022, *Telephone*: +91-22-2404 4477, *Fax*: +91-22-2404 4450, *Published*: weekly.

Chile Mining Report, Business Monitor International, Senator House, 85 Queen Victoria Street, London EC4V 4AB, United Kingdom, *Telephone*: +44 (0) 20 7248 0468, *Fax*: +44 (0) 20 7248 0467, *Published*: monthly.

Chile Telecommunications Report, Business Monitor International, Senator House, 85 Queen Victoria Street, London EC4V 4AB, United Kingdom, *Telephone*: +44 (0) 20 7248 0468, *Fax*: +44 (0) 20 7248 0467, *Published*: monthly.

China Chemical Reporter, No. 53, AnWaiXiaoGuan Street, Beijing, China, *Telephone*: (086) 010-64444031, 64421206, *Fax*: (086) 010-64421206.

China Food & Drink Report, Business Monitor International, Senator House, 85 Queen Victoria Street, London EC4V 4AB, United Kingdom, *Telephone*: +44 (0) 20 7248 0468, *Fax*: +44 (0) 20 7248 0467, *Published*: monthly.

China Insurance Report, Business Monitor International, Senator House, 85 Queen Victoria Street, London EC4V 4AB, United Kingdom, *Telephone*: +44 (0) 20 7248 0468, *Fax*: +44 (0) 20 7248 0467, *Published*: monthly.

Club Business International, International Health, Racquet Sports Association, 70 Fargo Street, Boston, MA 02210, *Telephone*: (800) 228-4772, *Fax*: (617) 951-0056, *Published*: monthly, *Price*: $74.95 one year.

Collision Week, Quandec Corporation, P.O. Box 538, Tannersville, PA 18372, *Telephone*: (570) 629-5920, *Published*: weekly, *Price*: $198 one year.

Colombia Telecommunications Report, Business Monitor International, Senator House, 85 Queen Victoria Street, London EC4V 4AB, United Kingdom, *Telephone*: +44 (0) 20 7248 0468, *Fax*: +44 (0) 20 7248 0467, *Published*: monthly.

Convenience Store News, VNU Business Publications USA, Inc., 770 Broadway, New York, NY 10003, *Telephone*: (847) 763-9050, *Fax*: (847) 763-9037, *Published*: 15x/yr., *Price*: $89 one year.

Cosmetics Business, HPCi Media Limited, Unit 1 Vogans Mill Wharf, Mill Street, London SE1 2BZ, United Kingdom, *Telephone*: +44 (0) 20 7193 1279, *Published*: monthly.

Crain's Chicago Business, Crain Communications Inc., 360 N. Michigan Ave., Chicago, IL 60611, *Telephone*: (312) 649-5411, *Fax*: (312) 280-3150, *Published*: weekly, *Price*: $61.60 one year.

Crain's Detroit Business, Crain Communications Inc., 1155 Gratiot Ave., Detroit, MI 48207-3187, *Telephone*: (888) 909-9111, *Published*: weekly, except semiweekly the fourth week in May, *Price*: $40.60 one year.

CRN, CMP Media, One Jericho Plaza, Jericho, NY 11753, *Telephone*: (877) 705-5559, *Published*: weekly, *Price*: free to qualified subscribers.

Croatia Telecommunications Report, Business Monitor International, Senator House, 85 Queen Victoria Street, London EC4V 4AB, United Kingdom, *Telephone*: +44 (0) 20 7248 0468, *Fax*: +44 (0) 20 7248 0467, *Published*: monthly.

CSP, CSP Information Group, 1100 Jorie Blvd. Suite 260, Oak Brook, IL 60523, *Telephone*: (630) 574-5075, *Fax*: (630) 574-5175, *Published*: monthly, *Price*: free to qualified subscribers.

Czech Republic Food & Drink Report, Business Monitor International, Senator House, 85 Queen Victoria Street, London EC4V 4AB, United Kingdom, *Telephone*: +44 (0) 20 7248 0468, *Fax*: +44 (0) 20 7248 0467, *Published*: monthly.

Czech Republic Telecommunications Report, Business Monitor International, Senator House, 85 Queen Victoria Street, London EC4V 4AB, United Kingdom, *Telephone*: +44 (0) 20 7248 0468, *Fax*: +44 (0) 20 7248 0467, *Published*: monthly.

D Business, 117 West Third Street, Royal Oak, MI 48067, *Telephone*: (248) 691-1800, *Fax*: (248) 691-4531, *Published*: bimonthly, *Price*: $9.95 one year.

Daily Star, 64-65, Kazi Nazrul Islam Avenue, Dhaka-1215.

Dairy Foods, 1050 IL Route 83, Suite 200, Bensenville, IL 60106, *Telephone*: (630) 694-4341, *Fax*: (630) 227-0527, *Published*: monthly, except semimonthly in August, *Price*: free to qualified subscribers.

Datamonitor Industry Market Research, Datamonitor USA, 1 Park Avenue, 14th Floor, New York, NY 10016-5802, *Telephone*: (212) 686-7400.

Dealernews, Advanstar Communications Inc., One Park Avenue, New York, NY 10016, *Telephone*: (212) 951-6600, *Fax*: (212) 951-6666, *Published*: monthly, *Price*: $43 one year.

Demoliton & Recycling International, KHL Group, Southfields, Southview Road, Wadhurst, East Sussex TN5 6TP, United Kingdom, *Telephone*: +44 (0) 1892 784088, *Fax*: +44 (0) 1892 784086, *Published*: monthly, *Price*: free, to qualified subscribers.

Detroit Free Press, Knight-Ridder, Inc., 600 Fort, Detroit, MI 48226, *Telephone*: (313) 222-6400, *Published*: daily, *Price*: $234 a year Detroit area.

Door and Window Manufacturer, 385 Garrisonville Rd. #116 Stafford, VA 22554, *Telephone*: (540) 720-5584, *Published*: 9x/year.

Drinks International, Reed Business Media, Shaw House, Pegler Way, Crawley, West Sussex, RH11 7AF, United Kingdom, *Telephone*: +44 (0) 20 8652 3500, *Fax*: +44 (0) 1293 474010, *Published*: monthly.

Drug Store News, Lehbhar-Friedman Inc., 425 Park Ave, New York, NY 10022, *Telephone*: (800) 216-7117, *Published*: 2x/mo., *Price*: $119 one year.

DrugStore Management, Millennium Media L.L.C., 3 Chaser Court, Holmdel NJ 07733, *Telephone*: (732) 888-0066, *Published*: annual.

Earth Imaging Journal, P.O. Box 336400, Greeley, CO 80633, *Telephone*: (970) 443-5211, *Published*: monthly, *Price*: free to qualified subscribers.

Editor & Publisher, 770 Broadway, New York, NY 10003-9595, *Telephone*: (800) 336-4380, *Fax*: (800) 654-5370, *Published*: monthly, *Price*: $99 per year.

EE Times, CMP Publications, 600 Community Drive, Manhasset NY 11030, *Telephone*: (516) 562-5000, *Fax*: (516) 562-5995, *Published*: monthly, *Price*: $280 one year.

eGroomer Journal, Find A Groomer Inc., P.O. Box 2489. Yelm, WA 98597, *Telephone*: (360) 446-5348, *Published*: quarterly, *Price*: free.

Egypt Telecommunications Report, Business Monitor International, Senator House, 85 Queen Victoria Street, London EC4V 4AB, United Kingdom, *Telephone*: +44 (0) 20 7248 0468, *Fax*: +44 (0) 20 7248 0467, *Published*: monthly.

Electronic Retailer, Electronic Retailing Association, 607 14th street, NW, Suite 530, Washington D.C. 20005, *Telephone*: (800) 987-6462, *Fax*: (703) 841-1751, *Published*: monthly.

Engine Yearbook, UBM Aviation, 3025 Highland Parkway Suite 200 Downers Grove Illinois 60515-5561, *Telephone*: (630) 515-5300, *Fax*: (630) 515-3251, *Published*: bimonthly.

ENR, McGraw-Hill Inc., Fulfillment Manager, ENR, P.O. Box 518, Highstown, NJ 08520, *Telephone*: (609) 426-7070 or (212) 512-3549, *Fax*: (212) 512-3150, *Published*: weekly, *Price*: $89 one year.

Entertainment Weekly, Time-Warner Inc., 1675 Broadway, New York, NY 10019, *Telephone*: (800) 828-6882, *Published*: weekly, *Price*: $38.95 one year.

Entrepreneur, Entrepreneur Media, 2445 McCabe Way, Ste. 400, Irvine, CA 92614, *Telephone*: (949) 261-2325, *Published*: monthly, *Price*: $12 one year.

Eurofresh Distribution, Av de Alicante, 1 -2° pta.5 46700, Gandia Spain, *Telephone*: +34 962 950 087, *Published*: monthly.

Feedstuffs, Miller Publishing Co., 12400 Whitewater Dr., Ste. 160, Minnetonka, MN 55343, *Telephone*: (952) 931-0211, *Fax*: (952) 938-1832, *Published*: weekly, *Price*: $144 one year.

Finance & Commerce, 730 2nd Ave. S., #100, Minneapolis, MN 55402, *Telephone*: (612) 333-4244, *Fax*: (612) 333-3243, *Published*: daily, *Price*: $229 one year.

Financial Stability Review, European Commercial Bank, Kaiserstrasse 2960311 Frankfurt am Main, Germany, *Telephone*: +49 69 13 44 0, *Published*: 2x/yr..

Financial Times, FT Publications Inc., 14 East 60th Street, New York, NY 21002, *Telephone*: (212) 752-4500, *Fax*: (212) 319-0704, *Published*: daily, except for Sundays and holidays, *Price*: $425 one year.

Flexible Packaging, Stagnito Communications Inc., An Ascend Media Company, 155 Pfingsten Road, Suite 205, Deerfield, IL 60015, *Telephone*: (847) 405-4000, *Fax*: (847) 405-4100, *Published*: monthly, *Price*: $95.22 one year.

Floor Covering Weekly, 50 Charles Lindbergh Blvd., Suite 100, Uniondale, NY 11553, *Telephone*: Tel: (516) 229-3600, *Fax*: (516) 227-1342, *Published*: weekly, *Price*: $61 one week.

Flow Control, Flow Control Magazine, Grand View Media Group, 200 Croft St. Suite 1, Birmingham, AL 35242, *Telephone*: (888) 431-2877, *Published*: monthly, *Price*: free to qualified subscribers.

Food & Beverage Packaging, 155 Pfingsten Road, Suite 205, Deerfield, IL 60015, *Telephone*: (847) 405-4000, *Fax*: (847) 405-4100, *Published*: monthly, *Price*: free to qualified subscribers.

Food Business News, Sosland Publishing Co., 4800 Main St., Suite 100, Kansas City, MO 64112, *Telephone*: (816) 756-1000, *Fax*: (816) 756-0494, *Published*: monthly, *Price*: free to qualified subscribers.

Food Engineering, 901 S. Bolmar Street, Suite P, West Chester, PA 19382, *Telephone*: (610) 436-4220, *Published*: monthly, *Price*: free to qualified subscribers.

Forbes, Forbes, Inc., 60 Fifth Avenue, New York, NY 10011, *Telephone*: (800) 888-9896, *Published*: 27x/yr., *Price*: $54 one year.

Fort Worth Star-Telegram, 309 West 7th St, Suite 1414, Fort Worth, TX 76102, *Telephone*: (877) 223-7355, *Published*: daily.

Fortune, Time Inc., Time & Life Building, Rockefeller Center, New York, NY 10020-1393, *Telephone*: (212) 522-1212, *Published*: twice monthly, except two issues combined into a single issue at year-end, *Price*: $139.72 one year.

France Telecommunications Report, Business Monitor International, Senator House, 85 Queen Victoria Street, London EC4V 4AB, United Kingdom, *Telephone*: +44 (0) 20 7248 0468, *Fax*: +44 (0) 20 7248 0467, *Published*: monthly.

Frozen & Dairy Buyer, 11472 S. Wilder St., Olathe, KS 66061, *Telephone*: (913) 481-5060, *Published*: monthly, *Price*: free to qualified subscribers.

Fuel & Lubricants International, F&L Asia Ltd., Room 2611-12, 26/F 302-308 Hennessy Road Wanchai, Hong Kong, *Telephone*: +852 8191 7449, *Fax*: +852 3753 5122, *Published*: $89.

Furniture Today, Reed Business Information, P.O. Box 2754, High Point, NC 27261-2754, *Telephone*: (336) 605-0121, *Fax*: (336) 605-1143, *Published*: weekly, *Price*: $159.97 one year.

Gear Technology, Randall Publications L.L.C., 1840 Jarvis Avenue, Elk Grove Village, IL 60007, *Telephone*: (847) 437-6604, ext 311, *Fax*: (847) 437-6618, *Published*: 8x/yr..

Global Cement, Pro Publications International Ltd., First Floor, Adelphi Court, 1 East Street, Epsom, Surrey, KT17 1BB, United Kingdom, *Telephone*: +44 (0) 1372 743837, *Fax*: +44 (0) 1372 743838, *Published*: monthly, *Price*: 150 euros one year.

Global Cosmetic Industry, Allured Publishing Corporation, P.O. Box 380, Mount Morris, IL 60154-0506, *Telephone*: (815) 734-1225, *Fax*: (815) 734-5887, *Published*: monthly, *Price*: free to qualified subscribers.

Globalization and Health, BioMed Central, 236 Gray's Inn Road, London WC1X 8HB United Kingdom, *Telephone*: +44 (0) 20 3192 2009, *Fax*: +44 (0) 20 3192 2010.

Golf Inc., Cypress Magazines Inc., 7670 Opportunity Road, Suite 105, San Diego CA 92111, *Telephone*: (858) 300-3201, *Published*: quarterly.

Government Fleet, 3520 Challenger Street, Torrance, CA 90503, *Telephone*: (310) 533-2400, *Published*: monthly, *Price*: free to qualified subscribers.

Greece Autos Report, Business Monitor International, Senator House, 85 Queen Victoria Street, London EC4V 4AB, United Kingdom, *Telephone*: +44 (0) 20 7248 0468, *Fax*: +44 (0) 20 7248 0467, *Published*: monthly.

Grocer, William Reed Publishing Ltd., Broadfield Park, Crawley, RH11 9RT, United Kingdom, *Telephone*: +44 (0) 1293 613400, *Published*: monthly, *Price*: £125.

Grocery Headquarters, Trend Publishing, One East Erie, Suite 401, Chicago, IL 60611, *Telephone*: (312) 654-2300, *Fax*: (312) 654-2323, *Published*: monthly, *Price*: free to qualified subscribers.

The Headliner, P.O. Box 3762, Christchurch New Zealand, *Telephone*: (03) 365 0301, *Fax*: (03) 365 4255, *Published*: monthly, *Price*: $36 one year.

HFN, Fairchild Publications, 7 W. 34th Street, New York, NY 10001, *Telephone*: (212) 630-4000, *Published*: weekly, *Price*: $109 one week.

Hoard's Dairyman, 28 Milwaukee Ave., W., P.O. Box 801, Fort Atkinson, WI 53538, *Telephone*: 920-563-5551, *Fax*: 920-563-7298, *Published*: 20 times a yar, *Price*: $18 one year.

Home Channel News, Lebhar-Friedman Inc., 425 Park Avenue, New York, NY 10022, *Telephone*: (212) 756-5000, *Published*: 22x/yr., *Price*: free to subscribers.

Home Media Retailing, 131 W First St, Duluth MN 55802, *Telephone*: (888) 527-7008, *Published*: 53x/yr., *Price*: $120 one year.

Home Textiles Today, Reed Business Information, 360 Park Avenue South, New York, NY 10010, *Telephone*: (646) 746-7290, *Fax*: (646) 746-7300, *Published*: monthly, *Price*: $170 per year.

Homeland Security Today, KMD Media, 6800 Fleetwood Road, Suite 1114, McLean VA 22101, *Telephone*: (540) 854-0910, *Fax*: (540) 854-0912, *Published*: monthly.

HomeWorld Business, ICD Publications, 45 Research Way, Suite 106, East Setauket, NY 11733, *Telephone*: (631) 246-9300, *Fax*: (631) 246-9496, *Published*: weekly, *Price*: free to qualified subscribers.

Hong Kong Telecommunications Report, Business Monitor International, Senator House, 85 Queen Victoria Street, London EC4V 4AB, United Kingdom, *Telephone*: +44 (0) 20 7248 0468, *Fax*: +44 (0) 20 7248 0467, *Published*: monthly.

Household & Personal Products Industry, Rodman Publishing, 17 S. Franklin Turnpike, Box 555, Ramsey, NJ 07446, *Telephone*: (201) 825-2552, *Fax*: (201) 825-0553, *Published*: monthly, *Price*: $65 one year.

Houston Business Journal, 1233 West Loop South, Suite 1300, Houston, TX 77027-9100, *Telephone*: (713) 688-8811, *Fax*: (713) 963-0482, *Published*: 56 issues a year, *Price*: $99 one year.

Hungary Food and Drink Report, Business Monitor International, Senator House, 85 Queen Victoria Street, London EC4V 4AB, United Kingdom, *Telephone*: +44 (0) 20 7248 0468, *Fax*: +44 (0) 20 7248 0467, *Published*: monthly.

Hungary Telecommunications Report, Business Monitor International, Senator House, 85 Queen Victoria Street, London EC4V 4AB, United Kingdom, *Telephone*: +44 (0) 20 7248 0468, *Fax*: +44 (0) 20 7248 0467, *Published*: monthly.

IDEX Magazine, 7 West 45th St., Suite 1602, New York NY 10036, *Telephone*: (212) 382-3528, *Fax*: (212) 382-2671, *Published*: monthly, *Price*: $240.65 per year.

Indianpolis Business Journal, 41 E. Washington St., Suite 200, Indianapolis, IN 46204-3592, *Telephone*: (317) 634-6200, *Fax*: (317) 263-5060, *Published*: weekly.

Instore Buyer, Sosland Publishing, 4800 Main St., Suite 100, Kansas City, MO 64112, *Telephone*: (816) 756-1000, *Published*: bimonthly, *Price*: free to qualified subscribers.

Insurance Facts and Stats, A.M. Best Co., Ambest Road, Oldwick, NJ 08858, *Telephone*: (908) 439-2200, *Published*: annual.

Investor's Business Daily, P.O. Box, 661750, Los Angeles, CA 9006, *Telephone*: (800) 831-2525, *Published*: daily, except weekends and holidays, *Price*: $299 one year.

Iran Telecommunications Report, Business Monitor International, Senator House, 85 Queen Victoria Street, London EC4V 4AB, United Kingdom, *Telephone*: +44 (0) 20 7248 0468, *Fax*: +44 (0) 20 7248 0467, *Published*: monthly.

Ireland Telecommunications Report, Business Monitor International, Senator House, 85 Queen Victoria Street, London EC4V 4AB, United Kingdom, *Telephone*: +44 (0) 20 7248 0468, *Fax*: +44 (0) 20 7248 0467, *Published*: monthly.

Japan Telecommunications Report, Business Monitor International, Senator House, 85 Queen Victoria Street, London EC4V 4AB, United Kingdom, *Telephone*: +44 (0) 20 7248 0468, *Fax*: +44 (0) 20 7248 0467, *Published*: monthly.

Jordan Telecommunications Report, Business Monitor International, Senator House, 85 Queen Victoria Street, London EC4V 4AB, United Kingdom, *Telephone*: +44 (0) 20 7248 0468, *Fax*: +44 (0) 20 7248 0467, *Published*: monthly.

Junior Scholastic, Scholastic Inc., 557 Broadway, New York NY 10012, *Telephone*: (800) 724-6527, *Published*: 24 issues, *Price*: $4.35 one year.

Kids Today, 7025 Albert Pick Rd. Suite 200, Greensboro, NC 27409, *Telephone*: (336) 605-1111, *Published*: 11 times per year, *Price*: $14.44 per year.

Laser Focus World, PennWell, 98 Spit Brook Rd., Nashua, NH 03062, *Telephone*: (603) 891-0123, *Published*: monthly, *Price*: free to qualified subscribers.

Latin Trade, Latin America Media Management LLC., 200 South Bicauyne Blvd., Suite 1150, Miami, FL 33131, *Telephone*: (305) 358-8373, *Fax*: (305) 358-9166, *Published*: monthly, *Price*: $39 per year.

LifeTips, LifeTips.com, Inc., 240 Commercial Street, Suite 3B, Boston, MA 02109, *Telephone*: (617) 227-8800.

Logistics Management, 225 Wyman Street, Waltham, MA 02451, *Telephone*: (781) 734-8000, *Fax*: (781) 734-8076, *Published*: monthly, *Price*: $110 per week.

Lube Report, LNG Publishing Co., Inc., 6105-G Arlington Blvd., Falls Church, Virginia, *Telephone*: (703) 536-0800, *Fax*: (703) 536-0803, *Published*: monthly, *Price*: free to qualified subscribers.

Malaysia Palm Oil Fortune, Malaysia Palm Oil Council, 2nd. Floor, Wisma Sawit, Lot 6, SS6, Jalan Perbandaran,47301 Kelana Jaya, Selangor Darul Ehsan,Malaysia, *Telephone*: 603 - 7806 4097, *Fax*: 603 - 7806 2272, *Published*: monthly.

Malaysia Telecommunications Report, Business Monitor International, Senator House, 85 Queen Victoria Street, London EC4V 4AB, United Kingdom, *Telephone*: +44 (0) 20 7248 0468, *Fax*: +44 (0) 20 7248 0467, *Published*: monthly.

The Manufacturing Confectioner, Manufacturing Confectioner Publishing, 175 Rock Rd., Glen Rock, NJ 07452, *Telephone*: (201) 652-2655, *Fax*: (201) 652-3419, *Published*: monthly, *Price*: $25 one year.

Marine Log, 345 Hudson Street, 12th Fl, New York, NY 10014, *Telephone*: (212) 620-7200, *Fax*: (212) 633-1165, *Published*: monthly, *Price*: free to qualified subscribers.

Marketing, Rogers Media Inc., One Mount Pleasant Rd., 7th Floor, Toronto, Ontario, M4Y 2Y5, Canada, *Telephone*: (416) 764-2000, *Fax*: (416) 764-1519, *Published*: 41 issues, *Price*: $120 one year.

Marketing News, American Marketing Assn., 250 S. Wacker Dr., Ste. 200, Chicago, IL 60606-5819, *Telephone*: (312) 993-9517, *Fax*: (312) 993-7540, *Published*: biweekly, *Price*: $110 one year.

MCV, Intent Media, Saxon House, 6A St. Andrew Street, Hertford, Hertfordshire England SG14 1JA, *Telephone*: 01992 535646, *Fax*: 01992 535648, *Published*: monthly.

Meatingplace, Marketing & Technology Group Inc., 1415 N Dayton Street, Chicago, IL 60622, *Telephone*: (312) 274-2122, *Published*: monthly, *Price*: free to qualified subscribers.

Medical Marketing & Media, CPS Communications, 7200 West Camino Real, Ste. 215, Boca Raton, FL 33433, *Telephone*: (561) 368-9301, *Fax*: (561) 368-7870, *Published*: monthly, *Price*: $96 one year.

Medical Product Outsourcing, Rodman Publishing, 70 Hilltop Road, 3rd Floor, Ramsey, NJ 07446, *Telephone*: (201) 825-2552, *Fax*: (201) 825-0553, *Published*: monthly.

Medical Textiles, International Newsletters Ltd., 9A Victoria Square, Droitwich, Worcs, WR9 8DE, United Kingdom, *Telephone*: +44 (0) 870 1657210, *Fax*: +44 (0) 870 1657212, *Published*: monthly, *Price*: $569 one year.

Metalworking Insiders Report, Gardner Publications, Inc., P.O. Box 107, Larchmont, NY 10538, *Telephone*: (914) 834-2300, *Published*: 24x/yr., *Price*: $449 per year in North America; $579 per year elsewhere.

Mexico Telecommunications Report, Business Monitor International, Senator House, 85 Queen Victoria Street, London EC4V 4AB, United Kingdom, *Telephone*: +44 (0) 20 7248 0468, *Fax*: +44 (0) 20 7248 0467, *Published*: monthly.

Middle East Economic Digest, Tower House Sovereign Park, Market Harborough, LE16 9EF, *Telephone*: +44 (0) 1858 438837, *Fax*: +44 (0) 1858 461739, *Published*: monthly, *Price*: $925 one year.

Milling & Baking News, Sosland Publishing Co., 4800 Main St., Suite 100, Kansas City, MO 64112, *Telephone*: (816) 756-1000, *Fax*: (816) 756-0494, *Published*: monthly, *Price*: $135 one year.

Model Railroad News, P.O. Box 1080, Merlin, OR 97532-1080, *Telephone*: (877) 787-2467, *Published*: monthly, *Price*: $34.95 one year.

Montreal Gazette, The Gazette, 1010 Ste-Catherine St. West, Suite 200, Montreal, Quebec, H3B 5L1, Canada, *Telephone*: (514) 987-2222, *Published*: daily.

MPN - Motorcycle & Powersports News, Babcox Media, 3550 Embassy Parkway, Akron OH 44333, *Telephone*: (330) 670-1234, *Fax*: (330) 670-0874, *Published*: monthly.

National Cattlemen, Naylor, 5950 NW 1st. Place, Gainesville, FL 32607, *Telephone*: (800) 369-6220, *Fax*: (352) 331-3525, *Published*: quarterly.

Nightclub & Bar, Questex Media Group, 275 Grove Street, Suite 2-130, Newton, MA 02466, *Telephone*: (617) 219-8300, *Fax*: (888) 552-4346, *Published*: monthly.

Non-Foods Management, Millennium Media, 3 Chaser Court, Holmdel, NJ 07733, *Telephone*: (732) 888-0066, *Fax*: (732) 888-0069, *Published*: annual, *Price*: free to qualified subscribers.

NonProfit Times, 201 Littleton Road - 2nd Floor Morris Plains, NJ 07950, *Telephone*: (973) 401-0202, *Fax*: (973) 401-0404, *Published*: semimonthly, *Price*: $65 one year.

Nonwovens Industry, Rodman Publishing, 17 S. Franklin Turnpike, P.O. Box 555, Ramsey, NJ 07446, *Telephone*: (201) 825-2552, *Fax*: (201) 825-0553, *Published*: monthly, *Price*: $48, or free to qualified subscribers.

Norway Telecommunications Report, Business Monitor International, Senator House, 85 Queen Victoria Street, London EC4V 4AB, United Kingdom, *Telephone*: +44 (0) 20 7248 0468, *Fax*: +44 (0) 20 7248 0467, *Published*: monthly.

Official Board Markets, 7500 Old Oak Blvd., Cleveland, Ohio 44130, *Telephone*: (440) 891-2730, *Fax*: (440) 891-2733, *Published*: monthly, *Price*: $270 one year.

Oil Daily, 5 East 37th Street, 5th Floor, New York, NY, *Telephone*: (212) 532-1112.

Oman Telecommunications Report, Business Monitor International, Senator House, 85 Queen Victoria Street, London EC4V 4AB, United Kingdom, *Telephone*: +44 (0) 20 7248 0468, *Fax*: +44 (0) 20 7248 0467, *Published*: monthly.

Optician, Quadrant House, The Quadrant, Sutton, Surrey SM2 5AS, United Kingdom, *Telephone*: (0) 1932 852 497, *Published*: monthly.

Oregonian, 1320 SW Broadway, Portland, OR 97201, *Telephone*: (503) 221-8327, *Published*: daily, *Price*: $26 one month.

Outreach Magazine, 2230 Oak Ridge Way Vista, CA 92081-2314, *Telephone*: 760-940-0600, *Price*: $29.95 one year.

Outside, 400 Market Street, Santa Fe, NN 87501, *Published*: monthly, *Price*: $24 one year.

Patriot Ledger, 400 Crown Colony Drive, P.O. 699159, Quincy MA 02269-9159, *Telephone*: (617) 786-7026, *Fax*: (617) 786-7025, *Published*: daily.

Prepared Foods, BNP Media, 1050 IL Route 83, Suite 200, Bensenville, IL 60106, *Telephone*: (847) 763-9534, *Fax*: (847) 763-9538, *Published*: daily, *Price*: $86 one year.

Prison Legal News, P.O. Box 2420, West Brattleboro, VT 05303, *Telephone*: (802) 257-1342, *Fax*: (866) 735-7136, *Published*: monthly, *Price*: $150 one year.

Private Label Buyer, Stagnito Communications, 155 Pfingsten Road, Suite 200, Deerfield, IL 60015, *Telephone*: (847) 205-5660, *Published*: monthly, *Price*: $95.18 per year.

Produce Retailer, 400 Knightsbridge Pkwy, Lincolnshire IL 60069, *Telephone*: (847) 634-2600, *Fax*: (847) 634-4379, *Published*: monthly, *Price*: free to qualified subscribers.

Professional Builder, Reed Business, 2000 Clearwater Drive, Oak Brook, IL 60523, *Telephone*: (630) 288-8000, *Fax*: (630) 288-8145, *Published*: monthly, *Price*: free to qualified subscribers.

Professional Deck Builder, 186 Allen Brook Lane, Williston, VT 05495, *Telephone*: (802) 879-3335, *Fax*: (802) 879-9384, *Published*: 6x/year, *Price*: free to qualified subscribers.

Progressive Grocer, 770 Broadway, New York, NY 10003, *Telephone*: (866) 890-8541, *Published*: 18 times per year, *Price*: $129 one year.

Publishers Weekly, Reed Business Information, 360 Park Avenue South, New York, NY 10010, *Telephone*: (646) 746-6758, *Fax*: (646) 746-6631, *Published*: weekly, *Price*: $240 one year.

Pulp & Paper International, Paperloop, 4 Alfred Circle, Bedford, MA 01730, *Telephone*: (866) 271-8525, *Fax*: (818) 487-4550, *Published*: monthly, *Price*: $140 one year.

QSR Magazine, Journalistic Inc., 4905 Pine Cone Drive, Suite 2, Durham, NC 27707, *Telephone*: (919) 489-1916, *Fax*: (919) 489-4767, *Published*: monthly, *Price*: free to qualified subscribers.

Quick Frozen Foods International, EW Williams Publishing Co., 2125 Center Ave., Ste. 305, Fort Lee, NJ 07024, *Telephone*: (201) 592-7007, *Fax*: (201) 592-7171, *Published*: monthly, *Price*: $42 one year.

Radio Ink, 1901 S. Congress Ave., Suite 118, Boynton Beach, FL 33426, *Telephone*: (800) 913-1299, *Published*: 20x/yr., *Price*: $147 one year.

R&D Magazine, Advantage Business Media, 100 Enterprise Drive, Suite 600, Box 912, Rockaway, NJ 07866-0912, *Telephone*: (973) 920-7000, *Published*: monthly, *Price*: free to qualified subscribers.

Redbook - A Supplement to Baking & Snack, Sosland Publishing, 4800 Main Street Suite 100, Kansas City, MO 64112, *Telephone*: (816) 756-1000, *Fax*: (816) 756-0494, *Published*: annual, *Price*: free to qualified subscribers.

Refrigerated & Frozen Foods, Stagnito Communications, 155 Pfingsten Road, Suite 205, Deerfield, IL 60015, *Telephone*: (847) 205-5660, *Fax*: (847) 205-5650, *Published*: monthly, *Price*: free to qualified subscribers.

Refrigerated & Frozen Foods Retailer, Stagnito Communications, 155 Pfingsten Road, Suite 205, Deerfield, IL 60015, *Telephone*: (847) 205-5660, *Fax*: (847) 205-5650, *Published*: monthly, *Price*: free to qualified subscribers.

The Republic, 333 Second Street, Columbus, IN, 47201, *Telephone*: (812) 372-7811, *Published*: daily.

Research Alert, EPM Communications, 160 Mercer Street, 3rd Floor, New York, NY 10012, *Telephone*: (212) 941-0099, *Fax*: (212) 941-1622, *Published*: biweekly, *Price*: $399.65 one year.

Research Studies - Freedonia Group, The Freedonia Group, Inc., 767 Beta Drive, Cleveland, OH 44143, *Telephone*: (440) 684-9600, *Fax*: (440) 684-0484.

Running Insight, 17 Barstow Rd # 407, Great Neck, NY 11021, *Telephone*: (516) 305-4709, *Published*: bimonthly, *Price*: free to qualified subscribers.

RV Business, P.O. Box 17126, North Hollywood, CA 91615-9925, *Telephone*: (303) 728-2267, *Fax*: (303) 728-7306, *Published*: monthly, *Price*: free to qualified subscribers.

San Diego Business Journal, 4909 Murphy Canyon Rd., Suite 200, San Diego, CA 92123, *Telephone*: (858) 277-6359, *Published*: weekly, *Price*: $69 per year.

San Francisco Chronicle, Hearst Communications, 901 Mission St., San Francisco, CA 94103-2988, *Telephone*: (415) 777-1111, *Fax*: (415) 536-5178, *Published*: daily.

Saudi Arabia Telecommunications Report, Business Monitor International, Senator House, 85 Queen Victoria Street, London EC4V 4AB, United Kingdom, *Telephone*: +44 (0) 20 7248 0468, *Fax*: +44 (0) 20 7248 0467, *Published*: monthly.

Screen Digest, Global Media Intelligence, Lymehouse Studios, 38 Georgiana Street, London NW1 0EB, *Telephone*: +44 (0) 20 7424 2820, *Fax*: +44 (0) 20 7424 2838, *Published*: weekly, *Price*: $1,000 one year.

Seafood Business, 121 Free Street, P.O. Box 7437, Portland, ME 04112-7437, *Telephone*: (207) 842-5500, *Fax*: (207) 842-5503, *Published*: monthly, *Price*: $57 one year.

Serbia Food & Drink Report, Business Monitor International, Mermaid House, 2 Puddle Dock, London EC4V 3DS, United Kingdom, *Telephone*: +44 (0) 20 7248 0468, *Fax*: +44 (0) 20 7248 0467, *Published*: monthly.

Seri Quarterly, Samsung Economic Research Institute, 8th floor, Kukje Center Bldg., 191 Hangangro 2-ka, Yongsan-ku Seoul 140-702, South Korea, *Telephone*: +82-2-3780-8131.

SGB Golf, 2151 Hawkins Street, Suite 200, Charlotte, NC 28203, *Telephone*: (704) 987-3450, *Fax*: (704) 987-3455, *Published*: monthly.

Singapore Food & Drink Report, Business Monitor International, Senator House, 85 Queen Victoria Street, London EC4V 4AB, United Kingdom, *Telephone*: +44 (0) 20 7248 0468, *Fax*: +44 (0) 20 7248 0467, *Published*: monthly.

Singapore Telecommunications Report, Business Monitor International, Senator House, 85 Queen Victoria Street, London EC4V 4AB, United Kingdom, *Telephone*: +44 (0) 20 7248 0468, *Fax*: +44 (0) 20 7248 0467, *Published*: monthly.

Slovakia Food & Drink Report, Business Monitor International, Senator House, 85 Queen Victoria Street, London EC4V 4AB, United Kingdom, *Telephone*: +44 (0) 20 7248 0468, *Fax*: +44 (0) 20 7248 0467, *Published*: monthly.

Solitaire International, Peninsula Spenta, 2nd Floor, Mathuradas Mill Compound, Senapati Bapat Marg, Lower Parel, Mumbai - 400013, India., *Telephone*: 91 22 24811010, *Fax*: 91 22 24811021.

Sosland Publishing Corporate Profiles - Milling & Baking News Supplement, Sosland Publishing Co., 4800 Main Street, Suite 100, Kansas City MO 64112, *Telephone*: (816) 756-1000, *Fax*: (816) 756-0494, *Published*: annual, *Price*: free to qualified subscribers.

Soundings, P.O. Box 546, Mt. Morris, IL 61054, *Telephone*: (800) 244-8845, *Fax*: (386) 246-0116, *Published*: monthly, *Price*: $14 one year.

Southern Africa Telecommunications Report, Business Monitor International, Senator House, 85 Queen Victoria Street, London EC4V 4AB, United Kingdom, *Telephone*: +44 (0) 20 7248 0468, *Fax*: +44 (0) 20 7248 0467, *Published*: monthly.

Spain Telecommunications Report, Business Monitor International, Senator House, 85 Queen Victoria Street, London EC4V 4AB, United Kingdom, *Telephone*: +44 (0) 20 7248 0468, *Fax*: +44 (0) 20 7248 0467, *Published*: monthly.

Sports Insight, Formula4 Media L.L.C., P.O. Box 2318, Great Neck NY 11023, *Telephone*: (516) 305-4710, *Fax*: (516) 305-4712, *Published*: bimonthly, *Price*: $24 one year.

SportsBusiness Journal, 1166 Ave of The Americas, 14th Floor, New York, NY 10036, *Telephone*: (212) 500-0700, *Fax*: (212) 500-0701, *Published*: monthly.

Spray, Technology and Marketing, 3621 Hill Road Parsippany, NJ 07054, *Telephone*: (973) 331-9545, *Fax*: (973) 331-9547, *Published*: monthly, *Price*: free to qualified subscribers.

StateWays, The Beverage Information Group, 17 High St., 2nd Fl., Norwalk, CT 06851, *Telephone*: (203) 855-8499, *Published*: monthly, *Price*: $20 one year.

Stores, 325 7th St NW, Suite 1100, Washington D.C. 20004, *Telephone*: (202) 626-8101, *Published*: monthly, *Price*: $120 per year to non-retailers.

Supermarket News, Fairchild Publications, 7 W. 34th St., New York, NY 10001, *Telephone*: (800) 204-4515, *Fax*: (212) 630-4760, *Published*: weekly, *Price*: $195 one year.

Switzerland Telecommunications Report, Business Monitor International, Senator House, 85 Queen Victoria Street, London EC4V 4AB, United Kingdom, *Telephone*: +44 (0) 20 7248 0468, *Fax*: +44 (0) 20 7248 0467, *Published*: monthly.

Talkers Magazine, 650 Belmont Ave, Springfield, MA 01108, *Telephone*: (413) 739-8255, *Fax*: (413) 746-6786, *Published*: 10 issues per year, *Price*: $75 per year.

Thailand Telecommunications Report, Business Monitor International, Senator House, 85 Queen Victoria Street, London EC4V 4AB, United Kingdom, *Telephone*: +44 (0) 20 7248 0468, *Fax*: +44 (0) 20 7248 0467, *Published*: monthly.

Tire Business, Crain Communcations, Inc., 1725 Merriman Rd., Ste. 300, Akron, OH 44313-5283, *Telephone*: (330) 836-9180, *Fax*: (330) 836-1005, *Published*: monthly, *Price*: free to qualified subscribers.

Tire Review, Babcox Publications, 3550 Embassy Parkway, Akron, OH 44313, *Telephone*: (330) 670-1234, *Published*: monthly.

Total Telecom, Terrapin Holdings, 4th Floor Welken House, 10-11 Charterhouse Square, London EC1M 6EH, *Telephone*: +44 (0) 20 7608 7030, *Fax*: +44 (0) 20 7608 7040.

Touch Panel, Veritas et Visus, 3305 Chelsea Place, Temple TX 76502, *Telephone*: (254) 791-0603, *Published*: 10x/yr., *Price*: $47.99 one year.

Turkey Telecommunications Report, Business Monitor International, Senator House, 85 Queen Victoria Street, London EC4V 4AB United Kingdom, *Telephone*: +44 (0) 20 7248 0468, *Fax*: +44 (0) 20 7248 0467, *Published*: monthly.

TV Veopar Journal, ADI Media, C-35, Sector 62, Noida - 201 307Uttar Pradesh (India), *Telephone*: 91-120-4021200, *Fax*: 91-120-4021280.

Twice, 360 Park Avenue South, 15th Floor New York NY 10010, *Telephone*: (646) 746-6980, *Fax*: (646) 746-7066, *Published*: weekly, *Price*: $143 one year.

United Kingdom Autos Report, Business Monitor International, Senator House, 85 Queen Victoria Street, London EC4V 4AB, United Kingdom, *Telephone*: +44 (0) 20 7248 0468, *Fax*: +44 (0) 20 7248 0467, *Published*: monthly.

Units, National Apartment Association, 201 N. Union Street, Suite 200, Alexandria, VA 22314, *Telephone*: (703) 518-6141, *Fax*: (703) 518-6191, *Published*: monthly, *Price*: $28 one year.

USA TODAY, Gannett Co., 7950 Jones Branch Drive, McLean, VA 22108-0605, *Telephone*: (800) 872-0001, *Published*: Mon.-Fri., *Price*: $146 one year.

Utah Business, 859 W. South Jordan Parkway, Ste. 101, South Jordan, Utah 84095, *Telephone*: (801) 568-0114, *Fax*: (801) 568-0812, *Price*: $40 one year.

Venezuela Telecommunications Report, Business Monitor International, Senator House, 85 Queen Victoria Street, London EC4V 4AB, United Kingdom, *Telephone*: +44 (0) 20 7248 0468, *Fax*: +44 (0) 20 7248 0467, *Published*: monthly.

Wall Street Journal, Dow Jones & Co. Inc., 200 Liberty St., New York, NY 10281, *Telephone*: (212) 416-2000, *Published*: Mon.-Fri., *Price*: $107 one year.

Window & Door, National Glass Association, 82000 Greensboro Ste 302, Mclean, VA, *Telephone*: (703) 442-4890, *Fax*: (703) 442-0630, *Published*: monthly, *Price*: $40 one year.

Wines & Vines, Hiaring Co., 1800 Lincoln Ave., San Rafael, CA 94901-1298, *Telephone*: (415) 453-9700, *Fax*: (415) 453-2517, *Published*: monthly, *Price*: $32 per year in U.S.; $50 per year internationally.

World Grain, Sosland Publishing, 48000 Main Street, Suite 100, Kansas, MO 64112, *Telephone*: (816) 756-1000, *Fax*: (816) 756-0494, *Published*: monthly, *Price*: free to qualified subscribers.

WWD, Fairchild Publications, 7 West 34th Street, New York, NY 10001, *Telephone*: (212) 630-4000, *Published*: Mon.-Fri., *Price*: $99 one year.

Your Convenience Manager, Fulcrum Media, 508 Lawrence Avenue West, Suite 201, Toronto, Ontario M6A 1A1, *Telephone*: (416) 504-0504, *Fax*: (416) 256-3002, *Published*: 6x/yr., *Price*: $91.15 one year.